R

Twentieth-Century Literary Criticism

**Excerpts from Criticism of the
Works of Novelists, Poets, Playwrights,
Short Story Writers, and Other Creative Writers
Who Died between 1900 and 1960,
from the First Published Critical Appraisals
to Current Evaluations**

**Dennis Poupard
Paula Kepos
Editors**

**Marie Lazzari
Thomas Ligotti
Associate Editors**

 **Gale Research Inc.** · DETROIT · LONDON

Guide to Gale Literary Criticism Series

When you need to review criticism of literary works, these are the Gale series to use:

If the author's death date is: **You should turn to:**

After Dec. 31, 1959
(or author is still living)

CONTEMPORARY LITERARY CRITICISM

for example: Jorge Luis Borges, Anthony Burgess,
William Faulkner, Mary Gordon,
Ernest Hemingway, Iris Murdoch

1900 through 1959

TWENTIETH-CENTURY LITERARY CRITICISM

for example: Willa Cather, F. Scott Fitzgerald,
Henry James, Mark Twain, Virginia Woolf

1800 through 1899

NINETEENTH-CENTURY LITERATURE CRITICISM

for example: Fedor Dostoevski, Nathaniel Hawthorne,
George Sand, William Wordsworth

1400 through 1799

LITERATURE CRITICISM FROM 1400 TO 1800
(excluding Shakespeare)

for example: Anne Bradstreet, Daniel Defoe,
Alexander Pope, François Rabelais,
Jonathan Swift, Phillis Wheatley

SHAKESPEAREAN CRITICISM

Shakespeare's plays and poetry

Antiquity through 1399

CLASSICAL AND MEDIEVAL LITERATURE CRITICISM

for example: Dante, Homer, Plato, Sophocles, Vergil,
the Beowulf Poet

Gale also publishes related criticism series:

CHILDREN'S LITERATURE REVIEW

This series covers authors of all eras who write for the preschool
through high school audience.

SHORT STORY CRITICISM

This series covers the major short fiction writers of all nationalities
and periods of literary history.

ISSN 0276-8178

Volume 29

Twentieth-Century Literary Criticism

**Excerpts from Criticism of the
Works of Novelists, Poets, Playwrights,
Short Story Writers, and Other Creative Writers
Who Died between 1900 and 1960,
from the First Published Critical Appraisals
to Current Evaluations**

**Dennis Poupard
Paula Kepos
Editors**

**Marie Lazzari
Thomas Ligotti
Associate Editors**

 *Gale Research Inc.*
Book Tower • Detroit, Michigan 48226

STAFF

Dennis Poupard, Paula Kepos, *Editors*

Marie Lazzari, Thomas Ligotti, *Associate Editors*

Joann Prosyniuk, Keith E. Schooley, Laurie A. Sherman, *Senior Assistant Editors*

Faye Kuzma, Sandra Liddell, Timothy Veeser, *Assistant Editors*

Jay P. Pederson, Debra A. Wells, *Contributing Assistant Editors*

Jeanne A. Gough, *Permissions & Production Manager*
Lizbeth A. Purdy, *Production Supervisor*
Kathleen M. Cook, *Production Coordinator*
Cathy Beranek, Suzanne Powers, Kristine E. Tipton, Lee Ann Welsh, *Editorial Assistants*
Linda M. Pugliese, *Manuscript Coordinator*
Maureen A. Puhl, *Senior Manuscript Assistant*
Donna Craft, Jennifer E. Gale, Rosetta Irene Simms, *Manuscript Assistants*

Victoria B. Cariappa, *Research Supervisor*
Maureen R. Richards, *Research Coordinator*
Mary D. Wise, *Senior Research Assistant*
Joyce E. Doyle, Kevin B. Hillstrom, Karen D. Kaus, Eric Priehs,
Filomena Sgambati, Laura B. Standley, *Research Assistants*

Janice M. Mach, *Text Permissions Supervisor*
Kathy Grell, *Text Permissions Coordinator*
Mabel E. Gurney, *Research Permissions Coordinator*
Josephine M. Keene, *Senior Permissions Assistant*
Eileen H. Baehr, H. Diane Cooper,
Anita Lorraine Ransom, Kimberly F. Smilay, *Permissions Assistants*
Melissa A. Brantley, Martha A. Mulder, Lisa M. Wimmer, *Permissions Clerks*

Patricia A. Seefelt, *Picture Permissions Supervisor*
Margaret A. Chamberlain, *Pictures Permissions Coordinator*
Pamela A. Hayes, Lillian Tyus, *Permissions Clerks*

Special thanks to Sharon K. Hall for her assistance with the Title Index.

The paper used in this publication meets the minimum requirements
of American National Standard for Information Sciences—Permanence
Paper for Printed Library Materials, ANSI Z39.48-1984.   ∞™

Library of Congress Catalog Card Number 76-46132
ISBN 0-8103-2411-3
ISSN 0276-8178

Printed in the United States of America

Published simultaneously in the United Kingdom
by Gale Research International Limited
(An affiliated company of Gale Research Inc.)

Contents

Preface

It is impossible to overvalue the importance of literature in the intellectual, emotional, and spiritual evolution of humanity. Literature is that which both lifts us out of everyday life and helps us to better understand it. Through the fictive lives of such characters as Anna Karenina, Jay Gatsby, or Leopold Bloom, our perceptions of the human condition are enlarged, and we are enriched.

Literary criticism can also give us insight into the human condition, as well as into the specific moral and intellectual atmosphere of an era, for the criteria by which a work of art is judged reflect contemporary philosophical and social attitudes. Literary criticism takes many forms: the traditional essay, the book or play review, even the parodic poem. Criticism can also be of several types: normative, descriptive, interpretive, textual, appreciative, generic. Collectively, the range of critical response helps us to understand a work of art, an author, an era.

Scope of the Series

Twentieth-Century Literary Criticism (TCLC) is designed to serve as an introduction for the student of twentieth-century literature to the authors of the period 1900 to 1960 and to the most significant commentators on these authors. The great poets, novelists, short story writers, playwrights, and philosophers of this period are by far the most popular writers for study in high school and college literature courses. Since a vast amount of relevant critical material confronts the student, *TCLC* presents significant passages from the most important published criticism to aid students in the location and selection of commentaries on authors who died between 1900 and 1960.

The need for *TCLC* was suggested by the usefulness of the Gale series *Contemporary Literary Criticism (CLC),* which excerpts criticism on current writing. Because of the difference in time span under consideration *(CLC* considers authors who were still living after 1959), there is no duplication of material between *CLC* and *TCLC.* For further information about *CLC* and Gale's other criticism series, users should consult the Guide to Gale Literary Criticism Series preceding the title page in this volume.

Each volume of *TCLC* is carefully compiled to include authors who represent a variety of genres and nationalities and who are currently regarded as the most important writers of this era. In addition to major authors, *TCLC* also presents criticism on lesser-known writers whose significant contributions to literary history are important to the study of twentieth-century literature.

Each author entry in *TCLC* is intended to provide an overview of major criticism on an author. Therefore, the editors include fifteen to twenty authors in each 600-page volume (compared with approximately forty authors in a *CLC* volume of similar size) so that more attention may be given to an author. Each author entry represents a historical survey of the critical response to that author's work: some early criticism is presented to indicate initial reactions, later criticism is selected to represent any rise or decline in the author's reputation, and current retrospective analyses provide students with a modern view. The length of an author entry is intended to reflect the amount of critical attention the author has received from critics writing in English, and from foreign criticism in translation. Critical articles and books that have not been translated into English are excluded. Every attempt has been made to identify and include excerpts from the seminal essays on each author's work.

An author may appear more than once in the series because of the great quantity of critical material available, or because of a resurgence of criticism generated by events such as an author's centennial or anniversary celebration, the republication or posthumous publication of an author's works, or the publication of a newly translated work. Generally, a few author entries in each volume of *TCLC* feature criticism on single works by major authors who have appeared previously in the series. Only those individual works that have been the subjects of vast amounts of criticism and are widely studied in literature classes are selected for this in-depth treatment. Franz Kafka's *The Trial* and Thomas Wolfe's *Look Homeward, Angel* are examples of such entries in *TCLC,* Volume 29.

Organization of the Book

An author entry consists of the following elements: author heading, biographical and critical introduction, list of principal works, excerpts of criticism (each preceded by explanatory notes and followed by a bibliographical citation), and an additional bibliography for further reading.

- The *author heading* consists of the author's full name, followed by birth and death dates. The unbracketed portion of the name denotes the form under which the author most commonly wrote. If an author wrote consistently under a pseudonym, the pseudonym will be listed in the author heading and the real name given in parentheses on the first line of the biographical and critical introduction. Also located at the beginning of the introduction to the author entry are any name variations under which an author wrote, including transliterated forms for authors whose languages use nonroman alphabets. Uncertainty as to a birth or death date is indicated by a question mark.

- The *biographical and critical introduction* contains background information designed to introduce the reader to an author and to the critical debate surrounding his or her work. References are provided to past volumes of *TCLC* and to other biographical and critical reference series published by Gale, including *Children's Literature Review, Contemporary Authors, Dictionary of Literary Biography,* and *Something about the Author.*

- Most *TCLC* entries include *portraits* of the author. Many entries also contain illustrations of materials pertinent to an author's career, including manuscript pages, title pages, dust jackets, letters, or representations of important people, places, and events in an author's life.

- The *list of principal works* is chronological by date of first book publication and identifies the genre of each work. In the case of foreign authors where there are both foreign language publications and English translations, the title and date of the first English-language edition are given in brackets. Unless otherwise indicated, dramas are dated by first performance, not first publication.

- *Criticism* is arranged chronologically in each author entry to provide a perspective on changes in critical evaluation over the years. All titles by the author featured in the critical entry are printed in boldface type to enable the user to ascertain without difficulty the works being discussed. Also for purposes of easier identification, the critic's name and the publication date of the essay are given at the beginning of each piece of criticism. Unsigned criticism is preceded by the title of the journal in which it appeared. When an anonymous essay is later attributed to a critic, the critic's name appears in brackets at the beginning of the excerpt and in the bibliographical citation. Many critical entries in *TCLC* also contain translated material to aid users. Unless otherwise noted, translations within brackets are by the editors; translations within parentheses or continuous with the text are by the author of the excerpt. Publication information (such as publisher names and book prices) and parenthetical numerical references (such as footnotes or page and line references to specific editions of works) have been deleted at the editors' discretion to provide smoother reading of the text.

- Critical essays are prefaced by *explanatory notes* as an additional aid to students using *TCLC*. The explanatory notes provide several types of useful information, including the reputation of a critic, the importance of a work of criticism, the specific type of criticism (biographical, psychoanalytic, structuralist, etc.), a synopsis of the criticism, and the growth of critical controversy or changes in critical trends regarding an author's work. In some cases, these notes cross-reference the work of critics who agree or disagree with each other. Dates in parentheses within the explanatory notes refer to a book publication date when they follow a book title and to an essay date when they follow a critic's name.

- A complete *bibliographical citation* designed to facilitate location of the original essay or book by the interested reader follows each piece of criticism.

- The *additional bibliography* appearing at the end of each author entry suggests further reading on the author. In some cases it includes essays for which the editors could not obtain reprint rights.

An appendix lists the sources from which material in each volume has been reprinted. It does not, however, list every book or periodical consulted in the preparation of the volume.

Cumulative Indexes

Each volume of *TCLC* includes a cumulative index listing all the authors who have appeared in *Contemporary Literary Criticism, Twentieth-Century Literary Criticism, Nineteenth-Century Literature Criticism, Literature Criticism from 1400 to 1800, Classical and Medieval Literature Criticism,* and *Short Story Criticism,* along with cross-references to the Gale series *Children's Literature Review, Authors in the News, Contemporary Authors, Contemporary Authors Autobiography Series, Dictionary of Literary Biography, Concise Dictionary of American Literary Biography, Something about the Author, Something about the Author Autobiography Series,* and *Yesterday's Authors of Books for Children.* Readers will welcome this cumulated author index as a useful tool for locating an author within the various series. The index, which lists birth and death dates when available, will be particularly valuable for those authors who are identified with a certain period but whose death date causes them to be placed in another, or for those authors whose careers span two periods. For example, F. Scott Fitzgerald is found in *TCLC,* yet a writer often associated with him, Ernest Hemingway, is found in *CLC.*

Each volume of *TCLC* also includes a cumulative nationality index. Author names are arranged alphabetically under their respective nationalities and followed by the volume numbers in which they appear.

New Index

An important feature now appearing in *TCLC* is a cumulative index to titles, an alphabetical listing of the literary works discussed in the series since its inception. Each title listing includes the corresponding volume and page numbers where criticism may be located. Foreign language titles that have been translated are followed by the titles of the translations—for example, *Voina i mir (War and Peace)*. Page numbers following these translated titles refer to all pages on which any form of the titles, either foreign language or translated, appear. Titles of novels, dramas, nonfiction books, and poetry, short story, or essay collections are printed in italics, while all individual poems, short stories, and essays are printed in roman type within quotation marks. In cases where the same title is used by different authors, the author's surname is given in parentheses after the title, e.g., *Collected Poems* (Housman) and *Collected Poems* (Yeats).

Acknowledgments

No work of this scope can be accomplished without the cooperation of many people. The editors especially wish to thank the copyright holders of the excerpted criticism included in this volume, the permissions managers of many book and magazine publishing companies for assisting us in securing reprint rights, and Anthony Bogucki for assistance with copyright research. We are also grateful to the staffs of the Detroit Public Library, the Library of Congress, the University of Detroit Library, the University of Michigan Library, and the Wayne State University Library for making their resources available to us.

Suggestions Are Welcome

In response to various suggestions, several features have been added to *TCLC* since the series began, including explanatory notes to excerpted criticism that provide important information regarding critics and their work, a cumulative author index listing authors in all Gale literary criticism series, entries devoted to criticism on a single work by a major author, more extensive illustrations, and a title index listing all literary works discussed in the series since its inception.

Readers who wish to suggest authors to appear in future volumes, or who have other suggestions, are cordially invited to write the editors.

Authors to Be Featured in Forthcoming Volumes

Twentieth-Century Literary Criticism, Volume 30, will be an Archive volume devoted to various topics in twentieth-century literature, including the Surrealist and Russian Symbolist movements, the New York Intellectuals and their journal *Partisan Review,* and the literature of German émigrés fleeing Naziism during the 1930s and 1940s.

Mikhail Artsybashev (Russian novelist)—Artsybashev was notorious for works promoting the principles of anarchic individualism and unrestrained sensuality. His erotic novel *Sanin* produced an international sensation and inspired cults dedicated to the destruction of social convention.

Henri Bergson (French philosopher)—One of the most influential philosophers of the twentieth century, Bergson is renowned for his opposition to the dominant materialist thought of his time and for his creation of theories that emphasize the supremacy and independence of supra-rational consciousness.

Edgar Rice Burroughs (American novelist)—Burroughs was a science fiction writer who is best known as the creator of Tarzan. His *Tarzan of the Apes* and its numerous sequels have sold over thirty-five million copies in fifty-six languages, making Burroughs one of the most popular authors in the world.

Samuel Butler (English novelist and essayist)—Butler is best known for *The Way of All Flesh,* an autobiographical novel that is both a classic account of the conflict between father and son and an indictment of Victorian society.

Willa Cather (American novelist and short story writer) Cather combined knowledge of Nebraska with an artistic expertise reminiscent of the nineteenth-century literary masters to create one of the most distinguished achievements of twentieth-century American literature. She has been compared to Gustave Flaubert and Henry James for her sensibility, emphasis on technique, and high regard for the artist and European culture, and to the "lost generation" of Ernest Hemingway and F. Scott Fitzgerald for her alienation from modern American society.

Anton Chekhov (Russian dramatist and short story writer) Praised for his stylistic innovations in both fiction and drama as well as for his depth of insight into the human condition, Chekhov is the most significant Russian author of the generation to succeed Leo Tolstoy and Fedor Dostoevsky. *TCLC* will devote an entry to Chekhov's plays, focusing on his dramatic masterpieces *The Seagull, Uncle Vanya, Three Sisters,* and *The Cherry Orchard.*

Stephen Crane (American novelist and short story writer) Crane was one of the foremost realistic writers in American literature. *TCLC* will devote an entry to his masterpiece, *The Red Badge of Courage,* in which he depicted the psychological complexities of fear and courage in battle.

Theodore Dreiser (American novelist)—A prominent American exponent of literary Naturalism and one of America's foremost novelists, Dreiser was the author of works commended for their powerful characterizations and strong ideological convictions.

Thomas Hardy (English novelist)—Considered one of the greatest novelists in the English language, Hardy is best known for his portrayal of characters who are subject to social and psychological forces beyond their control. *TCLC* will devote an entry to *The Mayor of Casterbridge,* a tragedy of psychological determinism in which Hardy introduced his belief that "character is fate."

Vicente Huidobro (Chilean poet)—Huidobro was among the most influential South American poets of the twentieth century for his formulation of *creacionismo,* a poetic theory that regarded poetry not as an imitation of nature but as an original creation.

William James (American philosopher and psychologist)—One of the most influential figures in modern Western philosophy, James was the founder of Pragmatism, a philosophy that rejected abstract models of reality in an attempt to explain life as it is actually experienced.

Nikos Kazantzakis (Greek novelist)—Kazantzakis was a controversial Greek writer whose works embodied Nietzschean and Bergsonian philosophical ideas in vividly portrayed characters, the most famous of which was the protagonist of *Zorba the Greek.*

Thomas Mann (German novelist)—Mann is credited with reclaiming for the German novel an international stature it had not enjoyed since the time of the Romantics. *TCLC* will devote an entry to his novel *Buddenbrooks,* a masterpiece of Realism which depicts the rise and fall of a wealthy Hanseatic family.

George Orwell (English novelist and essayist)—Designated the "conscience of his generation" by V. S. Pritchett, Orwell is the author of influential novels and essays embodying his commitment to personal freedom and social justice. *TCLC* will devote an entry to Orwell's first major popular and critical success, *Animal Farm,* a satirical fable in which Orwell attacked the consequences of the Russian Revolution while suggesting reasons for the failure of most revolutionary ideals.

Marcel Proust (French novelist)—Proust's multivolume *A la recherche du temps perdu (Remembrance of Things Past)* is among literature's works of highest genius. Combining a social historian's chronicle of turn-of-the-century Paris society, a philosopher's reflections on the nature of time and consciousness, and a psychologist's insight into a tangled network of personalities, the novel is acclaimed for conveying a profound view of all human existence.

Joseph Roth (Austrian novelist)—A chronicler of the last years of the Austro-Hungarian Empire, Roth is best known for his novels *Radetzky March, Job,* and *Flight without End.*

George Saintsbury (English critic)—Saintsbury has been called the most influential English literary historian and critic of the late-nineteenth and early-twentieth centuries.

Ernest Thompson Seton (American naturalist and author) Best known as the founder of the Boy Scouts of America, Seton was the author of twenty-five volumes of animal stories for children as well as books on woodcraft and natural history.

Italo Svevo (Italian novelist)—Svevo's ironic portrayals of the moral life of the bourgeoisie, which characteristically demonstrate the influence of the psychoanalytic theories of Sigmund Freud, earned him a reputation as the father of the modern Italian novel.

Mark Twain (American novelist)—Considered the father of modern American literature, Twain combined moral and social satire, adventure, and frontier humor to create such perenially popular books as *The Adventures of Tom Sawyer, The Adventures of Huckleberry Finn,* and *A Connecticut Yankee in King Arthur's Court.*

Thorstein Veblen (American economist and social critic) Veblen's seminal analyses of the nature, development, and consequences of business and industry—as well as his attack on bourgeois materialism in *The Theory of the Leisure Class*—distinguished him as one of the foremost American economists and social scientists of the twentieth century.

William Butler Yeats (Irish poet, dramatist, and essayist) Yeats is considered one of the greatest poets in the English language. Although his interest in Irish politics and his visionary approach to poetry often confounded his contemporaries and set him at odds with the intellectual trends of his time, Yeats's poetic achievement stands at the center of modern literature.

Additional Authors to Appear
in Future Volumes

Abbey, Henry 1842-1911
Abercrombie, Lascelles 1881-1938
Adamic, Louis 1898-1951
Ade, George 1866-1944
Agustini, Delmira 1886-1914
Akers, Elizabeth Chase 1832-1911
Aldrich, Thomas Bailey 1836-1907
Aliyu, Dan Sidi 1902-1920
Allen, Hervey 1889-1949
Archer, William 1856-1924
Arlen, Michael 1895-1956
Austin, Alfred 1835-1913
Bahr, Hermann 1863-1934
Bailey, Philip James 1816-1902
Barbour, Ralph Henry 1870-1944
Benjamin, Walter 1892-1940
Bennett, James Gordon, Jr. 1841-1918
Berdyaev, Nikolai Aleksandrovich
    1874-1948
Beresford, J(ohn) D(avys) 1873-1947
Binyon, Laurence 1869-1943
Bishop, John Peale 1892-1944
Blake, Lillie Devereux 1835-1913
Blest Gana, Alberto 1830-1920
Blum, Léon 1872-1950
Bodenheim, Maxwell 1892-1954
Bowen, Marjorie 1886-1952
Byrne, Donn 1889-1928
Caine, Hall 1853-1931
Cannan, Gilbert 1884-1955
Carducci, Giosuè 1835-1907
Carswell, Catherine 1879-1946
Churchill, Winston 1871-1947
Conner, Ralph 1860-1937
Corelli, Marie 1855-1924
Croce, Benedetto 1866-1952
Crofts, Freeman Wills 1879-1957
Cruze, James (Jens Cruz Bosen) 1884-
    1942
Curros, Enríquez Manuel 1851-1908
Dall, Caroline Wells (Healy) 1822-1912
Daudet, Léon 1867-1942
Delafield, E.M. (Edme Elizabeth Monica
    de la Pasture) 1890-1943
Deneson, Jacob 1836-1919
Diego, José de 1866-1918
Douglas, (George) Norman 1868-1952
Douglas, Lloyd C(assel) 1877-1951
Dovzhenko, Alexander 1894-1956
Drinkwater, John 1882-1937
Durkheim, Émile 1858-1917
Duun, Olav 1876-1939
Eaton, Walter Prichard 1878-1957
Eggleston, Edward 1837-1902
Erskine, John 1879-1951
Fadeyev, Alexander 1901-1956

Ferland, Albert 1872-1943
Field, Rachel 1894-1924
Flecker, James Elroy 1884-1915
Fletcher, John Gould 1886-1950
Fogazzaro, Antonio 1842-1911
Francos, Karl Emil 1848-1904
Frank, Bruno 1886-1945
Frazer, (Sir) George 1854-1941
Freud, Sigmund 1853-1939
Fröding, Gustaf 1860-1911
Fuller, Henry Blake 1857-1929
Futabatei Shimei 1864-1909
Gamboa, Federico 1864-1939
Glaspell, Susan 1876-1948
Glyn, Elinor 1864-1943
Golding, Louis 1895-1958
Gould, Gerald 1885-1936
Guest, Edgar 1881-1959
Gumilyov, Nikolay 1886-1921
Gyulai, Pal 1826-1909
Hale, Edward Everett 1822-1909
Hansen, Martin 1909-1955
Hernández, Miguel 1910-1942
Hewlett, Maurice 1861-1923
Heyward, DuBose 1885-1940
Hope, Anthony 1863-1933
Ilyas, Abu Shabaka 1903-1947
Imbs, Bravig 1904-1946
Ivanov, Vyacheslav Ivanovich 1866-
    1949
James, Will 1892-1942
Jammes, Francis 1868-1938
Johnson, Fenton 1888-1958
Johnston, Mary 1870-1936
Jorgensen, Johannes 1866-1956
King, Grace 1851-1932
Kirby, William 1817-1906
Kline, Otis Albert 1891-1946
Kohut, Adolph 1848-1916
Kuzmin, Mikhail Alexseyevich 1875-
    1936
Lamm, Martin 1880-1950
Leipoldt, C. Louis 1880-1947
Lima, Jorge De 1895-1953
Locke, Alain 1886-1954
López Portillo y Rojas, José 1850-1903
Louys, Pierre 1870-1925
Lucas, E(dward) V(errall) 1868-1938
Lyall, Edna 1857-1903
Machar, Josef Svatopluk 1864-1945
Mander, Jane 1877-1949
Maragall, Joan 1860-1911
Marais, Eugene 1871-1936
Masaryk, Tomas 1850-1939
Mayor, Flora Macdonald 1872-1932
McClellan, George Marion 1860-1934

Mikszáth, Kálmán 1847-1910
Mirbeau, Octave 1850-1917
Mistral, Frédéric 1830-1914
Monro, Harold 1879-1932
Moore, Thomas Sturge 1870-1944
Móricz, Zsigmond 1879-1942
Morley, Christopher 1890-1957
Morley, S. Griswold 1883-1948
Murray, (George) Gilbert 1866-1957
Nansen, Peter 1861-1918
Nobre, Antonio 1867-1900
O'Dowd, Bernard 1866-1959
Ophuls, Max 1902-1957
Orczy, Baroness 1865-1947
Oskison, John M. 1874-1947
Ostaijen, Paul van 1896-1928
Owen, Seaman 1861-1936
Page, Thomas Nelson 1853-1922
Parrington, Vernon L. 1871-1929
Paterson, Andrew Barton 1864-1941
Peck, George W. 1840-1916
Phillips, Ulrich B. 1877-1934
Pinero, Arthur Wing 1855-1934
Powys, T. F. 1875-1953
Prévost, Marcel 1862-1941
Quiller-Couch, Arthur 1863-1944
Ramos, Graciliano 1892-1953
Randall, James G. 1881-1953
Rappoport, Solomon 1863-1944
Read, Opie 1852-1939
Reisen (Reizen), Abraham 1875-1953
Remington, Frederic 1861-1909
Reyes, Alfonso 1889-1959
Riley, James Whitcomb 1849-1916
Rinehart, Mary Roberts 1876-1958
Ring, Max 1817-1901
Rivera, José Eustasio 1889-1928
Rozanov, Vasily Vasilyevich 1856-1919
Saar, Ferdinand von 1833-1906
Sabatini, Rafael 1875-1950
Sakutaro, Hagiwara 1886-1942
Sanborn, Franklin Benjamin 1831-1917
Sánchez, Florencio 1875-1910
Santayana, George 1863-1952
Sardou, Victorien 1831-1908
Schickele, René 1885-1940
Seabrook, William 1886-1945
Shestov, Lev 1866-1938
Shiels, George 1886-1949
Singer, Israel Joshua 1893-1944
Södergran, Edith Irene 1892-1923
Solovyov, Vladimir 1853-1900
Sorel, Georges 1847-1922
Spector, Mordechai 1859-1922
Squire, J(ohn) C(ollings) 1884-1958
Stavenhagen, Fritz 1876-1906

Stockton, Frank R. 1834-1902
Subrahmanya Bharati, C. 1882-1921
Sully-Prudhomme, René 1839-1907
Sylva, Carmen 1843-1916
Talvik, Heiti 1904-1947?
Taneda Santoka 1882-1940
Thoma, Ludwig 1867-1927
Tomlinson, Henry Major 1873-1958
Totovents, Vahan 1889-1937
Tozzi, Federigo 1883-1920
Tuchmann, Jules 1830-1901

Turner, W(alter) J(ames) R(edfern) 1889-1946
Upward, Allen 1863-1926
Vachell, Horace Annesley 1861-1955
Van Dyke, Henry 1852-1933
Villaespesa, Francisco 1877-1936
Wallace, Edgar 1874-1932
Wallace, Lewis 1827-1905
Walsh, Ernest 1895-1926
Webster, Jean 1876-1916

Whitlock, Brand 1869-1927
Wilson, Harry Leon 1867-1939
Wolf, Emma 1865-1932
Wood, Clement 1888-1950
Wren, P(ercival) C(hristopher) 1885-1941
Yonge, Charlotte Mary 1823-1901
Yosano Akiko 1878-1942
Zecca, Ferdinand 1864-1947
Zeromski, Stefan 1864-1925

Readers are cordially invited to suggest additional authors to the editors.

Leopoldo Alas (y Ureña)

1852-1901

(Also wrote under the pseudonym Clarín) Spanish novelist, critic, essayist, short story writer, dramatist, and journalist.

A Spanish man of letters, Alas was best known during his lifetime for his influential and controversial assessments of mid- to late-nineteenth-century Spanish fiction. Today he is chiefly remembered, both within his native country and abroad, as a satirical novelist, and his novel *La Regenta* is regarded as one of the most important works of Spanish literature to appear in the decades following Spain's revolution of 1868. This period of change in Spanish culture was marked in literature by the rejection of the romanticism and sentimentality that had been prominent features of early nineteenth-century fiction in favor of experimentation in the style of the literary movements of Realism and Naturalism then popular in much of Europe. In his literary criticism Alas praised those Spanish writers who were advancing Spanish literature in this way, and when Alas began writing fiction himself, he was largely influenced by Realism and Naturalism.

Alas was born in Zamora, the only son of a minor government official. He began attending a Jesuit school in León when he was six and proved a brilliant student, going on to study at the University of Oviedo at the age of eleven. During his school years Alas developed strong Republican political convictions, and as a graduate student in Madrid during the 1870s he joined several radical organizations. Most significantly he became associated with the *krausistas,* followers of the German religious philosopher Karl C. F. Krause, who propounded a form of syncretistic thought that combined belief in a divinity with liberal, progressive ideas in philosophy, pedagogy, and literature. *Krausismo* was enthusiastically accepted by young Spanish intellectuals and had a profound, liberalizing effect on Spanish culture of the time. Although Alas later satirized some aspects of *krausismo* in his fiction, the movement did affect his own early fiction and his outlook as a critic.

Believing that criticism could be an effective way to raise the intellectual and literary standards of his country, Alas began writing and publishing critical essays in the mid-1870s under the pen name of Clarín, which means "trumpet." He espoused literary Realism and Naturalism as exemplified in the works of Gustave Flaubert and Emile Zola. According to Frank Durand, Naturalism represented to Alas "an expansion of realism with new techniques, new subject matter, and a well-defined aesthetic end based on observed reality." As a critic of contemporary Spanish fiction, Alas championed the works of established and well-known Spanish writers—in particular the novelists Benito Pérez Galdós, Armando Palacio Valdés, and Emilia Pardo Bazán—who were writing in Realist and Naturalist styles, while almost invariably excoriating new, unproven writers regardless of their literary orientation. Known for antagonistic and uncompromising attitudes in his critical essays, Alas was disliked and feared, though grudgingly respected, within the Spanish literary and intellectual community. Upon graduating from the University of Madrid in 1877 with a law degree, he lost an opportunity to assume a teaching post for which he had been considered, in part because of the controversies surrounding his contentious literary pronouncements.

Early in the 1880s Alas became a professor of law, first at the University of Zaragoza and, in 1883, at the University of Oviedo, where he began work on the novel *La Regenta*. He was also writing and publishing satirical short stories at this time. When the novel appeared in 1884, readers readily identified the setting, a provincial town called Vetusta, with Oviedo, and were scandalized by Alas's unsparing presentation of small-town pettiness and sordid hypocrisy, particularly on the part of the town's "leading citizens" and church officials. The Bishop of Oviedo, in particular, charged that the novel was "saturated with eroticism, with infamous mockery of Christian practices and with slanderous allusions to highly respectable persons." A subsequent novel, *Su único hijo,* was similar in theme and plot to *La Regenta,* and it was similarly received by readers and reviewers. Despite his increasing involvement with fiction writing, Alas continued to produce a regular column of literary criticism in the Spanish press, and for the rest of his life he was one of the most influential, if controversial, literary critics of his time. His own fiction was almost always unfavorably reviewed, when it received contemporary attention at all—possibly, some commentators speculate, because critics were not disposed to treat gently a writer so prone to attacking the literary efforts of others—and in 1895 his social drama *Teresa* was poorly received. After suffering ill health for several years, Alas died at the age of forty-nine.

1

Noël M. Valis has called *La Regenta* "an extremely detailed and dense portrait of moral and social decadence on the collective and individual level." The novel tells the story of the young wife of an elderly retired Vetusta city official. She is the "regenta" of the title. Bored in the provincial outpost and neglected by her disinterested husband, she vacillates between religious devotion, encouraged by her confessor, and sexual fulfilment, offered by a local Don Juan. She eventually takes a lover; when her infidelity is revealed, her husband challenges the lover to a duel and is killed. The lover flees, and the regenta is made an outcast by members of a community equally guilty of unrevealed moral and social transgressions. Alas ruthlessly exposed the hypocrisy of the Vetustans, and almost as savagely lampooned ineffectual romantics who daydream that their lives resemble those of exciting fictional characters. At the novel's publication, Galdós called Alas a novelist of the first order. Most critics, however, reacted negatively, and Alas was even charged with plagiarism, since the novel so closely resembles Flaubert's *Madame Bovary.* More favorable assessments of *La Regenta* have predominated since the mid-twentieth century, and critics within Spain and abroad have come to regard the novel as an important developmental work in Spanish literature. It is among the first and best novels to eschew the romanticism and sentimentality of much earlier nineteenth-century fiction and to employ modern literary techniques, one of which, John Rutherford has noted, Alas especially commended in the works of Flaubert and Zola: "replacing the observations which the author often makes in his own voice about a character's situation by the character's own observations, using the latter's style—not, however, in the manner of a monologue, but as if the author were inside the character, and the novel were being created inside the character's brain." *La Regenta* has further been considered a fascinating social document valuable for its wealth of realistic detail about everyday life in Spanish society of the time.

La Regenta is the fictional work that is most fully informed by Alas's impatience with and desire to reform religious and moral hypocrisy and social decadence. In subsequent novels Alas tempered his implicit social criticism with more sympathetic depictions of character and situation. *Su único hijo,* for example, though similar in plot and theme to *La Regenta,* contains less satire and more neutral observation of the social situations that it portrays, while *Superchería* and *Doña Berta* explore the motivations of weak, self-deluding, and dishonest characters rather than merely describing and condemning their behavior.

Although he was enormously influential as a critic during his lifetime, more recent assessments of Alas have concluded that his criticism was too partial and too dogmatic to be considered truly great. Furthermore, in praising the best and most popular writers of his era, Alas was not breaking new critical ground. Nevertheless, his widely read commentaries on contemporary literature helped keep Spain's finest novelists before the reading public, and his place in world literature is secured by one extraordinary work: the novel *La Regenta.* As Raymond Carr has written: "If the limited oeuvre of Alas (he is essentially a man of two novels and a mountain of literary criticism) denies him the rank in Iberian fiction of Galdós . . . , *La Regenta* is the greatest single novel in modern Spanish literature."

(See also *Contemporary Authors,* Vol. 113.)

PRINCIPAL WORKS

Pipá (novel) 1879
Solos de Clarín (criticism) 1881

La literature en 1881 [with Aramando Palacio Valdés] (criticism) 1882
La Regenta. 2 vols. (novel) 1884-85
   [*La Regenta,* 1984]
Pipá (short stories and novel) 1886
Nueva campaña (criticism) 1887
Folletos literarios (criticism) 1888
Benito Pérez Galdós (biography) 1889
Insolacíon (novel) 1889
Su único hijo (novel) 1890
Cuesta abajo (novel) 1890-91
Doña Berta. Cuervo. Superchería. (novels) 1892
Ensayos y revistas (criticism) 1892
El señor y lo demás, son cuentos (short stories) 1892
Teresa (drama) [first publication] 1895
Cuentos morales (short stories) 1896
El gallo de Sócrates (short stories) 1901
Obras completas. 4 vols. (essays, criticism, short stories, and novels) 1913-29

Translations of Alas's short stories have appeared in the following anthologies: *Retold in English* (1905), *Short Stories from the Spanish* (1920), *Spanish Stories and Tales* (1954), and *Great Spanish Short Stories* (1956).

ROBERT AVRETT (essay date 1924)

[*Avrett is an American poet, educator, and critic. In the following excerpt, he discusses Alas's satirical attacks on the Catholic church and Spanish society in* La Regenta *and* Su único hijo.]

Although Leopoldo Alas, better known by his pseudonym of "Clarín," produced but two full-length novels, seldom has an author become the center of such heated controversy as was occasioned by the publication of *La Regenta* and *Su único hijo.* Clarín was admittedly a champion of naturalism in the novel, and he possessed to a remarkable degree the gift of satiric delineation of people, places, and institutions. (p. 223)

The naturalistic treatment of fiction lends itself readily to satire in all phases, from subtle irony to bluntly powerful sarcasm; and both novels of Alas, particularly *La Regenta,* fell strongly under the influence of naturalism. An examination of certain manifestations of Clarín's use of satire should prove illuminating, as indicative of the characteristics so bitterly attacked by his enemies and as stoutly defended by the admirers of the novelist.

La Regenta offers a comprehensive and intimate view of the lives of the principal persons in a Spanish provincial city (Oviedo, thinly disguised under the name of Vetusta); but the study extends much farther. The Church, or certain individuals in it, is made the target of devastating satire, along with the foibles and hypocrisies of society. The novelist exposes shams, intolerance, and injustice in the traditional naturalistic manner; but he drags in no obvious moral to hold up before his readers. Clarin is no soap-box reformer, but a searching analyst of the social structure of his times. (p. 224)

Since Vetusta lies literally and metaphorically in the shadow of the cathedral, it is inevitable that Clarín should treat of the ecclesiastical family; and with the single exception of the vacillating but kindly Bishop Camoirán, an appealing and at the same time a pitiable figure, the various clerics come in for caustic treatment. Scheming, jealous, ambitious of worldly preferment, fond of racy gossip, vindictive or domineering, each cathedral functionary is placed in an unfavorable light by the novelist. . . . Perhaps it may be going a trifle far to classify the purpose of Leopoldo Alas as definitely "anticlerical," but it is certain that the Church regarded the trenchant novelist as inimical.

With his major characters, Clarín is more deliberate and less sententious; because of their complexities of character and the number of events in which they figure, it is necessary to build up characterization more slowly and more subtly than in the case of lesser persons. But satiric elements are not lacking, although they may be less obviously elaborated.

Consider, for example, the Magistral Don Fermín de Pas, who holds the spiritual direction of Vetusta in the hollow of his hand, due to the dominant influence he exercises over the pious but weak-willed Bishop Camoirán. Don Fermín possesses tremendous vitality and great executive ability, but the priest's potential usefulness as a spiritual leader is largely nullified by the passions of the man. He craves power; consequently he misuses his position to enrich himself, and the fact that his mother, Doña Paula, drives him on unceasingly can serve as scant extenuation for his simony. The Magistral loves Ana Ozores, a married woman; and in order to spy upon her more effectively, Don Fermín does not hesitate to seduce her maid. In the delineation of the Magistral, Clarín presents the tragic irony of a strong character slowly destroying himself, together with the woman he loves, through the very strength of will that might have proved the salvation of both.

Ana Ozores, the Regenta, who wavers uncertainly between the spirit and the flesh, as personified respectively by the Magistral and Don Álvaro Mesía, may be termed a prototype of thwarted emotionalism. Orphaned at an early age, she is thrown upon the support of her two spinster aunts, who value her beauty merely as an aid toward marrying her off to a rich man. All her life Ana has yearned for a mother; and when she marries Don Victor Quintanar, a very respectable magistrate who is many years her senior, she is denied the motherhood which she feels would have appeased somewhat her own longing for maternal affection. The elderly Don Victor is kindly and generous, but certainly not the husband for a young girl of Ana's volatile and introspective temperament. Here again enters the incisive irony of Clarín: the husband who should have stabilized the malleable, emotional Ana is the unsuspecting cause of her partly mystical, partly physical infatuation with the Magistral, and of her final acceptance of the libertine, Don Álvaro, as a lover. (pp. 225-26)

The character of Don Victor throughout the novel is developed with satiric sureness, even though the man serves principally as a foil necessary to the formation of the tragic quadrangle composed of himself, Ana, the Magistral, and Don Álvaro Mesía. The portrayal of Don Victor presents a study in unconscious futility, and perhaps the reader comes nearer to sympathizing with him than with any other character in the novel. Quintanar's absolute faith in Ana and his pride in the company of Don Álvaro, the man who betrays him, afford an excellent opportunity for ironic treatment of the whole sordid complication. Don Victor has been a lifelong admirer of the drama of Calderón, but in the crisis of his own life the *ex-regente* is incapable of taking a truly Calderonian vengeance. For the first time the deceived husband realizes the immeasurable gulf that separates tragedy in real life from tragedy on the stage. (p. 227)

With the publication of *Su único hijo* in 1890, it was apparent at once that Leopoldo Alas had changed somewhat his outlook on life and his approach to the delineation of character in the novel. Although satire is abundant in the work, it is a softened, more kindly technique of satiric expression than that employed in *La Regenta*. Cutting sarcasm is almost entirely absent in *Su único hijo*, and naturalistic satirical censure has been softened in many cases to merely ironical appraisal of situation and character. Clarín holds in check his mordant wit, and characterization is developed with less of the impersonal incisiveness that is so noticeable in the two volumes of the earlier novel.

Bonifacio Reyes (called "Bonis" by his intimates) is the protagonist of *Su único hijo*, and he cuts a sorry figure in the beginning. He is a meek individual who long ago has been made to realize that his sole claim to importance lies in the fact that he has married the heiress Emma Valcárcel. Neglected by his shrewish wife and her family, and often treated with open contempt, Reyes finds solace in playing the flute and in daydreams of romance woven around himself as the hero. (pp. 227-28)

Bonis, torn between his passion for the singer Serafina and what he considers his duty toward his wife, toys with the intriguingly nebulous idea of renouncing the world and becoming a saint. (p. 228)

Occasionally a more robust satiric gibe, reminiscent of the scathing treatment applied to the *cursi* social element in *La Regenta*, finds expression in *Su único hijo*. Such a thrust is contained in the description of the method used by the German Koerner to gain the respect of his *montañés* associates. He wins acclaim by the simple expedient of eating at one sitting two dozen fried eggs, topped off by two seabream! Thus the redoubtable Koerner proves his superiority over a Spanish adversary, who is forced to stop with his eighteenth egg.

The character of Emma is a queerly jumbled composite of tyranny, vindictiveness, and sensuality—three traits that are used by the novelist to involve her in situations developed with frequent touches of irony. It is his wife's tyranny that drives Bonifacio to the arms of Serafina in the first place; and Emma's vindictiveness toward her uncle, who is mismanaging her property to his own advantage, takes the ironically illogical course of trying to squander the remainder of her fortune before her uncle can get possession of it. And the morbid sensuality with which she seems obsessed, quite as much as the desire to punish Bonis for his infidelity, involves her in a liaison with the baritone Minghetti. A certain satiric humor lies in the superstitious terror of Emma preceding the birth of her son, for she had accepted a lover with the comforting conviction that it was physically impossible for her to bear a child.

There is a trace of bitter irony in the fact that the son of Bonifacio has dreamed of and longed for comes to him under a cloud of general suspicion as to paternity, but the irony is elevated into something approaching sublimity by the persistent faith of Reyes that his son *is* his son. This belief is the one plank of salvation upon which Bonis resolutely stands. Perhaps this obstinate conviction is meant by Clarín as the crowning stroke of satire in the delineation of his protagonist; but it serves, nevertheless, to ennoble the character of Bonifacio Reyes. From a pitiable, timid weakling of negative personality, he has developed at last into a man worthy of respect.

Whether Leopoldo Alas may come generally to be considered one of Spain's great novelists is still a debatable point, for it is difficult for critics to appraise without bias the reputation of a man who has left behind him so small a novelistic production. (pp. 228-29)

Regardless of his ultimate place in the field of the Spanish novel, there can be no question of the mastery of Alas in the satirical presentation of places, customs, and people, whatever their station in life. Social satire is always a dangerous pathway to literary immortality, because institutions, uses, and abuses change from one period to another, carrying in these very changes the possibility that any given perspective may appear distorted when viewed by observers of later times. Assuredly, however, Clarín's gift of satire in varying nuances stands alone among the novelists of the naturalistic school in his own country. (pp. 229-30)

Robert Avrett, "The Treatment of Satire in the Novels of Leopoldo Alas (Clarín)," in Hispania, *Vol. XXIV, No. 2, May, 1924, pp. 223-30.*

WILLIAM E. BULL (essay date 1942)

[*Bull was an American educator and critic. In the following excerpt, he examines Alas's changing view of the theories, techniques, and underlying philosophy of literary Naturalism throughout his career.*]

One of the most interesting chapters in the literary career of Leopoldo Alas (Clarín) deals with his advocacy of naturalism and the creation and defense of his most famous original work, *La Regenta.* Early in his literary life Alas placed himself in the forefront of the Spanish followers of Emile Zola and for many years was one of the most vigorous advocates of naturalism in Spain. He came to the movement with abundant enthusiasm, defended it in many fiery polemics, but maintained throughout his life very definite reservations which reveal a Leopoldo Alas scarcely ever recognized by his contemporaries.

To his friends, and doubly so to his enemies, Clarín was a rash and tempestuous man who wielded his cutting pen in the vanguard of every literary innovation and who peered disdainfully with his myopic eyes at every conservative who crossed his path. Such opinions are always relative and depend on the point of view of the moment. Below the superficial aspects of his character and writings Alas was a somewhat different, if not totally distinct, person.

As early as 1876, when he seemed but little short of bearding the devil and was horrifying his father's conservative political friends and the much shocked clergy, he outlined in brief his philosophical *Weltanschauung,* which, if carefully analyzed, reveals a very serious and none too radical young man. He admonished the youth of the nation to pause in their headlong flight after new and dubious knowledge and to look back to see whether or not they were not losing something infinitely more valuable. He revealed a fundamental attitude characteristic of him throughout his life—and vague distrust of science and an essentially conservative philosophical outlook. (p. 536)

[Alas's writings] outline two of the reservations which Alas brought to the acceptance of naturalism. His doubts about positivism had their roots in his lack of knowledge of science, and as he grew older the doubt and the lack complemented each other. His lack of scientific knowledge led him to accept, partially at least, the vulgar notion of evolution.... Even while he conceded, when the *cuestión palpitante* ["burning question"] had him much on the defensive, that the Darwinian *Bible* was a book of much recondite "piety" and that man's

greatness might have its origin in the animal, he pointed to the noumenalogical possibilities as an alternative explanation.

In discussing Alas's attitudes toward naturalism it must be kept in mind that he never was, in the most latitudinous concept of the term, a man of science. In his university lectures he revealed no scientific preparation nor interest and in his private conversation he often ridiculed scientific endeavors. It pleased his fancy to call the work of the sociologists the "tortilla sociológica" ["sociological omlette"], and in his writings he fought the introduction of the sciences into the school system. Utilitarian subjects, he branded them, that ought not usurp the time devoted to the humanities. Such an attitude naturally fed his latent fear that science might destroy what he considered the ineffable values of civilization, and it kept alive and made more definite his opposition to positivism.

Whatever Alas's attitude toward naturalism was to be, it never in the slightest sense indicated his acceptance of any of the positivistic doctrines of the naturalists. The world of phenomena was never enough for him; noumena must exist in reality and, so, in art. Metaphysics, in its most exact Greek sense, must be considered a reality. In 1876, as we have seen, he feared that positivism was going to become general, and in 1880 the publication of Zola's *Le Roman Expérimental* elicited outright opposition to positivism. (pp. 537-38)

For Alas positivism only indicated a poverty of invention, a weakness of the faculties, and a censurable atrophy in those who subscribed to it, and he attacked it with vigor even at the height of his defense of naturalism.... The very thought of positivism made him sad and its influence was so great, in his sight, that he attributed the literary decadence of the 80's to it, and in 1901 he felt that it was gnawing at the very vitals of the people. (p. 538)

It is not at all surprising, in view of this evidence, that Alas never accepted the definition of naturalism in the French sense in so far as it included positivistic doctrine and that he declared, in his celebrated introduction to *La cuestión palpitante* of Pardo Bazán, that naturalism did not follow the procedural or experimental technique of Claude Bernard and that real naturalism did not follow Zola's systematic ideas on this score.... Alas's rejection of the positivistic aspects of naturalism clearly indicates that from the very beginning he imposed on the word *naturalism* a meaning that did not coincide with the definition of the term current at that time.

The meaning of the term was further changed in the mind of Alas by another reservation. By inheritance Alas was a Catholic, by disposition and personal inclination profoundly religious, and by preference a traditionalist. As might be expected with such a combination, the dogma of the church raised ideological barriers which made it necessary for him to reject scientific determinism and to hold to the doctrine of free will.

His attitude toward scientific determinism reveals a most complex state of mind. There is a wide gap between a superficial intellectual acceptance of certain aspects of determinism and the full appropriation of the whole theory. Alas never went beyond the first stage. In consonance with his syncretic attitude toward life he attempted to harmonize free will and determinism, and the false verbal harmony which he created led some to believe that he accepted the philosophic aspects of determinism. He attempted to create harmony where none existed. Really, he only departmentalized, and what might pass for determinism in his writings must only be considered the acceptance of the idea that environment stimulates persons to do certain things without actually determining that they shall do them. (pp. 538-39)

Sometimes Alas talked in the language of scientific determinism—he even explained social phenomena with its terms—but he always made the important reservation that the power of free will could overcome the circumstances which seemed to make actions inevitable. In this case his lack of scientific knowledge again played him false, for in his opposition to the theories of evolution and heredity he was willing to carry the doctrine of free will so far that he maintained that hereditary tendencies can be overcome. . . .

When Alas talked of actions being "inevitable" or being caused by the "forces of society" he did not at all mean to imply the same connotation given these words by the scientific determinist. It must always be remembered that the terminology of determinism had long been in use without the meanings given it by this scientific theory. Alas used the modern terminology with the old acceptations. In his discussion of Galdós's *El abuelo* and the problem of biological determinism and heredity he made a very open declaration of much importance in estimating his adherence to naturalism. He divorced himself quite completely from the determinists and, in consequence, from the fundamental philosophy of naturalism. (p. 540)

Since Alas, like Pardo Bazán, has been hailed as one of Spain's greatest naturalists and since **La Regenta** has been called "the leading example in Spain of naturalistic writing after the French Formula," it is important to observe how he deals with free will in his novel.

In contrast with the technique used by the French determinists, La Regenta, herself, frequently chooses a course of action which runs counter to fundamental urges. At fourteen, between a strong affection for her father and certain religious ideals she chooses the latter although one might expect a child starved for affection to accept the father in preference to vague abstractions. After the death of her father, when she has been physically and mentally ill, she is motivated to get well, even against her own inclinations, by the complaints of her aunts which she has accidentally overheard. . . . A chance conversation is made responsible for changes which the strict naturalist would have dealt with in detail and in which he would have implied some biological as well as psychological sources of stimuli.

Later, as a grown woman who is sexually starved, La Regenta is presented from the point of view of the non-deterministic psychologist. She is famous in Vetusta for her glacial attitude toward men in general, but as she is sexually frustrated Alas is required to provide elaborate motivations quite apart from her physical nature in order to explain her outward and inward attraction to Quintanar, Fermín de Pas, and Alvaro. Being a believer in free will Alas cannot allow the reader to suppose that, granted a certain character and a certain environment, certain actions will follow. Consequently Ana's attraction for Alvaro develops only after his long and carefully prepared siege forces him upon her. The voluptuous Ana, who lolls in her bed and plays with a tiger skin in an attempt to satisfy vicariously her basically animalistic desires, is not presented as being naturally attracted to Alvaro; and toward all other men she is cold. Yet this Spanish Nana, who is revealed in the manner of the stream of consciousness novel for hundreds of pages, exhibits no secret flutterings, no inward attractions for the opposite sex in general. Her biological urges are allowed to function only when Alas provides other specious motivation

for their expression. The possibility of activity which is not motivated directly by the author and which might have its origin in unstated deterministic impulses does not appear as a major factor in presenting her character. Consequently La Regenta is elaborately motivated to choose among alternatives—Quintanar and sexual starvation, sublimation in the Church, Alvaro and fulfillment—and many pages are devoted to describing the agony she goes through attempting to make that choice.

Alas, as a free-will psychologist, is more interested in depicting the choosing than he is in revealing the motivation for action provided by the stimulus of sexual frustration. The determinist would make Ana's actions appear inevitable, but Alas, since he does not believe that a naturally voluptuous and sexually starved woman will be seduced at the first propitious moment, finds it extremely interesting to spend more than half the novel keeping the reader in suspense about an action which is clearly anticipated some five hundred pages before it takes place.

The dénouement of the novel likewise indicates that Alas was not depicting his characters from the point of view of the determinist. It is brought about by fortuitous circumstances provided by the author and not by the direct actions of the main characters. Ana's maid, Petra, having secret ambitions of gaining a fine marriage through the influence of Fermín de Pas, who has seduced her, finds it to her personal advantage to inform de Pas of the clandestine meetings of Ana and Alvaro, and agrees, for the proper consideration, to force the crisis. This action serves as the means of bringing the story to an end. Petra sets Quintanar's alarm clock ahead; the latter gets up too early, catches Alvaro coming out of Ana's bedroom, and the whole affair is brought out into the open. The duel results, Quintanar is killed, Alvaro flees in a cowardly manner, and La Regenta is ruined and punished.

The catastrophe is brought about only by the indirect action of the main characters. They do not force the crisis by their actions; the crisis is forced upon them by an accident built up by the author. There is nothing inevitable in the dénouement; determinism plays no rôle at all. The hundreds of pages devoted to the actions of the main characters do not lead directly to the catastrophe that has been announced again and again; they lead only to the fortuitous solution made necessary by Alas's rejection of determinism.

The foregoing pages have demonstrated that Alas never believed in the basic philosophical tenets of French naturalism and especially the brand advocated by Zola. The "naturalism" which he proposed for Spain and which he followed in **La Regenta** differed from the French species in the one main essential which separates naturalism from realism. Alas's naturalism omitted scientific determinism and so differed from realism only in a matter of degree and technique.

Zola advocated what might be legitimately called a philosophy of novel writing; Alas admitted only in part the technique with which Zola put that philosophy into practice. (pp. 540-42)

Spanish naturalism, as Alas saw it, was to imitate French naturalism only in subject-matter and technique. There were still more reservations. The subject-matter had to be picked with a moral aim. . . . Alas's religious and philosophical preoccupations caused him to miss the point in the moral aim of Zola. Both Galdós and Alas believed in free will and they aimed to work on the individuals responsible for their own moral degeneracy. Zola never intended to change the individuals he wrote about by holding a mirror to their faces. He wrote his books for those powerful enough to bring about social change, and he hoped that they, seeing the degeneracy of the people about them, would do something to change the environmental conditions which cause that degeneracy. Alas distorted the aims of Zola, the determinist, to fit his own, those of a believer in free will. Zola sought to improve the environment; Alas aimed to improve the man.

This fundamental attitude explains a great deal of the critical aspects of **La Regenta**. *Nana, L'Assommoir, Germinal* and *La Débâcle* stress that there is much to be done before the world is improved and man made better. In **La Regenta** Alas does not present such a vast problem. He is dealing with a man of free will, a man (so much smaller than a world) whom one can reform, as Alas believed, by muck-raking his failures, publicizing his pecadillos. The characters of **La Regenta** are not individuals led to sin by society. In the novel and in Alas's mind the ills of society are represented as typified by certain individuals, people who make the world what it is, not the reverse, and people who should be condemned, censured, and held up to the public eye in hope of their changing their ways thereby. Alas aimed to reform certain types of characters and thus to improve society.... [It has been thought] that **La Regenta** might be more legitimately classified among the novels and plays of manners which aim to point out human foibles and to correct them by satire and by publicity.

This is in striking contrast with the philosophy behind Zola's naturalistic novels. As a scientific determinist Zola goes much deeper in his analysis. Socially undesirable types arise from profound environmental influences which include heredity. You cannot reform *them*, you must change the world so that it cannot produce them. One is back to the fundamental difference between Alas and Zola, and Zola, who takes a broader scientific view, presents a more pessimistic picture. For Alas a little crusading will change man; for Zola a world revolution is required. One might say that Alas would advocate preaching and jail terms for slum youths who had gone wrong; Zola would advocate slum clearance, health programs, vocational guidance, NYA, and paroles. Alas, being a believer in free will, would treat the man; Zola would eliminate the necessity of such treatment.

Alas's jubilancy over Galdós's *La desheredada* might indicate that in addition to his approval of the moral aim he also accepted the naturalist's notion that the novel should deal with life in all its details. Here again Alas brought further reservations to his acceptance of naturalism.

When the question of naturalism in Spain had gained enough importance to elicit from Pardo Bazán her famous *La cuestión palpitante*, Alas furnished an introduction in which he presented his longest and most formal defense of naturalism. After first complaining that the whole notion of naturalism had become vulgarized in Spain he began a series of negative definitions of naturalism headed by the statement that naturalism is not the imitation of whatever is repugnant to the senses. In practice and in his criticism Alas never went beyond the limits set by the realists. He became incensed over Alarcón's *Niño de la bola* and especially the actions of Soledad who was willing to commit adultery to satisfy her lover and who had married rather than become a nun since the bonds of matrimony may be disregarded more lightly than those of a nun. Alas complained indignantly about this depiction of moral degeneracy.... (pp. 543-45)

Alas's concept of realistic description never included anything that might offend a lady who did not use her imagination too

much. He maintained that naturalism was not the constant repetition of descriptions of ugly, vile, and miserable things. In practice he eliminated direct reference to anything capable of being labeled by these adjectives. (p. 545)

Alas's approach to slightly taboo subjects was always done by suggestion, and this technique frequently makes **La Regenta** appear a less wholesome book than the most explicit ones of the French naturalists. Alas was very squeamish about frank language and developed what might be called a euphemistic substitute for realism of language. (pp. 545-46)

Alas's reticence about dealing with certain subjects apparently prevents him from narrating (his favorite technique when he is afraid of outright description) either the seduction of Ana's maid by Fermín de Pas or the seduction of Ana by Alvaro. One does not learn that the latter major episode has taken place until some time after the actual event.... How roundabout this is in contrast with the direct method of Zola!

When Alas could bring himself to use realistic terms he frequently qualified them as bad and intruded himself into the narration in order to put the blame outright on the person using them.... **La Regenta** is full of such author criticism and condemnation of the language used by his own characters. Obviously Alas tried to hold fast to his statement that naturalism did not deal with unpleasant things, and when he was forced to be realistic he wanted the reader to be certain that he, the author, did not approve of such language. His preaching to the sin-type is made more evident by this technique.

Another contrast between Alas's method and that of the French shows up sharply in his description of La Regenta's illness in Chapter XIX of Volume II. There is no real description of Ana while she is sick. This treatment should be contrasted with the description of the death of Nana and Madame Bovary in which no detail is overlooked. Alas's very slight treatment of this subject shows how really different his technique is from that of the naturalists.

Only two of the negative definitions which Alas propounded in his introduction to *La cuestión palpitante* do not conflict with the French concept of naturalism. He announced that naturalism is not a closed doctrine which rejects other literary forms and that it is not a group of recipes for writing novels.

We shall not be exaggerating if we say that Alas defined away the very naturalism he was supposed to be defending in his introduction to *La cuestión palpitante*. Had he given up the term entirely and called *La desheredada*, for example, merely a realistic novel based on modern patterns, and had he called Pardo Bazán and himself realists, Spain's battle of the century would not have taken place.

The opponents of naturalism in Spain were attacking a theory based on positivism and scientific determinism. Pardo Bazán and Alas, especially the latter, denounced the same beliefs, but because they insisted on calling themselves naturalists and because they insisted on attacking those who denounced the very thing they themselves refused to accept they found themselves in the position of having to defend what most people already accepted in Galdós under the label of realism. The battle, once clear definitions are worked out, appears to have been only over terminology.

Since Alas's definition of naturalism stripped it of the characteristics which gave it separate identity, there is left the problem of determining what he called "naturalism" in his writings. His naturalism included a realistic approach, with reservations, to the depiction of life, more psychological study of motivations of characters than was common in Spain, some emphasis on details of human activities, but not on sounds, smells, objects, etc. which motivate those activities, a slightly more accurate imitation of the language of the people talking and a theoretical adherence to the experimentalist's technique in observation and recording. Thus when Alas applied the term *naturalism* to works of his contemporaries we must interpret it as meaning only some sort of modern realism for him.

For several years, however, he continued to identify more or less his brand of ''naturalism'' with the French without clearly realizing that his numerous reservations effectively put him outside the movement. In 1885, he declared, there were few Spaniards who understood naturalism. . . . But his own observation was indeed vague since he had not clearly explained what his concept of naturalism was. (pp. 546-58)

In the intervening four years [after 1889] his critical writings reveal a man groping in an attempt to concretize and verbalize his intuitive realization that he was really not so much in favor of naturalism as his previous utterances might have indicated. In 1885 he was still defending the term without giving it an explicit definition, but he showed by implication that he was not thinking of French naturalism. . . . The following year Alas could not give a clear notion of what he was talking about when he dealt with naturalism, and by 1887 he was openly attacking the Spanish ''naturalists.'' He took up the cudgels for *Amores de una santa* of Campoamor against the naturalists, and Zorrilla's *Cantar del Romero* provided him with another text to be read to them as an attack on their materialistic outlook. (p. 548)

The year of *Insolación* (1889) marks the awakening of Alas in his attitude toward naturalism. For the first time he clearly observed that Spanish ''naturalism'' had nothing much to do with French naturalism and that his articles were attempting to introduce the Spaniards to new ''aspiraciones literarias,'' especially a sort of neo-idealism. At the same time he seriously began to question Zola's scientific method and declared that it prejudiced Zola and interfered with his art. He denied that naturalism was dead in Spain but felt that there were new tendencies which were more legitimate and more opportune and that these should be cultivated without giving naturalism up completely.

By 1890 Alas was looking at his former naturalism as a sort of ''naturalistic measles'' from which he had suffered and he was then capable of considering *La cuestión palpitante,* which he once so vigorously championed, a superficial work, somewhat indelicate and vulgar. He had begun to use realist and naturalist interchangeably and put himself, Pereda, Galdós, Pardo Bazán, and Palacio Valdés in the group which he called ''realistas o naturalistas españoles.'' In 1891, when the second edition of *Solos de Clarín* came out, he carefully explained that his ideas had changed on the subject considerably in the intervening ten years. At this time Alas had reached what might be considered his most mature stage in his analysis of naturalism. What was unconsciously in his mind in the days of his violent defense of the movement had now become conscious and he verbalized it with considerable facility and accuracy. . . . Alas now turned to the new psychological, somewhat symbolical and sentimental novel which the reaction to naturalism was beginning to bring forth. He was happy to see that Galdós was moving into the new current and was beginning to deal with transcendental problems, ethics and religion.

Alas never gave up his position that naturalism (by now we should substitute realism) brought something worth while to the novel, a new technique, closer observation of the world in some respects, more accurate description, and all those things which we have come to consider part of realism and which were lacking in the romantic novels of the earlier years of the nineteenth century, but spiritually he moved farther and farther away from naturalism and even realism. (pp. 549-50)

[By 1901 the] fire of youth was ebbing from Leopoldo Alas and he was seeking no longer the harsh, sharp contrasts of the world; instead he was viewing it more and more from his basic metaphysical and traditional outlook. The reality of life was fast becoming something of the ''great beyond,'' literally and in the mystic sense that ultimate reality is found only in philosophic speculation. The forces that always kept Alas from accepting naturalism were becoming more dominant than ever and he was seeking a charm, an ease, and a sweet contentment that would make the days of a prematurely old, sick man more happy. . . . The doubts of youth had vanished, the syncretist's desire to harmonize conflicting beliefs had disappeared. There remained only one way of life. All others had been cast aside, and Alas was looking for a peaceful, quiet, untroubled world of nature which would provide a comfortable place to lay a head weary from many battles. (pp. 550-51)

> William E. Bull, ''The Naturalistic Theories of Leopoldo Alas,'' in *PMLA, Vol. LVII, No. 2, June, 1942, pp. 536-51.*

ALBERT BRENT (essay date 1951)

[*In the following excerpt, Brent examines Alas's eclectic use of different literary styles and theories of his day and discusses Alas's application of his literary theories to the novel* La Regenta.]

Regional literature is an outgrowth of the Romantic movement with its interest in national life and spirit manifested in popular types, customs, and local color. In Spain, where the historical novel was unsuccessful because of the Spaniard's inability to view his past objectively, as something detached from his present, the regional novel arose as a substantial substitute. The notion of time, as expressed by the historical novel in England, was, in Spain, transmuted into the notion of space. For the Spaniard, not interested in the past unless experienced as the present, the spatial depiction of contemporary life, broken up into different sections, was vital and significant. In other countries, regional literature has a less pronounced character. Outside of Spain, the regional writer tends to view his subject more or less objectively; the Spanish writer, on the other hand, usually identifies or relates himself in a personal way to his material. (p. 102)

Alas the student, the scholar, and the man of letters is everywhere present in [*La Regenta*] . . . as attested by its predominantly ''literary'' character. Books and literature are made to occupy an important place in the lives of many of the characters. They are the source of not a few of their ideas, topics of conversation, and ways of acting. In one case, they are the principal motivating force in the person's existence. A study of the style reveals, in addition, an extraordinary number of miscellaneous literary references and allusions which permeate the work, a great many of them appearing as figures of speech. The particular attention given to certain literary themes, such as that of Don Juan, confirms the knowledge that is had of the author's readings and literary preferences. Alas the literary critic is also in evidence in the criticism of certain works the characters read and of what they write. The cultural nature of the work, as it relates to the author, is further manifested by the many references to art and music.

In its presentation of the cultural, moral, and religious aspects of provincial society, *La Regenta* reveals much about its creator which is confirmed by the known facts of his life. His dominantly critico-satirical nature finds full expression in the analysis that he makes of the cultural and intellectual life of this society, whose members are shown by their speech, dress, manners, houses, customs, interests, and topics of conversation to be generally superficial, ignorant, and stupid. The important place given to the subjects of morality and religion, predominant over all other themes, is in keeping with Alas' life-long attraction to, and preoccupation with, these questions and with the moral, philosophical, and didactic intent which is the chief characteristic of all his writings. The most interesting manifestation, however, of the author's relation to his work, one which is presented in part as an hypothesis, is that demonstrated by the sardonic and censorious treatment of his material. In the severity of the judgment which is passed upon the intellectual and moral character of provincial society may be seen his inability or failure to locate himself normally in it. Furthermore, in the frustrated existence of his characters is undoubtedly reflected the major emotional problems of his own life. One might almost say that *La Regenta* came into being as the result of the conflict that existed between the author and the world about him. The antipathy and the resentment which Alas evinced toward his society, arising out of certain frustrations, was directed by him into creative efforts and converted into something affirmative and valuable, namely, a work of art. As Azorín has observed, an interesting relationship may be seen between the form and structure of the novel and the character of the author at this period of his life. *La Regenta* was Alas' first novelistic attempt and one of which he was exceedingly proud. As noted earlier, it had been originally contemplated as a much shorter work. As a critic, he considered diffuseness a defect in the novel of his time. Yet the idea of producing something big, important, and on a large scale doubtless attracted him as he wrote, and his novel came to acquire enormous proportions. Alas was always ambitious and his diffident nature craved recognition, particularly in the early stages of his career. But one feels that he attempted too much in his initial novelistic effort by trying to depict in so detailed a manner almost every aspect of provincial society. Splendid as it is, *La Regenta* frequently suffers from the lack of artistic unity. Certain themes introduced, such as the idea of heights associated with Fermín De Pas, are not sufficiently developed or carried through to completion as might have been done for the further enhancement of the work. The novel is crowded to overflowing with people, places, things, and ideas (much of it the ebullience of the author's erudition) which, while fascinating, are sometimes cloying and detract considerably from the forcefulness and dramatic effect of the major themes and figures. Nor can this be explained as due entirely to the influences of naturalistic techniques and methods under which Alas worked at this period, for it may be said to be characteristic to a certain degree of almost all his writing.

On the whole, *La Regenta* exemplifies very well its author's conception of what the contemporary novel should be. . . . It draws its materials from real life and, while remaining wholly within the artistic sphere, deals with a multiplicity of questions and problems of contemporary life as its author experienced them. One of those receiving major treatment in *La Regenta* is clericalism. In brief, the novel may be regarded as an un-

folding and an analysis of all the various elements contributing to the general cultural backwardness, the bigotry, and the low moral tone of provincial society around the middle of the nineteenth century. Although he sees in the novel an excellent vehicle for social and cultural reform, he is almost never explicitly didactic and succeeds admirably in conveying his ideas and feelings artistically. In this respect, he is much less *tendencioso* than was Galdós in the corresponding period of his novelistic career.

Throughout his literary life, Alas showed himself to be an eclectic, taking from each of the various literary movements and tendencies through which he lived whatever he thought to be worthwhile and adaptable to his own purposes and concept of art. *La Regenta,* of course, is the principal product of the so-called ''naturalistic period'' of his career. It is generally referred to in literary manuals as ''the most naturalistic novel in Spanish literature.'' Exactly what is meant by that designation is open to question. If it is taken to mean that *La Regenta,* more than any other Spanish novel, is concerned with the moral degeneracy of a society (in this case manifested as adultery), in which its members are shown to a certain degree to be the victims of their milieu, then that qualification is probably true. There are a number of elements, however, that keep the novel from being categorized according to the generally accepted idea of a naturalistic work. In the first place, the esthetic and spiritual aspects of life are far from being excluded; in fact, they occupy a considerable part of the work. In those cases where the sensual element is emphasized, Alas never becomes sordid or resorts to indecorous language. Actually, in its treatment of risqué themes, *La Regenta* is only mildly scandalous at the side of the majority of French naturalistic works. Furthermore, Alas does not depict his society as wholly corrupt. The best example of this is Tomás Crespo, the botanist and close friend of the Quintanares, who, through his close contact with nature, lives untouched by the corrupting influences all about him. Alas' solution to the problems he presents would appear to be one in which the individual must be changed rather than his environment. Finally, the characters of *La Regenta* are far from being deterministically conceived. Fermín De Pas and Ana Ozores are persons who possess a will of their own and who exercise it in the working out of their destiny. While the influences of French naturalism went into the making of *La Regenta* to a large degree, as well as other influences mentioned elsewhere, Clarín's first and principal novelistic work stands as a very distinctive expression of its writer's personality and view of life. (pp. 102-04)

> *Albert Brent, in his* Leopoldo Alas and ''La Regenta'': A Study in Nineteenth Century Spanish Prose Fiction, *The Curators of the University of Missouri, 1951, 135 p.*

SHERMAN H. EOFF   (essay date 1961)

[*In the following excerpt, Eoff compares* La Regenta *and Gustave Flaubert's* Madame Bovary *(1857), maintaining that both are examples of modern literary Realism, but with differently developed plots: Alas emphasized the comical and farcical aspects of life in his novel as well as the wretchedness of the human condition primarily emphasized by Flaubert.*]

Choosing as a setting [for *La Regenta*] the city of Oviedo (giving it the fictional name of Vetusta), the author builds up an oppressive environment of mediocrity and places in its midst a sensitive and refined woman who longs for liberation and wants above all to be loved. In general outline, then, *La Re-*

genta plainly recalls *Madame Bovary,* and there is little question that Alas had Flaubert's novel in mind when he mapped the basic framework of his narrative. He was writing, however, at a time when the realistic technique was at its height in popularity, and he indulged in an elaborate use of detail and collateral material, showing a greater interest than Flaubert in the relationship between environment and personality. In other ways, too, he engaged in a more ambitious task than Flaubert had undertaken. For one thing, he was interested in painting on a grand scale the portrait of an urban society in a materialistic age, and the sharpness of his satirical mood indicates how strong a motivation his antipathies were. In a leisurely, deliberate manner he presents numerous personal sketches that emphasize the trivial interests of almost everyone, including the clerics. The attention given to the activities of the numerous minor personages is so great that the community itself appears at times to be the protagonist. . . . In a further ambitious move, Alas introduces a second major character, a priest, to share with the heroine the burden of the narrative development. The subjects of religion and love are in this way brought into specific relationship. The scope of *La Regenta* is therefore broader and the technique less concentrated and precise than we find in *Madame Bovary,* but the fundamental ideas in each novel center on essentially the same subject: the heaviness of the material world and the failure of love as a means of liberation.

As the narrative begins, the reader is introduced to Don Fermín de Pas, *magistral,* or "master," of the Cathedral of Vetusta and the most powerful ecclesiastic in the city. A man of great strength, both physical and intellectual, he has gained his influential position at the early age of thirty-five by dint of hard work and a grim determination to erase the unpleasantness of his poor and obscure peasant origin. His ambitious drive has been reinforced and in good part directed by a mother of iron will whose compensation for an insecure place in society has been even more fierce than that of her son. De Pas feels a proprietary pride in his ecclesiastic command of Vetusta, ancient city of noble and honored past, but the loneliness and lack of affection that darkened his childhood persist with an intensity that can be pacified only by a woman's love. Sexual satisfaction alone will not suffice; the servant Teresina is available for that. Nor can De Pas be interested in an ordinary woman of high society, such as the frolicsome widow Obdulia, who was "exaggeratedly endowed by nature with the attributes of her sex" and who throws herself at men acquaintances, priests and laymen alike. Rather, he scorns the commonplace, holds himself aloof from the gossipy, envious clerics around him, and aspires to a companionship that will allow him to realize his emotional self at the highest possible level. The opportunity for such a companionship arises when the aged Don Cayetano withdraws as the confessor of Ana Ozores and recommends De Pas as his replacement.

The characterization of De Pas is from the outset a solid psychological portraiture and an excellent example of modern realism that takes into account the relationship between personality and environment while observing fully the special features that make the person stand out as an individual. The author is less fortunate in the portrayal of his heroine, apparently because he is less able—possibly less inclined—to measure than to cauterize the ethereal nature of her aspirations. Nevertheless, he relies on the contrast between her idealistic impulses and her material medium as the basis for his story. Ana Ozores is an aristocratic person, beautiful, refined, of spotless reputation. Like De Pas, she suffers the effects of a lonely youth devoid of affection. For she had never known a mother and had been left for the greater part of her childhood in the care of a hostile governess, whose major contribution had been to impress on the child an indelible sense of guilt for having on one occasion unavoidably spent the night in a boat on a river with a boy of twelve when they were unable to make their way back to shore. In her lonely adolescent years she withdrew into herself and sometimes, in a feverish physical state, felt strange mystic longings that caused her more uneasiness than peace, confused as she was by thoughts of the sinfulness of sex and the relationship of love and beauty to the idea of God. Receiving little sympathy from her aunts, with whom she lived after her father's death, she drifted into marriage with the ex-judge, Don Victor Quintanar, an upright and kind person but some twenty-five years her senior, rather careless in his appearance, and more alert to details pertaining to hunting than to the emotional—and sexual—needs of his wife.

Married to a neglectful husband and having no child on whom to lavish affection, Ana is lonely and bored, oppressed by the gloom of the Vetusta climate, and unable to find anything in common with the trivial acquaintances in her social circle. As she had done in her childhood, she caresses the pillows of her bed, feeling voluptuous pleasure in the touch of cold sheets and soft rugs, and daring now and then to think of the physically attractive Don Alvaro Mesía, skilled Don Juan of Vetusta. But the sense of guilt resulting from the boat episode of her childhood weighs on her still, and she lives in constant restraint of her natural impulses. Though rebellious at times, she actually increases her self-discipline to the point of taking martyr's delight in it, determined to resist the threat to her soul, which "was beginning to become infested" with the perfume of love left by the proximity of Mesía. Torn thus between spontaneous emotional-physical demands and the necessity for moral restraint, she is especially amenable to the thought of converting carnal love into spiritual love under the direction of the *magistral*, De Pas.

As the author brings the two principal characters together, then, he has prepared the way for a relationship that could become a tense psychological experience centering on an attempted sublimation of human love. Both persons are suffering from the absence of love, both are oppressed by the mediocrity of their surroundings, and each sees in the other an opportunity to rise above the immediacy of their prosaic existence. Hence the personal relationship which the author places in the forefront points to a struggle on the part of two people to liberate themselves from the bondage of circumstances by way of a Platonic partnership. In Ana's case the conflict will be essentially an effort to divert the demands of erotic instinct into an abstract mystic channel with the aid of a priest who, because of his profession, causes her no temptation in a physical sense. In the case of De Pas, the conflict will be more complicated. For in his burning desire to make Ana his exclusive spiritual possession there is a strong carnal attraction which he has to suppress, not only in deference to his profession but in bitter concession to the fact that Ana is not interested in him as a lover and is, instead, physically attracted to Mesía, the Don Juan. Conspiring against both persons are numerous gossipy "friends," a low level of moral values, and above all a social atmosphere redolently suggestive of carnal love. In this way support from the outside is assured for the interference of the third party, Mesía; and before the prospects of this uneven contest the reader finds himself pulling for De Pas to win. The latter, at least, is a man of flesh and blood, a troubled soul of complex emotions; while Mesía is merely a hollow symbol embodying little more than sartorial correctness and pride in the conquest of women.

The lurking presence of the third party tends to convert a potential drama of character into a contest for the favors of a woman, whose designation of a winner soon assumes more plot interest than the resolution of psychological complications. Ana wavers between the two men somewhat like a feather tossed to and fro by the wind, aspiring under the priest's tutelage to a mystic refinement of love and regarding her sensuous impulses toward Mesía as temptations befitting a test of her ability to achieve her exalted aim. Unfortunately, she tends more to caress the temptation than to nourish the aim, and her honest efforts to curb her physical impulses repeatedly produce in her a psycho-physiological cycle that traces a predominantly physical path.

A brief summary of chapters 16 to 19, inclusive, will illustrate this cyclical process, which constitutes the author's "psychological" method. Lonely, oppressed by the gloomy weather, pondering the monotony of her existence, Ana is inclined to forget the careful coaching of the *magistral,* feeling, rather, the strong pull of nature toward a danger that religion has somehow seemed unable to cope with. When Mesía happens to pass her balcony one day on a fine white charger, she is more desirous than ever of enjoying life and justifies her mental waywardness in the light of her unhappy past and her boredom in Vetusta. Encouraged by her husband and Mesía, now a welcome visitor in the Quintanars' home, she attends a performance of Zorrilla's *Don Juan Tenorio,* which she watches with a sensuous delight faintly refined by mystic sentiments. As she thus nears entrapment by a calculating Don Juan who needs only a propitious occasion to claim his prey, her sensuous deviation is brusquely interrupted by her spiritual adviser. De Pas is angry with his protégée for having gone to the theater on All Saints' Day without his permission, but he controls himself and sets about patiently trying to win her back to a religious path. Ana dutifully follows his directions, even accompanying him in some of his charitable enterprises. But neither charity nor the recommended religious readings provide the "poetic" experience that she longs for, and, confused and frustrated, she ends up by falling ill. Her husband watches over her solicitously for a while but misinterprets, or disregards, the sexual import of her nervous state and leaves her to tearful reflection on the cruelty of a world without love. When after a relapse and a long illness she recovers she accedes again to the ministrations of De Pas, who continues to be a counterbalance to the routine of the drawing room and the attentions of Mesía.

The drama of stifled, sex-laden love, which is thus enacted in the heroine is really more of a situational than a psychological conflict. It is, in fact, a tug of war between two men for a woman, who acts as a kind of physiological barometer indicating the fluctuating influences of the rivals. The Ana-De Pas relationship reaches an idyllic peak in the summer following Ana's long illness. Continually the *magistral* has conducted himself with an excruciating self-discipline, curbing his rebelliousness at the domination of his mother, at the restrictions of his profession in general, and particularly at the necessity for refraining from open conflict with an insignificant rival, whom he could easily vanquish in either physical or intellectual combat. Now, for a short time during the summer, when both his mother and Mesía are out of the city, he enjoys the luxury of freedom at home and the pleasantness of a peaceful relationship with his spiritual partner. The happy situation, how-

ever, is sharply disturbed by Mesía's return, and under the tension of the renewed contest De Pas makes the mistake of disclosing his love to Ana. Revolted at first, Ana feels compassion for her religious adviser and forcibly increases her zealousness, going to the extreme of walking barefoot in an Easter procession, only to react against this excessive display of self-punishment by an indulgence in the pleasures of a gay house party at the country estate of friends. Here, in an atmosphere of frivolity and pent-up sexual passion, the priest's rival has a tremendous advantage. After an episode in which De Pas is made to look somewhat ridiculous as he searches madly in the woods for Ana and Mesía, the attraction of the latter becomes irresistible. On the very last night of her stay in the country Ana finds herself alone with Mesía on a dark balcony. At last the *tenorio* has found the long-awaited coincidence of mood and circumstance.

The outcome of the tug of war, of course, has from its beginning been a foregone conclusion, discernible from obvious hints and especially from the repeated postponements of the decision. The author, in fact, has conducted a prolonged cat-and-mouse game which, for its continuous sameness, seriously taxes the reader's patience. That he has thus allowed the psychological quality of his story to become obscured by the elements of satire and suspense in a long drawn-out situational plot can be considered a technical weakness. Our complaint becomes less severe, however, when we realize that the narrative method is designed to enhance the farcical aspects not only of the local social scene but of life in general. The laughable features, therefore, belong to the life described and not to the description itself. For it is the author's intention to burden his heroine with the crassness of her situation; and in carrying out his plan he indulges in his own self-punishment, deriving a certain bitter-sweet pleasure from displaying the cruelty of a world in which love is either missing or debased. One cannot help remembering in this connection the circumstances, grim and farcical at the same time, attending Emma Bovary's love experiences. Probably the major distinction between *La Regenta* and *Madame Bovary,* to be found not so much in theme as in literary manner, lies in the preponderance (in the Spanish novel) of the comic element over the tragic—a fundamental distinction between the Spanish and the French literary genius.

This important difference, however, should not cause us to overlook the deep-lying similarity between the two novelists' motivations. As in *Madame Bovary,* the concluding section of the Spanish novel leaves a heavy impression of the meanness of the flesh and the futility of human aspiration. For a while after her surrender Ana experiences an ecstasy of physical love, becoming ever bolder in her relations with her lover. But De Pas, now consumed with anger and a desire for vengeance, contrives to reveal the love affair to Ana's husband, thus driving him to a duel and to his death. With the resultant scandal, the city of Vetusta turns against Ana. The women who have envied her beauty and reputation now gloat over her shame, and the typical reaction in her social circle is to condemn her for letting the situation get out of hand. "Nauseating," says the Marqués de Vegallana, who "kept in a country village all his illegitimate children." Thus deserted by almost everyone, including Mesía, who has fled to Madrid, Ana begins to think again about religion, and one day goes to the cathedral, hoping to gain the pardon of De Pas. The latter, still burning with the anger of frustration, rebuffs her in bitter silence, refraining with difficulty from striking her. As she lies on the floor after fainting, a sordid acolyte happens by and with lascivious impulse kisses her lips. She awakens, thinking she has felt "on her mouth the cold viscous belly of a toad."

The author thus concludes his story with emphasis on the wretchedness of the human situation after having followed the efforts of two people to rise above it via the idealization of love. The long tug of war has been, after all, only a means of displaying the human predicament. A lonely woman, unhappy in her marital relations, has tried in vain to convert erotic impulse into an intellectualized experience, only to be victimized by the bestiality of sex. Sharing with her the futility of this intellectual and aesthetic endeavor is the priest, himself wholly unable to disregard the physiology of love. And surrounding both of them is a hostile aggregate of humanity that looms like a diabolical conspirator breathing triviality and lasciviousness. The feeling of frustration, which has permeated the main narrative action and the psychology of the two principal characters, acquires in the end a climactic bitterness that underscores the tragic farce of an attempted exaltation of love. The final impact of the story thus recalls *Madame Bovary*. The similarity, of course, does not mean necessarily that Alas imitated Flaubert, but simply that he chose a basically similar problem as subject and followed it to its logical conclusion.

The particular kind of frustrated idealism found in *La Regenta,* which is inseparably linked with the question of a divine recognition of human love, can best be appreciated by thinking of a naturalistic philosophy colored with an ecclesiastical viewpoint that underscores the sinful aspects of love. Two considerations seem especially appropriate. If nature and God are one, the One recognizes only animal love and hence looks indifferently upon any attempt to idealize it into a fine sentiment suggestive of the word "divine." If God is independent of nature, He opposes human passions and chastises the human impulse to deify them. Both views, separately or together, exclude aesthetic and spiritual values from the concept of love.

The character portrayal of the heroine in *La Regenta* is particularly indicative, for it is in large degree a physical analysis in which sex satisfaction is the chief personality need. In this respect Alas was following naturalistic trends in the novel, possibly influenced by Zola, whom he greatly admired. *La Regenta* is, in fact, commonly considered one of the foremost examples of naturalism in Spain and may properly be so regarded if we think of the author's preoccupation with the heaviness of the natural world. As regards the fundamental question of relationship between environment and personality, however, it is scarcely more naturalistic than *Madame Bovary;* for Ana is neither a product of her environment nor a degeneration because of it. She is the victim of an irrepressible urge to love and be loved, which is only superficially explained by the absence of love in her childhood. Alas nevertheless occupies himself with physiology much more than Flaubert does, and his technique of portraiture reminds one at times of a clinical study that attaches great importance to the close relationship between the physical and the psychical. In this particular he reflects the prominence of an interest in physiological psychology, which was probably the most widely discussed scientific subject at the time *La Regenta* was written.

In view of the tendency in scientific circles to identify "soul" with the activity of the brain and nerve centers, it is understandable that one as alert to current intellectual trends as Alas should be affected to the point of depicting the suppression of love's sentimental and aesthetic aspects. Such a depiction, however, is carried out in a spirit of protest, and the protest is enacted in the heroine. Though falling prey to animal instinct,

Ana wanted to believe, like Emma Bovary, in a divine love big enough to embrace all creation: "love for all men and all creatures—for birds and beasts, for the grasses of the field and the worms of the earth." That she had in mind at the same time a personalized kind of love can be seen from her desire to believe that "God was in heaven presiding over and loving His marvelous work, the universe; the Son of God had been born on earth and for this honor and divine proof of affection the entire world was gladdened and ennobled." The fact that Ana's mystic longings are more obscured by carnal desires than is the case with Emma Bovary means simply that the delusiveness of sex, which is an unmistakable idea in Flaubert's novel, is given more space by the Spaniard.

The notion that love is merely a delusion working in the service of a "life force" was an attitude superimposed on biology by philosophy, and we should keep in mind that Schopenhauer and Von Hartmann were much discussed around 1880, in Spain as elsewhere. Some of Von Hartmann's remarks, in essential agreement with Schopenhauer, are relevant in the present connection; particularly his assertions to the effect that love is an evil to be endured for the sake of perpetuating the race: "The goal of the demon, then, is really and truly nothing but sexual satisfaction, and with a particular individual, and everything therewith, as harmony of soul, adoration, admiration, is only weak and false show, or it is something else, something next door to love." In the realm of self-conscious individuality, an aversion arises to sexual union as being "inadequate to the infinity of longing and hope, and unworthy of the unapproachable sublimity of the dreamt ideal." But, as Von Hartmann reminds us, alluding to Schopenhauer, the instinct of love performs its function as a "deceptive bait, by means of which the Unconscious deludes conscious *egoism,* and leads to the sacrifice of self-love in favor of the succeeding generation, which conscious reflection could never effect by itself." Von Hartmann's assertions take on a tone of harshness as he speaks further of the wretched consequences of love in general—the betrayals and sufferings, the bitterness and degradation associated with it; and though he would admit to being neither a Christian nor an ascetic, his attitude reminds one of asceticism when he lapses into an emotional discussion of sex.

Whether or not Alas was influenced by Von Hartmann, it is of interest to observe the parallel in which a philosopher, who called on the sciences, especially physiology, to support his theory, and a novelist, who showed respect for the sciences, assume an attitude toward love which harmonizes with a religious view that looks upon sexual enjoyment as sinful. Assuming that Alas was adversely affected by the implications of modern science, and was at the same time determined to cling to some kind of religious belief, he could logically be expected to make an adjustment by way of ascetic austerity. To such an unhappy compromise position he seems to have been driven, judging from *La Regenta.* For his heroine is trapped between asceticism and an urge to dignify her natural state with an aura of divinity. The idea of sinfulness in the relation between male and female, which was impressed on her in her childhood at the time of the boat incident, is combated by a constant desire to find, on the part of a "natural, affectionate, artistic religion," the sanction of "the profane emotions of love, of youthful joy." But she is forced to believe instead that life is all vanity and wretchedness, a view which she would be willing to accept if she could only visualize her distress in terms of beauty and emotion, unsoiled by "the prose and falsity and evil" of the world. Her husband, also, in his unhappiness over her infidelity, is driven to reflection on the wretchedness of life, recalling declarations of Thomas á Kempis on the necessity for suffering and mortification. Yet he affirms that nature is beautiful when free of the baseness imposed on it by man. It is as though the doctrine of original sin were merged with the theory of man's animal origin.

The attempt to sublimate nature thus becomes resignation to suffering, from which the artist, like his heroine, tries to extract the poetry befitting the lofty aim. The author's satirical, moralistic tone is the rougher aspect of this bittersweetness, which envelops the total narrative development in an expression of disappointment at not being able to validate the concept of love as a pleasurable, poetic sentiment by making it an attribute of the Supreme Being. The basic problem dramatized in *La Regenta,* therefore, seems unmistakably to be the human desire for a personal and sympathetic relationship with Deity. The problem is complicated, if not actually created, by the tendency in science and philosophy to emphasize the impersonal. Alas says of his heroine: "Perhaps this was the profoundest part of Ana's religious faith; she believed in God's direct, open, and individual attention to the acts of her life, to her destiny, to her pains and pleasures." This, at least, is the belief that Ana wants to embrace in the face of a skepticism that has originated she knows not where, perhaps in childhood while in the company of her father, a freethinker who associated with "philosophers" and scientists. Science and reason, the author indicates, have led to the replacement of a benevolent Father by an unfeeling, indifferent Power. Defeat thus leaves Ana in a state of sickening helplessness and De Pas in a mood of bitter resentment. Both are victims of a "universal indifference" which, as De Pas feels, envelops all things and all people. (pp. 71-83)

In the immediate background of *La Regenta* the ghost of Spinoza still seems to haunt the popular imagination, imbued more than ever with a suggestion of divine impassivity. With an expression of bitterness even more trenchant than that of Flaubert, Alas captures a mood befitting the vision of an indifferent Deity. The modernity of Flaubert's novel, it will no doubt be agreed, is particularly impressive at the present time; for Emma's anguish at being cut off from God's "personal" attention is fundamentally similar to the anxiety underlying the twentieth-century existentialist estrangement from Being. The same observation is not so clearly applicable to *La Regenta,* probably because Alas' metaphysics is less pointed in its implications and more complicated by religious attitudes. Nevertheless, the major dramatic force of Alas' novel originates in a conception of an impassive God out of reach of human love. The Spaniard bitterly scorns mass humanity while chastising himself, even more openly than Flaubert, with thoughts of the nullification of individual personality. The impression of cruelty in his novel, in fact, reminds one not only of Zola's naturalism but of certain twentieth-century novels in which Divinity is converted into an unfeeling—and terrifying—Force. . . . (pp. 83-4)

> *Sherman H. Eoff, "In Quest of a God of Love," in his* The Modern Spanish Novel: Comparative Essays Examining the Philosophical Impact of Science on Fiction, *New York University Press, 1961, pp. 51-84.*

FRANK DURAND (essay date 1965)

[*In the following excerpt, Durand expounds upon Alas's role as a social and a literary critic and demonstrates that Alas's critical purpose—to attack narrow-mindedness, mediocrity, and stupidity—is evident in the novel* La Regenta.]

Leopoldo Alas the novelist and Clarín the literary and social critic may seem to hold opposing views. The idealist who looks at life negatively, the critic who calls for utilitarian art and yet believes that a work of art must have a primarily aesthetic aim, would seem to be guilty of inconsistency or muddled thinking. Yet if we relate his ideas of social and literary criticism to his conception of art, especially as it is illustrated in *La Regenta,* it will become evident that the contradictions are more apparent than real, and that there is consistency in Alas' ideas and performance both as critic and as artist.

Clarín the critic, whose vitriolic pen was wielded by a tireless hand, became in a relatively short time the most feared man of letters in Spain. Probably no other critic has ever achieved such power or used it so effectively. With a single review Clarín was capable of damaging a writer's literary reputation or enhancing his career. His friendship was sought and cultivated by many, from writers of the stature of Galdós to novices such as the young Miguel de Unamuno, who in 1895 wrote to Alas enclosing some of his short stories so that Clarín might mention them in his articles.

Criticism, for Clarín, was a tool to be used to raise the cultural level of Spain, and the first necessary step in this direction was to eliminate the existing evils. Thus, in strongly sarcastic prose, Alas set out to attack and destroy every person, institution, and tradition which he felt was vulgar, unintelligent, shallow: Cánovas, for him the perfect example of a mediocrity taking a position of leadership in politics, literature, and scholarship; the disparity between the theoretical functions of an Academy and the horrid reality; the Spanish "tradition of tradition," the attitude that what had been, would be; the provincialism of the country as a whole, resulting from self-imposed isolation.

Much of Clarín's literary output was thus an angry indictment of the social and intellectual mores of his time. Such commentary, combined with the intense irony of which he was a master, would seem to imply a totally destructive view of the Spanish scene, yet his apparently negative attitude was actually positive. Through criticism he hoped to make Spaniards acutely conscious of the *medianías* who composed the higher strata of Spanish life; he would make possible the enrichment of the intellectual atmosphere of his country by exposing its present poverty. It was to this positive end—improvement—that his efforts were directed.

Intimately linked to his desire to raise the intellectual and literary standards of his country is the value he placed on intelligence *per se.* Intelligence became for him the supreme value of life: shield and weapon, inspiration and consolation, motivating force and ultimate goal. Without intelligence, life would become directionless, a merely physical phenomenon. Yet Alas's emphasis on intelligence did not correspondingly reduce in importance the life of the street. A preoccupation with things intellectual, to the exclusion of non-intellectual reality, was never part of his aim. If intelligence was supreme, it was so because it gave direction and purpose to every part of the process of living. Intelligence should suffuse activity of all kinds; the intellect was to operate not in spheres apart, but on the stuff of reality. In fields from politics to literature, intelligence should guide and govern. To realize this condition, he would, therefore, with intelligence as his yardstick and ridicule as his weapon, destroy the non-intelligent elements of Spanish culture, awakening his fellow Spaniards from their lethargic slumber: ". . . to wake the age into consciousness, creating in it the desire to be free from superstition and injustice and to raise its cultural and artistic level. How? By crying out against sectarianism, apathy, ignorance and mediocrity, by loudly proclaiming truth and beauty wherever and whenever he sees them."

In his condemnation of the Spanish scene, then, Alas was selective. His satire was reserved for the so-called elite class, and it ripped apart the supposedly intelligent groups, the leaders of the country—all those whose claims to distinction were, he felt, belied by their inherent lack of talent, intelligence, and honesty. Most irritating of all to him was the ignoramus with intellectual pretensions who prostituted great ideas and debased and vulgarized literature. . . . (pp. 37-9)

Clarín's writing reveals consistently his ideas of the functions of criticism as well as his own personal objectives: to separate the original from the imitative, the great from the mediocre; to criticize, ridicule, and destroy the pedestrian. Since great writers and great ideas were few, someone had to protect them from their imitators, who were plentiful. (p. 39)

If Clarín was exasperated by the number of second- and third-rate authors who abounded in Spain, he found it even more intolerable that these authors should be accepted and praised by the other critics of his time. It seemed that poor writers and critics gave each other a helping hand, and this served to encourage even more inferior writing. "The great increase in the number of people writing, caused by the mushroom growth of newspapers and magazines, the inevitable and consequent boom in inferior periodical scribbling, and the willingness of an un-tutored public to accept such offerings kept Alas in a state of constant perturbation over the future of Spanish letters" [William E. Bull, *Clarín: An Analytical Study of a Literary Critic* (unpublished Ph.D. dissertation)]. Such critics, he felt, represented the element most detrimental to the world of letters. Mediocre literary figures could be endured, but not mediocre literary critics. With praise from these critics, the otherwise short-lived fame of the minor writers was prolonged, and their works multiplied until they usurped the position of great works and exerted an unwarranted influence on the literary world. In this thought lay his justification for writing about third-rate authors. . . . Someone had to counterbalance the damage the critics of the time were doing, and Alas undertook the task. He felt he was performing a service of purification for contemporary literature, a service of *immediate* importance. That his criticism of these minor figures would not be remembered he knew, but the responsibilities of the critic were placed above personal ambition. To clear away the literary weeds was perhaps the most thankless of tasks, the least likely to bring fame, yet he performed it willingly in the hope of improving Spanish literature. . . . (pp. 39-40)

Criticism meant to Alas, then, intelligent and conscientious evaluation, with the aim of discovering the good and defending it from the bad. The evaluations of literary works as well as the existing irresponsible criticism of these works formed an important part of his social preoccupation, for these were both a reflection of the society that produced them and an influence on it. Just criticism was essential in maintaining, if not a high level of literary production, at least an accurate evaluation of that production. The critic was to become a judge and a policeman, rendering an invaluable service to art, and responsible critics with discriminating taste were desperately needed to police the increase in poor writing. . . .

His goals were not limited solely to the exposition of strengths and weaknesses, however. In addition to his function as "guar-

dia literaria," the critic should be the mentor who would educate the undeveloped tastes of the reading public to an appetite for good writing and an appreciation of it. (p. 40)

It should be clear, then, that Alas did not condescend to or condemn the elusive, hypothetical "average man"; some of his most delightful stories deal sympathetically with simple, ordinary realities in the lives of unexceptional people. In his creative works he has a strong tendency to portray the weak, humble characters with overwhelming pity, as in the case of Bonifacio Reyes in *Su único hijo.* . . .

This process of education could not, of course, be accomplished without the aid of the best in criticism. But the majority of the critics Alas saw succumbed to the influence exercised by editors, relatives, or friends—or they simply praised mediocre works out of kindness. This seemed to him a debasement of art, and the perpetrators were literary criminals. . . . (p. 41)

Clarín satirically advocated setting up fines to be imposed on such criminals. Kindness in literary matters, he felt, was not a virtue but a vice. It could not make a weak play into a work of art; it could only distort and eventually destroy the whole concept of art. Thus the attack on inferior writing was at the same time a defense of the best.

It was because he felt this need to prune the literary production of the time that Alas so highly esteemed sound criticism. In its utilitarian aspects, it was a servant of literature, a pragmatic means to an ideal end, perfection. Moreover, Alas's outlook on life, as well as literature, can best be characterized as critical, evaluative. As an intellectual perfectionist, he needed to write criticism in order to express his dissatisfaction with the status quo and his desire to see the rule of intelligence in all areas of human endeavor. Thus his critical attitude extended beyond literature to include all groups and institutions which laid claim to intelligence.

It would be unjust, however, to characterize his whole attitude toward literary criticism as utilitarian. In his views on *la crítica policíaca* he assigned criticism a utilitarian role because he realized the urgent need for this kind of "practical" criticism and, himself, gladly undertook the task. . . . Clarín accepted the necessity of certain specialized approaches to literature, but he insisted on not confusing them with true literary criticism. . . . There existed . . . for him, a form of literary criticism which rejected all extrinsic aspects of literature and concentrated its efforts exclusively on the study of the work of art; the requirements of such a study were the impartiality, the good taste, and the artistic sensitivity of the critic, whose province should be the work itself. Although Alas could hardly be called a nineteenth-century theoretician of the so-called "new criticism," it is certain that his approach to a definition of the critic's role is in some aspects similar. . . . (pp. 41-2)

Chiefly, however, Clarín was concerned in his own critical outpourings with the curing of immediate ills he had diagnosed in Spain's literature and society. The dominant pattern that emerges is a kind of mitigated nineteenth-century nihilism: attack and destroy in order to build more perfectly. And implicit in this is, of course, a profound and enduring concern for Spain—a passionate, if often ironically expressed, commitment to regeneration which compensated for the hardships and disappointments Alas suffered as a conscientious critic. The pessimism he often manifested, when the task he had set seemed impossible, vanished when he recalled his purpose. . . . The "powerful motive" which made his life work valid was precisely this concern with Spanish decadence, a concern which was soon to move the members of the generation of '98 and through them bring the regeneration of Spanish letters which Alas so fervently sought. (p. 42)

The vision of the author of *La Regenta* is the same as that of the critic: a hatred of mediocrity, hypocrisy, and general stupidity. If the action of the novel were somehow removed, one would be left with a long critical description of life in a provincial Spanish city best characterized by its narrow-mindedness, lack of intelligence, and rooted ignorance. There is thus a definite critical purpose in the presentation of Vetusta's intellectuals, a purpose evident in the ironic tone and the abundance of literary references in the novel. These references serve to emphasize the ignorance and shallowness of the Vetustans, orchestrating one of the major themes in the novel: the intellectual pretensions and the hypocrisy of the "cultured" class of the city. Because it is so successfully fused with subject, structure, and style, Alas's negative, critical view produces not a sociological tract or a reformer's tirade, but rather an added dimension of novelistic reality. Thus the moral, political, and literary issues taken up in the novel are as important to its ultimate artistic fullness as Ana herself. Yet at the same time, in accordance with theories expressed elsewhere, a utilitarian purpose is served: the exposition of Spain's cultural decadence in the hope of resultant improvement.

A study of the ideas reflected in Alas's criticism is thus of considerable importance in a thorough understanding of *La Regenta*. Neglect of this aspect of Alas's thought may lead to serious misinterpretations of both the novel and the novelist's world view. Two examples of such misinterpretations will illustrate the importance of this point. Professor Balseiro has suggested that Alas found it easier to create negative characters than to create admirable ones. Is this a fair and accurate estimate? I think not, for it seems to me impossible to divorce this aspect of the novel from the literary criticism, where intellectual hypocrisy is the major theme. More basically, of course, a critic should not take a novelist to task for omitting something which was not a part of the author's vision of reality. The critic may wish that this vision corresponded more closely to his own, but this is hardly fair ground for judging a work. We have already shown how Alas's negativism in the novel is based on a deep-rooted conviction that improvement is possible only after the destruction of the mediocre and shallow. The same is true of his satire in *La Regenta*, which thus has a utilitarian purpose: to expose the prevalent stupidity and superficiality of Spanish "intellectual" society. His irony is not superficial wit for the sake of wit, but rather the reflection of a whole complex of opinions and attitudes basic to his world view. The reader of *La Regenta* may be overwhelmed and amused at the gallery of stupid characters, but if he has read Alas's criticism he will realize that the author is simply presenting these people as he saw them; there will be no question of his presenting these characters negatively so as to avoid the difficulty of creating more positive ones (if, indeed, it *is* harder to write about the latter). It must also be remembered that not all the characters are depicted from a negative point of view. This is apparent in the treatment of Bishop Camoirán, "Atheist" Guimarán, and "Frígilis," as well as in the pathetic presentation of don Víctor when his dream of defending his honor becomes reality and he sees how ridiculous his posturing has been. The overall importance of Alas's negativism can hardly be overemphasized, however, because it is the key to understanding his thought and its reflection in the novel. It is through his negativism that we can arrive at the heart of his concept of life, for in his negative attitude is implicit his idealism and

his rebellious character. He could not have been so bitterly ironic over what he saw in Spanish life if he had not had a far different image of what it should be; dissatisfaction with the status quo implies the existence of a concept of a better situation.

Another interpretation of Alas's relentless attack on Vetusta's intellectual class has been offered by Albert Brent [see excerpt dated 1951], who gives as the "only" explanation the author's personal frustration. Once again, the interpretation is contradicted by the consistency of critical attitude clearly visible throughout the author's life. In addition, it is scarcely just to offer personal reasons as the only possible explanation of any author's criticism of society. By these standards, Voltaire wrote as he did because he was annoyed at not having an opportunity to light the first match at the burning of members of religious minority groups. The negative view in *La Regenta* has deeper and more significant bases than these two theories suggest, for it reveals the consistent world view of the author as it is expressed throughout his writings. In *La Regenta*, the novelist's attainment realizes the critic's aim, without doing violence to the highest goals of either. (pp. 47-9)

Frank Durand, "Leopoldo Alas, 'Clarín': Consistency of Outlook as Critic and Novelist," *in* The Romanic Review, *Vol. LVI, No. 1, February, 1965, pp. 37-49.*

FRANCES WYERS WEBER   (essay date 1966)

[*Weber is an American educator and critic. In the following excerpt, she examines the underlying unity between the alternating pursuit of spiritual and erotic fulfillment portrayed in the novels* La Regenta *and* Su Único hijo.]

Leopoldo Alas was mockingly critical of most of the intellectual tendencies of his time. In his two novels, *La Regenta* and *Su Único hijo,* the exposure of the failings of ideas and dogmas constitutes both a central theme and an ironic technique. Of course the traditional novel is essentially an ironic form, setting the simplifications of any interpretive scheme against the complexities of reality; its perennial subject is the great gap between beliefs and experience. The novelist's method is necessarily indirect, for he shows the lack of coordination between inner and outer life; he shows what is missing and offers no counterproposal as to how things ought to be. In his novels, Alas's humour destroys all pretensions to refined ideality, and his dramatic structure shows the tragic or pathetic plight of the protagonists whose private illusions are shattered by a vulgar social reality. I shall consider one favourite device for undermining the characters' fragile idealisms—the use of parodic religious symbols that level all values and demonstrate the unbreakable continuity of the physical and the spiritual. Religious patterns represent both the drama of love and the pursuit of sex.

The plot of *La Regenta* follows the heroine's oscillations between erotic temptation and religious enthusiasm. Her choice is not, as some think, between moral duty and immoral desire but between two apparently contradictory but really very similar ways of escaping the dull and confining routine of Vetusta—religious mysticism and non-carnal romantic love. As the two sentiments are intensified, they become more and more indistinguishable, and both alternate with momentary intrusions of bodily demands, sometimes in the form of physical or nervous collapse . . . , at other times in the promptings of a repressed sexuality. . . . Ana tries to overcome the limitations of the self either by mystical submersion in God or by amorous submersion in the soul of her lover. She imagines drowning in the divine essence . . . or in the delight of forbidden emotions. . . . That the two impulses are essentially identical is evident in the novel's resolution: it ends not with the death of the heroine, as do most nineteenth-century novels of adultery, but with her turning, after the disastrous love affair with Álvaro, to the emotional bond of religion and Platonic love that ties her to the *Magistral;* once again she goes to the cathedral seeking the consolations of the Church and of Fermín. The alternations seem to be fixed forever; she moves back and forth between two modes of the same endeavour.

Alas shows the underlying unity of Ana's two passions in subtle psychological descriptions and in the parodic patterns of the novel's action. Religious scenes turn into love scenes and vice versa. The whole structure of the plot reveals this fusion of motives. Part I, which takes place in only three days and which is filled with a wealth of descriptive and expository detail, focuses on two events, Ana's first confession with the *Magistral,* Fermín de Pas, and the supper at the Vegallanas' house. The confession initiates the action and provides, in Ana's preparation for it, the occasion for telling the story of the heroine's life up to the present (chapters III, IV, and V). In the two chapters that frame Ana's recollection of her past, gossip about her confession, first among the clergy (Chapter II), then among the habitués of the Casiono (chapter VI), contrasts the young woman's religious and emotional sensibility to the egotism, cynicism, and sexual libertinism of the Vetustans. The confession itself is not presented as a scene because its importance lies not in any immediate dramatic effect but in the reversal of religious values as the narrator moves from the inner life of the *Regenta* to the social world of the city, thus showing the impossibility of her aspirations in so degraded an environment.

In the novel's second episode, the supper at the Vegallanas', the religious theme becomes slowly transposed into an erotic one. Of course the two have already been set one against the other in the satire of types and customs in chapters I, II, and VI. But now the ironic shift from the protagonist's idealism to the concupiscence of upper class Vetusta is accompanied by Ana's own dim awareness of sensuality. The confession motif reappears charged with sexuality, innocently in Ana, with perverse intention in Álvaro. When the *Regenta* sees Fermín at the house of her friends, she blushes at the memory of her recently confided secrets. Then, thinking of the spiritual consolation the *Magistral* offers, she recalls not only the import of his words but the charm of his voice. . . . It occurs to her that the letter she wrote him that morning must be on his person and the thought of this physically shared object is vaguely voluptuous. But she believes that her salvation lies with Fermín because he can protect her both from Vetusta and from the "tentación francamente criminal" ["frankly criminal temptation"] of Don Álvaro. Significantly, she phrases this alternative with the word *entregar;* the word for sexual surrender is used to refer to its opposite, to the flight into pure spirituality. Álvaro is also present in the room, suspiciously watching Ana and the *Magistral,* but what he senses of the woman's psychological ambivalence is only the sensual direction. The author switches from the description of Ana's delicately balanced sentiments to Álvaro's simplifying views. . . . Mesía envies the priests because he is sure that women seek in their confessor "el placer secreto y la voluptuosidad espiritual de la tentación" ["the secret pleasure and the spiritual voluptuosity of temptation"]—the same voluptuous temptation that Álvaro himself represents to Ana. As a kind of revenge, he has imposed on his mistresses his own degrading version of the sacrament. . . . The theme of the inner life aspiring to an impossible purity (the impossibility is already evident in the mixture of the ideal and the sensuous in Ana's thoughts) has been replaced by the theme of the inner life as a source of lascivious pleasure. The principal organizing motif of the first volume moves between the poles of pure spirituality and pure materiality.

The extremes of religious devotion and erotic impulse are also developed in the characters' views of their roles. Ana sees the contest between Álvaro and Fermín as the confrontation between good and evil. She projects her dilemma on a cosmic scale: the two men are the antagonists in the great moral battle, Saint Michael and Lucifer. This vision is inverted by Álvaro who reduces God and religious devotion to the status of an opposing swain. Ana too tends to cast God and Álvaro in the roles of contending suitors, though at first she is repelled by this matching of the vulgar and sublime. . . . In this rivalry God and the *Magistral* merge into the single opponent of Mesía. Fermín becomes identified with Christ because he is persecuted by the calumny of the Vetustans. Ana in sacrificing herself for him will be like the Virgin at the foot of the cross. Fermín also links his suffering over Ana's betrayal to the Passion of Christ. For both Ana and Fermín the triangle would seem to be Ana, Álvaro, Fermín-Christ. Thus when the *Regenta* admits to herself the carnal nature of her attraction to Álvaro, she is remorseful. . . . (pp. 197-200)

The characters see no incongruity in the identification of their personal emotional problems with the Christian drama. The disparity between the two realms is the measure of the author's irony, and he develops this disparity in the arrangement of the novel's key episodes (most of which occur in Volume II, for Volume I is largely exposition, psychological analysis and description). The central action is an inner one: Alas traces with increasing tension the heroine's psychological oscillations between mystical exaltation and romantic love. External events are both a counterpoint and a stimulus to this conflict of sentiments; they are generally presented through scenes with dialogue (or through the memory of one of the characters) instead of through the narrator's summaries. Alas puts before the reader in dramatic form certain significant happenings and almost invariably the occasions are religious feast days and celebrations. Thus the very frame of the action lends itself to an ironic religious pattern.

The first chapter of Volume II (chapter XVI) takes place on All Saints Day and Alas makes of the traditional performance of *Don Juan Tenorio* a climactic and prophetic scene. The novel's three primary motifs—love, religion, physiology—are combined, reversed and fused in the interplay between Ana's reaction to the staged drama, the action of that drama and Álvaro's persevering attempts at seduction. On seeing Zorrilla's play, Ana is swept away by religious-erotic enthusiasm. Love is a "locura mística" ["mystical madness"] through which the soul is elevated to the realm of pure ideas. . . . In the drama and in Ana's emotional response, religion and eroticism blend; in the cross-purpose thoughts of Ana and Álvaro, they stand opposed to each other. Alas shows the romantic merging of the two sentiments and then humorously subjects this idealized fusion to Álvaro's simple-minded "realism." Both positions are undermined.

Most of the remaining dramatic scenes also join the erotic and the religious, and in their incongruous pairing, the narrator shows the unfortunate or comic results of the original separation of real and ideal. Those who would disengage themselves entirely from the material world are the victims of an absurd and impossible illusion; and those who accept only the physical as really real, are deformed and dehumanized. The carnal apes the spiritual, and the deficiencies of both appear through a kind of mutual contamination. Christian ceremonies become the framework for Ana's love story and for the presentation of certain determinedly materialistic or egoistic projects. In chapter XX, the gathering of twelve anticlerical friends who are plotting against Fermín mocks both the Last Supper and the sacrament of confession. The sexual connotation of the confession motif in chapter XIII is repeated and strengthened. . . . When the confessions of love affairs begin, Mesía's confidences are the ones most avidly followed. . . . Chapter XXIII, the Christmas Mass in the cathedral, like the *Don Juan* chapter, organizes the action into a contrasting pattern of devotion and sensuality, weaving back and forth between the inner drama of the heroine and the external farce of Vetustan piety. Ana's delight at the mingling of the sacred and profane in the organ music is set against the torpid sensualism of the Vetustans. . . . Chapter XXIV, the Carnival dance in the Vetusta Casino, presents, appropriately enough, the temporary and partial victory of Don Álvaro-Don Carnal. Chapter XXV, the celebration of the Novena to the Virgin of Sorrows, repeats the pattern of the Christmas scene, focussing now on Ana's inner conflicts, now on the grossness of the other worshippers. The Good Friday procession (chapter XXVI) is the final ceremonial occasion in which the author ties together his themes—eroticism and religion—and his subjects—the *Regenta* and the city. The episode also represents the height of Fermín's worldly power; the conversion of the atheist Pompeyo Guimarán had already marked his "apoteosis pagana" ["pagan apotheosis"]. . . . (pp. 200-02)

The religious experience seems to have degenerated into a vague psychic exaltation that can be induced by a variety of stimuli. Specifically Christian symbols and images are applied, consciously or unconsciously by the characters, with ironic intention by the narrator, to the transports of self-love or romantic love. Since any rapture of the soul may be religiously interpreted, spirituality and pseudo-spirituality are confused and all hierarchies are abolished. The protagonists' attempts to live in their own visionary world inevitably end in failure and the novelist underlines that failure by showing how the thoroughly materialistic pursuits of other characters imitate and mock the outward form of idealistic endeavours. But Alas's periodical ways certainly do not point to any other system of values that could replace these illusions. All values are under suspicion because no single abstract scheme can withstand the contact of reality. All the myths the Vetustans try to incarnate— the Calderonian, the romantic, the mystical, the positivistic— turn out to be equally delusive. Baquero Goyanes speaks of the "exaltación de lo vital" ["exaltation of the vital"] in *La Regenta,* but not even the non-literary or non-intellectual virtues are affirmed. The simple goodness of people like Caimorán or Frígilis is no match for the complicated evils of Vetusta. Nothing is exalted, and what might be of value is indicated only by its absence. The novelist presents the reverse of the desirable, the distorted image of the ideal.

For example, Alas refers indirectly in this novel to another kind of religion, a personal, humble cult, "la religión del hogar" ["the religion of the hearth"]. The atheist Pompeyo Guimarán discovers it just before his conversion to Catholicism (a conversion whose religious significance is anti-Christian because it leads to the Magistral's "apoteosis pagana"). Since all of Pompeyo's beliefs tend to be unconsciously pretentious, we cannot take his new-found faith with complete seriousness.

Yet throughout the novel, all descriptions of genuine affection are phrased in terms of familial relations. The best one can do in a debased world is to circumscribe the ideal, drawing in one's aspirations to the circle of the home. Faith is placed, not in promises of everlasting life for the individual soul, but in the anonymous immortality of family life, in the succession of fathers and sons. This religion becomes the subject of *Su único hijo.* And in the heightened satirical tone of that work, even this modest ideal is the object of ironic devaluation.

As in *La Regenta,* the vision that underlies Alas's second novel is the baseness of the material world and the futility of all attempts to escape from it into a purely spiritual realm. If in the first novel the author ridiculed the customs of the Vetustans through carefully detailed social scenes, in this one he reduces society to its dominating and most abstract feature—money. And the "ideal" in Clarín's second novel is a provincial romanticism nurtured on second-hand ideas and readings, an out-of-date, old-fashioned, literary pose, completely out of place in "modern" society in which the economic function takes precedence over all others and in which the erotic life has been debased to a mere diversion from money-making. The era of romanticism has passed, but it survives in the nostalgic reminiscences of the members of a *tertulia* that meets in a dry goods store. This circle lives at two removes from reality, seeing everything through a haze of romanticism that is itself diffused into a recollection of the past. In the Cascos' store they ruminate over an age when illicit love affairs flourished and were dignified with music and sentimental verses. Bonifacio Reyes, the novel's protagonist, . . . plays the flute and is fond of imaginary adventures. He is hopelessly unfit to cope with the machinations of the Koerners and Don Nepocemo who, as representatives of a new and more rational society, are scheming to build a chemical industry with funds swindled from Bonifacio's wife. Opposed to mercenary efficiency is an antiquated and ridiculous ideal (and both contraries alternate with perverted sexuality—Emma Valcárcel, Marta Koerner, and the members of the opera company).

The anachronism of an ideological or sentimental trend is thus paired with society's increasing materialism and the "modern" denial of all forms of idealism. . . . But woven into the theme of the incongruity of the new and the old-fashioned is another view of the past that stresses continuity and the transmission of love and affection. At the very beginning, Alas ties the topic of romanticism to the central theme of familial succession: the memories tenderly evoked in the *tertulia* are linked to Bonis's memories of his family; the *ubi sunt* of the *tertulianos* who recall and lament the illustrious figures of the 1840s leads him to the sad remembrance of his own past. The *tertulia* reminds him of his mother's lap. To this mingling of recollection, romanticism and motherly devotion is added, with the entrance of La Gorgheggi, the theme of sexuality. And for Bonis, the soprano's sexual attraction is almost indistinguishable from her maternal quality. . . . Serafina Gorgheggi is constantly present to him as an image of the mother. When he becomes her lover, he is charmed by her combination of ardour and spirituality, by the way she alternates between "transportes báquicos" [Bacchic frenzies] and maternal tenderness. . . . Eroticism and filial love are fused and both are inseparably linked with nostalgia for the past—the past as the Romantic Age or the past as childhood.

But then this complex of impulses and sentiments is turned from the past to the future. Bonifacio longs for a child. And this longing is climactically structured into a disconcerting scene in which the motif of "la religión del hogar" is presented through the unlikely image of Annunciation. Bonis is listening to Serafina sing. . . . Since it is after [Serafina's] recital that Emma first meets the baritone, Minghetti, future father of "Bonifacio's" child, the annunciation has indeed been an ironic foretelling. Bonis, in spite of his second-hand positivistic convictions, cannot help but remember that night as a revelation of his destiny. He sees a divine coincidence in the fact that the very day he ends his affair with Serafina, Emma's pregnancy is made known, but he does not grasp the meaning of the other coincidence, that of the increasing disorder of his household and the miraculous fulfilment of his hope for a child. So too, he is unaware of the irony of his sudden sense of sympathy for Saint Joseph.

The cult of the son is a true religion for Bonis, and a monotheistic one. . . . Fatherhood is a "sacerdocio"; the family is the only source and meaning of immortality. This "homey" faith will replace romantic raptures, and passionate love will give way to fatherly love. The home, not "Art" or romantic love, is the locus of ideality for humble spirits. . . . (pp. 202-06)

Bonifacio sees the world's unity in the succession of fathers and sons, a continuity that negates time and fuses the present with all past moments. He has an almost mystical vision of his entire past dissolved in a single plane of feeling in which sensory experience mixes with sentiments and memories. . . . All previous generations and the past and future of each individual exist simultaneously in the intuition of familial eternity. Bonis has a similar experience during a visit to the village where he was born (Raíces). The countryside, which Alas describes with truly romantic feeling, is melancholy and poetic, and Bonifacio feels united both with the landscape and with his own past. But from his character's romantic submersion in nature, Alas moves back to his peculiar appropriation of Christian image and to the irony of his fatherhood; the church bells ring the Angelus and Bonis remembers first his mother's evening prayers, then his own private annunciation. Planning for the future, he decides his son will fulfill all his own aspirations. . . . Alas has gone from the serious romanticism of the paragraphs describing the village and countryside to a burlesque of that romanticism in Bonifacio's sentimental delusions.

The novel's last scene takes place in the cathedral (the occasion is the baptism of Bonifacio's "only child") and, as in *La Regenta,* the setting enforces the cruelty of the ending. But now the Church represents not the Christian mysticism that Ana had tried to live but the private cult of the family: Bonis is impressed not by Catholic dogma, in which he does not believe, but by the Church's motherliness. When Serafina tries to disillusion him about his son, he asserts his faith in that child. Yet in spite of this affirmation, the line of succession is broken, and Bonifacio's faith is reduced to a will to faith. *La Regenta* ended with Ana's double failure, the failure of love and of exalted religiosity. And the conclusion of *Su único hijo,* more pathetic than tragic, shows the destruction both of the romantic ideal and of "la religión del hogar."

Baquero Goyanes has observed that not only is the romanticism of *Su único hijo* retrospective but that in general Clarín seems to be observing his century from the vantage point of ours. Alas consistently derided the philosophical movements of his time; the evolution and conflicts of ideas seemed to him meaningless changes of fashion. The theme of passing fads in ideas and ideologies occurs frequently in the novels and stories. Like the village priest in his story **"El sombrero del señor cura,"** Alas saw in the sequence of intellectual trends only senseless

reversals and repetitions: each system contradicts the preceding one, but eventually the wheel of fashion turns full round and the hat or belief ridiculed as out-of-date once again fits in with popular taste. Even his most obtuse characters are sensitive to the dictates of current style. . . . Romanticism, materialism, positivism, liberalism, vitalism are either disguises for unfashionable and disreputable ideas and actions (Marta Koerner dissembles her single-minded pursuit of money with declarations of romantic love) or handy explanations of personal and by no means philosophical convictions (Don Álvaro uses his meager grasp of science to rationalize his superstitious faith in his own sexuality. . .). Revolutionary political doctrines are nothing but new clichés to express an old resentment. . . . Alas stands aloof from his age because he sees all its ideologies as unstable, capriciously shifting fashions. And because of this instability, all ideals have become somehow impossible. The novelist indicates their inadequacies by applying the symbols and myths of Christianity to the paltry romantic idealism of his characters and by using those same images to describe a cynical and perverse carnality.

The reversal and parody of values is not an attack on religion or on any other specific ideal, but rather the exposure of the futility of all efforts to live solely by abstractions, of all attempts to deny man's compositeness. The materialistic and idealistic monisms of the nineteenth century had reduced the universe to either matter or mind, and the novelist finds both reductions equally unsuitable as guides to conduct. Alas confronts each abstraction with the phenomena that destroy it. In his world the degradation of matter is accompanied by the etherealization of the ideal which, completely cut off from reality, becomes thoroughly illusory. The "oscilación grotesca" ["grotesque oscillation"] between the physiological and the spiritual that characterizes the style and structure of both novels is matched by the confusion and levelling of all forms of ideality and by a grotesque mingling of symbols. In a sense we may see in the two aspects of this technique both a parallel and a counter-movement to the romantic fusion of real and ideal. In order to express its vision of nature as emblem of a hidden and mysterious infinity, romanticism sought to consecrate the humble, to "domesticate the marvellous." In these novels we observe an ironic exaggeration of this process: the marvellous is not only domesticated but made vulgar. Alas's novels give us a reversed image of a great romantic theme. What is revealed is not the desired indivisibility of spirit and matter but the spiritlessness of the modern world. Its ideals are no longer able to integrate experience. Life is split into the antagonistic aims of body and soul, and the novelist surveys the tragicomic results. The romantics sought the harmony of sensuousness and spirit; Alas, taking the round-about route of irony, shows the disharmony of what should be a single whole. Opposites are reconciled, lyrically in one case, satirically in the other. (pp. 206-08)

Frances Wyers Weber, "Ideology and Religious Parody in the Novels of Leopoldo Alas," in Bulletin of Hispanic Studies, *Vol. XLIII, No. 3, July 1966, pp. 197-208.*

THE TIMES LITERARY SUPPLEMENT   (essay date 1967)

[*In the following excerpt, the critic offers a reassessment of Alas's place in world literature, dismissing his literary criticism as unimportant and calling* La Regenta *a monumental novel in the tradition of nineteenth-century Realism.*]

The various literary reputations enjoyed by Leopoldo Alas, since he began to make a name for himself in the Spanish press as the columnist Clarín ninety years ago, make it almost obligatory to begin an appraisal of his work at this time by describing him as a conventional, second-rate literary critic, a facile, superficial journalist, a man of confused and vacillating political convictions, a writer of short stories of uneven and often poor quality, and the author of one monumentally fine novel in the best tradition of nineteenth-century realism. Obligatory not only because such a description represents the view of most modern readers of Alas's works, but also because it seems the proper way of redressing the balance of Clarín's spurious fame of earlier years.

Alas has never been an obscure figure in Spanish letters, but he has been esteemed—or despised, or feared—for what he was not: during his lifetime, as a great literary critic and as Spain's outstanding journalist; since his death in 1901, as a fearless, outspoken critic of traditional Spanish society, particularly of its clerical and politically conservative elements, the heir of Larra, the precursor of the Generation of 1898. In this latter respect it was remembered that he had written *La Regenta,* a scandalous novel slandering the clergy of his native Oviedo. The book was not easy to come by, and the legend grew. When Alas's eldest son died in the Civil War, people said (and say) that the Nationalists shot him because he was the son of the author of *La Regenta.* Some protested at the legend, among them a younger son, an ardent *franquista,* who insisted (chastened, perhaps, by his brother's fate) that his father had in fact been a man of the right; but meanwhile nobody read *La Regenta. . . .*

It is, of course, many things, as a novel of this length and depth can afford to be. At one level it is a malicious, satirical and often very funny account of the daily life of an actual society—Oviedo in the 1880s. When it was published in 1885, the Bishop of Oviedo publicly accused Alas of having written a book "saturated with eroticism, with infamous mockery of Christian practices and with slanderous allusions to highly respectable persons." In those more spacious days Alas could afford to be more amused than concerned about the anger of a prelate who had not read the novel, but there is no doubt about the substance of the Bishop's accusations of slander, and a good many of the jokes in *La Regenta* are specially for local consumption.

But this incidental aspect of the novel, far from limiting the interest of a modern reader, gives the book an almost exotic quality. The dense and massive authenticity of *La Regenta* makes it a fascinating social document. We get to know about things like the grass roots of Restoration politics, the local reality of that amazing national fraud on which the Spanish parliamentary system rested with such apparent security for so many years. We learn what books are read by the inhabitants of Vetusta—as Oviedo is rather needlessly called in the novel. We become familiar with every shade of popular ideology, from the opinions and style of argument of the freethinkers' club (one of whose solemn functions is to eat a meat dinner every Good Friday), to the kind of sermon currently favoured by the smart cathedral set. The first 300 pages of the novel advance the narrative by thirty-six hours. By that time we know exactly what it was like to live in Vetusta, with its eternal rain pouring from leaden skies and its tedious, claustrophobic, small-town life.

However, as is proper to the mature realist novel, all this is but the setting. Alas had no patience with the idea of realism for realism's sake, and he held firmly that writing novels was a business of selection and arrangement of elements of real life in order to communicate understanding. His documentation is anything but gratuitous. His disciplined technique requires him to spend half the novel immersing us in the setting, but only half the novel: after that he will proceed rapidly.

The understanding he has to communicate is of various sorts, and perhaps the most acceptable is the psychological sort, in which the novel is very rich. In the age of Zola, of whom he was an admirer with reservations, Alas is acutely aware of the extent to which we are the products of our circumstances, and he offers us meticulous, subtle, prolonged and yet in the end economical explanations of why his characters are as they are. As in all the great novels of this period, these explanations venture, often with great intuitive accuracy, into realms that were as yet scientifically unexplored, and thus afford the modern reader that special pleasure which might be crudely described as post-Freudian appreciation of pre-Freudian insights. But, special pleasures apart, all Alas's dissections of personality are masterly, in their humour, or their cruelty, or, more rarely in their compassion, and we quickly learn to appreciate his special talent for captivating portrayals of dull and unattractive people.

His insights are particularly interesting when he is dealing with elements that preoccupy him personally. *La Regenta* has that peculiar fascination of works which not only illuminate psychological depths, but also let us glimpse other depths of which the author himself is unaware, so setting up a kind of tension between the author and his material which provides an extra dimension of interest for the reader. The form this takes in *La Regenta* is that, as we read this devastating exposure of an outwardly respectable society, we gradually realize that the author, far from being the impassive, cynical critic we thought him to be at the beginning, is a crusading idealist, passionately involved in the outcome of his story.

All these priests, for example, at best ineffectual simpletons, but more often creeping predators, motivated by lust, greed or snobbery, what do they signify? They signify Alas's anger at what had become of the pure ideal of Christianity. Alas's famous anticlericalism turns out to be of a characteristically Spanish kind—indignation at the harm that unworthy ministers are doing to the Church. Compare his attitude to the other enemies of Christianity, the atheists, materialists, liberals, radicals and other clowns in the anticlerical circus: this lot give him no cause for anger or indignation, only for contemptuous amusement.

But this ruthless vision of Vetustan society is still not the novel's *raison d'être,* and those who have suggested that *Vetusta* would be an apter title overlook the message Alas urgently wishes to impart. Although the life of the town, its stifling boredom, its pettiness, its falsity, are essential to the development of events, the story of Ana Ozores, the judge's wife of the title, is a moral tale whose purpose is to indict the age in which Alas lived. It is the story of a superior, sensitive being, inexorably defiled and ultimately destroyed by a way of thought and life which Alas believed to be characteristic of a whole epoch, and with which he felt himself to be violently in conflict. Here again we feel the tension between the author and his material. *La Regenta* is not a detached study of a psychological predicament but an impassioned assertion of the validity of certain ideals. Ana Ozores is not presented as a neurotic crushed by the facts of life, but as a tragic heroine destroyed by a great evil.

Ana's type of aspiration is familiar enough. She believes in the validity of certain emotional experiences which seem to lift her above the gross reality of material existence. Vetusta revolts her because its inhabitants affirm, gleefully, that the gross reality of material existence is all there is. As one critic has observed, Ana is seeking to "dignify her vital needs," to find for them some kind of validity that will resist the intolerable insinuation that they are merely the needs of any attractive, intelligent young woman married to a decrepit, impotent, boring old man.

Alas allows her to have her doubts, which reflect his own awareness of the force of the materialist argument. But he also endows her with his own emotional conviction, and the ensuing drama is full of curious undertones which we learn to recognize as belonging to the personality of the author. We discover, for example, that Alas is one of those romantic idealists who cannot reconcile true love with physical sexuality. Indeed, for Alas, sex is so degrading that it is employed thematically as a symbol of the debasement of almost any ideal. Ana, deprived of love since birth, dreams of some vague, wonderful experience which will fill the void. Alas permits the aspiration to develop into what he believes to be its likely outcome in real life, as he involves her in a sordid and finally tragic seduction by the local Don Juan. But Ana also aspires to dignify her urges by way of religious experience. A reasonable project, one would have thought, in this ecclesiastical stronghold. But in the end she finds herself face to face with the same old monster: her spiritual director, in whom she thought she had at last found a kindred spirit, was merely, digustingly, in love with her. Wherever you look in Vetusta you find, either just beneath the surface or not even beneath it, lust, beastly carnal desire. What is Vetustan high society? A sexual orgy. What is this fashionable positivist philosophy? An excuse to throw off traditional moral restraint and to indulge in sexual licence. And what, above all, is religion, in this august Spanish cathedral city? A cover for furtive sexual activity, for excitement spiced by guilt. The deliberately unpleasant association of religion and sex throughout the novel is the measure of Alas's feelings about Vetustan Christianity. In the same way when we are presented with some beautiful, or holy, or otherwise moving experience (Christmas night Mass, the performance of *Don Juan Tenorio*, &c.), the mere juxtaposition of Ana's reaction and that of her neighbours is sufficient commentary in itself.

Ana is doomed to be dragged down to the level of the rest of Vetusta. That is the message. From time to time, Alas makes use of the image, or occasionally the actual presence, of a toad, as an expression of his feelings about the nature of the typical inhabitant of Vetusta. One senses a kind of mania in his wrath, in, for example, his assertion that the general public has defiled Zorrilla's well-known verses, "through endless repetition on lips slimy as toads' bellies." Defilement, that is, by mere popularity. The same loathing intensifies the cruelty of the novel's conclusion, where we meet the toad triumphant. At the end, Ana, utterly humiliated now, perceiving the full extent of her degradation, faints in the cathedral. A repulsive teenage acolyte comes across her in the shadows and takes advantage of her unconsciousness to kiss her on the mouth. This is how the novel ends:

> Ana came to her senses, tearing away mists of a nauseating delirium. She had the impression of having felt on her lips the slimy, cold belly of a toad.

As well she might. There is no further escape, no further excuse for hoping that life is anything but the disgusting existence of the toad-like inhabitants of Vetusta.

That is the novel's thesis, and many readers will find it unacceptable. It could, perhaps, diminish the art of a lesser artist. In the case of *La Regenta* it does not. Alas's personal problem was that his emotional convictions were incompatible with the scepticism forced on him by his liberal education. Whatever anguish this may have caused him personally, in creative terms the conflict was fertile, and resulted in a breadth of vision and of comprehension which would almost permit us, should we choose, to interpret Ana's ideals as mere illusions.

And when Alas is not dealing directly with subjects so close to his heart he leaves the reader to do the work, in the best tradition of the realist novel. Who is to say, for instance, what he intends by his treatment of those two famous archetypes of Spanish literature, Don Juan and the Calderonian husband, *el médico de su honra* (Mesía and Victor in the novel)? *La Regenta* is probably the first work in Spanish to tear these hallowed figures apart, and the demolition job is wholly convincing in human terms. But of what are we convinced? That the petty vulgarity of nineteenth-century materialism has extinguished these splendid types, or that the legends were always absurd fictions?

If Alas had provided the answers to these and a hundred other questions he would have written a simpler, duller, lesser novel. His art is an art of restraint, admirable for the way it respects both the complexity of its material and the intelligence of its audience. Any writer who masters this art as Alas does can surely be excused the odd tendentious presumption. Alas does not anyway really presume beyond insisting that we consider certain questions of great personal concern to himself—very little presumption to have to swallow in exchange for the novel's rewards.

"The Toads of Vetusta," in The Times Literary Supplement, *No. 3385, January 12, 1967, p. 26.*

CLIFFORD R. THOMPSON, JR.   (essay date 1969)

[*In the following excerpt, Thompson examines Alas's treatment of the themes of egoism and alienation in some of his short fiction and in the novel* La Regenta.]

The narrative fiction of Leopoldo Alas, more than that of any other writer of his generation in Spain, reveals an acute awareness of the isolation and loneliness of the human condition which we refer to today as alienation. Alas' intuitive recognition of this problem, which has received so much attention in recent years and has even been called the central problem of our time, contributes greatly to the relevance of his works for the twentieth-century reader. While our present more sophisticated consideration of alienation recognizes many varieties and complexities, it is essentially social alienation with which Alas is concerned. He does not, of course, use the term "alienated" to describe the isolated condition of his protagonists. The alienated character is referred to simply as being *solo;* he is cut off from meaningful contact with others.

Those of Alas' contemporaries who consciously sought the causes of social alienation tended to find them in physical changes imposed on man from without such as the industrialization of labor, the growth of cities and the increasing complexity of bureaucracy. Conversely, Alas sees alienation as fundamental to the human condition and closely associated with egoism, which he considers inherent in the nature of man and primarily responsible for the human predicament. Since this egoism-alienation duality is most simply and explicitly set forth in the stories, I shall first identify its appearance there before considering its significance to *La Regenta.*

Alas' most specific indictment of egoism is **"El pecado original,"** a story which satirizes the reaction of the human race to the discovery of a formula which will enable man to live forever. Although everyone in the world must contribute to the process by undergoing an extremely painful and costly operation, only one man, and subsequently his progeny, can be made immortal. All attempts to choose the one person to be given immortality are thwarted by egoism. An attempt to choose by ballot fails when each man votes for himself, and the idea of a lottery is rejected since no one will submit to the operation for the sake of another. . . . (pp. 193-94)

Looking beyond the legendary act of eating the forbidden fruit, Alas examines the attitude which prompted that act, asserting that it is man's selfish concern for himself and his lack of concern for others which caused his estrangement from God and which keep him from ever freeing himself from his imperfect condition.

With the earlier **"Cuervo,"** Alas had created a protagonist representative of the universal egoism to which he refers in **"El pecado original."** Don Angel Cuervo's egoism reveals itself specifically in his attitude toward death. Attending funerals is his greatest pleasure because the death of a fellow human being never fails to intensify his enjoyment of his own robust health. Alas constantly stresses the importance of egoism in determining the attitude of his protagonist and of those who share that attitude. (p. 194)

Cuervo's egoism is not unique; it is only extreme. . . . But even in an environment characterized by an egoistic indifference toward death, Cuervo surpasses the insensitivity of both man and nature in that he actually enjoys death, thriving on it, as his name suggests, like the proverbial crow of Spanish tradition. The alienation resulting from his inability to experience any emotion other than pleasure in the presence of death is underscored by the fact that the only person who shares this feeling is Antón, *el bobo,* a simple-minded youth alienated in the medical sense of the word, who accompanies him to every funeral.

While the reader is aware of the alienated condition of these two men, they themselves are not; for they are protected by their own egoism. An ironic aspect of alienation presented by Alas is that the egoism which contributes to it can, in some instances, be a very effective defense against it. As long as man is concerned exclusively with himself he will not be aware of his alienated state. Alas explores such a situation in **"El caballero de la mesa redonda,"** the story in which he most specifically relates alienation to egoism. Don Mamerto Anchoriz . . . is a light-hearted extrovert who enjoys being the center of attention but who does not really care about anyone. Secure in his own egoism, Anchoriz is not concerned that the interest which others show in him may be as superficial as his own. . . . (p. 195)

But the friendship of the other guests at a spa where he is staying is put to the test when he becomes seriously ill. Confined to his room he is soon ignored by his former companions who are interested only in the jovial amusing Anchoriz and quickly tire of the dying man, who is suddenly made aware that his own egoistic attitude is shared by others. . . . (p. 196)

Anchoriz now sees in new perspective the egoism which has been the principle of his life, for he has at last become the victim of that principle. Never having really cared about anyone he now finds that no one truly cares about him. Alas describes with great effect the increasing isolation and loneliness of the dying man as the season ends and guests and servants abandon the spa. The key word is no longer *egoísmo;* it is now *soledad* ["solitude"]. Anchoriz is saved from dying alone only by the presence of a rather ridiculous elderly woman whose romantic sentimentality, which Anchoriz had never shared, keeps her at his side.

Alas has presented his protagonist in a dual role: first as the complete egoist and then as the victim of egoism. This abrupt juxtaposition of roles focuses attention on the fact that man may be unaware of, or at least not concerned about, alienation as long as it is the result of his own attitudes and actions. Only when Anchoriz's illness makes him dependent on others does he become aware of his alienated condition. In Alas' stories the awareness of estrangement is usually reserved for the weakest members of society, for those whom illness or poverty or inferior social position has made particularly vulnerable to the egoism of others.

His most effective works are those which present the victims of an alienating society. As Ricardo Gullón has noted, stories such as **"Cuervo,"** in which the principal character represents an attitude of which Alas is critical, lack the lyric tension found in those stories involving characters to whose situation he is sympathetic. For this reason Gullón considers **"Cuervo"** a failure. Although **"Cuervo"** undeniably lacks the lyric tension to which Gullón refers, it has a very definite place in the total narrative production of its author, for it illustrates Alas' method of fulfilling the negative part of his rôle defined by Mariano Baquero Goyanes as defending the vital aspects of life and attacking the nonvital. **"Cuervo,"** like **"El pecado original"** and **"El caballero de la mesa redonda,"** is principally a study of an egoistic attitude.

The poetic quality lacking in these stories can be found in **"El dúo de la tos"** in which Alas presents characters estranged from society through no fault of their own. Like Anchoriz, in his final days, they are isolated by ill health. Alas begins this story by stressing the impersonality and anonymity of the hotel which provides the setting. The two nameless protagonists, a young man and a young woman each dying of tuberculosis, are referred to only as *bultos* ["baggage"] and are differentiated by the use of their room numbers.

Their loneliness and isolation are further emphasized by the constant use of the words *solo* ["alone"] and *soledad* ["solitude"]—Alas' way of referring to alienation—and it is the loneliness of their existence rather than their illness that they find difficult to endure. Their ill health is important to the story only in that it is responsible for their estrangement from society and is of secondary concern to the characters themselves. It is the fact of being alone that is primarily responsible for their unhappiness. Nowhere on their constant travels do they find sympathy or acceptance. . . . In this atmosphere of loneliness and indifference the coughing of number 32 and number 36 creates a sort of duo which gives each one the momentary illusion of companionship. By the following morning, however, the illusory moment has vanished and the two *bultos* resume their solitary travels.

With **"La conversión de Chiripa"** Alas presents a protagonist who encounters more than indifference; he is actually rejected by society. Chiripa . . . belongs to the very lowest social level and is therefore especially vulnerable. Alas introduces his protagonist at the moment when he is trying to find shelter from a storm knowing that he will be denied access to any public building because of his ragged and dirty condition. Being one of the least egoistic of Alas' characters, Chiripa is not concerned with social status or with possessing any of the material benefits of society. He scorns money, wanting only to be accepted by others. . . . (pp. 196-98)

Chiripa does eventually find the respect and acceptance which he seeks when he wanders into a church and discovers that there he receives as much consideration as the most distinguished members of society. The solution to his problem is only a partial one, of course, because the *alternancia* ["alternative"] which he finds within the church does not extend to the world outside. Chiripa is provided with a welcome refuge, but his social situation remains unchanged.

While the stories offer rather simple and easily identifiable aspects of the egoism-alienation duality recognized by Alas and reveal his constant interest in this problem, it is *La Regenta* which is his major exploration of the forces of egoism and alienation. Here the alienating society emerges as a theme in itself with egoism playing its usual decisive role. (p. 198)

[In *La Regenta*] Alas shows the humble members of society cast aside by the powerful; but it soon becomes evident that it is not just the poor who are estranged by the rich. Further description of Vetusta reveals that there are no meaningful relationships among those who live in the great mansions where exterior cordiality masks envy and rancor and where interest in one's acquaintances extends only to ferreting out their indiscretions and gossiping about them. Such is the social situation in which Alas places his protagonist.

While recent criticism has noted that Vetusta cannot be said to "determine" Ana's actions, it is generally agreed that they are at least in part dependent on and explained by her relationship to her environment. Frank Durand calls attention to an essential aspect of that relationship when he refers to Ana's "reactions against the nature of the city in which she lives" [see entry in Additional Bibliography]. I would stress the fact that her reaction is basically an egoistic one. Ana quite frankly despises the society of Vetusta and feels that she is superior to all the others. . . . (p. 199)

She sees herself as a victim of that society, as indeed she is, but unlike other of Alas' characters her estrangement is more psychic than physical. Although society's interest in Ana is superficial and insincere, her beauty and social position assure her being constantly sought after. Society does not in any overt way reject Ana; rather it is she who rejects social contacts which she finds meaningless and unsatisfying. Refusing to be like the people she scorns she sets herself apart from them, determined to follow a course of action which will distinguish her from her neighbors. . . . (pp. 199-200)

The egoism inherent in this decision further manifests itself in her attempt to find in religion or love a way out of an alienating environment in which she feels isolated and lonely. Alas refers specifically to the egoistic quality of her religious experience which causes her to feel that God looks on her with special pleasure and is satisfied with her. . . . She sometimes listens to De Pas . . . and while she speaks of making great sacrifices she nevertheless refuses to do anything which is at all inconvenient or unpleasant such as rising early as De Pas recommends.

Again it is egoism which is primarily responsible for Ana's downfall. She feels, in keeping with her belief in her innate superiority, that to resist Mesía is worthy of her. . . . She is so sure of herself, so certain that she will never submit to Mesía, that she will not deny herself the pleasure of seeing him. And as Alas points out, if she does have any doubts about her ability to resist, she follows the easy egoistic course of ignoring them. . . . (p. 200)

In spite of the egoism which leads Ana into adultery, the tragedy might have been averted had she been married to a man who adequately fulfilled the rôle of husband. But she is even more alienated from Quintanar than from society as a whole and so finds herself completely alone and highly susceptible to Mesía's attentions. Don Víctor, though solicitous at times, is frequently oblivious of his wife's existence. . . . (pp. 200-01)

Quintanar's egoism is of a different nature than Ana's, being more like that of the protagonists of **"Cuervo"** or **"El caballero de la mesa redonda"** in that it is protective and insulating. Unlike his wife, Víctor is not aware of being alienated; he never feels lonely. He is so absorbed with his own diversions, often shared with Frígilis, that he gives little thought to others. The fundamental characteristic of his egoism is selfishness. Conversely, Ana's egoism manifests itself primarily in conceit, causing her to see herself as a woman superior to her environment, worthy of God's personal attention and capable of enjoying but never yielding to amorous temptation.

Both conceit and selfishness are evident in the egoism of De Pas. He also despises Vetustan society and feels lonely and dissatisfied, and his interest in Ana is essentially selfish for his chief concern is not to help her but to satisfy himself. Just as Ana attempts to escape her alienated condition through religion, De Pas seeks escape through spiritual contact with Ana. But the satisfaction which he derives from their relationship only heightens his egoistic resolve to concern himself exclusively with his own gratifications. . . . (p. 201)

Mesía too seeks only personal satisfaction from his pursuit of Ana, which is not motivated by love but by egoism. Don Alvaro is anxious to make the ultimate conquest for the satisfaction of his vanity. . . . Throughout the novel pride plays a predominant rôle in the contest waged by these two men for dominance over Ana. When she fails to follow the advice of De Pas, he worries about what others will think; and on those occasions when she avoids Mesía, his first thought is for his reputation. The primary concern of each man is himself.

Of the four men who become significantly involved in the life of the protagonist only Frígilis is capable of disinterested action, and he is not precisely a member of Vetustan society with which he has almost no contact. . . . His reaction to Vetusta, though compassionate, has an element of the egoism which characterized the reactions of Ana and De Pas. He obviously considers himself superior to his environment, and except for his affection for Víctor and Ana, he shows no interest in others. Even his animated dialogues with the rural population outside the city are confined to discussions of crops and the weather, for he immediately ends any conversation which turns to topics which do not interest him.

While Alas, as narrator, does not specifically refer to him as an egoist his best friend does. . . . Víctor's thoughts reveal a lack of sensitivity in Frígilis to the feelings of others. While capable of genuine concern, his idea of helping people is to have them do as he thinks best, as when he arranged Ana's marriage to Víctor or as illustrated in his relationship with

Víctor in which it is always Quintanar who does what Frígilis wants to do. (pp. 201-02)

In *La Regenta* there is no love to transform and give meaning to the egoistic existence which estranges one individual from another, for *desamor,* as we see in **"El pecado original"** is one of Alas' synonyms for egoism. Instead of the *otroísmo* ["altruism"] which Galdós ascribes to Máximo Manse, there is only the *egoísmo* which Alas attributes not only to each of the principal characters but to the entire city of Vetusta. It is this egoism which is responsible for the alienated state of the characters and which prevents them from overcoming it. The tragedy, set against a background of collective egoism, is brought about by the individual egoism of Ana, her husband, her confessor and her lover, each of whom is primarily concerned with his own self-interest. (pp. 202-03)

Clifford R. Thompson, Jr., "Egoism and Alienation in the Works of Leopoldo Alas," in Romanische Forschungen, *Bd. 81, No. 1/2, 1969, pp. 193-203.*

NICHOLAS G. ROUND   (essay date 1970)

[*Round is an Irish educator and critic. In the following excerpt, he examines the novel* Superchería, *focusing on the development of the protagonist, Serrano.*]

Leopoldo Alas' achievement as a writer of short stories is clearly more sporadic in character than his success with the full-length novel; it is none the less real. The "novela corta" ["short novel"] *Superchería* is one of the peaks of that achievement. . . .

Strictly speaking, *Superchería* is not a *cuento* ["story"] but a *novela corta*—a distinction of whose nature Clarín himself was well aware. Its comparatively ample scale permits a degree of density in the characterization of Nicolás Serrano which would hardly have been possible in the shorter form. The very first paragraph initiates this process, informing the reader not only of Serrano's immediate circumstances, but also of aspects of his character which can later be used as points of reference to identify or anticipate his conduct. Thus Serrano's querulous dogmatism is acted out in his dealings with his doctor. . . . All this information is not merely given; what is important for an assessment of Clarín's art is the fact that it is fully fictionalized.

The *novela corta* form also allows a considerable variety of characters and settings. Clarín exploits these possibilities extensively here, yet the work is preserved from diffuseness by its concentration on the personal reality of its protagonist's life, a feature which ranges it with the short story, formally speaking, rather than with the novel. This concentration may have been easier for Clarín to achieve because Serrano's problem—how to be a philosopher in the world—was, in these general terms, a crucial one for his own life. Nevertheless, what is in question here is an exercise of artistic control: the successful realization as fiction of an individual life that is not Clarín's but Serrano's.

On the one hand Serrano is preoccupied by the desire for honesty and a purely intellectual integrity. On the other hand he is exposed, at first unwillingly, to the demands of his own appetite for emotional security and fruitfulness. Poised between these two sets of demands, he risks personal disintegration but a chance series of extraordinary events restores him to a measure of balance and wholeness. That is the substance of the tale in psychological terms, and its unifying simplicity is matched by a sturdy simplicity of narrative construction.

Essentially, the narrative moves through four phases. The initial episode of the nun's disappearance occupies the first two chapters. At this stage the mystery itself seems less important than the light which it throws on Serrano's personality. Chapter III and most of chapter IV deal with the early stages of his visit to Guadalajara. This makes it possible for him to attend a séance there; it also prepares him emotionally for the coming crisis. From here to a point midway through chapter IX there follows the account of the mind-reading session at which Caterina Porena startles Serrano by apparently divining the initial mystery and its importance for him. The final one and a half chapters explain her *acierto* ["success"] rationally and record Serrano's subsequent relationship with her. The maintenance of such a lucid structure in a work of this length without loss of subtlety on other levels is itself a major feat of craftsmanship.

The unity of the story is further reinforced by Clarín's careful control of the material point of view. Almost all the factual information in the story reaches the reader through the experience of Serrano himself. Even the exceptions to this are generally related to what is in his mind. The embarrassment of the nun at finding herself alone with him in the train is paralleled by his own embarrassment. Clarín gives details about Guadalajara society from a third person viewpoint but that society is firmly judged in its general outlines by Serrano himself. . . . Again, a narrative point like Caterina's starting up to help Serrano, who has fainted when she guesses his thoughts, and being restrained by Foligno coincides with Serrano's conviction that she cares for him but that her act is a *superchería* ["fraud"]. Two other exceptions—Antoñito's character and the final sentence of chapter II—seem to require further justification. Both are explicable.

Antoñito's importance lies in the fact that he is the character who most clearly embodies a temperament and attitude opposite and complementary to Serrano's own. Serrano suffers life as a series of cheats (*supercherías*); Antoñito practises it as such. Serrano is sceptical of all philosophical systems, Antoñito of all ideals. To establish such points of contrast and similarity, Clarín has to provide a certain amount of detail about Antoñito. But to make Serrano take detailed notice, at this stage, of his cousin's character and background would be psychologically implausible and would result in a loss of artistic concentration. Clarín is therefore obliged to introduce narrative material about Antoñito which is not covered by Serrano's immediate experience. (pp. 98-100)

To have placed Serrano at the centre of experience within the story was necessary if the mystery which so unnerved him was to be sustained without irksome authorial secretiveness. But Clarín also had to prevent his tale from being swamped at the outset by Serrano's own ideology. His initial state of unawareness and negativity . . . carries with it a closed system of judgement, incapable of assimilating events which, like the nun's disappearance, run counter to its premises. Obviously the reader cannot be invited to share in Serrano's refusal to respond to his experiences or he will simply abandon the story. Clarín has to provide a focus of judgement apart from his hero until Serrano's evaluation of his own nature and experience becomes more reliable. This is achieved by a judicious use of authorial commentary, prominent enough in the early chapters to enable readers to judge Serrano independently of his own inadequate frame of reference, and thereafter gradually withdrawn.

Yet even at the beginning, where it is most overt, third-person judgement is solidly grounded in the narrative. The evaluation of Serrano as a philosopher justifies itself in terms of psychological acuteness. It is the picture of a man whose philosophical idealism is a permanent obstacle to his ever making a gesture of practical idealism, for whom metaphysical anguish is hopelessly confused with digestive debility. And Serrano's actions in the course of the first two chapters confirm and amplify this assessment. (pp. 100-01)

Clarín is still very much present in the early stages of Serrano's visit to Guadalajara, noting, for example, the reasons for his resistance to nostalgic reverie. . . . But the philosopher himself is, by this time, on the point of abandoning this prejudice and confronting in his mind a wider area of his own experience. Once he has done so, authorial commentary recedes. The more involved Serrano becomes with Caterina, the closer Clarín comes to giving the reader his protagonist's unmediated experience until at last, after the crisis, he is allowed to tell of its aftermath in his own words. Even in the last chapter, which is third-person narrative once more, the sense that Serrano is now the source for both information and comment is still very strong. (p. 101)

This growing closeness to Serrano keeps pace with a developing insight into his character, and with changes in the mode of characterization through which he is presented. At the beginning, his character is established very largely through information about his past—appropriately enough, since his evasion of decisive action in the present is a product of past disillusion. Such information can readily be blended with authorial comment. In Guadalajara he begins to respond once more to present experience; the account of his personality, as well as Clarín's implicit assessment of it, can be focused through the dramatization of his relationships. By the closing chapters the relationship with Caterina has become all-important; the Nicolás Serrano to whom Clarín finally abdicates the telling of the story knows himself and is known to the reader through the nature of his contact with Caterina Porena.

The fact that Clarín is at last prepared to make Serrano into a focus of judgement as well as experience makes it clear that this development has the author's full approval. So do the overt comments on Serrano's condition at the start of the story. But Serrano's progress cannot be made to seem either credible or laudable by the mere fact of authorial approval alone. Whether it is credible will depend on the solidity of its fictional presentation. Whether it is morally acceptable will depend on the extent to which Clarín is able to establish that Serrano develops in a direction appropriate to his objective needs, as revealed in the fiction. In fact *Superchería* is a success on both counts. Serrano's development is adequately realized as fiction and is made to seem worthwhile in terms that are independent of Clarín's ideological hostility to rationalism and scepticism.

Serrano's initial trouble, indeed, is far wider than mere scepticism; it is an incapacity for committing himself to any scheme of thought or course of action. His refusal to be impressed by the landscape of Ávila, his dismissal of the extraordinary episode of the nun, and his later immobilization in Madrid . . . all illustrate the same pattern of behaviour. In each case Serrano is refusing to respond, not merely to something external, but to elements in his own nature. This is the basis of Clarín's case against his hero's rationalism. What he singles out for criticism in Serrano's philosophical memoirs is not their ideological viewpoint but the fact that they leave so much out. . . . This is more than an *a priori* condemnation of rationalism; it is a serious critique of a particular form which rationalism may take, effectively dramatized in Serrano's successive denials of his own nature. The trouble is not that he is a rationalist at

this stage in the story—he never, in fact, ceases to be one—but that he cannot be himself. He lacks personal wholeness and therefore, in a sense, he lacks integrity.

He does, of course, possess integrity in the sense of moral rectitude. . . . This means that his predicament is allowed a certain poignancy; he is more than a mere philosophical bad example. It also makes it plausible that he should, in the end, find a way out of his difficulties. There are various potential growing-points in his personality: the instinctive delicacy with which he reacts to finding himself alone in the carriage with the nun, the involuntary responsiveness to emotional impressions which he is at such pains to repress, and even the querulous and witty strain in his memoirs which hints at hidden reserves of toughness and vitality. The presence of such features early in the story and the resulting credibility of Serrano's development are evidence that Clarín wrote *Superchería* as a fictional artist, rather than as an antirationalist ideologue.

The precise means by which the first changes in Serrano's state of mind are brought about might, indeed, give rise to disquiet on just this score. It is disconcerting that his recovery should be initiated by a fit of nostalgia for his bookish and sentimental childhood days in Guadalajara. And the tone of conscious self-pity, so far from adding credibility to Serrano's eventual recovery of wholeness, recalls the indulgence with which Clarín, especially in his inferior short stories, was apt to treat such immature emotion. . . . (pp. 101-03)

Such a criticism would have more substance if this were the final stage of Serrano's development, approvingly contrasted with his rationalistic inertia. In fact it is an intermediate phase, representing a partial advance only. Both the reality of that advance in psychological terms and the relevance which it bears to his earlier condition are clearly established. Serrano has been incapable of commitment or of relationship, ultimately because he has refused to come to terms with his own nature. He now initiates his recovery with a new acceptance of self-relatedness. . . . [Serrano] recalling his childhood sojourn in Guadalajara, admits that there is a continuity between his past and present selves. . . . At this point at least he rises above mere self-indulgent musing and accepts a measure of responsibility for being himself which represents a positive gain in integrity.

Serrano's last extensive reminiscence about his past is not marked by any inhibition or self-consciousness in recalling past emotions. To that extent it is a further advance. But it, too, requires some kind of defence. In a long paragraph . . . Serrano, intrigued by the news that Tomasuccio's mother, besides being a professional mind-reader, is very like her son, recalls his own adolescent poem "El amante de la bruja" ["The Witch Lover"]. (pp. 103-04)

Serrano's thoughts of Caterina as a protective mother are merely an early stage in his recovery. They do not illustrate his mature reaction to her or even his thoughts on first meeting her; they arise long before that event takes place. And when he does meet her Serrano's reactions are a good deal more complex and remarkable. It is true that in the course of their few days' acquaintanceship he sees and admires her in her maternal role. But he then associates himself with her in a parental concern for Tomasuccio . . . rather than in a child-mother relationship. The idea of maternal "consuelo" ["comfort"] for Serrano is certainly present at an earlier stage in the story. But it is kept under control and soon give place to other ideas of greater maturity and appositeness to Serrano's condition.

Ideas of this sort, indeed, are implied by the very paragraph which first invokes the notion of consoling maternity. The witch-mistress of Serrano's adolescent poem is, after all, an odd incarnation of this quality. Though she offers her lover "amor puro, casto, ideal," ["pure, chaste, and ideal love"] she is still a Sevillan witch of a peculiarly depraved kind. . . . On one level this is simply a romantic cliché but on another the poem provides a valid and illuminating myth of Serrano's emotional needs. His dissociation from life ("alma solitaria, incomunicable") stems from his "desencanto"—a knowingness which "sees through" phenomena and so obstructs his becoming related to them. To recover his capacity for relatedness, and therefore for being fully himself, it is not enough for him to recapture childhood innocence. If he did only that, he would be recovering "integrity" by ceasing to be his true self—a dishonest conclusion to a contrived story. What he needs is to find a way of combining the world-abused knowingness which, in him, takes the form of rationalism with the emotional idealism which is also a part of his nature. Not an arbitrary escape into "innocence" but a renewal of the sense of innocence within experience. This at least is a mature aim, though "El amante de la bruja" is hardly a mature expression of it. Yet it is appropriate enough to the stage Serrano has reached. He is, in a sense, reliving his life; he has passed from childhood recollections to this reverie of adolescence, and is about to attend the séance where his adult philosophy will be challenged and its major crisis directly recalled by Caterina. Only at the end of this process will he reach ultimate maturity.

The later stages of his development are precipitated less by his new relationship with his past selves than by relationships with others. From the end of chapter III, when Tomasuccio appears, the story, hitherto concerned with Serrano in isolation, has begun to broaden out to include various subsidiary characters. Though Serrano is chiefly affected by Tomasuccio and Caterina, many of the other characters have an obvious relevance to his central dilemma. They remind the reader that there are many more ways of resolving the contradiction between innocence and knowingness than the one Serrano opts for. The magnetic mayor, possibly deluded by his own conceit, cheerfully imposes the result of that conceit, as a delusion, on others. Antoñito is content to lack innocence; to be knowing seems to him the way to get most fun out of life. Yet in another sense his wholehearted "living for the moment" might properly be described as innocent. Cesare Foligno, the professional illusionist, has abandoned innocence in order to make a living. The variety of these examples in itself helps to steer the story away from too doctrinaire a structure. By turning to account one of the advantages of the *novela corta* form—variety of characterization—Clarín is able to present Serrano's progress not philosophically, as the pursuit of the true synthesis, but imaginatively, as one of the varieties of human behaviour.

Even so, such an effect depends on these characters being more than exemplary. They must be, and are, fictionally adequate in their own right. Against Antoñito's type, it is true, Clarín seems to feel an obtrusively strong commitment. But even Antoñito is not judged in moralistic terms until some account has been given of his actual conduct. The mayor is a fine satirical vignette. Foligno is portrayed with a real command of perspective. He is seen almost exclusively through Serrano's hostility—an attitude accompanied by a fascination whose psychological significance is not lost on Clarín. . . . (pp. 104-06)

Yet Foligno's objective worth is clearly registered. The images of monarch, orator and actor, employed to describe him when he casts his first appraising glance at Serrano, evoke associations of both professionalism and dignity. His conversation with the philosopher in the interval of the séance compares favourably with Serrano's earlier boorishness in disrupting the performance. . . . Civilized, alien, expert, vulnerable and cunning, Foligno imposes both respect and conviction on the reader.

Tomasuccio and Caterina offer examples of contrary qualities reconciled which are more directly relevant to Serrano's condition. But in neither case is the fictional portrait which Clarín offers adversely affected by this relevance to the author's central preoccupation. Rather, the characters gain in solidity as a result. Tomasuccio's innocence and spontaneity are manifested in his ready acceptance of Serrano as a new friend; they are complemented externally by his golden ringlets and white clothes. (p. 106)

Clarín, no doubt for autobiographical reasons, was capable of writing embarrassingly badly about precocious and attractive children. But here, perhaps because they are childish rather than supposedly "spiritual" attributes, Tomasuccio's affectionate disposition, impulsive confidences and childish metaphysical puzzles are related without self-conscious unction. And once his part in the story—that of linking Serrano's recollections of childhood with his interest in Caterina—is over, Tomasuccio is kept firmly in the background. During most of Chapter IX, when Serrano is actually visiting Caterina, this attractive child is, very properly, asleep.

Knowingness and innocence are most completely and meaningfully reconciled in the person of Caterina Porena herself. It is part of her profession to be knowing, even disingenuous; her use of her memory of the disappearing nun episode to "read" Serrano's mind is anything but innocent. But Serrano finds in closer contact with her a rectitude and a practical purity of intention adequate to all his demands. She also gains in individuality for both Serrano and the reader in a way which carries her far beyond the fulfilment of the hero's secret wishes, or the author's ideal of safe, motherly womanhood. She is neither the idealized mother nor the fascinating witch, but someone whose experience of, and adaptation to, the harshness of life has left her dignity and moral sense intact. Serrano's relationship with her fulfils not the form of his immature wishes but the substance which lies behind them. The discovery of that relationship both changes and sustains him.

In some ways of course, Serrano is as much at a loss as he ever was. There is no hint that his philosophy is any more coherent; indeed his *angustia metafísica* ["metaphysical anguish"] is stated to be incurable. And though Caterina is the embodiment of something supremely important to him, any hope of a lasting contact with her is out of the question. When they meet in Madrid after Tomasuccio's death it is tacitly accepted that they will not see each other again. . . . And yet this episode, two years later than the main action of the story, is itself an index of Serrano's growth. At the beginning he is a divided personality, embittered by his failure to connect with realities he himself insists on destroying. Annihilated by the contradiction within himself, he still refuses to recognize it. At the end he voluntarily embraces the contradiction between his desire for Caterina and his moral sense by refusing either to forget her or to contemplate a love-affair with her. He does so, moreover, because he is able to envisage what she herself must be feeling; in balance with himself now, he can respond to another person's needs. At the beginning self-denial is a subject of academic speculation for him—"esta convicción no acababa de llegar" ["this conviction never caught on"]. By the end he has learned to give something up, possibly because he has found something worth giving up.

As for his philosophical difficulties, if he has not resolved them, he has at least put them in perspective—a perspective defined by the curious final episode of the dog. Serrano thinks the dog "mucho mejor filósofo que yo" ["a much better philosopher than I"]; it has, after all, achieved a view of the world exactly in accordance with most things in it: "tomaba los *fenómenos* como lo que eran, como una . . . superchería". ["it takes phenomena for what they are, like a . . . fraud"]. This is Clarín's last word in the story, as Serrano, walking away from his meeting with Caterina, follows the route the dog has taken. It has caused a certain amount of critical confusion. Serrano may follow, metaphorically, in the dog's rationalistic track; he may be no more trusting of phenomena than he ever was. But he acts like a man in possession of certainties of another kind. He is aware that besides phenomena there exist realities which are both meaningful and serious, even though they are also tragic and subject to time "quererse o lo que fuese" ["to love each other or else"] and the responsiveness to one another which dictates his and Caterina's forbearance. He is still less than a complete philosopher; to judge from his aside about the dog, he does not regard that as a particularly desirable thing to be. But he has become, in a sense in which he was not one before, a person. He is still given to prickly and sardonic reflections—about the dog, about Foligno—and subject to sudden floods of emotion. But this continuity of his character merely makes his growth the more credible.

The characterization of **Superchería,** then, supports the view that the theme of the story is Serrano's recovery of personal wholeness. This theme of integrity subsumes the philosophical question of appearance and reality, deepens the seriousness of the love-story and transcends Clarín's personal preoccupations with childhood and with maternal feeling. Its projection in terms of personalities emerges as neither schematic nor arbitrary. The characterization is strong in both psychological insight and fictional reality. But the working-out of the theme in terms of plot seems, at first sight, less satisfactory. Much—perhaps too much—depends on a series of unlikely coincidences. A story in which improbable events bring about unexpected changes in the protagonist's outlook runs the risk of appearing contrived and dogmatic. How does Clarín manage to prevent **Superchería,** with its manifold coincidences, from lapsing into a story of miraculous conversion?

In the first place, the actual treatment of Serrano's character clearly shows that his is a story not of conversion, but of growth. The influence of extraordinary events, then, is more oblique and gradual than it would have been had he undergone an abrupt conversion from "wrong" attitudes to "right" ones. Secondly, two of the major coincidences in the story—Serrano's decision to visit Guadalajara and his attendance at the séance—are explained in some depth. He goes to Guadalajara at his aunt's request and because of the attraction of his own memories of the town. He visits the séance at Antoñito's insistence and, presumably, because of his own fascinated curiosity about Caterina. These incidents at least are made to seem natural and uncontrived.

There remain two highly improbable phenomena: the nun's disappearance and Caterina's inexplicable awareness of that episode. These events are certainly coincidental and they certainly have a catalytic effect on Serrano's development. The crucial question, however, is the way in which that effect is exerted: whether Serrano is directly bludgeoned into a change

of view by these outrageous coincidences, or whether their impact on him is integrated into the more general pattern of his personal growth. The implications of the story's title for that process of growth are important here.

The word *superchería* has a wide range of connotations within the story: the professional charlatanism of the mind-readers, the mayor's amateur mesmerism and Antoñito's habit of selfishly imposing on all comers are all covered by the term in its literal meaning. But it has a still wider application. It can refer to an interpretation which the committed rationalist is liable to put upon all ostensibly significant realities. Thus Serrano, in his earlier memoirs, dismisses both his own philosophizing and other people's as an illusory masquerade. . . . The philosopher, on this view, is guilty of creating those very delusions whose victim he is. A little later Serrano, though desperate to find a rational explanation for the nun's disappearance, extends his scepticism to embrace the scientific outlook itself. . . . Any intellectual activity, any claim to vision, any experience comes under the same ban; everything is a form of trickery. As a result there is no foundation in any reaction to experience on which Serrano can build in order to act authentically or to come to terms with his own nature. The conviction that everything is a "superchería" robs him alike of wholeness and of peace.

Ultimately he escapes this predicament. He does so as his reactions to the nun's disappearance and to Caterina's extraordinary *acierto* gain in clarity and affirmative quality. But it is not these phenomena, interesting as they are in themselves, which provide him with his possibility of integrity. Initially both of them threaten him with total personal disintegration. His reaction when the nun disappears is a further withdrawal into defensive rationalizing. . . . He keeps insanity at bay by ferocious, clumsy, polemic rationalism: "abominaciones contra el milagro y la superstición, y a vueltas de todo esto la declaración de su miedo" ["abominations against miracle and superstition, and before everything this, the declaration of his fear"], as Caterina puts it. As for her mysterious awareness of the earlier incident, its immediate effect is to provoke a physical collapse on his part. Both incidents, by making his plight more extreme, break him up emotionally and thus prepare him for a new integration of his personality. But they do not themselves supply that integration.

Their effect on his philosophical attitudes is marginal. He consistently suspects that both episodes involve an element of falsity. His first reaction to the incident of the nun is to wonder if it is a hallucination and despite its disturbing implications he settles for this view. He is sceptical of the Folignos' telepathic powers from the outset. . . . He is inclined to explain the couple's successes in terms of an understanding that emanates from the sexual link between them—something of which he is jealously aware. When Caterina offers to read his past thoughts he still suspects her of deceit. . . . (pp. 107-11)

And as it turns out Serrano is quite right. Both of these extraordinary events have purely natural explanations. Both, consequently, contain an element of *superchería;* they amount to less than they seem to be. The vanishing nun was neither a vision nor a hallucination, but something of a comic figure; embarrassed at Serrano's presence, she elected to ride on the footboard of the train. Caterina did not employ telepathy to read Serrano's mind; she merely turned to account the coincidence of their meeting again, and the fruit of a curiosity she herself felt to have been discreditable. If Serrano's rationalism was barely shaken before, it is wholly vindicated by these revelations. But he himself has been changed—not as a philosopher but as a man. His indifference to these deflating explanations is one of the ways in which this change manifests itself.

For what matters to Serrano now is not Caterina's *acierto*, much less any possible explanation it may have, but Caterina herself and the fact of her contact with him. Her ''divination'' of his thoughts is, artistically speaking, a *coup de théâtre;* but it is also the perfectly logical culmination of his growth towards emotional responsiveness. The quickening of his atrophied emotions in Guadalajara, the meeting with Tomasuccio, the fantasy of ''El amante de la bruja,'' the actual sight of Caterina ''el amor . . . sin ojos'' [''love . . . without eyes'']—the eyes themselves that are brown and do not see him yet, his clumsily aggressive attempt to discredit her powers, the touch of her finger in the next experiment—all these stages lead him to the moment when, impinging directly on his inner life by her own action, she destroys him for a minute and he faints away.

When he recovers, it is to wonder urgently whether the experience was a real one; it is the sight of Caterina which guarantees its reality for him. From this moment onwards he begins to reintegrate himself through contact with another self, through Caterina's being unchallengeably, really there. . . . The marvellous element in this *supercheria* hardly matters now; no more does the rational explanation. The relationship with Caterina is established as the basis of Serrano's new-found peace and wholeness.

His discussion with Caterina on pp. 180-85 clarifies and confirms this account of the part played by extraordinary events in influencing his development. (p. 112)

His feeling for her does, of course, contain an element which can fairly be called idealistic. But even when she provides corroboration of his former fantasies of ideal motherhood, or of tender innocence coexisting with a sorceress's cunning, his account of her is centred upon the woman as she is, not on his own imaginings. . . . This ''honrada madre de familia'', he can now acknowledge, exists to serve her own dependents, not to gratify his daydreams. He can accept things in her which run clean counter to his own wishes. He accepts the limits which she sets to her frankness with him. . . . Her uncomfortably acute insight into his feelings at the nun's disappearance is no threat to him now; he can record, almost incidentally, her awareness that he was afraid. He can even accept and set down in his memoirs her rebukes to his own moral position. . . . Above all, he never wavers in his acceptance of the separation from her which they both know to be necessary. He speaks only of his love and respect for the family as a whole, never for her alone. Evading a direct declaration to her, he can take his leave of her with a sense that his responsibilities have been met. . . . He is not perfect in this relationship, as his disingenuous entry in Caterina's commonplace book and his obsessive curiosity when they part show. But he has become capable of making decisions in response to factors outside himself and his ideology, and has come, in practice, to order his life in response to the woman he loves.

Two years later, when they meet again, this is still apparent. There is a strong presumption that it is his contact with her which enables him to find a respite from his philosophical perplexities and to take pleasure in the Madrid spring. . . . Quite explicitly, he accepts their definitive separation after Tomasuccio's death because of the demands of his own moral nature and of hers. He does not resist, but welcomes as the best that life can provide, the prospect of living with memories of her,

even though he knows that they, too, will be blurred by time. This is an acceptance of his own past and his own needs which the Serrano of the earlier chapters could not have achieved.

In particular, it is an acceptance of the limitations of human existence. Serrano's philosophical awareness of these is at last in balance with the imperatives of his own life and emotional experience. Phenomena may be radically illusory but the mutual responsiveness which has existed between himself and Caterina is absolute in its value and authenticity. Awareness of others, a sense of responsibility to them, acceptance of his own nature and its objective conditions—these are the manifestations of that renewed sense of personal wholeness which Serrano has gained from his relationship with Caterina. The relationship is an idealistic one in the sense that it contains elements of self-denial, and also in that it has no physical consummation. It is not idealistic in the sense of insulating Serrano from contact with reality; in fact he is more in touch with the world outside himself now than ever he was in his earlier, cerebral phase. This is a distinction between types of idealism which Clarín was not always able to make.

Serrano, then, finds that relationship, even if begun from elements of childhood recollection and adolescent fantasy, can grow into something objectively immune to the charge of *supercheria*. He has remade himself by a process of reliving his life which is psychologically entirely plausible, free from ideological doublethink, and objectively impressive in its moral outcome. This, if it is an idealistic concept, is not one which forces an arbitrary shape on intractable fictional material; neither the role of coincidence within the story nor the introduction of themes and motifs which were personally significant for Clarín mars the autonomy and maturity of the tale. It arises from a mature understanding of the possibilities of human character, as they are presented in the particular character of Nicolás Serrano. It is this maturity of view which makes *Supercheria* the fine story it is; the other features which command respect—philosophical seriousness, psychological finesse, comic vigour, descriptive beauty, range and assurance of tone, skilled and intricate plotting, mastery of the particular form—are all dependent on this initial maturity. It is evidence of the highest artistry that a work successfully embodies in its form what it conveys in its meaning. *Supercheria* both treats of and exemplifies integrity. (pp. 114-16)

Nicholas G. Round, ''The Fictional Integrity of Leopoldo Alas' 'Supercheria','' in Bulletin of Hispanic Studies, *Vol. XLVII, No. 1, January, 1970, pp. 97-116.*

NOËL M. VALIS (essay date 1983)

[*An American short story writer, poet, and critic, Valis is the author of* The Decadent Vision in Leopoldo Alas *(1981). In the following essay, she discusses the ways that language, imagery, symbolism, and characterization in* La Regenta *combine to lend depth and complexity to the novel.*]

Reading the one thousand and more pages of *La Regenta,* by Leopoldo Alas (also known as Clarín), is an experience in entrapment. The more deeply we penetrate its reading surfaces the more exasperated and bewildered we as readers feel. Certainly like all novels, *La Regenta* refuses to be caught the first time around. Or the second or the third. The critical reader cannot keep the work complete and of a piece in his head; and as the sought for unity slips away, in its place a growing sense of despair and unease settles over him. Faced with such obstacles, he may even try to avoid, for a while at least, a text as disturbing and complex as *La Regenta.* Folded and double-folded in multiple layers, Clarín's novel has the fearful capacity to absorb, to pull the reader in. This of course is exactly what a great novel should do: it should uproot us from our unwanted and various selves and repot us in more conducive soil. But what if the reader-critic stumbles in his understanding and experiencing of the text, and finds that apparently smooth, even impenetrable surfaces, once tapped in the right place, break into disquieting fragments? What if the order sought for isn't any order at all?

"Order," Rudolf Arnheim says, "is a necessary condition for anything the human mind is to understand." The critical reader is of course that ordering principle which makes explicit an implicit order in literature. It is a natural inclination in the critic's soul to make sense of things. He wants to get on with it, to remove all that murk. He assures us he has examined his critical conscience—has not imposed a meaning, a unity—he does not want to invent the uninvented, only to make the thing invented, *la cosa inventada,* work—and work for him (and maybe for somebody else). So, having made our judgment, we hang the picture upside down—(sometimes)—and we get on with it: it being in this case *La Regenta* and meaning.

But meaning is inseparable from order. Indisputably *La Regenta* possesses order, the order of form. . . . Its highly organized specificity is unsurprising, given the fact that *La Regenta* belongs to the great mimetic tradition of novel writing. Its sophisticated verbal structure is infused with the real and the realness of objects, people, and places. What it says about them, however, is not very comforting, for this is a novel of betrayal: betrayal on both the human and spiritual planes of being. Centered around an emotionally confused though essentially decent, young married woman, Ana Ozores, and her desire to be loved, Clarín's recreation of a mean-souled, backwater town of late nineteenth-century Spain is an extremely detailed and dense portrait of moral and social decadence on the collective and individual level. Ana's inner instability, her loneliness, and sense of alienation from the rest of Vetusta—Alas's fictional universe—all these things will drive her, in desperation, first to the Church (specifically, to her confessor, the Machiavellian but also tormented Fermín de Pas), then to an adulterous affair with the shallow but attractive local Don Juan, Álvaro Mesía. Ultimately she will be betrayed by both, and ostracized by a world which ignores, adulterates, even perverts its own spiritual and moral values. One could describe the essence of Vetustan existence as an "unchanging core [that] paradoxically consists of an inauthenticity which itself is derived from lack of values and beliefs. . . . The very absence of beliefs—of a moral center—turns in upon itself and creates a static flurry of activity which never moves from its original spot, a stationary whirlwind. It is this deep sense of stagnation which partially accounts for the aura of decadence in the novel."

And yet to use decadence as an explanation of what *La Regenta* means is certainly insufficient in itself, for there is something in this text that eludes one, something that is and yet at the same time is not in the text. Rutherford put his finger on one significant aspect of *La Regenta,* on how "the language of *La Regenta* itself embodies [a] critique of language," for "the hidden, implied meanings, to which only literary competence gives access, are at almost every point of greater importance than what is actually stated" [see John Rutherford entry in Additional Bibliography]. It is also language that turns in upon itself to reveal the fakery, the incompleteness, even the disorder of language and of the manipulators of that language. Clarín's

ease in using for example parenthetical commentary to puncture the misuse of language and unclear thinking (Pepe Ronzal and his "espifor"), reiterated clichés to demonstrate the moral vacuity of Vetusta and the lethal effectiveness of the banal (the banquet scene in Ch. XX and Santo Barinaga's death scene), and fragmented sentences to reveal a loss of wholeness in personality and incoherent thinking (Ana Ozores' hysteria), all of these linguistic tricks point to the inherent duplicitous nature of language.

So words in *La Regenta* often appear not to possess substance. Still, as a critic I felt myself adrift, because what I was looking for was not there, at least, not in the language, the images, or characters, not, that is, in the text itself. What I wanted was the meaning beneath the textual surface, something below the verbal structure and (I hoped) probably implicated in it. How to see this, to explain it? Through an analysis of an early scene occurring in Chapter X, one which prefigures the disastrous consequences of Ana Ozores's future adulterous conduct. Alone, isolated, an outcast from dreamt of, better worlds, the *Regenta* steps out one night onto the balcony and stares into the face of the universe:

> Ana oía ruidos confusos de la ciudad con resonancias prolongadas, melancólicas; gritos, fragmentos de canciones lejanas, ladridos. Todo desvanecido en el aire, como la luz blanquecina reverberada por la niebla tenue que se cernía sobre Vetusta, y parecía el cuerpo del viento blando y caliente. Miró al cielo, a la luz grande que tenía enfrente, sin saber lo que miraba; sintió en los ojos un polvo de claridad argentina; hilo de plata que bajaba desde lo alto a sus ojos, como telas de araña; las lágrimas refractaban así los rayos de la luna.
>
> ("Ana heard the confused noises of the city, with their prolonged, melancholy resonances; cries, fragments of distant songs, barks. Everything faded in the air, like whitish light reverberating through the tenuous mist which wrapped itself around Vetusta, and seemed like the warm, soft body of the wind. She looked at the sky, at the great light which spread out in front of her, without knowing what she was looking at. In her eyes she felt a powder of argentine clarity; a thread of silver that descended from above to her eyes, like spider webs; it was in this way that her tears refracted the rays of the moon.")

Distance, fragments of sound, a tenuous light, shimmering objects metamorphosed in the night: all this sets the cosmic frame of an unstable, fragile reality.

Ironically, in an open space Ana feels closed in, as though she were suffocating, and with the intention of writing a letter to her confessor, Fermín de Pas, she goes back inside to her husband's study. "Se lo contraré todo, todo, lo de dentro," she says to herself, "lo de más adentro también" ("I will tell him everything, everything, all that's inside me, even my deepest feelings). Within,

> el despacho estaba a oscuras; allí no entraba la luna. Ana avanzó tentando las paredes. A cada paso tropezaba con un mueble. . . . Dio un paso sin apoyarse en la pared, siguió de frente, con las manos de avanzada para evitar un choque. . . .
>
> ¡Ay! ¡Jesús! ¿Quién va? ¿quién es? ¿quién me sujeta?—gritó horrorizada.
>
> Su mano había tocado un objeto frío, metálico, que había cedido a la presión, y en seguida oyó un chasquido y sintió dos golpes simultáneos en el brazo,

que quedó preso entre unas tenazas inflexibles que oprimían la carne con fuerza. Con toda la que le dio el miedo, sacudió el brazo para librarse de aquella prisión, mientras seguía gritando:

¡Petra! ¡luz! ¿quién está aquí?

Las tenazas no soltaron la presa; siguieron su movimiento y Ana sintió un peso, y oyó el estrépito de cristales que se quebraban en el piso. No se atrevía a coger con la otra mano las tenazas que la oprimían, y no se libraba de ellas aunque seguía sacudiendo el brazo. Buscó la puerta, tropezó mil veces; ya sin tino, todo lo echaba a tierra; sonaba sin cesar el ruido de algo que se quebraba o rodaba con estrépito por el suelo. Llegó Petra con luz.

("the study was dark; there, the moon didn't penetrate. Ana moved forward, feeling the walls. At every step she stumbled into furniture. She took one step without leaning on the wall, keeping dead ahead, with her hands stretched out in front to avoid a shock. . . .

"Ay! Sweet Jesus! Who goes there? Who is it? Who is holding me?" she cried out in horror.

Her hand had touched a cold, metallic object, which had given in to the pressure, and immediately she heard a crack and she felt two simultaneous blows on her arm, which was caught between rigid pincers tightly oppressing her flesh. With all the strength fear gave her, she shook her arm to free herself of this prison, and all the while she continued to cry:

"Petra! Light! Who is here?"

The pincers would not loosen their prey. They seemed to follow her movements and Ana felt the weight, and she heard the crash of crystal breaking on the floor. She didn't dare take hold, with her other hand, of the pincers which were crushing her, and she still couldn't free herself from them although she kept shaking her arm. She looked for the door, stumbling a thousand times; now, all caution gone, she let everything fall around her. All you could hear was the noise of something breaking or crashing with a great racket to the floor. Petra arrived with a lamp.")

The cold, metallic object Ana runs into turns out to be an animal trap, imperfectly fashioned by her husband Victor and their friend of long standing, Frígilis. Their intent: "tener bien sujeto al delincuente cogido infraganti" ("to hold tight the delinquent caught infraganti"). Ignorant of the machine's purpose, Petra and Ana have to wreck the mysterious artifact to free the *Regenta*'s bruised arm. "¡Qué! estropicio!" the maid exclaims, "apuntando a los pedazos de loza, cristal y otras materias incalificables que yacían sobre el piso." ("What a mess!. . . pointing to the pieces of crockery, crystal, and other unqualifiable objects that lay scattered on the floor"). And a few lines later: Petra "sentía un júbilo singular viendo aquella ruina de objetos que ella tenía que considerar como vasos sagrados de un culto desconocido" ("She felt a singular joy seeing the ruins of objects she was obliged to consider as sacred vessels of an unknown cult"). Clarín then reframes the scene in the same way he opened it, by suggesting a cosmic view of reality in Ana's subsequent walk through the garden. The moon, that solitary creature, seems to be falling into the abyss of a great dark cloud. In a panic of despair, the *Regenta* sees herself as the moon and the cloud, old age bereft of love, as Vetusta becomes engulfed in shadow and the cathedral transformed into "más sombra en la sombra" ("more shadow in the shadow").

What can we say about this scene? Like many other moments in *La Regenta* it operates on several levels. It is, first of all, extremely well constructed in the artful balancing of an interior scene between two exteriors, the balcony and the garden. This juxtaposition of outer and inner space suggests a layered and potentially expanding reality, as well as an implied tension between open-endedness and closed-endedness, freedom and constriction. Yet one strongly suspects this is a trap, not only for the participants but for the unwary reader as well. Freedom, Ana will discover, is an illusion. The fleeting liberation she will experience in her love affair with Álvaro Mesía is tangled in deceit and bonded to the bruised impotence of betrayed hearts. No freedom, only darkness, inside and outside. I have called this outer space a cosmic frame, a structural device to balance the scene. But there is also another kind of frame in this remarkable novel: the limits within which the characters function; in other words, the social space they move in, here, Víctor's study. What is significant is that within both the microframe of the social and beyond it, in the cosmic outlines of the heavens, darkness prevails.

This obscurity and Ana's subsequent literal entrapment in Víctor's things represent, it is evident, a symbolic rendering of the *Regenta*'s unilluminated and restricted existence. The scene also functions . . . as an implied metaphorical prefiguration of the novel's grim conclusion. Like the unsuspecting victims of Víctor's and Frígilis' trap, Ana will be caught infraganti; and Víctor will suffer the fate of his treasured objects. But even before that there are thematic and plot connections between this scene and others: I am thinking especially of the episode in Chapter XXVIII when Víctor and Fermín chase after the *Regenta* through the woods of the Marqués de Vegallana's summer estate. There they are in the middle of a violent thunderstorm, Fermín eaten away by a raging jealousy and Víctor completely bewildered. What are they doing here? Víctor wonders, while his half-opened umbrella runs into branches and snags itself in brambles:

> De rama en rama, de tronco a tronco, en todas direcciones subían y bajaban hilos de araña que se le metían por los ojos y boca al ex regente, que escupía y se sacudía las telas sutilísimas con asco y rabia.
>
> —¡Esto es un telar!—gritaba, y se envolvía en los hilos como si fueran cables, procuraba evitarlos y tropezaba, resbalaba y caía de hinojos, blasfemando contra su costumbre.
>
> ("From branch to branch, from trunk to trunk, in every direction, up and down went the spiders' threads, clinging to the eyes and mouth of the *ex-regente*, who in disgust and anger spat and brushed at the very fine webs.
>
> 'This is one great spider web!' he yelled, and he got all caught up in the threads as though they were cables. In trying to avoid them, he stumbled, slipped and fell to his knees, swearing, against his rule.")

Quintanar is caught in a web of circumstances and human weakness from which he is unable to extricate himself. The situation—humorous, yet also menacing—anticipates Víctor's later entrapment in his code of honor and public opinion. Similarly, De Pas "llevaba la boca y los ojos envueltos en hilos pegajosos, tenues, entremetidos" ("he felt his mouth and eyes entangled in sticky, tenuous, meddlesome threads"), for he too is trapped, the male animal imprisoned in the cassock of his priestly functions. So the two of them stumble, lost in a maze of spider webs, brambles, and thorns. De Pas "se perdía, confundía las señales, iba y venía . . . y don Víctor detrás, librándose de las arañas como de leones, de sus hilos como de cadenas'' (''he kept getting lost, he mixed up the signs, coming and going . . . and don Víctor behind him, freeing himself from the spiders as though they were lions, from their threads as though they were chains.'') And what do they find? A red silk garter—''una liga de seda roja con hebilla de plata.'' ''My wife's garter!'' Quintanar exclaims. Stupefied, De Pas learns a moment later that this unassuming object really belongs to Petra, the maid.

But what has Petra to do with all this? After all, she is a minor character in **La Regenta.** Let me make an apparent digression to one other moment in the novel, and then let us see if we can . . . only connect. Chapter XXIX: Víctor discovers he has been cuckolded. How does it come about? Through Petra. In reality, there is a chain of events and character interaction, irreversible and ineluctable in all likelihood, that has led to Quintanar's moment of truth. Fearful that Petra will tell Ana he has been fooling around with her, Víctor wants the maid to leave his household, but he is afraid to ask. Instead, Álvaro performs the dirty task; as a result, Petra goes to the Magistral and, together, they machinate the *Regenta*'s downfall. This linkage of events is reinforced by Petra's own Machiavellian awareness of her role in the Vetustan world. She sees the life of Quintanar and the others hanging by a thread, ''un hilo que tenía ella, Petra, en la mano, y si ella quería, si a ella se le antojaba, ¡zas! todo se aplastaba de repente . . . ardía el mundo'' (''a thread which she, Petra, held in her hand, and if she wanted, if she so desired, whoosh! Suddenly everything would be squashed . . . the world would burn''). And a few pages later, reflecting on her situation, she says to herself: ''¿Qué hacer? No cabía duda, ser prudente, coger el codiciado fruto, entrar en aquella *canonjía,* en casa del Magistral. Para esto era preciso echar a rodar todo lo demás, romper aquel hilo que ella tenía en la mano y del que estaban colgadas la honra, la tranquilidad, tal vez la vida de varias personas'' (''What to do? There was no doubt, she had to be careful, grab the coveted fruit, beard the Magistral's house, that canon's den. For this it was necessary to forget about everything else, break that thread which she held in her hand and from which hung the honor, the peace of mind, perhaps even the lives of several people''). And with a twist of her hand she sets Víctor's alarm clock ahead one hour, thus enabling him to see Álvaro Mesía climb down from Ana's balcony in the small hours of the morning.

What we see in these three distinct parts of the novel is a relatedness, a network of associations which thematically and structurally informs **La Regenta.** Petra herself provides a link in these scenes—as she also does, for example, in Chapter IX by escorting the *Regenta* through the masses of workers along *El boulevard.* In Chapter X she assists Ana in the destruction of Quintanar's trap while taking secret pleasure in the diminutive armageddon all about her. In Chapter XXVIII her red silk garter, once Ana's, becomes at the same time a cynical and mocking reproof of both Víctor's and Fermín's impotence before the downhill course of events and a portent of the *Regenta*'s imminent disgrace. (At the end of this chapter, one recalls, Ana's seduction will take place.) And in Chapter XXIX Petra, that thoroughly nasty yet captivating creature, deliberately breaks the thread precariously binding together the fragile texture of Vetustan relationships. And nothing can put it right again.

The interconnectedness we perceive in the example of Petra is further suggested in Clarín's use of specific images and objects.

The *Regenta*'s ''hilo de plata que bajaba desde lo alto a sus ojos, como telas de araña,'' as her tears refract the rays of the moon, anticipates the *telar* of spider webs and broken branches through which Quintanar and Fermín stumble many chapters later. It also stimulates an echoing and parallel response in another moment of the novel when Fermín, on the balcony, looks at the moon ''a través de unas telarañas de hilos de lágrimas que le inundaban los ojos. . . .'' (''Through spider webs of threads of tears which flooded his eyes. . .''). There is a figurative, sometimes even literal, thread running through these scenes: the *hilos* of light-dusted tears and spider webs, the garter with its obvious linking associations (*liga → ligar*), and Petra's final *hilo* of plot and counterplot. Thus things connect in **La Regenta,** they enmesh themselves within the fabric of Vetustan life.

But they also disconnect, come apart, unraveling lives and relationships. Let us go back once more to the scene in Chapter X. What if we looked at it from another perspective, from the point of view of the ruined objects themselves? Petra, we recall, regards them as ''vasos sagrados de un culto desconocido'' [''sacred vases of an unknown cult'']. What things are they anyway? Quintanar kindly enumerates them for us at the end of the chapter: ''. . .vio con espanto sobre el mueble los restos de su herbario, de sus tiestos, de su colección de mariposas, de una docena de aparatos delicados que le servían en sus variadas industrias de fabricante de jaulas y grilleras, artista en marquetería, coleccionador entomólogo y botánico, y otras no menos respetables'' (''. . . Horrified, he saw on the furniture the remains of his herbarium, his pots, his butterfly collection, a dozen delicate apparatuses that served him in his various activities as a fabricator of coops and cricket cages, as a cabinetmaker, as a collector, entomologist and botanist, and in other, no less respectable endeavors''). Víctor is an amateur botanist, ornithologist, inventor, hunter, gardener, everything, as Ana knows, except a husband. In many ways, Víctor himself—''de blanda cera'' (''like soft wax''), as Alas dryly observes—is a product of someone else's experimentation, namely, of Frígilis, that ''máquina agrícola'' (''agricultural machine'') to use the *Regenta*'s phrase, who has been patiently troweling year in and year out layer after layer of his ideas and interests onto Víctor's protean personality. Their enthusiasms reflect the nineteenth century's delight in things material and its obsessive tinkering with the mechanics of objects, with invention. Hence, Petra's ''vasos sagrados'' represent in their own small way the age of science and knowledge, the age of domination when men were confident they could order and manipulate the material and natural impulses of the universe.

That Ana's maid should fail to comprehend the nature of these objects, that she should gloat slyly over their ruin, is not at all surprising. Why should a poorly educated working girl bother with the invention of things, when the acquisition of those things is all that really matters? And surely Víctor's scattered objects reflect the comfort and leisure of a socio-economic class capable of devoting its time and resources to such scientific pursuits. I would suggest that Petra's willing participation in the destruction of Víctor's seemingly insignificant *cachivaches* represents an indirect attack of one social class against another, that it is an act of secret revenge of inferior against superior; and that her subsequent behavior bears me out in this view. There is evidently a kind of sympathetic magic at work here in these implications of class strife: destroy the object, destroy the class. In a word, if we interpret this scene as an artistic re-elaboration of social history, the resultant disorder is then a portentous sign of a world turned upside down, of hierarchical values ready to crack apart at any moment—at least from the point of view of the Spanish bourgeoisie, already fearful of lower-class encroachments.

But I think we underestimate Clarín's esthetic intelligence if we leave it at that. As I observed before, this scene works on different levels; and Alas's treatment of objects is witness to the complexity of approach in **La Regenta**. Remember how he first incorporates Víctor's trap into the text. It is a cold, metallic object. . . . Like Ana, the reader does not recognize the object. It has become, to use the Russian formalist Shklovsky's term, defamiliarized. "'. . . Art exists," he writes, "that one may recover the sensation of life; it exists to make one feel things, to make the stone *stony*. . . . The technique of art is to make objects 'unfamiliar,' to make forms difficult. . . . *Art is a way of experiencing the artfulness of an object; the object is not important*." In the darkness, Ana *hears* the click and *feels* the blows, as her arm becomes entrapped in the object. Dehumanized, she feels, she hears things crashing about her as, in her blindness, she wildly flails her imprisoned body. So we too feel not only the sharp pressure of metal against soft flesh, but the degrading effect of radical alienation between character and object. In making the *Regenta* and the reader as well feel and hear, but not see—how cleverly Clarín bounces verbs off and against the substantiveness of nouns—the acute entrapping qualities and consequences of the thing itself, the "trapness" of the trap, he simultaneously suggests estrangement from that very object. In defamiliarizing the object he makes us intensely aware of it, even physically linked to it, but also profoundly distanced from its very thingness.

Objects entrap. Yet things, I would suggest, are not hostile in themselves. It is only a piece of metal Ana has run into, after all. It is of course manmade, and in that sense, could be metaphorically construed as the trap of marriage, for despite all his good intentions, Frígilis the matchmaker has erred gravely. But it is Ana herself in her hysterical terror and confusion who wreaks havoc on Víctor's things. Immersed in feelings, she does not stop to think. Indeed, her intelligence seems to be of no use here. Indisputably, the *Regenta* is a woman of deep feelings, of refined sensibilities, superior to her fellow Vetustans, but her superiority is ultimately ill-founded, because she remains morally and emotionally confused. The real problem in this complex character creation lies not in the pull between carnality and spirituality, but in the inability to use her intelligence properly when confronted with overwhelming emotional needs. Readers know her mystical impulses nearly always take on a kind of sensual coloration. In truth, she cannot distinguish between the flesh and the spirit, because feeling in Ana has become a form of disorder, in the dual sense of the word. Neither romanticism run amok nor a growing hysteria is conducive to clear thinking. "Feelings, sentiments, values, and responses," says Richard Mitchell, "have causes, attributes, and consequences. We can *know* nothing of them, we can neither understand nor judge them, without the work of the intellect in the organization of minute particulars." Thus, feeling uninformed by intelligence is chaotic. It is destructive. Ultimately then, feeling is disorder.

I think this scene (and others as well) show us the unhappy consequences of emotional blindness. What Ana lacks is something that is largely absent in this novel (with the possible exception of the ambivalently conceived Frígilis) and what I think Clarín wanted: a thinking heart. So moments later in the garden, Alas observes, Ana finds herself "abstraída en su dolor, sueltas las riendas de la voluntad, como las del pensamiento

que iba y venía, sin saber por dónde, a merced de impulsos de que no tenía conciencia" ("lost in her pain, the reins of her will power loosened, like those of her thinking, which went this way and that, without knowing where it was going, at the mercy of impulses of which she was not aware"). The annihilation of Víctor's things forms an objective correlative to the chaos of the *Regenta*'s soul; and that alienation I mentioned before, that tension between object and subject, has resolved itself by spreading the inner anarchy to the external world as well. But are the fragments of an orderly material reality merely analogues to the unquestionable fragmentation of personality itself? In that case, they would function, as indeed they do, as symbolic images of human disorder. But these things are also things; they represent, as Sherman Eoff would put it, "the heaviness of the material world" [see excerpt dated 1961]. (Even here, of course, a thing must stand for something, it cannot simply be, when made verbal). Thus there is both a real and a symbolic significance to objects. Clarín the realist is adept, as we have seen, at making us feel the denseness of things. Objects cling to us; like spider webs, they literally stick. In the opening scene of **La Regenta,** deposits of gritty sand "se incrustaba para días, o para años, en la vidriera de un escaparate, agarrada a un plomo" ("were encrusted for days, or years, in the glass of a show window, clinging to a lead weight"). Hundreds of pages later, Edelmira "se incrustaba en la carne de su primo [Paco]" ("encrusted herself in the flesh of her cousin"). Sweets and other bits of food stick to the greedy fingertips of Visitación de Cuervo, that thieving magpie. The Vetustan world seems entangled in its own materiality.

What Clarín does, in truth, is float between the real and the symbolic, thus layering **La Regenta** in its own literariness. Sometimes he is quite explicit, telling us for example that Álvaro's disguised ladder for reaching Ana is in Víctor's view a "símbolo de su vida" ("symbol of his life,") or that doña Petronila's white cat "parecía un símbolo de la devoción doméstica" ("seemed like a symbol of domestic devotion"). And that Frígilis "semejaba el símbolo de la salud queriendo contagiar con sus emanaciones a la enferma (Ana)" ("seemed the symbol of health wanting to infect with its own emanations the sickly Ana"). At other moments, however, as in Chapter XIX when the *Regenta*, Quintanar, Mesía, and Frígilis picnic in the countryside, the novelist moves in the same scene from the delightful realness of "chorizos tostados, chorreando sangre, unas migas, huevos fritos, cualquier cosa; el pan era duro, ¡mejor!, el vino malo, sabía a la pez, ¡mejor!" ("roasted sausages streaming blood, fried crumbs and eggs, anything actually; the bread was hard, so much the better! The wine bad, it tasted fishy, even better!"), to a higher reality, "el ritmo recóndito de los fenómenos," ("the secret rhythm of phenomena"), and back again to eating with their fingers "salchichón o chorizos mal tostados, queso duro, o tortillas de jamón, lo que fuese . . . con los ojos clavados en la lontananza, detrás de la cual se veía el recuerdo, lo desconocido, la vaguedad del sueño" ("sausages big and small and badly roasted, hard cheese, or ham omelets, whatever . . . with one's eyes fixed on the horizon, behind which one saw memories, unknown things, the vagueness of a dream"). Like the very real seesaw in Chapter XIII, there seems to be a back and forth movement, a push and shove between reality and the image. And in this *vaivén clariniano* ("Clarinian fluctuation"), what consistently seems to happen is that the reality dissolves, and the symbol or image remains. To give an example: in the last chapter, the frightened and depressed Víctor, knowing Ana has betrayed him, stands in his doorway and says to Frígilis: ". . . comprende que ese aldabón me inspire miedo, explícate la razón que tengo para tenerle el mismo asco que si fuera de hierro líquido. . .'' (''. . . can you understand that this door knocker inspires fear in me, can you explain the reason why I feel the same disgust as though it were liquid iron. . .'').

What is left is the *sign* of dissolution. Thus, the objects smashed in the *Regenta*'s frantic movements become the symbols of their own destruction. Things have solidity, then they do not. Like the omnipresent rain in *La Regenta,* like a mind that is caving in, liquefying in its own confusion and despair, objects seem to melt away into an earlier, fundamental condition of formlessness. Is this anarchy of form, this reversion to disorder, essential to things? Scientists point out that, yes, there exists a Second Law of Thermodynamics, ''often formulated to mean that the material world moves from orderly states to an ever-increasing disorder and that the final situation of the universe will be one of maximal disorder.'' In Clarín's world, objects not only frequently are symbols of portending disaster and disorder; they sometimes even seem to participate in their own disorder, as in the example of Quintanar's and Frígilis' trap.

Roland Barthes has said that classical description ''sans doute, a su soumettre ses objets à des forces de dégradation . . . l'objet est porteur d'un mélodrame; il se dégrade, disparaît ou retrouve une gloire dernière, participe en somme à une véritable eschatologie de la matière. On pourrait dire que l'objet classique n'est jamais que l'archétype de sa propre ruine. . . .'' (''without doubt, has been capable of submitting its objects to forces of degradation . . . the object is the bearer of melodrama; it becomes degraded, disappears or experiences one last glory, participates, in short, in a veritable eschatology of matter. One could say that the classical object is nothing more than the archetype of its own ruin. . .''). Barthes was referring to the inexorable wearing away of time itself (''Chronos et sa faux'': ''Chronos and his scythe''). But the objects in Víctor's study are forcibly detached from their surroundings, spatially uprooted and left lying about in fragments, symbols of their own inadequacy. Whether you take this scene to mean historical, social, affective, or ontological disintegration—and I think it points to all of these manifestations of disorder—the most elemental aspect of it is that things are broken, the real *qua* real is destroyed. The dissolution of the real is, it seems to me, more than just symbolic. It is also real. And that is disturbing. The representational novel, as Auerbach, Scholes and Kellogg, and other critics have seen, has its referent in an external reality; and even if, as Lukács rightly observes, between that outside world and the individual's inner life there is a screen of relentless alienation (we think of Ana Ozores and, in particular, this scene), that parallel world still exists. What happens, though, when its fictional analogue shows signs of cracking apart? What is the novelist then saying about the nature of *our* world?

Or perhaps better: implying? ''You can tell novelists,'' writes John Fowles, ''quite as much by what they do not describe as by what they do—that is, by how well they use their art's exceptional facility for exclusion.'' I am well aware Clarín does not say the world he lived in, which is akin to saying the world we the readers live in, is doomed; but in art the gap between saying and meaning is usually prodigious. After all, what is *La Regenta* about? It is about absence. The absence of love, of friendship, of all things we hold dear as human values, the little that holds us together. *La Regenta* is the great novel of absence of the last century. And I would suggest that that very absence in its most radical (and paradoxical) expression ultimately points to the nothingness of our condition. By wreck-

ing the objects in Víctor's study, the artist wrecks our world. That is what is not written. It is the novel Clarín didn't write; but its meaning is there, beneath the text itself, in the fluctuation between connecting and disconnecting, in the tension between order and disorder implicit to all great art. I suppose you could say that in its rush toward entropy, *La Regenta* anticipates the twentieth-century novel.

Clarín's oscillation between the real and the symbolic also tells us something else: that within realism itself lie what some would call the seeds of its own dissolution and others, its transformation. The artist begins with the real. Goaded, however, by the insufficiency of the merely real, he searches for symbolic expression and in the process, he discovers that the symbols of order are just that: symbols. That the heart of the matter lies so deep it goes beyond objects, beyond symbols, to a wobbling and flickering center that is not a center at all. To the chaos within. What we see in *La Regenta* is the beginnings of a holocaustal imagination at work, something that in this century manifests itself more fully in such apocalyptic works as José Donoso's *El obsceno pájaro de la noche,* Gabriel García Márquez's *Cien años de soledad,* and in its own quite different way, D. M. Thomas' *The White Hotel.*

One can never utter the final word on a work as complex and disturbing as *La Regenta.* Like the open countryside beckoning deceptively and distantly to Ana at the end of the street, Clarín's work lays before the reader descending lengths of prose that promise freedom and instead entrap. Blinded by his own externality, the critic sets up barrier after barrier to the already existent circles of impermeability naturally present in any piece of writing. And like *Ulysses, La Regenta* is so dark a work that at times it seems obsidian. Impenetrable. It is an unsettling book, posing the unsolvable question of the role a lucid heart can play in an alien universe. Thus, it should not surprise us that in the end Ana fails herself just as others have failed her. Lost in that darkness, she is nevertheless a magnificent failure, for she, like *La Regenta* itself, enables us in our own quest for order and meaning to become, for a time at least, thinking hearts. (pp. 246-58)

> *Noël M. Valis, ''Order and Meaning in Clarín's 'La Regenta','' in Novel: A Forum on Fiction, Vol. 16, No. 3, Spring, 1983, pp. 246-58.*

JOHN RUTHERFORD   (essay date 1984)

[Rutherford is an English educator and critic. In the following excerpt, he argues that Alas was not a Naturalist but a Realist who utilized the narrative technique of free indirect speech.]

Although Alas was influenced by the theories of his eminent French contemporary, Émile Zola, *La Regenta* is a realistic novel rather than a naturalistic one. Unlike Zola, Alas was not impressed by the scientific discoveries of his time. The only extensive reference in his novel to nineteenth-century scientific materialism is a mocking one, when we learn of Don Alvaro Mesía's course of reading:

> Nevertheless, it would be a good idea to acquire some culture, to make a foundation for that materialism which accorded so well with his other ideas about the world and how to exploit it. He asked a friend for books which would prove materialism in a few words. What he first learned was that there was no longer any such thing as metaphysics, an excellent idea which did away with a number of puzzling problems. He read Büchner's *Force and Matter,* and some

books by Flammarion, but these upset him, for they spoke ill of the Church and well of heaven, God, the soul—and what he wanted was the precise opposite. Flammarion wasn't *chic*. He also read Moleschott, Virchow and Vogt, in translation, bound in saffron-yellow paper covers. He did not understand much of what they said, but he got the gist of it: everything was grey matter—splendid, that was just what he wanted to be told. His principal requirement was that there should be no hell.

The realistic novelist differs from his naturalistic counterpart in that he does not try to confirm theories but to explore experience. For the naturalist, the novel is an illustration of the validity of the scientific approach to knowledge; for the realist it is another kind of knowledge. Despite what naturalists such as Zola claimed, the realistic novel is both more objective than the naturalistic novel and more likely to stand the test of time; this is precisely because it is less influenced by the scientific ideas of its own period, which must, sooner or later, be superseded by others. So the novels of the naturalists are interesting in proportion as they wriggle free from the clutches of their own theory. So, also, the realistic novelist can make discoveries which psychologists only make many years later.

This is, I believe, what makes it possible for so much of the psychology of *La Regenta* to seem strikingly modern. I am thinking now, for example, of the descriptions of the symptoms of neurosis in general and hysteria in particular, in Ana's inner monologues, particularly in Chapters III and XXVII; and of the accuracy with which many of the inner monologues recapture the rapidity and illogicality of associative trains of thought (the last paragraphs of Chapter XV offer one of many examples). I am thinking, too, of the presence of sex as a principal (although often subconscious) motivator of action. *La Regenta* gives a detailed account of what psychologists call sublimation (in Ana, of course, but also in such minor characters as Visita, who sucks sweets as a substitute for sex), of the importance of the childhood trauma (the events after Ana's night on the ferry-boat with Germán, rather than the night itself), and of various sexual aberrations in inappropriate contexts, such as the latent foot-fetishism, sado-masochism and lesbianism of the procession on Good Friday in Chapter XXVI. The use of multiple perspectives for characterization makes the novel interesting from the standpoint of what is now called the psychology of interpersonal behaviour. In the book of that title by Michael Argyle . . . , many of the essential features of characterization in *La Regenta* are presented (without any reference to prose fiction, of course) as recent discoveries about human behaviour—for instance our creation of images of ourselves and our subsequent modifications of these images on the basis of what we think other people think of us; and our modeling of ourselves on our fellows and on ideal fictional figures. The chains of imitation in *La Regenta* are many and complex: for example, Paco Vegallana and Pepe Ronzal model themselves on Alvaro Mesía, who models himself on the Don Juan figure of Spanish literature and on the Parisian gentleman of his times; and lesser men in turn model themselves on Paco and Pepe. When I talk about the modern psychology of *La Regenta* I am also thinking of dreams and their interpretation, especially Ana's dreams in Chapter XIX and her interpretation of them in Chapter XXI, with its revealing blind spots: her suppressed wish for a sexual relationship with Canon De Pas is embodied in disguised form in her dreams, and still suppressed as she remembers them afterwards. There is also the functioning of memory, in Chapters III and IV, as Ana thinks about her childhood, and wonders about the validity of her remem-

brances: are they memories of events, or memories of memories, or memories of memories of memories? Personal relationships in *La Regenta* have all the intense complexity which we often associate with more modern writing, consisting, on both sides, of positive and negative feelings: attraction, admiration, love, goodwill, and at the same time repulsion, envy, hatred, malice (for example the relationships between Mesía and Ronzal, and between De Pas and Don Custodio). One especially striking feature of this novel is the non-verbal communication, both deliberate and unintentional, which takes place throughout. Here is a scene between Ana, her husband Víctor Quintanar, and their friend Alvaro Mesía, at the beginning of Chapter XXIX, which also shows characters occupied in one of their favourite activities, manipulating and playing games with each other:

> At dessert the master of the house became thoughtful. With furtive glances he followed Petra's comings and goings as she waited at table. After coffee Don Alvaro could see that his friend was impatient. Since the summer, when they had both stayed in the hotel in La Costa, Don Víctor had acquired the habit of having Don Alvaro as his table companion. He found him more talkative and agreeable at table than anywhere else, and often invited him to luncheon. But on other occasions, after chatting for as long as he felt like chatting, Quintanar would leave the table, walk around the garden, and go to dress, singing all the time—and thus leave Anita and his friend alone together for half an hour or more. And now—no, he wasn't moving. Ana and Alvaro looked at each other, and their looks asked what could be the reason for this novelty.
>
> Ana bent down to retrieve a napkin from the floor, and Don Victor made Mesía a sign which said, "She's in the way. If she left, we could talk."
>
> Mesía shrugged.
>
> Ana raised her head smiling at Don Alvaro and he, without Quintanar seeing, indicated the door with one movement of his eyes.
>
> Ana left.
>
> "Thank God!" said her husband, with a deep breath. "I thought the girl was never going."
>
> He did not remember that he was always the one who went.
>
> "Now we can talk."
>
> "I'm listening," replied Alvaro in a calm voice, puffing on his Havana so as to obscure his face; it being his habit to put up smoke-screens when it suited him.

If Alas had been much influenced by the psychological theories of his time, they would only have narrowed his vision and prevented his depiction of human behaviour from being as perceptive as it was. I am sure that only chronology has saved us from a shelf-ful of theses on "Leopoldo Alas's debt to Freud." Such theses would have made specific reference to Alas's treatment of that Spanish archetype Don Juan (and, by extension, of the whole ethos of machismo). For *La Regenta* was the first critical examination of Don Juan as a man whose valour, vigour and virility are far from what they seem to be, and so it anticipates the Freudian analyses of Don Juan by twentieth-century Spanish writers who have seen him as a man whose inability to love one woman alone is a result not of manliness but of its opposite.

La Regenta is also notable for the intensive and subtle use of many of the techniques developed by the realistic novelists of the nineteenth century. Alas identified one of them in his perceptive review of *La desheredada,* the novel written in 1881 by Benito Pérez Galdós under the influence of Zola's naturalistic theories. ''Another procedure employed by Galdós,'' wrote Alas, ''and now with more insistence and success than ever, is one used by Flaubert and Zola with very impressive results: replacing the observations which the author often makes in his own voice about a character's situation by the character's own observations, using the latter's style—not, however, in the manner of a monologue, but as if the author were inside the character, and the novel were being created inside the character's brain.'' So Galdós's novel brought the expressive possibilities of *sympathetic projection* to Alas's notice, and he used this technique in *La Regenta* much more insistently and for a wider range of characters than did Galdós or Zola or even Flaubert. In my *Leopoldo Alas: ''La Regenta''* [see Additional Bibliography] I have discussed Alas's skilful handling of this device, which he also called ''the underground speaking of a consciousness'' and ''*estilo latente*'' [''latent style'']. Many years later, French critics of Flaubert were to give it the name by which it is now commonly known, *style indirect libre* [''indirect free speech''] (and to create the myth that Flaubert invented it). *Estilo latente* made it possible for Alas both to give a panoramic view of a society and to explore the inner lives of its individuals. But it involves a frequent switching of viewpoint. In the following passage, for example, only a responsive reader will follow the movement of the point of view:

> Ana's attack of nerves was, as on the previous evening, melting into tears, into an impulsive pious determination always to be faithful to her husband. In spite of his infernal machines, Quintanar was her duty; and the canon theologian would be her aegis and protect her from all the formidable blows of temptation. But Quintanar knew nothing of this. The theatre had left him feeling awfully sleepy—he had not slept a wink the night before!—and full of lyrico-dramatic enthusiasm.

The subtleties of *estilo latente* were lost on readers accustomed to third-rate tales of adventure and romance, and bad translations of foreign novels (the Spanish novel was just beginning to be revived, after centuries of neglect). The principal difficulty of *estilo latente* is that it has no formal or grammatical identifying marks to distinguish it from authorial statement. In the passage I have just quoted, the reader has to make his own decisions about questions of style to attribute the first sentence to the (detached) narrator, the second to Ana, the third (as far as the end of the parenthesis) to Quintanar, and the last five words to the (now ironical) narrator. But judgements about style can seldom be definitive. We *could* attribute the whole passage to the narrator's voice, if we thought that this narrator speaks with an uncontrolled hotchpotch of styles and interrupts his story every so often to inform us of its future course (''and the canon theologian would be . . .''). The essential ambiguity of free indirect style has been exploited by many novelists. Jane Austen makes much use of it to report the thoughts of her credulous heroines in such a way that the reader is at liberty to take them for omniscient authorial pronouncements:

> Harriet certainly was not clever, but she had a sweet, docile, grateful disposition; was totally free from conceit; and only desired to be guided by anyone she looked up to. (*Emma*).

Yet in *La Regenta* we often find free indirect style complicated by a device the main effect of which is to destroy its ambiguity

and thus (when a character's thoughts are being reported) to increase the illusion of projection: enclosing it within speech-marks. This can at first seem strange, ungrammatical and confusing to modern readers:

> When, close to nightfall, as the horses dragged their coach uphill, the new presiding magistrate asked Ana if he was fortunate enough, perchance, to be the first man whom she had loved, she bowed her head and said, with a melancholy which sounded to him like sensual self-abandonment:
>
> ''Yes, yes, the first, the only one.''
>
> ''No, she didn't love him; but she would try to love him.''

The [quotation marks] around the last sentence force the reader to regard it as an account of Ana's thoughts just as in the following extract from *Emma* the [quotation marks] make it clear that the enclosed words report what the Coles say, not necessarily ''the truth'':

> The Coles expressed themselves so properly—there was so much real attraction in the manner of it—so much consideration for her father. ''They would have solicited the honour earlier, but had been waiting the arrival of a folding-screen from London, which they hoped might keep Mr. Woodhouse from any draught of air and therefore induce him the more readily to give them the honour of his company.''

(The first sentence of this extract is another example of ambiguous free indirect speech.)

The reader of *La Regenta* faces the problems of a bouncing narrative not only over point of view. Here is a description of the bank clerk's wife Visitación and the young widow Obdulia:

> When Don Alvaro was in the company of close friends he spoke of Visitación with disdain and grimaced with ill-concealed disgust. He affirmed that she had pretty feet and that her calves were much more handsome than one might suspect, but her shoes were shoddy, and her petticoats and stockings left a great deal to be desired—his listeners knew what he meant. And he wiped his lips with his pocket-handkerchief.
>
> Paco Vegallana swore that the woman used garters made of red tape and that he had once discovered her wearing one made of string. All this was to be mentioned only in the company of men, of course, and they were to be discreet about it.
>
> Obdulia's underclothes, on the other hand, were irreproachable; unlike her behaviour. But this was such common knowledge that nobody talked about it any more. To each successive lover, Obdulia herself denied all her previous affairs, except her affair with Alvaro Mesía. It was her pride and joy. The man had fascinated her, why deny it? But only him. She was a widow who never remembered her husband; it was as if she were really Alvarito's widow. ''She had no past but Alvaro!''
>
> That afternoon both women were looking very pretty, one had to admit it. At least the ingenuous Paco Vegallana admitted it.

Even the longer passages of ''the underground speaking of a consciousness'' are studded with interruptions as the outside world impinges on the attention of the character and redirects his train of thoughts. In this way, inner monologues become lively dialectics between the subjective and objective worlds.

Some of the features of Alas's restless writing are probably disconcerting to any reader. It is strange, for example—especially in a nineteenth-century novel—to find time handled with such freedom, to find that events are seldom related in chronological order, but that, instead, there are abrupt jumps forward, flashbacks, flashbacks within flashbacks. . . . In some places, tenses can seem disordered, particularly when the narrator switches between the viewpoints of a contemporary witness and a subsequent historian, between present and past tenses. Such disturbing qualities of *La Regenta* have caused some critics to find parts of it, at least, confused and cluttered. . . . Such attacks rest upon the assumption that a novel should, in its form and style at least, present the fewest possible problems to its readers, should be readily consumable (it is strange, incidentally, that many critics who welcome disturbing content reject disturbing form). It appears more likely to me that, on the contrary, it is one of the most important functions of literature to play games with the reader, frustrate his expectations, puzzle him and so invite him to re-examine his assumptions. *La Regenta* certainly does this. Restoration Spain, however, was not prepared to be ruffled.

The smug parochial society of Alas's Spain was quite unable, too, to appreciate the novel's deflating, satirical humour. *La Regenta* abounds in angry sarcasm, expressing Alas's exasperation at the mediocrity all around him:

> Don Robustiano had never read Voltaire, but his admiration for Voltaire was as intense as the abhorrence felt by Gloucester, who had never read Voltaire either.

But the novel also contains irony of a quieter kind: the turn of phrase which has something disturbing about it, the word which seems somehow odd or inappropriate, and to which the reader responds by wondering whether all is as it seems to be, whether an alternative ironical interpretation is necessary. Indeed the very first sentence, with its abrupt bathos and jingly rhythm after an apparently grandiose start, invites us to read the whole novel ironically.

La Regenta, rich in wit and humour, is also a work of intense moral seriousness. But Alas's audience, the Spanish middle and upper classes, was composed in the main of the same kind of shallow, frivolous, complacent people as *La Regenta* portrays. A novel which poses searching questions about our ability to control our destiny and find self-fulfilment, and about God's interest in our activities—and which suggests gloomy answers to these questions—could not be accepted in such an atmosphere.

The subject-matter of *La Regenta,* the life of a shabby Spanish provincial town in the late nineteenth century, might make it seem dated and parochial. But thanks to its universal themes, psychological insight and technical boldness it has proved itself to be worthy of the attention of modern men and women. *La Regenta* is ambitious—astonishingly so for a man of thirty-two writing his first novel. It is a big, rich novel in the nineteenth-century tradition—not just a long novel but an all-embracing one of many styles and moods, from broad humour to the most intense feeling, kept from degenerating into sentimentalism by Alas's controlling irony. (pp. 8-14)

John Rutherford, in an introduction to La Regenta *by Leopoldo Alas, translated by John Rutherford, The University of Georgia Press, 1984, pp. 7-17.*

ADDITIONAL BIBLIOGRAPHY

Boring, Phyllis Z. ''Some Reflections on Clarín's *Doña Berta.''* *Romance Notes* XI, No. 2 (Winter 1969): 322-25.
  Discusses the influence of both Gustave Flaubert's *Madam Bovary* and Miguel de Cervantes's *Don Quixote* on Alas's novel *Doña Berta.*

Bull, William E. ''Clarín's Literary Internationalism.'' *Hispanic Review* XVI, No. 4 (October 1948): 321-34.
  Explores Alas's knowledge of foreign literatures and the extent of foreign influences upon his writing.

———. ''Clarín and His Critics.'' *The Modern Language Forum* XXXV, Nos. 3-4 (September-December 1950): 103-11.
  Discusses the reaction of Alas's contemporaries to his literary criticism and the controversy caused by *La Regenta.*

Durand, Frank. ''Structural Unity in Leopoldo Alas' *La Regenta.''* *Hispanic Review* XXXI, No. 4 (October 1963): 324-35.
  Analyzes the plot structure of *La Regenta.*

———. ''Characterization in *La Regenta:* Point of View and Theme.'' *Bulletin of Hispanic Studies* XLI (1964): 86-100.
  Examines the importance of narrative point of view in understanding characterizations in *La Regenta.*

Griswold, Susan C. ''Rhetorical Strategies and Didacticism in Clarín's Short Fiction.'' *Kentucky Romance Quarterly* 29, No. 4 (1982): 423-33.
  Examines the purposes of different narrative styles in Alas's short story collection *Cuentos morales.*

Howells, W. D. ''*Doña Perfecta,* A Great Novel.'' In his *Criticism and Fiction and Other Essays,* edited by Clara Marburg Kirk and Rudolf Kirk, pp. 133-38. New York: New York University Press, 1959.
  Discusses some of Alas's literary opinions in a review of Benito Pérez Galdós's novel *Doña Perfecta.*

Ife, Barry W. ''Idealism and Materialism in Clarín's *La Regenta:* Two Comparative Studies.'' *Revue de litterature comparée* 44 (1970): 273-95.
  Compares Alas's presentation of individuals functioning within their society in *La Regenta* with that of George Eliot in the novel *The Mill on the Floss.*

Jackson, Robert M. ''Cervantismo in the Creative Process of Clarín's *La Regenta.''* *Modern Language Notes* 84, No. 2 (March 1969): 208-27.
  Compares the theme of romantic self-delusions derived from popular literature in *La Regenta* and Cervantes's *Don Quixote.*

Kronik, John W. ''The Function of Names in the Stories of Alas.'' *Modern Language Notes* 80, No. 2 (March 1965): 260-65.
  Discusses how character names in Alas's fiction function humorously, satirically, or as indications of true character.

Labanyi, Jo. ''City, Country and Adultery in *La Regenta.''* *Bulletin of Hispanic Studies* LXIII, No. 1 (January 1986): 53-66.
  Examines the thematic significance of rural and urban settings in *La Regenta.*

Nimetz, Michael. ''Eros and Ecclesia in Clarín's Vetusta.'' *Modern Language Notes* 86, No. 2 (March 1971): 242-53.
  Contends that confusion of gender roles in *La Regenta* is intended to suggest the decadence and sterility of both church and state in late nineteenth-century Spain.

Pyper, Stanton. ''Notes on a Spanish Writer.'' *The Dublin Magazine* 11, No. 1 (August 1924): 44-9.
  Discusses Alas's rejection of popular trends in Spanish literature.

Rivkin, Laura. "Extranatural Art in Clarín's *Su único hijo*." *Modern Language Notes* 97, No. 2 (March 1982): 311-28.
     Discusses Alas's use of different narrative styles in the novel *Su único hijo*.

———. "Melodramatic Plotting in Clarín's *La Regenta*." *Romance Quarterly* 33, No. 2 (May 1986): 191-200.
     Examines the plot structure of *La Regenta*, with particular emphasis upon chance, coincidence, and unexplained forces operating within the story.

———. "Clarín's *Cuesta abajo*: Anticipating Proust." *Modern Language Studies* XVI, No. 3 (Summer 1986): 255-63.
     Views Alas's unfinished novel, *Cuesta abajo*, as a self-reflexive work that anticipates many of Marcel Proust's literary themes and techniques.

Rogers, Douglass. "Don Juan, *donjuanismo*, and Death in Clarín." *Symposium* XXX, No. 4 (Winter 1976): 325-42.
     Examines Alas's use of a Don Juan figure in the novel *La Regenta* and the short story "El caballero de la mesa redonda."

Rutherford, John. *Leopoldo Alas: "La Regenta."* London: Grant and Cutler, 1974, 79 p.
     General overview of the themes, methods of characterization, and plot structure of *La Regenta*.

Sanchez, Elizabeth. "From World to Word: Realism and Reflexivity in *Don Quijote* and *La Regenta*." *Hispanic Review* 55, No. 1 (Winter 1987): 27-39.
     Extensive analysis of the way in which Alas depicted the characters in *La Regenta* by consciously modeling their behavior upon that of famous fictional characters and situations in world literature.

Sanchez, Robert G. "The Presence of the Theater and 'the Consciousness of Theater' in Clarín's *La Regenta*." *Hispanic Review* XXXVII, No. 4 (October 1969): 491-509.
     Examines an episode from *La Regenta* in which a central character attends the theater as a key to understanding the conflict between illusion and reality that permeates the novel.

Savaiano, Eugene. "An Historical Justification of the Anticlericism of Galdós and Alas." *The Municipal University of Wichita Bulletin* XXVII, No. 1 (February 1952): 3-14.
     Compares the anticlericism expressed in the works of Alas and in those of his contemporary, Benito Pérez Galdós.

Schyfter, Sara E. "'La loca, la tonta, la literata': Woman's Destiny in Clarín's *La Regenta*." In *Theory and Practice of Feminist Literary Criticism*, edited by Gabriela Mora and Karen S. Van Hooft, pp. 229-41. Ypsilanti, Mich.: Bilingual Press, 1982.
     Interpets the plight of Ana Ozores in *La Regenta* as representative of the repressed and stifled condition of women generally.

Thompson, Clifford R., Jr. "Evolution in the Short Stories of Clarín." *Revista de estudios hispanicos* XVIII, No. 3 (October 1984): 381-98.
     Chronological survey of Alas's short fiction demonstrating a shift away from the detached satire of his earliest works.

Valis, Noël M. *The Decadent Vision in Leopoldo Alas: A Study of "La Regenta" and "Su único hijo."* Baton Rouge: Louisiana State University Press, 1981, 215 p.
     Close examination of the relationship of Alas's two major novels with the Decadent movement in late nineteenth-century literature.

Weber, Frances. "The Dynamics of Motif in Leopoldo Alas's *La Regenta*." *The Romanic Review* LVII, No. 3 (October 1966): 188-99.
     Examines the theme of a dehumanizing division between spirituality and materialism that is presented in *La Regenta*.

Roberto (Godofredo Christopherson) Arlt

1900-1942

Argentine novelist, dramatist, short story writer, and essayist.

Largely neglected during his lifetime, Arlt is today recognized as an important Argentine novelist of the early twentieth century. He is particularly noted for works portraying the metaphysical anguish of the alienated individual in twentieth-century society. Premised on what he considered a breakdown of the philosophical and religious values of Western civilization, his fiction and dramas concern the plight of individuals contending with ''the inevitably crumbling social edifice,'' frequently depicting social unrest, urban alienation, deviant behavior, sexual maladjustment, and class hostility. Arlt believed that literature, if it is to express human experience, must not present a world more ordered than reality, which he saw as essentially chaotic and irrational. He therefore rejected the conventions of social realism, then popular in Argentina, to create a complex fusion of fantasy and reality in works replete with grotesque imagery and logical inconsistencies.

Arlt was born in Buenos Aires to German immigrants. His childhood was miserable, due in part to the militaristic discipline of his father, against whom Arlt rebelled. (They once went three years without speaking to each other.) Arlt's formal education ended at the age of eight when he was expelled from school, reportedly for writing to his teacher: ''Señorita, let us run away to the sea. Dressed in black velvet I shall carry you off to my pirate ship. I swear by the corpse of my hanged father that I love you. Yours till death. Roberto Godofredo, Knight of Ventimiglia, Lord of Rocabruna, Captain of the Whaler *Taciturn*.'' During the following years, Arlt read widely in both popular and classical literature, wrote short stories, and began his lifelong interest in science and mechanics. In 1916 he left home, and for the next decade he continued to write fiction while supporting himself as a bookstore clerk, mechanic, vulcanizer, and manager of a brick factory and of a small newspaper. In 1925 he became secretary to the prominent Argentine novelist and poet Ricardo Güiraldes, and in 1926 he published his first novel, *El juguete rabioso*. At this time, most Argentine writers were identified with one of two groups: the Boedo street group, known for social realism and proletarian concerns, and the Florida street group, known for avantgarde modernism. Reviewers of *El juguete rabioso*—most of whom found fault with Arlt's undisciplined, journalistic style—associated the realistic tone and lower-class setting of the novel with the Boedo street group. Arlt strengthened this association by spending much of his time in La Puñalada, a cafe frequented by underworld types, and writing sketches about its disreputable habitués. The individuals portrayed in these sketches served as prototypes for the characters of his next novel, *Los siete locos (The Seven Madmen)*.

In 1929 Arlt began writing a column, ''Aguafuertes porteñas'' (''Porteño Etchings''), for the Buenos Aires newspaper *El mundo*. This series was enormously popular, doubling the sales of the paper on the days Arlt's column was published. He continued to write prolifically for the rest of his life, publishing novels, short stories, dramas, and essay collections; at the same time he pursued his hobby as an inventor, eventually setting up a laboratory to develop hosiery that would not run and

establishing a business to produce his inventions. He sought through these ventures the financial means that would allow him to write without being compelled by financial necessity. In 1942 Arlt died suddenly of a heart attack, leaving behind a draft of his last play, *El desierto entra a la ciudad*.

Arlt's most important works, the novels *The Seven Madmen* and *Los lanzallamas,* tell the story of the aspiring anarchist Remo Erdosain and his vain struggle to give meaning to his life through participation in an absurd revolutionary group called the Society. Although Erdosain is an emotional and financial failure, having lost both his wife and his job, Arlt located the true source of his character's suffering not in personal misfortune but in a spiritual crisis afflicting twentieth-century society as a whole. Describing Erdosain and his partners, the author wrote: ''These individuals . . . are tied or bound together by desperation. The desperation in them originates, more than from material poverty, from another factor: the disorientation that, after the Great War, has revolutionized the conscience of men, leaving them empty of ideals and hopes.'' Arlt represented this disorientation in the novels by weaving into the narrative fabric the chaos and irrationality that are fundamental to Erdosain's (and Arlt's) perception of the world. For example, Arlt established the narrator of the novels as unreliable and erratic, never disclosing whether he is an omniscient author conveying his view of the human dilemma, a detached observer recounting what he has seen and heard, or a member of the Society participating in a plot against Erdosain. The narrative omits data important to an understanding of the plot, includes a plethora of irrelevant information, and contains footnotes that contradict the narrator's own text. The structure of the narrative also lacks unity and coherence: the time sequence is unclear and it cannot be determined whether certain events are real or imagined. As a result, the reader who searches for underlying meaning or logical consistency in the narrative is confronted with the irony that such a search for meaning parallels Erdosain's and that both are equally fruitless. Through the Society, Erdosain realizes new ideals and hopes and becomes in his own eyes the savior of humanity; however, his chosen path for arriving at salvation and meaning in his life leads him to sadism and crime. He states: "[If] tomorrow I throw a bomb, or assassinate Barsut, I become everything, the man who exists, the man for whom infinite generations of jurists will provide punishments, prisons, and theories. . . . Only crime can affirm my existence, as only evil affirms the presence of man on the earth." A similar theme appears in many of Arlt's short stories. In the stories collected in *El jorobadito,* for example, Arlt's narrators fabricate lies injurious to others or false confessions of crimes that they did not commit, all in order to secure recognition. Arlt's dramas, while similar to his fiction in their exploration of the irrationality and meaninglessness of existence, frequently focus not on the personal anguish caused by metaphysical anxiety, but on varying conceptions of reality and the problematic relationship between fantasy and reality. While Erdosain's fantasies are real only to himself and his accomplices, the fantasies of Arlt's dramatic characters become independent and equally viable realities. As is the case with all of Arlt's literary work, the underlying purpose of his dramas is to subvert any attempt to evaluate them according to rationalistic criteria of aesthetic, intellectual, or moral worth. Arlt sought to prevent the reader from relying on a rational interpretation of his works and, in the words of Naomi Lindstrom, to "persuade him to accept the irrational, the unexplained and the anomalous as predominant features of human existence. . . ."

The initial critical reception of Arlt's work was cool. Contemporary critics saw his work as being wholly realistic in intent and judged its complexities and unresolved conflicts, as well as Arlt's use of street language and ungrammatical prose, to be signs of an overweening and badly educated writer. In a parody of his critics, Arlt wrote: "Mr. Roberto Arlt keeps on in the same old rut: realism in the worst possible taste." More recent critics have reevaluated his work in light of the literary innovations of modern Latin American writers, and have found in Arlt's work the seminal development of many of the ideas that would preoccupy the literature of his continent after his death. Assessing the significance of his innovations, Jorge Lafforgue designated Arlt's works, with those of Juan Carlos Onetti, as "the beginnings of current Argentine-Uruguayan fiction"; Lafforgue's appreciation was echoed by Onetti himself, who stated: "If any inhabitant of our humble shores managed to achieve literary genius, his name was Roberto Arlt."

PRINCIPAL WORKS

El juguete rabioso (novel) 1926
Los siete locos (novel) 1929
  [*The Seven Madmen,* 1984]
Los lanzallamas (novel) 1931

El amor brujo (novel) 1932
Trescientos millones (drama) 1932
Aguafuertes porteñas (essays) 1933
El jorobadito (short stories) 1933
Aguafuertes españolas (essays) 1936
El fabricante de fantasmas (drama) 1936
Saverio el cruel (drama) 1936
La isla desierta (drama) 1938
La fiesta del hierro (drama) 1940
El criador de gorilas (short stories) 1941
*El desierto entra a la ciudad (drama) 1953
Novelas completas y cuentos. 3 vols. (novels and short
  stories) 1963
Teatro completo. 2 vols. (dramas) 1968

Several of Arlt's short stories have been published in English translation. These include "Ester Primavera," published in *Doors and Mirrors: Fiction and Poetry from Spanish America, 1920-1970,* edited by Hortense Carpenter and Janet Brof; "One Sunday Afternoon," published in *The Eye of the Heart: Short Stories from Latin America,* edited by Barbara Howes; and "Small-Time Property Owners," published in *Contemporary Latin American Short Stories,* edited by Pat M. Mancini.

*This work was written in 1942.

ROBERTO ARLT (essay date 1933)

[*In the following essay, which originally appeared in Arlt's newspaper column "Aguafuertes porteñas," Arlt responds to an editorial by the Argentine academician Monner Sans in which Sans criticized the widespread use of slang and abuse of grammar in Argentine Spanish.*]

Dear Mr. Monner Sans: Grammar is much like boxing. I'll explain it to you:

When a man takes up boxing and has no feel for it, all he does is copy the moves his teacher shows him. When another man takes up boxing and has it, and puts up a magnificent fight, sports writers exclaim: "He came at him from all sides!" Meaning, he's bright, so he finds a way around the textbook grammar of boxing. Needless to say, the one who finds a way around the grammar of boxing and lets fly "from all sides" wipes up the floor with the other guy, and that's how this phrase of ours got started: "European or show boxing," that is, boxing that's fine for show, but for fighting is no good at all, at least against our agrammatically boxing boys.

With peoples and with languages, Mr. Monner Sans, the same goes. Peoples with no brains keep reusing the same language forever, because, with no new ideas to express, they don't need new words or ways to say things; but, on the other hand, peoples that, like us, are continually evolving, come up with words from all sides, words that give schoolteachers fits, just as a European boxing teacher has a fit over the inconceivable fact that a kid who boxes all wrong wipes up the floor with one of his students who's technically a perfect boxer. All right: I see why you'd get upset. Go right ahead. . . .

A nation imposes its art, industry and business by imposing its language. Take the U.S. They send us their products with the labels in English, and we get used to a lot of English words.

In Brazil, a lot of Argentine words (slang words) are popular. Why? It's the superiority of language imposing itself.

"Last Reason," Félix Lima, Fray Mocho and others [folk humorists] have had a lot more influence on our language, than all the philological and grammatical flim-flam of a Mr. Cejador y Frauja, Benot and that whole dusty, cranky gang of book-worms, who just grub around in files and write memos that not even you, illustrious grammarians, bother to read, because they're so boring.

This phenomenon more than proves the absurdity of trying to straightjacket in a prescriptive grammar the constantly changing, new ideas of a people. When a crook who's about to stab his cohort in the chest says: "I'm gonna stick you but good," it's much more eloquent than if he had said: "I shall insert my dagger in your sternum." When a hood exclaims, when he sees a band of cops coming, "I had 'em eyeballed!" it's much more graphic than if he said "I had surreptitiously observed these officers of the law."

Mr. Monner Sans: if we paid attention to grammar, our great grandparents would have had to respect it, and so on backward, so it follows that, if our forebears had respected grammar, we, men of the radio and the machine gun, would still be using caveman speech. Most humbly yours, your obedient servant.

> *Roberto Arlt, in an excerpt from "The Language of Argentines," translated by Naomi Lindstrom, in* Review, *No. 31, January-April, 1982, p. 31.*

DAVID WILLIAM FOSTER (essay date 1975)

[*Foster is an American critic who specializes in Hispanic literature and linguistics. In the following excerpt, he discusses the social, political, and philosophical themes of* The Seven Madmen.]

Arlt possesses the dubious distinction of having earned during his lifetime the respect of only a few fellow-writers. He was, at the same time, being repudiated with emphatic distaste by the Establishment's critical voices for both his untutored approach to the genteel profession of letters and his sympathies with (but not his active membership in) proletariat and assorted Communist/anarchical movements in Argentina.

Los siete locos (The Seven Madmen), his most important novel, and the sequel *Los lanzallamas (The Flamethrowers)* are interesting precisely for their reflection of the *status animae* of the individual who, on the eve of the Great Depression, is identified with the vague underground currents of a Communist and/or anarchical stamp. The antihero Erdosain, at a time when the Argentine literary establishment is struggling to maintain the hegemony of an official literary-supplement gentility, becomes the first major embodiment of the flotsam and jetsam of twentieth-century Argentine society. Erdosain is the direct descendant of the spiritual waifs to be found in the naturalist novel of the first antiliberal reaction in the last decades of the nineteenth century.

It would be easy to conclude that Roberto Arlt was a spokesman for the concerns and the objectives of proletariat socialist realism in Argentina. As far as his actual work is concerned, nothing could be further from their meaning. It is true that Erdosain is the paradigmatic example of the alienated man of the twentieth century, obsessed by unnamed anxieties and irremediable inabilities to come to terms with society and existence. Within the novel these problems are given objective status by dismissal from his job for petty embezzlement and by his wife's cruel abandonment of him. Yet, despite Erdosain's almost mechanistic embodiment of the features of the perennial misfit, Arlt refuses to make him the standard-bearer for some nonexistent or external political activism that will neatly solve all of his problems and give him a functioning role in the order of the universe. Such a facile plot would produce only a work of propaganda. More significantly, Arlt possessed a spiritual alloy of Jewish and Mediterranean cynicism that prevented him, at least as far as his voice as a novelist is concerned, from subscribing to romantic leftist causes. By no means does this mean that Arlt was not sympathetic to these causes. His literature, while it cannot be easily read by a non-partisan as novelistic propaganda, cannot be read either as a defense of Establishment values or as a rejection of the anguish of the individual who did not belong to that Establishment.

Primarily at issue in Arlt's enigmatic novel is a concern with man's dilemma that is more metaphysical than political. In this sense, it would be easy to describe him as an existential writer, which has indeed been done often. But either the term is too broad and ill-defined as the epithet for any writer concerned with the problematic nature of modern man's sense of existence or it is too loosely applied to a writer who had no programmatic allegiance to the ethical idealism of existential thinkers. Arlt's concern, which he shares with innumerable contemporaries unable to discover a value system that would eradicate those anxieties, lies more closely to describing the essence of those anxieties and the curious modes of existence which they bring about. For the reader who may object that description is useless without prescription, one can only appeal to the cynical side of human nature, which denies prescriptive remedies and argues for the validity of an author's insights and their being keen enough to give adequate expression for the first time to what has since become a standardized image of man. And Arlt is all the more engaging for his capacity to maintain an ironic sense of humor in the face of the bleak, inevitable facts about man that his insights have revealed to him.

In another sense, we find in *The Seven Madmen* an impressive expressionistic conceit based on a sardonic attitude toward salvationist politics. Erdosain is the controlling consciousness of the novel, and he appears to be telling his story to some unidentified reporter who may or may not be the author. Thus, one interpretational problem is the omniscient knowledge of the narrator in the guise of information obtained from the central character. But Erdosain is in many ways less memorable than the Astrologer and his curious organization, which the protagonist joins. As the novel opens, Erdosain has lost his job, ostensibly for some petty thieving; either it doesn't matter or it's all part of an unnamed plot that, like so many incidents in the novel, is given a deliberately inadequate explanation. He then loses his wife, who seems to have seized the first opportunity to leave Erdosain. These two precipitate events, presented in a *deus ex machina* fashion that leads one to suspect either a mysterious plot against Erdosain or a deliberate undercharacterization of motivation for expressionistic reasons, lead Erdosain to turn to the Astrologer's Society and to devote all his energies to it.

The Society, allegedly modeled after the North-American Ku Klux Klan, is a group of individuals of specialized talents: Erdosain's contribution is a special process for the electrostatic plating of flowers. The Society is plotting to take over the country and to institute a utopia based on a dictatorially imposed euphoria that will solve the problems of the citizenry and ensure absolute rule for the Astrologer and his followers. Beyond an obvious parody of Socialist-Fascist utopian fantasies then current on both sides of the Atlantic, the full implications of the Society's aims are confusing. In the first place, there are many details which the reader is not permitted to know, and there is strong evidence that the whole business is a farce mounted by the Astrologer for his own entertainment at the expense of his followers. They are a motley collection of individuals who command his interest as misfits—gullible, faithful and frantic seekers after some promise—any promise—of a more perfect existence.

To the extent that one strand of Western civilization has come periodically under the sway of such promises—and the period of 1910-1940 was no exception—Arlt's conceit is essentially valid as one reasonable representation of a dominant side of human nature and only secondarily as a portrayal of specific utopian promises of modern history. Whatever the exact nature of the Society, the most important fact is Erdosain's relationship to it. Erdosain's own particular need for an order of existence that will free him from his persistent spiritual turmoil becomes the driving force of his behavior and, as a result, the narrative plot of the novel. A certain amount of attention to the Society is inevitable. There can be little question that it is a fascinating and conceitful creation, and the several unresolved questions surrounding its true nature, its actual constitution, and its real objectives make it a delightful topic of speculation. But such speculation should not detract from the central concern of the novel. To the extent that Erdosain is advanced as a controlling consciousness and to the extent that our doubts concerning the activities with which he becomes involved are also his own ignorance and naivete, a characterization of the work necessarily centers on the meaning of the individual and the rationale underlying his involvement with a project that is, from an outsider's point of view, a patently absurd and bogus operation.

A basic ingredient of *The Seven Madmen,* then, is an element of fantasy and surrealism quite disconsonant with the "committed" literature of social realism. The reader's first reaction to the novel is complete disorientation. He has little direct grasp of Erdosain as a person, since the man is presented only in vague terms of present actions and circumstances without any of the sustained background development associated with novels of character. He has even less understanding of the secret Society, of the Astrologer who directs its operations, and of the several individuals who, with their *commedia dell'arte* names and masks, are elusive faces of an elusive human order. And, finally, he has little help from the narrator, who calls himself the "commentator" on Erdosain's reportings. The narrator appears alternately to be (1) an omniscient author who organizes the entire spectacle as as expressionistic conceit on the human dilemma and man's piteous groping for a transcendent order; (2) a detached observer who favors the reader with Erdosain's comments on himself and his activities with the sect, ostensibly at some crucial point after Erdosain's *supposed* final act of involvement with the sect; and (3) another participant in the activities of the sect, part of the unnamed plot referred to above, unknown to Erdosain.

In this sense, therefore, the narrative fabric of the novel is very much a direct and maddening manifestation of Erdosain's own foggy peceptions. The reader is provided, via a few explicit comments by the narrator within the text and via at least nine disconcerting footnotes to the narrative, with some additional knowledge, such as the fact that the entire involvement of Erdosain the sect is in the end part of an elaborate hoax against him. But essentially we remain firmly anchored to the dark glass of Erdosain's consciousness, and we experience, step by step with him, the "sense" of his anguished existence. The conceit of the secret sect is given an explicit correlation with Erdosain in the form of his specific involvement with its activities. (pp. 22-7)

The key to an understanding of the novel lies in the essential nature of Erdosain as one anguished soul who may well be a figure of Everyman. For reasons that are not made clear, Erdosain is a haunted man, a man obsessed with his own corporeal senses, with their suffering, and with some intangible spiritual malaise that has become a pervasive obsession of his existence. To a certain extent the problem is strictly social, although not in any doctrinaire sense. Erdosain is the typical by-product of an exploitive urban society, a fact most clearly shown in the opening pages of the novel when he is fired from the sugar Corporation for petty embezzlement. It is clear that Erdosain's object in stealing the money was not to raise his standard of living, but simply to experience a few of the city's costly delights that are so inaccessible to the vast majority—a good meal, a good cigar, a good liqueur, a good movie, etc. This purpose may appear as petty as the theft itself, somewhat on the level of the waif's action when he finally manages to pilfer from the coveted wares of the candy counter. But it does become a succinct and brief correlative of Erdosain's sense of exclusion, of being an outsider, unable to participate on the most immediate, consumer-oriented level of modern life. Arlt does not belabor the point, and the novel quickly moves on to more profound disquietudes of his character.

After his dismissal without charges, Erdosain returns home to confront a wife who is abandoning him for another man. One of the most depressing scenes in the Argentine novel follows. Erdosain recalls his childhood and reflects on the failure of his relationship with a woman he still loves. His thoughts are expressed in terms of sexual fantasies that were taboo in the novel of the time and that earned the author the harsh censure of genteel critics who were unable publicly to admit the existence or the significance of such preoccupations. Erdosain, then, is presented as an individual who is first and foremost the synthesis of failure, both emotional and material. Failure is the common denominator of his character, and failure has become, by the time the novel begins, the motivating obsession of is existence. . . . (pp. 28-9)

The bulk of the novel chronicles, often hyperbolically, this individual's almost mystical quest for a meaningful substitute for the obsessive void, for a transcendent order that will satisfy the unnamed needs of those who have been cast aside by the established order and are part of the anesthetized masses. Erdosain's problem to a great extent is his ill-focused sensitivity and anguish over the incapacity of the existing order to cope with the material and spiritual demands of most men. For those who are unaware of the dynamics of society, their lot, to which they submit, is exploitation and a dreary and stultifying existence; such was Erdosain's lot up to the moment of the novel. For those who become self-conscious the only answer is establishment of a new order that will meet directly the needs of the obsessively aware. Such an order is precisely what the Society pretends to offer Erdosain. Thus, to a great extent, Erdosain is a functional psychotic; his fantasies and his attempt to live them through the Society are a flight from the unbearable reality of an existence that is nothing more or less than the excruciating burden of day-to-day living as the vast majority of mankind knows it.

It would be uninteresting to summarize point by point Erdosain's growing involvement with the Society as it is related to the reader. It is enough to characterize both the Society and Erdosain's involvement to underline Arlt's attitude toward such transcendent orders that offer themselves as alternatives to the admittedly destructive order of established society. The reader must absorb about two-thirds of the novel before he finally grasps the fact that the Society is a vast and brilliant hoax perpetrated by the Astrologer. Erdosain appears never to realize this falsity; to the end he is deadly serious in complying with his presumed role in a program that is to become the ultimate solution to man's dilemma. (pp. 30-1)

[The] Society offered sardonically by Arlt is aligned with the totalitarian social gospels prevalent in the late twenties. The Society is a brotherhood, and explicit comparisons are frequently drawn by the Astrologer with the Ku Klux Klan. Man will be given a sense of belonging, an organizational and self-sacrificing identity. And this, after the nature of such evangelical operations, will provide him with the necessary fervor and impetus to involve the rest of mankind.

There is, however, a mordant irony involved here. Erdosain appears not to realize that the objectives of the Society are precisely those of the world order from which he is fleeing, which he feels has cast him aside with repulsion. It is significant that the financial basis of the Society is to be the income from a chain of bordellos and that the power of the directorate is to derive from quasi-religious promises and illusions "greater than those dreamt of by any priest." Modern capitalist society has often been compared to a whorehouse in its enslavement of the unsuspecting masses for its own monetary ends, keeping the occupants dormant with meager consolations and the brutal threats of pimpish discipline. The metaphor is well known, and whether or not one subscribes to it, it is certain that Arlt—and his Astrologer—had it in mind in the sardonic and cynical creation and elaboration of an alternate order to Western society.

For Arlt, the irony of Erdosain's circumstance is based on his naivete, on an anguished awareness that is unaccompanied by any adequate perception of human and social experience. That characterization may be cynical and pessimistic with regard to Arlt's understanding of human nature, but it does reflect the implicit conviction expressed throughout *The Seven Madmen* that, although man is driven by idealistic desires for meaning, transcendence, order in his awareness of himself, the answers to those desires do not come from political and social ventures such as the Society. Not that Arlt condemns Erdosain for his involvement with the absurdities of the Society. Nor does he condemn the Astrologer for the hoax he perpetrates on the unsuspecting man. The trickery may actually work as good for Erdosain, who suffers from an acute case of intellectual myopia and is therefore unable to grasp the meaning of events around him. But the question remains whether the game in the long run is adequate even for Erdosain. It provides him with a momentary sense of identity and importance as he goes to witness the killing of Barsut in the name of his transcendent cause. But his shortsightedness, his inability to comprehend that he is only repeating in vain the gestures of the outside world he has rejected, undermine any permanent value for the hoax. At best, Erdosain is ignorant once again as to his own and human nature.

As for the Astrologer, he is only pandering to the existential whims of the Erdosains among us. Arlt seems to accept this standard justification and self-exculpation of the panderer. The Astrologer emerges as a clever and generous sort, willing to devote his time and energies to the allegedly selfless fabrication of an illusion of meaning for the life of a human derelict. . . . (pp. 33-4)

Despite the unquestionably deceitful nature of the whole program, despite Arlt's clear rejection of both the totalitarian solution and the fabulists, one cannot help but concede its profound and therefore justifiable importance to the dupe, Erdosain. While it would be easy to condemn the Astrologer for his deceit—and Arlt's condemnation of fascism is unquestionably one of the motives of the novel—one cannot overlook the validity of the relativist principle. As Luigi Pirandello was saying at approximately the same time as Arlt was writing, with the title of a work that has become a cliché of contemporary literature, "Così è, se vi pare": That's the way it is, if you think so. Leaving aside Arlt's opinion about the Society, leaving aside the Astrologer's ambiguous motivations in directing the hoax, leaving aside our own reactions toward Erdosain's crucial blindness, we are still left with the undeniable importance of involvement stupid or otherwise, for Erdosain himself. For this reason Arlt does not blush to elevate Erdosain to the level of a Christ figure who sees himself about to save his own soul and those of all mankind through the fulfillment of his commitment to the new order, even though that commitment involves the cruel killing of another man. . . . (p. 35)

For Erdosain this is the meaning of his existence, the ultimate gesture of an empty and sterile life, finally endowed with some virtue and significance. And finally, then, this meaning must be accepted strictly on Erdosain's own terms as valid, as somehow appropriate, no matter what the "objective reality" of the situation may appear to be to the reader and to the commentator. For Arlt and for the reader, the Society may be a cruel fascist hoax to exploit the disaffected, but for Erdosain it is his own and mankind's salvation. And herein lies the novel's axis of biting irony. From the point of view of novelistic structure, we can attribute to the notes of the commentator the tension between our contact with Erdosain and his peculiar neurotic reality and our superior information about the absurdity and futility of that reality. The author shows us both the essential value of Erdosain's commitment qua Erdosain and his own sardonic skepticism concerning any universal validity for such commitments. The tension resolves itself, but only imperfectly, since the author avoids Erdosain's ultimate confrontation of his deception by the new order in which he puts so much trust. The resolution comes in terms of the reader's conclusions concerning the futility of transcendent orders, the paradox of man's quest for them, and the inescapable truth that, like his God, if they don't exist, man will create them.

I would venture to say that it is for this reason that the commentator (who may or may not be the transparent mask of the author) is reluctant to take a firm stand concerning Erdosain's adventure. The adventure is over when the story is related, and Erdosain seeks refuge because of his crime in the house of the commentator. While the host demonstrates a superior attitude and shows through his notes his own successful investigations into the actual "truth" of the events that his guest relates, he confesses in the end to be as perplexed by Erdosain's character as is the reader:

> The chronicler of this story does not dare to define Erdosain, so numerous were the misfortunes of his life that the disasters brought about later in the company of the Astrologer can be explained only by the psychic processes undergone during his marriage.

> Even today, as I reread Erdosain's confessions, it seems incredible to me that I was a witness to such sinister revelations of shamelessness and anguish.
>
> I can still remember it. During those three days that he remained in hiding in my house he confessed everything.
>
> We met in an enormous room, empty of furniture, where very little light penetrated. . . .
>
> Impassively he piled one iniquity upon another. He knew that he was going to die, that the justice of men would seek him out mercilessly.

The impact of this comment upon the reader is to shake his confidence in the facile definition of Erdosain as simply a misdirected outcast and of his confession as the babblings of an inconsequential neurotic. Somewhere between the commentator's doubts and the Astrologer's ambiguous playing at God, between Erdosain's neurotic fantasies and the reader's recognition of his own secret image, lies the central meaning of the adventure of Everyman, of this forgotten Christ. He is neither a madman nor a savior, but a complex human consciousness, and the confusions of the narrative, its points of view and its meanings, are expressionistic correlatives of that complexity which cannot be resolved in easy formulas of truth. (pp. 37-8)

Clearly, Arlt's novel gains coherent form from the narrator's ironic attitude toward the series of events that surround Erdosain. They are events created only in part by the man himself; more effectively, they are the shape of an absurd pattern of a marginal life with which he can identify for the first time in his tortured, trivial existence. There are several levels of irony in the novel: the irony that characterizes the relationship between Erdosain and the Astrologer's secret Society; that which involves the unnamed narrator and Erdosain (recall that Erdosain tells his story to the narrator while he is in hiding to avoid arrest for the murder which he thinks has been committed); and finally, the irony that exists between the narrator and the reader to the extent that we are denied access to any significant explanation for certain circumstances and events.

One is tempted to sum up the ironic relationship between Erdosain and the Society (specifically, the Astrologer, for the question arises as to whether the other members are, like Erdosain, dupes of the hoax or are participants in the hoax at his expense) by reference to that commonplace of contemporary thought that man is the victim of an elaborate hoax by God. In *The Seven Madmen,* the man who is playing at God is the Astrologer, who claims that he is lending mankind an important service. To the extent that mankind seeks after grandiose universal designs of existence, both theological and social, and places his unswerving faith in the meager plans available for his choice, the individual capable of conceiving and executing a truly clever plan deserves to be congratulated at least by himself. We are, however, never quite sure what the Astrologer is trying to do, and this uncertainty is part of an irony at the reader's expense. But we are sure that apparently Erdosain is completely unaware of the Astrologer's machinations.

On one level, Arlt is understandably addressing himself to the power to enchant humble and bewildered Everyman by grandiose totalitarian designs of salvation and existential meaning. On a more significant level, concerning the reasons for having as the controlling consciousness of the novel Erdosain's muddled perspective on reality, the Society becomes, not the justification of his being and the release of his tormented soul from the bonds of a degrading existence, but, quite brutally and inescapably, just another placebo administered to man to keep him occupied and mildly content until his death. There is no question that, as the novel ends, Erdosain firmly believes he has fulfilled the all-validating mission of his life; he labors under the sacrificial delusion of Christ, as the several quotations selected from strategic points in the narrative make clear.

But the reader should not, like Erdosain, be deceived. (pp. 39-40)

The only clear conclusion to be drawn from the tone of the narrator's voice and from his ubiquitous footnotes is that it is only a matter of time until Erdosain discovers the extent of the cruel hoax. This revelation must mean that, once again, Everyman will find himself confronting not only the vacuousness of his existence but also the degrading humiliation of his fateful involvement with existence. In this sense, the novel is open-ended, implying a portentous sequence of events that are only hinted at in the work. The fact is that Arlt did go on to compose a sequel to *The Seven Madmen—The Flamethrowers.* But if we limit ourselves to Arlt's vision of man as it is expressed at one point in his works, we are justified in omitting reference to the Erdosain and the Society that are portrayed in the later and equally autonomous work. (p. 41)

Although we cannot know the exact intentions of the Astrologer, it is more important that we realize Erdosain's lack of any inkling of the plot in which he has become involved. No indication of any weakening in his faith is given in the novel, nor in his confessions to the narrator is there any hint that Erdosain is incapable of realizing that he is the victim of an elaborate deceit correlate with a vision of man as the perpetual object of such designs, divine or otherwise. Our knowledge about life, or the degree of our ability to possess that knowledge, is such that man is at best the victim of his own bewilderment and at worst the victim of deliberate hoaxes perpetrated by a being more intelligent than he. The obvious result of such thinking is that the hoaxers are in turn deceived by other hoaxers more intelligent than they: Both the Astrologer and God are in turn the victims of deceit. Arlt does not explore such a potential in his novel unless it is to imply that the Astrologer's ingenious game is the result of his awareness of a higher game that he is in turn but perpetrating on even lesser mortals—he is not an astrologer for nothing. (pp. 42-3)

Certainly one of the major points of departure for a deeper comprehension of *Los siete locos,* beyond the facile entertainment of the absurd story, is a realization of the overwhelming role of irony in the novel and the particular form that this irony assumes at the expense of the reader, who is, after all, approaching the novel with the same naive desire to "know" that characterizes Erdosain's own stumbling contact with the "reality" of the fictional world. Once the reader grasps this ironic framework, he can never be entirely comfortable with the novel. Its barely contained tensions threaten always to produce a total disintegration or annihilation of the logical coherency that we demand of life and of its fictional representations. The structural contradictions that even the careless reader of the work is able to discover (such as the tension between the narrator's authorial omniscience vs his supposed participation in the action itself, which would then render his omniscience unacceptable) have invited serious doubts about Arlt's competence as a writer. But once we see him within the framework of Kafkaesque expressionistic fiction of the early twentieth century, it becomes easier to accept contradictions, ironies, and the lack of clear fictional autonomy as techniques metaphoric of a singular conception of reality and of its description by the literary work.

In this sense Arlt's work is vatic in its peculiar way. There is no question that Erdosain deserves much empathy from both the narrator-author and the reader. Actually, however, the narrator, in a fashion symbolic of the sensible refusal of the artist to pretend he possesses universal and definitive knowledge about man and his circumstance, confesses his own utter bewilderment in the face of Erdosain's story. In this way, *The Seven Madmen* remains Arlt's nondoctrinaire statement concerning both the plight and the failure of the common man, who is unable to entertain himself with the genteel and aristocratic deceits of other men. And, surely, there is no better "artist" than the Astrologer.

It may be that Arlt's fiction can be read as a sympathetic portrayal of those segments of society which were called, in his time, the proletariat; certainly some spokesmen for social realism in Argentina have seen in Arlt one of the few sophisticated and satisfactory practitioners of that mode. Nevertheless, one searches in vain in his novel for any prophetic message for the redemption of the classes embodied in the Everyman figure of Erdosain. Indeed, here is precisely the point of the novel: that perhaps one of the most humiliating and degrading aspects of the plight of the Erdosains is their belief in transcendent promises—whether fascistic or socialistic—that are to save them from themselves. It is true that one can fault Arlt for the absence in his novel of a viable alternative. Certainly a fundamental aspect of social realism is the injunction to offer the specific mystical goal of its own beliefs as the alternative to the preliminary identification of the unacceptable circumstances of the lower classes. But if the critic is willing to content himself with understanding the writer's accomplishment rather than in proposing ends that he might have accomplished but did not, Arlt's novel is unquestionably significant for its characterization of Erdosain as the anguished Christ manqué and for the brilliant exposition of its vision in terms of an ingenious fictional artifice. (pp. 43-5)

> *David William Foster, "Roberto Arlt and the Neurotic Rationale," in his* Currents in the Contemporary Argentine Novel: Arlt, Mallea, Sabato, and Cortázar, *University of Missouri Press, 1975, pp. 20-45.*

JAMES J. TROIANO   (essay date 1976)

[*In the following excerpt, Troiano analyzes the complex relationship between fantasy and reality in the dramas* Trescientos millones, El fabricante de fantasmas, *and* Saverio el cruel.]

There are two recurring characteristic elements in the works of Roberto Arlt: his use of the grotesque tradition and his treatment of illusion and reality....

The principal motive behind Robert Arlt's propensity toward the fantasy world in his works is the playwright's dissatisfaction with the real world, which makes him search for something beyond the prosaic. There is a constant tension between the real and illusory world in Arlt's works, and the awakening to reality often rings with the harshness of an alarm clock or the shocking violence of a suicide. The grotesque literary tradition is utilized recurrently in order to accentuate the strain between the realms of reality and fantasy. (p. 7)

[In] the grotesque tradition there is a vision of the world as terrifyingly chaotic.... The many shocks and surprises one encounters in the grotesque tradition are created to plunge the spectator into acceptance of the artist's hallucinatory vision of the world. It is revealing to analyze how Arlt combines this fascination for the grotesque with his preoccupation for the interplay of reality and fantasy in his plays.

Arlt's first play, *Trescientos millones,* displays the author's propensity toward both fantasy worlds and the grotesque tradition in literature. The drama concerns a poor servant girl who escapes from prosaic reality by imagining an inheritance of three hundred million pesos and creating a chimerical world inhabited by characters who often appear more real than the character herself.

Arlt envisions, here, a fantasy realm which has an independent existence from people's imaginations. Characters have complete autonomy from their creators. Grotesque figures inhabit this fantasy realm, including a cubic man who longs to participate in a human relationship with someone and a Byzantine Queen who cannot be certain whether she is real or a *fantasma* (phantom). These supposed figments of dreamers' imaginations consistently refer to their "masters" as if the "fantasmas" actually maintained existences outside of their creator's imaginations. This is one of the many examples of Arlt's ambiguity and unpredictability as the playwright creates a grotesque world where no one or nothing is certain.

Parenthetically, Arlt presents Death in a very singular fashion in this work. The entrance of personified death would strike terror in the heart of anyone. Nevertheless, Death in Arlt's play carries a sense of humor. It first reprimands the servant for not offering a chair, consequently complains about the general untidiness of the servant's quarters, explains that the panacea for all ills is deviled ham, and then lecherously touches the servant's body. Death changes from an extremely fastidious complaining type to a lustful individual. In short, Arlt presents Death in a completely unexpected way, which accentuates the absolute unpredictability of the world.

The servant in *Trescientos millones* is drawn more and more deeply within her strange fantasy world. She is forced back to the real world by the harsh voice of her *patrona* and the shrill sound of the servant's bell. The fantasy realm is therefore a much more alluring and pleasant world for the servant. Arlt also longed to escape to a dream world as did his semiautobiographical characters, Silvio in *El juguete rabioso (The Rabid Toy)* and Erdosain in *Los siete locos (The Seven Crazy People)* and *Los lanzallamas (The Flamethrowers).* Roberto Arlt not only feels the attraction of the fantasy realm, but also clearly realizes the danger of a step by step departure from reality. The servant is drawn so deeply into her dream world that she cannot bear to return at the end of the play. The "patrona's" inebriated son attempts to enter her room and seduce her at the same moment she is about to meet her imaginary future son-in-law. The disparity between this significant moment and the vulgarity of the real world forces the woman to opt for suicide. Reality is constantly presented in the works as either tedious or coarse while fantasy is depicted as exciting or adventurous.... In Arlt's works the characters who depart on this journey are led to either death or madness.

Arlt, however, continues to astound the audience with his treatment of the interplay of fantasy and reality even after the servant's death. The characters that she enslaved now dance for joy, for they have finally been freed from her domination. There is, however, one exception: Rocambole, who has been transported from a series of novels by Ponson du Terrail into the servant's world. Rocambole respects the servant because he is closer to her than the other characters: she is a real character (fictional reality) while Rocambole is a fiction converted into a real character by Terrail and transposed into the fantasy world of the servant. The other *fantasmas,* on the other hand, do not appreciate nor understand the relationship between art and the imagination and therefore are hostile; that is why Rocambole asserts his superiority. Therefore, Rocambole pushes the ghosts aside in disgust and kisses the head of the dead servant. Once again Arlt uses the interplay of fantasy and reality to accentuate the ambiguity and complexity of a grotesque world where all reality is to be questioned.

El fabricante de fantasmas, like *Trescientos millones,* is an example of the fantastic grotesque with its bizarre characters and dream worlds, as well as the author's depiction of the lure and danger of the fantasy world. Here again the dream world and real world are blended together in a perplexing blur. The play begins in a very realistic fashion as Arlt presents the marital problems between an author named Pedro and his wife Eloisa. With no warning, the spectator is then cast into Pedro's fantasy world as the character-author is visited by two *fantasmas*. The two, one of whom is "el fantasma de Martina" (the ghost of Martina), the counterpart of his lover Martina, and the other a *galán* (lover) appear to produce a love scene for Pedro. Arlt presents the strange, bizarre love scene as if it were matter-of-fact reality, while he goes to all extremes to confuse the distinct realms of fantasy and reality. Martina even goes so far as to taunt Pedro on his relationship with his wife. Initially Pedro, as was the servant in *Trescientos millones,* is gradually led into a fantasy world which will be alluring at first, but soon perilous. His murder of his wife Eloisa commits Pedro to the dream world which becomes a bizarre specter of his distorted mind.

After the murder, Pedro's fantasy world becomes a nightmare. Pedro first encounters his conscience who tries to instill fear or remorse in the murdering author who responds that the fact he murdered his wife is of little importance to him. The scene becomes increasingly bizarre as Pedro and the conscience debate and threaten each other, until the possibilities of the role of the conscience on stage fill Pedro with enthusiasm and prompt him to inject into it an element of the grotesque: he threatens to transform the conscience into a hunchbacked monster. The conscience pleads that he does not want to suffer this fate for his entire life. What appears to be mere fantasy is converted into reality by the conscience acting as if it were a frightened person. The dramatist stresses here the absolute uncertainty of a truly grotesque world.

In *El fabricante de fantasmas,* Arlt's bizarre dream sequences acquire an even more nightmarish quality than in *Trescientos millones,* and the ambiguity between dream and reality is effectively presented. Two tense scenes illustrate this characteristic. The first dream depicts Pedro as relaxing at home, when his servant informs him that some visitors wish to see him. It appears to be a very real occurrence and the presence of a very real servant accentuates this. Nevertheless, the visitors are a grotesque group of characters from Pedro's works including: a hangman, a prostitute, a hunchback, and a cripple. The antagonism between the butler and the characters heightens the tension in the scene which borders on reality and chimera. The servant eventually departs upon hearing the bizarre group insist that they are Pedro's children. Arlt purposefully accentuates the vividly realistic details in the nightmarish scene stressing the inability to distinguish reality from fantasy.

The uncertainty between these two realms is even more apparent in a grotesque horror scene which occurs later in the play: Pedro attempts to escape from the *fantasmas* in Europe.

He feels confident that he is finally freed from these bizarre creatures which emanate from his conscience, when he meets a charming masked lady at a carnival and tries to convince her to unmask. She finally acquiesces and the horrified Pedro looks upon a face which is identical to his murdered wife. Later, when he unmasks the woman's husband he first finds the face of the judge who pursues him, and after that, he finds the face of the hunchback character who terrorizes him at home. The absolute initial tranquility of the scene is brusquely transformed into a horrifying inferno. The mask theme and carnival setting emphasize the unpredictability of the grotesque world. . . . In short, Arlt presents to the spectator a grotesque world permeated with terror, nightmares, and uncertainty.

El fabricante de fantasmas introduces a new element in the treatment of reality versus illusion; in this work the author Pedro is condemned and executed by his own characters. In contrast to the attitude of the servant in *Trescientos millones,* Pedro attempts to go beyond mere aspiration to escape from prosaic reality to actual execution, as he commits himself in an attempt to force reality to conform to liberated imagination. He realizes, however, that this forcing of reality can only be counterproductive, and this explains the fact that the *fantasmas* function as dreaded executioners, rather than sought-after entertainers, in this work. The significance of this development probably reflects the frustration of Arlt himself, who apparently found prosaic reality unbearable but inescapable, realizing that to go beyond mere aspiration to an attempted actual commitment inevitably must result in tragedy. Arlt's contradictory feelings toward the lure of the fantasy world and its dangers are not unlike Dante's sinners waiting for final judgment in *The Inferno* as they "yearn for what they fear."

In *Saverio el cruel* a group of wealthy young people are instigated by their friend Susana into creating a fantasy for the dairyman Saverio. It is apparently nothing more than a joke in rather poor taste. Saverio is told that Susana is victimized by the insane illusion that she is a princess who has been robbed of her kingdom and is pursued by a cruel colonel. Susana's friends inform the dairyman that the only way she can regain her sanity is by someone acting out the role of colonel; then they proceed to add that he should play the role to aid the unfortunate lady. Initially, the dairyman is skeptical, but he soon accepts. Saverio soon begins to accept his role as reality. He not only acts out the role alone, but with the servant, Simona, and Susana's friends. The dairyman, as colonel, even purchases a guillotine in order to maintain his power by eliminating his enemies. Thus an apparently rational person has become insane. Saverio, however, is informed by Susana's sister, Julia, that the entire plot concocted by Susana was a farce. Susana, however, insists that the fiction was real, finally shooting Saverio and exclaiming that he always was the colonel and merely disguised himself as a butter salesman.

Roberto Arlt has shocked the public in *Trescientos millones* and *El fabricante de fantasmas,* but in *Saverio el cruel,* his best play, Arlt victimizes his unsuspecting audience in an even more skillful manner, by lulling it into a belief in its own superior knowledge of the reality of the action as it unfolds. When the spectators see Susana's friends plotting against the dairyman and then Saverio alone with his private dreams, they are disposed to enjoy the farcical elements of the situation and are totally unprepared for the tragic denouement. Once again both characters and audience are unexpectedly thrown into a grotesque world, where no one can possibly see what may happen. Susana's acquaintances believe they are merely playing a cruel joke, yet in the space of a few hours Saverio is transported from an absolutely rational world to a chimerical realm in which his sanity and even his life are at stake. It is highly significant that in being submitted to the author's deceptive procedure, the spectators themselves are forced to share this grotesque vision of the world.

In his initial appearance, before becoming involved in the play-acting, Saverio appears weak and helpless. The absolute lack of imagination, his inability to see beyond the prosaic world of trivia, is evident, for example, in his constant references to the butter he sells, which he even suggests as a possible cure for Susana's madness superior to the foolishness of the invented play (''La manteca es una realidad, mientras que lo otro son palabras'') (''Butter is a reality, while the other thing is merely words'').

When Saverio views Susana peforming her role, he acts initially as a spectator, commenting on the part that she and her friend are playing. In doing so, Saverio thus maintains a certain aesthetic distance which is confirmed in his hesitation to involve himself. This situation is similar to that of Don Quijote when he views the puppets, taking a somewhat objective attitude at first, finally to jump wholeheartedly into the fantastic realm of the marionettes. Saverio readily enters into the role which he was previously hesitant to assume. He pretends that he is colonel when he is alone and more significantly, his imaginary world continues even when the servant enters. He goes so far as to compare himself with Hitler and Mussolini and insists that his role will lead him to real power. . . . When Saverio changes uniform from dairyman to colonel he is transformed from a timid, harmless figure into a violent and possibly dangerous man. It is as if the change from one figurative mask into another actually has created a different person.

Susana's friends' humorous reaction to Saverio soon changes to concern, as they begin to realize that Saverio's role as colonel is not pure fiction for the dairyman. The plotters' astonishment begins with Saverio's claim that he will need armaments. Saverio then makes a key statement which proves that his fictive role has become a real one for him: ''Entendámonos . . . de farsa para los otros . . . pero real para nosotros'' (''Let's understand, this is a farce for the others, but real for us''). Arlt stresses once again the fact that we are all play actors in life; what seems like mere pretense, ''farsa'' for others, is our only way of being.

In the third act it is clear that role playing has transformed the character. In marked contrast to the intitial woeful appearance of Saverio we are now told that ''su continente impone respeto'' (''his countenance imposes respect''). Saverio proceeds to astound characters and audience alike by telling them that the entire episode has been merely invented to amuse Susana and friends at his expense. Julia's declaration appears to have returned the dairyman to lucidity, a change to rationality which parallels Quijote in his final moments. The dairyman presents a logical analysis of what had occurred and shows self-deprecation as he returns to the simplemindedness of before. In this disillusioned awakening Saverio returns sadly to reality and the same petty preoccupation with his butter as before the transformation. Susana's actions after the dairyman's remarks then can only mystify the spectators. She continues the farce despite Saverio's rejection of it and then tries to inspire the dairyman to continue with the role. When Saverio reacts adversely, refusing to submit again to the appeal of the imagination, Susana shoots Saverio exclaiming: ''Ha sido inútil, Coronel, que te disfrazaras de vendedor de manteca'' (''It has been useless,

Colonel, to disguise yourself as a butter salesman''). The dying victim expresses the feelings of everyone as he gasps that this was no joke—Susana was really mad. Susana's derangement represents a new stage in Arlt for here a character goes beyond the real world into the fantasy world and is not brought back. The servant in *Trescientos millones* was constantly returned to reality by the service bell, the harsh voice of the *patrona* and finally the drunken son of the *patrona*. In *Saverio el cruel,* however, Susana continues the flight from reality to fiction, a restoration of the triumph of imagination over reality at the very point the opposite seems to have been established. In an existence which is a constant beginning and also the ultimate responsibility of the individual, there always exists the danger of the lack of outside controls and of carrying the imagination to the point of no return. Life, as a sort of tension between reality and fiction, is also one between sanity and madness. By feigning insanity, Susana has become mad.

The two grotesque dream sequences in *Saverio el cruel* indicate the author's animosity toward war. In the first dream, Saverio conjures up the image of a salesman who wears a mask which gives his face the appearance of a skeleton. The visitor is the representative of an armaments factory, which has sold heavily to numerous governments. Arlt's anti-military message in the dream constitutes a prelude to the vicious attack on the armament industry in *La fiesta del hierro (The Festival of Steel).* It is interesting to note that the salesman in Saverio's dream represents a corporation named Armstrong, precisely the name of the company in the later play.

In the second dream, Saverio imagines a loudspeaker which announces and comments on his belligerent actions. Saverio complacently remarks: ''Buena publicidad. El populacho admira a los hombres crueles'' (''Good publicity. The public admires cruel men''). As in his well-known short story **''La luna roja'' (''The Red Moon'')** and *La fiesta del hierro,* the playwright effectively captures the nightmarish tension of war as the loudspeaker accentuates each frightening detail of a world on the brink of destruction.

As I have illustrated, the grotesque tradition and the interplay of fantasy and reality are two major components of Arlt's *Weltanschauung.* For example, in *Trescientos millones* the servant escapes from reality into an alluring and yet dangerous fantasy world filled with innumerable astonishing surprises and bizarre creations from her prolific imagination. *El fabricante de fantasmas* deals with the relationship between author and character and the basic confusion between the essence of fantasy and reality. At the same time, there are bizarre characters and grotesque dream sequences, including carnival scenes and the mask and face theme. *Saverio el cruel* illustrates how fantasy can easily be transformed into reality as with Saverio and Susana, thus depicting once again the absolute relativity of reality. In addition, a grotesque world permeated with shocks, unexpected happenings, and strange dreams is also presented. Roberto Arlt is an author who ascertains that the real world is harsh and cruel and comprehends the common wish to escape into an alluring fantasy world, which he realizes can be a perilous journey. He fervently portrays the anguish of this enigma in his moving literary works. (pp. 9-14)

> *James J. Troiano, ''The Grotesque Tradition and the Interplay of Fantasy and Reality in the Plays of Roberto Arlt,'' in* Latin American Literary Review, *Vol. IV, No. 8, Spring-Summer, 1976, pp. 7-14.*

ADEN W. HAYES (essay date 1977)

[*In the following excerpt, Hayes analyzes structural and thematic elements common to the first-person narratives collected in* El jorobadito, *contrasting these narratives with works of conventional autobiography.*]

Roberto Arlt uses elements of the autobiographical form in nearly all his fiction—first-person narration in *El juguete rabioso,* confessions, diaries and interviews in *Los siete locos, Los lanzallamas,* and *El amor brujo*—but Arlt distorts and parodies many of the techniques of confessional autobiography in a series of short narratives, collected in 1933 under the title *El jorobadito,* which are mutually linked in form and theme. The stories which will concern us here all follow a similar narrative pattern, clearly exemplified in the first of them, **"Escritor fracasado"**; this story contains the basic structural elements employed in all the stories of the collection.

The narrator is a failed writer, an imposter, really, who has spent his adult life trying to convince himself and his reading public that he has creative talent, and is capable of artistic invention. Because he has no faith in himself or his abilities, he has adopted a series of poses—aesthetic experimenter, traditionalist, exigent critic, and detached, cynical observer of the literary scene—none of which represents his true feelings or interests. He is bored with this life of dissimulation, and ashamed of his failure to produce any work of lasting value. He has come to recognize that his artistic life (the life which he relates), is a sham, but he cannot define or interpret it, except with a few pejorative adjectives.

With this autobiographical story, in which he continues his practice of falsification, the writer emphasizes (consciously or unconsciously) the lying nature of art itself. By representing his artistic ventures as the sum total of his life (an acknowledged failure), the writer shows the reader the ultimately unsealable rift between art and physical experience, between the events of our lives and any representations of them. His story becomes a judgment of himself, rather than an explanation of his life.

In this writer's limited understanding of himself and of his literary work (including his autobiography), we may see an inversion of one of the reader's traditional expectations of the autobiographical form. The most coherent autobiographies are written from a point of view or an understanding which could not be reached while living the events, one which helps to define the narrative's focus, and to organize it. In this regard we may think of Croce, who, before he undertakes to recall and record his life as a critic, carefully sets out his reasons for writing, defines the format he will use, and explains why he has chosen to write this document in his fiftieth year. All this indicates a considered sense of purpose, makes clear the writer's convictions, and makes his text more convincing to the reader. Arlt's writer attempts none of this.

This is but one sense in which the elements of Arlt's text contrast to more ambitious and more purposeful monuments of confessional literature. Rousseau searches, through his mind and memory, and then through the construction of the *Confessions* itself, for his own identity. He seeks to bring meaning out of the disparate and seemingly contradictory elements of his life. . . . (pp. 192-93)

Arlt's writer, on the other hand, gives up interpreting his actions, and, very early in his story, admits that he doesn't understand the meaning of his life. This is simply reinforced at the end of his story when he adopts a nihilistic point of view which is an escape from thinking rather than a philosophy:

> ¿Para qué afanarse en estériles luchas, si al final del camino se encuentra como todo premio un sepulcro profundo y una nada infinita? ["Why busy oneself in sterile struggles, if at the end of the road one finds as the whole prize a deep grave and an infinite nothingness?"]

One of Rousseau's stated purposes for setting down his personal history was to show how exceptional he was, "like no one in the whole world," and it is in part this singularity which justifies the work. By contrast, Arlt's failed writer concludes that he is really no different from the public he had tried to dupe with his ersatz literature. . . . (pp. 193-94)

The failed writer is very like the narrators of the other stories of the collection, stories in which the elements of **"Escritor fracasado"** are used again and again, and always to achieve the same effect. These components can be isolated and enumerated: the narrator's attempted verbal manipulation of other characters through the fabrication of the appearance of a problem or crisis; the ultimate failure of that manipulative process; the subsequent exile or banishment of the narrator, and his physical isolation, or exclusion from social interaction; the narrator's confession of guilt—in the form of the story's text—a confession which, at least in part, pretends to be an explanation of circumstances and motives, but which is incomplete and obfuscating—an exercise in self-deception.

In each story under consideration, the narrator's desire to manipulate others is born of his sense of his own worthlessness and obscurity. The failed writer needs his public, as the other narrators need the characters around them, to confirm his sense of his own importance. A hostile reaction from his audience will not be, for him, a negative one, . . . because he fears that if he means nothing to them, if he provokes no response, no interest, then he truly is nothing. . . . (p. 194)

The narrator of another story, **"El jorobadito,"** explains that he tried to invent a social situation which would force his fiancée, Elsa, to recognize him as a person, rather than merely dealing with him as a presence in her house, as he plays out the social role of *novio* ["fiancé"]. He meets a hunchback in a bar, and convinces the little man to visit Elsa with him. The narrator asks her to prove her love for him by kissing the deformed man, hoping that this will provoke her to declare her love for the narrator only. But the plan is upset when the hunchback revolts against his role as pawn, takes out a pistol, threatens both Elsa and her *novio,* and the narrator strangles him.

"Ester Primavera" and **"Las fieras"** form a unit because the two stories have protagonists and plots which are nearly identical. The narrator of each reveals that he cynically convinced his girlfriend of his love for her, then broke off their relationship in order to make her suffer. The idea, established in the other stories, is evident here as well: through her suffering his girlfriend certifies his importance.

Ricardo Stepens, the protagonist of **"Noche terrible,"** tricks his fiancée, Julia, in the same way, but instead of announcing the end of their relationship, he allows it to continue until the night before their planned wedding, and then he runs away to Montevideo. Gustavo Boar, the narrator of **"El traje del fantasmas,"** seeks attention by showing up naked in downtown Buenos Aires; but his act is duplicitous in that he is trying to create a scene or a scandal, to divert public attention from the fact that he has just committed a murder, and to manipulate public opinion to accept him as insane.

The salient characteristic of all these attempts is the apparent failure of the verbal constructs to influence or regulate an exterior reality to the degree the narrators had hoped they would. The image which appears on the second page of the collection's first story, with which Arlt's writer describes his failures and ultimate helplessness, serves as a keynote for the plans and fates of all the protagonists:

> así como el inexperto viajero que se aventura por una llanura helada y repentinamente descubre que el hielo se rompe, mostrando por las grietas el mar inmóvil que lo tragará, así con el mismo horror, yo descubrí la catástrofe de mi genio, el deshielo de mi violencia.
>
> ["just as the inexperienced traveler who ventures out over a plain of ice and suddenly discovers that the ice is broken, showing through the cracks the motionless sea that will swallow him, so with the same horror I discover the catastrophe of my genius, the thawing of my violence."]

This attempt to manipulate by the imagination fails because it is antithetical to the exterior reality it seeks to influence and to mold; because it represents—as does any daydream, of which these are examples carried to an extreme that initiates action—a wish fulfillment; and because the narrators, that is, the perpetrators, are not clever enough to sustain this duality.

The paradigm of this kind of failure is presented by Eugenio Karl in **"Una tarde de domingo,"** a story which, like **"Noche terrible,"** is narrated only partly in the first person since, in each case, a third-person narrator introduces the protagonist's interior monologue, which constitutes the essence of the tale.

When his friend's wife Leonilda invites Karl to visit her on a Sunday afternoon, he privately envisions in great detail the process he will use to seduce her. His imagined methods are active and physical. But once inside her house, his technique becomes conversational. He tries to interest Leonilda in his past affairs, all failures, in which fantasy took precedence over reality. He feigned concern for his girlfriends' corporeal needs, but by merely discussing physical acts, by metaphorizing sex, he bored these women and they left him.

In turn, he bores Leonilda with the stories of these relationships while he fantasizes about having sex with her. He cannot control or coordinate the separate trains of thought, the conversational and the fantastic, and the effect of the combination of the two is psychically enervating and physically exhausting. He falls into a chair and feels as fatigued as a runner at the end of a race. His reaction parallels (and parodies) that of the sex act he wished to commit.

He no longer can dissimulate his intentions; the dichotomy of his fantasies and his social role becomes too great. He torpidly begins to define his own fantasies about Leonilda, by which he offends her; she orders him to stop talking. Ashamed of his failure, he decides to escape before her husband returns. He retreats from this defeat, physically, by returning to his solitary bachelor's existence, and emotionally, by trying to repress his libidinous interest in Leonilda. He pretends to understand her personality (and, by extension, her refusal of his advances), as the product of a monotonous, bourgeois, existence. He produces an aesthetic response to reality, distorting his experience (for himself, and for the reader), in a fictional version of his failure.

Living in exile, or in hiding, is the common fate of all the narrators of **El jorobadito,** primarily, as some of them hint, because of their fear of failing again. Ricardo Stepens takes refuge in Montevideo, where he is unknown. The failed writer retires and avoids his old friends and followers. The narrator

of **"Las fieras"** spends each day, bored and silent, sitting at a corner table in the Ambos Mundos bar; and the narrator of **"Ester Primavera"** is confined to a tuberculosis sanatorium in the Andean foothills. Both the narrator of **"El jorobadito"** and Gustavo Boar, of **"El traje de fantasma,"** are in jail.

It is from this vantage point of exile and isolation that they look back over their lives and make their confessions, in the form of the texts we receive. These are comparable to historical autobiography only in the broadest sense of a common format, but Arlt's works attack the assumptions of the reader who expects veracity and reliability from a first-person narrative.

Again, the story told by the failed writer provides our example for comparison. His autobiographical confession is partial, enigmatic, and deliberately destroys the confidence of the reader. This document is not, any more than the narrator's life was, based upon an understanding of exterior (social, historical) reality; in fact, it is anti-historical. Events of the text are only the events of the narrator's mind. Not a single date, historical occurrence, or artistic event is mentioned, and the narrator only confuses both his fictional reading public and the readers of his confessions with his cynical credo, the "Estética del Exigente, a base de un cocktail de cubismo, fascismo, marxismo y teología" ["Aesthetic of the Exigent, at the base of a cocktail of cubism, fascism, marxism, and theology"]. Whatever its sources, this "aesthetic" cannot be associated with any historical period or any coherent set of ideas. Like the remarkably similar doctrine proposed by the "revolutionaries" in Arlt's **Los siete locos,** it represents an impossible *ars combinatoria* designed to disorient, astound, or arrest the attention of his public, but above all to be penetrated, to be recognized for what it is, an invention.

The failed writer never mentions his own name (nor do the narrators of **"Ester Primavera,"** **"Las fieras,"** or **"El jorobadito"**), nor the names of any of his friends or followers. His life seems hollow and empty to us partly because it is not involved with any social process. There is no notion in his confessions of learning experienced over time. In fact, the importance of time itself is minimized by the lack of progression, or differentiation among the various phases of the artist's life. There seems to be no unity of events, in the sense of a direction or trajectory, because the narrator's thinking process does not correspond to our own. We never fully understand the reasons or motivations for his acts, which he prefers to describe partially and imperfectly.

The narrative focus, and therefore the presumed center of the narrator's life, is on his attempts to create new and beautiful art (as he calls it), and on the emotional pain which his failures to do this cause him. In the reader's understanding, then, the character is only his art, for in the end, his life is reduced to a vague and emotional literary text, a confession of errors.

This lack of precision and of thoughtful interpretation, and a concomitant emphasis on the narrator's personal reactions and feelings characterize all these narratives, and call into question the seriousness and exact nature of the sins or crimes of which each narrator feels he is guilty. Arlt here introduces another inversion of the confessional genre: these characters represent themselves as worse than other men because they want to be that way. For them, the confessional autobiography represents an opportunity to pursue the goals of social attention and recognition which earlier had concerned them so much.

This, in turn, prevents the adoption of a traditional technique of autobiographical works, whereby the narrator casts himself as a character, as he looks back on his life, by showing a disparity of understanding or motivation between the narrative voice and the personage it is describing. This is most clear, perhaps, in the picaresque genre, but it is true for other kinds of autobiographical literature as well. In these stories, however, the confessor tries to demonstrate a continuity between the character who, at sometime in the past, committed a nefarious act, and the narrator who uses that past event to bring attention to himself. In this respect, there is no difference in attitude between the figure in the text and the figure producing the text.

In this we must recognize Arlt's final, and most ambitious, reversal of the conventions of the confessional genre. These acts, or more precisely the results of the acts, which give them and their perpetrators importance, are not parts of any plot—a series of interactions among characters over a period of time—but are themselves the inventions of the narrators. They have their origins in the fantasies of these characters and, as such, are functions of the individual personalities rather than part of a fictional continuum of events.

The separation of author-invented reality and character fantasy is pointed out by the "Nota del autor" ["Author's Note"] appended to **"El traje del fantasmas,"** where it is explained that the tale is entirely the fabrication of the narrator, Gustavo Boar, that it is completely untrue, and is designed to deceive the public about Boar's sanity. This adventure story contains elements of the supernatural, the fantastic, and the pastoral romance, and it is autobiographical only insofar as it helps provide a psychological portrait of its inventor. More than anything else, it is Gustavo Boar's way of claiming to be exceptional, and is a call for the attention of the public which reads his narrative.

In **"Noche terrible"** Ricardo Stepens simply imagines the effects of the power he assumes that he has over Julia. Her suffering, her mother's embarrassment, and her brother's threats to shoot Stepens are included in the text only in the status of the protagonist's visions as he sits in a milk-bar in the Almagro section of Buenos Aires; they cannot be verified by any other character in the story. The narrator of **"El jorobadito"** believes he has disrupted or destroyed Elsa's life with his arranged farce, but this seems highly unlikely, since earlier he had complained that he doubted she really cared for him. The narrator never tries to reconcile these two ideas.

To break off with his girlfriend, the narrator of **"Ester Primavera"** simply sends a note by messenger to her house. In the note he mentions a sexual intimacy between Ester and himself which did not really exist. He imagines that this information will find its way to Ester's mother, and will then cause a crisis in the family, and endless problems for Ester. After he sends the note, he sees Ester only once, on the street, and for a minute he hopes she will come up and slap his face. But she simply looks at him for a moment, and walks on. The narrator is crushed, because her ignoring him proves the error of his fantasies of his own importance.

The failed writer imagines he has betrayed his friends, along with his talent, but we never see or know of any results of that betrayal. The narrator of **"Las fieras"** confesses to having committed an "horrible pecado" ["horrible sin"] in the past, but he refuses to define it more precisely; to do so, we come to realize, would only diminish its importance.

These protagonists reveal sins or crimes which they merely hope they have committed, and distress they wish they might have caused, rather than results they have witnessed and under-stood. They parody the apologia—by substituting self-condemnation for self-defense—and they refer in extravagant terms to their crimes or sins hoping to receive the reader's condemnation as well.

Both historical and fictional autobiography are taken to be based upon observation, not upon invention; but these narrators mock the reader's expectation of reliability, since their confessional narratives have their backgrounds, not in the exterior reality which the characters hated, feared and escaped, but in the imaginatively created interior reality which they have made their refuge. These confessional texts are Arlt's narrators' last defenses against the obscurity they fear. By reading them, the reader joins the public that each narrator seeks to validate his existence. (pp. 194-200)

> *Aden W. Hayes, "Arlt's Confessional Fiction: The Aesthetics of Failure," in* Journal of Spanish Studies: Twentieth Century, *Vol. 5, No. 3, Winter, 1977, pp. 191-201.*

NAOMI LINDSTROM (essay date 1977)

[*Lindstrom is an American critic who has written extensively on Latin American literature and has translated* Los siete locos *into English. In the following excerpt from her* Literary Expressionism in Argentina, *she analyzes the narrative devices by which Arlt intentionally introduced chaos into his fiction to convey the expressionistic belief that reality cannot be comprehended in a rational, orderly way.*]

Argentine expressionism . . . seeks to create a work of literature homologous in form to the universe it represents. As in the case of the German expressionists, the Latin American writers posited the existence of an incoherent universe, whose workings were not to be understood by rational inquiry and whose truths were not to be transmitted by rational discourse. Literature must dissuade the reader from his reliance on ratiocination and his insistence on being fully informed. It must persuade him to accept the irrational, the unexplained and the anomalous as predominant features of human existence, not to be explained away by a vigorous application of reason. Therefore, literature must refrain from presenting the reader with a fictional world more well-ordered than the world that we inhabit.

So we find Argentine expressionists resorting to many of the same disordering literary devices used by German expressionists. Data seemingly important to the understanding of the plot is omitted. Contradictory notions appear without any indication of which is more valuable or more correct. Characters and narrators forego a straightforward presentation of their statements, resorting to riddles, ambiguities, evasions, poetic effusions and unintelligible remarks. One character, Arlt's Astrologer, communicates partly by means of charades and news reports that have been fabricated for some rhetorical end. The overall structure of the work lacks unity and coherence. Frequently the time sequence is unclear, and it may be unclear whether some events take place at all, are imagined, fabricated or hallucinated. These formal devices reinforce the thematic assertions of expressionism concerning the nature of man's universe.

Roberto Arlt's deviant expression, long ascribed to his lack of education, leisure or personal stability, is now becoming recognized as a manifestation of Latin American expressionism. For instance, it is by now a commonplace that Arlt's Erdosain novels, **Los siete locos** and **Los lanzallamas,** are only superficially crime novels and fail to satisfy the exigencies of that genre. Commentaries on Arlt's work may list a number of ''loose ends'' in the plot, occurrences that are never fully explained or that appear inverisimilar in terms of other events in the story. The reader is thus alerted that he must read these apparent thrillers in quite a different spirit from that of the ''armchair detective'' or skilled reader of detective stories.

Going beyond this rather obvious lack of complete explanations for all occurrences, we find Arlt using a number of devices to undermine the reader's confidence in what the narrator has to tell him. Especially disconcerting is the use of footnotes that contradict the statements to which they refer. Such a footnote is appended to an episode occurring in a meeting of revolutionaries. The Astrologer, as leader of the cabal, introduces a new member as the Major, explaining that the man holds that rank in the Argentine military. Shortly thereafter, he announces that the Major is a mere civilian, introduced as a major in order to demonstrate the superiority of appearance over reality. The Astrologer's revelation is glossed, though, with the statement that the Astrologer first gave the man's true identity and then lied when he claimed to have lied about it. The footnotes and the text itself are both the words of the same narrator, a man who has taken it upon himself to reconstruct and chronicle the events of Erdosain's last days. Thus this self-appointed historian is telling the reader not to believe a statement that he himself has included in the text proper. The question of the Major's identity does not come up again in the novels. Such unresolved confusion frustrates any reader who attempts to read the novels as one would a novel of crime and detection. The matter of the Major's identity is a puzzle that simply has no solution.

''El traje del fantasma,'' a 1933 short story, again uses the footnote apparently to clarify a point, but really in order to create confusion. The text is an accused murderer's own account of the fantastic circumstances that will explain his connection with the corpse found in his room. His stated intention is to convince the reader that he did not kill the man and was not, as the popular press would have it, the dead man's lover. He asserts that a rapid succession of fantastic events befell him, including a sojourn in a land of skeletons. At the end of the accused man's deposition, a footnote appears. It warns the reader that the man's account is nothing more than an attempt to appear mad and thus escape responsibility for the murder. The reader has no indication whose work the footnote is. Thus he can equally well believe the footnote's statement that the prisoner was feigning madness or the prisoner, who says he does not want to be thought mad. If the footnote is wrong and the prisoner's deposition is a sincere effort, the events of the narrative may still be seen in more than one way. They may be not deliberately fabricated untruths, but rather the recollection of a series of hallucinations. If the story is a genuinely fantastic one, the prisoner's amazing story may have happened much as he tells it. Not only is the reader left unsure whether he has been reading clever lies, remembered hallucinations or fantastic adventures, but he is also unsure whether the story is principally naturalistic—the sordid tryst and subsequent murder, the workings of the criminal mind—or whether fantastic elements predominate, like the suspension of normal time and space, the voyage to a land populated by skeletons and the magic forces that determine the course of events. Through the highly ambiguous relationship between footnote and text, the entire tale becomes the indecipherable expression of a disordered universe, the world-as-madhouse of expressionism.

The footnote is also a device serving to decrease the reader's awareness of the fictional status of the work. At one point, ten days in Erdosain's life are left unaccounted for in the narrative. A footnote tells us that the narrator acknowledges this gap in his chronicle. He claims, however, to have heard Erdosain's account of those missing days, an account that would fill another book. Although considerations of space preclude immediate disclosure of that material, the narrator holds out to the reader the possibility of a disclosure ''posiblemente algún día'' [''maybe someday'']. Another footnote again suggests the existence of a body of material that has been withheld from the reader. One character has on his person a book of personal musings which may shed light on the part he plays in the events of the plot. As the text makes it clear how revealing the contents of that notebook may prove to be, a footnote is appended. The footnote says ''En la segunda parte de este libro daremos un extracto de la libreta de Barsut'' [''In the second part of this book we will give a summary of Barsut's notebook'']. These two footnotes do not contradict what has been said in the text itself. Rather they violate one's common-sense notion that characters in a work of fiction cannot have any existence outside that work. One can be certain of that idea and yet be tricked into believing that Erdosain has had ten days of activity that would fill an entire volume, or that Barsut's notebook was known to the narrator, but that this information is inaccessible to the reader. The narrator is himself a fiction, but he pretends to have more reality than his tale and to be able to withhold parts of his story when he feels so inclined. The reader can be convinced momentarily that this fictional being knows more about the characters in the novel than any mere reader can know.

In addition, footnotes that really do serve to clarify appear in the same text with the spurious ones. For instance, the publisher leaves a note to explain an obscure period reference and the author notes that he elaborated his plot before the occurrences of the sixth of September 1930, rather than fictionalizing history. The existence of such straightforward notes alongside those meant to generate confusion make the reader even more suspicious, to use Nathalie Sarraute's word.

Arlt's novels violate our notion that a story should be told in an elegant, accessible manner and should present narrative data at a moment when it will illuminate the emerging plot and its overall significance. The Arltian novel may either move too swiftly to facilitate comprehension or proceed so slowly as to cast doubt on the competence of the narrator. The Erdosain novels open and close with dispatch, but at various moments the story becomes becalmed amid a great deal of data that bear no obvious relation to the story proper.

For instance, Haffner's death agony occupies an entire chapter in *Los lanzallamas*. At this juncture in the plot, the reader is most eager to know why the conspirators have decided to eliminate Haffner. Indeed, Erdosain's motivation for deciding others shall die is a highly ambiguous point throughout the two novels and one that has attracted considerable critical attention. The reader would reasonably look to the description of Haffner's last moments for some clarification of this matter. After all, it is conventional in crime novels for betrayed gang members to name their murderers before dying. But in Arlt the reader is subjected instead to a rambling account of Haffner's life as a procurer. The account runs to great detail, such as how Haffner locked one prostitute out on a balcony all one winter night and failed to kill her in this fashion. This welter of trivia makes more evident the absence of any information relevant to the decision to murder Haffner. The insignificant is continually substituted for what is central and significant.

In the narration of Erdosain's death we find another such substitution. The plot is interrupted by a passage explaining how that character's unhappy childhood left him forever alienated. Not only has the reader had ample evidence of Erdosain's unhappiness and alienation, but he has already been told the story of Erdosain's childhood. One may well wonder why such a redundant passage should occur at the last moment before Erdosain's death. At the same time, information the reader wants is being withheld: why Erdosain acquired a stupid, cross-eyed mistress by degrading means, maintained her despite the revulsion she inspired in him and suddenly murdered her. The only purpose of this tardy retelling of Erdosain's early life is to be as painfully pointless as Erdosain's life was.

A third instance of irrelevant information encumbering the narrative occurs when Erdosain's wife, Elsa, leaves him. Taking refuge in a convent, she tells the story of her unhappy marriage to the nuns, for catharsis and to justify leaving the marriage. Elsa's account forms a chapter in *Los lanzallamas*. The chapter offers a fresh point of view on Erdosain's difficulties. However, Elsa proves to be another wildly erratic narrator. Like the unreliable central narrator of the novels, she congests her story with unimportant details and omits significant connections between events. She shares the central chronicler's disinclination to distinguish between what matters and what is peripheral. She violates our notion that there is a hierarchy of importance in which some things must be said and recognized, while others are less essential.

For instance, Elsa describes the stay of a young prostitute, Erdosain's guest, in their household. Of this stressful period, Elsa chooses to remember the difficulties she experienced trying to provide the girl with footwear and apparel. Elsa also mentions that one morning the girl began rooting aimlessly about in a little strip of soil near the house. This story, surely a peripheral anecdote, is related in detail. One learns how the girl acquired a digging tool and how Elsa tried to impose cosmos on chaos by suggesting the girl turn her rooting behavior into the cultivation of lettuce and tomatoes. Elsa mentions only briefly her conviction that the girl was eager to murder her reluctant benefactress, although most readers would consider murderous intention more important than vegetable gardening.

Elsa's too-detailed treatment of this episode bears witness to the severity of the girl's derangement. The world must be, indeed, a disordered place to produce such irrational behavior in young people. Yet the world's disorder manifests itself in a more alarming fashion in Elsa's mode of storytelling. Elsa is, after all, one of the more conventionally sane characters in the novels; one critic has called her ''la típica burguesita'' [''the typical bourgeoise''] for her adherence to existing norms. Thus if shoes, stockings, lettuce and tomatoes merit more attention in her story than does intent to commit murder, something very basic has gone awry. The general breakdown of values and beliefs that the novel depicts has swept away the devices by which human beings make sense of the world.

Paradoxically, some of the most disorienting passages in Arlt's fiction adhere superficially to generally-accepted norms for storytelling. In the context of a literary work that is often narrated in a wildly aberrant fashion, such conventionally related passages provoke yet further suspicion. The reader is given no indication in what spirit to read these apparently straightforward sections. One of Arlt's fictional conspirators describes this perplexing strategy in terms of chess. The character describes a chessmaster's genius as ''elasticidad del juego'' [''elasticity of the game'']. By this he means that the player ''no debe tomar un solo final del juego, sino muchos . . . porque así desconcierta de cien maneras al adversario'' [''shouldn't hold to a single end of the game, but many . . . because in that way he perplexes his adversary in one hundred ways'']. Indeed, the reader of Arlt finds himself the adversary of a narrator who will allow his purposes and goals to be grasped.

An example of such elasticity is the ending of *Los lanzallamas*. At first, the novel seems to draw to a close in a slow and eccentric manner. Erdosain's death is twice related, once as perceived by the sensational press and then in a more leisurely and accurate version reconstructed by the chronicler. The second telling includes elements that contradict the popular notion of how a wanted criminal must die. In the chronicler's version, Erdosain's mild appearance disturbs onlookers, for it disrupts their way of thinking about crime. . . . Erdosain seems to have died absorbed by the effort to remain decorously upright, rather than by reflections on the events that led to his death. Further incongruity comes with the appearance of an old man who spits on the dead Erdosain, pronouncing this curse and elegy: ''Hijo de puta. Tanto coraje mal empleado'' [''Bastard. So much courage used badly''].

While the narrator has up to this point been emphasizing the outlandish or disturbing aspects of Erdosain's death, he suddenly begins to tell his story in an especially conventional manner. He reveals briefly what happened to each of the other conspirators after Erdosain's death. Certainly it is a well-established novelistic convention to make known the fates of the various characters before closing. However, in a novel that withholds so much key information about its characters, such an abundance of specific information is puzzling.

However, the manner in which the story ends still precludes the reader's answering important questions: did the members of the cabal truly intend to put their revolutionary schemes into practice, and were they competent to do so? The newest recruits, who share the reader's curiosity, question senior members on these points. The answers they receive are enigmatic and evasive, not informative. (pp. 41-46)

Nor will the reader find a more definitive answer in the unfolding events of the plot. A swift succession of reverses results in the death, capture or disappearance of the cell members. Their grandiosely-elaborated schemes to foment insurgency are never put to the test. Thus it remains unclear whether these plans were intended to be carried out and whether the cell members could have been successful active revolutionaries.

Another question that has no one definitive answer is that of the precise nature of the characters' difficulties. Again, the characters themselves pose the problem to one another, formulating only cryptic answers in reply. Asked to provide an explanation for his erratic behavior, Erdosain says: ''Uno roba, hace macanas porque está angustiado'' [''One robs, tells lies because of anguish'']. He tells a questioner that the source of his unwise behavior is precisely ''lo que yo no sé'' [''that which I don't know''].

Critics, less willing than Erdosain to abandon the search for ultimate causes, have argued that the Arltian character suffers from the breakdown of the lower middle class, the loss of faith in God, existential terror, immigrant malaise, unresolved Oedipal complexes and simple poverty. Indeed, evidence can be found throughout Arlt's works to substantiate all of these diagnoses.

To examine this highly complex and ambiguous issue, let us reduce it to two simpler problems involved in specifying the nature of this Arltian uneasiness. To what extent does economic deprivation underlie the characters' unhappiness and to what extent is the urban environment at fault?

Economic well-being appears as both the *sine qua non* of happiness and a factor insufficient to bring satisfaction. A wealthy benefactor is the agent of fulfillment in Erdosain's recurring fantasies. In one version, a millionairess resolves his marital distress by pensioning off Erdosain's wife and taking the weary husband on a cruise to tropical lands. In another an eccentric millionaire ends Erdosain's career frustrations by agreeing to underwrite all his inventions. Elsa equates economic security with not only commitment, but with personal adequacy. . . . To justify abandoning Erdosain at a stressful moment in his life, she shows him her hands, witness to life without servants.

However, money brings Erdosain less fulfillment in reality than in his imaginings. He spends an embezzled sum "de una manera absurda" ["in an absurd manner"], contacting prostitutes of whom he requires nothing, purchasing luxuries he does not enjoy and yet not replacing his worn-out apparel. In an excess of despair, he treads a sum of money underfoot, finding no solace in what he once desired. Erdosain's musings on his unsatisfied needs for divine and for human communication cause many critics to consider him an existential hero. (pp. 46-7)

Similarly, the urban environment appears as both a genuine hell and as a convenient target for the characters' complaints. The best argument for the former point of view is made by Stasys Gostautas in his "La evasión de la ciudad en las novelas de Roberto Arlt." . . . He cites numerous instances of characters ascribing their problems to the unnatural rigors of city life.

However, one may also find examples of country life failing to satisfy. Hipólita, for instance, is a character who has carried out the fantasy of living in the provinces. She was horrified by what she witnessed there: "Era una vida bestial la de esta gente" ["The life of these people was bestial"]. . . . The Astrologer agrees: . . . "El dinero y la politica es la única verdad para la gente de nuestro campo" ["Money and politics is the only truth for the people in our countryside"]. The cell's revolutionary plans depend on the greed, gullibility, boredom and other negative features of the rural population. None of the conspirators objects to such an unflattering characterization of rural life, although it is hardly consonant with the notion that country living fosters spiritual purity.

In short, ambiguity is inherent in the characters' misery. At moments they believe that pastoral settings will revive their flagging spiritual energies. At other times, they accept a highly negative portrayal of country living. The events of the plot offer no indication as to which view is truer. Gostautas cites characters who believe the country could heal them. However, these characters are Arltian characters, masters of self-deception, self-contradiction and obfuscation. They do not realize their longings to live in a rural setting, so we cannot know whether a pastoral environment would have eased their anxieties. Again, the reader is left with too little definite information to decide how matters really stand in the plot.

Arlt's fiction also disconcerts the reader by appearing, at various moments, to belong to various varieties of prose fiction. The reader may make a classification that shortly turns out to be more illusory than real. In some cases the resemblance is altogether deceptive, for the Arlt work is radically unlike the form it superficially follows. In other cases, what is surprising is the multiple classifications to which one Arltian work lends itself, all categorization having a certain validity, but none the definitive characterization. The reader is put off his guard by his inability to presuppose what the fiction will "really" be about, what rules it will follow and in what spirit he ought to approach it.

For instance, *Los siete locos* and *Los lanzallamas* exhibit certain features of the naturalistic or documentary realistic novel. They do provide, to a certain extent, information about a certain social milieu at a certain moment. One critic finds in these novels a depiction of the stress experienced by those who found it difficult to remain in the middle class. In his analysis, the characters are torn between their need to present themselves as solidly middle class and the economic impossibility of doing so. He cites instances of sudden downward mobility, with its disorienting effect on the characters.

However, the novels break with the conventions of realism early on. As *Los siete locos* opens, Erdosain has embezzled a sum of money from his firm, which now knows of the crime. Called to account for his misdeed, Erdosain must surely, if he is a realistic character, plead dire necessity. Indeed, his clothes are ragged, his wife complains of his improvidence and he has no furniture in his house. Yet the embezzled funds went not to satisfy material needs, but rather to fulfill some obscure spiritual exigency. "Nunca se me ocurrió comprarme botines con este dinero" ["It never occurred to me to buy myself spats with this money"], he says, to which the narrator adds: "Y era cierto. El placer que experimentó en un principio de disponer impunemente de lo que no le pertenecía se evaporo pronto" ["And it was true. The pleasure he took from the principle of disposing with impunity of what didn't belong to him quickly evaporated"]. Certainly no realistically-portrayed character would act according to the demands of some undefined inner prompting, spending the stolen money capriciously. Thus Erdosain demonstrates to the reader that he is no ordinary realistic hero and that his difficulties are not altogether societal in origin.

After this initial display of deviance, Erdosain shows himself to have many problems suitable to the hero of a realistic work: his wife abandons him, apparently for a wealthier man, his job as a clerk is trivial and alienating, he cannot afford to develop working models of his inventions and he has poverty-induced tuberculosis. Yet his responses to these problems are atypical and disconcerting. When he finds his wife preparing to abandon him, just as he has been found out as an embezzler, he displays little outward despair or anger. Instead, he engages his wife's new protector, an army officer, in a discussion of his various inventions and proposed reforms. As Erdosain digresses onto such topics as his unhappy childhood and his scheme to market many-colored dogs, the officer gives every sign of being bored and unreceptive. Yet Erdosain continues to confess his innermost thoughts and most shameful experiences to this uncaring military man. The scene ends with Erdosain and his wife elaborating a fantasy of reunion, seemingly oblivious to the officer's presence. Any initial resemblance to realistic fiction is undermined and destroyed by this barrage of irrational behavior.

Arlt's prefatory remarks may create false expectations in the reader. For instance, the often-cited introduction to *Los lanzallamas* seems to be the apologia for an unflinching attempt to document certain unpleasant societal realities at the expense of esthetic considerations. Arlt satirizes an imagined reviewer's reaction: "El señor Arlt sigue aferrado a su realismo de pésimo gusto" ["Mr. Arlt continues stubbornly with his realism in the worst possible taste"]. The concern of the responsible author, according to this introduction, must be "los ruidos de un edificio social que se desmorona" ["the noises of the social edifice that is crumbling"], not "bordados" ["embroidery"]. . . . Similarly, Arlt dedicates *El jorobadito* to his wife with another apology for his esthetic sins, citing again the exigencies of honesty. While he would have liked to write a literarily satisfying work, he says, he could not in good conscience falsify human realities with "doradas palabras mentirosas" ["gilded lies"], but rather must remain "en contacto con gente terrestre, triste y somnolienta" ["in contact with terrestrial, sad, and drowsy people"]. Arlt seems to proclaim his adherence to the established tenets of social realism by his words of introduction. The aberrance of the works that follow thus become all the more startling as they violate these very tenets.

The beginnings of stories or of episodes in novels may also make one expect a particular kind of relation to follow, only to turn into something very different indeed. For instance, the title story in *El jorobadito* appears at first to be the anguished outpourings of an accused murderer who remains convinced that he has rid the world of an evil being. The narrator then proves most inept at substantiating his own thesis. While he gives many serious instances of his own cruelty to the murdered hunchback, his only example of the victim's alleged evil is the man's alleged beating of a sow. This eccentric, almost frivolous charge, never elaborated upon, suggests the narrator is an erratic, unreliable individual. One wonders how seriously to take his anguish or his claim to have vanquished an evil by killing his deformed friend.

The narrator further destroys the reader's confidence by departing entirely from his argument that his crime was justifiable. He relates instead the horrors of a middle-class engagement to a proper, chaperoned girl. Now his denunciation seems to shift from the evil in the world, represented by the hunchback, to the hypocrisy of a certain social milieu, exemplified by his fiancée and her vigilant mother. Only at the story's end do the two threads converge. Against the protests of the hunchback, the narrator insists his fiancée's first kiss be not for him but for the deformed man, as proof her love is stronger than revulsion and propriety. While the divergent elements of the plot meet, literally, the main rhetorical thrust of the story is still unclear. Does he care more to tell us about his justifiable crime or to show us the grotesque conventions of courtship and marriage? The reader is as bewildered as the audience of a German expressionist work in which numerous themes appear, develop in an erratic manner and come to no clear resolution. The world's disorder is not set to rights as part of the creation of a fictional universe. In fact, the unwieldiness of the literary work exceeds that of the real world in order to more firmly impress upon the reader the existence of unresolvable confusions.

The narrator of the stories in *El criador de gorilas* also raises expectations about his story that he does not fulfill. Though the stories at first resemble adventure stories in exotic settings, expressionistic confusions soon intrude. The narrator of the title story ostensibly sets out to give an eyewitness account of mutiny against the gorilla raiser. To this end he documents atrocities supposedly perpetrated by the gorilla breeder against his employees. Soon incongruous and whimsical elements make one doubt the reliability of the witness. The narrator, applying for work at the breeder's, is given a bottle of liquor and instructions to become drunk. The breeder finds his new employee three days later and, apparently satisfied with his drunkenness, gives him further orders. The horrendous or scabrous particulars of life on the gorilla farm occupy a prominent place in the *relation*, as does the narrator's insistence on his own unregenerate character. The chronology of the story is awry; the hiring anecdote follows several occurrences that the narrator could only have witnessed after gaining access to the farm.

One further doubts the value of the documentation of atrocities when the narrator commits a startling redundancy. After he has described in lurid detail the gorilla breeder's death, he informs the reader that "se lo comían vivo las hormigas" ["ants ate him alive"]. This event can hardly have escaped one's attention, and its reiteration seems to confirm the unbalanced nature of the narrator and the ramshackle construction of the world he inhabits.

Not only do Arlt's works confound one by conforming to and then violating the conventions of some familiar form, but they resist classification by conventional genres. It is frequently observed that *El juguete rabioso*, Arlt's 1926 novel, has more the features of a collection of short stories. Conversely, while *El jorobadito* is in format a book of short stories, Arlt himself refers to it as one of his novels. Indeed, the stories comprising it are closely linked by their urban settings, violent action and by the absence of a dependable narrative voice. The stories are all related in an exceedingly fragmented, cryptic and often chaotic fashion. Deformity, whether physical, spiritual or moral, is a constant theme in the stories; thus the title invites the reader to see them as all part of one fragmented portrait of societal and personality disintegration.

Moreover, it is difficult to say whether the 1929 *Los siete locos* and the 1931 *Los lanzallamas* constitute one novel or two. The two texts deal with the same characters and revolutionary conspiracy. Yet they have separate titles, and are not designated as parts one and two. *Los siete locos* presents difficulties to the reader by presenting the characters and plot situation in a sketchy, piecemeal and ambiguous manner. In *Los lanzallamas,* the plot is already set forth. Other, less esthetically intriguing difficulties greet the reader. Most notable of these is the exceedingly tortured syntax of certain passages. The latter novel also stuns one by including long political harangues by the Astrologer and Erdosain's plans and schemata for a poison gas factory, documents unlikely to have meaning for readers.

That the novels both are two halves of one work and two separate entities is the basis of an Arltian caprice. The Astrologer is left, at the end of *Los siete locos,* sitting speechless over a comparison between him and Lenin. *Los lanzallamas* whimsically opens with the Astrologer's reaction, which he has finally managed to verbalize. . . . Through this ploy, which strikes some readers as too frivolous, Arlt emphasizes the ambiguous status of the two texts: one more feature of his fiction which can never be fully grasped or defined.

All of these devices serve to prevent the reader from feeling he can determine what exactly he is reading and how he is to read it. The reader does not know many things he would like to know about the erratically unfolding plot. Nor does he know why he is given other bits of information that strike him as trivial or peripheral. He does not know to what extent he can believe the chronicler of the conspiracy in the Erdosain novels, nor who this chronicler is. Narrators in other Arlt works also exhibit erratic behavior that casts doubt on the veracity of their statements. Among the devices that indicate this irresponsibility are the use of footnotes that contradict the text or seem to violate the autonomy of the work, conventionally related passages juxtaposed with those of a wildly disordered nature, the creation of false expectations in the reader and puzzlng redundancies. In short, the form of the work of literature becomes as haphazard and baffling as the form of the world it represents: the expressionistic world-as-madhouse. (pp. 47-51)

> Naomi Lindstrom, "Narrative Garble in Expressionism," in her Literary Expressionism in Argentina: The Presentation of Incoherence, *Center for Latin American Studies, Arizona State University, 1977, pp. 39-65.*

ADEN W. HAYES (essay date 1980)

[*In the following essay, Hayes disputes the reading of Arlt's novels as autobiographical and examines the dichotomy of invention and reality in Arlt's works.*]

Critics have long recognized that Roberto Arlt's three novels—*El juguete rabioso, Los siete locos/Los lanzallamas* (a single novel issued in two parts), and *El amor brujo*—all contain innumerable autobiographical references, veiled fictionalizations of the author's personal experiences, and local and authentic details of Buenos Aires, the city which Arlt knew so well.... [Some] critics have tried to use these correspondences to equate Arlt's fiction to his personal life, to try to see the author in his characters, and to read his fictional texts as if they were simply compilations of the author's own adventures. (p. 48)

Of course, ... even true autobiography shares with fiction the processes of selection, emplotment and artistic shaping necessary to create it, and in no way can it be considered complete and untempered truth. Nor is there enough biographical information available even now (Arlt died in 1942), to validate such an approach. Finally, the imaginary world of any creative work eventually must be seen as autonomous, separated from its author's public life and communicating with its audience solely by way of its verbal constructs.... [Critics who use the autobiographical approach] tacitly discount the very different attitudes, outlooks and abilities of the three protagonists, and the different ways they cope with the bourgeois society which threatens them.

These are traditional arguments against biographical criticism. More interesting here, these arguments are corroborated by the statements in Arlt's fiction on the differences between real life and its representation in art, and the dangers of confusing the two. "Pensá" ["It may be"], Arlt wrote to his sister, "que yo puedo ser Erdosain, pensá que ese gran dolor (of his protagonist, Erdosain) no se inventa ni tampoco es literatura" ["that I could be Ersodain, it may be that that great suffering ... is not invented and is not literature"]. We must not reverse the components of the statement and read "yo puedo ser Erdosain" ["I could be Erdosain"] as "Erdosain could be me." Arlt enjoyed material, social and artistic success—in short, a *life*—which his character Erdosain, the victim of psychological and pecuniary limitations, could only dream of. Arlt here places in opposition two systems of reference and of presentation at work in his fiction: reality, and literature or invention. In all three novels, characters and narrators repeatedly express the idea that fiction, most particularly the novel, is not to be confused with reality. Fiction, in Arlt's work, is an illusion, an invention, and therefore not to be believed, or at

least not to be taken seriously; it is seen as unreal, misleading, even absurd. Examples abound.

In *Los siete locos,* after a meeting of the revolutionary society at the Astrologer's *quinta* ["villa"], Erdosain is disappointed to discover that the Buscador de Oro's report of gold in the Andes is false, that reality and its verbal representation do not coincide. The Buscador is more cynical, and tells Erdosain "supongo que no creerá en esa novela de 'placeres' " ["I suppose that you will not believe in that novel of 'pleasures' "], making *novela* synonymous with lie, with invention. Earlier on, Erdosain must repay six hundred pesos to his employers, or face arrest. His friends refuse to help him, but he receives a check from Haffner, the Rufián Melancólico, a stranger. The narrator comments that "el suceso era más absurdo que una novela, a pesar de ser él (Erdosain) un hombre de carne y hueso" ["the incident was more absurd than a novel, in spite of the fact that he (Erdosain) is a man of flesh and blood"]. Thus Erdosain is represented as a *real* man who is participating in an incident which itself is more absurd (that is, more unlikely), than that of a novel; and the narrator emphasizes that the *reality* of his character . . . , is not diminished by his participation in a seemingly fictional (that is, unreal), incident. As the novel develops, Erdosain more and more loses his grasp on reality and tries to retreat to a world of his own creation—a world in which he may live "sin perder su juventud, como el absurdo personaje de una novela inglesa" ["without losing his youth, like the absurd character of an English novel"]; perhaps he is thinking of Dorian Gray. Again, the contrast is affirmed: he hopes to exist outside reality; he is now a real person, later he will become like a fictional (unreal) character by divorcing himself from the constraints of quotidian reality. Needless to say, he does not achieve this divorce, except in his own mind, in his psychic isolation, and through his eventual suicide.

For Arlt's characters, "absurd" corresponds to Camus' use of the term some years later: the representation of a situation devoid of meaning, of characters cut off from referentiality, "the divorce between man and his life, the actor and his setting. . . ." Ionesco supplies a similar explanation: "absurd is that which is devoid of purpose . . . (and) cut off from his religious, metaphysical and transcendental roots, man is lost." Arlt, nearly thirty years earlier, had said basically the same thing about his own characters:

> Estos individuos . . . están atados o ligados entre sí por la desesperación. La desesperación en ellos está originada, más que por la pobreza material, por otro factor: la desorientación que, después de la gran guerra, ha revolucionado la consciencia de los hombres, dejándolos vacíos de ideales y esperanzas. Hombres y mujeres en la novela rechazan el presente y la civilización . . . quisieran creer en algo, arrodillarse ante algo, amar algo . . . aunque quieran creer, no pueden. Como se ve, la angustia de estos hombres nace de su esterilidad interior.

> ["These individuals . . . are tied or bound together by desperation. The desperation in them originates, more than from material poverty, from another factor: the disorientation that, after the Great War, has revolutionized the conscience of men, leaving them empty of ideals and hopes. Men and women in the novel reject the present and civilization . . . want to believe in something, kneel before something, love something . . . although they want to believe, they can't. As you see, the anguish of these men is born in their internal sterility."]

But Arlt's vision of his novel's characters is very different from that of his narrator, who represents himself and the other characters as real people who loathe and—at least initially—try to reject this burden of unreality and absurdity, which for them originates, and properly belongs only in fiction. These "people," in turn, judge fictional characters and situations as if they were something totally unlike and extraneous to themselves, and therefore absurd, devoid of meaning. For them the world of fiction—of the novel—is a world created of ideas, not of reality; and Arlt's characters feel bound to much more circumscribed and less marvelous conditions than those represented in fiction.

Erdosain, thinking about the plan to kill his nemesis Barsut, "lamentaba ya de que el plan fuera tan simple y poco novelesco" ["already lamented that his plan was so simple and so little novelistic"]. Erdosain's complaint confirms the equation: novel = imagination, illusion. When his friend the Astrologer asks him if he does not feel remorse for his part in the planned execution, Erdosain answers that life cannot duplicate art, "yo creo que eso sólo ocurre en las novelas. En la realidad yo he hecho acciones malas y buenas y ni en un caso ni el otro he sentido ni la mayor alegría ni el menor remordimiento" ["I believe that only happens in novels. In reality I have done good and bad actions and in neither case have I felt either the most happiness or the least remorse"]. Erdosain's confidante, the prostitute Hipólita, whose job necessitates the use of illusion, confirms that there can be only a tenuous link between real persons and fictional characters; that link is the imagined confidence, the fascination real people have for fictional personages and their adventures. But Hipólita finds, as Erdosain does, that art is richer in imaginative possibilities than is life. . . . Although they sometimes forget it, all the principal characters of *Los siete locos*/*Los lanzallamas* recognize the axiom that fictional situations and fictional solutions must not be applied to their "real" lives. So Hipólita fabricates illusions only to entertain her customers—not the "personajes de novela" ["novel characters"] of her imagination, but their infinitely more disappointing, real-life counterparts.

This dichotomy of reality and fiction is extended in Arlt's first and last novels. Both Silvio Astier (*El juguete rabioso*), and Estanislao Balder (*El amor brujo*), try to live lives inspired by characters in books. Silvio reads the adventure stories of Ponson du Terrail and Emilio Salgari, and dreams of becoming a famous bandit or pirate; but his limited, personal reality will allow him only to steal canes and billiard balls in Buenos Aires cafés, and poorly imitate dangerous adventure by betraying a crippled thief. His is an interesting case of "life" parodying art. Balder's sense of the limits of reality is confused by the "novelas que impresionaron su adolescencia" ["novels that influenced his adolescence"], and he tries to duplicate fictional situations and maintain them along with the reality of his own life. His relationship with his girlfriend Irene is based on falsification and illusion. In dealing with her, Balder constructs a series of fictions which both he and the narrator call a *comedia;* thus they categorize it as literature, as unreal, and as antithetical to the rest of Balder's life—that is, his reality. Balder becomes more and more desperate when he finds that the invented and the "real" aspects of his life are inimical opposites. Fabricating a transparent excuse, he breaks off the fictionalized relationship with Irene, returns to his family and job, and so resumes his poor, but reality-based existence as Estanislao Balder, bureaucrat, father, bored and alienated *porteño.*

In the world of Arlt's novels literature is linked to mechanical inventions in that both are constructs, made up instead of discovered. Silvio Astier, the inventor of a miniature cannon, a falling star counter, and a voice transcription machine, is thrown out of the Air Force because he is too bright, too inventive, and therefore seen as dangerous. His boss, Captain Márquez, after hearing about Silvio's inventions and his interest in literature—he reads Baudelaire, Dostoievski and Nietzsche—asks "¿no será un anarquista, éste?" ["won't he be an anarchist, this one?"]. The two pursuits, literature and invention, are linked in their production of what is unreal and unnatural. Throughout Arlt's fiction, inventions and machinery are shown to have gotten out of hand; they no longer serve their original purposes. Arlt's characters see modern civilization as an aggregate of mechanical inventions and the bourgeois society which uses them; both are uncontrollable in their constraint and oppression of the individual. Arlt's protagonists—Silvio, Erdosain and Balder—find that the one possible escape from this situation is to nature, that is, to a noninvented reality: to the delta of the Tigre river (Balder), to the Andes (Silvio), or to Ushuaia, in the extreme south of Argentina (Erdosain)—"allá se salvan las almas que enfermó la civilización" ["there the souls made sick by civilization are saved"]. But these characters never make good their escapes, for these are dreams, their own fictions within the fiction of Arlt's novels. The protagonists begin to reject their own, unacceptable, exterior reality and to retreat to an interior, fantasy existence in the mistaken belief that they can invent realities which suit them better than their own lives do. This invention, of course, is false—the life of the novel, not of the street. When these characters cease to discover their "real" lives and instead begin to *invent* them, they become characters in their own fictions; and fictions, in Arlt's work, are always misleading, unreal, and treacherous. (pp. 49-53)

Aden W. Hayes, "Reality and the Novel—The Case of Roberto Arlt," in Romance Notes, *Vol. XXI, No. 1, Fall, 1980, pp. 48-53.*

J. M. FLINT (essay date 1984)

[*In the following excerpt, Flint discusses the ways in which Arlt's characters turn to fantasy, crime, and gratuitous actions as an antidote to their suffering.*]

Several critics have insisted on the conscious, almost Dostoievskian act of humiliation and self-immolation to which Arlt's characters resort as an antidote to their suffering and anguish. Less attention has been paid to the role of fantasy in his writing and the exploration of the absurd and the gratuitous act as secondary palliatives. As his fiction matured, Arlt added to the somewhat puerile adventure episodes in the first part of *El juguete rabioso* a series of fantasmagoric visions and dreams, which were to become typical of his later fiction. His penchant for outlandish inventions, both in his life and in his works, is well established. The same tendency is manifest in his novels in the incidents woven around the invention of the "rosa metalizada" ["metal rose"], the idea for a chain of shops for dyeing dogs in various colours or even the proposal in *Los siete locos* to finance the "revolution" by economically run brothels and similar ill-starred ideas. As Raül Larra says of him: "Inventar es para Arlt condición divina; inventando el hombre se asemeja a Dios" ["To invent is for Arlt a divine condition; Man inventing resembles God"]. With Arlt, invention and fantasy go hand in hand. It was the gradual domination of his sense of fantasy and illusion which seems to have steered him away from the novel towards the theatre in 1932, following the publication of *Los lanzallamas* and *El amor brujo*. Whilst the keynote of his fiction is anguish and social oppression, the major theme of his theatre is the Pirandellian concept of a double reality and the interpenetration of fantasy and fact. Thus in *Saverio el cruel,* arguably his best play, a world of illusion is created for a poor commercial representative who becomes a colonel in a Ruritanian republic, an existence which is eventually more real for him than his own. The adolescent Susana, one of the instigators of the illusion, succumbs to her own invention and is finally the instrument of his destruction. *Trescientos millones* is set in what Arlt himself calls "una zona astral donde la imaginación de los hombres fabrica con líneas de fuerza los fantasmas que los acosan o recrean en sus sueños" ["an astral zone where the imagination of men fabricates with lines of force the ghosts that pursue them or delight them in their dreams"]. The play is a battleground for the struggle between the social deprivation of a servant-girl and the angelic innocence of her dreams which are shattered by the sexual advances of her employer's son. In *La isla desierta* a mulatto forces his way into a business office and fires the imagination of the desk-bound employees. Reality reasserts itself when the manager arrives to a scene of dancing and abandon. He dismisses the staff and orders the windows to be blacked out.

The problem of a double or shifting reality makes an earlier appearance in the novels. From *Los siete locos* onwards, footnotes are used to deceive the reader into assuming that the reality that he feels he has grasped is spurious. A classic example is the Major amongst the seven conspirators at the Astrologer's house. We first learn that he is an apocryphal major planted by the Astrologer to act out a farce and sow confusion. It is later revealed in a footnote that he is not apocryphal at all but a *real* major who is telling lies. On a reduced scale, we have here what Maldavsky calls "el vínculo de traición" ["the bond of treason"] between Arlt and his reader. Not only do the characters maintain a treacherous relationship with each other (as when Hipólita listens with compassion to Erdosain's harrowing confessions, all the while proposing to turn this knowledge to her own account) but the author-reader relationship is similarly based on a premise of mistrust. This may be seen as a manifestation of the co-existence of an invented "reality" and an idealized world that the characters seek to inhabit in their own mind, two worlds which between them form Arlt's universe. His characters are individuals who have fallen or are in some way degraded (literally fallen in the case of the Astrologer, for he has dropped over a bannister and castrated himself). They live in an ugly or warped world which he, the author, calls into question for its failure to live up to an ideal of clarity and truth. (pp. 63-4)

In novels and theatre alike, whenever their anguish becomes too acute, the characters plunge into daydreams and fantasies, which may, nevertheless, heighten their very anguish as happens with Erdosain's sexual fantasies about his wife and her lover after they have run off together. The Astrologer's ravings about the "revolution" are based on the principle that all men long for great imaginings. The "revolution" merely sets out to prove this and to provide it where it is lacking. In *El juguete rabioso,* the fantasies begin as a reconstituton of Arlt's childhood and adolescent reading but, by chapter II of this early work when it is peremptorily invested with an atmosphere of anguish, they assume their future role of revealing the urban hell that Man is creating for himself. One is reminded of Dalí's surrealist canvases. . . . This tendency towards abstraction persists and strengthens in the later works but is still accompanied

by innocent inventions that others might have left behind in their adolescence. Puerile dreams of deathrays (a constant of boy's magazines in the twenties and thirties), of becoming the captain of a super-dreadnought, of commanding great international conferences (presumably inspired by Versailles) exist side by side with abstract visions of the modern city and man trapped within it. . . . Arlt's creatures not only inhabit this grotesque world of the imagination but they may also be seen as a product of it, with their curious name and rabid philosophies. And yet, the black humour which underlies everything that he wrote is always at hand to turn the fantasy-world on its head, as Jean Franco has pointed out, by including references to "real" contemporary events in which reality outstrips fantasy. Gangsters slaughter each other, the Ku Klux Klan controls large areas of the USA, whilst the latter gobbles up the wealth of its southern neighbours. A ghoulish world where men gas each other or grind down their inferiors in industrial exploitation. . . . Needless to say, fantasy offers no lasting solace to the characters in their flight from their tortured existence; the end product is often death. It is ironic and no doubt deliberate that after his cruel visions of the nightmarish growth of urban technology, Arlt's protagonist should shoot himself on an electric train, a refugee from the real and fantasy worlds alike. As Noë Jitrik says: "*Los siete locos* y *Los lanzallamas* muestran un desgarramiento total y la pérdida total de las ilusiones. No hay nada que hacer para esa gente. Buenos Aires es una campana indiferente donde en cuestión de horas, más o menos, todos esos infelices serán exterminados." ["*Los siete locos* and *Los lanzallamas* demonstrate a total rending and a total loss of illusions. There is nothing for those people to do. Buenos Aires is an indifferent parish where in a matter of hours, more or less, all of those unhappy people will be exterminated."] However, Jitrik fails to notice that the few who *are* able to cling to their illusions survive (Barsut, the Astrologer and Hipólita), whilst those who are forced into an appraisal of their own reality either die or are killed (La Bizca, Erdosain, El Hombre que vio a la Partera, Elsa and the Rufián Melancólico).

Turning to the related concept of the absurd, we find a comparable picture. As is now recognised, the conquest of the absurd is one of the great contributions of existentialist writing to twentieth century literature. It was not to be expected that a "pre-existentialist" like Arlt, who had no formal philosophical knowledge, would handle this concept in a sophisticated manner from the mid-1920s onwards. However, in the atmosphere of the retreat from reason in the Buenos Aires of his day, he unfailingly highlights the contingency and absurdity of man's existence. With Camus, the conquest of the absurd is a first step towards man's realisation of his unique condition and his own fulfilment, since it makes of fate a human matter and of man "le maître de ses jours" ["the master of his days"]. Sysiphus, rolling the stone, becomes a symbol of a fate that is in the individual's own keeping. Quite contrary to this, Arlt's earlier reaction to the absurd is negative and thoughtless. For him, it is a source of suffering or wonderment but not a cause of philosophical speculation. Of course, it has a strong link with his exploitation of the gratuitous act, which we shall examine later. In Arlt, the absurdity of existence is manifest in the menial details of his characters' lives. Erdosain's debt of six hundred pesos, the sum stolen from his employer which lies at the heart of his first experience of anguish, is redeemed by an unsolicited gift from the Rufián Melancólico. He does not interpret this gesture as an act of friendship, or even of charity, but simply as an absurdity. . . . Erdosain maintains a steadfast attitude towards this event, saying to the Rufián:

"Quiero decirle esto: Que no le agradezco absolutamente nada el dinero que me ha dado" ["I want to tell you this: I am not grateful to you at all for the money that you have given me"]. However, he takes the money. Similarly, when Barsut has been sequestered at Temperley as a victim of the proposed "murder," Erdosain finds himself living, without apparent cause, in Barsut's lodgings. This is pure illogicality since, as far as he can remember, he has done nothing to bring it about.

Even in the early work *El juguete rabioso,* the same forces are seen to be at work. The protagonist Silvio joins the Air Force where all appears to go well for him. He is a model cadet with an extensive knowledge of explosives and scientific instruments. "Más que nunca se afirmaba la convicción del destino grandioso a cumplir en mi existencia" ["More than ever, the conviction of the grandiose destiny to be fulfilled in my existence is affirmed"]. But, for his pains, he is dismissed without cause or reason. So, too, when he visits the fortune-teller de Souza, who has promised to help him get on in life, the same absurdity operates against him and he is bundled out without ceremony. No reason is offered for this irrationality.

On a more serious level, Arlt seems to view Man's existence as a repetition of degrading mechanical functions, a notion which leads to some loathsome passages as his novel-writing advances. The recoil from reason and order obliges him to invent superhuman absolutes to account for this state of affairs. . . . (pp. 64-6)

On turning to his use of the gratuitous act, we enter deeper waters. It is not appropriate here to discuss the undeniably Dostoievskian influences at work in Arlt's exploration of the concept of humiliation and self-degradation: this is an area of his thinking which deserves lengthier enquiry. However, there are two further concepts in Dostoievksi which find an echo in Arlt's prose fiction which must concern us: the exploitation of crime as a means to self-inquiry and, closely-related, the use of the gratuitous act. Fromm considers the sadistic act of cruelty to be an attempt to attach ourselves to another person, to escape from our own sense of isolation. The *acte gratuit,* which so impressed Gide in Dostoievski, is a manifestation of the same urge, often, but not invariably, invested with sadistic cruelty. No doubt under the influence of his reading of Dostoievski at the height of the Florida/Boedo dispute in Buenos Aires during the early twenties, Arlt took this stratagem to great lengths in his novels and short stories. An incident from one of the stories, **"Ester Primavera,"** shows to what extent this concept had bitten deeply into Arlt's thinking. In this story, the unnamed narrator meets and apparently falls in love with Ester. He conceives the perverse idea of gratuitously shattering their relationship by telling a lie, stating that he is married when he is not. The girl is overwhelmed. To compound the injury, he dispatches a calumnious letter, heaping infamy upon the lie, in such a way that her family will receive it and read it. The motivation behind this senseless act is that she will be bound to him forever by the outrage. . . . It will be recalled that in Dostoievski's *Notes from Underground* the narrator similarly wounds Liza the prostitute. Having nurtured a friendly relationship with her and allowed her to believe that he has come to "save" her (this, too, occurs elsewhere in Arlt with a prostitute), he coarsely hurls the truth at her. Like Ester, the girl is heartbroken. The narrator is later gnawed by remorse, as is Arlt's character, but both remain steadfast in their contrariness. (pp. 67-8)

This is but one of the many gratuitous acts in Arlt's work; sometimes more mindless pieces of nonsense, as when Ergueta

decides to urinate on a passer-by. . . . Having perpetrated this stupidity, Ergueta dares the Basque Delavene to do the same to another person. He promptly does so but the victim draws a revolver and shoots him on the spot. Delavene's agony is long and painful, as is the narrator's in **"Ester Primavera"**; in the latter case, a lingering death by tuberculosis. And just as the incident lives on in his life, so too the Delavene incident remains in Ergueta's existence. ". . . cuando Ergueta estaba borracho y se nombraba a Delavene, aquél se arrodillaba y con la lengua hacía una cruz en el polvo." [". . . when Ergueta was drunk he would mention the name of Delavene, at which he would kneel and make a cross in the dirt with his tongue."] Could there be a more Dostoievskian out-come? Similarly, when Erdosain has been visiting the Espila family, whom he purports to help by having them produce his latest invention the *"rosa de cobre"* ["copper rose"], the daughter Luciana accompanies him down the road. She is filled with love and admiration, even to the extent of studying metallurgy to be more worthy of him. But as they talk the world bears in on Erdosain and his deep-seated need to wound her forces its way to the surface. As with the incident in Camus' *L'Etranger,* where the light oppresses Meursault and opens the way to the murder of the Arab, here the sounds and appearance of the world become unbearable and Erdosain is overwhelmed by his desire to commit some senseless act against the girl.

Sometimes, the characters' need to degrade and wound others is carried to loathesome lengths. On one occasion, Erdosain filthies a young woman's face in the dirt in an access of un-motivated spleen. . . . On another, he recounts to Hipólita a gruesome tale of how he once revealed to a little girl of nine ". . . el misterio sexual, incitándola a que se dedicara a corromper a sus amiguitas . . ." [". . . the sexual mystery, inciting her to the point of dedicating herself to corrupting her little friends . . ."]. Even as early as **El juguete rabioso,** senseless violence has its part to play. As a young writer, Arlt seems to have been uncannily aware of the workings of the warped mind. In one incident, social anger and abstract despair erupt in a mindless attack on an innocent victim who lies huddled in a shop-doorway, on whom Silvio throws a lighted match. When this mentality is turned against a person with whom the protagonist enjoys an intimate relationship, as it is at the end of **El juguete rabioso,** we are once again in a wholly Dostoievskian world. Silvio and El Rengo have planned a robbery against an engineer's house. On the day of the proposed break-in, Silvio conceives the perfidious notion of informing on his friend. . . . The motive for this betrayal is in no way economic; there is no question of personal gain as he demonstrates by refusing a reward. The motive is twofold, each carrying us forward into Arlt's later work. Firstly, the act of betrayal will permit Silvio to delve into his own conscience and discover its hidden depths: "La angustia abrirá a mis ojos grandes horizontes espirituales" ["The anguish will open grand spiritual horizons to my eyes"], he cries. "—Yo no soy un perverso, soy un curioso de esta fuerza enorme que está en mí" ["—I am not perverse, I am curious about this enormous force that is in me"]. Secondly, as with Ester Primavera, his victim will be tied to him forever. (pp. 68-9)

The first of these motives, the need to discover one's internal forces, leads naturally into a consideration of crime as an antidote to anguish. Not now the spontaneous *acte gratuit* but something monstrous and premeditated that will reveal the person to himself and allow him to *become* something, akin to the motives of Stavrogin in *The Devils:* ". . . if one were to commit some crime, I mean, something shameful, something really disgraceful, something very mean and ridiculous, so that people would remember it for a thousand years. . . .'' Or as Arlt puts it in one of his chapter headings, ''ser a través del crimen'' [''to exist through crime'']. To quote Fromm again:

> The basic need to fuse with another person so as to transcend the prison of one's separateness is closely related to another specifically human desire, that to know the ''secret of man.''

So says Erdosain, as the moment of the crime approaches:

> No estoy loco, ya que sé pensar, razonar. Me sube la curiosidad del asesinato, curiosidad que debe ser mi última tristeza, la tristeza de la curiosidad. O el demonio de la curiosidad. Ver cómo soy a través de un crimen.

> [''I am not crazy, since I know how to think, to reason. The curiosity of assassination comes over me, curiosity that should be my ultimate sadness, the sadness of curiosity. Or the demon of curiosity. To see how I am through a crime.'']

It is the same Dostoievskian motive that finds its echo in Gide, in the famous incident in *Les Caves du Vatican,* in which Lafcadio pushes his companion from the train. Gide's character declares: ''Ce n'est pas tant des événements que j'ai curiosité, que de moi-même'' [''It is not so much about the events that I am curious as about myself'']. In Arlt, the theme grows to major proportions and is allied to a general concept of evil as man's ultimate gesture of independence and self-assurance, this in its turn being a variant of the theme of deliberate remoteness from God.

> Y sin embargo si, mañana tiro una bomba, o asesino a Barsut, me convierto en el todo, en el hombre que existe, el hombre para quien infinitas generaciones de jurisconsultos prepararon castigos, cárceles y teorías. . . . Sólo el crimen puede afirmir mi existencia, como sólo el mal afirma la presencia del hombre sobre la tierra.

> [''And nevertheless, if tomorrow I throw a bomb, or assassinate Barsut, I become everything, the man who exists, the man for whom infinite generations of jurists will prepare punishments, prisons, and theories. . . . Only crime can affirm my existence, as only evil affirms the presence of man on the earth.'']

Thus, the urge towards self-knowledge, so fundamental in all existential thought, goes hand-in-hand with a death wish in Arlt. Injury done to others is an exteriorization of one's own wish for destruction. . . . ''El que les hace dano a los demás, en realidad fabrica monstruos que tarde o temprano lo devorarán a él'' [''He who does harm to others, in reality, makes monsters who sooner or later will devour him'']. After the incident in which he discovers his betrayal by his cousin Barsut, Erdosain determines that the latter shall be annihilated. Like Raskolnikov in *Crime and Punishment,* haunted by his feelings of utter despair and desolation, Erdosain concludes that he must perpetrate some act that will mobilise his will. In Raskolnikov's words: ''He had to make up his mind at all costs, do something, anything, or—renounce life altogether.'' Arlt's protagonist reaches an identical conclusion: each involves a gratuitous murder and both proceed with their plan in order to investigate their latent forces. As Erdosain later declares to Hipólita: ''¿Sabe? . . . todavía no he llegado al fondo de mí mismo . . . pero el crimen es mi última esperanza'' [''You know? . . . I still haven't arrived at the bottom of myself . . . but crime is my ultimate hope'']. The proposed ''murder'' has fired him with a great dream, an illusion, a grandiose project for his life.

''Es necesario hacer algo. Clavar un suceso en medio de la civilización que sea como una torre de acero'' [''It is necessary to do something. To nail an incident in the middle of civilization that would be like a tower of steel'']. The fact that the killing of Barsut is turned into a black farce by the Astrologer, from which the victim escapes unscathed, belongs to Arlt's view of the double reality of life and, significantly, the aborting of the murder is not revealed to Erdosain who continues to believe that his cousin is dead. In this way, the one great event which might have affirmed his existence is finally snatched from under his nose. The only path left open leads to his self-destruction. (pp. 69-70)

> *J. M. Flint, ''Fantasy, the Absurd and the Gratuitous Act in the Works of Roberto Arlt,'' in* Neophilologus, *Vol. LXVIII, No. 1, January, 1984, pp. 63-71.*

JACK M. FLINT   (essay date 1985)

[*In the following excerpt, Flint examines Arlt's depiction of women and relations between the sexes.*]

Arlt belonged to the vanguard in Argentina of those writers who were attempting to bring the individual to the centre of the stage, in the wake of the new existential thinking in the 1920s; he was the first to incorporate the theme of existential anguish into his narrative in a bold fashion; he was the first writer in Argentina to introduce the city as a major force in its own right into the novel, thus making a definite break with the lingering rural tradition in River Plate literature. He also carried fantasy, albeit crudely, to a level hitherto unknown in the Argentine novel, if not throughout Latin America, which was a sure pointer to future developments in the ''new novel'' in all parts of Spanish America in its flight from telluric themes towards a more urban-based literature. In this area of his work Arlt must now be regarded as an important precursor in a literary rebellion against traditional values and it is presumably for these reasons that writers like Cortázar and Onetti hold him so high in their esteem. It is therefore a curious and signal fact that in the area of his work connected with the role of sex and relations between the sexes (as opposed to sexual relations— hardly anyone has sexual relations in Arlt's writing!) he seems to turn a mirror to the society around him rather than open up any new adventures of thought or creativity. . . . [Whilst] Arlt had a great share in hammering out the new concept of the anguished and lonely individual trapped in his urban environment, his view of women (and therefore most of the female characters he created) seems to be governed by traditional Argentine values, if not by traditional *porteño* myths. On the other hand, his view of bourgeois marriage and the institutionalization of sexual relations is aggressive and iconoclastic. These concepts must be kept apart in our analysis, although, as in all Arlt's thinking, they intermingle and play upon each other, making neat definitions difficult to arrive at. (p. 50)

Whilst this was a period in which women were fighting for their rights all over the advanced world, a singular attitude subsisted in Latin America, and particularly in Buenos Aires, which has come to be known as *machismo*. The term is common coinage nowadays. It is too simple to write off this attitude as a mere desire for the continuance of male dominance in society, as an attempt simply to keep women ''in their proper place.'' The roots go much deeper in so heterogeneous a society as Buenos Aires and Argentina at large. . . . [Scalabrini Ortiz] discusses the strong historical reasons for the divisions between the sexes which became a characteristic of life. Firstly, as he says, one must take account of the simple numerical imbalance, since during the early years of immigration, men greatly outweighed women. He writes:

> (Buenos Aires) enclaustró a sus mujeres, ya insuficientes para la compañia de cientos de miles, de millones de hombres que arribaban solos, embarcados en una quimera de hartura corporal. . . . Buenos Aires no quería mujeres: las repudiaba, aunque el equilibrio sexual estaba ya seriamente comprometido y en un millón y pico de habitantes había ciento veinte mil mujeres menos que hombres. . . . Por la presión del ambiente enrarecido, la mujer veía en el hombre al timador de su honestidad. El hombre en la mujer, la enemiga de su lozanía instintiva. Los hombres quedaron desamparados.

> ["(Buenos Aires) cloistered its women, already insufficient for the company of hundreds of thousands, millions of men who arrived alone, pursuing a chimera of total bodily gratification. . . . Buenos Aires didn't want women, it repudiated them, although the sexual equilibrium was seriously compromised and with over a million inhabitants there were 120,000 fewer women than men. . . . Due to the pressure of the rarefied environment, women saw men as swindlers of their honesty. Men saw women as enemies of their luxuriance. Man remained abandoned."]

[This] paragraph might serve as an accurate résumé of the attitude assumed by Arlt's male characters towards their relationships with women—as necessary but dangerous and intrusive. According to Scalabrini, this situation had the inevitable result of sacrificing all normal, gentle relations between the sexes. All forms of *camaradería* were banished. Men who frequented women (other than in a spirit of conquest, presumably) came to be seen as unfaithful to their male relationships and thought of as *maricón* ["queer"] or *"caliente"* ["hot"]. (pp. 50-1)

To compound this situation and largely because of it, Buenos Aires became the city of rampant prostitution and the infamous *trata de blancas* ["white slavery"]. Without some knowledge of the degrading conditions to which the city had sunk by 1925, when Arlt began to write seriously, it is quite impossible to understand the creation of characters like the Rufián Melancólico (a travesty of Cervantes's "El rufián dichoso," of course), with his sadistic exploitation of the women he keeps or the proposals to finance the revolution by a chain of brothels. . . . Carella states that in the year of the Centenario (1910) thirty-seven per cent of women in Buenos Aires were involved in prostitution and that seventy-five per cent of all crimes were due to them. These figures may be open to doubt but there is no gainsaying the magnitude of the problem. Suicides were frequent and venereal disease and tuberculosis were rampant at the time Arlt was a young adolescent. Little wonder that prostitution and brothels figure so heavily in his fiction. (pp. 51-2)

The social condition of women in Buenos Aires during this period was not only one of inferiority but fraught, too, with economic distress, which was to be aggravated by the depression from 1929 onwards. Arlt admirably captures this moment of social stress in his *Aguafuertes* with his sketches of working-class women making ends meet by taking in washing and sewing. In his novels and stories, however, he is concerned with characters from the lower middle class where, if anything, the situation was even worse. As Arturo Jauretche points out, the women of the middle class were denied access to the menial solutions adopted by their social inferiors, their only possibility lying in teaching or matrimony. Against this background the behaviour of Arlt's Hipólita becomes much clearer.

A further reflection of the relations between the sexes may be found in the popular tangos of the period, in which the scheming woman is often depicted as the instrument of man's downfall, usually at the expense of his filial duties to his mother. The concept of woman as treacherous in love is a basic assumption of *El amor brujo* (whence the title) and a number of Arlt's stories display the *novia* ["fiancée"] invariably in league with her scheming mother, to the detriment of the man who is set up as the victim. . . . (pp. 52-3)

Arlt's approach to relationships between the sexes bears the stamp of the contemporary view of woman as the enemy of man's "lozanía instintiva" ["instinctive luxuriance"], but it is complicated by the recurrent theme of the purity of woman. . . . [These] are two sides of the same coin, one having its origin in *machismo* and social conditions, the other deriving from the general pursuit of an ideal which is apparent in his humiliated characters. For purposes of definition, we shall try to keep these two areas apart, although they inevitably react one on the other. It would be foolhardy to suggest that Buenos Aires invented *machismo;* man's sense of domination and his fear of woman as the destroyer of his liberty and inhibiter of his aspirations is presumably as old as the institution of marriage. (p. 54)

A consideration of this aspect of Arlt's writing carries us into *El amor brujo* and the stories published in *El jorobadito,* in which sexual relations are consistently interpreted as a snare. However, the theme is broached in one or two instances in the earlier works, which call for immediate investigation, for they are a key to his later thinking. In *Los siete locos,* Hipólita is the only character, apart from Erdosain, who is permitted the indulgence of exploring her own psychological state. Like him, she has suffered when young, been humiliated and experienced grave loneliness. Contrary to the other characters, most of whom are failed professional people, she appears to be of working-class origin. She has been a serving-maid in a wealthy household and this position has isolated her from the world. . . . She describes the first stirrings of her sexual awareness but, unlike the male characters, proceeds rapidly to the solution of her anguished condition *by means of sex.* She had once heard a young man on a tram propounding the hypothesis that an intelligent woman, even an ugly one, might become wealthy by taking up "la mala vida" ["the bad life"] and, provided she never fell in love, become "la reina de la ciudad" ["the queen of the city"]. . . . In the disconcerting way that Arlt's characters have of tackling their problems head on, she spends her next month's wages buying books about "la mala vida," but these merely turn out to be pornographic. . . . After visiting the law-courts to see if the truth is to be found there, she finally consults a doctor-of-laws. From him she ascertains, paradoxically, that by performing acts of love, purely for profit, she will be capable of liberating herself from her own body. More important than this theoretical discovery is her first sexual experience, from which she soon learns that a woman may exert total domination over a man through the sexual act; that a man, who at first seemed impregnable as a fortress, falls like a felled steer on achieving satisfaction. Thenceforward, she seeks a "lion" amongst men, whom she may admire. But all men fail her, save the Astrólogo. With him she achieves final satisfaction *because* he is castrated! The scene in *Los lanzallamas* in which he reveals his livid scar to her is a moment of great truth. "Sos . . . el único hombre" ["You are the only man''] she cries. Whilst it is possible to interpret this as typical of Arlt's penchant for black humour, it nevertheless provides a serious basis on which to judge his thinking about sex, from which we see that copulation is degrading to man, robbing him of his virility and leading to his ultimate domination by the female.

Maldavsky purports to see in Arlt a strong Oedipus complex which he claims is manifest in this aspect of his thought. . . . He affirms that castration anxieties predominate in Arlt over attraction to the opposite sex. What is certain is that there is a link in the novels between the drive towards sexual purity, which is merely a part of the general urge in Arlt's character to discover ideals and absolutes, and the frustration of the latter by the reality upon which they stumble. In this way, the anguish aroused in Erdosain by his sexual dissatisfaction must be seen as an important factor in his derangement rather than the main reason for it, as Maldavsky would imply.

A natural corollary of the tendency to see women as dominating man through sex is the attack on marriage as its end-product; that is, marriage as institutionalized amongst the middle classes. It is in this area that the male characters' fears are constantly exposed and it is here, too, that *machismo,* or at least its handmate, the fear of domination, may be seen at its most virulent. It is first hinted at in *Los lanzallamas* when Erdosain meets la Bizca and her mother. The latter is the first in a series of potential mother-in-law figures who not only strike terror into the male protagonists but are repulsive creatures in their own right. In a spirit of mockery, Erdosain proposes to establish relations with María la Bizca. This becomes possible because her mother has her eyes on the large quantity of money given to Erdosain by the Astrólogo. Protesting the while about her daughter's innocence and tender years and her own family lineage, she prepares to sell out. Arlt's description of her is typical of the many to follow and speaks of a deep-seated hatred of the sham that such individuals represent. . . . As Masotta points out, these mothers represent the instrument through which, generation after generation, society perpetuates itself. So, in *El amor brujo,* Irene's mother, Señora Loayza, maintains the same draconian control over her daughter, the difference being that this later novel has the problem of sexual relations and marriage as its major theme and the relationship between the male and female characters is even more ambiguous than in the previous works. There are effectively two couples in the novel: Irene and Balder (unmarried) and Zulema and Alberto (married). In each case, the men are finally deceived: Balder by Irene who maintained that she was a virgin, when she was not, and Alberto by Zulema, who sleeps with her dancing instructor. All four are made to waltz around the *éminence grise* of the novel, Señora Loayza. It is an oversimplification to state that Balder is deceived for, like all Arlt's male characters, he suspends the relationship before a final grave situation is reached. The novel is kept alive by his vacillation about Irene's supposed double-dealings and whether her sensuality is sincere or promoted from the background by her scheming mother. Unlike the case of la Bizca's mother, in *El amor brujo* the issue is never resolved and doubt is one of the important sub-themes of the work. Indeed, although it is mainly concerned with relationships between the sexes, the problem of doubt and the inability of Balder to achieve any firm knowledge about other persons' motives, or even about his own, is raised to quasi-philosophical levels. There even appears a character called El Fantasma de la Duda [''Doubt's Phantom'']. (pp. 54-7)

Let us now examine the view of marriage expressed in this last novel, for it provides a clue to the way in which the narrative

develops. In fact, given such hatred of middle-class conventions, *El amor brujo* could end in one way only,—in separation and disruption. Whilst in *Los lanzallamas* the attack on marriage is vituperative and mindless, here there is an advance towards more sociologically-based analysis. Having decided that his main theme was to be sex and marriage, Arlt seems to have determined to make his argument watertight. Thus the work contains long passages of painful but more objective comment on the attitudes of middle-class women. (Nowhere does he attack male value of *hombría* [''manliness''] and *machismo.* The man is always a potential victim. Arlt's criticism of the male bourgeois always relates to his petty materialism, of which the *tendero* [''shopkeeper''] is the prime and constant example.) Firstly, he is specific about the women he is discussing. They belong to the lower middle class . . . and to the generation born about 1900; that is, his own. Moreover, a further advance on the previous novel, their attitudes are now seen as a product of their circumstance. Formerly, the bourgeois woman was envisaged as wilfully and individually destructive of men; now she forms part of a group. . . . An understandable condensation takes place in Arlt's thinking following the publication of *Los siete locos,* from 1929 onwards. This is the moment of great crisis in Argentine and world economics. The whole range of his ideology becomes more specific, both in political and social values. He never achieves the completeness of a system, however, nor does he ever dominate total clarity of expression. . . . But it may be seen . . . that his point of view had by now taken on a more social orientation: women's attitudes are governed by the society in which they live. This marks a shift towards dialectical materialist principles, of course. Vituperation also gives way temporarily to deeper understanding, even to the extent of recognizing the denial of women's rights. (pp. 59-60)

Having established [a] quasi-scientific premise for his argument, his inherent nausea and spleen force their way to the surface again. Balder regards marriage itself as a lie and the family home as a pigsty. . . . Finally nausea gives way to compassion. He seems to realize something of the crushing conditions under which the *porteño* was living and he perceives the spiritual problem as paramount. The middle class has lost all sense of hope . . . and the workers below them survived on one overriding idea, that of becoming middle class themselves. Balder, in a final attack of gall, is described as ''uno de los tantos tipos que denominamos 'hombre casado.' Haragán, escéptico, triste'' [''one of those many who we called 'married man.' Lazy, skeptical, sad''].

Given this view of marriage in the middle class and Arlt's desire to hold it up to scorn, it was unlikely that *El amor brujo* could become a successful novel. It is too closely tied to its times, the circumstantial material is too insistent and, unlike the other novels, it is dated. Balder, like the others, is an anguished character, but the overwhelmingly social origins of his anguish are in sharp contrast with the metaphysical anguish of Erdosain. His failed marriage, his meeting with a young schoolgirl on a train and the impossiblity of any outcome of his affair are too slender a framework for a worthwhile comment on society. Arlt had thought to introduce an underlying irony at the beginning of the novel by inflating the euphoria that Balder experiences following his first meeting with the adolescent Irene and setting it against the ugly realities of bourgeois life and the threat that his relationship with the young girl constitutes to his integrity and manhood. But parts of the work slide into a maudlin novelette style and it is saved only by its lengthy examination of social *mores* and by his nauseated reaction to what he suspects to be the trap laid by Irene and her mother. It is probably most valuable for its documentation of one peculiar aspect of a society in the throes of economic distress, taking refuge in the proven means of survival.

Like Erdosain and Silvio, Balder is motivated by his sense of lost purity and by his striving to believe that the world cannot really be as black as it seems. . . . There is also an admixture of the problem of doubt and uncertainty of knowlege and the impossibility of achieving surety in human relationships, clearly an offshoot of the anti-positivist thinking of the times. . . . But this theme is never adequately elaborated. Arlt employs the diary technique to investigate the shifting sands of the protagonist's mind, groping for some measure of assurance in his life, but the psychological profundity of the previous novels is lacking. Indeed, therein lies the lack of success of *El amor brujo.* Whilst the author's technique in handling his material has visibly improved and whilst certain isolated passages are brilliantly composed, the work lacks the dynamism of the earlier novels because, ill-advisedly, he had moved away from existential anguish, in which he excelled, towards a more socially based criticism, in which his knowledge was too diffuse. Both elements are present in each of his novels but the different emphasis in *El amor brujo* accounts for the plummeting of the tone. His first efforts were being made in the theatre at the same time, concentrating on developing the theme already latent in the previous works,—the clash between the characters' dreams and the sordidness of the world around them. *El amor brujo* had begun to take him in a false direction and he abandoned the novel altogether. (pp. 61-3)

Mafud complained that women never achieve real status in Argentine fiction, Arlt included. However, it is not only to the fact that his novels are composed from a uniquely male point of view that the women owe their lack of substance, for they are intentionally projected into the male protagonists' lives in different ways at different times. As predators they are weak characters indeed. (There are no "doña Bárbaras" in Arlt's writing.) But, because they represent the social tendency to perpetuate institutions, they in their turn become the victims of the men. No woman in Arlt's fiction successfully subjugates her man; in every case the woman is abandoned. Manhood and liberty are invariably safeguarded at the expense of the female, whether she is guilty of laying snares or not. To see this merely as Arlt's tacit support for the male cause—which many of his female readers have done—is too simple a view, for there is evidence for a more elaborate understanding of the problem. Apart from the major instance of Balder's repudiation of Irene, because of her supposed lie about her virginity, there are a number of cases in his writing of the deliberate rupture of relations between men and women. This is a very different problem from that of reticence or refusal to enter into a relationship, as happens with Hipólita or Luciana Espila, although they have a similar cause: the resistance to betrayal of the ideal of feminine purity and the supposed degradation induced by sexual contact. (p. 63)

[In *El amor brujo*], Arlt uses the vagaries of the sexual situation to explore the ebb and flow of Balder's mind. The story-line is concerned with sex and the sexual attraction of an adolescent for an older man (as in Nabokov's *Lolita*), but an important underlying theme is the fallibility and precariousness of human reason in the apprehension of conflicting evidence. . . . Balder is the classic anti-hero, vacillating in his own mind, cut off from society, unable to affirm his own existence; the *abúlico* ["vacillator"] par excellence. The meeting with Irene and his

ensuing passion is the force applied to his circumstance to set the novel in motion, to allow the reader to explore the vicissitudes of his psychology as his reason grapples unsuccessfully with this new element in his life. In spite of its relative failure as a novel, this work is an obvious forerunner of Sábato's *El túnel.* Balder, engineer and architect, isolated, meets Irene and is infatuated; after a long struggle in which evidence and reasoning dance around each other, he severs the connection with the one person who might have given some meaning to his life. In Sábato's work, Castel, a painter, equally isolated, meets María Iribarne and, after a similar process involving the failure of his own reason, finally murders her, thus cutting himself off once again from mankind. She had been the only person in the world who had understood his paintings and he deliberately destroys her. Arlt uses the passionate relationship to mount an attack on bourgeois marriage, a social comment which is quite absent from Sábato's work, of course. (p. 64)

As Balder allows himself to be sucked further and further into the morass of his relationships with Irene, the motives behind his actions become clearer. It is identical to that which afflicted Erdosain: to discover what will happen to his soul when pursued to the limits of its endurance. . . . If he had been forewarned about the "millones de minutos de sufrimiento" ["millions of minutes of suffering,"] that lay before him, he would not have retreated from his desire to be dominated in his passion. The masochistic dualism of his nature is patently revealed: "¿Por qué anhelo la pureza y me revuelco en la porqueria?" ["Why do I crave purity and wallow about in filth?"] he asks himself. Ultimately, his desire for purity and his fear of final surrender, allied to his inability to discover firm knowledge of whether he is the victim of a trap or not, force him into the typical Arltian solution: the severance of the connection. This is the only instance in all Arlt's fiction where copulation is known to have taken place, although it is not described. Balder purports to have discovered that Irene was not a virgin. . . . He therefore abandons her in a spirit of self-justification. The technical reasons for her abandonment are to be found in *machismo;* a man who values his honour would not marry a sullied woman. But the deeper psychological causes are the valid ones: coitus has destroyed all hope of idealization, contact with reality has shattered all possible illusions. (p. 65)

A review of the relations between the sexes in Arlt's writing would be incomplete without reference to the problem of prostitution which figures so persistently. His male characters long for purity, amidst their very anguish, yet wallow the while in their own imperfections. Erdosain's immediate response to his anguish is not to bolt into the nearest brothel for relief but to drag himself from one to the other, searching for the most vile. . . . When he plunges into his fantasies about ideal women with whom sexual contact would be impossible, his imaginings are likely to end in a conflicting desire to become a "cafishio" (another *lunfardo* term for a pimp). In stories like **"Las fieras"** and **"Ester Primavera,"** not only do sexual perversities figure unashamedly but pimps and thieves abound. No doubt there is a deep-rooted desire to shock but Arlt also wishes to go further; his intentions are more serious. He seeks to demonstrate that evil and middle-class behaviour are not mutually exclusive. . . . Thus all his *rufianes* ["ruffians"] and *macrós* proceed from the middle class, along with the other characters. In fact, considerable emphasis—beyond that required for the normal creation of the character—is placed upon the fact that Haffner, the Rufián Melancólico, has been a teacher of mathematics. Seen from the present day, the picture that Arlt draws of Haffner's life seems to be from the depths of fantasy. In fact, it is one of the most realistic elements in the book. We have seen something of the gruesome conditions of prostitution in Buenos Aires in the 1920s. It was Arlt's self-appointed task to reveal this to the world, not out of a spirit of bravado (although he does not spare the details), but to establish how far society had gone in ensuring that reality should outstrip fantasy. Indeed, as Núñez points out, prostitution had become the career for the women who did not achieve the alternative of marriage. The figures we have quoted earlier would certainly bear out this supposition.

Haffner maintains three women who bring in two thousand pesos a month. His philosophy is a debased excrescence of *machismo,* an amalgam of cynicism and sadism. . . . The "mujer de la vida" ["woman of the night"] is the hardest and bitterest animal on earth, he contends, who complements with her masochistic attitude the sadistic exploitation of her body by her "man." . . . Arlt neither condemns nor condones this situation, although his character Erdosain is made to express a certain shock—even he! But what Arlt seeks to demonstrate is not the parlous state of morals in the city nor even the plight of women subjected to this kind of régime; his designs are more subtle. Through his picture of prostitution, with its "respectabilities," its hierarchical structure and its codes of conduct, he is able to show that other strata of society are none the less corrupt. (pp. 68-9)

We have tried to disentangle the ramifications of the problem of sexuality in Arlt, and in so doing we have seen that the urge to discover an ideal and pure relationship between man and woman is akin to the search for absolutes which operates throughout his creative process. Equally so, frustration of the ideal in its clash with reality may be expected to erupt in anguish. At the point where sexuality brushes against social concepts, we have discerned a dual tendency in Arlt. On the one hand, a reflection of stereotyped attitudes deriving from *machismo* and, on the other, a splenetic attack on marriage as a bourgeois institution. It is not too critical to say that Arlt's talent and originality do not lie in these areas. The attack on institutionalized sexual relations is age-old; he merely finds a niche in this worthy tradition. However, as the interpreter of the sexual *mores* of a given society at a certain time, he is invaluable. It is unlikely that he himself would have seen this as his first purpose, for he writes mainly from an indignant point of view. His outbursts, although scurrilous, are always enjoyable. They earned him the disrespect of many critics in his day. But, as Larra has said, in spite of his excesses, Arlt always remained on the side of moral honesty and human understanding. Constantly vanquished in their search for the

impossible, his characters never relinquish their drive towards something more noble than society can provide. (pp. 70-1)

> *Jack M. Flint, in his* The Prose Works of Roberto Arlt: A Thematic Approach, *University of Durham, 1985, 93 p.*

ADDITIONAL BIBLIOGRAPHY

Foster, David William. "Roberto Arlt's *La isla desierta:* A Structural Analysis." *Latin American Theatre Review* 11, No. 1 (Fall 1977): 25-34.
> Examines how the structure and language of the play serve to express its principal theme: the instability of reality.

Lindstrom, Naomi Eva. "The World's Illogic in Two Plays by Argentine Expressionists." *Latin American Literary Review* IV, No. 8 (Spring-Summer 1976): 83-8.
> Contends that a thematic affinity exists between Arlt's play *El desierto entra a la ciudad* and German Expressionist drama, both of which demonstrate the failure of reason to be a panacea for the ills of humanity.

——. Introduction to *The Seven Madmen,* by Roberto Arlt, translated by Naomi Eva Lindstrom, pp. v-ix. Boston: David R. Godine, 1984.
> Describes the changing critical reception of *Los siete locos* and notes the tone of uncertainty that pervades the novel.

——. "Arlt's Exposition of the Myth of Woman." In *Woman as Myth and Metaphor in Latin American Literature,* edited by Carmelo Virgillo and Naomi Lindstrom, pp. 151-66. Columbia: University of Missouri Press, 1985.
> Analyzes the character of Hipólita in the context of Simone de Beauvoir's theory about "the myth of woman." Lindstrom writes that Hipólita has "the power to provoke men to feats of extravagant mythmaking," and that Arlt "invokes the mythmaking process precisely in order to expose and to reveal its mechanisms and thus deconstruct it."

Review: Latin American Literature and Arts 31 (January-April 1982): 26-41.
> Section devoted to Arlt which includes the following: a chronology of Arlt's life and works by Lee Dowling; "Arlt: The Maverick" by David William Foster; translated excerpts from *Aguafuertes porteñas;* "Preface to *Los siete locos*" by Juan Carlos Onetti; a translated excerpt from *Los siete locos;* and "Live Language against Dead: Literary Rebels of Buenos Aires" by Naomi Lindstrom.

Troiano, James J. "Pirandellism in the Theatre of Roberto Arlt." *Latin American Theatre Review* 8, No. 1 (Fall 1974): 37-44.
> Traces the influence of Luigi Pirandello on Arlt's plays.

(Arthur) Joyce (Lunel) Cary

1888-1957

(Also wrote under the pseudonyms Arthur Carey and Thomas Joyce) Irish novelist, short story writer, essayist, and poet.

For further discussion of Cary's career, see *TCLC*, Vol. 1.

Cary is primarily known as a novelist whose varied works—which include comic novels, historical novels, and family sagas—portray complex and memorable characters embodying his personal philosophy. Most notably in the six volumes of his two trilogies, Cary's vividly realized protagonists illustrate his conviction that life, though profoundly unfair and arbitrary, can be a magnificent adventure for resourceful individuals who acknowledge no higher authority than their own vital and creative nature. Although many of his novels are so traditional in form that they have been compared to eighteenth-century classics, Cary is generally regarded as an innovative writer who employed modern literary techniques, including a first-person present-tense narrative that imparts a sense of immediacy to his fiction.

Cary was born in Londonderry, Northern Ireland, and was raised and educated in England. A shy and sickly child who suffered from pleurisy, asthma, rheumatism, and near blindness in one eye, he showed a precocious talent for writing and drawing. While on a sketching trip to France in 1904 he became enamored of Impressionism and resolved to become an artist. After completing secondary school, he pursued his art studies at the Board of Manufacturers School of Art (later the Edinburgh College of Art); however, he abandoned his studies after two years, convinced that he did not have the talent to be a successful artist. Redirecting his energies to writing, Cary sought financial support from his father by dedicating to him a collection of poetry, Cary's first published work, and by studying to become a lawyer, which was Arthur Cary's choice of a career for his son. Cary was an undistinguished law student at Trinity College, Oxford, and an indifferent writer of poetry. After graduating in 1912 with the lowest possible degree, he served with the British Red Cross during the Balkan War against Turkey, both because he supported the cause and because he was seeking experience for a novel. In 1913 Cary entered the Nigerian Service and for the next seven years served as an assistant district officer, a post that encompassed the duties of colonial administrator, tax collector, judge, census taker, and road builder, as well as troop leader in the West Africa Frontier Force during World War I.

Cary wrote prolifically during his years in Nigeria, but destroyed most of his attempted novels as failures. He found success, however, with his short stories, which were accepted by the lucrative *Saturday Evening Post*. Assured of a profitable outlet for his fiction, Cary retired from colonial service in 1920, resolved to write short stories for income and novels to satisfy his ambitions as a literary artist; however, his simple formula for commercial stories—"a little sentiment, a little incident, and a surprise"—became complicated by an increasing stylistic and thematic sophistication. By 1921 the *Post* found his stories too literary and he was able to publish very little of his work until 1932, when his first novel, *Aissa Saved,* appeared. During these years, Cary supported himself in a variety of ways and

read widely, seeking a comprehensive vision of life that would lend unity to his fiction.

Aissa Saved was the first of four novels set in Africa that dramatize the clash of European and African cultures during the British colonization, economic exploitation, and modernization of Africa. Although they had limited commercial success, the fourth of these novels, *Mister Johnson,* did gain critical recognition for its powerful portrayal of Africans corrupted by European values. Four years later, Cary published *A House of Children,* which received the James Tait Black Memorial Prize as the best British novel of the year. Based on Cary's childhood, this work was the first in which Cary utilized first-person narrative, a form he thereafter used in all of his major fiction and developed to great acclaim in the novels comprising his two trilogies. The third volume of the first trilogy, *The Horse's Mouth,* was a bestseller that finally brought Cary financial security. Following the completion of his second trilogy in 1955, Cary learned that he suffered from a form of fatal paralysis. During his last years he continued to produce a variety of works, the most important of which was *Art and Reality,* a respected collection of essays examining the creative process. He died in 1957.

Prominent among Cary's early works are his African novels—*Aissa Saved, An American Visitor, The African Witch,* and

Mister Johnson—which are based on his experiences in the colonial service and depict cultural and individual conflicts arising from the imposition of colonial rule on Africa. Emphasizing the dilemmas of Africans caught between two cultures, these works display a number of traits that remained typical of Cary's fiction: narrative inventiveness, copious action, and an objective portrayal of a wide variety of characters. Some critics have protested that Cary's extreme objectivity in presenting unpleasant behavior and violent events in the first three African novels resulted in works that lack a moral center, leaving the reader to make judgments about characters and situations that the author himself did not make. Critics have also complained that the first three of these early works are so densely packed with characters that none emerges with great force or clarity. By contrast, *Mister Johnson*, which is the most highly regarded of the African novels, focuses on a single and highly memorable character. Cary thereby avoided the diffuseness and confusion of his earlier books; furthermore, by writing in the present tense he imparted a sense of immediacy that critics have compared to the stream-of-consciousness narrative techniques of James Joyce, D. H. Lawrence, and Virginia Woolf.

Cary's two trilogies are his most successful and best-known works. The first comprises *Herself Surprised, To Be a Pilgrim,* and *The Horse's Mouth;* the second, *Prisoner of Grace, Except the Lord,* and *Not Honour More.* Each novel is narrated in the first person by a protagonist who appears in a subordinate role in the other two novels of the trilogy. In Cary's own estimation, the novels of the first trilogy "were not sufficiently interlocked to give the richness and depth of actuality that I had hoped for." The novels of this trilogy are loosely connected by the subjects of art, Protestantism in English history, and the struggle between freedom and authority. Barbara Hardy has written that the three volumes could not function together exactly as Cary wished because "when a major character in one action becomes a minor character in another he becomes an entirely different character. . . . He changes his relation to the reader." She maintains that such a shift in perception cannot be sustained over multiple novels, as it requires "more of a carry-over from one novel to the next than the formal completion of a good novel—not to mention lapse of time and shortage of memory—can permit." Other commentators, however, contend that reader comprehension of each character is enriched by the multiple perspectives provided by the different narrators. Hazard Adams, for example, maintains that "by having the three speakers of his trilogy tell about each other, each in his own way and with the full force of his assumptions about the world behind his interpretation, Cary extends the depth of our perception of all of them." The character Gulley Jimson, who narrates *The Horse's Mouth* and appears in *Herself Surprised* and *To Be a Pilgrim,* is considered one of Cary's finest creations. A disreputable individual but a committed artist, Jimson is considered the most interesting example of a recurring character type in Cary's fiction, described by Andrew Wright as "the man who rejoices in freedom: the anarch, the artist, the man who destroys in order to create, the man who ignores all claims but his own." Similar characters include the clerk Johnson in *Mister Johnson,* the unrepentant rogue Dick Bonser in *A Fearful Joy,* and the revolutionary Jim Latter in *Not Honour More.* Wright contends that Cary's most successful novels feature a representative of this character type—"the creator, the artist, the revolutionary."

The three novels of Cary's second trilogy—*Prisoner of Grace, Except the Lord,* and *Not Honour More*—are closely interre-lated by the immersion of all the principal characters in the complex world of politics. Benjamin Nyce has noted that the second trilogy expresses "Cary's belief that public politics is only the visible aspect of a pervasive politics, that the politics of marriage and the nursery are equally significant." Unlike the expansive and life-affirming characters of the first trilogy, those of the second are desperate, tense, and uncertain, and the strong individualism of the protagonists isolates them rather than bringing them into contact with others. Nyce maintains that the trilogy structure itself complements the political background of the three novels: "By giving over each novel to a separate speaker and by having each voice contradict and qualify the other voices, Cary achieved the ambiguity and sense of confusion he saw as cardinal characteristics of the atmosphere of political power." Because Cary does not promote one point of view over another, the contradictions in the narratives remain unresolved, and it is impossible for the reader to ascertain the credibility of each narrator. While some critics have objected to the absence of a moral authority in the second trilogy, Michael Rosenthal has observed that "the uncertainty of understanding and judging in the second trilogy indicates no shortcoming in Cary as a novelist: it is simply the final truth of the world as he came to see it." Many commentators have concluded that the novels benefit rather than suffer from Cary's failure to establish a single, clearly superior point of view, and that Cary's impartial presentation of differing points of view conveys a convincing and accurate picture of the world of politics.

Cary's personal philosophy informs all of his novels. Walter Allen has noted that "normally nothing is so much beside the point in the discussion of a novel as its author's beliefs," but that in the case of Cary, "his characters, along with the technical means he uses in order to render them in action, all originate in his beliefs about the nature of man." These beliefs include Cary's conviction that human beings exist in a condition of absolute freedom, and that creative imagination is the most valuable human attribute. Writing that "for good and evil, man is a free creative spirit," Cary maintained that the human tendency to create results in an uncertain and fundamentally unjust world of continuous change. Many of Cary's novels explore the conflict between the forces of creation and those of established order: for example, the painter Gulley Jimson in *The Horse's Mouth* steals and sells the property of others in order to finance his painting, and the revolutionary Jim Latter, in the third volume of the second trilogy, seeks to supplant the government supported by Chester Nimmo in the second volume of that trilogy. The conflict between creative freedom and established order is considered by many commentators to be the essential theme of Cary's career.

Cary's critical reputation grew steadily throughout his lifetime, and during his last years he was widely regarded as a major British novelist. Although he suffered some critical neglect for several years after his death, extensive critical studies in the late 1950s and the 1960s by Robert Bloom, M. M. Mahood, Malcolm Foster, and Jack Wolkenfeld sought to establish Cary's place in twentieth-century British letters. Such retrospective appraisals have examined Cary's treatment of philosophy, politics, society, religion, and above all his portrayal of character. Acknowledged to have dealt with crucial themes, such as human relationships, freedom of choice, and personal values, Cary is particularly esteemed for his exploration of these themes, not abstractly, but through the medium of masterfully depicted characters.

(See also *Contemporary Authors,* Vol. 104, and *Dictionary of Literary Biography,* Vol. 15: *British Novelists, 1930-1959.*)

PRINCIPAL WORKS

Verse [as Arthur Carey]   (poetry)   1908
Aissa Saved   (novel)   1932
An American Visitor   (novel)   1933
The African Witch   (novel)   1936
Castle Corner   (novel)   1938
Mister Johnson   (novel)   1939
Power in Men   (essay)   1939
Charley Is My Darling   (novel)   1940
The Case for African Freedom   (essay)   1941; revised
    edition, 1944
*Herself Surprised   (novel)   1941
A House of Children   (novel)   1941
*To Be a Pilgrim   (novel)   1942
The Process of Real Freedom   (essay)   1943
*The Horse's Mouth   (novel)   1944
Marching Soldier   (poetry)   1945
Britain and West Africa   (essay)   1946
The Moonlight   (novel)   1946
The Drunken Sailor   (poetry)   1947
A Fearful Joy   (novel)   1949
Prisoner of Grace   (novel)   1952
Except the Lord   (novel)   1953
Not Honour More   (novel)   1955
Art and Reality   (essays)   1958
The Captive and the Free   (novel)   1959
Memoir of the Bobotes   (memoir)   1960
Spring Song and Other Stories   (short stories)   1960
Cock Jarvis   (unfinished novel)   1974
Selected Essays   (essays)   1976

*These works were published as *First Trilogy* in 1958.

THE TIMES LITERARY SUPPLEMENT   (essay date 1932)

[*In the following review of* Aissa Saved, *the critic suggests that Cary's objective rendering of the novel's events gives the reader no moral point of view from which to evaluate those events.*]

One must assume that Mr. Joyce Cary, the author of *Aissa Saved,* knows the country and people that he is describing: the country is the Yanrin district of the Niger territory and the people are the native races inhabiting it, with the addition of three whites, Mr. and Mrs. Carr, of the mission at Shibi, and Bradgate, the District Officer of Yanrin. The common reader, however, being without the local knowledge that will enable residents in Nigeria to judge the events and personalities described, can only apply his ordinary standards; and these will probably lead him to the opinion that there is too much blood and cruelty here recorded to make this novel agreeable reading.

The main episode is the violent rioting that ensued after an attack by Christian natives upon the pagans who worshipped the goddess Oke, in which deeds that in Europe would be called extremely horrible were perpetrated on both sides. What leads to these excesses is a preliminary riot in the village of Kolu that occurred when Mr. Carr's mission went in a body to testify there on the occasion of a pagan festival. The missioner's pet boy, Ojo, and the missioner's wife's pet girl, Aissa, are the

chief causes of strife. Aissa, in particular, plays a leading part, for, after drinking beer and backsliding with her former love, she puts an old priest out of action with a canoe paddle, gets her own ankle broken and is thrown into prison: meanwhile the rest of the missioners have a hard fight for it to get away safe. The book seems to be the fruit of a humorous disillusionment on the subject of the white man's success in improving the morals of the black. Mr. Cary is never more successful than when contrasting the well-intentioned busyness of a district officer or the holy intentions of a missionary with the cynical remarks made by the natives upon the white men's actions and personalities. The Emir and other native functionaries who surround Bradgate, flatter him to his face and blandly disregard his orders in his absence are very amusing; and the boy Ali, a typical swelled-head, though brave as a lion, is a good piece of character-drawing. Aissa herself is a hysterical trollop who responds to any kind of strong suggestion, even to the length of hallucination. In the end she sacrifices her own child to the God of our faith exactly as, earlier in the story, a pagan woman, beside herself in ecstasy, had been induced to offer her baby to Oke. It is doubtless true that these things happen, and well that their possibility should be known; at the same time, when all their crudity is so vividly dwelt on, we have a right to expect some point of view in which to consider them. This is where Mr. Cary falls short. He is too objective. He seems ready to appreciate the good intentions of everybody, and to leave it at that; with the resultant spectacle of good intentions, aided by ignorance and stupidity on both sides, mutually thwarting one another in ludicrous but sanguinary manner.

A review of "Aissa Saved," in The Times Literary Supplement, *No. 1564, January 21, 1932, p. 42.*

CYRIL CONNOLLY   (essay date 1936)

[*Connolly was an English novelist and critic who reviewed books for the* New Statesman, *the* Observer, *and the* Sunday Times *from 1927 until his death in 1974. Considered a remarkably hard-to-please critic, he was the founding editor of the respected literary monthly* Horizon (1939-1950). *In the following excerpt from his favorable review of* The African Witch, *he commends Cary's sympathetic, insightful characterizations.*]

The African Witch is a novel on Nigeria. It is a long, solid, accomplished and interesting book. The author really understands natives and also paints a sympathetic picture of the Englishmen who govern them. He realises that, however we may have acquired Nigeria, the ordinary public-school type who go out there do not expect to make a fortune. Their worst crime is their inability to tolerate black men socially, and he has built up a plot from the predicament of a young Oxford-educated negro, possible heir to the river emirate of Rimi, and the bad impression he makes on the whites, who will not receive him, and on the blacks, who, devotees of ju-ju, a magical cult which makes no pretence to think human nature either good or capable of improvement, consider him a renegade and a Christian. It is an intelligent and fascinating novel. The descriptions of Elisabeth, the witch, and her ju-ju are remarkable, and so are the portraits of Louis, the coloured prince, intellectually and emotionally the superior of the white men, yet lacking their confidence and stability, of Burwash the affable, timid, and politic Governor, Rackham the intelligent but illiberal police commissioner, and the two women in his life. Mr. Cary does not give us types, although the life he describes is so obviously typical. He has no sympathy for the conventional product. (pp. 732, 734)

The African Witch has already been compared to *A Passage to India*. The difference is that Mr. Cary is a good novelist, and Mr. Forster is an artist; the similarity lies in the fact that both understand and are in sympathy with their respective natives, both appreciate the difficulties of the white rulers and realise that, although there is something inherently doomed and rotten in the possession of colonies, the era of native autonomy has not yet arrived. Mr. Cary does not accuse the British of exploitation, as Celine does the French, but rather of political reaction, preserving the political systems which they find, the small autocracies, rather than encouraging democratic education. But his achievement has been to make, as it were, the African figures in the crowd scenes of *Sanders of the River* separately intelligible. (p. 734)

> Cyril Connolly, in a review of "The African Witch," in The New Statesman & Nation, n.s. Vol. XI, No. 272, May 9, 1936, pp. 732, 734.

DONALD BARR   (essay date 1950)

[*Barr is an American educator and critic who has written extensively on educational issues. In the following excerpt from a review of* The Horse's Mouth, *he notes the primacy of character over plot in Cary's novels and discusses Cary's principal themes.*]

Of the two kinds of English comic novel—the mulled ale and the vinegar—Joyce Cary's belongs with the warm and the spiced. That is important enough, now that the two wars and the ruin of the spacious civilization of great country houses have soured most of English comedy. But what is more important, Cary's *The Horse's Mouth* is the best thing of its kind America has imported in forty years.

The Horse's Mouth is the autobiography of Gulley Jimson. Gulley is our old friend the artist at odds with society. Novels are full of painters and musicians and poets, and they are always at odds with society. And how gloomy and embarrassed about it they are! But Gulley, the bald, little, bandy-legged swaggerer humbly dedicated to art, meticulously painting The Fall of Man with the frayed stub of a rope and some stolen colors, threatening to cut the tripe out of a millionaire, forging his own works, and grandly blocking out his last huge masterpiece on a crumbling wall—Gulley is at odds with society in a new way, in dozens of new ways. Society hasn't a chance. This fellow enjoys being an artist. (p. 1)

Cary's success with the critics was until recently rather discontinuous. His reputation did not accumulate, but had to be renewed with every book. Why has this been? Probably because he is too versatile and too enjoyable.

Each of Cary's works has had to make its reputation afresh because each is a fresh work. He writes with equal zest and acumen about too many kinds of people; he will not specialize. Nevertheless, there are themes and characters that appear again and again. His stories abound with Faustian modern girls, bastards and their mothers—and their fathers, scoundrelly incarnations of the Life Force, carnal and alive, and yet somehow symbolic. Their very richness has befuddled some critics. The more they bounce, the more levity their creator is accused of. He has been thought an improviser, fertile but disorderly—"incapable of plot or profundity," as one admiring reviewer said.

On the contrary, Cary is a careful, even a profound, thinker. George Orwell, who does not suffer fools gladly, called him "an unusually independent mind, a man who has thought deeply over the problems of our time." It is true that his stories are picaresque, and one could not imagine Graham Greene doing anything so casually plotted as *The Horse's Mouth*. But Cary himself, writing in these pages recently, explained the novelist's job as one of bringing order to the dull chaos of experience, breathing a soul into brute reality—in short, pointing a moral.

With Cary, the ordering agent is not the metaphysical plot but the inspired Character. When we see this we sweep away the rock of misconceptions about his work. Of course nothing so abstract as a misconception could spoil one's enjoyment of a book like *The Horse's Mouth*. But to understand as well as enjoy Cary, we must group his two cardinal themes: Protestantism and the struggle between Freedom and Authority.

As one might expect of an Anglo-Irishman, he is intensely conscious of the Protestant tradition. His novels are crowded with all the varieties and outgrowths—some of them outlandish—of its spirit. To Cary English history is Protestant history.

Cary's crowning work on this theme is the trilogy of "English history, through English eyes for the last sixty years," of which *The Horse's Mouth* is the third book. The three can be read separately. Their narrators, Sara Monday, Tom Wilcher and Gulley Jimson, are as different as one can imagine. Sara is a brawny, pneumatic Devonshire cook, an earthy woman but with a deep biological cunning that makes her a veritable Alma Mater to a whole string of lovers. Of these, Wilcher, a deeply pious miser much given to indecent exposure and pinching strange girls, is one. Gulley is another.

Nevertheless, all the stories have the common theme of Grace. Cary is as seriously concerned with this (even if his books seem to make light of hell) as Graham Greene. Greene as a Catholic is concerned with the problem of evil. Cary as a Protestant is concerned with the problem of good.

Sara's autobiography, *Herself Surprised*, reminds every one of Defoe's *Moll Flanders*. But when Sara says—she is returning to her lover Jimson against her better judgment—"I am not a crying woman, but all the way back in the bus I was flooding with tears. They did not come out of my eyes, but my whole blood was swimming with their bitterness, and my heart was drowned under their salt," the prose accent goes back even beyond the Presbyterian Defoe to Bunyan's "Grace Abounding to the Chief of Sinners."

Wilcher's tale, *To Be a Pilgrim*, takes its name from the great hymn in *Pilgrim's Progress*. Wilcher, a lawyer who thinks in small type, has always yearned to be an evangelist. For all that he is a pettifogger, he is closer to being a Christian than a Mr. Legality.

And Gulley is a Mr. Illegality. As he tells his story in *The Horse's Mouth*, peppering it (but what condiment will spice spice?) with quotations from William Blake, we can find his place in the family of Protestantism. Gulley, who calls Blake "old Billy" and means "old billy-goat," is a modern Blake—in that sense, too. It would be hard to write a description of Blake—his quarrels with patrons, his great exhibition that failed, his cheerful indignation at neglect, his bawdiness—which would not remind us of Jimson. Blake, the great Apostle of Confusion, was a deeply Protestant apostle, and never more of a Puritan than when he raged against the moral law and glorified the Lineaments of Gratified Desire.

To Blake, artists were true saints afire with divinity. Gulley is wrong when, painting away at "The Fall of Man" in his leaky shed in Greenbank, he brushes aside a question with: "God knows. But he won't go into details. The truth is, *the old horse doesn't speak only horse. And I can't speak only Greenbank.*" It is not true, by Blake's gospel, that God speaks one language and Gulley another. Gulley Jimson, the artist, is the Horse's Mouth.

This brings us to the second of Cary's underlying themes: the conflict of freedom and authority, which has lately become a central problem in Cary's thought. It forms the titles of his political studies, ***Power in Men*** and ***Process of Real Freedom.*** It is allegorized in **"The Drunken Sailor,"** a ballad-epic written in a naïve, skipping rhetoric, which might almost be a commentary on *The Horse's Mouth.* For Gulley is an anarchist. Just as Blake rebelled against the cult of Reason followed by the rebels of his day, so Gulley cannot stomach the modern liberals' cult of government. And this, in Cary's view, is the ultimate—though not the proper—development of the Protestant spirit.

Cary himself, as a former magistrate in Nigeria, knows the other side; he knows that authority is equally necessary, equally creative. But obviously the cardinal rule of his art is to be objective, to present his characters in their own terms. And it is just this objectivity that gives the characters their enormous relish, their reality. By the very lawlessness of their energy it is the rogues who dominate the scene and the onlooker. Because nothing of these people has been withheld, or scaled down to a moral standard not their own, you become Sara, you become Wilcher—pinches and all. (pp. 1, 24)

Donald Barr, "For Gulley Jimson, Life Was Fun," in The New York Times Book Review, *January 29, 1950, pp. 1, 24.*

MARK SCHORER   (essay date 1950)

[Schorer was an American critic and biographer who wrote the definitive life of Sinclair Lewis. In his often-anthologized essay "Technique as Discovery" (1948), Schorer put forth the argument that fiction deserves the same close attention to diction and metaphor that the New Critics had been lavishing on poetry. He contended that fiction viewed only with respect to content was not art at all, but experience. For Schorer, only when individuals examine "achieved content," or form, do they speak of art, and consequently, speak as critics. Schorer also argued that the difference between content and art is "technique," and that the study of technique demonstrates how fictional form discovers and evaluates meaning, meaning that is often not intended by the author. In the following excerpt, he discusses A Fearful Joy *as a realistic social novel in the tradition of Daniel Defoe's* Moll Flanders *(1721).]*

When the English critic F. R. Leavis cited as exemplars of "the great tradition" in the English novel Jane Austen, George Eliot, Henry James, Joseph Conrad, and D. H. Lawrence, he pointed, perhaps, at the finest English novelists, but at the slimmest tradition. This is the tradition of the "morally intensive" novel, the novel that considers serious moral themes and is determined to define the exact quality of moral experience. When we say that it is the slimmest tradition in the history of the English novel, we mean, simply, that fewer novelists have chosen to write in this tradition than in any other.

Another tradition in the English novel is, in bulk, much greater. It is also more happily native to Great Britain. This is the tradition of what we may call the "socially extensive" novel, the novel that considers a large scene and is determined above all to encompass the quantity and only secondarily to define the quality of social experience. It is the great tradition of a downright gregariousness, the tradition that reminds us at all points that the British novel first of all was thought of not as vision but as fact; it was "news."

It came out of history and popular religion and political scandal and social reform. It came out of essays and letters; it came immediately out of books like Defoe's fictions of contemporary adventure. Its connections with romance, even popular romance, were so slight that it had no inclination to utilize even the debased remnants of ritual and myth to be found there. It was written, in fact, in the spirit of anti-romance. It came along with journalism; it was realism.

All this was, of course, of tremendous importance to the generic lines that were laid down for the novel: it created the great popular tradition with which we are most familiar in Smollett and Fielding, in Thackeray and Trollope and Dickens. Now that tradition is perhaps best represented in England today by the work of Joyce Cary, whose novel, **The Horse's Mouth,** attracted considerable critical attention in America.

The line from a book like *Moll Flanders* to a book like **A Fearful Joy** is so peculiarly direct that one might almost infer an intentional connection. **A Fearful Joy,** Mr. Cary's twelfth novel, is the history of a woman's life from birth to old age. It is packed with a miscellany of events that begins in the heart of the Victorian age and ends in Socialist England. Its scene shifts from pastoral village to Brighton, to Bohemian London, to the incredible squalor of a hut on an airfield.

It drives through all social levels, and its characters include rogues, scoundrels, prostitutes, and shopgirls; professional, literary, and academic types; industrialists great and small, politicians high and low, the gentry, the nobility. The book is as much the history of her times as it is of Tabitha herself, and we should judge it, perhaps, as we judge Defoe's books, as social revelation in a fictional guise, rather than as the finest novelistic art.

This is not at all to say that a good deal of "art" has not gone into Mr. Cary's racy narrative. Told in the present tense, the story impresses one from the outset with its tremendous pace. Before we have turned many more than a dozen pages, Tabitha has come into the world, has grown to young womanhood, has been "ruined" and then abandoned by a bounder, Dick Bonser.

In these few pages, too, her "destiny" has been fixed: it is Dick Bonser. And Dick Bonser, like Moll Flanders' Lancashire husband, appears and reappears throughout her long life, until at last he marries her. His appearance, in fact, gives the material some of that kind of progressive unity that is ordinarily the function of the plot.

Plot this novel does not have, but between Dick's appearances, many disjointed events occur in Tabitha's external life. She bears Bonser's child after she has become the mistress of a wealthy but foolish patron of the arts, and her salon grows famous as the center of discussion in the periods of "the decadence.". . .

Mr. Cary creates personalities rather than characters: with the exception of Tabitha herself, these are all clear and sharp, highly individuated and static. Like many of Dickens' persons, they seem the slaves of their own eccentricity, creatures driven and mauled not by circumstance or chosen purpose but by a distorted, compulsive energy. Tabitha is a different kind of creation—not clear, even vague. One cannot be certain whether this is a failure in Mr. Cary or an attempt to make of her a larger creation than the others—to make of her, in fact, the embodiment of the life force, which being everywhere, is likewise vague.

She is a kind of mindless being, true to her sensual destiny without ever quite choosing it, and seeming to assert that the one thing greater than either the fear or the joy, the suffering or the pleasure of life, is life itself. Thus she moves almost blindly through scenes that alternate between nearly insane cruelty and a crazy mirthfulness, and to both, as indeed to all experiences, she says, like Joyce's Molly Bloom, only "Yes."

The lesson would seem to be that here is a hundred years of uneven history, and that, trusting to our instincts, we may certainly expect to endure a hundred more. Such a lesson does not suggest a great or even a thoughtful novel, in Mr. Leavis' sense. *A Fearful Joy* is pure roast beef, served with Worcestershire sauce.

> Mark Schorer, "'Moll Flanders' Set the Pattern,"
> in The New York Times Book Review, October 8,
> 1950, p. 1.

RUTH G. VAN HORN (essay date 1952)

[*In the following excerpt, Van Horn considers the recurring themes of freedom and imagination in Cary's novels.*]

In an interview with Harvey Breit during Cary's visit to America in 1951, Arthur Joyce Lunel Cary, the English author, (now residing in Oxford, England), explained that he was able to work on several novels at one time because "all my ideas are part of the same system."

In search of this system, the reader of Joyce Cary's twelve novels, two non-fiction books, two books of narrative poetry, and various articles about writing itself, soon discovers that Cary's themes invariably revolve around two ideas, freedom and imagination. What is more, Cary has created a consistent philosophy on these subjects. It is a philosophy which can hardly be called simple and which is at times tragic in its import; yet it can serve as a strong and guiding light in these troubled times. (p. 19)

In the earlier novels, the Nigerian novels, Cary's canvases are too large, too full of people with too little emphasis and too much movement. One is disconcerted as one may be by a Breughel or Avercamp, until one finds that there is actually synchronization, in the case of Cary a synchronization which comes from his ideas on freedom and the imagination. In the later novels, particularly in the trilogy, Cary has found the form he needs and with it an even maturer expression of his philosophy. In all of Cary's novels, his opinions on imagination are inextricably woven into his opinions on freedom and the time-spirit, and in all we find his main thesis: the imaginative person lives with gusto and makes certain choices which are more than likely to bring him or her to a tragic end, because all freedom is only illusion and man must live in his environment, which is not only a personal environment but also the political, economic, social, religious, and aesthetic environment of the particular age in which he lives. In other words, the climate of opinion is a partial determiner of personal des-

tiny. Yet Cary is not a naturalist, for his individual does have freedom—in his imagination and in his privilege of choice.

In every one of the Nigerian novels, Cary is exposing the lack of imagination in British officials and missionaries, their lack of understanding of the need of proper education, and their callousness in denying the Nigerian freedom. In the later novels, Cary is dealing with the time-spirit and accounting for change. He says times change because man becomes bored with the old and his imagination begins creating new customs and practices. *Bored* is a favorite word with Cary. Many of his characters are motivated by their dread of boredom and their love of excitement. Their craving for excitement and their acting on the illusion of free will often bring tragedy, as in the case of Mister Johnson and Charley Brown.

Cary's thesis revolves on character; and his characters, however individualized, fall into two categories; the imaginative and the unimaginative. Like Shakespeare's, Cary's action develops from character. As Austin Warren says, "In art, seeming is even more important than being." And in Cary's novels, we see his men and women the way they seem to themselves and to each other. (pp. 21-2)

First, let us consider the characters and their imagination. In the novels, conversation does much to disclose character. Cary says of Cottee, one of the most imaginative of the men in *An American Visitor*, he "carried the furniture of two or three selves . . . but at present he was only conversation." (p. 22)

Just as Cary's affections center on his imaginative characters, so his contempt for the unimaginative, the reactionary, the narrowly conventional is shown in all the novels. As an example, in *The African Witch* even the conventional Rackham

> knew perfectly well that Aladai [the Negro] was worth six Honeywoods because Honeywood was a robot, a set of reactions, a creature ruled entirely by prejudice and a mass of contradictory impulses and inhibitions, which he called opinions and thought of as his character. . . . His brain did not seek to judge and know. . . . His will was the servant of nature, the crocodile in the swamp. He had no freedom. He was not a living soul, but a tumor. . . .

Second, let us consider the religious imagination, of which *Aissa Saved* is perhaps the most completely unalloyed demonstration; though this type of imagination is also preeminent in *The African Witch* and in *To Be a Pilgrim*. (pp. 23-4)

Louis Aladai, an Oxford educated Black Prince, is the hero of [*The African Witch*]; and Judy Coote, a lame Englishwoman, is the heroine. Both end tragically, as does Akande Tom, the handsome and not too intelligent lover of Aladai's sister Lisbet, who is a priestess. Tom is the precursor of Mr. Johnson, though his imagination is smaller, less poetic. Both Aladai and Tom, as well as Mr. Johnson, love to deck themselves out in white men's clothes. Cary writes, "No one can feel that happiness who has not been in Tom's position; a naked savage . . . only the most enterprising, like Tom—men of ambition and ideals—attempt to go over the gap." In other words, all progress is made first by the imagination. (p. 24)

Third, let us consider man's freedom and political action as they are affected by the imagination. *Castle Corner* and *A House of Children* present a different picture of Ireland than an American generally gains from James Joyce, Sean O'Casey, or the younger Frank O'Conner and Sean O'Faolain. *Castle Corner* opens with an eviction in Annish in the year 1890, a year before Parnell's death. It is important to note that Cary has been interested in the three most important questions confronting England at the turn of the century: the Irish question, imperial expansion, and economic decline. There is a change in the temper of Cary's works with his fifth novel, for he becomes absorbed in the philosophy of change, of the time-spirit. And his characters increasingly represent those who adjust to change, those who cannot change, and those who forward change. *Castle Corner* contains some of Cary's most important ideas. The accent is on freedom. (pp. 25-6)

Fourth, let us consider a summation of Cary's philosophy on freedom and imagination as they motivate men. *A House of Children* is the most beautiful of all Cary's books. From the first page to the last, it breathes with imagination of the rarest kind.

But with the trilogy, Cary's treatment of freedom and the imagination becomes at once more philosophical, more artistic, and more mature. It is in these three novels that Cary has perfected his technique of point of view. For these three novels alone, Joyce Cary could be called great.

Sara Monday writes the first of the trilogy, *Herself Surprised*. She is a lusty soul who has a style of expression all her own, a gift for quoting country adages and ending her sentences with an afterthought which expresses her nature; for instance, "Mr. W. loved the old ways, as I did. When the parlor maid came in, he pretended to have come about the dinner like a gentleman, dressed and bathed, with candles."

Wilcher, who continues the story in *To Be a Pilgrim*, escapes the day's problems by going back in time. The entire novel—which opens with the words: "People boast of their liberties nowadays, but it seems to me we have multiplied only our rulers"—becomes a work of Wilcher's imagination, for he reconstructs the past. The novel is a marvel of artistry, for Cary has managed to blend his theme into the novel's architecture, placing two ages in juxtaposition. His treatment is similar to Faulkner's. The past is always present. (pp. 26-7)

Gulley Jimson, the third writer in the trilogy who speaks so eloquently from *The Horse's Mouth*, uses a language far different from that of Wilcher, though both tongues are English and speak with Cary's own imaginative power.

Like Chekhov's plays, *The Horse's Mouth* begins with arrival and ends with departure. Gulley returns, after a month's sojourn in prison, to the leaking boat house where he had left his mural *The Fall*, and departs in the ambulance, presumably to heaven, for he had been painting the *Creation* on the condemned wall of an old chapel and, during his fall, he had seen angels. Seldom does one find such symbolism as this in contemporary literature. (p. 27)

The idea that Cary's novels follow the tradition of Defoe and Fielding, I should like to discredit. *Herself Surprised* or *A Fearful Joy* may be a second *Moll Flanders*, but Sara's and Tabitha's worlds are only one province of Cary's larger universe. . . . I feel that *The Moonlight* is the least imaginative book that Cary has published. In it Cary is war-weary. Yet the novel has style. And I hasten to add that despite his weariness and despair at the materialism of our post-war decade, despite his realization of the complexities which confront mankind today, Cary has kept his consistent, guiding philosophy.

Though I grant, with Mark Schorer, that we should judge *A Fearful Joy* "perhaps as we judge Defoe's books, as social revelation in a fictional guise, rather than as the finest novelistic art" [see excerpt above], I claim that Cary's novels are not

only "socially extensive" but also "morally intensive." Whether Cary belongs to what F. R. Leavis calls the "great tradition," I think hardly matters. Surely Cary does not stem from Jane Austen or Joseph Conrad, though there is something of *Heart of Darkness* in the Nigerian novels, and Cary told Breit that "the Russians and Conrad had great influence on me." Harrison Smith says, "Dickens himself could not have pulled *Mr. Johnson* out of the African bush." *To Be a Pilgrim* is not too wide a step from *Adam Bede* and Dinah Morris. Without question, Cary has that "free aesthetic life," the absence of which Henry James said was the weakest side of George Eliot's nature. And Cary's range is far greater than that of George Eliot or of his contemporary E. M. Forster, who is so well known in America. (pp. 29-30)

> *Ruth G. Van Horn, "Freedom and Imagination in the Novels of Joyce Cary," in* The Midwest Journal, *Vol. V, No. 1, Winter, 1952-53, pp. 19-30.*

WALTER ALLEN   (essay date 1953)

[*Allen is an English novelist of working-class life and a popular historian and critic of the novel form. In the following excerpt from his* Joyce Cary, *he considers various aspects of Cary's novelistic art.*]

In a famous passage in the *Biographia Literaria*, Coleridge isolates two opposed modes of the creative activity in their purest and most comprehensive expression. "While Shakespeare," he says, "darts himself forth, and passes into all forms of character and passion, the one Proteus of the fire and flood, Milton attracts all forms and things to himself, into unity of his own ideal. All things and modes of action shape themselves anew in the being of Milton; while Shakespeare becomes all things, yet for ever remaining himself." Coleridge is not making a value-judgement; he is contrasting the objective imagination with the subjective, we might say the extravert as artist with the introvert.

Few poets and novelists are so completely of their type as Shakespeare and Milton; between the two extremes are infinite gradations. Yet if one looks at English fiction during the past thirty years in the light of Coleridge's distinction, it is apparent that it has been predominantly Miltonic, subjective, introvert; so much so that the Shakespearian, objective, extraverted writer stands out with the novelty of the exceptional. He appears old-fashioned, or at least out of step with his time. The neat generalizations we evolve to sum up contemporary writing do not seem to apply to him. And this, perhaps, is the first thing that strikes us when we contemplate the novelist Joyce Cary against the background of his contemporaries. We are immediately aware of his *difference*, and the first difference is that pre-eminently he is "the one Proteus" of the English novel today. Like the poet as seen by Keats, he appears to have "no identity—he is continually in for and filling some other Body." So in turn, it seems without the slightest difficulty and with the greatest air of conviction, he becomes an African Negro warrior, an African native clerk from the mission school, an Irish landowner, an evacuee Cockney delinquent boy, a middle-aged domestic servant in prison for theft, a crotchety old lawyer, a painter of genius, the wife of a Radical politician. He is, to put it at the lowest, a superb impersonator, a truly protean actor. This in itself is much; but what gives him a value beyond this is the fact that his novels, taken together, are the expression of a view of life interesting and important in its own right, a view of life so considered and coherent as to be a whole system of belief. His novels are self-contained entities; Cary is as much "outside" his work as Flaubert was; so his system of belief is never explicitly stated in his novels, but it can be derived from them, and it is the sub-stratum of their being. (pp. 5-6)

Artistic development in the usual sense is absent from Cary's novels. One reason for this comes from his method of work. "I do not," he has said, "write one novel at a time. The process is more like collecting. . . . I have a great number of . . . manuscripts in every stage of development." Yet a general movement may be traced through his work, a movement from the treatment of the comparatively simple theme to that of the much more complex; and in retrospect, his novels seem to fall into four main groups, which may be loosely characterized as the African novels, *Aissa Saved, An American Visitor, The African Witch,* and *Mister Johnson*; the novels of childhood, *Charley Is My Darling* and *A House of Children*; the novels *Herself Surprised, To Be a Pilgrim,* and *The Horse's Mouth,* which relate the history of their time through the individual stories of three characters whose lives to some extent are intertwined; and the novels written since those, *The Moonlight, A Fearful Joy,* and *Prisoner of Grace,* in which Cary appears again as the historian of the past seventy years of English life as seen through significant characters. The classification is admittedly very rough, and the list omits *Castle Corner,* which was published during what one thinks of as Cary's African period and which seems to me, despite the extraordinary vividness, through a huge gallery of characters, of its description of Anglo-Irish life and the rise of colonial imperialism in the eighteen-nineties, to be a brilliant failure, an early attempt at the novel of contemporary or near-contemporary history he was to write so successfully a few years later.

All these novels, for all their great variety of scenes, actions, and characters, are of a piece; only Cary could have written them. Each is a metaphorical statement, a statement expressed through images of human beings in action, of his underlying beliefs about the nature of man and the universe, of his philosophy. (pp. 7-8)

The characters of every novelist or dramatist, no matter how protean his imagination, bear a family resemblance to one another. This is true even of Shakespeare's. Cary's too are plainly products of the same man's imagination. Black or white, rich or poor, male or female, they have certain outstanding qualities in common. . . . [All] the characters that seem typical of Cary are in the grip of what can only be called the creative imagination. Wilcher is in some ways an exception, but he recognizes its power in others, as when he says of his sister Lucy and her husband, Brown, the hellfire-and-damnation evangelist from the working class: "They were both people of power; life ran in them with a primitive force and innocence. They were close to its springs as children are close, so that its experiences, its loves, its wonders, its furies, its mysterious altruism, came to them as children, like mysteries, and gave them neither peace nor time to fall into sloth or decadence."

The creative imagination: Cary is its novelist and its celebrant. His characters are impelled by fantasies personal in the deepest sense, unique to each one of them, which must be translated into action. Life about them is, as it were, so much raw material that must be shaped according to their fantasies, which are never seen as fantasies because they are so fundamental to the characters who are moved by them. And the shaping fantasy, creative imagination, is something belonging to man by virtue of his being man. . . . Inevitably, since each man is unique and his shaping fantasy unique, his fantasies clash with those of

his fellows and, often, with the established order of society, the generally accepted scheme of things. For the individual the consequences may be tragic; equally, from the standpoint of society, they may be comic: in Cary's novels the comic and the tragic are different sides of the one coin.

An important part of Cary's main theme is the creative imagination of the individual in action in conflict with those of others or with authority. To begin with, in his African novels, he dramatized this conflict as the conflict between races and colours, between modes of being alien to each side and more or less incomprehensible to it. We are shown in these novels primitive peoples confronted with a new and almost wholly unintelligible civilization, taking what they want from the white man's religion and way of life and making of it a new thing satisfying to them but quite baffling to the white administrators and missionaries. One thinks especially of the mission scenes in these novels: the native who has "got" Christianity does not become as a result any more like his white Christian mentors; indeed, his interpretation of Christianity may appear to them as a blasphemous parody. But the "Christianized" native is in conflict not only with his saddened white teachers but also with his fellows who are still pagan and with those who are Moslem. The African world described, then, is one in which everyone is at cross-purposes with everyone else. Inevitably, the tragic and the comic are inextricably mingled.

As renderings and interpretations of primitive psychology, these novels are among the best we have in English, and an index of Cary's success in them is the fact that the white characters are revealed as no less essentially strange than the black: Cary enters the minds of both with an impartial gusto and sympathy, as E. M. Forster, for example, in *A Passage to India,* does not enter the minds of his English characters. (pp. 9-11)

As a novelist, Cary is generally spoken of as being much more traditional than most of the major novelists of our time. This does not mean that he practises his art precisely as the eighteenth-century novelists or the Victorians did theirs. Inasmuch as he renders human beings as unique individuals caught in their own fantasies, and often at the extremes of individuality, as Jimson is in *The Horse's Mouth,* it is understandable that he should draw characters in the minute particulars of eccentricity such as we find in Dickens. Again, in the furious pace of his comedy, in his later novels especially, as in his high spirits, he has obvious kinship with Smollett. Then, the first-person narration of *Herself Surprised,* and the overtones of the device, hark back to Defoe's *Moll Flanders.* Yet *The Horse's Mouth* could scarcely have been written by someone who had not absorbed into his own artistic being the "laboratory" work of James Joyce; and if there are affinities with Defoe, Smollett, and Dickens, those with D. H. Lawrence are hardly less plain.

Indeed, one of Cary's most considerable achievements is his success in grafting on to the trunk of our traditional fiction, with its stress on story, action, and broadly conceived character, technical devices first used in the experimental novels of this century, by Joyce, Lawrence, and Virginia Woolf particularly in their various ways. In classic English fiction for the most part—there are obvious exceptions, Richardson and Sterne the most conspicuous—the action of the novel is as it were completed before the reader picks up the book and reads. The action lies in the past, and the novelist's role is that of reporter of events already over; and as he reports his closed sequence of events he feels himself free to comment as he wishes on the action, to generalize and moralize on it, even to advise the reader which characters to admire, which to deplore. The reader is therefore at a distance from the characters of classic fiction: the author is in between. With Joyce and Virginia Woolf, and in a different way with Lawrence, this is not so; their aim was precisely to break down the old barriers between reader and character. The methods differ with each writer, but always the reader is taken right inside the minds of the characters. . . . These novelists were intent on rendering the moment of consciousness in itself; in their different ways they give us close-ups of consciousness; and as we read them we find ourself for much of the time—occasionally the author has to provide us with the equivalents of stage-directions—in what may be called a continuous present.

We experience much the same thing when we read Cary, at any rate after his early novels: while reading, we are at the cutting-edge of the present. Cary is incomparable among living novelists at pinning down the sense of life at the actual moment of being lived. He succeeds in capturing this even in his first-person novels, which, as fictitious autobiography, must be retrospective. (pp. 12-14)

Cary has another way of achieving the sense of the creative moment itself with the almost simultaneous generalization upon it: the use of first-person narration. It is here that his ability to feel himself into character, so that he becomes the character telling the story, is seen at its fullest. He has used first-person narration in the related novels *Herself Surprised, To be a Pilgrim,* and *The Horse's Mouth,* and in his most recent work, *Prisoner of Grace. Herself Surprised* is the first novel, as Cary has said,

> of a trilogy which was designed to show three characters, not only in themselves but as seen by each other. The object was to get a three-dimensional depth and force of character. One character was to speak in each book and describe the other two as seen by that person. Sara, the woman in a woman's world, was to see Wilcher and Jimson in that world, in relation to her own life and her own fortunes. She was to recall their history and the history of the times, as part of her own history. In practice this scheme, for technical reasons, did not come off.

The result was not a trilogy in the sense of *The Forsyte Saga* or Ford Madox Ford's Tietjens books, but rather three novels the stories of which touch at certain points, the link between them all being the character of Sara Munday, the narrator of *Herself Surprised.* The three novels, then, compose a group rather than a sequence.

They are probably Cary's finest work to date. It is, to say the least, a performance of extraordinary virtuosity that in successive novels he should have assumed so completely such diverse personalities as Sara Munday, Mr. Wilcher, and Gulley Jimson. (pp. 19-20)

I value first in Cary the emphatic power of his genius, his protean nature which enabled him, in his African novels, for example, most vividly to body forth the clash not so much of colour but the modes of being underneath the difference of colours. Then, accompanying the empathic imagination, is his exuberance of creation, not a common quality in the English novel to-day, which seems to reproduce, no less, the "daedal dance" of life itself. This exuberance cannot be separated from the comprehensiveness of his vision, which has enabled him to bring into his fiction a larger area of English life than any other living writer.

But fundamental to everything else is the nature of his vision. Cary has been described by a wit as the Protestant answer to Graham Greene: it would be as true to say that he is the English retort to the Existentialist writers, whether Christian or atheist; though it arises from sources very different from theirs, his view of life in its implications is just as Existential. But it is a very English Existentialism, and if, as I think is true, England and the English cannot be understood except by reference to the working of the Protestant, Nonconformist spirit, then a reading of Cary, of all living novelists, is essential to the understanding of the English. His great value for us now is that he has used all the resources of his art and talent to reinterpret in fiction an enduring tradition in our life and feeling, one without which England and the English would be very different from what they are. (p. 30)

> *Walter Allen, in his* Joyce Cary, *The British Council, 1953, 32 p.*

SAUL BELLOW   (essay date 1954)

[*Recipient of the Nobel Prize in literature in 1976, Bellow is one of the most prominent figures in contemporary American fiction. He is noted for upholding the traditional moral values of humanism and literary conventions of Realism, thus opposing the trend toward a modern literature that is nihilistic in temperament and experimental by conscious design. In the following excerpt, Bellow reviews* Except the Lord, *finding it too sketchy and episodic, and, in its assumption of the form of a personal record, less successful than Cary's comedic novels* Mister Johnson *and* The Horse's Mouth.]

It is always a pleasure to read a novel by Joyce Cary, though never twice a pleasure of the same degree. He is one of the most dexterous novelists now writing, with an enviable command of styles and a truly original point of view. You never can predict his next turn; he may decide to adapt to his peculiar need the voice of Moll Flanders or the voice of Matt Bramble or, as in the present instance, the tone of a nineteenth century memoir. This is a legitimate and commendable practice. There is no need for every writer to keep up the pretence that the art of the novel begins with him and that his originality is total, pure and godlike. Mr. Cary has his own sort of originality. Moreover, he is witty and he knows the world. A certain highminded desire for theory, perhaps of Puritan origin—that it is our duty to devote our minds to the study of ideas that will develop our abilities and benefit our lives, has had a wicked influence on the reading and writing of novels.

Luckily, Mr. Cary has almost entirely escaped this influence. He knows that what we require first of all is to be charmed by the novel, to be intrigued, to have our passions attached to the story. To be able to work his spell, a novelist must *know* something. Mr. Cary knows. He knows Africans, he knows colonial officials, he knows painters and their models. A novel cannot matter to us if it fails to inform us about the elementary circumstances of the lives of its characters. (p. 20)

Modern British comedy, whether that of Evelyn Waugh in the novel or of Alec Guiness in the films, tends to be satiric and sadistic. It is filled with violence and death, murder and corpses; its humor comes from the mixture of finesse, manners, niceness and hatred. It is nostalgic, also, and while it pokes fun at the Edwardian fathers it expresses a passionate envy of their stable dignity. Mr. Cary's comedy, in books like *The Horse's Mouth* and *Herself Surprised,* is not of this fashionable kind but is more tranquil and indulgent; it is far less social and class-conscious and it is devoid of snobbery. Liberal, humanistic, it accepts the contemporary, it defends the possibilities of the man of the present, denies that it is so very bad to be what we are or that we are born to be condemned with the times. It asserts that there are powerful and original natures to be found still, that genius exists, that striving is not necessarily monomania, happiness not extinct, hope not unjustified. "The marvel is that millions deny all hope and boast themselves wise," Mr. Cary's Nimmo earnestly says in *Except the Lord.*

There is no comedy at all in [*Except the Lord*], I am sorry to report. Of course, there is no reason why a novelist should be required to write always in his best vein. On the contrary, he should be encouraged to diversify his talents and deny himself no attitude or point of view, serious or comic. But this book, the story of the childhood and early manhood of the son of an evangelical West Country stableman, is not one of his best. Neither wide nor deep enough, it does not invite the reader's imagination to displace its full weight. No notable character emerges; the episodes are too brief. The book takes the form of the personal record of a national leader, and its style is more appropriate to a memoir than to a novel. I feel that Mr. Cary has accepted the convention too completely for the sake of its color; he ought not to have been so faithful to it. (pp. 20-1)

Nevertheless I read this book with admiration for Mr. Cary's power to create fictional situations out of a few hints, bits of knowledge and old memories.

Very good novels always give a sense of the pleasant harassment of the novelist. He has more information than the novel can accommodate, we are made to feel. If he omits the details of X's Saturday night it is not because he doesn't know what happened—he most certainly does—but because he has space in his holds for only the most important items of cargo. *Except the Lord* does not go down to the Plimsoll-marks, but it sails pretty well, all things considered. It is not, like *Mr. Johnson* or *The Horse's Mouth,* one of Mr. Cary's great successes. He is far better at comedies than at histories, though always admirable. (p. 21)

Saul Bellow, "A Personal Record," in The New Republic, Vol. 130, No. 8, February 22, 1954, pp. 20-1.

BARBARA HARDY   (essay date 1954)

[*Hardy is an English editor and critic who has explored narrative form in the studies* The Appropriate Form: An Essay on the Novel *(1964) and* Tellers and Listeners: The Narrative Imagination *(1975), among others. In the following excerpt, she examines narrative form and technique in Cary's novels.*]

It is no coincidence that two novelists of this century whose popularity may be called both highbrow and middlebrow—Graham Greene and Joyce Cary—have attempted the same kind of experiment. They have both made a transformation of a popular genre, a transformation which their admirers may greet as making the best of two worlds and their detractors as a fall between two stools. Graham Greene's adoption of the thriller is at once more obvious and more self-conscious than Joyce Cary's adoption of the less lively but no less popular form of the pseudo-saga, the chronicle of family life. One does not have to exaggerate Cary's talent in order to recognize the order he has restored to a shapeless literary tradition.

The popularity of the endless shapeless serials of Galsworthy, Walpole, and, to go a little lower, Mazo de la Roche, is as mysterious as it is certain. The formula is simple and unvaried: birth, love and death, in all their less interesting aspects. Mar-

riages are made, babies born, there is some allowed variety in the way of litigation, adultery and house-building, the babies grow up, marry, build, beget and die. The saga itself does not die, and it is its immortality, I suppose, which gives it the attraction of a specious realism. The kind of imagination which feels the need to pursue Beatrice and Benedick beyond the formal inevitability of their curtain has the repeated reassurance of a curtain which rises again and again. The kind of life which needs a substitute or a compensation for living has the satisfaction of a continued accompaniment almost as long as life itself. And to these extra-aesthetic pleasures is added the esoteric delight of recognizing familiar faces. The minor characters of one novel reappear as the heroes and heroines of another, not independently and reticently as in Zola, but often accompanied by baffling references to their earlier incarnations or, worse, by ill-disguised exposition of the past. What is a minor pleasure in reading Balzac, Zola, and Thackeray where the recurring characters are an essential part of a creation of a world with the realism of flux and diversity, becomes a major pleasure or a major distraction in Trollope and Galsworthy and all the less distinguished others who have helped to demonstrate the truth that where there is no form there is indeed no reason why there should ever be an end. This is the death of naturalism, the disappearance of the curtain, aesthetic damnation.

Galsworthy, of course, is making an attempt to do something as serious as Balzac or Zola, but his portrait of a social organism, growing, changing, inheriting, decaying, enduring, fails where Zola's succeeds because it puts an impossible weight on the external life. The attempt to shift the emphasis from the individual to the group seems to have been most successful where it has given a balanced prominence to individual sensibility and the distanced view of social process. The mere act of repetition from novel to novel is far less convincing as it is forced to bear the thematic burden in Galsworthy than the much less pretentious portrayal of family life in Ivy Compton-Burnett where a single novel can convince us of the life of a group: of the moral insulation of a family which can absorb the individual evil within itself. The serial of family life tries to substitute accumulation for symbolism and the game is hardly worth the candle.

The importance of length in the novel is certainly not a thing to be ignored, and the serial-sagas are attempts to compensate for the lack of distance which is so often the fault of the compression of many generations into one story. Even Virginia Woolf's *The Years* suffers from jerkiness and over-distancing and in Rose Macaulay's *Told By An Idiot* or Margery Allingham's *Dance of The Years* there is the maddening sketchiness of the bird's eye view without Virginia Woolf's compensating flashes of perception. The compressed saga depends on a reversal of the telescope. We never see enough of the characters to be sufficiently moved or involved. The slowly unrolled saga gives us time to be involved but, except for rare cases, has no form and therefore no significance. These two flaws of over-distancing and shapelessness are not inherent in the attempt to show the process of history or the social organism. *War and Peace* and *Middlemarch,* in their different ways, combine the microscopic view of the human heart with the larger view of a community or a country. *Ulysses* moves from the flux of the mind to the flux of the Dublin crowd; the individual sensation is laid bare and then merged in the anonymity of the city. But Joyce Cary, a very minor talent to be mentioned in the same breath as these three, treats the historical process in a way which is worth some mention.

Cary, like Galsworthy, sets out to show the flow of a family's life, but he has the initial advantage of a more assertive theme. In his most successful novels he has his eye not on the family but on the age. The conflicts, losses and gains of social change are criticized as they are chronicled, and the criticism is made directly through character and obliquely through form. The age is represented by a generation, the generation by two or more characters. Cary's representative characters are usually repeated and reinforced like Marlowe's and Jonson's humours, but they represent tendencies and not, like Zola's, varying social experience. As units of a social survey these repeated characters present too limited a vitality to make a carrying social symbol, but if we recognize the validity of an expression of opinion which does not pretend to be a complete document they make their point.

Cary's power of spawning characters has often been praised, rather oddly, for there is not a great deal of variety in his persons, either within single novels or in his work considered as a whole. One kind of sensibility is made to work overtime in Cary's novels and this is presented in terms of his visual preoccupation which enables him to show a crowd without losing the sense of the single lives which make up crowds. In some of his books, *Castle Corner* or *A Fearful Joy* for instance, vitality is not presented as a painter's joy of the eye but as a child's or a woman's joy in the living moment, but the evidence and method which establish the vitality is almost always visual. In these novels the sensibility gives life to a not greatly varied world—the lack of variety is perhaps unimportant, and I should not mention it if it had not been praised as the opposite of what it is. It is the dominant sensibility which gives order and simplicity to the novel, though in *Aissa Saved* and *An African Witch* it is not enough to triumph over a crowded and episodic form. But at his best—in *To Be A Pilgrim, The Horse's Mouth,* and *The Moonlight* there is not merely a painter's vision but the power of organizing the shifting life of pictures and conversations into a formal order which is both aesthetically pleasing and morally significant.

To Be A Pilgrim and *The Moonlight* share a theme and a pattern. In each book there is the conflict of human relations which have some socially representative force, and in each the action is carried on in counterpoint. Cary is showing the flow of generations not consecutively but contemporaneously, and thereby gains in compression, shape and thematic clarity. This formal transformation of the traditional saga is brought about by the use of another literary tradition, and not by experiment. Cary takes the flashback, the most overworked cliché in the film and the novel, and uses it realistically and functionally.

It is true that conventions do not need the excuse of realism, but the flashback is a necessity rather than a convention in Cary. It is the only way of making a certain statement. Wilcher in *To Be A Pilgrim,* and Ella, in *The Moonlight,* must be presented in flashback. Their life is the life they have lived rather than the life they are living. They participate in the past and look on in the present. The pattern of the novel is the intersection and interruption of past and present, the theme a fight between past and present. Here is significant form in Abercrombie's sense, the significance of the pattern being "the significance it gives to the matter it forms" and if it is here accompanied by too many explicit references to make it comparable in any fundamental sense with the suggestive accumulation of the great contrapuntal actions of *Anna Karenina* and *Middlemarch* there is the same kind of assertive pattern left in the memory. All four novels have individual form, order

as rigid and simple as that of a triangle, and as individual as a human face. It seems that novels need not have this formal assertion—it is an extra, though not a superfluous, pleasure of fiction.

Cary's world in these novels is small, and his use of form fairly simple. He is an excellent example of a writer as interested in form as the painter or musician, and it may very well be the influence of his painting which makes this conspicuous pattern-making. He seems to look on single characters and events with that double vision with which Jimson looks at his Adam and Eve. They are expressions of humanity: Eve leans away from Adam to fend off his first pass. They are also units in a pattern: Eve leans back because the composition demands it.

The counterpoint in *To Be A Pilgrim* and *The Moonlight* is obviously a source of psychological realism. It gives the characters that three-dimensional solidity which Cary hoped to create in the trilogy—*Herself Surprised, To Be A Pilgrim* and *The Horse's Mouth*—by showing the characters as they see themselves and as they see each other, as he explains in the prefatory essay to *Herself Surprised.* In practice, as he admits, this did not come off. Cary thinks that his plan may have failed because it imposed on Sara a consciousness of art and history which would have diluted her character, a consciousness which might be reconcilable with her character in reality but not in the limited world of the novel. But there is, I think, another reason for this failure.

When a major character in one action becomes a minor character in another he becomes an entirely different character. He may retain the given "characteristics" but he changes his relation to the reader. Such a shift can perhaps be workable only within one novel, as it is in *Middlemarch,* where it has many critical functions, or within one play, as in Shakespeare's romantic comedies where both unity and parody are achieved by the use of the major characters in the romance as the minor characters in the comedy, and *vice versa.* Where the change takes place between books it is more difficult for the reader to retain the relationship with the central character and this relationship is particularly intimate in Cary because of his use of first-person soliloquy and the more immediate stream of consciousness. C. P. Snow maintains his constant narrator as his actions shift but even so I doubt whether the reader can read more than one novel at a time. Both Cary and Snow seem to expect there to be more of a carry-over from one novel to the next than the formal completion of a good novel—not to mention lapse of time and shortage of memory—can permit. It may be that the novelist gains from a sustained but shifting exploration of a single world but the reader, for practical aesthetic purposes, has to read one book at a time.

The solidity which Cary hoped to achieve by the relation between the three novels of his trilogy has been achieved in a different way by the internal formal relations of the novels. The critical counterpoint, like Huxley's jugglings with time in *Eyeless in Gaza,* gives us ironical portraiture. Personality is seen as growth and as constancy. The doddering old man who misbehaves in parks was once an uncertain child, once an excited innocent wondering how one set about getting a mistress. And the reader sees them all at the same time. Both in Wilcher and in Ella continuity is given more emphasis than change. Age is only youth in a different body.

Indeed, age is often younger than youth in Cary's novels. The old man watches Ann, his niece, the old woman watches

Amanda, her illegitimate daughter, and their critical interference with the lives of the young is explained less by their own comments than by the silent commentary of their own interrupting youth. And not only Wilcher and Ella, but Ann and Amanda too are given definition and dimension by the novel's pattern. Their unsatisfactory loves, occupying months where the remembered past in the flashback occupies decades, are seen in ironical contrast with the flux of years. This time-scale has almost a symbolic function for while the new generation drifts and vacillates (desires and acts not, and breeds pestilence) the older generation, presented only at moments of selected crisis, is rushing with gusto through the cycle of birth, copulation and death.

The critical pattern is not merely the contrast between the slow day and the rapid years, between selected excitement and naturalistically displayed triviality. The counterpoint makes the criticism. The presence of the ghosts defines the living. The real action is not the attempt of the aged to force the past on to the young, nor Ann's pathetic imitation of the past, nor Amanda's dispassionate attempt to place herself in situations where circumstance will take the place of desire. Nor is it in their relations with Robert and Harry, two versions of Cary's almost Lawrencian farmer-hero whose lack of cerebral activity contrasts with the heroine's disastrous cerebral excess, and whose gross vigour contrasts, with shifting significance, with the departed grace and grandeur of the past. This is the stuff of the plot but the real action is the oblique criticism of the present by the past. What the present lacks, vitality, passion, grace, the past is shown to possess. Love, seduction, marriage, maternity, all are shown in past and present, the circumstances similar but the actors different. Again Cary provokes the comparison with *Middlemarch* where contrasts and parallels between persons and actions do much of the work of definition, and, more important, of judgment.

Cary is not a George Eliot and he sometimes makes judgment too explicit. Past and present show up each other's light and shade in a moving dance, but since the past is presented as memory it is hard for Cary to avoid explicit comparison. The pattern could say it all but since the past is contributed by Wilcher's memory, and since Wilcher, unlike Sara, is given the intelligence and the experience which can carry the weight of historical consciousness, his direct criticism is constantly supplementing the oblique comments of the juxtaposed actions. This is not true of *The Moonlight* for here there is no fixed *point d'oeil* and the reader does not receive criticism and impression through the sieve of an intelligent mind. And his use of a not particularly intelligent woman instead of an intelligent man has two advantages: there is a closer contrast with the heroine of the present, and there is no character within the novel who is in danger of drawing the reader's conclusions for him.

But in both novels there is yet another method of making the critical point, and this method is an obvious product of Cary's interest in painting. This is his brilliant use of scenic contrast, though once more he sometimes seems to err on the side of explicitness. He can make an almost symbolic use of scenes which are in the same contrapuntal relation as that in which the two actions are presented; as in *To Be A Pilgrim*, where Ann and Robert and the farm-girl carry patched lanterns to the mended boat on the lake which has shrunk to a pond and are faded-out while Wilcher's memory restores the grandeur and glitter of light, bowers, crowds and music which was the past they are trying to imitate. And he can turn to the facile symbolism of the threshing in the Adam room. Such scenes make just the visual point which the camera can make but in the novel it is extremely hard to make them direct, without annotation. It is only fair to say that if Cary's theme were cruder his visual symbols might seem more subtle. For his interpretation of the scenic symbol is often a modification. It is no simple measuring of bad new days by good old ones and he hastens to blur the simple boldness of the visual contrast. Perhaps the old grandeur, thinks Wilcher, was only another kind of make-believe. The water-parties and the crumbling Adam room cannot be left as suggestive scenes. Wilcher is made to accept the present, to accept the thresher's vigour and destruction.

The Horse's Mouth, like *To Be A Pilgrim*, has a similarly articulate mouthpiece, who is at times too explanatory, who puts the unnecessary words in the balloons when the picture has already said it all. It has a similar use of scenic symbol. The painting of Jimson's *Creation* on the chapel wall which is being demolished by order of the local authority sounds stagey when extracted from its context but it is, like the sonata in *The Moonlight* which becomes the expression of romance and passion, a private symbol, having accumulated its significance internally and gradually. Symbol is indeed a word I use with reluctance since Cary's symbols are not literary symbols, not imposed on the characters by the novelist, but are made by the characters out of the stuff of their living and working. The huge picture on the crumbling wall is too literally expressive of the fight of a man and an institution to be called a symbol. The wall and the Moonlight sonata are only symbols in the sense in which a gun is a symbol of death. They are symbols in so far as they are agents. But unlike the gun they have validity and intelligibility only within the novel. They are too particularized to be called symbols.

The crumbling wall-painting is only the sign of Jimson's vitality (he has desire and acts) and of that conflict which is the theme of *The Horse's Mouth*. Like *Mister Johnson*, the best of the African novels, and *Charley Is My Darling*, this book is about creative power and creative lawlessness. The emphasis varies. Mister Johnson is cheat first and poet after, Jimson is painter first and lawbreaker after, and Charley is both juvenile delinquent and infant prodigy. The characteristics are constant though the proportions vary. Johnson, Charley and Jimson all create, all destroy, and all have power, a power which is less the product of genius or courage or lawlessness than of vitality. Vitality was what Ann and Amanda lacked, and if we reduce the themes to the common element, this is it. What interests the novelist's imagination, Cary says in the preface to *Aissa Saved* is whatever makes man tick. His novels are not only dissections of some of the causes of human ticking—love, religion, politics, art—but are revelations of the nature of this ticking. Its intensity he demonstrates by showing us the Anns and Amandas whose vitality is missing.

Mister Johnson and *Charley Is My Darling* are portraits rather than pictures. *The Horse's Mouth* is both. Here Cary shows Jimson's ticking by a formal contrast very like that used in his chronicle novels. Once more the formal arrangement is carried out by an experimental use of someone else's experiment. What the revived cliché of the flashback does for *To Be A Pilgrim* the stream of consciousness or interior monologue does for *The Horse's Mouth*.

One of the excitements of *Ulysses* is the intersection of perception and action. Stephen and Bloom are shown in the normal human state of interrupted consciousness. Eye interrupts mind, ear interrupts eye, memory interrupts experience and friends and strangers force human intercourse and interrupt the private drift of thought and sensation. Most novelists have assumed, as a necessary selective premise, that the life of their characters shall be an unrealistic co-operation of perception of life and participation in life. Cary, following Joyce and Virginia Woolf, accepts and emphasizes the interruption and bittiness of life. Once more he has a double purpose. Jimson's interrupted consciousness creates a personality and a thematic pattern.

Jimson's vitality, his genius and his lawlessness put him in conflict with the law, with institutionalized man, with the Philistines who hate him and the admirers who love him at the wrong period or for the wrong reason. Like Wilcher he is intelligent and perceptive and acts as a sieve which deprives the reader of some of the pleasure of breaking the lumps for himself. Cary's direct method is too direct. But oddly enough it is once more employed with the oblique method. The interior monologue tells but it also shows. The monologue, or visual stream, provides an indirect expression of Cary's recurring theme of conflict, for the extractable plot is counterpointed, not against another plot, as in *To Be A Pilgrim* and *The Horse's Mouth*, but against Jimson's visual preoccupation. Everything which "happens"—Coker's attempt to get him to pay the money he owes her, the return of Sara, the occupation of the millionaire's flat by Jimson and the sculptor, Jimson's flight—all this is superimposed on the visual stream, whether this is Jimson's concern with the picture in hand or his perpetual falling in love with clouds, bits of body, spilt coffee or anything which makes pattern and colour. Everything in the book which is outside this visual preoccupation is made to define it. The story of the deaf girl is translated into form and colour, and things which defy translation point the struggle. Jimson is a character who is struggling against all the other characters, and the human struggle is narrated by the formal conflict between the stream of perception and the life of dialogue and action. It is a book which is a series of significant interruptions of character by character, of monologue by dialogue, of imagery by incident. It does not do to say that Cary is a painter writing novels; it is indeed musical analogy which seems more relevant than any other. It is the shaping of theme and character which states and proves visual sensibility, conflict, energy and change. The organic shaping is the thing which gives to the best of his novels the rare enough aesthetic pleasure of assertive form.

Cary's last novels, *A Fearful Joy,* and *A Prisoner of Grace,* seem to show the dangers of suggesting that he is preoccupied with form. *A Fearful Joy* has a naive enough structure of continuous flow. Past and present are there in two separate blocks since the point is less the life of past in present than the death of the past. *A Prisoner of Grace* has no formal assertion at all. Both novels, like *Herself Surprised,* are studies of the power and vitality of women, a power whose arbitrariness Cary conveys superbly, whose mystery and innocence he perhaps exaggerates. But, like *Charley Is My Darling,* they are not novels which force a pattern of conflict. The themes, more complex than I have suggested since they are also concerned with the innocent maker and spectator of history, demand and get a simple almost lyrical treatment. The only disadvantage of this in Cary is that it draws attention to the sameness of the human ticking he is studying. The causes vary but the vitality and the consciousness do not.

The important thing is the absence of formal assertion, an absence which does not destroy so much as draw attention to a deficiency. It is not a deficiency which concerns me here,

and I do not want to suggest that form is the life of fiction. Some novelists seem to need the pressure of forming a complex pattern. Others do not. Some themes force a pattern, some do not. Cary's form-making is organic in so far as it is necessitated by his theme of historical process. This has an inevitable emphasis of change and conflict and an equally inevitable shift from individual to environment, and it forces a formal correlative, but it is not the powerful thematic assertion of the counterpoint of *Anna Karenina* and *Daniel Deronda* where the shape of the narrative makes a statement which the characters are too blind to make and the novelist too wise. This is not to belittle Cary's achievement, merely to attempt to put it in perspective, and, since analysis seems more important than judgment, to discriminate between two very different uses of form. Perhaps the most significant thing is the recurrence, in great and minor talents, of a double aspiration of narrative, the aspiration towards the free life and flux of reality and the aspiration towards a formal order which has fixity and clarity. (pp. 180-90)

Barbara Hardy, "Form in Joyce Cary's Novels," in Essays in Criticism, *Vol. IV, No. 2, April, 1954, pp. 180-90.*

JOYCE CARY [WITH JOHN BURROW AND ALEX HAMILTON] (interview date 1954)

[*In the following excerpt, Cary discusses aspects of his novel-writing and his personal philosophy.*]

INTERVIEWERS: Have you by any chance been shown a copy of Barbara Hardy's essay on your novels [see essay dated 1954] in the latest number of *Essays in Criticism?*

CARY: On "Form." Yes I saw it. Quite good, I thought.

INTERVIEWERS: Well, setting the matter of form aside for the moment, we were interested in her attempt to relate you to the tradition of the family chronicle. Is it in fact your conscious intention to re-create what she calls the pseudo-saga?

CARY: Did she say that? Must have skipped that bit.

INTERVIEWERS: Well, she didn't say "consciously," but we were interested to know whether this was your intention.

CARY: You mean, did I intend to follow up Galsworthy and Walpole? Oh, no, no, no. Family life, no. Family life just goes on. Toughest thing in the world. But of course it is also the microcosm of a world. You get everything there—birth, life, death, love and jealousy, conflict of wills, of authority and freedom, the new and the old. And I always choose the biggest stage possible for my theme.

INTERVIEWERS: What about the eighteenth-century novelists? Someone vaguely suggested that you recaptured their spirit, or something of that kind.

CARY: "Vaguely" is the word. I don't know who I'm like. I've been called a metaphysical novelist, and if that means I have a fairly clear and comprehensive idea of the world I'm writing about, I suppose that's true.

INTERVIEWERS: You mean an idea about the nature of the world which guides the actions of the characters you are creating?

CARY: Not so much the ideas as their background. I don't care for philosophers in books. They are always bores. A novel should be an experience and convey an emotional truth rather than arguments.

INTERVIEWERS: Background—you said "background."

CARY: The whole set-up—character—of the world as we know it. Roughly, for me, the principal fact of life is the free mind. For good and evil, man is a free creative spirit. This produces the very queer world we live in, a world in continuous creation and therefore continuous change and insecurity. A perpetually new and lively world, but a dangerous one, full of tragedy and injustice. A world in everlasting conflict between the new idea and the old allegiances, new arts and new inventions against the old establishment.

INTERVIEWERS: Miss Hardy complains that the form shows too clearly in your novels.

CARY: Other complain that I don't make the fundamental idea plain enough. This is every writer's dilemma. Your form is your meaning, and your meaning dictates the form. But what you try to convey is reality—the fact plus the feeling, a total complex experience of a real world. If you make your scheme too explicit, the framework shows and the book dies. If you hide it too thoroughly, the book has no meaning and therefore no form. It is a mess.

INTERVIEWERS: How does this problem apply in *The Moonlight*?

CARY: I was dealing there with the contrast between conventional systems in different centuries—systems created by man's imagination to secure their lives and give them what they seek from life.

INTERVIEWERS: Didn't the critics call Rose a tyrant?

CARY: Oh, they were completely wrong about Rose. She was a Victorian accepting the religion and the conventions of her time and sacrificing her own happiness to carry them out. A fine woman. And no more of a tyrant than any parent who tries to guide a child in the right path. That religion, that system, has gone, but it was thoroughly good and efficient in its own time. I mean, it gave people good lives and probably all the happiness that can be achieved for anybody in this world.

INTERVIEWERS: Are the political aspects of your work controlled by the same ideas?

CARY: Religion is organised to satisfy and guide the soul—politics does the same thing for the body. Of course they overlap—this is a very rough description. But the politician is responsible for law, for physical security, and, in a world of tumult, of perpetual conflict, he has the alternatives, roughly again, of persuading people or shooting them. In the democracies, we persuade. And this gives great power to the spellbinder, the artist in words, the preacher, the demagogue, whatever you call him. Rousseau, Marx, Tolstoy, these were great spellbinders—as well as Lacordaire. My Nimmo is a typical spellbinder. Bonser was a spellbinder in business, the man of imagination. He was also a crook, but so are many spellbinders. Poets have started most of the revolutions, especially nationalist revolutions. On the other hand, life would die without poets, and democracy must have its spellbinders.

INTERVIEWERS: Roosevelt?

CARY: Yes, look what he did—and compare him with [Woodrow] Wilson. Wilson was a good man, but he hadn't the genius of the spellbinder—the art of getting at people and moving the crowd.

INTERVIEWERS: Is Nimmo based on Roosevelt?

CARY: No, he belongs to the type of all of them—Juarez, Lloyd George, Bevan, Sankey and Moody, Billy Graham.

INTERVIEWERS: Do you base your characters on people you know?

CARY: Never, you can't. You may get single hints. But real people are too complex and too disorganised for books. They aren't simple enough. Look at all the great heroes and heroines, Tom Jones, Madame Bovary, Anna Karenina, Baron Charlus, Catherine Linton: they are essentially characters from fable, and so they must be to take their place in a formal construction which is to have a meaning. A musician does not write music by trying to fit chords into his whole. The chords arise from the development of his motives.

INTERVIEWERS: In one of your prefaces you said, didn't you, that Jimson's father came from life?

CARY: I met an old man, an artist who had been in the Academy and a success, and was then ruined by the change of taste when the Impressionists created their new symbolic school. But I didn't use him in my book, I don't know anything about his character, only his tragedy. A very common one in this world. (*Suddenly*) The French seem to take me for an Existentialist in Sartre's sense of the word. But I'm not. I am influenced by the solitude of men's minds, but equally by the unity of their fundamental character and feelings, their sympathies which bring them together. I believe that there is such a thing as unselfish love and beauty. I am obliged to believe in God as a person. I don't suppose any church would accept me, but I believe in God and His grace with an absolute confidence. It is by His grace that we know beauty and love, that we have all that makes life worth living in a tough, dangerous, and unjust world. Without that belief I could not make sense of the world and I could not write. Of course, if you say I am an Existentialist in the school of Kierkegaard, that is more reasonable. But Existentialism without a God is nonsense—it atomises a world which is plainly a unity. It produces merely frustration and defeat. How can one explain the existence of personal feelings, love and beauty, in nature, unless a person, God, is there? He's there as much as hydrogen gas. He is a fact of experience. And one must not run away from experience. I don't believe in miracles. I'm not talking here of faith cures—but some breach in the fundamental consistency of the world character, which is absolutely impossible. I mean absolutely. (*With emphasis*) God is a character, a real and consistent being, or He is nothing. If God did a miracle He would deny His own nature and the universe would simply blow up, vanish, become nothing. And we can't even conceive nothingness. The world is a definite character. It *is*, and therefore it is *something*. And it can't be any other thing. Aquinas tells you all the things that God can't do without contradicting himself.

INTERVIEWERS: But about Existentialism.

CARY: Kierkegaard states the uniqueness of the individual and I stand by that.

INTERVIEWERS: That's what you meant, then, when you said that what makes men tick should be the main concern of the novelist? The character's principle of unity?

CARY: And action, their beliefs. You've got to find out what people *believe*, what is pushing them on . . . And of course it's a matter, too, of the simpler emotional drives—like ambition and love. These are the real stuff of the novel, and you can't have any sort of real form unless you've got an ordered attitude towards them.

INTERVIEWERS: But the fundamental beliefs are not always the most apparent, or, it seems to us, the most successful of the achievements in the novel. We were expecting, for instance, a much closer analysis of the religious beliefs of Brown in *To Be a Pilgrim*. But we felt, in fact, that what came across most successfully were the emotional responses of people to people—compelling, for instance, Lucy to follow Brown.

CARY: The details were there once. That is, Brown's arguments were there, and Lucy's response. But Lucy was only one character, one motive in the symphony. And also I was up against the problem of explicit statement. I may have cut too much, but the book is long and packed already. The essence of Lucy was her deep faith. She wasn't the kind of person who can float along from day to day like a piece of newspaper or a banana-skin in the gutter. And in the book, I had her feelings expressed. But I cut them somewhere in the rewriting. I rewrite a great deal and I work over the whole book and cut out anything that does not belong to the emotional development, the texture of feeling. I left too much of the religious argument in *Except the Lord* and people criticise it as too explicit or dull.

INTERVIEWERS: Do you find in those later stages that you're primarily concerned with the more technical side of "form"? With, for example, managing the flashback? And do you think, incidentally, that you owe that particular trick to the films? I believe that you worked on a film in Africa.

CARY: No, I don't really think it has anything to do with films. The flashback in my novels is not just a trick. In, for example, *The Moonlight*, I used it in order to make my theme possible. It was essential to compare two generations. You can't do that without a flashback contrast; the chronological run-through by itself is no good. (pp. 4-8)

INTERVIEWERS: Have you sympathy with those who most uncompromisingly pursue their own free idea whatever the opposition?

CARY: I don't put a premium on aggression. Oh, no, no, no. I'm no life-force man. Critics write about my vitality. What is vitality? As a principle it is a lot of balls. The life force is rubbish, an abstraction, an idea without character. Shaw's tale of life force is either senseless rubbish or he really means Shaw—Shaw as God's mind. The life force doesn't exist. Show me some in a bottle. The life of the world is the nature of God, and God is as real as the trees.

INTERVIEWERS: Which novelists do you think have most influenced you?

CARY: Influenced? Oh, lots. Hundreds. Conrad had a great deal at one point. I've got a novel upstairs I wrote forty years ago in Africa, under his influence. But I read very few novels nowadays. I read memoirs and history. And the classics. I've got them at my fingertips and I can turn up the points I want. I don't read many modern novels, I haven't time, but those I do read are often very good. There is plenty of good work being done, and in Britain the public for good work has enormously increased in my lifetime—especially in the last thirty years. (pp. 9-10)

INTERVIEWERS: Is there only one way to get a thing right? How close is form?

CARY: That's a difficult question. Often you have very little room for manoeuvre. See Proust's letter to Mme. Schiff about Swann, saying he had to make Swann ridiculous. A novelist is often in Proust's jam.

INTERVIEWERS: You are a determinist—you think even novelists are pushed by circumstances?

CARY: Everyone but a lunatic has reason for what he does. Yes, in that sense I am a determinist. But I believe, with Kant, that the mind is self-determined. That is, I believe intensely in the creative freedom of the mind. That is indeed absolutely essential to man's security in a chaotic world of change. He is faced all the time with unique complex problems. To sum them up for action is an act of creative imagination. He fits the different elements together in a coherent whole and invents a rational act to deal with it. He requires to be free, he requires his independence and solitude of mind, he requires his freedom of mind and imagination. Free will is another matter—it is a term, or rather a contradiction in terms, which leads to continual trouble. The will is never free—it is always attached to an object, a purpose. It is simply the engine in the car—it can't steer. It is the mind, the reason, the imagination, that steers.

Of course, anyone can deny the freedom of the mind. He can argue that our ideas are conditioned. But anyone who argues so must not stop there. He must deny all freedom and say that the world is simply an elaborate kind of clock. He must be a behaviourist. There is no alternative, in logic, between behaviourism, mechanism, and the personal God who is the soul of beauty, love, and truth. And if you believe in behaviourism, none of these things has any real existence. They are cogwheels in the clock, and you yourself do not exist as a person. You are a delusion. So take your choice. Either it is personal or it is a delusion—a delusion rather difficult to explain.

INTERVIEWERS: How do you fit poetry into this? I once heard you describe it as "prose cut up into lines." Would you stick to that?

CARY: Did I say that? I must have been annoying someone. No, I wouldn't stick to it.

INTERVIEWERS: Anyway, at what stage of your career did you decide to write novels rather than anything else?

CARY: What stage? Oh, I've been telling stories ever since I was very small. I always tell stories. And I've been writing them from childhood. I told them to other children when I was a child. I told them at school. I told them to my own children and I tell them now to the children of a friend.

INTERVIEWERS: *Aissa Saved* was the first one you published?

CARY: Yes, and that was not until I was forty. I'd written many before, but I was never satisfied with them. They raised political and religious questions I found I could not answer. I have three or four of them up there in the attic, still in manuscript.

INTERVIEWERS: Was this what made you feel that you needed a "new education"?

CARY: At twenty-six I'd knocked about the world a good bit and I thought I knew the answers, but I didn't know. I couldn't finish the novels. The best novel I ever wrote—at least it contained some of my best stuff—there's about a million words of it upstairs, I couldn't finish it. I found that I was faking things all the time, dodging issues and letting my characters dodge them.

INTERVIEWERS: Could you tell us something about your working methods?

CARY: Well—I write the big scenes first, that is, the scenes that carry the meaning of the book, the emotional experience.

The first scene in *Prisoner of Grace* was that at the railway station, when Nimmo stops his wife from running away by purely moral pressure. That is, she became the prisoner of grace. When I have the big scenes sketched I have to devise a plot into which they'll fit. Of course often they don't quite fit. Sometimes I have to throw them out. But they have defined my meaning, given form to the book. Lastly I work over the whole surface.

INTERVIEWERS: When does the process, the book, start?

CARY: Possibly years ago—in a note, a piece of dialogue. Often I don't know the real origin. I had an odd experience lately which gave me a glimpse of the process, something I hadn't suspected. I was going round Manhattan—do you know it?

INTERVIEWERS: Not yet.

CARY: It's an island and I went round on a steamer with an American friend, Elizabeth Lawrence, of Harper's. And I noticed a girl sitting all by herself on the other side of the deck—a girl of about thirty, wearing a shabby skirt. She was enjoying herself. A nice expression, with a wrinkled forehead, a good many wrinkles. I said to my friend, "I could write about that girl—what do you think she is?" Elizabeth said that she might be a schoolteacher taking a holiday, and asked me why I wanted to write about her. I said I didn't really know—I imagined her as sensitive and intelligent, and up against it. Having a hard life but making something of it, too. In such a case I often make a note. But I didn't—and I forgot the whole episode. Then, about three weeks later, in San Francisco, I woke up one night at four—I am not so much a bad sleeper as a short sleeper—I woke up, I say, with a story in my head. I sketched the story at once—it was about an English girl in England, a purely English tale. Next day an appointment fell through and I had a whole day on my hands. I found my notes and wrote the story—that is, the chief scenes and some connecting tissue. Some days later, in a plane—ideal for writing—I began to work it over, clean it up, and I thought, "Why all these wrinkles? That's the third time they come in." And I suddenly realised that my English heroine was the girl on the Manhattan boat. Somehow she had gone down into my subconscious, and came up again with a full-sized story. And I imagine that has happened before. I notice some person because he or she exemplifies some part of my feeling about things. The Manhattan girl was a motive. And she brought up a little piece of counterpoint. But the wrinkles were the first crude impression—a note, but one that counted too much in the final writing.

INTERVIEWERS: A note—

CARY: I was thinking in terms of music. My short stories are written with the same kind of economy—and no one would publish them. Some of them, now being published, are twenty years old. Because each note has to count and it must not be superfluous. A son of mine, a composer, wrote some music for the BBC lately. The orchestra was small, and the Musicians' Union wouldn't let him conduct. He heard one of the players ask the conductor what the stuff was like. The conductor, no doubt intending to warn the player, answered, "It's good, but the trouble is that every note counts." I suppose the editors who rejected me felt like that. They wanted a little more fluff.

INTERVIEWERS: You can depend around here on practically everyone's having read *The Horse's Mouth.* Do you think that's because it's less philosophical? Or just because it's a Penguin [an inexpensive paperback edition]?

CARY: *The Horse's Mouth* is a very heavy piece of metaphysical writing. No, they like it because it's funny. The French have detected the metaphysics and are fussing about the title. I want *Le Tuyau increvable*—the unbustable tip. They say this is unworthy of a philosophical work and too like a *roman policier* ["detective novel"]. I say *tant mieux* ["so much the better"]. But they are unconvinced.

INTERVIEWERS: A metaphysical work—

CARY: A study of the creative imagination working in symbols. And symbols are highly uncertain—they also die.

INTERVIEWERS: Gulley's picture on the wall then, which is demolished, is in its turn a symbol of the instability of the symbol?

CARY: That's what Mrs Hardy seems to think. But that would be allegory. I hate allegory. The trouble is that if your books mean anything, the critic is apt to work allegory in. The last scene of Gulley is a real conflict, not an allegorical one. And it was necessary to cap the development. It was the catastrophe in a Greek sense.

INTERVIEWERS: *The Horse's Mouth* was part of a trilogy. You're doing this again now, aren't you, in *Prisoner of Grace, Except the Lord,* and the third yet to come?

CARY: I was dissatisfied with the first trilogy. I've set out this time with the intention of doing better. I think I *am* doing better. The contrasts between the different worlds are much sharper. When I'd finished *Prisoner of Grace* I planned a second book on political religion, but contemporary religion. And I found myself bored with the prospect. I nearly threw in the whole plan. Then one of my children urged me to go on. And I had the idea of writing Nimmo's religion as a young man. This appeared to me as opening a new world of explanation, and also giving a strong contrast to the last book. So I got to work. And tried to get at the roots of left-wing English politics in evangelical religion.

INTERVIEWERS: And the third?

CARY: It's going to be called *Not Honour More.* In it, I deal with Jim—the lover in *Prisoner of Grace.* He is the man of honour, of duty, of service, reacting against the politician. But I'll show it to you in its present state. Upstairs.

We followed Mr Cary upstairs two storeys to his workshop. It was a room with a low ceiling. A window at the far end looked out onto trees. Where the walls downstairs had been covered with pictures, up here it was all bookcases, containing, it seemed, more files than books. Mr Cary went straight to his desk, pulling out sheaves of paper from the shelves over it. They were, one instantly observed, meticulously organised. The sheaves were numbered and titled, each chapter in its own envelope. Mr Cary explained that these were the "big scenes." Clipped on the front of each envelope was a sheet of memoranda indicating what still remained to be done within the chapter, what would be required to give the finished scene a more convincing build-up. These were the chapters of the embryonic **Not Honour More.** *(pp. 10-15)*

Joyce Cary, in an interview with John Burrow and Alex Hamilton, in Joyce Cary: Selected Essays, *edited by A. G. Bishop, Michael Joseph, 1976, pp. 3-18.*

GEORGE WOODCOCK (essay date 1956)

[Woodcock is a Canadian educator, editor, and critic best known for his biographies of George Orwell and Thomas Merton. He also founded Canada's most important literary journal, Canadian Literature, *and has written extensively on the literature of Canada. In the following excerpt, Woodcock examines four of Cary's novels,* Castle Corner, Mister Johnson, The Horse's Mouth, *and* Prisoner of Grace, *which he considers to display the chief characteristics of Cary's fiction.]*

In the present cautious age in English novel-writing, when the brittle verbal experiments of Henry Green and the shy probing into the irrational of P. H. Newby seem to set the patterns for the younger generation of fiction writers, when the meticulous miniature seems more aimed at than the bravura portrait, one of the most interesting phenomena has been the emergence into prominence of a writer whose work is so far removed from these tendencies, so robust (almost on a Fielding scale) as that of Joyce Cary. Equally interesting, in view of the fact that Cary is neither an *avant-garde* experimentalist nor an expert in the fashionable minutiae of psychological symbolism, is the wide range of acceptance that has been accorded to him. Not only the most perceptive English critics, but also practicing novelists as far apart as Philip Toynbee and Elizabeth Bowen and the late Hugh Walpole have given unstinted praise to his work. (p. 236)

Cary has published at least fourteen novels, and it would be unnecessarily overloading a relatively brief study to attempt a consideration of them all. I have accordingly chosen four which, considered together, will give a fairly comprehensive view of the main aspects of his work.

The first, *Castle Corner,* is an early novel which was published in 1938. It falls considerably short of the books Cary has written during the past decade, but I have chosen it as an important document of his formative period. My second choice, *Mister Johnson,* is a novel with an African setting, which was published in 1939. Next follows *The Horse's Mouth,* a tale of a disreputable artistic genius, which is probably Cary's best-known and best book yet; it was published in 1944. Finally, there is *Prisoner of Grace,* which portrays the career of a hypocritical political leader as seen through the eyes of his long-suffering and all-too-understanding wife; this appeared in 1952.

Castle Corner is the chronicle of an Anglo-Irish landowning family in Donegal during the last Victorian years, and of its relationship, on the one hand with the strongly nationalist Irish peasants, and on the other hand with the new-rich financiers of the era of Cecil Rhodes and their social hangers-on.

In scene, and doubtless to a great extent in action, it is autobiographical. Cary himself came from this north-western corner of Ireland, and thus he is one of the last of that brilliant line of Anglo-Irish writers which stretches from Swift and comes to an end in our own generation. Undoubtedly the stimulating qualities of the mixed Anglo-Celtic culture have contributed much to the peculiar vigour and irritability of Cary's talent—qualities which he shares with that otherwise very different Anglo-Irishman, Bernard Shaw. But the autobiographical points of contact go beyond mere family environment, for, like one of his characters, Cleeve Corner, Cary went to Oxford and, like another, Cleeve's cousin, Harry Jarvis, he spent a considerable time in West Africa.

Castle Corner is a sprawling work of the "saga" type, with an immense number of characters, and it loses direction in following too many individual threads of relationship and des-

tiny. The very plethora of material with which it is crammed is evidence of Cary's inventive fertility, but it is clear that his powers of discipline and selection are yet undeveloped. He is still too much under the influence of the discovery—relatively late in life—of his powers of vigorous prose composition. For this and other reasons I think we should regard *Castle Corner* as an apprentice work in which the writer was getting a great deal of autobiography out of his system and trying his hand tentatively at various fictional approaches.

It is particularly significant that more than one scene from *Castle Corner* appears again, polished and strengthened, in his later books; one of the characters, the nonconformist politican, Porfit, is actually a sketch for the hero of *Prisoner of Grace,* which was published fourteen years later. This anticipates a tendency that Cary shows repeatedly in his more mature career, to go back over situations a second—sometimes even a third—time from a fresh point of view. To give only one example, *Herself Surprised* shows the painter Gulley Jimson as seen by his mistress Sara Munday, while *The Horse's Mouth* gives, as its title suggests, a direct view of Gulley's interior landscape. Cary seems to work on the assumption that each situation has as many versions as there are participants.

I think the qualities of *Castle Corner* that would strike the reader **who came to it before any other Cary novel are to be found in its language** and its characterisation. As I have said, Cary is not an experimentalist in literary effect. His way of writing is lucid, fluent and straightforward; he achieves his effects by the muscular and forceful use of a language which is almost conventional in its vocabulary, but whose idiom and imagery are so fresh that, like the English of the great prose periods, they keep us always on that magic borderline between reality and fantasy.

In characterisation a similar shading off towards fantasy removes Cary from the school of realism in which the superficial verisimilitude of his descriptions might seem to place him. His characters are drawn vividly, but, like those of Dickens, they have always a touch of caricature, a floridity of colour and a flourish of outline which are not the attributes of real life. But perhaps the most significant thing about so many of these people is their tendency to revolt against what they are and to attempt, in defiance of the established state of things, at times even in defiance of the laws of nature, to raise themselves into something higher.

This spirit of almost Satanic revolt and self-assertion erupts in many of the people one meets in *Castle Corner.* (pp. 237-39)

Castle Corner collapses like the tower of Babel from the weight of [its] crowd of heaven defiers. There are too many positive and clamorous characters demanding our attention, and what might have been grandeur ends in confusion. This error Cary did not repeat, and in the novels he has written since that time the number of dominant characters has been strictly limited.

The result of this has been an immense increase in drive and a growth in the stature of the characters, until they do in fact seem to assume more than human proportions, and appear less as individual persons than as passionate symbols of human aspirations that are at everlasting variance with all the laws of god and man. His heroes are the amoral projections of liberated forces from the inner depths of the spirit which seek a fulfilment in human terms so vast that it takes on the proportions of anti-divinity, the pride of Satanism. In these more recent Cary novels, indeed, one has the feeling that here is the last and ultimate flowering of that concept of man as an autonomous force which was launched by the Renaissance, crowned by nineteenth century thinkers like Feuerbach and Nietzsche and Proudhon, celebrated by poets like Swinburne and Whitman in the high period of humanistic arrogance, and finally given this belated expression in the work of another wayward Irishman. Cary stands at the completely opposite end of the spectrum to Kafka, for, while Kafka's heroes are always defeated by the mysterious forces of the divine will, Cary's protagonists have an everlasting tendency to blunder their way through each defeat, physical or spiritual, and to end up triumphant in their own tragedy. Nowhere in the novel does one meet a more extreme or eloquent expression of the cult of humanistic individualism than will be encountered in the three remaining novels which I am about to discuss.

Mister Johnson was published only a year after *Castle Corner,* but there is a vast difference in quality between the two books. Where *Castle Corner* is sprawling and divided, *Mister Johnson* is tightly knit in form and condensed in direction, and out of this closer determination there emerges a new clarification of character and a simplified and strengthened style.

Mister Johnson returns to the African scene of parts of *Castle Corner,* but the period is now the inter-war era during which Cary himself knew the country. Johnson is a partly Europeanised Negro clerk in the government service who is pathetically anxious to take on the attributes of an Englishman. In fact, he belongs neither to the civilised nor to the savage world. At times he can lose himself in the dances and songs of his own people, but he is already too far removed by education to be other than a foreigner among the real children of nature, the drab, routine-minded village pagans from whom he buys himself a wife. On the other hand, he and his fellow clerks are unable to understand those concepts of responsibility which inspire the Europeans with whom they come into contact. In Johnson the result of trying to bestride two worlds is a violent tendency towards self-magnification. He believes that his position as a magistrate's clerk really constitutes a bond of alliance between him and the alien rulers, and he feels obliged by his position to enlarge his prestige by an extravagant campaign of hospitality. . . . Johnson is a figure of fun, a comic character, but under his comedy, as under the comedy of Falstaff, lies the dark ground of human tragedy.

According to the standards of his English superiors, he is an unreliable and dishonest man. He runs into debt to pay for his parties, he takes bribes from the officials of the native emirate, and he steals when he finds himself in difficulties. Yet he has a dynamic imagination, and when he realises the magnitude of the idea of building a road through the jungle that is haunting the mind of Rudbeck, his English superior, he devotes all his energies to achieving it, thinking up means of diverting funds to provide the cash a stingy government refuses and firing the imaginations of the native labourers with his own enthusiasm.

Yet these qualities, which result in the road being built against all the difficulties that are placed in its way by bureaucratic red tape, go unrecognised by Johnson's superiors when he is found to be involved in a muddled web of peculation, and he is dismissed from the service. But misfortune swells his self-glorification into a colossal defiance of circumstances, and he breaks into a great wave of hospitality which, since he is penniless, he finances by burglary from the local store. Eventually, he is caught by the white storekeeper and kills him in panic. He is tried by his former superior, Rudbeck, and sentenced to be hanged. Yet even in death he manages to shape his own fate, for he persuades Rudbeck to go against law and conven-

tion and shoot him. This he has asked because he prefers to die by the hand of the man who, despite everything, he regards as his friend, rather than being hanged by the alien hands of the soldiers.

Johnson moves on a level of comparatively simple impulse. Gulley Jimson, hero of *The Horse's Mouth,* is a much more complex character, a painter with a Blakeian exaltation, and with much intellectual involution under the amoral cunning with which he seeks the means to paint the symbolic visions that take shape within his mind.

Gulley, like Johnson, is at once inspired and preyed upon by ideas of a fantastic grandiosity. At one time he had been a successful painter, but the alterations of fashion have made him poor, and the cosmic message that is now his object is unpopular with the people who admired the Renoir-like nudes of his past. So Gulley, now an old man with the scheming crankiness of the aged, sets out like a guerilla warrior to fulfil his visions against all the obstacles society puts in his way. He tries threats and blackmail, which land him in prison, he steals and cadges and sponges on barmaids and baronets, until, after a Rabelaisian series of comic adventures, he finds a condemned chapel whose wall seems to have been made to receive his masterpiece. His work reaches a crescendo of frenzy when the municipality begins to tear down the old building. Now Gulley paints against time and destruction, working in a haze of brick dust to the sound of whacking picks and crashing masonry, undaunted and headstrong until the wall disintegrates under his very brush and he himself is carried off in the ambulance, evidently dying, his last work done in defiance of all the forces of disintegration. . . . (pp. 239-42)

Gulley tells his tale in the first person, with all the gusto and loud irritability, streaked with good humour, that are proper to his character, and I do not think Cary has ever written better than in *The Horse's Mouth.* One of its most interesting aspects is the way in which Gulley's painter's eye is used to illuminate and deepen the literary imagery. Cary himself studied painting, and one has the feeling, in reading this novel, that the kind of aims Gulley is after are just what his creator would have liked to achieve had he become a painter instead of a writer. It is significant that Jimson's final masterpiece should be, not a crucifixion, but a Creation. To take the very first act of the world, and, by giving it human form, by moulding it within the human mind, to endue it with a totally anthropomorphic symbolism—that, surely, is the last word in the glorification of man, in militant humanism. (p. 243)

Just as some mystics have been led to perform acts that seem outside ordinary morality in order to complete their visions, so Gulley Jimson is impelled to break every law and moral concept that may stand in the way of his achievement, yet that achievement remains positive and creative in character. But the urge that induces men to defy the gods can also take a malign and negative form, and in this sense Chester Nimmo, the hero of *Prisoner of Grace* is the antithesis—or is he perhaps the complement?—of Gulley.

Nimmo is the hypocrite *par excellence,* so consummate in his two-facedness that he deceives even himself and often completely fails to recognise the equivocal nature of his own actions or statements. Power is his preoccupation, and to achieve it he will use every means.

His story is told by his wife, Nina, a sprig of the aristocracy who gets into trouble with her cousin and is hastily married off to Chester, then a hectic young local preacher among the

Baptists and a rising politician at the county council level. For the Latter family it is a saving of face; for Chester it is a first long step on the journey of influence and intrigue that will lead him to eventual power. In human terms the cost of that journey is terrible; it involves the adoption of causes, not for their rectitude, but for the political capital that can be wrung from them, it involves the utmost cynicism in political manoeuvring, it involves the jettisoning of ideals at the psychological moment when they may become embarrassing, the abandonment of friends when their usefulness has been exhausted, the desecration and destruction of family relationships in the cause of personal advancement. (p. 244)

A great deal of the horror that emerges from this book arises from the glibness which Cary has been able to infuse into its writing as a means of suggesting the specious atmosphere in which the Nimmos lived. Nina is not basically a hypocrite like Chester, but thirty years of association with him have affected her way of thinking, and it is an illustration of the flexibility of Cary's writing that her account should have even in its idiom that taint of moral ambiguity which intensifies the atmosphere of intangible evil that hangs about her husband.

The creation of a character like Nimmo seems to show that Joyce Cary is intent on exploring all the aspects of rampant individualism. At the beginning of this essay, I compared his concept of humanistic individualism with that of the Renaissance, and it is significant that, just as the age of Michelangelo and Leonardo also produced Sigismondo Malatesta and Cesare Borgia, so the imagination of Cary has balanced a ferocious Renaissance-type artist like Gulley Jimson with a modern political *condottiere* like Chester Nimmo. Clearly, in his mind, there is no one way in which the form that human self-assertion takes can be predicted. It may be evil, and it may be good, but perhaps it is always necessary to take the chance if humanity is to live and grow.

It seems to me that in this re-assertion of the human individual we have, not merely the central core of Cary's attitude, but also, when united with his manifest gifts as a writer, the reason for the relative unanimity with which critics of so many different schools have hailed him as an important phenomenon in modern English literature. For it was faith in the inherent quality of man to impose his personality upon his environment that inspired the great novelists of the past, and it is perhaps safe to say that, if Cary has not yet shown himself a writer of the calibre of Stendhal or Dickens or Tolstoy, he certainly shares much of their attitude towards human character. That is, unfortunately, a rare and therefore an inspiring thing in an age which too often seems to advance, in the novel at least, into one of two impasses—either that of arid literary experiment, where the human character is caught in a net of self-conscious word spinning, or that of morbid psychological introspection, where man is lost in a labyrinth of spiritual agony. (pp. 245-46)

George Woodcock, "Citizens of Babel: A Study of Joyce Cary," in Queen's Quarterly, *Vol. LXIII, No. 2, Summer, 1956, pp. 236-46.*

ANDREW WRIGHT (essay date 1958)

[*Wright is an American educator, editor, and critic. In the following excerpt from his* Joyce Cary: A Preface to his Novels, *he discusses the importance of several recurring character types in Cary's novels.*]

[Although] as a novelist Cary is a rich—indeed a prodigious—inventor, his range is severely limited. He is often compared to Dickens, but Dickens draws a whole gallery of individuals because for him idiosyncrasy is the defining aspect of man; Cary portrays again and again the same three people because for him it is the commonness of the human dilemma which is compelling. The man who must create, the man who would preserve, and the woman who as female resembles both the one and the other but also differs from either—these are the types to which Cary mainly confines himself because, for all their singularities, they constitute in Cary's world the defining limits of human possibility.

The first and most interesting type is the man who rejoices in freedom: the anarch, the artist, the man who destroys in order to create, the man who ignores all claims but his own. There is the megalomaniac District Officer of *An American Visitor* who resists all authority, who wishes to rule his district as absolutely as Kurtz in "Heart of Darkness," and who suffers the same fate. There is Louis Aladai, the Oxford-educated young claimant to the Rimi throne in *The African Witch;* he begins by trying to introduce European standards into his native land, and ends by ordering his sister to take away his European clothes. In *Castle Corner,* the free man is fragmented into several characters; and fragmentation is the fatal flaw of that novel. In the novels of childhood there are Charley Brown and Evelyn Corner, both swimming with the revolutionary tide because in revolution is self-discovery and creation. Finally, and culminatingly, there is the artist, whose very vocation it is to foment revolutions. The artist is sketched out in the Mr Lommax of *Charley is My Darling,* in the holiday tutor Pinto of *A House of Children* and in the superb rogue Dick Bonser of *A Fearful Joy,* the endlessly inventive entrepreneur whose imagination makes bright worlds. In Gulley Jimson and in Chester Nimmo, the one a politician in art and the other an artist in politics, Cary's characterization of man as everlasting artificer becomes fully and, I think, triumphantly realized.

Opposed to the revolutionary is the man attached to the past because there can be found certainty, continuity, civilization; opposed to the revolution because in creating it destroys, but condemned, like Tom Wilcher, to be a pilgrim. If the artist most truly represents the first of Cary's types, the lawyer and the soldier, those guardians of the heritage, most adequately represent the second. Gore in *An American Visitor*—he is, I am sure, an early version of Tom Wilcher—tries endlessly to reconcile the claims of sound government with the aims of Monkey Bewsher, or rather he tries to reconcile Bewsher to obeying the rules. Cock Jarvis, the patriotic young soldier of *Castle Corner,* is the younger brother of the fanatical Jim Latter; the Latter of *Not Honour More* is simply young Cock Jarvis become middle-aged, disillusioned and desperate. Bill Wilcher the soldier and Thomas Wilcher the lawyer of *To be a Pilgrim* represent two facets of the conservative mind, the one accepting the world and doing his duty, the other entrapped by the past and sentenced to the dutiful life. (pp. 72-4)

Cary does not take sides. He presents his people disinterestedly. This is not, of course, because he is indifferent to the outcome but because his sympathies are so broad that he can feel the poignance of Tom Wilcher's defeat as keenly as he can Gulley Jimson's. But having been so objective in his presentation Cary does at last choose between them. He chooses the creative man. This is why Gulley's defeat is a triumph, and Wilcher's pathetic; this is why Chester Nimmo's defeat, for all that Cary makes us despise him, is a tragedy, and Jim Latter's fate sordid.

Mediating between these opposites is the female. Cary draws heavily on Blake for his idea of womanhood. The feminine principle is the completing and at the same time the destructive principle. "She nails him down upon a rock," Blake says in "The Mental Traveller," and "Catches his shrieks in cups of gold." It is the caught shrieks in the anguish of fulfilment which are the expressed creation of man. Cary's women perform the creative rites of temptation and seduction; having done so, they build nests and try, as Gulley says of Sara Monday, to domesticate their men. Aissa, the heroine of Cary's first novel, is so fully engaged in the war between Christianity and paganism that she has little time for domestic pursuits, but she understands Christianity only in exclusively female terms: her first communion means so much to her because she supposes that Jesus is having sexual intercourse with her; and when there comes a test of strength between the Christian doctrine to which she adheres fanatically and the female nature which calls her back to her lover Gajere, she does not hesitate to rejoin Gajere. Marie Hasluck of *An American Visitor* is to a certain extent de-sexed by her intellectual emancipation, but she succumbs at last to her female nature. She becomes the mistress, then the wife and finally the widow of Bewsher, from whom she learns that what she thought about life was simply thought about inexperience. Elizabeth Aladai, the African witch herself, is no doubt the most formidable of all Cary's women. She is so strong that she domesticates even her own brother, the young man with the English education, and she destroys one male after another in her insatiable greed for domestication of the male to her female needs. In *Castle Corner* all the women know and cherish their function as mistress, wife and mother, the Corner women no less than the Irish peasants and the African woman who becomes the sometime wife of Felix Corner. In the novels of childhood three girls stand out especially— the deaf and stupid Lizzie Galor, who knows simply by instinct that to love and succour Charley Brown is her rôle in life; and, in *A House of Children,* Frances and Delia, the one an easy cherishing mother and wife from her first maturity, the other, more vital, sparked by the imagination of Pinto with whom she elopes. And are not the women of Cary's later novels all of a piece? Sara Monday, the eternal Eve, the perpetual nest builder, the triumphant mother: the woman whose symbol and home is the kitchen; Ella Venn, of a different class, whose affirmation of sexuality is an affirmation of her female nature, even in an age which stresses duty at the expense of nature; Tabitha Baskett, possessed of greater intelligence than either Sara or Ella, but condemned like them both to make very much the same pilgrimage, though over different ground and at a faster pace; and finally Nina, the brightest and most complicated of them all, imprisoned by grace to a man whom she detests, imprisoned equally by a life-long love to a man whom she cannot respect.

Cary is one of the giants among twentieth-century novelists, but he did not become so until he invented the novel of the triple vision; nor, having made this discovery, was he at his best when he abandoned it—as he did in *The Moonlight* and *A Fearful Joy.* He began, like many other artists, conventionally; and, despite *Mister Johnson* and *A House of Children,* he did not hit his best stride until the interconnected *Herself Surprised, To be a Pilgrim* and *The Horse's Mouth.* But seven novels precede this first trilogy. For what Cary discovered was that his genius for impersonation exactly meshed with the idea which animates but does not always bring fully alive his earlier works. (pp. 74-6)

By the end of the 1920s Cary had worked out, very largely by himself, the idea of the world which is at the centre of all his novels. But, as his early work shows, he could not embody that idea fully because he could not make the novelistic form yield the kind of result which he sought. He had seen and understood but he could not create the characters who would embody, nor could he control the structure which could contain, his vision. Indeed, I think it is fair to say that the first four of his novels are all, as novels, unsuccessful experiments. In his fifth, *Mister Johnson,* he produced a small but nonetheless considerable masterpiece. However, it would be wrong to assert that thenceforward Cary worked with the cool certainty of having found adequate form for his intuition. He never stopped struggling and he never stopped failing: the trilogies are separated by a brace of novels, *The Moonlight* and *A Fearful Joy,* which simply cannot compare to the best of his works; and the forms of the two trilogies themselves, though they have the inevitability of great art, were painfully and uncertainly arrived at before they were seized upon.

Aissa Saved is dominated by Aissa, and I intend to consider her in due course, but there appears in that work no one man who can represent what always needs to be represented in a Cary novel—the creator, the artist, the revolutionary: the free man, making a free world for himself. But there are fragments of this man in the missioner Carr, who more than half stupidly but also kindly will impose a picture-book Christianity upon the Africans; in the District Officer Bradgate who plunges himself into the enterprise of building a bridge; and, above all, in the young African boy Ali who is en route by way of education to freedom. In fact, Ali was the germ of *Aissa Saved.* In the Carfax preface Cary records having known such a boy. He walked a hundred and thirty miles without sleeping, to help Cary make a map. This journey, which nearly killed the boy, was striking as "the effect of education on this rather shy and not very clever boy. . . . I was anxious to contrast Ali's standards and ideas with those above him. This, of course, involved questions of local ethics, local religion, the whole conflict of those ideas in a primitive community; and also the impact of new ideas from outside." But, in the course of writing the book, "Aissa gradually became the heroine because she was more central to a deeper interest, that of religion." Actually, I think Cary did not know how to handle Ali, who does not appear at all until nearly half-way through the book, and whose rôle is very small.

Ali, who is sixteen, is the son of the local Waziri—that is, the prime minister—and he has been to the government school. He explains to his fellow-countrymen who are anxious to make a sacrifice to the goddess of mountains and fertility, and who wish to put Aissa to death because they think she is a witch, that "witches had no power over rain which fell from the clouds when they were made cold, and besides all knew very well that it was a wrong thing to condemn anybody without a proper trial before judges." Ali indeed has his moments, but they are few. The most effective occurs at the riot, when he is reduced from a man of high moral dignity to a frightened boy. Ali will impartially save the life of a pagan as he has formerly saved the life of the Christian Aissa, because it is a matter of right; when he is struck down, he is so frightened that he crawls away saying, "Don't tell them—don't tell them." But Ali, sandwiched among some seventy characters in a very short novel, is given little opportunity to become more than a sketch for a portrait.

In *An American Visitor*, that uncomfortable juxtaposition of violence and colloquy, the creative man is represented not by an African but by the District Officer, Monkey Bewsher. He is a reckless, enthusiastic man in his forties, in love with the district over which he rules by the sheer force of his personality; or rather, like Conrad's Kurtz, he is in love with the power which he can exercise so freely in a remote district of Nigeria. He is motivated by no disinterested benevolence: he treats the natives like naughty children who must be subdued by the power of his imagination and the enlightenment of his superior knowledge. He prefers that they remain subdued.

In order to maintain his dominance he must outsmart not only the natives themselves but also the whites. He subdues Marie Hasluck, the American newspaperwoman, by communicating to her some of his own imaginative vigour; and she succumbs so far as to become his mistress and then his wife. He subdues the Governor by ignoring his urgent orders. He subdues a party of prospectors, despite their exclusive prospecting licence. "There's no reason on earth why they should come to Birri and smash up my whole show." He subdues, or tries to subdue, the missioners by proposing, among other things, that the pagan thunder god Ogun be transfigured into the Christian saint of Electricity and Vital Energy.

But Bewsher is doomed, as are all megalomaniacs, to defeat. He is killed by the very Africans over whom he has ruled with such magnificent skill. Indeed before the fatal battle he recognizes that there has come a term to his sway. This is sig-nalized by his willingness to shoot at the Africans, whom formerly he has triumphed over without force of arms. But Marie hides his pistol and he goes out to meet them armed merely with a pair of scissors. And his end has no tragic force. "Bewsher's own feelings as he lay on the ground with two or three spears in his body, though, of course, full of official indignation, was not empty of a kind of amusement as if some part of his mind were remarking to him, 'Well, old chap, the joke is on you. You're not going to get away with it this time.'" How near this is to the lightly uttered but equally despairing remarks of Gulley Jimson when he and Nosy Barbon flee in the rain to Sussex, toward the end of *The Horse's Mouth*. How near and yet how far. For Gulley's vision is so much more vast than Bewsher's megalomaniac dream; and Gulley lives to begin, though not to finish, his last and greatest painting.

In Cary's third novel, still another kind of man comes to represent the creator. He is Louis Aladai, brother to the African witch. Intelligent and well educated, his ambitions are not for himself but for his people. He says to the lame sometime don, Judith Coote, whom he knew in Oxford, "Rimi civilization. Do you know what it is?—ju-ju." He tells Judith that no one, except a small handful, is educated in Rimi. "It's too absurd— a million without schools—and Rimi civilization! Rimi! No, I love Rimi, and it is because I love it that I want to give it something worth calling a civilization."

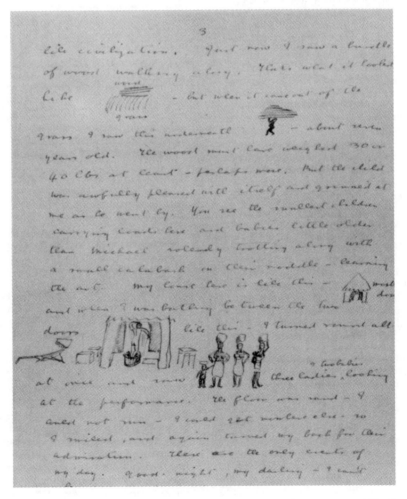

Illustrated letter from Cary to his wife, February 1919. Reproduced by permission of The Trustees of Joyce Cary's Estate, and The Bodleian Library, Oxford.

He soon discovers that there is nothing simple in the task of imposing European civilization upon his countrymen, and he learns eventually that the call of his own culture is stronger than the call of Europe. Thus one of his supporters, the Reverend Selah Coker, is a Christian whom Louis despises. Coker's "key word was blood, but it appeared in different connections: blood of Jesus—blood of sacrifice—blood of the wicked man— blood of the sinner—the baptism of blood." All of Louis' civilized instincts are revolted by the man; and yet, near the end of the book when Coker has made a sacrifice of the Schweitzer-like Dr Schlemm and has put his head on display, Louis feels the power and the temptation of this emphasis in religion.

In fact he becomes confused, and his confusion is not resolved by the behaviour of most of the whites at Rimi. He longs for civilization, for good talk; and one night he joins the company of the whites, all of whom depart and leave him sitting alone— even Judith Coote leaves, having been summoned by her fiancé, Captain Rackham. The only person besides the Resident who treats him well on this occasion is, ironically, the athletic Dryas Honeywood, a girl whose reflexes cause her to be polite, but who in fact despises all the natives.

The die is cast late in the book during the crisis about the emirate. Tempers are frayed. In public and therefore specially humiliating circumstances, Captain Rackham, who regards Louis as a "trousered ape," the more despicable because he has been educated, hits him and flings him into the river. When he is rescued, he is taken to his sister's house, where he orders Elizabeth to take his European clothes away and burn them. For, as he now says, "I am Rimi man." And he is killed in the riot, or war, which his sister foments.

What Cary does in his first three novels, therefore, is to explore the possibilities of delineating the hero as creator, and he moves in the direction of complexity. That Ali becomes Bewsher and Bewsher becomes Louis Aladai indicates a progress in the development of this character, and it is a considerable achievement. But Cary's next novel, *Castle Corner*, fails just because complexity becomes diffuseness. The creator becomes several characters, all of them minor. Indeed, there are no major characters in this long and populous novel, intended, as Cary has said, to be the first volume of a trilogy.

In *Castle Corner* the free man appears in such fragmentary characters as John Charles Corner, whose entire artistry is expended—and charmingly but trivially expended—upon a tandem race from the castle to the village and back again; in Theodore Benskin, the South African millionaire; in Robert Porfit, an ambitious lay-preacher who appears briefly. Above all, this type is personated in Felix and Cleeve Corner, father and son.

Felix Corner, the elder son of the patriarch of Castle Corner, is a fine piece of satirical portraiture. Imposing in physique, devoted to talk, utterly foolish in his wisdom, "his good sense, his wide knowledge, almost as much as his imposing figure and large beard, his bass voice and spectacles, made him respected wherever he went." He has the temperament but not the single-mindedness of an artist. He lays waste his life in a number of footless schemes, the most absurd of which is his involvement in the Mosi Trading Company, a West African enterprise which he is certain will make all the Corners rich again. When Felix goes to Africa he writes utopian reports to England, but before long he becomes entirely indolent and the Mosi Company becomes moribund. And so splendid is the ego

of the man that when he is persuaded by his native concubine to marry his stepdaughter, he does not suppose that he is going native. In short, Felix Corner is an artist without an art, and this characterization, although it must dispel the idea that Cary is a yea-sayer, a devotee of progress, is simply not substantial enough to succeed in a book containing nearly a hundred characters.

Felix's son Cleeve is more interesting. His disorientation is more fundamental, because his mother and father have travelled incessantly round Europe, and so he has missed the security of a centre, of a home. Yet this very deracination allows him to develop in more fruitful ways than either Felix or John Chass, more fruitful also than the other two boys of his generation who play prominent rôles in the novel: his cousin, Cock Jarvis, who becomes a soldier; and Philip Feenix, a neighbour of the Corners whose surrender to the idea of landlordship involves a crucial surrender of freedom that drives him to suicide.

Having left his public school and returned to Ireland as he thinks for ever, Cleeve tries unsuccessfully to write a novel about a Roman youth called Manlius—he comes to feel that Castle Corner is a backwater. He longs for Oxford, for London, for the season, and he makes his escape, a very young young man hungry for experience of life. When at last Cleeve goes up to Oxford he attaches himself to a succession of styles all of which enable him to explore the shape of the world. He becomes first a dandy in imitation of his friend Cobden Chorley, then an ardent reader of philosophy, until he is carried— to his father's disquiet—beyond Kant who is the fashion to more controversial philosophical standpoints. Cleeve Corner is clearly destined for a life in which intelligence will play a commanding rôle, and there is every prospect that his career will be more successful than his father's, for Cleeve's liberation is not the half-way house of apostasy. But whether Cleeve will fulfil his destiny is a question left unanswered at the end of *Castle Corner*, the longest of Cary's novels, and, paradoxically, the least developed.

Conscious of his failure, Cary returned to Africa for the setting of his next novel, *Mister Johnson*, a little masterpiece owing its force to the brilliant simplicity with which it is constructed. Arnold Kettle, in an excellent essay, calls this book a lyric. *Mister Johnson* does indeed sing—and principally through the characterization of that irresistible young African, Johnson himself. In portraying Johnson, Cary for the first time disclosed the scope of his great novelistic talent.

The book begins with a falling in love which is for the most part a construct of Johnson's lavish imagination, an imagination nourished by his youthful and poetic experiences of English civilization as he knows it through the colonial officers for whom he works. "The young women of Fada, in Nigeria, are well known for beauty. They have small, neat features and their backs are not too hollow." So begins this enchanting book, and Johnson falls in love with Bamu the ferryman's daughter, not only because of her beauty—"What pretty breasts—God bless you with them"—but because he has dreams of grandeur. He will make her into a government lady and in so doing will help to complete his idea of himself as a government gentleman. The relationship with Bamu is, however, less than half the story; the other, more important relationship is between Johnson and Harry Rudbeck, the Assistant District Officer. He treats Johnson, "his first clerk, with the ordinary politeness which would be given to a butler or footman at home," and Johnson adores him in return.

The pathos and humour of Johnson's position are indicated by its extreme precariousness, which is of course only a heightened version of the precariousness of the human situation anyway. Johnson has the capacity to forget which the reader is later to find in Sara Monday. His remorse, his despair—''Oh, Gawd, Oh, Jesus! I done finish—I finish now''—are real and agonized and short-lived. He immediately forgets his troubles when he starts to copy a report, for he delights in making capital S's. Indeed, Johnson's destiny becomes the more radiant as it becomes more uncertain. In difficulty with his creditors, he is charged with embezzlement. Furthermore, Bamu's brother, finding that Johnson cannot pay an instalment due on his sister, fetches her back to the ferry village. And, seeing the image of himself in the process of destruction, the boy gives himself to a suicidal despair. At last he is shown a way out of his difficulty: he becomes a paid spy for the Waziri. The rôle becomes possible, even desirable, because it is dangerous and therefore exhilarating. In order to get at the confidential files, Johnson must steal the key from underneath Rudbeck's pillow; when he has successfully done so, and when he has delivered to the Waziri the information desired, Johnson is so delighted with his new rôle as successful thief that he can hardly contain his joy.

So goes Johnson's splendid career from joy to sorrow and back again. It is a great piece of artistry; and, like all artistry, doomed in the very nature of things. His last great act is the greatest act of all, that of murder—it is a murder which he does not mean to undertake but which he is, in a way, trapped into committing. He kills Sergeant Gollup, who finds him stealing money from the cash-desk of Gollup's store. And since Gollup is a white, there can be no question about Johnson's punishment.

His trial is a tragi-comedy, because Johnson, observing Rudbeck's kindness toward him, is cheerful, indeed exuberant, in giving testimony. Rudbeck puts together a statement, to which Johnson agrees—he would in his gratitude agree to anything—that the killing was unpremeditated. Johnson is, however, ordered to be hanged, and Rudbeck must do the hanging. Rudbeck feels so defiant, and so torn by friendship, that he does not, until pressed, execute the order. When he weighs Johnson, the young clerk guesses his fate. He begs Rudbeck to shoot him rather than hang him. 'Oh, say, you my good frien'—my father and my mother—I pray you do it—I tink perhaps you shoot me.' And this in fact is what Rudbeck does. He tells his wife Celia—it is the last line of the book—'I couldn't let any one else do it, could I.' It is a cry of anguish, a tragic awareness no less moving than Captain Vere's awareness in *Billy Budd* of the conflict between personal and public loyalty. But *Mister Johnson* is not Rudbeck's book; it is Johnson's. The young African's intense and endless imagining, his creation of a glorious destiny, require that we rejoice in his triumph while we lament his defeat.

In his characterization of Mister Johnson, Cary moves in a new direction: he explores the destructive as well as the creative aspect of the free man. I think it fair to say, in fact, that as his novels improve so his idea of the world matures. Cary can realize in art the shape of his world as the shape of the world clarifies itself in his own mind. Or it may be that in the act of creation itself Cary's world develops the shape which is a realization in both senses of the word. At any rate, from *Mister Johnson* onward the hero as creator is also, though in varying degrees, a rakehell: the *genres* of these artists vary, but each ruins himself for his art.

This is certainly true of Charley Brown, the cockney adolescent who is the hero of *Charley is My Darling*. His adventures in the village to which he has been evacuated are disastrous and destructive. He paints a picture in which he is the hero-adventurer; so compelling is the self-portrait that he is led from theft and burglary to the destruction of a great country house in his efforts to create a world. As an artist he is a failure because he, like Mister Johnson, is only half-educated to life's possibilities; but, like Mister Johnson, he learns of the route to community. It is the route of love, which Johnson feels toward Rudbeck, and which Charley Brown feels toward the deaf Lizzie Galor. At the end of the book, Charley escapes from a remand home and collects Lizzie. But they are caught by the police. Before they part, Lizzie says, ''It's bin so lovely, I wish I could die.'' Indeed their parting is a little death, but it is not an annihilation: Charley Brown and Lizzie Galor have discovered separately because they have discovered together the bitter secret of human loneliness as they have discovered the sweet secret of human joy.

And in *Charley is My Darling* is Cary's first sketch of the man who is to become Gulley Jimson. In *Charley is My Darling* he is called Mr Lommax. He enchants the evacuees by his wild demeanour. When asked to conduct a drawing class for them, he reluctantly assents, 'Ah'll show em what it's about, if you like. but it won't do any good, you know, not a bit. They'll never learn anything. No one ever learns anything.' The boys are tantalized. As new-fledged leader of the gang, Charley explains that Mr Lommax ''aint a teacher, see, e's a real artiss.'' And he continues to enchant. He is untidy and tardy and unconventional. He praises Charley's drawings only when they become scatological.

When Charley is later put on trial for theft, Mr Lommax agrees to testify in his favour, for Charley is artistic. But, since Lommax thinks all children are artistic, it follows that he would testify for any other young miscreant. ''Can I say,'' asks the earnest young woman in charge of the evacuees, ''that you think him promising as an artist?'' To this Mr Lommax makes an altogether Jimsonian reply: ''Ah will come and swear it, if you like—perjury has no terrors for an artist—he is damned already.'' In *Charley is My Darling*, however, Cary had not yet learned—at any rate, he did not attempt—to draw the shape of his damnation.

The other novel of childhood, *A House of Children*, is a special case just because it is autobiographical. The central figure is the narrator Evelyn Corner, writing of the time when he was eight years old. Evelyn is Cary's *alter ego*: but it is a measure of the difficulty of translating life to art that Cary invents another character, Harry, to bear a part of the burden of recollection. ''I realized by some instinct (it was certainly not by reason) that the two together as a single character would be too complex for the kind of book I needed to write: a book full of that clarity, the large skies, and wide sea views, which belong to the vision of my childhood.'' Harry, the elder brother, the other aspect of Cary's *alter ego*, abandons art itself after the disastrous production of a play, a fact surely of great interest to those who would unlock the puzzle of Cary's own personality.

But Harry and Evelyn remain, at the end of the book, too young to have achieved even what Charley Brown achieves. Nevertheless, the free man appears in this book in the shape of Pinto, the holiday tutor, whose real name is actually Freeman. Pinto occupies a central position on the stage of their lives. Bored with teaching, quick-tempered, witty and imaginative, he appeals to their instinct to rebellion, their impulse to freedom. He speaks nonsense, which the children recognize as nonsense—for instance, "that policemen were the cause of crime and that the English had ruined India by stopping the widows from being burnt alive." But this nonsense is part of his sense, his shape of life. He is a utopian socialist, after William Morris; he is an artist and as artist anarchist, eternally at war with organization. He is interesting in this book not simply in himself but also as he prefigures Gulley Jimson.

There is, for instance, a simple rehearsal, in Pinto's story told against himself of pawning everything in a friend's flat, of Gulley Jimson's invasion of Sir William Beeder's flat. Pinto, the narrator tells us, "is an artist in description," and the story he tells is understatedly simple: "he described how he had been left to take care of a friend's, an artist's, rooms in London, but without money. The friend forgot to leave any and he had none. He therefore pawned a clock in order to telegraph for funds. But the telegram did not find its addressee, and no answer came. Meanwhile, according to Pinto, he had been obliged to pawn pictures, the cutlery, and at last the chairs and tables, till suddenly, while he was still hoping for funds to take everything out of pawn again, the friend himself had walked in and found him sleeping on a bare floor in the empty rooms."

The outline here follows almost exactly that of Gulley's occupation of Beeder's flat. But in *The Horse's Mouth* the incident is much elaborated. Gulley gets possession of the flat by a trick. He remains—for he is a real artist—to paint a wall, and he pawns all the furniture and fittings not so that he can eat, or rather not exclusively for this purpose, but so that he can paint. And when the owner returns, Gulley is sleeping on a floor, and must make an escape. While Pinto is "an artist in description," Gulley is an artist in fact.

After Pinto comes Gulley Jimson himself—Gulley at least as he is seen by Sara Monday; *A House of Children* and *Herself Surprised* were both published in 1941. And in the development of Gulley's character Cary delineates more fully than ever elsewhere his idea of man as creator, although in Chester Nimmo he embodies this idea with an impressiveness nearly equal to that of his realization in Gulley. These two characters, the heroes of the trilogies, must be treated separately, as the culmination of Cary's creative power, and they are the principal subject of the final chapter of this book. But I must say a word here about two works which were published between the two trilogies. They are *The Moonlight* and *A Fearful Joy*, both cast in the form of a chronicle, and each failing, as I have already suggested, for a different reason: *The Moonlight* because it has no central figure, *A Fearful Joy* because it attempts to chronicle too many of the revolutions in art and politics from the 1890s to the 1940s. These novels fail also, it seems to me, because they do not give Cary scope to explore the character of the free man. In *The Moonlight* there are only Geoffrey Tew, a young poet of the 'nineties who is an unsuccessful suitor of the romantic Ella Venn; and Ernest Cranage, somewhat weakly artistic in temperament, who is a science demonstrator and also Ella's seducer. The rôles of these two characters are very small. In *A Fearful Joy*, however, there is an important free man, the rogue Dick Bonser who is the heroine's tempter, seducer, husband and finally charge. He has, for Tabitha, real imaginative vigour. She cannot live without him, for she comes to recognize the need in herself of the sheer liveliness which he provides. At the end of the book, after his death in a Paddington brothel—even after this—Tabitha acknowledges what she owes the man. "He brought me to life again; it was like a resurrection from the dead." In fact, she reflects, Bonser, "that danger and burden, has also been the ground and the sky of her life." But Bonser, for all his pyrotechnics, plays a rôle in *A Fearful Joy* altogether subordinate to that of Tabitha; and this, it seems to me, is the wrong way round. Besides, Dick Bonser's artistry consists neither in the creation of works of art, like Gulley Jimson's paintings, nor in the creation of a government, which is Chester Nimmo's political ambition: Dick Bonser is a mere rogue, and after some hundreds of pages he becomes to the reader, if not to Tabitha, a bore.

Although Cary sets over against the free man another type of character, the man attached to the past, to stability, to achievement rather than to experiment—although Cary does this, he is not simply juxtaposing opposites in order to exalt the one and depress the other. Cary is, I think without any question, on the side of the free man; but he is extremely sympathetic to the gallery of conservatives who people his novels. For, besides recognizing the fact that this type exists, Cary acknowledges not only the appeal but also the necessity of such a temperament in a world blessed or doomed—"as you please"— with freedom. Furthermore, he manages to show that these contrasting characters are not opposite at every point. Even the most rooted of Cary's conservatives must do battle in their own souls with the impulse to create—and some of these characters actually do create, within certain limits. So Cock Jarvis in *Castle Corner* romps enthusiastically into a forbidden territory, and precipitates an international crisis. And the most fully realized of all the conservatives, Thomas Wilcher in the first trilogy, comes to acknowledge that creation and preservation, though always at war with each other, go hand in hand, willy-nilly.

Of course, it is true that all Cary's novels turn upon this war, but it is frequently fought out in terms that do not require the figuration of the conservative man. Thus *Aissa Saved* centres on the liberation—and this phrase is no tautology—of the free spirit, in religious terms. For Aissa this means a pull in opposite directions: toward her pagan lover Gajere and toward the Christianity taught by the missioners. But there does not appear in that novel any substantial character embodying the conservative spirit. Furthermore, Cary often chooses to dramatize his theme in the more purely Blakean terms of male versus female. *The Moonlight* and *A Fearful Joy* are both of them altogether too schematic in this dramatization. In *The Moonlight* it is Rose who resists, and Ella who succumbs to, the creative impulse; in *A Fearful Joy* Tabitha repeatedly comes to recognize that she cannot live without the rascally Bonser; and he for his part always returns to her because she offers his creative spirit a completion equally necessary.

But in the best of the novels—in *Mister Johnson* and the two trilogies—the conservative character plays a prominent rôle. Indeed, there are two kinds of conservatives in the canon, and each is given an ultimate characterization in the trilogies. There is the conservative by intellectual and spiritual commitment figured in the lawyer Thomas Wilcher, and there is the conservative by instinct figured in the soldier Jim Latter. But the lines cross; these are not pure types worked out according to a grand preliminary plan. They are, on the contrary, discovered in the course of writing a number of novels. In Cary's early work I find sketches and half-portraits of these conservatives.

There is, first of all, Harry Gore in *An American Visitor*, an intellectual who has found his way to Africa. Nicknamed the Stork "because of his long thin legs, his long neck and long face and long beak," he resembles even in physique the character who is to become, ten years later, Thomas Wilcher. Gore's rôle as a colonial officer is to forestall, mediate and arrange. Everyone else in the book is passionately committed to a positive course of action: Marie Hasluck to militant pacifism, Monkey Bewsher to assertion of his authority, the prospectors to pressing their claims, the Africans to maintaining their authority and identity. Harry Gore's rôle is simply preventive. In order to keep the peace he lends Marie money, attempts to maintain intercourse between Bewsher and the prospectors, urges the prospectors to press their claims tactfully, and endeavours to avoid a war between blacks and whites. Gore is accused by one of the prospectors of playing at life, and so thoroughly does he understand the other man's nature that he rather sympathizes with the prospector. At the end of the book he realizes that all his management has not prevented alteration in the status quo. He becomes gloomy and pessimistic. "For Gore the world was going to the devil. A new dark age of persecution, superstition, tyranny and general wretchedness impended. Glory and loveliness stood on their last legs." And thenceforward the book becomes a kind of essay by Cary on the necessity of recognizing the fact that the world is always in a state of revolution. *An American Visitor* becomes a thesis and thus ceases to be a novel. And what is interesting in a man like Gore is not so much what leads up to his disillusionment as what afterwards impends. Perhaps, therefore, it was necessary for Cary to write Harry Gore into a novel before he could make him into Thomas Wilcher.

The other conservative—the soldier who becomes at his best Wilcher's loyal and simple-minded brother, Bill, at his worst the paranoid Jim Latter of the second trilogy—is prefigured variously in the early novels. The first appearance of this man is in *The African Witch* in the person of Captain Rackham, a young Irishman who is Assistant Police Commissioner in the Nigerian district of Rimi. He is full of gaiety, bounce and charm. He has an old-fashioned devotion to duty and he closes his mind to the political movement in Nigeria. He supposes his duty to consist in maintaining British supremacy in the colony, and he therefore resents such a man as the claimant to the Rimi throne, Louis Aladai. Rackham, indeed, flings him ignominiously into the river. This act spells the end of Rackham's career, the end of his engagement to Judith Coote and the end of his residence in Africa. The narrator tells of the young man's departure for England, where he is to keep a training stable in Berkshire; and there surely he will become, though the book does not say so, embittered for the same reasons that Jim Latter becomes embittered when he retires from Africa. To see in Rackham an early version of Jim Latter is to be reminded of the sympathy which Cary would invoke even for that murderous man. For Rackham is not unattractive; his very real quality is indicated in the nature of his response to the lame and sensitive Judith Coote, to whom he is for a time betrothed.

In *Castle Corner* both kinds of conservative appear—the soldier in Cock Jarvis, the intellectual in Philip Feenix. Jarvis's destiny is that of empire-builder. From a boy he displays the soldierly virtues of solemnity, reckless courage, simple patriotism. . . . As an enthusiastic officer in the West African Frontier Force, he subscribes to what the narrator calls "the master faith of the age; the idea of the struggle for existence; the survival of the fittest; the idea that some power in nature itself, a scientific providence discovered and proved by Darwin, had ordained progress by universal war." It is thus perfectly natural that he should, against government orders and against private orders, invade the Daji emirate, and thus precipitate an international

crisis. His enterprise requires not only great daring but great endurance. But his spirit is invincible, and his soldierly intelligence superb. And though no one knows how to take the news of his victory, he comes back to England a hero: his triumph coincides with the Boer agitation, and chauvinism is the style of the hour.

But since the *Castle Corner* trilogy remains unfinished, Harry Jarvis's career is not fully detailed. The career of Philip Feenix, however, is interrupted by suicide at the end of *Castle Corner* itself. Son of a colourless Protestant clergyman and nephew of a domineering and doting uncle, he is doomed to the mere pathos of mere failure. Tied by the strings of responsibility and love to his dynamic uncle, James Slatter, he surrenders again and again his chances for freedom. His uncle intends him to possess Castle Corner, and for years awaits the opportunity to take it over from John Chass, so that he can give it to his beloved Philly. But the opportunity never comes, and in the meantime Philip passes by the opportunity to go to Cambridge, or to go away from Ireland and become a missioner. He acts as Slatter's agent and secretary, and without knowing the cause of his dissatisfaction with life, turns to drink, lethargy and finally torpor. (pp. 77-96)

In *Mister Johnson* there are two conservatives, Harry Rudbeck and Sergeant Gollup. I have said enough about Rudbeck, who is, like Gollup, only lightly sketched out: for the book is almost altogether Johnson's. But Gollup must be dealt with here. He is an old soldier, a cockney with a sense of order who has built a good business in Fada. He is a man with a murderous temper, but he quickly forgets his anger. He likes Johnson, and the boy, perceiving this, likes him in return. Besides, Gollup is a man of imagination. On Sunday afternoons he gets drunk and becomes a philosopher. He talks about England and the regiment. "Gollup has the usual hatred of the old soldier for the rich and their women, and in fact for all those who live easy and self-indulgent lives without risk or responsibility, that hatred which has made all countries with conscription inclined to violent revolution." He is an empire man, a sort of working-class Jim Latter whose passionate luridness Johnson responds to without understanding it.

Finally—for the novels of childhood do not deal with the conservative temper except as it is potential in the children themselves—there are the conservatives in the two trilogies. In the Thomas Wilcher of the first trilogy (complemented by his soldier brother) and in the James Latter of the second are the penultimate embodiments, and they are first-rate characterizations altogether. But the ultimate embodiment is Chester Nimmo, who in the course of his career is transmogrified from the free to the unfree man: so tantalizing, so difficult, and so repellent that Cary tried in *The Moonlight* and *A Fearful Joy* to do without this kind of man. He did not fully succeed, for the life-defeated James Groom of *The Moonlight* and the life-defeated son of Tabitha in *A Fearful Joy* belongs to this type. But partly because they are sketchy, the books are sketchy. Cary's map of the world requires a map in depth of the conservative man. Such a map is to be found in Wilcher, in Latter and in Nimmo.

In every single one of Cary's novels there is a woman of impressive moral stature—impressive because she recognizes by instinct if not by ratiocination a rôle in life of some considerable magnitude. Generally, the moral stature of these women is matched by physical bulk, the outward and visible sign of their specially female grace. And all of them possess the splendid vigour which stems from certainty. This is not to say that they are unperplexed. Indeed—to take the most complex of them all—Nina in the second trilogy becomes from time to time so perplexed that she tries to take her own life: she becomes perplexed just because she is so certain that her rôle in life is to be Chester Nimmo's spouse, and she can hardly bear it. Above all, the Cary heroines exist not independently but dependently—upon the men whom it is their destiny to cherish; and when, as in *The Moonlight,* female sexuality is denied, the female nature becomes contorted. Cary draws women well. His skill derives in part, I think, from his thoroughly masculine comprehension of what is, despite all emancipation, still the opposite sex. In fact, Cary's women are often better than his men.

So it is Aissa who saves *Aissa Saved:* she who redeems it from mediocrity, she who makes it a first novel of promise. Among the central figures in Cary's novels, Aissa is certainly the simplest. Less educated even than the Ali who was originally meant to be the hero of this novel, Aissa is neither so intelligent as the Elizabeth of *The African Witch* nor so sophisticated as the almost entirely unsophisticated Sara Monday. Aissa's character can be drawn only in bold relief, because she is elemental; and she is therefore no doubt an excellent choice for the heroine of a first novel. Her ultimately fatal effort to create a life out of the materials given her is recorded with Cary's altogether characteristic sympathy for the human impulse to love, to create, to fulfil.

Aissa's devotion to Christianity springs initially from gratitude: she has come to the Shibi Mission as a refugee from her native village, and she makes Christianity into a substitute for what she has already discovered by instinct to be the foundation of her life: Christ becomes the father of her child and even, as she supposes when she is taking the sacrament of the Lord's supper, her husband. Such perplexity as she often feels is instantly resolved when surrogate and actuality meet: Aissa breaks off her singing of a hymn when she spies her husband Gajere, and she runs to his embraces. Nor will she return to the mission while she and Gajere can be together. Much of her life is spent protecting her child, who is more important to her than belief, more important than life itself. Toward the end of the book, reunited with Gajere after a long separation and after a number of scarifying experiences, Aissa asserts very practically, 'I do plenty good for Jesus. . . . Jesus, he do plenty for me. Good-bye now—all done finish.' But when, having been dragged off to the ants' nest to die, she is forever separated from Gajere, she turns to Jesus again, as substitute husband. "Jesus . . . had taken her, he was carrying her away in his arms."

The heroine of *An American Visitor* is, though extremely ignorant and naïve, more sophisticated than Aissa. Marie Hasluck, the American visiting Nigeria, is an anarchist; she has a faith, but it is an educated faith. As a newspaperwoman who has come to Africa to write a series of articles on native culture, she wishes to substantiate her prejudices in favour of what she takes to be noble savagery; and the book is a record both of her disillusionment in this respect and of her discovery of a faith differently based, a faith based on a truer apprehension of her own nature and thus of human nature altogether. At the beginning she is thought to be "a very dangerous agitator." This is because, as one of the prospectors explains, she is "teaching self-determination to bare-arsed apes." Another replies that if he "was an Amurcan girl brought up on Freud and the fourteen points mixed in with Valentino and turned loose in a wilderness of notion salesmen and ward politicians, he'd be Bolshy. But the fact was that the poor bitch didn't know what she was or what she wanted. That was the trouble." This is indeed Marie's trouble, although she does not discover the fact for some considerable time. At first, and despite evidence to the contrary from the beginning, she reads Africa through the eyes of Rousseau.

The common ground which Marie and Monkey Bewsher find is a mutual distrust of civilization. For different reasons each dislikes the idea of the "encroachment" of civilization upon native culture. On the evening after both of them have nearly been killed by the natives, they argue with Frank Cottee, one of the prospectors, while Gore attempts to make conciliatory remarks to both parties. Cottee attacks Marie as an anarchist, and Marie is secretly frightened; she "was liable to these fits of doubt and dreaded them. They had a physical effect upon her nerves. She felt sometimes as if the actual ground had wavered and sunk beneath her. It was for a moment as if the most solid objects were illusory, as if there was nothing secure, nothing fixed, permanent and trustworthy in the whole world; no peace, no refuge."

There is indeed no refuge in the beliefs which she has brought as baggage to Africa with her. But she finds her way confusedly and certainly to the female destiny of wife to Bewsher; and shedding the impedimenta of anarchism she attaches herself to him in such domestic dependence that she can as easily dispense with ungrounded faith as Aissa herself. It is not simply the facts of Africa that overturn Marie Hasluck's beliefs: it is the overwhelming fact of female life.

With his customary daring, Cary makes Elizabeth Aladai, the African witch, the moral centre of his third novel. Tall, bulky, strong, this woman of "monumental dignity" is a ju-ju priestess and she dominates *The African Witch:* dominates her brother Louis Aladai; dominates Judith Coote, the lame and lively don who has come to Nigeria because she is engaged to the equally lively though not so talented Assistant Police Commissioner Jock Rackham; dominates the Reverend Selah Coker, whose idea of Christianity centres on sacrifice; dominates the Mohammedan claimant to the throne—and even causes the most powerful white man in the area, the Resident, to walk several miles because she has declared a woman's war.

Her first appearance is especially impressive. She comes to the door of her ju-ju house and "she almost filled the opening which framed her with sunlight streaming into the yard behind. She was a woman who seemed, in her height and proportions, bigger than the largest and most powerful men. In fact she was probably about five foot ten in height, and fifteen or sixteen stone in weight—not of fat, but of bone and muscle." (pp. 96-101)

Elizabeth is powerful not only in her own realm, the ju-ju house and its surroundings, but within the entire purview of the novel. *The African Witch*'s plot turns on a struggle for the succession to the emirate of Rimi. The two chief contenders for the throne are a Mohammedan leader named Salé and Elizabeth's brother Louis, who is a Christian. Since Salé's accession would threaten her because it threatens ju-ju, she supports her brother's claims, not because he tolerates ju-ju, but because he is "a fool boy. She could manage Aladai at any time."

Elizabeth's greatest triumph is the women's war, of which she is instigator and commanding general. She undertakes it because she wishes to support her brother's royal claims. At one point she is saved by her female nature. She is captured and imprisoned. When she refuses bribes, her captors feed her poisoned chicken and put her into a hole in the bush to be eaten by hyenas. In such circumstances a more ordinary mortal would die. But not Elizabeth. She is rescued, taken back to her compound, and delivered of a baby. Before long the women's war is resumed, and although it is brought to an end quickly when the troops are called out by the Resident, Elizabeth herself is not defeated. Indeed she has her most complete triumph of all when her paramour Akande Tom, who has tried to escape from her and who is attempting with the help of Judith Coote to "learn book," returns to her in misery and terror. Elizabeth works her ju-ju on him and he crawls to her on all fours. He is whipped "and he no longer tries to be a white man, or to learn book."

Elizabeth Aladai is perhaps the most stunning of Cary's females, and female she is. She is woman triumphant rather than woman subdued. She acts out the rôle described in "The Mental Traveller," for she binds iron thorns around the heads of her men, and conquers them. Because she is stronger than any of the men within her orbit she succeeds to fail: the process described in Blake's poem requires a man to rend up his manacles. Elizabeth, therefore, is Sara Monday or Nina Nimmo victorious; the two Englishwomen are luckier in that the material with which they have to work is adamant, and so their female destinies are, paradoxically, more thoroughly fulfilled in submissiveness.

Castle Corner and the two novels of childhood mark a transition, it seems to me, from the starkness of Africa to the complexities of the English scene depicted in *The Moonlight, A Fearful Joy* and the two trilogies. I am arrested in *Castle Corner* by the figure of Helen Pynsant, the not altogether respectably fashionable woman who is in a way a sketch for the Tabitha of *A Fearful Joy,* although Helen is a colder and less sympathetic figure. In *Charley is My Darling* there is Lizzie Galor, the adolescent girl to whom Charley becomes attached, a girl whose devotedness is as deep and instinctive and complete as that of every other Cary heroine. And there is in *A House of Children* the general favourite Delia, a sixteen-year-old girl the very violence of whose personality grips the imagination. "Even when she was sitting still, she had the air of intense activity within; of rapid and concentrated thought or vigorous feeling or both." Against her the phlegmatic Frances, who marries early and respectably and not for love but for motherhood, is a fine contrast. But none of these females is realized in the transitional novels as well as they are elsewhere.

In *The Moonlight* female nature is the very subject. The intended commanding centre of the book is Miss Ella Venn, the seventy-four-year-old younger sister of Rose and the mother (though this fact is not acknowledged until quite late in the book) of Amanda. It is a happy choice of viewpoint. For Ella both as younger sister and as mother is a mediator between the generations. Rose as a Victorian lives for duty; Amanda as a child of the twentieth century lives in the atmosphere of emancipation; and Ella, who understands female nature better than either of them, tries to reconcile both her sister and her daughter to a more accurate version. Ella is inarticulate—she is supposed by her relations to be a romantic—but she has that splendid vitality and instinctive commitment to female nature so characteristic of Cary heroines. The book fails not because of the rôle of Ella Venn but because of faults of construction and viewpoint: because, as a thesis-novel in answer to a thesis-novel, it forgets to be novel at all.

Of Tabitha Baskett in *A Fearful Joy* nearly enough has already been said. The daughter of a suburban doctor, she is "a small thin girl with large, too prominent eyes, a thick mouth, a snub nose, and a heavy clubbed pigtail of brown hair. And she was still remarkable for nothing but a certain violence of ordinariness." After her father's death Tabitha becomes severely and perfervidly religious. She is devoted to her elder brother Harry "because she knew that he was good;" he is not an affectionate man and he lectures her; but she hates his wife Edith—"handsome, sensual, rather blowsy, fond of bright colours and rich food, critical, like a woman much loved, of her husband." Tabitha embraces the idea of being a missioner in China, until a missioner dares criticize ladies who ride bicycles. She then determines to become a concert pianist, and practises six hours a day for over a year. But she becomes restless. She says to herself, "Oh—oh—oh, if only something would happen!"

At once—in consonance with the rules of melodrama—she becomes involved with Dick Bonser, the handsome young man who has been black-balled from the local tennis club; who is in debt, but who expects a large inheritance as soon, he says, as a law case is decided in his favour. Bonser tells her fascinating things about himself—for instance, that he is the illegitimate son of "a nobleman of the highest rank and a countess." He declares great love for Tabitha and a few days after proposes marriage to her. Tabitha cannot say no, and she runs away with him.

Such is the beginning of Tabitha's first adventure with Bonser, and it establishes the pattern of all the others. She is drawn to him irresistibly from girlhood because of the radiance and the fertility of his imagination. The duplicity in his character, the bombast of his speech, the fatuousness of his grandiose schemes eternally madden her, but throughout the course of her life she is vitalized in spirit by this restless, roguish, animated man. Even after he dies at a great age, the memory of the man, and the reincarnation of his spirit in his granddaughter by Tabitha, renew the old woman's life.

Cary's vision is tripartite, and the three figures on the landscape of his world require one another. When, as in *The Moonlight* and *A Fearful Joy* the female dominates, the whole picture becomes inadequate because distorted. The men of *The Moonlight* never come forward—or if they do they are soon made to beat a retreat before the person and then the ghost of Rose Venn. Nor can Dick Bonser take his place in *A Fearful Joy;* the book is too thoroughly Tabitha's, and he has no complement as do both Gulley Jimson and Chester Nimmo. But Sara and Nina are both torn between the free and the unfree man, which is simply to say that their complicated female natures demand a complexity, in fact a contradiction, in response. Sara and Nina succeed as characters by virtue of their relationships. They succeed also—and this is perhaps putting the same matter in other words—because they can tell their own stories, which can be corrected in their turn by the stories of their men.

To notice . . . how often Cary repeats himself, is not, I trust, to suggest by way of derogation that he is a limited writer. Limited he surely is—and so is everyone else by culture, temperament, intelligence, experience. Cary differs, as all artists differ, from other people in coming to have a sense of the scope of his limitation. And he differs also in that the richness of his culture, the sturdiness of his temperament, the acuity of his intelligence, the catholicity of his experience made possible the writing of novels representing something worth representation. What I have been saying in this chapter shows something else as well: that the literary artist's endeavour is not simply to work with the variously tractable medium of language and the variously tractable medium of structure. The artist's endeavour must be to know himself. (pp. 102-06)

Andrew Wright, in his Joyce Cary: A Preface to His Novels, *Chatto & Windus, 1958, 186 p.*

HAZARD ADAMS   (essay date 1959)

[*Adams is an American educator and critic who has written extensively on William Blake's poetry. He is the author of* Joyce Cary's Trilogies: Pursuit of the Particular Real *(1983), a close examination of the philosophical ideas implicit in Cary's two trilogies. In the following excerpt, he discusses the shifting perspectives provided by the three different narrators of the novels in the first trilogy.*]

Cary is not a slavish copier of early twentieth-century modes, and his own writing about literature is remarkably devoid of the literary cliches of our time. Nevertheless, it is clear that he would not have written as he did had his immediate predecessors not written as they did. It should be obvious to any reader of the *First Trilogy*, for example, that Cary is most interested in the minds (how his characters imaginatively construct their worlds) rather than the actions of his characters; this preoccupation as well as his treatment of focus of narration to reveal minds is quite twentieth-century, though on the surface he may adopt older techniques. Cary's interest in mind is so predominant and so clearly based upon contemporary attitudes toward our knowledge of each other that we can say Cary's allowing the three speakers of his trilogy to see and comment on each other is an outgrowth of present attitudes toward experience. (pp. 108-09)

In *To Be A Pilgrim,* the second novel of the trilogy, we have neither the continuous present of Joyce and Woolf nor a tale told completely in retrospect. We have instead a man writing a journal. What Tom Wilcher writes at the beginning or at any given moment cannot be affected by later acts. At times he seems to have written immediately or a few hours after the events have occurred. In the midst of these more immediate responses are long passages of reminiscence colored by events in the near present which have given rise to them. These reminiscences are not treated in chronological order, but instead depend on the mind of Wilcher in the continuous present of the actual writing. On the surface the device is similar to that of Samuel Richardson's *Pamela,* but made far more complicated and revelatory by this constant emphasis upon the mingling of recent and old memories. Cary's device provides several advantages. If he gives up some immediacy of response to specific experience, he gains in depth some of the character's memory and formulating imagination. But more important, he can present Wilcher in a particular way, which symbolizes his central concerns, for Wilcher's compositional problem is an analogue of his whole emotional problem: to strike a balance between the present and his attachment to the past.

Of the three central characters of the trilogy, Wilcher is most introspective. Unlike Sara Monday of *Herself Surprised,* he is tortured by doubts about his own place and the validity of his own emotions. He has been brought up a conservative in all things, but, growing old, he has come to think conservatism an impractical spiritual ideal. He learns that change is the rule and that to live by it is a necessity, but he is tied to the past. In order to express this tension between past and present in Wilcher's mind, Cary chose the device of the journal, because in it we can see Wilcher's finished, most complete attempt to meet his problem rationally while at the same time overpowering emotional complications shine through the effort. So if at first Cary here appears to be concerned mainly with that part of the mind that moves above the surface, it becomes clear as

we proceed that in Wilcher's pathetic and moving attempts to deal with his problem by writing it out we discover much more about Wilcher than even he is aware of. He confesses to more than he realizes, in attempting to bring his actions under some rational explanation, he discloses a gap between action and analysis. Wilcher does not really lie to us. Except for the sin of omission he is as candid as his emotions will allow, but his life itself is a contradiction. As his journal proceeds, we realize that his eccentric brother and sister, Edward and Lucy, are really parts of himself suppressed in odd, unexpected ways. We see also that although he appears to accept the future and therefore the disappearance of the past and present he cannot see that future except in the image of Sara Monday:

> "Yes," I thought, "that was the clue to Lucy, to my father, to Sara Jimson; it is the clue to all that English genius which bore them and cherished them, clever and simple. Did not my father say of Tolbrook which he loved so much, 'Not a bad billet,' or 'Not a bad camp?' And Sara. Was not her view of life as 'places,' as 'situations' the very thought of the wanderer and the very strength of her soul? She put down no roots into the ground; she belonged with the spirit; her goods and possessions were all in her own heart and mind, her skill and courage."
>
> And is not that the clue to my own failure in life?

Sara comes to represent to him what he somehow cannot come to be. His tragedy is that for him Sara is not the true future but the past—something else that must simply be uprooted, merely an *image* of stability which he confuses with real, moving time.

The first novel of the trilogy, **Herself Surprised,** has very obvious affinities to *Moll Flanders* and in this sense might be thought of as old-fashioned, if it were not for the immensely greater insight into herself with Sara Monday unwittingly divulges. There is absolutely no confusion apparent in Cary's aims, while we are never certain whether Defoe is fully in control of his material. Cary's method is not that of the journal but of the retrospective confession. Sara writes it in jail previous to the action which is the present of the third novel, **The Horse's Mouth.** Here Cary wanted to provide us less with immediate reaction to sheer events than with actions filtered through and shaped by an imagination viewing all things retrospectively. The journal of a constantly introspective person would be impossible for Sara, who has no powers of introspection and no other inclination to keep such a record. Her "confession" is being written for money. The important thing here is that Sara be allowed to review her past, that we see the speaking, moralizing Sara, the supposedly repentant Sara as no different from the Sara she describes.

It is totally through the language she uses that the present Sara is revealed. She, of course, does not realize how much her literary style reveals about herself. In fact, she does not even realize that there is that much to reveal. Neither an introspective person nor a rationalist, she is a *survivor* who, as Wilcher understands, is able to ride the wave of time. Quite clearly Sara colors most of the facts, and her moralizations are convenient to her. She often verbalizes in the most sentimental and hackneyed fashion. She constantly draws lessons from actions, but we know by the distance between her language and the actions she describes that these lessons remain isolated in a world of theory which never impinges on the time world. She instinctively knows that the flesh is always weak; her confession, though outwardly pious, ends as its own apology:

I deserved no less, as the chaplain said, for no one had better chances and more warnings. Neither had my luck left me, for just when I was fretting for our quarter day at Gulley's and Tommy's bills on top of that, this kind gentleman came from the news agency and offered me a hundred pounds in advance for my story in the newspapers, when I come out. Paid as I like. So that will pay the school bills, at least, till I'm free, and I've no fear there. A good cook will always find work, even without a character, and can get a new character in twelve months, and better herself, which, God helping me, I shall do, and keep a more watchful eye, next time, on my flesh, now I know it better.

It might be argued that the real Sara has never been represented, that her language provides too opaque a surface, and the only alternative to revealing merely that surface would be a Molly Bloom soliloquy or something similar to Woolf's technique in *The Waves*. But it seems to me that Cary's method in the long run really does with language what the symbolists constantly claimed to do, that is, to express linguistically by suggestion depths which cannot be expressed by direct representation. It might be argued, furthermore, that Joyce's and Woolf's soliloquies were *by comparison* naive attempts to represent directly in language something that can only be approached—the unspoken areas of mind where linguistic structure dissolves into something expressible only indirectly. Cary's alternative is to use language in a true imitation of perceivable action and yet point through it to a depth of meaning.

Of the three characters who narrate the novels to us, Gulley Jimson is most conscious of himself and his motives. He is also, because of this, in greatest control of what he cares to reveal. His exaggerations are consciously contrived and a key to what lies behind them. Cary's technique here is to let the speaker actually speak, dictate his story to someone else (that someone is never named, but it is probably Nosy Barbon; surely it is not Gulley's biographer Alabaster). The advantage is one of fidelity to the total representation, and with Gulley as the speaker certain advantages of the two preceding methods have been combined. The book is not a journal, as is Wilcher's, but it has an immediacy consistent with Gulley's painter's eye, and the immediate events are those which take place during only about one year's time (further shortened by Gulley's failure to tell us much about his experiences in jail and hospital during this period). It is in no respect a confession even in surface gesture, as is Sara's, and in only a very limited sense is it a personal apology (Gulley calls it a "memoir"). It is as if we were present at a long dramatic monologue, for Gulley treats his own story with art. There are passages (for example, the opening of the book) which closely resemble stream-of-consciousness technique, but these passages are *by* Gulley, who is an early twentieth-century artist using early twentieth-century forms. The novel is about a man who is familiar with the techniques of discontinuity and interior monologue and uses them naturally. Gulley casts his whole story into the form of what is now commonly called "soliloquy." Cary's aim is to show Gulley's experience consciously shaped by his own imagination, not an unconscious reflection of his experience. We cannot imagine Gulley keeping a journal, and pure stream of consciousness is not to Cary's purpose, for Cary wishes to develop Gulley as a kind of apologist for the position of symbolist artists in general. The exaggerations and prevarications of Gulley are therefore more impersonal than those of Sara and Wilcher even though they are more carefully contrived. Gulley is not, like Sara or Tom, an unconscious ironist. He is instead a very conscious one.

It would *appear* that Gulley is more concerned with conceiving works of art in the imagination than actually in completing them. This is partly true, but it is also in part the artist's defense against a hostile world. Apparently Gulley is a true son of the imagination, in Coleridge's sense of the term: the shaping spirit is an aspect of mind, the canvas being a representation of it. Gulley's epic paintings are seldom finished, and if they are they are usually covered over or mutilated. Of course he hates this—he occasionally slips and reveals to us indirectly (it is also Sara's view of him) that he *would* like the fame that comes from creating a lasting work. But he needs a defense against time and its powers to destroy, and part of his glorification of the activity of art is a shoring up against ruin. He tries to think of his own imaginings as the important things, and he tries to be content with them. His resilience in the face of wholesale destruction is marvelous to behold. When his great work is used by Mrs. Coker to patch the roof, it is Nosy who is outwardly indignant, not Gulley. It is obvious that Gulley is rationalizing the situation, but on the other hand there is truth to his argument that one must always "give way to gaiety" (the words here are particularly revealing of Gulley's gesture; a thinner mask would have required one *not* to have given way to *morbidity*). In his facetious argument against Nosy's hysterical indignation, Gulley indicates that all art is eventually destructible, that real artistry is work, activity, creation—not the dead product. Gulley argues that Mrs. Coker's action is unfortunate mainly because it prevents him from work.

Gulley exaggerates and prevaricates as a defense against a world which resents the artist and the creative spirit, but these prevarications are also truths in which he almost believes. Speaking to Nosy and to his own youth, he seems to be defeating his own position. The point is that Gulley attacks Nosy not for the wrongness of his views, which are right enough, but for the uselessness of arguing in such a fashion when as an old man it is only to waste time. The important thing is again *work* and not to let the destruction of the past destroy the future. The idealism of the true artist, who knows what he is doing, is to get on with the job, and almost all of Gulley's actions are traceable primarily to this desire. It is of course convenient if while one is getting on with the job one can also gain some revenge against the Philistine, but such play is incidental to the greater end.

Both the comedy and the tragedy of Gulley's situation as artist are heightened by Cary's allowing Gulley to dictate his memoir, for throughout the novel we find Gulley trying publicly to keep to his own ideals. With Gulley speaking, the tragic necessity of his comic resiliency is always before us, constructed by himself.

By having the three speakers of his trilogy tell about each other, each in his own way and with the full force of his assumptions about the world behind his interpretation, Cary extends the depth of our perception of all of them. At the same time the indirection of his focus upon them is increased. Each character is a kind of crystal, and the reader's vision of each is complicated by the fact that he is invited to look through one crystal into another. Invariably, each crystal observed reflects the crystal through which it is observed.

In *The Horse's Mouth*, Gulley Jimson reveals himself. He also reveals something of Sara, just as he says that his painting revealed "some of her, anyhow." But of course the aspect of her which he does reveal is that part which fits into his own vision of things. Not that this perspective is insignificant. Jimson looking at Sara reveals Jimson as if we could see in Sara a reflection of him which he himself cannot see; but Jimson also gets at something of the real Sara. The reader then must resolve this Sara, discounting Jimson's excesses and perhaps inaccuracies, with the Sara which she reveals to us as well as the Sara which is revealed by Wilcher. Then, just to complete a regress almost long enough to please J. W. Dunne, the reader must weigh all of these views against his own conception of human nature.

Cary has spoken of Sara as the central figure by which the three novels are linked, and in his introduction he has stated how the three views of her differ:

> Sara regards herself as a tenderhearted creature whose troubles are due to her good nature. This estimate is true. Wilcher sees in her an easygoing mistress who will cherish him in his decrepitude. He is quite right. Gulley calls her a man grabber, and he is also right. All the ideas of the three about each other are right from their point of view.

This is an introductory simplification, adequate enough for Sara's view of herself, which is less important than what she *reveals* of herself; but Wilcher sees more than this in her and so does Jimson. We may take as examples Wilcher's and Jimson's attitude toward Sara and religion. There is a considerable disagreement between Wilcher and Jimson about this, but transcending this disagreement is a curious accord. The disagreement between them reveals not Sara but their own particular selves, while their agreement reveals Sara. The best indication of the difference is expressed by Jimson in his account of the meeting between himself and Wilcher:

> "A truly religious woman," said Mr. W. using *vox humana.*
>
> "Yes, you might say Sara had some religion, female religion."

By his answer Jimson relates Sara to the natural earth-mother archetype of Blake's prophetic books, from which he is always quoting. The comparison is meant to be anything but complimentary to Sara's *formal* religion, which he interprets as hypocritical. Elsewhere he says, "Sara was a God-using Christian that went to church to please herself and pick up some useful ideas about religion, hats and the local gossip." Jimson sees Sara's constant moralization as a form empty of religious content.

Wilcher, on the other hand, sees her quite differently:

> One forgot the thick coarse figure, the rough features, in the light of a spirit which gave always encouragement. From the beginning I had noticed one good quality in Sara, her regularity at prayers and church. But I knew she had been well brought up by a God-fearing mother and thought her piety merely habitual. I came to discover how strong and rich a fountain of grace played not only in the energy of her religious observance but in everything she did, and in her most casual remark. All was colored by these country maxims, so often in her mouth which rise from a wisdom so deep in tradition that it is like the spirit of a race.

What we notice at once in Wilcher is a tendency himself to use well-worn morals, frayed cliches, and in general a rhetoric now considered devoid of sincerity (though for him it is sincere). It is no wonder that Sara's language appeals to a man who would use the term "fountain of grace" and put together the phrase "a spirit which gave always encouragement." It is no wonder that, following up this hint, we discover the maxims of Sara which Wilcher quotes to be far more trite than those

Jimson recalls and even more trite than those Sara herself uses. (pp. 109-15)

But in spite of these obvious differences in attitude, Jimson and Wilcher each discover something similar in Sara, though they might not themselves be aware of the similarity. They both see in her some basic strength. (p. 115)

In the end we see that through the expression of their views of Sara both Wilcher and Jimson reveal much of themselves. Sara helps reveal for us Wilcher's immense difficulty in bringing his image of her into line with his moral sense, and yet we understand the necessity of his doing so. When Wilcher comes to see her as a schemer, he convinces himself that she had to scheme and thus formulates an excuse for her. Jimson sees her as a schemer but sees also no reason to defend her against a moral code which he rejects. With Wilcher there is some resentment to be overcome, a resentment which arises out of his attachment to other ideals. When he sees Sara for the last time, this resentment comes to the fore, and he accuses her of duplicity. But later he regrets having done so. Jimson, whose world is far larger than Wilcher's, can become enraged at Sara, can suspect her always, but is not at war with himself over her.

And yet neither is wrong about Sara, even if each may be wrong to put her so neatly into his own frame (and this wrongness is human nature). Nor are they in such disagreement over her as their language suggests. If Wilcher reads freedom of spirit in Sara's trite maxims, Gulley reads it in her scheming. And each is right, though each must see through his own crystal of ideas and beliefs to that other person who is never more or less than his own formative powers can make her. (p. 117)

In looking at someone else each character reveals primarily himself. Jimson's comment upon Wilcher is brief but pithy. We have already suggested that the formal principle of Jimson's world is Blakean. If Sara is by turns the true and false female of Blake's "Mental Traveller," Wilcher is the villainous image of abstraction and generalization which Blake called the "spectre." In Wilcher, Jimson sees the irrationality and viciousness of Reason:

> Yes, a regular Boorjwarrior. London is full of them. Infuriated blackcoats. Lying low in some ambush with a dagger in one hand and a bomb in the other. And the fires of death and hell burning under their dickies. When you meet them, they're all clockwork bows and hems and how-de-do's, until they've got you where they want you, and then out come the claws, and bang, they're at your throat like a Bengal tiger.

Fitting Wilcher to his own pattern, Jimson nevertheless confirms something about Wilcher that *To Be A Pilgrim* also suggests: Wilcher is torn between his reason and his emotions in a way that Sara never, and Jimson seldom, is. Jimson, as is natural to him, clearly sees this in Wilcher as a great danger to others. In Wilcher's own story we see that the greater danger is to himself.

But although Jimson in his way is quite right about Wilcher as regards any conceivable relations between *them*, Sara sees a side of Wilcher which the suspicious Jimson can not afford to notice. In reflecting upon Wilcher, however, she too reflects herself:

> As for those who said Mr. W. was a hypocrite to make so much of church and then run after young girls, I thought of his boils and his hot blood, and I

thought, too, of my past deeds. And it seemed to me
that I might have been called a hypocrite, when I
was going to church in my best, knowing that Hickson and several more men were looking upon me
with lickerish eyes.

For Sara it is live and let live, and when Wilcher displays
himself naked in the hall she simply thinks, ". . . if the master
had that whim, to show himself, it was no harm in the world,
except to idle heads and bad tongues."

Except for giving us some factual information (she, incidentally, is very inaccurate about dates), Sara does not tell us
much about Wilcher that we do not know from *To Be A Pilgrim*.
But she does, in contrast to Jimson, suggest that Wilcher's
outward gentility has some real merit: she sees that he is capable
of kindness.

We can dismiss Wilcher on Jimson quickly. Characteristically,
he would prefer not to dwell on unpleasantness and therefore
refrains from much comment. To think of Jimson, perhaps, is
to think of Sara in a way which prevents him from seeing her
as a symbol of his release.

But Sara on Gulley is much more rewarding. Sara likes to
mother her men, and she accepts the bad in them with the good
in order to retain this pleasure.

It is fairly obvious that Sara liked Gulley a great deal. We
know this mainly because she is always comparing Matt and
Tom with Gulley to the latter's detriment. Matt and Tom were
in her eyes weak (as to her, all men are), so she praises them.
But in at least one respect Gulley was strong. She says of him,
"If I ever loved Gulley, it was for his never grousing and never
spoiling a joy in hand with yesterday's grief or tomorrow's
fear." . . . Her commentary upon Gulley's virtues confirms
that Gulley lives the Blakean life which he is constantly talking
about, even though the odds against the artist's doing this are
extreme. Furthermore, Sara's own judgment of Gulley is a
convincing reminder that Sara too is strong and that Wilcher
is as right as Jimson about her basic strength.

In observing what these three speakers tell of each other, we
notice that as a binding force Sara is the central figure of the
trilogy. it is she who plays the greatest part in the stories outside
her own. It is she who reflects the others most brightly, but
she does this by her presence in their stories, not in hers. If
we were to subtract *Herself Surprised* from the trilogy, we
would lose less of all the characters, than if we subtracted
either *The Horse's Mouth* or *To Be A Pilgrim*. Sara is a marvelous character in her own story, but in the other two alone
she vindicates Cary's method: she *reflects* Jimson and Wilcher
better in their stories than she describes them to us in her own.
We can conclude from this that Cary's aim is still the modern
one of exploring the minds of his characters. From *Herself
Surprised* through *The Horse's Mouth* all experience becomes
images in the minds of his speakers. And the greatest of these
images is Sara Monday.

These points prove, I think, what Cary says in his introduction
about his characters: "Each of us is obliged to construct his
own idea, his own map of things by which he is going to find
his way, so far as he can, through life." This is what Cary's
people do and fail to do in the novels. Woolf and Joyce in
their most extreme efforts attempted to explore the minds of
their characters below the level of statement. Cary chose to
explore what the minds of his characters can articulate, how
conscious they are of their own self-revelations, how careful
they are in trying to suppress what they think they have not

revealed. Adopting also a triple focus, he sometimes seems to
have created a world similar to the mirror house of an amusement park. But this creation has the sanction of modernity
every bit as much as do Joyce's interior monologues—both
suggest that the problem of our age is the isolation of mind.
If Cary's method often has some obvious affinities to those of
Defoe and Samuel Richardson, in another respect he has done
from the level of articulate speech of his characters what Joyce
and Woolf did from below the level of articulation. In moving
beyond the eighteenth century, he exhibits a more careful control of the said to reveal the unsaid. In moving back from Joyce
and Woolf, he has reasserted that the surface of speech as well
as that which moves below it reveals mind. It is an axiom that
a new step in literature is also a re-examination and use of the
past.

A final point: It is perhaps Cary's disarming simplicity, his
magical ability, as Walter Allen has pointed out, to become
his characters that has put off critical analysis of his work. We
recall that, as a follower of Blake, Cary's Gulley Jimson was
an English symbolist. Perhaps one of these days someone will
follow the suggestion that in at least some respects Cary was
too. When that time comes, Cary will indeed "baffle nobody."
Criticism is prepared for *that*. (pp. 117-20)

Hazard Adams, "Joyce Cary's Three Speakers," in
Modern Fiction Studies, *Vol. V, No. 2, Summer,
1959, pp. 108-20.*

ROBERT BLOOM   (essay date 1962)

[*Bloom is an American educator and critic. In the following excerpt, he maintains that critical neglect of Cary may be attributed
to the faulty conception of reality in which the novels are grounded,
rendering them devoid of meaning and order.*]

Any admirer of Joyce Cary must feel uneasy about the neglect
that Cary has suffered at the hands of serious critics of contemporary fiction, and somewhat disconcerted, as well, by the
extravagant recognition that he has had from his most enthusiastic admirers. The injured tone that Hazard Adams takes in
his recent survey of Cary criticism [see Additional Bibliog-
raphy], as he contemplates the "woefully small" body of intelligent and detailed comment now available, threatens to become the characteristic way of thinking about, and dealing
with, Cary. We have come to a point, at any rate, where to
approach Cary's novels at all is to be concerned inescapably,
if not woefully, with his failure, by and large, to interest the
best critical minds of our time. The present study attempts to
explore and to explain what I take to be the basis of this failure.
The fault, we shall see, lies less with the critics than with Cary
himself.

Cary's consistently impressive performances in the sixteen novels that he wrote in the period from 1932, when his first novel,
Aissa Saved, appeared, to 1959, when the posthumous *The
Captive and the Free* was issued, are enough to assure us that
a problem exists. The fiction produced in England during this
period does not, on the whole, make Cary's work suffer by
comparison, and will not, in any event, entirely explain the
silence about him in high places. The explanation, I think,
must rather be looked for in the particular conception of reality
in which his novels are grounded. It is this conception which
gives them their shape, their purport, and their vitality. But
more importantly, . . . it is this same conception which is responsible for Cary's frequent failure to impose genuinely meaningful shape on his fiction—a failure that has made his novels,

despite his extraordinary gifts, fall short of the best work done in this century. (pp. vii-viii)

In 1920, when he was thirty-two years of old, Joyce Cary settled at Oxford with his wife and began a course of study to prepare himself for writing novels. . . . From 1920 to 1932, when his first novel, *Aissa Saved,* was issued, Cary published nothing but worked steadily at re-educating himself, repairing his intellectual omissions, and achieving an "integrated idea of the world." His success was sufficiently meaningful, to himself at least, to allow him, in the interval from 1932 to his death in March 1957, to produce sixteen novels, more than thirty-five short stories, four political treatises, a book on aesthetics, some twenty-five literary essays and another twenty-nine on general subjects, together with an attic full of manuscripts which remain, for one reason or another, unpublished. Having solved his intellectual problem, his only difficulty since 1932, he tells us, was to choose what he should write next, what aspect of the rich world he should explore.

In discussions of his own work, Cary has repeatedly insisted upon this close connection between his systematic thought and his ability to write his mature fiction. He has been careful too, however, to point out that the novel is by no means a form which accommodates itself easily to philosophical discourse. "I don't care for philosophers in books," he says. "They are always bores. A novel should be an experience and convey an emotional truth rather than arguments." (pp. 1-2)

In one of his most succinct formulations of this idea, Cary says,

> The world loves its own creation, which is its life. Not merely the artist, but every man and woman, begins from childhood to create for himself a world to which, as creator, he is deeply attached. Each of these worlds is highly complex and extensive. One man, for instance, does not create for himself only a home, a business, a family, but a religion, a political idea, a nation, a world idea. He creates them in his imagination, and lives in them. Deprived of them, or even any large part of them, he would wither and die.

Cary is not talking about an insurmountable metaphysical or epistemological isolation that cuts men off completely from one another. "Men are together in feeling, in sympathy," he says, "but alone in mind." Still, the isolation in mind is formidable and quite irremediable: "We are alone in our own worlds. We can sympathize with each other, be fond of each other, but we can never completely understand each other. We are not only different in character and mind, we don't know how far the difference goes."

We can readily trace, if we wish, this notion of the private world through most of the fiction that Cary has produced since 1932, along with the essentially objective or dramatic cast that it gives to his work. He has been content, in what has come to seem the best modern manner, to remove himself as author from his novels and stories and allow his characters to convey their own unique, individual worlds. His very first novel, *Aissa Saved,* involves Cary's remarkable entry into the mind and world of a primitive African girl who commingles missionary Christianity and pagan worship until they yield her a culminating apocalyptic vision. Of this novel Cary says that it "deals with individual religion, that is to say, the beliefs or unconscious assumptions which actually govern conduct. These assumptions are very different in every person. That is to say, everyone has his own faith. Of course each great religion does

draw large numbers of people together in general rules of conduct, and general statements of belief. But each person makes a particular application of the rules drawn from all kinds of sources." In *Aissa,* then, Cary's notion of a personal and private reality is dealt with primarily in religious terms. He continues to render the African religious sensibility and the world that it shapes brilliantly in *The African Witch,* with its close scrutiny of juju. The other two African novels are similar achievements of empathic penetration. In *An American Visitor* Cary deals with the evolution of Marie Hasluck, an American visitor to Nigeria, from a vague, unrealistic liberalism to a genuine grasp of African life, a growth which is brought about chiefly by her increasing intimacy with Bewsher, a somewhat Africanized District Officer. Marie's world, in effect, undergoes correction and amplification under the tutelage of Bewsher and Africa. In *Mister Johnson* Cary deals once again with a native formulation of reality, this time the spontaneous, childlike world of a young African clerk who moves, during the course of the novel, from joyfulness and song to a touching death, as a result of his imperfect assimilation of British culture and his unconquerable naïveté. His simple created world does not accord sufficiently with imperialistic complexities to see him through his life. In Cary's novels of childhood, *Charley Is My Darling* and *A House of Children,* this same leading idea is in force. The first of these deals with a group of London children evacuated to rural England during the Second World War. It is concerned particularly with young Charley Brown's adolescent world and the place that delinquency and love have in it as it brushes against the harsh adult universe. *A House of Children* is an evocation of the childhood world of the novel's narrator, Evelyn Corner, set down with compelling tenderness and sensitivity. It is here that Cary introduces first-person narrative into the novels, although the autobiographical context—Cary's own childhood in Northern Ireland is the source of the book—makes the technique rather a different thing from his later use of it in the trilogies. The two women's novels, *The Moonlight* and *A Fearful Joy* are devoted to the same kind of exploration, this time of feminine worlds; and a number of Cary's best short stories are also grounded in the idea.

It is in the trilogies, however, that the created worlds of individual human beings receive their fullest exposition. In order to exploit this conception as fully as possible, Cary, not content with a mere Jamesian limited third-person objectivity, all but obliterates himself as author. He does so by creating six different authors, all of whom write their own novels in the first person. As a result, he is in a position to allow his narrators an unstinted autonomy in the projection of the worlds that they have shaped for themselves, as well as six different styles in which to do so. *Herself Surprised* is concerned with Sara Monday's domestic world and with the womanly force that sustains it. *To Be a Pilgrim* is Thomas Wilcher's account of politics, society, and family in the coherent world of Edwardian England, which is for him the only reasonable, sensible reality, and by which he gauges the decadence of the present. *The Horse's Mouth* is Gulley Jimson's testimony to the world of spirituality and art, threatened perpetually by stupidity, indifference, and hatred, preserved by an exertion of heroic, but almost inhuman, energy and dedication. His driving need to create new paintings, new forms, new modes is directly at variance with Wilcher's hostility to innovation; the private world which rests upon constant renewal clashes with the world of loving conservatism. In the second trilogy, Nina Latter reveals, in her narrative, *Prisoner of Grace,* her confused world of political expediencies, questionable loyalties, and burgeoning duplicity—all of it shaped during thirty years of marriage to Chester Nimmo. Chester advances his own surprising religious view of human affairs in *Except the Lord*. And Jim Latter presents his plea for his doomed world of honor and duty, along with his ranting hatred of Chester and political machination, in *Not Honour More*. (pp. 4-7)

The notion of a private universe which each man creates for himself, and without which he cannot continue to live, raises questions—even if, as Cary maintains, men are alone only in mind rather than feeling—about ultimate reality and truth. If each man construes experience subjectively, we may wish to know whether there is a verifiable external and objective reality, whether men have access to the true nature of things, or must rest content with narrow individual fantasies. Does one man's created world, we may ask, approximate such an objective reality more closely than another's? Can we, that is, refer to some criterion of adequacy by which to measure the scope and accuracy of a man's grasp of experience? On the whole, Cary does not occupy himself extensively, even in his nonfiction, with these questions. He is not directly or centrally concerned with this kind of judgment. As a result, the doctrine of private worlds becomes a way of avoiding real commitment to any particular private world. Cary tends to rest content with an account of the possibilities of diverse belief, so that his outlook is implicitly relativistic.

His own world, on the other hand, suffers from none of the narrowness that he assigns to other men. In both his speculative thought and the practice of his art, he is exempt from his own formula. The mere conception of a multiplicity of private worlds immediately frees Cary, in mind as well as feeling, from the confines of such a limited world. And his extraordinary skill at rendering, in novel after novel, the subjective worlds of African natives, children, women, and an array of men quite unlike himself—all unmistakably from within—bespeaks a transcendence, again both in mind and feeling, of his own doctrine. The trilogies alone shatter it at one blow. It is as though, in his own life, he was intent upon escaping the limitation that he found inherent in the human condition itself. Whether he was aware of such an intention or not, we can trace manifestations of it in the cast of his mind as he considered a variety of political, philosophical, and aesthetic problems. Out of a dissatisfaction with narrowness, he fashioned his own uncommonly spacious universe. He did so by fending off commitment, or by committing himself, in large measure, to a relativism founded on multiplicity, inclusiveness, and indeterminateness. (pp. 7-8)

[Regardless] of the subject engaging Cary, and quite apart from the specific problem which he is considering, his mind tends naturally to respond to the multiplicity of things. Some of the good consequences, for the trilogies, of this susceptibility are obvious enough. The rich profusion and interaction of attitudes, personalities, things, historical periods, ideas, social stations—the whole extraordinary range and diversity that distinguish the novels—have their source in this tendency. But less fortunate consequences occur as well. (p. 17)

Cary's reluctance to be confined by his own schema of the private world gives him a taste for multiplicity. The same kind of reluctance takes him from multiplicity to a desire to incorporate into his thinking a number of dualities and antitheses. Being so sensitive to the manifold possibilities of reality, he is loath to choose among them. We can trace some of this characteristic inclusiveness, once again, regardless of the specific matter in hand. Politically, for example, Cary's positive definition of liberty as the power to realize oneself and one's

desires is aimed, largely, at his wish to reconcile freedom with government intervention. In this perspective, the English factory acts and the increasing state regulation of the Liberal government of 1902-1914 do not so much represent restraints on the liberty of employers as they do a significant increase in the real liberty of the British population at large. Just as his thinking comprehends both liberty and regulation, it is prepared to deal with another of the everlasting political contrarieties. "Competition and co-operation," he says, "are both instinctive to man, they are both rooted in the nature of his liberty and freedom, and they are both essential means of his realization and his progress." Cary's more general conceptions are equally inclusive. Within the first seven pages of *Art and Reality* he touches on the existence in the universe of both chaos and law, matter and spirit, a subjective and an objective reality, and—rejecting Croce's aesthetic—intuition and expression. The world, furthermore, is for Cary both determined and free: "Although all events are determined, those that are ideas for action formed in some mind are partly self-determined and unpredictable. This brings uncertainty into every chain of causation where one link is the human will." (pp. 17-18)

The moral evasiveness and indifference of the trilogies is related as much to Cary the reader as to Cary the novelist. Both as reader and writer, Cary is prepared to recognize the fictional character as a moral being, but not quite so ready to claim as much for the author. The latter . . . tends to withdraw morally as well as technically when the novel moves from Victorian intrusion to modern objectivity.

Cary's fears for other readers of fiction and their capacities also tend toward moral neutrality. He feels that it will not do to state a case with all its necessary qualifications, in fiction, "because to do so is to appeal to the intelligence alone and to break the emotional continuity." The great writers "do not preach," he says elsewhere. "If they did they would bore." Indeed, Cary has it that the novelist must wheedle and bribe his reader in order to accomplish his real ends:

> The artist has no weapon that will penetrate the most delicate material carcass. He deals with the persons, with the souls, with the ghost in the machine. He must catch it when it is not aware of itself as a mind, a person, or character, when it has no practical aim or will, and when it has taken off the armour of its conceptual judgment, its conventional ideas, the tension of fear and hate, in order to relax. In this state it does not want to hear sermons; nine times in ten it does not want to learn anything at all, it wants only enjoyment, self-forgetfulness. And he must give it—the dream. He must transport this lounger into another existence, and make him know what he wants him to know, as an experience, as a realisation that simply happens to him. So when a passing headlight shows a landscape both unexpected and familiar, it is not for a long time that this glimpse reveals itself to him as an important event.

Very little moral communication or commitment is likely to emerge from this combination of cajoling novelist and pleasure-seeking reader. Such moral ideas as are transmitted through the dream must, Cary maintains, take the form of experience. That is, they must be embodied in an action in which the reader can share. He makes choices, then, along with the characters, guided by his own moral judgment. The novel exists to give him "a certain experience of moral beings in action." This notion, however, is another of Cary's means of moral eschewal. It is certainly true that such participation and evaluation on the part of the reader are indispensable in fiction. It is true, as well, that the reader proceeds by comparing the fictional representation with his own sense of reality and conduct. Cary's formulation is quite accurate: "We can intuit the facts in the actuality of our daily life. We check our fiction by our own direct knowledge. That is to say, we can check the fundamental presentation of moral character. . . ." However, the corroboration—which is the reader's only means of apprehending the moral purport of a novel when that purport is transmitted solely as "experience"—is not feasible in the context of Cary's thought. For the "actuality of our daily life" and "our own direct knowledge" are wide-ranging variables in Cary's private-world system, with its heavy emphasis on subjective value. While on occasion he does assert that "at a certain primitive level, all men agree," his case for the opposite view is a good deal more persuasive. Consequently, at this juncture at least, Cary's inclusiveness—his desire for both a private and a universal reality—cannot quite provide for an "experiential" novel's explicit moral communication. If the solution, then, must be that every reader makes his own personal moral estimates of the characters' circumstances and choices, without significant help, either direct or indirect, from the novelist, we have a fairly accurate anticipation of the conditions that obtain in the trilogies, and that begin to manifest themselves even in Cary's earliest novels.

Novelists have traditionally afforded the reader a good deal more help than Cary suggests in these remarks on morality or . . . than he offers in the trilogies themselves. And Cary himself, as an astute student of the novel, recognizes elsewhere that the great writers of the past have never obscured their intention, the view of life which they sought to convey. Such clarity, Cary maintains, is necessary for the novel because of the chaotic nature of existence:

> Life, as it occurs, has no meaning. It is too full of chance, too stupid. We give it meaning by choosing from it significant patterns. I don't mean that we make those patterns, we find or think that we find them [a characteristic qualification] among the mass of nonsense as a man sees from a plane the track of a Roman road under crops and chicken runs; or a beach-comber goes out for drift wood to a certain bay at a certain hour of a certain month.

Such a pattern, or theme, Cary says, is what the novelist endeavors, in the face of the apparent meaninglessness of life, to express in his work:

> Trollope found in life what we all find, a mass of detail without meaning, of useless cruelty, stupid evil, blind fate, fools doing accidental good and well-meaning saints doing immense evil; what he did was what every writer does, even those modest writers who frankly work for the pay: he created a work of art to give a certain kind of experience.

> He said in effect: "This is the shape of things under the confusion of appearance; these are the forces which really move people to action." His whole story, however complex, was designed to illustrate and develop a theme.

Cary does not, typically, lay much stress here on moral value as a component of the novelist's theme, contenting himself instead with a conception of the novel as a revelation of underlying truth, the actual "shape of things." This emphasis on insight rather than judgment is a fairly persistent strain in his theory. . . . In contrast to Tolstoy, Hardy, Flaubert, and James, whose themes, by [Cary's] own admission, consist of specific evaluative judgments to which these writers are un-

mistakably committed, Cary's theme is evasively vague and generalized. It is not a moral commitment at all. Instead of composing "a picture of the world and of what is right and wrong in that world," he is content to assert that it is "intensely dynamic, a world in creation"; and he does not have conviction enough even about this to express disapproval of the characters in his novels, like Wilcher, who resist change. By offering us a world in which we navigate "in a sea without charts" he delineates not the "shape of things under the confusion of appearance" so much as the underlying confusion of things, with which, as human beings, we are presumably already too familar. Cary's greatest failing as a novelist—and his greatest strength as well—is his submission to the variety and multiplicity of experience. In the novels he is only too ready to abandon his own view and assert merely that there are many views. Indeed, in the trilogies, where this tendency has its culmination, each of the six novels is entirely given over to the exposition and defense of a different view of life, no one of them entirely congruent with Cary's own. As a result, the kind of ordering which a novelist's particular and precise belief can supply is largely absent in each trilogy as a whole. This, of course, is not to say that Cary's broad sympathies, sensitivity to multiformity, and remarkable objectivity are necessarily intellectual vices. On the contrary, they make him a refreshing and significant, if somewhat reluctant, intelligence; and they offer us the best means we have of taking hold of his novels, of understanding how they are made and what they are about. However, they also create formidable problems of a moral and aesthetic nature. . . . (pp. 33-9)

Cary himself is hardly unaware of the difficulty:

> I had tried to be objective; and this is not always very easy when one is entirely convinced that the world is such and such a kind of reality and not at all what some character believes it to be. One is always in danger of thinking, "But if I allow such things to be said, and to happen, the reader will suppose that they are true, that they ought to happen, and so make nonsense of the book."

In general, Cary feels that it is only too easy for anyone, including the author himself, to make nonsense of a book. Uncertainty about the meaning of novels is yet another form that his indeterminate impulse takes. Thus, speaking about the writer's need to assess his own work as he writes, Cary says, "I am speaking as a professional when I say that the great difficulty here is not only to see the objective clearly as it is, to value your achievement with an unprejudiced eye, but to know what it is all about. You are faced with a mass of words, and a story like many other stories, your characters and your general theme. But what is the meaning of it all, the real meaning?" In addition, Cary points out that the novelist's original intuition and intention may undergo serious alteration during the actual composition of a book, sometimes quite uncontrollably. This, he says, happened to Dostoevsky when he allowed Ivan Karamazov the more crushing arguments in the Grand Inquisitor sequence of *The Brothers Karamazov*, though the plan had been to allow orthodox dogma to triumph. "So that [Dostoevsky's] scheme for that chapter," Cary maintains, "his concept *a priori* of what the chapter would mean, was completely ruined." The elusiveness of meaning is at least equally troublesome for the audience, in Cary's opinion: "No two people can possibly see the same picture in the same way, or read the same book. In short, there are as many personal meanings in a work of art as there are persons to appreciate, and each can find there his own truth." And Cary is aware that this ordinary variation and uncertainty about a book's meaning becomes especially notable in a first-person narrative. (pp. 40-1)

In most of [the trilogy novels], instead of an indiscriminate, irresolute permissiveness, we get a deeply committed first-person narrator pronouncing on life, condemning and cherishing values, trying to make sense of the world both to his own sensibility and intelligence and his readers'. In writing each of these novels, Cary qualified his general, encompassing ideas of diversity and indeterminateness sufficiently to create six brilliant narratives. But his suspension of generalized disbelief is only partially successful, because the shadow of his overarching noncommittal tendencies, and of the surrounding novels of the trilogies as well, falls disturbingly on each of the component works. Remarkable as they are, Sara's, Wilcher's, Gulley's, Nina's, Chester's, and Jim's narratives are sustained by a factitious commitment—not Cary's own, but his exploitation of a possible, hypothetical view—a view which is necessarily a mere pose. When we compare their conviction to the earnest moral concern of James, Conrad, Lawrence, or even the Joyce of the *Portrait,* we must feel uneasy, as though, in the trilogies, we are in the hands of an ultimately irresponsible intelligence, indifferently, yet bewitchingly, contriving the whole standpoint of each novel. But these are misgivings, fortunately, that come after our pleasure in each individual book. Cary's failure on the level of the trilogies cannot altogether do away with his achievement in each volume. And, in the end, we could not have one without the other, for both his achievement and his failure derive from the same persistent strain of multiplicity, inclusiveness, and demurral that runs through his thinking. It is an affinity that makes his greatest work both feasible and vulnerable. (p. 42)

> *Robert Bloom, in his* The Indeterminate World: A Study of the Novels of Joyce Cary, *University of Pennsylvania Press, 1962, 212 p.*

MALCOLM PITTOCK   (essay date 1963)

[*In the following excerpt, Pittock maintains that Cary was unsuccessful in his attempt to depict the processes of social change in* A Fearful Joy, *instead presenting a crude and oversimplified view of history in the novel.*]

It is obvious . . . that in *A Fearful Joy* it is Cary's aim to trace the process of social change in this century, but though I agree that he deserves some commendation for essaying a task which few novelists have attempted he hasn't succeeded in carrying it through; indeed he hasn't come within measurable distance of doing so.

What immediately strikes me about this novel is the way in which the complex transformations of history are simplified to the level of a strip cartoon or to a B.B.C. parody of one of its own historical documentaries. Cary's jazzed-up history reminds me in some ways of Waugh, but whereas Waugh is deliberately exaggerating to make a satirical point, Cary apparently believes himself to be delineating reality. Perhaps the easiest way of illustrating the simplified falsity of Cary's portrayal of history is to quote one of the many potted summaries of social change integral to Cary's purpose in *A Fearful Joy.* The Liberals have just won the 1905 election:

> there is a feeling of revolution in the air, and as in all revolutions, a sudden intensification of moral violence. The neurotics, the cranks of every shade of opinion, believing that the millennium has come,

when their special whim will be achieved, are shouting at the tops of their voices that the Empire is Chinese slavery and also a divine trust; the British worker is a serf, and the fountain of wisdom; vaccination is a crime, but science is the hope of the world; marriage is bondage, but divorce is the cancer of the state—notions which renew themselves in a certain kind of brain for ever and ever. It is like an earthquake, when sewer pipes tower like steeples and college towers fall down.

I shouldn't have thought that any serious reader could have been led astray by Cary's casually amused yet lordly tone, his smart antitheses and the general violence of statement which culminates in the self-assured but inept comparison of that last sentence really to think that this was anything but a comically distasteful travesty of that gradual alteration in social and political attitudes which had its modern beginnings early this century.

The same crudity manifests itself in Cary's attempts to show how social changes affect the lives of his characters: he seems to think that this can only be done by directly involving them with people and institutions at the centre of such changes. This is exemplified very clearly in the fortunes of his central character, Tabitha Baskett. Is it the Naughty Nineties complete with decadent poets and artists?—then Tabitha has to be the mistress of a fashionable art critic, assistant editor of a coterie magazine, and the hostess of an exclusive salon. Is it the ascent of Captains of Industry to new heights of power and prestige with the First World War?—then Tabitha must be married to one of them and that the most spectacular. Is it the Gay Twenties with their lax morals?—then Tabitha must be the wife of a speculator in road-houses who makes a fortune out of exploiting the increased mobility of young people and their liking for good, not so clean fun. Is it the development of provincial universities?—then Tabitha's son must be a leading light at one of them. And so it goes on.

Further: Cary often puts explicit statements about social developments in the mouths of his characters in a way that often reminds me of instructional books for children told in story form. We have this kind of thing:

> Manklow's dream is to start a paper of his own, any kind of paper. "Look at the opening. All these board schools teaching kids to read. That's the big thing, Tib, nowadays, education. The country's rotten with it. Now's the time to get in." . . .
>
> (pp. 428-30)

Many of his characters indeed are merely ludicrously exaggerated type figures. There is Boole, that impossible epitome of all decadent poets:

> a little wizened old man with a thin grey beard and a long blue nose . . . "Yes, I have been drunk, I have been drunk beyond dreams; I have lived in the uttermost realms of the drunken."
>
> (p. 430)

Indeed any kind of verisimilitude is sacrificed in the interests of Cary's simplified, sensationalised portrayal of social change. Many of the incidents are, as presented, quite incredible and there is no kind of consistency in the delineation of character. Tabitha's various metamorphoses, for example, consist of such a tissue of absurdities that it is almost egregious to pick out one rather than another. But let me take one at random from many similar. Tabitha is presented as having little interest in reading (she "rarely opens any book"), yet, apparently, she is able to shine, as I have mentioned, as hostess at a salon where literary and artistic people congregate and to assist in editing an esoteric paper. (pp. 430-31)

Indeed the more I consider *A Fearful Joy* the more obvious to me it is that Cary has no real sense of history at all because he doesn't grasp what it is like for people to be set within a living context of beliefs and attitudes. Tabitha as a young Victorian girl from a middle class home can run away from it and live first as Bonser's and later as Sturge's mistress not only without any sense of guilt but with virtually no sense of even outraging the conventions. And again, although Cary has given us a great deal of potted history concerning the emancipation of woman and the changes in relations between the sexes, he can present Tabitha's grand-daughter, who, when younger has been one of the coolest and most emancipated of customers herself, as pathetically anxious to humour the selfish brute she has married and to put up cheerfully with all the humiliations he loads on her, for all the world as if she had been born a hundred years earlier.

It is remarkable that so inept a performance—it is representative of the Cary I have read—could gain a serious hearing. How was it done? First of all, as I said at the outset, Cary gets far more credit than he deserves merely for attempting a worthwhile task which so many novelists must have shrunk from, especially, as anyone who reads the Carfax preface can see, he is so pretentious about it. Second, I can see that the very contradictions in his characters, mediated as they are through the casual self-assurance of his writing with its smack of a self-protective irony which so often give an appearance of smartness to what is inept, can be mistaken for evidences of subtle insight—a realisation that people can combine within themselves opposed traits much more readily than most novelists have realised. And then his technical innovations can be admired too—his use, for example, of a historic present tense

Cary at his desk. Popperfoto.

which is obviously intended to give his narrative a greater immediacy and a sense of the moment to moment life of his characters, but which proves to be the merest trick. But even allowing for the effects of these different ways of throwing sand in the critics' eyes, I marvel at Cary's success in blinding them. (p. 431)

Malcolm Pittock, "Joyce Cary: A Fearful Joy," in Essays in Criticism, Vol. XIII, No. 4, October, 1963, pp. 428-32.

BENJAMIN NYCE   (essay date 1971)

[*In the following excerpt, Nyce examines the differing viewpoints presented by the multiple narrators of Cary's second trilogy, commending Cary's portrayal of the subjective vision of individual characters.*]

In *To Be A Pilgrim,* the second novel of Joyce Cary's first trilogy, one of the characters says:

> No one has written a real political novel—giving the real feel of politics. The French try to be funny or clever, and the English are too moral and abstract. You don't get the sense of real politics, of people feeling their way; of moles digging frantically about to dodge some unknown noise overhead; of worms all driving down simultaneously because of some change in the weather, or rising gaily up again because some scientific gardener has spread the right poison mixture. You don't get the sense of limitation and confusion, of walking on a slack wire over an unseen gulf by a succession of lightning flashes. Then the ambitious side is always done so badly. Plenty of men in politics have no political ambition; they want to defend something, to get some reform—it's as simple as that. But then they are simple people, too, and it is the simple men who complicate the situation. Yes, a real political novel would be worth doing. I should like to do for politics what Tolstoy has done for war—shown what a muddle and confusion it is, and that it must always be a muddle and confusion where good men are wasted and destroyed simply by luck as by a chance bullet.

The speaker is Edward Wilcher, a former politician who has enjoyed brilliant success but has let himself drift into a political backwater from which he will never return. He never writes the novel he speaks of so well. We may take his words as Cary's own, however, for in 1952, ten years after the publication of *To Be a Pilgrim,* the first novel of Cary's political trilogy appeared. The emphasis in *Prisoner of Grace* is upon the feeling of "real politics." In this novel, and in the trilogy as a whole, Cary managed brilliantly to convey the atmosphere of confusion, mistrust, violence, and enthusiasm which permeates the world of a man who uses political power like an artist. After nearly a decade of reading political novels by the score, I know of no fictional effort which presents the atmosphere of political power so convincingly. (pp. 89-90)

In the political trilogy the chief device of meaning is the trilogy form itself. By giving over each novel to a separate speaker and by having each voice contradict and qualify the other voices, Cary achieved the ambiguity and sense of confusion he saw as cardinal characteristics of the atmosphere of political power. Moreover, the trilogy form accurately reflects Cary's mixed view of his central figure, Chester Nimmo. As in the first trilogy, two opposed men are mediated by a woman who loves and understands them both. I propose to begin by looking closely at Nina Latter, not only as she appears in her own narration, *Prisoner of Grace,* but in the trilogy as a whole. The political trilogy is a unit; it benefits from being read as a whole even more than the first trilogy. . . . (p. 90)

Nina's character has perplexed some readers. She is depicted as an unreliable, wishy-washy narrator, whose account verges upon the downright dishonest and, what is more serious, the unintelligible. If one grasps a few basic characteristics of her novel, however, she becomes entirely understandable, if not always open and clear. First, she occupies a middle position between two highly dissimilar men who desire her; and because she loves both men and understands both, she is subjected to stresses which upset her and naturally affect her narrative. Second, the purpose of her novel is to present Nimmo at the height of his career from a domestic and feminine point of view, giving both a criticism and an understanding of him. And finally, this criticism and understanding are largely comic in nature.

As in all of Cary's best fiction, beginning with *Mister Johnson,* the style of *Prisoner of Grace* is a perfect reflection of the narrator. In its scattered, self-qualifying patterns, in its mixture of candor and guile, of outright falsehood and wisdom, of half-truth and euphemism, Nina's style demonstrates the excitement and confusion and torment that result from a life spent in the atmosphere of power. The movements of her equivocal voice present the reader with verbal equivalents for the comic postures she strikes in her precarious balancing act. In order to survive, she must hide from herself and re-create herself.

One side of her truly hates the conniving and underhandedness of public politics, but she proves herself adept at the private variety and just as truly believes that relationships need attention, or, as she puts it, that "relations need managing." One side of her despises Nimmo's double-dealing and callousness, but the other allows him to bribe and threaten her with the material rewards of his power. She loves Latter's inflexible honesty, but knows that his rigidity leads him into foolish and intemperate behavior. Merely in order to hold herself together, she must find refuge in a series of partial truths. As long as we are aware of this characteristic, there is no reason why we should regard Nina uneasily as an unreliable narrator. In fact, it is because of her doubleness, because of her feminine ability to hold contraries in some sort of equilibrium, that her insights are more varied and complex than either Nimmo's or Latter's and that her picture of politics is the most engrossing and convincing of the trilogy.

In her struggle with Nimmo, Nina is essentially a passive agent. Her own personal happiness and pleasure are the chief goals of her politics. She does not want power for its own sake. In her innermost nature she is a drifter, a compromiser, a hedonist—a veritable Cressida waiting to get "roped in" by circumstances. Nimmo controls her by practicing his hell-fire and damnation politics upon her. He keeps her under his control by making her a "prisoner of grace" and by establishing himself as the chief purveyor of grace. As Jim Latter puts it: "Nimmo could play on her like a piano. On her cleverness and her pride. Even her bad opinion of herself. Building her up as a noble free soul and knocking her down as a light woman." But Jim sees only half the picture because he idealizes Nina and wishes to put her in the role of victim to his hated rival. He fails to see that Nina and Nimmo are both prisoners of grace and that they are equally infected by the virus of political behavior. (pp. 90-2)

Nina's sense of damnation, her repudiation of politics, is only the other side of her commitment (galvanized by Nimmo) to

the political method. Thus her defense of Nimmo's behavior is also an apology for her own. . . . (p. 92)

The full ambiguity of the political trilogy is represented by the continuing relationship between Nina and Jim and Nimmo. If we take the whole of *Prisoner of Grace* alone, however, Nina's tormented condition properly suggests the unresolved nature of the argument and the mixed view Cary has of it. Her highly ambivalent outlook tells us far more about politics than Nimmo's self-righteousness or Latter's truculence and explains why *Prisoner of Grace* is naturally the first novel of the trilogy.

The Nina of *Prisoner of Grace* is somewhat different from the Nina of *Not Honour More.* True, both novels underline her repugnance to Nimmo's politics and suggest the deleterious effects of a life spent in the pursuit of power. But where *Prisoner of Grace* attempts to persuade us that Nina has been deeply uneasy with politics from the start, Jim Latter shows us her intense support of Nimmo to the very end (she is quite willing to ruin a policeman named Maufe in order to protect Nimmo). Moreover, we are constantly aware that Nina is manipulating Jim in the most artful way. She is, in a sense, practicing on Jim what she has learned from Nimmo. The more one looks at Nina in terms of the whole trilogy, the more one is aware that it is she who wants to perpetuate the threesome. Her ability to wean the early Nimmo away from strict evangelicalism and teach him to like high living and at the same time to hold Jim's affections is as great a political triumph as any of Nimmo's in the public sphere. She is an expert in domestic politics, an area of political behavior which for Cary is as important as public politics.

Still, one should not imply that Nina's task is an easy one for her. She is trapped in her middle position. When she sees at the very end that Jim is preparing to kill her, she makes no struggle but acts like a damned soul who goes to her death as if she too accepts it as the judgment Jim insists it is. Her death is the logical result of her tormented and ambiguous position. (p. 93)

Jim Latter, the narrator of *Not Honour More,* is designed to contrast with Nimmo. He is an idealist while Nimmo is a pragmatist. He is a man of direct action while Nimmo is a temporizer and manipulator. He is a career officer in the British army, with all of the rigid aristocratic outlook one associates with the type, while Nimmo is a civilian, a commoner, a liberal, and a flexible man by nature. He is a conservative maker of England's past and empire, while Nimmo is a modern democrat. His conservatism is based upon personal loyalty, upon a desire to preserve the forms of the past, and upon a strong belief that relations should be conducted in an open, aboveboard fashion. He relishes the hearty, man-to-man relationships he has experienced in the army, and sees no reason why they, and other army conditions, cannot be perpetuated outside the service. His narrative style is terse, speedy, colloquial, quite without art when compared to Nimmo's own narrative in *Except the Lord.* His style is, once again, a perfect image of himself—a man of action rather than of contemplation, of strong feeling uncomplicated by thought. Quite naturally, the atmosphere that Nimmo creates frustrates him. (p. 94)

Jim's strength, as well as his weakness, is that he acts almost immediately on the most basic levels of emotion. His obsession with honor and duty makes him as simple as Nimmo is complex, and as easy to get around. A great deal of the humor in his novel comes from watching Nimmo and Nina manipulate him. As in *Prisoner of Grace,* the politics of the threesome is the microcosm and central focus of a larger politics.

Jim's satire of Nimmo's political techniques is accurate and often hilarious. He fails to see, however, that Nimmo's ability to calm a dangerously violent crowd by talk is infinitely preferable to inciting it to bloodshed by some direct, provocative action, such as sending in the police to lay about with truncheons. His difference from Nimmo defines the politician and favors the politician's methods over his own. (p. 95)

In his simplicity and his absolutist's approach to truth, Jim comes very close to fascism. He may hate fascism in the person of Nimmo's enemy Brightman, but he often sounds like a fascist. He does not understand the democratic system and its necessary disorderliness, its need for a free, partisan press and even for the "mob." His failure to bring to the surface and examine the political ideas which underlie his strong feelings presents us with his major weakness. He is dangerous because he considers himself above politics—particularly democratic politics. He is a good illustration of the adage that in a political situation a rejection of politics is in itself a political act—and not a wise one.

There is another side to Jim, however. Throughout *Not Honour More* he stands with the small, ordinary man and his innate distrust of politicians (his very colloquialness comes from the same fondness for common, ordinary experience). His colorful behavior and man-to-man code of conduct make him an excellent military leader. The special police he commands during the general strike fight like demons to protect him. Other people (the newspaper reporters, the Oxford students) are compelled into friendship for him by his candor and strong feeling. In many instances something in Jim causes politics to fly out the window, and the reactions of those who confront him are placed on a purely personal basis. They seem compelled to return to him the dedication he shows to the numerous small individuals who are hurt by the political juggernaut. From his lament in the opening pages for his friend Pickett, whom Nimmo shoves off the Emergency Committee in order to get a place for himself, to his sympathy for Potter, whose age-old family boatyard is ruined by the General Strike, to the policeman Maufe, and finally to his friend Varney (who, one suspects, is much more of an old tough than Jim is willing to admit), Jim's narrative is filled with instances of personal suffering. His judgment of Nimmo from a purely personal and private standpoint has merit, but we must resist the urge to let it assume a larger weight than it should have. Cary's picture of politics is a complete one because it includes a full measure of cruelty and suffering. To refer to Jim simply as a madman, as Andrew Wright has done, is not really accurate. His statements may be wild and vituperative, and his actions often violent, but he is deeply committed to personal loyalties which transcend politics—as Nimmo's loyalties almost never do. And yet Jim's judgment is denied the full weight he intends it to have because it disregards politics so completely. Jim in himself is the best reason for the necessity of politicians like Nimmo. But without men like Jim, the Nimmos might take over completely. The two, it seems, are fated to oppose one another.

From the standpoint of purely personal and private morality, Jim's judgment of Nimmo would have more weight if the foolishness of his public efforts were counterbalanced by a certain wisdom and sanity in his private life, but this is not the case. He is a lamentably poor representative of the excellences of the private life because of his total disregard of politics. His intransigence and inflexible naïveté make for innumerable domestic fights. Even his closest personal friends have reason to fear his loyalty because he is apt to include them in the consequences of his foolhardiness. A gigantic innocence lies at the root of Jim's character. In his tortured raging, it expresses itself in images of animality, filth, disease, coarse and repugnant sensuality, which remind one of nothing so much in English literature as the painful ragings of Jonathan Swift— another innocent totally unfitted for politics who found himself in a political milieu.

Chester Nimmo is the central figure of the political trilogy. He is the only character who figures largely in all three novels. The trilogy is designed to give us his life history and to suggest the atmosphere of power which surrounds him. Each novel presents us with the public incidents of his rise to power, as well as the private politics of the threesome, though the latter receives the major emphasis. *Except the Lord* shows his childhood in an evangelical family, his early commitment to politics during the failure of the trade union movement in England in the 1870s and 1880s, and his repudiation of political action and return to evangelical preaching. Nina's narrative gives us a Nimmo who has returned to politics and is establishing himself as a major political figure by swinging from a platform of pacifism during the Boer War to the position of Minister of War during World War I. Jim's story shows us a maddened and tortured Nimmo who has been thrown out of office and is trying desperately to get back in power by exploiting the turmoil which nearly paralyzed England during the General Strike of 1926. As a whole, then, the trilogy is designed to chart Nimmo's rise to power and to show the disintegrating effects of power upon a masterful politician. (pp. 96-8)

Except the Lord is the second novel of the trilogy. Speaking of his narrative, Nimmo says: "This book is not the history of political events but of a boy's mind and soul, of one who came so near perdition that his escape still seems to him like a miracle." Nimmo would convince the reader that his narrative is a spiritual history, not a political document. But we must remember that he is composing his story at the very time he is trying to recover power. *Except the Lord* must be considered in the light of Nina's and Jim's depictions of Nimmo the politician. Cast out of office and embittered, the old politician may be in the mood to confess his wrongs, but he is calculating that the confessional nature of his book will win him political supporters. *Except the Lord* illustrates Nina's comment about Nimmo: "It did not prevent his religion from being 'true' that he knew how to 'use' it."

The style of the novel is biblical and rhetorical. Cary has succeeded admirably in capturing the voice of a man who took his early training in evangelical preaching. . . . Unlike Nina's confused and equivocal style, Nimmo's style shows that he is a verbal artist; he knows how to write for effect, and his judgment of events is bold and sure. As he looks back upon his childhood and early manhood, he paints a portrait of a young man who is idealistic and deeply religious, loyal and loving to his family. It is, of course, a sympathetic portrait, and it is also a convincing one, for it is marked by surprisingly candid judgments by the old man upon the young. Once again, Cary took pains to give us a narrator who, on the whole, is plausible. Still, the reader must admit that the political lecher of Jim's and Nina's stories is perhaps too absent, and that, for Nimmo, the narrative style is only one-half the man. (pp. 98-9)

Except the Lord, as Robert Bloom has noticed [in his *The Indeterminate World: A Study of the Novels of Joyce Cary* (1962)], depicts a young man "whose deepest instincts, curiously enough, are not political at all.'' The book is as much a family chronicle as it is a personal confession. Indeed, Nimmo's tendency to measure his transgressions by the standards of family loyalty is a major theme. He reveals a strong sense of moral inferiority to his father and to his brother Richard. It is interesting that the only person in the family to whom Nimmo does not feel inferior is the one who has by far the most influence upon him. He is most easily understood when one examines his relationship with his sister Georgina. Both are proud, tough, passionate, and unwilling to accept their condition on earth as only God's to change. Thus they are often torn between their allegiance to the visions created by their own strong egos and to a strict religion which damns these visions as prideful agents of the devil. The spirit of their father's religion cannot dry up in them as it does in Richard. (pp. 99-100)

The other ''noble woman,'' besides Georgina and his mother, to whom Chester refers in the opening paragraph of the book is, of course, Nina. *Except the Lord* covers the period prior to his relationship with Nina, but Nimmo cannot keep from inserting a few remarks about her, and it is here that we can recognize most easily the Nimmo of *Prisoner of Grace*. The reference to Nina is, in fact, designed to link the two novels. Her absence in *Except the Lord* (in contrast to her absorption with Nimmo in her own narrative) is understandable because the novel covers Nimmo's earliest years, but it also suggests Nimmo's monumental egotism, the genius for self-absorption, which is perhaps the most important characteristic of the politician and which enables him to risk himself time after time in the political arena. When Nimmo interrupts the narrative of his youth to talk about Nina or to damn his detractors, the comic dimension of *Prisoner of Grace* returns, and we are sure that we are listening to the same man and confronting the same mixture of truth and falsehood. The very few appearances of Nimmo in old age suggest, nevertheless, that the differences between what he is saying and what he is doing, and between what he is and what he was, are great indeed. The whole of chapter 47 of *Except the Lord* is a brilliant peroration on the beauties of the home, of motherhood, of woman's love of peace and security. On the surface, it is only the pious political oratory we have become used to; but if we remember the situation at the end of *Prisoner of Grace,* we are suddenly aware that underneath it all Nimmo is half asking, half warning Nina to stay by him, submissive to his power. The trouble is that the dominant tone of *Except the Lord* is so different from that of *Prisoner of Grace* that it takes an almost forced act of recollection to realize that Nimmo is making frenzied sexual attacks upon Nina (which she accepts) at the same time he is dictating his memoirs. We are confronted with the problem we noticed at the beginning: are the Nimmo of *Prisoner of Grace* and the Nimmo of *Except of Lord* the same, or are they so different as to leave us unable to see them as aspects of one changing man?

The trilogy form is somewhat at fault here. In order to make the narrative of Nimmo's early life a reliable one, Cary was forced to keep the older Nimmo's oratory and obfuscation firmly in the background. The spirit of moral reaction, in which the older Nimmo is left as a result of his final political defeat, insures Cary's success, for the old man is in a confessional mood. The recollection of his youthful political transgressions intensifies his confessional desires, and we are given passages of great openness and honesty, such as the declaration that he would have approved Pring's policy of violence even if he had first recognized it as such. The danger, however, is not that Nimmo will deny his sins, but that he will seem too much the

repentant sinner when, and if, he is not so. Thus, we have the unusual inclusion by Nimmo of a heartless report he made to Pring's union on the beating up of two strikers. Since he is readying himself for another political campaign at the time he is writing his memoirs, it is odd that he should want to include such a damning piece of information. His desire to tell the truth is deep, but it does not run counter to his political ambitions. The intrusive presence of this information is necessary to qualify Nimmo's narrative and to remind us that the young man's story is about the old man, too. These incidents point up Cary's pains to remedy Nimmo's tendency to give a too-partial portrait of himself.

There is in *Except the Lord* no narrator, such as Nina, in whom all points of view are met and who could show some of the richness and complexity of the Nimmo we see in *Prisoner of Grace*. But even if there were, would we get a full and varied portrait of the young Nimmo? The young Nimmo has not yet reached the variety and complexity of the mature man. This, coupled with the overreliance on the memoir technique, is the major reason for the thinness of the book. The complexity of the mature man is the result of a successful effort somehow to assimilate amoral politics into a religion of passionate nonconformism and hellfire and damnation. In the full year of moral disgust and self-doubt which Nimmo experiences after he ends his connection with the union movement and before he becomes a lay preacher like his father, we have a rejection of politics which would seem severe enough to be permanent. If we ask how the Nimmo of *Except the Lord* becomes the Nimmo of *Prisoner of Grace*, we must admit that we are given no description of his ten years as a preacher and that the trilogy might have benefited had it become a tetralogy. This gap in the treatment of Nimmo's career is the one major weakness of the trilogy. (pp. 100-02)

It is chiefly in the attitude of moral reaction and repentance that the old and young Nimmos can be seen as one character, but that a changing character. We will not understand Nimmo's compulsive and tortured condition at the end unless we see that the young man's sense of sin is all mixed in with the old man's sense of political failure. Politics has become his religion, and though he continues to be hurt by a feeling of sin, his truest salvation would come by being returned to power. He is still vital (his sexual vitality seems almost undiminished), still full of ideas. As Wright has said, ''*Except the Lord* sets out to rediscover the roots of Chester's own religion, his orientation in the world.'' The old Nimmo needs to recapture the spirit of his youth. He needs to summon once again his essentially religious energies. Exiled after his political downfall, he repeats the same ritual of repentance he acted in his youth. His sermons to Nina, as he dictates his memoirs to her, are full of the same intensity, the same penitential spirit (plus all the cunning he has learned) as the sermons we may imagine he gave as a preacher. Nevertheless, *Except the Lord* is still a political *Grace Abounding to the Chief of Sinners*. It shows us a man whose freedom is qualified—a man who is in part his own best ''prisoner of grace.'' (pp. 102-03)

Our final view of Nimmo must rely on Jim's and Nina's narratives more than on his own. The effects of total commitment to the pursuit of power are more visible in their stories. Nina's explanation of Nimmo, that ''his religion stirred up his politics and his politics stirred up his religion,'' is fully dramatized in *Prisoner of Grace*. She shows a shrewd operator who can use the class issue to keep her in line, and who can, under the banner of pacifism, exploit violence at the riots at Chorlock and Lilmouth to advance his fortunes. She shows a man who is nimble enough to make a successful switch from pacifism to Minister of War. In her description of Nimmo's relationship with his son Tom, we see the suffocating atmosphere that surrounds a great man and stifles Tom's growth. Her description of Nimmo's relationship with his backer Gould gives us the distinction between the money magnate and the power magnate. Most important, Nina and Jim show us the results of living a long time in the atmosphere of power. Her description of Chester after he is thrown out of office is meaningful:

> It was impossible any longer to reach him. He had,
> so to speak, in thirty years of war, made such dev-
> astation round himself that to talk to him at all was
> like calling across a waste full of broken walls and
> rusty wire and swamps of poisoned water. . . .

The battlefield is a brilliant metaphor to describe the solitary end of a savage political fighter and Minister of War. Jim's satirical descriptions of Nimmo's vigorous efforts to return to power do not conceal the tragedy of Nimmo's disintegration. His vitality and imagination seem as strong as ever, but he is a representative man who has lived beyond his time (significantly, Nina describes his style of dress as old-fashioned).

Nimmo represents the liberal man who stands for the "everlasting revolution," as he calls it. He is the man who can adapt to change, who demands change, even though change reduces him to a comic-tragic position at the end of his life. His vitality expresses itself in a politics of Protestant dissent and nonconformism. The belief that "there is only one true religion—between a man's own soul and his God" and the hatred of dogma he expresses when he says that "mechanism is everywhere the enemy of joy" enable him to combine his politics and his religion in a way which helps him operate effectively in the rough-and-tumble of a democratic system. As Nina says, "freedom . . . was always an exciting word in Chester's mouth."

Cary's successful restriction of his personal viewpoint in the trilogy may make us wonder what his attitude is at certain moments, but it does not deprive us of an essential knowledge of where he stands, as I hope I have demonstrated. That is why it is surprising to read in the fullest study yet published on the trilogy—Robert Bloom, *The Indeterminate World: A Study of the Novels of Joyce Cary* [see excerpt dated 1962]—that the novels are damaged by a refusal on Cary's part to commit himself to a single point of view and that his created world suffers from a hurtful indeterminateness. When Cary speaks of his world of the creative free individual, he is speaking as a writer for whom the multiplicity and changefulness of the world are as important as its permanent and lasting features and more interesting. As a liberal and nonconformist, he seeks the intensity and uniqueness of the personal visions of his characters. To blame him for withholding his own personal vision is to miss what is perhaps his major strength: the great lack of egotism which allows him to assume so many different roles, to populate a world so rich and varied, to suggest a multiplicity of truths (all true because each is personally felt, perceived in the minutest detail—not in the abstract). This absence of egotism is the prime quality of any great character actor, and it is the basis of Cary's mimetic technique. More important to this study, Cary's so-called indeterminateness is the very quality which enabled him to write a great series of novels about politics, to capture so brilliantly the ambiguity which lies at the center of the best political novels.

Cary's world is democratic; it demands freedom, openness, the primacy of the personal, subjective vision; it asserts the secondary importance of correctness, the necessity of dissent. To put it into plain terms, Cary cared more about being read with intense personal involvement than he cared about being read correctly. One can imagine him anticipating with some humor the varying reactions to his work and saying to not a few of his readers, "Your understanding says as much about you as it does about my work." His unwillingness to force complexities into unnatural resolutions means that he will be read from varying viewpoints and that his fiction will maintain its richness and vitality.

Cary's belief that public politics is only the visible aspect of a pervasive politics, that the politics of marriage and the nursery are equally significant, is the direct result of his interest in the whole man and his ability to dramatize that interest in his fiction. For Cary, the public gesture and the private gesture are never far apart, with the result that his political trilogy has a resonance lacking in so many other treatments of politics. His political fiction does not suffer from an overreliance upon the rational and the didactic as does the fiction of Koestler and Orwell. It is not lamed by a lack of knowledge of the workings and atmosphere of politics as is James's. It does not suffer from Conrad's sometimes ill-concealed prejudice or his desire to shove politics aside in favor of the dark, eternal verities of man's soul. Unlike Turgenev and Dostoevsky, who in their political fiction focus on a group of revolutionaries on the fringe, Cary concentrates his attention on a man who commands central power and is subject to a variety of complex demands because of his central position.

What Cary's political trilogy does do (and that magnificently) is to keep a sharp vision of a practicing politician's world in front of the reader. It differs from other novels about politics in its refusal to obey what Irving Howe has called the "apolitical temptation." It refuses to retreat into a mordant irony (as in *The Secret Agent*), or into pastoral fantasy (as in Orwell's *Coming up for Air*), or into some notion of universal redemption or destruction (as in *Nineteen Eighty-Four*). Cary does not carp or browbeat, nor does he throw up his hands in despair and frustration. He keeps a sane and steady eye upon the workings of politics, and shows both the value and the culpability of his politician. He refuses to back away from politics because some aspects are repugnant. Though he admits charges of cruelty and egotistical blindness against Nimmo, he deprecates the fastidious cleanliness of those who subject Nimmo to wholesale criticism (for political ideas are nothing if not ideas in contact with soiled reality). His political world is violent, ambiguous, confusing, exciting, and vastly absorbing. It is politics as it is, not as it should be. (pp. 103-06)

Benjamin Nyce, "Joyce Cary's Political Trilogy, the Atmosphere of Power," in Modern Language Quarterly, *Vol. 32, No. 1, March, 1971, pp. 89-106.*

MICHAEL ROSENTHAL (essay date 1971)

[*Rosenthal is an American educator and critic. In the following excerpt, he discusses Cary's four comic novels,* Mister Johnson, Charley is My Darling, Herself Surprised, *and* The Horse's Mouth, *all written at about the midpoint of Cary's career and constructed around conflict between the hero and conventional society.*]

Growing out of [the] same conditions Cary sees as responsible for man's tragic destiny—his isolation, his inability to communicate, his precarious status in an absurd universe—his comedy makes the conditions endurable by transforming them into the stuff of laughter. Comedy becomes Cary's defiant response to the intolerable facts of human suffering and defeat. Cary has a detachment, Hazard Adams suggests, perhaps absorbed from Blake, "that sees the comic in the tragic, rather than the tragic in the comic." (pp. 340-41)

But laughter does not predominate in Cary, and we must now try to place the comic novels in the context of the rest of his fiction. To begin with, Cary's comic novels fall roughly in the middle of his career. Neither the African novels at the beginning nor the second trilogy at the end of his career, taken by themselves, would suggest very much about Cary's comic tendencies. Cary moves into his richly comic manner with *Mister Johnson* in 1939, and sustains it through *Charley Is My Darling* (1940), *Herself Surprised* (1941), and *The Horse's Mouth* (1944). Though substantially different from one another these novels do share certain qualities that set them apart from his other work.

Cary's comic novels are all built around the conflict Northrop Frye has designated as archetypally comic: the opposition between the hero and the conventional society from which he is alienated. Sadly lacking in respectability, Cary's heroes are outcasts, rejected by a society that does not understand them. Mister Johnson, Charley, Sara, and Gulley manifest their unfitness for social living in various ways: they are impoverished, frequently immoral, invariably criminal—cheating, lying, and stealing their ways through the world. And yet, although frayed at the edges and rather seedy, they clearly embody those life-giving virtues of spontaneity, kindness, and imagination in which Cary believes. They are all immoral rogues who, in their joyous embracing of life, come closer to the secrets of it than the decorous representatives of society who frown at them and put them in jail.

However disreputable, these characters are redeemed by their essential goodness and, more important, by their absolute commitment to the job of living. Gulley's insistence, repeated throughout *The Horse's Mouth,* that he must "get on with the job," refers not just to the creation of his art, but to the creation of his life as well, and in this latter sense becomes the obligation felt by all the comic heroes. The job of living is the work to which all dedicate themselves. Their doing this job, in the face of innumerable obstacles, provides the simple structural pattern of the novels.

Cary's comic heroes, then, have much in common with the "picaresque saints" R.W.B. Lewis feels are the most representative figures in contemporary fiction [*The Picaresque Saint* (1961)]. Cary's heroes, like Lewis' rogues, are "outsiders—criminals to be pursued, escapees on the run, strangers in an alien world." Like these rogues, Cary's figures, morally unacceptable in conventional terms, transcend in human value those who condemn them: "It is exactly in their impurity—whether it is reckoned by official morality or by any other kind—that the saintly characters achieve, and in fact incarnate, that trust in life and that companionship that the contemporary novel so emphasizes. They are outsiders who share; they are outcasts who enter in."

And finally, the adventures of Cary's heroes, struggling to live, are cast in the same episodic form Lewis feels has become peculiarly modern—the picaresque: "The tragic fellowship I speak of is accomplished in narrative terms by a series of encounters—encounters between the hero and the beings and customs it is his purpose to outwit. . . . The genre of fiction which has emerged to carry the adventures of the picaresque saint is the old and sometimes disreputable genre of the pic-

aresque novel—the traditional account of the journeying rogue."

Part of the success of the comic novels comes from the certainty with which Cary draws and distinguishes between living values and respectable ones. There is no ambiguity about the conflict: we are not faced with a moral dilemma in sympathizing with Sara, because, although we know quite clearly that she occasionally steals and lies, we also know that she cannot be judged by what she does, and what she is simply transcends conventional terms of approbation and censure. The "facts" that lead Sara, as well as Charley, Mister Johnson, and Gulley into court never sway our estimate of them: however guilty they are according to the law, they still retain their essential innocence for us. The comic novels thus present two distinct orders of behavior—the respectable and the roguish—and clearly opt for the latter.

The confidence with which Cary moves in these novels has important implications. In his unqualified admiration for the rogue heroes, Cary suggests that individuals have a reality which transcends actions and words, and that it is possible to intuit that reality directly. Sensing "straight from the horse's mouth" the true worth of his comic heroes, we are not disturbed in the least by their frequently disreputable behavior. Cary's mastery in negotiating the discrepancy between what people are and what they do dispels any confusion.

The world of Cary's picaresque novels is thus a world of certainty. And the fact that there is certainty, that the outsiders can achieve and maintain their unequivocal, if peculiar quality of saintliness contributes to the affirmation in the comic novels. The comic heroes' belief in themselves is seen as an absolute good and establishes their innocence in our eyes, an innocence that is most fully realized when they are wholeheartedly "getting on with the job of living." The moments when they are doing so become the most significant moments in the novels, for if they are ultimately defeated in the quest for fulfillment, they nevertheless temporarily achieve it precisely by managing to be themselves and asserting their rights to live as they will.

Clearly cut off from a society that oppresses them, the rogues turn their isolation into a comic struggle for survival. Innocence confronting respectability becomes the comic conflict, during which innocence does not hesitate to employ all manner of devious methods to bait its enemy. The gaiety of the battle overshadows neither its seriousness nor the ultimate defeat of the innocent, but that there should be gaiety at all sets the comic novels significantly apart from the rest of Cary's fiction.

Such gaiety, as I have said, is lacking at the beginning and, though for different reasons, at the end of his career. Cary's first three novels—*Aissa Saved, An American Visitor,* and *The African Witch*—are clearly exploratory novels in which Cary is attempting to discover for himself "the landscape of existence." The abstractness of the novels, the attempts to deal with a large number of issues and personalities without the anchor of an individual consciousness, the third-person method of narration—all show Cary's not having found as yet his novelistic way. The themes of isolation, of the difficulties of communication, of the prevalence of injustice, though present in these novels, are not realized with anything like the fullness of his later work because Cary is not yet certain of their significance and of their implications for man. That is, Cary's point of view, both "moral" and technical, remains unformed.

The terrible violence and suffering of the African novels—they abound in murder, torture, and bloody sacrifices—are thus unredeemed by any pervasive gaiety or humor because Cary has not yet fully integrated the facts of human suffering into a coherent world view. Once Cary is able to impose an order on the welter of violence and injustice of the African novels, to see clearly their tragic implications for the individual, the comic affirmation follows. The broad, overcrowded canvas of the three African novels does not allow such an untrammeled vision; it is not until he focuses on the destiny of a single creative soul that Cary reaches the balanced understanding necessary for his comedy, and the first product of this understanding—*Mister Johnson*, published in 1939—becomes the best of Cary's early novels, at once poignant and funny.

If Cary's comic response emerges with his sharpened awareness of the tragic conditions of human life, it is ultimately subdued by that awareness. Cary's final trilogy is somber and grim, totally lacking the gaiety of the comic novels. His vision of reality is much darker here; the certainty with which he was able to establish value in his comic work is gone, and gone with that certainty is the precarious transcendence of circumstances previously granted his rogue heroes. A world in which it is no longer possible to distinguish between right and wrong, in which people's actions cannot be confidently understood or their motives analyzed, is not a comic world.

Though critics discussing the second trilogy have endlessly tried to explain the enigma of Chester's behavior—immoral charlatan seeking only power or genuinely God-possessed soul wanting only to serve?—no one has attempted to understand the reasons for the uncertainty, as well as for the frequently odd behavior and uncertain moral status of Nina and Jim. Cary has been accused of "novelistic dereliction of duty," in not making clear choices, in not preferring the good Jim to the bad Chester (or the good Chester to the bad Jim), in not making obvious exactly to what degree each is self-deceived. But the difficulty of unequivocal moral evaluation is precisely the point of the novels: we are presented with a world of moral confusion, somewhat like that of *The Good Soldier*, a world in which knowledge of men and motives no longer seems feasible. Whereas there was never any difficulty in seeing through the words and actions of Sara and Gulley to the people beneath, now the words and actions of Chester and Jim *become* their reality and we find it difficult to say with assurance what lies beneath. And the uncertainty of understanding and judging in the second trilogy indicates no shortcoming in Cary as a novelist: it is simply the final truth of the world as he came to see it.

The world of the second trilogy is considerably more desperate than the world of the comic novels. The absolute belief in themselves through which the rogue heroes achieve their innocence has a corrupting, debilitating effect on the more proper narrators of the second trilogy. Jim's fanatic righteousness, his conviction that he is the last bastion of morality in a decaying society, rather than redeeming him in any way, turns him into a near lunatic, unable to cope with reality, and finally, into a murderer. If Jim's fervent morality leads him to prison awaiting the scaffold, Chester's evangelicalism leads him to an ignominious death in a bathroom after a life of enormous obscenity and deceit. Hedging, lying, concealing at every turn, Chester, in spite of or even because of his piety and arguments of political necessity, ends by stripping himself of human dignity.

But it is not only belief that ultimately proves corrupting. Salvation is not given Nina either, whose parenthetical style reflects her parenthetical character. Unable to extricate herself from the muddle of conflicting sympathies into which her pas-

sivity has led her, Nina finally compromises herself to destruction. Her lack of belief proves as fatal as the beliefs of Chester and Jim.

The murky, uncertain world of the second trilogy thus stands in sharp contrast to the clarity and gaiety of the comic novels. The change in tone and mood is accompanied by a change in structure: the focus, in the comic novel, on the conflict between the outsider and society—a conflict which as I have said, produces the humor—now shifts to individuals caught within the web of society. Nina, Chester, and Jim are all concerned with (if they do not necessarily embody) respectability and morality. Unlike alienation, entanglement is not comic: people here are more caught up in circumstances, less able to achieve any kind of inner serenity. Living becomes a burden, not a delight. Human isolation in the second trilogy is much more terrible than the isolation in the first precisely because people are superficially more involved with each other in the second. The complex relationship of Nina, Chester, and Jim, has no parallel in the comic novels—nor does the enormous gulf of misunderstanding existing between them, a gulf that annihilates any possibility of real communication. If sympathetic understanding sometimes occurs among the outsiders in the comic novels, as, for example, between Charley and Lizzie, or Coker and Gulley, it is totally missing among the last trilogy's insiders. Language only deceives in these novels, and the characters have no other way of communicating.

As Cary was unable to finish *The Captive and the Free* before his death, the second trilogy constitutes his last completed fictional statement about the world. It is a disturbing world, lonely and grim. The gaiety of the earlier novels is gone, as if Cary no longer had the faith or energy left to sustain it in the face of the shipwreck "of so much that was beautiful, true, delicate" around him. Cary's last novels are filled with a terrible sadness for which there is no comic solace. In them we feel, to borrow Christopher Fry's words, that the intuition of innocence responsible for Cary's best comic achievements has finally been worn thin by the grating facts of experience. (pp. 342-46)

Michael Rosenthal, "Joyce Cary's Comic Sense," in Texas Studies in Literature and Language, *Vol. XIII, No. 2, Summer, 1971, pp. 337-46.*

DENNIS HALL (essay date 1983)

[*In the following excerpt, Hall examines contradictions between Cary's avowed personal philosophy and the worldview expressed in his novels.*]

[The] biggest obstacle to the understanding of the novels of Joyce Cary is Joyce Cary. He regarded himself as a man with a message. He believed that he was conveying it in his books. He was distressed that nobody seemed able to realise what it was and, towards the end of his life, sought to explain, at first in various articles and interviews and finally in *Art and Reality*. Presumably he died satisfied that he had made his point at last. Certainly, one hopes so.

To me, however, his explanations are not always helpful, and in certain respects obscure the issue rather than clarify it. As I see it, there were two Joyce Carys. One of them was the thinker who, puzzled as we all are by the phenomenon of human existence and needing a faith to live by, succeeded after several years of intense effort in producing a creed that, so far as he was concerned, accounted for that phenomenon satisfactorily.

The other was the artist who produced the novels and who, in certain important respects, had different ideas. He knew, for example, that there is no satisfactory explanation. Cary himself was not aware of this. It never occurred to him that his novels might not—did not—if I am right—fully match his consciously held ideas and that his explanation of their meaning might therefore be misleading. He knew what he meant to do, and he was convinced that he was doing it.

Having said this, I want to emphasise that I do not believe that Cary the novelist was entirely at variance with Cary the thinker, or that the latter's ideas should be disregarded altogether. On the contrary, a knowledge of the essential points of Cary's thinking is a valuable and sometimes necessary tool for the interpretation of his works. It is a fault of his method that he sometimes succeeded so well in his avowed intention of keeping the subjective viewpoint from which he was writing out of his books that there is no means of knowing what it is without reference to his thinking. The point is that Cary was not an impressive metaphysical thinker and he did not always realise the implications of his thought. He needed certainty in an area—the nature and meaning of human existence—in which certainty is impossible, and succeeded in persuading himself that he had achieved it. (pp. 1-2)

Cary really did have a curiously divided mind. He believed devoutly in a personal God, but logically he ought to have been an atheist. He was convinced of the existence of transcendental values, but he ought to have been an existentialist. He was convinced that man is free, but for practical purposes he was a determinist. He was similarly convinced that man is moral, but his world is essentially an amoral one. He was a man who could not consciously face the consequences of his own thinking, and who found it necessary to disregard its plain implications (by no means a rare achievement, of course) in order to make life intelligible, explicable and, therefore, manageable. He knew perfectly well that life as we experience it is a chaos, and said so, but at the same time insisted that it made sense.

However, the part of him that wrote the novels, the artist, did accept the implications of the thinker's ideas and worked accordingly and it is this that makes Cary the theorist such an uncertain guide to the novels. How, then, are they to be interpreted?

There can be no doubt, I think, that Cary's primary concern is with freedom. He wrote: "All my books deal with the world which, as I see it, is the consequence of this situation [the 'fact' that man is free]. I once had a plan to call the books the Comedy of Freedom . . ."; and on another occasion: "My world is that of the free soul in a society in which the permanent qualities of affection are realised in a situation of continuous change. . . . All my books deal with different facets of this dilemma." His conscious purpose as an artist was thus centred on the problems that the individual encounters in trying to 'create his own world', to make his life what he personally wants it to be; and he set out in his books to explore and depict the situation that results from the efforts of different kinds of people, with different needs, in different social contexts, to achieve this kind of satisfaction. In fact, the sole concern of all Cary's fictional major characters (excluding, that is, those in *A House of Children,* who are based upon real people) is the pursuit of self-satisfaction, when self-satisfaction is defined as the product of doing what you like. There are always wider issues involved, of course: art in the first trilogy and politics in the second, to take the two most obvious examples; and

these issues are treated seriously, but they never constitute the major centre of interest.

Passionately as Cary believed in freedom, he cannot be doing what he thought: depicting human beings who, in spite of constraint, are undeniably free; since it is not possible, without recourse to fantasy, to portray convincingly in fiction a state of affairs that cannot be shown to exist in reality. Moreover, a reading of his novels that is coloured neither by knowledge of his intentions, nor by the influence of any of the criticism that is based upon his statements, does not, in my opinion, leave the impression that his people are free. The opposite is the case. Cary's characters are never seen deciding what the larger purposes of their lives are to be, as one would expect if their minds are indeed to be regarded as first causes. What motivates them is always given and can always be accounted for by inherited factors and a plausible response to the environment. They never change courses or become in any substantial way different people as a result of their experiences. Rather, they go on pursuing the same ends until their deaths, which are often premature and usually a direct consequence of their conduct. In effect, Cary determines in advance what sorts of people his characters are and never lets them develop. The only freedom he allows them is that of selecting whichever seems best of the available means of attaining their ends, which is hardly an adequate demonstration of the 'fact' that man's will is a first cause.

In a writer who wants his characters to be seen as free, this is astonishing. The power of self-determination, if only on occasion, and the ability to change as a result of it are the minimum effects such a writer must create if he is to have any chance of success. It is not astonishing, of course, that Cary should have failed, since, as I say, success in his self-appointed task was in any case impossible. The astonishment arises from the complete oppositeness of the effect he produces. In *A Fearful Joy,* for example, he deliberately portrays the child of the third generation, Nancy, repeating her grandmother Tabitha's behaviour pattern, and in *The Horse's Mouth,* Gulley Jimson . . . is clearly portrayed as a compulsive painter. It is plain enough that the thinker and the artist are not in step. There is nothing unusual, of course, about a writer who does not fully understand the nature of his own work and gives inadequate or misleading explanations of it. But as D. H. Lawrence pointed out, it is the tale, not the teller, that must be trusted.

That Cary should have been obliged to explain was, as I have said, a direct consequence of his method. He wanted his books to strike his readers as felt experience and intended that they should draw for themselves from his portrayal of life the same conclusions about what he called "the nature of things" as he himself had drawn from life itself. That the task was beyond him, apart from the fact that he was asking a great deal, is mainly a consequence of the further fact that no book can provide the same range of information and experience that life provides. Again, he knew this and said so, but he did not take adequate steps to supply what was missing. He asked too much of his method, and did not appreciate the extent to which what was so obvious to him needed to be spelt out to his readers. In *Aissa Saved,* for example, God speaks directly to Aissa, but there is no indication in the book as to how the reader is intended to take it. Once it is known, however, that Cary denied God the power to intervene in the workings of the physical universe, it at once becomes clear that Aissa's experience must be seen as purely subjective. It is on occasions like this that a knowledge of his thinking is essential. (pp. 5-7)

There really can be no doubt that in Cary's world man is an amoral being whose ends are pre-determined, whose freedom is so circumscribed as to be scarcely worth the name, and whose sole motivation is self-satisfaction. But because he could not consciously accept this, any more than he could subconsciously reject it, what Cary did in his novels was to search for a means of alleviating this intolerable situation, for a means, that is, of salvation. Lionel Trilling, in his essay "On the Teaching of Modern Literature," expressed the opinion that "the questions asked by our (i.e. modern) literature are not about our culture but about ourselves. It asks us if we are content with ourselves, if we are saved or damned—more than anything our literature is concerned with salvation." Cary is a case in point. As an artist, he both asks and answers the question: "Given that our lot is what it is, what must we do to be saved?" And in fact his first book, *Aissa Saved,* apprentice work though it is, is concerned with exactly that. It was published at the end of twelve years of continuous effort and in it, as he said himself, he succeeded for the first time both in clarifying his ideas and satisfying himself that they were valid and would translate into the novel form.

In embryo, everything he had to say is present in this book, and he spent the remainder of his life exploring the implications of his answer. One is reminded of Einstein, who announced his famous theory at the beginning of his career and then spent the remainder of his life exploring its implications. However, Cary's solution was not original; nor, of course, is this surprising. In science, there are no doubt innumerable discoveries still to be made, but in philosophy the fundamental problems are all insoluble, and it is likely that all possible solutions have been canvassed several times over. Certainly, Cary was no original thinker, and the answer he arrived at, in fact, is that true freedom, or perhaps the illusion of it, can only be found in complete, voluntary subjection to the will of God. It is this discovery that Aissa makes, and it is this that causes her to die in happy acceptance of her dreadful fate.

Cary, however, did not appreciate what his achievement was and, since, as he says in the preface to the Carfax edition, he edited out the thinking on which the book was based, it is hardly surprising that nobody else did either. Much was said about colonialism and missions; Cary himself, in the same preface, talks about the impact of ideas on cultures not prepared to receive them; and all these things the book is about, but they are not central. What happens to Aissa is; for she achieves freedom, complete and utter freedom, in the only way that is open to man. That is why the book is called *Aissa Saved.*

Having succeeded in stating his message (Cary held that all serious artists have one), he then settled down to explore its implications. The road to freedom that Aissa took is open to few. She is potentially a saint and has the illusion of direct access to God. But what of the rest of us? Cary saw two big obstacles that somehow have to be coped with. The first is youth, together with its concomitants, ignorance and inexperience. Aissa herself suffers badly in this respect. The second is what he called "the fixed in nature," by which he meant primarily those human characteristics that are inherent and involuntary . . . , and secondarily the fact that "the world is this kind of world and not that". In other words, in spite of his conviction that man is free, he recognised that determinism exists and is a factor that cannot be ignored.

The first stage of his development is therefore an examination of the problems that youth experiences. It stems directly from *Aissa Saved* and includes *An American Visitor, The African*

Witch, Mister Johnson, Charley Is My Darling and *A House of Children.* All these books deal with aspects of this problem. All the protagonists, except Bewsher in *An American Visitor,* are very young adults, adolescents or children. Bewsher, it is true, is in his forties, but his behaviour is persistently boyish and he is decidedly immature. His physical and mental ages do not coincide. All these protagonists come to grief as the result of the single-minded pursuit of their own ends (of trying, that is, to do what they like), carried on with a profound lack of appreciation of the fact that other people as individuals, and society as a corporate phenomenon, also have their own given characteristics and are also engaged in the pursuit of their own ends, which must be both allowed for and, when necessary, deferred to. They do not understand what true freedom is; they lack the understanding necessary to cope with life as they encounter it, and disaster strikes them down before they have a chance to acquire it.

The final book in this group, *A House of Children,* is different in that it constitutes Cary's response to the problem: the necessity of education. It is autobiographical and it depicts the loving upbringing of the young that Cary himself experienced and that brought him successfully to adulthood. He was much concerned with the care of the young.

In the next stage, which contains the First Trilogy, *The Moonlight* and *A Fearful Joy,* Cary turns his attention to the problems confronting men and women who survive their immaturity and have come to terms with their own natures, that part of themselves that, free or not, they cannot override without nullifying their own identities. In fact, the change of emphasis is not unheralded. Having rounded off his discussion of the problems of immaturity, Cary harked back to *Mister Johnson,* who, as a character, fits equally as well into the second stage as into the first; for like all the protagonists in the novels that constitute the second group, Johnson is a type-character rather than a credible representation of a real human being. Cary described him . . . as "the artist in life," just as he described Sara as "the nest builder," Wilcher as "the conservative," and Gulley as "the Artist." Similarly, he conceived the four women in *The Moonlight* as types of womanhood and Tabitha in *A Fearful Joy* as making an unvarying response to life. . . . (pp. 8-11)

There can be no doubt that the creation of type-characters was not what Cary intended. In the much-quoted letter to Mark Schorer in reply to what he considered to be a faulty interpretation of *A Fearful Joy,* Cary proclaimed his hatred of allegory and said, "my characters are real people in a real world or they are nothing," but he was wrong. These protagonists are fixed quantities, quasi-allegorical characters designed to enable Cary to explore the problems encountered by the human qualities they personify, such as the artistic temperament in the case of Gulley Jimson, and they have to remain fixed since, if they changed, Cary's purpose would be frustrated. There is no choice, it seems to me, but to conclude that in this respect too Cary did not fully understand the nature of his own work: his purpose and method are simply incompatible with his assumption about the nature of his characters.

The third stage of Cary's exploration of his view of life is to be found in the Second Trilogy. It is interesting to note in passing that as he worked towards the final, full re-statement of the solution to the problem that is embodied in the novel that alone constitutes the final stage, *The Captive and the Free,* so Cary worked through the lives of his protagonists. Starting with childhood, adolescence and young adulthood in stage one, he covered the whole lives of most of the protagonists in stage two, whilst in stage three, all three protagonists are near to, and know themselves to be near to, the ends of their lives. This is significant, I think, in that Cary's primary concern at this point is no longer with the constraints on freedom that have to be coped with, but with the need for justification that men and women feel as their lives begin to close in, the approval of their fellows for what they have achieved, the assurance that they have behaved worthily—a need that increases as death approaches.

It is as if the artist in Cary, having achieved Gulley Jimson, was acknowledging that doing what you like, and surely Gulley comes as near to that as anybody can, is not enough. Man does not and cannot exist in isolation. Gulley works only because he is a personification and not a "real" human being. . . . For all his immense vitality and his metaphysics too, he is not plausible because of his total self-sufficiency. Transfer him to *Peer Gynt* and he at once becomes a troll. But the stage three protagonists are once again people, and they have the human being's need for sympathy and approval. At this point, then, Cary the theorist's notion of freedom breaks down and is seen to be inadequate. In practice it is not merely external constraint that prevents man from doing what he likes but human nature. The way is now open for the artist to replace it with the definition that is implicit in *Aissa Saved:* freedom is not doing what you like, but doing what God likes.

The third stage thus follows organically from the second, as that did from the first. The callow youth gives way to the adult who seeks to express what is in him. The type-character adult who has done what he liked to the extent of his powers and circumstances gives way to the credible adult character who desperately needs approval. The development is natural and convincing. So too is the characterisation. One remembers Gilbert Phelps's observation that Chester Nimmo's career "is related with such calm conviction that it is often difficult to remember that it is not an actual biographical study." And once again, just as the second stage novels did not develop straight off the end of the first stage books, Cary going back to *Mister Johnson* and picking up for development an aspect that he had touched upon in passing, so now Cary goes back to *To Be a Pilgrim* and takes Wilcher as his point of departure, for he alone of the second stage protagonists feels the need to justify himself. Though conceived as a type and functioning as one, he nevertheless has this human characteristic. One cannot imagine Gulley asking for approval, nor, although their cases are less blatant, any of the others.

The stage three characters all fail in their quest, and one does not have to seek far for the reason. Man is a fickle and often irrational creature. His opinions are various and his judgements are inconstant, and in any case facts are often extremely difficult and sometimes quite impossible to establish to universal satisfaction. To look for justification to one's fellow men with the expectation of more than limited success is unrealistic. Full and permanent justification can only be based upon standards that are not merely fixed and unalterable, but infallible; and for such one must look to God. Thus, with the unfinished *The Captive and the Free,* we find ourselves back with Aissa. Syson, who is her counterpart, like her achieves a vision of God that sets him free, because for him too, doing what God wants and doing what he likes becomes one and the same thing. There is one great advance though. Aissa could only achieve freedom at the cost of life. Syson is not required to pay such a heavy price. He lives to explore the possession of freedom, though Cary, sadly, did not. One wonders what more he would have had to say. (pp. 11-13)

Dennis Hall, in his Joyce Cary: A Reappraisal, *St. Martin's Press, 1983, 162 p.*

ABDUL R. JANMOHAMED   (essay date 1983)

[*In the following excerpt, JanMohamed maintains that Cary's African novels can be best understood as "racial romances" rather than as realistic fiction, because they are infused with Cary's antipathy toward many aspects of African culture and his acceptance of common stereotypes that prevented him from fully developing African characters.*]

It has been universally assumed that in his African novels Joyce Cary was writing realistic fiction. Though critics have questioned the mimetic adequacy of the novels, they have insisted that Cary's portrayal of Africans is "authentic," and consequently they have tended either to apologize for Cary's colonialist viewpoint or to reproach him for it. Most of this criticism is substantial and useful in its own way, but I believe we can better appreciate these novels if we treat them as romances rather than as realistic fiction. (p. 15)

In attempting to define the precise nature of Cary's racial romances and in tracing their ideological sources, we have to consider both the general opposition between white/good and black/evil poles of his fictive societies as well as the contradictions that influence characterization and organization in his works. Northrop Frye's general definition of romance is applicable on the whole to Cary's African fiction:

> The essential difference between novel and romance lies in the conception of characterization. The romancer does not attempt to create "real people" so much as stylized figures which expand into psychological archetypes. It is in romance that we find Jung's libido, anima, and shadow reflected in the hero, the heroine, and villain respectively. That is why the romance so often radiates a glow of subjective intensity that the novel lacks, and why a suggestion of allegory is constantly creeping in around its fringes.

> . . . [Where the novelist deals with *personae* and stable society the] romancer deals with individuality, with characters *in vacuo* idealized by revery, and, however conservative he may be, something nihilistic and untamable is likely to keep breaking out of his pages.

Cary's romances conform to these criteria. Only a few of Cary's "pagan" Africans, in *An American Visitor,* are portrayed as individuals against specific social backgrounds of the tribe. The vast majority of his Africans, particularly the "acculturated" blacks, exist in a social vacuum—in their attempt to emulate European culture they reject native societies but are themselves ignored or rejected by white colonialists. The characterization of these blacks is based on stylized elaboration of similes such as the African as a child, as a savage, and as an emotional, irrational dependent being, and so on; they are at once archetypes and stereotypes. They are also shadows or demonic parodies of civilized whites—the pagans are uncivilized and the acculturated are "bad copies of English gentlemen." The subjectivity of the romances manifests itself in the narrators' opinionated assertiveness about questions of racial characteristics, in their tendency to drop their objectivity and become protagonist-reporters, and in the coincidence of the white characters' and narrators' attitude toward blacks. The intensity of the subjective antipathy results in gratuitous violence toward blacks that recalls the nihilistic tone of Kurtz's hatred in *Heart of Darkness:* "Exterminate all the brutes." However, Cary's racial romances vary from the traditional pattern in the presentation of both blacks and whites.

Cary's Africans are generally characterized through similaic association with children and animals and by metonymic reduction. However, the narrators' very conception of black characters is determined to some extent by metaphoric transference. For instance, because both Ali (in *Aissa Saved*) and Johnson are teenagers and because Aladai is about twenty, they cannot help behaving immaturely. Yet the narrators expect them to behave like adults and mock them when they fail to do so. To the extent that characterization is determined by the absorption of metaphors into the structure of ideological perception and conception, Cary is much closer to myth, albeit racial myth, than to the central tradition of romance. Similarly, the contradictions in the colonialist attitude to Africans result in the presentation of "accultured" blacks as schizophrenics, which becomes another departure from traditional romance patterns.

The most significant variation, though, is that the white/good society is depicted in a realist-satiric manner. The refusal to idealize the English administration can be traced back to Cary's bitterness toward colonial government and to his belief in the democratic/egalitarian imperative of English society which allows and even obliges him to criticize his own culture, whereas his negative idealization of Africans can be traced back to his dislike of and paranoid feeling toward the blacks in Nigeria and to the imperialist/autocratic imperative which demands that Africans be seen as a subhuman group. However, Cary's criticism of the white/good society does not alter significantly the good-evil polarity of romance, for in contrast to his condemnation of the African savagery and evil, the white colonial society, with all its faults and the heroic D.O.'s, who are blameless, virtuous, good samaritans, seems pure and enlightened.

Even if we take these variations into account, it is clear that Cary's African fiction is still essentially a version of romance. His novels do not fit into the mainstream of English romance but are part of a subgenre, the "racial romance" that flourished in the English empire. We can understand their nature as romances better if we take into account what Frantz Fanon has called the manichean structure of colonial society. Only then can we see that the allegory that lurks behind Cary's romances is essentially the same as the one that defines such a society: it is the allegory of white and black, of civilization and savagery, of superiority and inferiority, of good and evil, of the elect and the damned, of the self and the other.

That such a society should facilitate, and (as we shall see later) even demand, the writing of "racial romance" is not surprising. For if the "social affinities of the romance, with its grave idealizing of heroism and purity, are with the aristocracy," then the feudalistic colonial society, with its Europeans as aristocrats and its blacks as serfs, provides the ideal conditions. If the essential raw materials for romance are magic and otherness, then the "ju-ju" in Africa provides the former and the savagery and blackness of Africans provide the latter. If romance flourishes in transitional periods when society is torn, when alternatives are grasped as hostile but unrelated worlds, and when social order is in the process of being undermined and destroyed by other nascent movements, then again colonial society fulfills all these conditions. In the 1930s, when Cary was writing his racial romances, the social order imposed by colonialism was beginning to be challenged by nascent nationalistic movements, and European society too was beginning to experience the conflict between democratic and fascist forces.

Given these social conditions and the subsequent necessity for "racial romance," the socio-political function of Cary's African fiction was not to demonstrate a genuine purification of black/evil society, not to show the complete triumph of colonialist order over African anarchy, but precisely to maintain the colonial status quo by achieving a compromise between the two forces. The elimination of "accultured" Africans at the end of all his romances leaves only the "pagans," who still need to be "civilized," thus insuring the perpetuation of colonialism. Cary's criticism of the colonial government does not affect the maintenance of the status quo, for, as we have seen, he never questions the fundamental purpose of colonialism but only satirizes bureaucratic inefficiency. What Frye calls "kidnapped romance," that is, the absorption of romance into the ideology of an ascendant class, attempts to justify the social function of that class and to idealize its acts of protection and responsibility. Cary's "racial romances" do in fact justify the perpetuation of colonialism even if they do not wholeheartedly idealize the ruling bureaucracy.

Cary himself was troubled by a vague awareness that colonialist ideology, or, as he viewed it, the African setting itself, compelled him to write a certain kind of fiction. On the one hand, he found the African setting very useful because it permitted a certain kind of simplification. "The attraction of Africa is that it shows these wars of belief, and the powerful often subconscious motives which underlie them, in the greatest variety and also in very simple forms. Basic obsessions, which in Europe hide themselves under all sorts of decorous scientific or theological or political uniforms, are there seen naked in bold and dramatic action." Although this setting is attractive, Cary tells us in the . . . preface to *The African Witch* that after he had completed *An American Visitor* he did not want to write any more fiction about Africa and that he particularly wished "to avoid the African setting which, just because it is *dramatic, demands* a certain kind of story, a certain violence and coarseness of detail, almost a *fabulous* treatment, to keep it in its place . . .".

Obviously the "simplicity" is not endemic to African societies but is an inherent component of colonialist perspective and ideology. Therefore, slight and temporary changes in Cary's perspective of and attitude toward the colonial endeavor produce significant variations in the configuration of his novels; they do not all uniformly fit the above definition of "racial romance." The configurational variations clarify the extent to which these romances are determined by certain ideological components and by Cary's affective attitudes. As we have seen, Cary's sympathy for traditional "pagans" and his antipathy for "accultured" Africans respectively lead to the normative presentation of individuals and society in *An American Visitor* and to a stylized presentation of stereotypically reduced characters and social institutions in the other three novels. The bifurcation of sympathy and antipathy, which correlates quite systematically with the need to perpetuate colonialism by suppressing the "accultured" Africans, leads to the major variations: those novels dominated by pure antipathy tend to be closer to the ideal racial romance, while those dominated by sympathy tend to be removed from the ideal.

Thus Cary's first novel, *Aissa Saved,* which is marked by the narrator's antipathy toward the religious aspirations of Aissa and other Christian converts, shows signs of the simplification that is so necessary for romance. Even when Cary's thematic concern is focused on religious consciousness and even though he had researched the "watch-tower movement" in West Africa, he is unable to interpret adequately the complexity of his material. In this novel he presents the material as the ''commandments'' of a native revivalist, messianic movement. The ''orders of the Kingdom of Heaven, by Ojo, servant of God'' run as follows:

> No one is to have or keep any property which is abolished.
>
> No one is to use money which is abolished.
>
> No one is allowed to marry as fornication is forbidden.
>
> It is forbidden to drink beer, gin, whiskey.
>
> All judges are abolished including the white judge. Only God is judge. All laws are abolished except the law of God written in His book. All books are to be destroyed except God's book.
>
> Those who do not become Christians are to be killed, and the white men who are not Christians shall be driven away.

Now, in a colonial society where channels of political protest or action are completely blocked for the natives, the transference of political reactions to religious activity is common; religions become to some extent smoke screens for politics. Such revivalist movements express opposition to racial discrimination by exaltation of African values and a corresponding rejection of European values; their resort to the Bible allows them utopian visions which alleviate their present misery; and their direct appeal to God allows them to bypass colonial and church authorities and even to justify rebellion against them. Thus their prime function is to overcome the insecurity created by economic, political, and cultural domination of the colonizers. Clearly the above ''orders'' mentioned by Cary are designed to fulfill some of the same political-religious functions. Yet Cary is not at all interested in the complexity of this combination of religion and politics. He only interrupts the narrative in order to cite these ''orders'' as a ''curiosity'' that was later sent to the governor. Even though Cary convincingly shows that Marie (the American visitor in his second novel) turns to religion out of social and personal insecurity, he is unable to apply the same insight to African religious movements. The process of simplification is of course accompanied by the portrayal of acculturated natives as wild, hyperemotional, uncontrolled, bloodthirsty, cruel savages. Thus by rendering them as directly antithetical to the civilized Europeans, Cary produces an almost perfect racial romance in *Aissa Saved*.

However, Cary's next novel, *An American Visitor,* which does not contain any threats to colonial stability from aspiring blacks, is least like a romance. As we have seen, the natives in this novel are quite content to exist within their traditional culture and the D.O. is anxious to protect them from external encroachment. Thus the absence of *political* antagonism between the Africans and the colonial administration leads to a corresponding lack of aesthetic stylization and opposition between the white/good and the black/evil worlds. The harmony of purpose allows Cary to present the two worlds in a more realistic manner. In comparison to *Aissa Saved, An American Visitor* is essentially a benign novel full of authorial guilt about the whole colonial endeavor. However, the very accurate criticism of the duplicitous structure of colonialism is diffused and masked by its relegation to outsiders like the American Marie and ''exploiters'' like Cottee, while the guilt is expressed indirectly through Bewsher's attempt to protect Birri territory

from the English mining interest that represents the commercial arm of colonial enterprise.

But in his next novel, *The African Witch,* Cary reverts to the romance structure of *Aissa Saved.* Once again the colonial administration is criticized for its inefficiency, confusion, and ignorance, while the Africans who emulate Europeans are portrayed as apes, and the traditional natives are presented normatively and realistically. Aladai, who wishes to establish a school for native children, reverts to savagery as soon as he comes into contact with his own people, and Cocker, who aspires to become a Christian minister, reverts to ju-ju and human sacrifice. Cary's antipathy for these acculturated natives is best exemplified by his description of Cocker's ''natural or primitive religion'' which is nothing more than

> herd communism, herd fear, herd love, blood ties and race hatreds.
>
> Such a religion is pre-human, even in its ritual of blood. Beasts fear blood, and drink blood. It has a special significance for them.

This description, which shows neither objective accuracy nor intellectual rigor, is remarkable for its violent negative emotions. Cary's antipathy, which forms the basis of his racial romances, finally manifests itself through the fact that he subjects such characters to the same degree and kind of violence that they themselves are supposed to embody. The configuration of the racial romances is produced by the projection of Cary's hostility.

Mister Johnson is also defined partly by such projection, but it is a rather ambivalent novel that combines antipathy and guilt. Johnson too attempts to emulate the Europeans, and consequently he becomes the recipient of his share of physical punishment: he is beaten by various Africans and, finally, apparently mercifully shot by Rudbeck. However, instead of using violence, Cary manifests his antipathy toward Johnson's imitation of Englishmen by ridiculing his attempts. In order to succeed in presenting Johnson as a buffoon who incongruously and absurdly ''apes'' English values and tastes, Cary has to withhold his own sympathy and intellectual understanding from his protagonist's aspirations. By thus distancing himself from his character, Cary is able to portray the hysterical, hyperemotional, and absurd Johnson as the complete antithesis of the typically controlled, calm, and dignified Englishman; the ridiculousness of Johnson's behavior is directly dependent upon the tacit agreement between author and reader that civilized people conduct themselves in a manner diametrically opposed to that of Johnson. Although the opposition and distance between the ''evilness'' of Johnson and the ''goodness'' of the civilized person is not, strictly speaking, a *moral* one, the sense of superiority that Johnson's antics afford the reader is, in its psychological payoff, really no different. However, Cary's antipathy is accompanied by a powerful guilt that is particularly evident at the end of the novel. When Johnson has been condemned to death for stealing from and murdering Gollop, Rudbeck, who is entrusted with his execution, repeatedly asks Johnson to absolve him from his possible indirect responsibility for the clerk's predicament. Rudbeck is afraid that his denial of a salary advance and his negative recommendation of Johnson may have respectively led to theft and the harsh sentence. Such a sense of accountability is understandable to some extent, but when Rudbeck asks for complete acquittal, when Johnson repeatedly insists that the blame is entirely his own, when the hero all too willingly absolves his master and then asks, as a personal favor, to be executed by Rudbeck himself, and, finally, when the latter willingly does so and is later proud of it, one begins to suspect the *function* of Rudbeck's powerful desire for absolution and Johnson's abject but apparently genuine humility. This ending clearly identifies Cary's own sense of guilt and his desire to be forgiven some unnamed trespass, but nevertheless he still portrays Johnson as a buffoon and eventually kills him. The same ambivalence is revealed by the dedication of the novel to Musa, Cary's assistant in Nigeria, which is followed by the motto "Remembered goodness is a benediction." But if Johnson represents Musa, then clearly the remembrance of the latter's moral "goodness" through the representation of him as a buffoon, a thief, and a murderer, that is, as the antithesis of civilized human behavior, defines Cary's deep ambivalence about his African experience which, in combination with the moral judgment that underlies the manichean structure of colonial society, produces the bifurcated structures of Cary's racial romances.

The point that I wish to stress here is not that Cary should be faulted for inadequately representing African reality, but that his belief in the nexus of values and ideas that comprise the colonialist ideology limits his perception and determines the shape of his fiction. The power of this influence is demonstrated by the simple fact that when Cary turned his attention to British settings he stopped writing romances and began producing realistic novels. His English novels, which take up some of the same themes as his African romances, do much greater justice to the intricacies of character and theme; they contain neither the narrative shifts nor the contradictions of the romances. Yet, whereas his realistic British novels represent some of the complexities of English society, his African romances reveal not the complexities of *African* cultures but rather the "worldness" of the colonialist world; the "racial romances" reveal the "horizons" of colonialist ideology—they are an indirect manifestation of the shape and strength of that ideology. (pp. 41-8)

> Abdul R. JanMohamed, "Joyce Cary: The Generation of Racial Romance," in his Manichean Aesthetics: The Politics of Literature in Colonial Africa, *The University of Massachusetts Press, 1983, pp. 15-48.*

KINLEY E. ROBY (essay date 1984)

[*Roby is an American educator and nonfiction writer. In the following excerpt, he assesses Cary's place in English literature.*]

To place Cary among the other novelists of his period is to see how highly differentiated his brand of fiction is. In some respects, of course, he maintained the tradition of the novel. He was profoundly middle class in his preoccupation with respectability. That this preoccupation is expressed in opposition, such as Gulley Jimson's struggle against the forces of order in his world, against the Beeders' wealth, Hickson's conservatism, and Sara's desire for a first class funeral, only serves to underline his obsession. In every novel from *Aissa Saved* to *The Captive and the Free* the broad foundations of his fictive worlds are built on the middle-class values of order, respectability, moral responsibility, and conventional values.

Over and over again his protagonists come to grief against the adamantine walls of propriety, social conservatism, and cultural Philistinism. But he is not, like Aldous Huxley in such novels as *Point Counter Point,* a social satirist. Even in his political trilogy he is not a political novelist in the sense that George Orwell is in *1984* or *Burmese Days.* In his African stories Cary is not primarily concerned to show the major

configurations of African life as Leonard Woolf sets out to do in *The Village And The Jungle.* The closest he comes to writing this sort of novel of cultural exploration is in *Castle Corner,* an attempt that was only partially successful. One has only to mention such writers as Thomas Hardy, Arnold Bennett, and John Galsworthy to understand how different was the flow of Cary's artistic genius.

Neither can it be said that Cary was a particularly experimental writer. His occasional excursions into the use of the first person or any of the minor structural experiments in his novels are modest efforts. Considering the work of Conrad, Ford, and Joyce, who came before him, or that of Samuel Beckett, a contemporary, or Henry Green and Ivy Compton-Burnett, one can see that Cary obviously was not primarily interested in remaking the form of the novel. There is little in Cary's novels that would appear strange, so far as form is concerned, to a nineteenth-century reader, especially one familiar with George Meredith or Laurence Sterne.

He is quite different from a chronicler of English life like Anthony Powell in his *Music of Time* series or C. P. Snow who, in his *Strangers And Brothers* novels, strives to explain the grave dangers to our society posed by the division between scientist and nonscientist. One can read all of Cary's novels without encountering an overview of English life. This is not to say that one does not encounter vivid and memorable renderings of English and Irish life in Cary's novels. Chester Nimmo's childhood, life at Castle Corner, Gulley Jimson's London are only a few examples of the vitality of Cary's ability to convey a sense of place and time. But such effects, powerful as they may be, are not the heart of his fiction.

Does he, then, belong to any tradition in English literature? The answer is yes, but it is not one closely of his time. From the time of William Langland in the fourteenth century onward, there have appeared at intervals writers whose work has been the product of intense and powerfully compelling visions of reality. Langland's *Piers the Plowman* is an early example of the type and John Bunyan's *The Pilgrim's Progress* is another. It may seem strange to compare Cary to Langland and Bunyan, but the strangeness is soon overcome when one begins to think about the sources of their inspiration.

William Blake, Bunyan, Langland, and others of their kind wrote out of a conviction that they had encountered the truth and were God-bound to reveal it. A modern reader may be made uncomfortable by a close encounter with a writer claiming to be a voice from the horse's mouth, but that is only because he no longer lives in an age of faith. Even Cary's vision, when it came to him, came in a secular revelation that he called truth and not God. Still, his vision was of such force that it accounts for the shape of his art and, indeed, all of his life thereafter.

Cary believed that he had discovered the fundamental truth about human existence. This truth reveals man condemned to freedom in a universe that is contantly changing. The nature of the change is that the old is broken up to make way for the new and that the only way the new can be formed is through the destruction of the old. All attempts to preserve anything, whether it is a custom or a castle, are doomed to failure. Nothing survives. Everything changes; and man must, as long as he lives, continuously make choices in his life that cause him to change also. In this sense Cary's universe is fated.

Such a view of things might, conceivably, have led Cary to preach a stoic indifference toward the monstrousness of life.

But his vision led him, in fact, in quite another direction. The freedom that man has had thrust upon him allows him to shape his own life. This is regarded by Cary as a great opportunity for man to develop his moral nature. Of course it also provides him, as well, with the opportunity to develop the satanic aspect of his nature.

The characters in Cary's fiction are often engaged in the task of building their souls. The problem is that this development does not go on smoothly. Tempted by greed, selfishness, power, and complacency, characters backslide, go sideways, and fall from grace. Even the best of Cary's characters fail to avoid all of the pitfalls laid in their paths. Aissa runs away from the mission to be with her lover. Jim Latter becomes a murderer. Chester Nimmo cannot resist the attractions of power. Sara Monday constantly surprises herself with her failures.

The worlds that Cary creates in his novels are also systematically destroyed. In the African novels, the native culture is ploughed up and the tribes broken. In *The Horse's Mouth,* the wall on which Gulley paints his last picture is bulldozed into rubble. The Corner house goes out of the family. In *To Be A Pilgrim* Wilcher cannot prevent Tolbrook from being wrecked or Tenacre from being stripped of its trees and hedges and ploughed into a faceless field, where machines can labor unimpeded by lanes or copses or laborers' cottages. In the novels nothing remains unchanged.

In this chaos has Cary found any abiding values? Several. They are all connected with the way in which people deal with one another. Clearly, family life was important to Cary. It can be seen in his own personal history as well as in its representation in his work. It is particularly evident in his evocation of childhood in *Charley is My Darling, Castle Corner, A House of Children, Prisoner of Grace,* and elsewhere. Children in particular in his fiction are sustained by love and harmed by its absence.

Love among the adults in his novels tends to run to a formula. Cary's women are victims or tyrants. And the clear implication is that women who are not suppressed, by physical force if necessary, will become tyrants. His view of women is, in my opinion, the least appealing part of his comprehensive vision. His men are either creators such as Mister Johnson and Gulley Jimson who destroy the old world, or conservative men such as Hickson, Latter, and Wilcher who vainly strive to maintain the old world. Cary's women love both varieties of men and are often ground between them.

Today, Cary has lost much of the popularity that he worked so arduously to win. He certainly qualifies for the epithet of neglected writer. To be great, a writer must demonstrate a breadth of vision and a universality of appeal that will make him accessible and attractive to a wide range of readers. He must both be of his time and transcend his time. He must be copious enough to have created in his work a picture of the world that is rich and complex. He must give a clear vision of life. He must be a consummate storyteller.

By these measures Cary is a great novelist. He meets every condition set down. He is neglected, perhaps, because in the last analysis readers demand to hear what the great myths and the lowly folk tales tell them, that life is a struggle between life and death and that life wins. In Cary's novels the struggle ends in a draw.

It is quite possible to point out that, over and over again in European literature, we find life being defeated. In Ibsen, Zola,

Flaubert, the reader sees the dream crushed, the blossom blown. Indeed, the blossom can be observed withering in Hardy's *Jude The Obscure* and in *Tess.* But Hardy is an exception. In the tradition of the English novel, from Defoe to Iris Murdoch, life wins. Evil is cast out like winter's garment to be burned in the purifying flame of spring's rebirth.

Cary does not give his readers that ritual cleansing, but he gives them much else. His novels are brimming with life, the lines dance with energy, and his characters have sufficient force to march, frequently, straight off the page into our memories. Gulley Jimson, to name only one, is a permanent addition to English literature's pantheon of fictional immortals. Cary was a great writer and a great visionary. The neglect which now afflicts his work will be amended, and he will once again be brought forward to stand in the first rank of English novelists. (pp. 119-21)

> *Kinley E. Roby, in his* Joyce Cary, *Twaine Publishers, 1984, 137 p.*

ADDITIONAL BIBLIOGRAPHY

Adams, Hazard. "Joyce Cary: Posthumous Volumes and Criticism to Date." *Texas Studies in Literature and Language* I, No. 2 (Summer 1959): 289-99.
> Surveys Cary's critical reception, which Adams considers inappropriately slight, focusing upon reaction to two posthumously published works, *Art and Reality* and *The Captive and the Free.*

————. *Joyce Cary's Trilogies: Pursuit of the Particular Real.* Tallahassee: University Presses of Florida, 1983, 280 p.
> Maintains that Cary's two trilogies contain one overriding idea—"the importance of the continued presence of the particular and unique in any artistic creation"—and examines the presence of this idea in the novels.

Battaglia, Francis Joseph. "Spurious Armageddon: Joyce Cary's *Not Honour More.*" *Modern Fiction Studies* XIII, No. 4 (Winter 1967-68): 479-91.
> Summarizes critical disagreement about the reliability of the narrators of Cary's second trilogy and contends that Jim Latter, from the third novel, *Not Honour More,* is the least reliable of the trilogy's three narrative voices.

Bettman, Elizabeth R. "Joyce Cary and the Problem of Political Morality." *The Antioch Review* XVIII, No. 2 (June 1957): 266-72.
> Examines the ways that Cary's second trilogy explores the uses of creative imagination in the politics of public and private life.

Brawer, Judith. "The Triumph of Defeat: A Study of Joyce Cary's First Trilogy." *Texas Studies in Literature and Language* X, No. 4 (Winter 1969): 629-34.
> Suggests that Gulley Jimson's three great paintings described in *The Horse's Mouth* illustrate Cary's belief that creation is the imagination's response to destruction and provide the thematic framework of the entire first trilogy.

Burgess, Anthony. "Great Individuality." In his *The Novel Now: A Guide to Contemporary Fiction,* pp. 72-80. New York: W. W. Norton & Co., 1967.
> Briefly surveys Cary's career, noting the recurrence of some primary themes, such as conflict between different cultures and the importance of human imagination, in the major novels.

Christian, Edwin Ernest. "Joyce Cary's Major Poems." *Ariel* 17, No. 2 (April 1986): 33-46.
> Demonstrates that Cary's poems "Marching Soldier" and "The Drunken Sailor" "share many themes, particularly the themes of the injustice of life, the necessity of freedom, and the world's creative character," with the novels.

Collins, Harold R. "Joyce Cary's Troublesome Africans." *The Antioch Review* XIII, No. 1 (March 1953): 397-406.

Discusses the characterization of Africans in Cary's novels, concluding that "if we make allowances for the satirical tone of Cary's African novels, we may be confident that they give an authentic view of the conflicts between white men's authority and black men's aspirations in modern Nigeria."

Cook, Cornelia. *Joyce Cary: Liberal Principles*. London: Vision Press, 1981, 242 p.

Examines the representation in Cary's fiction of late nineteenth- and early twentieth-century British political and philosophical Liberalism.

Echeruo, Michael J.C. *Joyce Cary and the Dimensions of Order*. New York: Barnes & Noble, 1979, 175 p.

Examines Cary's ideas regarding metaphysics, politics, and aesthetics, maintaining that the relation of Cary's philosophy to his fiction should be the primary concern of critics.

Fisher, Barbara. *Joyce Cary: The Writer and His Theme*. Atlantic Highlands, N.J.: Humanities Press, 1980, 414 p.

Uses unpublished material as well as published works to explicate Cary's personal philosophy, which the critic contends is essential to understanding his writing. Fisher appends a complete primary and secondary bibliography.

Foster, Malcolm. *Joyce Cary: A Biography*. Boston: Houghton Mifflin, 1968, 555 p.

Critical biography exploring the bearing of events in Cary's life on the development of the philosophical ideas that shaped his literary works.

Fraser, Keath. "Potboiler to Artist: Joyce Cary and the Short Story." *Studies in Short Fiction* VII, No. 4 (Fall 1971): 617-26.

Discusses the development of Cary's short fiction from the early potboilers of the 1920s to the later, more sophisticated and artistically accomplished short stories of the 1940s.

French, Warren G. "Joyce Cary's American Rover Girl." *Texas Studies in Literature and Language* II, No. 3 (Autumn 1960): 281-91.

Discusses Cary's implicit condemnation of the undisciplined idealism of the character Marie Hasluck in *The American Visitor* and, by extension, all such inadequate attempts to bridge cultural gaps.

Goonetilleke, D.C.R.A. "Joyce Cary: The Clash of Cultures in Nigeria." In his *Developing Countries in British Fiction*, pp. 199-244. Totowa, N.J.: Rowman and Littlefield, 1977.

Examines Cary's presentation of conflict between native Nigerian and colonial British cultures in his African novels. Goonetilleke commends Cary's depiction of Nigerian culture.

Hicks, Granville. "Joyce Cary Concludes His Trilogy Tragically with *Not Honour More*." *The New Leader* XXXVIII, No. 24 (13 June 1955): 21-2.

Favorably assesses Cary's second trilogy in a review of the final volume. Hicks praises Cary's creativity and his ability to convey the unique vitality of each human life that he treats.

Hoffman, Charles G. "The Genesis and Development of Joyce Cary's First Trilogy." *PMLA* LXXVIII, No. 4 (September 1963): 431-39.

Draws from published and unpublished sources to determine Cary's techniques and intentions as he developed the novels of his first trilogy or "multiple novel."

Hopwood, Alison L. "Separate Worlds: Joyce Cary's Nimmo Trilogy." *Texas Studies in Literature and Language* XIII. No. 3 (Fall 1971): 523-35.

Close study of Cary's second trilogy focusing on the sharp distinctions between the three novels that are accomplished by the extreme differences in the narrators.

Johnson, Pamela Hansford. "Joyce Cary." In *Little Reviews Anthology*, edited by Denys Val Baker, pp. 200-09. London: Methuen & Co., 1949.

Biographical and critical sketch surveying Cary's career through *The Moonlight*.

———. "Three Novelists and the Drawing of Character: C.P. Snow, Joyce Cary, and Ivy Compton-Burnett." In *Essays and Studies 1950*, edited by G. Rostrevor Hamilton, pp. 82-99. London: John Murray, 1950.

Favorably compares Cary's character delineation with that of major nineteenth-century satirists Fielding, Smollett, Sterne, and Dickens.

Kanu, S.H. *A World of Everlasting Conflict: Joyce Cary's View of Man and Society*. Ibadan, Nigeria: Ibadan University Press, 1974, 300 p.

Examines the theme of a creative individual in conflict with society in Cary's novels *Aissa Saved, The African Witch, An American Visitor, Mister Johnson, Charley is My Darling, A House of Children*, and *Prisoner of Grace*.

Kerr, Elizabeth. "Joyce Cary's Second Trilogy." *University of Toronto Quarterly* XXIX, No. 3 (April 1960): 310-25.

Considers the presentation of major characters from different points of view the central device of Cary's second trilogy.

Larsen, Golden L. *The Dark Descent: Social Change and Moral Responsibility in the Novels of Joyce Cary*. New York: Roy Publishers, 1966, 202 p.

Examines Cary's worldview as evidenced in his novels.

Mahood, M.M. *Joyce Cary's Africa*. London: Methuen & Co., 1964, 206 p.

Two-part study that combines a factual account of Cary's years in Nigeria with critical examinations of the African novels in an attempt to avoid the tendency to identify incidents from Cary's life too closely with the novels.

Majumdar, Bimalendu. *Joyce Cary: An Existentialist Approach*. Atlantic Highlands, N.J.: Humanities Press, 1983, 220 p.

Chronologically arranged examination of the development of existentialist themes in Cary's novels.

McCormick, John. "Tradition and the Novel: England." In his *Catastrophe and Imagination: An Interpretation of the Recent English and American Novel*, pp. 135-69. London: Longmans, Green, and Co., 1957.

Notes that several aspects of Cary's novels, in particular his characterization, belong to nineteenth-century British literary tradition.

Mitchell, Giles. "Joyce Cary's *Prisoner of Grace*." *Modern Fiction Studies* IX, No. 3 (Autumn 1963): 263-75.

Close study of the function of the first-person narrator in *Prisoner of Grace*, examining discrepancies between the narrator Nina's stated intention and the actual effect of her account. Mitchell concludes that the chaotic narrative style is a metaphor for the narrator's moral confusion.

———. *The Art Theme in Joyce Cary's First Trilogy*. The Hague: Mouton, 1971, 136 p.

Examines the nature and the role of the artist in Cary's first trilogy, which, Mitchell contends, contains and explicates Cary's fundamental beliefs about the role of art in human existence.

Monas, Sidney. "What to Do with a Drunken Sailor." *The Hudson Review* III, No. 3 (Fall 1950): 466-74.

Analyzes the relative effectiveness of the different first-person narrative styles of the novels composing Cary's first trilogy. In a similar examination of narrative structure in *A Fearful Joy*, Monas finds that the novel achieves extraordinary effectiveness through its unusual third-person present-tense narrative.

Obiechina, Emmanuel. "Background to the West African Novel." In his *Culture, Tradition, and Society in the West African Novel*, pp. 3-28. Cambridge: Cambridge University Press, 1975.

Considers Cary's African novels handicapped by his point of view as a colonial administrator, stating that Cary lacked essential understanding of the African way of life and presented only ''the Africa of the European imagination.''

Ola, Virginia U. ''The Vision of Power: Joyce Cary and African Women.'' *Ariel* 9, No. 1 (January 1978): 85-97.
    Provides a close study of Cary's presentation of female African characters in the novels *Aissa Saved* and *The African Witch*. Ola contends that Cary's ''obsessive fear of the power of African women'' led him to portray them as unstable, contradictory, and overly emotional.

Pritchett, V.S. Review of *Herself Surprised, To Be a Pilgrim,* and *The Horse's Mouth,* by Joyce Cary. *The New Statesman and Nation* XLII, No. 1077 (27 October 1951): 464-65.
    Favorable review of Cary's first trilogy, especially praising his characterizations.

Raskin, Jonah. *The Mythology of Imperialism: Rudyard Kipling, Joseph Conrad, E. M. Forster, D. H. Lawrence, and Joyce Cary.* New York: Random House,1971, 335 p.
    Provides character studies of Johnson from the novel *Mister Johnson* and Gulley Jimson from *The Horse's Mouth,* maintaining that both protagonists were vividly depicted but imperfectly understood by Cary, and assesses Cary's political analysis *The Case for African Freedom* as ''a whitewash of imperialism, an attack on African civilization, on Black nationalism.''

Rosenfeld, Isaac. ''Popular Misery.'' *The New Republic* 127, No. 16 (20 October 1952): 27.
    Professes not to understand why Cary's novels—which are ''written in a minor key and bear a load of squalor and frustration''—are popular and successful.

Salz, Paulina J. ''The Philosophical Problems in Joyce Cary's Work.'' *Western Humanities Review* XX. No. 2 (Spring 1966): 159-65.
    Contends that Cary possessed a tragic view of life that is implicit in his fiction and explicit in many of his nonfiction works.

Starkie, Enid. ''Joyce Cary.'' *The Virginia Quarterly Review* 37, No. 1 (Winter 1960): 110-34.
    Appreciative reminiscence by a friend of Cary who recounts how aspects of his personality are evident in his novels.

Teeling, John. ''Joyce Cary's Moral World.'' *Modern Fiction Studies* IX, No. 3 (Autumn 1963): 276-83.
    Discusses Cary's views on morality as expressed in his works.

Wolkenfeld, Jack. *Joyce Cary: The Developing Style.* New York: New York University Press, 1968, 200 p.
    Pronounces Cary a wholly original literary figure ''who created his own work in his own way,'' and dismisses comparisons with either nineteenth- or twentieth-century literary traditions as of little value in understanding him.

Bernard DeVoto

1897-1955

(Also wrote under the pseudonyms John August, Cady Hewes, Richard Dye, Fairley Blake, and Frank Gilbert) American historian, critic, essayist, biographer, novelist, and short story writer.

DeVoto is chiefly remembered for three volumes of American history, *The Year of Decision: 1846, Across the Wide Missouri,* and *The Course of Empire.* These works comprise a detailed, complex, and vividly presented overview of the importance of the frontier experience in shaping American culture, politics, and national character. However, during a long career in which he wrote prolifically in several genres, DeVoto frequently attracted less attention as a historian than as a literary antagonist. He often contended that his critical works—most prominently his biography *Mark Twain's America* and the essays collected in *The Literary Fallacy*—functioned as "correctives" to prevailing critical thought, and he did not hesitate to castigate in print anyone whose opinions, beliefs, and literary theories were contrary to his own.

DeVoto was born in Ogden, Utah, to a Roman Catholic father and a Mormon mother. Neither parent was actively religious, and DeVoto grew up acutely aware of his family's differences from their predominantly Mormon neighbors. After excelling in high school, he attended the University of Utah for a year and then enrolled at Harvard in the fall of 1915. DeVoto quickly came to love New England and to regard his home state with disfavor. Nevertheless, after graduating from Harvard in 1920—as part of the class of 1918 whose studies had been interrupted by armed service during World War I—he returned to Utah and taught history at Ogden Junior High School for a year before obtaining a teaching position at Northwestern University in Chicago. There, in 1923, he married one of his students, and the following year published his first novel, *The Crooked Mile.* Over the next several years DeVoto wrote magazine articles, short stories, and a second novel, and in 1927 moved to Cambridge, Massachusetts, where he devoted his full time to writing. DeVoto enjoyed being part of the New England literary community and quickly rose to a place of prominence within it. He joined the faculty of Harvard in 1929, first as an instructor and then as a lecturer, and edited the *Harvard Graduate's Magazine* from 1930 through 1932. In 1935 he became editor of *Harper's* "Easy Chair" column, and his often controversial pronouncements on politics, education, literature, automobile travel, and the perfect martini, among other topics, appeared monthly until January 1956. For two years, from 1936 through 1938, DeVoto added to his other duties the editorship of the *Saturday Review of Literature.* His novels, histories, volumes of criticism, and collections of essays appeared regularly throughout his life, some to high acclaim, particularly his historical study *Across the Wide Missouri,* which received the Pulitzer Prize in history for 1948. Much of his later life was devoted to conservationist issues. DeVoto died unexpectedly at the age of fifty-eight.

DeVoto's career was shaped largely by his fascination with the history of the American western frontier, and this pervasive interest can be seen in his fiction and criticism as well as his histories. His historical concerns became evident first in his

novels, a number of which were popular works published under the pseudonym John August. DeVoto published under his own name the five novels that he considered his best: *The Crooked Mile, The Chariot of Fire, The House of Sun-Goes-Down, We Accept with Pleasure,* and *Mountain Time.* The first three employ aspects of American frontier history either directly or indirectly in their plots. *The Crooked Mile* and *The House of Sun-Goes-Down* follow several generations of families descended from early American pioneers, while *The Chariot of Fire* is an unflattering depiction of Mormonism and religious fanaticism in the West. Critics generally agree that DeVoto included historical elements in these novels to dispel common myths about the frontier as a place of lawless adventure and to provide what he considered far more interesting information about the complex daily lives of frontier dwellers involved in establishing a new culture and civilization. DeVoto's final two novels, *We Accept with Pleasure* and *Mountain Time,* are semi-autobiographical works that deal with complicated personal and professional relationships in the turbulent 1920s. Although most of DeVoto's novels appeared to favorable reviews, none received sustained critical or popular interest.

DeVoto's reputation as a literary antagonist began in 1932 with *Mark Twain's America,* an "essay in the correction of ideas" written in response to Van Wyck Brooks's *The Ordeal of Mark Twain* (1920). In his biography of Twain, Brooks described the West as uncouth and culturally barren and contended that Twain's early development in this environment was responsible for his later failure as a serious literary artist. DeVoto objected strongly to what he considered both an undervaluation of Twain's talents and a historically inaccurate view of the American West. Arguing that Twain is properly appreciated as a humorist, DeVoto maintained that he was typical of the real frontier, which was a lively, stimulating place that helped shape his fertile imagination and literary genius. Not content merely to expound his own views, DeVoto dedicated much of *Mark Twain's America* to attacking Brooks and others whom he considered to have an imperfect understanding of the frontier and who were therefore unable to present faithfully either that phase of American history or the lives of those born and raised in the West. DeVoto's denunciations—not confined to the chapter entitled "The Critics of Mark Twain" but scattered throughout the book—were so prevalent that one reviewer, Percy H. Boynton, expressed his regret that such a valuable study should be "becluttered" with invective against others.

Although many commentators took exception to the way DeVoto dismissed the theories of other critics while asserting that his own were unimpeachable, *Mark Twain's America* was hailed as a significant new approach to understanding Twain, and it inaugurated a resurgence of scholarly interest in his work. This attention netted DeVoto an unexpected return: in 1938 he was made curator of the Mark Twain papers held by Harvard's Widener Library. Over the next eight years he edited and arranged for the publication of two important new Twain collections: *Mark Twain in Eruption* (1940) and *Letters from the Earth* (1962). However, while the curatorship gave DeVoto access to information previously unavailable to any critic or biographer, it was an unpaid position that absorbed a great deal of his time. Furthermore, Twain's daughter and a lawyer she hired to oversee the estate presented DeVoto with continual difficulties arising from their attempts to keep from publication anything that would portray Twain as bitter or irreligious. In 1946 DeVoto resigned as curator, partly out of annoyance at the restrictions placed on his use of the papers, and partly because he felt he had learned all he could from them and had written all he wanted about Mark Twain. His second major study, *Mark Twain at Work,* had been published to enthusiastic reviews in 1942.

With *Mark Twain's America* and *Mark Twain at Work* DeVoto became a historian of the frontier as well as a literary biographer, developing a historical method based on the accumulation and interweaving of every known fact that could be marshalled about a time or place, and he used this method to write his volumes of American history: *The Year of Decision: 1846, Across the Wide Missouri,* and *The Course of Empire.* These three works describe and explain different aspects of the impact of the frontier experience on American history. The first volume summarizes the important events of one year in an eventful decade. Constructed much like a novel, *The Year of Decision* weaves personal accounts taken from firsthand sources such as journals into a complex narrative that deals with nearly every major event of that year and touches the activities of numerous prominent people of the period. *The Year of Decision* was widely praised by reviewers. *Across the Wide Missouri* also appeared to uniformly positive reviews, and since that time has been acknowledged as DeVoto's finest historical work and one of the best American histories ever written. A study of the fur trade between 1832 and 1838, the book is more narrowly focused than DeVoto's other major histories, concentrating on several dominant figures in this

industry. *The Course of Empire* is the broadest in scope and most ambitious of DeVoto's histories, covering the three centuries of westward migration across North America, again making effective use of firsthand documents. The focus of the book is the often striking contrast between the actual geography of the North American continent and the imprecise, frequently inaccurate conception of the land recorded by those who crossed it.

In April 1944 the *Saturday Review of Literature* published an essay by DeVoto entitled "They Turned Their Backs on America," which was later reprinted in his essay collection *The Literary Fallacy.* In the essay and subsequent book, DeVoto charged that works produced in the 1920s, as well as those written later about this decade, greatly misrepresented American culture, depicting it as decadent and brutish during a time when American life was actually creative and energetic. Writers, DeVoto maintained, should have presented the renascent aspect of American life; the negative portrayal of America, he protested, was not only historically inaccurate but also contributed to the low esteem in which much of Europe held the United States. *The Literary Fallacy* generated many angry responses and remains the focal point of much critical and biographical discussion of DeVoto. One of the strongest replies came from Sinclair Lewis, who in an article entitled "Fools, Liars, and Mr. DeVoto " denounced *The Literary Fallacy* as "prosily dull, carelessly planned, presenting nothing but Mr. DeVoto's bellows about his own importance." Most other responses to *The Literary Fallacy* were similarly negative, though few were so personally abusive as Lewis's. Many commentators assessing the book conclude that DeVoto was simply wrong to assume that it was possible for the work of any writer to encompass the entire reality of the American experience during that time. Some found him guilty of what Malcolm Cowley termed a "critic's fallacy": assuming that the writers of the twenties failed because they did not provide a historically correct representation of the period, when in fact many authors had different intentions for their works and fulfilled their own purposes admirably.

DeVoto remains a controversial figure in twentieth-century American letters for the belligerence with which he set forth his critical opinions, asserting his infallibility, especially in historical matters, while assuming that no one else possessed his comprehensive knowledge of literature and history. Prolific in many genres, he left his lasting mark as a historian of the American frontier and a student of the development of Mark Twain. Commentators often note that DeVoto combined novelistic techniques with primary sources to compose histories that have the structure, form, and engrossing interest of a skillfully plotted novel. For these works he remains highly regarded as an author who contributed to the understanding of the frontier experience and its impact on American history.

(See also *Contemporary Authors,* Vol. 113, and *Dictionary of Literary Biography,* Vol. 9: *American Novelists, 1910-1945.*)

PRINCIPAL WORKS

The Crooked Mile (novel) 1924
The Chariot of Fire (novel) 1926
The House of Sun-Goes-Down (novel) 1928
Mark Twain's America (biography) 1932
We Accept with Pleasure (novel) 1934
Forays and Rebuttals (essays) 1936
Troubled Star [as John August] (novel) 1939

THE NEW YORK TIMES BOOK REVIEW (essay date 1924)

[*The following review assesses DeVoto's first novel,* The Crooked Mile, *as an overly ambitious and flawed work.*]

The Rocky Mountains figure in *The Crooked Mile,* by Bernard De Voto, as a rebuke to the flimsy industrial civilization which has, according to the novel, sprung into being at their base. Mr. De Voto states that "the mountains dwarfed the people, who had not lived up to them, who had not returned beauty and power for their lines, their sweep, their distances." His people are the third generation since the pioneers; they have lost the dangers and excitements of those first-comers, seeking for gold, and have slumped away from their virility into sloth, with nothing left but the original greed and hard materialistic values, stripped of the pathfinders' daring glories. The mills and machines which were their answer to the opulence and generosity of nature have sterilized the wills, and blanked the visions of their descendants. Such feeble twinges of awe and primitive fear as may have energized the early settlers into rare, brief moments of superhuman splendor have been evaded by the comforts of good plumbing and country clubs; Mr. De Voto's characters look at the mountains without seeing them.

Mr. De Voto's drama of the gradual impoverishment of the spirit is crystallized in the Abbey family. The grandfather ventured into the wilderness to find some escape from the growing exactions and restrictions of the older communities of the nation. The father fought, all his life, the encroaching stupidities of the herd: he was a flaming discontent in the midst of the smug, unscrupulous "empire builders." The son, Gordon Abbey, is the central character of Mr. De Voto's novel: Abbey's heredity is given as a sort of symbol of the trend of succeeding generations under the mountains.

Abbey is traced through childhood, youth, years in Harvard, and flounderings to find orientation in a wilderness of timidities and ineffectualities, opportunism and downright crookedness. He is given to self-conscious speculation on life, the pioneer, the moving-picture theatre, religion, war, love, liquor, the country club, his destiny and all his friends and acquaintances. It is somewhat adolescent in its overwhelming cynicism, yet it has a certain pathos of frustration. Mr. De Voto gives an intimate sense of the community of Windsor, Abbey's home; each character has its family, financial and social background, as well as its careful and sometimes convincing personal exposition. The town of Windsor, with its cheap politics, its unscrupulous business men, its liberal crusaders, its slightly ridiculous "art patrons," its vacuous, even vicious, "society,"

and its hastily constructed class distinctions based on wealth, might be a cross-section of almost any thriving city.

Abbey's dilemma, in the uncongenial atmosphere of his city, is of mind and temperament divided against himself. He takes refuge in a deceptive armor of contemptuous acquiescence. He experiments with the forging of new modes of thought via the newspaper, new expressions of industry via the railroad and the mill, and sounder inflections in the politer realm of the country club and the ballroom, and is each time defeated by his own disbelief. He tries drink and the seduction of women, and his restless abundance of vitality is once more reduced to bored bewilderment.

Mr. De Voto's design is a bit too inclusive: his novel is too long as a result, and the sharpness of his effects is considerably blurred. Many of the conversations are obviously clever epigrams and paradoxes, and others strain after crushing finalities; most of the dialogue, in fact, is somewhat stilted. The author has set himself a huge task and has failed gallantly in the larger aspects of his intention without diminishing a lively sense of acute penetration and virile creative ability. In spite of his missing the centre of his mark he leaves a definite impression of a vigorous intellect which is not afraid to come to grips with the actual conditions of his life and his art. He will undoubtedly synthesize out of the two a valuable contribution to American literature.

"Social Life of the Rockies in a New Novel," in The New York Times Book Review, *October 5, 1924, p. 8.*

ALLAN NEVINS (essay date 1926)

[*Nevins was an American historian and biographer who is particularly noted for his Civil War history* The War for the Union (1959). *In the following essay, he favorably reviews DeVoto's second novel,* The Chariot of Fire.]

[In *The Chariot of Fire*] Mr. De Voto has written of the frontier fanatic who thought himself a new Messiah. He has taken the same theme which William Dean Howells treated in *The Leatherwood God* and made of it a novel which, if less mellow, wise, and penetrating in its portraiture than Howells's, is more dramatic and spirited. The subject is difficult. It requires a thorough knowledge of backwoods society, a firm grasp of frontier psychology, to make the mere basis of the story convincing. Mr. De Voto has to explain how the Illinois prairie of the twenties or thirties could bring forth a mystic with visions of God and revelations from him, and how he could recruit followers by the score. He has to exhibit the inevitable clash of the new religionists with the equally fanatical Christians of the Peter Cartwright school, and within this clash he must find the personal elements of his narrative. It is a very different task from that involved in the ordinary objective historical novel.

The central achievement of Mr. De Voto is his study of Ohio Boggs, the village drunkard who gets religion at a great orgiastic camp meeting, and begins preaching the imminent Day of Judgment, with his own power to save the chosen few. Boggs, who gathers scores of disciples about him, is a greater villain than Howells's Messiah, Dylks. But he is treated rather more charitably. He is a sot, an adulterer, and a murderer. He slays his wife when she interferes with his purposes, and uses his position to prey upon the women he wants. His most effective revelations are cunning counsels of crime. By virtue of these counsels his holy city of Lo-Ruhamah ultimately becomes a den of robbers, supporting themselves by raids upon the nearest hamlets and farms. Sometimes these raids are bloody, and Boggs rejoices in the death of the Philistines. But the great merit of Mr. De Voto's character study is the skill with which he shows that Boggs was no conscious impostor. He was self-deluded before he deluded others; his illiterate, drink-dimmed, religion-fuddled brain is convinced of his righteousness. Obscene and ugly as he is, he is comprehensible, not intolerably repulsive, and at times even pitiable.

The story moves at a rapid pace, and follows a logical pattern. Seceding from the rest of their frontier community, the Boggsites soon find themselves in direct hostility to it. Even families are rent asunder. A smouldering feud springs up between the extremists on both sides, and a brutal raid of the Boggsites, with four farmers slain, converts the feud into open war. Among Ohio Boggs's followers is a lovely but foolish girl, whom Boggs himself comes to fancy—a girl whom he has rescued from death by one of his "miracles"; on the other side is the girl's lover, a promising youth. These characters might be called conventional, but the girl is treated with real understanding—her waverings between the prophet and her suitor, between common sense and religious hysteria, are made genuinely real. Still another character is conventional; the free-thinking judge who acts as a tragic chorus for the drama, offering his sardonic comments upon its various phases. But he also takes on individuality when he becomes captain of the Christians who march against the Boggsites. With the battle between the two forces the story reaches a well-planned climax. The girl, the lover, the judge, and Ohio Boggs all play important parts in a rather unexpected dénouement.

Mr. De Voto has written an able study of religious frenzy and of the temperament of the religious fanatic and organizer; he has combined it with a good, if not highly distinguished, picture of frontier life and a well-knit love story. The result is a novel of varied interest and a real addition to the fiction of pioneer society.

> Allan Nevins, "A Prairie Prophet," in The Saturday Review of Literature, Vol. III, No. 12, October 16, 1926, p. 194.

MARK VAN DOREN (essay date 1932)

[*Van Doren was one of the most prolific men of letters in twentieth-century American writing. His work includes poetry (for which he won the Pulitzer Prize in 1939), novels, short stories, drama, criticism, social commentary, and the editing of a number of popular anthologies. In the following essay, Van Doren maintains that despite DeVoto's contention to the contrary, he in fact advances several literary theories in Mark Twain's America, and further, that aspects of the book are not completely accurate. DeVoto responded privately to Van Doren (see letter below).*]

"I have no theory about Mark Twain," says Mr. De Voto in his foreword [to his ***Mark Twain's America***]; and goes on in a loud, angry voice to develop several theories about Mark Twain and mid-nineteenth-century America.

If he ever reads the second half of the foregoing sentence he will be angrier still, for he hates literary theories as other men hate wrist watches. He would not be caught dead with one on him if he could help it. I am sure he would have burned the manuscript of this book if it had been disclosed to him that one reviewer would accuse him of possessing general ideas. I do so accuse him, and will point them out.

His original anger is at Van Wyck Brooks, whom for three hundred pages he kicks around for having written *American's Coming-of-Age* and *The Ordeal of Mark Twain*—more particularly, of course, the latter—and for having inspired Waldo Frank and Lewis Mumford to write similar nonsense. None of these gentlemen, he says, knows anything about Mark Twain or about the America which produced him. He knows, however. He is a "literary skeptic"; impatient with literary ideas, he merely gathers "facts" and studies them until they yield "the truth"; and here are "the facts" about Mark Twain.

"It is not only that Mark Twain never became anything but a humorist, realist, and satirist of the frontier; he never desired to be anything else." This is stated as a fact, and is the thesis of Mr. De Voto's book. But how does Mr. De Voto know what Mark Twain's desires were? Mr. Brooks thought he knew; he psychoanalyzed Samuel Clemens. And Mr. Brooks is anathema to Mr. De Voto for thinking he knew. How, I wonder, does Mr. De Voto know? For he does act as if he knew. He describes Mark Twain's books in such a way as to make his statement plausible. He rather waves away, for instance, the romantic chapters which introduce *Life on the Mississippi*; and he puts the *Personal Recollections of Joan of Arc* in their place. He does seem to make the facts fit. But that is it. Fit what? A theory: "Mark Twain never became anything but a humorist of the frontier and never desired to be anything else."

Of course it is necessary for him then to say a good deal about the frontier which Mr. Brooks knows nothing about. I agree that Mr. Brooks knows little about it. But I cannot agree with Mr. De Voto that he knows enough to justify the swagger he puts on; and I doubt very much whether the America he describes with so much learning would recognize itself in his pages. For one can be learned about the past and still be far from understanding it. Mr. De Voto knows old American humor as well as anybody does, and he knows the wilder aspects of frontier life: the brawling, the bawdry, the dances and the songs, the tall tales and the merry ones. But that this was America is, I submit, a theory, just as Mr. Brooks's account of a nation starved in brain and heart was a theorist's account.

Mr. De Voto would have written a better book if he had known the kind he was writing, if he had known that in his book, too, thought was required. Charging blindly into the territory which Mr. Brooks has long dominated by virtue of a beautiful and sinuous intelligence, he leaves himself open on every side. And he never really answers Mr. Brooks, since the only thing that can answer a theory consciously held is another theory consciously held. Mr. De Voto thinks he is meeting a theory with facts, but as is usual in such situations he only gets tangled in a profusion of data. His data concerning American humor and the humor which Mark Twain wrote actually support the contention of *The Ordeal* that something better had been possible. And his proof that the pioneer democrat thought pretty regularly about sex fits fatally well with Waldo Frank's notion that he was aware of sex in the wrong way. Perhaps it was the right way after all. Mr. De Voto does not see that he might so argue.

He sees nothing, indeed, but the mass of information he has collected. It is a big mass, for his energy is enormous, and it has its value. But it must wait for someone less cantankerous than he, and more willingly intellectual, to establish what this value is. (pp. 370-71)

> Mark Van Doren, "De Voto's America," in The Nation, New York, Vol. CXXXV, No. 3511, October 19, 1932, pp. 370-71.

BERNARD DeVOTO   (essay date 1932)

[*In the following letter to Mark Van Doren, DeVoto contends that Van Doren misrepresented* Mark Twain's America *in his review of that work (see essay above).*]

Dear Mr. Van Doren:

I must ask leave to bore you dreadfully over some pages. It happens that a half-dozen reviews of my book, *Mark Twain's America,* seem to me to have misrepresented it, and that I select yours to examine in detail. I shall make no reply to the others. The authors of some of them seem to me to have no authority to pass judgment on the book. The authors of the rest interest me so little that I do not care what they say. You, however, have a position of unquestionable authority, and I happen to respect your mind. So I ask your patience while I examine your review and describe what seems to me its misrepresentation. I risk a further offense by deciding that, since you have authority in its field, your misrepresentation cannot be the result of either ignorance or accident.

Let me make clear that I do not question any of your opinions about the book's merits or success or failure. Nor do I question any judgment of me or my motives that you derive from my book—though, having in part written it to exhibit the folly of deriving psychological theories from literary works, I cannot believe that any you may form about me will be realistic. I shall argue one or two matters with you, but as opinion only and with no conviction that argument is important. My principal point raises a question of fact and of a reviewer's responsibility toward fact.

I begin with the fourth paragraph of your review where, after you have diagnosed what it amuses you to call my anger and loudness, you assert that I am wrong when I say I have no theory about Mark Twain. I cannot believe that you misunderstand the method used in my book. I find it equally hard to believe that an elementary difference between two ways of thinking is unknown to you, or that you intend to quibble about mere words. The method my book objects to is the derivation of conclusions *a priori*—the deductive method, if you will, specifically the psycho-analytical method of Mr. Brooks. That is the method of theory, and I am quite sure that my definition of it is both accurate and clear. It has proved accurate and clear enough to be satisfactorily reported by men whose intelligence is unquestionable. The method of my book is exactly the opposite. It is to assemble all the facts I can find that relate to Mark Twain's books—if you want to substitute the word "data" for the word "facts," I do not object—and then to state the conclusions they indicate. It is, if you will, the inductive method. There is an irreconcilable difference between the *a priori* method, the theory, and the empirical method, the conclusion from data. I think that my method succeeds—I should not have published the book if I didn't think so. But—here enters the question of a reviewer's integrity—though you are certainly free to decide that it fails, are you free to misrepresent my book by describing its method as similar to the one it attacks, when in fact it is not similar? I cannot believe that you misunderstood so elementary a difference. But if you didn't, does not this paragraph avoid the reviewer's obligation to describe fairly the book he is reporting on?

The next paragraph. "I doubt very much whether the America he describes . . . would recognize itself in his pages." I do not fully understand that. It appears to be a cautiously phrased declaration that I am wrong about the frontier. But just how and where? When you tell a historian—permit me to call myself one for the moment—that he is wrong, you must specify the nature and extent of his error, or your accusation will be meaningless. In my book I make no unsupported statement about what I describe as Mr. Brooks', Mr. Mumford's, or Mr. Frank's mistakes. I quote or summarize what they actually say and then set against their statements a bulk of "data" which allows the reader to compare them with the facts. That is the only way in which accusations of error can be given responsibility. You make no effort to identify my errors; you say I am wrong and let it go at that. Unless one assumes your infallibility, as I see no reason to do, your accusation is irresponsible.

Were the readers of the *Nation,* I among them, supposed to regard your review as a report of my book for which you accepted responsibility? Then point out to me the facts, the "data," about America in my book that are erroneous.

The paragraph goes on, in support of your assertion, with misrepresentation that cannot possibly be inadvertent. You say that I knew "the wilder aspects of frontier life—the brawling, the bawdry (you rather make a point of the bawdry, but just where do I?), the dances and the songs, the tall tales and the merry ones." You immediately add, "But that this was America is, I submit, a theory. . . ." No possible wrenching of words will make your two sentences anything but an assertion that I say this was America. If you have read my book and if your phrase "wilder aspects" is to be taken as meaning what it says, then you very seriously misrepresent what the book says. I do not say that you misrepresent it from malice—I avoid subjective interpretations—I here assert that you falsify its obvious intention and its actual content.

Did you read the second chapter, the fourth chapter, the fifth, seventh, tenth and twelfth chapters? I must assume that you did—how otherwise would you have ventured to review it? But if you did, then you read a constant insistence on qualities of frontier life as different as possible from the "wilder aspects." You read about music, the jubilees, the hymns, the theater and the concert hall and the minstrel stage. You read about a pleasant rural society and its schools, churches, quilting and fanning bees, the developing social organization—its constant attempts at decent human intercourse. You read my repeated declaration that the frontier had leisure and peace and quiet as well as energy and turbulence. You read my tiresomely repeated description of various idyllic "aspects" of the frontier, my long analysis of the beauty and freedom of frontier life as they are reflected in Mark Twain's books. Furthermore, you knew when you wrote the review that this effort to present hitherto disregarded and specifically denied "aspects" of the frontier, not "the wilder aspects," was the principal effort of my book. I presume to write that last sentence as a statement of fact on the basis of an induction: everyone with whom I have been able to talk about the book and two hundred reviewers recognize it as the principal effort. Your review makes no mention of that effort, but specifically and by implication denies that it is made. I repeat: you are entitled to any opinion about my book that you may care to express but if there are standards of critical integrity, you are not entitled to falsify it.

I use such words as "misrepresent" and "falsify" with complete deliberation. Only an explanation of the discrepancies I here point out can convince me that I am wrong in using them.

Your next paragraph. I do not understand your argument very well here, and your statement that "the only thing that can answer a theory consciously held is another theory consciously held" seems to me mere nonsense. But I do understand that you believe my book "open on every side." Yes? Are my facts, my "data" subject to overthrow? One interpretation of your sentence would be that you think they are. If they are, then the book certainly fails, as you say it does. But which "data" are subject to overthrow, and why do you not overthrow them? You say I am wrong but you do not show wherein I am wrong. Your assertion is irresponsible until you do. Make the effort, point out where my "data" err, designate those which are mistaken or unrepresentative. If you do, I will modify the book in later editions, for I respect data more than you do. If you prove unable to do so, then this part of the review is another misrepresentation.

"His data . . . actually support the contention of *The Ordeal* that something better had been possible." This is said unequivocally as a statement of fact. Well, which data? Better than what? Data I supply, you say, prove me wrong. Name them, point them out, specify page and line, or quote the words that phrase them. Until you do, your assertion is frivolous—the reviewer's cheap dismissal of authority on his unsupported statement. And "better" than *Huck Finn*, do you mean? "Better" than the passages I have called the best things in American fiction? The data I use to prove *Huckleberry Finn* the best of our native literature really prove against these very data, that better stuff than *Huckleberry Finn* was possible? I cannot see in this notion of yours anything but uncontrolled theorizing, and I shall be unable to see anything else in it until you point out which of my data support it. I accept it as a revelation of your sentiments, but it is irrelevant in a discussion of my book.

"And his proof that the pioneer democrat thought pretty regularly about sex. . . ." Another falsification. There is no such proof, no such assertion or suggestion in my book. Here I deny as flatly as possibly what you say: you are distorting my book in a manner that nothing can excuse. If you can support your statement, please do so at once in a letter to me. But if you can't support it, then this is one more serious misrepresentation. If your desire was to report to your readers what I said about sex on the frontier, then you should have reported it correctly. You should have said that I opposed to the idea that sexual repression characterized frontier life a certain number of facts, "data," and drew two conclusions from them. One conclusion was that the sexual customs of the frontier were freer than those of the seaboard. The other conclusion was that "the relations of men and women remained the relations of men and women" on the frontier—an assertion that they were normal relations. I nowhere said or suggested that "the pioneer democrat thought pretty regularly about sex." Your obligation was to report correctly what I said before you began to argue about it. I cannot see that you fulfilled the obligation by attributing to me almost the exact opposite of what appears in my book.

I do not raise the question of criticism. The standards of criticism, I believe, would have required you to examine the content of my refutation instead of dismissing it in epithet. They would have required you to appraise the method I offer in substitution for the one I attack—to pass judgment on "data" you dismiss. They would have required you to tell readers that I examine Mark Twain's books in relation to my "data" and then to appraise what I say about my books. They would have required you to discuss the validity of my appraisal of Mark Twain—in short, to criticize the results I reach. Instead, you announced that you agree with Mr. Brooks. You are certainly entitled to agree with him, but, I think, you are not entitled to offer a distortion of my book in support of your agreement. But I am concerned solely with that distortion, not with what

you might have said. I have made herein certain assertions that you have misrepresented my book. So, this question: are my assertions true?

The convention that forbids a writer to reply in print to a reviewer is, I think, a healthy one. At least it is one I do not care to violate. But it does not proscribe a private answer and this is one. This is an effort to hold you to accountability for what you have said in public about my book. My conclusion has been stated: for motives I do not venture to guess about, you deliberately misrepresented my book to the *Nation*'s readers. I do not know whether you will care to answer me. If you do, and if it appears that I owe you a retraction, I will make one. Otherwise, consider that this letter offers you, uncalled for, my opinion about the value of your judgment of my book. (pp. 62-6)

Bernard DeVoto, in a letter to Mark Van Doren on October 17, 1932, in his The Letters of Bernard DeVoto, *edited by Wallace Stegner, Doubleday & Company, Inc., 1975, pp. 62-6.*

CONRAD AIKEN   (essay date 1937)

[*An American man of letters best known for his poetry, Aiken was deeply influenced by the psychological and literary theories of Sigmund Freud, Havelock Ellis, Edgar Allan Poe, and Henri Bergson, among others, and is considered a master of literary stream-of-consciousness. In reviews noted for their perceptiveness and barbed wit, Aiken exercised his theory that "criticism is really a branch of psychology." His critical position, according to Rufus A. Blanshard, "insists that the traditional notions of 'beauty' stand corrected by what we now know about the psychology of creation and consumption. Since a work of art is rooted in the personality, conscious and unconscious, of its creator, criticism should deal as much with these roots as with the finished flower." In the following excerpt, Aiken tempers his general approval of DeVoto's* Forays and Rebuttals *with criticism of the antagonistic attitude expressed in many of DeVoto's critical essays.*]

[Mr. DeVoto] belongs to the school of the gentlemanly essayist—though he might not like to be told so. "Tough guy's essays" might be his own term for these truculent and forthright papers [gathered in *Forays and Rebuttals*], which range in subject from a study of the origin and evolution of the Mormon Utopia to appraisals of New England and culture and examinations of the theory of biography and criticism. In history, Mr. DeVoto wants us to remember—and very sensibly too—that we are dealing with a pluralistic world, about which it is dangerous to dogmatize on restricted evidence. In biography, he wants us to stick to facts, and nothing but facts—just the documents, no guesswork, no psychoanalytical reconstruction or recreation or interpretation—which leaves just about nothing at all. (In this connection, Mr. DeVoto makes the dogmatic statement that "psychoanalysis cannot come into effective relationship, into any relationship, with a dead man." Which we modestly suggest just ain't true.) In criticism, he would like to see a sociological or functional check on esthetic and popular judgments, as on evolutions in taste or fashion—not an original idea, but worth saying often. In short, Mr. DeVoto *is* sensible, a lot of the time, but is inclined to be a little angry and repetitive about it, and a little too sure that nobody else is as sensible as himself.

Conrad Aiken, "The Gentlemanly Essayist," in The New Republic, *Vol. LXXXIX, No. 1155, January 20, 1937, p. 364.*

EDMUND WILSON   (essay date 1937)

[*Wilson, considered America's foremost man of letters in the twentieth century, wrote widely on cultural, historical, and literary matters, authoring several seminal critical studies. He is often credited with bringing an international perspective to American letters through his widely read discussions of European literature. Wilson was allied to no critical school; however, several dominant concerns serve as guiding motifs throughout his work. He invariably examined the social and historical implications of a work of literature, particularly literature's significance as "an attempt to give meaning to our experience" and its value for the improvement of humanity. Although he was not a moralist, his criticism displays a deep concern with moral values. Another constant was his discussion of a work of literature as a revelation of its author's personality. In* Axel's Castle *(1931), a study of literary symbolism, Wilson wrote: "The real elements, of course, of any work of fiction are the elements of the author's personality: his imagination embodies in the images of characters, situations and scenes the fundamental conflicts of his nature." Related to this is Wilson's theory, formulated in* The Wound and the Bow *(1941), that artistic ability is a compensation for a psychological wound; thus, a literary work can only be fully understood if one undertakes an emotional profile of its author. Wilson utilized this approach in many essays, and it is the most-often attacked element of his thought. However, though Wilson examined the historical and psychological implications of a work of literature, he rarely did so at the expense of a discussion of its literary qualities. Perhaps Wilson's greatest contributions to American literature were his tireless promotion of writers of the 1920s, 1930s, and 1940s, and his essays introducing the best of modern literature to the general reader. In the following excerpt from an essay that originally appeared in the* New Republic *in 1937, Wilson discusses some of DeVoto's strong points and shortcomings as a critic and calls for DeVoto to explain the premises of his social and literary criticism.*]

It is unfortunate that there is nobody nowadays to uphold the conservative point of view. The academic background of the older critics had certain decided advantages. They had the scholarly habit, for one thing, of doing a thorough and careful job, and could never have adapted themselves to the kind of miscellaneous monthly reviewing that even the better-grade critics—such as Mary M. Colum in the *Forum* and John Chamberlain in *Scribner's*—have recently been reduced to: a kind that can have little weight because it imposes the necessity of grouping together a number of books that may have nothing whatever in common except simultaneity of publication. The featured reviewer who dealt regularly, from a definite point of view, with subjects of serious interest seemed to have become extinct.

Then a conspicuous exception appeared in the shape of Mr. Bernard De Voto, the new editor of the *Saturday Review of Literature*.

Mr. De Voto is evidently something new, and he deserves our respectful attention. First of all, it must be said that it is pleasant to find regular weekly reviewing done by a man who can write, who ranges widely and observes acutely, who studies an author's whole work and attempts to sum it up, and who is truculently independent. Mr. De Voto has already succeeded in making the *Saturday Review* quite interesting. The whole magazine is coming to bear the stamp of the new editor's ideas and special interests, and it gets from them a force and an accent that it never has had before. Mr. De Voto is a Westerner who has been trained at Harvard but who has never repudiated the West. On the contrary, he has stuck to it stubbornly, making use of the lessons he has learned from it in dealing with the rest of the world, and championing its cultural importance. He

has written some interesting papers on Mormonism (Utah is his native state); and in his book on *Mark Twain's America,* he has thrown some new light on the life of the frontier and on Mark Twain's literary sources. Among the literary phenomena of his own time, he has maintained a toughness of mind that has become more and more uncommon. No popular reputation passes current with him till he has attempted to assay its worth for himself; and he seems to shed fashionable shibboleths as easily as a really good raincoat sheds water. Furthermore, he has the academic training which has enabled him, for example, to clean up without remorse on the psychoanalytical biographers who have been aping Lytton Strachey. We must, therefore, be thankful for Mr. De Voto. He is trying to do something in the *Saturday Review* that nobody else has been doing, and he has qualifications for doing it well.

Yet precisely because Mr. De Voto has undertaken this kind of responsible criticism, we expect of him more than he has given us yet. We expect of him an intelligible basis of taste and an intelligible general point of view. He *sounds* as if he were being discriminating in his discussion of the relative merits of books, yet the standards by which he judges them remain obscure; he *sounds* as if his strictures on other people's doctrines were based on some solid philosophy of which he was very certain; and yet, though we keep on reading him in the interested expectation of being told what that philosophy is, its outlines never appear. On the surface, Mr. De Voto is positive and plainspoken, but when we try to go below the surface, we find ideas that seem confused and erratic.

Mr. De Voto as a critic may be examined most satisfactorily in his book on *Mark Twain's America,* which is the most elaborate of his literary studies and typical of his methods and habits of mind. This "essay in the correction of ideas" somewhat labors under the disadvantage of being one of those books that have been written, not primarily to present the author's own view, but to combat somebody else's. This is characteristic of Mr. De Voto, who always seems to approach his subjects with a chip on his shoulder. In this case, the writer with whom Mr. De Voto is trying to pick a quarrel is Mr. Van Wyck Brooks, the author of *The Ordeal of Mark Twain.* Now, it is true that Mr. De Voto is able to correct some minor errors on the part of Mr. Brooks, and at least one serious one: the assumption that, in the last century, when the country was full of communities organized by socialist and religious groups, Americans had taken no part in the movements represented, as Mr. Brooks says, by "the Tolstoys and the Marxes, the Nietzsches and the Renans, the Ruskins and the Morrises." And he is able to correct the lugubrious picture that Mr. Brooks painted of the old Far West by filling in the more cheerful aspects. But one ends by deciding that Mr. Brooks is a kind of King Charles's head for Mr. De Voto: an obsession which is not altogether rational.

For, after all, by the time Mr. De Voto is done, he seems to have supplied evidence himself for most of Mr. Brooks's points: that the life of the frontier was savage and taxed the pioneer's endurance and that Mark Twain's humor (as a consequence of this, according to Mr. Brooks—Mr. De Voto deplores the phenomenon but he does not attempt to explain it) tends to run to the disgusting and the horrible; that the genteel tradition of the East had an emasculating influence on letters and that, for Mark Twain, this influence, as represented by Boston and Hartford and Olivia Clemens, imposed an ordeal of another sort. Where Mr. De Voto attempts to ignore Van Wyck Brooks's findings, he obviously exposes himself. He is, for example, quite ready to throw out all the literary deadwood that is the basis of Brooks's contention that Mark Twain did not mature as an artist; but he hardly touches at all on the rankling indignation at institutions which is Brooks's very striking evidence that there was an undeveloped social prophet in Mark Twain. And, though Brooks's psychoanalytic interpretations may sometimes seem a little far-fetched, he does at least try to establish a relation between Mark Twain's choice of subjects and his methods of treating them and his character and social background; whereas De Voto is content to exclaim that Mark Twain was a great artist and a fine old boy, and, aside from tracing some of his sources, to leave his relation to his work unexplained.

It may possibly be true that Mr. Brooks has attached too much importance to the incident related by Mark Twain's biographer, in which the young Sam, much given to mischief, is made to swear by his mother at his father's deathbed that he will always thereafter be a good boy. But the duality that Mr. Brooks attributes to Mark Twain is there in his work as plain as day—in the antagonism, for example, represented for Huckleberry Finn by Miss Watson and her world, on the other hand—to which Tom Sawyer is more or less committed—and the Nigger Jim and the raft, on the other; and this duality does account, as Mr. De Voto scarcely attempts to do, and scoffs, in fact, at the notion of doing, for the dualities of *Pudd'nhead Wilson* and the Siamese twins in *Those Extraordinary Twins*.

What is more serious is that Mr. De Voto completely evades the central question which Mr. Brooks is most impressive in illuminating: the question of Mark Twain's pessimism. Mr. De Voto's explanation of this pessimism is simply that Mark Twain had seen a good deal of life and that, being no fool, it had made him gloomy. But so had Dickens and Dostoevsky and a great many other people, who did not, nevertheless, become pessimists. The pessimism of Mark Twain is surely one of the blackest cases on record. Such documents as his thoughts on the death of his daughter, which Mr. De Voto does not mention, are rare in the history of Western civilization. We know that there were special causes for the pessimism of a Swift or a Leopardi; and Mr. Brooks is certainly well advised in looking for a special cause for the pessimism of Mark Twain. He is perfectly convincing, it seems to me, in finding it in causes similar to those that evidently operated in the cases of Leopardi and Swift: in a cripplingly insurmountable frustration. Involved with all this is Mr. De Voto's failure to give an adequate account of *Huckleberry Finn*. Mr. Brooks may have praised that book too scantily, but he did put his finger on its meaning; whereas, if you believe Mr. De Voto, it is simply a marvellous story about floating down the Mississippi. Mr. De Voto devotes eleven pages to *Huckleberry Finn* and yet manages never to mention the theme which gives the book its emotional force and makes it something more impressive than a mere picaresque novel: the contrast between Huck's natural instincts and the distortions of civilization.

The truth is that Mark Twain's books, though funny, are in general, sad—just as that other great Westerner, Lincoln, who was also funny, was sad; and Mr. De Voto never explains or even faces this fact. Of course, the Far West of the sixties and seventies was more hilarious and more exciting than Mr. Brooks, in his earlier and dolorous phase, was able to represent it, and Mr. De Voto's correction is in order; but the kind of whooping it up for the good old days that Mr. De Voto attempts in his chapter called "Washoe" is just as emotional and just as "literary," that is to say, just as poetic, as Mr. Brooks's bitterness.

In one of the essays in his collection called *Forays and Rebuttals*, Mr. De Voto denounces literary "fantasy," which he opposes to historic "fact": "The fantasies of the literary historian are frequently beautiful and nearly always praiseworthy, but they are a form of protection or of wishful thinking, a form of illusion and even of delusion," etc. Yet in what sense is Mr. De Voto's vision of a mining-town in Mark Twain's day "fact" that would make Mr. Brooks's vision "fantasy"? Mr. De Voto's book is full of rhetoric—the "incandescence" of the West, for example, which is always being brought in to do duty for more exact description. Parts of it sound, in fact, as if they had been written for declamation. There are moments when it suggests a Hollywood picture made from a novel by Fannie Hurst. Mr. De Voto is even capable of throwing out Mark Twain's own testimony when it does not fall in with his own conception; and at one point he seems to be wanting us to accept bear-and-badger-baiting as evidence that the life of the pioneer was not devoid of gaiety and charm. (pp. 650-56)

As for Mr. De Voto's main grievance, it seems to me largely unfounded. He complains that American criticism has written down Mark Twain as a failure and insufficiently appreciated his work; whereas the fact surely is that the period he complains of has been that in which Mark Twain has been appreciated most. The older critics tended to exclude him from serious literature; but, beginning with William Lyon Phelps's essay and going on through John Macy and Mencken, the respect for Mark Twain has been growing. Stuart P. Sherman's chapter on him in *The Cambridge History of American Literature*, published in 1921, though rather uninspired, certainly takes Mark Twain seriously. Even Brooks does not belittle Mark Twain: he dignifies him by making him tragic; and the negative influence of Brooks and those who have followed his line has been negligible in comparison with the influence of Mark Twain's writings themselves. Ernest Hemingway and Sherwood Anderson have amply acknowledged their debt to Mark Twain; and the main stream of American humor has followed the channel he deepened. It is certainly not true in general that the Croly-Brooks view of the frontier has dominated in the writing of our period. On the contrary, the folklore and romance of the West have, if anything, been overdone. Haven't we all heard enough by this time about Sutter and Paul Bunyan and Billy the Kid? The Wild Bill Hickoks and Calamity Janes are now the heroes and heroines of Hollywood; and the demand for American folk humor has actually now reached a point where the author of *Caleb Catlum's America* has found it profitable to produce it synthetically.

What, then, is Mr. De Voto's real grievance? This indignation at other people's errors which seems to prevent him from stating his own case, this continual boiling-up about other people's wild statements which takes a form not merely wild but hysterical, have been characteristic of all his criticism.

Well, this may be partly due to the Westerner's grudge against the Easterner; and I should say that a certain amount of it was due to the peevishness of the literary professor against the writer outside the academic enclosure. Stuart Sherman behaved in very much the same way till he himself came to work in New York. It is a combination of disapproval, often on sound enough grounds, of what seems to them cheap and superficial in the work of writers ignorant of the classics and with no training in the standards of scholarship, and of envy of the freedom of the non-academic. The critic who is or has been a teacher cannot seem to help adopting toward his readers the tone he has acquired in the classroom. That Bernard De Voto has been somewhat conditioned by the academic environment is indicated, I think, by the fact that, in his essays on education, where he is dealing with a world in which he has lived, whose difficulties and hopes he has shared and whose victories he has helped to win—even in criticizing that world severely—he gives out both heat and light; but that whenever he encounters, for example, the graduates or denizens of Greenwich Village, which has also had its hopes and its hardships, its ignominies and its victories, he stiffens with the distrust of a stranger.

Yet De Voto, I should say, fundamentally, has nothing of the supercilious professor. There is evidently some other reason for his attitude toward his contemporaries; but the difficulty is to imagine from what point of view it is possible to charge them all with a common guilt. In his review of Carl Van Doren's *Three Worlds,* he seemed to sweep them all together and accuse them of "misrepresenting" America; he seemed to ascribe to each one all the opinions of all the others. He must have mastered some precious secret which the rest of us badly need if he is not to be included himself in this general potpourri (he belongs to the same generation as the writers of the twenties he denounces, and he has been publishing novels for years)— if he can claim the privilege of standing apart and knowing that he is saved, while he looks on at the plunge of the Gadarene swine.

But what *is* this point of view, this secret? Mr. De Voto never lets us know. He only hints, and on the basis of his hints one is unable to construct anything that hangs together. One gathers that he is definitely opposed to certain tendencies that he regards as prevalent and which he characterizes variously as "progressive," "Utopian" and "religious." These tendencies evidently have to do with the desire to see the economic system modified in such a way as to safeguard human society against the social inequalities, depressions and wars which, visibly in Europe, as Mr. De Voto writes, are destroying civilization itself. Mr. De Voto's antagonism to Mr. Brooks seems, in fact, to have been primarily inspired by the latter's concern about these problems. Well, of the people that Mr. De Voto lumps together, some are no doubt Utopians; but others are Marxists, and Marx and Engels exploded Utopian socialism almost a century ago. Yet all of them, one gathers from Mr. De Voto, have in some way been untrue to America. And not only the ones who want to get rid of capitalism—equally those who, like Sinclair Lewis, simply stayed at home and criticized. All the works of this period, apparently—Lewis's caricatures, Hemingway's idyls, Brooks's diagnoses, O'Neill's tragedies, Dos Passos's social webs, Fitzgerald's drinking-parties, Sherwood Anderson's waking dreams, Edna Millay's lyrics—had it in common that they betrayed America.

But in the interests of what is Mr. De Voto speaking? Who or what has been betrayed? A group, so far as one can gather, that Mr. De Voto calls the middle class. These middle-class people, it seems, have been going about their business, taking care of the country's essential work and maintaining its moral soundness, while our writers of the twenties and thirties have been jeering at them and leaving them in the lurch and attempting to bemuse them with Utopian visions. It is hard to understand why this solid middle class should have bought and read so many copies of the books of the above-named writers, who have blasphemed their American heritage.

What then? All is dim after that. Fitful chinks in the clouds of words show principles leaning at unexpected angles, which seem to change between the chinks. For example: "Revolutions are always struggles between special groups; only propaganda

tries to make them seem the will of the people in action. The people remain mostly unharried by them, neither willing nor acting, and in the end pay tribute to the old group, victorious, or to the new one which has cast it out. Even agrarian revolt has little to do with the agrarians in a mass.'' Then another barrage against the intellectuals, under cover of which no troops seem to advance. Then a vision—very vivid and convincing, this one—of the rise of the Mormon community in Utah: we are shown how, beginning with something that was in some ways very similar to communism, it developed a privileged hierarchy and succumbed, in the long run, to the financial and industrial interests. From this, some kind of moral seems supposed to be drawn. But what is it? Something about dictatorship and how all dictatorships must take the same course? Something about the enslaving effects of capitalism? Does he mean to suggest that Salt Lake City exhausts the possibilities of human society? One would think that the absorption of the communism of the Mormons in the expansion of the capitalist system precisely proved the Marxists' case. There are any number of questions that we should like to put to Mr. De Voto. Since we do not understand his premises, it is difficult to know how to debate with him. He seems content to tear his hair and, lumping us all together like one of those composite pictures that does not resemble anybody, pretend he is arguing with us.

I am sure that I am being unfair to Mr. De Voto, but I have written in the hope of smoking him out. He has been influenced by the Italian sociologist Vilfredo Pareto, and, since I have not myself read Pareto, I haven't this key to his system. I *have* read the number of the *Saturday Review* that Mr. De Voto devoted to Pareto, but the articles, including his own, threw very little light on the subject. I gather that the discipline of Pareto enables you to detach yourself from social groups and to study them objectively and dispassionately. Is that what Mr. De Voto is trying to do when he becomes so madly excited about the life of the American frontier?

Let him stand and unfold himself. What does he want? If he does not believe in the improvement of society, to what does he look forward, then?—and where do the values of literature come in? Let him not merely refer us to Pareto. Let him not merely tell us we are Easterners (especially since a good many of us are Westerners) who will never understand the frontier. It is a long time since anybody new in this field has really had anything to say to us; and if Mr. De Voto has something to say, he may be sure of an attentive audience. (pp. 656-61)

Edmund Wilson, "American Critics, Left and Right: Bernard DeVoto," in his The Shores of Light: A Literary Chronicle of the Twenties and Thirties, *Farrar, Straus and Giroux, 1952, pp. 650-61.*

F. O. MATTHIESSEN   (essay date 1942)

[*Matthiessen was an American educator and literary critic whose major studies examine American writers and intellectual movements. As a critic, he believed that analysis of a given work of literature must also consider the social and historical context of that work. Concerning his study of American literature, Matthiessen stated: "I wanted to place our master-works in their cultural setting, but beyond that I wanted to discern what constituted the lasting value of these books as works of art." His works include* American Renaissance *(1941) and* Henry James: The Major Phase *(1944). In the following excerpt from a 1942 review of* Mark Twain at Work, *Matthiessen maintains that DeVoto's study reveals a deeper critical understanding than the earlier* Mark Twain's America.]

DeVoto and his wife, circa 1941. Photograph by James Woolverton Mason.

[In *Mark Twain at Work*] Bernard DeVoto continues to present his findings from the Mark Twain manuscripts. As usual he throws his weight around. He tells us that he has seen no reason to revise any of his conclusions of a decade ago; that these essays might well be enlarged except that he is a writer "who always has more books ahead of him than he will ever write"; and that even this fragment of a volume has involved for himself and his secretary "a long, laborious, exhausting and fantastically minute study." Despite all this pointless bluster and despite an equally unnecessary display of showy and rather amateur scholarship, the new material he offers us is of real interest. And whether he likes it or not, DeVoto's judgment has deepened since he wrote *Mark Twain's America* in 1932.

Familiarity with the manuscripts, which came into his hands four years ago, has enabled him to round out the story of Twain's impulsive and sporadic methods of composition. He prints for the first time a sketch written about 1870 which he believes to be its author's first attempt to go beyond casual anecdotes to the production of sustained fiction. Significantly this sketch begins to tap the material which was to be its author's one enduring source of creative vigor. It is told by Billy Rogers, who numbers among his friends a Tom Sawyer. It seems unquestionably the germ of the latter's adventures, and foreshadows both Twain's strength and weakness. Told in the first person, it has occasional passages in the firm native idiom that was to be Twain's great contribution to American

style; but the mawkish story of Billy's hopeless love for Amy Johnson quickly breaks into the flat burlesque of his own characters that Twain could not entirely escape even in *Huck Finn*. These series of fragmentary notes for that book throw quite a bit of light on the way Twain, after having left the manuscript lying around unfinished for half a dozen years, worked out its final structure. They also reveal, as DeVoto says, how Twain's creative improvisation was nearly always linked uncritically with extravaganza.

The manuscripts have also enabled DeVoto to write a definitive note on the subject that so outraged the 'twenties, the enforced expurgations. These all seem to have been small but significant concessions to a ludicrous propriety: "as mild as Sunday school" had to become "as mild as goose-milk," such words as "putrid," "rotten," "bowels" had to be blotted out, and the Duke's denunciation of the King had to sacrifice one thoroughly appropriate epithet "you unsatisfiable tunnel-bellied old sewer." Magazine standards and Livy's [Twain's wife Olivia] nerves were doubtless responsible for most of this weakening of the language, but DeVoto puts the question into new perspective by insisting that the "sexual timidities" were Twain's own. No matter what his conversation may have been, when it came to writing for a general audience, he was demonstrably more prudish than Howells. DeVoto cites as evidence the whole range of Twain's work, the notable fact that only in *Pudd'nhead Wilson* are we aware of sexual desire as a human motive, and then it is in "the forbidden world" of the Negro slaves. Elsewhere Twain could create the middle-aged women of the frontier, but his young heroines—not excepting Joan of Arc—are "pasteboard." It is revelatory also that in spite of his deep penetration into the fantasies of boyhood, he closed his eyes to anything that Huck knew about sex.

Such reflections show wherein DeVoto has extended his equipment. He now makes recurrent use of Freudian analysis, the validity of which for biographical studies he formerly found highly debatable. His final essay ends up where Van Wyck Brooks began, meditating on the symbols of Twain's despair. He still angrily denies that his work and Brooks' have anything in common, and, to be sure, he does not saddle Twain with Brooks' rigid thesis of the artist frustrated by society. But he experiments none the less with analytical technique, especially in probing the suffering of Twain's last years. His own thesis is that Twain was plunged into a compulsive anxiety by the series of family and financial disasters which overtook him in his middle fifties, and that he finally brought himself back to wholeness, after long years of frustration, by the therapeutic act of writing *The Mysterious Stranger*. This thesis, though supported by much interesting detail from unfinished manuscripts, seems hardly persuasive, since *The Mysterious Stranger* is itself such a truncated and immature work, and since DeVoto presents no evidence to show that Twain's despair was appreciably less after its completion.

Where DeVoto's psychological knowledge serves him in better stead is in his comprehension of the complex image of boyhood which Twain's best work presents us. This is an image compacted both of enchanted freedom and of haunted terror, and thus corresponds profoundly also to the environment which Huck knew. DeVoto is very shrewd in remarking that all of Twain's richest fiction springs from Hannibal, that it might all be grouped under the title which Twain gave to some autobiographical notes, "Villagers of 1840-43." But when he talks in social rather than psychological terms, DeVoto does not yet profit to the full from what he has learned of ambivalence. In his scorn for the detractors of frontier life, he sometimes talks as though the idyllic village of some of Twain's reveries had really existed, as though its remote serenity was really the historical fact "of what we once were, of what it is now more than ever necessary to remember we once were." Yet Twain, on nearly every page of Huck's epic procession, yields a more relevant image of social actuality of reminding us that the joy and freedom of the frontier were never long separate from the violence and the cruelty.

When DeVoto is not attempting to defend any thesis, either about Twain or the frontier or himself, he gives us some of the ripened insights that can come only through years of devoted attention to an author. Then he observes how much of the folk-mind itself is revealed through Huck's eyes, the folk-mind of a period that was shaped by "the tremendous realities of conquering a hostile wilderness and yet shadowed by the unseen world." Then, too, he stresses the democratic significance of the fact that Twain's most heroic character is Nigger Jim. We can be grateful for these insights, even though DeVoto seems determined to prove through his tub-thumping exaggerations that he possesses every temper except the critical temper. (pp. 227-30)

F. O. Matthiessen, "The Effort to Repossess the Past: Mark Twain at Work," in his The Responsibilities of the Critic: Essays and Reviews, *edited by John Rackliffe, Oxford University Press, 1952, pp. 227-30.*

MALCOLM COWLEY   (essay date 1944)

[*Cowley has made several valuable contributions to contemporary letters with his editions of important American authors (Nathaniel Hawthorne, Walt Whitman, Ernest Hemingway, William Faulkner, F. Scott Fitzgerald), his writings as a literary critic for the* New Republic, *and above all, with his chronicles and criticism of modern American literature. Cowley's literary criticism does not attempt a systematic philosophical view of life and art, nor is it representative of a neatly defined school of critical thought. Rather, Cowley focuses on works that he considers worthy of public appreciation and that he believes personal experience has qualified him to explicate, such as the works of the "lost generation" writers whom he knew. The critical approach Cowley follows is undogmatic and is characterized by a willingness to view a work from whatever perspective—social, historical, aesthetic—that the work itself seems to demand for its illumination. In the following essay, he suggests that in criticizing the writers of the 1920s in* The Literary Fallacy, *DeVoto fell victim to "a critic's fallacy": "projecting an imaginary purpose for works of literature, quite different from the actual purposes of their authors, and then condemning the authors . . . because they failed to achieve it."*]

No other period in American literature has been denounced more vehemently and persistently than the 1920's. Not to mention the early attacks against *This Side of Paradise* in 1920 and against *Three Soldiers* in 1921, there were the professional insults of the Humanists and, all through the depression, the continued jeers of the proletarian critics. These were followed, after the beginning of the Second World War, by the exhortations of MacLeish as a reformed poet lecturing his comrades in sin, and by the anathemas of Van Wyck Brooks, who spoke as a moralist deeply concerned for the future of literature and his country; both were threatened, he believed, by roving bands of unrepentant writers. Still other voices joined in. The attacks were made by men of different literary and political faiths, who invoked a mixture of conservative, radical, reactionary and liberal-democratic standards; but in general they brought forward the same charges: that the literature of the 1920's was superficial, immoral, negative, and had failed to depict the healthier side of American life.

Bernard DeVoto restates and magnifies these accusations. In his new book, ***The Literary Fallacy,*** he asserts that the authors of the 1920's were "ignorant, inaccurate or foolish—or frivolous or corrupt." They completely misunderstood the society of their time—which, he says, "was rugged, lively and vital; but literature became increasingly debilitated, capricious, querulous and irrelevant." And DeVoto ends by saying:

> Never in any country or any age had writers so misrepresented their culture, never had they been so unanimously wrong. Never had writers been so completely separated from the experiences that alone give life and validity to literature. And therefore, because separation from the sources of life makes despair, never had literature been so despairing, and because false writing makes trivial writing, never had literature been so trivial. . . . Seeking for a phrase which will convey the quality of that literature, history may sum it up as the Age of Ignominy.

But you wonder, reading his book, how it came about that such an ignorant, foolish, debilitated, querulous, trivial and utterly ignominious literature had managed to survive this series of attacks. Why do young writers still imitate Wolfe or Crane or Fitzgerald, in preference to Willa Cather and Robert Frost? Why do flyers back from New Guinea and Australian war correspondents in the Middle East write novels in Hemingway's early manner? Might it be that the continuing attacks against these writers are another testimony to their life and power? Even Bernard DeVoto, who belabors them from any convenient angle; who is now a sociological critic, now a wise anthropologist, now a historian, now a moralist, now (briefly and inadvertently) an esthetician, now radical, now conservative, now speaking in behalf of the American scholar and now rallying the crowd against him—even DeVoto proclaims the vigor and art of these writers by his need to use all weapons against them.

In his attacks, he is not always careful to preserve the appearance of consistency and fairness. Thus, he indicts *The Flowering of New England* and *New England: Indian Summer* on two principal counts: that they fail to consider national affairs or the opening of the frontier, and that they neglect economic trends "in showing us the delicacies of minds absorbed in the fascinating task of writing books." Forgetting that the two works together were planned as a literary history of New England, he insists on judging them as a social and cultural history of the nation at large. In his second chapter, he condemns writers for their careless use of the word "fascist." "Except in a small number of cases," he says, and with good reason, ". . . the epithet 'fascist' applied by writers to one another has meant one or the other of two things. It has meant either 'I disagree with him' or 'He does not like my books.' " In his fourth chapter, however, he forgets this wise observation in his rage at Hemingway. "From the beginning up to now," he says, "both implicitly and explicitly, with a vindictive belligerence, Mr. Hemingway has always attacked the life of the mind, the life of the spirit and the shared social experience of mankind. . . . It is a short step from thinking of the mob to thinking of the wolf pack, from the praise of instinct to war against reason, from art's vision of man as contemptible to dictatorship's vision of men as slaves." In other words, Hemingway is a short step from being a fascist. Either DeVoto disagrees with him or he doesn't like DeVoto's books.

A graver fault than this unfairness or inconsistency—of which I could give many other examples—is the author's failure to define his subject strictly in his own mind. He says that his book is an examination, "reasonably detailed but far from complete, of certain ideas, dogmas and conclusions which appear and reappear in much American literature of the 1920's, particularly in the work of writers who were then widely held to be most characteristic of the time and most expressive of its spirit." Elsewhere he mentions these writers by name: they are H. L. Mencken (born in 1880), Sinclair Lewis (1885), Ernest Hemingway (1898), John Dos Passos (1896), William Faulkner (1897), Thomas Wolfe (1900), T. S. Eliot (1888) and Van Wyck Brooks (1886). Most of these men belonged to one of two different categories. Either they were the writers who *dominated* the 1920's (along with Dreiser, Anderson, Cabell and Hergesheimer) or else they were the men who *appeared* in the 1920's, existed as a group in opposition to the dominant trends and did their best work in the following decade. Brooks was the one exception. He detested the 1920's and, for a time, he wrote nothing whatever; all his best work was done before and after the period that DeVoto claims to be treating. When he collects the faults of two hostile generations while neglecting their virtues, the result is an interesting amalgam of literary crimes, but it bears little resemblance to what actually happened in American letters.

The principal crime of which DeVoto accuses both generations together is that of indulging in what he calls "the literary

fallacy." This he defines as, "essentially, the belief that literature is the measure of culture." But in that case, why confine himself to the 1920's, considering that writers of all ages have held a similar belief? And why confine himself to literature? There is also an agricultural fallacy, which consists in believing that agriculture is the measure of culture. There is a plumbing fallacy: that bathrooms are the measure of culture. At all times men have sought to glorify their own professions; you might almost call it the human fallacy. It is a pardonable failing, and it causes less damage than might be expected, considering that human culture is a unity, something that can be approached and penetrated from almost any angle; men often start from such different fields as fiction, agriculture, science and even plumbing to reach the same truths about life as a whole. There is also a critic's fallacy, however, and it is somewhat less innocent than the others we have mentioned. It consists in projecting an imaginary purpose for works of literature, quite different from the actual purposes of their authors, and then condemning the authors jointly and separately because they failed to achieve it. DeVoto writes as if to illustrate that fallacy. He takes for granted that the authors of the 1920's should all have been cultural historians and should all have depicted American civilization as DeVoto now sees it; then he charges them with offering only a false or fragmentary picture. Quoting Emerson, he orders them back from their special interests to "the meal in the firkin, the milk in the pan."

But when I came to reread "The American Scholar," I found that Emerson's words had a different application from the one that DeVoto was trying to give them. They were a plea, not for writing great treatises on American civilization based on years of study in the library, but rather for understanding our immediate surroundings. "What would we really know the meaning of?" Emerson asked. "The meal in the firkin, the milk in the pan; the ballad in the street; the news of the boat; the glance of the eye; the form and gait of the body; show me the ultimate reason of these matters . . . and the world lies no longer a dull miscellany and lumber-room, but has form and order; there is no trifle, there is no puzzle, but one design unites and animates the farthest pinnacle and the lowest trench." He way saying almost what Hemingway said at the end of "Death in the Afternoon": Let those who want to [do so] change the world, if you can get to see it clear and as a whole. Then any part you make will represent the whole if it's truly made." There is no sign in this quotation—although there are a few signs elsewhere—of the violent anti-intellectualism that DeVoto imputes to Hemingway. There is every sign of an intellectual purpose he shared with other members of his generation: to deal only with the parts of the world they knew best, in the conviction that those parts would reveal the whole world. They hated eloquence, even of Emerson's homely sort; but instinctively they agreed with him that "one design unites and animates the farthest pinnacle and the lowest trench."

Hemingway, for example, didn't write about America the Vastly Beautiful, as DeVoto would have liked him to do; he wrote about the Michigan woods, about Paris cafés and fighting on the Isonzo and bull-fights in Spain; these were his meal in the firkin and his milk in the pan. Faulkner wrote about a single Mississippi county in book after book dealing with hundreds of different characters; by now he has composed what is our nearest approach to a *comédie humaine*. Fitzgerald wrote about his wealthy neighbors on Long Island and the Riviera, investing them with a false glamor and carefully explaining its falsity. Wolfe wrote badly at times, worse than any other American author of distinction, but he also gave us the poetry of the adolescent who feels infinite possibilities in himself and sets out from a back-country town to conquer the world—or rather, his part of the world. All these authors wrote about parts of the world; Dos Passos and Hart Crane were the only exceptions, the only men of their generation who tried to deal with America as a whole. Crane's attempt was a failure—as a whole; but he is marvelous in his treatment of specific scenes: the Brooklyn Bridge, the subways, the Mississippi. Dos Passos wrote from the special view of the traveler, the man who continually meets new people, hears their stories briefly, and travels on. That too was a part of the world: a cross-section taken horizontally rather than in depth.

The parts of America that appear in their novels and poems are not in general the smiling parts, the broad farmlands, the big Sunday dinners after coming home from church, the bouncing optimism that Mr. DeVoto finds everywhere. As a matter of fact, these authors were rebelling against another picture of American life that was dominant and accepted, that was preached in the churches, proclaimed at Rotary luncheons and romanticized by the *Saturday Evening Post*. Nobody was misled by them at the time they were writing: if anybody wanted the antidote to Dos Passos, let us say, he could find it in every magazine at his dentist's office and almost every novel in the loan library at the corner drugstore. But a curious thing has happened in the intervening years. The orthodox, optimistic, forward-looking literature of the 1920's has disappeared so completely that DeVoto doesn't even remember it. The literature of the rebels and renegades has survived and has come to be taken as a complete picture of the period. It had the strength to live.

Today it is time for us to see these authors in perspective, with their great faults—which are not always the faults DeVoto imputes to them—set beside their great virtues; their lack of broad vision set beside their power in depicting what was close at hand; their injustice to certain phases of American life set beside their emotional depth and lyricism. It is much too soon to assign them their separate ranks, and I should greatly question whether any of them will ever be placed on the same level as Emerson or Thoreau or Melville; yet together (and with a dozen contemporaries almost equally gifted) they represent a great period in American letters, the greatest since Concord in the 1850's. To them and to their critics I would apply what Gide said recently about Victor Hugo, after mentioning his faults one after another: "But instead of demanding qualities from people that we could easily find elsewhere, should we not take them for what they are: the titans for titans, the dwarfs for dwarfs, and the pedants who attack Hugo for fools?" (pp. 564-65)

Malcolm Cowley, "In Defense of the 1920's," in The New Republic, *Vol. 110, No. 17, April 24, 1944, pp. 564-65.*

WALLACE STEGNER   (essay date 1948)

[*Stegner is an American novelist, historian, and critic who won a Pulitzer Prize for his novel* Angle of Repose *(1971) and the National Book Award for* The Spectator Bird *(1976). His works often concern ethical problems and frequently use the American West as their setting. A close friend of DeVoto, Stegner collaborated with him on some aspects of the historical research for* The Literary Fallacy, *and his* The Uneasy Chair: A Biography of Bernard DeVoto *(1974) is the most extensive study of DeVoto's life and works. In the following excerpt, Stegner favorably assesses* Across the Wide Missouri *as an excitingly told, fresh approach to the history of the fur trade.*]

Bernard DeVoto's investigation of the origins and growth of what he calls the "continental mind" has been persistent and brilliant. *Mark Twain's America* displayed Manifest Destiny in its peak years, the period closed and symbolized by the meeting of the rails at Promontory. *The Year of Decision* went back in time to trace the complex lines of force that in 1846 made inevitable the pattern of western settlement, the war between the states, the eventual triumph of the continental idea. [*Across the Wide Missouri*] goes still farther back, into the closing years of the mountain fur trade. In his next he will deal with Lewis and Clark, back in the years when the West was still Louisiana or Mexico, and the idea of a continental nation had just been born.

Provocatively, excitingly, with wide and curious learning Mr. DeVoto gives us in *Across the Wide Missouri* a history of the twilight years of the fur trade. He is at pains to project present into future and indicate the obscure beginnings of later and greater things. The period he treats contains the beginning of the end of the Plains Indians, the virtual end of the mountain trappers, the first trickles of empire down California and Oregon trails. (p. 122)

Merely because of the freshness of its approach and its large use of primary sources, especially the diaries of travelers, this book is an important addition to such standard history as Chittenden and Coues. But because of its constant cross-reference and its restless curiosity in a very wide context, it becomes something more: the kind of intelligent study of social dynamisms that not too many historians are capable of.

Probably there will be objectors to Mr. DeVoto's judgments on all the early missionaries except Marcus and Narcissa Whitman, yet his charges of narrowness, inflexibility, jealousy, petty rancor, are based in the main on quotation from their own journals. His treatment of the Indians too is likely to seem mercurial to some, and he may seem to grow too ribald about their stone age superstitions, too skeptical of their often-celebrated courage, too dubious of their savage skills and intelligence. On the whole, he likes the Crows and the Nez Percés best: the Nez Percés were the best horse breeders and bowmakers in the West, and the Crows were the most skillful thieves.

Mr. DeVoto admires skill, in other words; he admires the mountain men for the same reasons, for their perfect adaptation to a given set of conditions. No laws, even moral laws, can survive a basic alteration of those conditions, and that is one of the firmest lessons of this big rich book: How fast the mountain men went out, how fast the Indians followed them, when the conditions changed and the forts along the western trails became not trading posts but way stations on the road to Oregon. By the end of the book, the mountain man has been overtaken by the settler, and a period of the West's brief and furious history has come to an end. The story has never been more excitingly told than it is here. (pp. 122, 124)

Wallace Stegner, in a review of "Across the Wide Missouri," in The Atlantic Monthly, *Vol. 181, No. 1, January, 1948, pp. 122, 124.*

PHILIP RAHV   (essay date 1949)

[*Rahv was a Russian-born American critic. Focusing on the intellectual, social, and cultural milieu influencing a work of art, his critical writings are intellectually eclectic and non-ideological. According to Richard Chase, "What one admires most about Rahv's critical method is his abundant ability to use such tech-*

niques as Marxism, Freudian psychology, anthropology, and existentialism toward his critical ends without shackling himself to any of them.'' In the following essay, Rahv blasts DeVoto for promulgating in The Literary Fallacy the ''reactionary fantasy'' that literary dissidence and experiment weaken a country politically, and demonstrates the extent to which DeVoto and one of his chief antagonists, Van Wyck Brooks, share similar opinions.]

In this country we have been largely spared the vicious campaigns against *Kulturbolschewismus* by which art and literature have been undermined in several European countries. The second World War did not pass, however, without provoking in America too a nationalist reaction in writing which was of course part and parcel of the world-wide attack on all cultural forms of dissidence and experiment. Bernard DeVoto's ***The Literary Fallacy*** is the leading document of this reaction, and it is as mindless a tract as any produced by those who have set themselves the task of subverting the critical spirit of the modern period. It deserves to be noticed, if only to keep the record straight.

First, as to the reactions to DeVoto. Some counterblows were struck, but the most widely-read reply—that of Sinclair Lewis in the *Saturday Review of Literature* [see Additional Bibliography]—turned out to be little more than a lively exercise in vituperation. For what was Lewis doing if not playing possum when he denied that the literature of the nineteen-twenties was dominated by any specific movement or tendency? And what point was there in his dragging in the names of people like Booth Tarkington and Edith Wharton? Such names in no way prove that the creative work of the twenties is without unity and that DeVoto was therefore attacking something without real existence. The representative figures of that decade are well known to everyone. Lewis's strategy showed him up as belying his own past, as repudiating the very movement in the absence of which it is inconceivable that he could have written either *Main Street* or *Babbitt*. He rejected implicitly what his seeming antagonist, DeVoto, rejected explicitly. Like Van Wyck Brooks and, for all one knows, DeVoto too, Lewis is a fugitive from an earlier self.

But for sheer brashness in proclaiming philistine values, DeVoto beats all comers; and he is a terrible show-off besides. Familiar as he is with a great many details of American history, he insists on exhibiting his knowledge, regardless of its degree of relevance to the subject at hand. Thus he writes a really incredible chapter—and that in a book of six short chapters—in which he goes on page after page telling us with a straight face all about the advances made by American medical men in the treatment of burns and about John Wesley Powell, a geologist who helped develop the Forest Service, the National Park Service and several learned societies, and who wrote, among other books, a *Report on the Lands of the Arid Regions of the United States*. ''Mr. Brooks has not heard about it,'' gloats DeVoto, ''nor Mr. Mumford, nor Mr. Stearns, Mr. Lewisohn, Mr. Frank, Mr. Parrington, or Mr. Hicks, not even Mr. Edmund Wilson or Mr. Kazin.''

Perhaps none of those ill-assorted gentlemen ever ''heard about it,'' but if DeVoto had any sense of method in handling ideas he would have kept the treatment of burns out of it, and Powell too. If his point is, however, that ours is a great and wonderful country precisely because of such phenomena, then he must be laboring under the delusion that America has a monopoly on medical scientists and public-spirited geologists. Furthermore, neither Brooks nor any other critic of American life has ever complained of our insufficient progress in applied science and technology. On the contrary.

It is DeVoto, also, who gives us the true-blue American version of the reactionary fantasy that it is writers of the type of Proust that caused the fall of France to the Nazis. He declares that it is the ''description of the United States as a pluto-democracy and its people as degenerate'' in the writing of the twenties ''which forms the basis of Hitler's understanding of America in *Mein Kampf* and elsewhere. . . . The correspondence is so obvious, so often an identity, that there must be a causal relationship between them.'' Here you have the essence of what our retrograde times have produced—the *amalgam* palmed off as the leading argument and as the answer to all questions. As for the ''literary fallacy''—defined by DeVoto as the overvaluation of literature as against life—who holds to it more than he does, when he attributes to the work of literary men so much political weight and influence?

Among the writers he belabors is T. S. Eliot, whom he accuses of having written disrespectfully of such ''little people'' as the young man carbuncular and the typist home at teatime. He asserts that since people of that sort stood up to the London blitz, the author of *The Waste Land* must now hang his head in shame. But even if we grant DeVoto his O.W.I. test of poetic truth, he still must account for the fact that the German young man carbuncular and the German typist also stood up to the blitz—a fact which, in his terms, would tend to prove that fascism is as good as democracy.

Where his worst philistinism comes out is in his attitude toward the war. He sees the war as a spiritual triumph that once and for all gave the lie to the criticism of modern life contained in modern literature. It never occurs to him that the virulence and pessimism of that literature have been completely justified by the war. No wonder he maintains that whereas American society was ''rugged, lively and vital'' in the twenties, American writing ''became increasingly debilitated, capricious, querulous and irrelevant.'' Writers repudiated their country and shut themselves off from its realities. Now a charge of this kind could be substantiated, it seems to me, only in one way, and that is by analyzing some of the typical and outstanding works of that decade (say *Babbit, The Great Gatsby, The Triumph of the Egg, Beyond the Horizon, The American Tragedy*, etc.) so as to show that there is no correspondence between them and the national life, that their revelation of the national character and conduct is either false or irrelevant. Yet this DeVoto fails to do. For the most part he is content merely to hurl accusations and ''to glow belligerently with his country,'' to borrow a phrase aimed by Henry James at the DeVotos of a past age. And whenever DeVoto does come down to cases he unknowingly proves the reverse of what he set out to prove.

This becomes particularly clear in his dealings with Brooks. The latter is an obsessive theme with DeVoto, and a gratuitous one besides, since he and Brooks are actually comrades-in-arms. For DeVoto locates the source of the literature of the twenties in the early work of Brooks—a notion patently nonsensical. A literature of such dimensions and variety can hardly be characterized otherwise than as an organic expression of American society. To be sure, the early Brooksian thesis influenced a good many writers, but DeVoto falls into sheer fantasy when he blames Brooks for the faults of novelists like Lewis and Hemingway. The truth is that it is exactly the Brooksian thesis which best explains those faults. The lack of ''maturity of mind, maturity of emotions, maturity of character and experience'' in both Lewis and Hemingway is not to be explained in terms of any literary fallacy, for no two authors are less addicted to making literature the measure of existence; it can be adequately accounted for only in relation to those forces in American life, charted by Brooks in such studies as *Letters and Leadership* and *America's Coming of Age,* which frustrate the artist and arrest his development. These forces are still at work in American civilization, and a critic like DeVoto is helping to perpetuate their dominance when he assaults the writers who at one time tried to overcome it.

When it comes to evaluating the literary art of the modern age Brooks and DeVoto now see eye to eye. Brooks, looking to poor dear old Whittier for his salvation, is more archaic in his approach. DeVoto is not quite so predisposed to favor the past. In his judgment the best American writers of our times are Carl Sandburg, E. A. Robinson, Willa Cather, Stephen Vincent Benét, and Robert Frost. The real trouble with him, one suspects, is that he loves literature not at all. (pp. 161-64)

> *Philip Rahv, ''De Voto and Kulturbolschewismus,''
> in his* Image and Idea: Fourteen Essays on Literary
> Themes, *New Directions, 1949, pp. 161-64.*

ORLAN SAWEY   (essay date 1969)

[*Sawey is an American educator and critic. In the following excerpt from his biographical and critical study* Bernard DeVoto, *he discusses DeVoto's interest in the American West as exemplified by his early novels and his three important histories:* The Year of Decision: 1846, Across the Wide Missouri, *and* The Course of Empire.]

In spite of the comments of his friends and enemies to the contrary, DeVoto always considered himself a novelist, though not always a popular or successful one. The dates of his novels (his last was published in 1947) indicate his continued interest in fiction.

As a novelist, DeVoto continually sought to explain the West to his readers. Of his . . . five novels—*The Crooked Mile, The Chariot of Fire, The House of Sun-Goes-Down, We Accept with Pleasure,* and *Mountain Time*—the first three deal with the Western Movement and the influence of the frontier on American civilization. The fourth, *We Accept with Pleasure,* describes the intellectual life in the East of some of the relatives of John Gale, DeVoto's frontier historian; and it contrasts the effete Eastern civilization with the more meaningful life of the West (or at least the Middle West). The fifth, *Mountain Time,* is partially set in the West. The basic theme, the redemption found in separation from the degrading forces of the East, is in keeping with DeVoto's general attitude. (p. 18)

Relatively unknown, the novels are significant revelations of DeVoto's ideas.

The first novel, *The Crooked Mile,* a careful study of the frontier town of Windsor, shows the deterioration in the third generation of a frontier family, the Abbeys, and describes the new West, a West controlled by rapacious corporations which have destroyed or at least emasculated the frontier ideal. The second novel, *The Chariot of Fire,* pursues a side issue, frontier religion, in a description of the religious fanatic previously written about by William Dean Howells in *The Leatherwood God.* The third novel, *The House of Sun-Goes-Down,* describes the earlier phases of frontier development as seen in the lives of the first two Abbeys and in the history of a frontier town, Windsor.

Although DeVoto's general theme is the validity of the frontier ideal, he is more interested in an analysis of the mind of the frontiersman than in the pursuit of a historical thesis. He never

forgets that he is a novelist, writing about real people. His novels are intellectual; he develops his main characters—Pemberton Abbey, Gordon Abbey, John Gale, and Hope Gale—by tracing their thinking and reproducing their conversations. Action is slowed by long philosophical discussions; but, at the same time, character is more clearly revealed. After all, people do discuss ideas, sometimes at boring lengths. But DeVoto succeeds admirably in avoiding boredom.

In DeVoto's novels the Westward Movement is revealed in the lives of men of three generations of the Abbey family. The frontier is shown as a place of hardships and problems. The wife of James Abbey, the patriarch of the Abbey family, never became reconciled to frontier life. The struggle in the first generation was against the land itself; in the second generation, against the encroachment of a tainted capitalism; in the third generation, against a highly-organized, dominant capitalism. In DeVoto's plots violence is minimized, and human relationships are emphasized. Few Western novelists have as clearly avoided the usual clichés about Western Life. (p. 19)

One of DeVoto's main problems was to arrive at a method of discussing facets of frontier philosophy and still to write a novel. The conventions of the modern novel discourage long digressions for the purpose of discussing ideas. DeVoto partially solved this problem by removing John Gale, contemporary of Pemberton Abbey, from his native New England and setting him down in Windsor, where he devoted most of his life to writing a history of the frontier. DeVoto used excerpts from these imaginary histories as introductions to sections of *The Crooked Mile.* He had Pemberton Abbey, Gordon Abbey, and other characters in the novels discuss Gale's writing with him. In these discussions, a natural part of the novels, the various concepts of the frontier emerge. (pp. 20-1)

DeVoto even provided John Gale with a fictional bibliography, a quite believable one. The first volume was entitled *The Goisute Indians* (1897); its subtitle indicates that it was a discussion of the organization, culture, and folklore of an American tribe. The work of Gale's most often quoted by DeVoto is *The Diaspora: A History and Criticism of the Frontier Movement in America.* Volumes I and II were published in Boston by the Laurel Press in 1908 and volumes III and IV by the same press in 1910. *The Frontier Ethos: Essays in Western History* was published in 1911 and *Religious Colonization: A Study of Catholic and Calvinistic Civilization in Western America* in 1914. Gale also published a biography of the great populist, Henry Clay Bryce, but this date of publication is unknown.

These ''histories'' considerably add to the realism of DeVoto's frontier novels. They serve as a basis for questioning the importance of the frontier in American civilization. DeVoto made Gale an iconoclast, a New England puritan who ruthlessly pushed aside romantic concepts of the frontier and described social development from the detached viewpoint of the scientific historian. DeVoto said of Gale that he laid forever the myth that human freedom had any more existence on the frontier than elsewhere. He had Gale say that the frontier was only a ghost, that most frontiersmen blindly obeyed necessity, and that frontiers of courage and of creation never existed—they were only mysterious and occult delusions.

Although Louis Farrand, Gale's son-in-law, believed that ''the kingdom of heaven was in process of establishment on the frontier'' and that all that remained was the education of certain politicians, John Gale's books announced that no millennium would spring from the frontier; energy had declined. Gale insisted that the pioneer was "not a superman dominated by visions of empire, but a hell-ridden calvinist driven west by economic pressure." Moreover, "Not God's whisper urged him out, but bankruptcy among his stronger brothers. He sought not something lost behind the ranges, but free land by which he might repair his fortunes."

In the introduction to Part II of *The Crooked Mile* DeVoto quoted from *The Diaspora,* making Gale insist that there was no real frontier—there was no freedom, opportunity, and virtue; there was "only an advancing fringe of dubious civilization where men repeated the unchanging cycle of their race. There were inheritors of fear and barrenness and frustration." (pp. 22-3)

The early novels show a preoccupation with the frontier, a desire to explain what happened there, that DeVoto never lost. This interest embroiled him in controversy over Mark Twain and eventually led him into battle with other critics. His interest in frontier ways led to the writing of three full-length histories and many other essays on the West. It led into combat with the private-enterprise industrial forces which he felt had plundered the West and were attempting to continue to do so.

Finally, his experience as a fiction writer was a continual influence on DeVoto's other works. The narrative techniques of the novelist were used in *Mark Twain's America* and in the histories. The style of DeVoto, the historian, was continually being influenced by the imagination of DeVoto, the writer of fiction, although his love for "the facts" kept his imagination under strict control. Nevertheless, DeVoto's writing of novels has contributed greatly to the art and the interest of his histories. (pp. 33-4)

Bernard DeVoto was always a historian of the American West, even when the history was disguised in fiction or in social criticism. He began his appraisal of the impact of the frontier on American life in his first novel, *The Crooked Mile,* in the scholarly histories written by the fictional historian, John Gale. Of DeVoto's first four books, as has been noted, the first three are novels, concerned with the American frontier complex, and the fourth, *Mark Twain's America,* is social history, an impassioned defense of the West and its impact on American institutions and American writers. (p. 73)

Mark Twain's America is probably the most significant of DeVoto's works. It was . . . the cause of his becoming in 1938 the curator of the Mark Twain papers, and it also contributed to his conflict with contemporary critics and to *The Literary Fallacy.* The chief contribution of *Mark Twain's America,* however, was its providing a technique for DeVoto for the writing of history. In his foreword to the book he stated that Arthur Schlesinger, Sr., had suggested that the book was the social history of Mark Twain; but DeVoto insisted that the book was not comprehensive enough to be history. Nevertheless, the broad, sweeping description of the frontier from the Mississippi River to the Pacific Ocean, as it was during Twain's time, is social history of the finest kind; for the account is filled with minute detail about the daily life, the attitudes, and especially the humor of the frontiersmen. (p. 74)

[*The Year of Decision: 1846, Across the Wide Missouri,* and *The Course of Empire*], which form the bulk of DeVoto's historical writing, are really a trilogy which explains the impact of the frontier on American civilization. *The Year of Decision,* as the title indicates, is a complete picture of what happened in all parts of America in the most interesting year of the century's most significant decade, the 1840's. Not only did DeVoto relate historical events, but he drew vigorous conclu-

sions, also. For instance, he concluded that "at some time between August and December, 1846, the Civil War had begun."

The "Calendar for the Years 1846-1847" at the beginning of the book relates only the most important events of a nineteen-month period. These events include Fremont's activities in California (where gold at Sutter's fort was soon to be discovered), The Mexican War, the Mormon trek west, the Magoffins' trip to Sante Fe, the Donner tragedy, Francis Parkman's sojourn among the Sioux, and the Mormon Battalion's trip to California. The book itself touches on the lives of almost every important person living in 1846, from Abraham Lincoln to the Brook Farmers, from Jim Bridger to Henry David Thoreau. DeVoto made an attempt to give a complete picture. In a note he expressed regret (almost anguish), that the stories of J. W. Abert, Lewis Garrard, and George F. Ruxton could not be woven into the narrative. If books did not have to end, he wrote, all three accounts would have been included.

In his preface, DeVoto rationalized his method of narration. His original purpose, he said, was a literary one: "to realize the pre-Civil War, Far Western frontier as personal experience." However, when he began the book he found that his "friends and betters," the professional historians had failed him because they had done only specialized studies—all except Paxson. Nobody had tried to fit the parts together; for the stories to have literary value, their orientation had to be made clear. **Hence, DeVoto had to become a historian to provide the background. (pp.75-6)**

DeVoto's *original* purpose in writing *The Year of Decision* was literary, for he did not in 1943 consider himself a historian but a literary man. (pp. 76-7)

It is impossible to summarize *The Year of Decision* because the book is itself a summary. DeVoto did succeed in his avowed purpose; he did picture the Far Western Frontier as "personal experience." He used the technique of the novelist, and he planned and described his settings carefully. He described his characters fully; he reproduced them from original primary sources and from the records of those who were present. For example, Susan Magoffin's own journal was the basis of **DeVoto's full-length portrait of her. (pp. 77-8)**

Using the technique of the omniscient novelist, DeVoto brought together his cast of characters and fitted them all into his structure, or plot—the picturing of the parallel events of 1846, events which led to the forming of the nation: the Mexican War and the Westward Movement. (p. 79)

If history is merely a compilation of dates and events, then *The Year of Decision* is history. Too frequently the writers of history are bound by these facts of history; and the result is dusty, dry, and unpalatable. DeVoto said that "most historians and most scholars appear to write with something between a bath sponge and an axe." Sometimes the would-be historian, repelled by the taste of the dry-as-dust history, engages in wild flights of fancy, imagines the thought of his characters, and repeats conversations heard only by the conversers. But DeVoto wrote neither of these kinds of history. In *The Year of Decision,* a broadly projected and carefully executed history of one year in America, DeVoto, without distorting his material, used his skill in narration and in character development to write history that is *alive.* Few people of importance who lived in 1846 are ignored; all are fitted into the main stream of the events of that crucial year. (p. 81)

The major literary figures of the time, wrote DeVoto, did not express the tenor of the time; but "Stephen Foster caught it dead center. . . . The way to understand the persons who were about to fight an unpremeditated war and by building new homes in the West push the nation's boundary to the Pacific— is to steep yourself in Stephen Foster's songs." "Doo-Dah Day" and "Oh Susanna!"—not "Passage to India," "Eldorado," or "Roger Malvin's Burial"—are DeVoto's chapter headings.

One must read carefully *The Year of Decision* in order to understand its completeness and to appreciate its vivid characterization and narration. DeVoto's mind and his wit were constantly active; his prejudices frequently appeared. He was bemused with Francis Parkman's lack of perception. He was constantly seeking an evaluation of the contributions of the Mormons, for whom he had no love, to Manifest Destiny. He analyzed the political and military battles in depth. He presented the attitudes of the Mexicans, especially the Californios, to American occupation. He sought an explanation of the horrors experienced by the Donner Party. He defended Stephen Watts Kearney's actitivies in California and wrote with scorn of the politics of John C. Fremont and his father-in-law, Thomas Hart Benton. He defended (and used) Walter Prescott Webb's discussion of the importance of Samuel Colt's revolver in the winning of the West. He speculated that the source of the Civil War rebel yell was the "cry of the cattle range, a wild, unnerving sound deep in the bass which climbed to a full-throated, deafening falsetto" produced by Texans of Taylor's army who "had worked the great herds of Texas longhorns."

DeVoto was not afraid of tearing down idols and of disagreeing with the critics. He spoke of "Hawthorne's exquisitely engraved melancholy" and of "the cheap gloom of Edgar Poe." He praised Clarence King who, he said, survived "as a name to be mentioned in appraisals of our civilization through his friendship with a person of considerably inferior intelligence, Henry Adams. . . ." He praised Ferdinand Vandiveer Hayden, an obscure geologist who made many maps for the Geological Survey headed by John Wesley Powell, another unappreciated "prime intelligence." He admired one of Powell's assistants, Clarence Edwards Dutton; and he slyly accused Charles Dudley Warner, John Muir, and John Burroughs of plagiarizing Dutton's works: in copying whole pages exactly, they were "too absorbed to inclose them in quotation marks."

After describing Congress' declaring a war which already existed, DeVoto wrote, "The muse of history does not sleep: that day an organization of superintendants of insane asylums convened in Washington." On the other hand, in quite another vein, DeVoto described the westering pioneer thus:

> So he had found the West and given it to the United States; now he faced the labor of subduing it and building in it a farther portion of the United States. To that labor would be addressed the rest of Bill Bowen's life and the lives of his children and their children. Christmas along the Sacramento and the Willamette, the Bay of San Francisco, the lower Columbia, was Christmas in a strange land firelit by memories of Christmas back home in the States but also heightened by the realization he had achieved. Beside these waters that fell into the Pacific there was a hope about the future that has become a deed within our past.

The second work in DeVoto's trilogy is more than a history; it is a work of art. It is, as the preface indicates, a treatment of "the Rocky Mountain fur trade during the years of its climax and decline"—the period between 1832 and 1838. The book contains a separate chronology of the mountain fur trade; a separate article entitled "The First Illustrators of the West"; notes at the back, chapter by chapter, similar to those in *The Year of Decision;* and, most important, an extensive bibliography of works about the mountain fur trade. In addition, the book contains reproductions, some in color, of eighty-one paintings by Alfred Jacob Miller, Charles Bodmer, and George Catlin, artists who were in the West during the time covered by the book and who painted forts, mountain men, Indians, the flora and fauna of the Rockies, and the beautiful scenery.

Two facts must be taken into consideration in the analysis of this work which, as art, is the best book of the trilogy. First, DeVoto disclaimed any attempt to write a comprehensive history; he stated that Chittenden's *The American Fur Trade of the Far West* (1902) was out of date because of the uncovering of much new material, and that it was time for someone to write a modern historical synthesis. But, he insisted, *Across the Wide Missouri* was not such a history: "Instead I have tried to describe the mountain fur trade as a business and as a way of life: what its characteristic experiences were, what conditions governed them, how it helped to shape our heritage, what its relation was to the western expansion of the United States, most of all how the mountain men lived.

DeVoto did admit, in his preface, that he was a historian; but he also insisted that his book was written to entertain the general reader. As a historian, he had been interested in the "growth among the American people of the feeling that they were properly a single nation between two oceans: in the development of . . . the continental mind." He was especially interested in relating the fur trade to westward expansion as a whole: "I shall have succeeded if the reader gets from the book a sense of time hurrying on while between the Missouri and the Pacific a thousand or so men of no moment whatever are living an exciting and singularly uncertain life, hurrying one era of our history to a close, and thereby making possible another one, which began with the almost seismic enlargement of our boundaries and consciousness of which I have written elsewhere.

The second fact that one must consider in order to evaluate DeVoto's statements about his own work is that this book, unlike *The Year of Decision,* does contain an extensive bibliography. In the first book DeVoto stated in general what his sources were, but he insisted that a complete bibliography was impossible. The implication was that this kind of history, if it were history, needed no bibliography. In *Across the Wide Missouri,* however, DeVoto provided what was unfortunately missing in the first volume. (pp. 81-4)

In spite of the disclaimer in his preface, *Across the Wide Missouri* is history of the finest kind, not the "dry bones moved from one graveyard to another" (J. Frank Dobie's definition of a doctoral dissertation, with which DeVoto would agree). And DeVoto again brought to history the techniques of the novelist. The story of the mountain fur trade was constructed around the experiences of Sir William Drummond Stewart, with whom Alfred Jacob Miller traveled. Stewart was in the area for six years, from 1833 through 1838. At the beginning of the book DeVoto gave a "Dramatis Personae," a list of those involved in the business during the years which the book covers. The list reads like an honor roll (if *honor* is the right word) of the "mountain men," the Rocky Mountain beaver trappers, who were as nearly savage as any group on the frontier. Among those listed are Francis Chardon, Jim Beckwourth, Jim Bridger ("Old Gabe"), Tom Fitzpatrick, Joe Meek, Louis

Vasquez ("Old Vaskiss"), Kit Carson, the Sublettes, Doc Newell, and Joseph Thing. More respectable and less savage were Kenneth McKenzie of Astor's Company, Dr. John McLoughlin of the Hudson's Bay Company, Captain Benjamin Louis Eulalie de Bonneville of the United States Army, Nathaniel Jarvis Wyeth (Yankee businessman with eager beaver aspirations), Dr. Benjamin Harrison, Captain Stewart . . . , and the painter, Alfred Jacob Miller.

DeVoto described the setting of his narrative well (the paintings help); the narrative has unity since most of the events are related directly to Stewart's experiences. The point of view of the narrative is as consistent as is possible in an effort of such a broad scope. Although De Voto has been criticized for presenting a confusing story, a careful examination of the material reveals a tight, systematic organization. The approach is as chronological as he could make it, especially if one considers the mass of the material presented.

And in characterization DeVoto again used his skill as a writer of fiction. Captain Stewart is fully-drawn, as is Captain Bonneville (DeVoto is one of the few American critics to recognize the value of Washington Irving's Western chronicles, especially his *Captain Bonneville*). Perhaps the trapper himself, as typified by Jim Bridger, Joe Meek, and Kit Carson, could have been better drawn; but Irving and Ruxton had already described these men fully. Also, modern novelists, such as Oliver La Farge and A. B. Guthrie, Jr., have utilized Ruxton's and Irving's works in describing the mountain man. (pp. 84-5)

In the third book of his historical trilogy, *The Course of Empire,* DeVoto came closer to being a historian's historian than in the other two books. In his "acknowledgements" he admits to being a historian of the Westward Movement, but in his preface he calls the book the "last of three narrative studies." There is a difference, however, between the third volume and the other two: *The Year of Decision: 1846* covers less than a two-year time span; *Across the Wide Missouri,* about seven years; *The Course of Empire* (DeVoto says), a period of two hundred seventy-eight years, evidently from 1527, when Cabeza de Vaca began his long trek, to 1805, when Lewis and Clark reached the Pacific Ocean. This extended span of time made DeVoto's previous narrative approach not so "biddable." The difference in time, he wrote, made necessary "the use of different conventions, historical as well as literary, and a different method." But DeVoto still insisted that literary method was a part of his approach to writing history.

This different method was a switch from the chronological narrative structure to a thematic structure; but as much as is possible with such a mass of material, the book is still a chronological history. DeVoto described his thematic method as follows:

> There are minor themes but the principal ones are these: [1] the geography of North America in so far as it was important in the actions dealt with; [2] the ideas which the men involved in those actions had about this geography, their misconceptions and errors, and the growth of knowledge; [3] the exploration of the United States and Canada, so much of it as was relevant to the discovery of a route to the Pacific Ocean; [4] the contention of four empires for the area that is now the United States; [5] the relationship to all these things of various Indian tribes that affected them. Let me repeat: the meaning is not the themes in themselves but their combination.

The different literary conventions are apparent. Individual characters could not be analyzed as minutely as in the other book,

and theme rather than chronology had become the basis of structure. There is also less of the personality of the narrator in this book; in a literary sense, DeVoto had become more objective. On the other hand, there is a difference in the historical approach. In the first two books DeVoto was avowedly careful to document his statements, mainly from primary sources. In his preface to *Course of Empire* he admitted that only some of his historical facts had been established without question and that often he had given summaries of events about which there was no certainty. He had, he said, tried to be accurate; and generally, when uncertainty was present, he admitted it. In spite of this honest admission of DeVoto's (or perhaps because of it), *The Course of Empire* is more "historical" than "literary." DeVoto's fifth theme by itself would make this a valuable history since few books have dealt so thoroughly with Indian troubles and Indian migrations.

According to DeVoto, the theme of all three books in the trilogy is found in Lincoln's second annual message to Congress, December 1, 1862. In this message Lincoln insisted that there was no possible national boundary in the United States which could be used for dividing the country. The line between slave and free country, Lincoln said, consisted merely of surveyors' lines or rivers easy to cross. The interior of the nation was the "great body of the Republic." Eastern, Northern, Southern, and Western outlets were necessary for trade. No boundaries were possible. DeVoto quoted in italics the following passage from Lincoln: "Our national strife springs not from our permanent part; not from the land we inhabit; not from the national homestead. There is no possible severing of this but would multiply and not mitigate evils among us. In all its adaptations and attitudes it demands union and abhors separation. In fact it would ere long force reunion, however much of blood and treasure the separation might have cost. Our strife pertains to ourselves, to the passing generations of men. . . ."

This statement of Lincoln's is, of course, a restatement of the Manifest Destiny idea of 1845, the theme of DeVoto's first two books. By the time of the Civil War it was obvious, according to Lincoln, that the United States, from the Atlantic to the Pacific Ocean, from the Canadian to the Mexican border, was destined, because of the nature of its geography, to be one nation. All five of DeVoto's themes, even the Indian migration theme, are directly related to geography; and Manifest Destiny was a geographical concept.

DeVoto also explained the apparent contradiction between Thomas Jefferson's feeling that the United States should not extend from ocean to ocean and his actions in preparing the way for such an extension to take place. DeVoto said that, if one examines Jefferson's actions in chronological sequence, from his reports on the Northwest Territory for the Congress of the Confederation to the Louisiana purchase, he must decide that, although Jefferson may sometimes have *thought* that the nation could not permanently fill its continental system, he *acted* as if, manifestly, it could have no other destiny.

In 1953 DeVoto extended this thesis in an article in *Collier's.* There was significance, he thought, in the fact that Jefferson, before the purchase, secretly asked Congress to authorize the exploration of the Western area to the Pacific Ocean. (*The Course of Empire* really ends with the arrival of Lewis and Clark at the Pacific.) Moreover, Jefferson's idea that such a large area could not be governed was soon made obsolete by American inventions and development: the invention of the steamboat that could travel "in a heavy dew—or a light one, when necessary"; the development of the westward trails, such as the Santa Fe Trail, for commerce; and eventually the building of the railroads.

In *The Course of Empire,* bound by the enormity of his task and by an unwillingness to ignore the facts, DeVoto nevertheless filled his account with minor mysteries and marvels. He described in detail the pursuit of many ephemera, will-o'-the-wisps such as the "Seven Cities," the "Welsh Indians," and other strange creatures just over the horizon. The frontiersmen of the French, Spanish, and American frontiers are described well. He emphasized the great curiosity of the mountain men, the trappers, and the westering pioneers as to what lay behind the mountains. He posed the question of obstructions to moving west, such as the ranges of the Appalachians, and dramatized the overcoming of such obstacles. He also dramatized the Indian wars and wondered that "The Indians resisted decadence as well as they did, preserved as much as they did, and fought the whites off so obstinately and so long. For from 1500 on they were cultural prisoners." He emphasized the Indian adaptation to the horse and buffalo culture. He wrote of their use of iron in their own weapons; of the white man's adoption of the Indian's mode of transportation, the birch-bark canoe; and of the destruction of entire tribes by the white man's diseases (as when the Mandans were wiped out by smallpox).

The Course of Empire, for which DeVoto received the 1952 National Book Award for nonfiction, is good history; and it is readable and interesting. (pp. 90-3)

As a historian DeVoto never managed (if he wanted to) to escape his literary background. To say that he was a literary historian would be in error; this term has been widely used to describe another type of writer, and DeVoto would not want to be so designated. Instead he was a historian constantly influenced by the literary way of thinking. While he was careful to make his history factual, he was always affected by an irrepressible imagination. Perhaps, although he would sneer at the classification and doubt its necessity, he was a belletristic historian or a belletrist surrounded by the world of historical fact. (p. 95)

> *Orlan Sawey, in his* Bernard DeVoto, *Twayne Publishers, Inc., 1969, 146 p.*

WALLACE STEGNER   (essay date 1985)

[*In the following excerpt, Stegner discusses the controversial nature of much of DeVoto's literary career.*]

From the time in the mid-Twenties when he published his first essays in H. L. Mencken's *American Mercury,* [Bernard DeVoto's] career had been controversy. He had broken spears against the progressive schools and the football colleges, against Van Wyck Brooks and the young intellectuals, against the literary censors of Watch and Ward, against the Communists and Popular Fronters, against J. Edgar Hoover and the FBI, against Senator McCarthy, the Reece Committee, and other official enemies of civil liberties, against academic historians and southern revisionists, against the "beautiful thinking" of the literary who hunted in pack, against western stockmen and their political backers. To some he seemed merely contrary: when the public weathervane veered Left, he veered Right; when it veered Right, he veered Left. In the 1930s the *Daily Worker* called him a fascist. By the 1950s, the *Worker* was quoting his Easy Chairs with approval, old antagonists such as F. O. Matthiessen and the editors of *New Republic* were his

somewhat astonished allies, and Senator McCarthy was denouncing "one Richard DeVoto" as a communist.

Early in 1937, pondering DeVoto's aggressive editorship of the *Saturday Review of Literature* [see excerpt dated 1937], Edmund Wilson found him difficult to label, and rather plaintively called on him to stand and declare himself in the ideological struggles of his time. Who was he? What did he believe in? What did he want? Why was he so angry?

Some of the questions were rhetorical, some unanswerable. DeVoto could never have explained why he was so angry, any more than a fish could have explained why it breathed through gills. And Wilson had to know who DeVoto was—he had been around for considerably more than a decade, in postures of constant challenge. But there was every reason why Wilson could not understand DeVoto. There were enough differences of background and belief to make them incomprehensible to one another, though Wilson was probably more comprehensible to DeVoto than DeVoto was to Wilson. For DeVoto was a westerner, something easterners have seldom understood, and a belligerent westerner at that. Moreover, he was a shirtsleeve democrat, almost a populist—a Declaration-of-Independence, Bill-of-Rights, Manifest-Destiny American democrat, inhabiting intellectual territory that the then-reigning arbiters of opinion thought uninhabitable. (pp. 151-52)

In his Foreword [to *Mark Twain's America*], DeVoto had rejected the temptation to explain Mark Twain simply or according to any formula, as he accused Brooks of doing [in *The Ordeal of Mark Twain*]. "I do not believe in simplicities about art, artists, or the subjects of criticism," he wrote. "I have no theory about Mark Twain. It is harder to conform one's book to ascertainable fact than to theorize, and harder to ascertain facts than to ignore them. In literature, beautiful simplicities usually result from the easier method, and, in literature, the armchair assertion that something must be true is the begetter of unity."

There, if Wilson had looked, was the explanation of DeVoto. Throughout his career, while opponents accused him of flipping back and forth, he held to the tests of fact and experience. Viewed in retrospect, his principles reveal themselves as completely consistent. He was a rock in the surf of changing minds, fickle fashions, liberal hesitations, doubts, recantations, and gods that failed. Though his interests moved steadily away from literature and toward history and politics and conservation, he distrusted *a priori* thinking wherever he found it, and his nickname among his colleagues at the Breadloaf Writers' Conference, where he taught for a good many summers during the 1930s and 1940s, was Ad Hoc.

Over a period of three decades, his writings say it in a hundred contexts. In a double editorial in the *Saturday Review* for February 13, 1937, he said it for Edmund Wilson, who had complained about his lack of "articulated ideas."

"This," he said, 'is a demand for a gospel, and I have been acquainted with it since my earliest days. I was brought up in a religion which taught me that man was imperfect but might expect God's mercy—but I was surrounded by a revealed religion founded by a prophet of God, composed of people on their way to perfection, and possessed of an everlasting gospel. I early acquired a notion that all gospels were false and all my experience since then has confirmed it . . . I distrust absolutes. Rather, I long ago passed from distrust of them to opposition. And with them let me include prophecy, simplification, generalization, abstract logic, and especially the habit of mind which consults theory first and experience only afterward.''

In a time which spent much of its intellectual and emotional energy debating whether America would go communist or fascist, and when most of the literary leaned left, that pragmatic, skeptical, equilibristic stance was glaringly unorthodox. Distrusting New York as the nest where all the current orthodoxies were laid and hatched, DeVoto consistently earned New York's dislike and disapproval. He refused all the fashionable hooks, however attractively baited. In 1943 he said, ''Politically, I am a New Dealer on Election Day and a critic of the New Deal at other times.'' In 1950 he said, ''I am a half-Mugwump, 60 per cent New Dealer, 90 per cent Populist dirt-roads historian.'' In 1944, in a last charge against accepted literary opinion, he put together some lectures delivered at the University of Indiana under the title *The Literary Fallacy,* in which he again defended American society from the commonplace assumption that it was a ''great gaslighted barbarity'' that destroyed its artists. He said instead that its artists had betrayed and misrepresented their society, and called down on his head the wrath of all the literary, especially Sinclair Lewis, whose attack in the *Saturday Review* of April 15, 1944 will probably persist in our literary history simply by virtue of its *ad hominem* virulence [see Additional Bibliography].

Through the literary unrest of the Twenties, the leftist temptations of the Thirties, the crisis patriotism of the war years, and the demoralizing witch-hunts of the late Forties and early Fifties, DeVoto reiterated, in woodwinds, strings, and brass, the declaration of belief to which he had been forced by Wilson; and as the political air darkened, so did the DeVoto analysis. Ideas as systematic constructs, ideas unresponsive to the facts of a nation's history and the habits and needs of people, were not merely intellectually offensive but politically dangerous, no matter whether well-meant or ill-meant. (DeVoto's one-time intimate and surrogate father, Robert Frost, put it succinctly in a comment on Henry Wallace. ''Henry,'' he said, ''is bound to reform you whether you want to be reformed or not.'')

To a mind as truculently independent as DeVoto's, all dogma, whether in religion, literature, history, teaching, or any other endeavor, suppressed thought. In politics, it was a constant threat to freedom. Passionate political dogmas led to machine-gun government; and ''idealism, whether moral or metaphysical or literary, may be defined as a cross-lots path to the psychopathic ward, Berchtesgaden, and St. Bartholomew's Eve. Absolutes mean absolutism.''

In the pre-War and War years when left-leaning intellectuals had more or less cornered American publications (with the marked exceptions of *Harper's* and *The Saturday Review*) DeVoto was as completely anathema to the political intellectuals as he had earlier been to the literary. He got his revenge, and could not resist airing it, when the faithful began to recant and fall off the Moscow Express, as Malcolm Cowley put it, after the Moscow Trials and especially the Hitler-Stalin pact. In a 1951 Easy Chair entitled **''The Ex-Communists,''** DeVoto commented on these born-again democrats: ''The road to an understanding of democracy crosses the communist east forty. Before you can add a column of figures correctly you must first add them wrong. He who would use his mind must first lose it. Various ex-communist intellectuals are offering themselves on just that basis as authorities about what has happened and guides to what must be done. Understand, I am right now *because* I was wrong then. *Only* the ex-communist can un-

derstand communism. Trust me to lead you aright now *because* I tried earlier to lead you astray. My intelligence has been vindicated *in that* it made an all-out commitment to error.''

In DeVoto's view, the ex-communist had arrived, proud of his mistakes, at precisely the place where any non-communist American had stood all along. ''Where, for God's sake, was he when they were distributing minds?'' One thing he could be sure of—he himself had been more stoutly at the barricades than the twice-born ones. During the war he had repeatedly tried to free the hands of his friend Elmer Davis, then head of the Office of War Information, to disseminate information instead of soothing syrup and propaganda. ''The way to have an informed public opinion is to inform the public.'' And in the October, 1949 Easy Chair he had capped his long career in defense of civil liberties with **''Due Notice to the FBI,''** an essay that made him stronger and more lasting friends than all his controversies together had made him enemies. He would no longer, he said, discuss anyone in private with any FBI operative. If it was his duty to do so, he would discuss anyone, but only in court, and in the presence of his attorney, not for the dubious uses of a system of informers and secret police.

''I like a country where it's nobody's damned business what magazines anyone reads, what he thinks, whom he has cocktails with. I like a country where we do not have to stuff the chimney against listening ears and where what we say does not go into the FBI files along with a note from S-17 that I may have another wife in California. I like a country where no college-trained flatfeet collect memoranda about us and ask judicial protection for them, a country where when someone makes statements about us to officials he can be held to account. We had that kind of country only a little while ago and I'm for getting it back.''

That was who Bernard DeVoto was, and had been, and would continue to be—as dedicated a cultural patriot as the country has had since Emerson, light years away from the literary and political coteries with their Anglophile, Francophile, or Russophile addictions, and 90° divergent from H. L. Mencken, under whose enthusiastic Booboisie-thumping tutelage he had begun. In spite of its frequent failure to live up to itself and its willingness to listen to siren voices, America was what he believed in. He believed in its political principles and its democratic strength, in its always-tumultuous present and its probably-distracted future, and he was stimulated and invigorated by its past.

His enemies called him a philistine. He did not mind—he even embraced the role. And before he was done he would make three major contributions to the American tradition. 1) His essays on civil liberties and public affairs (see especially those in **The Easy Chair**), stand re-reading better than the work of any commentator of his time except E. B. White, who for some years shared the pages of *Harper's* with him and helped make it the most influential magazine of the period. A few of those essays, such as **''Due Notice to the FBI''** and **''Guilt by Distinction,''** belong among the very best statements of the American gospels. 2) His essays on the West, especially those written during the late 1940s and early 1950s in an almost-singlehanded and spectacularly successful attempt to forestall a grab of public lands by western resource interests, explained the West and the public lands to the rest of the nation as no one else had succeeded in doing, and gave him unquestioned leadership in the modern conservation movement. And 3), his histories, among which one should probably classify *Mark Twain's America,* finally won him the praise and recognition that his novels had failed to win him, including the Pulitzer and Bancroft prizes and the National Book Award. (pp. 154-57)

> Wallace Stegner, "Bernard DeVoto," in Western American Literature, *Vol. XX, No. 2, August, 1985, pp. 151-64.*

ADDITIONAL BIBLIOGRAPHY

Bowen, Catherine Drinker. "The Literary Fallacy." *The Saturday Review of Literature* XXVII, No. 23 (3 June 1944): 19.
> Letter to the *Saturday Review* concerning *The Literary Fallacy.* Bowen contends that the volume's overwhelmingly positive affirmation of humankind transcends "all DeVoto's name-calling earlier in the book."

————. "Bernard DeVoto: Historian, Critic, and Fighter." *The Atlantic Monthly* 206, No. 6 (December 1960): 69-75.
> Favorable assessment of DeVoto as a historian, noting and approving his impatience with histories written "from intuition or from deduction or from the argument a priori and the flowery heights of what he castigated as 'the literary mind'" rather than from fact.

Boynton, Percy H. Review of *Mark Twain's America,* by Bernard DeVoto. *The New England Quarterly* VI, No. 1 (March 1933): 184-87.
> Regrets that an "otherwise clear, rational, and convincing" account is "becluttered" with invective against other critics.

Butterfield, L. H. "Bernard DeVoto in the Easy Chair." *The New England Quarterly* XXIX, No. 4 (December 1956): 435-42.
> Approbatory assessment of DeVoto's monthly "Easy Chair" column in *Harper's* from 1935 through 1956.

Canby, Henry Seidel. "Mark Twain Himself." *The Saturday Review of Literature* IX, No. 16 (29 October 1932): 201-02.
> Review of DeVoto's *Mark Twain's America,* addressing many of the specific points of contention between DeVoto and Van Wyck Brooks.

————. "Mr. Bernard DeVoto." *The Saturday Review of Literature* XXVII, No. 19 (6 May 1944): 16.
> Reviews *The Literary Fallacy,* maintaining that DeVoto was wrong to assess literature from a historian's standpoint.

————. "Bernard DeVoto's Novel of Character." *The Saturday Review of Literature* XI, No. 10 (22 September 1934): 125.
> Largely favorable review assessing *We Accept with Pleasure* as an engrossing novel with somewhat static characterization.

Cowley, Malcolm. "Marginalia." *The New Republic* 110, No. 16 (17 April 1944): 537-38.
> Questions the validity of DeVoto's critical position—"as a spokesman for the disadvantaged against the too easily successful and for the hard-working scholars against the esthetes"—in light of his high standing in academic and editorial circles.

Flint, R. W. "Smear and Whitewash." *The Kenyon Review* VI, No. 4 (Autumn 1944): 669-72.
> Strongly worded negative review of *The Literary Fallacy,* describing DeVoto as a minor critic who has mistaken the purpose and value of art and suggesting that "there are perhaps personal frustrations involved" in DeVoto's censure of the writers of the 1920s.

Jones, Alfred Haworth. "The Persistence of the Progressive Mind: The Case of Bernard DeVoto." *American Studies* XII, No. 1 (Spring 1971): 37-48.
> Outlines the controversies that were instigated by *The Literary Fallacy.*

Kazin, Alfred. "By America Obsessed." *The Saturday Review* 2, No. 16, (3 May 1975): 24-5.
> Unfavorable assessment of DeVoto's career.

Lemons, William. "Bernard DeVoto and the West." *South Dakota Review* 21, No. 2 (Summer 1983): 64-112.
> Discusses "DeVoto's thirty-five years of paradoxical thinking, feeling, and writing about the frontier experience and the West" in his novels, histories, and "Easy Chair" columns.

Lewis, Sinclair. "Fools, Liars, and Mr. DeVoto: A Reply to *The Literary Fallacy.*" *The Saturday Review of Literature* XXVII, No. 16 (15 April 1944): 9-12.
> Strongly worded attack on *The Literary Fallacy* that occasionally ventures into personal attack on DeVoto.

Matthiessen, F. O. Review of *Mark Twain's America,* by Bernard DeVoto. *The Yale Review* XXII, No. 3 (March 1933): 605-07.
> Praises DeVoto's "vigorous knowledge" of the "shaping forces" of Twain's life, but notes that oversimplification and inaccurate depictions of much American history outside of DeVoto's realm of expertise—the western frontier—detract from the work.

Mizener, Arthur. Review of *The Literary Fallacy,* by Bernard DeVoto. *The Sewanee Review* LII, No. iv (October-December 1944): 597-600.
> Disparaging review dismissing *The Literary Fallacy* as a superficial treatment of American literature of the 1920s.

Nelson, Raymond. *Van Wyck Brooks: A Writer's Life,* pp. 138ff. New York: E. P. Dutton, 1981.
> Discusses DeVoto's attacks on Brooks's Twain scholarship and DeVoto's contention that Brooks had a pernicious influence on American literature of the 1920s.

Schlesinger, Arthur M. "Bernard DeVoto and Public Affairs." In his *The Politics of Hope,* pp. 155-82. Boston: Houghton Mifflin and Co., 1963.
> Favorable assessment of DeVoto's life and career by a friend.

Stegner, Wallace. "Benny DeVoto's America." In *The Papers of Bernard DeVoto,* by Bernard DeVoto, edited by Julius P. Barclay, pp. 7-28. Stanford, Calif.: Stanford University Press, 1960.
> Chronologically arranged biographical and critical sketch outlining the salient features of DeVoto's career.

————. *The Uneasy Chair: A Biography of Bernard DeVoto.* Garden City, N.Y.: Doubleday & Co., 1974, 464 p.
> Comprehensive biography exploring all facets of DeVoto's life and career. Stegner had access to unpublished DeVoto papers and established a close working relationship with DeVoto's widow during the book's composition.

————, ed. *Four Portraits and One Subject: Bernard DeVoto.* Boston: Houghton Mifflin, 1963, 206 p.
> Sketches and reminiscences of DeVoto as a writer and a friend by Stegner, Catherine Drinker Bowen, Edith R. Mirrielees, and Arthur M. Schlesinger, Jr., as well as bibliography of DeVoto's writings by Julius P. Barclay.

Williams, Stanley T. "Counterblast." *The Yale Review* XXXIII, No. 4 (June 1944): 747-49.
> Raises some mild objections to DeVoto's conclusions in his "lively, savage monograph" *The Literary Fallacy.*

W(illiam) H(enry) Hudson

1841-1922

(Also wrote under the pseudonym Henry Harford) Argentine-born English essayist, novelist, short story writer, and autobiographer.

Hudson was a field naturalist who wrote essays and fiction that expressed both scientific understanding and emotional appreciation of nature. His essays consist primarily of detailed observations of nature, at times including philosophical and mystical reflections on the relationship between human beings and the natural world. He is slightly less esteemed by critics as a fiction writer, for although his fiction contains scenes of great intensity and conveys a sense of the overwhelming power and beauty of nature, Hudson could seldom sustain plot or character in a full-length narrative. Nevertheless, his prose style was greatly admired by his literary peers, including such writers as Joseph Conrad, Ford Madox Ford, and Ezra Pound, and the passionate love of nature prominent in all of his works has won him a loyal readership.

Hudson was born on the pampas, a vast unsettled plain surrounding Buenos Aires, to immigrants from the United States. He received very little formal education and was left free to explore the lands around his parents' ranch and to associate with the local gauchos. From an early age he was fascinated by nature, especially birds, and through observation he became an expert in the local flora and fauna. When he was fourteen, Hudson was given a copy of Gilbert White's *Natural History and Antiquities of Selborne,* and this book strongly influenced his decision to pursue a career as a field naturalist. A year later, he was severely afflicted by rheumatic fever and was left with a permanently weakened heart; doctors said that he could die at any moment. He later wrote that living with a constant awareness of imminent death intensified his love of life and made him savor even more the simple beauty of nature.

Little is recorded about Hudson's early adulthood. He spent some time assisting his father with the work of the ranch, and he also wandered the countryside observing the wildlife and talking with people. In 1866, the director of the Natural History Museum in Buenos Aires helped Hudson receive a commission from the Smithsonian Institution to collect bird skins for scientific purposes. This assignment brought Hudson to the attention of Dr. P. L. Sclater of the Zoological Society of London, and they began to correspond about the birds of Argentina. Sclater published Hudson's letters in the Society's *Proceedings,* and Hudson was given the title Corresponding Member. Hudson's association with the Society undoubtedly influenced his decision, in 1874, to move to England.

Hudson had expected to support himself in England by writing about nature, but he discovered that without a formal scientific background, and without any expertise in English wildlife, his talents were in small demand. He lived in extreme poverty, often finding himself with nowhere to sleep but a park bench. In 1880 he met Morley Roberts, his future biographer, who gave Hudson the mental stimulus that he had been lacking and who introduced him to English literary society. He also encouraged Hudson to contribute essays to popular literary journals, exposing his work to a wider audience. During this time

Hudson wrote his first novel, *The Purple Land That England Lost,* which was unfavorably received upon its publication in 1885. He achieved his first popular and critical success seven years later with the essay collection *The Naturalist in La Plata,* establishing himself both as a naturalist and as an author. Hudson traveled widely in rural England and made close observations of English wildlife, which he described in *Birds in a Village* and subsequent books. In 1900 he became a naturalized British citizen, and the following year friends secured for him a small pension that left him free to travel and write. In 1904 he published what was to become his most famous novel, *Green Mansions,* and even though few copies were sold at the time, his style was admired by some of the most prominent literary figures of the period. During the next two decades Hudson continued publishing fiction and nature studies. In 1915 he became ill with bronchitis and during his convalescence wrote a book about his childhood, *Far Away and Long Ago.* He finally achieved financial success with an American edition of *Green Mansions,* published in 1916, and the popularity of this novel prompted a demand for Hudson's other works. He continued to write until his death in 1922.

The most widely appreciated feature of Hudson's work has been his prose style. He has been called a poet in prose, with many critics maintaining that the elegant simplicity of his style gives the impression of being effortless. Joseph Conrad, for example, said that "you may try forever to learn how Hudson got his effects and you will never know. He writes down his words as the good God makes the green grass to grow, and that is all you will ever find to say about it if you try forever." However, Hudson's apparently simple style is now known to be the result of meticulous revision and rewriting.

Hudson's nature essays convey his passionate love of nature and demonstrate his intimate knowledge of wildlife. Intellectually, he was influenced by Charles Darwin and Herbert Spencer, but he disagreed with their attempts to explain nature in terms of scientific theories with no regard for the beauty of nature. Instead, he advocated an approach to nature that combined both intellectual and spiritual understanding. Pound called Hudson a "priest of nature," and Edward Garnett wrote that Hudson acknowledged the "mysterious force of being" that scientific writers denied. Hudson idealized nature, and although his descriptions are accurate, they are characterized by a tone of admiration and wonder. Leonard Woolf noted that this tone contrasted with the bitterness and misanthropy evident in Hudson's letters and concluded that Hudson felt an attraction for only those things that he could cover with a cloud of romance: nature and his childhood in Argentina. Hudson recounted his childhood experiences in his autobiography, *Far Away and Long Ago*. Critics compare this work to William Wordsworth's poem *The Prelude* (1799-1805) in that both describe a growing appreciation of nature and both portray early childhood as a time of purity and innocence, a condition that allows the child to view nature as benevolent. Hudson's last book, *A Hind in Richmond Park*, which sums up his life as a field naturalist and as a writer, compares the sensory experience of animals to that of humans and includes discussions of music, poetry, and art. Hudson believed that art was a manifestation of creative energy deriving from an innate sense of beauty. As such, it was not restricted to human endeavors, but was akin to natural phenomena such as the singing, dancing, color, and plumage of birds. He also believed that the beauty of art could not surpass the beauty of nature, and he therefore felt that the greatest aesthetic experience was not the production or appreciation of art, but the direct perception of the beauty of nature.

Hudson's fiction similarly stresses the power and beauty of nature. *The Purple Land* recounts the adventures of Englishman Richard Lamb in Uruguay and his gradual conversion to the morality of the natives of the Banda Oriental (Uruguay). Many critics have found fault with the loose, almost picaresque, structure of the novel. However, Hudson's depictions of gauchos are praised as vivid and accurate, as are his descriptions of the Uruguayan wilderness and the revolutionary fervor of nineteenth-century Uruguay. Hudson's next novel, *A Crystal Age*, depicts an English time traveler who finds himself unable to adapt to a futuristic utopian society whose members live in intimate harmony with nature. The relationship between humans and nature is further explored in Hudson's most popular novel, *Green Mansions*, which many critics consider to be his finest. The novel tells the tragic story of Abel, an explorer who falls in love with Rima, a fantastic being who is half bird, half human. Hudson creates the illusion of reality by narrating his story in the first person and by elaborately detailing scenes and characters. He uses imagery from nature to describe Rima, a technique that underscores her affinity to nature. Critics view Rima more as an embodiment of passion than as a woman, and consider Abel's love for her a symbol of human yearning for perfect love and beauty. Rima's death is a vision of the

encroachment of humans on the world of nature: the result is the destruction of what is most beautiful in the world.

Hudson witnessed the beginning of the settlement of the wild Pampas and the resulting extinction of ever-increasing numbers of animal species. The beauty of nature was being destroyed and would never return: this is a leading motif in Hudson's writing and a major preoccupation of his life. He tried to preserve what was most precious to him by stimulating in others the love of nature that he keenly felt, writing of his own experience of nature which, as H. J. Massingham wrote, "unified the precise and speculative habit of the field naturalist with poetic sensibility, a passion for the many-colored pageant of life, and a melancholy-mystical apprehension of its fantasy."

(See also *Contemporary Authors*, Vol. 115 and *Something about the Author*, Vol. 35.)

PRINCIPAL WORKS

The Purple Land That England Lost   (novel)   1885; also published as *The Purple Land*, 1904
A Crystal Age   (novel)   1887
Argentine Ornithology. 2 vols. [with P. L. Sclater] (essays)   1888-89; also published as *Birds of La Plata* [abridged edition], 1920
Fan [as Henry Harford]   (novel)   1892
The Naturalist in La Plata   (essays)   1892
Birds in a Village   (essays)   1893; also published as *Birds in Town and Village* [enlarged edition], 1919
Idle Days in Patagonia   (essays)   1893
Nature in Downland   (essays)   1900
Birds and Man   (essays)   1901
El Ombú   (short stories)   1902; also published as *South American Sketches*, 1909, and as *Tales of the Pampas*, 1916
Hampshire Days   (essays)   1903
Green Mansions   (novel)   1904
A Little Boy Lost   (novel)   1905
The Land's End   (essays)   1908
Afoot in England   (essays)   1909
A Shepherd's Life   (essays)   1910
Far Away and Long Ago   (autobiography)   1918; revised edition, 1931
Dead Man's Plack and an Old Thorn   (short stories)   1920
A Traveller in Little Things   (essays)   1921
A Hind in Richmond Park   (essays)   1922
Collected Works. 24 vols.   (novels, short stories, and essays)   1922-23
153 Letters   (letters)   1923; also published as *Letters to Garnett*, 1925

THE SPECTATOR   (essay date 1893)

[*In the following excerpt, the critic reviews* Idle Days in Patagonia.]

Mr. Hudson is already well known as the author of a delightful volume entitled *The Naturalist in La Plata*, and on the ornithology of South America he may be regarded as an authority. Not only has he observed much, but he has the art of describing what he sees in a singularly attractive style,—a gift not always bestowed upon men of science. It is interesting to meet with an author who has an unfeigned passion for the subject upon which he writes, and when the reader discovers that this enthusiasm is based upon experience, it will claim his respect even where it fails to awaken his sympathy. Mr. Hudson's days in Patagonia [described in *Idle Days in Patagonia*] would have no charm for a Sybarite, but neither the ordinary nor the extraordinary annoyance of travel appear greatly to trouble him; and when the steamer stuck fast in the sand and he waded on shore with some companions, many miles from their destination, he relates that he felt the sense of relief and exhilaration "which one experiences in a vast solitude, where man has perhaps never been, and has, at any rate, left no trace of his existence." The heat was great, and there was not a tree on those level plains to shelter the travellers from the sun; they were without water and without food, and the ravenous mosquitoes gave them no rest. After twelve hours' walking the travellers were still far from their wished-for bourne. At night, Mr. Hudson's comrades supped on armadilloes, but his thirst was so great that he was afraid to eat. Before daybreak, they were on the road again, and although the stars were still shining, a little bird broke out into a song marvellously sweet and clear:—"The song was repeated at short intervals, and by-and-by it was taken up by other voices, until from every bush came such soft delicious strains that I was glad of all I had gone through in my long walk, since it had enabled me to hear this exquisite melody of the desert." Not daring to rest, the travellers trudged doggedly on for six hours before they were rewarded by a sight of the Rio Negro, and "never river" says Mr. Hudson, "seemed fairer to look upon; broader than the Thames at Westminster, and extending away on either hand until it melted and was lost in the blue horizon, its low shores clothed in all the glory of groves and fruit-orchards, and vine-yards, and fields of ripening maize."

It is not, however, on the fruitful banks of the Negro that the traveller discovers the characteristics of Patagonian scenery. They are to be seen in the boundless expanse of its plains, without water, without trees, without hills,—plains uninhabited and uninhabitable except by a few nomads. And yet, if the experience of Darwin and Mr. Hudson may be trusted, there is in this lonely level an inexpressible charm. The voyager of the *Beagle* attributes this charm to imagination; the later traveller thinks it is owing to our primitive nature. In the Patagonian solitude, he avers, a man escapes from the repression of civilised life, his higher faculties are suspended, "he is in perfect harmony with Nature, and is nearly on a level mentally with the wild animals he preys on." The dream of living as a noble savage allures the author's fancy, but Mr. Hudson carried his culture with him to the wilderness, and probably had to thank that culture for all the pleasure which it yielded. If he had not been a naturalist, we may safely say that he would have found but slight charms in Patagonia; but the days of his solitude were spent in a close observation of every natural object; and so universal was his taste that, on discovering a venomous serpent, which had taken shelter under his cloak during the night, he rejoiced to think "that the secret, deadly creature, after lying all night with me, warming its chilly blood with my warmth, went back unbruised to its den." (pp. 177-78)

Some chapters in this work, reprinted from periodicals, appear to have been inserted in order to add to its bulk. Interesting and suggestive though they be, their place in a volume on Patagonia is not very apparent. (p. 178)

"A Naturalist in Patagonia," in The Spectator, *Vol. 71, No. 3397, August 5, 1893, pp. 177-78.*

EDWARD GARNETT (essay date 1903)

[*A prominent editor for several London publishing houses, Garnett discovered or greatly influenced the work of many important English writers, including Joseph Conrad, John Galsworthy, and D. H. Lawrence. He also published several volumes of criticism, which are characterized by thorough research and sound critical judgment. In the following excerpt from an essay originally published in 1903, he stresses the artistic and spiritual vision that informs Hudson's observations of nature.*]

[We] prize those original minds among us whose talents are, as it were, new variations of our ordinary mental vision, talents which carry us some little way beyond the over-worked channels of our busy human interests, and make us penetrate into that vast archipelago of nature's life where man's being and doing appear as merely one sort of phenomena, as the human speck in the universal ocean of life. W. H. Hudson has one of these creative minds, and he is the chief writer on nature's life, today, whose spiritual vision is inspired by some elusive strain of Merlin's fabled power.

At first sight all the great secrets of the future would seem to belong to the scientific students, to the calm, "passionless" observers equipped with the ever-increasing marvellous instruments that Science places daily in their hands, but at first sight only. Admitting that the discoveries of the great captains of Science, and the observations of the vast band of humble workers, have immeasurably increased our knowledge of nature's laws and indeed revolutionized our conceptions of the formation and evolution of the material universe, it is obvious that the scientists themselves cannot escape the great law of the specialization of functions, and that their angle of vision, no matter how adjusted or to what ends directed, can never serve them as a magical glass harmonizing and uniting all the manifold human visions in general. The scientific view has in fact its strictly defined sphere of applications, and has little power to enter into, for example, the fields of vision of seers, such as the poets, the musicians, the painters, the philosophers, or the great religious teachers. Indeed, in recognizing the triumph of Science in explaining the working of vast ranges of nature's laws, we cannot help seeing that our whole human understanding of life has not come to us through any "scientific method" of observation, and that the "scientific method" can only be used as the auxiliary tool of our instinctive perceptions. For example, the great scientist when he wishes to comprehend his wife's feelings about him does not employ a scientific method to determine them! So we are justified in turning round on the scientific men, and saying to them: "What you tell us is of extraordinary light-giving value, but you will be the first to admit that your demonstrations of fact can never synthesize the most important fact of all? You tell us countless facts about the laws of life, but the actual spirit of life, its living feeling, which is the essential volatile principle of life, can never be fully assessed by you." "Quite so," the scientific men will rejoin; "we don't pretend to be able to analyse feeling, except in some of its physiological causes and psychological effects, and therefore our descriptive studies nearly always leave it on one side as an indeterminable force."

Now the surprising characteristic of Mr. Hudson's writings is that this mysterious force of feeling, ever present in nature's life, which modern scientific writers agree to leave out, Mr. Hudson puts in. "Ah! but he puts his own human feelings into his descriptions, and that is unscientific," the reader may exclaim. Wait a little. Himself a scientific student he has an instinctively poetic and artistic method of his own in examining living nature, a method which interprets for us "the facts" of the trained observers, and synthesizes for us the living creature's *spirit*—a method which is indispensable to any spiritual comprehension of nature. Our knowledge of the workings of the human mind and of human life that the great creative artists, from Homer to Shakespeare, have brought to us may be "unscientific" in this sense, that it is not demonstrable of proof, but it is none the less knowledge. The key that has unlocked the gates of the vast regions of spiritual life is our mysterious instinctive *feeling* about life. (pp. 17-20)

We cannot actually comprehend nature's life without being emotionally affected by it, *i.e.,* our comprehension *is* largely the emotion it excites in us. So face to face with nature's wild life "scientific observation" must be supplemented and inspired by artistic and poetic methods of divination. To comprehend sentient life we must employ all the old emotional tools of the human mind, all those shades of æsthetic sensibility and of human imagination by which the great artists and poets seize and apprehend the *character* of life. The scientists are in their element in investigating the working of physical laws, in determining the properties or the functions of living organisms, but a knowledge of these laws no more qualifies them to apprehend the character, nature, or spirit of the life of nature's wild creatures under the open sky than a perfect knowledge of anatomy can make a man a Praxiteles.

And wild nature's life being a natural drama of instinct, an unceasing play of hunger, love, battle, courtship, fear, parental emotion, vanity, and most of all, perhaps, pure enjoyment of physical powers, it is obvious that every man who is irresponsive in his feelings, or possessed of a dull artistic imagination, or weak æsthetic sensibilities, must remain practically aloof from wild nature, and its infinite feast of characteristic displays. He will not see or feel what is going on in forest and meadow, and so, remaining blind to the whole force and spirit of nature, he will not be able to pronounce on its *life*. (pp. 23-4)

Now Mr. Hudson's method face to face with nature, this curious mingling of scientific curiosity to know all about her, with artistic susceptibility to her charms, derives its inner inspiration from what is essentially a poet's spiritual passion to lose himself in contemplation of her infinitely marvellous universe. Though it is indeed largely by the gleams and flashes of light arising from the poets' communion with nature that man's spiritual sense of the great Universe flowing around him has best found its expression, the poets in general (some of the great poets excepted) have only tentatively explored the vast archipelago of nature's life that exists for itself outside man's world of thought, though it exists indeed in invisible relations with it. It is Mr. Hudson's distinction, however, to have sought and followed these mysterious realms of nature's life, not as a scientific specialist, as a botanist, or zoologist, studying natural laws of structure, habit, or environment, but in the same spirit of creative enjoyment with which the great poets examine and search human life, *i.e.,* with a sense not only of what this life's *character* is as life, but of what all this absorbing drama of nature's eternal fecundity signifies spiritually to man. Any adequate treatment of Mr. Hudson's writings would therefore have to analyse the extreme originality with which he enlarges both the poets' and the scientists' horizons, at one and the same time, by showing the poets new worlds to conquer, and by showing the scientists that their methods, though indispensable, do not carry us far enough. We cannot pursue this analysis in detail here beyond saying that Mr. Hudson's work as an ornithologist has been to cut away, as it were,

whole sections of dead and petrified lore, from our shelves, and replace them by a series of the most delicate living studies of the character, habits, and genius of bird-life. Nor have we space to dwell here on what we chose to call, a little arbitrarily, his artistic feats of delineation, by which he has drawn away with a magician's hand the heavy veils of misunderstanding with which our dull ordinary brains, scientific or otherwise, cloak the actual life led, with the rich zest of instinct, by the great non-human populations of squirrels, jays, weasels, hornets, moths, spiders, adders, stag-beetles, shrew-mice, crickets, dragon-flies, moles, snails, and the thousands of other little creatures to whom nature has given the earth no less than to us. The two books, **Hampshire Days** and **Nature in Downland**, contain, as it were, *la vie intime* ["the intimate life"] of all these independent tribes of creatures, and chronicle their wars, their loves, their hates, their prejudices, and the countless agitations of their days, with all the insight, grace, whimsical humour, and delicious freshness that the true artists employ in fashioning our human chronicles. (pp. 26-8)

The secret fascination of Mr. Hudson's outlook, the real force of his spiritual vision arises from his *refusal to divide man's life off from nature's life*. Civilized man as he exists today, in his present stage of mental development, may be defined as nature's unruly independent child, who, having thrown off the instinctive stage of babyhood, thinks, because he has learnt to stand alone, and feed himself, that his reason is greater than his mother's wisdom. All nature's realm is now for *his* interests, all her creatures are to serve *his* purposes, for use and food, all exist for him to spoil, slay, maim, extirpate—just as he pleases. This brutal callousness to the value and beauty of life other than his own (and he does not scruple to hunt out of existence the inferior races of man) is in fact an inherited instinct of those days—not long back, and indeed hardly past yet—of stern necessity, when every hour was a struggle for bare existence. Nature herself has implanted in man, as in all her creatures, this imperious instinct for conquest, nature herself who in all ranks of creation is full of intestine wars, with her great law of the strong species preying on the weak. But man having gained the mastery over all other of earth's creatures, man having gained the supreme dictatorship by the superior force and subtlety of his mind, will never be able to supplant nature's laws, and put himself to reign in his mother's stead. On the contrary, as the struggle for bare subsistence becomes less and less intense, he rises higher and higher, by understanding her laws, by studying and admiring her miracles. And as his mind develops, Earth's teeming fecundity of living things, each gloriously fashioned and framed, becomes less and less a mere arena with man entering as their bodily conqueror, to spoil and slay. The great law of conquest is applied more and more to mental spheres, where man, by his creative intelligence, can contemplate nature's life as the supreme, inexhaustible spectacle; and in losing himself in contemplation of the external ocean of the Universe flowing round him, man enters into nature, and becomes one with her more absolutely than in his earlier stage of preying on and slaughtering all other of her creatures.

Now the force and fascination of Mr. Hudson's vision of Life, as we have said, is that he reveals to us more than any modern writer man's true spiritual relation to the vast world of created sentient things in earth and sky, that free life of wild nature whose beauty cannot yet content our souls, but we must harass, mutilate, and exterminate them, or scientifically catalogue and "collect." Everybody must have felt at some time or other in his heart stir a vague faint feeling of love or struggling pity for some poor "brute beast," or captive bird fluttering at its cage's bars. And it is by the force of this mysterious love, by the intensity of the feeling with which he enters spiritually into communion with wild nature's life, that in Mr. Hudson's wrathful pleading against man's shortsighted brutality we hear the voices of hundreds of thousands of people scattered throughout the earth who, like him, also love and rejoice in the wild creatures' life. He is their spokesman. And so it is that it is not surprising that Mr. Hudson, who, flinging off the soiled dust of our human thoroughfares, and going into nature's wilderness to escape the sight of the "pale civilized faces," with the mean round of petty human interests of their "artificial indoor lives," it is not surprising that Mr. Hudson, who has written the finest invective ever penned against the yearly carnival of bird-slaughter, is the same man who has given us one of the tenderest and deepest and saddest stories of human life that our readers can name. It is not surprising either that in his nature books, taken together, there are hundreds of passages in which man's life is presented to us as a beautiful thing when seen *as a part of nature*, with all its strong ties, visible and invisible, to the earth that sustains and nurtures him, and to the firmament in which he draws his breath. Even as Mr. Hudson refuses to believe that the birds of the air can be in truth "scientifically" studied by shutting them up in boxes, or by dissecting them in class-rooms, or by stuffing their dead bodies, and arranging them on museum shelves, and holds that if you wish to comprehend what the lark's life *is* you must go into the fields and hear his ecstatic song of the sun, the driving winds, and the rustling grass; so does he take no pleasure in seeing man in that predominant aspect which the modern world conspires to place him in—the aspect of a stuffy town animal, leading an unnaturally artificial gaslight existence. Man of course can be examined truthfully from a thousand angles of vision. You can, for example, study the labourer simply as he appears in the tap-room, and you can study him at his work in the fields. The finer, however, is the writer's field of vision the more does his picture of life suggest not merely the visible limitations of its immediate phase, but its permanent relations with the great background of human life, into which it is continually being dissolved, and out of which it is continually emerging reshaped. It has been reserved for "modern thought," temporarily intoxicated by its hasty draught of "scientific discoveries," to fail (where no age has ever failed before) to lay stress on man's spiritual dependence on the world of nature round him. The great minds, the great poets, philosophers, and religious teachers of all ages, from Homer to Virgil, from Shakespeare to Turgenev, from the Hebrew prophets to Buddha, have never shared in this materialistic trick of human vision, of seeing man out of perspective. Now owing to Science's materialistic discoveries obscuring our field of spiritual vision, nearly every writer today is, as it were, trying to see nature's life, *without* the medium of human emotion, and *in vacuo*, as it were. It is Mr. Hudson's distinction to have shown by his superior penetration into wild nature's life that though the material gain to Physical Science of studying nature *in vacuo* may be great, the supreme inexhaustible field that lies before man lies outside the narrow province of pure reason, lies outside his utilitarian interests, lies in his own spiritual absorption in the vast drama of nature's myriad activities. Man, in short, Mr. Hudson shows us, can only enter into the vast world of her myriad sentient life by employing all the old emotional tools—his sense of mystery, love of beauty, poetic imagination, and human love—to supplement and vivify the "impassive" truths of Science. So shall he develop his innate Merlin power of sympathetic *feeling*, and comprehend better

and better that mysterious essence or spirit of life which is itself inseparable from feeling. Thus man may slowly become one in thought with nature, and more and more shall he comprehend the beauty of the eternal ocean of life flowing around him. (pp. 30-5)

*Edward Garnett, "W. H. Hudson's 'Nature Books',"
in his* Friday Nights: Literary Criticisms and Appreciations, first series, *Alfred A. Knopf, 1922, pp. 15-35.*

JOSEPH CONRAD (essay date 1904)

[*Conrad is considered an innovator of novel structure as well as one of the finest stylists of modern English literature. In his preface to* The Nigger of the "Narcissus" *(1897), an essay that has been called his artistic credo, Conrad explained that "art itself may be defined as a single-minded attempt to render the highest kind of justice to the visible universe, by bringing to light the truth, manifold and one, underlying its every aspect. It is an attempt to find in its forms, in its colours, in its light, in its shadows, in the aspects of matter, and in the facts of life what of each is fundamental, what is enduring and essential—their one illuminating and convincing quality—the very truth of their existence.... My task which I am trying to achieve is, by the power of the written word, to make you feel—it is, before all, to make you see." In the following excerpt from an essay written in 1904, he notes the "pure love of the external beauty of things" that is evident in* Green Mansions.]

I have been reading two books in English which have attracted a good deal of intelligent attention, but neither seems to have been considered as attentively as they might have been from this point of view. The one, *The Island Pharisees,* by Mr. John Galsworthy, is a very good example of the national novel: the other, *Green Mansions,* by Mr. W. H. Hudson, is a proof that love, the pure love of rendering the external aspects of things, can exist side by side with the national novel in English letters. (pp. 133-34)

The innermost heart of *Green Mansions,* which are the forests of Mr. Hudson's book, is tender, is tranquil, is steeped in that pure love of the external beauty of things that seems to breathe upon us from the pages of Turgeniev's work. The charming quietness of the style soothes the hard irritation of our daily life in the presence of a fine and sincere, of a deep and pellucid personality. If the other book's gift is lyric, *Green Mansions* comes to us with the tone of the elegy. There are the voices of the birds, the shadows of the forest leaves, the Indians gliding through them armed with their blowpipes, the monkeys peering sadly from above, the very spiders! The birds search for insects; spiders hunt their prey.

> Now as I sat looking down on the leaves and the small dancing shadow, scarcely thinking of what I was looking at, I noticed a small spider with a flat body and short legs creep cautiously out on the upper surface of a small leaf. Its pale red colour, barred with velvet black, first drew my attention to it; for it was beautiful to the eye....

"It was beautiful to the eye," so it drew the attention of Mr. Hudson's hero. In that phrase dwells the very soul of the book whose voice is soothing like a soft voice speaking steadily amongst the vivid changes of a dream. (pp. 136-37)

Joseph Conrad, "A Glance at Two Books," in his
Last Essays, *Doubleday, Page & Company, 1926, pp. 132-37.*

JOHN GALSWORTHY (essay date 1915)

[Galsworthy was an English novelist who is best remembered today for a series of novels known collectively as The Forsyte Saga *(1906-22). In the books of* The Forsyte Saga, *he employed a Victorian setting to explore the theme of the evil that can be brought about by ungovernable greed. In the following excerpt from his foreword to the 1916 edition of* Green Mansions, *he extols Hudson's vision of natural beauty and human life as an antidote to the maladies of industrial civilization.]*

I take up pen for this foreword with the fear of one who knows that he cannot do justice to his subject, and the trembling of one who would not, for a good deal, set down words unpleasing to the eye of him who wrote *Green Mansions, The Purple Land,* and all those other books which have meant so much to me. For of all living authors—now that Tolstoi has gone—I could least dispense with W. H. Hudson. Why do I love his writing so? I think because he is, of living writers that I read, the rarest spirit, and has the clearest gift of conveying to me the nature of that spirit. Writers are to their readers little new worlds to be explored; and each traveller in the realms of literature must needs have a favourite hunting ground, which, in his good-will—or perhaps merely in his egoism—he would wish others to share with him.

The great and abiding misfortunes of most of us writers are twofold: We are, as worlds, rather common tramping ground for our readers, rather tame territory; and as guides and dragomans thereto we are too superficial, lacking clear intimacy of expression; in fact,—like guide or dragoman—we cannot let folk into the real secrets, or show them the spirit, of the land.

Now Hudson, whether in a pure romance like this *Green Mansions,* or in that romantic piece of realism *The Purple Land,* or in books like *Idle Days in Patagonia, Afoot in England, The Land's End, Adventures among Birds, A Shepherd's Life,* and all his other nomadic records of communings with men, birds, beasts, and Nature, has a supreme gift of disclosing not only the thing he sees but the spirit of his vision. Without apparent effort he takes you with him into a rare, free, natural world, and always you are refreshed, stimulated, enlarged by going there.

He is, of course, a distinguished naturalist, probably the most acute, broad-minded and understanding observer of nature living. And this, in an age of specialism, which loves to put men into pigeon-holes and label them, has been a misfortune to the reading public, who seeing the label Naturalist, pass on and take down the nearest novel. Hudson has indeed the gifts and knowledge of a naturalist, but that is a mere fraction of his value and interest. A really great writer such as this is no more to be circumscribed by a single word than America by the part of it called New York. The expert knowledge which Hudson has of Nature gives to all his work backbone and surety of fibre, and to his sense of beauty an intimate actuality. But his real eminence and extraordinary attraction lie in his spirit and philosophy. We feel from his writings that he is nearer to Nature than other men, and yet more truly civilised. The competitive, towny culture, the queer up-to-date commercial knowingness with which we are so busy coating ourselves, simply will not stick to him. A passage in his *Hampshire Days* describes him better than I can:

> The blue sky, the brown soil beneath, the grass, the trees, the animals, the wind, and rain, and stars are never strange to me; for I am in and of and am one with them; and my flesh and the soil are one, and

the heat in my blood and in the sunshine are one, and the winds and the tempests and my passions are one. I feel the "strangeness" only with regard to my fellow men, especially in towns, where they exist in conditions unnatural to me, but congenial to them. . . . In such moments we sometimes feel a kinship with, and are strangely drawn to, the dead, who were not as these; the long, long dead, the men who knew not life in towns, and felt no strangeness in sun and wind and rain.

This unspoiled unity with Nature pervades all his writings; they are remote from the fret and dust and pettiness of town life; they are large, direct, free. It is not quite simplicity, for the mind of this writer is subtle and fastidious, sensitive to each motion of natural and human life; but his sensitiveness is somehow different from, almost inimical to, that of us others, who sit indoors and dip our pens in shades of feeling. Hudson's fancy is akin to the flight of the birds that are his special loves—it never seems to have entered a house, but since birth to have been roaming the air, in rain and sun, or visiting the trees and the grass. I not only disbelieve utterly, but intensely dislike, the doctrine of metempsychosis, which, if I understand it aright, seems the negation of the creative impulse, an apotheosis of staleness—nothing quite new in the world, never anything quite new—not even the soul of a baby; and so I am not prepared to entertain the whim that a bird was one of his remote incarnations; still, in sweep of wing, quickness of eye, and natural sweet strength of song he is not unlike a super-bird—which is a horrid image.

And that reminds me: This, after all, is a foreword to *Green Mansions*—the romance of the bird-girl Rima—a story actual yet fantastic, which immortalises, I think, as passionate a love of all beautiful things as ever was in the heart of man. Somewhere Hudson says: "The sense of the beautiful is God's best gift to the human soul." So it is; and to pass that gift on to others, in such measure, as herein is expressed, must surely have been happiness to him who wrote *Green Mansions.* In form and spirit the book is unique, a simple romantic narrative transmuted by sheer glow of beauty into a prose poem. Without ever departing from its quality of a tale, it symbolises the yearning of the human soul for the attainment of perfect love and beauty in this life—that impossible perfection which we must all learn to see fall from its high tree and be consumed in the flames, as was Rima the bird-girl, but whose fine white ashes we gather that they may be mingled at last with our own, when we too have been refined by the fire of death's resignation. The book is soaked through and through with a strange beauty. I will not go on singing its praises, or trying to make it understood, because I have other words to say of its author.

Do we realise how far our town life and culture have got away from things that really matter; how instead of making civilisation our handmaid to freedom we have set her heel on our necks, and under it bite dust all the time? Hudson, whether he knows it or not, is now the chief standard-bearer of another faith. Thus he spake in *The Purple Land:* "Ah, yes, we are all vainly seeking after happiness in the wrong way. It was with us once and ours, but we despised it, for it was only the old common happiness which Nature gives to all her children, and we went way from it in search of another grander kind of happiness which some dreamer—Bacon or another—assured us we should find. We had only to conquer Nature, find out her secrets, make her our obedient slave, then the earth would be Eden, and every man Adam and every woman Eve. We are still marching bravely on, conquering Nature, but how weary and sad we are getting! The old joy in life and gaiety of heart have vanished, though we do sometimes pause for a few moments in our long forced march to watch the labours of some pale mechanician, seeking after perpetual motion, and indulge in a little, dry, cackling laugh at his expense.'' And again: ''For here the religion that languishes in crowded cities, or steals shamefaced to hide itself in dim churches, flourishes greatly, filling the soul with a solemn joy. Face to face with Nature on the vast hills at eventide, who does not feel himself near to the Unseen?''

> Out of his heart God shall not pass,
> His image stamped is on every grass.

All Hudson's books breathe this spirit of revolt against our new enslavement by towns and machinery, and are true oases in an age so dreadfully resigned to the ''pale mechanician.''

But Hudson is not, as Tolstoi was, a conscious prophet; his spirit is freer, more willful, whimsical—almost perverse—and far more steeped in love of beauty. If you called him a prophet he would stamp his foot at you—as he will at me if he reads these words; but his voice is prophetic, for all that, crying in a wilderness, out of which, at the call, will spring up roses here and there, and the sweet-smelling grass. I would that every man, woman, and child in England were made to read him; and I would that America would take him to heart. He is a tonic, a deep refreshing drink, with a strange and wonderful flavour; he is a mine of new interests, and ways of thought instinctively right. As a simple narrator he is well-nigh unsurpassed; as a stylist he has few, if any, living equals. And in all his work there is an indefinable freedom from any thought of after-benefit—even from the desire that we should read him. He puts down what he sees and feels, out of sheer love of the thing seen, and the emotion felt; the smell of the lamp has not touched a single page that he ever wrote. That alone is a marvel to us who know that to write well, even to write clearly, is a woundy business, long to learn, hard to learn, and no gift of the angels. Style should not obtrude between a writer and his reader; it should be servant, not master. To use words so true and simple that they oppose no obstacle to the flow of thought and feeling from mind to mind, and yet by juxtaposition of word-sounds set up in the recipient continuing emotion or gratification—this is the essence of style; and Hudson's writing has pre-eminently this double quality. From almost any page of his books an example might be taken. . . . He seems to touch every string with fresh and un-inked fingers; and the secret of his power lies, I suspect, in the fact that his words ''Life being more than all else to me. . .'' are so utterly true.

I do not descant on his love for simple folk and simple things, his championship of the weak, and the revolt against the cagings and cruelties of life, whether to men or birds or beasts, that springs out of him as if against his will; because, having spoken of him as one with a vital philosophy or faith, I would not draw red herrings across the main trail of his worth to the world. His work is a vision of natural beauty and of human life as it might be, quickened and sweetened by the sun and the wind and the rain, and by fellowship with all the other forms of life—the truest vision now being given to us, who are more in want of it than any generation has ever been. A very great writer, and—to my thinking—the most valuable our age possesses. (pp. 147-58)

> *John Galsworthy, ''Foreword to 'Green Mansions','' in* Castles in Spain and Other Screeds, *Charles Scribner's Sons, 1927, pp. 145-58.*

THEODORE ROOSEVELT　(essay date 1916)

[*Roosevelt was the twenty-sixth president of the United States as well as a great conservationist and outdoorsman. In the following essay, written as an introduction to the 1916 edition of* The Purple Land, *he lauds Hudson's portrayal of gaucho life and the wilderness of the pampas.*]

It is well worth while to bring out a special edition of ***The Purple Land.*** I wish that the edition could be extended to include *El Ombú*; and also those delightful books, *Idle Days in Patagonia* and *The Naturalist in La Plata,* wherein the birds and small beasts of Argentina are brought before the reader so that ever afterwards he knows them as he knows the familiar living things of Old World song and story. On the whole *El Ombú* is the most noteworthy of all these books, for it gives the very soul of the land; and nowadays the soul is changing as rapidly as the land itself.

Hudson's work is of great and permanent value. He combines the priceless gift of seeing with the priceless gift of so vividly setting forth what he has seen that others likewise may see it. He is one of a very limited number of people—which include Knight, the author of the *Cruise of the Falcon,* and Cunninghame Graham—who have been able not only to appreciate the wild picturesqueness of the old time South American life, but to portray it as it should be portrayed. His writings come in that very small class of books which deserve the title of literature. To cultivated men who love life in the open, and possess a taste for the adventurous and the picturesque, they stand in a place by themselves. Herman Melville did for the South Sea whaling folk, and Ruxton did for the old time Rocky Mountain trappers, much what Hudson has done for the gaucho. He brings before us the wild rider of the pampas as Gogol brings before us the wild rider of the steppes. In addition he portrays the life of bird and beast as in more quiet lands they have been portrayed by White of Selborne and John Burroughs. The men, the horses, the cattle, the birds of the vast seas of grass, all are familiar to him. We see the rough work of the horsemen, and their rough play; the long, low, white house of the great ranch owner, solitary under the solitary ombu tree; and the squalid huts where the mounted laborers live and the squalid drinking booths where they revel. We see also the Indians standing erect on the bare backs of their horses to look across the waving plumes of the tall grass clumps; and we listen to the tremendous choral night-chant of huge bustard-like water fowl, whose kind is unknown in any Northern land. He tells of the fierce and bloody lawlessness of revolutionary strife. Above all, he puts before us the splendor and the vast loneliness of the country where this fervid life is led. (pp. ix-x)

> *Theodore Roosevelt, ''An Introductory Note,'' in* The Purple Land: Being the Narrative of One Richard Lamb's Adventures in the Banda Oriental, in South America, as Told by Himself, *by W. H. Hudson, E. P. Dutton and Company, 1916, pp. ix-x.*

ARTHUR COLTON　(essay date 1917)

[*Colton was an American novelist and poet. In the following excerpt, he attributes Hudson's genius not to his writing style, but to his extraordinary capacity of perception.*]

The chapter which especially caught my attention in the *Idle Days in Patagonia,* as it probably has that of most readers of the book, was the thirteenth. It appeared that the idler, riding in the gray monotonous waste, found himself each day falling into a singular mental state, and remaining there until his return at nightfall to the river and the habitations of man. He concluded afterward that it must have been the mental state of the pure savage or quasi-animal, a case of atavism and return to an ancient prime, induced by the hypnotism of the desert. His ''mind had suddenly transformed itself into a machine for some other unknown purpose. To think was like setting in motion a noisy engine in my brain. . . . My state was one of suspense and intense watchfulness—the state seemed familiar rather than strange, and accompanied by a strong feeling of elation. . . . A revelation of an unfamiliar nature, hidden under the nature we are conscious of, can only be attributed to a reversion to primitive and wholly savage mental conditions.'' Every day, as soon as he entered the desert, he fell back into this condition of habit and instinct, blank of reason, empty of idea, the higher faculties suspended, the senses strangely alert, the general feeling one of ''intense watchfulness.'' Every noon he came without knowing why to the same bunch of trees and rested there.

The fascination of Mr. Hudson's writings asks for some explanation. There is no glitter and brilliancy about them. He moves habitually at a footpace. The nervous intellectual virility of Thoreau, the grace of Mr. Burroughs, the mellow humor and vast knowledge, carried so simply, of Henri Fabre,—none of these are characteristics here. The first explanation that arises is the occasional occurrence of such passages as the above. There is one towards the end of the twenty-eighth chapter of **The Purple Land,** on the theme that liberty is better than good order. It is not a prose style of any distinction, but it is significant thinking. I do not understand Mr. Galsworthy's saying ''as a stylist, Mr. Hudson has few if any living equals'' [see excerpt dated 1915]. As ''style,'' if the thing can be separated, it does not seem to me an adequate style. The ''styles'' of Ruskin and Chateaubriand, of Thoreau and Izaak Walton, are adequate to the temperament behind, but the ''style'' of Mr. Hudson, like that of Richard Jefferies, seems relatively ordinary, sometimes even fumbling and crude, inadequate to a temperament behind, which is somehow extraordinary, subtle in a sense, almost mystic.

Passages and chapters, however, do not explain Mr. Hudson. There is a fundamental unity about him, an essential and peculiar quality which is everywhere, but which the half dozen volumes on English country life, the work of later years, bring out more clearly than do the South American books—*A Shepherd's Life* is one of those volumes. It is full of descriptions of Wiltshire downs and lonely villages, anecdotes of dogs, life stories of shepherds, women, and families, given not because there was any particular point in them, but because they interested him, and were so. His gaze on nature and man is a slow ruminating gaze, a primitive wilderness kind of gaze, motionless, intense, inclusive, undistracted, and long. The village of Winterbourne Bishop and the life of Caleb Bawcombe, are mirrored in minute and patient chronicle. He watches them as he watches a bird in the grass. Any ornithologist, who can sit motionless and long, with his eyes and mind fixed on a single object, has trained himself to a habit and capacity that belongs to primitive hunters and animals that lie in wait. But with Mr. Hudson the characteristic has given to his writings their main peculiarity. William James noted it as ''a love of pure sensorial perception,'' but it is also a capacity for the practice of that kind of perception, and of conveying into a book a sense of that long watchful gaze, that crystal receptivity. This faculty is the phenomenon which, intensified by the hypnotism of the Patagonian desert, seemed to Mr. Hudson a ''reversion.'' But this ''suspense and intense watchfulness,'' this ''pure perception,'' and the love of it for the sense of

elation that it gives, appear to have been habitual and characteristic to a degree comparatively extraordinary. Is not this the real secret of the power which one feels to be somehow there and at first is at a loss to explain, which some commentators have attempted to explain by attributing qualities that do not appear to be there? (pp. 856-58)

A Crystal Age is a Utopian romance of a world organized by houses, something like beehives, each with a queen bee at the centre. Mr. Hudson remarks in his Preface of thirty years after that ''it is colored by the little cults and crazes and modes of thought of the 'eighties; I have not stood still while the world has been moving''; but that, if he were to compose another such dream, though the habit and form of the book would be different, it would still be a dream in the same spirit.

The Purple Land is only perfunctorily a novel. Its values differ from those of the *Idle Days in Patagonia* in that it deals less with nature and more with men, with the men and women of revolutionary Uruguay. As a picture of those men and women, of that place and time, for vividness and truth, I suppose it is unique; and I suggest again that the uniqueness here, as in all Mr. Hudson's books, has for the most part the same source, that the characteristic or faculty which made possible his extraordinary experience in Patagonia, is the same characteristic or faculty which gives his books their extraordinary fascination. (p. 858)

Arthur Colton, ''The Quality of W. H. Hudson,'' in The Yale Review, *Vol. VI, No. 4, July, 1917, pp. 856-58.*

EZRA POUND (essay date 1920)

[*Pound, an American poet and critic, is regarded as one of the most innovative and influential figures in twentieth-century Anglo-American poetry. He was instrumental in obtaining editorial and financial assistance for T. S. Eliot, Wyndham Lewis, James Joyce, and William Carlos Williams, among other poets. His own* Cantos, *published throughout his life, is among the most ambitious poetic cycles of the century, and his series of satirical poems* Hugh Selwyn Mauberly *(1920) is ranked with Eliot's* The Waste Land *(1922) as a significant attack upon the decadence of modern culture. Pound considered the United States a cultural wasteland, and for that reason, he spent most of his life in Europe. In the following excerpt, he argues that Hudson's appreciation of sensory perception and of beauty runs contrary to the degradation of man and the destruction of nature that is characteristic of modern society.*]

Hudson's art begins where any man's art is felicitous in beginning: in an enthusiasm for his subject matter. If we begin with **The Naturalist in La Plata** we may find almost no ''art'' whatever; there are impassioned passages, naive literary homages, and much unevenness, and a trace of rhetoric in the writing. **The Shepherd's Life** must, at the other end of the scale, be art of a very high order; how otherwise would one come completely under the spell of a chapter with no more startling subject matter than the cat at a rural station of an undistinguished British provincial railway.

Hudson is an excellent example of Coleridge's theorem ''the miracle that can be wrought'' simply by one man's feeling something more keenly, or knowing it more intimately than it has been, before, known.

The poet's eye and comprehension are evident in the first pages of **The Naturalist:** the living effigies in bronze rising out of the white sea of the pampas. (p. 13)

One may put aside quibbles of precedence, whatever the value of evidence of man's fineness, and in an age of pestilence like our own there is little but the great art of the past to convince one that the human species deserves to continue; there can be no quarrel between the archæologist who wishes to hear the "music of the lost dynasty," or the gracious tunes of the Albigeoius, and the man who is so filled with a passion of the splendour of wild things, of wild birds which:

> Like immortal flowers have drifted down to us on
> the ocean of time . . . and their strangeness and beauty
> bring to our imaginations a dream and a picture of
> that unknown world, immeasurably far removed,
> where man was not; and when they perish, something
> of gladness goes out from nature, and the sunshine
> loses something of its brightness.

The voice is authentic. It is the priesthood of nature. Yet if an anthropologist may speak out of his pages to the "naturalist," it is not only the bird and furred beast that suffer. A bloated usury, a cowardly and snivelling politics, a disgusting financial system, the saddistic curse of Christianity work together, not only that an hundred species of wild fowl and beast shall give way before the advance of industry, i.e., that the plains be covered with uniform and verminous sheep, bleating in perfect social monotony; but in our alleged "society" the same tendencies and the same urge that the bright plumed and the fine voiced species of the genus anthropos, the favoured of the gods, the only part of humanity worth saving, is attacked. The milkable human cows, the shearable human sheep are invited by the exploiters, and all other regarded as caput lupinum, dangerous: lest the truth *should* shine out in art, which ceases to be art and degenerates into religion and cant and superstition as soon as it has tax-gathering priests; lest works comparable to the Cretan vases and Assyrian lions *should* be reproduced and superseded.

There is no quarrel between the artist and Mr. Hudson, and he is right in saying that there would be more "wail" over the destruction of the British Museum than over the destruction of wild species. Yet how little the "public" cares for either. And how can it be expected to care so long as so much of it is "at starvation level," so long as men are taught that work is a virtue rather than enjoyment, and so long as men render lip service to a foul institution which has perpetuated the writing of Tertullien and of men who taught that the human body is evil.

As long as "Christendom" is permeated with the superstition that the human body is tainted and that the senses are not noble avenues of "illumination," where is the basis of a glory in the colour-sense without which the birds-wings are unapprehended, or of audition without which the bell-cry of the crested screamers is only a noise in the desert.

"Their strangeness and their beauty" may well go unheeded into desuetude if there be nothing to preserve them but usurers and the slaves of usury and an alleged religion which has taught the supreme lie that the splendour of the world is not a true splendour, that it is not the garment of the gods; and which has glorified the vilest of human imaginations, the pit of the seven great stenches, and which still teaches the existence of this hell as a verity for the sake of scaring little children and stupid women and of collecting dues and maintaining its prestige.

My anger has perhaps carried me away from Hudson who should have been my subject; yet his anger is germane to it. Mediæval Christianity had one merit, it taught that usury was an evil. But in our day Rockefeller and the churches eat from the one manger, and the church has so far fallen into vacuity that it does not oppose "finance," which is nothing but a concatenation of usuries, hardly subtle, but subtle enough to gull the sheep and cow humans.

And for the same system man is degraded, and the wild beasts destroyed. So I have perhaps not lost my subject after all, but only extended my author's exordium.

The foregoing paragraphs can hardly be taken as introduction to Mr. Hudson's quiet charm. He would lead us to South America; despite the gnats and mosquitoes we would all perform the voyage for the sake of meeting a puma, Chimbicá, friend of man, the most loyal of wildcats. And, as I am writing this presumably for an audience, more or less familiar with my predilections, familiar with my loathing of sheep, my continual search for signs of intelligence in the human race, it should be some indication of Hudson's style that it has carried even me through a volume entitled *A Shepherd's Life,* a title which has no metaphorical bearing, but deals literally with the subject indicated. (pp. 14-16)

John B. Yeats has written somewhere: "I found that I was interested in the talk, not of those who told me interesting things, so much as of those who were by natural gift truthful tellers"; a phrase which is as good a qualification of Hudson's work as I can find. Hudson's books are indeed full of interesting things, of interesting "information," yet it is all information which could, like all information whatsoever, have been made dull in the telling. But the charm is in Hudson's sobriety. I doubt if, apart from the *Mayor of Casterbridge,* and *The Noble Dames,* and the best of Hardy, there is anything so true to the English countryside as Hudson's picture. F. M. Hueffer must not be forgotten; there is his *Heart of the Country,* and passages in other of his books to maintain the level; and Hueffer is perhaps at his best when he approaches most closely to Hudson's subject matter; when he is least clever, when he is most sober in his recording of country life.

This is not however an arranging of hierarchies and an awarding of medals for merit. Hudson touches Hueffer when dealing with England and Cunninghame Graham in dealing with La Plata. And it is very foolish to wail over the decadence of English letters merely because some of the best work of these three men is possibly ten years old.

It is perhaps faddism and habit that causes people still to gossip of Poe, when *El Ombú* has been written, not as a grotesque but as tragic elegy, as the ordered telling of life as it must have happened. And then Poe's prose? Poe's prose is as good as Hudson's in places, and Hudson is indubitably uneven; relieved if not by *hokkus* at least by the sense of the "special moment" which makes the hokku: thus his trees like images of trees in black stone.

This image-sense is an enrichment, perhaps "dangerous" to the unity of his style, but very welcome to the lover of revelation. And to balance it there is the latent and never absent humour as in **"Marta Riquelme."**

"What is, is; and if you talk until to-morrow you can not make it different, although you may prove yourself a very learned person." (p. 17)

*Ezra Pound, "Hudson: Poet Strayed into Science,"
in* The Little Review, *Vol. VII, No. 1, May-June,
1920, pp. 13-17.*

JAMES V. FLETCHER   (essay date 1933)

[*In the following excerpt, Fletcher studies Hudson's worldview in terms of his misanthropy and Wordsworthian romanticism.*]

W. H. Hudson was a sworn enemy of the literary humanism of his age. This may invite protests from those who know him only through *Green Mansions, The Purple Land,* and *Far Away and Long Ago,* for the true color of his faith can be seen in those books only by the reader who comes to them sensitized by a knowledge of the passion that is more openly displayed in his less known works. Yet, though Hudson's antipathy to contemporary humanism is unmistakable, those of his literary comrades who have toasted him so royally have been charmed by the magic of his style out of all desire to criticize his heterodoxy. Had his eulogists fixed their attention on his anti-humanistic creed rather than on his style, he might not today hold his high place of honor among modern English writers.

Hudson dedicated his life, not to writing South American romances, but to a knightly defense of Dame Nature against the hostile spirit of a humanitarian and scientific age. To aid him in this losing battle he borrowed both the creed of the nature worshippers of the early nineteenth century and Meredith's melioristic faith in the principle of evolution. The result is a crazy-quilt of ideas in which the pantheistic mysticism of Wordsworth, the Rousselian doctrine of natural education, the romantic conception of the noble savage, and the Meredithian glorification of the struggle for existence are all pieced together. The patchwork is somewhat unified, however, by the central block about which it is built, for all of Hudson's ideas were mothered by his one ruling passion—an unreasoning love for wild life and a corresponding conviction that nature could do no wrong.

He went back directly to the romantics to borrow the ritual which they used in their worship of the green goddess; but he was content to take only their naturistic ideas, leaving them their humanistic idealism. By making Nature the absolute center of his thoughts and attentions, and by letting his fellow men and their "petty interests" succeed as best they could, he far eclipsed his precursors as a lover. Zealous as the romantics were in their worship of Nature, they did after all regard her as mediate. What they desired most of her was that she should take them by the hand and lead them into the high places of human happiness, Hudson's love was far more disinterested. "To sit by her, and have her hand to hold," and to remain there in adoration for a long lifetime was as much of the highest good as he desired. In order to express his passion, he gleaned all of the handsome compliments to Nature that two generations of poets had produced. To the romantic enthusiasm for scenery and the noble natural man Hudson married the Victorian apotheosis of evolution and the commensalism of all life which Meredith before him had made a subject for art. His system is the legitimate and fascinating child of that union even though to many modern spirits it may seem a monstrous birth. (pp. 24-5)

In spite of his poor heart Hudson seemed to have the gift of eternal youth. His intense eagerness for living and for observing nature never slackened. His finest book, *Far Away and Long Ago,* was written at the age of seventy-five. His unbounded appetite for life—he believed that a million years would scarcely suffice him—probably derived much of its intensity from the knowledge that life might be snatched away at any moment. The melancholy undertone of his writings, ill-suited to the fundamental optimism of his thinking, was the product of his reluctant admission of the fact of death. That was a law of nature that not even he could call good. His sorrow in the presence of death is the subject of some of the most exquisite passages in his books, of which **"The Return of the Chiffchaff"** in *A Traveller in Little Things,* is perhaps the finest. His boyhood joy in nature was continually interrupted by feelings of intolerable sadness at the thought of death. It was always this thought, whether concerned with the loss of friends or of animals, that brought the discords in. His solution of this conflict was to spend his precious little of existence in the observation of all forms of life, and in the worship of the great mother of life. This compensatory attempt perhaps helped to drive him to his extreme nature-centric attitude.

In Jung's classification of psychological types Hudson would be categorized as the extraverted sensation-feeling type. The sensuous apprehension of external nature represented to him the fulness of living, and he reënforced this basic attitude with all the drive of a tremendous libido. To lose his own identity in the pluralistic wonder of landscape was his greatest joy. This attitude is in contrast with the adjustment of such an introverted nature poet as Shelley, for instance, who tried to find an absolute unity in nature such as he found in his inner experience. Schiller would have called Hudson the naive, and Shelley the sentimental, poet. Had Hudson not been maimed by his youthful sickness, he would perhaps never have gone into literature for a livelihood, for it is in the active life of the world that such a temperament usually finds its satisfaction. His aversion to intellectual idealism and scientific abstractions is clearly traceable to his temperamental bias toward sense experience. The same predilection made it easy for him to set certain animals above the human level of excellence for the keen sense perceptions which they manifest. His mysticism too, one feels, is not the necessary and intimate experience of Blake, but a spasmodic and aberrant manifestation of the recessive thinking and intuitive functions. In the remainder of this discussion, the reader will notice many freakish turns of Hudson's thinking which mark his inability to let reason be his guide. Sensations and feelings were invariably the materials of which his best writing was made, and the passages prompted by reflective thought are unexceptionally his worst work. To what extent the psychological explanation should supplant an historical explanation of Hudson's thought is difficult to determine. It is certainly clear that neither one nor the other alone is sufficient. In discussing the historical influences, therefore, it will be well to remember the temperament that selected only those ideas in its intellectual heritage which conformed to its genius.

Hudson's naturalism is not completely romantic. The scientific thinking habits of the very age he condemned made him loth to read transcendental meaning into nature; and the same current brought him to a primary interest in animals where the romantics had been interested above all in scenery. But the blood and tissue of Hudson's doctrine is romantic. No exposition of his thought which disregards that element can hope to explain anything. All of his other ideas are offshoots from that root. The spirit of wonder is the guiding star, and the ghost of Wordsworth stands at the helm.

It is to Wordsworth that we must go to find a kindred spirit for Hudson. Wordsworth found a chaos of ideas concerning nature at a time when the world needed a new deity. Out of that chaos he formed a pantheistic god, and gave to his English contemporaries a new ethical creed. To speak of the romantic nature tradition is virtually to speak of the Wordsworth tradition, inasmuch as he stood at the center of the movement and crystallized the guiding doctrines of the cult.

Nature is right. That faith, nurtured by a century of belief in the perfection of the Newtonian world-machine, and first enunciated with full vigor by Rousseau, was wrought into great English art by Wordsworth. Hudson, writing at a distance of a hundred years, accepted the creed as a foregone conclusion. Nature was to him infallibly good, and he accepted without a murmur Wordsworth's dictum that "Nature never did betray the heart that loved her." This implicit trust lay at the very heart of his thinking, and most of his songs of praise are variations of this theme. The main theme is apparent enough to the most casual reader of Hudson. To find him following the lead of the masters in some of its variations is more surprising.

For the proper worship of their goddess all true romantics require solitude. Byron is perhaps the most striking example of the romantic refugee from the "busy hum of cities," seeking salvation in the waste places of nature untouched by man. But in a less obvious way the same impulse was the inspiration of Wordsworth's best poetry. He was a great individualist, not primarily a social thinker. His constant purpose was to search out the truth of the mystical relation between the individual perceiver and collective soul of nature. The most magical effects of his verse gain their charm from the shadowy moods of the inner life as it is influenced by the massive stillnesses of lonely scenes. He believed, with the other romantics, that Nature withholds her most blessed moods from populous cities and villages, and unveils her shining sacredness only to those who journey alone to her inmost shrine in the untrod places of the earth. Hudson, in keeping with the tradition, was also a lover of solitude, searching constantly for lonely landscapes "where a lover of solitude need have no fear of being intruded upon by one of his own species." Nothing in our literature captures "the breathing and the balm" of the earth's waste places so surely as the chapter in *Idle Days in Patagonia* entitled "The Plains of Patagonia." Elsewhere in the same book he confesses,

> To my mind there is nothing in life so delightful as
> that feeling of relief, of escape, and absolute freedom
> which one experiences in a vast solitude, where man
> has perhaps never been, and has, at any rate, left no
> trace of his existence.

Nothing could be further from the norm of contemporary literature which, with Whitman, says

> Keep your splendid silent sun, . . .
> Give me faces and streets.

Our literature is increasingly social, and Hudson's attitude is stridently discordant to the social ear.

Once alone with Nature, Hudson achieved the mystical consummation of his love in true Wordsworthian fashion. The glory and the dream of the mystical ecstasy came to him, as to Wordsworth, through the spiritualized sense-perception of natural beauty. The Wordsworthian mystic differs from others in this respect: instead of renouncing the flesh for the elation of the spirit, he exercises the senses to the limit of their powers until the natural world is transfused into spiritual substance. Hudson attained his raptures standing erect and drinking in natural beauty with open eyes. (pp. 25-9)

Hudson denied the validity of the abstract Victorian science as stubbornly as Wordsworth had revolted from the sterility of the age of reason, because it shut out wonder from the natural world and prized too highly the abstracted generalizations of its own analysis. And to Hudson and Wordsworth not only the

Postcard written by Hudson to Morley Roberts in 1918. From Idle Days in Patagonia, *by W.H. Hudson. J.M. Dent & Sons Ltd., 1923. By permission of the publisher.*

suffused and monistic spirituality of nature stood in danger of being murdered by dissection;—the individual spirits of nature's organic creatures were also threatened with death by analysis.

Pervading the experience of both Hudson and Wordsworth, giving rise to and augmenting this anti-intellectualistic strain in their thinking, was a kind of primitive animism that imbued their perceptions with a naive, sometimes playful, yet unshakable belief in the sentient nature of "mute, insensate things." It was Wordsworth's faith "that every flower enjoys the air it breathes." For him the daffodils, fluttering and dancing in the breeze, "out-did the sparkling waves in glee." Again,

> The Moon doth with delight
> Look round her when the heavens are bare.

His delight in nature came not from the æsthetic pleasure that characterizes the modern love of scenery, but largely from an underlying conviction that "there is a spirit in the woods." A similar atavistic belief prevails in Hudson's writings. He recognized, as Wordsworth apparently did not, that the belief in the spirits of things arises from the human tendency to project the self into nature, but this realization in no way disturbed his keen pleasure in the exercise of the faculty. Hudson, as well as Wordsworth, experienced the animistic emotion most powerfully in childhood. The chapter on "A Boy's Animism" in *Far Away and Long Ago* is the best description of his early experience. It is a counterpart of the first book of the *Prelude* in its expression of the haunting influence of natural objects on the boyish emotions. In the same chapter he expresses a liking for Wordsworth's animism, and a distaste for most eighteenth century literature because it lacks that emotion. He makes it plain that

> the survival of the sense of mystery, or of the super-
> natural, in nature, is to me in our poetic literature
> like that ingredient of a salad which "animates the
> whole."

Because such primitive feelings were so dear to them, Hudson and Wordsworth, with other adherents to the faith, looked with mistrust at strictly rational thinking and analytical science. They believed with Keats that "the mere touch of cold philosophy" would rob all natural charms of mystery. In *The Book of a Naturalist* Hudson inveighs against the false science that kills, dries, weighs, and catalogs a snake, thinking thus to describe it truly. The cold, glistening, fiery spirit of a snake was to him its real spiritual self, or, in Wordsworth's phrase, its "beauteous form." The attempt to preserve the organic integrity of objects is at least as old as Leibnitz and as recent as Whitehead. Indeed Whitehead in *Science and the Modern World* commends Wordsworth's attitude as a welcome reaction to the composition theory of reality current in eighteenth century thought. The abstracting habits of Victorian science were as inimical to the proper apprehension of reality as the eighteenth century theory, and Hudson's dogged refusal to dissect nature may be considered a contribution to modern realism, as well as evidence of his essential romanticism.

In general, the attempt of the romantic nature worshipper was to endow the landscape with the finest qualities of the human spirit, and in turn to make nature a measure of human goodness. In the age of Wordsworth and before, although there was a vital interest in animal life, the insensible elements of scenery provided the best base for philosophical reflection and the best background for arcadian idealizations of human life. After Lamarck and Darwin, however, literary interest in the lower animals increased, and found fullest poetic expression in Meredith. Animal life, rising as it does much closer to human life than rocks and stones and trees, provides a far more convincing interlinkage of nature and man than the romantic landscape. Hudson recognized this, and the realization gladdened him because it provided for the union of his two driving passions: his love for animals, and his utter faith in nature, romantically conceived. (pp. 29-31)

But this creed is, as Hudson realized, the expression of a high desire, not the statement of an accomplished fact. Since 1850 there have been few literary men who have steered their thinking course by nature, and during his writing life Hudson was virtually the only one of consequence in England. Acknowledging his isolation in the midst of what he caustically labeled "this enlightened, scientific, humanitarian age," Hudson took up the cudgels for his brotherhood of beasts and birds.

In two books particularly, *The Naturalist in La Plata* and *A Hind in Richmond Park,* he poured his fire hot on the flanks of the humanists. In almost every comparison he makes between man and the animals, man comes out second best. He admits, to be sure, the unquestionable mental superiority which man holds over the brutes. The human species specializes in brains, and holds its dominant position by virtue of that specialization. But to the extent that the animal man has eclipsed his brothers in mental capacity, they in turn have surpassed him in other respects. "But we, poor human creatures, the weaklings of the animal world, are surpassed in the same way in all physical powers and keenness of senses," thought Hudson, betraying his temperamental bias towards sensation and away from thinking. What is more, he, the creator of the exquisite Rima, had no doubt whatever that the lower animals excel the human being in "beauty of form and colouring, grace of motion, and in melody."

There is nothing startling or new about these ideas. It is only the strong feeling with which Hudson enunciates them that makes them significant. But, not content to give the animals qualities of strength, beauty, and sense that would place them on or above the human level, he went further, and found in them the attributes of love, artistic sensibility, and spirituality, which if not so highly developed as the same capacities in man, are made of the same stuff and force man to recognize his deep-founded kinship with the animals.

In *Adventures among Birds* Hudson professes a belief in love between animals. He mentions with scorn some "lordly minded person" who said that it is a misuse or an abuse of the word to describe as friendship the distinct preference for each other's company and the habitual consorting together of two individuals among the lower animals. (pp. 31-2)

He tried with equal zeal to show that artistic sensibility and the impulse toward creative expression are strong in the lower animals. This idea perennially fascinated him, and after devoting a chapter to the subject in the early *Naturalist in La Plata,* he returned to it again in the last chapter of *A Hind in Richmond Park* thirty years later. He scorned the Darwinian notion that mating songs and certain formal dances that appear during the mating season are mere devices of the male to secure the approval of the female bird. He believed that there is an over-plus of energy in the animals that finds expression in play, in songs, and in dances, which has nothing to do with their survivalistic activities. Art is the outcome, he thought, of a universal sense of beauty, and the natural desire of the animal to share the experienced beauty with others. This desire first finds expression, both in animals and man, in a cry that calls attention to something seen, and forms itself finally when the animal becomes a man, in words: "I see something beautiful and interesting—come and look at it!" Thus far could Hudson stray from the path of scientific method in the service of his darlings, the beasts and birds.

The same doctrinaire tendency prompted him to discover in the animals a capacity for spirituality. How easy it has been, thought Hudson, for men with their complex mental states to look down upon the other animals and mark their spiritual blindness. The roots of spirituality, he tells us, lie far lower than the lowest level of human consciousness. (p. 33)

"All that is in our minds is also in theirs." That, in brief, was Hudson's creed, the passionate belief that colored all his observations and drove him into a naturalistic bog.

His fervent prejudices prevented Hudson's success either as a naturalist or as a thinker. He said of himself that he was a better observer than a thinker. The fact is that he was neither, scientifically speaking. He was a poet of nature. He observed nature with an artist's eye for beauty of form and color and with a great human affection for personalities in all species, from the human down. His observation, in other words, was not impartially scientific and interested in the detailed workings of nature, but highly selective in the artistic sense. The dullest passages in his books are his attempts at original scientific investigation or speculation. His very language was ill adapted to abstract reasoning. It lost all its transparency and grace the moment he started to think. But once he returned to the lyric vein, the rippling cadences of his true style came obediently back to his command.

It was not for nothing that Hudson chose to write almost exclusively about birds. Birds are, beyond all comparison, the most romantic members of the animal kingdom, and make the best subjects for poets' songs. Of all animals they combine to the utmost the grace of movement and melody with splendour of form and coloring; and they combine in a unique way the qualities of freedom and beauty. Significantly enough, the romantic poets favored birds over other animals, apparently because they appealed most to their ideal of beautiful freedom. Hudson, our romantic, when describing a beloved or especially rare or beautiful bird, is Hudson at his singing best. These descriptions are not scientific notations, nor are they quaint or curious sketches in the Gilbert White or John Burroughs vein. They are close to Shelley in lyric intensity, with the added objectivity and self-free delight characteristic of Hudson's joy in nature. In no portion of his writing did Hudson ever forget his great love for birds. When trying to describe odd human beings he likened them to birds. When he wished for a concrete symbol of courage, or beauty, or freedom, birds provided the illustration. And of course, when he fashioned Rima, his dream woman, he endowed her with a bird-like voice and an ethereal grace and freedom of movement. Hudson's creation of Rima after a natural model was in keeping with his general practice of deducing human ideals from his broad, dogmatic conceptions of natural ethics. His system, so conceived, is unique in contemporary letters.

Hudson's effort to find a place for man in nature, though always subordinate to his worship of nature, continued through all of his writing life. His conception of the good life, as one would expect, was based, in some form or other, on a return to nature. His mind had been hospitable to such diverse systems of natural thought, however, that at different periods he held different views, and was never able to fuse them into a unified system. On his romantic side he dreamed of Arcadian peace and simplicity, of a time when human beings would forgo their vain strivings after scientific and artistic progress, and learn from nature the art of living. But Darwin and Meredith and Huxley had driven home the truth that peace means decay, that the improvement of life is bought only with ceaseless struggle. One view tempted him as much as the other, so finding a synthesis impossible, he shifted constantly from one to the other. Thus in *Idle Days in Patagonia* he extols the savage and his way of life as highly as in *Green Mansions* he condemns him and dotes on the peaceful child of nature; and *A Crystal Age*, an Arcadian utopia, was written despite Hudson's conviction that peace, as there presented, would mean retrogression.

Although both these notions were parts of one romantic attempt to discover a nature-man harmony, the longing for peace and concord was the definite Wordsworthian element in his ethics. Of the creatures that he believed to be perfectly adjusted to nature,—animals, savages, peasants, and children—the peasants and children belonged to the more idyllic side of his theory. Hudson created two great children of Nature, Rima and himself, in the pages of his two best books, *Green Mansions* and *Far Away and Long Ago.* Rima's most immediate ancestors are Wordsworth's Lucy, Shelley's Cythna, and Meredith's exquisite girl of *Love in the Valley.* Like her forebears she was conceived and reared in the midst of natural beauty to be the imaginary sweetheart of a nature-loving poet. Hudson never found in the flesh the kind of woman he could love because it was only a compound of bird and woman beauty that would satisfy him. His only alternative to no passion being imaginary passion, he created Rima. Like Lucy, Rima ''dwelt unknown'' in the heart of a virgin forest, where she and her lover might attain to a mystic union with nature. Somehow Nature had endowed her, in addition to ethereal beauty and an other-world voice, with a love for beauty and a moral sense fine enough to entrance a man of old-world culture. In a word, she was Hudson's conception of Nature's perfect child. But both she and Lucy, being the embodiments of an unattainable ideal, died just when Nature had completed her work. Few passages in either Hudson or Wordsworth approach their expressions of sorrow at the deaths of their created sweethearts.

Hudson believed himself to be a counterpart of Rima, her rightful mate, a male child of Nature. The portrait of himself as a boy and a youth given in *Far Away and Long Ago,* while it of course lacks the silken delicacy of his Rima, is in many ways quite as ideal as she. This is not to say that Hudson falsified the true picture of his early life; he was truthful just as Wordsworth was truthful in the *Prelude.* The ideality is owing, in both cases, to a careful selection of experiences that would illustrate most clearly the influence of nature on the growing boy. The number of pure romantic, and especially Wordsworthian, themes that appear in the book is surprising. The animistic sense of the supernatural in nature, presented in the chapter on ''A Boy's Animism,'' is similar to Wordsworth's emotion described in the first book of the *Prelude.* Hudson never outgrew, nor ever wished to outgrow, his boyish vision of nature presented there. As with Wordsworth, his boyish imagination seemed to him to be ''the foundation light of all his day.'' Having had only a modicum of formal education in his, to him ideal childhood, he championed the Rousselian doctrine of natural education. He could not but look with abhorrence upon the lives of city children, ''pressed into a mould or groove by schoolmasters and schools,'' preferring a young mind to be ''a forest wilding rather than a plant, one in ten thousand like it, grown under glass in a prepared soil, in a nursery.'' With the romantics again, he believed fervently in the goodness of childhood. The child, not yet weighted with the incidental baggage of existence, seemed to him to be most natural and free, to lie ''in Abraham's bosom all the year.'' Whenever he wrote about children, and especially in *A Traveller in Little Things,* he lavished on them the full measure of his immense tenderness.

Akin to his belief in Nature's benign influence on the child was his belief in the superiority of the life of the peasant over the life of the city-dweller. The life of a downland shepherd, Caleb Bawcombe, appealed to him most. Here was a life in which the springs of affection had not been dried up in a world of materialistic ideals, in which the machine age had not undermined the bodily tone and destroyed the healthy optimism of nature, and in which an artificial culture had not jaded the appetite for sheer living. Here, in short, was man with nature harmonized. But Hudson felt that such lives are rare as they are excellent, and that encroaching city life is increasing their rarity. Whenever he found some urban influence insinuating itself to change for the worse the lives of the simple country folk, he cried out with Wordsworth,

> Is then no nook of English ground secure
> From rash assault?

All this is romantic doctrine through and through. But into this warm green fabric of essential romanticism Hudson wove a pattern of crimson. He indulged in poetic dreams of the peaceful reconciliation of man and nature, but felt certain that the path of strife was the only way to virility and progress for the race. *Idle Days in Patagonia,* an early book, is dominated by the idea that the instinctive life of the savage, being closer to natural purpose, is superior to the life of civilized man. This passage sounds the keynote of the book.

> He [the savage] thinks little, reasons little, having a surer guide in his instinct; he is in perfect harmony with nature, and is nearly on a level, mentally, with the wild animals he preys on, and which in turn sometimes prey on him.

(pp. 34-7)

The message of this book is that the only real, practicable way of returning to nature is to accept her first law of life,—struggle. Hudson rationalized the struggle for existence in the same way that Meredith did before him, if indeed he did not actually get the notion from Meredith, who was one of his idols. Nature is right. Her basic principle is the law of strife. Therefore, to struggle is to achieve harmony with her. So far did this idea carry Hudson away from humanistic tradition that near the end of his life he expressed a distrust of all idealisms and actually welcomed the war because it seemed to him to show that the race was still virile, and because he believed it would act as a social purgative. (p. 38)

It cannot be too much emphasized that Hudson in his thinking held himself apart from human life. However much Morley Roberts [see Additional Bibliography] and Edward Garnett [see excerpt dated 1903] may declare Hudson's immense humanity, even they admit that he spent the greater share of his tenderness on Nature and her children of the wild. It was only towards human beings that he could act bitter and critical; animals were beyond reproach. (p. 39)

In his studies of English life he rarely sentimentalizes over human beings, with the exception of children or unusually naturalized peasants; but sentimentality is the rule for his descriptions of birds. In a way he never got beyond the second stage of Wordsworth's intellectual development, when to the earlier writer nature was "all in all." He never got into the main stream of the English humanistic tradition. He was a professed enemy of the arts and a disbeliever in the value of science. Not only was he an alien to his own age but to every other age in our literary history. But despite these treasons we honor Hudson. Why?

Our age is short on magic. The spirit of wonder has been until recently in disrepute. We found the daylight of science more revealing than the starlight of faith and credulity, and promptly illuminated all the shadowy corners, even in the arts where they were doing no harm. But we have repented our sins, and we are learning once again to have faith in the magic of romanticized art. We did not sin against human idealism as Hudson did, but neither did he sin against living beauty as we did. He fought a man's fight for the faith of the child in the wonder of the world, and in learning to wield his literary weapon he became one of the great prose masters of his generation. So deft is his poetic skill that sympathetic readers are all but persuaded to worship his mistress Nature; and the least friendly are compelled to admire her charms. (pp. 39-40)

> James V. Fletcher, "The Creator of Rima: W. H. Hudson, Belated Romantic," in The Sewanee Review, Vol. XLI, No. 1, January-March, 1933, pp. 24-40.

FORD MADOX FORD   (essay date 1937)

[*Ford was an English man of letters who played an important role in the development of twentieth-century realistic and modernist literature and art. In 1908, he founded the* English Review, *a periodical generally considered to be the finest literary journal of its day during Ford's brief tenure as editor. Much of the journal's renown was due to Ford's display of acute editorial perceptiveness in publishing works by such writers as Henry James, T. S. Eliot, H. G. Wells, Thomas Hardy, and Ezra Pound, in addition to his discovery of both D. H. Lawrence and Wyndham Lewis. Another contributor, Joseph Conrad, had earlier collaborated on two novels with Ford. Although these experimental works have received little critical attention, scholars recognize the significance of the collaboration in shaping impressionistic techniques that characterized later, highly regarded works by both authors. Many years after resigning the editorship of the* English*

Review, *Ford established the* Transatlantic Review, *to which James Joyce, Gertrude Stein, and Ernest Hemingway contributed. Among Ford's own writings,* The Good Soldier *(1915) and the tetralogy* Parade's End *(1924-28)—novels generally concerned with the social, political, and moral decline of Western civilization—are considered masterful examples of the modern psychological novel. In the following excerpt, Ford describes the admiration that he and his literary friends had for Hudson's style.*]

In the days when there were still gods—and that was indeed far away and long ago, for if you ran a thousand years with the speed of the victor of Atalanta you would never discover that vanished place or overtake those receding minutes—in those days, then, there was Hudson. (p. 38)

And there was no one—no writer—who did not acknowledge without question that this composed giant was the greatest living writer of English. It seemed to be implicit in every one of his long, slow movements. (p. 44)

He was, at any rate in England, a writer's writer. I never heard a lay person speak of Hudson in London, at least with any enthusiasm. I never heard a writer speak of him with anything but a reverence that was given to no other human being. For as a writer he was a magician. He used such simple means to give such gorgeous illusions. It was that that made him the great imaginative writer that he was. If you read his *Green Mansions* you feel sure that he had an extraordinary intimacy with the life of tropical forests and, indeed, once you had read it you couldn't, when you met him next, fail to believe that he was the child of some woodland deity. You could not rid yourself of the belief even when he snapped at you half contemptuously that he had never been in a forest in his life. That was probably a fact, for he said over and over again that, until he came to London at the age of forty, he had never been off the pampas except to go—but very rarely—to Buenos Aires. . . . And this because of a weakness, real or supposed, of a heart that nevertheless contrived to do its work until he was eighty. (pp. 44-5)

[It] was in the hinterland of Venezuela that the scene of *Green Mansions* was laid. But *Green Mansions* differs from Hudson's other masterpieces—*The Purple Land, El Ombú, Nature in Downland,* and *Far Away and Long Ago*—in that it is a projection of a passion. *The Purple Land* is Romance; it is Romance as it was never before and never again will be put into words. But, like *El Ombú*, its situations are got in by rendering redolences of the soil, of humanity and humanity's companion, the horse, and of man's plaything, woman. It is full of laughter and broad stories and the picaresque spirit and hot youth and reckless fugitive passions.

If I have heard one, I have heard twenty of Hudson's rivals, from Conrad to Maurice Hewlett, or from Galsworthy to the much-too-much-forgotten George Gissing, say that *The Purple Land* is the supreme—is the only—rendering of Romance in the English language; and if I have heard one I have heard twenty say that *Green Mansions* is Anglo-Saxondom's only rendering of hopeless, of aching passion. There was, therefore, as Hudson felt with his sure instinct, no need for localization; indeed, topographical exactitudes would have been the fifth wheel on a coach that was the story of a man's passion for a voice that sang in the green house of a tree's boughs . . . and nothing else. And his instinct for covering his tracks, for retaining a veil of secrecy over his past, was also a motive for setting his story in a wilderness of forest that had never been explored. And no doubt there were material reasons for the change of the locale because there is also no doubt and no reason for preserving secrecy as to the fact that Hudson had once, far away and long ago, nourished an intolerable passion for a being who had had a beautiful voice and sang from the gleaming shadows of the green mansion of an *ombu*. It had eaten into his life; it had made him take to expressing himself; it had driven him from the limitless plains of his manhood and youth to the sordid glooms and weeping gaslit streets of . . . Bayswater!

The Purple Land, on the other hand, was a projection rather of other people's reckless lives in a revolutionary South. He was obviously not old enough to have ridden with Bolivar, but in his boyhood all South America rang with fables of the exploits of the Liberator. And his anecdotes of that heroic theorist were so vivid that you actually saw him galloping a black horse into the smoke from the lines of the Royalists. You saw it yourself and, as not until long after his death was the date of his birth ever established, you thought him a hundred years of age. And it all added to the romantic Hudson legend of the frequenters of the Mont Blanc.

Actually Bolivar the Liberator was an inspiring theorist of liberty, rather than a hat-waving horseman—a thin, nervous, Spanish revolutionary of genius. And his personal ambition was so small that when by the middle eighteen-twenties he had liberated the whole of South America from the European yoke and was going on to the founding of the confederation of Latin America, he suddenly resigned his power. He was too sensitive to stand the possible accusation that he aimed at dictatorship. He was born in 1783—about the year when Hudson's paternal grandfather came to the State of Maine—and died in 1830, eleven years before Hudson was born. But such a man leaves after him such an aura of legends that it was no wonder that, brought up amongst peons and peasants who had all seen the Liberator in the flesh, Hudson should be able to convey to you the idea that he too had ridden with Bolivar and known the rollicking life of a heroic spurred-and-saddled pampas era.

And it was that faculty above all that made Hudson take his place with the great writers. He shared with Turgenev the quality that makes you unable to find our how he got his effects. Like Turgenev he was utterly undramatic in his methods, and his books have that same quality that have those of the author of *Fathers and Children*. When you read them you forget the lines and the print. It is as if a remotely smiling face looked up at you out of the page and told you things. And those things become part of your own experience. It is years and years since I first read *Nature in Downland*. Yet . . . the first words that I there read have become a part of my own life. They describe how, lying on the turf of the high sunlit downs above Lewes in Sussex, Hudson looked up into the perfect, limpid blue of the sky and saw, going to infinite distances one behind the other, the eye picking up one, then another beyond it, and another and another, until the whole sky was populated . . . little shining globes, like soap bubbles. They were thistledown floating in an almost windless heaven.

Now that is part of my life. I have never had the patience—the contemplative tranquillity—to lie looking up into the heavens. I have never in my life done it. Yet that is I, not Hudson, looking up into the heavens, the eye discovering more and more tiny, shining globes until the whole sky is filled with them, and those thistle-seed globes seem to be my globes.

For that is the quality of great art—and its use. It is you, not another, who at night with the stars shining have leaned over a Venice balcony and talked about patines of bright gold; you,

not anyone else, saw the parents of Bazarov realize that their wonderful son was dead. And you yourself heard the voice cry *"Eli, Eli, lamma sabacthani!"* ["My God, my God, why have you forsaken me!"] . . . because of the quality of the art with which those scenes were projected.

That quality Hudson had in a supreme degree. He made you see everything of which he wrote, and made you be present in every scene that he evolved, whether in Venezuela or on the Sussex Downs. And so the world became visible to you and you were a traveller. It is almost impossible to quote Hudson *in petto* ["in the heart"]. He builds up his atmospheres with such little, skilful touches that you are caught into his world before you are aware that you have even moved. But you can't, just because of that, get his atmospheres fully without all the little touches that go to make them up. The passage that follows I selected by a process akin to that of the *sortes Virgilianae* ["Virgilian lots"] of the ancients. I went in the dark to the shelf where my Hudsons are kept, took the book my hand first lighted on, and pushed my index finger into the leaves until it stopped on the passage I have written down here. It is from *Hampshire Days* and it is appropriate that it should be about his beloved birds. For Hudson watched birds with a passion that exceeded anything that he gave to any other beings . . . except to Rima of *Green Mansions*.

> The old coots would stand on the floating weeds and preen and preen their plumage by the hour. They were like mermaids for ever combing out their locks and had the clear stream for mirror. The dull-brown, white-breasted young coots, now fully grown, would meanwhile swim about picking up their own food. The moorhens were with them, preening and feeding, and one had its nest there. It was a very big and conspicuous nest, built up on a bunch of weeds, and formed, when the bird was on it, a pretty and curious object; for every day fresh, bright green sedge leaves were plucked and woven round it and on that high, bright green nest, as on a throne, the bird sat. . . . And when I went near the edge of the water. . . .

Don't you wish you knew what came next!. . . And don't you see the extraordinary skill with which the picture is built, and won't that picture be a permanent part of your mind's eye from now on? I don't suppose you would ever take the trouble to wade through rushes to the edge of clear water and stand for hours watching water birds in their domesticities. I know I never should, though I am never happy if I have not wild birds somewhere near me. But I have that picture and know now how water birds comport themselves when, like men after work sitting before their cottage doors, they take their ease in the twilight. And indeed, before I had half-finished transcribing that passage, I knew what was coming. I cannot have re-read *Hampshire Days* since just after it was republished in 1923, a year after Hudson's death. But when I had got as far as "and had the clear stream for mirror" I knew what was coming— the high mound of the moorhen's nest decked out with bright green leaves.

Conrad—who was an even more impassioned admirer of Hudson's talent than am even I—used to say: "You may try for ever to learn how Hudson got his effects and you will never know. He writes down his words as the good God makes the green grass to grow, and that is all you will ever find to say about it if you try for ever."

That is true. For the magic of Hudson's talent was his temperament, and how or why the good God gives a man his temperament is a secret that will be for ever hidden . . . unless we shall one day have all knowledge. It is easy to say that the picture is made for you when those words "and had the clear stream for mirror" are written. But why did Hudson select that exactly right image with which to get in his picture? His secrets were too well protected.

I once or twice went through his proofs for literals after he had gone through them himself and was not feeling well, when I had called to take him for a walk in the park. And you learned nothing from his corrections. He would substitute for the simple word *grew* the almost more simple word *were*. *When the hedges were green* for *when the hedges grew green*, not so much with the idea of avoiding alliteration as because there is an actual difference in the effect produced visually. You do not see hedges grow, but you do see that they are green. And I suppose these minute verbal alterations, meticulously attended to, did give his projected scenes their vividness. I fancy, too, that his first manuscript drafts may have been rather florid, as if he made in them a sort of shorthand of his thoughts immediately after seeing something that interested him. But I was never able to make out even a few words of his first drafts. From a whole scratched-out page you cannot discern a single whole phrase . . . *As to art my feeling is that* . . . and then three lines scratched out and two illegible; then the words *money value*, and, in the middle of the last paragraph on the page, *in August*, and three lines lower, *may develop*, which I know he afterwards changed into *may become*, because I saw it in the proofs of the article which he wrote for one of the heavier magazines. . . . And the curious thing is that I can hardly remember at all what the article was about, except that it contained on the side some reflections on the value of the arts to the public: yet I remember perfectly well his making that change—or rather seeing that he had made that change.

I am glad that the question of Hudson's attitude towards the Arts has come in thus almost accidentally, for most writers about Hudson—and Hudson gave them ground enough for the idea—have written that he cared nothing about the Arts as arts, but considered himself, as so many Anglo-Saxon writers do, a man of action before he was a writer. I am convinced that this is wrong. It was with him a sort of humility; he was, as it were, as astonished that the writers of the Mont Blanc should take him seriously as a writer as they were that he should notice anything as dingy as that poor imitation of a Paris *bistrôt* and its occupants. Because one's astonishment every time that he appeared there gave place in the end always to the feeling that he would surely never come there again. But if at the end of three or four hours' conversational labour one had convinced him that he was really a very great writer, he would express a sort of grim and sardonic satisfaction, wrinkling up his nose more than ever and from far above your head letting out humph-humphs and well-wells. And would then contentedly listen to a great deal of praise. (pp. 45-50)

Ford Madox Ford, "W. H. Hudson," in his Portraits from Life: Memories and Criticisms, *1937. Reprint by Greenwood Press, 1974, pp. 38-56.*

JORGE LUIS BORGES (essay date 1941)

[*An Argentine short story writer, poet, and essayist, Borges was one of the leading figures in twentieth-century literature. His writing is often used by critics to illustrate the modern view of literature as a highly sophisticated game. Justifying this interpretation of Borges's works are his admitted respect for stories that are artificial inventions of art rather than realistic representations of life, his use of philosophical conceptions as a means*

of achieving literary effects, and his frequent variations on the writings of other authors. Such characteristic stories as "The Aleph," "The Circular Ruins," and "Pierre Menard, Author of the Quixote" are demonstrations of the subjective, infinitely various, and ultimately indeterminate nature of life and literature. Accompanying the literary puzzles and the manipulations of variant models of reality, there is a somber, fatalistic quality in Borges's work which has led critics to locate his fictional universe in close proximity to the nightmarish world of Franz Kafka and the philosophical wasteland of Samuel Beckett. In his literary criticism, Borges is noted for his insight into the manner in which an author both represents and creates a reality with words, and the way in which those words are variously interpreted by readers. With his fiction and poetry, Borges's critical writing shares the perspective that literary creation of imaginary worlds and philosophical speculation on the world itself are parallel or identical activities. In the following excerpt from an essay first published in Spanish in 1941, he places The Purple Land *in the tradition of the picaresque adventure novel and praises the book as a superior example of gaucho literature.*]

This novel [*The Purple Land*], Hudson's first, is reducible to a formula so ancient that it can almost comprise the *Odyssey;* so fundamental that the name formula subtly defames and degrades it. The hero begins his wandering, and his adventures encounter him along the way. *The Golden Ass* and the fragments of the *Satyricon* belong to this nomadic, random genre, as do *Pickwick* and *Don Quixote, Kim* of Lahore and *Segundo Sombra* of Areco. I do not believe there is any justification for calling those books picaresque novels: first, because of the unfavorable connotation of the term; second, because of its local and temporal limitations (Spain, sixteenth and seventeenth centuries). Further, the genre is complex. Disorder, incoherence, and variety are not inaccessible, but they must be governed by a secret order, which is revealed by degrees, I have recalled several famous examples; perhaps all show obvious defects. (p. 141)

The most elementary of the sort of novels I am considering aim at a mere succession of adventures, mere variety: the seven voyages of Sinbad the Sailor are perhaps the best example, for the hero is just an underling, as impersonal and passive as the reader. In other novels (which are scarcely more complex) the function of the events is to reveal the hero's character, and even his absurdities and manias; that is the case in the first part of *Don Quixote.* In others (which correspond to a later stage) the movement is dual, reciprocal; the hero changes the circumstances, the circumstances change the hero's character. That is the case with the second part of the *Quixote,* with Mark Twain's *Huckleberry Finn,* with *The Purple Land.* The latter actually has two plots. The first, the visible one: the adventures of the young Englishman Richard Lamb in the Banda Oriental. The second, the intimate, invisible one: the assimilation of Lamb, his gradual conversion to a barbarous morality that reminds one of Rousseau a little and anticipates Nietzsche a little. His *Wanderjahre* ["years of travel"] are also *Lehrjahre* ["years of apprenticeship"]. Hudson was personally acquainted with the rigors of a semibarbarous, pastoral life; Rousseau and Nietzsche knew such a life only through the sedentary volumes of the *Histoire Générale des Voyages* and the Homeric epics. The foregoing statement does not mean that *The Purple Land* is flawless. It suffers from an obvious defect, which may logically be attributed to the hazards of improvisation: the vain and tedious complexity of certain adventures. I am thinking of the ones near the end of the book: they are so complicated that they weary the attention, but do not hold it. In those onerous chapters Hudson appears not to understand that the book is successive (almost as purely successive as the *Satyricon* or the

Buscón) and benumbs it with useless artifices. This is a common mistake; for example, Dickens tends toward similar prolixities in all his novels.

The Purple Land is perhaps unexcelled by any work of Gaucho literature. It would be deplorable if we let a certain topographical confusion and three or four errors or errata (*Camelones* for *Canelones, Aria* for *Arias, Gumesinda* for *Gumersinda*) conceal that truth from us. *The Purple Land* is essentially Creole, native to South America. The fact that the narrator is an Englishman justifies certain explanations and certain emphases required by his readers, which would be anomalous in a Gaucho accustomed to such things. In Number 31 of *Sur*, Ezequiel Martínez Estrada wrote:

> Never before has there been a poet, a painter, or an interpreter of things Argentine like Hudson, nor will there ever be again. Hernández is one part of the cosmorama of our life that Hudson sang, described, and explained. . . . The final pages of *The Purple Land* express the maximum philosophy and the supreme justification of America in the face of Western civilization and the refinements of culture.

As we see, Martínez Estrada did not hesitate to prefer Hudson's total output to the most notable of the canonical books of our Gaucho literature. Incomparably more vast is the scope of *The Purple Land*. The *Martín Fierro* (notwithstanding the canonization proposed by Lugones) is less the epic of our origins—in 1872!—than the autobiography of a cutthroat, adulterated by bravado and lamentation that seem to prophesy the tango. Ascasubi's work is more vivid, it has more joy, more passion, but those traits are fragmentary and secret in three incidental volumes of four hundred pages each. In spite of the variety of its dialogues, *Don Segundo Sombra* is marred by the propensity to exaggerate the most innocent tasks. No one is unaware that the narrator is a Gaucho; and therefore to indulge in the kind of dramatic hyperbole that converts the herding of bulls into an exploit of war is doubly unjustified. Güiraldes assumes an air of solemnity when he relates the everyday work of the country. Hudson (like Ascasubi, like Hernández, like Eduardo Gutiérrez) describes with complete naturalness events that may even be atrocious.

Someone will observe that in *The Purple Land* the Gaucho has only a lateral, secondary role. So much the better for the accuracy of the portrayal, we reply. The Gaucho is a taciturn man, the Gaucho does not know, or he scorns, the complex delights of memory and introspection. To depict him as autobiographical and effusive is to deform him.

Another of Hudson's adroit strokes is his treatment of geography. Born in the Province of Buenos Aires in the magic circle of the pampa, he nonetheless chooses to write about the purple land where the revolutionary horsemen used their first and last lances: the Banda Oriental. Gauchos from the Province of Buenos Aires are the rule in Argentine literature: the paradoxical reason for that is the existence of a large city, Buenos Aires, the point of origin of famous writers of Gaucho literature. If we look to history instead of to literature, we shall see that the glorification of the Gaucho has had but little influence on the destinies of their province, and none on the destinies of their country. The typical organism of Gaucho warfare, the revolutionary horseman, appears in Buenos Aires only sporadically. The authority falls to the city, to the leaders of the city. Only rarely does some individual—Hormiga Negra in legal documents, Martin Fierro in literature—attain, with the rebellion of a fugitive, a certain notoriety with the police.

As I have said, Hudson selects the Banda Oriental as the setting for his hero's escapades. That propitious choice permits him to enlist chance and the diversification of war to enrich Richard Lamb's destiny—and chance favors the opportunities for vagabond love. Macaulay, in the article about Bunyan, marveled that one man's imaginings would become, years later, the personal memories of many other men. Hudson's imaginings remain in the memory: British bullets that resound in the Paysandú night; the oblivious Gaucho who enjoys his smoke of strong tobacco before the battle; the girl who surrenders to a stranger on the secret shore of a river.

Improving the perfection of a phrase divulged by Boswell, Hudson says that many times in his life he undertook the study of metaphysics, but happiness always interrupted him. That sentence (one of the most memorable I have encountered in literature) is typical of the man and the book. In spite of the bloodshed and the separations, *The Purple Land* is one of the very few happy books in the world. (Another, which also is about America, also nearly paradisaic in tone, is Mark Twain's *Huckleberry Finn*.) I am not thinking of the chaotic debate between pessimists and optimists; I am not thinking of the doctrinal happiness the pathetic Whitman inexorably imposed on himself; I am thinking of the happy disposition of Richard Lamb, of the hospitality with which he welcomed every vicissitude of life, whether bitter or sweet. (pp. 142-45)

> Jorge Luis Borges, "About the Purple Land," in his Other Inquisitions: 1937-1952, *translated by Ruth L. C. Simms, University of Texas Press, 1964, pp. 141-45.*

ROBERT HAMILTON   (essay date 1946)

[*In the following excerpt, Hamilton explains why he considers* The Shepherd's Life *to be Hudson's most stylistically perfect work and describes Hudson's social views presented in the book.*]

A Shepherd's Life is Hudson's best known essay, and probably his best known book after *Green Mansions*. It is already regarded as a classic; and I can think of no other book of his that approaches it in sustained beauty and serenity. Although almost everything he wrote contains something of value, his work, like that of most great men, was uneven; but *A Shepherd's Life* stands apart in being of even quality throughout. It is not, perhaps, his greatest, but it is certainly his most perfect book—a flawless thing, unique, complete, and final. Its quietude never becomes dull, and though it lacks the emotional intensity and intellectual fecundity of some of the other works, it is pervaded by a glowing coolness that imparts to it the quality of an autumnal sunset. (p. 87)

The setting of *A Shepherd's Life* is a Wiltshire village called by Hudson "Winterbourne Bishop." He never disclosed the real name of the village, but gave Roberts a clue when he told him there was a Bustard House and a Bustard Down near by. Recently, however, there appeared in the correspondence columns of *The Times Literary Supplement* an interesting letter purporting to give, not only the name of the village, but also of the shepherd around whom the book is written—Caleb Bawcombe, as Hudson called him. (p. 88)

Much of the book is made up of stories told by Caleb Bawcombe relating to the history and occupations of his family and neighbours in the village and surrounding countryside. The incidents recorded are simple enough, and concern mainly the everyday work, loves, sorrows, and joys of the country people;

but they are transformed and transmuted within the crucible of Hudson's imagination. He does not invent anything: he takes what is already there and, in the mere act of taking, transforms it. More than any other book of his, *A Shepherd's Life* bears out the truth we considered earlier on in connection with Morgan's words on treatment. Superficially, it could be described as a faithful record of Wiltshire life, written with sympathy and charm. Such a description would be correct—and totally inadequate. It would tell us nothing of the art that turned each trivial narrative into a thing of beauty, and made of the whole a flawless unity.

The human note is predominant in *A Shepherd's Life,* which contains many fine examples of character drawing, some of the most memorable done with a few strokes of the pen. Hudson never strains after effect in describing human personality. Sometimes he does not describe directly at all and the personality emerges obliquely from a number of impersonal incidents. All the characters of this book live unforgettably for us—Caleb and his brothers and sisters, his father Isaac, Liddy, old Elijah Raven the "dictator" of the village, and, for me especially, Tommy Ierat who shepherded up to the age of seventy-eight. (p. 90)

Hudson is far less discursive than usual in this book: most of the stories and incidents radiate from the village and the shepherd. There are stories of the old people of the village and of their youth long ago, many of them dealing with poaching and deer-stealing. In those days the agricultural labourer was underpaid and underfed, and though he was, in the main, honest and steady in his work, he did not regard the taking of animal flesh for the needs of his family as theft. He risked much, for the penalties were heavy. Reading some of the stories of poverty and oppression recorded in *A Shepherd's Life* we are filled with admiration for the endurance of the countryman of the early and middle nineteenth century. Yet in spite of his sufferings he succeeded in living a full and happy life—as Caleb Bawcombe's words bear so eloquent a testimony:

> "I don't say that I want to have my life again, because 'twould be sinful. We must take what is sent. But if 'twas offered to me and I was told to choose my work, I'd say, Give me my Wiltsheer Downs again and let me to be a shepherd there all my life long."

Caleb's philosophy is Hudson's also; that is why, in writing of a shepherd's life, he brings such inspired conviction to the task. He, too, wanted nothing but to live always close to nature and to enjoy the simple things; hence he was able to enter imaginatively into the shepherd's mind and feel at one with him in his hardships and sufferings.

The power of the countryman to rise above the most terrible hardship proceeds from his faith and courage—for it is not hardship that makes for unhappiness, but a drying up of the human spirit. The simple faith of the villagers gave them hope, and the constant presence of nature stabilized and strengthened them. Nothing else could have enabled them to live down such experiences as Hudson relates—the political struggles and riots in the early days of mechanization, and the cruel sentences of unfeeling judges who deported numberless men for life, never to see their loved ones again. In these pages Hudson comes nearer to the expression of a sociological attitude than anywhere else in his work. We have seen that he was, broadly speaking, a conservative; but his fundamental sociological attitude was more akin to what is called distributism; and the ideal that emerges from this book, older than any political system and to some extent entering into them all, is the ideal of well-distributed property and of small ownership, with its protest against monopoly in any form, capitalist or socialist. In the nineteenth century the countryman was everywhere attacked by machinery, the law, and the State, and much of *A Shepherd's Life* is a melancholy record of the encroachment of these forces and a protest against them. The protest is all the more effective because cast in aesthetic form; for where the abstract political treatise fails, a "human story," told with sympathy by a man of genius, will succeed.

Hudson's sympathy with the poor and illiterate countryman did not prevent him from appreciating the good points of the squire. He was able to feel at home with both shepherd and squire. The primitive and aristocratic appealed to the two sides of him which were revealed in his appearance, with its mixture of ruggedness and sensitive courtesy. His keen interest in human nature made it possible for him to get on with almost every type of man, no matter what his outlook or calling; but the most difficult for him to approach were the industrial proletarian and the business man. In the country labourer at one end, and the squire, artist, or man of letters at the other, he found elements of his own nature. H. J. Massingham has remarked on the affinity which unites the humblest agricultural worker with the squire. It is, he says, the land itself. Centuries of contact with the land have bred in each a love of a common thing that unites them beyond any distinctions of class or station. Hence rural societies seldom rebel, for between the squire and his men there is, in a literal sense, a natural bond, a bond of nature, whereas between the capitalist and the dispossessed proletarian there is only the antagonistic relation of impersonal economic forces.

Hudson was not blind to the dark side of the "squire-archy." Roberts observes that "those who have read *A Shepherd's Life* will see how bitterly indignant he could be with the abuses that are too commonly connected with the ownership of land. He had seen tyranny in action. The type of Conservative landowner who was to him a noble and desirable animal to preserve was one who preserved the peasant and preferred healthy children to many head of game: one who did not encourage the breed of gamekeepers: who did not collect or destroy birds, who hated a pole-trap and an owl or a jay-murderer worse than a trespassing old woman seeking fallen firewood: one who was an ideal, kindly gentleman who thought more of humanity than of sport, who gloried in the varied life possible upon his estate and sought to increase it. It may be left to others to determine how many there are of the kind that appealed to him, as they and their fellows are displaced by rich men without the authority of ancestry or of manner or any true culture in their veins." One would agree with Roberts in lamenting the displacement of the best type of aristocratic landowner by the rich; but it is not so much the rich man "without the authority of ancestry" who had made things difficult for the countryman and, indeed, for the poor everywhere, but his successor, the bureaucrat, neither aristocratic nor wealthy, but powerful with all the power the State can confer.

A Shepherd's Life contains several intimate and charming portraits of squires, who, with all their faults and eccentricities, are, to my mind, the best of England. At the other end of the social scale are the sketches of gypsy life on the downs. The gypsy always fascinated Hudson. To many people he must have appeared something of a gypsy himself—a wanderer over the countryside, a rugged, weather-beaten figure, unique, beyond the artificial distinctions of class. He felt a genuine affinity with this ancient people, who, like himself, possessed an extraordinary sharpness and brightness of the senses. He was always happy and at ease in their company, and relates how he haunted their camp and had many talks with them. It is not difficult to understand their attraction which, for most of us, probably derives from the fact that they embody the hidden longing for lawless freedom and a life of primitive simplicity that exists deep in the human heart. We are no less attracted by the element of mystery revealed in their folk-lore and melancholy music, and in their strange prophetic powers to which Brian Vesey-Fitzgerald pays so remarkable a tribute in his book, *British Gypsies*. For centuries the gypsies of Britain have wandered up and down the length and breadth of these islands, watching men and civilizations come and go. But they remain; and in a sense they are the true natives of Britain, akin to those ancient men who built their lonely barrows and monoliths long ago on the high, windswept hills.

In his chapter on the gypsies, Hudson raises again the question of racial type and distribution which he discussed more fully in *Hampshire Days* and *The Land's End*. The chapter, called "The Dark People of the Village," contains some interesting speculations on the subject, and some charming stories of dark people told him by Caleb. Hudson distinguished three types of dark people of three distinct races in the Wiltshire downs— the brown-skinned gypsy type with high cheek-bones, the white-skinned, round-headed type probably the descendants of the Wilsetae, and the very dark, oval-faced descendants of the ancient British race.

As a naturalist, Hudson tended to view people anthropologically; but as a man he approached each individual with sympathy and understanding as the manifestation of a unique self hood. For him, man, though he may exist in many spheres of being, religious, social, anthropological, psychological, is primarily an individual—a view in which he differed from so many of his contemporaries who tend to ignore individuality and to see man exclusively in one or other of these spheres. Where the sense of individuality is lost, freedom and responsibility vanish, and human life becomes cheap, as we see in the totalitarian countries. Nevertheless, man's individuality is ineradicable, since it is of the very essence of his nature. In the lowest forms of life individuality hardly exists; but as we ascend, there is increased differentiation, first in families, then in genera, then in species, until the advent of man, a creature in whom individuality is so highly developed that each person is, in a sense, a complete species in himself. The totalitarian movements of our time represent the attempts of the forces of reaction to arrest the terrifying thrust forward into greater individuality; man is frightened and bewildered by the development of his self-hood (a development greatly accelerated by the rapid increase of his knowledge and experience in the last three hundred years), and instead of seeking a deeper integration in God and nature takes blind refuge in the mass. Nevertheless, individuality must continue to develop, though totalitarianism may cause a great deal of misery, and last for a very long time. The environment depicted by Hudson in *A Shepherd's Life* is a fertile breeding-ground for human personality. Contact with nature and the rhythm of the seasons nourishes the individual soul. The men and women who emerge from this book are poor and ignorant and often down-trodden; but they are unmistakably individuals. (pp. 91-6)

A Shepherd's Life is a book of deep satisfaction, a book full of kindliness and peace. Shepherds and sheep-dogs, and the lonely downs in sun and wind and rain; family life; hardship and sorrow, joy and thankfulness—these are the strands from which its "rich tapestry" is woven. The charm of the book is indefinable, but may derive partly from its enshrinement of memory at one remove. It is permeated, not by the direct remembrance of Hudson's own experience, but by the memories of the shepherd, remembered again by Hudson and transformed in the light of his imagination. Memories of memories; and the passing of things that shall be no more. (p. 98)

> *Robert Hamilton, in his* W. H. Hudson: The Vision of Earth, *J. M. Dent and Sons Ltd., 1946, 148 p.*

RICHARD E. HAYMAKER (essay date 1954)

[*In the following excerpt, Haymaker explicates* Green Mansions.]

For its conception, **Green Mansions** owes something, though not so much as has been claimed, to Lady Morgan's *Missionary*. Since the present age does not find nymphs in streams or dryads in woods, one of the chief means of giving human poignancy to an experience that belongs essentially in the realm of fantasy, as scarcely any artist need be told, is to set it in a region that will stimulate the imagination without sacrificing the sense of reality—preferably one just beyond the farthest reach of exploration. For the enactment of his story, Hudson chose an outlying part of the Guayana jungles, which had long captivated the European imagination, both scientific and literary, and improvised its topography to suit his special purposes.

Of great help in creating the illusion of reality is the choice of the hero as the teller of his own story. Though the restriction of the point of view has its disadvantages—Rima's death, for instance, cannot be presented dramatically—the feeling of intimacy that it gives makes the plotting seem less palpably invented. The introduction of the narrator is rather awkwardly managed, but, besides evoking an immediate sense of mystery with the mention of an ornamented cinerary urn kept in a darkened room, it provides, as in the novels of Conrad, an occasion for the telling. The choice of Abel as the hero is also a happy one, for he is well oriented to social and cultural life and, though young, competent as a naturalist, both in the observation of plants and animals and in that of such human fauna as the Indians of the jungles. Who could be better qualified to report accurately a unique experience?

In order to make some of the sensational elements in his story less nakedly romantic, Hudson gives a good deal of attention to the accumulation of circumstantial details. Each of the various stages of Abel's journey from Quarico to the Parahuari mountains is carefully motivated. He flees to the jungle because of complicity in an abortive revolution. His wanderings as a naturalist, which take him to the headwaters of the Orinoco, are brought to an abrupt end by a severe bout of fever and the loss of his journal. After he convalesces at one of the Maquiritari settlements, the old conquistatorial lust for gold lures him toward still more remote outposts. Upon reaching the small village of Runi and his tribe, Abel realizes that his pursuit has been that for a will-o'-the-wisp, but, impressed by the "rare loveliness" of the landscape, the poet that is also in him takes possession, and he decides to give himself up, for a season at least, to the pure enjoyment of nature. The Indians with whom he now fraternizes are made psychologically real—sullen Runi, thawed out of his hostility by casserie and the desire for revenge on a neighboring tribe; impetuous Kua-kó, an easy target at foils; and, especially, garulous old Cla-cla, youthful in spirit despite her snow-white hair and innumerable wrinkles. Thus, before Abel crosses over the savannah to the patch of woodland under the *pax rimae* ["peace of Rima"], our disbelief has been completely suspended.

As should be, there is little description of nature until Abel arrives at Runi's village. The depiction of its setting (the stream fringed with verdure and scattered dwarf trees, the brown savannah sloping upwards to a rocky ridge, the forests and mountains beyond) and particularly Rima's enchanted paradise (the clouds of greenery, the glades filled with mysterious half-lights, the impenetrable, creeper-laden undergrowth, the great variety of plant and animal life) is one of the chief attractions of *Green Mansions*. In such descriptions as those of the song of the campanero and the vista from the dominating landmark of the region, the "dark cone of Ytaioa," Abel shows himself very much the poet, and hence precisely the person to be most sensitive to Rima's preternatural beauty. The primitive vastness of the landscape, as well as the constant threat of the savages, gives poignancy to the brief drama they enact together. Since Hudson had never seen the tropical jungles, his picture of them, which has impressed no less an expert than Beebe, is indeed a triumph of the imagination.

Rima, who is more a passion than a woman, is very subtly introduced. Her status in the savage mind as "the daughter of Didi" prepares us for an extraordinary creature, one enveloped in an aura. To Abel, she is at first only a mysterious bird-melody coming from a tangle of bushes. Later, after detecting with his keen ears an element of human feeling in it, he suspects a human embodiment. When the song keeps accompanying him on his saunterings about the forest, he becomes conscious of being an object of friendly interest. Yet, until actually getting a glimpse of her behind a "light leafy screen," he is uncertain whether the possessor of the song be human or avian; and that ambiguity, emphasized by her search for an interpreter of her ancestral tongue, is never allowed out of our consciousness. Gradually we come to see and to know Rima better—her Ariel-like figure; her arachnidian silk dress; her loose-flowing, iridescent hair and dark eyes lighting up with the fire of the ruby; the transparency of her skin, reflecting the shifting colors around her; her childlike innocence and birdlike brightness of mind; the reflection in her character of all that is best in wild nature—but her full story, like that of her spiritual cousin, Atala, is withheld until it is necessary to provide a motive for the tragic ending.

The portrayal of so elusive a figure as Rima, particularly when done in detail, is extremely difficult; yet, on the whole, Hudson succeeds. As in many oriental tales, the difficulty is to some extent overcome by the use of imagery from nature, especially from birdlife. Thus, her "quick, passionate gestures" are likened to the flirting of a bird's wings; her swift and soundless gliding about the forest, to that of a great low-flying owl; her anger, to that of a wasp, "every word a sting"; her appearance as she lay in a deathlike swoon in Abel's arms, to that of the Hata flower, whose transcendent beauty has given rise to a legend. The comparison most employed and, except for the want of song, the most appropriate is to the hummingbird: in the hut, this wood nymph is like one of these "fairy-like" creatures perched on a twig in the shade; in the forest, like one "moving about in an aerial dance among the flowers—a living prismatic gem that changes its colour with every change of position. . . ." So thoroughly is she identified with nature that we feel no discordancy when she is even likened to a snake. Essentially, of course, Rima is indescribable, and best imagined through the incandescent passion she inspires in Abel.

Up to the time of the dramatic scene on Ytaioa, which is the turning-point of the plot, the action of *Green Mansions* progresses leisurely. It takes a while for Abel to become acquainted with so shy a creature as Rima, and to remove the barriers between their love. Though the dialogue is at times formal and even operatic, Hudson shows considerable skill in the unfoldment of love within her—an unfoldment complicated by an imperfect medium of communication and her inability to comprehend the meaning of the tumult in her heart. To prevent too continuous a strain upon the romantic sensibilities, relief is provided by shifting the scene either indoors, where Rima loses much of her charm, or to the Indian village, toward which Abel occasionally turns his steps, and by the sardonic portraiture of cunning old Nuflo, with his harpings on "God's politics." In the meantime, Hudson has been carefully preparing, as with Kua-kó's eagerness to train Abel in the use of the blow-pipe, for the tragedy that is soon to close in upon them.

With the inclusion of Riolama in the Whitmanesque panoramic survey from "everlasting Ytaioa's granite throne," the action gathers momentum and intensity. The eighteen-day journey to the cave where Nuflo discovered Rima's mother is indeed interrupted by the insertion of the story of these last two survivors of a mysterious race, but, actually, it serves to increase our sense of the distance being traversed. Hudson does not shirk the difficult scene that soon takes place: Rima's anguish and despair at not finding her people, who might have given her guidance, her long, deathlike swoon, and her awakening to the realization that love is "the flower and the melody of life." Beseeching Abel not to regret the journey to Riolama, she touchingly declares that all she wished to know of her kinsfolk she has now found in him. There is some mere capriciousness in Rima's resolve to return alone to her forest home and in those familiar surroundings prepare for the coming of her bridegroom, but it is not inconsistent with her character. The scene of her appalling death, though of necessity presented indirectly, has in it "the pang of all the partings gone, and partings yet to be."

One of the chief merits of *Green Mansions* is its intensity, an intensity rare in English fiction, and comparable to that in *Wuthering Heights*, in many Elizabethan plays, and in some of the oriental romances made popular by F. W. Bain about the time of its writing. There is passion in the appreciation of nature, as when Abel drops to his knees in thankfulness for the beauty of the enchanted woods, and throughout the love scenes, especially that in which Abel identifies his beloved with the mystic Hata flower. The intensity that makes the greatest impression comes after Rima has fallen, with her lover's name upon her lips, into the voracious sea of flames. Abel's grief, sharp as a dagger-thrust, is so excruciating that it drives him to the killing of Runi and all his kindred and even to the cursing of God. Night after night, like Heathcliff, he embraces in waking visions a spirit-bride, the wraith of Rima. Pangs of remorse for his killing of the Indians and the animals sacred to his beloved, epitomized in the recurring images of dead Clacla's staring eyes and blood-dappled hair and the lidless white eye of a serpent's severed head, bring him to the verge of madness, the feeling that he has been "dwelling alone" for thousands of years "on a vast stony plain in everlasting twilight. . . ." Extraordinarily effective is the incident in which a moth flutters into his hut and, after resting for a while on the thatch directly over the fire, falls into the white blaze—an incident that has the power of the sleep-walking scene in *Macbeth* to revivify the most terrible part of the previous action.

The intensity is superbly sustained: the main thing supporting Abel on his headlong, Orestean flight to the coast, pursued by phantom Indians and a tremendous ophidian head, is his resolve to find a repository for Rima's ashes, so that his own might ultimately be mixed with them. Since Hudson had the same instinct as the Greeks for the quiet ending, the novel comes to a close with the hero's re-discovery of the "everlasting freshness and beauty" of the earth.

Without doubt, there is profound autobiography in *Green Mansions,* Rima being for her creator the incarnation of his longing for a woman who would be "the sustentation" not only of his body but likewise of his "higher winged nature." But, by the transmuting power of poetry, she becomes at the same time something more universal. She is, indeed, *das Ewig-Weibliche* ["the divine in woman"] that draws men to her and leads some of them on to a higher plane of being. (This is perhaps the reason that *Green Mansions* means more to men than to women.) And implicit in Rima's death is a tragic vision of the world as a whole. In the life of man, so exquisite a love as that between her and Abel cannot be more than a brief interlude. In the life of nature, much that is most admirable—especially the more ethereal elements—is continually being destroyed by the evil in the heart not only of man but of Nature herself. Whenever a Rima, in whom "all the separate and fragmentary beauty and melody and graceful motion found scattered throughout nature [are] concentrated and harmoniously combined," arouses the resentment of a Runi and the likes of him, her fate is sealed. Such a belief brings to a piercing note a leading motif in all of Hudson's writings: the beautiful vanishes and returns not. (pp. 331-36)

Richard E. Haymaker, in his From Pampas to Hedgerows and Downs: A Study of W. H. Hudson, *Bookman Associates, 1954, 398 p.*

JOHN T. FREDERICK (essay date 1972)

[*An American critic and novelist, Frederick was the founding editor of the literary journal* Midland *(1915-33). In the following excerpt, he discusses* A Crystal Age *and* Tales of the Pampas.]

A Crystal Age, Hudson's second novel, is an anomaly in the whole body of his work; but it also expresses some of his most profound attitudes and beliefs. A dream-romance, the vision of a utopia, it relates the experience of one Smith—the name deliberately identifies him as a representative Englishman of Hudson's own time—who awakens from a mysterious sleep which is subsequently shown to have lasted thousands of years. Though Smith remembers only a fall while on a hunting expedition and finds himself still clothed in a woolen outdoor suit that has grown musty with time, no effort is made by Hudson to explain the circumstances in realistic terms.

As Smith wanders across a countryside recognizably English, yet strangely altered, he encounters a group of beautifully clothed and personally beautiful people who are engaged in a burial service. He is immediately seized by a profound admiration and passion for one of the number, seemingly a young girl, whose name is later revealed as Yoletta. He is keenly embarrassed by the contrast between his soiled and unlovely clothing and the beautiful attire of these strange people—and he immediately desires to be accepted by them. He is kindly accepted by the group, is fed and lodged, is promised new garments, and is given work to do to pay for them—the sovereigns he offers are rejected—in plowing a field with a primitive plow. Genuine humor appears in Hudson's treatment of this and other early experiences of Smith in *A Crystal Age:* when he displays his ignorance, the horses harness themselves to the plow; and they quit when they feel they have worked long enough.

Gradually, Smith learns something of the society into which he has come. Its center is the House: it is an extremely ancient and extremely beautiful structure, rich in the most exquisite and elaborate works of art and craftsmanship. The people speak English, but their writing is totally different from English script or printing, and Smith has to be taught to read the magnificently illuminated volumes which recount their history and beliefs. The House is ruled by a Father, the only bearded man of the community, who is said to be almost two hundred years old.

Smith learns that the whole world is now possessed only by widely separated comparable houses that are known to one another from the reports of pilgrims. Belatedly, Smith finds that there is also a Mother, the real ruler and principal person of the community. The reader, rather than Smith, comes to see that sexuality is absent from this society except for the Father and the Mother, who alone have the responsibility of perpetuating it. Except for these two, sexual love is replaced by kindliness, by creation of things of beauty, and by reverent enjoyment of the beauty of the earth and cultivation of its fruits. Smith is constantly embarrassed by his blunders, and constantly he more deeply and passionately loves the girl Yoletta—who he learns is a woman of thirty-one.

As the book nears its end, the reader gradually perceives that the Mother, Chastel, who is very ill—in marked contrast to the perfect health of the other members of the community— has taken a special interest in Smith and that he is under consideration as a new Father of the House, with Yoletta as the Mother and his bride. But, even as Smith glimpses this prospect, he is reading ancient books of the community that cause him to have a profound desire to wipe from his memory all that remains of his earlier life and all that he has known before entering the Crystal Age. When, as result, he drinks the liquid in a flask labeled "Drink of me and be cured," he dies.

A Crystal Age draws its not inconsiderable dramatic strength from the characterization of Smith, who is sufficiently consistent as an ordinary modern Englishman in his bewilderments, blunders, and passion for Yoletta, as well as in his schemings and his bafflements, to gain a substantial measure of empathy. There is a measure of dramatic reality also in the Father and a large measure in the Mother, Chastel, in her physical suffering and in her gradually developing interest in Smith after she learns that, with his hand on her forehead, she can sleep. In some measure recognizably human and alive also is Edra— the friend and mentor of Yoletta—and Yoletta herself; the other members of the community (who number only a dozen or so) are colorless and undifferentiated.

The whole effect of the book, obviously, is to project against the mass misery, frustration, and futility of the modern world, which are concretely realized in the thoughts and conduct of Smith, the vision of human beings living in complete harmony with the earth and with each other. Some years after the publication of *A Crystal Age,* Hudson defended certain aspects of the book in a letter of August 17, 1893, to an American friend, Louise Chandler Moulton, who had apparently objected to the death of Smith and also to the characterization of Chastel as inconsistent with the general pattern of life in *A Crystal Age:*

> You are keenly appreciative of whatever is good in the book, & kindly say nothing of its faults, which are not few. But about poor Smith, what was to be

done with him? He, a commonplace, modern, "bank-holiday sort of young man" could never have got himself into any sort of harmony with that serene passionless social atmosphere into which he was thrown. It was better that he should die accidentally and escape from a false position. And as for Chastel: well, I could do nothing with those quiet-minded humans of the future, they seemed so unlike ourselves, & so was obliged to introduce one tempestuous pain-racked soul to preserve something of human interest in the narrative.

Stylistically, *A Crystal Age* is as distinctive as its material. There are long passages, especially in speeches of the Father, which are marked by a Ruskin-like eloquence of great beauty. Other passages of natural description are akin to Hudson's most characteristic in later writings, recording his own actual experience, in their power and beauty.

A Crystal Age owes little to its immediate predecessors in the history of utopian romance. The immediate suggestion for such a work may have come from Richard Jefferies' *After London,* for Hudson knew and admired Jefferies' books about nature. But *After London* has nothing in texture or substance to align it with Hudson's work. The widely read *Erewhon* (1872) of Samuel Butler is a more probable source, for in *Erewhon,* as in *A Crystal Age,* sickness is a crime that is punishable—though the correlated idea, that crime is an illness and is to be given sympathetic medical treatment—is not suggested at all. Moreover, *A Crystal Age* has not the slightest suggestion of the savage irony of Butler's treatment of religious and educational institutions.

A Crystal Age is wholly antithetical to the most popular of the utopian romances which succeeded it, Edward Bellamy's *Looking Backward,* in which machinery, which has been destroyed or reduced to the simple forms of a primitive plow and an ax in *A Crystal Age,* has become the means of solving the material problems of man and of freeing him for the development of his intellect and soul. Hudson's romance also has nothing of the intention of immediate social criticism and commentary which mark either Bellamy's work or William Dean Howells' *A Traveler from Altruria* and his *Through the Eye of the Needle* (1907). *A Crystal Age* is most closely approached in structure, in tone, in the nature of the utopia described, and in style, by William Morris' *News from Nowhere* (1891), and I think it wholly probable that Morris knew Hudson's book.

Lewis Mumford has made in his *The Story of Utopias* [see Additional Bibliography] the most discerning comment on *A Crystal Age* that work has yet received. He sees that the most significant literary relationship of *A Crystal Age* is to the original *Utopia* of Sir Thomas More: "Mr. W. H. Hudson returns upon More; and in *A Crystal Age* the farmstead and the family is the ultimate unit of social life." Mumford also defines clearly the biological concept which underlies the picture of society presented by Hudson: a single female, the Mother, is chosen for the sole function of reproduction and the perpetuation of the family; and a single male is likewise selected as her mate:

> To the objection that this sort of utopia requires that we change human nature, the answer, in terms of modern biology, is that there is no apparent scientific reason why certain elements in human nature should not be selected and brought to the front, or why certain others should not be reduced in importance and eliminated. So, for all practical purposes, there is no apparent reason why human nature should not be changed, or why we should not be prepared to believe that in times past it has been changed . . . a

utopia which rests upon the notion that there should be a certain direction in our breeding is not altogether luny; indeed, is nowadays less so than ever before, for the reason that it is possible to separate romantic love from physical procreation without, as the Athenians did, resorting to homosexuality.

> If *A Crystal Age* opens our minds to these possibilities, it is not to be counted purely as a romance, in spite of the fact that as a romance it has passages that rival *Green Mansions*. Between the individual households and common marriages, the utopia of the beehive is a third alternative which possibly remains to be explored.

Mumford's analysis of the central idea in *A Crystal Age* is confirmed by a passage in a letter of June 10, 1917, from Hudson to Edward Garnett, in which he said: "The sexual passion is the central thought in *A Crystal Age*: the idea that there is no millennium, no rest, no perpetual peace till that fury has burnt itself out, and I gave unlimited time for the change. It is . . . the social model of the beehive with the queen mother in its centre. Because of this letter's statement about the beehive and the queen mother, the initial conception of *A Crystal Age* may have come from a passage in Thomas Belt's *The Naturalist in Nicaragua* (1874), which was well known to Hudson. It is cited more frequently in Hudson's own first book of essays on nature, *The Naturalist in La Plata,* than any other recent scientific work except Darwin's—and Belt's ideas are always given approval. Belt, after commenting on his observations on the conduct of several species of communal ants (similar to that of bees), enumerates in detail the aspects of their behavior which are strikingly illustrative of cooperation and fruitful community action. He then quotes at length from Sir Thomas More's *Utopia* his account of a reformed human society: "there is no unequal distribution, so that no man is poor nor in any necessity, and though no man has anything, yet they are all rich. . . ." Belt's comparison of an insect society with the human, to the discredit of the latter, and especially his quotation from More, justify the suggestion that this message may have influenced, or even initiated, Hudson's conception of the society pictured in *A Crystal Age*.

It remains to note the significance of *A Crystal Age* as expressive of Hudson's religious view and position. Although the relatively limited critical writing about Hudson includes various attempts to define his religious position, with much employment of such terms as animism, Hudson's religion was actually relatively simple; it is clearly expressed in and through the whole body of his work. It was earth worship: reverence and sympathy for every form of life and for all living things, reverence for the earth itself as the source and sustainer of all life, and reverent acceptance of the conditions and limitations of the life of every creature. This religion is also that of the people of *A Crystal Age,* as it is revealed through the imperfect and gradual perception of Smith. (pp. 40-5)

Hudson's best short fiction, collected under the title *El Ombú,* was first published in 1902 by the London firm of Duckworth and Company. . . . Duckworth published the volume again in 1909, with no changes in the text but with a new title, *South American Sketches.* When the success of *Green Mansions* created a demand for Hudson's work in the United States, Alfred A. Knopf brought out the volume under still a third and a better title, *Tales of the Pampas,* adding to it a very early, inferior, and previously uncollected story and also a long narrative poem.

Of the four stories included in the two Duckworth editions, **"The Story of a Piebald Horse"** was an unintegrated chapter taken from *The Purple Land;* the story of a mysterious disappearance in the violent pampas life is explained by a first-person narrative: the family of the man who has disappeared cause his piebald horse to be kept tethered at a wayside tavern, and eventually a man who recognizes the horse appears and tells the story which explains the mystery. "**Nino Diablo**" is marked by humor of a high order and by strong suspense. The widely feared killer and outlaw, the *nino diablo* ["devil boy"], is appealed to by a despairing rancher whose wife has been captured by Indians; later, he listens unrecognized to the abuse and threats uttered against him by another visitor to the same *estancia.* He steals the braggart's horses and succeeds in rescuing the rancher's wife.

The major achievement of the volume is found in the two longer stories—the title story and "**Marta Riquelme.**" "**El Ombú**" is a story told in the first person, with a single brief introductory paragraph:

> This history of a house that had been was told in the shade, one summer's day, by Nicandro, that old man to whom we all loved to listen, since he could remember and properly narrate the life of every person he had known in his native place, near to the lake of Chascomus, on the southern pampas of Buenos Ayres.

The narrative which follows—one of violence, death, insanity, and love—is perfectly controlled and integrated by the quiet, slightly formal, explicit style of the narrator. Its effect is one of massiveness; of intense human experience rendered only the more poignant by the narrator's consistent simplicity and understatement. Few works of fiction of comparable length, in English or in any other literature, equal it in essential power or in completeness of achievement.

In the first paragraph Hudson sketches swiftly, with details which remain in the reader's memory as background until the end of the story, the physical setting as it is at the time of Nicandro's recital of the people and events associated with the place:

> In all this district, though you should go twenty leagues to this way and that, you will not find a tree as big as this ombú, standing solitary, where there is no house; therefore it is known to all as "*the* ombú," as if but one existed; and the name of all this estate, which is now ownerless and ruined, is El Ombú. From one of the higher branches, if you can climb, you will see the lake of Chascomus, two thirds of a league away, from shore to shore, and the village on its banks. Even smaller things will you see on a clear day; perhaps a red line moving across the water—a flock of flamingos flying in their usual way. A great tree standing alone, with no house near it; only the old brick foundations of a house, so overgrown with grass and weeds that you have to look closely to find them. When I am out with my flock in the summer time, I often come here to sit in the shade.

Nicandro first tells the story of Don Santos Ugarte, an early owner of the *estancia* called El Ombú because of its one enormous ombú tree (like the twenty-five of Hudson's first home), which is visible for many miles. Ugarte, who is known to be the father of many sons in the neighborhood, is ironically unable to have a son of his own name though he has three times married. When a slave, an intelligent and gentle boy who has been especially favored by Ugarte, saves his money until he has enough to buy his freedom and offers it to Ugarte, his master kills him, goes into self-imposed exile to escape punishment, and never returns to the estate. He dies, an old man, as a suicide by drowning.

Nicandro then turns to the story of more recent occupants of the *estancia,* Nicandro's beloved friend, Valerio, and his family. Valerio has a happy marriage and an idolized little son, Bruno. Both Nicandro and Valerio are conscripted to serve in the forces of one Colonel Barboza. When the troops are discharged, Barboza cheats them of their pay, and Valerio is chosen to present a protest. Barboza first sentences him to be flayed alive but then reduces the punishment to two hundred lashes. Valerio, all but killed by the flogging, is conducted back to El Ombú by Nicandro, but he dies as he is being greeted by his wife and child.

The widowed mother, Donata, takes into her arms a deserted child, a girl named Monica, who grows up with Bruno. She is very beautiful, kind, and gentle, and the two learn to love each other. But, when he is grown, Bruno learns for the first time the circumstances of his father's death; and, in spite of Nicandro's efforts to dissuade him, leaves secretly with the purpose of revenge, and all efforts to find him fail. Donata takes into her house at El Ombú a penniless and dispossessed old couple; shortly thereafter she dies, leaving Monica with them. Monica rejects all suitors, waiting for Bruno's return.

After years, a returning soldier tells Nicandro and Monica of the final insanity and strange death of Barboza, following an attempt to assassinate him in which he kills the would-be assassin. At the end of his story, he names as an afterthought the man who had tried to kill Barboza—Bruno de la Cueva. On hearing these words, Monica falls senseless to the floor, and thereafter she has no memory and no reason. When the old house at El Ombú is torn down "for the sake of the material which was required for a building in the village," Monica is taken by the old woman whom Donata had befriended to live with relatives at a nearby town, and she remains with them after the old women's death. The people of the town "are kind to her," Nicandro says, "for her story is known to them, and God has put compassion into their hearts."

The final paragraph of Nicandro's narrative illustrates the concreteness, the simplicity, and the tinge of formality which mark Hudson's style and tone of the narrative:

> To see her you would hardly believe that she is the Monica I have told you of, whom I knew as a little one, running barefoot after her father's flock. For she has grey hairs and wrinkles now. As you ride to Chascomus from this point you will see, on approaching the lake, a very high bank on your left hand, covered with a growth of tall fennel, hoarhound, and cardoon thistle. There on most days you will find her, sitting on the bank in the shade of the tall fennel bushes, looking across the lake. She watches for the flamingos. There are many of those great birds on the lake, and they go in flocks, and when they rise and travel across the water, flying low, their scarlet wings may be seen at a great distance. And every time she catches sight of a flock moving like a red line across the lake she cries out with delight. That is her one happiness—her life. And she is the last of all those who have lived in my time at El Ombú.

In some ways even more remarkable is the other long story, "**Marta Riquelme,**" which was first published in the edition of 1902. It is told in the first person by a Roman Catholic missionary who is sent to a remote village at the foot of the Andes, where the people, nominally converted, are actually still under the dominion of the ancient heathen gods. The young cleric, struggling against himself, falls in love with a girl of Spanish blood whose name gives the story its title; and he watches her tragic life until she becomes at last a *Kakue*, a birdlike demon of the forest. Because of the agony resulting from his witnessing this transformation, the narrator returns to Spain, to his beloved Córdoba, expecting to die there. Instead, he regains his health and is sent again to the remote village of his earlier ministry, where he finally regains a measure of his former faith.

The narrative is as consistent in its integrity of revelation as is that of **"El Ombú"**; but the essential intent of **"Marta Riquelme"** is that of swiftly intensifying psychological anguish. The very firm specification of place and character in the earlier part of the story makes inevitable the reader's extreme measure of participation in the climax of Martha's agony and in that of the priest when she rejects the crucifix and is claimed by the powers of evil. Narrower in its emotional range than **"El Ombú"** and perhaps less within the emotional grasp of some readers, **"Marta Riquelme"** is another great story and one that is all but unique for Hudson in its psychological realism.

[The] two items added to the original group in *Tales of the Pampas* are far inferior to the four of the earlier collection. They are a prose narrative, some forty pages in length, entitled **"Pelino Viera's Confession"**; the fortunately shorter narrative in verse is **"Tecla and the Little Men."** Both are frankly supernatural in material. Neither constitutes an addition of value to the earlier volume or to Hudson's literary achievement. (pp. 47-51)

> *John T. Frederick, in his* William Henry Hudson, *Twayne Publishers, Inc., 1972, 150 p.*

BRIAN FINNEY   (essay date 1985)

[*In the following excerpt, Finney examines* Far Away and Long Ago.]

The circumstances leading to the composition of Hudson's childhood autobiography bear a resemblance to the kind of vision sometimes granted to religious mystics as a crucial turning point in their lives. At the age of seventy-four Hudson was suffering from one of his recurrent bouts of severe illness that periodically afflicted him as a result of the rheumatic fever which had nearly killed him when he was sixteen. Recovering in a convent nursing home at Hayle in Cornwall during November and December 1915, he suddenly had what seemed like total recall of the childhood he had spent in Argentina. The "vision" continued and during his six weeks' confinement in bed he wrote a long first draft of the autobiography. Aware of the possibility that he might die of his illness, he was struck all the more forcefully by the effect of these memories of his happy childhood which appear to have acted as a form of self-cure, just as visions frequently precede religious conversion in seventeenth-century autobiographies. Throughout the next three years of the war he revised and shortened his original draft which in its longer version was too formless for his liking. Published October 1918, *Far Away and Long Ago: A History of My Early Life* was immediately greeted as a masterpiece in its genre.

Prior to his moment of recall Hudson had been reading with great admiration Aksakoff's *Childhood* to which he twice alludes in his own autobiography. In his opinion Aksakoff was quite exceptional in that, unlike most people, he was able to re-create the feelings of childhood uncontaminated by the distortions of an adult's memory, so that "in his case the picture was not falsified." Hudson claimed that he also had never outlived his childhood experience, especially of nature, so that his autobiography likewise relives the past "in its true, fresh, original colours." Hudson has a strong personal motive for wishing to believe that his childhood memories flood back to him unmediated by an adult consciousness. It is because he has a Romantic's worship of the child's proximity to the marvels of the natural world which he wants to retain into later life. At the same time he is well aware of the generic need to select, arrange and shape this material, even if he refers to it in distinctly negative terms. Normally, he writes, "unconscious artistry will steal or sneak in to . . . falsify the picture." The fact is that he felt compelled to "reshape" his first draft. He also justifies the hiatus of three years over which he skips prior to the last three chapters by explaining the need "to bring [the book] to a proper ending." His references in the book to the classic childhood autobiographies of St. Augustine, Leigh Hunt and Aksakoff in themselves point to Hudson's consciousness of the generic tradition to which he was contributing. So he uses all the guile of an autobiographer to create the impression of a guileless recorder of his past. (pp. 210-11)

Far Away and Long Ago has a rather awkward, idiosyncratic shape to it. But the autobiography is held together by the older Hudson's unusual sense of continuity with his childhood self and especially with his childish sensitivity to and joy in the feelings that nature in the wild aroused in him. The opening chapter offers a sample of the sort of experiences from which he constructs most of the book. There is the description of the farmhouse where he was born with its distinctive row of twenty-five Ombú trees followed by a disquisition on the nature of these and other trees native to the region. There are also loving evocations of his dog, his mother, and two grotesque occasional visitors to the house. We appear to be reading the childhood account of an unusually perceptive naturalist. But in what way is it a spiritual history of the self? Hudson is careful to prepare for his later introduction of those animistic beliefs which became for him a religion in adult life. He does this by emphasizing his unusual capacity as an adult to recapture his childhood feelings with all their original strength when in the presence of nature. (pp. 211-12)

His autobiography confirms him in his belief that he has lost none of his childhood responses to the natural world. In 1893 Hudson published *Idle Days in Patagonia*, a semi-autobiographical collection of essays based on his sojourn there during 1870-1. In it he expresses most openly his conviction that in early childhood we come closest to the emotions experienced by our primitive ancestors in a state of nature. Citing Thoreau's description of his exuberant desire to seize a woodchuck stealing across his path and eat it raw, Hudson comments: "In almost all cases . . . the return to an instinctive or primitive state of mind is accompanied by this feeling of elation, which, in the very young, rises to an intense gladness, and sometimes makes them mad with joy, like animals newly escaped from captivity." Hudson's description of his childhood in his autobiography attempts to recapture this sense of an animal's unthinking enjoyment of an uninhibited existence in the wild. Compared to the numerous chapters devoted to his adventures in the pampas, the few descriptions he offers us of his mother and the family home make one realize that he felt his first home was out of doors. . . . (p. 212)

It is interesting that Hudson is more explicit about these most intimate feelings in **Idle Days** than in **Far Away and Long Ago** where they act as an implicit thematic element that helps hold the book together. I would argue that the autobiography is structured on the gradual replacement of home and parents by the world of nature.

Opposed to nature in the wild stands civilization. For Hudson "the civilized life is one of continual repression." This is how his spasmodic experiences of schooling are received in the book. Trigg, his first tutor, seems to the young boy's eyes a Jekyll and Hyde figure, loved by the adults but a tyrant in the schoolroom. "For," Hudson explains, "he was a schoolmaster who hated and despised teaching as much as children in the wild hated to be taught." Trigg, in fact, is as oppressed by the civilization whose values he is attempting to transmit as are Hudson and his brothers. Civilization is given its most potent symbolic expression in Hudson's description of Buenos Aires, the capital of a country torn by civil wars which seem to erupt from the city and spread like plagues across the plains until they exhaust themselves in bouts of pointless bloodletting. Even his first visit there in his sixth year left him shocked by the behaviour of the ideal young gentlemen who baited the laundresses and nightwatchmen for a pastime and the savage beggars that infested the streets. But his later stay there when he was fourteen provides the excuse for a diatribe against the evils of civilization in general. The city he remembers is contaminated by the stench of rotting cattle flesh from the slaughtering grounds at its southern end. He compares these open abattoirs to the worst scenes in Dante's *Inferno,* pervaded by "the smell of carrion, of putrefying flesh, and of that old and ever-newly moistened crust of dust and coagulated blood." Nowhere else in the book is his language quite so violent as in this description of Buenos Aires as "the chief pestilential city of the globe." As a child of nature he inevitably falls victim to this city of infection by catching typhus. His early conviction that "our loss in departing from nature exceeds our gain" receives personal confirmation in the near-fatal illness he succumbs to.

In the major portion of the autobiography chapter after chapter vividly evokes the plant and animal life that Hudson spent much of his childhood observing and entering into. Repeatedly trees or birds are treated as fellow beings with a life of their own that is quite as thrilling to the young boy as the human fauna he encounters on the plain. Even the trees assert their individuality as Hudson wittily demonstrates in the case of a rare acacia: "Of all our trees this one made the strongest and sharpest impression on my mind as well as flesh, pricking its image in me, so to speak." Similarly his passages of natural description are intended to prick the presence of animate nature into the consciousness of the reader. Birds gave him most pleasure as a child, "not only because birds exceed in beauty, but also on account of the intensity of the life they exhibit." In describing the bird-song of linnets he finds harmony where by rights there should be dissonance, but harmony of a higher order than any produced by mere man: "It is as if hundreds of fairy minstrels were all playing on stringed and wind instruments of various forms, every one intent on his own performance without regard to the others."

Just as non-human life forms are seen in human terms, so humans are shown to display the attributes of their fellow creatures, especially the birds. This technique is employed with particular intensity in the chapter describing his first visit to Buenos Aires. The large collection of fashionably dressed people that gathers outside the church on a saint's day reminds him of "a flock of military starlings, a black- or dark-plumaged bird with a scarlet breast." The negro washerwomen covering the beach of the River Plata with their white flapping linen while they chatter and laugh with one another make him think of "the hubbub made by a great concourse of gulls, ibises, godwits, geese and other noisy waterfowl on some marshy lake." Birds of prey naturally occur to this hater of cities. The raucous cries of the nightwatchmen sound like "the caw of the carrion-crow." Most of the beggars are ex-soldiers "thrown out to live like carrion-hawks on what they could pick up." This capacity to discern the animal in the human is exercised, if less concentratedly, throughout the book. Yet it rarely obtrudes. (pp. 212-13)

All this is a subtle stylistic preparation for the introduction of animism two-thirds of the way through the autobiography. Throughout Hudson describes his own boyish self as he does all the other humans by similar comparisons to the bird life that captivates his young imagination, a process which culminates in his desire for the wings of a great-crested screamer: "If I could only get off the ground like that heavy bird and rise as high, then the blue air would make me as buoyant and let me float all day without pain and effort like the bird!" If this longing of his is only occasionally gratified indirectly in dreams in which he is levitating, he does finally forge out of his longing to belong to life in the wild a philosophy of life, a personalized religious belief in the existence of animal and vegetable intelligence. He distinguishes what he means by the term "animism" from cultural anthropologists who understand it to mean "a doctrine of souls that survive the bodies and objects they inhabit." As Hudson first explained this concept in **Idle Days,** for him animism is "the mind's projection of itself into nature, its attribution of its own sentient life and intelligence in all things." Hudson first became conscious of "this sense of the supernatural in natural things" at the age of eight and claims that "the feeling has never been wholly outlived." His unusual retention of this childlike feeling gave him the confidence to apply his adult perceptions and his immense skill as a prose stylist to the formative experiences of his childhood in his autobiography.

The effect which animism has on him, he writes, is both pleasurable and at times frightening. For the spirit of nature which he had been observing and communing with from infancy struck him as cruel as well as beautiful. The early chapters of the book are scattered with instances of nature's cruelty and violence. There are the "paroquets" who strip off the peach blossom to make themselves a perch. There are the "thistle years" when giant thistles cover the plains, restricting the movement of man and beast alike and threatening them with death by fire. Or there is the storm in which half-inch-thick hailstones batter down the crops and kill or injure hundreds of cattle. Deer die locked solidly together by their horns. And the cruelty extends to men. Hudson is both horrified and fascinated by the barbaric behaviour of the gauchos whose heartless method of slaughtering cattle he describes in considerable detail. Nor does he exclude himself from this less pleasant side to nature. Shooting birds for the table he seems to think is justified. Yet when he is pursuing a golden plover, because when cooked it is one of his father's favourites, he recalls his humiliation at being reproved for "chasing away God's little birds" by, of all people, an uncouth gaucho. Just before his discovery of his belief in animism he learns to stop persecuting serpents and is rewarded by a near-mystic vision of a black snake, so representative in his dual nature of all life in the wild. The snake, which had

Drawing of Hudson by W. Rothenstein. Courtesy of Hispanic Institute, Columbia University.

crawled over his foot while he had remained frozen with horror, had left in him "a sense of mysterious being, dangerous on occasion as when attacked or insulted, and able in some cases to inflict death with a sudden blow, but harmless and even friendly or beneficient towards those who regarded it with kindly and reverent feelings in place of hatred." Hudson continued throughout his early manhood to have ambiguous feelings about killing the birds he collected for a living and sent off to various museums. But his close observation of the workings of nature convinced him that life in the raw necessarily entailed an eternal conflict between predator and prey, nature and man: "It is a principle of Nature that only by means of strife can strength be maintained. No sooner is any species placed above it, or overprotected, than degeneration begins."

Hudson sees modern urban civilization as the product of such degeneration, an atrophied state which is infinitely inferior to the risk of death in the wild which makes life there so much more vivid. The autobiography employs death as a recurrent motif for just this purpose, to help Hudson convey to the reader the intensity of his early life which he shared with the wild life of the pampas. Chapter I associates the house in which he was born with the ghost of a former negro slave who had been scourged to death for daring to declare his love to the mistress of the house. He never saw that ghost, but he did come across an apprehended murderer tied to a post in the great barn of his new home, "The Acacias," described in Chapter 2. In the next chapter comes the death of his old dog, Caesar, and his

tutor's speech over his grave in which he pointed out that we all end up dead and buried like Caesar. The young Hudson is devastated by the thought and immediately sees his condition as similar to that of the murderer awaiting a possible sentence of death. When his mother explains the Christian belief in the immortality of the soul he "wanted to run and jump for joy and cleave the air like a bird." He is restored to his primitive enjoyment of an unthinking life of the senses. Yet, for all the reassurances that his mother gives him, the frequency of death in his world soon brings back his life-long fear of it, as the rest of the chapter shows. Death threatens the continuation of his wild animal self for which no talk of the soul can compensate him.

The theme recurs in Chapter 8 where the young Hudson is taken by a shepherd boy to see a bloodstain on the ground belonging to an officer of Rosas's defeated troops who had been murdered by his own men. This incident introduces his horrified description of the blood lust of the gauchos who cannot resist slitting a long white neck when they see one, a perversion of nature as Hudson understands it. These repeated references to man's mortality are skilfully drawn together in the coda consisting of the last three chapters. On his fifteenth birthday Hudson is for the first time brought face to face with the end of his boyhood and the likelihood that manhood would mean abandoning his rapturous life amidst nature in favour of "that dull low kind of satisfaction which men have in the set task." The thought is almost as bad as the prospect of dying itself since both manhood and death mean a loss of his intense immersion in the natural world. Next he falls ill of rheumatic fever and his case is pronounced hopeless by the doctors. He is traumatized at the thought of losing forever his intense life of the senses and feels once again like the captured murderer or "like any wretched captive, tied hand and foot and left to lie there until it suited his captor to come back and cut his throat or thrust him through with a spear, or cut him into strips with a sword. . .," a reminder of the gaucho's method of killing an opponent. He reverts to the terror he felt after the death of his dog Caesar.

But this time Christianity fails to offer him even temporary consolation and he describes his gradual loss of faith following the arguments of a disillusioned old Roman Catholic landowner, his reading Darwin's *The Origin of Species* and his mother's unexpected death. So the book is framed by this motif of death which occurs in the first and last chapters. His abandonment of Christianity has been prepared for in the chapter, "A Boy's Animism," where he claims that the animistic instinct is usually repressed by Christians with their belief in an implacable anthropomorphic deity continuously watching and judging them, condemning any feelings of the supernatural amidst the natural as sinful temptations of the devil. In *Idle Days* Hudson uses a powerful metaphor to justify his belief in the superiority of the animistic spirit to Christian denials of the barbaric element still lurking within us. This primitive element Hudson compares to "a hidden fiery core" the heat from which "still permeates the crust to keep us warm." This state, he adds sarcastically, "is, no doubt, a matter of annoyance" to those who wish to be rid of their brute instincts and "to live on a cool crust and rapidly grow angelic." Hudson prefers us to be what we are, "a little lower than the angels." The combination of geological and Christian imagery here shows Hudson restoring to the natural world the religious feelings appropriated by Christianity.

Eventually Hudson emerges from his own dark night of the soul convinced that his animistic perception of nature will survive his loss of boyhood and that it matters more to him than a belief in immortality. Death is his true enemy because it will bring what he calls his "earth life" to a complete end. He concludes the book with the bare assertion that throughout his life he has felt "that it was infinitely better to be than not to be." His spiritual quest has ended with a defence of life on earth that is lived so intensely that material existence reveals the supernatural within itself. In showing that the author has retained contact with his powerful experiences of nature as a child his autobiography acts as a vindication of his subsequent life—especially of his achievement as a naturalist and writer. The childhood vision that led to his conversion to animism in his later teens is responsible, he considers, for the books he has subsequently written and the life he has subsequently lived with the vision undiminished in his mind. So that *Far Away and Long Ago* turns out to be an apology for (which is nearly always a vindication of) a life and belongs to that long line of religious apologies starting with Augustine and stretching to Newman. Hudson's true reader is himself looking for validation to himself as writer for his continuing dependence on the formative drama of a childhood in his case lived in the depths of nature from which his writing draws its inspiration and vision. (pp. 215-19)

Brian Finney, *"The Spiritual History of the Self,"* in his The Inner I: British Literary Autobiography of the Twentieth Century, *Oxford University Press, 1985, pp. 207-26.*

AMY D. RONNER (essay date 1986)

[*In the following excerpt, Ronner examines Hudson's philosophy as expressed in his works.*]

Even after **Green Mansions** made him a famous novelist, as Hudson explained to Ford Madox Ford, he did not like to be called an artist: "I'm not an artist. It's the last thing I should call myself. I'm a field naturalist who writes down what he sees."

This vocation derives in part from Hudson's pronounced affiliation with the work of Gilbert White who in 1755 resigned his fellowship at Oriel College, Oxford, and settled as Curate at Selborne.... Hudson repeatedly declares himself akin to Gilbert White, whose *Natural History of Selborne* was given to him at age sixteen, just the "right thing to get for that bird-loving boy out on the pampas." White's compilation of letters became for Hudson a holy writ to which he pays tribute in nearly every collection of out-of-door essays. (p. 75)

Hudson's most extensive discussion of the early naturalist occurs in **Birds and Man** where every detail of Selborne calls forth his image. Hudson explains:

I thought of White continually. The village itself, every feature in the surrounding landscape, and every object, living or inanimate, and every sound, became associated in mind with the thought of the obscure country curate, who was without ambition, and was "a still quiet man, with no harm in him—no, not a bit," as was said by one of his parishioners.

While wandering through the village, Hudson feels that White's memory is "interwoven with living forms and sounds." He says, "It began to seem to me that he who had ceased to live over a century ago, whose Letters had been the favourite book of several generations of naturalists, was, albeit dead and gone, in some mysterious way still living." This "continual sense

of an unseen presence" leads the narrator into a dialogue in which he discusses the "marked difference in manner, perhaps in feeling between the old and new writers on animal life and nature." Hudson perceives a modern disposition to emphasize the more aesthetic and emotional aspects of nature. The new naturalist is more than an amateur scientist collecting facts, but he is a spiritualist with "a kind of subsidiary conscience, a private assurance that in all [his] researches into the wonderful works of creation, [he is] acting in obedience to a tacit command, or, at all events, in harmony with the Divine Will." Through assuming the first person plural, Hudson defines this new breed of nature writers for the figurative ghost of Selborne.

We are bound as much as ever to facts; we seek for them more and more diligently, knowing that to break from them is to be carried away by vain imaginations. All the same, facts in themselves are nothing to us: they are important only in their relations to other facts and things—to all things, and the essence of things, material and spiritual. We are not like children gathering painted shells and pebbles on a beach; but whether we know it or not, are seeking after something beyond and above knowledge.

This definition of a post eighteenth century naturalist who investigates all things "material and spiritual," who quests for unity in the universe, counters Hudson's other persona, the ordinary outdoor man with a professed interest in mere surfaces.

On one level, the more complex voice of W. H. Hudson is one of a field naturalist who is also a religious philosopher. His outdoor study brings about a mystical experience where the self merges with the ceaseless cycles of Nature and provides the soul with a sense of immortality, which for Hudson seemed far more tenable than the Christian after-life. On another level, the field naturalist is an artistic philosopher. Hudson emphasized the active relationship between the mind and Nature, one that results in mythmaking and the creation of metaphor which is central to both fiction and "science." Hudson saw art as the universal "instinct" to express beauty which in its highest form reflects the very spirit and breath of Nature. Hudson also believed that the true field naturalist transcends both the spheres of art and science: he is an individual independent of both and free to embrace the whole world as his subject matter.

Related to Hudson's definition of the field naturalist is his refusal to associate himself with any organized faith. (pp. 76-7)

In *Far Away and Long Ago* Hudson explores the dawning of his religious atheism. After his serious illness Hudson plunges into religious literature in an attempt to convince himself of the possibility of salvation. Once after reading Richard Baxter's *The Saint's Everlasting Rest*, the young naturalist, "assailed by lawless thoughts," finds himself envious of the "eternally damned." This reaction, at the time seemingly blasphemous, eventually became the foundation for his mature philosophy.

If an angel, or one returned from the dead, could come to assure me that life does not end with death, that we mortals are destined to live for ever, but that for me there can be no blessed hereafter on account of my want of faith, and because I loved or worshipped Nature rather than the Author of my being, it would be, not a message of despair, but of consolation; for in that dreadful place to which I should be sent, I should be alive and not dead, and have my memories of earth, and perhaps meet and have communion there with others of like mind with myself, and with recollections like mine.

His hope for immortality of the soul drives the young Hudson into theology, sermons and meditations which only bring him more disputation and doubt. He claims, "The worst of it was that when I tried to banish these bitter, rebellious ideas, taking them to be the whisperings of the Evil One, as the books taught, the quick reply would come that the supposed Evil One was nothing but the voice of my own reason striving to make itself heard." Hudson describes his encounter with a neighboring gaucho who tells him that although he is supposedly a Roman Catholic and the Hudsons are Protestants, a minority considered to be heretics in that area of the world, there is really no difference since both orthodoxies are false:

> "You see all this with your eyes," he continued, waving his hands to indicate the whole visible world. "And when you shut them or go blind you see no more. It is the same with our brains. We think of a thousand things and remember, and when the brain decays we forget everything, and we die, and everything dies with us."

Although Hudson initially rejects the gaucho whom he feels is sadly deluded, in later life he returned to accept this view.

The clearest spokesman for Hudson's feelings about church establishments and the followers is the carpenter, Mr. Cawood, who in *Fan* sounds a great deal like the author's own "voice of reason." This man "known to be temperate, a good husband and father, and a clever industrious mechanic" is approached by the narrow-minded fanatic, Mrs. Churton, who arrives at his home to persuade him to save his soul and attend church. Her lecture on the "truth of Christianity" culminates in advice—"to search the scriptures, to worship in public, and humbly seek instruction from our appointed teachers." Cawood remains unmoved and heroically asserts his independence.

> I think we are free to do good or evil; and if there is a future life—and I hope there is—I don't think that anyone will be made miserable in it because he didn't know things better than he could know them. That's the whole of my religion, Mrs. Churton, and I don't think it a bad one, on the whole—for myself I mean; for I don't go about preaching it, and I don't ask others to think as I do.

Once Cawood exempts himself from the debate over faith and turns to his own instinct as his authority, Fan, who is listening, feels "like a bird newly escaped from captivity." After months of enduring Mrs. Churton's tirades, Cawood's neutrality released her and spoke to "her disposition and humble intellect." The author apparently sides with Cawood and his saint-like heroine since the final speech of the carpenter sounds like Hudson's own voice.

> For here am I, neither for one thing nor the other. On one side are those who have the Bible in their hands, and tell us that it is an inspired book—God's word; on the other side are those who maintain that it is nothing of the sort; and when we ask what kind of men they are, and what kind of lives do they lead, we find that in both camps there are as good men as have ever lived, and along with these others bad and indifferent. . . . I thought it best to give it all up, and give my mind to something else.

Hudson also abandoned the notion that there exists a Judge outside the self. Like the message Rima's apparition delivers to the nearly insane Abel, Hudson believed that people must grant their own peace and redemption.

> Think not that death will ease your pain, and seek it not. Austerities? Good works? Prayers? They are not

seen; they are not heard, they are less than nothing, and there is no intercession. I did not know it then, but you knew it. Your life was your own; you are not saved nor judged; acquit yourself—undo that which you have done, which Heaven cannot undo—and Heaven will say no word nor will I.

It is not until Abel realizes that Rima, the soul of Nature, endures as part of his own soul that he releases himself from guilt. He comes to see self condemnation for what it is—a cruelty worse than Rima's incendiary death: "for they had but tortured and destroyed her body with fire, while I cast this shadow on her soul—this sorrow transcending all sorrows, darker than death, immitigable, eternal." Once he stops looking for forgiveness in the outside forces, he exorcises the fever from his brain and finds the "everlasting beauty and freshness of nature" completely restored. Through Abel's revelations in *Green Mansions* Hudson shows how peace is attained through the awareness of a connection between the I and the infinite.

Hudson's spiritual communion with Nature comes alive in his letter to Morley Roberts, dated November 10, 1920.

> I never had such a sense of oneness, as when I was once on the Downs near Burlington Gap. It was a beautiful day, the sky was a deep wonderful blue, and before me there was a great spread of thinly growing viper's bugloss, such as I had seen on the pampa. It was so wonderful a sight that I *became* the blue of the sky and the bugloss and the air! Why I didn't seem to walk, I just floated, floated! Have you ever felt like that?

This is what Hudson called the "natural mystical feeling" where the character or narrator himself attains this "oneness" with Nature. In *A Traveller in Little Things* Hudson defines this as the "perfect harmony," when the self extends into the surrounding space, and likens this event to spiritual revelation.

> Sky and cloud and wind and rain, and rock and soil and water, and flocks and herds and all wild things, with trees and flowers—everywhere grass and everlasting verdure—it is all part of me, and is me, as I sometimes feel in a mystic mood, even as a religious man in a like mood feels that he is in a heavenly place and is a native there, one with it.

In these moments away from the artificiality of city life when he feels in tune with the earth, Hudson passes into this "mystic mood" where the surroundings become a part of and a reflection of the self. In his writings Hudson frequently echoes the scriptures to invest Nature with a religious significance: Smith of *A Crystal Age* compares the "translucence and splendour" of light filtering through the foliage to the effect of "stained glass in the windows of some darkening cathedral." Abel, after a period of exile, returns to the Christian settlement like a prophet bringing new knowledge "of *his* world—the world of nature and of the spirit."

At Selborne Hudson, conversing with the emanation of Gilbert White, brings up the ever evolving awareness of a unity in all living things as the central concern of the nineteenth century naturalist: "For we are no longer isolated, standing like starry visitors on a mountaintop, surveying life from the outside; but are on a level and part and parcel of it; and if the mystery of life daily deepens, it is because we view it more closely and with clearer vision." The highest attainment for the new naturalist is this perception of an ongoing commensalism in Nature. The naturalist becomes like a priest imparting "not only the thing he sees but the spirit of his vision" and finally, his own relationship to it.

Far Away and Long Ago contains two contrapuntal motifs which are in the end reconciled, one being the child's growing animistic relationship with all living things, the other, an increasing awareness of mortality threatening to tear young Hudson away from the delights in Nature. In the third chapter, Hudson remembers the response of his tutor to the death of the family dog: "That's the end. Every dog has his day and so has every man; and the end is the same for both. We die like old Caesar, and are put into the ground and have the earth shovelled over us." This pronunciation throws Hudson into a depression which is temporarily alleviated by his mother's religious teachings. But the relief is interrupted by several other occurrences that keep "the thoughts and fear of death alive." There are the semi-human cries of cattle being slaughtered, the visitor who almost perishes in the ravine, and the death of the young servant girl, Margarita. The theme climaxes near the close of the autobiography when sixteen year old Hudson is informed that because of his permanently injured heart, he could "drop down at any moment," a diagnosis which he feels is the obliteration of the entire universe.

> This visible world—this paradise of which I had had so far but a fleeting glimpse—the sun and moon and other worlds peopling all space with their brilliant constellations, and still other suns and systems, so utterly remote, in such inconceivable numbers as to appear to our vision as a faint luminous mist in the sky—all this universe which had existed for millions and billions of ages, or from eternity, would have existed in vain, since now it was doomed with my last breath, my last gleam of consciousness, to come to nothing.

Even the beauty of the outdoors could not ease these fears.

Hudson found in nature, particularly "the autumnal migration," a mingling of two contrary sensations, "intense joy" and "ineffable pain." Eventually as his health improved, he learned to accept the momentary pleasure derived from Nature as his peace. He explains at the close of his autobiography his decision to focus on happiness in the present tense.

> When I hear people say they have not found the world and life so agreeable or interesting as to be in love with it, or that they look with equanimity to its end, I am apt to think they have never been properly alive nor seen with clear vision the world they think so meanly of, or anything in it—not a blade of grass.

Instead of continuing with his struggle to have faith in the possibility of an after-life, Hudson channeled his hopes for peace into this life. In *Far Away and Long Ago* he closes with a reaffirmation of life: "In my worst times, when I was compelled to exist shut out from Nature in London for long periods, sick and poor and friendless, I could yet always feel that it was infinitely better to be than not to be."

It is characteristic of Hudson that in the midst of describing some natural phenomenon, he introduces the subject of death. Hudson came to believe that the encroachment of the end could intensify one's appreciation of Nature. In *Nature in Downland* he explains how the yearly decline of life can bestow on us a feeling of immortality.

> For these innumerable little lives quickly pass while ours endure. Furthermore, the brief life which they have is but one, and though their senses be brilliant they see not beyond their small horizons. To us the Past and the Future are open, like measureless countries of diversified aspect, lying beyond our horizon; yet we may see them and are free to range over them

at will. It may even happen that the autumnal spectacle of the cessation of life on the earth, nature's yearly tragedy brought thus suddenly and sharply before the mind's eye, may cause us to realize for the first time what this freedom of the mind really means. It multiplies our years and makes them so many that it is a practical immortality.

The mind observing cycles in Nature with this broad perspective will separate the self from the "innumerable" deaths and "all at once begin to abhor the sickly teachings of those who see in nature's mutations, in cloud and wind and rain and the fall of the leaf, and the going out of ephemeral life, nothing but mournful messages, dreary symbols, reminders of our mortality." By detaching oneself from these minor cessations of life and instead by identifying oneself with the vernal rebirths, one can triumphantly cry, "I shall not die, but live!"

In the **"Return of the Chiff-Chaff"** the speaker demonstrates how he may turn to Nature for the sense of immortality. He begins by expressing his wish "to divest himself of himself—that second self which he has unconsciously acquired—to be like the trees and animals, outside of the sad atmosphere of human life and its eternal tragedy." He feels haunted by images of departed friends, in particular, his wife, who brings about his somber mood: "The sweet was indeed changed to bitter, and the loss of those who were one with me in feeling appeared to my mind as a monstrous betrayal, a thing unnatural, almost incredible." Hudson then traces his gradual return to peace through enchantment with Nature.

> Then little by little the old influence began to reassert itself, and it was as if one was standing there by me, one who was always calm, who saw all things clearly, who regarded me with compassion and had come to reason with me. "Come now," it appeared to say, "open your eyes once more to the sunshine; let it enter freely and fill your heart, for there is healing in it and in all nature. It is true the power you have worshipped and trusted will destroy you, but you are living to-day, and the day of your end will be determined by chance only. Until you are called to follow them into that 'world of light,' or it may be of darkness and oblivion, you are immortal."

The narrator animates Nature which appears in the form of a "mysterious mentor" advising him to immerse himself in the "unchanging call" of the Chiff-Chaff, a song from which the speaker separates himself, for "the small bird exists only in the present; there is no past, nor future, nor knowledge of death." Once detached, the speaker finds relief from the "intolerable sadness—from the thought of springs that have been, the beautiful multitudinous life that has vanished." He realizes that his own moods are as mutable as the seasons and that "Nature herself in her own good time heals the wound she inflicts." He discovers that the power of his mind to project his loss even upon the resplendence of spring makes the disappearances of his loved ones seem less final: "They are not wholly, irretrievably lost, even when we cease to remember them, when their images come no longer unbidden to our minds. They are present in nature, through ourselves, receiving but what we give, they have become part and parcel of it and give it an expression." In contrast, the loss serves to intensify the beauty once it is restored: "As when the rain clouds disperse and the sun shines out once more, heaven and earth are filled with a chastened light, sweet to behold and very wonderful, so because of our lost ones, because of the old grief at their loss, the visible world is touched with a new light, a tenderness and grace and beauty not its own." Hudson believed that our interactions with the visible world, our study of its ongoing life and death cycles, can help us see that our stay on earth is prolonged and can grant us a feeling of immortality.

In "A Boy's Animism," the heart of his account of his early years, Hudson recalls the shape and appearances of Nature evoking more powerful sensations than his mother's most profound religious teachings.

> These teachings did not touch my heart as it was touched and thrilled by something nearer, more intimate, in nature, not only in moonlit trees or in a flower or serpent, but, in certain exquisite moments and moods and in certain aspects of nature, in "every grass" and in all things, animate and inanimate.

Hudson explains that this sense of "something" in Nature is due to "animism," a process defined at the start of the chapter: "by animism I do not mean the theory of a soul in nature, but the tendency or impulse or instinct, in which all myth originates, to *animate* all things; the projection of ourselves into nature." This leads to the "sense and apprehension of an intelligence like our own but more powerful in all visible things." In a chapter suggestive of Wordsworth's *Prelude,* Hudson traces the development of his "sense of the supernatural in natural things," a feeling which begins with the sensuous appreciation of the outdoors.

Hudson recalls his first association with Nature as a physical delight—"the blue of the sky, the verdure of earth, the sparkle of sunlight on water, the taste of milk, of fruit, of honey, the smell of dry or moist soil, of wind and rain, of herbs and flowers." This first appreciation is Edenic, a state prior to the infiltration of complex knowledge with its creative, spiritual and factual levels. Hudson describes a change in his eighth year when he became conscious of "something more than this mere childish delight in nature. . . . It was as if some hand had surreptitiously dropped something into the honeyed cup which gave it at certain times a new flavour." Hudson defines a mystery tempered both with pleasure and fear, a feeling he found most powerful on late night rambles.

> Yet on the very next night I would steal out again and go to the spot where the effect was strongest, which was usually among the large locust or white acacia trees, which gave the name of Las Acacias to our place. The loose feathery foliage on moonlight nights had a peculiar hoary aspect that made this tree seem more intensely alive than others, more conscious of my presence and watchful of me.

These early experiences of animism are equated with divine appearances—"similar to the feeling a person would have if visited by a supernatural being." Although the projection of the self onto Nature brings about the apprehension of a like intelligence, the force itself remains invisible, mute, indifferent. It stands "silent and unseen, intently regarding him, and divining every thought in his mind," yet takes "no visible shape nor speak[s] to him out of the silence." The imagination, of course, may grant this being a shape and a voice, but apart from the mind or the resultant myth, it remains a nebulous mystery.

Hudson distinguishes his animism from pantheism or superstition. Animism is the process underlying all nature worship, superstitions and myths, a faculty that expresses itself in the deification of the forces and laws of the universe: "This faculty or instinct of the dawning mind is or has always seemed to me essentially religious in character; undoubtedly it is the root of all nature-worship, from fetishism to the highest pantheistic

development." In "The Quality of Whiteness," a chapter in *Idle Days in Patagonia,* Hudson argues that animism is independent of any one system of beliefs; it is a universal foundation for both primitive and civilized philosophies that perceive this living soul in Nature. Hudson sets himself apart from the anthropologists, Robertson, Smith, and Frazer, and speaks of Tyler who in his *Primitive Culture* uses the term to mean "a theory of life, a philosophy of primitive man, which has been supplanted among civilized people by a more advanced philosophy." According to Hudson, "the mind's projection of itself onto nature, its attribution of its own sentient life and intelligence," is really a "primitive universal faculty on which the animistic philosophy of the savage is founded," one which hasn't been and cannot be extinguished.

> When our philosophers tell us that this faculty is obsolete in us, that it is effectually killed by ratiocination, or that it only survives for a period in our children, I believe they are wrong, a fact which they could find out for themselves if, leaving their books and theories, they would take a solitary walk on a moonlit night in the "woods of westermain," or any other woods, since all are enchanted.

This "latent animism that is in all of us" manifests itself in various forms, from the sailor navigating a ship which he believes is "alive and intelligent" on a sea which is "no mere expanse of water, but a living conscious thing" to the types of tree-worship "found existing among a few of the inhabitants in some of the rustic villages in out-of-the-world districts in England." But sometimes communion with Nature and a personification of the visible world results in the apprehension of a spirit which at times seem harshly indifferent to the human world. Hudson's description of the spirit of winter illustrates this seeming impersonality.

> There is no longer any recognition, any bond; and if we were to fall down and perish by the wayside, there would be no compassion: it is sitting apart and solitary, cold and repelling, its breath suspended, in a trance of grief or passion; and although it sees us it is as though it saw us not, even as we see pebbles and withered leaves on the ground, when some great sorrow has dazed us, or when some deadly purpose is in our heart.

Hudson's relationship with Nature based on the active link between the mind and the external world brings about the recognition of an Unseen Being along with a sense of its separation from the self, and at times, its lack of sympathy with the small human world.

In *Far Away and Long Ago* Hudson claims that he never lost this animistic faculty nurtured on the pampas. In fact, animism is a key to his books: in almost every work he includes the animistic experience of Nature in all its stages. Smith of *A Crystal Age* delights in the flight of buzzards and recalls "how often in former days when gazing up into such a sky, he had breathed a prayer to the unseen spirit." In *Afoot in England* the narrator at Stonehenge describes "the unbedding of the lark," by animating the voices that "were not human nor angelic, but passionless," and by emerging from the experience with a sense of something other-worldly. Rima, whose voice is both human and supernatural, becomes Hudson's most complete animistic creation, the imaginative embodiment of Nature.

For Hudson, poetic language is the outcome of the same process, the animistic activation of the visible world. Hudson specifically renames the process of making a metaphor as animistic excitement.

> Let us remember that our poets who speak not scientifically but in the language of passion, when they say that the sun rejoices in the sky and laughs at the storm; that the earth is glad with flowers in spring, and the autumn fields happy; that the clouds frown and weep, and the wind sighs and "utters something mournful on its way"—that in all this they speak not in metaphor, as we are taught to say, but that in moments of excitement, when we revert to primitive conditions of mind, the earth and all nature is alive and intelligent, and feels as we feel.

In his own treatment of nature, Hudson too shows us this reversion to the "primitive condition of mind." In *A Little Boy Lost* when Martin murders a spoonbill, he finds his own guilt and remorse reflected in the very hues and shapes of the landscape.

> Swifter and vaster, following close upon the flying shadow, came the mighty cloud, changing from black to slaty grey; and then, as the sun broke forth again under its lower edge, it was all flushed with a brilliant rose colour. But what a marvellous thing it was, then the cloud covered a third of the wide heavens, almost touching the horizon on either side with its wing-like extremities; Martin gazing steadily at it, saw that in its form it was like an immense spoonbill flying through the air! He would gladly have run away then, to hide himself from its sight, but he dared not stir, for it was now directly above him; so, lying down on the grass and hiding his face against the dead bird, he waited in fear and trembling.

Martin's own sense that he has committed a crime and his desire for punishment which has transformed the sky itself, culminates in a "great cry of terror" from "all the wild birds." Through Martin and his first transgression, Hudson not only reveals the active relationship between mind and Nature, but also demonstrates the workings of animistic mythmaking.

Hudson also finds a place for animism in his naturalist writings and ornithology. In *Birds and Man* it takes the form of a quest for human likenesses in nature:

> We have but to listen to the human tones in wind and water, and in animal voices; and to recognize the human shape in plant and rock, and cloud, and in the round heads of certain animals, like the seal; and the human expression in the eyes and faces, generally, of many mammals, birds and reptiles to know that these casual resemblances are a great deal to us.

Hudson believed that emphasizing these resemblances to human beings could in its final impact express his vision of Nature and her workings with more accuracy. The best example occurs in *Birds in Town and Village* when a search for the wryneck, the source of a "strange penetrating call," modulates into a myth.

> First heard as a bird-call, and nothing more, by degrees it grew more and more laugh-like—a long far-reaching, ringing laugh; not the laugh I should like to hear from any person I take an interest in, but a laugh with all the gladness, unction, and humanity gone out of it—a dry mechanical sound, as if a soulless, lifeless, wind instrument had laughed. It was very curious. Listening to it day by day, something of the strange history of the being, once but no longer human, that uttered it grew up and took shape in my

mind; for we all have in us something of this mysterious faculty. It was not bird, no wryneck, but a being that once, long, long ago, in that same beautiful place, had been a village boy—a free careless, glad-hearted boy, like many another.

Leaving the bird behind, Hudson tells the tale of a child whose innocence is shattered by a too sudden awareness of death. This knowledge brings about extreme suffering and progressive deterioration until a spirit or witch introduces him to the antidote to mortality, a diet consisting solely of ants: "If any person should be able to overcome his repugnance to so strange a food so as to sustain himself on ants and nothing else, the effect of the acid on him would be to change and harden his flesh and make it impervious to decay or change of any kind. *He would, so long as he confined himself to this kind of food, be immortal.*" After much anguish, the child adjusts to the new food and undergoes a Lamarckian transformation: "As his strength increased so did his dexterity in catching the small active insect prey; he no longer gathered the ants up in his palm and swallowed them with dust and grit, but picked them so deftly and conveyed them one by one to his mouth with lightning rapidity." Hudson describes him after his many years of bodily adaptation as a "lean grey little man, clad in a quaintly barred and mottled mantle, woven by his own hands from soft silky material, and a close-fitting brown peaked cap on his head with one barred feather in it for ornament, and a small wizened grey face with a thin sharp nose, puckered lips, and a pair of round brilliant startled eyes." After leading the reader away from the bird into the history of an odd man who haunts rural villages looking for ants, Hudson returns to the origin of his myth.

> I looked and beheld the thing that had laughed just leaving its perch on a branch near the ground and winging its way across the field. It was only a bird after all—only the wryneck; and that mysterious faculty I spoke of, saying that we all of us possessed something of it (meaning only some of us), was nothing after all but the old common faculty of the imagination.

Through the language of myth, a child's metamorphosis, Hudson communicates information about the voice, diet and habits of the real wryneck. This is not intended to be a sugar-coated deliverance of ornithological facts. Instead, Hudson hoped to express the feeling the creature excited in him, something he felt was as important as the facts. Hudson believed that the animistic faculty behind pantheism, hylozoism, nature-worship and behind the creation of Rima should also express itself in the work of a field naturalist. One who studies "the life and conversation of animals" has license to transform the wilds in order to reveal this consciousness and unity pervading all life.

What Hudson objected to most was specialization, the exclusive obedience to any one authority, and what he saw as the modern tendency to construct impenetrable boundaries between art and science. In **"The Serpent in Literature"** Hudson complains of the scientist who through his elaborate system of classification and nomenclature extinguishes the beauty and mystery of life.

> When the snakists of the British Museum or other biological workshop have quite done with their snake, have pulled it out of its jar and popped it in again to their hearts' content; weighed, measured, counted ribs and scales, identified its species, sub-species, and variety; and have duly put it all down in a book, made a fresh label, perhaps written a paper—when all is finished, something remains to be said; some-

thing about the snake; the creature that was not a spiral-shaped, rigid, cylindrical piece of clay-coloured gutta-percha, no longer capable of exciting strange emotions in us—the unsightly dropped coil of a spirit that was fiery and cold.

This approach to the creature, one that is devoid of emotion, causes Hudson to direct his reader elsewhere for the more complete picture. "The poet does not see his subject apart from its surroundings, deprived of its atmosphere—a mere fragment of beggarly matter—does not see it too well, with all the details which become visible only after a minute and, therefore, cold examination, but as a part of the picture, a light that quivers and quickly passes, that we, through him, are able to see it too, and to experience the old mysterious sensations, restored by his magic touch." After listing those who have caught the fear and magic of "snakiness"—Matthew Arnold, Gordon Hake, Shakespeare, Browning, Tennyson, Meredith, and Keats, the naturalist decides that Oliver Wendell Holmes's *Elsie Venner* is the "best presentation of serpent life" in prose because he views it "at a distance and as a whole, with the vision common to all men, and the artist's insight added."

Hudson's praise of Holmes's treatment of the snake is consistent with his definition of the evolving field naturalist. Hudson informs the ghost of Gilbert White that modern books about Nature are moving in the "direction of a more poetic and emotional treatment of the subject." Hudson demonstrates this approach in his own autobiography when he mingles his refutation of the notion of the serpent as mute with his memories from childhood.

> A long sibilation would be followed by distinctly-heard ticking sounds, as of a husky-ticking clock, and after ten or twenty or thirty ticks another hiss, like a long expiring sigh, sometimes with a tremble in it as of a dry leaf swiftly vibrating in the wind. . . . I, lying awake in my bed, listened and trembled. It was dark in the room, and to my excited imagination the serpents were no longer under the floor, but out, gliding hither and thither over it, with uplifted heads, in a kind of mystic dance.

Also, in *Green Mansions* the serpent is both a real and imaginary creation, beautiful, enticing and yet suggestive of the fall.

> It was a coral snake, famed as much for its beauty and singularity as for its deadly character. It was about three feet long, and very slim; its ground colour a brilliant vermillion, with broad jet-black rings at equal distances round its body, each black ring or band divided by a narrow yellow strip in the middle. The symmetrical pattern and vividly contrasted colours would have given it the appearance of an artificial snake made by some fanciful artist, but for the gleam of life in its bright coils.

In his books, both fiction and nonfiction, Hudson intertwines fact and emotion: he refuses to estrange any creature from its natural environment and imitate the enemies under attack in his campaign against "Feathered Women." Any creature without life, amputated from its habitat, could no longer activate the animistic faculty or excite the kind of imaginative soarings Hudson claims to experience on the downs: "I can almost realise the sensation of being other than I am—a creature with the instinct of flight and the correlated faculty; that in a little while, when I have gazed my full and am ready to change my place, I shall lift great heron-like wings and fly with little effort to other points of view."

Although Hudson did attack the methods of the laboratory, he refrained from blaming science alone for the uglification of the wilds. Instead, he found a more general target, the tendency in both science and art to pull away from the earth. An artist whose excursions into a supernatural realm seem irreversible is as culpable as the scientist whose systems of classification make him lose sight of the magic and mystery within the real form in nature. The new field naturalist who makes room for emotion and fantasy may take imaginative flights in order to shed light on the actual scene, but should, like the bird, always return again to the ground. In *A Hind in Richmond Park* Hudson explains the importance of being in touch with the very essence of the object.

> Apart from the aesthetic feeling which the object or scene or atmospheric conditions may rouse, and from the sense of novelty, the lively interest we experience at times in what we see and smell and hear and feel, and from other things operating in us, there is a sense of the *thing itself*—of the tree or wood, the rock, river, sea, mountain, the soil, clay or gravel, or sand or chalk, the cloud, the rain, and what not—something, let us say, penetrative, special, individual, as if the quality of the thing itself had entered into us, changing us, affecting body and mind.

In "A Serpent Mystery," a chapter of the autobiography, Hudson demonstrates his ideal approach, the transformation of the subject without loss of the "thing itself." He recounts his boyhood fascination with a unique black snake which appeared to be a "coal-black current flowing past [him]—a current not of water or other liquid but of some such element as quicksilver moving on in a rope-like stream." He, in constant pursuit of this rarity, attributes to it human reactions and emotions: "The serpent might come upon me unawares and would probably resent always finding a boy hanging about his den." In later life he unearths facts which partially explain the mystery of the ophidian's unusual color: "Eventually I heard of the phenomenon of melanism in animals, less rare in snakes perhaps than in animals of other classes, and I was satisfied that the problem was partly solved. My serpent was a black individual of a species of some other colour." In this anecdote Hudson follows his own pattern: he describes the creature, analyzes the sensations evoked by it, animates it and then closes with the snake itself and a hypothesis informed by science.

Hudson remembers that as a boy he felt an almost inexplicable dissatisfaction with Gilbert White's *Selborne:* he sensed that something central to his own experience of Nature was missing.

> I read and re-read it many times, for nothing so good of its kind had ever come to me, but it did not reveal to me the secret of my own feeling for Nature—the feeling of which I was becoming more and more conscious, which was a mystery to me, especially at certain moments, when it would come upon me with a sudden rush. So powerful it was, so unaccountable, I was actually afraid of it, yet I would go out of my way to seek it. At the hour of sunset I would go out half a mile or so from the house, and sitting on the dry grass with hands clasped round my knees, gaze at the western sky, waiting for it to take me. And I would ask myself: what does it mean? But there was no answer to that in any book concerning the "life and conversation of animals."

According to Hudson, the new naturalist is not only more mystical, more emotional, but also a rebel who refuses "to take one branch of life and give all his attention to that" and knows that "to specialise is to lose your soul." To Hudson, this did not mean combining art and science or even attempting to reconcile seemingly disparate fields. He felt that real change can only come about when the artist and the scientist begin to feel "antagonistic" toward their respective niches and declare their independence of both.

> If there are any signs of change, they are in the minds of those who are outside of the artistic world. And outside of the scientific world as well, seeing that in both cases the reflex effects of their vocation on their minds is to distort the judgment. I refer to those only who are outside both fields, whose reasoning and aesthetic faculties are balanced, whose interest is in the whole of life, and who have succeeded in preserving perfect independence of mind in a herd where those who have captured the first places dominate the others and impose their perverted judgments on them.

The new naturalist should strive to transcend both the spheres of art and science, should work to be "untied, unconfined in a groove, free and appreciating his freedom, intensely interested in life in all its aspects and manifestations," and should aspire to worship Nature and imitate its infinitude. (pp. 76-97)

> *Amy D. Ronner, in her* W. H. Hudson: The Man, the Novelist, the Naturalist, *AMS Press, 1986, 127 p.*

ADDITIONAL BIBLIOGRAPHY

Aldington, Richard. "The Prose of W. H. Hudson." *The Egoist* 1, No. 10 (15 May 1914): 186-87.
> Describes the "great literary pleasure" that Aldington felt while reading Hudson's fiction, but doubts whether there is enough human sentiment in his natural history books for them to be classified as literature.

Bennett, Arnold. "W. H. Hudson." In his *Books and Persons: Being Comments on a Past Epoch, 1908-1911*, pp. 278-79. New York: George H. Doran Co., 1917.
> Praises Hudson's literary talent.

Brown, Christopher. "Hudson's *Far Away and Long Ago:* The Uses of the Past." *Research Studies* 49, No. 4 (December 1981): 221-30.
> Comments on the style and major themes of *Far Away and Long Ago*.

Charles, R. H. "The Writings of W. H. Hudson." *Essays and Studies* XX (1935): 135-51.
> Attributes the charm of Hudson's works to their expression of Hudson's personality and his accurate, tolerant, and patient method of observing nature.

Curle, Richard. "W. H. Hudson." *Fortnightly Review* 118, No. DCLXX (2 October 1922): 512-19.
> Appreciation of Hudson's life and works by a friend.

De la Mare, Walter. "Naturalists." In his *Pleasures and Speculations*, pp. 47-65. London: Faber and Faber, 1940.
> Argues that there are three distinct perspectives in Hudson's writing: the field naturalist, the human-naturalist, and the supernaturalist.

Douglas, Marjory Stoneman. "W. H. Hudson: Monuments to His Green World." *The Carrell* 15 (1974): 1-16.
> Describes various monuments to and paintings of Hudson as well as his contributions to naturalism and literature.

"The Work of W. H. Hudson." *The English Review* 2 (April 1909): 157-64.
> Praises Hudson, his work, and his poetic spirit.

Fairchild, Hoxie N. "Rima's Mother." *PMLA* LXVIII, No. 3 (June 1953): 357-70.
> Traces the literary roots of the character Rima, concluding that Arthur O'Shaughnessy's *Colibri* was the main source of the character.

Galsworthy, John. "Four More Novelists in Profile: An Address." In his *Candelabra: Selected Essays and Addresses*, pp. 249-69. New York: Charles Scribner's Sons, 1933.
> Explains why he considers *The Purple Land*, *El Ombú*, and *Green Mansions* to be masterpieces.

Garnett, Edward. "W. H. Hudson: An Appreciation." *The Academy and Literature*, No. 1572 (21 June 1902): 632-34.
> Praises *The Purple Land* and explains why it received little recognition after its first publication.

Gilbert, Ariadne. "William Henry Hudson: Wild and Gentle." In her *Over Famous Thresholds*, pp. 329-48. New York: Century Co., 1929.
> Describes the development and manifestation of Hudson's affection for nature.

Goddard, Harold. *W. H. Hudson: Bird-Man*. New York: E. P. Dutton & Co., 1929, 80 p.
> Sympathetic assessment of Hudson's worldview as presented in his works.

Gorman, Herbert S. "W. H. Hudson." In his *The Procession of Masks*, pp. 107-22. Boston: B. J. Brimmer Co., 1923.
> Defends Hudson against J. C. Squire's criticism that his works are memorable only for the style of their prose.

Graham, R. B. Cunninghame. "The Purple Land." *The Saturday Review* 98, No. 2562 (3 December 1904): 695-96.
> Discusses Hudson's appeal to exclusively English tastes and the critical underestimation of *The Purple Land*.

———. Introduction to *Far Away and Long Ago*, by W. H. Hudson, pp. v-ix. London: J. M. Dent & Sons, 1951.
> Recognizes that the apparent ease of Hudson's style is actually the result of strenuous and deliberate effort, argues that Hudson was at his best when writing about the pampas, and comments on the lasting fame of his works.

Hammerton, J. A. "On and in *The Purple Land*." In his *Memories of Books and Places*, pp. 280-303. Freeport, N. Y.: Books for Libraries Press, 1928.
> Compares Hudson's description of the country and people in *The Purple Land* with the author's own experience in Montevideo.

Harper, George McLean. "Hardy, Hudson, Housman." In his *Spirit of Delight*, pp. 70-91. New York: Henry Holt and Co., 1928.
> Notes the many similarities between the works of Hudson and Thomas Hardy.

Hueffer, Ford Madox. "W. H. Hudson: Some Reminiscences." *The Little Review* VIII, No. 1 (May-June 1920): 1-12.
> Recounts his friendship with Hudson and describes him as a master of English prose.

Hughes, Merritt Y. "A Great Skeptic: W. H. Hudson." *University of California Chronicle* XXVI, No. 2 (April 1924): 161-74.
> Examines Hudson's skepticism of science and art and his profound belief in direct observation of nature as the way to an experience of truth and beauty.

Looker, Samuel J., ed. *William Henry Hudson: A Tribute*. Sussex: Aldridge Bros., 1947, 169 p.
> Collection of essays and reminiscences about Hudson by friends and naturalists including James Guthrie, Arthur Wilde, Violet Hunt, and David Dewar. Also includes thirty-two illustrations.

Mackenzie, Compton. "Great Individuals." In his *Literature in My Time*, pp. 175-83. Freeport, N. Y.: Books for Libraries Press, 1934.
> Hails Hudson as the best writer of English prose in his day.

Massingham, H. J. "W. H. Hudson." In *The Post Victorians*, edited by W. R. Inge, pp. 255-71. London: Ivor, Nicholson & Watson, 1933.

Studies Hudson's views on life, society, and nature, and maintains that his greatest achievement was to expose the fallacy of the nineteenth-century belief in the cruelty and purposelessness of nature.

Moore, John. "The Eagle and the Caged Bird." In his *Country Men*, pp. 170-90. Freeport, N. Y.: Books for Libraries Press, 1935.
    Describes Hudson's attitudes toward life, nature, and humanity.

Mumford, Lewis. Chapter Nine in his *The Story of Utopias*, pp. 171-90. New York: Boni and Liveright, 1922.
    Maintains that the utopia created by Hudson in *A Crystal Age* resembles Thomas More's *Utopia* in that both describe the farmstead and the family as the central units of social life. Mumford also discusses the organization of sexual and social roles in *A Crystal Age*, which he argues are patterned after those of bees.

Nicholson, Mervin. " 'What We See We Feel': The Imaginative World of W. H. Hudson." *University of Toronto Quarterly* XLVII, No. 4 (Summer 1978): 304-22.
    Maintains that the imaginative power of the essays collected in *Nature in Downland* equals that of *Green Mansions* and notes that the major themes of the two works are similar.

Rees, John. "A Reading of *The Purple Land*." *Kansas Quarterly* 14. No. 2 (Spring 1982): 135-48.
    Explicates the five major themes in *The Purple Land* and describes how Hudson's comic sense modifies the romantic melodrama of the novel.

Rhys, Ernest, ed. "A Rare Traveller: W. H. Hudson." *Modern English Essays*, pp. 233-45. London: J. M. Dent & Sons, 1922.
    Describes Hudson as a discoverer of nature and extols his ability to reveal wonderful aspects of nature that had previously gone unnoticed.

Roberts, Morley. *W. H. Hudson: A Portrait*. New York: E. P. Dutton and Co., 1924, 310 p.
    Biography of Hudson written by a close friend.

Swinnerton, Frank. "Travellers: R. B. Cunninghame Graham, W. H. Hudson, Joseph Conrad, H. M. Tomlinson, Norman Douglas." In his *The Georgian Scene; A Literary Panorama*, pp. 131-67. New York: Farrar & Rinehart, 1934.
    Evaluates Hudson's major works.

Thomas, Edward. "W. H. Hudson." In his *A Literary Pilgrim in England*, pp. 190-99. New York: Dodd, Mead and Co., 1917.
    Maintains that Hudson's passionate love of life allowed him to be both a poet and a man of science, and that his work is valuable for its contribution to the study of nature as well as for its profound humanity.

Tindall, William York. "Myth and the National Man." In his *Forces in Modern British Literature 1885-1946*, pp. 360-86. New York: Alfred A. Knopf, 1947.
    Criticizes Hudson for being overly sentimental about nature, but concedes that in the works where his sentimentality is less obtrusive, such as *Far Away and Long Ago*, his style is perfectly suited to his subject.

Tomalin, Ruth. *W. H. Hudson: A Biography*. London: Faber and Faber, 1982, 314 p.
    Comprehensive biography.

Walker, John. " 'Home Thoughts from Abroad': W. H. Hudson's Argentine Fiction." *Canadian Review of Comparative Literature* X, No. 3 (September 1983): 333-76.
    Analyzes Hudson's place in British and Argentine literature and argues that his short fiction is superior to his longer narratives.

————. "W. H. Hudson, Argentina, and the New England Tradition." *Hispania* 69, No. 1 (March 1986): 34-9.
    Examines the influence of New England writers, such as Ralph Waldo Emerson, Henry David Thoreau, Herman Melville, and Nathaniel Hawthorne, on Hudson's nature essays.

Ward, A. C. "Travellers and Biographers." In his *Twentieth-Century Literature 1901-1940*, pp. 222-44. New York: Longmans, Green and Co., 1940.
    Maintains that Hudson was at his best in his autobiography and nature essays, in which he was most able to express "his extraordinarily acute faculty of observation."

West, Herbert Faulkner. *For a Hudson Biographer*. Hanover, N.H.: Westhold Publications, 1958, 37 p.
    Contains Morley Roberts's letters to R. B. Cunninghame Graham written soon after Hudson's death, Hudson's *London Times* obituary, and a copy of his will.

Weygant, Cornelius. "The Out-of-Doors Essays of W. H. Hudson." In his *Tuesdays at Ten*, pp. 255-77. Philadelphia: University of Pennsylvania Press, 1928.
    Criticizes Hudson's fiction for weak characterization but notes that his essays capture more of the beauty and joy of nature than those of any other writer.

Woolf, Leonard. "A Traveller in Little Things." In his *Essays on Literature, History, Politics, Etc.*, pp. 72-80. New York: Harcourt, Brace and Co., 1927.
    Discusses why Hudson's popularity developed so slowly and compares Hudson's disposition as it appears in his literary works with how it appears in his letters to Edward Garnett.

Franz Kafka

1883-1924

Austro-Czech novelist, short story writer, and diarist.

The following entry presents criticism of Kafka's novel *Der Prozess*, first published in 1925 and translated into English in 1936 as *The Trial*. For a discussion of Kafka's complete career, see *TCLC*, Volumes 1 and 6; for a comprehensive discussion of his novella *The Metamorphosis*, see *TCLC*, Volume 13.

The Trial is considered one of the most brilliant and enigmatic novels in modern literature. The narrative relates the arrest of Joseph K. by warders from a mysterious court; his year-long trial, during which he is unable to determine the crime of which he is accused or build an effective defense against the unknown charges; and his ultimate execution. An unfinished novel published posthumously, *The Trial* is composed of discrete chapters often bearing little relation to one another, and scholars debate the order in which these chapters were arranged by Kafka's friend and editor Max Brod. Most commentary on the novel, however, revolves around the existence and nature of K.'s guilt, which has been interpreted from a variety of perspectives, especially those relating to psychology, philosophy, and religion. Through its nightmarish juxtaposition of realistic and fantastic elements, *The Trial* is often considered to presage the breakdown of traditional beliefs and values in the twentieth century.

The Trial was written in the months following the termination of Kafka's marital engagement to Felice Bauer. Kafka had met Bauer two years earlier in 1912, and immediately began a voluminous correspondence with her. Two days after he initiated this correspondence, Kafka wrote the highly regarded short story "The Judgement" in a single eight-hour sitting, an event that is considered his first major artistic breakthrough. Although Kafka was apprehensive about marriage, fearing the effect it would have on his writing, he and Bauer eventually became engaged, a decision that initiated a tumultuous process in which he repeatedly attempted to convince Bauer of his unfitness for marriage. Kafka backed out before the engagement became official, and afterward became romantically involved with a friend of Bauer's, Grete Bloch, who had originally acted as an intermediary between Kafka and Bauer. Although Kafka had been the one to discontinue the engagement, and he and Bloch were falling in love with each other, he felt rejected by Bauer and tried to win her back; when she accepted and the two became formally engaged, Kafka attempted to continue his relationship with Bloch, stating that neither engagement nor marriage would lessen his affection for her. He refused Bloch's requests that he return her letters, and wrote to her at length of his objections to marrying Bauer, yet did not end the engagement. Soon after his thirty-first birthday, when Kafka arrived in Berlin to visit Bauer and Bloch, he was confronted by them in his hotel room, along with Bauer's sister Erna and Kafka's friend Ernst Weiss. Bloch had told Bauer of Kafka's indiscretions and complaints, and during the following hours Bauer conducted what Kafka later termed a "law court," with Bloch and Erna as witnesses and Weiss as an advocate for Kafka. The engagement was once again dissolved, and a month later Kafka began work on *The Trial*.

Although in explicating *The Trial* many critics point to Kafka's difficulties in his relationship with Felice Bauer, and specifically to the "law court" in the Berlin hotel, the novel lends itself to far more expansive interpretation. It begins with the sentence, "Someone must have traduced Joseph K., for without having done anything wrong he was arrested one fine morning." K. is arrested on his thirtieth birthday by two "warders" named Franz and Willem, and neither they nor the inspector who questions K. are able to inform him of the crime of which he has been accused. They do not take him into custody, stating that the arrest is merely to inform K. of his status as an accused man and to record his reaction, nor do they provide evidence that they have the authority to arrest him, treating the justice of his arrest as self-evident and his objections as incomprehensible and irrelevant. The Court that arrests K. is unrelated to the ordinary criminal court system: the offices are located in the attics of slums, the actions of Court officials and employees toward K. are bizarre and impenetrable, and the information offered to K. by those from whom he solicits help is contradictory. After his arrest, K. attempts to ignore his trial, refusing to recognize the court's authority over him; as the trial advances, however, he is forced into progressively greater involvement with his defense, hiring a lawyer at the insistence of his uncle, neglecting his duties as a bank employee even though the advancement of his career had formerly been his most important goal, and finally becoming so obsessed with the trial that he regards his work as an impediment to his defense.

As K. becomes frustrated by the apparent lack of progress effected by his lawyer, he begins to search for other avenues of assistance. One who offers a lucid but despairing picture of the Court is the painter Titorelli, who claims to have important connections with many Court judges. Titorelli outlines for K. three avenues of defense corresponding to three desired outcomes: definite acquittal, ostensible acquittal, and indefinite postponement. A definite acquittal may be granted only by the Court's highest judges, whose inaccessibility prevents their verdicts from being influenced by anyone, including the accused. Moreover, no records exist of a definite acquittal having ever been obtained, although there are "legends" about such acquittals, according to Titorelli. To secure an ostensible acquittal one must procure a number of judges' signatures on an affidavit of the accused person's innocence, after which the case is officially dropped and the defendant is free, although the trial may be resumed and the accused re-arrested at any time. Indefinite postponement requires a strategy of keeping the case from advancing beyond its initial stages, thereby preventing a verdict from being reached and sentence from being passed. While critics variously interpret the allegorical meanings of the three defenses, these supposed alternatives are generally regarded as the most obvious example of the many meaningless choices K. confronts in the course of his trial.

A more enigmatic insight into the workings of the Court is offered in the chapter "In the Cathedral." When K. discusses his case with a priest, who reveals his identity as the prison chaplain for the Court, the priest attempts to correct K.'s "delusion" about the Court by telling him a parable from the "writings that preface the Law." The parable, "Before the Law," was the only part of the novel published by Kafka during his lifetime, and forms a microcosm of *The Trial* itself. In the parable a doorkeeper stands before the Law, and when a man comes seeking the Law and asks to be admitted, the doorkeeper tells him that he cannot "at present" admit him. The man then sits and waits for years, asking the doorkeeper questions and even trying to bribe him, but is never admitted. As he is dying, he asks the doorkeeper why, if everyone seeks the Law, he was the only person who came asking for admittance. The doorkeeper replies, "No one but you could gain admittance through this door, since this door was intended for you. I am now going to shut it." In *The Trial*, the recitation of the parable is followed by a discussion of its meaning between the priest and K. The priest contradicts K.'s assumptions, and demonstrates by references to the text that the doorkeeper may have been both deceptive and honest, above and below the man in status, kind and cruel to him, and knowledgeable and ignorant concerning the Law. K. is left with no definitive interpretation. Many discussions of *The Trial* center on "Before the Law," which demonstrates both K.'s dilemma and the difficulty of interpreting an ambiguous text. In the final chapter, K. is broken in spirit and compliant in his execution. He finds himself waiting for the executioners on the evening before his thirty-first birthday and leads them to the place of execution. Unable to bring himself to obey the executioners' implied demand that he himself carry out the sentence through suicide, however, he reaches out toward an illusory hope just before the end and dies in shame, "like a dog."

The progress of K.'s psychological deterioration throughout *The Trial* raises the question of chapter organization in the novel. The unfinished novel was given to Max Brod as a collection of separate chapters, the order of which Brod reconstructed by examining internal evidence and by recalling the order in which Kafka had read him his work-in-progress. In the third German edition of *The Trial*, Brod included an appendix containing fragments of chapters that Kafka had left unfinished as well as an afterward explaining how the chapter organization had been determined. In 1953, Herman Uyttersprot proposed an alternative chapter arrangement that inserted the fragments into the body of the narrative and moved two chapters to earlier positions in the novel. Uyttersprot's primary criterion for determining order was the progression of seasons throughout the novel: since K.'s trial lasts for one year, seasonal references should follow their usual sequence. Having thus arranged the chapters, Uyttersprot found that the novel appeared less episodic and more consistently portrayed K.'s mental breakdown and submission to the Court. Critics are divided in their reaction to Uyttersprot's reorganization of the chapters. Although some strongly agree with his conclusions and base their readings of *The Trial* on his organization, others point out textual inconsistencies introduced by the rearrangement, as well as aesthetic objections raised by positioning the fragment "Prosecuting Counsel" at the beginning of the novel and placing "In the Cathedral," the penultimate chapter in Brod's arrangement and one of the most crucial sections in *The Trial*, two chapters earlier. In general, Uyttersprot's suggestions have met with limited critical interest, and no edition of *The Trial* has been printed using his arrangement.

Erich Heller has remarked that "there is only one way to save oneself the trouble of interpreting *The Trial*: not to read it." Interpretation of the novel revolves primarily around the mysterious crime of which K. is accused. While he protests his innocence, he nonetheless divulges feelings of guilt through his comments and actions. When asked by the inspector if he is surprised by his arrest, he replies with characteristic ambivalence, "I am surprised, but I am by no means very much surprised." After storming out of his first interrogation shouting, "I'll spare you further interrogations," K. dutifully returns the following week, even though the Court has not called him, and finds that the Court is not even in session. K.'s guilt, whether real or imagined, has been analyzed according to the methodologies of various disciplines, including psychology, theology, philosophy, and social criticism, as well as by diverse combinations and derivatives of them.

In the psychological approach, the Court becomes an externalized symbol of K.'s superego, related to Kafka's fear of his father, irrationally condemning K. for his weekly visits to a prostitute or for his growing sexual desire for a fellow tenant at his boardinghouse, Fräulein Bürstner. Psychological critics emphasize that K.'s age at the time of his execution is only a few weeks younger than Kafka's when his engagement was broken; that in Kafka's manuscript Fräulein Bürstner's name is shortened to F. B., the initials of Felice Bauer; and that the German word *bürsten* is a slang term for sexual intercourse. K. appears both obsessed with and derisive of Fräulein Bürstner, absurdly mishandling his incipient relationship with her, and critics take note of K.'s infantile relations with women throughout the novel, as well as his deference to and resentment of such father figures as his uncle, the lawyer Huld, and the omnipotent spectre of the Court itself, with its mysterious high judges to whom he can never appeal. Kafka's *Letter to His Father* reveals his fear and awe of his father, a strong-willed, successful merchant incapable of comprehending his son's literary ambitions and melancholy temperament. Kafka's work abounds in images of the powerful, domineering father, and critics see the Court of *The Trial* as an abstraction of the same image. In interpreting the Court as K.'s superego, critics question its objective reality, considering it either a hallucination undergone by K. or an intermediate reality that does exist independently of K. but is also partially controlled by his expectations or fears. In demonstrating this position, critics cite evidence suggesting that K. precipitated his own arrest, showing that at his first interrogation the Court begins at the time he had guessed that it would and emphasizing the importance of the surrealistic chapter "The Whipper," in which K. opens the door of an unused storeroom at the Bank to find the two warders who arrested him being beaten by order of the Court because K. had filed a complaint against them at his first interrogation. When K. opens the door the following day, he is again confronted by the two warders and the whipper, exactly as he had seen them the day before, suggesting that such scenes occur only within his own mind and that K. in fact unconsciously arrests, prosecutes, judges, and sentences himself.

Theological critics view the Court as a representation of God's justice, incomprehensible to humans, and the Law as the moral law, of which all have fallen short. Some critics emphasize the profound influence on Kafka of Danish theologian Søren Kierkegaard, while others stress Kafka's Jewish heritage, his later interest in Hasidic Judaism and Zionism, and passages of his work which contain clear references to Hebrew scripture, the Talmud, or rabbinical writings. In the theological view, K.'s guilt is assumed, and is construed either as original sin or as his ignorance of the moral law. All protest against his trial is not only ineffectual but actually damages his case; the only course of action that would help him would be to confess his guilt and throw himself on the mercy of the Court. While secular readings of *The Trial* view the groveling of the tradesman Block, another accused man, before the attorney Huld as a parody of religious devotion and its ineffectiveness, theological critics regard K.'s submission to his execution in the final chapter, "The End," as indicative of his changed perspective and acceptance of guilt, although his ambivalence throughout the chapter and his inability to carry out the sentence himself divide critics over whether K. is finally justified or condemned.

Similar to theological readings of *The Trial* are those that adopt a more broadly philosophic, and specifically existentialist, view of the novel. However, existentialist readings tend to view the Court as an image of a malevolent, rather than beneficent, God who is entirely inaccessible and whose existence, like that of the highest levels of the Court hierarchy, is doubtful. In the existentialist view, K. suffers guilt because of his inability to justify his existence, the world of the Court is absurd and without meaning, and differing interpretations of *The Trial* are futile attempts to discover meaning in a text which this view sees as inherently meaningless. Among other readings of *The Trial* are those that emphasize the surface resemblances between Kafka's fictional world and life under twentieth-century totalitarian governments. Most critics, however, dismiss a strictly political interpretation of *The Trial*, noting inconsistencies that preclude this approach, such as the fact that the Court seems to function independently of the State. Many critics nonetheless view K.'s guilt as his acceptance of bourgeois values, his lack of concern for others, and the subordination of his individuality to the advancement of his career at the Bank. The location of the Court offices in the city's slums and K.'s disgust with this area and the people who live there become evidence of his guilt.

Although some early critics interpreted *The Trial* by means of a single methodology, and the majority of modern critics select one or two approaches as more relevant than others, most now consider the novel a profound work that supports various and even mutually exclusive interpretations, a possibility Kafka himself demonstrated in the chapter "In the Cathedral." The adaptability of this novel to a variety of differing interpretations suggests that it conveys truths that defy rational analysis. Through its nightmarish portrayal of the persecution of Joseph K., *The Trial* remains unique in world literature as a profound study of human guilt.

(See also *Contemporary Authors,* Vol. 105.)

HERMANN HESSE   (essay date 1925)

[*Recipient of the Nobel Prize in literature for 1946, Hesse is considered one of the most important German novelists of the twentieth century. Lyrical in style, his novels are concerned with a search on the part of their protagonists for self-knowledge and for insight into the relationship between physical and spiritual realms. Critics often look upon Hesse's works as falling into the tradition of German Romanticism, from the early bildungsroman* Peter Camenzind *(1904) to the introspective* Steppenwolf *(1927) to the mystical* Das Glasperlenspiel *(1943;* Magister Ludi*), his last major work.* Magister Ludi *is generally held to epitomize Hesse's achievement, delineating a complex vision which intermingles art and religion to convey a sense of harmony unifying the diverse elements of existence. This work, along with such earlier novels as* Siddhartha *(1922), established Hesse's reputation as an author who to many readers and critics approximates the role of a modern sage. In the following excerpt from an essay originally published in German in 1925, Hesse offers his comments on* The Trial.]

The Trial: what a strange, exciting, original, and delightful book this is, like the others of this poet: a web of gossamer, the construct of a dream world created with such immaculate technique and force of vision that a haunted and distorted mirror image of pseudoreality is evoked. This oppressive and fearful nightmare image persists until gradually the hidden significance dawns on the reader. Only then do his wilful and fantastic evocations radiate their redemption, only then do we understand that contrary to their appearance as carefully wrought miniatures their significance is not artistic but religious. They are expressions of piety and elicitations of devotion, even reverence.

The Trial is no exception. A man is arrested one morning in his room; he suspects nothing, is guilty of nothing. Later he is subjected to a series of fantastic bureaucratic formalities, cross-examined and intimidated, later released, and still later brought back again. An invisible and terrible secret tribunal seems responsible for this tortuous trial that begins as a farce and gradually gains in force until it drains and consumes one's very life. For it is not the existence of this or that dereliction which has brought the accused before the court but the original and inescapable guilt of life itself. And most of the accused are convicted after their endless trials, a very few fortunate ones are said to have been acquitted in earlier times, others receive a "conditional acquittal" that can at any time result in a new trial and imprisonment.

In short, this "trial" is none other than the guilt of life itself. The "accused" are the afflicted ones among the unsuspecting, harmless masses that have a dawning awareness of the terrible truth of all life, an awareness that is gradually strangling their hearts. Their redemption is in reach—via the path of submission, of pious devotion to the inevitable.

This is the moral proclaimed in the *Trial,* a moral achieved solely with the means of pure poetry and not by explanations or crude allegories. The reader is enticed into the atmosphere of a dreamlike unreal world and caught in the cobwebs of chaotic dreams, suspecting dimly and from afar that in this image of the fantastic dreamscape he is actually viewing earth, hell, and heaven. (pp. 482-83)

Hermann Hesse, *"Eine Literatur in Rezensionen und Aufsätzen,"* in his *Gesammelte Werke Vol. 12, Suhrkamp Verlag, 1970, translated for this publication by Noel K. Barstad, 1988.*

MAX BROD (essay date 1937)

[*Although best known as the editor of the posthumously published works of Franz Kafka, Brod was also a prolific novelist, dramatist, biographer, and nonfiction writer whose works were highly regarded in Europe during his lifetime. His novels were judged rich and powerful, though occasionally flawed by a tendency to moralize on his growing attachment to Judaism and Zionism. His biography* Franz Kafka *(1937) is prized by scholars for the unique insights provided by his close friendship with Kafka. In the following excerpt from that work, Brod relates the circumstances in which Kafka wrote* The Trial *and examines the novel from a religious perspective.*]

In September [of 1914 Kafka] read aloud to me the first chapter of the novel *The Trial,* and in November, **"In the Penal Colony."** They are documents of literary self-punishment, imaginative rites of atonement. What K., the hero of *The Trial,* had done is never said. By ordinary civil standards he is undoubtedly innocent. There is "nothing, or at least not much that can be said against him." And yet he is "diabolical in all his innocence." Somehow or other he has not lived up to the laws of the good life. He is called to account by a mysterious court, and finally the sentence on him is carried out. "On the eve of his thirty-first birthday," says the last chapter. As a matter of fact Kafka, when he began his novel, was thirty-one. There is a girl who appears in the book several times, Fräulein Bürstner—in his manuscript Kafka generally writes this character's name abbreviated to Fr. B., or F. B., and then the connection [to his fiancée Felice Bauer] is surely quite clear. At the end, K. is still trying to keep the bailiffs off. "Then in front of them, from a little alley that lay deep in the shadows, up a short flight of steps, Fräulein Bürstner came out into the square. It was not quite certain that it was she, the resemblance was certainly great. Whether it was really Fräulein Bürstner or not, however, did not matter to K.; the important thing was that he suddenly realized the futility of resistance." It is really of no importance whether the apparition is Fräulein Bürstner or is only like her. The whole failure of his attempt to get married, indeed, was important for the life of Kafka, as will soon become clear, as a pattern, and not individually—independent of the person of his fiancée—or rather as a pattern that, as the last year of his life shows, could be broken through by the personality of a woman of unusual character. (p. 146)

For all his mourning over the imperfection and intransparency of human actions, Kafka was convinced that there were truths which could not be assailed. He did not express this in words, but he did so by his whole behavior all his life. It was for that reason that in spite of all the depression he exuded, one felt

infinitely well in his company. The "Indestructible" made its presence felt, Kafka's unobtrusively quiet but firm behavior was at the same time a pledge for the everlasting laws of love, reason, and kindness. He was admittedly limitlessly skeptical and ironic. But there was, for instance, for him no skepticism about the substance and heart of Goethe. Well then, after all not "limitlessly skeptical"? No, the limit was there—a very distant limit, but a limit nevertheless.

Belief in an absolute world—but we go astray, we are too weak, we do not grasp it. Next to his belief in the Absolute stands for Kafka his consciousness of human insufficiency. This feeling of weakness Schoeps explains by the special situation of the Jew today, who does not follow the traditional law of his religion. There is also an explanation from the Catholic side; the Jew who does not accept Christ. But as a motive in this feeling of weakness, we must not forget Kafka's many private, accidental failings and sufferings, beginning with his youthful impressions and the "education that went wrong"; they all condition the feeling of God's "farness" which expresses itself so insistently in his works. Through this one grasps real life and truth better than through theological interpretations. "To be near God" and "to live rightly" were identical for Kafka. As a member of a race without a country one cannot live properly. This almost realistically Jewish interpretation of Kafka, in which Zionism is accepted as a way of life of almost religious relevance, I shall endeavor to develop later on.

But let us first establish the general religious side.

The Absolute is there—but it is incommensurable with the life of man—this would seem to be a fundamental experience of Kafka's. From the depth of his experiences it takes on ever new variations; in the bitterest irony, in despair, in unexampled self-abasement, and in a tender hope that sings through all his savage skepticism, not often, but all the more unmistakably, here and there. The chief theme remains the enormous danger that we may lose the right way, a danger so grotesquely out of proportion that it is really only an accident—*"gratia praeveniens"*—that can bring us to the point of entering into "The Law," i.e. the right and perfect life, into "Tao." How much more probable it is, on the contrary, that we miss the way altogether. "Once you have followed the false alarm of the night-bell—you can never put it right again." The eternal misunderstanding between God and man induces Kafka to represent this disproportion again and again the picture of two worlds which can never, never understand one another—hence the infinite separation between dumb animals and men is one of his chief themes in the numerous animal stories which his works contain, not by accident. The same is true of the partition wall between father and son. This writer's gaze rests with the endless pity of understanding on everything that expresses incommensurability, and brings it into silent relation with the most fatal and greatest of all misunderstandings, the failure of man in the sight of God.

This perception undoubtedly has its kernel in the feeling that there is a world of the Absolute, Freedom from sin, Perfection—that is that which the faithful call "God." This feeling for the "Indestructible" was for Kafka an immediate certainty, at the same time—equipped as he was with the sharpest of eyes of the soul—he did not overlook a single one of the countless, wretched backslidings, not one of the sins, not one of the absurdities with which men embitter each other's lives, make each other's lives impossible indeed, and which cause them to wander farther and farther away from the fountain of life. A good life is prescribed for us, but we are incapable, through faults in our innermost being, of comprehending this life. For this reason the divine world becomes for us a transcendental territory, and in the truest sense of the words, strange, uncanny. To our ears the will of God sounds illogical, that is to say opposed to our human logic in a grotesque fashion. Since the Book of Job in the Bible, God has never been so savagely striven with as in Kafka's *The Trial,* and *The Castle,* or in his **"In the Penal Colony,"** in which justice is presented in the image of a machine thought out with refined cruelty, an inhuman, almost devilish machine, and a crank who worships this machine. Just the same in the Book of Job, God does what seems absurd and unjust to man. But it is *only* to man that this seems so, and the final conclusion arrived at in Job as in Kafka is the confirmation of the fact that the yardstick by which man works is not that by which measurements are taken in the world of the Absolute. Is that agnosticism? No; for the fundamental feeling remains that in some mysterious way man is nevertheless connected with the transcendental kingdom of God. Only the usual, flat, rationally understandable kind of connection it just isn't. And the terrible wound of doubt that Kafka's ever-fresh wit, and Kafka's ever freshly creating, bizarre fancy, deal our moral system, cannot be healed by phrases, by sanctimoniously lifting up one's eyes, and patching things up with evil, not by belletristic anointings, but only by a tremendous, mounting feeling for the positive that dares bid defiance to all this undisguised negation. To have registered the negative and fearfully defective sides of nature without veiling them in any way, and yet at the same time to have seen continually from the depths of his heart the "World of Ideas," in the Platonic sense—that was the distinguishing feature of Kafka's life and of his works, that was the thing that proclaimed itself to his friends, without a word being said about it, as a kind of revelation, peace, certainty, in the midst of the storm of suffering and uncertainty.

Perhaps there have been men who have had a deeper, that is to say, a less questioning faith than Kafka's—perhaps also there have been men with even more biting skepticism—that I don't know. But what I do know is the unique fact that in Kafka these two contradictory qualities blossomed out into a synthesis of the highest order. One might gather its importance into this sentence: Of all believers he was the freest from illusions, and among all those who see the world as it is, without illusions, he was the most unshakable believer.

It is the old question of Job. But Kafka stands almost completely on the side of man. That is how it is in the story, "Before the Law." The doorkeeper has deceived the man who demands admission, or he is too simple. To close the argument, K., to whom the legend is related, says, "It turns lying into a universal principle." It is true that that is also not the last word. The priest argues against it, protests by word and deed. Thus the justice of the highest court (in his novel *The Trial*), the possibility of a good life in accordance with the divine command, "The Law" in fact, is not denied—but this possibility is not a certainty. Everything remains hanging in the air. Darkness and light hold the scales against one another. In what time is this "timeless" novel set? One minute before the creation of the world. Will it succeed, or not? A terrible fear of doubt, of uncertainty, fills one's heart.

What is the reason? Why man does not achieve the real, the true, that, with the best will in the world, he wanders from the path like that country doctor who followed the "false alarm of the night-bell"? Kafka, by the very nature of his being, was not inclined to give any promises, or any directions for the happy life. He admired everyone who could—he himself remained in suspense. But just this suspense would have been empty and bare, had he not felt the Absolute as something inexpressible (αρρητον) in himself. In his uncertainty one felt a distant certainty, through which alone this uncertainty is made possible and preserved. I have already said that this positive trait appears perhaps less strongly in his writings—and that is why they have been found depressing by many readers—than it was to be felt in his personal calm and serenity, in the gentle, considered, never hasty, character of his being. But also he who reads Kafka's works with care must again and again catch a glimpse through the dark husk of this kernel that gleams, or rather beams gently through. On the top lie distraction, and despair in that which is related—but the ease and minuteness of detail with which it is related, the "copy fever" which is in love with detail, that is, with real life, and with descriptions true to nature, the humor in the compressed structure of his sentences, which often has the effect of a short circuit, in so many tricks of style—the debtors "have become extravagant, and are giving a party in the garden of some inn, and others are breaking their flight to America for a little while to attend the party"—all this points, already *through the form alone,* to the "indestructible" in Kafka and in the human-being-in-general that he recognizes.

When Kafka read aloud himself, this humor became particularly clear. Thus, for example, we friends of his laughed quite immoderately when he first let us hear the first chapter of *The Trial*. And he himself laughed so much that there were moments when he couldn't read any further. Astonishing enough, when you think of the fearful earnestness of this chapter. But that is how it was.

Certainly it was not entirely good, comfortable laughter. But the ingredients of a good laugh were also there—alongside the hundred ingredients of uncanniness, which I shall not try to minimize. I am only pointing out the fact that is otherwise so easily forgotten in studies of Kafka—the streak of joy in the world and in life.

What he reproached himself with was, in fact, just that his belief in life wavered, that life was not strong enough in him. And he admired the things of the country, an admiration expressed as early as in his (unpublished) youthful letter to Oskar Pollak: "Have you already noticed how the soil comes up to meet the cow as she is grazing, how intimately it comes up to meet her? Have you already noticed how heavy, rich, arable earth crumbles at the touch of fingers which are all to fine, how solemnly it crumbles?" It is still more clearly expressed in the diary he kept of his stay in Zürau, which says among other things, "General impressions of the farmers: noblemen, who have found salvation in their farming, where they have arranged their work so cleverly and humbly that it fits without omission into the whole, and will keep them safe from every wavering and sea-sickness until their happy death. Real citizens of the earth." But naturally his admiration did not stay confined to country folk alone. He writes in just the same style, 10/20/1913, in his diary, about a completely urban author, who was sure of his path: "Have just been reading the case of Jacobsohn. This strength to live, to make decisions, to set one's foot with joy in the right spot. He sits in himself as a first-class oarsman sits in his own boat, and would sit in any boat."

The scale of values that Kafka applied becomes clear from notes such as that. He loved an efficient vitality, but only one which stood at the service of what is good and constructive.

(A twofold demand hard to satisfy!) He always found fault with himself for "never having learned anything useful." He complains in his diary, 10/25/1921, that "the current of life has never caught me up, and that I never broke away from Prague, was never put on to any game or trade." He often reproaches himself with coldness, incapacity for life, lifelessness, as we frequently find in his letters, and in the last chapter of *The Trial*. The two black mysterious bailiffs only carry out a sentence that has already been carried out. As they lead K. away, they form together with him "one unit, such as almost only lifeless matter can form." He is dead already: that is to say, dead to real life. That is the real reason why the ghostly appearance of Fräulein Bürstner has such a paralyzing effect on him. He wants to see her, not because he promises himself any help from doing so, but "in order not to forget the warning that she holds for him." K. had not married, remained a bachelor, had allowed himself to be terrified by the reality of life, had not defended himself against it—that is his secret guilt, which had already, before his condemnation, shut him out from the circle of life. "There would be nothing heroic about it if he did resist," is therefore the final conclusion: "if he were now to make difficulties for the gentlemen [the bailiffs], if he tried now by defending himself to enjoy the last appearance of life." K. died of weakness in living, is already dead from the beginning of the book—from the moment of the arrest, which Kafka must have written in a kind of trance, in a moment of clairvoyance, or did there exist then, in 1914, the tight-fitting black uniforms with buckles, pockets, buttons, and belt? Admittedly weakness is a relative idea, and if you translate the novel back into the autobiographical from which it came, then one must not forget that Kafka's life can only be considered as tainted with weakness when measured by the heroically moral, in fact monumental demands he made on himself. But what would not be weakness in this case? A feeling of this comes to life in the unbearably moving passage at the end of *The Trial,* where "the responsibility for this last misdoing" is thrust off, where K, rears up, reaches after a far-away, unknown, indistinct person. "Who was it? A friend? A good man? Someone who sympathized? A man who wanted to help? Was it an individual? Was it everybody? Was there still help? Were there objections one had forgotten to raise? Surely there were some. Logic is, of course, unshakable, but it cannot withstand a man who wishes to live. Where was the judge he had never seen? Where was the high court before which he had never appeared?"

The old problem of Job.

Kafka's fundamental principle: pity for mankind that finds it so hard a task to do what is right. Pity, half-smiling, half-weeping pity. Not the fulminating excommunication of the "theology of the crisis" which knows so exactly where mankind has gone wrong. (pp. 173-80)

> *Max Brod, in his* Franz Kafka: A Biography, *translated by G. Humphreys Roberts and Richard Winston, Schocken Books, 1947, 236 p.*

JOHN KELLY   (essay date 1940)

[*In the following excerpt, Kelly analyzes* The Trial *as an artistic representation of the Calvinist theology of Søren Kierkegaard and Karl Barth.*]

An eschatological novel—an allegory of man's relations with God in terms of a Calvinistic theology—is unique in our time, or in any time; and Kafka's production of such a work in a style palatable to an unspecialized group of readers is the climax of his bizarre explorations into the fate of man. *The Trial* sets forth in the form of an elaborate parable the basic principles of a modern system of theology, erected on the startling teachings of the Danish philosopher and psychologist of religion, Soeren Kierkegaard. Kierkegaard's opinions were so antipathetic to the ordinary philosophic and religious atmosphere of the nineteenth century that the recognition he has received in the writings of the "Existenz" philosophers and the exponents of the so-called Theology of Crisis amounts to a resurrection. This body of thought, probably the most interesting intellectual product of the War, is associated with the name of its most forceful and uncompromising exponent, the greatest living Protestant theologian, Karl Barth. Critics have noted in a very sketchy manner the influence of Kierkegaard upon Kafka; but his close affinity with the thought of Karl Barth has been overlooked. This is understandable because of the absence of any formal association between the two disciples of Kierkegaard; for though they were working at the same time under the Dane's influence, they were quite unaware of each other. A comparison of Kafka's religious views with those of Barth is a distinctly more fruitful approach to him than the customary attitude, that he is to be treated as a remarkable psychological case, or a social oddity. (pp. 748-49)

Karl Barth's celebrated *Commentary on the Epistle to the Romans,* the keystone of his thought, is contemporaneous with Kafka's *Trial.* Strongly influenced by Kierkegaard as was Kafka at this time also, it expounds with technical clarity all the ideas which are perceived through a glass darkly in Kafka's own book. Conceived in the milieu of the War, and in an atmosphere of defeat, Barth's theology is characterized by a sweeping rejection of man and all his works: "Over against man's confidence and belief in himself there has been written, in huge proportions and with the utmost clearness a *mene, mene, tekel*" [The writing on the wall of Belshazar's banqueting hall (*Daniel* v. 25-8): "God hath numbered thy kingdom and finished it; thou art weighed in the balances, and art found wanting: thy kingdom is divided"]. This is the theme of Barth's social consciousness, and Kafka, when he wrote the allegory, had reached very much the same conclusions. Barth repeatedly attacks the idealism and humanism active in nineteenth- and twentieth-century Protestantism, its consequent absorption in social problems, and simpering endeavor "to supply society with an ecclesiastical cupola or wing." He disparages philosophy, science, art, aesthetics, and any performance in which he detects anthropomorphic premises. To him the attempted synthesis of Christianity and the philosophy of Plotinus, suggested by Troeltsch as the "way out" for religion, is as absurd as it is irreligious. That Plotinianism which Dean Inge takes for the honey of Hymettus to Christianity is to Barth just a sugary decoration on the tower of Babel—a particularly vicious example of the oversimplification inherent in all religious "solutions." "Simple to us is neither Paul's Romans, nor the present situation in theology, nor the present world situation, nor man's situation in general toward God——Hard and complicated is man's life today in every direction." Such a position defines accurately the nature of Kafka's own "pessimism" (which Max Brod naïvely supposes did not exist, because Kafka was occasionally gay, and bore suffering heroically!)—a pessimism which is only partial; which is a gloomy, but not a cynical feeling about man's fate; which recognizes the hardness of his lot, but in that very hardness finds a basis for positive affirmations, for a belief that there is a *hard,* a "crucial" solution.

Barth and Kafka search for the key to salvation in terms of the events on the road to Damascus, and in the experience of the Jewish prophets. St. Paul's conversion remains the chief clue to the action of God; Calvin and Kierkegaard are, for the crucial theologians, the foremost expounders of this action. Barth totally rejects *human* activity as a way to God. Any assistance in the quest for the Absolute, alleged to be found in philosophy and art, is a complete delusion, for there is no way from man to God; there is only a way from God to man. The theology of crisis knows no "flight of the alone to the alone," no "satisfaction for the yearning soul in finding the Infinite." In the true Church, according to Barth, all cultural values are nil in terms of the Absolute. (pp. 750-51)

Among humanitarian and idealistic thinkers, the fallen state of man is usually considered, when its existence is recognized at all, to be the result of his failure to realize his inherent possibilities, or the "wickedness" or "inhumanity" of certain individuals or groups. Barth, on the other hand, asserts that man's state "is a perplexity felt by man simply by virtue of his being a man, and has nothing to do with his being moral or immoral, spiritual or worldly, godly or ungodly." And again, "man from the viewpoint of the good is powerless." Kafka, as is well known, was deeply and peculiarly involved in a quest for "the good," and for "the right way of life." "Men want to hear a word they can rely on and live by," observes Barth. Neither Barth nor Kafka was able to find a right way of life in any of the recognized ethical systems they found about them, whether religious or philosophic. Barth considered every ethical system to be either the product of cynical determinism, or of enthusiastic ideology. "Human ethics are impossible to both, for one removes responsibility and freedom, the other guilt and entanglement." Kafka bestows these four qualities upon his hero in abundance; they dominate the hard solution at which the allegory arrives. Joseph K. is entirely free, entirely responsible, wholly guilty, hopelessly entangled. His only escape is the way of "crisis."

The "crisis" is Kierkegaard's most striking concept. From him Barth and Kafka develop it elaborately, starting from his premise: "Finitum non capax infiniti—There is an infinite difference between time and eternity; God is in heaven, man on earth." God is transcendent and absolute—*ganz anders* ["wholly other"]. Religious experience, therefore, can be grounded only in a direct speech from God to man. Any quest for Him on the part of man is pointless, for there is no way up to Him. He reveals Himself to man or He does not. All ideas of God's immanence, from Wordsworth's crude pantheism to the refined raptures of Plotinus, are ruthlessly set aside. "God cannot be known by his active presence in the world, but is regarded as hidden, so that what God is is not revealed" (Emil Brunner). God speaks and commands; man hears and obeys—or turns away from the command to his own destruction. This revelation of God is the crisis in the man's life—the turning point of his existence, the beginning of a struggle, in which he can be saved only by making the right turn, in the right way.

"God's command is the categorical imperative of absolute urgency, of absolute stringency. He who is claimed by God knows nothing of 'Still we have time' (the evolutionary view); of 'Not-yet' (growing perfectibility); of 'gradually, or more or less' (the metaphysical view); or a 'Not-now' (the moralist's view). It is a 'No-longer!'" (Karl Barth). This is the Barthian view of Kierkegaard's great "Either-Or"—the starting point of the neo-Calvinist's Vita Nuova. After this crisis, all that has existed before in the life of the "claimed" man must be discarded. "There is absolutely no continuity between the natural life and the new one, and in consequence a complete breach with the natural human development takes place. . . . One can no longer seek God, by falling back on the past and one's true self" (Kierkegaard). "No moment is not a turning-point in the drama, in which every victory or defeat, standing or falling, living or dying, is indicated, a Jacob's flight in which man is necessarily wounded in the thigh, if the matter is to go on—every moment with the character of once-for-allness and non-repetition. Entirely to associate with God truly in this relation is claiming the stake, the risk of man's existence at every moment" (Karl Barth). All this is a perfect commentary on the career of Joseph K. from the moment of his arrest, and on the struggle which the mysterious command forces upon him.

Does Joseph K. accept his "trial"? The Barthian theology teaches that every man at the time of crisis is free to take another turn, free to reject the struggle at any point. At first, Joseph K., quite rationally, contemplates some resistance to this unauthorized arrest:

> Who could these men be? What were they talking about? What authority could they represent? K. lived in a country with a legal constitution, there was universal peace, all the laws were in force; who dared seize him in his own dwelling? He had always been inclined to take things easily, to believe in the worst only when the worst happened, to take no care for the morrow even when the outlook was threatening. *But that struck him as not being the right policy here . . . his very first glance* at the man Franz had decided him for the time being not to give away any advantage that he might possess over these people . . . if this was a comedy he would insist on playing it to the end [italics mine].

From that moment of decision, Joseph K., entirely by his own manipulation, remains in the grip of the Law. Bit by bit, the continuity of his life is broken down, and all his reliances, habits, and safeguards cease to operate. More and more completely he becomes absorbed in the processes of the Law, in discovering how it works, and in its relationship to him and his "case." "Here are my identification papers." "What are your identification papers to us?" sneer the minions of the Law. So begins the Jacob-fight to the death.

What is the Law? What must a man do to be saved? Kafka works out his hero's problem by basing his allegory on the prophetic writings of the Old Testament, and on Calvin's Pauline Christianity, absorbed through Kierkegaard. The most bewildering problem which confronts Joseph K. after his arrest is that of his "guilt." In the court offices, K. encounters some other "claimed" men. "They did not stand quite erect, their backs remained bowed, their knees bent, they stood like street beggars. K. waited for the Law-Court Attendant, who kept slightly behind him, and said: 'How humbled they must be!' 'Yes,' said the Law-Court Attendant, 'these are accused men, all of them are accused of guilt.' 'Indeed!' said K. 'Then they're colleagues of mine.'" Thus sarcastically, humorously, tentatively, K. fumbles with the notion of his own "guilt" for a time; but, in the end, he is so convinced of it that he wills his own destruction in expiation. He evolves into a Pauline Christian. "And I lived sometime without the law. But when the commandment came, sin revived, and I died. And the commandment that was ordained to life, the same was found to be unto death to me" (Epistle to the Romans).

But he becomes still more, a Calvinist; for the Law of Wrath by which K. is bound is elaborately discussed by Calvin in his *Institutes*.

Let us examine what sort of righteousness can be found in men during the whole course of their lives. Let us divide them into four classes. For either they are destitute of the knowledge of God and immersed in idolatry.... [Joseph K. is clearly this first class, so we halt in it.] In the first of these classes judged according to their natural characters, from the crown of the head to the sole of the foot there will not be found a single spark of goodness; unless we mean to charge the Scripture with falsehood.... But if any among them show that integrity in their conduct which among men has some appearance of sanctity, yet since we know that God regards not external splendour, we must penetrate to the secret springs of these virtues, whatever they may be, or rather the images of virtues, if we wish them to avail anything to justification.... The observation of Augustine is strictly true—that all who are strangers to the religion of the one true God, however they may be esteemed worthy of admiration for their reputed virtue, not only merit no reward, but are rather deserving of punishment, because they contaminate the pure gifts of God with the pollution of their own hearts.

This elaborate and terrifying view, discreetly laid to rest for some centuries by liberal Protestants, has been revived with great emphasis by the Barthian theologians; and Kafka is again on their side, by way of Kierkegaard. "Guilt and transitoriness are the characteristics of even our best deeds. Just here, we can do nothing else than confess: 'Surely what we do is to no profit, even in the best life.' And it is just the converted man who can say that" (Karl Barth).

It is characteristic of the thinking of the time that the problem of guilt and forgiveness has been pushed into the background and seems to disappear more and more.... There are even today, a great many people who understand that man needs salvation, but there are very few who are convinced that he needs forgiveness and redemption.... Sin is understood as imperfection, sensuality, worldliness—but not as guilt.... Man can do nothing to remove guilt.... No continuity of action, no accomplishment of works can create anew the broken connection [Emil Brunner].

This, in short, is the lesson which Kafka teaches in his allegory. Every experience of Joseph K. demonstrates the futility of human endeavor to remove this primordial "Guilt."

Such is the framework of the hero's struggle: to establish a connection with the higher authority, to understand his guilt, to be freed from it, if possible. This is an enterprise which is foredoomed to failure by the terms of this theology, in so far as the hero attempts it by his own efforts. Even when he has come so far as to accept his guilt, we find him still hatching schemes to free himself from it. Only at the end has he reached the full realization of the futility of this conduct. His first defense is the naïve one that he is ignorant of the Law. "'I don't know this Law,' said K. 'All the worse for you,' replied the warder. 'And it probably exists nowhere but in your own head,' said K.... 'You'll come up against it yet.' Franz interrupted: 'See, Willem, he admits that he doesn't know the Law and yet he claims he's innocent.'" Eventually K. acquires the services of an advocate to assist him with the Law. In the advocate's milieu he encounters the cheapest sort of graft; but the advocate is a fairly good Calvinist. In passages which achieve unparalleled heights of humor, the nature of the court and its judgments are discussed. "The advocate was always working away at the first plea, but it had never reached a conclusion, which at the next visit turned out to be an advantage, since the last few days would have been very inauspicious for handing it in, a fact which no one could have foreseen." The reasons for all this shuffling on the part of the advocate are alleged to derive from the peculiar character of the court. Actually the ultimate character of the court is as hidden from all the advocates and officials connected with it as it is from Joseph K., himself:

... the legal records of the case, and above all the actual charge-sheets, were inaccessible to the accused and his counsel, consequently one did not know in general, or at least did not know with any precision, what charges to meet in the first plea; accordingly it could only be by pure chance that it contained really relevant matter.... In such circumstances the Defence was naturally in a very ticklish and difficult position. Yet that, too, was intentional. For the Defence was not actually countenanced by the Law, but only tolerated, and there were differences of opinion even on that point, whether the Law could be interpreted to admit such tolerance at all ... the whole onus of the Defence must be laid on the accused himself.

It soon becomes clear that all this legal defense is the sheerest quackery, and that only the most menial officials of the court can be approached at all. A case in its higher stages cannot be followed by anyone, not even the accused himself. Yet far from displaying any rebelliousness or dissatisfaction with a court of this shifty and arbitrary character, the advocates and the officials regard it as a paragon of unerring justice. In this they follow Calvin who observes (in a chapter attractively entitled, "The destined destruction of the reprobate procured by themselves"):

We, who know that all men are liable to so many charges at the Divine tribunal, that of a thousand questions they would be unable to give a satisfactory answer to one, confess that the reprobate suffer nothing but what is consistent with the most righteous judgment of God. Though we cannot comprehend the reason of this, let us be content with some degree of ignorance where the wisdom of God soars into its own sublimity.

In a conversation with the court painter, the question of Joseph K.'s innocence is discussed, without much consolation for the unfortunate defendant.

"Are you innocent?" he asked. "Yes," said K. . . . "That's the main thing," said the painter. He was not to be moved by argument, yet in spite of his decisiveness it was not clear whether he spoke out of conviction or out of mere indifference. K. wanted first to be sure of this, so he said: "You know the Court much better than I do, I feel certain, I don't know much more about it than what I've heard from all sorts and conditions of people. But they all agree on one thing, that charges are never made frivolously, and that the Court, once it has brought a charge against someone, is firmly convinced of the guilt of the accused and can be dislodged from that conviction only with the greatest difficulty." "The greatest difficulty?" cried the painter, flinging one hand in the air. "Never in any case can the Court be dislodged from that conviction. . . ."

For the Court, he explains, while not impervious to proof in general, is distinctly impervious to any "proof which one brings before the Court." Acquittals are, of course, entirely possible, he adds; but

> The final decisions of the Court are never recorded,
> even the judges can't get hold of them, consequently
> we have only legendary accounts of ancient cases.
> These legends certainly provide instances of acquit-
> tal; actually the majority of them are about acquittals,
> they can be believed, but they cannot be proved. . . .
> I myself have painted several pictures founded on
> such legends.

Thus the allegory is provided with a hierarchy of saints, of
persons who are supposed to have won through this trial to
something like acquittal. The painter's attitude towards Joseph
K. does not indicate that he numbers him among these elect.

Meanwhile K.'s break with his old existence becomes as complete as the Barthian theology requires. His old social, business, and sexual lives slip away from him. Despite his contempt
for the milieu of the Court, his thoughts turn more and more
to the "final result of the case." He neglects his work at the
bank as much as he can, and becomes increasingly indifferent
to the other persons in his lodging house, who have interested
him for one reason or another at the outset of the trial. He
even becomes cautious and patient. Women cease to concern
him. His regular mistress of whom he has been quite proud
drops out of his life fairly early in the proceedings. Promiscuity
naturally continues for a while, for the most part with the
advocate's strange servant, Leni. She is a sort of Thaïs of the
scullery, to whom "accused men" are particularly appealing.
"She makes up to all of them, loves them all, and is apparently
loved in return," observes the Advocate.

> If you have the right eye for these things, you can
> see that accused men are often attractive. It's a re-
> markable phenomenon, almost a natural law. . . . It
> can't be a sense of guilt that makes them attractive,—
> for—it behooves me to say this as an advocate at
> least—they aren't all guilty, and it can't be the justice
> of the penance laid on them that makes them attrac-
> tive in anticipation, for they aren't all going to be
> punished, so it must be the mere charge preferred
> against them that in some way enhances their attrac-
> tion.

This is, of course, the old "eternal feminine" indispensable
in any Germanic work; but in K.'s behaviour there is a close
suggestion of Calvinism. It is his exclusive devotion to the
progress of his trial which induces him to give up Leni. Calvin
declares that continence is a peculiar gift of God, bestowed
upon a few, who have been "called," and notes that Christ
himself has mentioned "a certain class of men, who have made
themselves eunuchs for the kingdom of Heaven's sake,—that
is, that they might be more at liberty to devote their attention
to the affairs of the Kingdom of Heaven." K.'s abandonment
of sex is a strong hint that his trial is nearing its climax.

"Joseph K." A priest's voice rings through the Cathedral. K.
has been decoyed there by the customarily confused methods
of the Court. He goes under the assumption that he is to show
the Cathedral to an Italian client of the bank; but the court has
by now taken control of the external forces surrounding him,
and subverted every element in his normal existence. Hearing
his name called out through the darkening and empty Cathedral,
"K. started and stared at the ground before him. For a moment
he was still free, he could continue on his way and vanish
through one of the small dark wooden doors that faced him at
no great distance. It would simply indicate that he had not
understood the call, or that he had understood it and did not
care." This insistence on K.'s freedom of choice throughout
the allegory is absolutely essential to the theological concepts

with which he is working. Even at the end of the shattering
colloquy with the priest which ensues, and during which the
imminence of his fate becomes apparent, K. is told: "The Court
makes no claims upon you. It receives you when you come
and it relinquishes you when you go." Man is always free to
make his choice, to hear and obey the word, or to turn away.

The parable and exegesis which occupy this section of the novel
is probably the most important statement of Kafka's theological
views. The actual story of the parable is clear enough. A man
comes from the country and seeks admission to the Law; he
is stopped at the gate by a keeper and told he cannot enter "at
this moment." The man sits down by the gate to await permission to enter. He waits all his life. Near the end he perceives
a "radiance that streams immortally from the door of the Law."
Whereupon, all the experience of his life condenses into one
question which he puts to the doorkeeper.

> "What do you want to know now?" asks the door-
> keeper, "you are insatiable." "Everyone strives to
> attain the Law," answers the man, "how does it
> come about, then, that in all these years no one has
> come seeking admittance but me?" The doorkeeper
> perceives that the man is at the end of his strength
> and that his hearing is failing, so he bellows in his
> ear: "No one but you could gain admittance through
> this door, since this door was intended only for you.
> I am now going to shut it."

The exegesis of the parable which the priest offers is highly
confusing to K., which is natural enough, for it reveals the
paradoxical character of the Kierkegaardian theology in a satiric
manner. The priest points to two important statements in the
parable, the first that the doorkeeper cannot admit the man at
the moment, the second, that the door was intended only for
the man. Here the doorkeeper is speaking in the character of
the church of Calvin, with its emphasis on man's eternal election by God, but his inability to procure it by any activity of
his own, and the final uncertainty as to whether he is really
elected and saved. Even Calvin is rather timid on this important
point:

> The discussion of predestination—a subject of itself
> rather intricate—is made very perplexed and there-
> fore dangerous by human curiosity, which no barriers
> can restrain from wandering into forbidden laby-
> rinths, and soaring beyond its sphere, as if to leave
> none of the divine secrets unscrutinized or unex-
> plored. As we see multitudes everywhere guilty of
> this arrogance and presumption, and among them
> some who are not censurable in other respects, it is
> proper to admonish them of the bounds of their duty
> on this subject. First, then, let them remember that
> when they inquire into predestination they penetrate
> the utmost recesses of Divine wisdom, where the
> careless and confident intruder will obtain no satis-
> faction to his curiosity, but will enter into a labyrinth
> from which he will find no way to depart . . . to those
> whom he devotes to condemnation, the gates of life
> are closed by a just and irreprehensible, but incom-
> prehensible judgment.

Thus Calvin scares away the inquirer, very much as the priest
puts off Joseph K.

The second statement, that the door was intended only for the
man, brings one face to face with the great riddle of Kafka's
novel. Is Joseph K. saved or damned? At the beginning of his
discourse with the priest, K. is still in a hopeful frame of mind.
"I am going to get more help," he announces. "There are
several possibilities I haven't explored yet." The priest natu-

rally disapproves of this attitude. "'Can't you see anything at all?' It was an angry cry, but at the same time sounded like the involuntary shriek of one who sees another fall and is startled out of himself." But in the ensuing discourse, the tremendous complexity of his position is brought home to Joseph K. Rational truth he discovers is useless to him. "It is not necessary to accept everything as true, one must only accept it as necessary," says the priest. "A melancholy conclusion," replies K.

It is possible to treat the final, brutal dispatch of K. as really a "melancholy conclusion," representing his damnation; but the preponderance of evidence derived from inspecting the theological background indicates that this execution represents in reality his salvation. Calvin gives some valuable hints on this problem:

> The declaration of Christ that many are called and few chosen, is very improperly understood, for there will be no ambiguity in it, if we remember what must be clear from the foregoing observations, that there are two kinds of calling. For there is a universal call, by which God, in the external preaching of the word, invites all, indiscriminately to come to him, *even those to whom he intends it as a savour of death, and an occasion of heavier condemnation.* There is also a special call, with which he, for the most part, favours only believers when, by the inward illumination of his Spirit, he causes the word preached to sink into their hearts.

Which of these calls has been given to K.? At first glance it might seem that he was one of the outstanding victims of the Calvinistic God's brutal sport, one called in the "savour of death." This seems to be the opinion of the priest and the court officials. But there is more to be said for K.'s position by Calvin and the Barthians. Calvin says further: "Now the elect are not gathered into the fold of Christ by calling, immediately from their birth nor all at the same time. . . . Before they are gathered to that chief shepherd, they go astray, scattered in the common wilderness, and differing in no respect from others, except in being protected by the special mercy of God from rushing down the precipice of eternal death." There are many more grounds for assigning K. to this fortunate class. Luther, for instance, says that there are no perceptible signs by which the senses can discern the work of grace. Karl Heim, of the Barthian theology, elaborates this: "The divine accent that falls upon the Yea does not depend upon an enhanced feeling of happiness, nor upon the strength of the religious emotions—nor upon the visionary irruptions from another realm, which could be established in William James' sense, nor upon any attestable sign whatever, by which the affirmation could be empirically given preference over the denial." Barth holds, moreover, that faith, itself, "is never given, never ready, never secured; seen from psychology, it is ever and ever anew the leap into the unknown, into the dark, into empty air."

So far there is at least a negative case to be made out in favor of Joseph K.'s salvation; and the signs that he is a man about to undergo a frightful doom may be read in an entirely different light. The doom may be really his salvation, his peculiar call from the Absolute. This view is made certain, when the nature of his death is inspected. In his death Joseph K. makes what is considered by Kierkegaard the greatest gesture toward salvation it is within the power of man to make. This gesture is the famous "teleological suspension of the ethical." This principle appears to be not too well understood, as may be gathered from Mr. R. O. C. Winkler in *Scrutiny*, who makes an egregious error with regard to it:

> The most obvious of temptations that offer themselves is a discussion of Kafka's philosophy. The Kierkegaardian system of belief that was responsible for much of the form and content of Kafka's novels is sufficiently remote from contemporary English habits of thought for an account of it to give an appearance of throwing light on the novelist's apparent obscurities. . . . For whether or not we care to admit from a doctrinal point of view the possibility of a teleological suspension of the ethical, there can be no doubt that something of this kind is assumed whenever one asserts the universality of a work of art [see excerpt by Winkler dated 1938 in *TCLC*, Vol. 2].

This passage is not much more confused than most contemporary English criticism, being notable only in that it crams more errors into less space than is usual. In the first place, the principle of the teleological suspension of the ethical has no more to do with art, universal or otherwise, than Boyle's Law of Gases, or Gresham's Axiom that "bad money drives out good." Secondly, there is no question of our admitting it or not admitting it, for it is primarily a descriptive phrase for that conduct which results from our acceptance of a spiritual prompting, to disobey the established ethical standards of our personal or social lives, as a direct command from God, taking precedence over these ethical standards. The great type of this sort of behavior is Abraham's sacrifice of Isaac in obedience to Jehovah's command. An account of the Kierkegaardian system, moreover, *does* throw light on Kafka's obscurities, which are much more than merely "apparent." (By *apparent*, Mr. Winkler must have meant *obvious*, unless he contends that the novelist's difficulties can be resolved without reference to Kierkegaard. In any case, he has given a clear demonstration of just how remote Kierkegaard is from contemporary "English habits of thought.")

Kierkegaard scandalized Copenhagen by the elaborate manner in which he broke off his engagement to be married. He announced that this was the offering of all that was dearest to him to God, whereby he hoped to experience the double action of infinity, the paradoxical character of God's love, that by giving up all he should receive all. The real reasons for this performance were probably considerably less exalted; but, in any case, he regarded it as a case of the teleological suspension of the ethical, and considered it his greatest bid for salvation. At the end of the allegory, Joseph K. is in the same position. In this case, the offering is an even more striking one, his own life.

A great change has come over Joseph K. since his interview with the priest. He has abandoned all attempts to escape from the jurisdiction of the Court, and is in a mood to go forth joyfully and meet its sentence. He accepts his guilt and responsibility; he longs for escape from the Barthian "entanglement," and he hopes for forgiveness. His executioners arrive to lead him away; he is expecting them. He had hoped that the final scene would be more elegant; but these executioners are two coarse, fat, creatures, as shabby and unsavory as all the other officials of the Court. As he marches along the street between these two, the appearance of a policeman offers him a last chance of escape; but he rejects it and delivers a final judgment upon himself. "Am I to leave this world as a man who shies away from all conclusions? Are people to say of me after I am gone that at the beginning of my case I wanted it to finish, and at the end of it wanted it to begin again? I don't want that to be said.'' With such finality does he now will his own sacrifice that he hustles his executioners along, and does all he can to assist them in their unsavory job.

The final scene is even conceived in an atmosphere of ritual: the ceremonial attitude of the executioners, the questions of precedence that arise between them, the pains taken to find a suitable sacrificial stone. Kafka introduces a very novel element here, possibly to reveal his whole purpose. For the first time a personal and singular term is used to designate the authority pursuing him, instead of a reference to the Court in general. ''He could not completely rise to the occasion, he could not relieve the officials of all their tasks; the responsibility for this last failure of his lay with *him* who had not left him the remnant of strength necessary for the deed.'' It is further suggested that Joseph K., having at last abandoned his entire will and personality to ''him,'' is brought face to face with God, his Judge, and his potential Saviour, as was Abraham at the moment of his great sacrifice. ''His glance fell on the top storey of the house adjoining the quarry. With a flicker as of a light going up, the casements of a window there suddenly flew open; a human figure, faint and insubstantial at that distance and that height, leaned abruptly far forward and stretched both arms still farther. Who was it?'' Hope and shame are the last feelings of Joseph K., as the knife is plunged into his bosom. The Barthians say that sin, while so awful, is only known when it is forgiven.This is the source of Joseph K.'s final, overwhelming shame. But adds Barth: ''In God . . . forgiveness and penalty.'' Joseph K. has reached the only solution possible for man's perplexity, the violent and hard solution, prescribed by the theology of crisis, the complete surrender of one's self to the will and punishment of God. The Absolute has come to Joseph K.; it has come, as usual on its own terms, thwarting all his efforts to uncover its secrets, and careless of all his values, destroying his life, but offering its own peculiar salvation.

In all modern literature, Kafka's performance probably most deserves the term, Dantesque; not for his scope, or varied technical power (actually he is very limited), but for the pitch of his profundity and the strength of his intellectual background. *The Trial* is as firmly grounded in the rigid and elaborate theology of crisis, as was *The Divine Comedy* in the Scholastic theology and philosophy; and Kafka adheres as faithfully to his intellectual standards as does Dante. Most modern writers either do not adhere faithfully to any standards of this sort, or the standards to which they do adhere are relatively shallow. In the former class might be placed novelists such as Proust, Joyce, Thomas Mann, and their followers; in the latter, mostly poets, Yeats and Eliot, representing the real poets, and the vast horde of poetasters. These three novelists are probably all greater than Kafka; they are much larger figures. But they do not invade the realm in which Kafka is supreme, the world of man's doubt and perplexity. Kafka realized that in religious writings were to be found the most careful analyses of man's reflections on his ultimate fate. He proceeded to master the content of religious teaching, and did not employ it as mere decor in his writings. In fact, religion does not appear at all on the surface of his work. His overwhelming seriousness as compared with almost any other modern writer is emphasized most by this fact. Yeats and Eliot, for instance, have distinctly religious elements, and exhibit a great amount of what might seem at first sight to be Barthian ''perplexity.'' But both are chiefly concerned because the Kingdom of God is not on this earth. Yeats' religion is merely an attractive compound of whimsy and theological quackery. Eliot's performance is no more re-

ligious than a troop of nuns crossing the stage in an opera; his perplexity is the perplexity of a ballerina Queen of Swans, alarmed at the approach of the Huntsmen.

Poetry, says I. A. Richards, will save us. In one way or another, most modern writers accept this view, or exhibit pretensions implying that they do, or that their work is somehow part of the historical program by which man's salvation is to be accomplished. Kafka, Barth, and Kierkegaard are far removed from this nonsense. Their ''pessimism'' derives chiefly from their profound conviction that man can in no way save himself. (pp. 752-66)

John Kelly, ''Franz Kafka's 'Trial' and the Theology of Crisis,'' in The Southern Review *(Louisiana State University), Vol. IV., No. 4, Spring, 1940, pp. 748-66.*

ALBERTO SPAINI (essay date 1946)

[*In the following essay, Spaini discusses* The Trial *as a symbolic account of an individual's confrontation with death and examines the manner in which Kafka created a moral drama from this confrontation.*]

In discussing the very strange work of Franz Kafka, one is apt to get lost in comments and interpretations, each making the text more difficult and incomprehensible, a text which is, however, very clear despite all appearances, provided one relies only on the letter and that natural extension of it, that symbolic echo which is tied to the letter. But if we attempt to take a book by Kafka, *The Trial* for example, or *The Castle* which seems a second version of *The Trial,* as an allegorical work to be interpreted step by step and word by word, very probably every lyric and poetic value will be lost from it.

Among contemporary German writers there is none who can even remotely be compared with Kafka. If we had to trace back the origins of his work, we would probably be very perplexed, since all the associations which come to mind most readily we perceive to be completely superficial and actually foreign to the spirit of Kafka. Max Brod has for some time been occupied with a circle of ideas which can be related to Kafka's, but the broad spirituality which prevails in the plot of some of his novels, such as *Tycho Brahe,* becomes pale and scanty before that one basic thought on which the construction of Kafka's books rests. Nor would it be a matter of evoking memories like Meyrink's *Green Face,* where mystic and magical elements are used like devices in a detective story and are stripped of every intimate value. On the other hand, the mystic literature of the Jewish writer, Martin Buber—to anticipate one or two considerations which we presently will make regarding the Hebraism of Kafka—is frankly religious and transcendental and lacks that mysterious fascination which is truly Kafka's, namely the complete dissimulation of mystic elements within the plot of the novel.

We like Kafka precisely because it is superfluous to interpret him. We like him for his ultra-realistic way of describing things which a good average citizen would call, taking the words from our mouth, ''things of the other world.'' Things of the other world which happen in this, with all the schemes, the causes and the effects of this world. Like Joseph K., the protagonist of *The Trial,* we too feel that we are completely disloyal when we are surprised at what happens to him. Nor is anything understood of the trial against Joseph K., as he likewise understands nothing of it; but we too, just as he, are intimately persuaded that everything is in order and that it is well that it

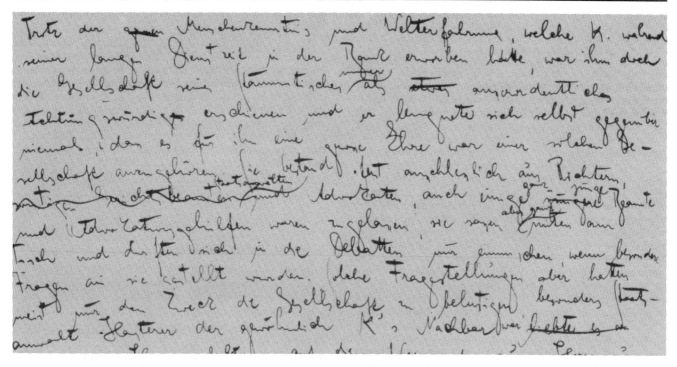

Part of the manuscript of The Trial. *From* Franz Kafka: Pictures of a Life, *by Klaus Wagenbach. Translated by Arthur S. Wensinger. Pantheon Books, 1984. English translation copyright © 1984 by Random House, Inc. Reproduced by permission of Pantheon Books, a Division of Random House, Inc.*

is thus. Nor do we escape the trial even if we do not know why we are on trial or who is the tribunal before which the trial is taking place. That is Kafka's strength: to make us accept as indispensable a whole story which contrasts with the elements of daily life, and yet is woven together solely and exclusively of these elements. Not the story only, but every episode and the connection of the various episodes and the characters and the connections between them and little by little the things which they do and say. Everything is perfectly in place, and everything is incredible. But "in the beginning is the word" and Kafka had the gift of that word which in the center of our life evokes and enchants events of which an instinct or an illumination tells us that they can only be the echo of higher worlds.

If we wished to try our hand at some interpretations, there is one that we might perhaps accept, especially since it offers a means of casting a glance at the way Kafka's narrative art functions, and the interpretation would be materialistic or psychological. What is the trial against Joseph K.? In terms of our knowledge of the duty and the law of men, the trial is not explained. One would have to imagine that it deals with a mysterious secret tribunal, a type of unconsecrated Sacred Wheel, which is inquiring into and judging our private life, those actions of ours which can appear before one tribunal only, that of our conscience. Then, however, the construction of the tribunal as it is depicted in the novel would appear too arbitrary and subtle. Instead things appear quite different if we imagine that Joseph K. has not been accused before a tribunal, but that this is only a symbolic way of expressing another situation; for example this: that K. has been struck by an incurable disease, and that he is awaiting death. Imagine all the first steps of a man in this situation, and the successive states of mind through which he will pass: you find them precisely in K. It is enough to enumerate one or two of them: his obstinacy in

not wanting to "confess" (that is to admit to being sick); his idea that if instead of being arrested in his house, in the morning when he was hardly awake, he had been arrested in his office "he would not have let himself be taken by surprise" (that is the attachment to active life, which seems of itself to deny the possibility of death); the fact of not having taken the trial seriously at the outset, of almost not having thought of it, and then, bit by bit, to live entirely in its midst, never to be able to detach himself from it, to have to abandon every activity....
This interpretation is very beguiling, not only because it gives to the book a very logical and transparent symbolism, but also because it explains to us the spontaneous mood with which Kafka constructs his tale, thinking constantly of a series of hidden events, which still are not actually uttered, which take place on a parallel plane with those which are set forth. And thus it is that the story is told "with the trial as the key" while in reality all the events, the psychological conditions, the sentences which most successfully give form to the events, are thought of "with sickness as the key." The uninterrupted transposition, executed with a technical and almost mechanical perfection which is amazing, explains to us without doubt Kafka's stylistic secret, and it is not inconsiderable.

But this interpretation is likewise very suggestive for a third reason which without doubt would bring joy to a psychiatrist: Kafka was actually the victim of an incurable disease, he really expected death. Was it not natural that in the very delicate and sensitive poet this dramatic situation should be translated into a series of nightmares, that sickness should in fact become for him a trial (an image also suggested even by colloquial language, which describes an incurable as one "condemned")? In the memory of us all there is an infantile nightmare which makes it almost worth supposing that even the ideas of responsibility and of justice are innate in us. Where is the seven-year-old child who has not awakened some night howling with terror because he saw the most horrible thing which he had ever met up to that time or had succeeded in imagining, and which now, being rocked and consoled, he no longer succeeds in explaining? Then frequently this nightmare returns, until one day he succeeds in understanding it: the little dreamer had made a promise, an unbounded promise, which surpassed all his strength and which he never in the world would have been able to keep; but he had given his word and there was no way to turn back. Nor is it known what catastrophe followed this broken promise but it was an inevitable catastrophe, and we ourselves had provoked it, with a spontaneous act of our will. We would not have been able to fulfill this act, this promise: but now we had created from nothing a world (which then was the world of our moral duty) and we were its prisoners.

The psychologists give a thousand beautiful explanations of the dream, and more than one of them could be very well adapted also to *The Trial*. What is more natural than this completely spiritual reaction in a man like Kafka to the nightmare of sickness? The events of the physical world he transposes into the moral world (or rather uses their scheme to give to his story a material solidity which augments the mystery and the mystic fascination of it) and by the repression of physical terror in the face of evil is derived precisely its sublimation in the work of art. That is why psychology might perhaps furnish a very fine and plausible interpretation. But if, instructed by this interpretation, we begin to read Kafka's novel, we find it even more mysterious; now that we *know* everything, we *understand* much less than before. For this reason we were on our guard against the tendency to "interpret" Kafka. For whatever interpretation be given to this account, one fact remains that doesn't change and that has no need of interpretations. In our dream, the first cosmic and tragic terror is born in us out of the consciousness of a destiny which we have created with our will. Thus in *The Trial*, it is not the fate of Joseph K. which is of greatest importance, but the moral conduct which he assumes before this fate. As we read it "with illness as the key," or, in the case of *The Castle*, under the veil of social and political ambition, Kafka's novel appears to us only outwardly as an episode of our struggle against destiny. In substance K. does not fight against destiny, he fights against himself; Kafka has imposed upon himself the superhuman task of making this struggle moral. And there is the point. The struggle against destiny reduces man to an animal level, to that of a blind corpuscle crushed by the imponderable mass which weighs heavily above and beyond us. Man's secret is that of forcing destiny onto a spiritual plane. Man's life must take place exclusively in that world over which man has power: his own spirit. Whatever blow may come upon us from the outside (K.'s arrest) must find us unassailable within our spirituality. "The fact that only one world of the spirit exists, takes hope from us and leaves us certainty": those are words of Kafka in which extreme renunciation is mingled with extreme triumph.

Joseph K., our hero, was not the man most ideally suited to sustain that part in life. And indeed the first reaction to the events of which he will be the victim is one of rebellion. "Someone must have been telling lies about Joseph K., for without having done anything wrong he was arrested one fine morning." That is Kafka's first sentence. His first impulse is to deny having done anything wrong and his first thought is that of being the victim of a false accusation: he succumbs, that is, to destiny; he wants to struggle. And the second from the last chapter (but which can be considered the last, since the end is really an epilogue) closes with this sentence: "This Court makes no claims upon you. It receives you when you come and it relinquishes you when you go." Destiny has completely disarmed; it no longer takes place in the material order of facts, but in the moral activities of man. But this withdrawal from destiny onto a more remote plane, from which it no longer has any power over us, lasts only as long as our capacity to remain firm and enclosed within ourselves survives. Has Joseph K. ever reached it? And if he has reached it, has he known how to preserve it? It seemed to him that the shame of it would probably outlive him, so Joseph K. dies without that halo of glory which for a moment or two we believed we saw shining again behind his head; he did not know how, finally and completely, to renounce hope and he did not attain certainty. He dies "like a dog."

In the struggle against destiny therefore he conquers destiny, but the man remains inferior in respect to his duty to create an indestructible moral universe. Joseph K. did not raise himself above the animal level, and even less prepared to meet the serious task which awaits him is the protagonist of *The Castle*. Kafka did not succeed in conceiving an optimistic affirmative situation with his plot (apparently so monotonous); his every attempt toward liberation ended fatally in a tragic catastrophe. Some have chosen to see in this spiritual torture of Kafka a reflection of his Jewish psychology, so frequently gloomy and pessimistic (Weininger, Michelstaedter). It is not so much the search for God which characterizes the Hebraism of Kafka, as Enrico Rocca has noted a cabalistic structure beneath the plot of *The Trial*, or to perceive some relationship between his so painfully realistic symbolism and that of chassidic literature. Is Kafka's dialectical despair Hebraic? But then all philosophy and all the modern world are Hebraic: from the time when we renounced hope in a God who intervenes by his grace to save us, certainly our Jehovah has re-acquired some of the ineluctable characteristics which He of the Old Testament had; his strength is no longer infinite, but it is exactly limited by the strength of our spirit. He hasn't one gram more power than we are able to give him.

Joseph K., when he reaches the threshold of knowledge, in the chapter about the Cathedral, does not dare to ask either the priest or God for help. Suddenly the priest also identifies himself as a member of the court. Consolation, grace thus become impossible. Once again K. is driven within himself. Only his shame will live after him. Here, at this extreme limit, the inexorability of Ancient Law and of modern idealism become equivalent. But it is a coincidence which has been recorded because Hebraism is in style, or precisely because Kafka was Jewish.

But the last word on Kafka seems to us rather what has been said by Groethuysen: "The not-I is before the I." *The Trial* is, to be content with the ugly expression, the poem of the not-I; it is a miraculous effort to understand and to encompass within precise words the not-I, so that we can recognize the limits which separate our personality from the world, and we can prohibit the world from passing across them. The way of speaking which all of Kafka's characters have, from Joseph K. down to the humble Frau Grubach, from the priest who offers his mercy in vain to the guard who has grown fat eating the prisoners' breakfasts, is that of people who are obsessed with one idea, with one idea whatever its type, and must circumscribe it, very exactly. K.'s style creaks under this ferocious task of enclosing all mysteries in everyday words; no shade must remain outside his formulas, all the more besetting since they are of every day. Thus it is with a man's life: "Was help at hand? Were there some arguments in his favor that had been overlooked? Of course there must be. Logic is doubtless unshakable, but it cannot withstand a man who wants to go on living.'' It is this irresistible logic, a release of vitality, which is behind Kafka's style and truly gives strength to those mannerisms of his, so extremely plain, smooth and phlegmatic; it is the desperate phlegm of the man who knows how to be lost if he loses his calm only for a moment.

Hence the morbid fascination of Kafka's novel. The image of the catastrophe hangs above the whole tale; the most everyday and insignificant events, under this spectral light, become strangely plastic, acquire the unreal reality which is a characteristic of nightmares. But all this would perhaps have disappeared in the great night which encompassed the still very young author without the balance of his language which is poised on ample and airy planes indispensable in supporting such disagreeable burdens. The philosophical undertaking, the symbolic flooring, the romantic and sometimes decadent nature of the visions, the realistic construction of the tale—all passive things in the work of Kafka—are sustained without effort by the style, which, transfiguring these disparate elements, constitutes the originality of his work. (pp. 143-50)

Alberto Spaini, ''The Trial','' translated by John Glynn Conley, in The Kafka Problem, *edited by Angel Flores, New Directions, 1946, pp. 143-50.*

HERMAN UYTTERSPROT (essay date 1953)

[*In the following excerpt from an essay originally published in German in 1953, Uyttersprot notes inconsistencies in Max Brod's arrangement of the chapters in* The Trial *and deduces an alternative order which better represents K.'s mental deterioration during the year of his trial. For reactions to Uyttersprot's arrangement, see the excerpts by H. S. Reiss (below) and Gary Handler (1969).*]

It has often been stated that the sequence of chapters in *The Trial* is not fixed; it has indeed been asserted that several chapters are interchangeable like building blocks. Is this contention tenable? Is it impossible to trace a continuous thread? Must we abandon from the start all attempts to find a logically developed, plausible plot?

If we are not, indeed, to abandon such attempts, our first step must be to question the present arrangement of the chapters, an arrangement for which Max Brod, not Kafka, is responsible and upon which Brod himself (in the epilogue to the third German edition) has thrown some doubt. If we begin with the first four chapters, we soon discover a relationship between Chapters I and IV so intimate as to suggest that IV should actually appear between I and II.

In Chapter I, on the evening of the day of Joseph K.'s arrest, he argues angrily with his landlady, Frau Grubach, over her suspicions concerning Fräulein Bürstner, with whom he would like to become better acquainted. Then follows the conversation with Fräulein Bürstner in her room at 11:30 that night, abruptly interrupted by their realization that the landlady's nephew, the Captain (still nameless at this point), is an involuntary eavesdropper. This realization evokes anxiety in Fräulein Bürstner, and in Joseph K. vague feelings of guilt and concern. Now Chapter IV—as shown by indications of time, events that occur, and the emotional state of the protagonists—constitutes a direct continuation of this incident. It begins with the information that ''in the next few days K. found it impossible to exchange even a word with Fräulein Bürstner.'' And he at first refuses to speak to Frau Grubach, but on Sunday he ends his

sulking. In so doing he relieves the suspense under which she has lived, fearing that he was permanently angry; and he discovers that the Captain has betrayed nothing to her about the conversation with Fräulein Bürstner, thus dispelling his own fear on that score. These two questions raised in Chapter I are, then, resolved in Chapter IV; and Frau Grubach's statement in IV—''I kept asking myself''—ties in directly with I. Furthermore, K. meets the Captain for the first time in Chapter IV— ''This was the first time that K. had seen him close at hand''— a fact which is difficult to explain if there are more than a few days between the two chapters; for otherwise K. would surely have met him previously in the small boardinghouse, where ''on Sunday almost all the boarders had their midday dinner. . . .''

The indications are, then, that the Sunday in Chapter IV, the Sunday upon which K. ends his sulking and speaks to Frau Grubach, is the first Sunday after the day of his quarrel with her and of his conversation with Fräulein Bürstner—which was, of course, the day of his arrest. Yet at the beginning of the present Chapter II we learn that the first interrogation in K.'s trial is to take place ''next Sunday''; and when that Sunday arrives, he says, ''Some ten days ago I was arrested. . . .'' This, in other words, in Chapter II, is the *second* Sunday after the arrest, apparently one week *after* the events of Chapter IV. And it is worth noting that only something of this kind can account for K.'s ability in Chapter II to invent a joiner called Lanz—''the name came into his mind because Frau Grubach's nephew, the Captain, was called Lanz''—even though, in the present arrangement of chapters, he learns the Captain's name for the first time in Chapter IV.

Let us now turn to the fragment (perhaps a brief chapter) called ''The District Attorney,'' which Brod believes should have followed immediately upon Chapter VII—its ''opening lines are written on that sheet which contains a copy of the final sentences of that chapter''—and to another fragment called ''Journey to His Mother.''

Careful analysis will show that ''The District Attorney'' actually belongs at the very beginning of the novel: it could even serve as the first chapter or as a kind of prologue. The atmosphere that pervades it might be described as that of a pre-trial stage; for there is no hint of danger, no suggestion of a trial. Joseph K.'s position in life and at the bank seems entirely normal and unshaken. The circle of friends in his favorite tavern, as depicted in this fragment, corresponds exactly with that of the beer hall mentioned in Chapters I and II and nowhere else; and nothing in the novel seems to demand the sudden reappearance of these friends five chapters later at the end of Chapter VII, where Brod would put them. Precisely the same is true of the influential Hasterer, who appears in the fragment and to whom Joseph K. refers as to a personal friend in Chapter I and whom the Deputy Manager mentions as one of K.'s friends in Chapter II; with the additional, surprising fact (if we are to imagine this as part of Chapter VII) that in the fragment the Manager expresses surprise upon hearing of the friendship between the two: surely by this time he would know about it.

Furthermore, in ''The District Attorney'' we are informed that Joseph K. ''was deprived of his mother's affection, who, half-blind, was living out of town, and whom he had last visited two years ago.'' If we compare this with the first lines of the unfinished chapter ''Journey to His Mother,'' we can easily derive the exact chronology of the novel:

> Suddenly, at lunch it occurred to him that he wanted
> to visit his mother. Now *spring was almost over* and

with it the *third year* since he had seen her. She had begged him at that time to visit her on his *birthday;* despite many obstacles he had acceded to her wish, and he had even promised to spend every birthday with her, a promise, however, which he had *twice* failed to keep. Therefore he did not now want to wait until his birthday, although it was only a matter of *two weeks,* but rather to visit her at once. . . . His mother's eyesight was almost totally gone, but Joseph K. had been prepared for this for several years by the doctor's reports. (My italics.)

According to "The District Attorney," then, Joseph K. last saw his mother two years ago, when she was half blind. In "Journey to His Mother" it has been nearly three years since he saw her, and she is now almost totally blind. There is, therefore, an interim of about a year between the two fragments—namely, the fateful year, the year of the trial, which began with K.'s arrest on his thirtieth birthday and ended on the "evening before [his] thirty-first birthday. . . ." "The District Attorney" therefore cannot be inserted after Chapter VII as suggested by Brod, for at that point Joseph K. has at most a few months of life left him: Chapter VII takes place on a morning in winter, and Joseph K. dies in the late spring or the first days of summer—as we know from the above passage (where two weeks before his birthday spring is "almost over"), from a specific reference to spring in the first chapter ("That spring K. had been accustomed to . . ."), and from descriptive details in the last chapter ("the foliage of trees and bushes rose in thick masses").

Strong proof that the birthday mentioned in "Journey to His Mother" is indeed his thirty-first and that at this time he therefore has only thirteen days to live resides in K.'s emotional state throughout the fragment, where we see him as a person nearly destroyed by the arduousness of the trial in its final stages. He is guilty of a "general plaintiveness and an endeavor to indulge in all his desires." He is sentimental at a time when it might cause him to miss something important—that "opportunity for intervention [personal intervention in the trial] which might now occur any day, any hour" and for which, in Chapters VII and VIII, there is such a fervently expressed need. There are also indications here of that constantly growing and clearly realized inability to maintain, in the face of his trial, his position at the bank and in everyday life, the inability which constitutes the heart of his difficult inner struggle in Chapters VII and VIII. "Now much occurred against his wishes," which is to say that his position at the bank has been weakened (just as his reputation has suffered). He consoles and deceives himself: "Joseph K. still was one of the most important officials at the bank . . . he still could take away a letter from one of the officials, by name of Kullich, who even had connections with the court, and without any excuse, tear it to pieces." Yet Herr Kühne, a subordinate clerk, rudely accepts Joseph K.'s directives with his face turned sideways—"As if he were condescending to permit this ordering about on the part of Joseph K. only from the goodness of his heart."

These two fragments—one dealing with the days before the arrest, the other with the final stages of the trial—lead us on to discover, with surprising completeness, the rest of the chronology. We are now able to arrange all but one of the important events in their proper order. "The District Attorney" belongs not after Chapter VII, where in its present form it would destroy the coherent development of the action, but at the beginning of the novel, either as a prologue or as Chapter I. In all probability "Journey to His Mother" was intended as the penultimate chapter: Joseph K., condemned to death, tearful, self-indulgent, abandoned even by his mother, presumably receives neither help nor consolation from her. All that now remains is mute resignation to his fate, the calm acceptance of the inevitable, shown by the composure with which he receives his executioners in the last pages of the novel. And the basic, overall chronology is clear. On his twenty-eighth birthday K. visits his mother for the next-to-last time, and he agrees to visit her each year on this day. On his twenty-ninth birthday he fails to keep his promise. On his thirtieth birthday, the day of his arrest, he fails again. Two weeks before his thirty-first birthday he wants to make up for his neglect, and presumably he pays his visit. Thirteen days later he is executed.

The next step is to determine the order of events—and thus the order of the chapters and fragments—within the year of the trial. We know, to begin with, that this year begins and ends in late spring (or, perhaps, very early summer). We can, on the basis of hints about the season that we have already noticed, place K.'s birthday—the beginning of the trial (Chapter I) and the end of it (Chapter X)—towards the end of May or the middle of June, shortly before the summer solstice. If we examine the other chapters for similar hints, we get, with one exception, a perfectly consistent picture of seasonal progress through the year.

In Chapter IV, which for other reasons we have inserted after Chapter I, there is nothing (beyond one reference to a house standing in the sun) to help us here.

Chapter II takes place, as we have seen, about eleven days after the arrest and puts us into the early part of summer: as K. hurries along to the suburb he sees men in shirtsleeves leaning out of open windows, women at other windows airing the bedding, children playing in the street, a man with bare feet reading a newspaper, a young girl in her night-jacket at the well, laundry being hung up to dry, a fruit-dealer crying his wares to the people at the windows. It is the picture of a suburb in summer.

That Chapter III is precisely a week later is clear from the opening sentences: "During the next week K. waited . . . and when no appointment was made by Saturday evening, he assumed that he was tacitly expected to report himself again at the same address and at the same time. . . . [Now the interrogation chamber] was really empty and in its emptiness looked even more sordid than on the previous Sunday." And the summer weather is suggested by the comment that "the sun beats on the roof here and the hot roof-beams make the air dull and heavy."

Chapter V (which in the new arrangement follows III) begins "a few evenings later," but there are no references to the weather or the seasons.

The hints in Chapter VI are slight, yet they suggest that we are still in summer: K.'s uncle wears a Panama hat and stands for several hours in a light rain with no mention, in his bitter complaints, of being cold.

Chapter VII, however, takes place "one winter morning." The season is twice specifically designated as winter (though it is also once inexplicably called "an awful autumn"), and there are numerous comments upon the cold and the snow. It is furthermore apparent that K., in his musings at the beginning of this chapter, looks back upon a fairly long association with the advocate whom he first met on that summer evening in Chapter VI: now "it was more than a month since Huld had sent for him, and even during the first few consultations. . . ."

There is no clear reference to weather or season in Chapter VIII, but the commercial traveler (Block), who almost prides himself upon having a trial already five and a half years long, says to K., ''Your case is six months old, isn't it? Yes, that's what I heard. An infant of a case!'' This would of course place the action of the chapter in December.

Thus far everything has moved as it should. But the episode in Chapter IX—which in the old arrangement falls between a day in December (Chapter VIII) and a day in late spring (Chapter X)—takes place in autumn: the ''prevailing wet autumnal weather'' is very much in evidence. Either this chapter is out of place or there is a *two-year* period between the arrest on K.'s thirtieth birthday and his execution the evening before his thirty-first birthday! The following tentative solution, based simply upon the progress of the seasons, suggests itself: Chapter IX should appear immediately before Chapter VII.

But does such a change hold up under closer scrutiny and, if so, how does it alter our understanding of the novel? There are at least two important arguments in favor of the old arrangement: Max Brod, Kafka's intimate friend and literary executor, established it; and a cathedral (the scene of Chapter IX), a blessed, solemn place, seems at first glance to provide a peculiarly ideal background for K.'s last struggles and an ironic contrast with the action of the final chapter. Brod himself, however, destroys the value of the latter argument when he says, in his epilogue to the American and the first German edition, ''Franz Kafka regarded the novel as unfinished. Before the final chapter . . . various further stages of the mysterious trial should have been described.'' If this is true, then any purely aesthetic notions we may have about the juxtaposition of Chapters IX and X must give way. And there are of course some fragments—''Struggle with the Deputy Manager,'' ''Journey to His Mother,'' and ''The House''—which seem in fact to be Kafka's attempts to describe those ''various further stages'' of the action related to the trial. ''Journey to His Mother,'' especially, with its precise information about the time—only thirteen days before the execution—fits smoothly into the novel immediately before Chapter X. ''The House,'' we know, must follow the unit composed of Chapters VII and VIII; for it deals with Titorelli, the painter whom K. met on that winter morning in Chapter VII, and it speaks of him as K.'s close, almost intimate friend, thereby suggesting that a reasonably long period of time has passed since the December day of Chapter VIII. Yet there is still no evidence other than the autumnal setting of Chapter IX to suggest that the cathedral scene does not belong even closer to the end of K.'s life than does his journey to his mother. We must look more closely at the substance of the novel.

Whatever might be the meaning of the novel, it is certain that the year-long struggle between the incomprehensible trial and normal life—between those powers that would destroy and those that would preserve life, or, reduced to simpler terms, between the court and work (K.'s duties at the bank)—is the axis around which everything revolves. Until his thirtieth birthday Joseph K. lives for his work, his position, without any obstacle and with all his powers. We have already seen how the fragment called ''The District Attorney'' shows him as the completely unhampered and successful head clerk. On his thirtieth birthday the trial appears (the disintegrating delusion, the persecution complex, the obsession, the neurosis?); but at first, for months even, the danger is underestimated as it only slowly undermines the ability to work, the joy found in work. For example, even as late as the last lines in the fragment ''To

Elsa,'' which probably belongs between Chapters V and VI, K. has the power to forget about the court: ''thoughts about the Bank began, as in former times, to absorb him completely.''

K. resists the corrosive power of the court at first mildly, carelessly, in high spirits, even challengingly (see ''To Elsa''), then more and more frequently and violently. But the trial slowly overpowers him, paralyzing his ability to resist, inducing at last a state of apathy and lack of will. At first K. recognizes what is happening, but the recognition grows fainter until he succumbs to the hostile power of the court ''without knowing. . . .'' If this struggle, with K.'s resulting disintegration, is progressive, close attention to it should tell us something about the sequence of chapters; and, indeed, if we read Chapters VII and IX carefully, we are struck by the fact that the disintegration is far more pronounced in VII than in IX.

In Chapter IX K.'s position with the bank is still safe, basically unaffected by the trial. He is still considered an efficient clerk whom his superiors trust not only with ''honourable'' business missions but with the responsibility (''that K. would once have felt to be an honour'') of entertaining an Italian colleague whose ''influential connections . . . made him important to the Bank. . . .'' K. is, to be sure, deeply troubled. He knows that he is no longer ''able to make the best use of his office hours,'' he sees himself ''continually threatened by mistakes intruding into his work from all sides,'' he thinks ''now that all his energies [are] needed . . . to retain his prestige in the Bank,'' and he cannot help ''suspecting that there [is] a plot to get him out of the way while his work [is] investigated. . . .'' But nothing in the chapter suggests that his superiors are actually aware of his decreasing value to them; and he cannot know ''if there [is] even the smallest ground for his suspicions. . . .'' The fear he has of not being allowed, after a business trip, to return to the bank is ''a fear which he well knew to be exaggerated. . . .'' His worries are, in other words, great; but he knows that he must fight against exaggerated and even unfounded apprehensions, that he must exert himself, force himself to work. Furthermore, he still has the necessary energy, the will to fight. In front of others—though not before his own conscience—he still asserts himself with determination. On the whole, it is his work and not the trial which as yet forms the center of his activities. Even when away from the bank he thinks about his duties there, aware, as he is, of his weakening ability to work properly. This is of course a sign that he is no longer normal, is already pathological: before the trial he could freely enjoy his leisure. Still, until the conversation with the priest late in the chapter, a conversation in which K. becomes involved almost against his will, there is little mention of the trial as such. His thoughts revolve around his duties at the bank.

Now let us turn to Chapter VII, where in contrast to IX, we find a shattered, tortured, self-torturing individual, one who is irresolute, apathetic, wholly unable to work. Consider the very first lines: ''One winter morning—snow was falling outside the window in a foggy dimness—K. was sitting in his office, already exhausted in spite of the early hour. To save his face before his subordinates at least, he had given his clerk instructions to admit no one, on the plea that he was occupied with an important piece of work. But instead of working he twisted in his chair, idly rearranged the things lying on his writing-table, and then, without being aware of it, let his outstretched arm rest on the table and sat on with bowed head, immobile.'' The following pages are concerned with K.'s thoughts as he sits there shamelessly neglecting the interests of the bank and its clients, interests which were once so close to his heart. He is unable to rouse himself until eleven o'clock: "he had wasted two hours in dreaming, a long stretch of precious time, and he was, of course, still wearier than he had been before." When at last he grants one of the long-waiting clients (the manufacturer) an interview, he is unable to pay attention, though he knows this to be an "important piece of business"; and he is actually relieved when the hated Deputy Manager steals the client away, a theft that he would never previously have allowed. But now he is glad to be alone: "he had not the slightest intention of interviewing any more clients [there are several who have been waiting all morning for him] and vaguely realized how pleasant it was that the people waiting outside believed him to be still occupied with the manufacturer, so that nobody, not even the attendant, would disturb him. He went over to the window, perched on the sill, holding on to the latch with one hand, and looked down on the square below. The snow was still falling, the sky had not yet cleared. For a long time he sat like this, without knowing what really troubled him. . . ."

Chapter VII shows us a man who is no longer able to keep his mind on anything but himself, his own difficulties. Things have gone so far that it is no longer, as in Chapter IX, the trial which seems to him to interfere with his work but precisely the other way around: "While his case was unfolding itself, while up in the attics the Court clerks were poring over the charge papers, was he to devote his attention to the affairs of the Bank?" In Chapter IX the priest had to remind K. of the trial, and could do so without really upsetting him. They were able to discuss the court and its proceedings calmly and objectively, and, so far as K. was concerned, even indifferently at the beginning. But in Chapter VII the trial overshadows everything: "the thought of his case never left him now." The man who in Chapter IX was still willing and able to work and who was perfectly aware of the need to fight *against* the trial is here convinced of the need to fight *for* the trial. All the energy that he had previously mustered for his work is now devoted to the trial, which has literally cast a spell over him, has pushed aside everything else, all pleasures, all normal ambitions. The decisions he now reaches, "the decision which might prove valuable," have nothing to do with forcing himself to work, as was still the case in Chapter IX; they involve, for example, the question of whether to keep or to dismiss his lawyer; they have value only in connection with the trial. And though such decisions are the sole result of his wasted working hours, they give him satisfaction: "the Court would encounter for once an accused man who knew how to stick up for his rights."

Only once in this long chapter—by far the longest in the novel, sixty-four pages, with a direct continuation in Chapter VIII—does he momentarily remember that especially at this time he "should be devoting his mind entirely to work"; and only once does he pause briefly over the fact that should he continue to abandon his work so completely (he is about to rush off to see Titorelli, the painter, leaving three more clients to the Deputy Manager) "his prestige in the Bank would suffer irreparable injury." Such thoughts have no power over him: "almost elated," he pursues the course he knows will ruin him at the bank. The prestige which he here sacrifices so consciously was, we remember, intact in Chapter IX, and K. was still fighting to retain it. Furthermore, in Chapter IX K. only imagines as a fearful possibility what in Chapter VII actually happens. "In his mind [in Chapter IX] he saw the Deputy Manager, who had always spied upon him, prowling every now and then into his office, sitting down at his desk, running through his papers,

receiving clients who had become almost old friends of K.'s in the course of many years, and turning them against him. . . ." In Chapter VII the Deputy Manager actually does come into K.'s office, he does run through K.'s papers—searches "through his files as if they belonged to him" and even carries a huge package of documents off to his own office—and he does, with not so much as a murmur of complaint from K., take for himself four of K.'s clients. Yet as K. leaves the bank immediately after this defeat, which would once have been insufferable, he is "almost elated at the thought of being able to devote himself almost entirely to his case for a while. . . ."

It seems clear enough on the basis of the evidence already presented—-Kafka's references to weather and to the seasons and his handling of the conflict between work and trial within K.'s mind—that Chapter IX must precede Chapter VII. And if we examine the highly important conversation between K. and the priest which forms the last half of Chapter IX, we find that it, too, suggests the accuracy of the new arrangement. It is, to begin with at least, oddly vague and mild if we are to imagine it as coming after the long, even tedious, complicated characterizations of the court and of the possible judgments that flow from Huld (the advocate), Block (the commercial traveler) and Titorelli (the painter) in Chapters VII and VIII. The mildness of the priest's warning—"Do you know that your case is going badly?"—and K.'s reply—"I have that idea myself"—would perhaps seem more appropriate if they preceded instead of followed the far more pessimistic remarks (by a variety of characters, including a bank attendant, K.'s uncle, and Leni) to be found in the earlier chapters. The priest appears, furthermore, to know nothing about the ways in which K. has, in Chapters VII and VIII, conducted his defense. He says, "You cast about too much for outside help . . . especially from women." Now it is true that K. has sought for help from Fräulein Bürstner in Chapter I and the wife of the Law-Court Attendant in Chapter III and that he has found help without asking for it from Leni in Chapter VI, all of which would give the priest's remark real force if Chapter IX followed immediately after VI. But in Chapters VII and VIII, and in the fragment "The House," we learn about the discussions between K. and the advocate and about his attempts to obtain help from Block and Titorelli. It is in these chapters that we find the greatest detail and the deepest penetration; it is from these gentlemen that K. obtains the insight into the court, into its functions and procedures, that he has until then sought in vain. Yet in all of Chapter IX no mention is made, by the priest or by anyone else, of Huld, Block, or Titorelli. Is not such a silence difficult to explain unless Chapter IX does in fact precede Chapters VII and VIII?

This limited knowledge on the part of the priest has its counterpart in K.—in the conception he has here of the Court, which, he says, "consists almost entirely of petticoat-hunters. Let the Examining Magistrate see a woman in the distance and he almost knocks down his desk and the defendant in his eagerness to get at her." It is a conception based entirely upon his experiences in Chapters II and III. He shows here neither fear nor respect; his remarks reveal only scorn and indignation and almost haughty indifference, which is of course familiar to us from that part of the novel which precedes Chapter VII. But in Chapter VII there arises a genuine longing on K.'s part to "study" the court, and this longing is stimulated by K.'s relationship with the experienced Block in Chapter VIII. Titorelli, in Chapter VII, notices it at once: "You want to find out something about the court. . . ." But there is not the slightest intimation of it anywhere in Chapter IX.

The priest makes a good impression upon K., and at one point K. says to him, "You are very good to me. . . . But you are an exception among those who belong to the Court. I have more trust in you than in any of the others, though I know many of them." By the end of Chapter VI the final pronoun would refer to the guards, the bailiff, the examining magistrate, the student, the attendant, the usher, the young lady, the advocate, the chief clerk, and several subordinate officials. But if Chapter IX follows Chapters VII and VIII, the pronoun must also refer to Titorelli. He, too, must be one of the "others" in whom K. has little trust. This does not, I think, seem likely, for K. learns a great deal from Titorelli; yet the possibility raises a most important matter: the real significance of the painter.

K. first meets Titorelli on a winter forenoon in Chapter VII; and after a long talk K. leaves, promising to return soon. "'But you must keep your word,' said the painter . . . , 'or else I'll have to come to the Bank myself to make inquiries.'" And his next-to-last words are "till our next meeting." By the time of the fragment "The House" there have apparently been many meetings: K. and the painter have become close, almost intimate friends. This fragment, if nothing else, demonstrates that the Titorelli relationship was not conceived to end with Chapter VII; it seems, on the contrary, specifically designed (with "Journey to His Mother") to fill out the really large gap between Chapters VII-VIII (winter) and Chapter X (late spring or early summer). Here—and here in particular—the incompleteness of the novel makes itself felt in a most regrettable manner. There are of course a number of people who give K. information as he investigates the court and tries to clarify his case and discover the nature of his guilt; but the individual whose central position is most strongly emphasized is Titorelli. None other gives K. as deep an insight into the mysteries or makes him as familiar with the functions and the apparatus involved as does the painter.

The priest, to be sure, warns him against mistaken judgments; yet he affords him no better insight, not even through the parable "In the Eyes of the Law." Whatever may be the meaning of this legend, K. does not understand it, refers to it as something completely unknown to him, as he does with the other explanations of the priest, which are completely unsatisfactory and constantly digress from the point at issue. Can they, in fact, really be called "explanations"? Are they not rather a somewhat cowardly way of evading the subject? Perhaps significant in this connection is a passage which Kafka deleted from the novel: "It occurred to him that he had now talked about and criticized a legend; he didn't even know the work from which this legend came, and just as unfamiliar to him were the explanations. He had been drawn into a train of thought that was completely unfamiliar to him. Was this clergyman like all the others after all? Did he wish to discuss his affair only in hints, perhaps deceive him thereby, and remain silent at the end?" Whatever the answer to such a question, the interview with the priest leaves K. in the cold, perhaps more so than he has ever been before, especially after the priest's meaningless last words—"The Court makes no claims upon you. It receives you when you come and it relinquishes you when you go"—which provide the whole rhetorically arranged chapter with a most insipid finale and form an almost brusque contrast with what in the old arrangement is the immediately following execution.

K.'s need for instruction, for an understanding of the mysterious authorities is satisfied no better either by the lawyer, who purposely deceives him by giving him a partially false picture of the court and of his true situation, or by the helpless Block, who does, however, demonstrate in his own person what happens to those who are accused and not sentenced: they become dogs, weakened and worn out by years of torture, robbed of all their human dignity, cringing in doglike, debasing humility, ready for any act of servility.

Between Block, the victim, and the lawyer stands the painter, the true warner. It is from his lips that K. learns everything: the inexorability of the court and the exact nature of the various possibilities open to the accused. It follows that K. must see in Titorelli the only one who does not, "like all the others," dismiss him with vague hints but, instead, gives him the insight he craves. In Chapter IX, with the priest, an occasional monumental sentence betokens a general and valid insight; in Chapter VII, with Titorelli, such insights follow each other in rapid succession to form an impressive total: "Never in any case can the Court be dislodged. . . . everything belongs to the Court. . . . A single executioner could do all that is needed." And there are many more. Titorelli knows that there are only two real alternatives to being sentenced—"ostensible acquittal and indefinite postponement"—and he leads K. to understand that while they do "save the accused from coming up for sentence," they also "prevent an actual acquittal." At which observation, Titorelli says, "You have grasped the kernel of the matter." The kernel, the heart! In other words, here is the concisely phrased significance of the painter's long, excessively long, speech (perhaps it is also Kafka's final philosophy, the only lesson to be found in his writings, a lesson of defeat): there is absolutely no way out, there is no hope. Of the one alternative, Titorelli says, "The second acquittal is followed by the third arrest, the third acquittal by the fourth arrest, and so on. That is implied in the very idea of ostensible acquittal." And of the other alternative K., in the next chapter, meets a concrete example: Block, who has experienced, over five and a half years, all that the painter describes as a possibility; his trial has gone on and on, and nothing points to a possible solution, to a possible end. This is what we recall when we are watching K.'s death, for he too recalls it. He approaches death calmly, almost joyfully, for he refuses to bear what Block has suffered. His pride intervenes: "am I to show now that not even a whole year's struggling with my case has taught me anything? Am I to leave this world as a man who shies away from all conclusions? Are people to say of me after I am gone that at the beginning of my case I wanted it to finish, and at the end of it wanted it to begin again? I don't want that to be said." He has, in effect, made the decision that Titorelli defined for him by describing the various possibilities.

We have reached our goal. The structure of *The Trial* is represented by the following new arrangement of chapters and fragments (Arabic numerals for the new numbering, Roman numerals for the old):

The District Attorney (fragment)

1 (I)
2 (IV)
3 (II)
4 (III)
5 (V)
To Elsa (fragment)
6 (VI)
7 (IX)
8 (VII)
9 (VIII)

Struggle with the Deputy Manager (fragment)
The House (fragment)
Journey to His Mother (fragment)
10 (X)

(pp. 127-40)

In opposition to the commonly accepted opinion that Kafka consciously aimed for chaos and confusion as elements productive of magical effects, the chronology we have discovered in the text seems to show that he in no way wished to create a chaos, a magical jumble. On the contrary, it seems to show that he envisaged a well-planned, orderly structure, determined by a compact time schedule, whose evolution is marked outwardly, so to speak, by birthdays, while the logical succession of the seasons guarantees a natural development in the factual and emotional course of the events. The whole is marked by directness, by an almost schematic rigidity. It is in the same direct manner that Kafka wished to plan and shape the core of his story, the battle between work and court, between intellectual and emotional health and sickness, between the sense of reality and fever-ridden fancies. (p. 141)

> Herman Uyttersprot, "'The Trial': Its Structure," translated by Konrad Gries, Edmund P. Kurz, and Inge Liebe, in Franz Kafka Today, edited by Angel Flores and Homer Swander, The University of Wisconsin Press, 1958, pp. 127-45.

H. S. REISS (essay date 1956)

[*Reiss was a German educator and critic. In the following excerpt, he analyzes Herman Uyttersprot's arrangement of the chapters in* The Trial *(see excerpt above).*]

[Uyttersprot's] considerable alterations of the sequence [of chapters in **The Trial**] seem all the more impressive since Uyttersprot has also been able to find the appropriate place in the novel for the fragments. He is, however, aware that a solution of the questions about temporal sequence does not by any means answer all of the questions regarding the structure of the novel, and he proceeds to examine in detail the questions raised by the rearrangement of chapters. He begins by noting, in all fairness, that we are under the spell of Brod's arrangement of the structure of the novel, and that Brod, after all, had the manuscripts at his disposal while editing the book, as well as enjoying the "inestimable privilege of having been Kafka's intimate friend and having heard (how many?) readings from the novel."

Uyttersprot then proceeds to investigate the question of the close organic connection between the chapter "In the Cathedral" and the concluding chapter. This connection Uyttersprot disputes, in the first place because Brod himself admitted the possibility that other sections could have been contemplated for inclusion between these chapters, and in the second because the fragment "Trip to Mother's" belongs for factual and atmospheric reasons after the cathedral chapter. And Uyttersprot maintains that part of these sections to be inserted are contained in the chapter "Advocate—Manufacturer—Painter" and in the fragment "Struggle with the Deputy Manager." In the cathedral chapter, moreover, Josef K.'s position is still relatively secure, whereas by the chapter "Advocate—Manufacturer—Painter" K. is already deranged, purposeless, unwilling to work, and obsessed by the idea that he is being scrutinized. Indeed, his condition has deteriorated so far that he thinks his obstacles are at the bank rather than as a part of his trial; in

the cathedral chapter, he has to be reminded by the priest that there is a trial.

Uyttersprot perceives in the novel an exact order of things which he compares to the image of a balance: "At first the one scale—the scale of work—is heavily laden and stands below, while the other—the scale of the trial—is free and empty. Gradually the work scale empties, becoming lighter and rising, while the trial scale, originally empty, increases in weight from everything it has taken over from the first and now stands still at the bottom, having gone down as far as it can. At the beginning of the novel, on K.'s thirtieth birthday, the scale of life (of work, of the bank) is lower; by the conclusion—the thirty-first birthday—it is the trial scale which is lower: the scale of death and execution."

If we examine the cathedral chapter in the light of this metaphor, Uyttersprot maintains, it will be evident that the priest has only the most sketchy knowledge of the court, and his remarks about K.'s search for help have nothing really concrete to say about Titorelli, the advocate, and Leni. They could, in other words, appear in the story after the cathedral chapter without causing any complications for the plot. All of these details serve to underscore the correctness of Uyttersprot's hypotheses. He also mentions, however, the fact that the priest speaks in such a way as to suggest that Josef K.'s trial is in its later stages, which would tend to support Brod's arrangement, although Uyttersprot does not consider this detail to be of great moment.

Another of Uyttersprot's conclusions is that Kafka did not deliberately set out to describe chaos and confusion for the sake of magical effect, as a majority of interpreters maintains, but rather "seems to have had a well-thought out, articulated plan in mind." This plan "was linked to the rigid temporal framework of which the birthdays form the external boundaries, as it were, while the logical sequence of seasonal changes authenticates the natural development in the course of the external and internal or psychic events." On the other hand, Uyttersprot also points out that a confusing exception to the chronological development occurs in Chapter 7, where in the course of a winter day described in detail the manufacturer suddenly makes a remark about the "awful autumn." This Uyttersprot considers to be merely a casual remark or a slip of the pen.

Uyttersprot's discussion is extremely illuminating. His examination of the chronology is so clear and so fundamental that one cannot help asking why none of the innumerable Kafka scholars undertook to do so earlier. One explanation—that may be understandable if not compelling—is that the ambiguity and inexhaustibility of Kafka's oeuvre have prevented this essential aspect from being examined more closely. There is, then, no question of Uyttersprot's achievement; and yet one cannot completely dispel certain reservations.

Although Uyttersprot has admitted that Brod's arrangement, because of his privileged situation, cannot be completely discounted, it is possible that he has not taken Brod's view sufficiently into account. This is perhaps inevitable, inasmuch as it was his skepticism of Brod's arrangement that provided him with the initial thrust of his own examination. But Brod's statements cannot be merely discounted and his arrangement put aside. Uyttersprot's arrangement of the chapter sequence, based on the chronology, undoubtedly represents *one* version. But is it the only possibility? Could there not have been others?

Kafka had left the novel unfinished and had entrusted the manuscript to Brod before his death. It is possible that Kafka had planned different versions at various times, and that Uyttersprot's version represents the structure of the earlier form of the novel, while Brod's represents a later arrangement which he did not rework again. It is equally possible that Kafka had originally planned to include the cathedral chapter before the conclusion, and that Brod knew of this plan, but that Kafka did not discuss it with him afterwards, since we know that he disliked discussions of his work in progress. As we do not know how many times Kafka reworked the novel, if indeed he reworked it at all, nor whether earlier versions and additional chapters existed that were later destroyed, such questions remain unanswerable.

There are several indications which support Uyttersprot's hypothesis of a linear progression in the novel that proceeds from the complete independence of Josef K. at the outset to his complete subjugation to the judicial process at the end. F. D. Luke has noted the architectonic perfection of the *Metamorphosis* and substantiated his argument in detail. This is a work which was published during Kafka's lifetime in completed form. And a stylistic examination of my own of two (admittedly unpublished) short stories of Kafka showed in the one instance ("The Knock at the Manor Gate") a linear progression similar to that in the *Trial,* leading from a state of mind of confidence and trust to one of despair. The second story ("The Test") also demonstrates a type of development, it is true, but one that is neither continuous nor linear and has a sudden jump toward the end.

Because these two sketches were unpublished their evidence is of lesser import, but their examination demonstrates that the continual shift of mood, and the vacillation of thoughts characteristic of Kafka's style reflect a similar attitude of the writer. This indecisiveness and shift of stance can explain in part the various alternate versions of the novel. The fact that Kafka did not complete the novel shows that he was dissatisfied with it as a work of art. The shape of the novel, since it was never completed, must therefore remain a matter for conjecture, and Kafka's dissatisfaction with its structure may well have been one of the reasons why he did not finish it.

> *H. S. Reiss, "Eine Neuordnung der Werke Kafkas? Zu zwei Aufsätzen von Herman Uyttersprot" in his* Franz Kafka, *ergänzter Neudruck, Verlag Lambert Schneider, 1956, translated for this publication by Noel K. Barstad, 1988.*

RENE DAUVIN (essay date 1958)

[*In the following excerpt, Dauvin interprets the characters in* The Trial *as externalized aspects of K.'s psyche and the trial itself as the consequence of K.'s guilt for having chosen a superficial mode of life.*]

The Trial is so mysterious, so vague, that many interpretations are possible. As we stand on the threshold of Kafka's work, we feel uneasy, disoriented. The very form and structure of the novel amaze us, for it escapes all classification and transports us into an atmosphere of hallucination and strange disquiet. There seems to be no apparent continuity in this world. Did Kafka, then, abandon himself to the meanderings of dreams? I do not think so. We must take Joseph K. to be the alter ego of Kafka. The author of *The Trial* and his hero are both obsessed by strange visions which haunt their sleep. How can one rid himself of these anguished specters that inhabit the most diverse layers of the subconscious and which are ready to rise to the surface the instant awareness of reality flags? Psychoanalysis tells us that this can be done by an effort of the consciousness which brings these specters out into the light. And that is precisely what Kafka does. Literary composition was for him a sort of catharsis. That is why *The Trial* is a plunge into the night, a long nightmare which takes us through the stifling atmosphere of the darkest regions of Kafka's ego.

Joseph K. is arrested one morning after getting up. This is the hour, according to Kafka's *Diaries,* when "healthy men disperse the phantoms of the night." But with him, "the phantoms return as the night wears on, and in the morning they are all there, only they are not recognizable." Thus, K.'s arrest is the beginning of a nightmare or, more exactly, of a series of nightmares. The action, therefore, takes place in Kafka's soul, and the plot is symbolic of manifest or repressed tendencies. The characters of *The Trial,* whether they argue with K. or agree with him, are aspects of his ego. The novel is a dialogue Kafka has with himself; it is not by chance that one of the police inspectors actually bears the name "Franz." In his dreams, Kafka becomes aware of the deep antagonisms which tear his being apart. But he is not the master of his nocturnal visions. He allows himself to be guided by them, a fact that explains the alogical composition of the novel. These nightmares haunt him at night and on Sundays—in other words, during those hours when the congeries of daily toil no longer spreads a protective screen of banal tasks over the subconscious. That is why Joseph K. is summoned to court either at night or on Sundays. Furthermore, Joseph K., more aware than Kafka's other characters, knows very well that this mishap could not have happened to him at the office. "In the Bank, for instance, I am always prepared," said Joseph K., "nothing of that kind could possibly happen to me there. I have my own attendant, the general telephone and the office telephone stand before me on my desk, people keep coming in to see me, clients and clerks, and above all, my mind is always on my work and so kept on the alert." What, then, are these long, stifling corridors leading nowhere, these ghostlike judges with their phantom beards, these dark attics, if not the nocturnal universe of Kafka or Joseph K.? Now we know the climate in which the novel unfolds. The dream-key is the one that opens the door to this world. (pp. 145-46)

Up to his thirtieth year, Joseph K. was a man like other men. He led the life of an automaton and found peace and security in the world of daily routine and work. He would stay at the office until nine; then he would take a little walk, alone or with colleagues, and round out the evening at the café, where he stayed until eleven usually at a reserved table in the company of older men. There were exceptions to this regime: the Manager of the Bank who thought highly of his work occasionally invited him to take an automobile ride or for dinner at his villa. Once a week K. visited a young lady named Elsa who was night waitress at a café and during the day entertained her visitors from her bed. One cannot imagine a more impersonal, anonymous existence. His name, reduced to a simple initial, is symbolic from the outset, Joseph K.'s life is a superficial one, like the lives of all those who, in an attempt to escape the anguish of original dereliction, take refuge in an arbitrary system of the world. They organize raw existence, laden with menace, and transform it into an intelligible, reassuring world. But this involves a precarious construction of the intellect which eliminates the mystery of the world and interprets everything from the practical point of view. Of course, in exchange, such men lead a calm existence; but they buy that tranquillity at the price of what is deepest in them, since they base their interpretation of themselves only on things. Everything that compromises the security of the average man is relegated to the subconscious and he lives unauthentically. In the end he no longer knows his own soul and thinks that it is that thin solidified crust under which a world of deep chaotic tendencies slumbers. He becomes incapable of fulfilling his own possibilities. Obsessed by the material world he wishes to master, concerned only with the practical problems, he no longer sees the totality of his soul and interprets himself only in the light of categories he has created to make his environment subserve his needs. He is, then, only a thing among things, and because of the hypertrophic development of his intellect, his true being becomes strange to him. Only the impersonal dictatorial "they" subsists. Joseph K.'s life seems to coincide with the portrait Heidegger paints of unauthentic man.

But sometimes, as in the case of the hero of *The Trial,* it happens that the reign of the "they" is upset. Joseph K.'s arrest is a call issued from another region of being. It is a parliamentary question that has surged up from the depths of the original chaos existing in man in a latent state, overladen and concealed by preoccupation. Joseph K. has fled his destiny, the responsibility he had not had the strength to shoulder. His deepest "I," which is truer to him than he is to himself, reveals itself in the form of fear and trembling. If Franz and Willem proceed to arrest Joseph K. in Fräulein Bürstner's room, and not in his own, it is not a chance occurrence. Joseph K. is being torn from his world and transplanted into a world which, in its terrifying strangeness, is his own. Joseph K. had lived in bad faith: obliged to choose between two existential possibilities, he had chosen unauthentic existence and betrayed what was deepest and most personal in him for the benefit of a superficial and reassuring way of life. He is guilty because he had not taken his total "I" into account. He therefore cannot be arrested in his own room which is part of his "environmental world." He is arrested in Fräulein Bürstner's room, for it represents a world foreign to K., and yet close to him: it is the dark, subconscious part of his "I." Joseph K. had, in effect, consented to live a "fallen life" and suddenly in anguish, personified by Franz and Willem, he becomes aware of this divorce in his being which, up to that point, had been frozen in the familiar world of everyday interpretations. Joseph K. is guilty towards this deepest and original "I" which is no longer content to turn up in his sleep. Anxiety invades his life. His happy indifference is compromised by the sudden eruption of dark powers which summon him to their Court.

How can he escape this accusation, this anxiety? By becoming the champion of "infinite surrender" like Kierkegaard's Abraham, and living in a new world of being, a higher level of consciousness; by integrating into himself all the virtualities of his "I," the demoniac powers he fears, the terrifying aspect of the original absolute world. He would have to assume his personal destiny and understand the call that comes from the depths of the mutilated, travestied being. This hidden "I" is all-powerful; it is found behind all unforeseen acts which drag Joseph K. from the regular paths he had been passively following before his arrest.

The workmen's quarter which on Sunday is swarming with disorderly primitive life, Fräulein Bürstner, the girl who is so near and yet so remote, the sheriff's wife, the nurse Leni, simply represent the repressed demoniac forces that constitute a constant threat to everyday life, but are also the promise of a higher, regenerated, richer, sincerer life than the spiritless one led by the proxy, Joseph K.

The court, which represents the Synagogue of Prague, is also a manifestation of this vague feeling of basic guilt. Demoniac characters appear. They stand on a plane superior to normal existence. On that level, only being is of importance. It scarcely matters whether one is the proxy of a great bank or a house painter. These are attributes whose values exist only in a humanized world. But K., in spite of all warnings, remains a stranger to this world of being and assumes a deep guilt with regard to it. He does not understand the warning that was issued him. His servitude to the world of unauthenticity is too powerful for him to be able to free himself and understand, as Leni tells him, that all accused men are handsome, since their fate is of the elect, a fate enhanced by the tragic beauty of metaphysical anxiety. He protests that Franz and Willem have eaten his bread and butter, his honey, and have stolen his linen on the pretext that they would hold it in trust. But was that not an invitation to turn away from the human world of preoccupation and focus his attention on a world of real values, rooted in the most authentic aspects of man himself? It is at the price of such surrender that he might escape from a banal life and become like Abraham a "Champion of the faith." But he does not wish to escape from the hold of this average banal world; he clings to it and makes use of all human means to regain the sweet calm that had deserted him.

He tells Fräulein Bürstner all the details of his arrest. What does he really expect? To free himself from that anxiety which, once described and translated into everyday language, will, he hopes, cease being disquieting and unique. He accepts the suggestions of his uncle who, as a man of action, sees in Joseph K.'s arrest a threat to the entire family since it holds the unauthentic life up to doubt. He will therefore seek out a lawyer, a pale symbol of dogmatic human intelligence, one who is content with describing and remaining in the domain of the finite and foreseeable. The light which the lawyer sheds on the affair is as pale as the light of his candle. His world is at odds with the world of the Court; for Huld personifies abstract and general knowledge. He describes, without even questioning Joseph K., and moves in the sphere of the finite, without ever being able to suggest a solution for the problem of human destiny. Intellect is powerless; it cannot put an end to the trial which is a strictly personal affair and can be won by the accused only. Besides, the new forces that have been aroused in Joseph K. and have given birth to his anxiety are so imperious that he escapes, leaving his uncle and lawyer to dispose of him as of something inanimate, and follows Leni, the symbol of tendencies that cannot be reduced to the intellect.

He grows tired of his lawyer; since human reason cannot in any way help him, he will seek out the artist. Perhaps human art will bring back to him the peace he wants at any price. The solution suggested is of very little consolation. The painter lives in appearance and cannot obtain any definite acquittal. Only "apparent acquittal" and "unlimited delay" exist for him. The solution is only temporary. The painter is simply a merchant of illusions. He does not live in the world of being; his world is one of appearances. Thus Joseph K. cannot turn to anyone, he is always brought back to himself, for salvation resides only in him, in a courageous decision to shoulder life.

We therefore see the unfortunate Joseph K. oscillating between two worlds: he comes back to the Court although he has not been summoned, because he, like Frau Grubach, has the feeling that his happiness is somehow involved. Yet he still turns his back on the solitary life and seeks in the community a remedy for his anxiety; but the human community henceforth rejects him. Frau Grubach, as well as the two inspectors, refuses to shake his hand. He is at home neither in unauthentic society nor in the world of original contingency represented by the Court that is located in attics and sits only at night and on Sundays in a dehumanized region exempt from the workaday world and abstract categories.

Joseph K. is like the ape in **"A Report to an Academy"**: in order to escape the darkness of his cage, the ape abdicates his simian nature and immediately learns to shake men's hands. He, too, gains security and freedom from care only at the price of a betrayal, by shouldering a destiny that is not his. But Joseph K. lives on the border of two worlds and in his confusion finds no lifebuoy he can hold on to.

Only now can we understand the numerous reasons why Joseph K. is sentenced to death. He must die because he does not seek out the Law. He finds it by chance, in the cathedral, but does not understand the deep causes of his anguish.

Besides, he is a selfish bachelor, arraigned by a society which condemns celibacy. According to Kierkegaard, is there any greater debt than owing one's life to a man? The *Talmud,* which Kafka quotes, proclaims that without children a man does not deserve to be called a human being. Even Kafka's father finds that he is rehabilitated because he is, in a sense, the living example of the Law obeyed. Did he not raise five children? No matter what direction Joseph K. takes, he finds himself in an impasse, and there is no way out for him other than death. He is such a model of a "utilitarian world" that he rebels against the world of authentic being and in his struggle has recourse to all operations of an all-too-human logic. If Joseph K. must die, Kafka, on the other hand, has a right to bachelorhood which, for him, is not a criminal exception. He has a right to live, also, for his books are an escape from the artificial world which will not liberate Joseph K. When, several moments before Joseph K.'s execution, Fräulein Bürstner is seen at the turning of a side-street, his executioners' hold relaxes on Joseph K., for he starts to follow her. But he does not understand the warning; he gives up his pursuit and the executioners tighten their hold. He had had no right to celibacy, for the goal of his life had not been the personal search for a new God who demands solitude.

Kafka therefore appears to us as having the characteristics of a melancholy Narcissus viewing himself in a double mirror: on the one hand, he faces Joseph K.; on the other, the more flattering face of the priest. Joseph K. is without doubt the image which Kafka's family and friends had of him and the image he had of himself when he doubted his mission. Besides, is not the day chosen for Joseph K.'s execution his birthday, the day when, thirty-one years earlier, he had received from his parents a name, the symbol of all the misunderstanding that had accumulated around his person? The priest is therefore probably the authentic portrait of Kafka as he saw himself, an idealized portrait of days of happy exaltation. His mission requires solitude, and celibacy is required of the Catholic priest. Since he too sought God and since the kingdom of God is not a kingdom that can be entered in company, Kafka had as much right to celibacy as did the Catholic priest, the rather mysterious priest who made of his quest for the Law the object of his meditations in the lonely cathedral.

In addition, Kafka had for a long time hesitated between celibacy and the married state, which was to him like the two-faced Janus. In fact, marriage might have been for him a way of understanding himself better; unknown tendencies of his spirit might have been revealed to him and might have restored him to a complete authentic personality. Fräulein Bürstner, from this point of view, doubtlessly personifies an unsuspected part of Joseph K.'s soul. Of course, the priest reproaches him for seeking out the help of women too much, for not depending on himself sufficiently to win his case. He tells him not to spread himself too thin; it is clear he wants to make him understand that he ought to give up women for one woman who will give him a more comprehensive awareness of his being. In so doing, the priest echoes Leni's suggestion to Joseph K. that a girl like Elsa was incapable of sacrificing herself for him, for he had come to her by chance and not because of an inner need. But marriage can be a yoke constraining free development of the personality. Kafka came to a clear decision only when he was struck down by illness and saw in that ordeal a Providential warning to the effect that he must give up his fiancée and devote himself to the quest of the new Law. Joseph K., on the other hand, is not aware of this dilemma. He is too much attached to the material world to discover the meaning of his anxiety. He is therefore guilty towards society and the Law.

Is this Law that Kafka must seek out inaccessible? On this count, we discern a certain hesitation in his thought. Sometimes it is the unknowable: "It is not," says Kafka, "because his life was short that Moses did not enter the promised land, but because it was a human life." The absolute, then, seems to him to be heterogeneous to weak, limited human life, and he humiliates himself before the grandeur of the Divine. But more often, he seems to believe in a "heaven of fixed stars" to which men may have access.

What is this Law, then? "It is," says Kafka, "that which is indestructible, and to believe is to free the indestructible in oneself, to be indestructible, or more exactly, to be." To be himself, without remorse, without anxiety, was the ideal Kafka tried in vain to achieve. He felt that his oddity was a sin, and then one day he understood that it was a crushing but inestimable privilege. To be oneself is the final message of the writer who never ceased hoping. To be oneself, to give up the impersonal life which men lead and ascribe even to their God, a vain and lifeless abstraction.

From this point of view, the cathedral scene is rich in meaning. Time seems to be in abeyance, transformed into a Platonic eternity. The years spent by man standing before the gates of the Law roll by rapidly in contrast with the duration that is so charged with events and constitutes the substance of the other chapters. We are, in effect, in the "heaven of fixed stars," which is an inner heaven, hidden in the deepest recesses of the individual soul. Shortly before he dies, man is astonished and asks his doorkeeper: "Everyone strives to attain the Law, how does it come about, then, that in all these years no one has come seeking admittance but me?" The doorkeeper bellows into the ears of the dying man: "No one but you could gain admittance through this door, since this door was intended only for you. I am now going to shut it." Somewhere in his notebooks, Kafka points out the analogy between the German words *sein* and *Dasein,* thus giving us to understand that life should not be anonymous but personal. Each man should seek out his Law and become himself, even if he has to struggle against society, its fixed ideals, its bloodless codes, its thingness. The doorkeeper himself is simply the symbolic representation of the world as obstacle in the path of the quest of our deepest, unconditional personality. It knows no Law; it turns its back on the Law and is naïve, as naïve as realistic doctrine. It is interested only in attributes, in the accidents of substance; it cross-examines man about the parish he lives in, asks a thousand banal questions, and accepts his gifts. Man asks his question only when he is about to die, when he is about to shake off the hold of the material world and become pure spirit, freed from artificiality. Joseph K. does not understand this parable. He is not sufficiently detached from the material world. The light of the Tabernacle counteracts the light of his electric lamp and prevents him from noticing the carvings on the altar. The lamp which the priest gives him to hold goes out in his hand.

But the priest tells Joseph K. that there are holes in the character of the guardian of the Law. That is why one can, in this life, have access to the world of truth and the absolute. This truth is one which must be discovered phenomenologically because it is hidden; its depths are covered over. "The magnificence of life," says Kafka, "is all around us in its entirety, but its depths are covered over, invisible."

To penetrate that region of feeling, one must be able to give up this world: like Abraham, one must sacrifice what is earthly. But Isaac was restored to Abraham and Abraham was twice joyous when he received his son for the second time. Job, too, after his ordeal, received everything twice, says Kierkegaard in his *Rehearsal*. This would also have been true of Joseph K., but he understood nothing about the mysterious nature of his anguish. He did not understand that it was no question of theft but of custody when Franz and Willem carried away his linen. He did not understand that everything earthly would be given back to him when he found his Law and built his life on solid foundations.

At the end of his life, Kafka became cheerful and optimistic. He had faith in the future and believed in an earthly paradise. We have been expelled from it, say the Scriptures, but it was not destroyed. In a way, the expulsion was a good thing, for if we had not been ejected, paradise would have had to be destroyed. The happiness that awaits us is therefore of this earth, for we shall find paradise again. The Messiah will come. Kafka is certain of that. "He will come as soon as an individualism of the most uncontrollable faith becomes possible. Towards that end, it will be necessary for the mediator in each man to come alive again." Kafka seems to reconcile the Jewish and Christian concepts of the Messiah, for the Messiah will come only one day after his arrival: that is, he will be truly among us the day his message becomes universal truth.

It was not without suffering that Kafka rose to this optimistic view of the world. He had to struggle, and his novels are an echo of the struggles that led him to the very heart of despair.

Of course, Kafka's world is almost entirely pervaded by the lugubrious light of a black sun, because he really wishes to free himself from the world of doubt and uncertainty that prevents him from saying "Yea" to existence. It very often involves therapy. "I have a hundred thousand false, horrible feelings," he says, "the good ones make their appearance only in rags and they are quite weak." He therefore seems to hate his work and orders Max Brod, his literary executor, to burn it. He fears, perhaps, that he is imposing on his readers that obsessive world which he himself identifies as contrary to the ideal. But his friend's pious disobedience saved these books which one should read against the current as one does the *Notebooks of Malte Laurids Brigge*. His premature death deprived us of works which certainly would have been the contrary of this nocturnal hallucinatory, absurd and contradictory world. The **Diaries** evoke this reconciled world, based on a

deep individualism enlightened by the dazzling light of indestructible Law, the secret home of any human personality worthy of that name. Joseph K. dies because, like the son in **"The Judgment,"** he is protected neither from on high nor from behind, neither by God nor by an existence established on the deep foundations of the authentic being. His life is therefore no longer based on the absolute. Faith is dead; men, whether Jews or Christians, had killed it. Life is set adrift. Man is nothing more than a wreck; he must find his reason for being in himself, at the very core of his existence which intellect has reduced to the condition of an abstract category. He must rediscover the meaning of life. The Court is in this respect, like many symbols in the novel, a polyvalent symbol. It represents the fallen Synagogue and the New Law, constructed on the depths of being. Joseph K. lives in an anguish that does not create new values because he is not able to discern its meaning clearly. He sinks into absolute nihilism, because he cannot find a remedy for this anguish either in religion or the inoffensive world of day-to-day existence. He cannot find himself, although summoned by his anguish to the Court of his deepest "I," which aspires to be, totally and absolutely, an ultimate instance. He ought to kill himself. But this would give meaning to life. So he lets himself be executed by his two executioners, and run-of-the-mill humanity seems to heave a sigh of relief when Joseph K. dies. The alarm is over. Life has ceased being problematic, for K.'s anxiety was really a threat that compromised the tranquil existence of "intelligent men, those intruders remorselessly present like a splinter in the flesh of an illegal poacher." The same thing is true of *The Metamorphosis*. As soon as the corpse of the cockroach which was once Gregor Samsa is thrown into the dustbin, the everyday world becomes calm again: cheerful heedlessness is restored and Gregor's sister blooms into a pretty girl with a good figure.

But the indestructible will reign one day. Kafka was firmly convinced of that; his hope was invincible. "To find happiness," he says, "I must raise the Universe to the Pure, the True and the Definitive." To achieve such an ideal of perfection, man will have to have the courage to be in his life what he is in his deepest self; he will have to surrender bad faith in favor of authentic being.

Kafka is therefore not a prophet of the absurd; his optimism is all the more unshakeable for his having risen above total despair and for having slowly developed a lucid, tenacious will. Gide's adaptation conceals this meaning of *The Trial,* for the parable of the Law has been eliminated, and we have only a long, hallucinatory series of reasons for despair. In reality Kafka's work is, I repeat, full of Messianic hope. A fervent admirer of Goethe, Kafka always hoped for a life made possible by an ideal human community that safeguarded the irrefutable rights of the individual. That is the lesson taught us by his books. It is a message we should meditate upon, especially at a time when the individual may be eliminated by collectivism. The individual, out of fear of loneliness, is only too prone to take refuge in a group and lose himself. Even if he triumphed over his existential anguish and made an effort to affirm himself towards and against all the rest, he would risk being wiped out, gagged by powerful collective entities. We can only hope that the meaning and the resonance of Kafka's work will be understood and will inspire man to lead his life with the courage it requires to be himself, for there is no real culture without respect of the human being as something unique and irreplaceable. (pp. 151-60)

René Dauvin, "'The Trial': Its Meaning," translated by Martin Nozick, in Franz Kafka Today, *edited by Angel Flores and Homer Swander, The University of Wisconsin Press, 1958, pp. 145-60.*

FREDERICK J. HOFFMAN (essay date 1960)

[*Hoffman was an American educator and critic who wrote extensively on twentieth-century American literature. In the following excerpt, he argues that K. unwittingly colludes with the Court in his own destruction.*]

The opening scene of Kafka's *The Trial* describes a quite unexpected interruption in the life of its hero. An upstanding, virtuous and efficient man, he has reached his thirtieth birthday and is well established as an Assessor at the Bank. This morning, however, instead of being greeted with good wishes and his breakfast, he is confronted by a stranger, who announces his arrest. This introductory shock is of the utmost importance to the impression the novel will ultimately have. It suggests the intrusion of the absurd into a world protected on all sides by familiar assurances and securities. Joseph K. is especially well acquainted with these comforts; his life is dedicated to an almost endless calculation, by means of which he helps to assure that society will function smoothly. The break in routine at first seems a trick, perhaps a birthday joke, which he will surely soon discover and dismiss. The strategy of this opening scene is to give the reader a brief acquaintance with an unfamiliar world. After all, he understands K., sympathizes with him, and is in many ways his double. There are rules, there is the law; people have long known how to take care of unexpected intrusions. It is unreasonable to expect that the disruption is more than temporary.

This is the first contribution of the novel to Kafka's analysis of modern circumstance. The element of surprise in human relationships may last only so long; it cannot in any case be permitted to alter the design of human security, or that design will change. Surprise is an indispensable element of the fact of violence in modern life. A carefully plotted pattern of expected events has always been needed to sustain a customary existence. A sudden break in the routine challenges the fullest energy of man's power of adjustment. Suddenness is a quality of violence; it is a sign of force breaking through the design established to contain it.

Another oddity of Kafka's opening scene is that the interruption is not a distortion of the setting in which it takes place. It is the same lodging house in which K. has lived for some years. The arrest takes place in the rooms, and the warders are ordinary citizens. No monster crashes into the scene, to split it to fragments. Instead, Kafka describes the warders' appearance with the meticulous care that is one of his trademarks. One of the essentials of modern literature is that it should define and describe the violent disruptions of conventional life in a conventional way. No work of Kafka lacks this precision. This quality of style means that the enormity, the incredible event, in modern life is represented in conventional terms. The unexpected is therefore "usual." It needs no Gothic trickery, no monstrous or surreal properties, to make its effects.

Kafka's skill in presenting the scene as precisely recognizable has another important effect. The scene and the personality at its center are in no genuine sense disparate. They possess a reciprocal status. The hero makes the scene possible; the scene reflects the hero's status. This interaction of scene and hero suggests a profound way of explaining the source of modern violence. We are in a very real sense the heirs of the nineteenth century, in that modern attitudes toward force were originally formed then, and the illusions of protective containment of force were gradually established in that time. The only way to understand violence—beyond superficial devices for merely admitting it as a fact of modern life—is to assume it as somehow the result of our willed interference with the balance of force and power in the human economy. We live constantly in a world in which this power is being extended. Many decades ago the instruments used for propelling force first exceeded the strength of man physically to contain or endure it. Almost daily now the means are improved to increase the disparity of force and personality and to lengthen the distance between assailant and victim.

The warders who have come to inform Joseph K. of his arrest are persons like him. They are, as K. is to discover much later, phases of himself, parts of the intricate conscious and subconscious pattern that is the totality of K. In any scrupulous analysis of K.'s situation, we shall have to say that K. has been interrupted by—K., that his neatly efficient life has been interfered with by himself. In the spirit of a half-recognition of this shared impulse, K. takes his stand on a question of protocol, of form: by what right do these men invade his privacy; on whose orders? The warders as well manage the arrest in terms of rules: K. is supposed to stay in his room, he is not allowed to wander about the house, he must wait for the Inspector to arrive. (Politeness is the ironic tone throughout. In the end K.'s executioners bow ceremonially and fastidiously attend to protocol.) This is to suggest that the rules for order are not vastly different from the rules for disorder. They are both a part of the same man, of his will and of the way he exercises it in society. Manners are flexibly pertinent to each expression of human motive. One of the most persistent challenges to literature in an age of violence is that of accommodating human manners to violent occasions. The grammar of violence is achieved through a realignment of the grammatical terms of peace. In the modern war novel, for example, both the descriptions of violence and the matter of accommodation to it are given within the same range and scope of human intercourse.

I have suggested in other essays that modern literature of violence may best be seen in terms of the metaphor of the assailant and his victim. The economy of this relationship may be defined as the distance achieved between the two. It is generally true that the range of psychological resources is best and most clearly employed in violent situations in which the distance between the assailant and the victim is so limited that the two protagonists are within sight of one another. In any violence there is a form of collaboration of the two involved in committing the act. The assailant strikes with force; the victim receives the force. The basic changes in the relationship occur when the distance becomes too great to allow for moral and emotional visibility as an element of the experience. It is only when that visibility is no longer possible that violence can be called "surprising." K. is surprised by his arrest, not because the warders are invisible but because they are not the real assailants. He finds it all but impossible to adjust to the rules and regulations governing his arrest because he cannot see the source of it or the motive for its having happened. *The Trial* is made up largely of scenes in which K. searches energetically for his assailant. He never knows who he is, and dies without a glimmer of comprehension of his complicity as victim. This desperate circumstance is repeated in a thousand ways in modern literature. The great energy of modern tragedy lies not so much in the carnage which is its established feature but in the uncertainty about causes and motives, the extreme difficulty in determining the victim's relationship to the act of violence.

K. is at liberty in the days following his arrest. The initiative of establishing the reality of his case is left to him. And at first he tries to hold to the idea that the whole thing is after all a hoax, or at worst so flagrant an injustice that he will need only to be firm and honest to have the affair exposed. His new role of criminal is at first only moderately recognized by the men and women around him. The *idea* of criminality is communicated at first in terms of atmosphere and scene. There are no machines at present at the disposal of an assailant. Since the assailant is not known, to the Court, to K.'s friends, or to K. himself, nothing is specified in the usual sense. The elaborate devices used for criminal detection, with which any reader or viewer of murder mysteries is familiar, do not exist. Instead, the Court and its subordinate functions are found in rooms, located in buildings not unlike K.'s rooming house.

On one Sunday morning K. makes his way to such a house and is surprised that the scene provides no sign of its function as a court building. Once inside, he is again puzzled and annoyed that they should not have given him more definite information: ". . . these people showed a strange negligence or indifference in their treatment of him, he intended to tell them so very positively and clearly." This dismay over the absence of conventional signs is closely related to the bewilderment over the accusation itself: who made it, why has it been made, how can he defend himself if he is so vague about its character? "His mind played in retrospect with the saying of the warder Willem that an attraction existed between the Law and guilt, from which it should really follow that the Interrogation Chamber must lie in that particular flight of stairs which K. happened to choose." This is his first real insight into the nature of the crime; it is of the very substance of himself, and therefore the course of his discovering what it is follows the line of his will and choice. He is, however, by no means convinced of his guilt, as his speech in the Chamber attests. Innocent persons are accused of guilt, he tells his audience, "and senseless proceedings are put in motion against them, mostly without effect, it is true, as in my own case."

No great exercise of the imagination is needed to grasp the significance of this remark, made as it is in a crowded room, the atmosphere "fuggy" and unclear, the audience divided in its view of the case. It stresses once again the role of the irrational in modern literature. The majority of literary reactions to the first World War were primarily expressions of shock, disbelief, extreme anger over the "unreasonableness" of the proceedings. This literature is clear at least on the question of the sources of violence. They are linked closely to the "fuggy" atmosphere created by force employed in the functioning of our economy. But beyond that, and more subtly, the mist, fog, smoke of the scene are of our own making. K. is talking into the dim and dirty atmosphere of his own mind as he strikes out at the unreasonableness of his circumstance. But he speaks as the Bank officer, setting that aspect of himself off from the other selves that may inhabit him. The scene of his protest is thus unreasonable: he finds it difficult both to see into it and to determine what if any part of his audience is sympathetic to him.

Moral tragedy has two major determinants: the matter of the hero's complicity, as assailant or victim, or a fusing of both; the matter of his state of awareness of his complicity. Hemingway's Lt. Henry, at first maddened by the irrationality of the Caporetto front, ends by saying that the war did not have

anything to do with him. The worst fear haunting the protagonist of the *Waste Land* is that of his involvement as a sacrifice to the necessities the scene describes. Anger and fear are variously interrelated in modern literature, to suggest the deep bewilderment of the modern soul over the question of his precise relation to the criminal circumstance in which he lives. In his own confident expansion of the possibilities of force, he has pushed assailant and victim further and further apart, until the instruments of violence have acquired such overwhelming force as to make the distinction all but impossible. The scene of the violence becomes the sole remaining evidence of motive and its relation to force; the assailant is the scene itself, and the scene includes the victim. The most extreme of our literary efforts to encompass a violence so shockingly out of hand describes painstakingly the deterioration of the victim, to the point where he resembles the assailant and is to all intents and purposes indistinguishable from it. This condition is in part revealed by the fact that the modern hero is not distinguishable from his fellows; or, if he is different, it is only in the degree and detail in which he externalizes his inner violence. The hero is a man of inner and outer violence, moving from one to the other according to the disposition of the author toward the scene. Throughout there is a sense of the dim, strange, "fuggy" atmosphere that defines the condition at the same time as it prevents a clear grasp of the meaning of the violence.

The progress of Kafka's hero is in terms of such a metaphoric scene of diffused violence. K. steadfastly refuses to admit the scene as part of himself. He comes back one day to the Interrogation Chamber and, finding it unoccupied, looks about him. He picks up a volume of what he assumes are law books, but finds in it an indecent picture, crudely drawn, of a man and woman sitting naked on a sofa; another bears the title, *How Grete Was Plagued by Her Husband*. Surely, he thinks, the Courts must be more corrupt than he had guessed; to give his own case more than the most perfunctory and contemptuous attention would surely mean contributing to an already bad situation. He turns to a woman in the room and finds her also involved in the corrupted scene. Quite without clearly recognizing the irony of his position, he is shortly engaged in wooing her support for his case, in terms of the very corruptive influence he has just recently scorned: "And probably there could be no more fitting revenge on the Examining Magistrate and his henchmen than to wrest this woman from them and take her himself." He is at once the outraged victim and the conniving collaborator of the situation. Throughout the progress of the novel, this dual role suggests itself in trivial acts and gestures; K. makes his way toward his death, never fully suspecting the force of his own role in causing it.

The most brilliantly revealing scene in this connection is the episode of the flogging. The two warders who had first arrested K. have been sentenced to be whipped because of a complaint he is said to have made about their behavior (they had tried to appropriate some of K.'s private belongings). But, K. insists, he hadn't intended to have them whipped; he was "only defending a principle." In any event, he is shocked that the scene should be taking place in the Bank building, and most disturbed that the noise might rouse the attention of the men still there. Here he is directly forced to see that he can be an agent of violence, and the sight disgusts him. In what way is a man involved in the sufferings of others? The disparity of principle and human incident is here eloquently presented. The intricate and complex wavering of principle and chance in our moral life causes incidental and sometimes violent pain to others. (pp. 89-95)

K. is gradually brought to a partial awareness of the seriousness of his circumstance, but he does not relinquish the privilege of righteous immunity. There are always extenuations: the corruption of the Court, the venality of lesser officials, the protective images of the security his position in the Bank provides, and so forth. At no time is the crime specified; at no time are the officials or minions of the Law made to look like monsters or grotesques. They are common variants of the human condition, of which K. is himself the central image. *The Trial* is in this sense a parable of man's grudging journey to moral awareness. Above all, it stresses the fatal deficiency of common moral safeguards. We are aware of their failure only when, suddenly and without warning, they fail us. One of Kay Boyle's recent novels, *The Seagull on the Step,* describes a busload of passengers on a routine journey in southern France soon after the end of the second war. Her attention is dispersed throughout the crowded bus and only occasionally focuses upon the driver, who strikes one as the most trustworthy of the tribe. A brake failure at the last plunges the vehicle down a cliff to destruction and death.

This melodramatic instance simply points up an obvious fact which is all but willfully neglected. K.'s concern for his innocence is only gradually moved from the center of his belligerent confidence in conventional rectitude. His uncle arrives from the country, profoundly disturbed over the news of K.'s arrest and even more upset that he should not have more scrupulously attended to his case. On one of his visits to the Advocate whom his uncle has engaged on his account, K. finds a commercial traveler, named Block, already there and apparently in constant, eager attendance upon the Advocate's every word. Block is an example of the force of unrelenting piety, the parody of a narrow moralistic self-concern. His submission to the most ludicrous of requirements does not testify to his being in any sense a righteous man, but rather suggests an energetic passivity, almost a ruthless drive toward self-involvement in guilt. While K. holds the Court guilty of a malicious miscarriage of procedure, Block submits to whatever may be with a diligent persistence. His action suggests a soldier hurrying from skull to skull, in search of whichever one had once been his head. When K. visits the Advocate, it is with the intention of telling him he no longer wishes his services, that he feels he will now go on his own. The contrast of Block and K. describes the range of earnestness in the moral life. Surely the political implications of this range are obvious enough.

If only because the demands upon his time have made him weary and listless in his performance as Bank Assessor, K.'s quest of definition shows obvious signs of absorbing his attention more and more. Without relinquishing his firm belief in innocence, he nevertheless improvises strategies of self-defense. On one occasion he visits a painter, Titorelli, who makes a poor enough living doing portraits of minor officials. The scene of Titorelli's quarters is itself a revealing image of the moral landscape. It is even a poorer neighborhood than that in which the Court holds its meetings.

> . . . the houses were still darker, the streets filled
> with sludge oozing about slowly on top of the melting
> snow. In the tenement where the painter lived only
> one wing of the great double door stood open, and
> beneath the other wing, in the masonry near the ground,
> there was a gaping hole out of which, just as K.
> approached, issued a disgusting yellow fluid, steaming hot, from which a rat fled into the adjoining canal.

Like many other Kafka scenes, this may be taken to suggest a variety of meanings. Surely it is in itself identifiable as a disheartening and disgusting slum, whose chief distinguishing marks most candidly define the body's private functions. As the relationship of men to space diminishes, the chance of either hiding such functions or breathing good air all but disappears. K. may be said here to have undertaken a journey to the ugliest sector of his moral world. Within the tenement he encounters three ugly, bold-faced young girls; one of them ''nudged him with her elbow and peered up at him knowingly. Neither her youth nor her deformity had saved her from being prematurely debauched.'' When K. finally finds his way to Titorelli's room, he finds the air here even more atrociously hot and foul than that of the courtroom he had visited. The entire scene clearly defines the décor of human evil. It is not an evil of commission, but an evil of disregard, of the impurities which the body's efforts for survival create in an imperfect and vulgarized atmosphere.

In another sense it is an atmosphere of purgation. The foul smell, the darkness, the constriction of space are all elements identifying the character of the body, its emission of impurities in the ordinary course of its progress toward inevitable corruption. K., in entering it, may almost literally be said to be journeying toward death, for the smell of death is about him and the space he occupies is not much larger than the space of a tomb. In such an atmosphere, K. discusses his case with Titorelli. He is unregenerately convinced that the whole affair is an elaborate injustice, but he is also aware that the ways of justice are skillful, subtle, and devious: ''And in the end, out of nothing at all, an enormous fabric of guilt will be conjured up.'' This remark and the scene in which it is made are available to numerous interpretations, but none of them is free of some suggestion of the idea the novel as a whole supports. The intricacies of human justice and intelligence are a composite of many fragmented decisions and their underlying motives Evil is subtly and slyly intermixed with the good; indeed, the good is scarcely to be defined by itself, since a just impulse can easily react painfully upon a weaker self.

The portrait Titorelli shows K. gives an ambiguous impression of Justice and Victory combined; though a trick of light and shadow also bring out the impression of ''a goddess of the Hunt in full cry.'' The passion for ''right feeling,'' for a principled life, might easily be confused in the chance admixture of aggression, so that one portrait reveals all three. The impression should convince the hero that he cannot longer expect surface good will to save him from the crime of which he is accused. One strong impression this scene gives is that the human will is never free of the taint of arrogance or ambition; nor is a human act ever free of the chance of causing pain, however indirectly. Quite aside from the very real service K.'s visit to Titorelli performs, by way of making him more fully aware of the seriousness of his case, the scene is itself the most powerful literary image of the landscape of violence. Here there is no real discrimination between assailant and victim. In submitting to the indignities of this setting, K. is in a real sense examining himself, or seeing the capacity of the self for absorbing the filth of its own making. One of the most obvious of the discrepancies noticeable in modern life is that between the nobility of appearance and the disorder of underlying reality. There have been many Potemkin villages in the history of the modern soul. But the most effectively shocking of modern scenes is that in which the disorder of the soul is imaged in a disarray of objects scattered in space. Man's power of calling forth violence, or of enduring within a landscape of its effects, is suggested again and again in modern literature.

More than that, the victim of this violence is himself an initiator of it. K.'s will and soul are here set forth most uncompromisingly. As he discusses the legal possibilities of his case, he remains at the very center of the disorder to which the officials ordering his arrest had originally hoped to call attention. In this very effective way, Kafka shows him growing toward an awareness of his situation at the very time when he is most earnestly exploring the chances of evasion. (pp. 97-100)

In the next to last of the novel's scenes, K. finds himself in the Cathedral, where he is awaiting a visitor whom the Bank has asked him to entertain. The event has been carefully prepared, and is eligible to much easy allegorical interpretation. One can say that K. has come to the Cathedral to hear still another version of his case; or that he is there because of the connivance of the Law officials, who are after all designers of his conscience. Whatever the meaning of the plans, K. is in the dark interior and, waiting for his guest, looks about him. He is curiously drawn to the altar-piece of a small side chapel which appears to contain near its outer edge the picture of a huge armoured knight.

> He was leaning on his sword, which was stuck into the bare ground, bare except for a stray blade of grass or two. He seemed to be watching attentively some event unfolding itself before his eyes. . . .

The center of the picture is a conventional enough portrayal of Christ being laid in the tomb, but K.'s attention now aroused, he searches further. His eyes are finally drawn to a small pulpit of plain stone, so small as scarcely to accommodate the preacher whom he now sees for the first time.

The scene is a sharply realistic addition to the parable of K.'s life. Once again he finds himself within a setting that is closely identified with his moral circumstance. The huge armoured knight he had examined so curiously guards the tomb; the small side chapel is the site chosen for his meditation on his "case"— that is to say, on his willed intervention in the affairs of men and his resistance to confession of the guilt. The priest who stands in the pulpit is the prison chaplain, there to discuss his present disposition to the case. The chaplain's fable brings the scene into the discourse itself: before the Law stands a doorkeeper in guard, he says. This man is specially designated for the moment of death. One must await one's turn and be present at precisely the right spot when it comes. But, while the man of the fable has awaited the moment patiently, he has not actively sought it, and the chance is lost. He had taken no initiative in seeking the way, but had passively assumed his fate would be decided and announced to him. But of course K. considers the tale ridiculous and leaves the Cathedral uninformed. Not only has he not sought out the verdict, but he has throughout resisted going the full way to acknowledgment of guilt.

There is nothing left to do now but send K. to his death. Kafka has conscientiously attended to every conceivable scenic effect, and K.'s soul has been quite exhaustively examined. A year after his arrest, on the eve of his thirty-first birthday, two men call at his lodging. Once again their appearance is grotesquely inappropriate to one's expectation of killers on a mission: "In frock-coats, pallid and plump, with top-hats that were apparently uncollapsible." The circumstances of violence are to the very end the same as those of normality. The men are polite to excess: "Tenth-rate old actors they send for me," K. grumbles. "They want to finish me off cheaply." Still firm in his disbelief, convinced of his innocence, K. walks between and slightly to the front of these grotesquely proper persons, like

servants perhaps, doormen or carriage attendants: ". . . the only thing for me to go on doing is to keep my intelligence calm and discriminating to the end." As the walk progresses, K. quickens the pace; and the two executioners, their arms tightly clasped to his, run with him. The death occurs on the outskirts of the town, near an old stone quarry, though there is also "a still completely urban house" nearby. One of the men draws out a long, thin, double-edged butcher's knife, and the two of them pass it to each other across K.'s body. "K. now perceived clearly that he was supposed to seize the knife himself, as it travelled from hand to hand, and plunge it into his own breast." But he does not do so, and the partners collaborate in the death, one of them holding K.'s throat, the other thrusting the knife into his heart.

> With failing eyes K. could still see the two of them, cheek leaning against cheek, immediately before his face, watching the final act. "Like a dog!" he said; it was as if he meant the shame of it to outlive him.

Just before this act, K. had turned his head to one side and in the direction of the distant dwelling. He saw, or thought he saw, a man reaching outstretched arms to him. Even at this moment of extremity, his hopes were stimulated. Could the man be offering help? Was there still some evidence that might save him? Is it possible that the man was an intermediary, who had the power to call off the execution? But the death does occur, the most ambiguous of conclusions of a baffling case. K. is alert to the end to the shame of his death, to its lack of dignity. It is unworthy of him; it has been committed at the level of an animal cruelly tortured to give sadistic pleasure.

The killing is the final ambiguity which follows correctly from a succession of ambiguous scenes. K. is a superb example of the modern moral hero, whose two great and striking characteristics are that he proclaims his innocence while in the act of willing his guilt, and that as a victim of a scene of violence he conspires with the assailant in the act of his death. There is no clear separation of the assailant from the victim in this case. The elaborate, scenic meditation of which the novel consists portrays modern man willing his guilt as he asserts principle, most tragically of all perhaps unable or unwilling to discriminate between the satisfactory reason and the ambiguous cause. While men have always fought wars for a cause and have invoked principle in defense of violence, they have not been altogether clearly vindicated in either case. Events culminating in violence lead after their conclusion very quickly to retrospective doubt. (pp. 101-03)

The over-powering image left at the end of K.'s struggle is of the victim conniving with the assailant in his own destruction. The assailant is no longer a single, identifiable, fingerprinted criminal, whose act can be related to the clear circumstances of a victim's death; the two, in the complex of moral implications described in *The Trial,* are joined in the landscape of violence itself. It is only in this sense that we can understand the paradox of cruelty committed "without cruel intent," or of Eliot's statement that ". . . Unnatural vices / Are fathered by our heroism. Virtues / Are forced upon us by our impudent crimes." (pp. 104-05)

Frederick J. Hoffman, "Kafka's 'The Trial': The Assailant as Landscape," in Bucknell Review, Vol. IX, No. 2, May, 1960, pp. 89-105.

DONALD M. KARTIGANER (essay date 1962)

[*In the following excerpt, Kartiganer compares* The Trial *with the biblical Book of Job.*]

At its most basic and universal level Franz Kafka's *The Trial* may be considered as a history of the hero in search of the father—to confront him, and, if necessary, to conquer him; in Joseph Campbell's words, to *atone* with him. According to this myth of the hero, when his time has come, the son elects to leave the security of the mother and venture forth to seek the father—his source and his rival. Once he has begun this quest, however, he must be prepared to endure the arduous tests of initiation prescribed by the male parent. When he has undergone these labors, when he has submitted to an unintelligible cruelty, inflicted seemingly for its own sake, when he has died his death of humility and the acceptance of pain, and has been reborn to a new understanding and perception—then, and only then, is his journey done, and he is one of the masters of the world. He is Phaeton, who has come not only to the porches of the sun, but has driven the chariot of Apollo safely across the sky. What he has discovered, of course, is not only the father, but that even more complex enigma, himself.

Constructed with an acute awareness of the nature of this hero myth, *The Trial* seems to be, more specifically speaking, a conscious parallel of the Book of Job, as well as containing additional—less vital—allusions to the stories of Abraham and Isaac, Jacob, Joseph and Christ. Not separate from these parallels, indeed pertinent to an incisive understanding of the myths themselves, is a web of psychological behavior patterns, as constructed in the theories of Freud. But clearly the guiding myth for Kafka, a man deeply versed not only in Biblical literature but in Talmudic commentary as well, is the story of Job, the archetypal image of the apparently innocent sufferer at the hands of the father. Job, without benefit of understanding the nature of his crime, endures tremendous punishment, from the loss of his family to physical affliction, yet clings steadfastly to a rod-like integrity and courage, descends to a death of patience and resignation, and is restored to an even greater wealth and fulfillment than he had known before. Like Job, Joseph K. has been burdened with the unspecified accusations of an incomprehensible authority, and compelled to withstand excruciating mental torment and anxiety. Yet, when he has appeared to arrive at Job's own solution to his inhuman affliction, that of courageous, dignified resignation to an authority which cannot be fathomed, he tragically relinquishes the gains he has made, and sinks to a death beyond which there is nothing but an everlasting shame. The novel's concluding sentence is a pitiful parody of Job's resurrection to completion, for it is only Joseph K.'s shame that survives him, that *lives on:* "es war, als sollte die Scham ihn *uberleben.*"

In reading *The Trial* in terms of the Job situation, one must be careful to point out the obvious sense of parody and irony that is at work in the novel—as in scenes of the oppressive Court, supposedly a Seat of Judgment, or in the tedious, sophistical discussions of law and procedure. It is also clear that there are several character differences between the Biblical Job and Kafka's whining hero, as well as great similarities. Yet the mythical pattern which underlies the events of the novel provides those differences with a heightened sense of imminence, humor, and, ultimately, tragedy. Doubtless the possibility exists that Kafka is working, through the medium of irony, in opposition to the Book of Job, bitterly castigating its message, condemning not his own belabored hero who fails his mission, but the vicious system which engenders that failure. I do not believe that this is the best reading of *The Trial,* in spite of what Kafka's own biography may imply regarding his attitude toward the relationship between fathers and sons. It is my feeling that Kafka, in the final analysis, is working in essential harmony with the Book of Job; that Joseph K.'s failure—however pitiful, however touching—is failure nevertheless; and that this weakness in K. becomes particularly meaningful for the reader, and for Kafka himself, when compared with the mythic strength of Job. (pp. 31-2)

The Trial, from the very first scene in the novel, reveals a dramatic framework very close to that of the Book of Job. The attributes of Job's three friends and "comforters" are initially embodied in the two warders who make the arrest, and their inspector (later these are replaced by the Uncle, Huld, and Titorelli, as more concrete references to Zophar, Eliphaz, and Bildad). The warders, like Job's friends, uphold completely the justness of the Law. A man is accused only if he is guilty; there can be no error. In his first speech Eliphaz says:

> who that was innocent ever perished?
> Or where were the upright cut off?

Like the warders, Eliphaz can imagine no other reason for human suffering than some preceding sin. That God may have some higher, more complex motive is incomprehensible to him. K.'s reply to such immediate assumption of guilt foreshadows his dismissal of the lawyer Huld later in the novel, and is similarly an allusion to Job's impatience with his unsympathizing friends. K. thinks to himself: "Must I . . . let myself be confused still worse by the gabble of those wretched hirelings. . . . Plain stupidity is the only thing that can give them such assurance. A few words with a man on my own level of intelligence would make everything far clearer than hours of talk with these two." Job replies with a similar scorn:

> worthless physicians are you all
> Oh that you would keep silent,
> and it would be your wisdom!

He too speaks of a face to face meeting with a more intelligent being:

> But I would speak to the Almighty,
> and I desire to argue my case with God.

In this first assertion of innocence we find a bravado and assurance similar to K.'s, but that will subsequently become in Job a quieter, firmer courage. The object of both Job and K. is, of course, to confront the awesome father, but only on their own terms. They do not yet know that the justice of the father is beyond the understanding of the son, and that revelation of its workings can come only as the culmination of successfully endured brutality. At the beginning neither is willing to face him without some form of alleviating condition. This unwillingness on the part of both heroes to approach the father naked and unarmed parallels what is probably the most difficult phase of the search: the necessary detachment from the mother that must precede it. This act of departure, this stripping oneself of all mediatory helps and aids, is the hero's farewell to security and dependency, and to all parental indulgence. It is an act necessary to the final confrontation of the father and the ultimate test, resulting in annihilation or resurrection.

At the outset of the novel K. is a kind of pre-adolescent, still relying on the care and affection of others, a status suggested several times by his relations with Frau Grubach and Fräulein Bürstner. It is clear that part of the business of the Court is to shatter this refusal to be independent. For surely, if one thing is evident about the nature of the Court, it is that all the lawyers, women, ushers, and painters solicited by K. cannot exert one whit of influence upon his case. An example of this penchant on the part of the true members of the Court to encourage K. to stand alone occurs in the opening chapter. As soon as K.

becomes aware of the fact that he is being accused of some crime, his first reaction is "I'd better get Frau Grubach—." " 'No,' said the man at the window, flinging the book down on the table." Later, when K. proposes calling his lawyer Hasterer, the Inspector replies, "Certainly . . . but I don't see what sense there would be in that, unless you have some private business of your own to consult him about." The task of the hero is to reject the temptation to insert a mother-image, such as Frau Grubach or the washerwoman, between himself and the Court, or to find a less stringent and forceful father-image, such as Huld, as a substitute for the true father, the only one who has the power to unite the hero with the self. But K., of course, is slow to learn this lesson. He spends the bulk of the novel collecting various advocates and aids, highly-sexed women to utilize their wiles on his behalf, lawyers to draft affidavits and formal pleas, confidants of the Court to enhance his status with bribery and cajolery. His is a continual search for mediation.

Nor is Job, for all his boasting of his innocence, quite prepared to face the Lord without some mitigation of the inherent disadvantages of being only a human being. He sets up various conditions that he wishes to see in effect before he will be willing to greet the face of God.

> For he is not a man, as I am, that I might answer him,
>   that we should come to trial together.
> There is no umpire between us,
>   who might lay his hand upon us both.
> Let him take his rod away from me,
>   and let not dread of him terrify me.
> Then I would speak without fear of him.

Later he is still desirous of a little extra consideration:

> Only grant two things to me,
>   then I will not hide myself from thy face:
> withdraw thy hand far from me,
>   and let not dread of thee terrify me.
> Then call, and I will answer;

It is this desire for mediation, for some divine interference from a savior, that must be put aside by both Job and K. before the last meeting can occur.

There is little doubt as to precisely what it is that the father will demand from the son as final payment for understanding. That final demand is death: in the Book of Job this concluding punishment is symbolized in the hero's repentance in "dust and ashes." In *The Trial* it is drawn in far more vivid terms, with the butchering of the hero in the lonely, moon-lit quarry. The difference is that one is a case of self-sacrifice, while the other is simply murder when suicide becomes too difficult a task.

Further parallels between the two stories are the frequent self-pitying comments made by both Job and K. regarding their alienation and mistreatment at the hands of their fellows. Job complains:

> I call to my servant, but he gives me no answer;
>   I must beseech him with my mouth.
> I am repulsive to my wife,
>   loathsome to the sons of my own mother.
> Even young children despise me;
>   when I rise they talk against me.
> All my intimate friends abhore me,
>   and those whom I loved have turned against me.

Each and every one of these complaints is dramatized in *The Trial,* as either an actual occurrence or the product of a guilt-ridden mind. The novel begins, of course, with the servant who fails to answer: "His landlady's cook, who always brought him his breakfast at eight o'clock, failed to appear on this occasion." Secondly, K.'s sexual difficulties, first with Fräulein Bürstner, then with the washerwoman of the Court, serve as examples of the abhorrence in which potential lovers hold him, once his initial attraction has worn off. The reasons for this abhorrence contain much of the psychological meaning of *The Trial;* it is a meaning that is hardly touched upon in the Book of Job yet seems implicit in the progress of its events. K.'s essential problem with women is that he is driven to them solely out of his own insecurity. He comes to them not as an adult lover, a completely masculine being, but as a child, interested only in alleviating the guilt of incestuous mother-love by transferring his desires to another woman. He does not possess fully-developed sexual passion. It is no coincidence that when K. first goes to the Court he claims he is looking for Lanz, the joiner. In German *Lanz* means "lance": He is a symbol of the virility and phallic potential which K. is trying desperately to attain.

Until K. achieves adult masculinity, his attempts at love must prove abortive. His desire for Fräulein Bürstner in Chapter I is a purely childish one. He is annoyed with the mother-image of Frau Grubach, and desires a replacement, if only to make the former mother jealous, and it is obvious that K. clearly enjoys the pain that his affair with Fräulein Bürstner causes Frau Grubach. There is absolutely no sexual desire in K. as he waits in his room for Fräulein Bürstner to come home. "He felt no special desire to see her, he could not even remember how she looked, but he wanted to talk to her now." He wants her not as a lover, but as a mother, to whom he may reveal his sorrows of the day. Instead of confronting her in the hallway, K. hides behind his door and whispers to her through the crack: "It sounded like a prayer, not like a summons." It is clear, on the other hand, that Fräulein Bürstner would have no aversion to a sexual advance, if only K. had the maturity to make one. She smiles warmly, invites him to her room, presses her palms caressingly aginst her hips, and whispers to him: "I'm so tired that I'm letting you take too many liberties." Finally, after a half-dozen invitations have flown past K.'s innocent brow, and his chance has gone by, he does make a clumsy attempt to accost her. "K . . . kissed her first on the lips, then all over the face, like some thirsty animal lapping greedily at a spring of long sought fresh water." The imagery is that of a dog licking from a stream; and it is as a dog, not a lover, that he has approached her. Her disappointment and boredom with his actions are to be expected.

In similar fashion K.'s lust for the Court washerwoman is again the lust of a child for its mother. His initial interest in her is solely for the aid which she can provide him; it becomes a jealous rage when she is stolen from him at the behest of the Examining Magistrate. K.'s reactions to this affront are appropriately juvenile, as he punches the student in the back, and thinks: "There could be no more fitting revenge on the Examining Magistrate and his henchmen than to wrest this woman from him and take her himself." His passion for the woman is obviously not invoked by her attraction for him as a lover, but only for her position as a mother-image, to be stolen from the father-image of the Examining Magistrate.

His third and final affair is with Leni, the lawyer's maid, and it is here that K. begins to show the first signs of progress toward maturity. Although he is first drawn to her (again the woman is clad in the apron, a mother symbol) for the help she promises to give him, he allows himself to be seduced by her. The kiss he plants on her webbed fingers is symbolic of the kissing of the frog king: the discovery of latent desire and the passing into a new realm of human experience. When Leni gives him the key to her door, and the instructions to "come whenever you like," it is evident that K. has made a certain advancement, at least in the ways of physical love and manhood.

In his brief catalogue of complaints (of which his repulsiveness to his wife is only the second) Job has referred to the "loathsomeness" with which he feels the "sons of his own mother" regard him, a lament which parallels the incessant conflict K. has at the Bank with the Assistant Manager. In this case the Bank, a kind of symbol of security, is the mother-image for which he is competing, a fact emphasized by the continual anxiety expressed by K. in his suspicions that the Assistant Manager is subverting his influence and prestige. Lastly, the young children who despise Job correspond to the hateful glares of the children K. confronts on the stairway to the courtroom as he interrupts their play, and also the children who adore Titorelli.

K.'s efforts throughout the novel to solicit effective aid from his various acquaintances roughly suggest the relations in the Book of Job between the hero and his so-called comforters, who counsel him in his plight. Certainly the total effect of these advisers is the same in both works: the counselors are a significant part of the trials which the hero must endure. All are equally convinced that their client is guilty and that only supplications, connections, bribery, and similar expediencies can provide acquittal. All begin with the assumption that the Court or father-image is just, and that the defendant is sinful. In this sense they are allied with the Court, and are meant to harass, not to help, the hero. The role of the three comforters as an integral part of the trial itself is evident in the dramatic sequence of the Book of Job. Following each of the two visits from Satan, the second of which is climaxed by the disgust Job's wife feels for his afflicted body, the hero refuses to exclaim against his misfortune. Then his three friends come forward to observe his suffering: "After this Job opened his mouth and cursed the day of his birth."

Eliphaz, Zophar, and Bildad to some degree correspond to Huld, Uncle Karl, and Titorelli. These sets of advisers have definite conceptions of what constitutes correct procedure in such cases. In **The Trial** their long dissertations on judicial maneuvers in the Court are ultimately of little use, being utterly casuistic and self-contradictory. They solve nothing. So too is the advice of Job's three friends, who emphasize his guilt, foolishly maintain a cause-effect relationship between wickedness and punishment, and, most of all, are totally devoid of sacred pity for the man who undergoes such torment. In any case, the counsel of all six advisers has a common denominator of half-truth entangled in a web of misconceptions, doubletalk, and delusion. There is only one that really knows the truth of the hero's situation.

Eliphaz and Huld are the least vicious of the three pairs. They are older men, more experienced and less assured than the others. They are calm and reasonable in their treatment of the suffering hero, although their counsel is ultimately of little value. Eliphaz cannot understand the wrath of Job over his undeserved afflictions; he feels that Job should be able to endure this domination by the Lord without a whimper of denial or rebellion:

> Is not your fear of God your confidence,
>   and the integrity of your ways your hope?

In similar fashion, Huld is incapable of understanding why Joseph K. should be so impatient at the meagre advancement of his case. Neither counselor can tolerate the idea of rebellion, of accosting the father face to face and demanding justice. Eliphaz urges:

> Agree with God, and be at peace;
>   thereby good will come to you.
> Receive instruction from his mouth,
>   and lay up his words in your heart.

Huld, not through any malevolence, but only because of his blindness, would have every client be a Block, a cur, crawling about on his hands and knees, kissing the hands of the mediator, pleasing the Court with his wretchedness. "The client ceased to be a client and became the lawyer's dog. If the lawyer were to order this man to crawl under the bed as if into a kennel and bark there, he would gladly obey the order."

Both Eliphaz and Huld are totally ignorant of the problem and task of the hero-son. The duty of the latter is not to give in to an accusation which he feels is unjust; his duty is to honor and maintain his integrity as long as he believes he is right. His duty is to persevere in his own innocence until the father has shown him a greater truth, has revealed it to him through the cleansing fire of ultimate initiation. Combined with this insistence upon innocence, however, must be the courage to accept punishment and affliction in spite of the fact that the hero cannot comprehend the reasons behind such torture. In short, he must be prepared to accept what he deeply feels to be injustice: neither to confess a guilt he does not believe is his, nor to curse the father who brutally indicts him. It is only by this combination of acceptance and courage that the hero may discard the child's skin of youthful innocence and assume the sacred robes of understanding and wisdom.

Zophar and Uncle Karl are also of a kind. Both bear the nature of the zealot, quick, short-tempered, brutal in their condemnation of resistance to the father. Zophar is far more blunt than his companions:

> Should your babble silence men, and when you mock,
>   shall no one shame you?

> • • • • •

> Know then that God exacts of you less than your
>   guilt deserves.

Uncle Karl is particularly violent when Joseph leaves the lawyer's room in the middle of their first conference for a rendezvous with Leni, Huld's new maid. This first successful physical relation with a woman, and the implied rebellion against the standard Court procedure of total submission to a lawyer, brings down the wrath of the uncle: "[He] seized him by the arms and banged him against the house door as if he wanted to nail him there. 'Boy!' he cried, 'how could you do it! You have terribly damaged your case, which was beginning to go quite well'." The images of crucifixion, and the consequent reference to Christ as rebel, can hardly be missed.

The connections between Bildad and Titorelli are not as strong as in the other pairs, for although certain similarities exist in the advice they give the hero, the fact remains that one is as foolish as his colleagues, while the other is as wily and cunning as Satan himself. With the characterization of Titorelli Kafka takes his greatest departure from the Job myth by including in the heart of his story what in the Book of Job is only a part of the prologue: a Satanic figure. We are given a very slight preparation for the introduction of such a character in the scene with the manufacturer, immediately preceding the meeting with Titorelli. The Assistant Manager and the manufacturer are leaning against K.'s desk talking: "it seemed to K. as though two giants of enormous size were bargaining above his head for himself." It is the only suggestion in *The Trial* of the bet between God and the Devil in the prologue of the Book of Job. It is the manufacturer who gives K. Titorelli's address, with the additional information that he is a painter, that his name is a pseudonym, and that he is a chronic liar.

The painter's studio is "almost at the diametrically opposite end of the town from where the Court held its meetings," clearly suggesting Hell, a suggestion which is strengthened by additional description: "There was a gaping hole out of which, just as K. approached, issued a disgusting yellow fluid, steaming hot, from which some rats fled into the adjoining canal. At the foot of the stairs an infant lay belly down on the ground bawling, but one could scarcely hear its shrieks because of the deafening din that came from a tinsmith's workshop at the other side of the entry." With the inclusion of the shrieking, deformed, and debauched little girls the picture of Hell is complete. To be sure, Titorelli's studio connects with the offices of the Court itself, but even in the Book of Job Satan was not a stranger in heaven.

The interesting aspect of the coupling of Titorelli and Bildad is that both give remarkably similar counsel, but one speaks in order to condemn the audacity of the hero, and the other to delude him. Bildad, like Eliphaz and Zophar, believes firmly in a cause-effect relationship between guilt and punishment. In mocking Job, Bildad speaks of what God will do for him provided he is innocent:

> if you are pure and upright,
>   surely then he will rouse himself for you
>   and reward you with a rightful habitation.

It is a passage notably similar to Titorelli's comments on innocence and acquittal, the irony being that the latter actually comprehends the truth of what he is saying: "The only deciding factor seems to be the innocence of the accused. Since you're innocent, of course it would be possible for you to ground your case on your innocence alone. But then you would require neither my help nor help from anyone." But Titorelli combines with this important statement a long, esoteric, and completely meaningless discussion on the difference between ostensible acquittal and indefinite postponement. His purpose appears to be to mislead the hero. Of definitive acquittal—the *only* kind of acquittal which the hero-son can be contented with and still prevail—Titorelli adds: All that remains of these cases are myths and legends, which "can be believed, but . . . cannot be proved." And yet, "they must have an element of truth in them, and besides they are very beautiful." To the soundness of this advice K. foolishly replies: "Mere legends cannot alter my opinion."

The Devil has won a victory. He has deceived K., temporarily at least, into rejecting the best counsel he has received so far, for surely this is the path to the father: the preservation of one's own integrity, and the willingness to stand alone, to stand and accept the punishment inflicted, neither to confess, nor to curse its source. And where have the histories of such instances been collected but in the myths and legends of human memory? Titorelli then proceeds into his long treatise on the other two kinds of acquittal, which have one characteristic in common: "They prevent the accused from coming up for sentence." Indeed they do. They are a fool-proof preventative from ever arriving at the gates of the father and speaking to his very face,

from succumbing before the final initiation in "dust and ashes," in order to ascend to the majesty and grandeur of adulthood. Those like Block, who live lives of cowardice and desperation, seeking only continual postponement and delay, can never arrive at the final initiation.

The turning point of the novel occurs in the chapter following the Titorelli section, titled "Dismissal of the Lawyer," which was never completed by Kafka. K. is outraged at the spectacle of the tradesman Block humiliating himself before Huld, and it appears as if he is about to sever relations with the lawyer when the chapter breaks off. That Kafka fully intended such a parting of the ways to occur, however, seems apparent in the title of this section. The violent sense of shame which comes over K. in witnessing the blatant obsequiousness of the tradesman is evidence of the progress he has made. He does not seem to remember his own dog-like kisses, or the dog-like cries of Franz in the lumber room. What is most important is that he recognizes the truth that it is not dignified for a man to crawl about on his hands and knees. This scene with Huld is the closest Kafka comes to portraying the transformation of K. from a state of ceaseless, yet ineffectual struggling against the indictment of the Court, to one of quieter, firmer acceptance, but acceptance without the loss of dignity.

The next time we see K. he has attained that status of acceptance which Job reaches just before the speech of Elihu. No longer is Job requesting some kind of advantage for being only a man, no longer does he ask for mediation because of his imperfect form compared with that of the Lord. Job has become a true hero, ready for the final test, confronting the father.

> (Here is my signature! let the Almighty answer me!)
>   Oh, that I had the indictment written by my adversary!
> Surely I would carry it on my shoulder;
>   I would bind it on me as a crown;
> I would give him an account of all my steps;
>   like a prince I would approach him.

The imagery is clear; Job is ready to be crucified. Following the passages of Elihu, God speaks to Job out of the whirlwind.

K. is also ready, awaiting his execution, dressed in black coat and gloves. He and his companions begin the final journey. Although his executioners are not the earlier warders, Franz and Willem, they fulfill a similar function: they illustrate the personality now united: "In complete harmony all three now made their way across a bridge in the moonlight, the two men readily yielded to K.'s slightest movement, and when he turned slightly towards the parapet they turned, too, in a solid front." Suddenly a remnant of his earlier cowardice, not wholly shed even yet, is revealed in his desire to resist. But miraculously Fräulein Bürstner appears before him. It is a divine intervention, *unsought*. He quickly realizes that resistance is futile, that the important thing is acceptance: to accept this reality of execution, and in accepting it quietly and courageously, to conquer it.

> . . . the only thing for me to go on doing is to keep my intelligence calm and analytical to the end. I always wanted to snatch at the world with twenty hands, and not for a very laudable motive, either. That was wrong, and am I to show now that not even a year's trial has taught me anything? Am I to leave this world as a man who has no common sense? Are people to say of me after I am gone that at the beginning of my case I wanted to finish it, and at the end of it I wanted to begin it again? I don't want that to be said.

Now it is K. who is leading his companions up the mythical hill, out to the deserted quarry. And then at the final moment, he fails his quest. It is the instant of initiation, of the barbaric ritual of self-destruction. He is to wrest the knife from the hand of the executioner and plunge it into his breast, to renounce the shameful sacrifice of the scapegoat, and approach his father like a prince. But once again, in a scene of powerful human tragedy, K. cries out for a mediator, a savior: "He could not completely rise to the occasion, he could not relieve the officials of all their tasks." He sees the faint image of a figure in a window overlooking the quarry, perhaps a savior, perhaps an angel to stay the murderous hand of the intrepid patriarch, and release the child from the altar, and K. "raised his hands and spread out all his fingers" in an ignominious thrust of human fear. Once more the despicable dog imagery; Joseph K., unlike the heroic Job, will approach his father on his hands and knees. (pp. 33-43)

Donald M. Kartiganer, "Job and Joseph K.: Myth in Kafka's 'The Trial'," in Modern Fiction Studies, *Vol. VIII, No. 1, Spring, 1962, pp. 31-43.*

KEITH FORT (essay date 1964)

[*In the following essay, Fort discusses the relationships between reality, meaning, and style in a literary work, and postulates the worlds of the Bank and the Court in* The Trial *as two visions of the same world, one objective and pragmatic, the other subjective and frightening.*]

Kafka has been dead almost forty years, and during that time **The Trial** has been examined and re-examined in such detail that today there is at least a degree of agreement on the essential points of the novel's meaning. However, there is almost total disagreement about what the "Court" is and why it has the nightmarish quality of unreality that has made Kafka's name synonymous with any unreal, mysterious force which operates against man. We find ourselves faced, in studying **The Trial,** with a situation like seeing the roof of a house without being able to see the walls.

The meaning of the novel comes from a study of the character of Joseph K., his shifting attitudes and hopes, and eventually his death. But the *reality* of the world that K. is in is not understood. Murray Krieger [in his *The Tragic Vision: Variations on a Theme in Literary Interpretation*] is one critic who notes the importance of discovering the relation between the bank world that K. lives in and the court world; but Krieger admits that he does not himself understand what this relation is. Most critics who deal with Kafka take an implicit stand on this question and can be separated into two groups. The first group hold that the court has subjective reality; i.e., the court is a psychological allegory as in a dream. They say that Joseph K. has the need for self-expression, and his subconscious creates objects that are analogous to his need. These objects, the court and its creatures, are projections of K.'s imagination. In studying the novel these critics use a method not unlike dream analysis, where X in the dream is equal to Y in K.'s mind. The second group maintain an exactly opposite viewpoint. They say that the court is real within the novel. It has its offices in attics of suburban tenements of a large city and has its officers and agents. This court actually accuses K. and eventually executes him. This group of critics naturally believe that the court is totally independent of K.'s mind, and its form is consequently unrelated to any state of K.'s mind.

Certain theoretical questions are by implication raised in an approach to the question of the reality of the court. When any object is described in a work of art, its reality is instantly defined. We are accustomed to accepting pragmatic reality as the essential quality of objects. If an author uses the word "chair," it is assumed that the reality of the object he is describing is "an object for men to sit in." But this is only one way of defining the chair. I have read of a schizophrenic who would not sit in a chair because he believed that the chair would attempt to squeeze him to death. For the normal man and for the schizophrenic, the reality of the chair is quite different; if each tried to describe the chair, he would use a different style to express this reality. We would probably understand what the normal man means because the essence he is trying to express is one that we accept. The schizophrenic would, on the other hand, have a hard time making us understand that the essence of the chair for him was something else. In the end he would have to resort to the use of private symbolism, meaningful only to himself.

For both, the ultimate cause for the reality which they recognize would be a value system which they hold. The normal man, in expressing the pragmatic essence of the chair, is reflecting his belief that "use" is the prime value of the chair. The schizophrenic would be trying to show the essence of the chair in relation to some values, personal and esoteric, which are important to him.

Dante, for example, in *The Divine Comedy* describes things (characters and objects) in such a way as to show the relation of the object he is describing to God. The essence of the thing is determined by its relation to God. I wish to be careful here to avoid overstatement. I do not mean that objects cannot have pragmatic reality in *The Divine Comedy*, for, of course, they do. But when Dante is describing objects that have a pragmatic essence, he has no real need for the devices of literature, for he can simply state the word that represents the object, and its essence is assumed to be pragmatic. However, when he is trying to show what things *really* are, he needs to have a style which can describe them so as to bring out their real essence— their relation to God. The object, represented by words, is compressed by literary devices until it reveals this reality. Structure, symbols, and all aspects of Dante's literary technique are tools which force a thing to reveal its religious reality. The unity of style, form, structure in a given age grows up because the values held can best be realized by particular kinds of literary devices and techniques.

It is traditionally, therefore, *meaning* which determines *reality*. Style is the basic tool for causing a meaning to be shown as the essence of reality. Yet the modern way of looking at the world may be said to have begun at the moment when the general acceptance of value and meaning began to crumble. With the gradual death of values, the nature of reality crumbled also. We were left with varied systems of thought (religion, art, science, etc.) with varied values. With the different values came differing realities, which in turn meant that words which once referred to the same reality now had to refer to different realities. The breakdown in communication in our time comes largely from the fact that the same old words are used very differently. The only common denominator that allows general communication is pragmatic reality, which is less a reflection of value than it is a reflection of our failure to have value.

With the passing of a generally accepted value system a new artistic process came into being. The artist was presented with dead appearances and dead words, and he had to go through appearances to a perception of Being which would, he hoped, reveal meaning to him. Meaning no longer determines reality, but rather reality determines meaning. With an understanding of this reversal, we see how style is catapulted into an importance in modern literature that it never before had. Style has passed from being a tool for the expression and realization of meaning into a tool for the discovery of meaning. Today, instead of showing how value is present in the world, style—the way in which objects are described—will determine value.

Ultimately a belief underlies much of serious modern literature that there is a correspondence between words and the essence of objects and that the act of understanding is conducted through words, so that, as style is purified, the essence of objects is revealed. Correspondingly, as the essence of objects is revealed, the style is necessarily purified. This "complementation" might then be carried to a point where the words become Word and objects become Being. However, language always seems to break down almost before this mystical process can be begun.

Henry James's time-worn cliché that writers must render and not report is an implicit understanding that every time a modern author puts pen to paper he must redefine his reality. The styleless writer is one who accepts pragmatic reality without thought; i.e., author and reader agree that the reality of objects is their usefulness. However, more serious writers usually offer a "new" reality which is defined with their work. Physical details in a story or novel have as their essential reality their relation to the theme of that particular work. But we would not go so far as to suggest, because a character in a story has his hair parted in the middle and the story is about the need for balance in human affairs, that the essence of parted hair is balanced personality.

The giants of our time have not been content to let their style create an immanent reality which is valid only within one story. They are seekers after the absolute. They hope not only to redefine reality within the limits of a particular work, but also to define reality in life itself by using fiction as a means to pass beyond appearance into a perception of Being itself, which will be true not only within the story but without as well. Hemingway, for example, describes a world where reality is stripped of its pragmatic qualities so that objects exist in themselves without meaningful relations to man. His style accomplishes one of the most difficult and frequently faced tasks of modern fiction—the depiction of non-significant objects. When we consider how deeply ingrained in our minds is the concept of reality as pragmatic, we can have some idea of the enormity of the problem faced. Once this nature of reality has been shown in Hemingway's works, the despairing conclusions at which they arrive follow necessarily. His definition of reality determines a major part of the meaning of his novels.

The origins of the great experiments in style in the past three-quarters of a century have been highly personal, intense searches for paths which might lead through appearances towards Being. These experiments have lit arcs of great beauty across the literary sky, but the attempts to force objects to reveal Being and words to reveal the Word have failed—in the blank pages of Mallarmé, the confusion of *Finnegans Wake,* the silence of Rimbaud, the reasonable obscurity of Pound, the jumbled dreams of surrealism. These have all become *ex post facto* erections of dead-end signs on a few of the infinite number of roads that lead outwards from cliché towards ultimate meaning.

One more important contention in my theory of style must be presented before returning to *The Trial.* Style is intention. An artist looks at the world in a certain way so that he notes certain details in the objects he sees. Thus Dante looked through the world towards God and found it to be good or evil depending upon the nature of its relation to the value he held. Reality which is defined by style must be seen as the result of looking at the world in a certain way, towards a value.

Now we can return to an examination of *The Trial.* Joseph K. seems to live in two worlds. On the one hand is his bank world and on the other the world centered around the court. The bank world is apparently "real." Its reality is a pragmatic reality which we simply accept as real because it imitates what is our accustomed way of looking at the world. When Joseph K. is in his bank world he sees objects as useful, related to the future, etc. What then is the court?

The court is composed of the same objects that make up the world in which K. lives. It is the same world which we recognize so easily when its reality is defined within the bounds of the pragmatism to which we are accustomed. But it becomes the court when it is looked at in a new way and its reality is redefined. This redefinition occurs when K. reflects upon his daily life and sees that its essence is not the harmless, even benign, reality which he assumed it to be. He sees instead that the essence of the world is the court. This new reality is defined by another level of K.'s being, other than the conscious, rational, future-regarding intellect which he uses with the bank. It is very close to being his subconscious, but "subconscious" has connotations which are not exactly applicable. For example, in "The Whipper" chapter K. passes quickly and often between these two ways of looking at the world. On the one hand, the reality of the action is probably a simple reprimand to two clerks, a reprimand that would insure the smooth functioning of the bank. On the other, the essence of the action is a cruel, inhuman representation of the evil at the heart of K.'s bank world. It is, therefore, not exactly accurate to say that K.'s world is a court when he sees with the eye of the subconscious and a bank when he sees with the eyes of the conscious. Perhaps it is more accurate to say that the world as a bank is seen by K. the functionary, and the world as a court is seen by K. the human being.

We might imagine that the redefinition of reality by K.'s innermost being would result in symbols unintelligible for us. This is not true; however, *The Trial* offers proof of the fact that there is a degree to which all modern men share in the subconscious or existentialist idiom which allows Kafka's personal interpretation of his world to be at least partially intelligible.

There is now one more important step in understanding why the court takes the peculiar form it does. Style defines reality in relation to value, but Kafka is writing from within the total anxiety caused by the absence of absolute value. He redefines his world with his subconscious, looking through appearances, measuring them against his need for an absolute. K. redefines objects in relation to the presence or absence of absolute meaning. When absolute meaning is not found, incoherence and chaos emerge as the ultimate reality of Joseph K.'s world. So Kafka in *The Trial* creates a world which is relatively significant (to K.) but absolutely insignificant. This is, of course, a vision similar to the one created by a great deal of so-called "absurdist" art in our time. The reality which Kafka creates by his style is the reality of chaos.

Although the level of K.'s being involved with the court is broader than the "subconscious," it has more affinities with the subconscious than with the conscious. This distinction is important in *The Trial* in explaining a great deal of the action. K.'s mind defines his life in terms of the court, but he does not himself necessarily understand the meaning of that definition. When Joseph K. goes to the court or has any dealings with it, he is bringing his conscious mind to bear upon an insight that has been intuited by his subconscious. Although this device sounds like dream analysis, it has one great difference from that method. In a dream there is no real subject matter upon which the subconscious operates. It simply discovers or creates symbols that reflect itself. This is not so with Joseph K. He actually analyzes his life with the subconscious, so that the subject matter on which he works is composed of the real actions and objects of his life.

I refer again to my analogy with the chair to clarify this point. If a normal man defines a chair for me as ''something to sit in,'' he will be using his rational mind. If I analyze the style of his definition, I will understand something about the way this man's mind works. If the psychotic, on the other hand, defines the chair as a thing which will kill him, he is defining the chair with his subconscious. If I am lucky, I may also learn something about the way his mind works from analyzing his statements. Suppose, however, that the psychotic suddenly recovers and remembers how he defined the chair and wants to understand himself as well as the chair. He will then present himself to the image he had of the chair as a potential murderer, and in understanding that picture will understand something of himself and of the chair. Thus, when Joseph K. goes to the court he is trying to rationalize and understand a subconsciously intuited truth about the real world around him.

The Trial can be thought of as a huge extended metaphor in which Kafka states, ''K.'s world is a court.'' Both parts of this metaphor (bank world and court world) are expanded and extended so that we have a fairly complete picture of both kinds of reality. One of the most basic kinds of metaphors presents a particular object in relation to an idea so that the object and the idea complement each other, as in Marvel's famous ''vegetable love.'' It would have been possible for Marvel to take the connotations of ''vegetable'' and the connotations of ''love'' and extend and expand them until each half of the metaphor became an entire world, as Kafka has done in *The Trial*. The idea of the meaning of the world is expanded until it takes on the form of another real world. [In his study *Franz Kafka*] Gunther Anders calls this technique the use of ''a literal metaphor.'' He recognizes that Kafka's method is to translate meaning into picture: ''The objects in his world [court] are frozen truths, objects created out of truth about objects in our world.''

Upon the morning when K. is arrested, he is awakened from his sleep by two warders, who are later joined by an inspector. K. soon realizes that there are also three clerks from his bank in the house, who have come to take him to work. Later, on the way to the bank with the clerks, he notices:

> the inspector had usurped his attention so that he did not recognize the three clerks, and the clerks had in turn made him oblivious of the inspector.

He cannot see them at the same time, for they are the same figures looked at in a different way. I do not mean to imply that there is a point-by-point equation between K.'s bank world and his court world, i.e., that an object in one world will receive a new definition in the next chapter or on the next page. If K. were to recall his entire life on both planes, then such an equation should be possible; but the novel is fragmentary, and

we find many instances where one side of this metaphorical equation is developed and the other side is not.

The court to which Joseph K. goes is simply and directly described as though the world were actually as it seems to be in the novel, and it is Kafka's contention that the world really is that way. The simplicity of the description is a further tribute to the fact that Kafka was totally immersed in his new reality as he was writing. We might imagine ourselves in Joseph K.'s position. Suppose that we were suddenly wakened from sleep to go to work. It is likely that the deeper levels of our being would start to feel that the call to work was the call from some hostile, meaningless force which was making us perform a futile act. Almost immediately, however, we would repress this vision and reconsider the call with our usual, practical way of looking at the world. We would recognize that we had to go to work to make a living, etc. But Kafka does not repress his existential way of looking at the world. He continues with this deeper vision until he has seen that the reality he lives in is not the harmless, reasonable, practical thing that habit has accustomed him to but is instead the frightening, meaningless, hostile reality of the court. (pp. 643-51)

Keith Fort, ''The Function of Style in Franz Kafka's 'The Trial','' in The Sewanee Review, *Vol. LXXII, No. 4, October-December, 1964, pp. 643-51.*

CARL S. SINGER   (essay date 1965)

[*In the following excerpt, Singer discusses narrative perspective and characterization in* The Trial.]

Anyone who still feels obligated to offer an opinion on the much discussed case of the Court *vs.* Joseph K. is well advised to begin with a declaration of impartiality. Anyone, that is, who has remained convinced of the sense and legitimacy of treating *The Trial* as a work of art. In general, of course, the critic is not required to disavow explicitly all commitment to non-aesthetic doctrine; but with reference to Kafka—in view of the already awesome accumulation of interpretation contributed by established psychologists, theologians, etc.—the critic must call attention to the fact that he is voluntarily confining himself to literary questions, if only to remind himself of his amateur status in all other matters. The anguish and distress implied in the titles of many books on Kafka—*The Kafka Problem, Kafka and the Labyrinthic* are typically unsettling examples—have both generated and thrived on just such amateurism. But there is little point in further taxing those whom Kafka has driven to a frenzy of overextension. Instead I think it will prove valuable to investigate the causes of the frenzy, the qualities of Kafka's work and of *The Trial* in particular, that are disruptive of the calm prerequisite of critical detachment.

Undeniably, there is much in *The Trial* that is so unfamiliar as to disorient even the most determined literary approach. We cannot fasten upon Kafka's method of character development, for the simple reason that none of his characters are ''developed''—what we see and hear of them is not intended to give us the comforting sense of acquaintance by an eventual yielding of essence. Again, we cannot discern in *The Trial* the workings of a plot, or even note a specific arrangement of events that leads to the hero's undoing, because the arrest that opens the book occasions, precisely, the cessation of purposeful activity on the part of Joseph K.: his subsequent undertakings are not so much in vain as irrelevant. Finally, to close this series of subtractions provisionally, what are we to make of the milieu of *The Trial?* Here also Kafka thwarts standard critical procedure, though by giving not too little but rather too much. The description of K.'s city has the oppressive density of a movie viewed a few feet from the screen: minor, seemingly random details present themselves with an unwarranted insistence while the picture as a whole remains blurred. The more intently we peer, the less distinct becomes the composition of the background. Speculation on "the significance" of the unpredictable stream of objects that catch K.'s eye—dust in the attic court chambers, wash hanging on a clothes line—tends to be, consequently, somewhat embarrassing. In short, Kafka's apparent disregard for the conventions of the novel results in a considerable formal inaccessibility. And this, I believe, accounts for the liberties taken by many of his interpreters, who, often with the best of intentions, entirely neglect the matter of style. The attempt to establish and appreciate Kafka's own novelistic conventions must, however, be made, since it is likely to disclose more of his elusive meaning than that which survives in the various doctrinaire translations of his writings.

Since there is no magic key to Kafka's work, we must be content to operate with prosaic tools. The critical concept of "point of view" is the most effective one at our disposal. The shape reality assumes depends on who is looking at it, and when the shape is as confused as in *The Trial,* the only reasonable course is to determine whose eyes (what sort of eyes) are responsible for the confusion. And in this particular at least *The Trial* poses no problems whatsoever, for Kafka's employment of point of view is remarkably pure and straightforward. A single pair of eyes fixes reality in *The Trial*—and they belong not to the author but to Joseph K.; as we read we are aware only of what is registering upon his consciousness. Thus Kafka's narrative technique aims at, and doubtless achieves, the opposite of omniscience: there is only K.'s eternal ignorance, the recital of his failures to obtain information. The author totally absents himself; he supplies no commentary to K.'s thoughts and actions, nor does he reveal the motives and judgments of the other participants in the proceedings. It is this unrelieved immediacy of presentation that compels us to participate in what is commonly referred to as K.'s *Angst.*

The recognition that we are in the midst of Joseph K.'s world admittedly does little to order the chaos of *The Trial.* The question becomes, what manner of man is it whose imagination peoples the attics of dilapidated tenements with examining magistrates? Lukács suggests that Western writers, in response to the total lack of purpose and direction in their culture, have gotten into the habit of considering psychopaths and idiots the best-qualified witnesses of life; and Kafka is for him the foremost exponent of this habit. The claim, despite its unduly harsh wording, is not easily refuted. Certainly K. is forever thinking of those bright days when, in his capacity as a high bank official, he acted with spectacular cunning and dispatch. Yet the K. we see "in action" is incapacitated—unable to defend his position in court and office alike. But whether or not K.'s fate after the arrest should be labeled pathological is not, for our purposes, an issue of primary importance; we have to come to terms with the vision of reality that Kafka transmits in the testimony of his incapacitated witness. Only then can we assess its validity.

I have said that Kafka refuses to develop his characters, that no matter how much we come to know of them, we never get to know them. This apparent anti-technique is really the substitution of one technique for another: Kafka subordinates characterization to point of view. Joseph K. not only cannot com-

pete with Balzac and Dickens in cataloguing human types, he simply cannot catalogue at all. Not that he doesn't try. In fact, although he worries a good deal about the possibility of a premature judgment giving a disastrous conclusion to his own endeavours, he doesn't scruple to pass immediate judgment on others. Invariably, however, people refuse to conform to his first impressions of them, they force him to change his mind—and to keep on changing it—with their every gesture, almost their every word. And, since we have no way of bringing this fluctuation of opinion to a standstill, we are necessarily as baffled by these "characters" as K. himself. None of K.'s conjectures are shown to be blatantly false—for this would give us a resting point. The trouble is rather that the individual traits he seizes upon are never exhaustive but simply elements of a series—a series which K. cannot integrate. Unable to discover the continuum which defines personality, K. finds that the most casual of meetings are apt to turn into nightmares.

To measure the effects of this aspect of K.'s incapacitation, we should first consider a character whom K., before his arrest, had always thought totally unmystifying—the Uncle. Sensing a certain bustle outside his office, K. recalls the manner of this long-awaited visitor with the ease of a man accustomed to handling his fellows in a superior, condescending fashion.

> He had often pictured him just as he appeared now, his back slightly bent, his dented straw hat in his left hand, stretching out his right hand from afar and thrusting it with inconsiderate haste across the desk, knocking over everything in sight. His uncle was always in a hurry, for he was plagued by the unhappy idea of accomplishing, during his regularly only day-long visits to the city, everything he had planned, without at the same time neglecting whatever offered itself by chance in the way of conversations or business deals or enjoyments. . . . "The ghost from the country," K. usually called him.

There is a satisfying, near Dickensian precision about this portrait. We smile at this bumptious harassed provincial; here at last is someone who need not be taken seriously. But K. soon realizes that the old caricature no longer really contains the Uncle's character. Inexplicably, the "ghost from the country" seems to be an initiate in the very matters his cosmopolitan nephew is at a loss to understand—to K.'s dismay, and our own astonishment, he becomes a person to be reckoned with. There can be no doubt that the Uncle remains a perfect clown of social ineptitude; yet all the while that K. is trying to laugh, his uncle's questions and revelations, shouted out for all the world to hear, are making him shudder. In a final effort to silence this booming harangue, K. announces with affected coolness that his case has nothing to do with the regular courts, isn't connected with his work in the bank, and really is of no importance whatsoever. But the Uncle knows better:

> "That's bad," said the Uncle. "What?" K. said and stared at his uncle. "I mean that it's bad," repeated the Uncle. . . . "I thought," said K., "that you would attach even less importance to this whole business than I do, and now you are taking it so seriously." "Joseph," cried the Uncle . . . "you are completely changed, you always had such a keen mind, and it's abandoning you?—now of all times. Do you want to lose your case? Do you know what that would mean? It would simply finish you. And the whole family would be pulled down with you, at the very least our name would be dragged through the mud. Joseph, pull yourself together. Your indifference is driving me crazy. Looking at you I'm almost tempted to

believe the old saying: to have such a case is the same thing as losing it.''

K.'s startled exclamations, the matter-of-fact tone of the Uncle's remarks (his proverb, a truly staggering specimen of folk wisdom, leaves no room for argument)—these are notes typical of all the conversations in *The Trial*. The people K. comes in contact with always manage to overwhelm him by their self-assurance; they know what they're about and K. does not. His notions that they are silly, flighty, infirm, humble, or stupid are well founded but of no value to him when he tries to anticipate what they will say or do. Of course, as readers we have what would appear to be a great advantage over Joseph K., who is perhaps too busy or upset to figure things out. We can close the book whenever we wish and attempt to decide once and for all whether, for instance, the Uncle is really an officious country bumpkin or instead a knowledgeable counselor whose advice should be heeded. But we quickly see that no amount of reflection solves the problem. We have only K.'s contradictory impressions to go on, and there is no evidence in the text to show which of them is right, or even more right. Opening the book again, we may be struck by the Uncle's suggestion that K. consult Advocate Huld; but whether this is worthwhile advice or merely foolish boasting of not-at-all-powerful connections depends upon whether or not Huld can be of any use to K., and this, in turn, depends upon whether Huld really intends to defend K., or simply hopes to use such a famous case to boost his reputation, or perhaps actually means to betray K.'s interests in return for special favors from the Court, and all this, in turn, depends upon whether or not Huld's activity can have any effect one way or the other, since the Court does not officially countenance the mediation of lawyers in the first place, and so on. But to perform such an analysis is the same thing as becoming Joseph K. (my apologies to the Uncle). Suffice it to say that we have no means of correcting or steadying K.'s evaluation of his uncle, just as, for the most part, we cannot claim to understand *The Trial* better than K.

K.'s women constitute still greater torments—despite, or rather because of, the degree of intimacy he achieves with them. People simply have a way of exploding in K.'s face, and, naturally, the closer the contact the more devastating becomes the shock. Thus the bank executive, running true to form, even finds himself routed by the wiles of a scrubwoman. In fact, K.'s abortive affair with the court attendant's wife is so exemplary a demonstration of the ''Kafkaesque'' that it will be well to linger awhile on its vicissitudes. The woman first comes to K.'s attention as the object of that clamorous sexual assault which gave a disastrous ending to K.'s first hearing. Understandably little disposed in her favor, K. is quite surprised to learn that she considers herself a respectable married woman. But she is convincing in her reply to K.'s sarcasm, and he is soon ready to accept her version of the regrettable disturbance. '''Are you alluding to the incident in the last assembly through which I disturbed your speech?' the woman asked. . . . 'It wasn't to your disadvantage that your speech was interrupted. It was judged very unfavorably afterwards.' 'That may be,' said K. to change the subject, 'but that doesn't excuse you.' 'I am excused before all who know me,' the woman said. 'The one who attacked me on that occasion has been persecuting me for a long time'.'' A few minutes later, however, this unfortunate but faithful wife again surprises K. by remarking on the exceptional beauty of his eyes and inviting him to take a good look at her legs (under the pretext of showing what nice stockings the examining magistrate has given her). K.'s reaction is eminently reasonable: ''So that's what it's all about, K. thought.

She's offering herself to me. She's corrupt like all of them here. She's had enough of the Court officials, which is certainly understandable, and so she greets any stranger that happens along with compliments about his eyes.''

But when she freely talks of the examining magistrate's nascent passion for her and promises to use her influence over him in K.'s behalf, K. is, of course, again mollified. To be sure, he doesn't have much of a chance to savor the idea of commanding a fifth column, for his new-found helpmate shows no inclination to act in accordance with her new role. At the appearance of the law student who had ''attacked'' her at the hearing, she darts away from K. with a speed that is, at the very least, disconcerting, and announces: ''I have to go with him now . . . .'' Yet, without allowing him any time to express his surprise, she blithely, if incomprehensibly, continues: ''But I'll come back right away and then I'll go away with you, if you'll take me. I'll be happy if I can get away from here for as long as possible. The best thing, of course, would be to get away for good.'' Stunned, then gladdened by these assurances of devotion, K. manages to adjust his sights once again: if she means to abscond with him, there is no sense in her going to the judge first; indeed what sweeter revenge could there be than to leave the judge waiting—forever. Accordingly, K. sets off to free the woman from the clutches of the law student, whose loud kisses he now construes as positive evidence of the persecution she had complained of before. But now the scrubwoman stupefies K. with one more surprise: she isn't resisting the student's embrace at all. '''You don't want to be freed!' K. screamed, and placed his hand on the shoulder of the law student who snapped at it with his teeth. 'No!' cried the woman and pushed K. back with both hands. 'No, no, anything but that, what are you thinking of! That would be my ruin. Leave him alone, oh please, just leave him alone. He's only following the orders of the examining magistrate. He's carrying me to him.' 'I don't care where he's going and I don't ever want to see you again either,' K. said . . . '' And K., trembling with rage and disappointment, watches the happy couple until they scamper out of sight.

In following the burlesque *péripéties* of this romance, we recognize the characteristic form of the frustration experiences that abound in Kafka's work. But what, exactly, is the cause of this frustration? Clearly, not so much the hero's failure to effect his designs as his failure to discover what his designs should be. For to discover what may reasonably be expected and asked of other people, one must first have some idea of what these people are really like, and, as we have seen, K. is forced to discard one such idea after another. And if he regards his rejection as the ''first unequivocal defeat'' he has suffered at the hands of the Court, we must admit that we cannot conceive how he might have avoided this defeat. The court attendant's wife is, after all, an incredibly trying character. Just how trying becomes palpable in a rehearsal of the stages of K.'s confusion. Was he right in his original distrust of her? Not if she really was the helpless victim of the law student's ardors. Was he then right in his later sympathy for her? Not if she really is prone to random promiscuity. Was he then foolish in taking her offer of help seriously? Not if she really is tired of the court officials. Was he then right in fighting for her? Not if she really is at the examining magistrate's beck and call. And so on. K. has been vanquished by a collection of characters who all call themselves the scrubwoman, a collection which is disparate and, apparently, inexhaustible. ''The woman waved to K. as he looked after her, and sought to show by moving her shoulders up and down that she wasn't responsible for this abduction, although her movements did not evince a great deal of regret. K. stared at her as if she were a stranger, without expression. He didn't want to betray either that he was disappointed or, on the other hand, that he would easily be able to get over his disappointment.'' This last sentence, defying the law of the excluded middle, eloquently circumscribes K.'s position. In the attempt to meet all contingencies—to do justice to all the contradictions he cannot resolve—K. inevitably becomes absurd. As he himself realizes, only by staying at home, only by renouncing all designs, could he possibly have preserved his dignity. Ultimate passivity, death, is the sole conclusion the logic of *The Trial* permits.

At this stage in the proceedings, however, K. still consoles himself with thoughts of those segments of his life upon which the Court is powerless to intrude. He imagines how badly this despicable law student would fare in his own domain, for example, in a confrontation with K.'s once-a-week beloved Elsa. Actually, Elsa invariably occurs to him in the midst of his self-immolating adventures with the women who know of his case; small wonder, since she is dependably, payably one-faced, while the others seem to be veritable functionaries of the Court in their delight at dumbfounding him through protean elusiveness. Even Leni, who by virtue of her lust presents herself in a comparatively monolithic fashion, turns out to be a person of treacherous depth. She leads K. away from his would-be lawyer with the challenge, ''Must you always be thinking of your case?'' She changes direction in her next admonishment: ''. . . don't be so adamant. After all, one can't defend oneself against this court; one simply has to make a confession. Just make your confession the first opportunity you have.'' And she comes full circle in a comment she makes on another occasion: ''You haven't been to see us in so long, even the lawyer has been asking after you. Don't neglect your case!'' But behind these mere inconsistencies of speech is the riddle itself of her oppressively militant desire for K. At first she fairly compels K. to regard himself as the unique object of a glorious passion, though after a while, especially in the light of Lawyer Huld's none-too-delicate hints, she emerges as a curiously selective nymphomaniac who asks of her men only that they be ''accused.'' (Whether Huld is hinting at the truth or instead trying to humiliate K. is another insoluble question.) And finally there is Fräulein Bürstner, the perennially fascinating ''little typist.'' . . . I think it can be said that K. experiences her first as a vaguely loose seductress, then as a woman mindful of her reputation and strict in matters of morality, and, ultimately, as the lame, everyday Miss Montag (German for Monday). In short, the women are bewildering. And yet the distress they bring K. into does not really differ in kind from that which he feels in his encounters with his uncle, lawyer, etc.: all are open characters, people who worry K. because he cannot define them.

Elsa and the assistant manager are the only conventional characters in *The Trial,* for they alone submit to the control of K.'s reason. Then again, they are both representatives of the business world, which is ordered by reason. But with his arrest K. has become aware of, and captivated by, another world, one which is so little amenable to reason that a bank executive's perceptions of it resemble those of ''an idiot.'' I use Lukács' term, but with reservations, since I think most of us would admit to being, at least now and then, almost as idiotic as K. in our nonofficial contacts with other people. Only when reading ''for pleasure'' do we expect that isolated gestures and chance speeches will prove to be reliable indicators of character; in real life we recognize that the deeper our involvement

with a particular person is, the more laborious and protracted the process of definition and understanding is apt to become. But, by confining us to the insights of his emphatically non-omniscient hero, Kafka makes of us the unaccustomed demand that we apply the same process to characters in a book, i.e., he evokes the pains and embarrassments associated with reality instead of affording us the pleasures of fiction. (pp. 182-92)

Carl S. Singer, ''The Examined Life,'' in Approaches to the Twentieth-Century Novel, *edited by John Unterecker, Thomas Y. Crowell Company, 1965, pp. 182-217.*

HEINZ POLITZER   (essay date 1966)

[*Politzer is an American poet and critic who has written extensively on Franz Kafka. In the following excerpt, he argues that in* The Trial *the Law violated itself in arresting Joseph K., and examines the parable ''Before the Law'' for similarities to and divergences from K.'s trial in view of this violation.*]

''Someone must have denounced Joseph K., for without having done anything wrong he was arrested one morning.'' This first

Sketches by Kafka. From Franz Kafka: Pictures of a Life, *by Klaus Wagenbach. Translated by Arthur S. Wensinger. Pantheon Books, 1984. English translation copyright © 1984 by Random House, Inc. Reproduced by permission of Pantheon Books, a Division of Random House, Inc.*

sentence of the novel points to the paradox of the Law. But it remains hidden from the reader until he hears the last words the Chaplain speaks in the Cathedral scene. Here, at the high point of what is to be considered the climactic chapter of the book, the clergyman formulates the law of the Law. His words contain the only statement about the Trial which is no longer the guess of an outsider, the gossip of a meddler, or the doubtful hint of an incompetent intermediary, but a declaration of principles made by the Court about itself. "Do you realize who I am?" asks the priest. K., impatient and tired from a long-winded conversation, replies, "You are the Prison Chaplain." The clergyman retorts, "This means I belong to the Court." Underscoring the authority of the initiated, he also reveals the close connection his chaplainship has with the prison and the Law. Then the priest adds: "So why should I want anything from you? The Court wants nothing from you. It receives you when you come and dismisses you when you go."

This characterization of the Court is accurate but for one thing. In majestic patience the Trial has enveloped K.'s life; yet it still allows him to come and go as he pleases. "You are under arrest, certainly," he had been informed in the beginning, "but this need not hinder you from going about your business. Nor will you be prevented from leading your ordinary life." In this respect, the Trial resembles the Cathedral, the scene of this revelation: the church is always there but only for him who enters of his own volition; its doors are open equally for those who come and those who go, as K. will realize when he leaves. It, too, wants nothing from him.

Although K. is not used to worship and this particular visit has been planned as a tour, he enters the Cathedral voluntarily. He even enters it twice: the first time he is driven through the portals by the rainy day outside. "The Cathedral Square was quite deserted.... On a day like this, this was even more understandable than at other times. The Cathedral seemed deserted too." He has stepped in, automatically and unconsciously, while he was immersed in his thoughts. The moment of entry has not been registered in the narrative. Therefore he has to go back to the entrance and make the circuit of the building once more before the tale continues: "Since he was tired he felt like sitting down, went into the Cathedral again ... and sat down." Here he knows what he is doing; the language dwells on the act of his entrance (he "went ... again"); and the tiredness which prompts him to do so is, as we have learned at the beginning of the chapter, no momentary feeling of lassitude but the exhaustion caused by his yearlong occupation with the Trial. Consciously he enters now upon the scene in which the Court is to disclose to him the Law of its actions.

But if it is the law of the Law to receive those who come, dismiss those who desire to go, and otherwise remain unmoved and unmovable, then the Court has broken this Law by the very act of arresting K. It has singled him out and separated him from the others; it initiated the action when it forced him to start on the way that leads to the Cathedral, and eventually to his execution. This Law is at variance with another law, which was announced by the tall warder in the hour of K.'s arrest: "Our officials, so far as I know them, and I know only the lowest grades among them, do not by any means go hunting for the guilty ones in the populace, but, as the Law decrees, are drawn toward the guilty and must then send us warders. This is the Law." The limitations and qualifications of this statement should not deceive us; they are due to the warder's desire to avoid any responsibility for what he has said, an attitude typical of the servants of this Court. The Law itself,

which "must" dispatch its emissaries and is "drawn toward" the criminals it persecutes, has lost its supremacy. No longer does it rest impassively above the humans who come and go; it reacts, it acts, it arrests. When K. admits, "I don't know this law," he refers of course to the "legal constitution" of the country in which he lives. But the higher constitution under which, according to the Chaplain, the Law of this Trial operates is contradicted by this arrest. Even the Chaplain violates the fundamental laws by calling K.'s name as soon as he sees him, thus summoning him once more. And when K., who senses a contradiction between the spirit of the Law and its administrators, suggests to the priest: "You may not know the nature of the Court you are serving," the Chaplain cries, "Can't you see one pace before you?" Here the sovereign indifference of the Law gives way to its urge to seize the man, to direct him, to keep him back, and to impart itself to him. The narrator adds by way of elucidation: "It was an angry cry, but at the same time sounded like the unwary shriek of one who sees another fall and is startled out of his senses." In this moment of terror the Law unmasks itself. Showing concern for K.'s despair, it also admits the responsibility for the arrest which caused him to despair in the first place.

This basic paradox, inherent in the nature of the Law, may contribute to our understanding of the intermediaries whom the Court uses in its attempts to communicate with K. These officials, attorneys, and women appear stricken with guilt of one kind or the other because the Law which they pretend to know or to represent has committed a crime: it is guilty of having violated itself. By contradicting himself the priest proves his association with the Court more clearly than by his robe or his words. Since *The Trial* never proceeds beyond the sphere of these intermediary figures (among whom the Chaplain is the most advanced in rank and the most confusing), it is their paradoxical nature rather than the nondescript character of K. which seems to have fascinated Kafka. (pp. 167-70)

If the paradox of the Law is accepted as the central point of interest for Kafka in *The Trial*, it follows that the central figure in the parable "Before the Law" is not the man from the country but the doorkeeper who denies him entrance. There is some textual evidence to support this assumption. The doorkeeper is introduced in the first sentence of the parable, the man only in the second. The language itself establishes his priority. The doorkeeper is described in detail, "in his furred robe, with his huge pointed nose and long thin Tartar beard"; even the "fleas in his fur collar" do not go unnoticed. The man from the country, on the other hand, remains as impersonal as K., to whom he is meant to serve as an example. The doorkeeper is mentioned twenty-three times during the very brief narrative, the man only eleven times (in the German original, nine times), and of these only twice with his full title, the "man from the country." This word count betrays the priest's—and the Law's—intention to sidetrack K., to divert his attention from the man and direct it to the doorkeeper by means of his frequent appearance in the text.

The doorkeeper seems to have been there since time immemorial, just as does the Law which is introduced before the keeper ("Before the Law stands a doorkeeper"); the man on the other hand has to undertake a long and troublesome voyage to appear before the door. Human time and eternity seem to meet before the gate of the Law. A first discrepancy appears: according to "the very words of the scriptures" the Law has precedence over the doorkeeper, and yet the latter behaves as if the Law were there for his sake and not the other way around.

He interferes between the man and the Law when he says that he cannot admit him at the moment. Immediately afterward he contradicts himself: he steps aside and grants the man entrance to the Law, which "stands open as always." Just as confusing is the next information he gives the man: "I am powerful. And I am only the lowest doorkeeper." Almost literally the doorkeeper repeats here the words that the tall warder had spoken to K. in the first chapter. Although he was powerful enough to arrest K., he immediately betrayed his insignificance before the higher grades of the Court's officials. The way that led K. from his arrest to the Cathedral is mockingly extended into infinity when in the parable the doorkeeper continues to enlighten the man: "From hall to hall, doorkeepers stand at every gate, one more powerful than the other. And the sight of the third of them is more than even I can bear." As was the case with the warder, the doorkeeper seems to impart this information to the man partly to impress him with the magnitude of the Law, but partly also to escape a full measure of responsibility. Visually we can grasp the double role he is playing when we realize that, while addressing the man, he has to turn his back upon the Law he represents. His words are spoken simultaneously with regard to the Law and with disregard of it. His actions betray a similar ambiguity: he interrogates the man but merely as a routine measure. He accepts his bribes but only "to keep you from feeling that you have left something undone," thus adding compassion to corruption. Finally he roars at the man whose hearing is failing him: "No one but you could gain admittance through this door, since this entrance was intended only for you. I am going now to shut it."

This amazing statement concludes the parable "Before the Law" just as the law of the Law is pronounced at the very end of the Cathedral scene itself. This structural parallelism establishes the corresondence between the doorkeeper and the Chaplain: they are both intermediaries between Law and man; they both act as deterrents rather than as helpers; and the priest is defending his own role when he subjects the doorkeeper to an "exegesis." It also relates, by way of a contradiction, the last words of the doorkeeper to those spoken by the Prison Chaplain. By pronouncing his final verdict, the doorkeeper speaks counter to the scriptural passage according to which the door is open "as always." Furthermore, he belies the principle, announced by the priest, that the Court "receives you when you come." Finally, an authority such as the Court described by the priest, which is prepared to dismiss the man who wants to go, does not need a door, and certainly not a closed one. Put into the context of the whole chapter, the parable shows that the doorkeeper is speaking and acting quite independently of the Law. His independence, however, works to the detriment of the man from the country.

Martin Buber has discussed at some length the contribution which Kafka has made to the "metaphysics of the 'door'": "Every person has his own door and it is open to him; but he does not know this and apparently is not in a condition to know." Expanding from the parable "Before the Law" to the whole of *The Trial*, Buber says that the novel describes

> a district delivered over to the authority of a slovenly bureaucracy without the possibility of appeal. . . . What is at the top of the government, or rather above it, remains hidden in a darkness, of the nature of which one never once gets a presentiment; the administrative hierarchy, who exercise power, received it from above, but apparently without any commission or instruction. . . . Man is called into this world, he is appointed in it, but wherever he turns to fulfil

> his calling he comes up against the thick vapours of a mist of absurdity. . . .—it is a Pauline world, except that God is removed into the impenetrable darkness and that there is no place for a mediator.

Buber's reading reverses the point of view taken by most critics of *The Trial*. Whereas the story is usually analyzed with Joseph K.'s predicament foremost in the mind of the reader, Buber interprets the novel—and judges its hero—from the heights of the Law, the very Law that Kafka proclaims has been lost to the world. Textual evidence, however, suggests that Kafka was interested less in the Law and the man from the country than in the doorkeeper. The doorkeeper, in turn, stands for the other emissaries of the Court whom Buber calls, with great insight, "extremely powerful bunglers." Bunglers conduct the Trial and stand trial in it.

The "exegesis" of the parable turns right away to the doorkeeper and occupies itself with him almost exclusively. "'So the doorkeeper deluded the man,' said K. immediately, who was strongly attracted by the story." He falls into the trap set for him by the wording of the narrative. With his first remark he misses the one dialectical advantage he had: by concentrating on the man from the country instead of the doorkeeper, he could have denied the relevance of the parable for his particular situation. He could have stressed the fact that the man from the country had come to the Law out of his own volition, whereas he, K., had been sought out and overtaken by the Court. However, K. is as spellbound by the doorkeeper in the parable as he had been fascinated before by the warders when they appeared in his bedroom. Quite generally, the parable serves as a symbolic master plan for the novel as such. The initial situation of the novel is repeated here; this time it is couched in the form of an intellectual exercise, rather than as a part of the plot. K. loses out both here and there.

Actively supported by K., the Chaplain now "interprets" the doorkeeper instead of the man. Accordingly K. fails to learn anything from this "exegesis" which he could not have gathered previously from his meetings with the other intermediaries. Like them the doorkeeper is simultaneously dutiful and negligent of his duty, both patient and impatient, compassionate and condescending, free and bound, a deceived deceiver, "extremely powerful" and yet "a bungler." He is the visible representative of an invisible authority which even he cannot comprehend fully, precisely because he is visible. He shows the same ambiguity that K. had noticed in his dealings with the warders, the Examining Magistrate, the lawyer, and Titorelli, who appear superior to him but have to obey a higher authority, deriving, on the other hand, a considerable degree of freedom from the fact that they are not able to comprehend fully the command under which they operate. Like the doorkeeper, they stand before the Law, turning their backs upon it, unaware of the radiance that streams forth from it. Yet they need not see it, since they take part unconsciously and mysteriously in the proceedings of the Court.

The Chaplain is prepared to support this paradox with a note from the commentators: "The right perception of the matter and a misunderstanding of the same matter do not wholly exclude each other." It is the one little word "wholly" that protects this statement from any attack and renders it at the same time useless for K. It explains that the doorkeeper can misunderstand the Law and still have the right perception of the order he serves. The command given him may even have been meant to be misunderstood by him. Only at the very end of the "exegesis," when the figure of the doorkeeper has vanished behind a multiple web of pettifogging sophistry, does K. voice the claims of the man from the country, which are also his claims: "Whether the doorkeeper is clearsighted or deluded does not decide the question. I said the man is deceived." Now he has let go of the intermediary; it is, at long last, the man who matters. Compare the introductory statement, "So the doorkeeper deluded the man," with K.'s last formulation, "The man is deceived": the man has turned from object to subject, and the phrase has changed from a noncommittal active to a truly tragic passive voice. K. adds imploringly, "You must not forget that the doorkeeper's delusions do himself no harm but harm the man a thousandfold." The priest has now been challenged and nothing remains to this "interpreter" but to withdraw behind the authority of the Law: "Whatever he may seem to us [the doorkeeper] is yet a servant of the Law; that is, he belongs to the Law and as such is beyond human judgment. . . . It is the Law that placed him at his post; to doubt his dignity is to doubt the Law itself." This commentary means, on the basis of K.'s past experiences, that the warders whose selfishness and greed he had castigated vociferously had acted under the authority of the Court, although the same Court had also responded to K.'s complaint and sent out the whipper to punish the derelict servants. By the same token he rebels against the Law when he questions the dignity of the Examining Magistrate, whose books contain obscene drawings. Therefore he dismisses as a lie the priest's concluding remark that "it is not necessary to accept everything as true; one must only accept it as necessary." This blatant paradox contains the truth. Although it is not a truth that would profit K. in his Trial, it reveals the true nature of the Court: K.'s arrest had become necessary since it offered the Court the only opportunity to communicate with him. By this "necessity" the Law explains the offense it committed against itself. For its "truth" rests in itself, consists of itself, is "beyond human judgment" but also beyond the Law's ability to communicate with man.

The words of the priest throw light on the Court and its proceedings. It is, however, a light that leaves K. in the dark about himself and his guilt. For this paradox Kafka has found a poignant image introduced shortly before K. is summoned by the Chaplain:

> K. happened to turn round and saw not far behind him the gleam of another candle, a tall thick candle fixed to a pillar. . . . It was quite lovely to look at, but completely inadequate for illuminating the altarpieces, which mostly hung in the darkness of the side chapels; it actually increased the darkness.

The light shines to reveal the depth of the darkness. Hope is there for man to fathom his despair. Even the radiance that in the priest's parable "streams inextinguishably from the door of the Law" starts up only when "the man's eyes grow dim and he does not know whether the world is really darkening around him or whether his eyes are only deceiving him." One thing has become clear after the reflection of this radiance has played across his deadly tired eyes: "Now he will not live much longer." Also K.'s life is drawing to a close after he has perceived, in the words of the Chaplain, a ray of the mortifying light of the Law.

The light of the Law only illuminates the depth of the abyss in which it appeared to K. (pp. 177-82)

Heinz Politzer, in his Franz Kafka: Parable and Paradox, *revised edition, Cornell University Press, 1966, 398 p.*

GARY HANDLER   (essay date 1969)

[*In the following essay, Handler points out inconsistencies in Herman Uyttersprot's arrangement of the chapters in* The Trial *(see excerpt dated 1953).*]

In his well-known chapter rearrangement of Franz Kafka's uncompleted novel, ***Der Prozess,*** Herman Uyttersprot suggests that Max Brod's designation of "In the Cathedral" as the ninth chapter is erroneous. Uyttersprot maintains that it should properly precede "Lawyer, Manufacturer, Painter" (Brod's Chapter Seven). However, if we read these two chapters in the English edition using Uyttersprot's order, we must deal both with a narrative technique uncharacteristic of Kafka in this *Roman* and an unproductive repositioning of textual events.

Early in the chapter entitled "In the Cathedral," the narrator comments on K.'s relations with the bank's Assistant Manager. This man "had *always* spied upon him, prowling *every now and then* into his [K.'s] office, sitting down at his desk, running through his papers, receiving clients who had become almost old friends of K.'s in the course of many years, and luring them away from him . . . [italics mine]." These comments, in the light of what happens in "Lawyer, Manufacturer, Painter," may seem reasonable, for there is virtually perfect accord between what had passed "every now and then" and what passes between the Assistant Manager and manufacturer in Chapter Seven. But a close look at the narrator's remarks as K. hastily prepares to abandon his work for a chance to speak with Titorelli, the painter, will leave some doubt as to the frequency of the Assistant Manager's "prowling."

The narrator tells us that K. hesitates momentarily to leave the bank knowing that "his prestige . . . was suffering irreparable injury," and his present neglect of two clients would certainly do his reputation further harm. The narrator even conjectures that K. might have postponed his departure for a short time, had he not "caught sight of the Assistant Manager *himself* in K.'s *own* room searching through his files as if they belonged to him. *In great agitation* K. approached the doorway of the room . . . [italics mine]." Are we to assume from this description and the one quoted from "In the Cathedral" that although K. is accustomed to having his files looked through by the other man, his obvious shock and anger registered in the latter account are only a result of his momentary preoccupation with other affairs? Rather, from the force of the emphatic words, "himself," "own" and "great agitation," this is the first instance of such "prowling." Whether the Assistant Manager "had always spied upon him" becomes irrelevant in the face of this unpleasantly new and startling experience confronting K. in "Lawyer, Manufacturer, Painter."

The effect of reading an account of a specific sort of harassment by the Assistant Manager directed at K., and then many pages later confronting the first instance of this harassment is confusing. Not only is the technique of explicit foreshadowing unlike Kafka, but we are also surprised and puzzled by Joseph K.'s "great agitation" with the Assistant Manager's actions in "Lawyer, Manufacturer, Painter," because we have already been told ("In the Cathedral") that they are not new to him. But reversing the quotations (thereby reinstating Brod's order) permits us a satisfying recognition and understanding of the general state of K.'s affairs in terms of a specific instance presented earlier. (pp. 798-99)

Gary Handler, "A Note on the Structure of Kafka's 'Der Prozess'," in MLN, *Vol. 84, 1969, pp. 798-99.*

ANTHONY THORLBY (essay date 1972)

[*Thorlby is an English educator and critic. In the following excerpt, he focuses on* The Trial *as a linguistic document which explores the relationships between reality, words, and meaning.*]

It is tempting to return to the facts of Kafka's life for a fuller explanation of the mystery [of the *Trial*]. This novel is all about a "trial," albeit in a most unusual court of law; but the "court of law" *(Gerichtshof)*, as Kafka called it, was also most unusual when sentence was passed on him—as he felt—in the Berlin hotel, the Askanischer Hof, on the occasion of his breaking off his engagement to Felice Bauer. We know also that this novel was written in the months following that break and would appear, with its obsessive theme of some private guilt, to have been largely inspired by it. A modern critic, accustomed to the dependence of a work of art on the psychology of the artist rather than on the reality of the world, will inevitably start to notice such "revealing" details as that the initials of Felice Bauer are the same as those of the girl who, at the start, means a lot to Joseph K. in his trial, Fräulein Bürstner; or that a minor but attractive part is played in the novel by a girl called Erna, which was the actual name of Felice's sister; and so on. Yet this kind of information does not help us very much, for the obvious reason already given, that Kafka has made such a strange use of whatever autobiographical material he may have incorporated in the novel, and it is precisely the significance of this strange use that we should be endeavouring to understand. (pp. 56-7)

The problem the novel raises for us is indeed connected with the significance of names, persons, and even events in Kafka's life; but the problem is a linguistic, rather than a biographical or even psychological one. What do the words mean with which Kafka has represented what happened in his life, thereby distorting it so strangely? This is a problem of truly general, and essentially philosophical interest, for it makes us wonder at the process by which language makes experience comprehensible to ourselves and communicable to others. How well do the words we use actually "fit" the reality of what happens in the world? This is a question to which we must have an answer—or else a sense of trust that conventional language does mean something—and yet we ultimately cannot answer it. Kafka is writing in this novel, and to some extent in all his work, about this problem: about what words "really" mean, about their conventional meaning often smooth with well-worn metaphorical usage, and about the dark, inscrutable background that lies behind this reassuring facade.

When Joseph K. discovers the scene of a beating in the office store-room, he not only slams the door on it, he goes over to a window and gazes out. He has had a glimpse of some deeper reality and now he tries to penetrate its meaning—"to pierce the darkness of the courtyard," or more explicitly in German: "mit den Blicken in das Dunkel eines Hofwinkels einzudringen." Let us not labour the symbolism of what "court" [*Hof*] this now is, but simply ask what K. is trying to do in this moment of penetrating contemplation, when we might have expected some more conventional action from him. He is making "a vow not to hush up the incident," a phrase that does not reveal to an English reader what Kafka's commonplace German expression plainly states: "Er gelobte sich, die Sache noch zur Sprache zu bringen"—to put the thing, or case, or cause, into words. It is a matter of language.

Inasmuch as this is what the novel explores, namely, the linguistic, and not the legal or moral, essence of K.'s case *(Sache)*, a great deal of its significance gets lost in translation. Even the title of the book is misleading, for although the English "trial" has more than one meaning, the connotations of the word are different from those of the German one. *Der Prozess* is cognate, of course, with the English "process," and Kafka uses the term interchangeably with *das Verfahren*, which means "procedure," but also has undertones of "entanglement" and even "muddle." Joseph K.'s trial is thus a verbal process, the process whereby we try to investigate with language what the matter with our lives is, getting hopelessly entangled "in the process."

It is, as James Joyce knew, quite simple to construct an "action" out of plays on words, but it is probably impossible to produce the same pattern of verbal "cases" with English words as with Kafka's original German one. For instance, it is just as easy for an English as for a German reader to see that the initials for Fräulein Bürstner are the same as Felice Bauer's, but no amount of ingenuity can communicate the sexual echoes of *bürsten*, a word that Kafka would surely have known as a vulgar expression for intercourse. Similarly, the mysterious "authorities" who try Joseph K. symbolize verbally the spiritual predicament a man finds himself in as soon as he asks questions about language. For the German *Behörde* has a philological groundwork, a foundation in a more "real" reality, which is of the greatest interest. Cognate with it is the word for "to belong" *(gehören)*, which in turn goes back to the basic word for "to hear" *(hören)*, and to words describing ancient conditions of servitude *(Hörer, Hörigkeit)*; *gehörig*, on the other hand, is a common modern word for "appropriate" or "relevant," with legal overtones of competence and admissibility.

The authorities before whom K. stands, therefore, are a symbol for some of the most fundamental questions raised by man's capacity to reflect about his position as a thinking, word-using animal in the world. To whom does he belong, who hears him, what words are appropriate to his situation, whom should he obey and who is competent to judge him? The consistent way in which Kafka's language creates an appearance of concrete action and character out of his basically spiritual, abstractly philosophical preoccupation with the "world" of consciousness, becomes still more apparent when we look at other words closely connected with the above. K., for instance, is subjected to cross-examination, which in German is *Verhör*, with undertones of hearing incorrectly. Yet another train of words is based on the process of exploration downwards *(untersuchen)*, as well as on concepts of what is right, embodied in persons K. only hears about but never meets *(Untersuchungsrichter)*.

Once we assume that this is in part what *The Trial* is "about," we can go on to interpret various aspects of the "action" and of the "characters" accordingly. For example, Joseph K. has to decide whether to get a lawyer to represent him, and then when he grows dissatisfied with this character's ability properly to represent his case, whether and how to get rid of him. Who is this character and why is he presented as a sickly, bedridden old man, who would be of no interest to K. at all if he did not have a sexy girl in his house to look after him? The answer is that he represents a character called in (ad-vocatus) to represent K.'s case; this he is too feeble to do, however, because K. is instinctively interested less in tiresome discussions of meaning than in its dependence on sex, which seems to have some intimate relationship with it. The lawyer thus "represents" a character in a new sense: he represents Kafka's feeble reliance on characters (other than his hero's—and not even on his in any naturalistic sense) to further the "action" of his unique kind of spiritual inquiry. Kafka uses the word *Vertreter* (representative) interchangeably with *Advokat* (lawyer), and we learn that there is a "difference between a lawyer for ordinary legal rights and a lawyer for cases like these. . . . The one lawyer leads his client by a fine thread until the verdict is reached, but the other lifts his client on his shoulders from the beginning and carries him bodily without once letting him down until the verdict is reached, and even beyond it."

There are many clues in this chapter to show the reader that this passage, and the characters and situation described in it, represent different kinds of literary, rather than legal, practice. One of them lies in the word *Eingabe* (petition), which it is the representing lawyer's task to handle; a very similar German word from the same root means "inspiration" *(Eingebung)*. K.'s attitude towards his representative is unconventional, by comparison with that of an ordinary client like Kaufmann Block. The word *Kauf-mann* (business or tradesman) is given overtones of venality, because Block has apparently bought the services of many representatives; he is like a hack novelist, always looking for a new way to put his case. And the kinds of representatives that he chooses are doubtless the ordinary ones referred to above, who lead him on through a rather tenuous tale. Kaufmann Block is simply a rather poor writer—his "petitions (inspirations) turned out to be quite worthless"—who turned to matters like these only late in life, after his wife had died. He has no business to invoke the help of an *advocatus* like K.'s, who has specialized in the much more difficult kind of "practice, in which after a certain moment nothing essentially new ever occurs."

K.'s *Advokat*, however, is surely one of those lawyers who wants to "lift his client on his shoulders and carry him bodily, without letting him down, until the verdict is reached and even beyond it" (. . . trägt ihn, ohne ihn abzusetzen, zum Urteil und noch darüber hinaus). This is a description of Kafka's "practice," or at least of the one he has been looking for from the beginning, and it recalls details from the stories, from the early **"Description of a Fight"** in which his first characters rode one upon the other's back, to the inescapable verdict of **"The Judgement,"** where there was no longer any possibility of being "put down" again on to the ground of common-sense reality; a world in which metaphor, the process itself of language, becomes a nightmare-reality in its own right.

In ordinary literary terms the verdict to which a writer is exposed is merely the verdict of the public on his work. He does not "do" anything criminal, but simply goes on with the process of writing, and this "process"—as the priest explains to K. near the end—"gradually passes over into a judgement" (geht allmählich ins Urteil über). In Kafka's case, we know that this verdict, which essentially he passed on himself, however he might represent it in writing (as being, for instance, the "judgement" of his father), had the force of a "life-sentence"—a play on words that is not possible in German but comes near to the spirit and goal of Kafka's work, just as it does to that of James Joyce whose *Finnegans Wake* is also a kind of never-ending "life-sentence."

It is significant that Joseph K., like his author, declares that he is not interested in knowing "the meaning of the sign" that causes his public, at his first interrogation, to applaud or to hiss. He is aiming (like his author) at something more serious than ordinary literary success. He has a spiritual cause to champion: the cause, the case, of all individuals who have been "arrested" like himself. For here everybody and "everything belongs to the Court," even though most of the people he meets seem quite unconcerned at the fact, even unaware of it. (Kafka evidently thinks like Kierkegaard that all men are in despair and anguish at their human condition no matter whether or not they realize it.) But the fact that all men are subject to the process of living, which most of them do not think about enough to realize that it is (metaphorically) a nightmare, does not make the plight of the individual less grievous. The more desperately he pursues his case, the more inevitable the verdict becomes.

Thus, K. cannot make common cause with other men: "combined action against the Court is impossible," which is to say that mankind cannot achieve through the solidarity of some public convention or belief any release from each man's private "trial." Nor can he dissociate himself from other men entirely. As with the animal in **"The Burrow,"** who can neither stay up above in the world or down below on his own, so Joseph K.'s case is inextricably bound up with his having a public existence which he keeps up right to the end: "had he stood alone in the world, there would have been no case." In other words, he realizes the nature of his own individuality through contact with other people. They have a part to play in the process through which the fateful verdict is reached. It is through this relationship to the others that the self realizes what it is.

It is not solely through a relationship to another person that we come to realize the unique character of the self as a state of consciousness; we may discover it more immediately through our relationship to our body. This is now Joseph K. first discovers it. For the figures who break in on him one morning, eat his breakfast and steal his clothes, are certainly not secret-policemen but rather representatives of his own body. They beg K. to stop protesting about his position and asking for their "warrant" for being there. Why on earth, they exclaim, "can't you accept your position and why are you so intent on pointlessly annoying us, who are probably closer to you than any of your fellow human beings!" The symbolism could scarcely be more obvious, and it is supported by many associated details, that call attention to the base, bodily character of these men, "bodyguards" *(Leibwächter)* of the spirit, who later have to be ascetically punished and chastised for taking liberties to which they are not entitled. The liberty that K. desires is a pure, spiritual freedom, a total *Freisprechung* (absolution) through words. It was, of course, Kafka's own desire as a writer, an aspiration to emerge victorious over the monstrous "process" (trial?) of being a thinking, speaking person in a world where language does not ever seem to "apply."

This novel is about the futility of man's "applications" (*Bittschriften*—indeed, the novel is itself a *Bittschrift*), and about the very serious consequences to his body of repeatedly making them. We know how ruinous to Kafka's health writing was, and how he associated literature with illness; K.'s health similarly suffers as the "process" continues—and in the last scene he is put to death "like a dog." These famous final words suggest that it is a bodily fate, which he cannot control, that at last overtakes him, even while his mind is battling to argue still and hope. The last thing he sees are his strange executioners observing the *Entscheidung*, an almost untranslatable word in this context, for it means the outcome of the story, but also suggests a decision or judgement of some kind, and has undertones of division and separation. The separation is between K.'s mind and body; the decision is his own; the outcome inevitable. The logic of this situation is "unshakeable" (*unerschütterlich*—the word Kafka used to describe his sense of "judgement" on looking again at Felice Bauer), but "it cannot withstand a man who wants to go on living." Alas, the novel has made it quite clear that K. did not simply want to go on living; he wanted to know. The outcome, decision, separation was for Kafka inevitably fatal.

The style of the final chapter—to the extent to which it is finished—is particularly grotesque. Two more men are sent to execute K., who are less realistic, more absurd characters than the warders who came to arrest him in chapter one. They look to K. like "tenth-rate old actors," then again like tenors. Outside in the street they grapple hold of him in such a way that the three become a unity—"a unity such as almost only lifeless matter can form" ("wie sie fast nur Lebloses bilden kann"). The trio move wherever K. wants to go; he catches sight of Fräulein Bürstner, or a girl resembling her, and like a single man they follow her: "that he might not forget the warning that she signified for him." The lesson is plainly stated: "he suddenly realized the futility of resistance. There would be nothing heroic in it were he to resist . . . to snatch the last appearance of life by struggling." So K. does not resist, but co-operates, even getting himself and his executioners past a policeman who might have intervened. Only at the last he cannot seize the knife, "as it was his duty to do . . . and plunge it into his own breast. . . . He could not relieve the authorities of all the work, the responsibility for this final mistake lay with him who had denied him the last bit of strength necessary for the deed."

While a biographical interpretation could explain this scene perhaps by reference to the grotesque "performance" in the Berlin hotel, when Kafka's fateful separation from F. B. was conducted largely by others, the question still remains why Kafka has presented it like this at the end of *The Trial.* From a literary point of view, the scene is a travesty, a deliberately non-heroic ending. The executioners who are even more closely linked with K.'s person than the warders, symbolize his rapidly ailing state. When K. was first "arrested" *(ver-haftet),* his spirit was brought to a halt in mid-career; both the German and the English word suggest this coming to a standstill and being held fast. Throughout Kafka's writing there is a constant play on images (often very common words) of movement and standstill; their conflict is as fundamental as that between freedom and imprisonment, or silence and noise. What is ambiguous is which is the better state. This last chapter describes a series of sporadic movements as K. half runs to meet his fate, half tries to stop it still. But since, after a year of futile "trial," he no longer knows what he wants to stop it for (certainly not for F. B.), he can only acquiesce as his body performs the inevitable last act. In just this way Kafka was to describe his outbreak of tuberculosis three years later: as his lungs taking on the burden of suffering which his spirit could no longer bear. (pp. 57-64)

In making this kind of interpretation, we are beginning to distinguish between what "is" (or stands for) body and what is spirit in Kafka, between reality and consciousness, in a way that his manner of writing renders finally impossible. Thus, the ubiquitous organization that has arrested K., with its endless hierarchies of officials, can be looked at symbolically as meaning either or both of two totally different things. One interpretation might see these authorities as symbolizing the infinite ramifications of consciousness, with airless corridors of thought, and impenetrable realms of speculative inquiry. Why else should people wear cushions on their heads, if not to symbolize the pressure upwards of the mind, always eager to break out of any constriction?

Many other details concerning the Courts suggest, however, that they are anything but a symbol of man's spiritual state. Their law-books are obscene, their practices corrupt, especially in their claims on women. The reactions of the women themselves, both in this novel and in *The Castle,* are equally ambiguous. They seem to have intimate connections with the courts, even belonging to them in some ill-defined sense; at the same time they fall in love with men who are accused and "arrested," i.e. men who are in conflict with the Courts. Finally, the attitude towards women of the hero in each novel confirms this ambiguity. K. finds Fräulein Bürstner and Leni—later it will be Frieda and Pepi—attractive because he has been arrested and the women seem (at first) to offer something that he deeply needs. This something could be the solace and promise that have always been associated with love; but Kafka's love scenes give a more sordid impression of mindless sex.

Now, again, we have to be clear about what is original in Kafka's representation of ambiguity in the nature of love, and more broadly in the nature of reality. It is not the ambiguity itself, but Kafka's way of representing it, that disturbs us. Indeed, by making it appear to be totally a problem of representation, he makes it appear quite hopeless, irrational, and fatal. That is to say: we do not need to look very far in literature to discover that love has another side that is hostile to the spirit—"the expense of spirit in a waste of shame." Nor (to be more precise) that a writer will be particularly sensitive to the question: "What boots it with uncessant care / To tend the homely slighted Shepherd's trade, / And strictly meditate the thankless Muse? / Were it not better done as others use, / To sport with Amaryllis in the shade, / Or with the tangles of Naera's hair?" But the problem that confronts K. no longer appears in this light, and it is Kafka who has changed the lighting.

The biographical experience from which he started, of uncertainty and even incapacity concerning marriage, is not in itself so extraordinary—to the extent to which we can talk of an experience "in itself" apart from a man's reaction to it—as Kafka well knew from reading of similar experiences in the lives of Grillparzer, Kierkegaard, and Flaubert. Kafka places this experience in a new and unrecognizable light, and in so doing puts it beyond man's moral control or even rational comprehension. All forms of moral or rational presentation assume that we can recognize what is right and wrong, better and worse, in the world; even if we make the wrong choice, we can know when we do. And this in turn assumes that the character and meaning of reality does not depend entirely on our interpretation of it; that the world is distinct from human consciousness, which can thus hope to penetrate and master its laws. Kafka's writing totally undermines these assumptions. we are no longer sure what is "there" in reality, and what exists in K.'s mind. Does he confront a symbol of the natural world, physical existence in its sordid, obscene inscrutability? Or a symbol of his own consciousness, a projection outwards of his own muddled nature, which takes on a semblance of evil reality? Kafka's literary achievement consists in his having made it possible to distinguish between these two things. His symbolism is, as we have said, total, and leaves nothing outside itself to which it can confidently be referred, or on which a distinction between reality and consciousness can be based. (pp. 65-7)

The impenetrability of the world's law is summed up most brilliantly in this novel in the separate story. . . . "Before the Law," which is preached by a priest to K. as a parable. He has already been warned by the artist, Titorelli, that the court before which he is being "tried" is "completely impenetrable by argument" or more exactly: "Impenetrable by arguments that one brings before the court. . . . It is quite a different matter with one's efforts behind the public court, that is to say in the consulting rooms, in the corridors, or for instance in this very studio." The word "impenetrable" is in the German *unzugänglich*, which the first translator (Edwin Muir) rendered as "impervious." Whatever undertones an English reader may find in these words, it is important to notice how much more readily concrete the German *Zugang* is; it can mean an entrance or gateway, as well as "access" in a more metaphorical sense. In Kafka's parable this situation is visualized concretely: a man waits before the entrance to the law all his life, and never gains admittance. The situation seems hopeless partly because the man insists on waiting for access. But when, after the parable has been told, K. himself tries to argue his way into the meaning of the story, he is unable to base any conclusive arguments on it, i.e. to reach any conclusion in either a negative or a positive sense.

K. cannot even prove, for instance, that the man who waits away his life has been deceived; that would at least establish a rational criterion of truth external to the story. However, at the same time that no truth can be established literally, so that in this representative symbol (if it is one) the mind's situation before the law of existence is hopeless, the story itself captures this very situation perfectly—and that, as the artist says, "is quite a different matter." This parable is preached to K. for a *good* reason: it is his story. Literally speaking, in terms of the novel as a whole, this parable does not do K. any good; it does not help him to evade his fate, does not procure for him the total "acquittal" *(Freisprechung)* he seeks.

What, after all, would total release from the "charge" of living mean? "The documents relating to the case are said to be completely done away with, they vanish entirely from the proceedings, not only the charge, but the trial and even the acquittal itself is destroyed, everything is destroyed." It sounds like Kafka's wish that his own manuscripts should be destroyed! But even while he knew that literally his writing could not save him, Kafka could imagine perfectly the hopelessness of desiring that it should. This parable represents a moment when the mind totally grasps its own situation, a moment of pure freedom such as the animal dreams of in **"The Burrow,"** an impossible and "untenable" position like the Archimedean point only to be reached on condition that it is turned against its possessor. At this point in the book, the meaninglessness of the whole "trial," the process not only of writing—as we have provisionally interpreted *Der Prozess* here—but of existing consciously at all, is concretely symbolized. The novel grasps itself in a symbol that passes beyond any interpretable meaning, for it symbolizes the impossibility of interpretation. "The text is unalterable and the opinions [of critics] are often only an expression of despair at this fact." (pp. 67-8)

Anthony Thorlby, in his Kafka: A Study, *Rowman and Littlefield, 1972, 101 p.*

ERICH HELLER   (essay date 1974)

[*Heller is a Czechoslovakian-born English educator and critic. In the following excerpt from an essay originally published in 1974, he discusses the ambiguous nature of* The Trial *which both invites and resists efforts at interpretation, concluding that the novel is a failure because of the unspecified nature of the protagonist's guilt.*]

There is only one way to save oneself the trouble of interpreting *The Trial:* not to read it. Not reading it would be, moreover, the only available manner of fulfilling Kafka's wish that all his unpublished writings should be destroyed. For to take advantage of the contrary decision made by Max Brod and to read the book is to become an interpreter; and this in a much more radical sense than applies to all intelligent reading. Goethe, in the Preface to his *Theory of Colours,* says about any experience of the mind: "Looking at a thing gradually issues in contemplation, contemplation is thinking, thinking is establishing connections, and thus it is possible to say that every attentive glance which we cast on the world is an act of theorizing." For the same reason one may say that every attentive glance at a text is an act of interpreting. But this, Goethe adds, ought to be done with the consciousness that it *is* an interpretation, and therefore, "to use a daring word, with *irony*"—a quality oppressively absent from the minds of many literary commentators who go through their texts with the professional air of policemen searching for the "meaning" as if it were contraband or stolen property. Their findings more often than not tend to provoke the question: If *this* is what the author meant, why did he not say so?

In the case of Kafka, and *The Trial* in particular, the compulsion to interpret is at its most compelling, and is as great as the compulsion to continue reading once one has begun: the urgencies are identical. For Kafka's style—simple, lucid, and "real" in the sense of never leaving any doubt concerning the reality of that which is narrated, described, or meditated—does yet narrate, describe, or meditate the shockingly unbelievable. While it is in the nature of Biblical parables to *show* meaning, through concrete images, to those who might be unable to comprehend meaning presented in the abstract, Kafka's parables seem to insinuate meaninglessness through nonetheless irrefutably real and therefore suggestively meaningful configurations. "The most wondrous poetic sentences are those which make us see, with indisputable certainty and great clarity, the physically impossible: they are true descriptions through words," Hugo von Hofmannsthal said with regard to Novalis. It might carry even greater conviction if it were applied to Kafka, perhaps with the rider that in his case the "physically impossible" makes us see not the miraculous, as sometimes happens with Novalis, but infinite expanses of meaninglessness endowed with whatever meaning its "true description through words" is capable of yielding.

Yes, it is so! is what Kafka's reader is made to feel, only to look up and add, "It cannot be." It is the most sensible vision of an insensible world that produces this dizzying simultaneity of Impossible! and Of course! That Gregor Samsa of *The Metamorphosis* wakes up one morning to find himself transformed into a giant insect is reported without the slightest vestige of the fuss usually accompanying the fantastic. Does the narrated event, therefore, persuade us to suspend our disbelief? Not in the least; but as if we watched an unheard-of natural phenomenon, we are forced to ask: What does it mean? Again like an unheard-of natural phenomenon, it defies any established intellectual order and familiar form of understanding, and thus arouses the kind of intellectual anxiety that greedily and compulsively reaches out for interpretations.

"The right perception of any matter and a misunderstanding of the same matter do not wholly exclude each other." This is what the priest in *The Trial* affirms—talmudistically to the point of caricature—concerning the flawed understanding which the doorkeeper in the legend "Before the Law" has of his duty (which consists in keeping watch at the gate leading to the interior of the Law). Of the many divergent opinions which interpreters of the legend have entertained, the priest says: "The text is unalterable, and the interpretations are often merely expressions of the despair engendered by this." Did Kafka make him say this, prophetically, also of his own texts and their future interpreters? The legend "Before the Law" is at the heart of the novel and harbors its secret in the way Kafka's best stories harbor their secrets: unyieldingly and only occasionally allowing for those glimpses of illumination that blind rather than enlighten.

Joseph K., high official of a Bank, mysteriously tried by a sordidly mysterious Court of Justice for a mysterious offense he is accused of having committed against a mysterious law, has been waiting in the Cathedral for an Italian businessman to whom he was to show the artistic monuments of the city. His waiting has been in vain. (With Kafka *all* waiting is futile, although it is also right to say of it what a character in the novel says: that it is not the waiting that is useless but only action; or, as the prophet Daniel pronounces: "Blessed is he that waiteth.") The guided tour of the Cathedral is not to take place. In any case, it would have been impossible to see the works of art inside the Cathedral for the darkness of the winter morning is growing ever darker and is finally impenetrable; the reader joins K. in wondering whether winter clouds are its sufficient cause. The blackness soon reveals its symbolic character when the priest (who turns out to be the Court's prison chaplain), angered by K.'s persistent defamatory remarks about the Court, shouts at him, "Can you not see two steps ahead of you?"

"You are Joseph K.," says the priest from his pulpit, and then warns him of the bad prospects of his trial. "Yet I am not guilty," K. once again maintains. This time he adds the question of whether guilt has any place at all in human affairs: "We are all human beings here, every one of us," implying: human beings with their inevitable failings. "True," replies the cleric, "but this is how the guilty tend to speak." When K. complains about the bias of the Court and once again about its corruption, the priest, descended from the pulpit, admonishes him not to misjudge the character of the Court—after the fashion of his misjudging the doorkeeper in the legend "Before the Law" which he now narrates.

The legend, which according to the priest is part of the prefatory explanations introducing the Law itself, tells of a man from the country who arrives at the entrance gate of the Law. There he encounters the doorkeeper. He asks to be admitted. The doorkeeper refuses: "Not now," he says. "Perhaps later?" asks the man. "It is possible," is the doorkeeper's reply, "but not now." There never will be "now." The man from the country is kept waiting forever. Having vainly entreated and even bribed the doorkeeper, and having become so familiar with him that he knows "even the fleas in his fur collar," he is, after years and years, about to die. He asks his final question:

> "Everyone strives to attain the Law . . . how does it come about, then, that in all these years no one has wanted to be admitted but me?" The doorkeeper recognizes that the man is approaching his end and in order to reach his hearing that fails, he bellows in his ear: "No one but you could gain admittance through this door, since this door was meant for you alone. I am now going to shut it."

The parable "Before the Law" is the only part of *The Trial* that Kafka, with infallible discrimination, published himself.

Despite its familiarity, it has retained its terrible charm and shows all the characteristic features of Kafka's art at its most powerful—possessing, that is, the kind of power that is in the gentle wafting of the wind rather than in the thunderous storm, and is the more destructive for it. Parodying Biblical simplicity, *sancta simplicitas,* it expresses the most unholy complications of the intelligence and raises hellish questions in the key of the innocently unquestionable. Its humor is at the same time tender and cruel, teasing the mind with the semblance of light into losing itself in the utmost obscurity.

It may have been from sheer benevolent consideration for the reader that Kafka did not let the parable, as its own aesthetic will seems to demand, stand by itself. In *The Trial,* he supplemented it with pages of exegesis that encroach upon its sovereignty but for once forestall any interpretative maneuvers: the writer himself demonstrates their futility. For instance: Has the doorkeeper deceived the man from the country? Joseph K. feels immediately certain he has, but the priest exhorts him not to judge too rashly and above all not to venture outside the text; the text allows for no such condemnation of the doorkeeper; all that we come to know is that the man is not permitted to enter *now,* even though this particular entrance is meant only for him. It is not the doorkeeper's fault that the moment never comes which would redeem the supplicant as well as the very existence of the door. (Doors in Kafka's writings appear to be an architectural invention for the purpose of preventing people from entering.)

There is not the slightest hint to be found anywhere in the text that the doorkeeper—humble because he is only the lowest in the hierarchy of the Law, and yet powerful because he is, after all, in the Law's service—violates his commission by not admitting the man at that particular moment or at any particular time. It has to be assumed that he acts in accordance with the Law. Why should he act otherwise? From a capricious dislike of the man? On the contrary, it may be from kindness that— at least in the opinion of many learned interpreters—he goes beyond the call of duty by allowing the man to know that at some future time his request may be granted. Or is he corrupt in accepting gifts? The text does not support the conclusion that such acceptance is against the Law, although it would not doubt be against the Law if the doorkeeper let himself be seduced by bribes. Is there any reason for not believing him when, with the accent of Kafka's wit and the logic of the Hapsburg bureaucracy, he says that he only takes the man's presents to comfort the giver with the certainty that he has tried everything in his power? And so the exegetical dialogue between Joseph K. and the priest continues, leaving no pebble of interpretation unturned, and then throwing all of them away as worthless missiles, unfit to make so much as a dent in the armor of the mysterious futility. "The text is unalterable, and the interpretations are often merely expressions of the despair engendered by this."

Is there any fissure in it, undetected by Joseph K. and left unprotected by the priest? It seems there is not. We have heard the priest say that the correct comprehension of any matter *and* its misunderstanding are not entirely incompatible; and this paradox—like all good paradoxes, a splendid performance of the mind, induced by the castration of logic—was prompted by the observation that the doorkeeper was both right and wrong with regard to his office. In this respect he gives the impression of being simple-minded as well as conceited. True enough, his power is considerable, yet his manner suggests that he is unaware of the measure of his subordination. He conducts himself after the fashion of "great men" and does not seem to recognize that in some respects the man from the country might well be superior to him; he is free and has made the journey on his own volition, possessed as he is by the desire to come to know the Law. The doorkeeper, on the other hand, has long since accepted (if indeed it has not always been a matter of indifference to him) his lack of courage in not daring to face even the third of the many other doorkeepers on the way to the Law, not to mention the fact that he is bound by the Law to stay in the place assigned to him, while the man from the country is free to leave if he so wishes—like Joseph K. himself, from whom, in the parting words of the priest, "the Court wants nothing. . . . It receives you when you come and it dismisses you when you go." The doorkeeper does not even know the Law that he so obediently serves—just as the Whipper of the Court, in one of the most disquieting episodes in this disquieting book, cruelly and incorruptibly beats the "culprits" assigned to him without questioning the assignment, and responds to Joseph K.'s attempt to ransom the victim by saying: "I refuse to be bribed. I am commissioned to whip, and whip I shall" (an anticipation of that evil honesty and conscientiousness which later was to beget the most abhorrent deeds in the regions of Kafka's birthplace).

Compared even to the pitiable condition of the man from the country, shrunk and blind and deaf in the end, the doorkeeper is an obtuse creature. The story does not record that, with his eyes intact, he has ever seen what the man in his blindness perceives: the immense radiance streaming forth from the Law. Also, as some of the fictitious commentators of the legend believe, he may be deluded or be bragging or be cruelly determined to inflict grief and regret upon the man in his last moments when he tells him that now, in the hour of the man's death, he is going to shut the door that was meant only for him. Has he the power to do so? Has it not been said at the beginning of the parable that the entrance to the Law is always open? This "always" cannot possibly be affected by the death of the individual. Nevertheless, despite all his failings, the doorkeeper is, as the priest affirms, a servant of the Law and as such "beyond human judgment." Therefore it ought after all not be assumed that he is really inferior to the man from the country. To be enlisted by the Law, even as the lowest of doormen, is incomparably more than to live freely in the world; and to doubt this guardian's worthiness is to doubt the Law itself. Thus speaks the priest—not unlike K.'s lawyer, who advises him early in the novel that often it is better to be in chains than to be free. But at this point Joseph K. disagrees with the priest; if he were right, one would have to believe that everything the doorkeeper says is true; and has not the priest himself proved that this is impossible? No, the priest replies, one need not accept everything as true, "one must only accept it as necessary." K. calls this a "melancholy opinion": it holds that the order of the world is based upon a lie. This Joseph K. says "in conclusion," but Kafka sees to it that it is "not his final judgment." "The simple story had lost its clear outline, he wanted to put it out of his mind and the priest, who now showed great delicacy of feeling, suffered him to do so and accepted his comment in silence, although undoubtedly he did not agree with it."

Kafka's art of conclusively stating inconclusiveness is unsurpassed and probably insurpassable, and unbreachable seem the fortifications he builds to protect the mystery from the onslaughts of dogma, opinion, or conviction. Merely to protect the mystery from them? No, to deprive dogmas, opinions, and convictions of the air they need for breathing. And if they were

as firm as rocks they would become like the sand of the desert, blown hither and thither by the wind and blinding even the most determined believer. Yet there is one certainty that is left untouched by the parable as well as by the whole book; the Law exists and Joseph K. must have most terribly offended it, for he is executed in the end with a double-edged—yes, double-edged—butcher's knife that is thrust into his heart and turned there twice. Three years before Kafka began to write *The Trial,* he had, on November 11, 1911, entered in his diary: "This morning, once again after a long time, I took pleasure in imagining that a knife was being turned in my heart," and as late as 1921 (October 20) he recorded a dream in which there was " . . . happiness . . . in the fact that I welcomed so freely, with such conviction and such joy, the punishment when it came." But there is no joy in *this* punishment; it comes to Joseph K. in a deserted quarry on the periphery of the city, while the casements of a window on the top floor of a neighboring house fly open and a human figure stretches his hands out toward the scene of horror. The questions, evoked by this apparition and presumably issuing from Joseph K.'s mind, might be taken to point toward a miscarriage of justice: who was the person at the window? "A friend? A good man? . . . Someone who wanted to help? Was it one person only? Was it mankind?" The friendliest impulses of mankind, then, may well be working against the Court's administration of justice and may side with its unhappy victim. But, on the other hand, the gestures of the figure up there might be mere projections of K.'s will to live, rising up in vain against the secret logic of the case, this logic being unshakable—and yet, we read—"it cannot withstand a man who wants to go on living."

Alas, it can, and Joseph K. dies "like a dog!" These are his last words; and if the reader's terrified revulsion leaves him capable of reflecting, he might find them somewhat inappropriate. For this is not how dogs are killed. Rather does it resemble the matador's way of killing the bull; and although no perfect metaphor is perfectly fitting, we come a little closer to it by remembering the episode with the painter Titorelli, the amiable charlatan and lover of children, confidant of Court officials and their only licensed portraitist, who adorns his portraits of the judges with the allegorical figure of Justice in a kind of personal union with the winged and dynamic goddess of victory. "Not a very good combination," says K. "Justice must stand still, or else the scales will waver, and a just verdict will become impossible." But still worse, after a few more strokes of Titorelli's crayon there emerges, dominating the previous image, the goddess of the hunt. But this is in blatant contradiction to what one of the warders, who come to arrest Joseph K., says of the Court: its officials "never go hunting for guilt in the populace but are drawn toward the guilty . . . and must send out us warders."

There is no end to such contradictions and ambiguities in *The Trial.* No end: the novel was doomed to remain a fragment and, as a novel, had to fail, even though Kafka did write the final chapter. As a conclusion to whatever might have been the whole work, it too is a failure, despite its superbly sustained, quietly sensational tone of narration, which is a little reminiscent of the last pages of Stendhal's *Le Rouge et le noir.* It fails in aesthetic and—which in this case is the same—ethical logic. For a nightmare will not become a novel even if it is pursued and elaborated through episode after episode. And an ending, unquestionable in its stark finality, is aesthetically and ethically offensive if it is supported only by a sequence of arbitrarily protractile scenes, all showing a presumed culprit who, not knowing the nature of his guilt, helplessly casts about for help; or the sordidness and corruption of the judiciary order (at least in its lower echelon, and we come to know only this); or the clownish irresponsibility of those who claim to be able to assist the accused in his desperate struggle for acquittal. What *is* his guilt? What *is* the Law?

It is the secret of Kafka's art almost to silence such questions. They are laughed out of court, as it were, by demons mischievously squatting in the empty spaces between the questions and the sought-for answers. Boorish curiosity in the company of tragic subtleties! And do such questions not miss the very point of *The Trial*? Yet, such is the mechanism of the moral and aesthetic sensibility that even the most accomplished description of a death sentence carried out with studied violence by two men looking like "tenth-rate old actors"—"What theatre are you playing at?" K. asks them—must affect us, in the absence of any answers to those questions, like the indiscretion of a sadistically bad dream told in public. (pp. 71-82)

> *Erich Heller, in his* Franz Kafka, *edited by Frank Kermode, 1975. Reprint by Princeton University Press, 1982, 140 p.*

WALTER H. SOKEL (essay date 1976)

[*Sokel is an Austrian-born American educator and critic specializing in German literature and the writings of Franz Kafka. In the following excerpt, Sokel analyzes the conflict between what he terms the "Oedipal" view of* The Trial, *which finds Joseph K.'s guilt a reflection of Kafka's self-condemnation for leading an unworthy life, and the "existentialist" view, in which Joseph K.'s undefined guilt serves as the impetus for his free investigation into its meaning.*]

The crucial circumstance about K.'s trial is the fact that the charge against him is never specified. The existence of a guilt—some guilt—is assumed, but its nature is left undefined and remains unknown both to the protagonist and to the reader. The conclusion is often drawn that this kind of unspecified guilt corresponds to the theological concept of original sin. However, the doctrine of original sin holds everyone guilty; this does not seem to be the case with K.'s court. The court "arrests" only some persons, while many others are free. Manager and Deputy Manager of the bank where K. works, his landlady, Fräulein Bürstner, the manufacturer in Chapter Seven, K.'s uncle and girl cousin—they all are free of the accusation which has befallen only some characters in the work. Thus the analogy between K.'s guilt and original sin does not get us very far.

What else can unspecified guilt indicate? One possibility is that it implies the accused's guilt is his whole way of life at the time of his arrest. Such guilt cannot be specified because it is total. Unlike original sin, it is a particular kind of life, the one lived by K., that is equated with guilt. It is the existence of a representative bourgeois, atypical only on account of his extreme representativeness, most of whose relationships before his arrest are based on the cash nexus or on a superficial need for diversion. The little we can learn about the other defendants does not contradict the inference that K.'s type of existence is considered guilt.

If the guilt of the accused is his whole life, his punishment can only be death. This view is expressed by K.'s uncle when he says that having such a trial amounts to having lost it, and that in turn amounts to being erased. I would call this view the Oedipal view of the trial. In his most coherent attempt at an autobiography, the famous **"Letter to his Father,"** Kafka

presented his own life in terms closely corresponding to the Freudian Oedipus conflict. A father incomparably stronger than the son aroused infinite guilt in him and burdened him with the conviction that he lived a life totally unworthy, or nearly so, when judged in the light of his father's standards and example. No matter what Franz would or would not do, he was guilty: beginning with his totally inadequate body, his whole existence, next to his father's, was guilt. In Kafka's early tale, **"The Judgment,"** a father condemns his son to die, in *Metamorphosis* he mortally wounds him with an apple, in *America* he brutally exiles him into a highly dangerous and uncertain fate. In *The Trial,* written two years after these works, the situation is abstracted from the family context, of which only remnants, such as K.'s uncle and mother, are left. The son has become the accused and the father has been generalized, depersonalized, and elevated into an accusing court. But the basic structure is the same as the one articulated in Kafka's **"Letter to his Father"** and the earlier family tales. (pp. 1-2)

[The] inference which lies at the bottom of the Oedipal view—that K.'s guilt is his life—is not the only possible inference to be drawn from an accusation left unspecified. An undefined guilt may also imply that the accused has to discover what his guilt is. From this perspective, the arrest is the alerting of the accused, and his trial is the invitation to discover himself in his search for his guilt. "Not to show you what is wrong with you but that something is wrong with you," so runs one of Kafka's aphorisms that seems like a commentary on this view of guilt in K.'s trial. Many details point to the structure of *The Trial* as a travelogue, an aborted voyage of discovery. It is no coincidence that the first member of the court to appear to K. seems to be wearing travelling clothes, and that K., in pursuing his trial, continuously discovers unknown locales, unfamiliar districts, unsuspected circumstances, etc. According to this inference, the trial should be considered a process of exploration and questioning. The double meaning of the German title, *Der Prozess,* meaning both trial and process, would lend support to the view that the trial is, or should be, the process of the discovery of K.'s guilt. (pp. 3-4)

The obvious policy of the court is to allow K. to reveal himself by this freedom to choose. This existential policy differs markedly from the Oedipal strategy of breaking the self and its will. It tends to make K. the free arbiter of his fate. There is, within the court system itself, a conflict between the two views of the trial. This conflict is explicitly stated by the law student Berthold who severely criticizes the examining judge for allowing K. "to run around so free." He calls it a "mistake," about which he had complained to the judge. "Between the interrogations at least, [K.] should have been held captive in his room." The student's view of K.'s trial conforms to the Oedipal pattern of Kafka's earlier story, *Metamorphosis,* in which Gregor's family keeps him prisoner in his room. The student would make confinement the policy towards the arrested. He would not seek K.'s free commitment, but his captivity, the repression of his ego, the reduction of his vital capacities, a harsh and severe education towards inwardness, and ultimately a preparation for the grave. The student's policy would conform to the treatment accorded to the prisoners in **"In the Penal Colony,"** in that golden age of the Old Commander's rule which the Officer so nostalgically evokes. The plot of **"In the Penal Colony"** shows the decline and breakdown of this older system. Begun shortly before and continued after **"In the Penal Colony,"** *The Trial* presents the older system, as desired by the student, countermanded and superseded by the judge's new policy of physical freedom for the accused, which changes the whole concept of the trial from an Oedipal to an existential intent. For the student, the new policy, as represented by the judge, is "incomprehensible."

We are dealing, in *The Trial,* with two contrasting layers of intention, which explains a good deal of the particular obscurity and ambiguity of this novel, which is extreme even for Kafka's opus. This duality conforms to Kafka's development, which makes *The Trial,* like **"In the Penal Colony,"** a work of transition and evolution from the harsh Oedipal law of the family tales of 1912 to the ironic existentialism of his late phase, as represented by *The Castle,* **"A Hunger-Artist"** and **"Investigations of a Dog."** *The Trial* shows a primitive layer, expressed by the lower court organs—the warders and the student—advocating physical coercion, being contravened by the higher and official law of the court, enunciated and practised by the Inspector and the Examining Judge, which insists on the accused's freedom to commit himself to his trial. In composing *The Trial* Kafka made the Oedipal law of *Metamorphosis* and the penal machine be literally superseded by the new law of *The Trial* as a series of existential decisions. The structure of self-alienation is very similar to that of *Metamorphosis,* but the difference is even more significant. In *Metamorphosis* Gregor is physically forced into his alienation before the action starts. Extremely limited options remain to him. But in *The Trial,* the Inspector expressly states that the arrest only serves the function of "informing" Josef K. of his condition and seeing "how he has received it," leaving him the freedom to continue his previous life, and to neglect his trial or to concentrate on it, as he chooses. This difference in intent makes for a difference in form between the two works. The fatalistic realism of *Metamorphosis* in which the initial event inexorably determines the outcome, in a tight plot, gives way, in *The Trial,* to a loose sequence of scenes reminiscent of old morality plays. In these, the protagonist has to choose between several options. *The Trial* is not, like Gregor Samsa's metamorphosis, a determining condition from the start. It is a series of challenges. The protagonist's reactions to or evasions of them determine the structure. This structure corresponds to the existential policy of the court. (pp. 6-7)

Titorelli reveals . . . [the] juxtaposition of the existential and the Oedipal view of the trial. Titorelli makes it clear to K. that real acquittal can never be obtained through helpers, but must be based solely upon the defendant's innocence. Innocence is an inner certainty which is not in need of external confirmation. Where innocence is involved, acquittal flows naturally from it, and judges cannot be influenced. But real acquittals lie outside experience. They are rumoured from ancient legends and no proof exists of their attainability. In fact, holding out for real acquittal is an enormous risk precisely because of the Oedipal nature of the lower court, which is the only one accessible to empirical experience. For Titorelli the actual court—in contrast to the unknown and unknowable Highest Court, which alone has the power to acquit—has the appearance of a merciless Oedipal power of horrifyingly wrathful divinity. Like the penal colony under the Old Commander, the known court takes guilt for granted in any accused. Never can it be dissuaded from its conviction of guilt. "If I paint all the judges in a row here on a canvas," says Titorelli to K., "and you'll defend yourself before this canvas, you will be more successful than if you stand before the real court." Faced with such a court, the dream of gaining real acquittal can only be a wish for suicide or else an overwhelmingly strong and venturesome faith of the self in itself. Like the entrance into the law, in the legend of the priest, it can only be the kind of faith that would bear

out Kafka's dictum, "Believing means: to liberate the indestructible in oneself, or better: to liberate oneself, or still better: to be indestructible, or better: to be." K.'s way of going about his trial, therefore, appears ironic from Titorelli's perspective, because K. says he is innocent and yet searches for helpers in his trial.

Titorelli's comments on the court show the same contradiction in its programme as is revealed by the lawyer's intimations. Titorelli admits the possibility of a defendant's innocence and complete acquittal. This possibility conflicts flagrantly with the guilty verdict for every accused which Titorelli assumes with certainty on the basis of his own and all known experience with the court. However, if the trial is interpreted as a choice between one's faith regardless of consequences, and precautions for one's survival, the contradiction falls away. For then the defendant is free to commit himself or not to commit himself to his faith in himself. In these terms innocence appears as a resolve. It is a choice of being—of being innocent. Such a choice of the self precludes, of course, the usefulness of any helpers.

When K. considers dismissing his lawyer and making his plea by himself, he seems to be veering towards such a course. He decides never to admit guilt under any circumstances. Yet this is only an apparent convergence between K.'s plan and the court's programme. For his refusal to admit guilt would not be at all the same as the innocence of which Titorelli speaks. Refusal to admit guilt would be a device, a strategy in a struggle with the court; unlike innocence it would not be a commitment to be.

However, according to Titorelli, innocence and real acquittal are legendary exceptions to the rule of human reality. For the real, i.e., the regular case, Titorelli recommends two other courses—ostensible acquittal and indefinite procrastination. The assumptions on which these two possibilities rest are diametrically opposed to the assumptions of innocence. For them guilt or innocence is not the issue. In relation to these options, the trial is conceived as an attack upon the accused against which he has to protect himself for his survival. Therefore, helpers, compromises, and subterfuges are necessary as a matter of course.

Thus there issue from Titorelli two mutually contradictory concepts of the trial—the trial as self-choosing and the trial as self-defence. One is concerned with being, the other with surviving. The former is the existential, the latter the Oedipal view.

While the existential interpretation always pertains to official and explicit court policy, ascribed to the unseen high court, the Oedipal view is based upon the weaknesses and limitations of the lower judges. According to Titorelli's advice, the existential possibility, real acquittal, can issue only from the highest court, while the subterfuges of ostensible acquittal and procrastination exist by virtue of the corruptibility of the lower court members. In all instances, the existential meaning of the trial relates to the genuine and pure essence of the court whereas deviations and corruptions on the lower levels support the pattern of an Oedipal struggle.

This by no means invalidates the reality and seriousness of the Oedipal aspect of the trial. The trial operates on two levels at once, and both are necessary to an understanding of it. The existential aspect of court policy as described by the lawyer can, for instance, easily be interpreted as an extreme of Oedipal intimidation. The defendant is to be isolated and deprived of all human fellowship and comfort in order to be more quickly destroyed. The text certainly allows for such a reading.

This co-existence of two opposed levels of meaning, however, intensifies the protagonist's necessity to choose between different interpretations of his situation. Interpretation must precede choice as choice must precede action. Interpretation is a careful weighing of the various meanings implied in a situation. One of these the protagonist has to choose in order to act. Thus his reading of his situation must be the antecedent of his acting on it. K.'s whole trial, from the moment of his awakening, is a single challenge to him to read, and interpret, and then to act. K.'s arresting warder, Willem, reads a book when K. first sees him. This sign seems to tell K. that he is asked to read. Both warders and the Inspector explicitly admonish K. to listen more and to talk less. They ask him to concentrate and to reflect, they advise him not to jump to hasty conclusions, and warn him that great efforts are in store for him. All that points to the fact that he will be asked to find the meaning of his trial by himself. It is in the same vein when we hear Frau Grubach refer to K.'s arrest as "something scholarly . . . which does not have to be understood," i.e., for which there does not seem to exist a meaning prepared for the accused. Huld by implication, and Titorelli explicitly, make clear to K. that it is he who has to choose what meaning he will give to his trial by choosing a course of action from the several possibilities outlined to him. Basically the choice boils down to one of two interpretations—the existential and the Oedipal—the choice of treating his trial as a commitment to self-exploration or as a struggle in self-defence. Both are possible and both are applicable according to Titorelli. The main point is the choice itself. Its urgency cannot be overlooked in Titorelli's insistent admonitions to K. to make his choice soon. Regardless of what it will be, the choice itself must not be deferred.

This necessity to choose culminates in the necessity to interpret with which the prison chaplain confronts K. It is no accident that the trial culminates in a parable to which the listener, K., seems to be called upon to supply the key and make the application to his own case. The legend of the doorkeeper who stands before the law abstracts the challenge which the trial itself represents.

The priest tells K. the legend of the doorkeeper as an illustration of K.'s delusion in regard to the court. This delusion is explicitly stated in the text of the parable. At the end of his life, the man from the country asks why no one else has come to ask for the entrance, although everyone strives to enter the law. The doorkeeper answers that this entrance was destined for this man alone. The man's delusion consisted in the belief that entrance into the law is something universal.

This delusion is implicit in the parable from the beginning. It is so strong that it easily escapes the reader because it is built into the man's perspective, which the reader, like K., tends to share. The delusion is implied in the man's initial reaction to finding the doorkeeper blocking his way. The text says the man has "not expected such difficulties," for he assumes "that the law is supposed to be accessible at any time." The man, in other words, has come with the expectation that entrance into the law is an automatic right available to everyone and at all times. To be sure, he does ask for permission to enter, but assumes that the permission will be a formality.

The doorkeeper says that he cannot allow the man to enter "now." The word is crucial because it is intimately tied to the man's expectation that the law would be open at any time. The

doorkeeper's "not now" proves this expectation is the man's primary illusion. The implication in his answer is this: At the moment of his asking for permission the man is not allowed to enter. Left open is the possibility that he might be able to enter if and when he does not ask for permission. This implication becomes explicit almost immediately. The doorkeeper suddenly steps aside and laughingly invites the man to go in despite his prohibition. Now "the door," the text tells us, "stands open as always." That is, no physical force whatsoever prevents the man from going in. The doorkeeper underlines the man's freedom by his jocular invitation. To be sure, in the same breath, he warns him of the frightening appearance of further doorkeepers inside.

Now there is nothing in the man's way except his fear. It is not the doorkeeper, but the man's fear that keeps him from entering. His desire for the law is great, but his fear is greater. To enter would involve a grave risk. The man decides not to take this risk. Intimidated by the doorkeeper's words and looks, he prefers to wait for permission. And this permission never comes.

The timing is a decisive key to the understanding of the parable. Entrance into the law is possible only at a definite, unique moment, which the man allows to pass by unused. The unique moment is linked to the unique individual for whom alone this entrance is destined. Uniqueness of moment and uniqueness of person are united in the free decision that is necessary to enter the law. No one else can make the man's entrance possible since it is *his* alone, and the one single moment for it must be seized by him who is to enter. If the doorkeeper were to grant the entrance, it would not be the man's entrance. It would be a gift bestowed on him by another or it would be a general right belonging to anyone and everyone. Furthermore, the entrance can truly belong to the man alone only if it results from his own free decision. Given the absolutely individual nature of the entrance, the man must lose it from the moment he fails to choose it. We are reminded of Kierkegaard's *Fear and Trembling* in which the individual's relation to the Absolute—in terms of Kafka's parable "the law," i.e., that which everyone strives for—can only be individual, i.e., completely and utterly unique.

The function of the doorkeeper as a figure of denial is necessary for the existential meaning of the parable. The obstacle is essential to the quest. Significantly the text does not begin with the man, but with the doorkeeper standing in front of the entrance. If there were no doorkeeper, the entrance would be a simple wish fulfilment. Only by overcoming difficult resistances can the entrance become the man's entrance. For that, the nay-saying authority is necessary. This explains the priest's later remark that one does not have to accept everything the doorkeeper says as true, but only as necessary. Whether there really are such horrible doorkeepers inside the law, i.e., the truth, is impossible to ascertain. However, the fear aroused by them is necessary to make the entrance a true decision.

With his challenge to the man to try the entrance in the face of possibly terrifying odds, the doorkeeper imposes the existential meaning on the parable. For he burdens the man with the necessity of making a decision which will determine his further existence. His choice will reveal what he is. Like Heidegger's *Dasein*, Sartre's *réalité humaine,* and Kierkegaard's eternal self, the man before the law creates himself by his choice. He is free to put his passion for the law above his life, which he would risk if the inner doorkeepers were really what the doorkeeper says they are. But at the same time, he is also free to place his life above the law and wait. In fact, he would even be free to leave his quest altogether and go home. Thus the doorkeeper makes the man choose himself before our very eyes. And the man, carefully deliberating, does make his choice. Among his three possible existences he chooses himself as one who rejects his freedom and waits for the permission of another. He has chosen himself for all his life as a dependent and supplicant and thereby literally cheated himself of his true existence, his authentic life.

The man from the country is K.'s mirror image. K. too has decided to seek his law, i.e., his trial, by choosing the court over the yacht. But, like the man from the country, he then refuses to accept the paradox of the self-determined entrance. He wants the court, *his* doorkeeper, to relieve him of his own self-discovery and hand him his acquittal, or else take the blame for murdering him. Listening to the parable, K. mistakes the Kierkegaardian paradox of a law of freedom for an authority figure's dirty trick. He takes an Oedipal view of the doorkeeper, as he does of his trial. The doorkeeper appears to him as an oppressive deceiver, withholding and denying the man's right to enter. K. completely ignores the intent of the law, the uniquely personal nature of the entrance into this law, even though the parable itself had explained it to him.

Thus the doorkeeper legend illustrates K.'s delusion in regard to the court. K. views his trial as an unjust attack by illegitimate power figures. He misunderstands the fact that the trial is his own choice, in which acquittal cannot come from another, even as the doorkeeper cannot give the man an entrance that belongs to the man alone. K. experiences his trial as a fight inflicted upon him by a vicious antagonist, and therefore he looks for aid. Although he does not go as far as Block or the man from the country in enslaving himself to helpers, he cannot see his way without them, either. The parable "Before the Law," like the degrading spectacle staged by K.'s lawyer and Merchant Block, illustrates the priest's warning to him, "You are looking too hard for the help of others . . . Don't you realize that it is not the true help?" But K. fails to connect the priest's clear warning with the "legend" that illustrates it. Otherwise he would be able to see that it is not the doorkeeper's malice, but the man's fearful dependence that cheats him of his entrance into the law.

It is K.'s Oedipal perspective that blocks his understanding of both the parable and his own trial. He sees the court as a gang of corrupt lechers who, if a woman is shown to them, "would overrun the bench and the defendant to get there in time." The image drastically conveys the Oedipal sense of the trial in which a feeble defendant is literally victimized by the sex drive of his judges. This view seems to appal the priest, as though it were not only blasphemous, but a most dangerous misapprehension. He shouts at K., "Can't you see two steps ahead?" Yet, even though the priest seems to consider it a fatal blindness, K.'s experiences in the novel do not contradict his Oedipal view. The priest himself contributes to the Oedipal atmosphere of *The Trial* when he singles out the help of women as a particularly illusory form of help. Here we come up once more against the two meanings of the trial as, on the one hand, an Oedipal assault upon the defendant's male adulthood and ego, and on the other, an existential challenge to choose and define oneself. K. himself has to find his own interpretation as the man has to find his own entrance into the law.

Hermeneutics, or the art of choosing the appropriate understanding of a text, and the trial, or the process of choosing the appropriate reaction to one's condition, are forms of one an-

other. This explains the crucial importance of the priest's observation on hermeneutics in his discussion with K., "I only show you the current opinions," he says to K. "You must not pay too much attention to opinions. The text is unchangeable and its interpretations are often only expressions of despair over that fact." In the context of the parable, this remark is not an absolute discouragement of the hermeneutic attempt, as it is usually interpreted, but the opposite, a forceful suggestion of the necessity to find one's own interpretation. In his discussion of the legend, the priest behaves like a careful New Critic, restraining a hasty student from identifying the text's meaning with the protagonist's point of view. He always seeks to bring K. back to the text and points out the need to be faithful to the literal wording. Furthermore, although he shows all sorts of interpretations, he never offers his own, or any definitive one. K. himself has to find *his* interpretation, just as the man from the country has to find *his* entrance into the law. Text and doorkeeper parallel each other. The unchangeable text stubbornly retains its ambiguities and withholds its meaning, functioning like the doorkeeper who withholds permission.

As we have seen, interpretation is the necessary first step in the process of deciding on a course of action. The parable tells of a man who has to interpret the doorkeeper's words and gestures. He has to weigh one meaning—the invitation to go in—against another which contradicts it. To which should he give preference? He has to choose his interpretation before he can decide his action. He has to choose between his own desire for entrance and his fear of the possible consequences. In fact, there is no way for the man to discover the true meaning of the doorkeeper prior to his own action. Only by attempting the entrance can the man find out the truth or falsehood of the doorkeeper's statements and the truth about the law. Before he can understand doorkeeper and law, the man must reveal himself by his choice of action. (pp. 11-18)

Beyond K., and beyond his creator, the court reaches out to the parable's reader—ourselves. Like the man before the door, the reader assumes that a definitive entrance into the law, or into the text, is to be offered by the proper authority, and he assumes that this entrance is general and relatively easy to obtain—one and the same door for every seeker, one and the same meaning for every reader. But the text resists the attempt at unambiguous understanding. The events depicted and the statements perceived remain contradictory. K.'s preliminary interrogation takes place in Fräulein Bürstner's room. Is the meaning of this to punish K. for his desire for the girl? Or is it the opposite, a signal drawing him to a more personal form of eros, which his weekly visits to Elsa have drowned in routine? There is no answer given, only the unchangeably ambiguous text. But the open question challenges us, as it challenges K. There does not seem a way to meaning except by a choice entailing the risk of error. K.'s guilt remains impenetrable because the only access to it is interpretation, which is risk, instead of revelation, which gives certainty. (p. 21)

> *Walter H. Sokel, "The Programme of K.'s Court: Oedipal and Existential Meanings of 'The Trial',"* in On Kafka: Semi-Centenary Perspectives, *edited by Franz Kuna, Barnes & Noble Books, 1976, pp. 1-21.*

DAVID I. GROSSVOGEL   (essay date 1979)

[*In the following excerpt, Grossvogel contends that* The Trial *produces a sense of mystery and provokes thought because in it*

Kafka created a fictional world that draws attention to its artificiality.]

A century after Poe, what might have been his private nightmares have become considerably less private. Much of the century's writing assumes that the reader feels less comfortable in a world that seems more alien even as it is better known. When Kafka takes his turn as chronicler, he does not describe the aberration of a single consciousness; rather, he describes the aberration of a world that mocks the obdurate sanity of a single consciousness. The reader recognizes Kafka's strange world in his own familiar malaise, but that very familiarity is strange—it is unable to allay the reader's sense of estrangement. Evolution from the private world of Poe to the public world of Kafka suggests that the specialized probing of the psychoanalyst has become less necessary for an understanding of the author behind his text: Kafka is closer to his reader by virtue of what has happened to that reader since Poe. The affinities between author and private awareness, which the fiction of Poe may well mask for the lay reader, appear on the surface of Kafka's text. Kafka has no story to tell; he conveys a mood, an anxiety—*his* anxiety. He does not comment on the mystery: he and his book are a part of it. . . . When Kafka contrives a text that discloses Kafka rather than a fiction, he shows again that the impossibility of knowing is within the one who wants to know. . . . [The] reader reads himself in the man writing because even after the veil of Kafka's fiction has been thinned into evanescence, the mystery is still not disclosed—only the author stands revealed as another kind of text to be deciphered within the unending process of reading.

Blanchot, who is not necessarily in disagreement with this "reading" of Kafka, begins nevertheless with a challenge: since the art of writing creates at best a surrogate self, are we not indulging in loose talk when we substitute the man writing for his text? How can I write "I am unhappy," asks Blanchot, without turning misery into *calculation* through the contrivance of a text that *states* my misery? An answer (though not quite the one Blanchot proposes) is that a wholly impersonal contrivance by the author is just as impossible. The least personal statement—the most fictional—is an idiosyncrasy: the voice of the writer is in his words whatever those words say. Blanchot, who concludes that writing can only sham life, also concludes that writing is impossible: the writer's voice, as that voice, cannot sham. And Kafka writes stories whose only subject is Kafka.

The paradox begs the question of Kafka's intent; Kafka is not just an anxious man transcribing an anxiety: no act of transcription is innocent. However much the man Kafka is caught up in his act of transcription, that transcription remains a conscious strategy that is distinct from the intimate sense that impels it. That strategy is affected by the strange persistence of the reader's hope—the reader's desire for his text to have a meaning (that is to say an *end*) that corresponds to his need for his world to have a meaning, to *signify*. The modern reader appears to remain as thralled by his expectation as did previous readers who could assume more legitimately that the book might finally be *closed* and its truth contained, though so much of modern fiction subverts the possibility of closure, resists the possibility of a metaphysical assertion even within the boundaries provided by the physical space of the text.

The success of that strategy can be seen in *The Trial*, a text about the confusion of critics and other readers that adroitly confuses critics and other readers. *The Trial*'s story (before Kafka finally wears out the veil of the story) looks like those of the most fraudulent, and hence the most comforting, of fictional appropriations of mystery—the mystery story. Even when his predicament cries out for K. to ask "why?" he insists on asking, as any ordinary detective might, "where?" or "who?": condemned by a perverse metaphysics, the victim argues all aspects of his case except the metaphysical. [This] refusal to internalize is necessary for the dissemination of the "unheimliche" ["the uncanny"]: Kafka is conjuring not a metaphysics, but its climate.

That climate results from a world described as a surface (the resistance to interiorization begins in this kind of description): it is a staged, artificial, but generally nonsymbolic world; it has the partially comic, partially frightening rigidity of any nonhuman imitation of life. The staged artificiality suggests a self-consciousness, the felt presence of an observer. "One fine morning," when the day begins as innocuously as any other for K., he notes among many familiar reminders "the old lady opposite, who seemed to be peering at him with a curiosity unusual even for her." K.'s angered exclamation at the presence of the warders confirms their being and their presence as a dominative intrusion: "It occurred to him at once that he should not have said this aloud and that by doing so he had in a way admitted the stranger's right to superintend his actions." The strangeness of K.'s circumstances results from his attempt to enact everyday gestures on what is becoming more and more definitely a stage: "The old woman, who with truly senile inquisitiveness had moved along the window exactly opposite, in order to go on seeing all that could be seen." "At the other side of the street he could still see the old woman, who had now dragged to the window an even older man, whom she was holding round the waist." "In the window over the way the two old creatures were again stationed, but they had enlarged their party, for behind them, towering head and shoulders above them, stood a man."

K.'s sense that the gaze of another is on him represents largely his altered perception of the world around him; he now subjects what would be otherwise an unperceived continuation in his existence to the disjunction of analysis so that what should seem natural appears to be contrived, as when he hears the intimate talk between Leni and Block: "K. had the feeling that he was listening to a well-rehearsed dialogue which had been often repeated and would be often repeated." Only very occasionally does the strangeness of this staging derive from an actual alteration of K.'s world, as when the warders first appear in his bedroom, or when, walking along a hall in his bank, K. discovers those same warders being whipped in a closet.

Because the event is staged, it *contains* the actor and limits him. The metaphysical constraint is forever being echoed in the comic reductiveness of functional gestures that have become problematic—as when K. tries to hurry his loud and indiscreet uncle out of the bank: "'I thought,' said K., taking his uncle's arm to keep him from standing still, 'that you attach even less importance to this business than I do, and now you are taking it so seriously.' 'Joseph!' cried his uncle, trying to get his arm free so as to be able to stand still, only K. would not let him, 'you're quite changed'." But the implications of this comic constraint extend into the implication of a menace: any attempt at a disengagement from this constraint, however successful the attempt appears to be, leads only to further constraint. Direct confrontation of the impediment may cause it to recede, not to disappear:

> "Here's a fine crowd of spectators!" cried K. in a
> loud voice to the Inspector, pointing at them with his

finger. ''Go away,'' he shouted across. The three of them immediately retreated a few steps, the two ancients actually took cover behind the younger man, who shielded them with his massive body and to judge from the movements of his lips was saying something which, owing to the distance, could not be distinguished. Yet they did not remove themselves altogether, but seemed to be waiting for the chance to return to the window again unobserved.

The futility of even modest gestures to achieve an intended purpose demonstrates through comic reduction the metaphysical verdict of the Court that Titorelli spells out for K.: he is ''provisionally free''; definite acquittal is out of the question; only the possibilities of ostensible acquittal and indefinite postponement can sustain the balance of hope and frustration that define the victim once he has begun to question his circumstances.

The comic quality of this artificial world eventually turns into what it was all along—the horror of inhuman motion, a supreme illogicality resulting from the only logic that is possible: somewhat in the manner of Munch's cry frozen within the silence of his canvas, Kafka arrests within the frieze of his denouement K. moving at an ever accelerated pace, and finally at a run, to his own death. What accounts for the comic and the horror is the man at the center, K., not simply an initial but an anthropocentric obduracy, the persistent belief in a world that cannot be subverted ''one fine morning'' by agents of the unknown; a world in which a sense of boundaries and control makes the question ''where?'' possible and gives it meaning—along with all other aspects of existence. K. is more than the evidence that Kafka assumes the same expectations in his readers: K. is the encouragement for them to persist, as does K., in those expectations. Kafka's whole strategy of disquietude depends on his ability to counterstate the obdurate normalcy of K. and of a reader who, like K., obdurately requires that normalcy. Kafka thus presents and subverts simultaneously the reassuring surfaces of a familiar world. Henry Sussman [see Additional Bibliography] notes that this duality reaches the heights of irony in K. himself, whose everyday existence absorbs within its unvarying pattern the magnitude of the abnormalcy that has invaded it: K. goes as far as to abet the conspiracy of which he is a victim whenever he can. K.'s outburst to Frau Grubach (an exclamation later reinterpreted by Groucho Marx) is a comic synopsis of the duality that acknowledges his victimization even as he makes an attempt at self-assertion by assuming the point of view of the victimizers: '''Respectable!' cried K., through the chink in the door; 'if you want to keep your house respectable you'll have to begin by giving me notice'.'' (pp. 148-53)

What marks [Kafka] as a modern author is his refusal to let the reader find refuge within that last perimeter of his control—the book. Like Borges or Poe, Kafka replaces the *idea* of an alien world with the objective *evidence* of a text. This inhibiting and contrived world is, after all, a real book that rehearses, within the one who wants to know, the impossibility of fully knowing. The reader cannot *contain* Kafka's text even though it presents itself as the form (the mystery story) that most readily contains mystery.

The evidence of the text is confirmed by the central image: the Law is a world of books; K. is convinced that if he could read them, he would win his case—possession of the Word being, perhaps, less problematic than possession of an other: K. responds to the sexual blandishments of the Court usher's wife in order to possess the books that are in the library of the Law

(only to find in their stead, as we have seen, further instances of an unappealing and frustrating sexuality). These books are not, of course, available to K.: those behind whom the Law hides are the sole repositories of a textual secret. The Examining Magistrate has, as his only distinguishing prop, a single notebook:

> But the Examining Magistrate did not seem to worry, he sat quite comfortably in his chair and after a few final words to the man behind him took up a small notebook, the only object lying on the table. It was like an ancient school exercise-book, grown dog-eared from much thumbing. ''Well then,'' said the Examining Magistrate turning over the leaves and addressing K. with an air of authority, ''you are a house painter?''

Writing is a lingering activity, even within the deserted Court offices: ''Some of the offices were not properly boarded off from the passage but had an open frontage of wooden rails, reaching, however, to the roof, through which a little light penetrated and through which one could see a few officials as well, some writing at their desks.'' Because he is a part of the Court, Titorelli is the scribe of a tradition, even though he is a painter. Because he uses a different language, he *paints* Court legends:

> [W]e have only legendary accounts of ancient cases. These legends certainly provide instances of acquittal; actually the majority of them are about acquittals, they can be believed, but they cannot be proved. All the same, they shouldn't be entirely left out of account, they must have an element of truth in them, and besides they are very beautiful. I myself have painted several pictures founded on such legends.

What Titorelli's paintings have in common with other texts that represent the Law is that they cannot be grasped, that they possess no efficacy, no firm or reliable substance; like the very text given the reader, the texts of the Law are adequate only to sustain for a while the hope of the one who inquires of them, not to reward that hope.

But texts persist in the persistence of the decipherer's hope of possessing his text: one of the many ways K. is tempted to join the world of his persecutors is by turning into a writer of his own script—creating the arcane document that will *stand for him*:

> The thought of his case never left him now. He had often considered whether it would not be better to draw up a written defense and hand it in to the Court. In this defense he would give a short account of his life, and when he came to an event of any importance explain for what reasons he had acted as he did, intimate whether he approved or condemned his way of action in retrospect, and adduce grounds for the condemnation or approval. The advantages of such a written defense, as compared with the mere advocacy of a lawyer who himself was not impeccable, were undoubted.

Writing would represent a new aspect of the same quest for K.: it would be a way for the patient reader, which the victim—K. or Block—has already become, to seize his text, instead of being reduced, like Kafka's own reader, to read those reading (writing), unable as he is to read the text those readers read (or write).

Whatever object the quest may posit, through whatever subterfuge, that object remains elusive. The word *God* is absent from Kafka's fiction, but the Jewish mystical tradition. . .equates for Kafka the impossible revelation and the revelatory letter: it is within scripting signs that the unknowable shows and conceals itself. The word, as mystical mediator, as initiate, is caught up in the dialectical process that affects the way in which all initiates are perceived: it can only state its failure to reveal but in so doing is suffused with intimations of the mystery it has attempted. The Kabalah believes in the occult meaning of the letter, the presence of God in the sign of His word: instead of making God apprehensible, this presence makes the letter awesome. We have noted in our reading of Borges how, in time, this awesome signifier becomes little more than an amulet, a container suggesting a reversal of the original denial by offering as *possible* the appropriation of a final and absolute mystery. But a sacredness attaches to even the ineffectual amulet (it is for that reason that no amulet is wholly ineffectual).

In Kafka's fiction, the missing term *God* is replaced by His letter, the Law, an ironically scripted form of the absolute, in the same way as the letter of this text is informed by the presence of its own *deus absconditus*—Kafka. "Everyone strives to attain the Law": K.'s hope, and the reader's, are sustained by an awareness—the importance of the part of themselves that is concealed by the fiction of their text. For both, the integument of the mystery that cannot be uttered (as cannot be uttered the name of God) will be the *parable*, the traditional reduction of that mystery as allegorical fiction.

The parable, a mode in which Kafka showed an abiding interest, acknowledges intellectual slippage, a failure of the mind to apprehend its object. The parable is a *substitute*, a simile. The German word *Gleichnis* also means simile; its root, *gleich*, evidences the perplexity of knowing: it means both *same* and *resembling*—that is to say, identical and different. It is not improbable that Kafka favored the parable because he was most intent on demonstrating this slippage, on making the reader experience the impossibility of locating his world anywhere else but in this slippage. In his ***Parables and Paradoxes,*** he says, "All these parables really set out to say is merely that the incomprehensible is incomprehensible." The parable also contains the tone, the tradition, and the manner of the failure of the hidden god to become manifest. And when the parable comments on the failure of the parable, it merely returns to literature a traditional concealment of god as text.

Long before Kafka turns formally to the parable, he has already constructed a fiction that proves, in the multiple instances of its own slippage, to be more than a mere fiction. And in this endeavor, he is seconded by an ironic fate: none of his major fiction is complete in the form we have of it; in *The Trial,* the very ordering of the chapters is not necessarily Kafka's. It is on this shifting ground that contrives the deceptive revelation of a parable whose magnitude is equal to the totality of the fiction that Kafka establishes a central parable that his fiction treats as a problematic text—a parable whose lesson is the doubtful nature of parables. (pp. 155-58)

In the house of God, and in the accepted manner of any solemn handing-down, a voice calls K. from the pulpit: the ultimate mystery, like lesser ones, states clearly its relation to its object and little more. The voice acquires its resonance not only from the spiritual acoustics of the Cathedral but because it belongs to a young priest who knows K.: he is connected with the Court. Intuiting the ambiguity of what will follow, K. responds only when he has been able to make the unequivocal summons seem ambiguous:

But if he were to turn round he would be caught, for that would amount to an admission that he had understood it very well, that he was really the person addressed, and that he was ready to obey. Had the priest called his name a second time K. would certainly have gone on, but as everything remained silent, though he stood waiting a long time, he could not help turning his head a little just to see what the priest was doing.

With comic obduracy, and true to his mode, K. tries to reduce the intrusion of a transcendental revelation to the mundane level of his everyday life: "I came here to show an Italian round the Cathedral." So K. must be told what the reader knows already, that this normalcy is "beside the point." The point is that K. is presumed guilty. For one of the few times in his life, K. rebels: if he is guilty, then no man is innocent: "If it comes to that, how can any man be called guilty? We are all simply men here, one as much as the other." The priest acknowledges this similarity but reminds K. that this is nevertheless the talk of guilty men; the condition is not circumstantial and is therefore not subject to rational rejection. The *trial* (in German, *der Prozess*), which is never a trial but simply a *process*, turns into guilt as part of the process: "The verdict is not suddenly arrived at, the proceedings only gradually merge into the verdict." In the *process* of our existence, our *arrest* is nothing more than our awareness, our *trial* the result of that awareness.

This concomitance denies the possibility of melioristic gestures and human contact. The priest is supposed to bring comfort, but however good his intentions, he is likely to harm K. Still, K. is drawn to this figure of good: "With you I can speak openly." The priest's answer is ambiguous: "Don't be deluded"; it may refer to what K. was saying previously, it may refer to what K. has just said. K. attempts to clarify the ambiguity; in response, the priest delivers Kafka's parable, the similitude that instances an *otherness*, the periphrase whose elaboration confuses.

The parable reinforces within this context notions of mystery, elevation, and final revelation. In a story about the impossibility of passing beyond, the Door (the traditional gateway to a supernatural realm) and the Law loom (like the word of God) before the man from the country. For the reader, the parable also borrows biblical cadences in order to tell about the Door—the uttermost extension of the human possibility, informed with the terrible mystery that it proclaims and protects.

The doorkeeper is the traditional intercessor similarly haloed (though here in a comic mode) by his proximity to the unknown and, in the manner of all intercessors, utterly ineffectual. The doorkeeper, like the Door itself, like the priest who tells the story, like the very story of which that story is a part, is on *this side* of the impenetrability: he can only be a distracting focal point. Moreover, he does not keep out the man from the country, and the door is always open; the inability to enter is in the one seeking admission. The priest's critical analyses may be confusing in their catholicity, but they are not necessarily wrong:

He allows the man to curse loudly in his presence the fate for which he himself is responsible.

The man from the country is really free, he can go where he likes, it is only the Law that is closed to him, and access to the Law is forbidden him by only one individual.

> There is no lack of agreement that the doorkeeper will not be able to shut the door.

It is the necessary ineffectiveness of the intercessor that allows him even to be kind: "The doorkeeper gives him a stool and lets him sit down at the side of the door"; "The doorkeeper often engages him in brief conversations, asking him about his home and about other matters." The kindness of the doorkeeper, like the consolation of the priest, are of the same order as the impediment that may be forced temporarily to recede, but not to disappear, or the human gesture that achieves an immediate end mocked by the metaphysical dilemma that constrains it.

The man from the country can do only what man has always done before the unknowable: fasten on the figure of the intercessor. Like Oedipus, like Block, like K. himself, the man becomes a close reader of the surface of an impenetrable text: "In his prolonged study of the doorkeeper he has learned to know even the fleas in his fur collar." As the mystery asserts its impenetrability, man acknowledges his failure to know by deifying the unknown: in an ultimate and self-deriding attempt to contain what cannot be contained, he makes of the mystery God: "In the darkness he can now perceive a radiance that streams inextinguishably from the door of the Law."

But Kafka is concerned, of course, with an entirely different text—there is no man before the Door: there is only a reader, Kafka's, before *his* text. The parable that complicates the complex fiction within which it is set will now be turned into an object lesson—literally, a parafictional object on which the reader will perform the exercise suggested by the fictional characters. The priest, who belongs to the Court, has charitably entertained all of K.'s unanswerable questions; the priest, as critic of the text, will entertain sufficiently numerous and contradictory interpretations to show the impossibility of reading.

The "scripture" related by the priest is both holy and full of holes: it is given as the comfort of a truth recaptured, an absolute that can be comprehended. But modern fiction, perhaps starting with Kafka, opens fiction unto the unknown deliberately, offering itself as experience rather than imitation. The priest is not content to set forth a parable about the impossibility of knowing; he will not lose the reader within the diverse and contradictory possibilities afforded by the genre. Though he is the only speaker of the parable, he cautions K. against hasty interpretations: "Don't take over someone else's opinion without testing it." But there is no "someone else": K. has only the priest's text, just as the reader has only Kafka's; the suggestion is inescapable: though the priest has told "the story in the very words of the scriptures," the very text as text is suspect.

Once doubt has been cast on the body of orthodoxy, its absolute assertion is no longer commensurate with absolute revelation. Any interpretation is possible: "The commentators note in this connection: 'The right perception of any matter and a misunderstanding of the same matter do not wholly exclude each other'." The scripture therefore invites a gloss that is supposed to provide further steps towards the unknown. But as the gloss is the intercessor of an intercessory text, it represents in fact a step back, a greater distance from the inaccessible truth. Even though K. was admonished by the priest because he had "not enough respect for the written word," that "disrespect" comes from the only posture that is possible before the text: utmost respect; through overly close scrutiny, K. has analyzed the only surface allowed him into meaninglessness. It is through this same kind of gloss-making that the priest now leads Kaf-

ka's reader. As the reader is drawn through the maze of the text, he is drawn through another part of his awareness; forced to proceed tentatively through the text, he rehearses the tentative nature of his being, the tentative nature of an existential process of which the book he is reading is now only a part.

For neither K. nor the reader can there be any ultimate revelation. There is only description, necessity: "I don't agree with that point of view," said K., shaking his head, "for if one accepts it, one must accept as true everything the doorkeeper says. But you yourself have sufficiently proved how impossible it is to do that." "No," said the priest, "it is not necessary to accept everything as true, one must only accept it as necessary." "A melancholy conclusion," concludes K., "It turns lying into a universal principle." But such "lying" results only from a confrontation with the absolute; the priest is more philosophical and relativistic—he is, after all, only a part of the shifting boundaries that defeat the possibility of any human grasp.

K.'s light, which the priest gave him to hold, has long since gone out; small loss: it was more limiting than revelatory. Kafka snuffs it out three times: in the cathedral, in the death of K. (our confused eye within this particular text), in the text itself. Like K., and for the duration of the fiction we share, we have been kept at arm's length from something that is important to us and that we can sense only by circling around it. But in our circling we have become K., and we also have been reading about ourselves reading—hopelessly. Starobinski notes a similarity between Dostoevsky and Kafka in that the characters of each no longer have a "chez soi"—they have been expelled from their rightful home, they are in exile from themselves. Kafka's purpose is to make us aware of our own exile, but in the process we have entered his book, we have entered into his sense of the unenterable; we now inform the pale surfaces of his story as he first did. (pp. 160-64)

David I. Grossvogel, "Kafka: Structure as Mystery (I)," in Mystery and Its Fictions: From Oedipus to Agatha Christie, *The Johns Hopkins University Press, 1979, pp. 147-64.*

ADDITIONAL BIBLIOGRAPHY

Anderson, David. "The Self and the System." In his *The Tragic Protest: A Christian Study of Some Modern Literature*, pp. 104-23. Richmond, Va.: John Knox Press, 1969.
> Examines the existential despair portrayed in *The Trial* and *The Castle* and posits that Kafka's protagonists fail because they attempt to achieve their goals through the incorrect means of rationalism.

Barthes, Roland. "Kafka's Answer." In his *Critical Essays*, pp. 133-37. Evanston: Northwestern University Press, 1972.
> Discusses semantics and allusion in Kafka's works, arguing that Kafka's technique is his meaning.

Berg, Temma. "Text as Meaning in *The Trial*." *PMLA* 93, No. 2 (March 1978): 292-93.
> Response to Henry Sussman (see entry below) equating the process of writing to K.'s trial, and the verdict of the Court to the critical reaction that Kafka's work would receive if published.

Berkoff, Steven. "*The Trial*." In his *The Trial and Metamorphosis: Two Theatre Adaptations from Franz Kafka*, pp. 9-81. Ambergate, England: Amber Lane Press, 1981.
> Drama based on *The Trial*.

Borges, Jorge Luis. "Kafka and His Precursors." In his *Other Inquisitions 1937-1952*, pp. 106-08. Austin: University of Texas Press, 1964.
> Points out earlier works that contain "Kafkaesque" elements.

Bryant, Jerry H. "The Delusion of Hope: Franz Kafka's *The Trial*." *Symposium* XXIII, No. 2 (Summer 1969): 116-28.
> Discusses the modernity of Joseph K. as a literary figure, comparing him to the "absurd hero" of Albert Camus and the "knight of faith" of Søren Kierkegaard.

Buber, Martin. "Existential Guilt," translated by Maurice Friedman and Ronald Gregor Smith. In *Guilt: Man and Society*, edited by Roger W. Smith, pp. 85-116. New York: Anchor Books, 1971.
> Examines the inability of Jeseph K. in *The Trial* to admit guilt or to see it within himself.

Carrouges, Michel. *Kafka versus Kafka*. Tuscaloosa: University of Alabama Press, 1968, 144 p.
> Biography of Kafka emphasizing his Jewish heritage and his interest in Zionism during the final year of his life.

Church, Margaret. "Dostoyevsky's *Crime and Punishment* and Kafka's *The Trial*." *Literature and Psychology* XIX, Nos. 3 and 4 (1969): 47-55.
> Psychoanalytic comparison between *The Trial* and *Crime and Punishment*.

Cohen, Sandy. "Kafka's K. and Joseph K.: A Confusion Eliminated." *Germanic Notes* 2, No. 6 (1971): 45.
> Submits textual evidence that Joseph K.'s name was meant to be Joseph Karl.

Diller, Edward. " 'Heteronomy' versus 'Autonomy': A Retrial of *The Trial* by Franz Kafka." *CLA Journal* XII, No. 3 (March 1969): 214-22.
> Analyzes *The Trial* from the social and theological perspective of theologian Paul Tillich, concluding that K.'s "crime" is to oppose the urbanized and secularized world, and his failure to transcend such a world is due to his opposition on merely rational grounds, rather than those of love or faith.

Dyson, A. E. "Trial by Enigma: Kafka's *The Trial*." In his *Between Two Worlds: Aspects of Literary Form*, pp. 114-34. London: Macmillan Press, 1972.
> Demonstrates that *The Trial* portrays the consequences of the loss of faith in modern civilization.

Emrich, Wilhelm. "The World as Court of Justice: The Novel *The Trial*." In his *Franz Kafka: A Critical Study of His Writings*, pp. 316-64. New York: Frederick Ungar Publishing Co., 1968.
> Detailed examination of *The Trial* and its symbolism from the premise that K.'s ignorance of the Law is his guilt.

Feuerlicht, Ignace. "Omissions and Contradictions in Kafka's *Trial*." *The German Quarterly* XL, No. 3 (May 1967): 339-50.
> Discusses contradictory elements and omitted information that create the enigmatic effect of *The Trial*.

Friedman, Maurice. "The Problematic of Guilt and the Dialogue with the Absurd." *Review of Existential Psychology and Psychiatry* XIV, No. 1 (1975-76): 11-25.
> Explicates *The Trial* as the convergence of an absurd world, the Court, with the existential guilt of K.

———. "Crisis of Motives and the Problematic of Guilt." In his *Contemporary Psychology: Revealing and Obscuring the Human*, pp. 164-75. Pittsburgh: Duquesne University Press, 1984.
> Contains a discussion of *The Trial* as an example of the combination of neurotic guilt and existential guilt.

Goodman, Paul. "Self-Destruction." In his *Kafka's Prayer*, pp. 139-82. New York: Vanguard Press, 1947.
> Psychoanalytic interpretation of *The Trial* as a paranoid delusion arising from repressed homosexuality.

Gray, Ronald. "*The Trial*." In his *Franz Kafka*, pp. 103-25. Cambridge: Cambridge University Press, 1973.

General essay discussing various aspects of *The Trial*, including the nature of K.'s guilt, the humor and dreamlike atmosphere of the novel, and important sections such as "The Whipper" and "In the Cathedral."

Grossvogel, David I. "Kafka: *The Trial*." In his *Limits of the Novel: Evolutions of a Form from Chaucer to Robbe-Grillet*, pp. 160-88. Ithaca, N.Y.: Cornell University Press, 1967.
> Summary and examination of the plot elements and disconcerting intrusion of the unreal into the real in *The Trial*.

Gunvaldsen, Kaare. "The Plot of Kafka's *Trial*." *Monatshefte* LVI, No. 1 (January 1964): 1-14.
> Jungian psychoanalytical interpretation of *The Trial*. Gunvaldsen discusses the novel as a refutation of Freudian psychoanalysis, and as Kafka's attempt to resolve conflicting feelings concerning his engagement to Felice Bauer. In addition, Gunvaldsen refutes Herman Uyttersprot's reorganization of the novel (see excerpt dated 1953), postulating that the final chapters consist of attempts by K. to implement the painter Titorelli's options of "definite acquittal, ostensible acquittal, and indefinite postponement."

Handler, Gary. "A Textual Omission in the English Translation of *Der Prozess*." *Modern Language Notes* 83 (1968): 454-56.
> Offers textual evidence that Chapter 4 of *The Trial* is meant to be the second chapter, agreeing with Herman Uyttersprot's ordering of the chapters (see excerpt dated 1953).

Hayman, Ronald. *Kafka: A Biography*. New York: Oxford University Press, 1982, 349 p.
> Biography focusing on the relation of Kafka's life to his works.

Heller, Peter. "Kafka: The Futility of Striving." In his *Dialectics and Nihilism: Essays on Lessing, Nietzsche, Mann, and Kafka*, pp. 227-306. Amherst: University of Massachusetts Press, 1966.
> Examines the demand in Kafka's work for various interpretations.

Hobson, Irmgard. "The Kafka Problem Compounded: *Trial* and *Judgement* in English." *Modern Fiction Studies* 23, No. 4 (Winter 1977-78): 511-29.
> Includes examples of what Hobson considers mistranslations in the English text of *The Trial*.

Hyde, Virginia M. "From the 'Last Judgement' to Kafka's World: A Study in Gothic Iconography." In *The Gothic Imagination: Essays in Dark Romanticism*, edited by G. R. Thompson, pp. 128-49. Pullman: Washington State University Press, 1974.
> Examines elements of Gothicism in Kafka's fiction.

Jaffe, Adrian. *The Process of Kafka's "Trial."* Lansing: Michigan State University Press, 1967, 150 p.
> An analysis of literary theory and its assumptions using *The Trial* as a case study.

Kavanagh, R. J. "The Optimum Velocity of Approach: Some Reflections on Kafka's *Trial*." In *Structure and Gestalt: Philosophy and Literature in Austria-Hungary and Her Successor States*, edited by Barry Smith, pp. 195-210. Amsterdam: John Benjamins B. V., 1981.
> Argues that Kafka's descriptions of motion in *The Trial* reveal Joseph K.'s ambivalence to the Court and that his excessive concern with appearances obstructs his efforts to gain knowledge.

Kirchberger, Lida. "*The Trial* or Fly-by-Nights." In her *Franz Kafka's Use of Law in Fiction: A New Interpretation of "In der Strafkolonie," "Der Prozess," and "Das Schloss,"* pp. 43-118. New York: Peter Lang, 1986.
> Explication of *The Trial* from a legal viewpoint, distinguishing between the law of the State and the secret law that prosecutes K. Kirchberger considers this law to be the work of a powerless, illegal subculture which brainwashes K. and forces him to participate in his own destruction.

Kontje, Todd. "The Reader as Josef K." *The Germanic Review* LIV, No. 2 (Spring 1979): 62-6.
> Demonstrates that the experience of the reader responding to *The Trial* is comparable to that of Joseph K. as he undergoes his trial.

Kuna, Franz. *"The Trial."* In his *Franz Kafka: Literature as Corrective Punishment*, pp. 99-135. Bloomington and London: Indiana University Press, 1974.
> General discussion of *The Trial* that includes biographical information about Kafka and Felice Bauer and views K.'s trial as a spiritual quest enacted on two planes of reality.

Lasine, Stuart. "Kafka's *The Trial.*" *The Explicator* 43, No. 3 (Spring 1985): pp. 34-6.
> Compares the merchant Block in *The Trial* with the Old Testament character Balaam.

Leopold, Keith. "Breaks in Perspective in Franz Kafka's *Der Prozess.*" *The German Quarterly* XXXVI, No. 1 (January 1963): 31-8.
> Lists passages from *The Trial* in which Kafka departs from Joseph K.'s viewpoint and adopts that of an omniscient narrator.

Lesser, Simon O. "The Source of Guilt and the Sense of Guilt—Kafka's *The Trial.*" *Modern Fiction Studies* VIII, No. 1 (Spring 1962): 44-60.
> Analyzes psychoanalytic, religious, ethical, and sociopolitical interpretations of *The Trial*.

McGowan, John P. "*The Trial*: Terminable/Interminable." *Twentieth Century Literature* 26, No. 1 (Spring 1980): 1-14.
> Argues that *The Trial* could not have been completed without the text having supported one of the painter Titorelli's strategies of defense: definite acquittal, ostensible acquittal, and indefinite postponement.

Neumann, Erich. "Kafka's *The Trial*: An Interpretation through Depth Psychology." In his *Creative Man*, pp. 3-112. Princeton: Princeton University Press, 1979.
> Study of K.'s psychology, positing that the Court inhabits an intermediate reality between the world outside of K. and his own psyche, and an examination of the chapter "In the Cathedral."

Pawel, Ernst. *The Nightmare of Reason: A Life of Franz Kafka*. New York: Farrar, Strauss, and Giroux, 1984, 466 p.
> Biography utilizing psychoanalytic theory to interpret Kafka's life and work.

Pearce, Richard. "*The Alazon*: The Theme of Intrusion in *Great Expectations* and *The Trial*." In his *Stages of the Clown: Perspectives on Modern Fiction from Dostoyevsky to Beckett*, pp. 26-46. Carbondale: Southern Illinois University Press, 1970.
> Examines Dickens's *Great Expectations* and *The Trial* as novels in which the main character is an intruder and is expelled from the world into which he has intruded.

Rahv, Philip. "The Death of Ivan Ilych and Joseph K." In his *Literature and the Sixth Sense*, pp. 38-54. Boston: Houghton Mifflin, 1969.
> Compares *The Trial* with Leo Tolstoy's novella *The Death of Ivan Ilych* to demonstrate that Kafka's writing is not entirely anomalous in world literature.

Rhein, Phillip H. *The Urge to Live: A Comparative Study of Franz Kafka's "Der Prozess" and Albert Camus' "L'Etranger."* Chapel Hill: University of North Carolina Press, 1966, 123 p.
> Compares the themes, characters, and philosophies expounded in *The Trial* and Camus's *The Stranger*.

Robertson, Ritchie. "The Intricate Ways of Guilt: *Der Prozess* (1914)." *Kafka: Judaism, Politics, and Literature*, pp. 87-130. Oxford: Clarendon Press, 1985.
> Construes K.'s guilt as his ignorance of the Moral Law, examines various religious and social approaches to the problem of guilt, and finds in "Before the Law" references to Judaism that are probed more deeply in later works.

Sewall, Richard B. *"The Trial."* In his *The Vision of Tragedy*, pp. 148-60. New Haven and London: Yale University Press, 1980.
> Argues that K. achieves a self-awareness in the final chapter of *The Trial* that renders his death tragic.

Sokel, Walter H. *Franz Kafka*. New York and London: Columbia University Press, 1966, 48 p.
> Includes a discussion of *The Trial* in which Sokel argues that the difficulty in understanding the novel is due to the irresolution with which Kafka viewed his subject.

Spann, Meno. "Punishments." In his *Franz Kafka*, pp. 89-107. Boston: Twayne Publishers, 1976.
> Overview of *The Trial* containing biographical information, a plot summary, and a discussion arguing that K. cannot be viewed as a representative of humanity as a whole.

Spender, Stephen. "Franz Kafka." *The New Republic* LXXXXII, No. 1195 (27 October 1937): 347-48.
> Early review examining the internal logic of *The Trial* and *The Metamorphosis*.

Spiro, Solomon J. "Verdict—Guilty! A Study of *The Trial*." *Twentieth Century Literature* 17, No. 3 (July 1971): 169-79.
> Discusses the priest, K.'s lawyer Huld, and the painter Titorelli in *The Trial* as representatives of religious, psychoanalytic, and artistic methods of responding to the problem of guilt.

Sussman, Henry. "The Court as Text: Inversion, Supplanting, and Derangement in Kafka's *Der Prozess.*" *PMLA* 92, No. 1 (January 1977): 41-55.
> Discusses the Court of *The Trial* as a "text," the incomprehensible actions of which are variously interpreted by the diverse characters K. enlists as aids. K.'s inability to form a lucid conception of the Court thus becomes analogous to the reader's inability to form a rational interpretation of *The Trial*.

Tauber, Herbert. *"The Trial."* In his *Franz Kafka: An Interpretation of His Works*, pp. 77-120. New Haven: Yale University Press, 1948.
> Religious analysis of symbolic images and episodes in *The Trial*.

Torok, Andrew. "Kafka's *Der Prozess.*" *PMLA* 92, No. 3 (May 1977): 495-96.
> Challenges Henry Sussman's (see Additional Bibliography entry above) use of etymological evidence that would not be noticed by a native German speaker. Following the article is Sussman's reply.

Ziolkowski, Theodore. "Franz Kafka: *The Trial*." In his *Dimensions of the Modern Novel: German Texts and European Contexts*, pp. 37-67. Princeton: Princeton University Press, 1969.
> Discusses Kafka's distortions of time and physical reality, K.'s guilt and denial of guilt, and the fragmentary and circular structure of *The Trial*.

Dmitry Sergeyevich Merezhkovsky

1865-1941

(Also transliterated as Dmitri, Dmitriy, Dmitrij, and Dmítry; also Sergeevich and Sergéevich; also Merezhkovski, Merezhkóvsky, Merezhkovskij, Merežkovskij, and Merejkowski) Russian novelist, poet, critic, philosopher, biographer, essayist, and dramatist.

Merezhkovsky was one of the most influential voices in Russian philosophy and literature at the turn of the century. He is especially known for his leadership of the Russian Symbolists, the group of artists that initiated the Russian Modernist movement in the 1890s, and for his later development of a neo-Christian philosophy which attempted a synthesis of Russian Orthodox Christianity and ancient Greek paganism. The evolution of Merezhkovsky's personal philosophy may be traced through his writings, inasmuch as his poetry, fiction, and criticism served primarily as a vehicle for the expression of his philosophical ideas. His greatest literary work, the trilogy *Khristos i Antikhrist* (*Christ and Antichrist*), successfully combines philosophical speculation with striking portrayals of three important historical figures: the Roman emperor Julian, Leonardo da Vinci, and Russian czar Peter the Great, each of whom exemplifies Merezhkovsky's synthesis of Christian and pagan ideals.

Born in St. Petersburg to a family descended from Ukrainian nobility, Merezhkovsky received his secondary education at the Third St. Petersburg Classical Gymnasium and in 1884 entered the University of St. Petersburg to study philosophy. Subject to chronic depression, he found existence a burden and sought a system of belief that would give purpose to life and yet satisfy his critical intellect. Merezhkovsky became well versed in the current positivist philosophy represented in the works of Auguste Compte, but he was averse to the positivists' hostility toward metaphysics and to their preclusion of the importance of art and imagination. In 1888 Merezhkovsky received his degree, published his first collection of verse, *Stikhotvoreniya, 1883-1887,* and spent a year traveling in the Crimea and the Caucasus, where he met and married the poet Zinaida Hippius. The couple settled in St. Petersburg and became active in literary and intellectual circles.

In the early 1890s Merezhkovsky embraced the nihilistic philosophy of Friedrich Nietzsche, which he had earlier rejected as cruel and barbaric in its avowal of "will to power" as the ultimate motive of human life, but which affirmed aestheticism and sensual pleasure as justifications for existence. In 1892 and 1893 Merezhkovsky accepted this view of aesthetics while denying the Nietzschean premises that life is purposeless and art is merely a distraction from this purposelessness. During this period he made his two most important contributions to the Russian Modernist movement: *Simvoly,* a volume of poetry that introduced the term "symbolism" in its modern sense into Russian literature, and a critical study entitled *O prichinakh upadka i o novykh techeniyakh sovremennoy russkoy literatury* (*On the Reasons for the Decline, and the New Currents, in Contemporary Russian Literature*), which came to be regarded as a manifesto of the nascent Russian Symbolist movement. During his association with the Symbolists, Merezhkovsky looked to art as a guide to transcendental truth but instead found that

aesthetics failed to provide him with a coherent system of belief. By 1894 Merezhkovsky had fully espoused nihilism and attempted to pattern his life after Nietzsche's character Zarathustra, living in full knowledge of the meaninglessness of life. However, within five years his abandonment of all supernatural doctrines of faith had led him to the brink of suicide, and he announced a "turn to Christ." In 1900 Merezhkovsky began propagating a "New Religious Consciousness" that attempted to blend Christianity, which emphasized the spirit, with Greek paganism, which accentuated the flesh. Merezhkovsky's views attracted the attention of St. Petersburg intellectuals who were religiously inclined. With Hippius and a close friend, D. V. Filosofov, he organized the "Religio-Philosophical Society," which stimulated religious speculation and debate and published a magazine that encouraged a religious consciousness in Modernist literature. During this time Merezhkovsky published the final two volumes of his *Christ and Antichrist* trilogy, *Voskresshie bogi: Leonardo da Vinchi* (*Leonardo da Vinci*) and *Antikhrist: Petr i Aleksey* (*Peter and Alexis*), as well as an influential essay on Leo Tolstoy and Fyodor Dostoevsky, all of which reflect Merezhkovsky's changed religious views.

Merezhkovsky's thought included the expectation of a worldwide religious revolution originating in Russia, and when a populist rebellion took place in 1905 he enthusiastically supported it. Although the revolt ended with the adoption of a written constitution and an elected parliament, the czar remained in power and the political climate in Russia was essentially unchanged. Finding these conditions unacceptable, Merezhkovsky went into self-exile in Paris. During this time he wrote several books, some with Hippius and Filosofov, attacking the czar and the Russian Orthodox church. Within a few years Merezhkovsky returned to Russia and in 1917 supported the February revolution against the czar, but bitterly opposed the October seizure of power by the Bolsheviks. His denunciation of the regime led to his imprisonment for two years, and upon his release in 1919 he again fled Russia, spending a year in Poland before returning to Paris. Merezhkovsky continued to evolve and propagate his New Religious Consciousness until his death in 1941, and in his later writings combined religious subjects with virulent attacks on communism.

Merezhkovsky's reputation rests on his prominent role in the development of the Russian Symbolist movement and on his neo-Christian philosophy. His involvement with the Symbolists was restricted primarily to the early 1890s, before his full acceptance of nihilism. In his essay *On the Reasons for the Decline, and the New Currents, in Contemporary Russian Literature,* Merezhkovsky advocated a rejection of the literary realism that had dominated Russian literature during much of the nineteenth century. In this essay Merezhkovsky identified symbolism as a profound aspect of art that expressed idealistic conceptions by transcending the literal meanings of such literary elements as images, characters, settings, and words themselves. Working partly from the model of the French Symbolists, the Russian Symbolists considered the physical world an illusion behind which existed a higher reality that could be approached only artistically, through the use of symbols from the material world. The Symbolists' work was inherently allusive and indirect, and as such was obscure and often unintelligible, even among fellow artists. Discovering no answers to his philosophical questions through the Symbolists' view of art, however, Merezhkovsky abandoned the movement.

Following his disillusionment with aesthetics and nihilism, Merezhkovsky attempted to construct a system of belief which would combine those elements he considered positive from the various philosophies he had studied. The basis of his new philosophy was his assumption of a great antithesis between pre-Christian paganism and Christian asceticism. In Merezhkovsky's view the historical Christian church had denigrated sexual intercourse as a necessary evil only justifiable as a means of reproduction, while the Greeks had exalted it as a form of worship. Following Nietzsche, Merezhkovsky advocated the Greek affirmation of sensuality and worship of the flesh, especially in the area of sexuality. In abandoning the nihilistic aspects of Nietzsche's philosophy, however, Merezhkovsky also affirmed Christianity's attention to the spiritual needs of humanity, provision for transcendental truth, and affirmation of life's purpose and worth. Merezhkovsky wished to unify these antitheses in a synthesis that would exalt both body and spirit in a single concept of "holy flesh," and would affirm sexuality as humanity's closest approach to transcendent experience and to the androgynous existence Merezhkovsky believed would prevail in the afterlife. This theological outlook, which Merezhkovsky developed and propagated throughout the rest of his life, is reflected in his fiction, criticism, and view of politics and history.

The trilogy *Christ and Antichrist,* written during the years of Merezhkovsky's most intense religious searching, comprises the first literary expression of his New Religious Consciousness. The first volume, *Julian the Apostate,* recounts the life of a late Roman emperor who unsuccessfully attempted to revive the worship of the ancient pagan deities in the Christianized Roman Empire. *Leonardo da Vinci,* long considered the most successful volume of the trilogy, presents the great Renaissance artist and inventor as torn between Christian devotion and pagan sensuality. The final volume, *Peter and Alexis,* examines the eighteenth-century Russian czar Peter the Great, who Westernized the Russian empire and took control of the Russian Orthodox church. These three novels, whose settings are separated by centuries, are unrelated except for the antithesis between Christianity and paganism that underlies each volume and the progression from the Emperor Julian, who despite his paganism is portrayed as fulfilling the essence of Christianity, to Peter the Great, who in spite of his avowed faith in Christ appears as a figure of the Antichrist in his attempt to effect secular domination of the Russian Orthodox church. This trilogy is considered Merezhkovsky's greatest literary work, his later novels representing lesser vehicles for his religious ideas.

In the area of literary criticism, Merezhkovsky first developed his theological ideas in *L. Tolstoi i Dostoevskiy* (*Tolstoi as Man and Artist, with an Essay on Dostoievski*). In this study, which has greatly influenced criticism on the two Russian masters, Merezhkovsky posited a dichotomy between Tolstoy as the consummate artist of the flesh, or sensual and physical reality, and Dostoevsky as the supreme artist of the spirit, or transcendental reality. While early critics believed that the essay ultimately exalted the spirit over the flesh, more recent scholars have emphasized the equal importance Merezhkovsky attributed to both aspects of life. Merezhkovsky's later critical articles also pursue the concept of antitheses between authors, with Alexander Pushkin, whom Merezhkovsky considered to be the last Russian author to fully combine flesh and spirit, held up as an ideal.

After completing *Christ and Antichrist* and *Tolstoi as Man and Artist,* Merezhkovsky continued to develop his religious and philosophical ideas in many literary, critical, biographical, and theological works. One of the most fully developed areas of Merezhkovsky's thought is his dialectic view of history. Merezhkovsky divided history into three parts, each of which represented both a member of the Trinity and a stage in the Hegelian dialectic pattern of thesis, antithesis, and ultimate synthesis. Merezhkovsky considered pre-Christian theory the "dispensation of the Father," epitomized by Greek paganism and worship of the flesh. The Christian era represented the "dispensation of the Son," when sensuality was denigrated and spirituality exalted. Merezhkovsky considered the function of the Son to be nearing its end, and would be completed in a religious revolution originating in Russia and spreading worldwide, in which "holy flesh," or the unity of flesh and spirit, would be recognized as the synthesis of the two former beliefs. This "dispensation of the Holy Spirit" would signify the end of history as the resolution of humanity's disparate religious longings, after which people would live in peace and love.

Critics consider Merezhkovsky a crucial participant and leader in Russia's "Silver Age," a cultural awakening which took place during the two decades preceding the Communist Revolution. His influence is marked in the ascendancy of the Symbolist movement and in the religious revival among Russian intellectuals in the early twentieth century. Although he is overshadowed by other writers of fiction and poetry, Merezh-kovsky remains an important theorist, critic, and philosopher whose works are essential to the understanding of early twen-tieth-century Russian literature.

PRINCIPAL WORKS

Stikhotvoreniya, 1883-1887   (poetry)   1888

Simvoly   (poetry)   1892

O prichinakh upadka i o novykh techeniyakh sovremennoy russkoy literatury   (criticism)   1893
   [*On the Reasons for the Decline, and the New Currents, in Contemporary Russian Literature* (partial translation) published in *The Russian Symbolists*, 1986]

Novye stikhotvoreniya, 1891-1895   (poetry)   1896

Smert' Bogov: Yulian Otstupnik   (novel)   1896
   [*Julian the Apostate*, 1899; also published as *The Death of the Gods*, 1901]

Vechnye sputniki   (essays)   1897
   †[*The Life Work of Henrik Ibsen*, 1907; *The Life Work of Montaigne*, 1907; *The Life Work of Pliny the Younger*, 1907; *The Life Work of Calderon*, 1908; *The Life Work of Flaubert*, 1908; *The Acropolis*, 1909; *Marcus Aurelius*, 1909; *The Life Work of Dostoievski*, 1912]

Voskresshie bogi: Leonardo da Vinchi   (novel)   1901
   [*The Romance of Leonardo da Vinci, the Forerunner*, 1902; also published as *The Forerunner*, 1902]

L. Tolstoi i Dostoevskiy   (criticism)   1901-02
   [*Tolstoi as Man and Artist, with an Essay on Dostoievski*, 1902]

Antikhrist: Petr i Aleksey   (novel)   1905
   [*Peter and Alexis*, 1905]

Gogol' i chort   (criticism and biography)   1906

Gryaduschiy Kham: Chekhov i Gor'kiy   (criticism and nonfiction)   1906

Prorok russkoi revoliutsii: k iubileiu Dostoevskago   (nonfiction)   1906

Pushkin   (criticism and biography)   1906

‡*Le Tsar et la révolution* [with Z. N. Hippius and D. V. Filosofov]   (nonfiction)   1907

Ne mir, no mech   (essays)   1908

Pavel I   (drama)   1908

Aleksandr I   (novel)   1913

Polnoe sobranie sochineniy. 24 vols.   (novels, poetry, drama, criticism, biography, and nonfiction)   1914

Chetyrnadtsatoe dekabrya   (novel)   1918

Tsarstvo Antikhrista [with Z. N. Hippius, D. V. Filosofov, and V. Zlobin]   (nonfiction)   1921

§*December the Fourteenth*   (novel)   1923

Rozhdenie bogov: Tutankamon na Krite   (novel)   1925
   [*The Birth of the Gods*, 1925]

Tayna trekh: Egipet i Vavilon   (nonfiction)   1925

Messiya   (novel)   1926-27
   [*Akhnaton, King of Egypt*, 1927]

Tayna Zapada: Atlantida-Europa   (nonfiction)   1930
   [*The Secret of the West*, 1933; also published as *Atlantis/ Europe: The Secret of the West*, 1971]

Iisus Neizvestnyy   (nonfiction)   1931
   [*Jesus the Unknown* (partial translation) 1933; *Jesus Manifest* (partial translation) 1933]

Pavel, Avgustin   (biography)   1936

Frantsisk Assisskiy   (biography)   1938

Zhanna d Ark   (biography)   1938

Dante   (biography)   1939

‡*Luther*   (biography)   1941

‡*Pascal*   (biography)   1941

‡*Calvin*   (biography)   1942

*These three volumes comprise the trilogy *Khristos i Antikhrist* (*Christ and Antichrist*).

†Translated essays from *Vechnye sputniki* were published separately.

‡These volumes were originally published in French.

§*December the Fourteenth* is a translated and abridged compilation of *Aleksandr I* and its sequel *Chetyrnadtsatoe dekabrya*.

HERBERT TRENCH   (essay date 1901)

[*Trench was an Irish poet, playwright, and critic. In the following excerpt, he discusses the philosophical content of the trilogy* Christ and Antichrist.]

Dmitri Mérejkowski is perhaps the most interesting and pow-erful of the younger Russian novelists, the only writer that promises to carry on the work of Tolstoi, Turgeniev, and Dos-toievski. His books, which are already numerous, are animated by a single master-idea, the Pagano-Christian dualism of our human nature. What specially interests him in the vast spectacle of human affairs is the everlasting contest between the idea of a God-Man and the idea of a Man-God; that is to say, between the conception of a God incarnate for awhile (as in Christ) and the conception of Man as himself God—gradually evolving higher types of splendid and ruling character which draw after them the generations.

The novelist's own doctrine seems to be that both the Pagan and the Christian elements in our nature, although distinct elements, are equally legitimate and sacred. His teaching is that the soul and the senses have an equal right to be respected; that hedonism and altruism are equals, and that the really full man, the perfect man, is he who can ally in harmonious equi-librium the cult of Dionysus and the cult of Christ.

Mérejkowski conceives that European civilisation has been born of the tremendous conflict between these two main ideas. And he has embodied this conflict in a trilogy of novels,—three historical romances. The first is entitled **The Death of the Gods,** and deals with the extraordinary career of the Roman Emperor, Julian the Apostate, who in the fourth century A.D. sought to revive the worship of the Olympians after Christianity had been adopted by Constantine the Great as the official religion of the Roman Empire.

The historical novel, pure and simple, exists no longer. Writers of genius who seem to write historical novels in reality are only transferring to the stage of the world a drama which is being played in their own souls. They transfer thither that drama in order to show that the struggle which is now going on in us is eternal. Mérejkowski sees the question, which is of su-preme interest to us, being asked by the great spirits of a wealthy and imperial civilisation closely resembling our own, in the fourth century. And, what is of more interest still, he not only sees the momentous problem and places it before us with remarkable lucidity, but he also seems, in his own fashion, to arrive at a solution. Moreover, this novelist, this psychol-ogist, is also an artist and a poet, possessed by what he some-where calls the "Nostalgia of the Distant." With an ardour as of Flaubert in *Salammbo*, and with perhaps more skill than

Sienkiewicz in *Quo Vadis,* the author of *The Death of the Gods* has succeeded in re-creating the wonderful rich scenes and characters of that remote epoch. We see the racing stables of the Hippodrome of Constantinople, battles with wild German warriors round Strasburg, the interior of the baths at Antioch, dinners of epicures and men of letters at Athens, pictures of a Roman Emperor at his toilet-table, or of a lovelorn child in the Temple of Aphrodite. Before writing this first of his great romances Mérejkowski himself travelled through Asia Minor and Greece, visited Constantinople and Syria, and gathered everywhere living impressions to serve his art and his thought. He was besides admirably prepared to handle a subject which had attracted him from youth. A delicate Hellenist, his first appearance in literary life was as a harmonious translator of Æschylus and Sophocles. Later, the Gnostics, the Fathers of the Eastern Church, the Greek Sophists (who represented the last throes of expiring Paganism and already dreamed of reviving it), were the young poet's objects of study. Thus was born the romance of *The Death of the Gods,* which he has continued later in *The Resurrection of the Gods* (of which Leonardo da Vinci is the hero), and completed by *The Anti-Christ,* portraying the savage figure of Peter the Great, the creator (despite all natural obstacles) of St. Petersburg and of modern Russia.

In the first romance of the three the new Christian spirit is seen invading the soul of Julian himself, the last champion of expiring Paganism. It can even be seen in the little treatises, *The Sun King* and the *Mother of the Gods,* which Julian wrote in his feverish nights to defend his lost cause. Soon there remained to this singular man of all that first ardour but a feeling of impotent rage and unbridled pride—the Napoleonic lust of conquering the world. And so we see him in this book, in the midst of the mad expedition against Persia, where he was to meet his death, oversetting the altar of the gods who had betrayed him, and exclaiming: *"The gods are no more; or rather, the gods do not yet exist. They are not. But they will be. We shall all be gods. We have but to dare!"* A few days later he falls, vanquished by the Galilean, whose image haunts his deathbed. But at that last hour it is not the fierce God of the Arians (who educated Julian the Emperor) that he sees. He whom delirium calls up is Christus Pastophorus,—the Good Shepherd,—the Spirit of gentleness and love. It is that Spirit who has dethroned the Olympians.

But the gods do not perish utterly. Centuries pass, and from the bosom of the waters, like Aphrodite, from the bosom of the earth, like Cybele, they come forth again, serene and impassive. Popes, kings, great nobles, simple Florentine merchants welcome them, brought by galleys from the coasts of Hellas, or discovered by patient excavators of the antique soil. Their marble glory shines anew. The rays of Helios penetrate the soul of artists. The fires of Dionysus kindle the blood of the young men and the young women. It is the dawn of the *Renaissance.* Has then the God-Man conquered the Man-God? No; because, see, Savonarola is defying the gods of Olympus and the gods of the earth. The latter destroy him, but the Christ has reappeared, and the problem of the two forms of wisdom continues to be set in a form more august and more painful than ever before. (pp. iii-vi)

And since then, as before then, as at all times, at every fresh crisis, at every renewal of the creative process taking place within human consciousness, the two principles reappear. They struggle too in the soul of the strongest. Look at Peter the Great, whom old believers used to call "The Anti-Christ." He

will be the hero of the third romance of the trilogy. We shall see therein the tragedy of the gentle Tsarevitch Alexis, servant of the Galilean and immolated victim of the new god; victim, that is, of human will incarnate in the genius of Peter, lifting itself above good and evil. (pp. vi-vii)

Herbert Trench, in an introduction to The Death of the Gods *by Dmitri Merejkowski, translated by Herbert Trench, G. P. Putnam's Sons, 1901, pp. iii-vii.*

T. E. PAGE (essay date 1902)

[*In the following excerpt, Page unfavorably reviews* The Romance of Leonardo da Vinci.]

[*The Forerunner*] is a medley of history, biography, fiction, art, science, religion, philosophy, and mysticism. There is no real plot, and the story ranges over a period of twenty-five years (1494-1519 A.D.), while the number of personages introduced bewilders the mind, including as it does, among countless minor characters, such great figures as Charles VIII., Louis XII., Francis I., Alexander VI., Leo X., Cæsar Borgia, Ludovico Sforza and his wife Beatrice, Savonarola, Macchiavelli, Michael Angelo, and Raphael. In order to introduce them all the author arranges a series of brilliant, though somewhat garish, *tableaux vivants,* which are loosely linked together by being all associated with the life of Leonardo da Vinci, the painter of *The Last Supper,* and the development of an idea which it is only possible to explain imperfectly because no ordinary mind can understand it.

As in his previous novel, *The Death of the Gods,* the writer selected the era of Julian the Apostate in order to set forth the victory of Christianity over Paganism, so here he has chosen the period of the Renaissance to depict what he calls, in the Russian title of his work, *The Resurrection of the Gods.* As Julian with his cry *"vicisti, Galilæe"* acknowledged the triumph of "the God-man," so the Renaissance represents the struggle for supremacy of "the Man-god," of the man, that is, who instead of humbling himself before high heaven seeks Titan-like to scale it. *Ecce Deus* is what Leonardo da Vinci wrote beneath his great statue of Francesco Sforza, "that son of a peasant, strong as a lion, astute as a fox, who attained by sagacity, by crime, and by great exploits, the summit of power," and his own life is represented as a continuous effort to rise, through knowledge, above the level of humanity. He seeks to know and understand all things, to discover not only the exact laws of art, but also the exact laws of all science. When we first meet him he is "putting the angle-measure to the fair lips" of a newly-discovered statue of Aphrodite—a favourite goddess in this volume—and explaining that he "generally divides the human face into degrees, minutes, seconds, and thirds, a third being $\frac{1}{48823}$ of the whole face," and also, one would think, an awkward unit of measurement. Then we see him sketching Savonarola "with superb composure," as after a thrilling sermon "pressing his white lips on the crucifix he knelt and burst into sobs" while "the long agonised wail of penitents . . . rose to heaven." Or, again, he is standing by the deathbed of Beatrice Sforza, and there, since "the look of supreme suffering in a human face was to his eyes a rare and beautiful manifestation of nature . . . , not a wrinkle, not the quivering of a muscle escaped his passionless, all-seeing eyes." Nor does this strange devotion to art absorb all his powers. He rejoices in the study of mathematics as the perfect expression of those laws by which "The Prime Mover," or "Thrice-Marvellous Necessity," rules the universe; he has written 120 volumes dealing with natural science; he is an adept in mechanics, having invented a long catalogue of warlike engines as well as "a new mincing machine for sausages." And yet he is a kindly man withal, adopting orphans and doing good deeds manifold, for it is the great article in his creed, which he asserts in capital letters, that "Perfect knowledge of the universe and perfect love of God are one thing and the same."

In fact, however, failure awaits him, his work, and his theories. He finds the mildew, which will ultimately destroy it, beginning to spot his great fresco; the wings for flight to which he has devoted a life's labour (and which are typical of his ambition) prove faulty and cripple the faithful servant who attempts to use them; his pupils turn on him, and the favourite among them, distracted between his old religious beliefs and his master's new teaching, takes refuge in suicide; he himself dies in poverty and exile. For he is only "the Forerunner." But of what? Of whom? That indeed it is hard to say. Just before his death, however, he paints a picture "of a naked youth, womanish, seductively beautiful," but which is not, as might be thought, the heathen Dionysus, "for instead of the leopard's skin he wore a garment of camel's hair; instead of the thyrsus he carried a cross," pointing to it "with a subtle smile." The figure, it seems, symbolises that blending of Paganism with Christianity to which apparently the author looks forward as the ideal religion of the future, and in the Epilogue a young Russian painter rhapsodises over the work, and declaims about "the third Rome, the new Zion," and "a Woman in shining garments" who is "Hagia Sophia, the wisdom of God," and will appear "over the land of Russia." What the meaning of these dark sayings is none can tell; but the third volume of this "trilogy," which is entitled *Anti-Christ,* and deals with Peter the Great, will perhaps bring the interpretation.

Before such a work as this sane criticism is dumb. Those who admire most what they understand least will doubtless applaud it, and the fact that the writer commands readers in several countries is fresh evidence how prone the human mind is to mysticism. Perhaps, however, it is not its eccentric teaching which commends the book so much as its vivid realism. Merejkowski has mastered the history of the period he deals with, and he paints his scenes with full details, and in the strongest colours. Sometimes he is genuinely effective, and it would be difficult to illustrate the spirit of that strange age more forcibly than he does in his sketch of the "historiographer" Merula exulting over a palimpsest on which, beneath a monkish copy of a penitential psalm, he has discovered a Greek hymn to Aphrodite, and then getting as drunk as Porson in his scholarly rapture. But too often his style displeases by excess, and it needs a strong stomach to assist at a banquet where "there is served up a naked Andromeda, made of the breasts of capons, bound to a rock of cream-cheese, and about to be loosed by a winged Perseus of veal," while, if anyone desires unmitigated and nauseating horror, he has only to turn to the chapter entitled "The Witches' Sabbath."

The book is not one which will commend itself to any but the crudest literary taste. It is interesting in places—for anyone who writes with knowledge about such a period must be interesting—but the flavour it leaves in the mouth is not always pleasant, and the effect of the whole is cloying. A great number of historic personages appear upon the stage. Their costumes are splendid, and the background of each scene is brilliant, but the figures that pass before the eyes do not seem to be alive, and the intelligent reader, as he closes the book, will experience the feeling of one who steps into the fresh air after a long afternoon at Madame Tussaud's. (pp. 25-6)

T. E. Page, in a review of "'The Forerunner'," in The Bookman, *London, Vol. XXIII, No. 133, October, 1902, pp. 25-6.*

EDWARD GARNETT   (essay date 1903)

[*A prominent editor for several London publishing houses, Garnett discovered or greatly influenced the work of many important English writers, including Joseph Conrad, John Galsworthy, and D. H. Lawrence. He also published several volumes of criticism, which are characterized by thorough research and sound critical judgments. In the following excerpt, Garnett offers a mixed review of* Tolstoi as Man and Artist.]

Every fresh book on Tolstoy is a gain, because however inadequate a critical study on him may, nay, must be, Tolstoy's colossal life work is seen and felt afresh behind each critic's conclusions, much as a great mountain is seen looming up behind the driving mists. [*Tolstoi as Man and Artist*] is decidedly interesting, none the less because there is a personal note of jealousy in it which the author has not been able to conceal. Merejkowski, himself a Russian, is best known to the English reader by his novel *The Death of the Gods,* a study of the life of Julian the Apostate, which reveals the author as a clever scene painter of picturesque historical drama, with but little original temperament, and no special creative insight. Merejkowski is a learned and clever man, but the English critics who have hailed him "as a worthy successor to Tolstoy and Dostoievski" might as well affirm that Alma Tadema is a worthy successor to Rembrandt. Merejkowski decidedly has talent, but he is not a creative genius, not a creator. In *Tolstoi as Man and Artist,* Merejkowski now comes before us as a critic and man of culture, who has been not a little influenced by Nietzsche, and has a semi-Nietzscheian theory of Pagan *v.* Christian art. The first half of the book, dealing with Tolstoy the man, reads like the work of a dilettante who, jealous that Tolstoy's fame should overshadow all his contemporaries, is trying to say all that he can to belittle it; but in the second half of the book the author seems to become conscious that he has gone too far, and he tries to establish firmly his critical argument and free it in a measure from the clouds of his personal feeling. In the picture of "Tolstoy as Man," Merejkowski rather cleverly dwells on various inconsistencies in Tolstoy's character and conduct, and seeks to throw ridicule on him for living in a comfortable home while he is preaching "self-denial" and "asceticism" to the world, but Merejkowski's tone is so spiteful as to betray malice. In his lecture to Tolstoy teaching the great man how to live, Merejkowski becomes at times both a little offensive and a little ridiculous:—

> Does the worm gnaw at his heart? Is he pursued and harassed by the consciousness that he has not done the bidding of Christ, that while the body is gratified the soul is mortally troubled? Is it not dreadful that even this man, who has utterly thirsted for truth, who has so remorsefully found fault with himself and others, should have admitted such a crying deception to soul and conscience—such a monstrous anomaly? Despite all appearances, the smallest and the strongest of the devils, the latter-day Devil of Property, of Philistine self-content and neutral pettiness, has won in this man his last and greatest victory.

> Will he at last realise that here there is nothing high nor low, that paths diverse, yet equally true, lead to one and the same goal; that in reality all paths are one; that it is not against and not away from things earthly, but only through things earthly that we attain

the more than earthly, not in conflict with, or divested of, but only through the bodily that we attain the spiritual.

His illness is shown by a gradually-increasing silence, callousness, decline, ossification and petrification of the heart, once the warmest of human hearts. It is because his ailment is inward, because he himself is scarcely conscious of it, that it is more grievous than the malady of Dostoievski or the madness of Nietzsche. . . . And Tolstoy, too, has deserted us.

In like vein Tolstoy is gravely reproved because his wife puts a sachet of scent among his linen; because he sleeps tranquilly on a "ventilated leather bolster"; because the "thin mutton broth which he loves is scarcely less tasty than the most expensive and complicated soups"; because he jumped over a hedge to get away from a peasant who begged for a foal, etc., etc. That Tolstoy has sacrificed the spirit within him for the sake of worldly ease, and that the spirituality of his teaching is invalidated by the fact that he "loves" thin mutton broth, and is particular about his gaiters, this assertion may please petty-minded people who judge great men by themselves, but it is given the lie by the whole meaning and effort of Tolstoy's life. Leaving, then, "Tolstoy as Man," an attack which recoils on its author's head, let us turn to the critical argument in Merejkowski's book.

The critical argument is original, but very paradoxical. Tolstoy, in Merejkowski's eyes, is the great Pagan representing the preponderance of the flesh over the spirit, while Dostoievski, as the great Christian, represents the preponderance of the spirit over the flesh. Tolstoy, our author argues, is unequalled in depicting the human body, the greatest analyst, known in literature, of bodily sensations. "His sensual experience is inexhaustible, as if he had lived hundreds of lives in various shapes of men and animals." "He fathoms the unusual sensation of her bared body to a young girl, before going to her first ball"; he understands the sensations of a nursing mother "who has yet not severed the mysterious connection of her body with that of her child"; he knows "the feelings of a woman old and worn out with child bearing, who shudders as she remembers the pain of her quivering breasts"; and lastly, the sensations and thoughts of animals, as in the case of Levin's sporting dog, and the whole range of the consciousness of man's animal nature possessed by war, sport, love, work, etc.; all this it is Tolstoy's triumph to have explored. "Tolstoi is the greatest depicter of this physico-spiritual region in the natural man; that side of the flesh which approaches the spirit, and that side of the spirit which approaches the flesh, the mysterious border-region where the struggle between the animal and the God in man takes place. Therein lies the struggle and the tragedy of his own life. He is a 'man of the senses,' half-heathen, half-Christian; neither to the full." But if he essays the opposite region: "human spirituality, almost set free from the body, released from animal nature, the region of pure thought (the passionate workings of which are so well embodied by Dostoievski and Tiutchev)," the power of artistic delimitation in Tolstoy "decreases and collapses." "But within the limits of the purely natural man, he is the supreme artist of the world." When Tolstoy, however, abandons the life of the body, for the life of the soul, says Merejkowski, "we get a crystallised, lifeless abstraction, a moral and religious vehicle for a moral and religious deduction. Thus Nekliudov, the hero of *Resurrection,* is "a dreary megaphone, through which the 'gentleman author' behind proclaims his theorems to the moral universe." Dostoievski, on the other hand, "has an accumu-

lating superfluity of vitality, a carrying over to the utmost limit of the refinement, acuteness, and concentration of spirituality." "To Dostoievski the revealing light comes from within." All his life he sought out what was most difficult, disastrous, hard, and terrible, as if he felt suffering necessary to the full growth of his powers. In Siberia he wrote to his brother, "This is my cross, and I have deserved it." "The fire of love penetrating and purifying Dostoievski glows even in his most commonplace acts." Dostoievski is "superior in tragedy" to Tolstoy, superior in "his characters' conversation," in their "mental life." Finally, Merejkowski argues that the two great Russian writers represent two halves of the Russian soul, two diverse sides of the Russian nature, each incomplete without the other:—

Tolstoi and Dostoievski are the two great columns, standing apart in the propylaeum of the temple—parts facing each other, set over and against each other in the edifice, incomplete and still obscured by scaffolding, that temple of Russian religion which will be, I believe, the future religion of the whole world.

That there is a great deal of very able criticism and many brilliant observations in Merejkowski's analysis of Tolstoy's art, no critic of intelligence would wish to deny. There is, in fact, much penetration shown throughout, and some illuminating pages . . . , which more than counterbalance some bad pages . . . , where Merejkowski either draws unfair comparisons, or is borrowing from Nietzsche wholesale, and gets out of his depth. It is not our author's insight that is at fault, not the threads of his criticism, but the fabric that he weaves out of them. His main conclusion—that Tolstoy is the great Pagan, that he fails in depicting "the life of the soul," that it is only within the limits of the purely natural man "he is a supreme artist," is little but a great paradox. For what is "the natural man"? And who are the "Christian" artists? To conclude that Dostoievski is more "spiritual" than Tolstoy, because the latter deals with our actual bodily sensations, whereas the former dwells chiefly in the rich world of his own hallucinations, is an absurdity. And what does "pagan" mean in the connection? If the antithesis between "pagan" and "Christian" can hold good, then Plato and Sophocles are far more Christian, in the sense of representing the preponderance of the spirit over the flesh, than nineteen out of twenty Christian writers. If, on the other hand, a perfect equipoise between the body and the spirit is the mark of the great pagan writers, then Turgenev is a great pagan. But Turgenev's work is far more "spiritual" than Dostoievski's work, and yet the latter is held up as being predominantly spiritual! The fact is that Merejkowski's argument, though ingenious and presenting strongly interesting half-truths, rests on a very partial interpretation of the word "spiritual." A great writer may indeed, as Tolstoy does, in analysing human life, show us the preponderance of the body over the spirit, but he may be far more deeply "spiritual" in his attitude to life than the writers who show us the preponderance of the spirit over the body. It is not by shutting off from us, by avoiding, or by being incapable of understanding, the world of man's animalism, that a writer proves his spirituality. Tolstoy's very penetration into life springs chiefly from his moral dissatisfaction with it. We cannot, therefore, see in Merejkowski's thesis anything beyond a convenient platform which serves his purpose of showing some of Tolstoy's artistic defects, and of exalting Dostoievski. "As a matter of fact," says the author, "I only wished to pull back and fairly adjust the rope, too far strained by the popular Christianity of Tolstoy and of Europe to-day." "I own from the first chapter of my inquiry the reader has cause to suspect me of a prejudice against Tolstoy, and in favour of his contemporary." The attempt is an interesting one, and though the impression that remains after finishing the book is as though some clever sculptor had been trying his chisel on the face of some great antique bas-relief, and had found the marble uncommonly hard, and the proportions impossible to alter, still we are not sorry Merejkowski should have attempted it, if for his remarks on Dostoievski alone. (pp. 166-67)

> Edward Garnett, "Merejkowski on Tolstoy," in The Bookman, *London, Vol. XXIII, No. 136, January, 1903, pp. 166-67.*

STEPHEN CHALMERS   (essay date 1906)

[*Chalmers was a Scottish novelist and poet. In the following essay, he discusses the historicity of* Peter and Alexis *and Merezhkovsky's treatment of the title characters.*]

Dimitri Merejkowski's *Peter and Alexis* is his first novel on a purely Russian theme, and it would not be surprising if it were the last, for in *Peter and Alexis,* which is the third novel of a trilogy on one underlying idea, the author seems to have used up the study of a lifetime, and, in fact, left little untold that is of world interest on the subject of Russia, its Government, its ignorance, depravity, struggles to redemption, religions, and superstitions.

As one reads this semi-biographical novel one is struck by the similarity between conditions as they existed at the time of Peter the Great and as they obtain in Russia to a great extent today. Although the capital which Peter founded has advanced as the Czar prophesied, the rest of Russia seems to have jogged along in the same old way. The picture presented by Dimitri Merejkowski, compared with the similar conditions existing at the beginning of the recent war, (which has threatened to revolutionize everything,) should leave in the mind of the careful reader an interrogation point after the word "Finis."

That 200 years should pass over Russia and bring little change seems well-nigh impossible. Yet it is a fact, unless perhaps one asserts that Dimitri Merejkowski has taken present conditions as he has studied them, and pictured the same as in the time of Peter. It might also be asserted that in the Alexis of the early eighteenth century the author has painted the lineaments of Nicholas II, for they are practically one and the same.

Such assertions, however, would be unfair under the circumstances. The fact that Russia and its lower classes are where other nations were five hundred years ago is proof enough that two hundred years ago Russia was a great deal worse than Dimitri Merejkowski paints it. The impression is that he has carefully erred on the safe and generous side of coloring. As the prefatory note says: "It is a simple and earnest psychological study, . . . a sketch, vivid and true, of classes and conditions, of Court and society, of peasants and wild religious beliefs, in Russia at the beginning of the eighteenth century."

It is decidedly a book for men and women of deep and serious thought. There are scenes in it that excel in literary excellence and other things the festal scene in *Quo Vadis?* But it is such scenes in *Peter and Alexis* that bring out, like a brilliant light against a black shadow, and vice versa, the remarkable character of the great horny-handed Czar and the vacillating moods of the effeminate Alexis. In both are to be seen the characteristics of the Romanoff family—the fury that has more than once appalled Europe; the weakness that has astonished the world; the power that has shaken itself to pieces.

In Alexis we find a character, or lack of it, that is familiar to all who have read the newspapers in the last two years. He is a young man born to the best of intentions, gradually growing despondent in the shadow of existing conditions, hoping against hope that, when he comes to the throne, things will be different. That he does not come to the throne, but is flogged to death by his own father, (the brute flogging the better self and the better self looking upon its own corpse aghast,) does not affect later history. Alexis has reigned more than once, and the result is apparent.

Peter the Great! There is the figure in the book. Little wonder his presentation on the stage has ever failed. Here, in a few extracts, is this extraordinary man:

> It is his custom, (says the diary of a maid of honor,) when all are drunk, to double the guards and let no one pass out of the door. At the same time the Czar, who is never drunk, much as he may take, tries purposely to provoke quarrels among them. He then learns what he could never have known otherwise. . . . The banquet develops into a public inquiry into character . . . . The human faces all looked beastlike; the Czar's the most terrible of all. . . . Calm and disdainful, his look was clear and piercing. He alone had remained sober; and was now with curiosity peering into the vilest mysteries, into the bared soul of human beings. . . .

Add to this, the man had a passion for blood. He took an active part in executions. On one occasion he showed an executioner in practice the neatest way to lop off a head. When he was not at this recreation Peter performed autopsies, even upon his deceased relatives. So great was his pride in his surgical skill that the Court feared to betray illness, for in that event he would immediately get out his instruments and cut up the whole body to discover what was wrong. But here is the more admirable side of the man:

> At 6 in the morning he began to dress. Pulling on his stockings, he noticed a hole; he sat down, got a needle and a bail of wool, and began darning. Ruminating about a road to India, in the footsteps of Alexander of Macedonia, he darned his stockings.

> He began to dictate ukases as to a fit place for the deposit of manures; on the substitution of hair sacks for sacks of matting in which to carry biscuits to the galleys; and barrels, or linen bags, for grain and salt, "mats should on no account be used"; on the saving of lead bullets used at practice firing; the preservation of forests; "the prohibition of hollowed-out trunks for coffins," which were to be made of planks. "N.B.—England to be written to for a model."

A few notes from his memoranda suggest queer trains of thought:

> Exposed foundling infants to be educated.

> The fall of the Greek monarchy was caused by contempt of warfare.

> Buy the secret of making German sausages.

> Chemical secrets for testing ore.

> Engage foreign comedians at high pay.

The progress of Christianity is the underlying theme in this novel, as in the other two of the trilogy, *The Death of the Gods* and *The Forerunner.* Around this are painted pictures, terrible and extraordinary. But nothing is so powerful in the book as its character studies.

Stephen Chalmers, ''Merejkowski's Tale of 'Peter and Alexis','' in The New York Times, *February 10, 1906, p. 78.*

D. S. MIRSKY (essay date 1926)

[*Mirsky was a Russian prince who fled his country after the Bolshevik Revolution and settled in London. While in England, he wrote two important histories of Russian literature,* Contemporary Russian Literature *(1926) and* A History of Russian Literature *(1927). In 1932, having reconciled himself to the Soviet regime, Mirsky returned to the USSR. He continued to write literary criticism, but his work eventually ran afoul of Soviet censors and he was exiled to Siberia. He disappeared in 1937. In the following excerpt from a chapter originally published in* Contemporary Russian Literature, *Mirsky affirms Merezhkovsky's talent and central position among Russian Modernists, especially praising* Tolstoi as Man and Artist, *but denigrates his overuse of antithesis in his philosophical, theological, and literary works.*]

The principal figure of the ''modern'' movement in literature during its first stages was Dmítry Sergéyevich Merezhkóvsky.... As early as 1883, verse over his signature began to appear in the liberal magazines, and before long he was universally recognized as the most promising of the younger ''civic'' poets. When Nádson died (1887), Merezhkóvsky became his lawful successor. His early verse (collected in book form in 1888) is not strikingly above the level of its day, which was a very low one, but it shows a greater carefulness for form and diction; it is tidier and more elegant than that of his contemporaries. His reputation as the most promising poet of the younger generation was further enhanced by his narrative poem **''Véra,''** written in a style that is the distant descendant of Byron's *Don Juan* but had been sentimentalized and idealized out of recognition by two generations of Russian poets. It is a story of self-disbelieving love, and it ends on a vaguely religious note. It was admirably adapted to suit the taste of the time and had a greater success than any narrative poem had had for several decades. About the same time Merezhkóvsky married Zinaída Híppius, a young poetess of outstanding talent, who later became one of the principal poets and critics of the symbolist movement.

New ideas were in the air, and the first indication had appeared in 1890 in the shape of Mínsky's ''Nietzschean'' book *By the Light of Conscience.* Merezhkóvsky soon followed suit and abandoned the colors of civic idealism. In 1893 he published a collection of essays, **On the Causes of the Present Decline and the New Currents of Contemporary Russian Literature,** and a book of poems under the aggressive and modern title **Symbols.** Together with his wife, with Mínsky, and with Volýnsky, he became one of the staff of the *Northern Messenger,* which came forth as the champion of ''new ideas.'' These ''new ideas'' were on the whole a rather vague revolt against the positivism and utilitarianism of orthodox radicalism. In **Symbols** and **On the Causes,** Merezhkóvsky is as vague as Volýnsky, but soon his ''new ideas'' began to take definite shape and to form themselves into a religion of Greek antiquity. Henceforward he developed that taste for antithetic thinking which finished by ruining both himself and his style. This antithetic tendency found its first striking expression in his conception of **Christ and Antichrist,** a trilogy of historical novels, the first of which, **Julian the Apostate,** or **The Death of the Gods,** appeared in 1896. It was followed in 1901 by **Leonardo da Vinci,** or **The Resurrection of the Gods,** and in 1905 by **Peter and Alexis.** The last of these belongs to already another period of Merezhkóvsky's evolution, but the first two are char-

acteristic of that stage of his activity which was parallel to the Westernizing action of Diághilev and Benois. **Julian** and **Leonardo** are animated by a pagan ''Hellenic'' feeling, and the same spirit animates all he wrote between 1894 and 1900. This includes a series of **Italian Novellas;** translations of *Daphnis and Chloë* and the Greek tragic poets; and **Eternal Companions,** a collection of essays on the Acropolis, *Daphnis and Chloë,* Marcus Aurelius, Montaigne, Flaubert, Ibsen, and Púshkin. All these writings are centered in one idea—the ''polar'' opposition of the Greek conception of the sanctity of the flesh, and of the Christian conception of the sanctity of the spirit, and the necessity of uniting them in one supreme synthesis. This central antithesis dominates a number of minor antitheses (such as the Nietzschean antithesis of Apollo and Dionysos), so that the general impression of his work as a whole is one of significant contrasts and relations. The identity of opposites and the synthesis of contrasts dominate all this world of interconnected poles. Every idea is a ''pole,'' an ''abyss'' and a ''mystery.'' ''Mystery,'' ''polar,'' and ''synthesis'' are his favorite words. Οὐρανὸς ἄνω, οὐρανὸς κάτω is his favorite maxim, and its symbol the starry sky reflected in the sea. This new world of his, with its mysterious connecting strings and mutually reflected poles, attracted the tastes of a public that had been for generations fed on the small beer of idealistically colored positivism. Merezhkóvsky's popularity became very great among the advanced and the young, and for about a decade he was the central figure of the whole ''modern'' movement. At present all this symbolism seems to us rather puerile and shallow, lacking in those qualities which make the work of the genuine symbolists more than a mere checkerboard of interesting straight lines. He has neither the subtlety and saturated culturedness of Ivánov, nor the intense personal earnestness of Blok, nor the immaterial Ariel-like quality of Bély. His style also lacks charm. Even more obviously than his philosophy, Merezhkóvsky's prose is nothing more than a network of mechanical antitheses. But in spite of this, all his work is historically important and was for its time beneficent. It introduced to the Russian reader a whole unknown world of cultural values; it made familiar and significant to him figures and epochs that had been only names in textbooks; it gave a life to objects and buildings, to all the material side of bygone civilizations, which is loaded with such portentous symbolism in Merezhkóvsky's novels. This shallow symbolism is dead, but it has done good educational service. After Merezhkóvsky, Florence and Athens became something more than mere names to the Russian intellectual, and if they are now living entities he owes it very largely to the sophistications of **Julian** and **Leonardo.**

In 1901 Merezhkóvsky began publishing (in monthly instalments in *Mir iskússtva*) his most important work, **Tolstóy and Dostoyévsky.** The first two of its three parts—*Life, Writings,* and *Religion*—are the most intelligent and readable thing he ever wrote. His interpretation of the personalities of Tolstóy and Dostoyévsky dominated Russian literature for many years. Like all his conceptions, it is a more or less cleverly constructed antithesis, which is developed in the most thoroughgoing way to explain and bring into order the minutest details of the life, work, and religion of the two great writers. Tolstóy, in Merezhkóvsky's interpretation, is the great pagan and pantheist, the ''seer of the flesh'' (*taynovídets plóti*)—a half truth there was some merit in discovering in 1900. Dostoyévsky is the great Christian, ''the seer of the spirit'' (*taynovídets dúkha*)—another half truth it was less difficult to discover. The book may still be read with interest and profit, but the simple-minded reader who is uninitiated into the mazes of Merezhkóvsky's mentality will either be repelled by its geometrical seesaw of contrasts or fall too easily into the carefully woven nets of his sophistry. *Tolstóy and Dostoyévsky* marks the transition of Merezhkóvsky from West to East—from Europe to Russia, from the Greek to the Christian ideal. The "great pagan" Tolstóy is consistently belittled before the "great Christian" Dostoyévsky, and the messianic mission of Russia is everywhere emphasized. *Peter and Alexis* (the third part of *Christ and Antichrist*), written immediately after *Tolstóy and Dostoyévsky* and published in 1905, is a further vindication of the "Russian" and "Christian" cause against the Western and pagan spirit of "Antichrist" embodied in Peter the Great. (pp. 412-15)

There is no need to deal in any detail with Merezhkóvsky's numerous books of "philosophical" prose published after *Tolstóy and Dostoyévsky* (*Gógol and the Devil, The Prophet of the Russian Revolution, Not Peace but a Sword, Sick Russia,* essays on Lérmontov, on Tyútchev and Nekrásov, and so on). In them he retains, and even exaggerates, the fundamental characteristic of his style—an immoderate love of antithesis. But whereas his early works are written in a reasonable and "tidy" manner, from about 1905 he developed a sort of verbal hysteria that has made all he wrote after that date utterly unreadable. Every one of his books and essays is a seesaw of mechanical antithesis sustained from beginning to end in the shrillest of hysterical falsettos. This style developed when he grew conscious of himself as a great philosopher and prophet, and its appearance is roughly simultaneous with the time his teaching took its final form. This teaching styles itself Third Testament Christianity. It insists on the imminence of a new revelation and on the approach of a new religious era. But his mysticism is not concretely personal like Soloviëv's; it represents the universe as a system of variously interconnected ideas reflected in individual and material symbols. His Christ is an abstraction, not a person. His religion is not based on personal religious experience, but on the speculations of his symmetry-loving brain. Judged by religious standards, his writings are mere literature. Judged by literary standards, they are bad literature.

Merezhkóvsky's fame outside Russia is mainly based on his novels. The first of these, *The Death of the Gods* (*Julian the Apostate* . . .), is also the best. Not that it is in any sense a great novel, or even a novel at all in any true sense of the word. It is entirely lacking in creative power. But it is a good work of popularization, an excellent "home university" book that has probably interested more Russian readers in antiquity than any other single book ever did. The same may be said of *Leonardo da Vinci,* but this time with some reservation. In *Julian* the material is kept in hand and the "encyclopædia" side is not allowed to grow beyond all measure; *Leonardo* is already in danger of being stifled by quotations from sources and by the historical bric-a-brac, which is there only because Merezhkóvsky happens to know it. Besides, both these novels are disfigured by the artificiality of the ideas that preside over them, which are of his ordinary crudely antithetic kind. Both *Julian* and *Leonardo* are inferior to Bryúsov's *Fire Angel.* Merezhkóvsky's novels on Russian subjects (*Peter and Alexis, Alexander I, December the Fourteenth*), as well as his plays *Paul I* and *The Romanticists,* are on a much lower level of literary merit. They are formless masses of raw (sometimes badly understood, always wrongly interpreted) material, written from beginning to end in an intolerable hysterical falsetto, and saturated *ad nauseam* with his artificial, homuncular "religious" ideas. Merezhkóvsky is a victim of ideas. If he had never tried to have any ideas, he might have developed into a good novelist for boys, for even in his worst and latest novels, there is always

a page or two that reveals him as a creditable and vivid describer of events. Thus, in the dreary *December the Fourteenth,* the scene in which a mutinous battalion of the guards rush down the street with bayonets lowered, its officers brandishing their swords, breathless with running and Revolutionary excitement, might have been quite in its place in a less sophisticated narrative.

To sum up, Merezhkóvsky's place in literary history is very considerable, for he was the representative man of a very important movement for more than a decade (1893-1905). But as a writer, he scarcely survives, and the first part of *Tolstóy and Dostoyévsky* remains his only work that will still be read in the next generation. (pp. 416-17)

D. S. Mirsky, "The New Movements of the Nineties," in his A History of Russian Literature Comprising "A History of Russian Literature" and "Contemporary Russian Literature," edited by Francis J. Whitfield, Alfred A. Knopf, 1949, pp. 407-29.

P. W. WILSON   (essay date 1934)

[*Wilson was an English biographer, novelist, and critic who wrote extensively on religious themes. In the following excerpt, he discusses the unorthodoxy and forcefulness of Merezhkovsky's theology as put forth in* Jesus the Unknown.]

In the person of Merejkowski there is concentrated the surviving mysticism of a Christendom that has been secularized. The prayers of saints, the songs of angels, the preaching of evangelists, the faith of the fathers—all of this is unquenchable in his sincere and reverent being. Like Paul before Nero, there he stands, undaunted by denials, unconquered by doubts and unafraid of Nazis or Fascists or Communists or whoever they be that seek to stamp out the divine spark which transforms the soul of man into a shrine of the eternal.

In a moving passage Merejkowski refers to his New Testament—"a small book in 32mo, 626 double-column pages of small print, bound in black leather" which has been in his possession for thirty years. He says:

> I read it daily and shall continue to read it as long as my eyes can see, and by every kind of light, by rays coming from the sun or from the hearth, on brightest days and in blackest nights, happy or unhappy, sick or well, full of faith or of doubt, full of feeling or devoid of feeling. And it seems to me that there is always something new in what I read, something unfathomed, and that I shall never plumb its depths or reach its end.

Of that New Testament he also writes:

> The gilt edges of the leaves are tarnished, the paper is yellow, the leather binding is coming to pieces and the back has come unstuck. Some of the pages are loose . . . it ought to be rebound, but I cannot find it in my heart to send it away; indeed, the thought of being separated from it for even a few days frightens me. . . . What shall be buried with me in my coffin? The Book. With what shall I rise from the grave? With the Book. What did I do on the earth? I read the Book.

Armed with a weapon that is mighty in his hands, Merejkowski challenges a civilization that, despite his Leonardo, knows him not. He pities the "poor soul" of Nietzsche, "bound in its earthly hell of insanity." He denounces Renan, who "has no rival" in the deadly "arts," defined as an ability "to mingle poison with honey, to conceal needles in bread pellets.'' He ridicules the "scientific dementia" or "mythomania" that dismisses Jesus as "a wraith, a composite personality created by Seneca and Josephus Flavius." Against the perception that is limited to sight of what can be seen, there are leveled the uncompromising shafts of that insight which, with more penetrating rays than visible light, reveals the unseen.

The method of Merejkowski is symphonic. He takes what he means by "the gospel" as his theme and elaborates around it a varied orchestration. The variations are at times bewildering and, like the dissonance of other contemporary classics, even cacophonous. But, amid the uproar, the theme is dominant.

A true exile never ceases to be himself and the manner of this composition is Russian. Here is no fugue by Bach in which every note harmonizes with the rhythmic music of revolving spheres. The symphony is in the manner of Tchaikovsky—reverent yet barbaric, tender amid tornadoes; reiterating the clangor of major chords yet subduing sudden climaxes into swift and startling silences. In the heights, some lonely flute sings what is left of its song; and in the depths, the grumbling thunder of the drum mutters obstinate rebellion against tranquillity.

Of Brahms, it is said that his masterpieces are better than they sound whereas Tchaikovsky's sound better than they are. The merits of this literary Tchaikovsky are uneven. He is not merely graphic. He is paragraphic and, like stanzas of a poem, the paragraphs are numbered. It is arithmetic that, as a thread, prevents the pearls from scattering.

A strong man in his strength strains after a supreme significance, amid which struggle materials are thrown, hither and thither, into a disarray of allusion and argument, narrative and description, lapses into scholarship and leaps into mysticism, verbless sentences, rhetorical questions and exclamatory outbursts.

Amid intensity of enthusiasm there is apt to be sacrificed an exactitude of meaning. On the Transfiguration, we have this:

> Cold as death was the flame of His glance, and His face shone darkly, like the sun before an eclipse.

Whatever be true of a gaze, the glance reveals life, not death; a flame cannot be cold; no face or anything else has shone darkly; and "before an eclipse" suns and moons shine exactly as usual. What sounds so splendid is not easily translated into sense.

How long and earnestly Merejkowski has wrestled with his Wellhausens and his Weizsäckers is indicated by multitudinous "notes." But erudition, so acquired, has its perils.

In the ancient creeds there is declared the dogma of the Virgin birth. At Rome, in the year 1854, there was promulgated the dogma of the Immaculate Conception. As every theologian is aware, these dogmas are frequently confused. But we hardly expected that, on two occasions, one term should appear in these pages where, as it seems to us, the other term was clearly intended. In one enveloping "mystery," to use the word that is standard throughout Eastern churches, the distinctions over dogma, so sharply defined by the schoolmen, are adoringly absorbed.

As an interpreter of the New Testament, which he knows by heart, Merejkowski is impregnably entrenched on his own ground. It is when he proceeds from what he calls the known

Christ to the unknown—from "the Book" to the "agrapha," or unwritten life of Jesus—that questions arise.

Merejkowski emphasizes the importance of the tradition out of which the canon of Scripture was, as it were, consolidated. He quotes at length from records that the early church held to be apocryphal. Nor does he exclude the hostile or pagan witness. As it seems to us, though not always to our author, these fragments as a whole show that the evangelists in their selections picked the best.

But it is one thing to gather up ancient legend. It is quite another thing to seek to create a new legend, that had no existence prior to the twentieth century. From time to time Merejkowski joins the company of the numerous writers—usually inferior to himself—who, like medieval artists, seek to fascinate by fiction. They portray the Christ of their own imagination.

In Scripture we are told, simply and clearly, that Jesus was led into the wilderness to be tempted of the devil. Let us see how this appears in a typical "agrapha." We read:

> He who was in the white raiment crossed, as though on wings, to the other side of the torrent, stepping from stone to stone over the foaming whirl, and began to mount the steep goat path which led up the almost perpendicular cliff. Here, too, he seemed to fly; the white raiment darted in and out of the dark green heather.

And "Simon, with a last sobbing breath, sighed heavily" and said, "He is gone—he is gone."

Some people admire a painting of the Temptation by El Greco. Others are less appreciative. But, in any event, all know it to be El Greco. What we have quoted is Merejkowski. For Simon's last sobbing breath, for his heavy sigh, for his ejaculation, "He is gone—he is gone," there is no shred of evidence.

The art of the exile is apocalyptic. Ezekiel "among the captives by the river of Chebar"—Daniel as a prisoner in a Babylonian palace—Bernard, the monk of Clairvaux—Dante driven forth from Florence—Blake—abnormal amid the normalcies—and Lewis Carroll segregated at Oxford from the nineteenth century—all of them were aviators, winging their way through space, with no support save the invisible. To the infinities, Merejkowski—crying, "O marvel of marvels, O unending wonder"—holds the eternal passport. Of the kingdom that is from everlasting to everlasting, he is a citizen.

The aviator surveys a landscape with which he has ceased to be in contact. Roads where men travel are to him direction. Homes are roofs, flat as the map is flat. There is no foreground to him that flies—not a hint in these pages of the Paris where Merejkowski has been domiciled. In the "heavenly atmosphere" there is only distance, and "the farthest point seems near."

Nor is there any ecclesiastical map on which we may locate the exile amid his apocalypse. To what spire of a cathedral, to what peak of a sacred mountain, can the aviator raise his eyes? Catholic and Protestant, modern and ancient, are absorbed in the universal. "The inner tumults of man," we read, "are as obedient to Jesus as those of the elements." It is the liturgy of those who worship neither at Jerusalem nor on Georgim but in spirit and in truth.

The vision of the apocalyptic may be remote from earth. But it is unobstructed. He sees East and West, past, present and future, in one comprehensive panorama. It is on mankind as a whole that he delivers judgment. We read:

The world, as it now is, and the Book cannot continue together. One of two things: either the world must become other than it is, or the Book must disappear from the world.

At a moment when "the Book" is either rewritten or suppressed or ignored, these are provocative words.

The question is "whether Jesus is above history, or whether history is above Jesus," and that question, according to this Tolstoy of orthodoxy, is ethical. "It would never enter any one's head," he declares, "to ask whether Jesus had lived unless, before asking the question, the mind had been darkened by the wish that he had not lived," and in evangelic fervor, he adds:

> The thief requires that there should be no light: the world that there should be no Christ.

It is easier to hear this from a Russian than from a revivalist. But it is precisely the kind of thing that the Rev. William Sunday has been saying whenever he preaches.

Like all apocalyptic seers, Merejkowski peers into the future. "Yes," he cries, "terrible as it may be for us, we are the men of the End, of the Second Coming, nearer than any for two thousand years of Christianity to seeing His face" which countenance is "Lightning—the lightning that burns the world to ashes." Once more,

> The world is very evil,
>   The times are waxing late,
> Be sober and keep vigil,
>   The Judge is at the gate.

Of Merejkowski, the Russian mystic who is excommunicated by Moscow, that is the ultimatum to civilization as he sees civilization on the Continent of Europe. Savonarola would have understood it. Loyola would have understood it. Moody would have understood it. Dr. Buchman understands it. It is inherent in the utterances of Pope Piux XI. It is visualized in armies and navies and the collapse of the League of Nations.

Is the world coming to an end? Despite apocalypses, it did not end—as Merejkowski reminds us—in the first century when the temple on Mount Zion vanished in conflagration. It did not in the fifteenth century when Constantinople was overwhelmed. Will it end in the twentieth century? Colosseums are crumbling. But are there no catacombs? Below the surface of publicity, unknown disciples of the Christ unknown are still building the foundations of the kingdom that has yet to be. (pp. 7, 16)

> *P. W. Wilson, "Merejkowski's Mystical but Impassioned Life of Jesus," in* The New York Times Book Review, *February 25, 1934, pp. 7, 16.*

HARRY M. CAMPBELL   (essay date 1948)

[*In the following essay, Campbell reevaluates Merezhkovsky's trilogy* Christ and Antichrist, *praising it for skillfully incorporating psychological and philosophical analysis and for realistically depicting its historical characters.*]

Merezhkovsky's great trilogy of novels entitled *Christ and Antichrist* were once considered to be among the best of the minor classics in Russian fiction. Now, however, of the three books—(1) *The Death of the Gods: Julian the Apostate* (2) *The Forerunner: The Romance of Leonardo da Vinci,* and (3) *Peter and Alexis: A Romance of Peter the Great*—only the *Leonardo* receives much attention. The neglect of this important trilogy

can be explained, to a great extent, by Prince D. S. Mirsky's vehement condemnation of it in his very learned book entitled *Contemporary Russian Literature* . . . [see excerpt dated 1926]. Prince Mirsky's reputation as a historian and critic of Russian literature seems to have induced many readers to trust his judgment, even when, as in his criticism of this trilogy, it is not supported by very convincing logic. Prince Mirsky says simply of *Julian the Apostate* that "it is not in any sense a great novel, or even a novel at all in any true sense of the word. It is entirely lacking in creative power." But even so, he thinks, it is better than *The Romance of Leonardo da Vinci,* because *Leonardo* "is already in danger of being stifled by quotations from sources, and by the historical bric-a-brac which is there only because Merezhkovsky happens to know it." And *Peter and Alexis* he dismisses as a "formless mass of raw material, written from beginning to end in an intolerable hysterical falsetto, and saturated *ad nauseam* with his [Merezhkovsky's] homuncular 'religious' ideas." Perhaps because he found Merezhkovsky's art "in danger of being stifled by quotations from sources," Prince Mirsky carefully avoids any quotation from these books which he attacks so viciously. Indeed he gives no proof whatsoever beyond the somewhat explosive, name-calling remarks quoted above and a few others like them. The truth of the matter, as this paper attempts to demonstrate, is that the original, contemporary high praise of all these books was far more nearly correct than Prince Mirsky's pontifical condemnation of them.

In each of these novels, to be sure, the opposition and then the attempted reconciliation of "the truth of the Titan and the truth of the Galilean" does point to what Prince Mirsky calls a chaotic eclecticism, but the philosophical chaos is in the historical situation and not in the artist, whose only obligation is to present dramatically the great and confused conflict. The dramatist does seem to hope that the opposing forces may be reconciled in some Nietzschean Superman, but he recognizes that all such attempts in the past have failed. The reconciliation has always been blocked by the tragic conflict between Christians and pagan characters, and between Christian and pagan qualities within individual characters. It is this great conflict which unifies the vast and complicated tragedy that covers three of the most troubled periods in human history.

This mighty conflict appears, first of all psychologically, in the complex and often inconsistent personalities of the three main characters in the trilogy—Julian the Apostate; Leonardo da Vinci and Peter the Great. Instead of simplifying these historical characters for dramatic purposes, Merezhkovsky has made exciting mental drama out of this very complexity. Julian the Apostate, for example, though hating Christianity passionately, often proves to be essentially more Christlike than the Christians, and, for that reason, says his prophetic adviser Maximus, is destined not to succeed in restoring the pagan gods. ". . . these gods of thine," says Arsinoe to Julian, "have been seduced by the fishermen of Capernaum,—weak, meek, ailing, dying from their pity toward men,—inasmuch as, dost thou see, pity toward men is deathly for the gods." Leonardo da Vinci, an even more complex character than Julian, seems to have so many characteristics of both Christ and Antichrist, often in such appalling juxtaposition, that Giovanni, his puzzled and devoted Christian student, worries himself into insanity and dies of brain fever. "How can it be?" says Giovanni "The same man,—he that bestoweth his benediction, with a guiltless smile, upon the pigeons, like to St. Francis; and he, of the smithy of hell, the inventor of the iron monster with the ensanguined spider's paws,—the same man? . . . the Usurper!" And Peter the Great, in the concluding volume, though ardently

interested in what he considers to be the welfare of his countrymen, is so cruel in his treatment of them that to many of
them, especially after he has tortured and killed his own son,
this self-styled "Russian Christ" seems to be in very truth
Antichrist.

In presenting such complex characters as these, Merezhkovsky
succeeds because he uses the direct dramatic technique always.
He does not lecture the reader, like Thackeray or Fielding, but
presents philosophy or profound psychological analysis in realistic conversation or illustrates it by vivid action. This is a
technical trick that he seems to have learned from Dostoievsky,
and his handling of it seems indeed not unworthy of the master.
Again it must be emphasized that it is the skill of the dramatization and not the soundness of the philosophy underneath
that should determine our judgment of the work as art. Consider, then, Merezhkovsky's treatment of a subject that would
appear to be very dry and abstract—religious heresies. Flaubert, in *The Temptation of Saint Anthony*, gives a straightforward and exhaustive recital of the various heretical sects that
tempt Saint Anthony; but Merezhkovsky (as skillfully here as
Dostoievsky handling similar material) arranges and manipulates his actors on a stage—the Atrium of Constantine, to which
the Emperor has summoned representatives of the various sects
for an ecclesiastical council. An acute observer explains to his
companion the beliefs of the different sects as he points out
their representatives stalking in hostile fashion about the Atrium:

> The blue morning sky seemed dark against the daz-
> zling whiteness of the double colonnade surrounding
> the court. . . . White pigeons were fluttering here and
> there in the sky, with gleeful beating of wings. In
> the centre of the court stood the statue of Venus
> Callipyge, in warm and beautiful marble. The monks,
> passing by her, turned away, hiding their eyes, but
> the tender temptress remained, for all that, in their
> midst. . . . The dark robes of the religious appeared
> blacker still, their starvation-dulled faces more meagre.
> Each strove to wear an air of indifference and pre-
> sumption, feigning not to see his enemy at his elbow,
> yet casting stealthy glances of curiosity and con-
> tempt.

> "Holy Mother of God, what is this? Whither are we
> fallen?" said the old bishop Eustace, with profound
> emotion. "Let me pass out, soldiers!". . . .

> "By the will of Augustus, everybody here has come
> to the council," responded Daglaif, inflexibly keep-
> ing him back.

> "But this is not a council, it is a den of thieves!" . . .

> Juventinus noticed that the Caecilian bishop who was
> passing in front of Purpuris brushed the vestments of
> the Donatist with the corner of his chasuble. The
> latter turned fiercely round, with a growl of disgust,
> and, taking the stuff between two fingers, shook it
> several times before the eyes of everybody.

> Evander informed Juventinus in a low voice that when
> a Caecilian happened to enter a Donatist congregation
> he was hunted out and the flags touched by his feet
> were washed with salt water.

> Behind Purpuris, dogging him step by step, walked
> his faithful bodyguard, an enormous half-savage Af-
> rican . . . armed with a cudgel, gripped tightly in his
> nervous hands. He was an Ethiopian peasant, be-
> longing to the self-mutilating sect called Circumcel-
> lions.

Besides his ability to make each scene an intense drama in
itself, Merezhkovsky is able to unify an enormous variety of
scenes by making them all illustrations of the great struggle
between Christianity and paganism. Apparent digressions, like
Julian's raping his wife during his expedition into the Germanic
forest, prove to be directly and climactically connected with
this central theme:

> She was trembling and leaning against the wall; he
> approached and put his arm round her waist.

> "What are you doing? Let me go, let me go!" She
> tried to cry out, to call the servant.

> "Why are you calling? Am I not your husband?"

> She began to weep bitterly.

> "Brother, this must not be. . . . I am the bride of
> Christ! . . . I believed that you . . ."

> "The bride of the Roman Caesar cannot be the bride
> of Christ!"

> "Julian! . . . If you believe in Him . . ."

> He smiled.

> "I abhor the Galilean!"

> In a supreme effort she strove to repulse him, ex-
> claiming. "Away, Devil! . . . Why hast thou aban-
> doned me, Lord?"

> With his impious hands he tore off the black vest-
> ment. His soul was full of fear, but never before in
> his life had he known such intoxication in evil-doing.
> Ironically, with a smile of defiance, the Roman Cae-
> sar gazed at the opposite corner of the cell, where in
> the feeble flicker of the lamp-light hung the great
> black crucifix. . . .

Merezhkovsky uses the technical device of shifting from scene
to scene with impressionistic rapidity to parallel the historical
intermingling of the two great forces, hostile to each other and
yet confusingly related often in the same person or place: pictures of bacchanalian revels by the side of the Madonna and
Child in Duke Moro's palace; Pope Alexander VI praying sincerely and fervently at Mass and then going immediately to
witness an amatory contest involving harlots and powerful male
slaves; Leonardo working at the same time with equal devotion
on "The Last Supper" and on "Leda and the Swan," one of
the most voluptuous pictures ever painted; Leonardo finally
completing as his last work a figure whose clothing, staff, and
general bearing proclaim him to be St. John the Baptist but
who has the face of Bacchus. With the opposing forces so
bewilderingly mixed, the traditional type of orderly progression
of events would hardly have been appropriate—or possible.

But with all this complexity the most rigid unity is maintained,
even in *The Romance of Leonardo da Vinci*. I am unable to
find in this remarkable work what Prince Mirsky calls "bric-
a-brac which is there only because Merezhkovsky happens to
know it." It would be helpful if Prince Mirsky had been more
specific in this and his other pontifical judgments; but surely
he could find nothing more nearly bric-a-brac than the Witches'
Sabbath. Yet, in spite of the ornateness of Merezhkovsky's
description, he transforms this curious piece of folklore into a
masterpiece of imaginative prose that is as functional in his
story as the Porter Scene in *Macbeth* which De Quincey analyzed so brilliantly. Without implying that Merezhkovsky's
dramatic power is worthy of a full comparison with Shakespeare's, one can see that the Sabbath, like the Porter Scene,
enhances the central tragedy at the natural level by transferring

it briefly to a carefully conceived supernatural setting. In this Russian *Walpurgisnacht* the superstitious perversions of Christianity in the Middle Ages merge into the resurrection of the gods of Hellas—a poetic reinforcement of the pagan resurrection theme that unifies the book:

> Around the Goat of the Night, *Hyrcus Nocturnus,* enthroned in state on a crag, thousands upon thousands whirled by, like rotted leaves of autumn,— sans beginning, sans end.
>
> "Garr! Garr! Glorify the Goat of the Night! . . ."
>
> High and hoarse skirled the bag-pipes, made of hollowed dead men's bones; and the drum, drawn over with the skin of men who had met their end on the gallows, thumped with a wolf's tail, throbbed and rumbled, muffled and even, *toop, toop, toop.* In gigantic cauldrons a horrible mess was coming to a boil, unutterably delectable, even though unsalted, for the Host of this place detested salt.
>
> "Let us dance!" Aunt Sidonia was impatiently tugging Cassandra.
>
> "The horse-trader might see us!" exclaimed the girl, laughing.
>
> "May he be food for the dogs, this horse-trader!" answered the old woman.
>
> They both dashed off, and the dance carried them off like a gale, with din, howling, squealing, roaring, and laughing:
>
> "*Garr! Garr!* Right to left. Right to left!" . . .
>
> Suddenly they all stopped . . . and grew deathly still . . .
>
> And the miracle was wrought.
>
> The goat's hide fell from him [the Goat of the Night], even as the shed skin sloughs from a snake, and the ancient Olympic god Dionysos appeared before Monna Cassandra, with a smile of eternal rejoicing on his lips, holding a thyrsus uplifted in one hand, a cluster of grapes in the other; a leaping panther strove to lick this cluster with its tongue.
>
> And at the very same instant the Devil's Sabbath was transformed into the divine orgy of Bacchus; the old witches into youthful maenads; the monstrous demons into aegipedal satyrs; and there, where the dead bowlders of chalky cliffs were, sprang up colonnades of white marble, illuminated by the sun; between them in the distance, the azure sea began to sparkle, and Cassandra beheld in the clouds the entire sun-clad throng of the gods of Hellas.

Then, as in the Porter Scene, we are brought back to reality by a knocking from the outside. The doltish trader, who has come to claim the hand of Cassandra, knocks on the door in the rain, shouting that he has brought a calf as a present for her uncle and guardian. Cassandra, who detests the trader, recalls the interrupted merriment of the Sabbath and reflects:

> "Was this in a dream, or in reality? Probably, in a dream. But that which is taking place now,—that is reality. After Sunday, Monday . . ."
>
> "Open up! Open up!" vociferated the trader, by now in a voice grown hoarse and desperate.
>
> The heavy drops from the water-spout plashed monotonously into a dirty puddle. The calf lowed piteously. The monastery bell tolled dismally on.

Leonardo himself is portrayed quite as vividly as the large number of less complex characters around him; but not even in presenting this most enigmatical of characters does Merezhkovsky have to resort very often to straight forward, omniscient-author analysis. Leonardo's personality appears vividly, if not altogether clearly (for he never understood himself very clearly), in his actions and in his conversations, especially those with his friend Machiavelli. Leonardo devotes much of his time and genius to reviving and improving upon Hellenistic culture; but ironically, in his last days, though he does not believe in the doctrines of the Church and would have preferred to die "as he had lived,—in freedom and truth," he accepts the ritualistic ministrations of the priest to avoid disturbing the peaceful faith of his devoted pupil Francesco. The thoughts of the dying Leonardo are presented very effectively in stream-of-consciousness mental drama.

The great struggle of the trilogy is resumed some two hundred years late (in the third volume) with Peter the Great representing Hellenism and Western culture, and his son Alexis favoring the traditionally Christian part of the Russian nation. Again there is an ironical intermingling of the two opposing forces, and the same merciless psychological dissection of the frailties of both groups, presented directly through conversation and action, or from the point of view of minor characters like the German secretary of Alexis' German wife. The point of view changes but is usually limited rather than omniscient-author and is never confused. Additional unity comes from Peter's interest in bringing to Russia the results of the Hellenistic revivals to which Julian and Leonardo had contributed so much. Peter brings to Petersburg, for example, the beautiful statue of Venus by Praxiteles which had been unearthed near Florence by Leonardo in a memorable scene from the second novel of the trilogy. The following passage, though similar to the oratorical art criticism of Élie Faure, performs an important technical function: it relates this book, obviously but effectively, to the first two and evokes very vividly the ominously changed atmosphere in which the great struggle will continue:

> She [the statue of Venus now in Petersburg] was the same now, as on the hillside in Florence where Leonardo da Vinci's pupil had looked at her with superstitious fear; or, yet earlier, when in the depths of Cappadocia, in the forsaken temple near the old castle of Macellum, her last true worshipper had prayed to her, that pale boy in monk's attire, the future Emperor Julian the Apostate. She had remained the same innocent yet voluptuous goddess, naked and not ashamed. From that very day when she arose from her millennial tomb far away in Florence, she had progressed further and further, from age to age, from people to people, halting nowhere, till in her victorious march she had at last reached the limits of the earth, the Hyperborean Scythia, beyond which there remains nought but chaos and darkness. And having fixed herself on the pedestal she for the first time glanced with a look of surprised curiosity around this strange new land, these flat moss-covered bogs, this curious town, so like the settlements of nomads, at this sky, which was the same day and night, these black, drowsy, terrible waves of Styx. This land . . . seemed as hopeless as the land of Oblivion, the dark Hades. Yet the goddess smiled as the sun would have smiled had he penetrated into Hades.

The rococo liveliness of diction in background passages like this becomes real vigor and solid strength in the fateful narrative that reaches its climax in the execution of Alexis by his own father. The immense gusto and vitality of the narrative are restrained by the very carefully ironical balancing of the two opposing forces. The inconclusive ending of the trilogy is necessary in the interest of truth, for neither side has ever won in this eternal struggle. The irony apparent in the final chapter, entitled "The Coming Christ," is certainly artistically superior to the ending of a novel often judged superior to Merezhkovsky's trilogy—*Quo Vadis.* In the sentimental view of Sienkiewicz, the Apostle Peter's death represents the eternal triumph of Christianity already achieved: ". . . though its Emperors and the hosts of the barbarians and the succeeding ages would pass away, the reign of that aged man in Rome would last until the end of time." Merezhkovsky, on the other hand, ends his trilogy with a dramatic presentation of an ironical and a tragic truth: neither Hebraism nor Hellenism, to use Arnold's terms, has won, or perhaps can win, and they have never been satisfactorily reconciled. The result of course is philosophical chaos, but, once more, the chaos is in the situation and not in the artist who is honest enough to portray it as it really is. In spite of too many rococo and even Bulweresque passages, Merezhkovsky has presented a powerful story that vividly dramatizes important problems still harassing our own variant of a Götterdämmerung civilization. (pp. 44-51)

> *Harry M. Campbell, "Merezhkovsky's 'Christ and Antichrist'," in* The Western Review, *Vol. 13, No. 1, Autumn, 1948, pp. 44-51.*

RALPH E. MATLAW (essay date 1957)

[*In the following essay, Matlaw summarizes Merezhkovsky's critical essay* On the Causes of the Present Decline and the New Currents of Contemporary Russian Literature *and discusses its importance to the Russian Symbolist movement.*]

D. S. Merežkovskij's *On the Causes of the Present Decline and the New Currents of Contemporary Russian Literature,* written during the four years preceding its publication in 1893, is a curious literary document. Any attempt to break with tradition is bound to meet opposition, particularly in a "committed" literature like Russia's. To attack the idols and ideals of a militantly partisan reading public is a dangerous undertaking: the new movement had to be initiated circumspectly. Consequently, much in the essay is understated or overqualified; some of the most important issues are completely avoided. While the essay traces the decline of Russian literature in the 1880's with considerable insight, it contains egregious errors in evaluating tradition, interpreting contemporary achievements, and stating future needs. (p. 177)

The essay readily divides into two sections, each comprising three chapters; the first is devoted to the decline of letters, the second to new literary currents. After a general discussion of literature and culture, Merežkovskij attributes the decline to current public tastes, monetary rewards and the system of publication, public demands, the decline of language, and the inadequacy of criticism. The last three chapters designate tendencies inherent in Russian literature which Merežkovskij would emphasize in what he calls the "new literary direction": "new idealism" in Turgenev, Gončarov, Dostoevskij, and Tolstoj; love for the people (Ijubov' k narodu) in Kol'cov, Nekrasov, Uspenskij, Maxajlovskij, and Korolenko; the achievement of the current literary generation, Garšin, Čexov, Fofanov, and Minskij; and new directions in the criticism of S. A. Andreevskij and Spasowicz.

Merežkovskij sees a prophetic view of the decline of Russian letters in Turgenev's death-bed letter urging Tolstoj to return

to literary activity, for "language is the incarnation of the national spirit; therefore the decline of the Russian language and its literature is at the same time the decline of the Russian spirit." Merežkovskij anticipates the objection that to consider literature as being in decline is a commonplace of criticism, by retorting that such strictures are usually malevolent and represent the attack on new achievements by older generations. Another objection, attributing literary decline to an absence of genius after the era of Turgenev, Gončarov, Dostoevskij, and Tolstoj requires a more elaborate answer. Literature must be delimited from poetry: "poetry is a primordial and eternal force, an elemental one, an immediate and involuntary gift of God" while literature "is really the same poetry, seen not from the point of view of individual works of various artists, but as a force moving whole generations, whole nations in a certain cultural direction, as a succession of poetic phenomena, handed from century to century and joined by a great historical beginning." Literature can exist only in a receptive setting and tradition. All cultural creations, therefore, represent the genius of the nation (*narod*).

The next problem is to ascertain whether Russia has a "literature" rather than a succession of great poets and writers. Puškin had complained about the hopeless loneliness of the writer in Russia, and other literary giants had suffered similarly. While writers with temperamental and literary affinities have had some intellectual and aesthetic communication, they have done so in isolated, doctrinaire "circles" which are an even greater evil than loneliness, since they avoid productive and stimulating interchange. Under various guises all Russian writers manifest the same fundamental "flight from civilization" (*begstvo ot kul'tury*) so typical of Tolstoj. Without a culture one may be, like Tolstoj, a great poet, but not a man producing "literature." Nevertheless, "poetry" and "literature" need not remain apart. Goethe, for example, managed to combine the two. He did not fear that science and culture would set him apart from nature and from his fatherland, but rejoiced when a higher degree of culture was attained, since it also indicated a greater nationality (*narodnost'*). Therefore, "no matter how many writers of genius may appear in Russia, while there is no literature of its own, it will not have its own Goethe, its own representative of the national spirit."

The first chapter, in attempting a definition, indicates a critical as well as historical anachronism. Many ideas in Merežkovskij, such as his definition of poetry, are commonplaces of German romantic criticism. They may be found, for example, in A. W. Schlegel's *Vorlesungen über die dramatische Kunst und Literatur,* which Merežkovskij, then engaged in translating Greek drama, might be echoing; religious and nationalistic pronouncements smack of F. Schlegel and Novalis. Even Belinskij, in his *Literary Reveries* of 1834, had lamented the absence of a national literature, maintaining that Deržavin, Puškin, Griboedov, and Krylov are merely four outstanding literary "talents." Almost 50 years later—with considerably less justification—Merežkovskij still fails to see what Russian culture or nationality may be, and how its giants had shaped and expressed it. It is strange indeed that after Dostoevskij's Puškin Day speech Merežkovskij should refuse to acknowledge that a Russian "literature" corresponding to his definition does exist and has existed, or that the individual writer necessarily depends upon literary and national traditions and himself furthers them. Similarities among writers, or even the exacerbated battles between literary camps and between Slavophiles and Westerners, themselves indicate the existence of a vital and developing cultural tradition. But Merežkovskij, perhaps in order to strengthen the polemic value of his essay, refuses to acknowledge that tradition.

He next examines three causes of linguistic deterioration in Russia. The first involves the particularly ironical—almost colloquial—mode of expression used by Russian criticism. Pisarev had used it as an extremely effective weapon and had dazzled the critics of the 1860's with it. However, whereas Pisarev used such language as a source of power, contemporary critics are merely coarse. Pisarev's irony has been turned into an insulting familiarity with the reader; his simplicity, into a lack of concern for all decorum. The second factor in the decline of language is "that special satirical manner Saltykov called 'a slavish Aesopic language'." Merežkovskij, aware that no adverse criticism of Pisarev or Saltykov would be tolerated by liberal readers and polemicists, hastens to add that this language is successfully used by Saltykov, but is senseless and repugnant in critics who lack his artistic organization of material. The third, and most important, reason for decline is the public's and critic's "increasing ignorance." One critic informs the reader that Ibsen's *Doll's House* was first performed in Weimar under Goethe's direction, another calls Leconte de Lille "Count de Lille." Merežkovskij himself provides the best example of the extent to which this ignorance has pervaded literary men when he refers on the next page to an English writer called Samuel Ben Johnson.

Another factor in the decline of literature is the system of paying honorariums to authors. Writers, as "the last remnant of impractical people, the last dreamers" give their work to the public without remuneration. While this statement is obviously false if one considers the dependence of Puškin, Dostoevskij, and to a lesser extent Turgenev and Tolstoj, on the income from their works, or the rise of professional literary men in the 1850's (Nekrasov, Fet, Pisemskij, Ostrovskij, et al.), Merežkovskij's real intention is to convey that an artist's work *cannot* be rewarded financially. "When honorariums cease having an ideal meaning, when they cease being a symbol of the public's gratefulness, but become remuneration for work done, then honorariums become harmful." The use of the word "symbolic" in this context (and the earlier reference to a "symbolic story from the Acts of the Apostles" is, as we shall later see, indicative of his use of the word, and his attitude toward the concept of symbolism. There are, Merežkovskij claims, only two ways of pleasing the public: the first is to write a work of genius—which happens, at best, once or twice in a generation; the other method is to cater to the public's low tastes, and honorariums are an inducement to such pandering. He refutes in two ways the idea that honorariums are a necessity to literature and illustrate the dependence of literature on capital. First, he cites Puškin's statement that Russian writers are members of the highest social class and therefore demand respect for their work (which was certainly no longer true in 1890), and then he claims that unlike other countries, Russia has no intellectual aristocracy capable of appreciating great literature. Honorariums, and the concomitant system of "thick journals," create a public of low intellectual caliber and therefore low literary demands.

A corollary to the system of honorariums is the fact that writers do not dare to publish a work in book form. Books receive little attention and the writer must necessarily come to the journals for honorariums. The editors of these journals are servants of public taste, and will publish nothing that risks public disapproval. In the Western world, Merežkovskij claims, books are held in greater esteem and therefore standards are

not relaxed. Here again he distorts the reality of publishing conditions and fails to consider achievements in serial publications of writers like Dickens in the West or Dostoevskij and Tolstoj in Russia. However, he concludes, honorariums and journals are only external manifestations. The most important single factor in the decline of literature is Russian literary criticism.

Merežkovskij sees two types of critics in Western Europe. Critics like Taine attempt to apply a strict "scientific" system to criticism, but their work is not fruitful since too little is as yet known about the psychology of aesthetics. The second type is the "subjective-artistic" critic who, in certain pages, himself becomes a poet—Sainte-Beuve, Herder, Brandes, Lessing, Carlyle, Belinskij. Merežkovskij commends these critics, since the world of literature plays the same role for them that reality does for the creative writer. Books for them are like living people, calling forth likes and dislikes, suffering and exaltation. The implied polemic against utilitarian criticism is unmistakable. Nevertheless, Merežkovskij fails to point out differences in critical approaches in this extraordinary—and motley—collection of names and, perhaps out of ignorance, perhaps for polemical purposes, disregards critical schemes like Sainte-Beuve's, which, if not as limited as Taine's, are no less rigorous.

"Subjective-artistic" criticism deals with two problems. The poet-critic is interested in the beauty of language rather than the beauty of reality. In its highest form this may be termed the "poetry of ideas," a creation of the nineteenth century's infinite spiritual freedom and "insatiable affliction of knowledge." A second line of development for this criticism may, in the future, lead to explanations of the creative process itself. A chance remark by Puškin, Stendhal, or Flaubert may reveal greater psychological insight than long articles by well-meaning professional critics. Russian criticism, however, with the exception of several articles by Belinskij, Grigor'ev, Straxov, Turgenev, Gončarov, Dostoevskij, and Puškin, has always been anti-scientific and anti-artistic, primarily because Russian critics have been insufficiently artistic and scientific. The publicists who invaded and appropriated criticism did not even possess Pisarev's and Dobroljubov's protective attitude toward philosophy and science. Yet even they were necessary as popularizers of the most common and ordinary ideas. At the moment (1893) Russian criticism can offer only Protopopov and Skabičevskij. While the latter has fewer publicistic tendencies, he compensates for this virtue by his banality and concessions to public taste. These critics see only the banality of tragic occurrences, not real tragedy, and argue the scholastic question "does art exist for life or vice versa?" without realizing that neither can exist without the other. "The highest *moral* meaning of art does not lie in affecting moral tendencies, but in the selfless, incorruptible veracity of the artist, in his fearless sincerity." The only immorality art recognizes is distortion and vulgarity. Critics like Skabičevskij and Protopopov, unaware of the real issues in art, unknowingly cause a decline of letters by their work. Their criticism destroys the literary future of writers who might, under different conditions, have developed into good critics, writers like Burenin and Volynskij. But despite all shortcomings in criticism and literature there is a slight indication of a new trend. The remainder of Merežkovskij's essay is devoted to an investigation of its first signs.

When, in 1886, I. S. Aksakov attempted to characterize the poetic and linguistic problems of the 1830's and the earlier decline of poetry, he attributed the fault to tendentiousness, to making art a means rather than an independent entity. The parallel with the 1880's is clear:

> It seems to us that the impression of *historical necessity* and personal sincerity is no longer evident in our poetry because the historic mission of poetic creation, as we see it, has been accomplished. Contemporary poets may be, and really are, talented to a greater or lesser degree, but they either echo the familiar past, which now lacks its previous enchantment, or they introduce external tendencies, foreign to art, into their works.

> Incidentally, because of the abnormal course of Russian social development, because our enlightenment failed to express the life of our national spirit, because not all strings of the national soul were sounded, because the very forms of our poetry are borrowed, it may be that a renaissance of Russian poetry, expressed in a new, hitherto unknown, individual, more national form, will begin. *Perhaps*; it is not a certainty, only a guess.

Merežkovskij's observations are more militant, and attempt to concretize and explain the tendencies that gave Aksakov a vague premonition of a new movement. He first examines what he calls the "beginning of new idealism" in the works of Turgenev, Gončarov, Dostoevskij, and Tolstoj as a tendency that may help resuscitate Russian literature. The basic taste of the public is realistic, and artistic realism corresponds to scientific positivism and materialism. But another theory, idealism, is held just as strongly and comes into bitter conflict with materialism. Its proponents, among them the French symbolists, are asserting themselves in a new movement. Merežkovskij quotes Zola's opposition to the *symbolistes* from Huret's *Enquête sur l'évolution littéraire en France* but takes issue with him. Not quantity but quality is the criterion: even four lyric lines may have greater literary value than a long series of novels. He contrasts Zola in position, wealth, and health with the "chief of the idealist poets—Paul Verlaine" and notes that the strength of the "idealists" lies not only in their poetry, but also in their revolt. The success of their venture, their revolt against the oppression of positivism, will continue regardless of their poetic achievement, since this revolt is vital. Indeed, this kind of idealism had been stated considerably earlier, by no less a figure than Goethe, who, according to Eckermann, claimed that the work of art is beautiful in proportion to its inaccessibility and incommensurability.

By next noting Goethe's dictum that a work of art must be *symbolic*, Merežkovskij reaches the center of his argument. He now defines the symbol, by example rather than in a formula. Symbolism is a higher, or deeper, aspect of art. Although a scene in a bas-relief of the Parthenon depicts life realistically, even with naturalistic detail, its effect does not correspond to that of a realistic work. "You feel in it the impress of the ideal of human culture, a *symbol* of the free Hellenic spirit." The bas-relief depicts a scene of everyday life but it also reveals the divine aspect of our souls. All Greek art produces the same effect. Similarly, in Ibsen's *Doll's House,* a light is brought on stage and "the replacement of physical darkness by light acts on our inner world; under the realistic detail an artistic *symbol* is hidden." Merežkovskij does not pretend to know how this symbol acts on the reader, nor why it affects him. He merely reiterates "one feels that this happens." "These symbols must pour out naturally and involuntarily from the depth of reality," and since they always do so in great writers like Flaubert and Ibsen, one feels another, a deeper movement in addition to the direction of the thoughts formulated by words.

So far Merežkovskij has not used the words *symbolist* and *symbolism* to correspond to their meaning in French symbolist theory, or even that aspect of suggestion and nuance propounded by Mallarmé in reply to Huret's *Enquête*. Rather, he uses these words to indicate a higher level in the interpretation of an artistic work, a level which is clearly present in every work that does not simply reproduce reality mechanically. Zola himself partakes of this kind of "symbolizing" process, and in Merežkovskij's usage might be called a symbolist. In his discussion of poetry, however, Merežkovskij approximates Mallarmé's *suggérer, voilà le rêve* or the tenets of Verlaine's *Art poétique,* although he does so by means of Tjutčev's romantic ideology. "A thought expressed is a lie" (Mysl' izrečennaja est' lož'), the famous line from Tjutčev's *Silentium!,* serves as the text upon which Merežkovskij bases his conception that whatever is not stated, whatever glimmers through the beauty of a symbol, acts more strongly on the reader than that which is expressed by words. Critics should not even attempt to transmit the meaning of symbolic characters (Faust, Don Quixote), for words only limit and define an idea while symbols express its unlimited aspect. Once again Merežkovskij's irrational extension of anti-positivism is closer to Schelling's or Novalis' concept of the art as the infinite finitely expressed (a commonplace of German Romanticism), than to symbolist theory.

The necessity to widen the realm of experience, to deal with hitherto unknown, fleeting sensations, is for Merežkovskij a necessary adjunct to the extension and change of affective means. The beautiful, as Poe and Baudelaire had pointed out, must to some extent amaze, must be unexpected and rare. This quality has been more or less successfully labelled "impressionism" by French critics. Thus the three requisites of the new art are a widening of artistic apprehension (impressionism) combined with mysticism (idealism) and symbols. Merežkovskij now, however, wishes to emphasize that Russian letters are not derivative nor dependent upon French theory, and that the achievements of the four great Russian prose writers (Turgenev, Gončarov, Dostoevskij, Tolstoj) parallel French developments. He illustrates the three qualities in Turgenev, whose greatest contributions to art were not his tendentious novels but his "poetic" descriptions, his opposition of ideal (fantastic) female types to the vulgarity of life around them. Gončarov and Gogol' used symbols, perhaps to a greater degree than any other writer, primarily in the juxtaposition and delineation of characters. Merežkovskij sees Dostoevskij's contribution to Russian literature as that combination of pity and cruelty which critics still are unable to handle adequately. Dostoevskij and Tolstoj increased the mystical content of literature and showed Europe Russia's free religious feeling. In the footsteps of these "symbolist artists" must follow the new generation, which Merežkovskij aptly names "post-greats."

Merežkovskij requires still another quality in symbolism (and its concomitant "impressionism" and "mysticism") in order for there to be a truly national literature. This quality, which is very similar to his idealism, may be called populism (*narodničestvo*). Kol'cov's verse reflects the discontent, the unlimited desire for freedom that characterizes folk-poetry; he has only one predecessor, Lermontov, whom Merežkovskij considers an idealist and a scorner of all utilitarian ideas. All folk-poetry is essentially religious, and there is but one road to God, a road that leads through the people, the great Christian folk of Russia. Nekrasov's greatness, the beauty that lies in his lyrics, thoroughly reveals his soul. His civic verse is second-rate, but Nekrasov is also an idealist and "more or less like all Russians, a mystic.'' His best poems may be viewed as the highest form and freest expression of religion, and they demonstrate his profound tie with the people. Again and again he reiterates his love for the Virgin and Mother Russia and, indeed, both images frequently fuse in his poetry. "Is not such poetry religion?" asks Merežkovskij. Similarly, *Makar's Dream* contains a breadth of life and of the Russian people, and illustrates that Korolenko, as an idealist, a mystic, a believer, is a great poet. Gleb Uspenskij is ordinarily ashamed of beauty and writes as a publicist rather than as a poet attempting to reach the reader's heart. But Uspenskij, too, becomes a poet when love for the people appears in his work. Populism is even apparent in Mixajlovskij, in his articles on Darwin and Spencer. All Mixajlovskij's originality lies in his deep, ardent populism and subjectivity.

The last chapter of Merežkovskij's essay is devoted to the contemporary literary generation. Its first representative is Garšin, who follows in the realists' footsteps but in essence returns to the romantic lyric poem—expressed in prose. He describes feelings he has himself experienced; his method of making characters immediate, comprehensible to the reader, consists of eliminating psychological motivation and analysis, and a refusal to dwell on minor circumstances. Thus the story *Three Days* achieves its effect primarily by the symbolic juxtaposition of two people, one alive and the other dead, an executioner and a victim, the symbols of *Man* and *War*. The corpse rotting in the sun becomes the embodiment of all war's horror; the wounded man beside the corpse is the embodiment of rational humanity, going to war in the name of an elemental love for one's fatherland. Everything experienced by the protagonist assumes a profound meaning "and the naturalistic description of bodily disintegration creates a series of poetic symbols; a realistic tale turns into a lyric poem."

Garšin, unlike his contemporary Čexov, does not really know people, nor is he interested in them. Čexov presents impressions of life and nature, while Garšin presents Petersburg scenes. Čexov, like Garšin, eliminates everything superfluous, making his stories compact as a lyric, but since his artistic expression is remarkable for its simplicity, apparent artlessness, and brevity, his return to an ideal form of art cannot be called a return to the subjective lyric, like Garšin's, but rather "a little narrative *epic* poem in prose."

The same impressionism can also be found in verse, in Minskij and the city poetry of Fofanov. The eternal questions sounded by the great Russian writers, and their concern for social problems have not disappeared in this generation, but have merely been transferred to a different arena, that of the city.

The new critic possesses perhaps the rarest quality in Russian literature, real respect for the writer's moral freedom and the *highest cultural tolerance*. Traces of these gifts appear in S. A. Andreevskij and in Spasowicz, who realize that artistic criticism of literature takes precedence over the artisan work of criticism itself. Spasowicz particularly manifests a European culture, and a higher stage of culture permits greater philosophical breadth in literary criticism. Also, the new generation possesses in Vladimir Solov'ev a writer who illustrates that deep religious feeling can be combined with a concern for social issues and need not be reactionary. The required new idealism is felt in all great Russian writers. The task of Russian literature, then, is to strike out from its period of creative poetry, of direct and elemental work, and enter a critical period, a conscious and cultural one that will prepare Russia for greater achievements in literature.

It seems hardly credible, in view of the foregoing summary, that the early symbolists should have considered Merežkovskij's essay as the manifesto of their movement. He cannot be said to propose a cogent platform for them; his statements pale beside Jean Moréas' manifesto in the *Figaro* of September 18, 1886, or the more radical statements on the function and method of art in the symbolist periodicals *Mir iskusstva* and *Vesy* a decade later, statements by Brjusov and Belyj, culminating in the latter's *Symbolism* (1910). Indeed, Merežkovskij deliberately minimizes the role of French symbolists and their predecessors, whose work had been accorded a comprehensive review in the *Vestnik Evropy* in 1892 by Z. Vengerova.

Part of the explanation lies precisely in those conditions Merežkovskij delineates in his third chapter. The reading public of the 1880's and the critics directing them were essentially at the intellectual level indicated by him. Although his essay was not published in the "thick journals"—where even the apparently innocuous statements about Russian letters would not have been tolerated—support for a more violent "slap in the face of public taste" did not yet exist. Furthermore, in view of the traditional responsibilities of Russian literature, it would have been dangerous to affiliate the new movement too closely with its French counterpart and its pejorative *décadence*. The essay, therefore, was thought to contain the strongest possible reaction of utilitarian literature and criticism.

Merežkovskij's essay is only the manifesto of the new movement. Obviously it could not anticipate the poetic practices of individual artists, nor was Merežkovskij temperamentally suited to lead them through turbulent literary battles such as those provoked by Brjusov's poems and translations from Mallarmé and Verlaine in his *Russian Symbolists* (three fascicles, 1894-95). Yet Merežkovskij does indicate several salient features that were to differentiate Russian symbolism from its European counterparts. Perhaps because his essay owes so much to German Romanticism the new direction was to be nationalistic and religious. It was to express the Russian spirit, particularly its folk spirit, but, as Merežkovskij saw it, it was to continue the best features inherent in the works of the older Russian writers. Between the lines, however, one may also see the influence of French poetry and critical theory. Thus Merežkovskij asks for greater interest in and concentration on the aesthetic qualities of a work; he conceives of the poet as seer at least in Baudelaire's sense if not in Rimbaud's; he shifts the locale to the city; he sees beauty in the commonplace and the ugly. And in minimizing or glossing over the poetry of Tjutčev and Fet he indicates the urgent necessity for remedying the shortcomings of Russian literature.

The hasty and undocumented criticism in the essay is symptomatic of Merežkovskij's superficial analysis of the literary basis for the movement and of his ideological formulations. Nevertheless, its protest against outdated forms and themes represents the first clear break from the tradition he attacked, and thereby prepares the scene for the first efforts of the new movement. (pp. 177-89)

Ralph E. Matlaw, "The Manifesto of Russian Symbolism," in Slavic and East European Journal, *Vol. XV, No. 3, Fall, 1957, pp. 177-91.*

C. H. BEDFORD (essay date 1963)

[*In the following excerpt, Bedford presents a detailed analysis of Merezhkovsky's religious beliefs.*]

The main development of Dmitry Sergeyevich Merezhkovsky's thought during the first two decades of the 20th century was of a political and social as well as of a religious nature, concerned primarily with the establishment of a universal humanity in the universal church as the basis for the kingdom of God on earth. Yet Merezhkovsky did not wholly put aside the purely religious contemplation which he had begun in **Tolstoy and Dostoyevsky,** the first work devoted to his religion of the Trinity. On the whole, he remained faithful to what he proclaimed at that time regarding resurrection, sex and historic Christianity. There were, however, four new premises which entered his religious programme, and from which in turn the major portion of his post-revolutionary writings evolved.

The first of these innovations was his plan of the evolution of religion, which he likened to the three stages of dialectical development.

> To the triplicity of mystical cognition corresponds the triplicity of metaphysical cognition at three moments, which are brought about by the law of dialectical development and in which is revealed the deepest essence of life accessible to human reason: the first lower synthesis, the unconscious unity of life and consciousness—I am I—divides into thesis and antithesis, subject and object, I and not-I, an internal and external world, in order to be completed by a final higher synthesis, by a final conscious union, which is required by the metaphysical and is brought about by mystical cognition. From the first unity through bifurcation to the final union, from one in one through two in one to one in three—such are the three moments of dialectical development.

The three stages of the religious development of humanity correspond to his concept of the three Testaments—of God the Father, God the Son, and God the Holy Ghost—and were centred on the problem of the flesh and the spirit.

The first stage, that of God the creator as the absolute being and the only God, was exemplified by Israel, for as early as 1907 Israel came to represent for Merezhkovsky a religion of the flesh. Moreover, he considered that the one God of Israel was the one God towards whom all paganism with its multiplicity of gods strove. Human sacrifice symbolised for him the unity of God the One in One. He ascribed human sacrifice to all ancient religions (later he excluded Greek and Roman paganism), and while it did not take place in Israel, the possibility of it was apparent in God's commanding Abraham to sacrifice Isaac. Above all, he observed it in the Hebrew rite of circumcision.

> A relic of these human sacrifices, in which the deepest metaphysics of all objective religions was manifest in former times, is preserved in circumcision—the sacrament of the First Testament, of the first unity of the Creator with the creature, of the Spirit with the flesh.

> The ultimate symbolisation of objectivity for human consciousness is the tangible outer substance, since the flesh of man himself—his flesh, as well as cosmic flesh—is matter. This is why the first stage of religious evolution is primarily *a religion of the flesh.*

God the Father, who presented the reality of the flesh, offered the first thesis. The second stage, which revealed the Son as the second hypostasis, separated the first lower unity into two higher elements: the spirit and the flesh. This was the religion of the Two in One, in which by Christ's resurrection all men received absolute life in God's being.

Merezhkovsky ceased to be as bitterly opposed to historic Christianity as he had formerly been, now that he acknowledged it as a necessary stage in the evolution of religion. He himself did not accept Christianity as the final religion; he still complained that it failed to surmount the contradiction of its two elements, flesh and spirit, and resulted not in a synthesis but in the absorption of the thesis by the antithesis, that is the flesh by the spirit. It was this that caused the duality which plagued humanity.

> The religious problem of the spirit and the flesh, of the polarity of the abysses, of duality, does not spring from the ontological dualism of human nature, but from the greatest mystery for us of God's division into two Countenances and the relation of this divarication to the plural world which emanates from God.

Nonetheless, he at least conceded that Christianity was necessary in order to attain the religion of the Trinity. Indeed, his own religion derived essentially from Christianity, for, as he admitted at this time, his Coming Christ would have been impossible if it were not for the Christ who had already come; therefore, the Church of the Second Coming, apocalyptical Christianity, would accept the Church of the First Coming, historic Christianity, for there was truth in the latter, but not the whole truth.

He was also adamant in his opinion that brotherly love was not the basis of Christianity.

> Indeed, Christianity is not at all based on love for one's neighbour, as is usually thought—this love is present in the law of Moses and also in all ancient teachers of wisdom from Socrates to Marcus Aurelius, from Confucius to Bodhisattva—not on the righteous life and crucifixion of Christ, but on the real possibility, which has been proven by experience, of physical resurrection.

Consequently, this resurrection of the flesh was the first and most important point of Merezhkovsky's new world order, which was the third and final stage of the religious evolution of humanity. This was the kingdom of the Holy Ghost, in which the thesis and antithesis, the flesh and the spirit, would be synthesised, and in which the Three in One would be realised.

> At the present time the religious consciousness of mankind has risen to this stage. Christianity is coming to an end, because it has fulfilled itself to the end, just as 'the law and the prophets' were finished with the advent of Christ. Christ *did not violate, but fulfilled* the law. And the Holy Ghost *will not violate, but will fulfill* Christianity.

Thus Merezhkovsky continued to aver that the end was at hand.

Resurrection of the body was of cardinal importance in the religion of Merezhkovsky. The problem of the victory of life over death continued to be a source of anxiety to him, and he constantly returned to it. Death represented for him the destruction of the individual—an unacceptable fact to this epitome of individuality, for "if death exists, then there is nothing but death; if death exists, then all is nothing." Christ, the absolute individual, vanquished death; this was a long-standing belief held by Merezhkovsky. To strengthen it, he added his newly formulated conviction in the power of love over death, for his God was a God of love. Love, he declared, was the main action of life, for it was the affirmation of existence. From this he drew the following conclusion:

> Not to exist is not to love; only the one who does
> not love may accept death as non-existence. The one
> who loves loves the living person of the beloved.
> Love is the will to the immortality of the personality.

The importance of love for Merezhkovsky cannot be overlooked. He himself had loved deeply only once—the object of
his love, his mother, was long since dead; yet he had to believe
in her continued existence and sought it through his love for
her.

> For the one who loves there is no death, because love
> is the absolute affirmation of life. Absolute negation
> is destroyed by absolute affirmation, death is de-
> stroyed by love. Love is life; he who loves is alive;
> and inasmuch as he loves, inasmuch is he alive, is
> immortal—"is risen from the dead." Love is not a
> superficial virtue, not the strength of the soul, but
> the soul itself. Love is unable not to love; the soul
> cannot avoid living in love, not only the future life
> beyond the grave, but also the present life of this
> world; which is not the abstract "immortality of the
> soul," but a real resurrection of the flesh and the
> spirit in the perfect unity of the personality. Love is
> not the road from this world to the other, but the
> absolute revelation of the other world in this—the
> perfect union of the two worlds. Love is not the
> knowledge of God, love is God.

In this way Merezhkovsky not only indicated the power of
love, but also its holiness and its necessity for the immortality
of the individual.

It was in connection with sex, fleshly love, that he at last
proclaimed a conclusion that had long been germinating in his
mind, since the time when he had commented on the female
qualities of his hero, Leonardo da Vinci. He decided that the
individual, the complete individual, must contain both male
and female elements, since sex was a division, a splitting into
two halves. Here, too, Merezhkovsky's habitual desire to achieve
a synthesis is apparent.

> Not only according to Christian metaphysics, but also
> according to common sense, the personality, *indi-*
> *viduum, is indivisible,* is whole; sex is a half, a bi-
> section (two sexes), a division, a fraction of the per-
> sonality. The perfect human being, the perfect
> personality is not a man, *only* a man (male) and not
> a woman, *only* a woman (female), but something
> more . . . in every man there is the feminine, and in
> every woman the masculine. The union of male and
> female—not in the sexual act, outside the person-
> ality, but within it—is the basis of personality.

Merezhkovsky expressed this opinion in 1913. He was to take
it up again in an expanded form as one of the bases for his
later religious convictions. It is interesting to note that Merezhkovsky considered sex for the propagation of the species
to be the death of individuality. He felt that sexual love of this
nature was basically lust and not, as it should be, a love for
the spiritual "glorified" flesh. The complete union of the sexes
could only occur in a more exalted love, which Merezhkovsky
termed *vlyublennost'* to distinguish it from ordinary love (*lyu-*
bov').

From this point, *vlyublennost',* sprang Merezhkovsky's concept of eternal womanhood. Once again he came close to Vladimir Solov'yov, but there is a considerable difference both in
the method by which each adopted this symbol, and the contents of it. Solov'yov derived his eternal woman from three
visions which he is reputed to have had of St Sofia, the divine
glory of the cosmos, whom he presented as the salvation of

the world. Merezhkovsky himself pointed out the essential trait
of Solov'yov's eternal woman: it was heavenly—too heavenly
and too Christian in comparison with his own.

Merezhkovsky's eternal feminine was not the result of a vision,
but, like the whole of his work, was the product of a more
rational contemplation and was a symbol of the uniting of
heaven and earth. One might trace the origins of his eternal
woman back to Venus-Aphrodite, whose statue played such an
important rôle in his first trilogy, *Christ and Antichrist (The*
Death of the Gods: Julian the Apostate, The Resurrection of the
Gods: Leonardo da Vinci, and *Antichrist: Peter and Alexis).*
This was a purely earthly woman, and he needed a heavenly
one as well, in order that earth and heaven could be synthesised
in one heavenly-earthly woman, the symbol of his Church of
the Second Coming. He was not content with the eternal woman
either as Venus or as divine beauty; eternal womanhood was
synonymous with eternal motherhood, and in this lies the main
difference between Merezhkovsky and Solov'yov. Here, also,
may be seen once again the influence of Merezhkovsky's undying love for his mother, who apparently represented for him
the ideal of womanhood—motherhood. This, together with the
important position ascribed to Mary, the Mother of God, both
in the Orthodox and in the Roman Catholic faiths, also influenced his judgment. He found a link between the Mother,
petitioning Christ in the interest of mortals, and the Holy Ghost.

> At the last judgment the Mother intercedes with the
> Son for the convicted; but the Spirit, which *intercedes*
> *for us with unuttered* sighs, is this not also Eternal
> Motherhood? The first appearance of Eternal Wom-
> anhood is the Mother of God in Christianity; the last
> in the Apocalypse—the woman clothed with the sun—
> is the revelation of the Holy Spirit, the Holy Flesh,
> the Church as the Kingdom, the God-Man in God-
> Humanity.

The eternal mother, who therefore appeared in the beginning
and the end, led him to conclude that: "Eternal Motherhood
and Eternal Womanhood, that which existed before birth and
that which will exist after death, become one."

Merezhkovsky then examined the popular concept of the Mother
of God. He found that this was inextricably bound up with the
concept of the Mother-Earth, which he himself had upheld for
some time. Earthly and heavenly were thus joined, as far as
Merezhkovsky was concerned, and therefore God the Father
and God the Son could be reconciled by the Holy Ghost—the
Eternal Womanhood-Motherhood—just as Merezhkovsky and
his father had been reconciled on numerous occasions by the
intervention of his mother.

> Christianity separated the past eternity of the Father
> from the future eternity of the Son, the earthly truth
> from the heavenly truth. Will they not be united by
> that which comes after Christianity, the revelation of
> the Spirit—Eternal Womanhood, Eternal Mother-
> hood? Will not the Mother reconcile the Father and
> the Son?

Only this revelation of the Third Testament offered the solution
to the enigma of the earth and heaven, the flesh and the spirit,
in the Holy Ghost as the eternal woman, who contained both
love-motherhood (*vlyublennost'-materinstvo*) and love-virgin-
ity (*vlyublennost'-devstvennost'*), the uniting of the earthly and
the godly in one Virgin-Mother.

There were the contemplative elements which were evolved
simultaneously with Merezhkovsky's more active socio-political ideals during the first twenty years of this century. Together

with his belief in universal humanity, they formed the basis for his writings as an exile in France.

The last twenty years of Merezhkovsky's life proved to be no less prolific creatively than any comparable earlier period. They were years in which were published two novels—*The Birth of the Gods: Tutankhamen in Crete* (1925) and *The Messiah* (1925): a religious study in the form of a trilogy—*The Secret of the Three* (1925), *The Secret of the West* (1930) and *Jesus the Unknown* (1931); and a series of interesting and unusual biographies—*Napoleon* (1929), *Paul-Augustine* (1936), *Francis of Assisi* (1938), *Joan of Arc* (1938) and *Dante* (1939). (pp. 144-49)

The preoccupation with sex, which had been growing in Merezhkovsky from the time when he had sanctioned Bacchic pleasures in his early poetry, finally came to the fore in the writings of these two decades. He was not unaware of the almost complete uniqueness of his position in writing about sex as he did, when he remarked, referring to humanity at large: "we are silent, we are ashamed to speak of it." Nonetheless, he felt obliged to break the bond of silence, for, he explained: "We will never understand that sex is a holy or accursed point, the gates of heaven or hell, but a profundity and not a level. With all its weight our world, our hell, leans upon these gates, lest they open." The problem of sex was therefore of the utmost importance in Merezhkovsky's religious programme, and was to be dealt with thoroughly in his works.

The primary motif of the majority of his compositions in this period was the presentation of all pagan antiquity, which represented the religion of the flesh, as pointing the way to the coming of Christ. (p. 150)

Merezhkovsky was dissatisfied with the accepted "scientific" interpretations of antiquity. He considered that pagan religions should be approached with sympathetic religious experience: a method which he could follow, but which was, he believed, beyond the limitations of "godless scholars." Merezhkovsky was indeed sympathetic to all ancient religions, for he did not agree with the opinion that they were no more than beliefs in non-existent gods and myths. He accepted myth as fact, declaring that: "The truth of the myth is in the mystery; its secret is in the sacrament. The key to pagan mystery was Christian sacrament, and it was in the light of this belief that he examined pagan antiquity, for he was convinced that if Christianity was truth, so was paganism. He agreed with Schelling's statement that mythology was a religion, hence all gods exist; but he was not content to remain at this premise, and he continued this reasoning to the point of declaring that there were no false gods and that all gods were true.

It was his contention that all humanity was under the sign of the cross, and it was with a view to proving this that he examined all pre-Christian antiquity. He discovered deep similarities between the life of Christ and the myth-mysteries of pagan dying and resurrected gods.

> History is the mystery, the sacrament of the cross, and all nations participate in it. The way from Bethlehem to Golgotha is already the path of paganism, of pre-Christian humanity. There are many nations, "tongues," and there are many myths, but there is only one mystery—the mystery of the God who died and was resurrected.
>
> Egyptian Osiris, Babylonian Tammuz, Canaanite-Egyptian Adonis, Attis of Asia Minor, Iranian Mithras, Hellenic Dionysos—in all of them is He.

He was so convinced of the truth of his theory that these gods were indeed precursors of Christ, that he formulated the following concept:

> In each earthly age, each eon, the dead body of one Man is preserved undecayed; when the new age comes, it rises from the dead, and That Man becomes God; then he again dies, again is resurrected,—and so it is for all time. In all ages—in all eternities—he is like the sun in drops of dew.

Merezhkovsky did not merely base his deductions on the superficial similarity that is most clearly apparent: that Osiris, Tammuz, Dionysos, Mithras, Adonis, and even Quetzalcoatl (whom he later included), as well as Christ were gods who became incarnate on earth, suffered in order to save mankind, perished and again rose from the dead. He sought more obscure evidence. He found theophagy in the Eleusinian mysteries and in the religion of Osiris. In the latter instance, for example, he decided that since Osiris was the spirit of wheat, then by eating bread the Egyptians ate their god, just as in the Christian Eucharist; "So the shadow comes in contact with the Body: the shadow—Osiris—falls at the feet of the Lord." He also declared that the concept of the shepherd-god extended from Babylon to Israel in the person of Tammuz-Adonis-Adonai (Merezhkovsky considered these three to be in essence one God, just as he asserted that Tammuz and Osiris were one), and from Israel to the end of time in the person of Christ.

Besides stressing these and other similarities, Merezhkovsky placed great emphasis on the mystic number three, which was the basis of his own form of Christianity. He sought, and found, in pagan religions this same trinity of gods which exists in Christian teaching. He ascribed evidences of it to Samothrace, in the worshipping of the Father, heavenly Zeus; the Mother, Demeter the earth; and the son of earth and heaven, Dionysos. In a somewhat different order he found it in the Eleusinian cult of Dionysos as the Father, Demeter as the Mother and Iacchus as the Son. In Canaan they were represented by Baal, Astarte and Adonis; in Babylon by Ea, Ishtar and Tammuz; and in Egypt by Osiris, Isis and Gor. These trinities of deities corresponded, for Merezhkovsky, with the Christian Trinity of God the Father, God the Son and God the Holy Ghost—Merezhkovsky's "Mother-Spirit."

Merezhkovsky was attempting to show by these analogies the importance of the Trinity throughout all humanity. He hoped, of course, to attract humanity once more to the Trinity, for he declared that in the past three centuries, and in particular the preceding twenty or thirty years, man had forgotten the Three in One, although he saw reflections of it in all aspects of life. He stated that man thinks threefold—but failed to show how this takes place; that space and time are threefold: space because it is made up of length, width and depth, and time because it comprises past, present and future. He found the Trinity in physics and chemistry, and cited the law of chemical reaction as an example. The biological field also provided indications of it. In this case he pointed out the external symmetry and duality of organs, such as the eyes and ears, and the inner unity of their functions; but even greater was the trinity visible in sex: "two sexes, two poles, and between them is the eternal spark of life."

Merezhkovsky's attitude to the importance of sex in religion at this period of his development and also his whole concept of the religion of God the Father closely approached that of Rozanov. Rozanov had preached a natural (one might even term it 'phallic') religion since the end of the 19th century, even before Merezhkovsky had embarked on his first pronouncements on sex. At that time, in the early years of the 20th century, Merezhkovsky disclaimed any kinship with Rozanov, and opposed the latter's views on the importance of the family and progeny. So antagonistic had Merezhkovsky been to Rozanov that he had seized every opportunity to denounce him in the Religio-Philosophical Society. V. F. Botsianovsky reported on Merezhkovsky's seeking personal quarrels with Rozanov and cited the following instance as an example:

> "We," Bishop Sergiy interrupted him [Merezhkovsky], "are not speaking about Rozanov, but about marriage. . . ."
>
> "No," Merezhkovsky persisted, "we must talk about Rozanov. . . ."

While not accepting Rozanov's teachings as a whole at this latter date, Merezhkovsky's attitude toward his former antagonist altered considerably, to the extent that after Rozanov's death in the Soviet Union in 1919 Merezhkovsky conceded that he was a great Russian writer; and even quoted frequently from Rozanov's works in his *Secret of the Three*. Like Rozanov before him, Merezhkovsky now proclaimed the holiness of the phallic religions of pre-Christian antiquity; but while Rozanov merely stated that Christianity, too, should be at least in part based on sex, Merezhkovsky went further, for he believed that it was originally so and would be again.

Merezhkovsky was one of the most vehement protagonists of the holiness of sex and its transcendental mystery. Not only did he declare that "sexual craving is the craving for knowledge, curiosity towards the transcendental," but he also stated:

> For man sex is the only possible flesh-and-blood "contact with other worlds," with transcendental essences. Here, in sexual love, is birth, but here also is death, for everything that is born dies; death and birth are two roads to the same place, or one road to and from it.

Sex was the godly Trinity in the human body: "sex is the first, primordial, flesh-and-blood touch of God the Three in One." From it flowed the whole of the Testament of the Father—paganism.

There is little need to examine (as Merezhkovsky did) all the pagan manifestations of holy sex, from the "divine" prostitution of the worshippers of Ishtar to the "godly" bestiality which, like Rozanov, Merezhkovsky felt was one of the secrets of Egypt and was quite permissible, for he not only proclaimed the animal in God, but also stated that the animal was closer than man to God, since the heavenly joy of earth (sex), though extinguished in man, still shone in the animal. Although he found evidence of the holiness of sex in all pre-Christian religions, he continued to maintain that the greatest revelation of it was circumcision. This concept, too, Merezhkovsky had borrowed from Rozanov.

> Circumcision is the flesh-and-blood betrothal of man to God, a Testament of marriage, a conjugal union, the sexual copulation of man with God.

Thus sex, the most ardent point of the flesh, was consecrated in God.

Merezhkovsky did not agree with Rozanov that Christ was a refutation of the Father, and the New Testament a break with the Old. Following up his line of thought that circumcision was the marriage of God with humanity, he decided that Christ, who was circumcised according to Hebrew rites, welded both

covenants with the blood of circumcision; he also added his belief in the references to Christ as the bridegroom and the Church as his bride as further justification of this acceptance of sex. He also discovered a new significance in Christ's healing of the woman with the issue of blood:

> She approached from behind, because she was ashamed of her illness; she hid it from people, just as all conceal from one another their eternal "shameful wound"—sex.

Merezhkovsky's interpretation of this act of healing was that by it Christ took on Himself the "shameful wound" of sex and therefore accepted the whole Testament of the Father.

All paganism, Merezhkovsky asserted, showed the way to resurrection through sex. This was but a further development of his concept that "the secret of love is Resurrection." Not only did he see evidence of this in pagan cults: Osiris resurrected by Isis, Tammuz by Ishtar and so on; but he also sought to find it in Christianity, in Christ's resurrection. Very significant in Merezhkovsky's opinion was that the resurrected Christ was seen first by a woman, Mary Magdalene. He took this as proof that Mary's love for Christ had been stronger than death, and that Christ's resurrection was a miracle of love. As for human sexual love, he declared:

> Sexual love is the unended and unending path to resurrection. Vain is the striving of the two halves to the whole: they unite and once more fall apart; they wish to, but cannot rise from the dead—they always give birth and always die.
>
> Sexual enjoyment is the anticipation of the resurrecting flesh, but through bitterness, shame and fear of death. This contradiction is the most transcendental in sex: I take pleasure and I am repelled.

He continued this line of thought and stated his belief that "the wholeness of sex, the wholeness of the personality is life and, at the final limit, eternal life is resurrection."

Before beginning an analysis of Merezhkovsky's concept of the androgyne as the perfect individual, it is first imperative to examine the rôle of the mother as the third member of the Trinity, for Merezhkovsky's deductions regarding bisexualism hinge in part on the latter. He had already written on the Holy Ghost as the Eternal Woman-Mother, who would save the world. Now he turned his attention to a detailed study of the mother goddess, whom he found throughout the world, from Babylon ("'Ishtar Mami'—'Mama,' Babylon lisped in the earliest baby talk, and this will be taken into account for it in the ages and in eternity") through countless stone-age idols depicting a mother and child, discovered in various parts of Europe, Asia Minor and Africa, to the Apocalypse: "The woman, clothed with the sun, and the moon under her feet, and upon her head a crown of twelve stars. And she being with child" and "pained to be delivered."

This convinced Merezhkovsky that humanity's first and last thought was about the Mother; he went on to state that "Mother Earth is more ancient than the Heavenly Father." He was certain that God the Mother was an integral part of Christianity, as of all other religions, for God the Father, he argued, could not give birth to the Son without a female divine being. While he attached great importance to the earthly mother of Christ, he regarded her as an earthly symbol which only pointed the way to the heavenly Mother, who alone could complete the Trinity: "The Trinity in God begins and ends with the Mother-Spirit." The basis for his belief in the Holy Ghost as the Eternal

Mother was not derived exclusively from his own logic, but from an apocryphal source in which Christ speaks of "My Mother, the Holy Ghost."

God is therefore Father and Mother, male and female—a bisexual Supreme Being. This was one of the two concepts responsible for Merezhkovsky's preoccupation with the androgyne. The other was his belief that in each of the human sexes there are traces of the other.

> In each man is the secret woman; in each woman the secret man. The unearthly charm of man is femininity; of woman—masculinity. Empiric sex is opposed to the transcendental.

Bisexualism was a divine state. Not only did Merezhkovsky find it in pagan deities: Isis and Osiris, Ishtar and Tammuz, bearded Venus, the portrayal of the heads of Hera and Zeus joined to one neck on an ancient coin; but he also believed that the same bisexualism was apparent in the one God of Israel. He seized on the fact that *Elohim*, the Hebrew word for God, is in the plural, and deduced that this revealed that God was dual—consequently male and female. This was corroborated for Merezhkovsky by the creation of man in God's image; since God created both Adam and Eve, male and female, then God is two in one: "Elohim, He and She—the Man-Woman"; and "two sexes in one being—that is what is meant by 'the image of God in man'." Conversely, since God at first created Adam in his own image, Adam was a divine creature, an androgyne. Merezhkovsky drew the same conclusion from other myths and decided that in each case the androgyne had been split into two sexes because he rivalled the gods.

Not only was the male-female revealed in pagan deities and in the God of Israel, but also in Christ. Merezhkovsky did not rely on the Gospels for his evidence, for in them Christ is represented as asexual; he once again drew on apocryphal sources to establish Christ's beauty, which he declared to be infinitely greater than any other manifestation of human beauty since it was neither masculine nor feminine, but a harmonious blending of the two. God the Father was bisexual, and so was God the Son, for in the divine order the Son and Father were one. Merezhkovsky added:

> If the birth of the Son is not empty abstraction, by which the very dogma of God Incarnate would be destroyed, then the Son is born in the Father of the Spirit-Mother. Or, speaking in our coarse and feeble tongue, all three Countenances of the Divine Trinity unite, giving birth to each other and being born of each other, in the Maternal-Paternal-Filial, ineffably conjugal love.

Christ had to be male and female to fit into Merezhkovsky's concept of resurrection as being the return to the state of the complete individual and the whole sex, the androgyne. As the final proof of the holiness of, and the eventual uniting of the sexes into one bisexual being, Merezhkovsky cited Christ's words (found in an apocryphal source, the writings of Clement of Alexandria) that His Kingdom would come:

> when the two are one . . .
> male is female,
> and there is neither male nor female.

Merezhkovsky saw traces of this "third sex" in contemporary humanity in the hermaphrodite and also in unisexual love.

> Men love men, women love women, because for the former the female is visible in the male, and for the latter the male is visible in the female; it is as if a

golden deposit of initial bisexualism—of the whole Man, the Androgyne, who is more than the present-day man, cleaved into two, into man and woman—gleams in the dark ore of two separate sexes.

> It is possible that in unisexual love it is something greater, the primary whole, the complete, which fascinates "the people of the moonlight."

Yet he warned against physical manifestations of unisexual love, for this was opposed to spiritual bisexualism. He viewed the openness of homosexuality, Sodom, with alarm, for he considered it to be the reflection of divine bisexualism—such as is revealed by his "Christ the Unknown"—in the devil's mirror. "Europe is Sodom," he declared, for the spirit of unisexualism predominated. In the east, in the Soviet Union, communism represented a purely feminine oneness, for all were comrades, neither men nor women, and consequently impersonal and sexless. In the west he found an equal impersonality and sexlessness in masculine militarism. The result would be war—the destruction of humanity.

It was with the intention of preventing this destruction by warning the world of the danger which faced it, that Merezhkovsky wrote of the first humanity, Atlantis. If one is to adopt a scientific approach to Merezhkovsky's writings on this subject, then one is apt to dismiss them as of no value, for the author indulged in complicated and extremely speculative theories on the historical existence of Atlantis. He examined myths and legends which he found in Greek, Babylonian, Egyptian and Hebrew sources, correlated them and accepted them as fact, reiterating his belief that myth was but a veil for higher truths. He invaded the realm of the archaeologist and the anthropologist to justify his claim, drawing conclusions from the vaguest of similarities. He declared, for example, that Mayan pyramids, Babylonian ziggurats and Egyptian pyramids showed a common Atlantean origin, that the symbol of the snake found among the Aztecs and Hebrews must also have originated in Atlantis; and that samples of soils brought up from the bottom of the Atlantic Ocean matched the colour of the houses of Atlantis as reported in Plato.

Although Merezhkovsky revealed his belief in the actual existence of this mythical land, it is its symbolic meaning that is of importance, for Atlantis represented antediluvian humanity. Since he contended that man was at first bisexual, it was his contention that the Atlantes were androgynes, living in Paradise in divine love and peace. They were not divine, however, and in their pride considered:

> that they had reached the summits of wisdom, knowledge, power, greatness, beauty; in the words of Plato, these unfortunates considered themselves "all-beautiful," "all-blissful,"—"men-gods." Each one of them considered himself to be God and was prepared to sacrifice all to himself alone.

War and Sodom resulted, and Atlantis was therefore destined to perish in the Flood. It is interesting at this point to compare the opinion of another Russian exile, G. Golokhovastov, on the same theme. In his narrative poem "The Destruction of Atlantis" he puts forward the thesis that Atlantis perished because it strove to become androgynous and thus become divine: a view directly opposed to that held by Merezhkovsky.

It was Merezhkovsky's theory that Atlantis was the origin of Europe, and that the first humanity and the second were inextricably linked. In an endeavour to establish the historical truth of his deduction, he again ran counter to more scientific theories, for he stated that the European races moved from west to east, from Atlantis to Crete, and from there to the rest of the ancient world. Once more it is necessary to overlook Merezhkovsky's error as an historian and to examine the metaphysical significance of this theory. Atlantis bequeathed to Europe a knowledge of divine bisexualism. Merezhkovsky saw this clearly in Cretan paintings, in which he could not distinguish man from woman. Yet the greatest link between Atlantis and Europe, in his estimation, was contained in the Gospels, for by his baptism Christ became the second Adam: "the former man, the first Adam, as it were, drowns, dies, in the watery grave of the font; and there rises from it, is born, the new man of the new humanity, the second Adam."

The second, and equally important uniting of the first and second humanities, and also the third humanity, Merezhkovsky discovered in the Gospels.

> If the myth of the flood, "Atlantis,"—the end of the first humanity,—is religiously and, perhaps, prehistorically significant, then "the second Adam," Jesus, speaks to the second humanity in the tongue of the first.

> In the 11th century B.C. Aramaic was just as universal as a thousand years later was the vulgar, *Common—Koinê*—Hellenic language of Alexander the Great and the God Dionysos—the shadow of the Sun, of the coming Son. The Gospel unites both universalities into one, both humanities into one: the second and the first into the third. And here again is the thesis, antithesis and synthesis; the Father, the Son and the Holy Ghost: the Gospel resounds with the same music of the Trinity, as a shell with the noise of the waves of the sea.

Yet Merezhkovsky believed that Atlantis also bequeathed the greatest evil of all to Europe—war: "the first humanity began and the second continues everlasting war." It was this which caused Merezhkovsky to declare that Europe, the second humanity, was doomed to perish like the first. Consequently, he regarded the approach of the second world war with apprehension, for he felt that it would be the end of the world, "the second Flood, no longer of water, but of blood and fire." He saw no salvation in the second humanity, but put his faith in the Apocalypse, in the third humanity. In his last literary work, which was published in 1939 on the eve of the second world war, he made his last declaration of his faith: "the fearful knot of social inequality, which especially in our time threatens to tighten into a noose of death and to strangle humanity, may be untied only in the Third Testament—in the Kingdom of the Holy Ghost."

Perhaps Merezhkovsky himself realised, at the end of his long and strenuous efforts to present humanity with the means for salvation, that his work was not "of his own time," as Demidov had remarked earlier. Perhaps he hoped that it would be of value to future generations, the third humanity of which he wrote. If he did not succeed in accomplishing his chosen task, it was not through lack of desire or the sparing of his resources. It was because the world, bound up in positivist materialism, was not prepared to heed his words. Yet his religious search, reflected as it was in his works as well as in his life, produced one positive result. It guaranteed for Merezhkovsky immortality on earth, both as a religious thinker and as an author. (pp. 151-60)

C. H. Bedford, "Dmitry Merezhkovsky, The Third Testament and the Third Humanity," in The Slavonic and East European Review, *Vol. 42, December-June, 1963-64, pp. 144-60.*

BERNICE GLATZER ROSENTHAL   (essay date 1974)

[*In the following excerpt, Rosenthal analyzes the influence of Friedrich Nietzsche's philosophy on Merezhkovsky's religious development and on the form of Christianity he espoused.*]

[Dmitrii Sergeevich Merezhkovsky] was one of the chief proselytizers of Nietzscheanism in Russia. In his lectures, poems, novels, and critical essays he related Nietzsche's ideas to the cultural problems of Russia and brought Nietzsche to the popular consciousness. Highlighting the existential questions that populism, positivism, and Orthodoxy had failed to solve, his works disseminated a conviction that a radical new faith was needed. A cultural impresario, Merezhkovsky introduced Russians to French symbolism and, almost singlehandedly at first, fostered an appreciation of beauty and culture for their own sake. Even those hostile to him testify to his influence in shaping the culture of the "silver age." (p. 432)

Torn between independence and need for love, between intellect and emotion, Merezhkovsky was a deeply unhappy and lonely man. Although he was convinced that faith would integrate all conflicts in a greater whole, his questing intellect barred actual belief. Finding existence a burden, he sought some reason to go on living. But pleasure eluded him, and devoting his life to "the people" as the populists advocated was not the answer either. "And I want to, but cannot love the people," he admitted. Fear of death ruled out suicide; more important, it made the question of what happens after death the most significant question of all. Secular philosophies could not answer it. Merezhkovsky was isolated from both "the people" and his fellow intellectuals; neither Russian Orthodoxy, which proscribed the intellect as a form of vanity, nor secular materialism, which overlooked the spiritual and emotional dimensions of man, could satisfy what Merezhkovsky called a "thirst for faith."

Merezhkovsky's discovery of art, beauty, and culture completed his estrangement from the belief systems of his time. Positivism was indifferent to art and hostile to imagination; through science and reason the problems of life would be solved. Populism and Orthodoxy required the artist to bend his vision to serve a higher goal. Furthermore, they demanded a degree of self-effacement which the egoistic Merezhkovsky could not accept. The faith he sought would provide happiness on earth, guarantee personal immortality, and still withstand a rational critique. Stressing "personality," a concept that includes heart and soul, as well as mind and body, Merezhkovsky belonged neither to the traditional right, which condemned the body, nor to the revolutionary left, which ignored the soul.

During the eighties Merezhkovsky and his friend Minsky (N. Vilenkin) began to study "problems of individualism." A mutual interest in individualism brought Merezhkovsky and his future wife, Zinaida Hippius, together in 1888. He was twenty-four at the time. While a student at St. Petersburg University, he had become familiar with Herbert Spencer's philosophy. Rejecting Spencer's economic individualism, Merezhkovsky also demanded to know the individual's place in the cosmic scheme. At the same time, accepting Schopenhauer's conviction that the ego is the source of suffering, he tried, unsuccessfully, to deaden his own sense of self.

Though the exact date of Merezhkovsky's first reading of Nietzsche is not known, by 1890 Nietzschean themes are evident in his works. His drama *Sylvio* deals with a would-be superman, a bored Renaissance prince whose only goal is to fly like an eagle (one of Zarathustra's two animals) and whose greatest joy is battle. But Merezhkovsky rejected Nietzsche. The unhappy prince is saved by a humble Christian woman who teaches him to love "the people." Merezhkovsky had not yet made a break with populism. His first impression was that Nietzscheanism was a crass and bloodthirsty creed unsuited to sensitive souls. Shortly before, Merezhkovsky had rejected the idea of art as religion. Using the French novelist Gustave Flaubert as an example, Merezhkovsky argued that conscious craftsmanship and minute examination of one's own emotions destroy both spontaneity and love, thereby negating the possibility of happiness itself.

In 1891, however, Merezhkovsky changed his views; he accepted Nietzsche's emphasis on art, beauty, and sensual pleasure. A trip to Greece and Rome was the catalyst. There Merezhkovsky found a form of art which combined feeling and intellect and celebrated life itself. He specifically stated that the Parthenon of Athens was a revelation, beauty incarnate, the ideal become real. Its effect on him was overwhelming. Nero's Colosseum, he said, is only "the dead greatness of overthrown power. Here [in the Parthenon] is living eternal beauty. Only here, for the first time in life, I understood the meaning of *beauty*. I had never before thought of it, never desired it. I did not weep, I was not glad, I was content. . . . It seemed that this moment was eternal and will be eternal." For the very first time Merezhkovsky had achieved a sense of inner peace. So completely was the Parthenon in harmony with its natural setting that it appeared to have risen from the soil in accord with divine laws. But the fact that it was created by men testified to human powers and demonstrated what it is possible for bold men to achieve. The nude goddesses, he said, were "naked beauty itself," flesh become spirit. The body was no longer an object of shame.

Greece became Merezhkovsky's symbol of harmony. Through beauty, Greek culture fused heart and mind, body and soul, religion and life, into an integrated whole. Aesthetic creativity appeared in a new light. Beauty became more than just an intellectual exercise, a means to withdraw from the real world; it was the way to make life meaningful, to give man the courage to go on living. The influence of Nietzsche's *Birth of Tragedy* is obvious; Nietzsche had stated that "existence can be justified only in aesthetic terms." Through art, man can face the horrors of existence, "without turning to stone."

Rethinking the issues, Merezhkovsky accepted Nietzsche's glorification of the pagan virtues and seconded his call for a new way of life based on art. In **"Acropolis,"** a critical essay written in 1891, he called for a "new Parthenon," to be created by "Godlike men on earth." Liberated from the slave morality, he implied in a poem of the same period, men will account to no one but themselves; they will live "only for happiness . . . for life."

But Merezhkovsky was not yet a Nietzschean; he could not accept Nietzsche's statement that "God is dead," nor could he believe that art is *only* an illusion. Desiring happiness on earth, he was still unable to abandon the hope of eternal life. His mother, to whom he was extremely attached, had just died. Torn between love for beauty and desire to be reunited with her in heaven, he asked:

Where then is the truth . . . in death, in heavenly love and
    suffering?
Or in the shadow of the gods, in your earthly beauty?
They quarrel in the soul of man as in this divine temple,
Eternal joy and life, eternal mystery and death.

Between 1891 and 1893 Merezhkovsky's Nietzscheanism co-existed with a romantic semireligious mysticism which viewed art as a path to the world soul. Attracted to the symbolism he discovered in France because of its mystical yearning for "other worlds than ours," he hoped that aesthetic intuition would lead to the new truths, the new faith, he needed.

In 1892 he published *Symbols,* a collection of verse influenced by modern French poetry. A mixture of religious and pagan themes, it exalts both pagan and biblical heroes. There is a long poem, **"Vera,"** whose theme is that "love is stronger than death," a conventionally romantic tribute to nature, **"Hymn to Beauty,"** and a semipagan poem, **"Laughter of the Gods."** Valerii Briusov, who became a leading symbolist writer, recalls that the appearance of *Symbols* was an "event" in his life; it became his "handbook" (*nastol'naia kniga*), and he knew "Vera" by heart. Other poems lauded the citizens of Ancient Rome as the "equals of the gods," and admired the "free spirit" of the Roman Republic. **"Future Rome"** embodies Merezhkovsky's hopes for a new faith that would restore human greatness and unify the world:

Rome is the unity of the world; in the ancient Republic
    A stern pagan spirit of freedom united the tribes.
Freedom fell, and wise Caesar, subjugated the entire world to
    Eternal Rome,
    In the name of the good of the people.
Imperial Rome fell, and in the name of the All-Highest God
    The Church wanted to gather all humankind in the temple of
    Peter.
But following Pagan Rome, Christian Rome perished.
    Faith died out in our hearts.
Now in ancient ruins, we wander around full of grief.
    O can it be we will not find such a faith that would again
Reunite all tribes and people on earth?
    Where are you, O Future Rome? Where are you, O
    Unknown God?

Arguing against blind imitation of ancient forms, Merezhkovsky warned against superficial Hellenism. The poet A. N. Maikov, he said, focused on the serenity of the Ancient Greeks without understanding their consciousness of suffering, tragedy, and evil. Mere form is useless as a guide to life. Cultures must be studied in depth, their eternally valid principles separated from their obsolete forms; an entirely new faith must be created.

Reason has failed man, Merezhkovsky insisted; the new faith will be based on art. In an 1892 lecture, *On the Causes of the Decline and on the New Trends in Contemporary Russian Literature,* Merezhkovsky set forth his view that populism, materialism, and science could not answer the needs of Russia. True enlightenment consists of spiritual transformation; it demands a new culture to unite intelligentsia and people on a higher level. A declaration of war against populism and science, the lecture exalts symbolist art as the vehicle leading to higher truths. Mystical, introspective, and imaginative, symbolism explores both the human soul and the cosmos; it enables the artist to penetrate through the veil of illusion to the eternal forms inaccessible to the ordinary man. His intuition and imagination are divine gifts. As the artist provides the materials for a new faith, the gulf between secular intelligentsia and believing peasants will be ended. Quite influential for many young poets, the lecture, which was published the following year, was their first exposure to French symbolism.

The lecture was a mixture of symbolist mysticism and Nietzsche. The Nietzschean aspects emphasized art as the highest form of human activity, imagination as the highest faculty, and the artist as the explorer of the human soul. The mystical aspects were strikingly reminiscent of romantic ideas in general and of Soloviev in particular—beauty is an expression of the soul's yearning to reach the Ideal, and art is the means to divine truth, the glimpse of eternity visible to man on earth.

The epistemological and metaphysical premises of Nietzscheanism, however, Merezhkovsky brushed aside. He did not even discuss them at length until 1915. In 1893 he simply refused to accept the Nietzschean idea that the world is meaningless and ultimately incomprehensible. Nietzsche's conviction that higher truths do not exist (there are only more beautiful illusions) was still in the background of Merezhkovsky's consciousness; he had grasped and concentrated on the Nietzschean celebration of beauty and life. The essential thrust of Nietzscheanism, in particular its "affirmation of the earth," its concentration on life in this world, was in direct contradiction to Merezhkovsky's desire to use art as a theurgy to reach other worlds. A common concern for the truth of man, a hope of ennobling him, and a mutual love of beauty were the points at which the conflicting orientations intersected. And both found the world of Philistines repulsive. But a true synthesis had not been achieved; one or the other element was bound to prevail.

In the space of only two years Merezhkovsky opted for Nietzscheanism. His earlier hopes that symbolist poetry would enable the artist to reach the people and create a new national culture were clearly not being fulfilled. Symbolist art was far too esoteric to serve as the basis for any popular movement. Even artists had difficulty understanding one another's work. Nietzscheanism provided theoretical justification for Merezhkovsky's failure to reach "the people"; it permitted him to acknowledge his secession from populism with finality and conviction and to proclaim proudly the individualism and elitism which had formerly been a source of embarrassment and guilt. The poet was not only a prophet; he became a hero—a "hero of contemplation." His creativity was the "highest form of action." Opposing materialism and economic progress, Merezhkovsky insisted that the frenetic activity of economic man deals with trivia. It is the artist who destroys the old life and creates the new; a warrior for true culture, his field of action is the human spirit.

Between 1894 and 1896 Merezhkovsky exalted Nietzschean values and mocked Christian asceticism and humility. Militant and strident, these writings constituted his answer to social changes which threatened to leave artists in a backwater. Directed by Finance Minister Sergei Witte, the government's industrialization drive was succeeding. By 1896 a wave of industrial strikes signaled the advent of the "proletariat"—to Merezhkovsky, the urban "mass man." Nietzscheanism enabled Merezhkovsky to affirm his own importance, to set himself off against the vulgar "herd." A creed of defiant, asocial individualism, Merezhkovsky's Nietzscheanism exalted the creator in revolt, Zarathustra leaving the marketplace.

During these years Merezhkovsky attempted to make himself into a superman—to live according to Zarathustra. Symbolism had not led to faith. Deliberately turning his back on "other worlds," he set about overcoming the "fear of life" which had enveloped him since childhood. Determined to forget the "mystery in all things," the "eternal darkness and horror," he would strive for earthly joys instead. "Remain faithful to the earth," Zarathustra had counseled. "Do not believe those who speak of otherworldly hopes! Poison mixers are they, whether they know it or not! Despisers of life are they, decaying and poisoned themselves. . . . so let them go! . . . To sin against

the earth is now the most dreadful thing. . . ." Obeying Zarathustra's dictum, "Learn how to laugh," Merezhkovsky also sought Zarathustra's "dancing god."

Soul became psyche as his search for higher truths assumed a secular form. Art and sensuality would make life bearable. Man would create himself, transcend his present human limitations. Beauty became Merezhkovsky's god, and he based a new way of life on its worship. Featuring adoration of the flesh and defiance of established verities, beauty's pioneer was the artist. Integrity to the artist's personal goals and courage to defy convention were the only virtues; banality and ugliness, the only sins. All other forms of morality were obsolete. "For the new beauty," Merezhkovsky proclaimed, "we will break all laws, transgress all limits." No constraints, no inhibitions to aesthetic expression would remain standing. For the artist, "all is permitted."

Julian the Apostate is Merezhkovsky's most famous work of this period. Essentially a Nietzschean tract, its central figure is based on the Roman emperor who attempted to restore paganism, and it exalts courage, worship of beauty, and defiance of death. Originally entitling the work *Outcast*, Merezhkovsky refused to call Julian an apostate. For him Julian was the prophet of a new faith. A successful novel in terms of sales, it was quickly translated into the major European languages. But basically it was a *succès de scandale,* and its characters only vehicles for ideas—thus its present oblivion.

Julian was obviously Merezhkovsky, or more exactly, the new man Merezhkovsky hoped to become. Julian's paganism resulted from his having fallen in love with a statue of Aphrodite while still a young man (an allusion to Merezhkovsky's experience in Greece). Hating the Christians who smashed such statues, Julian determined to destroy them. He referred to Christians as the "crows of Galilee," and condemned them, their slave morality, and their obsession with death and suffering. Julian saw their symbol, the cross, as an instrument of torture; it did not merit the worship of free men. To their sickly religion, Julian counterposed his own—worship of the "living soul of beauty." Based on self-exaltation and joyous love, the bright happiness it brings men will eliminate all shadows, all anxious questioning. "Despondency, fear, sacrifice, and prayer" will all become superfluous. Man will decide his own destiny, create his own meaning. Aesthetic gratification and the excitement of battle and struggle will bring man such ecstasy that he will cease to think of death. "Eternal Olympian laughter" will drive out the sound of weeping in a new world where men themselves are gods: "Do not say: the gods *already* are no more, but rather, the gods, *as yet* are not! They are not but they shall be, not in the heavens but here on earth. We shall all be as gods—only it is necessary to possess great daring such as no one on earth has had, not even the hero of Macedon himself."

Julian teaches man how to conquer the fear of death. Meeting it courageously on the field of battle, he proclaims, "Let the Galileans triumph, we shall conquer later on. The reign of Godlike men, eternally laughing like the sun, will be on earth." Laughter is Julian's leitmotif. A symbol of lightheartedness, it has been considered the weapon of the devil by many Christians, including Baudelaire.

The Nietzschean exaltation of sensuality ("Sex, for free hearts, innocent and free, the garden happiness of the earth . . ."), muted in Julian, is the theme of Merezhkovsky's introduction to his 1896 translation of Longus's *Daphnis and Chloe.* Sec-

onding Nietzsche, Merezhkovsky charged that Christian asceticism was directly responsible for man's misery; it had forced
him to deny his most vital instincts. Physical love, he said, is
not sinful; it is "the eternal return of the human essence to
nature, to the bosom of unconscious life. Love and nature are
one and the same; love is the passionate flight of the soul to
primordial spontaneous health from that artificial cultivated
sickness which we call culture." The entire essay lauds "guiltless and natural love" and bewails its absence from the life of
intellectuals. Eros, Merezhkovsky claimed, has departed from
the cities; it has retreated to "the quiet fields of the shepherds,
with goats and sheep in desolate gardens, where one can hear
the buzz of the bees and the fall of ripe fruits through the
branches, [to] the empty shores of the sea, in forgotten corners
of nature where, to this very day, people are still like gods
and beasts. And here they still lead their childish untaught play
which reveals the secret meaning of universal life. The voluptuousness of Pan . . . pure nymphs helping him, sheep and goats
copulating . . . teach the children love. Here love moves rivers,
the breeze breathes love." But the natural and spontaneous life
is gone; old forms cannot be resurrected. New forms, suiting
modern life, must be created.

Man still does not know what those new forms are. But they
cannot emerge until the old order has been destroyed; destruction, therefore, has priority. But destruction is a task for supermen. Only they are capable of authentic rebellion, of pushing
forward into the void. Lesser men do not have the strength to
maintain their revolt; they lack staying power and cannot bear
the loneliness of long-term rebellion. They do not possess the
courage to proclaim their own goals. Seeking social acceptance
and security, after a brief show of defiance, they backslide to
conventional behavior.

New Verse exalts heroes who challenge tradition, who wrestle
with God, in order to create a truly new culture. Michelangelo,
in particular, is lauded as a lonely superman, a tragic hero,
whose stubborn attempt to dethrone old values was unceasing
and uncompromising:

> You [Michelangelo] cursed art, but while your mouth,
> Without faith, in torment summoned God,
> Your soul was morose and empty.
>
> And God did not alleviate your sadness.
> And you did not wait for salvation from people.
> Your mouth, with contempt, fell silent forever.
>
> You no longer prayed or grumbled,
> Embittered in lonely suffering,
> You perished, not believing in anything.
>
> And there you stood, unconquered by fate.
> You, a proud face, bowed before me.
> In despair, and peace, and profundity.
>
> Like a demon, hideous and great.

"Song of the Bacchanal" glorifies the Bacchanalian orgies,
symbol of the elimination of all restraints. The Dionysian
(ceaseless flux, instinct) overpowers the Apollonian (structure,
reason), thus liberating the inner man. Through ecstasy, he
achieves oblivion and overcomes the fear of death:

> Do not be ashamed of nudity.
> Fear neither love nor death.
> Do not fear our beauty.
> . . . To you, O youth
> Despondency is the greatest sin.
> There is one exploit in life—joy.

> There is one truth in life—laughter.
> Our groans are just like laughter.
> Approach, all powerful Bacchus, dare
> Break all limits and all laws
> With innocent laughter.
> We will drink the nectar of life,
> To the dawn, like gods in the heavens.
> With laughter we will conquer death.
> With mad Bacchanal in our hearts.

The line "Our groans are just like laughter" suggests that
Nietzscheanism had not enabled Merezhkovsky to overcome
suffering. Arsinoe, a character in *Julian,* is the spokesman for
Merezhkovsky's continuing reservations. Having led Julian to
the forbidden Greek statues, Arsinoe is directly responsible for
his paganism; therefore, her subsequent conversion to Christianity is crucial. Paganism had failed to bring her happiness;
it had not obviated her distaste for life. Life, she tells Julian,
is "more terrible than death." Desiring to be reunited with her
recently deceased sister, she is converted to Christianity. Happiness *after* death, at least, will be hers. Determined to squelch
her intellect, she will achieve belief. "Intelligence is more
seductive than any passion," but through belief, life and death
will become equal. She will then be immune from life's vagaries. Arsinoe's statements indicate that at the very height of
his rebellion, in a book celebrating an antichrist, Merezhkovsky
was still unable to overcome his fears and enjoy life. The poem
"De Profundis" (after Oscar Wilde) also reveals the confusion
and conflict raging within him:

> I love evil, I love sin.
> I love the daring of crime.
>
> My enemy scoffs at me.
> "There is no God; ardor and prayer are fruitless,"
> I bow low before You.
> He answers, "stand and be free."
>
> I run once again to Your love.
> He tempts proud and evil.
> "Dare taste the fruit of knowledge,
> You will have strength equal to mine."
>
> Save, save me! I wait.
> I believe. You see, I believe in a miracle.
> I do not fall silent. I do not go away.
> And I will knock at your door.
>
> In me burns a desire for blood.
> In me is a hidden seed of decay.
> O give me pure love.
> O give me tender tears.

In this poem, Nietzschean revolt, Christian love, *fin de
siècle* decadence, and Schopenhauerian quietism ("But sometimes it seems that joy and sadness / and life and death are
one and the same / Peacefully to live, peacefully to die / That
is my final consolation") all clash. Though no single world
view emerged victorious, the desire for Christian love is most
prominent.

Works written between 1896 and 1899 indicate Merezhkovsky's growing reservations about Nietzscheanism. While still
living a life devoted to art and worship of the flesh, Merezhkovsky was inwardly groping for new values. Beauty was not
enough. The pessimism of "Children of the Night" betrays
his disillusion with Nietzscheanism as a guide to life:

> Children of grief, children of the night.
> Wait, our prophets will approach.

With hope in our hearts,
Dying we yearn
For worlds not yet created.
We have a presentiment of the future.

Our speech is daring,
But we have been condemned to death.
Too early forerunners
Of a too slow spring.

· · · · ·

We are hanging over an abyss.
Children of darkness, waiting for the
    sun.
The sun will come, and like shadows,
We will die in its rays.

Nietzsche had stated that the first generation is a sacrifice. Presumably, Merezhkovsky and his contemporaries were the unfortunate casualties of a transition era; they would not live to see the new world.

His treatment of Greek culture shifted to an emphasis on its tragic aspects, and he tended to regard its joy as almost inconsequential. Apparently the emotional gratification he had sought in Nietzscheanism still eluded him; his life (like Nietzsche's) remained basically ascetic. As his doubts about pure paganism increased, he immersed himself in its art even more and translated additional Greek tragedies. His version of Sophocles' *Oedipus at Colonus* appeared in 1896. In his prefatory remarks he stated that the issue was that Oedipus posited himself against the entire world order, attempting to make himself a god. But the ending, he noted, was almost Christian in its tenderness. His translation of *Antigone* appeared in 1899; he considered it a tragedy of voluptuousness and wisdom which prefigured the Christian theme of sacrifice for an ideal. Through these comments and translations Merezhkovsky made knowledge of the culture of classic Greece and Rome part of the cultural baggage of the era.

With all his doubts, he was still in love with beauty. Between 1896 and 1900 he and Hippius made several trips to Greece and Italy. The Italian Renaissance particularly interested him as an attempt to combine pagan and Christian ideals. An article on Leonardo da Vinci appeared in 1897 and a biography of him, *The Resurrection of the Gods,* in 1900. Merezhkovsky also wrote several imitations of Italian novellas of the fifteenth century; **"Love is Stronger Than Death"** is typical of the Neo-Platonism which began to predominate in his works. Directing his sensuality to visual enjoyment, he withdrew ever more from society and became almost indifferent to real life. As before, his associations were confined to fellow artists.

Eternal Companions is a collection of essays, many published previously, which reveal Merezhkovsky's misgivings about Nietzscheanism as a creed. Still convinced that art is the means to truth, he read extensively in the classics of world literature. (This was unusual for the time; the intelligentsia did not value culture.) Treating each author as an exemplar of the consequences of a particular world view, Merezhkovsky counterposed love to struggle, balance to extremism, and purpose to endless flux and moral chaos. Inner harmony remained his ideal, and he became less hostile to Christianity. The essays on Flaubert, Ibsen, and Dostoevsky clarify his disillusionment with Nietzscheanism as a guide to life, and the essay on Pushkin set forth his criteria for a new creed.

To Merezhkovsky, Flaubert symbolized the failure of art as religion. Flaubert sought oblivion in aesthetic creativity; he "fled from the world to art as a hermit flees to a cave." But Flaubert was unsuccessful; his pursuit of beauty ceased to be an abstract principle and became a mania. Seeing both himself and others only as objects to be studied, Flaubert lost his capacity for feeling and his moral sense. Sacrificing happiness and love, he created his own loneliness. Unable to love, he became fascinated with evil and depravity; virtue seemed boring. Merezhkovsky concluded that genius unguided by love will "devour the heart" and destroy the artist himself. Probably he was aware of the fate of artists such as Rimbaud whose experiments with their own sensations led them to madness.

Ibsen is Merezhkovsky's symbol of the negative aspects of individualism—its stance of perennial revolt. All Ibsen's heroes, Merezhkovsky noted, are essentially alone and unable to achieve either inner peace or social integration. Though they do overcome restrictions, the defiant rebel within them is insatiable. Uncommitted to anything or anyone, they lead lives that will always lack meaning. Hedda Gabler epitomizes this nihilism; she demonstrates that a person needs a positive goal, that it is "not possible to live this way." Ibsen himself died lonely and unhappy. Unwittingly, Merezhkovsky concluded, Ibsen proved that revolt cannot be a way of life, that affirmation is also necessary.

The essay on Dostoevsky continues this theme; his characters all testify to the failure of secular individualism. Ivan Karamazov was responsible for the death of his father and was himself ruined. Kirillov consented to Shatov's murder and killed himself, and Raskolnikov actually murdered two old women. Although Raskolnikov was ultimately saved, it was love, not intellect, that saved him. The instrument of his salvation, moreover, was not a superman but a humble prostitute. Intellect, Merezhkovsky warns, must be guided by an ethical ideal, by love for one's fellow man. Otherwise it results in the "passion of fanaticism," the tendency to disregard human life when it obstructs the fanatic's abstract goal.

According to Merezhkovsky, Dostoevsky was the only writer with the courage and vision necessary to identify the problems of modern man. He neither ignored the complexities of modern life nor advocated a retreat to simpler times. His characters live in the city; they grapple with the very same problems afflicting all men today: "He is us, with all our thoughts and suffering . . . , he knows us . . . knows our most secret thoughts, the most criminal desires of our hearts." (Note Merezhkovsky's allusion to his own decadence.) Dostoevsky had realized that freedom could be a curse. Unchecked by faith and love, it could lead to all sorts of horrors. Dostoevsky had also foreseen the advent of the superman. Calling him the "man-God," he had specifically warned against him and advocated a return to religion. Only through religion, he said, can man achieve inner wholeness; only the consciousness of brotherhood under one Father in heaven can enable man to love. Although Dostoevsky himself wavered between the ethical idealism of Father Zosima and the cynical realism of the Grand Inquisitor, he posed the problem—the relation of Christianity to life in this world—which, Merezhkovsky insisted, must be answered.

The essay on Pushkin marks the beginning of Merezhkovsky's life work—the unification of paganism and Christianity in a higher synthesis. Each, he said, embodies an "eternal principle," each is half of a yet unknown truth. "Paganism" is love of the earth; Christianity is love of the sky, man's search for an Ideal. Paganism strives for happiness on earth; it values freedom, beauty, culture, and prosperity and is individualistic, realistic, and practical. Christianity strives toward eternal life.

Scorning this world, it values asceticism, humility, and altruism. Christians refuse to accept the idea that anything is impossible; they are imbued with a limitless search for the "eternal and endless." The "golden mean" is foreign to them. Neither paganism nor Christianity is sufficient in itself; paganism denies the soul, and Christianity denies the body. The struggle between these two "eternal principles," Merezhkovsky argued, gives history its dynamic. Nietzscheanism, positivism, and utilitarianism are merely variants of secular paganism.

Only Pushkin was able to unify the two principles. Paganism accounts for the beauty and clarity of his poetry, for his love of life. But his love of all people, his compassion for those who are suffering, is Christian. Though Pushkin admired Peter the Great, he sympathized with Peter's victims. (Merezhkovsky refers to Pushkin's poem *The Bronze Horseman*. The statue of Peter comes to life during a flood and tramples a humble clerk to death.) Pushkin's idealism is also Christian; his *Eugene Onegin* holds the life of the "superfluous man" up to scorn. Pleasure is not enough. Merezhkovsky stressed Pushkin's love of freedom, his hatred of tyranny in all its forms—autocracy, conventional morality, and mob rule. This too, he said, derived from a combination of Christianity, which frees the soul, and paganism, which frees the body.

But the means by which Pushkin combined the "two truths" is not known; their unity was unconscious. Unable to follow him, his successors in Russian literature gravitated to either the pagan or the Christian pole. The pagans were atheists and materialists; the Christians rejected art, sensuality, and even worshiped suffering. The generation of the sixties combined the worst features of both worlds; they were pagan in their materialism but Christian in their asceticism. If Russians could fathom Pushkin's source of inner strength, they would be able to resolve all conflicts including the perennial problem of Russia and the West. Pushkin, Merezhkovsky claimed, was a universalist, but he never advocated Russia's losing her own identity. His successors, however, were either Westernizers, who would make Russia into a copy of Europe, or Slavophiles, who resisted all change and made the primitive peasant their ideal. (pp. 432-46)

In 1899 Merezhkovsky decidedly rejected Nietzscheanism and announced his "turn to Christ." In 1900 he, Hippius, and Filosofov began their attempt to create a new Christianity based on the Second Coming of Christ as prophesied in the Apocalypse. The New Christianity had a marked Nietzschean touch. Arguing that "historical Christianity" was incomplete because the New Testament contained only part of Christ's full message, Merezhkovsky retained the individualism, aestheticism, and sensuality of his Nietzschean period. Exactly how to combine them with Christianity was yet to be revealed. The Christian tenets of his new faith were love and eternal life; apropos the latter, Merezhkovsky insisted that both the body and the soul would be resurrected. The New Christianity was a direct, though implicit, response to Nietzsche's shortcomings as Merezhkovsky perceived them. For the rest of his life Merezhkovsky tried to meet the challenge to religious faith posed by Nietzsche, to combine the best of both worlds in a new creed. He still advocated destruction of the old order and based his new views on the Apocalyptic prophesy of "a new sky and a new earth."

Though Merezhkovsky began to speak, in general terms, of the failure of aesthetic individualism, he waited until 1915 to describe the inner turmoil Nietzscheanism had caused him. *Two*

Secrets of Russian Poetry: Tiutchev and Nekrasov . . . reveals the personal anguish he experienced during the nineties. Aestheticism, he admitted, had brought him to the verge of suicide. The fault was Tiutchev's. It was Tiutchev's, not Nietzsche's, because by 1915 Merezhkovsky had become so Christian that he denied his former views. (Tiutchev did influence the symbolist poets, but that is beside the point.) As early as 1908 he described Nietzscheanism as "a childhood sickness . . . fatal to adults," and denied that he was ever "seduced by that chaff." By 1911 and 1914 he had deleted passages offensive to Christianity in the two editions of his collected works. By 1915 Merezhkovsky had positively reevaluated the populist poet Nekrasov, who had been the symbol of everything Merezhkovsky had previously detested in art. Now sympathetic to the Socialist Revolutionaries, Merezhkovsky exhorted Russian artists to learn from Nekrasov.

Tiutchev's spirit, Merezhkovsky proclaimed, was a sickness; it was poisoning Russia:

> The sick man knows his pain better than all the doctors because he knows it from within; thus we know Tiutchev better than all the critics. . . . Today in Russia, suicide and suicidal loneliness are as much an everyday occurrence as capital punishment. Who has done this? Russian decadents, Balmont, Blok, Briusov, Bely, Z. Hippius? Yes, they, but through them . . . Tiutchev. . . . And the suicides themselves do not know that the cyanide of potassium with which they poison themselves is *Silence, Silentium.*
>
>> Keep quiet, conceal and hide
>> Your feelings and dreams.
>> Be able to live only in yourself.
>
> This is our sickness—individualism, loneliness, asociability. . . .

The aesthetes of the nineties, Merezhkovsky explained, tried to carry out Tiutchev's idea of solitude. Accepting Tiutchev's conviction that communication between people is impossible and that friendship does not exist, they secluded themselves. Hoping to become invulnerable, they tried to make themselves into supermen, to take God's place. But only God is invulnerable; as human beings the aesthetes still suffered. Indeed, loneliness increased their suffering. Withdrawing even further from the world, they tried to obliterate consciousness by either overstimulating or deadening their senses and retreating from activity and life.

The atheism of the aesthetes, Merezhkovsky emphasized, could only lead to despair. A world predicated on the absence of God cannot have any order or meaning. With no higher good, conflicting human will becomes the only law; struggle becomes the only constant. Such a world is too frightening for man to accept. To preserve some meaning, he invents an impersonal God and calls it "blind will," "dionysian flux," the mystical "All," or some other form of pantheism. But names do not solve the problem of meaning. God himself is lost in the chaos; chaos becomes God. Pantheism's denial of personal immortality removes all source of hope. The brief period of earthly self-affirmation fails to compensate for eternal death. Happiness, sensual enjoyment, and beauty—all pale at the thought of the abyss that lies ahead. Furthermore, in a meaningless universe, nothing is sacred. If the universe is unknowable, moral standards are impossible. Without a referent, good cannot be distinguished from evil. Indeed, if God is All, he must sanction evil and suffering themselves. Evil thus becomes acceptable, even predominant. Men cease to regard one another as brothers of one father: "At night all cats are gray; in pantheism all gods are demons." In a world of unchecked evil, existence is indeed a curse, Nirvana or nothingness, a deliverance. Suicide again becomes attractive.

Realizing all this, Tiutchev still hesitated to admit his preference for darkness, his love of evil, and his belief that since the world is illusion, action is futile. Thus his "Silentium." "Poor Tiutchev, poor us," Merezhkovsky concluded. "He only related what went on in most of us."

Nietzscheanism failed to bring Merezhkovsky happiness, and it did not deliver him from fear. Instead, it actually increased his misery and made him actively desire death. Tiutchev's alleged conclusion, "There is no need to strive for chaos because life is already chaos, no need to strive for death because life is already death," was Merezhkovsky's testimony to his own despair. His previous allusions to criminal thoughts and to the fascination of evil become clear. (Devil worship existed in avant-garde circles of the *fin de siècle* in both East and West. Both Hippius and Briusov affected a demonic pose.) Again referring to himself, Merezhkovsky said that from his desperate conclusion Tiutchev, "having recoiled in horror, grasped at Christianity like a drowning man at a straw." Merezhkovsky's attempt to create a life centered on art crumbled before the prospect of the abyss that loomed ahead of him. Reluctantly he realized that he was not a superman, that he could not sustain a philosophy of self-exaltation in a cosmic void. Thus he began to seek a specifically Christian faith with absolute values and eternal life.

Taking upon himself the role of Christian prophet, Merezhkovsky called on the aesthetes (whom he now called decadents) to follow him in his New Christianity. Russia, he said, is like a dry forest; the life-giving sap of faith is gone. The decadents are the highest branches of the trees. When the inevitable lightning strikes, it will hit them first. From them, the entire forest will go up in flames. In answer to Zarathustra's statement, "The people . . . are becoming weary of themselves and languish even more than for water—for fire . . . herald of the Great Noon," for Merezhkovsky the "Great Noon" was the Second Coming of Christ. Having been through the abyss (the term is used by both Dostoevsky and Nietzsche, but the imagery here is Nietzsche's), man thirsts for truth—for the Word of God and for the establishment of the Kingdom of God on Earth. Again answering Nietzsche, Merezhkovsky insisted that the universe is not ceaseless flux; it has a definite meaning, a definite beginning, and a definite end:

> [We] believe in the end, see the end, want the end . . . ,
> at least the beginning of the end. In our eyes is an
> expression which has never before been in human
> eyes—in our hearts, feelings which people have never
> before experienced. . . . We have been on the very
> edge of the abyss, on too great a height where nothing
> grows. There below in the valleys, high oaks leave
> roots deep in the soil. . . . And we, weak, small,
> hardly visible from the earth, open to all wind and
> storms, almost deprived of roots, almost withered.
> From the early morning and from the heights of the
> oaks still surrounded by fog—we see that which no
> one else sees; we are the first to see the Sun of the
> Great Day already shining; we are the first of all to
> say to Him, "Aye, approach, O Lord."
>
> (pp. 446-49)

Bernice Glatzer Rosenthal, "Nietzsche in Russia: The Case of Merezhkovsky," in Slavic Review, *Vol. 33, No. 3, September, 1974, pp. 429-52.*

ADDITIONAL BIBLIOGRAPHY

Bedford, C. H[arold]. "D. S. Merezhkovsky: The Forgotten Poet." *The Slavonic and East European Journal* 36 (December-June 1957-58): 159-80.
    Examines the expression of Merezhkovsky's religious and philosophical thought in his poetry.

————. *The Seeker: D. S. Merezhkovsky.* Lawrence: University Press of Kansas, 1975, 222 p.
    Detailed analysis of Merezhkovsky's fiction, poetry, and religious and political thought.

Clowes, Edith W. "The Integration of Nietzsche's Ideas of History, Time and 'Higher Nature' in the Early Historical Novels of Dmitry Merezhkovsky." *Germano-Slavica* 3, No. 6 (Fall 1981): 401-16.
    Traces the influence of Friedrich Nietzsche's philosophy in Merezhkovsky's trilogy *Christ and Antichrist*.

Jahn, Gary R. "A Note on the Concept of the Artist in Thomas Mann and Dmitry Merezhkovsky." *Germano-Slavica* 11, No. 6 (Fall 1978): 451-54.
    Demonstrates that Merezhkovsky was an influence on Mann and compares their similarly dualistic conceptions of the artist.

Kalbouss, George. "The Birth of Modern Russian Drama." In *Russian and Slavic Literature,* edited by Richard Freeborn, R. R. Milner-Gulland, and Charles A. Ward, pp. 175-89. Cambridge, Mass.: Slavica Publishers, 1976.
    History of modern Russian drama discussing Merezhkovsky and Nikolai Minsky as the chief theorists, critics, and promoters of Symbolist theater.

Lednicki, Waclaw. "D. S. Merezhkovsky, 1865-1941." *The Russian Review* I, No. 2 (April 1942): 80-5.
    Obituary lauding Merezhkovsky's personal accomplishments and literary works.

Levitzky, Sergei. "An Unnoticed Anniversary—On Merezhkovsky's Role in Russian Culture." *The Russian Review* 27, No. 3 (July 1968): 321-26.
    Biographical article written to commemorate the centennial of Merezhkovsky's birth.

Lossky, N. O. "Philosophical Ideas of Poet-Symbolists." In his *History of Russian Philosophy,* pp. 335-44. New York: International Universities Press, 1951.
    Contains a summary of Merezhkovsky's religious beliefs.

Maslenikov, Oleg A. "The Early Phases of the Symbolist Movement in Russia" and "Andrey Biely and the Merezhkovskys." In his *The Frenzied Poets: Andrey Biely and The Russian Symbolists,* pp. 9-32 and 128-45. Berkeley and Los Angeles: University of California Press, 1952.
    Synopses of Merezhkovsky's role in the origination of the Symbolist movement and of his and Zinaida Hippius's position in the religio-philosophical group in St. Petersburg.

Padelford, Frederick Morgan. "Merejkowski: A Prophet of the New Russia." *The Sewanee Review* XXVI, No. 4 (October 1918): 385-406.
    Examines Merezhkovsky's belief that Russia would lead the world in embracing his "New Christianity" after the Bolshevik Revolution.

Persky, Serge. "Dmitry Merezhkovsky." In his *Contemporary Russian Novelists,* pp. 246-73. 1913. Reprint. Freeport, N.Y.: Books for Libraries Press, 1968.
    Assesses Merezhkovsky as a poet, novelist, critic, and philosopher.

Poggioli, Renato. "Modernism and Decadence." In his *The Poets of Russia: 1890-1930,* pp. 46-88. Cambridge, Mass.: Harvard University Press, 1960.
    Contains a discussion of Merezhkovsky's leadership of the Modernist movement.

Rosenthal, Bernice Glatzer. *Dmitri Sergeevich Merezhkovsky and the Silver Age: The Development of a Revolutionary Mentality.* The Hague, Netherlands: Martinus Nijhoff, 1975, 248 p.

Examines the cultural renaissance in Russia at the turn of the century and the political implications of its aesthetic ideals. Rosenthal writes, ''Merezhkovsky and the revolutionary mentality he represented and fostered constitute both a symptom and an indirect cause of the uprootedness that led to the Bolshevik Revolution of 1917.''

————. ''Eschatology and the Appeal of Revolution: Merezhkovsky, Bely, Blok.'' *California Slavic Studies* XI (1980): 105-39.

Contains a summary of Merezhkovsky's thought concerning religion and social revolution.

Salgaller, Emanuel. ''*Dmitrij Samozvanec*—A Dramatic Fragment by D. S. Merezkovskij.'' *The Slavic and East European Journal* VII, No. 4 (1963): 392-400.

Discusses an unfinished play written by Merezhkovsky concerning an early seventeenth-century impostor of a Russian prince.

Scanlan, James P. ''The New Religious Consciousness: Merezhkovskii and Berdiaev.'' *Canadian Slavic Studies/Revue Canadienne D'Etudes Slaves* 4, No. 1 (Spring 1970): 17-35.

Analyzes Merezhkovsky's religious belief and its variant form advocated by Nikolai Berdiaev.

Slonim, Marc. ''Mystics, Philosophers, and Marxists.'' In his *Modern Russian Literature: From Chekhov to the Present*, pp. 103-24. New York: Oxford University Press, 1953.

Includes a biographical essay tracing the development of Merezhkovsky's thought.

Stammler, Heinrich A. ''Russian Metapolitics: Merezhkovsky's Religious Understanding of the Historical Process.'' *California Slavic Studies* IX (1976): 123-38.

Examines Merezhkovsky's mystical view of history.

Ricardo Palma

1833-1919

(Born Manuel Palma) Peruvian short story writer, dramatist, historian, poet, and nonfiction writer.

Palma is credited with creating the literary form of the *tradición,* a type of short story in which fictional elements are combined with historical fact to produce a humorous and often satirical narrative. The majority of Palma's *tradiciones* are set in Peru's colonial period, which lasted from the early fifteenth century through the nineteenth. A social and political liberal, Palma frequently satirized the Roman Catholic clergy, the legal profession, and selected political figures. Although other Peruvian writers have written *tradiciones* in imitation of Palma's, critics agree that none equal them in effectiveness and wit.

Palma was born in Lima in 1833, less than a decade after Peru won independence from Spain, and throughout his youth attended various schools, including the Convictorio de San Carlos. There he became part of a group of young writers who embraced the new literary movement of Romanticism, in reaction to the Neoclassicism that had previously dominated Peruvian literature. Palma published his first poem in the newspaper *El comercio* when he was fifteen years old, and his first play, *La hermana del verdugo,* was performed in 1851. At the age of twenty Palma entered the navy, and it was during a prolonged stay on the Chincha Islands that he discovered the classics of Spanish literature, most importantly the works of Miguel de Cervantes and Francisco de Quevedo. By 1860 Palma had left military service and was writing liberal invectives against the policies of Peru's president Ramón Castilla; in November of that year, he indirectly participated in an unsuccessful assassination attempt on the president and, threatened with imprisonment, fled to Chile. In 1863, after a newly elected president declared amnesty for all political exiles, Palma returned to Peru and was appointed to the Brazilian consulate. He eventually ascended to the Peruvian senate, where he served from 1868 to 1872 under the presidency of José Balta. Following the election of 1872, in which Balta lost the presidency to Manuel Pardo, four of Balta's generals temporarily seized power and murdered Balta, an action that destroyed Palma's faith in the efficacy of politics and prompted his interest in writing *tradiciones,* through which he could, by his own acknowledgement, "live in centuries now departed."

Between 1872 and 1877 Palma compiled four volumes of *tradiciones* and one volume of poetry. In 1879 his work was halted by the War of the Pacific between Peru and Chile, during which the Peruvian National Library was destroyed. At the end of the war Palma began a thirty-year career as director of the National Library, restoring much of the former collection and adding an additional 35,000 volumes. Palma continued to write *tradiciones* and various historical articles until 1909, when his doctor advised him to discontinue writing because of the strain it placed on his health. He died in 1919.

Palma's popular appeal and critical reputation are based on *Tradiciones peruanas,* the *tradiciones* he wrote and published between 1872 and 1909. Their settings range in time from A.D. 1180 to the years of Palma's childhood, and in place from Latin America to Spain, France, Italy, and England. The

characters depicted are drawn from all social classes, occupations, and personality types. The majority of the *tradiciones* are set in the city of Lima during Peru's colonial period, and they present an informed picture of that time. Displaying a strong sense of regional pride, Palma's *tradiciones* often portray Limean women as more beautiful, Limean men more brave, and the city residents generally more clever than visitors from abroad. The *Tradiciones peruanas* are written in a lively, humorous style which incorporates considerable dialogue, short and smooth sentences, little or no extraneous description, and abundant irony and satire. Critics affirm Palma's ability to use a few precise details with natural action and dialogue to create living, realistic characters. In his later years, Palma attributed the popular success of the *Tradiciones peruanas* more to their form and style than to their content. He wrote, "I believe that the secret of the 'tradición' lies, above all, in the form. It should be narrated the way stories are narrated. The pen ought to glide lightly and it ought to be sparing in the use of details."

After Palma left politics in 1872, his liberal principles found expression in the social and political satire of the *Tradiciones peruanas.* His most frequent objects of ridicule were Roman Catholic priests, monks, and mystics; lawyers, judges, and officials of the court; and political figures. Opposed to hypocrisy, injustice, corruption, and suppression of freedom, he satirized the people and institutions that he considered most guilty of such offenses. His wit, although thought-provoking, was nonetheless gentle, in keeping with the lighthearted atmosphere characteristic of his conception of the *tradición;* as he wrote, "A severe style in the *'tradición'* would be as appropriate as the magnificat during the matins; that is to say it would not be suitable at all." Apart from satirizing various institutions, Palma succeeded in constructing a detailed and colorful portrait of Peru during its period of colonization. The degree of historical accuracy in Palma's *tradiciones* has been debated, but critics agree that he reproduced the character and atmosphere of colonial Peru masterfully.

Critics often contend that in his *tradiciones* Palma articulated the irony and humor of the Peruvian national spirit. His work inspired a much-imitated literary form in Latin American fiction, and captured both the popular imagination and critical respect. For his evocative style and honest opposition to hypocrisy and corruption, Palma is considered one of Peru's greatest writers.

PRINCIPAL WORKS

La hermana del verdugo (drama) 1851
La muerte o la libertad (drama) 1851
Rodil (drama) 1852
Anales de la inquisición de Lima (history) 1863
Armonías: Libro de un desterrado (poetry) 1865
Pasionarias (poetry) 1870
Tradiciones. First series. (short stories) 1872
Tradiciones. Second series. (short stories) 1874
Tradiciones. Third series. (short stories) 1877
Tradiciones. Fourth series. (short stories) 1877
Verbos y gerundios (poetry) 1877
Perú: Tradiciones. Fifth series. (short stories) 1883
Perú: Tradiciones. Sixth series. (short stories) 1883
Refutación a un compendio de historia del Perú (history) 1886
Poesías (poetry) 1887
Tradiciones: Ropa vieja. Seventh series. (short stories) 1889
Tradiciones: Ropa apolillada. Eighth series. (short stories) 1891
Filigranas (poetry) 1892
Tradiciones peruanas. 4 vols. (short stories) 1893
Neologismos y americanismos (nonfiction) 1896
Recuerdos de España (memoirs) 1897
Tradiciones y artículos históricos (short stories and history) 1899
Cachivaches (short stories) 1900
Papeletas lexicográficas: Dos mil setecientas voces que hacen falta en el diccionario (nonfiction) 1903
Mis últimas tradiciones peruanas y Cachivachería (short stories) 1906
Apéndice a mis últimas tradiciones peruanas (short stories) 1911
Poesías completas (poetry) 1911
Tradiciones selectas del Perú. 2 vols. (short stories) 1911
Tradiciones peruanas. 6 vols. (short stories) 1923
The Knights of the Cape (short stories) 1945
Epistolario. 2 vols. (letters) 1949
Tradiciones peruanas. 6 vols. (short stories) 1951
Tradiciones peruanas completas (short stories, poetry, history, and nonfiction) 1952
Cartas inéditas de Ricardo Palma (letters) 1964

†*Tradiciones en salsa verde* (short stories) 1973

*This volume comprises thirty-eight translated *tradiciones.*

†This volume was written and privately circulated in 1901.

ALFRED COESTER (essay date 1916)

[*In the following excerpt, Coester discusses the form, content, and humor of Palma's* tradiciones.]

In Ricardo Palma (born 1833), Peru may claim the inventor of a new form in literature, the tradition, to give it the name which the author himself employed. It is nothing more than the historical anecdote, frequently only a bit of scandal, a sensational or unusual crime, a practical joke, just such things as appear in the newspapers every day, but Palma's traditions were gleaned from the historical chronicles of Peru. Though he vouched for their accuracy they were written in such a vein of humor with the striking points so skillfully brought out that his critics accused him of falsifying history without succeeding in producing a novel. None of his imitators ever quite caught the trick of style which made his work popular in all the periodicals of Spanish America for thirty years. The inimitable was probably the dash of Peruvian wit. Besides he ransacked so thoroughly both the oral and written traditions of Peru that he left little in that field for anybody else.

Palma, when scarcely twenty years of age, was banished for participation in a political plot. Accordingly, in Paris he published a volume of verse, ***Armonías, libro de un desterrado.*** While it contained enough laments in romantic tone to justify the sub-title, the most original poems were certain "cantorcillos" miniatures in verse of his later traditions in prose.

In the first series of traditions, Palma, aiming more at the historian's task, related the acts of the viceroys; but as the number of the series lengthened into nine between 1863 and 1899, any sort of anecdote afforded him material. Consequently he played upon a great diversity of emotion from the thrill of horror to the broad laugh, and introduced members of every class of society from the viceroy to the slave. Being somewhat skeptical himself, he delighted in stories referring to religious superstitions, belief in ghosts or tales dealing with loose living by friars. At the same time he paid willing tribute to heroism, as in the story of Fray Pedro Marieluz, who died rather than reveal the secrets of the confessional even when his political sympathies would have persuaded him to do so.

But to excite laughter was Palma's chief aim. As an example take the tale of the skeptical Andalusian shopkeeper, who did not believe in hell. A fanatic priest wished to buy some provisions of him on credit. The man refused to sell, saying discourteously: "I won't trust you in order to be paid in hell, that is, never." The priest accused the shopkeeper of being a heretic because he did not believe in hell and so worked on the sentiment of the villagers that the shopkeeper had to flee to save his life. The priest incidentally excommunicated him. To lift the decree of excommunication, the shopkeeper betook himself to the archbishop in Lima. The latter imposed as penance marriage with a certain young woman of ill repute, daughter of a famous vixen. After the shopkeeper had been married a short time, he admitted to a friend that the priest was right in affirming the existence of hell "because I have it at home."

The plastic character of Palma's traditions owes much to his constant effort to cull the homely phrase or the picturesque turn of expression from the speech of the people or from old books. He put together some observations of this sort in his **Papeletas lexicográficas,** a continuation of Paz Soldán's *Diccionario de peruanismos.* As a result of this careful documentation and Palma's resolve not to inject into the narrative any fancies of his own, the reader of his traditions feels that the vivid picture of colonial times and ideas possesses historic value and is thankful that Palma has wiped from it the dust of ages. (pp. 254-57)

> *Alfred Coester, "Peru and Bolivia," in his* The Literary History of Spanish America, *Macmillan Publishing Company, 1916, pp. 244-63.*

G. W. UMPHREY (essay date 1936)

[*In the following excerpt, Umphrey discusses Palma's poetry and prose writings and examines historical and stylistic aspects of the* Tradiciones peruanas.]

Although the reputation of Palma rests mainly on his **Tradiciones peruanas,** his other literary work should not pass unnoticed. It was not until he reached the middle years of his long life that he discovered the path by which he was to attain enduring fame as a *tradicionista,* and already he was widely known for his poetry and historical investigations, not to speak of three romantic plays that were given a warm reception on the stage, but that, in the opinion of the author, were not worth preserving in print. An excellent introduction to his early literary life as well as to the whole romantic movement in Peruvian literature is to be found in **"La Bohemia de mi tiempo,"** a reprint of **"La Bohemia literaria de 1848-1860,"** written by Palma in 1887 as a prologue to his collected poems. In this sympathetic, although humorous, account of the literary ambitions and accomplishments of the group of writers to which he belonged in his youth, the strong points of the Peruvian romanticists are stressed; their weaknesses become only too apparent to the impartial student of their writings. Romanticism was incompatible with the national character and in much of the poetry of that period the lack of individuality and sincerity is apparent. Palma, so thoroughly Peruvian and Limenian in his sprightly wit, in his ironic subtlety and in his natural tendency to jest at anything and everything, was a romanticist because of literary contagion and not by temperament. His best poetry was written after romanticism had ceased to be the dominant literary tendency and he was permitted to give free rein to his natural inclinations. His early poems in the romantic manner are now seldom read, whereas several poems of his later collections, **Verbos y gerundios** and **Nieblas,** find their way into all popular anthologies of Peruvian poetry. The harsh judgment that he passed in his old age on his own poetry is not acceptable to other critics, and no less a poet than Rubén Darío has said of him that "en cuanto a sus versos ligeros y jocosos, pocos hay que le aventajen en gracia y en facilidad. Tienen la mayor parte de ellos un algo encantador, y es la nota limeña" ["in all of his light and comical verses, there are few that are surpassed in grace and ease. The greater part of them have something delightful, and it is the mark of Lima"].

Aside from the **Tradiciones,** his prose writings consist of historical studies, journalistic articles on matters political and literary, impressions and sketches, philological discussions. Soundness of scholarship and seriousness of purpose are evident in spite of the witty manner of presentation. As literary critic he possessed good taste and a wide knowledge of literature; his genial nature and benevolence made him too tolerant of the weaknesses of his fellow writers and too generous with his praise. The longest of his historical studies, **Anales de la inquisición de Lima,** is of slight historical value compared with the much more exhaustive work of the great Chilean historian, José Toribio Medina, in the same field. Its value is also weakened by the author's prejudices in all matters connected with church history; his anticlericalism and especially his hostility toward the Jesuits are apparent in it as in his other writings. His shorter historical articles are notable mainly for their literary qualities. Palma was primarily a literary artist; the great mass of material that he gained by patient and laborious research, passing through his creative imagination, took permanent form in his inimitable **Tradiciones.**

It is in Palma the *tradicionista* that we find the happy combination of the best that was in him as poet, historian, archeologist, and genial critic of life and literature. Keenly interested in the social and political life of Peru from the earliest times down to his own day, he familiarized himself with all the available documents in print or in manuscript; with the creative imagination of a poet he converted the dry and lifeless details that he gained by careful historical and archeological research into scores and even hundreds of living pictures. (pp. xvi-xviii)

[The] *tradición* is a literary type that lies midway between history and prose fiction. The historical novel or the short story dealing with some historical event or person belongs to the same middle ground. The shortness of the *tradición,* varying from one page to ten or twelve pages, prevents any possible confusion with the historical novel. Its differentiation from the ordinary short story of historical import is less apparent; there is, however, an essential difference, a difference that may become clear in the course of this study. For the present, we shall give our attention to a brief comparison of the methods followed by the *tradicionista* and the historian in the attempt to reconstruct the past on the basis of documentary evidence.

The historian is concerned with the main current of national life and with the logical development of social and political institutions; he gives his attention to events and persons of outstanding importance, and he is concerned with them only in so far as they are related to the main current of events or to the growth of institutions or customs. Palma's purpose was not to give the connected history of Peru or of the city in which he was born and in whose present and past he was so intensely interested. It is true that most of the important events in the history of his country and of his native city are covered in his **Tradiciones,** but only incidentally, as it were; they serve mainly as the historical background for the *tradiciones,* and are usually presented with concise brevity in the distinct division of each *tradición* that is frankly historical in content. It is true, too, that the incident, custom, legend, or anecdote that forms the nucleus of the *tradición* may have to do with some important historical event or personage, but it is treated always as an incident or custom that is interesting in itself and not because of its relation to important events or personages. Just as in modern journalism reporters gather news that is worth being printed merely for its "human interest" and not for its real importance, so Palma in his historical research and archeological investigations always sought out the "human interest story" that could be expanded into a *tradición* by the addition of fictitious elements. Some of his material he got from printed histories; as for the greater part, the small details and incidents that the serious historian is likely to overlook or to pass over

TRADICIONES

POR

RICARDO PALMA.

LIMA
IMPRENTA DEL ESTADO.
1872.

Title page of Palma's first volume of tradiciones.

consciously as matters relatively unimportant, this material Palma obtained from moth-eaten manuscripts and from dusty archives; or, in the case of more recent material, from the lips of those who had gained it through personal experience or by tradition.

The scores of *tradiciones* contained in six large volumes give a complete, though disconnected, series of pictures that place vividly before our eyes the life of Peru and particularly of Lima from the early 15th century down to the war with Chile fifty years ago. They do not follow each other in chronological sequence, because of the casual manner in which the variegated themes attracted the attention of the author. The amorous escapade of a viceroy; a miracle performed by a saintly priest; a royal edict prohibiting the wearing of the *saya* and *manto;* the origin of a curious proverb; a traditional superstition; an unusual street name; a bit of folklore; some old custom of strange beginning; the caprice of a Limenian lady of many years ago; the first introduction of some fruit or grain; the discovery of the medicinal qualities of quinine or Peruvian bark; these and many other similar incidents and minor details of history became the objectives of his investigations and the themes of his *tradiciones*. Whatever he was unable to discover for the completeness of his picture was supplied by his fertile imagination, controlled by his intimate knowledge of the social and political life of the period in question. Human frailties, rather than heroic deeds, gave him the material that he could use to best advantage, so that the life he presents bears some resemblance to that of picaresque fiction.

> Para mí el mundo pícaro es poético,
> Poco en el hoy y mucho en el ayer.

["For me the mischievous world is poetic,
A little in the present and much in the past."]

Every period in Peruvian history is represented more or less completely in the ten series of *Tradiciones.* Among the first that he wrote are some that go back to the Pre-Hispanic period, such as **"La gruta de las maravillas," "El hermano de Atahualpa," "La achirana del Inca."** The conquest and the first years of the colony under Francisco Pizarro are represented by **"Granos de trigo," "La casa de Pizarro"** and others. The Civil Wars (1538-1554) that followed close upon the subjugation of the Incas and that divided the Spanish conquerors and colonists into two warring camps offered a rich store of picturesque incidents that served as nuclei for several *tradiciones;* thirteen of them have to do with Francisco Carvajal, *El demonio de los Andes,* whose steadfast loyalty to his friends, reckless bravery and ready wit compensated to some extent for his unrestrained passions and vices. With the viceroyalty of the Marqués de Cañete the colony settled down to a peaceful routine of existence that lasted without interruption for two centuries and a half. During the first part of this period, that is, from about 1550 to 1700, life in Peru was merely a pale reflection of the life of Spain. Because of its unbroken monotony, its futility and pettiness, it is, from the historical point of view, the least interesting period in Peruvian history, and the ordinary historian does little more than enumerate the many viceroys that were sent out from Spain one after the other in long succession, with brief comments upon their good and bad points. That Palma was able to discover material for many interesting *tradiciones,* **"Una aventura del rey poeta," "Los polvos de la condesa," "Una vida por una honra,"** to mention only three of them, is proof of his originality and genius as a story teller. More to his individual taste, however, was the 18th century; his ironical skepticism, his irreverence and Voltairean wit found in it a completely congenial atmosphere. The steady growth of criollismo ["creolism"] throughout the 18th century, resulting in the increasing differentiation between Peruvian customs and those of the mother country; the rivalries and enmities that were becoming more and more common between Peruvians of Spanish descent, the *criollos,* and the newcomers from Spain, the *peninsulares* or *chapetones;* the growing spirit of skepticism and anti-clericalism; in these changing conditions and tendencies he found the inspiration and material for many of his best *tradiciones,* among which might be mentioned **"Capricho de Limeña," "La camisa de Margarita," "El cigarrero de Huacho," "La gatita de Mari-Ramos que halaga con la cola y araña con las manos."** Coming down to the 19th century we find several *tradiciones* dealing with persons and events connected with the War of Independence, the political struggles and civil wars that followed the gaining of national independence, and the war with Chile. They are interesting for the sidelights that they throw on important events and for the glimpses that they give us into the private lives of the outstanding military and political leaders, but, as *tradiciones,* they are less artistic than those treating of customs, persons, and events that were sufficiently removed from Palma's own time to be veiled with the poetic glamor that belongs to the past.

Because of the great diversity of treatment it is difficult to make a general statement regarding Palma's method of procedure. Usually the *tradición* is divided into three or more short chapters; the first chapter introduces the historical or legendary incident about which the author embroiders his fictitious details; then, having awakened the reader's interest, he leaves the story in suspense and in the second chapter gives a comparatively sober account of the historical background of the period; in the following chapter or chapters he carries the story to its conclusion, sometimes with extreme rapidity, sometimes with many rambling digressions. In this methodical separation of fiction and history, a separation so distinct that an intimate knowledge of Peruvian history is not needed to enable us to separate the fact from the fiction, lies one of the chief differences between the *tradición* and the short story or novelette. Another dissimilarity is Palma's indifference to a progressive and logical development of his story. The action is interrupted on the slightest provocation; something reminds the author of a related incident or anecdote and with or without an apology he pauses to tell it, and before he returns to his story he has entertained us with many witticisms or amusing comments. This personal contact between author and reader is one of the interesting characteristics of the *Tradiciones.*

Much of Palma's success as a *tradicionista* was due to his mastery of a prose style in complete harmony with the content of his *tradiciones.* To the rich store of picturesque words and idioms that he got from the writers of Spain he added the equally picturesque words and idioms that he had garnered from the language of everyday speech in Lima and from the old documents with which he became so familiar. Over the surface of his prose there ripples incessantly a spontaneous wit of the Andalusian variety, tinged with maliciousness and often decidely picaresque; it becomes even salacious at times. The tendency to jest at anything and everything leads him frequently into witticisms that seem sacrilegious to many readers. Fortunately, his good literary taste usually kept these natural tendencies in check, so that he can rarely be charged with vulgarity in his facetiousness, and if his shafts of wit are sometimes tipped with malice and irreverence, they are rendered harmless by the pervading spirit of benevolence. Subtle irony underlies many of the *tradiciones,* irony so subtle that it might easily be missed by the casual reader. The ingenuous candor of many of his stories treating of miracles and superstitions cannot be taken at its face value; the alert reader is well aware of the genial skepticism permeating the apparently candid story and ingenuous comments.

Many Spanish-American writers have written *tradiciones* in imitation of those of Palma. They have studied his formula and have adopted his methods with more or less success, but the qualities that give to the *Tradiciones peruanas* their essential novelty and that constitute the literary individuality of Palma cannot be transferred at will from one writer to another. Palma is still without an equal in the type of literature that he created and in which he was so productive. He is, as José de la Riva Agüero says of him in his *Carácter de la literatura del Perú independiente,* "el maestro insuperable de las evocaciones coloniales, el que sabe resucitar una época entera hasta en sus mínimos pormenores" ["the insuperable master of the colonial evocations, he who knows how to revive an entire epoch even in its smallest details"]. The *Tradiciones peruanas* offer us a vivid and interesting picture of the social and political life of Peru for more than three centuries; in the excellent prose in which they are written are to be found the literary qualities that, according to Peruvian critics, are most characteristic of their national literature. In Ricardo Palma we find, to quote again from Riva Agüero, the "raro concierto del criollismo y de la cultura. . . . Posee, más que nadie, la chispa, la maliciosa alegría, la fácil y espontánea gracia de esta tierra. . . . Palma es el representante más genuino del carácter peruano, es el *escritor representativo* de nuestros criollos" ["rare concert of creolism and culture. . . . He possesses, more than anyone, the

spark, the artful glee, the easy and spontaneous wittiness of this land. . . . Palma is the most genuine representative of the Peruvian character, is the *representative writer* of our Creoles"]. (pp. xx-xxvii)

G. W. Umphrey, in an introduction to Tradiciones peruanas *by Ricardo Palma, edited by G. W. Umphrey, Benj. H. Sanborn & Co., 1936, pp. xv-lviii.*

HARRIET DE ONIS (essay date 1945)

[*De Onís edited and translated* The Knights of the Cape, *a collection of Palma's* tradiciones. *In the following excerpt, she discusses the historical background of the* tradiciones *and Palma's literary style.*]

In presenting to the American public [a] selection from Ricardo Palma's *Tradiciones peruanas,* one of the classics of Hispanic letters, it would be helpful if we could find the author's counterpart in our own literature and thus, following the best pedagogical precepts, proceed from the known to the unknown. But, unfortunately, he has none. The nearest approach would be Washington Irving. Both loved to evoke the past in its intimate and legendary, rather than strictly historical, aspects, to seek out the bright threads that give the web of history warmth and color. Irving's legends and tales belong, in broad classification, to the same genre as the *Tradiciones.* But Washington Irving was of the romantic school; realism was in the ascendancy when Palma began his *Tradiciones,* and that tendency of the times was reinforced by his own skeptical, satirical, Voltairean turn of mind. Moreover, the mediums with which the two men worked were completely opposed. It was the placid, homespun countryside of the Hudson Valley, the charmingly conventional halls of Merry England, the Alhambra through whose gardens wandered the shade of unhappy Boabdil as against the pomp and circumstance, complexity, violence, intrigue of Lima, "the thrice-crowned City of the Kings," from its earliest days to our own times.

If the mountains that ringed the bountiful farms and sleepy villages of the Dutch patroons harbored certain malign, mischievous spirits of forgotten Indian chieftains and old comrades of Hendrik Hudson who vented their spleen against intruders by blowing up sudden storms or causing henpecked husbands to develop amnesia, spirits of quite a different caliber brooded over the scene of Palma's tales. The fratricidal wars between Huascar and Atahualpa, the heir and the usurper of the throne of the Incas, the sudden, paralyzing stab of the conquest, the civil wars between the conquistadors, the establishment of the pompous vice-royalty, the jockeying for power among the different religious orders, pirate attacks, earthquakes, tidal waves, saints, miracles, the Independence—all these form the teeming cyclorama of history from which Palma has taken the materials for his tales that have been the delight of the Spanish-reading public since he first began to publish them in 1872. Series followed series, to the number of six; in 1889 came the "last," which turned out to be the seventh; then came another last, the eighth. In 1910, nine years before his death, came *Apéndice a mis últimas tradiciones,* which, to his readers' regret, brought the series to a close. It is doubtful that any work by a Spanish American writer has enjoyed greater popularity. Palma belonged not to Peru alone but to the entire Hispanic world. There was nothing parochial about his work, despite the fact that its horizons were the "four winds" of his native land and, principally, the city of Lima during the colonial epoch. But so penetratingly has he portrayed this world that it acquires continental stature. Allowing for unimportant differences, the life of Lima was the life of Bogotá, Quito, Mexico City, La Paz, where the same elements had combined to produce that mixture of splendor and squalor, refinement and degradation, mystic withdrawal and hypocritical libertinism, piety and superstition which Palma has so deftly portrayed.

Palma is no hero-worshipper; like the protagonists of the Spanish picaresque novels he knew so well, he took the ant's-eye view of humanity. Familiarity with the great, whose acquaintance he had made in the dust-covered archives over which he pored with such avid delight and whom he had come to know "as well as if he had given birth to them," had bred a tolerant contempt in him. The viceroys and beruffed members of the Royal Tribunal are not presented in their moments of statesmanship or weighty decision; a casual reference suffices for this. It is their human, frailer side that interests Palma, when these escutcheoned representatives of His Catholic Majesty, muffled in dark capes, prowl the streets of Lima like amorous tomcats, follow some beautiful unknown from church to church, run afoul of the Inquisition, or forgather with spies in dark, deserted squares. One sees Francisco Pizarro, probably the greatest of the conquistadors, not in his role of captain winning battles against overwhelming odds by his brilliant strategy and courage, but cutting the first figs in his garden in Lima, the swineherd become a fine gentleman, chatting with his page and meeting an absurd death in his own house at the hands of traitors. Even the saints and aspirants to sainthood, in which Lima abounded, are shown in their less exalted attitudes. We see St. Rose of Lima, not in a mystic rapture with the Divine Spouse or suffering the self-imposed martyrdom of her crown of nails, but establishing a non-aggression pact with a swarm of troublesome mosquitoes. Her contemporary the Blessed Martín de Porres performs such humdrum miracles as pulling a fresh smelt out of his sleeve to tempt the prior's appetite or persuading a dog, cat, and mouse to eat out of the same dish.

Every rank of society is represented in this pageant. Great lords and ladies, bishops, judges, friars haughty and meek, fortune-hunters who had struck it rich at Potosí or had discovered hidden Incan treasures, gamblers, cut-throats, Spaniards, Creoles, Negroes, Indians, half-breeds. . . . And, above all, the ladies, those daughters of Lima, beautiful, fascinating, capricious, unmanageable, with a finger in every pie, from every walk of life and every profession, including the oldest. All of them come to life at Don Ricardo's magic touch. Miguel de Unamuno, who admired him greatly, made this shrewd observation: "Ricardo Palma could have fittingly applied to himself Ernest Renan's words: 'This world is a spectacle a god has staged for his own enjoyment. We can assist the great choreographer in his designs by helping to make the performance as brilliant and as varied as possible.'"

There is no doubt that Palma enjoyed to the fullest this world he really created, for it was he who brought it back to life from the dust of oblivion under which it lay. No detail was too insignificant to escape his notice, and he infused his creations with his own gaiety, mirth, irony, and impudent charm. He gave them not only life but immortality as well.

Included among the historical legends are various old folk tales, which are known throughout Spanish America, but which Palma has told in his own incomparable manner, filling them with droll anachronisms, slang, and irreverent asides. The best example of these is **"Where and How the Devil Lost His Poncho."**

No study of Palma, however insignificant, would be complete without a word about his style. He has had many imitators, but it can be said of them as Mark Twain told his wife when she attempted to outswear him in the hope of breaking him of his profanity: "You've got the words, my dear, but not the music." No one else has been able to catch the rich, robust flavor, the irony, the tongue-in-cheek sanctimoniousness, the mockery, the hilarious double meanings that are the delight of the reader and the despair of the translator. Few writers have had a greater sense of language than Palma. He was steeped in the Spanish classics; like all the young men of his day he had drunk deep at the fountains of romanticism, Scott, Chateaubriand, Byron, Heine, Hugo, Lamartine. . . . But his ear was always closely attuned to the living language, that of the streets, the market-place, the old wives' tales to which he had listened with delectation as a child and which he never forgot. His style is a mosaic of all these elements, embellished with his own Puckish inventions. (pp. xi-xv)

The number of the founders of Lima is said to have been thirteen. It should be increased to fourteen, for Palma was as surely one of them as were Pizarro and his twelve companions. If they founded it, he has perpetuated their creation. To it and to himself he has left a monument more enduring than brass. And the heaven his roguish, skeptical, tolerant spirit would have welcomed as the reward for its sojourn on earth—assuming that having lived in Lima were not reward enough—would not have been that conception of the hereafter in which one lies in the bosom of Abraham and knows the reason of all things, but resting on some softer bosom and knowing the inside story of all things. (p. xv-xvi)

> *Harriet de Onís, in an introduction to* The Knights of the Cape and Thirty-Seven Other Selections from the "Tradiciones peruanas" of Ricardo Palma, *edited and translated by Harriet de Onís, Alfred A. Knopf, 1945, pp. xi-xvi.*

ENRIQUE ANDERSON-IMBERT   (essay date 1963)

[*In the following excerpt, Anderson-Imbert examines the various sources Palma drew from in writing the* tradiciones *and evaluates his skill as a literary artist.*]

Ricardo Palma . . . was the great figure of lagging Peruvian Romanticism. He wrote dramas in verse which he condemned later as "abominable monstrosities" and many verses (four volumes) which he called, with manifest disinterest, "rhymed lines of writing." In the entertaining, confidential notes of *The Bohemian Life of My Time (La bohemia de mi tiempo)* Palma tells of the Romantic literary excesses of the years 1848 to 1860. Disappointed and mocking, Palma withdrew from Romanticism; but only after he had lighted one of his torches to illumine romantically the Peruvian past. The romantic sympathy for the past took possession of certain literary genres. A born narrator, Palma must have felt the attraction for all of them: the historical novel, the sketch of customs, the legend, the short story. He did not submit to any of them, but taking a little from here and a little from there, he created his own genre—the "tradition." Already in 1852 he was writing stories on traditions; ten years later these "traditions" were taking on definitive configurations, and from 1872, the long series of *Peruvian Traditions (Tradiciones peruanas),* in perfect form, are published. From 1872 to 1883 there were six series which were followed by others with different titles: *Old Clothing (Ropa vieja); Moth-eaten Clothing (Ropa apolillada); Knick-*

knacks and Traditions and Historical Articles (Cachivaches y tradiciones y artículos históricos); Appendix to My Latest Traditions (Apéndice a mis ultimas tradiciones) already in print in 1911. (We have read the manuscript of **"Off-Color Sauce"** [**"Tradiciones en salsa verde"**], still unprinted, and scarcely printable because of its pornography.) With the years, Palma became aware of his originality and recorded the formula of his invention in several places: in his letter to Pastor S. Obligado, in the prolog to Clorinda Matto de Turner's *Traditions,* in the introduction to his **Old Clothing,** in the frequent allusions to his theory and to the method of the traditionalist, diffused in the *Traditions* themselves. From these we extract one: "A dash or two of lies, and an equal dose of truth, no matter how infinitesimal or homeopathic it may be, a good deal of nicety and polish in the language, and there you have the recipe for writing Traditions...". The socio-geographical-historical-psychological tapestry he offers us in his *Traditions* is quite extensive: from the beggar to the viceroy; from Tucumán to Guayaquil; from the time of the Incas to contemporary events in which Palma himself had a role; from the idiot to the genius.

But in the center of the tapestry, and woven with a fine thread, is the resourceful viceregal society of eighteenth-century Lima. The sources are numberless and at times unrecognizable: edited and unedited chronicles, histories, lives of saints, books on travel, pasquinades, wills and testaments, tales by missionaries, convent registries, verses, and, in addition to the written word, the oral one of the proverb, the cliché, the couplet, superstition, legend, popular stories. The structure of the *Traditions* is also complex. The combination of historical documentation and narrative action is disarranged, shifting, free. At times there is no structure at all; the events moulder and smother the narrative. Or, in one tradition, there are many other minor traditions inserted one into the other. The granary of plots, situations, and interesting characters is so abundant that a whole family of short story writers could feed there. One sentence might be the kernel of a possible story. Even Palma's spirit unfolds on two planes. He was in Herderian sympathy with the voices of the people, but also indulged in Voltairian mockery of them. But the person who influenced his humor was not so much Voltaire as Balzac and his *Contres drolatique.* He has the multiplicity of perspectives of the bantering skeptic, and even his protestations of impartiality—"I don't subtract or add anything"—are ironic needlings at the absolutism of the Church and State.

He was a liberal, and only took seriously the right to a free conscience, and the sovereignty of the people and the moral values of good, honor, and justice. His dominant tone is one of mischievous, picaresque jesting. And he even keeps the smile on his lips when he relates the poetical miracle of **"The Scorpion of Friar Gómez"** (**"El alacrán de Fray Gómez"**) or the dramatic sacrifice of **"Mother Love"** (**"Amor de madre"**). This latter "tradition," one of his best, enthused Benito Pérez Galdós so much that, according to what he tells in a letter, it gave him the desire to write a drama "like *El abuelo.*" Nevertheless, because of that semi-mocking, semi-compassionate smile of Palma, **"Mother Love,"** more than drama in the Galdós manner, would lend itself to the grotesque theater of the Italians Chiarelli and Pirandello. Tragi-comic farces, and not tragedies, would be found in Palma's vein. Despite his carelessness, he was a good narrator. He knows how to make us wait for the denouement. There is not a single virtue of the short story writer that Palma did not have. He presented his characters gracefully, especially the women; he selected strange conflicts, tangled them, and then untangled them. But there is not a single

"tradition" that is really a short story. His joy at being an antiquarian causes him to collect facts; and to make room for them, he interrupts, deviates, and constantly alters the course of the story. His handling of historical facts keeps his hands so occupied that he cannot give the action that final tweak for a surprising wind-up. He is attracted not only by the action, but also by the historical atmosphere in which it occurs; and that atmosphere is composed of particles of archival dust. The facts float in the air, loosely and wildly. As with Montalvo, Palma's prose is something of a linguistic museum in which words and tropes are squeezed into the smallest spaces. However, in contrast to Montalvo, Palma's language is more American and more popular. In this instance Palma, who as a member of the Peruvian Academy, corresponding to the Spanish, had worked in lexicography, responded to a linguistic theory: that the vocabulary enriches itself by allowing free entry to Americanisms, archaisms, neologisms, cultured and popular words; but that one must conform to the syntax studiously and zealously. In the *Traditions* the oral and written language, the Spanish and Hispanic-American language, the popular and cultured language constantly interchange their thrusts, movements, cadences, words, and syntax. Since these undulating ideals of expression had joined, separated, and then joined again in literary histroy, even Palma's artistry has a good deal of the colloquial, and in turn, his manner of conversing, a good deal of literature. On the whole, his prose is enchanting for the way it vitalizes hackneyed expressions and for raising popular expressions to the category of artistic monuments. (pp. 209-11)

Enrique Anderson-Imbert, "1860-1880," in his Spanish-American Literature: A History, *translated by John V. Falconieri, Wayne State University Press, 1963, pp. 195-228.*

KESSEL SCHWARZ   (essay date 1975)

[*In the following excerpt, Schwarz examines linguistic experimentation in Palma's work and compares his use of language with that of the modern Spanish novelist Juan Goytisolo.*]

Andrés Bello, José Martí, Manuel González Prada, Rufino Blanco Fombona and many other Spanish Americans have written cogently about the Spanish language. José Martí believed that American writers who used new words to augment the American scene could justify each new linguistic innovation only through a complete knowledge of the language in order to "separate themselves from rules promulgated by the orthodox academies of language, art, and literature."

From the 1960's on, the question of language in literature has taken on added importance, especially in the development of what some critics term "novels of language" by novelists concerned with the transformation of narrative linguistic reality itself. In this attempt to create a new language with a quality and form corresponding to its interior mystery, they create puns, neologisms, non-sentences and non-paragraphs. The same evolution may be seen in the works of Spain's leading novelist, Juan Goytisolo, vitally interested in language, as his collections of essays and novels and his many interviews reveal.

Guillermo Cabrera Infante states: "In the speech of Cubans Spanish is being converted every day into something different not only in its phonetics . . . but also in its syntax." Essentially, Cabrera's well known *Tres tristes tigres* may be viewed as an attack on literature and a defense of language through its negation of the established lexicon, use of ambiguity and allusions, and parody of conventional language.

No doubt Cabrera Infante's novel influenced the language of Juan Goytisolo's own masterpiece, *Reivindicación del conde don Julián,* which contains sarcastic references to well-known literary figures, a scathing and iconoclastic attitude toward literature, and a disassembling and reassembling of words in a syllabic, semantic game, much in the manner employed by Bustrófedon, Cabrera Infante's linguistic protagonist. Indeed, Goytisolo acknowledges the influence of Cabrera Infante in the foreword to his own novel.

These experiments have been accepted as something totally new and refreshing, perhaps akin to the poetic reformation a half century earlier by Vicente Huidobro and others. Yet except in degree and the inclusion of syntax as part of the focus of Goytisolo's irreverent attitude, one may find what at first glance seems to be a rather improbable ancestor of Goytisolo in Ricardo Palma, fascinated by language. Peruvianisms, proverbs, folkloric expressions, epigrams, Indian words, and neologisms. In his studies such as *Neologismos y americanismos* and *Papeletas lexicográficas,* which includes about 2,700 words missing from the Royal Academy Dictionary, as well as in works such as *Recuerdos de España* and in his correspondence, he constantly attacked what he considered to be a moribund Royal Academy while at the same time professing his love of language: "A devotee, as I am, of linguistic studies. . . ."

Palma, while ostensibly digging into archaic linguistic forms, was rejecting artificial and stilted Castilian for a special mixture of neologisms and Peruvianisms, a combination of the *castizo* and the *americano* through which he managed to emphasize "curious and personal idiomatic creations." He proposed fitting the language to multiple views, gave it meaning on many levels of abstraction, much in the fashion of contemporary writers, and created variants and curious turns and twists of language to meet his artistic purposes. His blend of "words, phrases, and turns, taken alternatively from the mouth of the common people who swarm in markets and taverns, and from the books and other ancient writings of the sixteenth and seventeenth centuries," reveals that like Goytisolo, who professes to profane classical texts, he had to have a great knowledge of classical language and popular speech in order to be able to reproduce the living document and to restore the original force of words.

Palma offers us the same kind of burlesque of official Peru found in Goytisolo's mockery of a static Spain. He uses the equivalent of associative chains, irony, and malicious portraits in satirizing literary and linguistic intransigence, although the contemporary writer's devotion to lavatory graffiti is matched, in Palma's case, only by his insistence on new and funny words. A master of locutions, Palma delights us, as does Goytisolo, with his semantic and phonetic implications. He believed that an author, in order to convey humor, had to know the very nature of language and "to make a serious study of the structure of sentences, of the euphony and rhythm of words. . . ." His tolerant contempt for some figures of the past matches that of Goytisolo for the giants of his country's literature, and he also uses irony, tongue in cheek puns, and words with double meanings. His attacks on what he calls "the impropriety, unsuitability, and vulgarity in the form of our bureaucratic communications" reflect, in a more traditional way, Goytisolo's reproduction of Don Alvaro's discourse in *Reivindicación del conde don Julián.* Goytisolo differs in the intensity, to the point of irrationality, in his persecution of the "marvelous

language of the Poet, vehicle necessary for betrayal, your beautiful language,'' and in his insistence on the need for multilevel and ambiguous expressions through which to launch an attack on the social and political *status quo.* Goytisolo feels the need to destroy linguistic myths as part of his forays against cultural and historical values and that his duty, as a modern writer, is "that of being myth destroyer." Palma also saw the need for change and realized that the younger generation in his country "neither loves nor hates Spain; it is indifferent to her." Both writers picked up the sound of the adolescent of the street and the unique verbal contours of living Spanish, but Goytisolo is aggressively ideological and Palma is not.

Ricardo Palma, at various times in his speeches and writings, mentions his efforts to preserve the purity of the language in spite of giving it a contemporary flavor through his use of current dialect, but his love for linguistic purity seems reserved almost exclusively for Spanish syntax: "The spirit, the soul of language, lies in its syntax more than in its vocabulary. Enrich the latter, revere the former, that is our doctrine." He repeats this refrain a number of times. "For me, purity must not be sought through vocabulary but rather through correct syntax, for syntax is the soul, the characteristic spirit of all tongues." (pp. 138-39)

Palma, in spite of professing love for the syntactical integrity of his native tongue, chides those who strive for a virginal Castilian, for languages, he claims, "are not virgins: they are mothers, and fecund mothers who are always providing from the claustrum of their brain through the opening of their lips new children to the world of love and human relations." He rejects the "anemic lexicon of Castile" and reiterates that one must be prepared to sacrifice the purity of Castilian to be truthful to a living Spanish. He argues that one should have the right to create any word necessary to convey an expression and to realize the peculiar potentialities of his native speech, that Peruvian is not Castilian, and that new flexibility and meanings are needed to have a living and not a dead language. This revolution in language, "an irresistible imposition of the twentieth century," is imperative because a "liturgical language is a language condemned to die.''. . .

The Royal Academy is a favorite target for both Goytisolo and Palma. In *Neologismos y americanismos, Recuerdos de España,* and in a series of letters, Palma complains about Academy intransigence to changes in language or the acceptance of Americanisms. He laments the fact that the only potential tie between Spain and the New World is language, a fact the Royal Academy refuses to recognize, to its sorrow; for new expressions and forms will prevail because "to exclude or condemn them there exists no institution sufficiently powerful or authorized. . . ." He praises the American spirit of Castelar for accepting new modes of expression in spite of an "intransigent academic majority"; contends that language, independent of all rules, will survive, "in spite of the Academicians . . .''; rejects the Academy dictionary as "a *cordon sanitaire* between Spain and America" and as a "restrictive measuring stick''; and states that usage and not "the doctors . . . those who impose such and such a word" will prevail. He rejects the Academy view that languages are vestal virgins whose purity they are charged to preserve as ridiculous as the Academy itself, for him "of slight importance." He reiterates that Academy authority simply turns writers and young Americans away from the study of language and literature. Fifty million Spanish Americans are the true owners of the language because, in truth, Castilian has become, even in Spain, little more than a regional tongue. (p. 140)

Carlos Fuentes sees the search for language as "a temporal return to the fount of language . . . to encounter a language which is at long last the answer of the writer as much to the exigencies of his art as to the needs of his society, and I believe that herein lies the possibility of contemporaneity." One may accept the anticultural aspects of Goytisolo's fiction and the contention of critics like Rodríguez Monegal about the creation of new relationships between the modifications of the individual and his reality while at the same time insisting that, linguistically speaking, the search for artistic authenticity among contemporary writers differs only in degree from that of other generations. Palma was responding in the nineteenth century to invariable artistic exigencies through his language and unusual connotations, much as Goytisolo, in his experimentation with new form, was reacting to what he termed linguistic myths. In the final analysis, both, true artists, rejected the concept of language as something inherited or definitive, adapted words and sentences to each nuance of content, and created a highly original, metaphorically informative, and authentic language, as they explored their transmuted realities in compelling and stylistic interpretations of society and history. (p. 141)

Kessel Schwarz, *"Language and Literature: Ricardo Palma and Juan Goytisolo,"* in The International Fiction Review, *Vol. 2, No. 2, July, 1975, pp. 138-42.*

PHYLLIS RODRIGUEZ-PERALTA   (essay date 1981)

[*In the following excerpt, Rodriguez-Peralta praises the wit, irony, and humor of the* Tradiciones peruanas.]

Palma's ***Tradiciones peruanas*** touch four centuries of Peruvian history, but he focuses mainly on the viceroyalty. This fact has been the basis for considering him a colonialist who regretted the loss of courtly splendor and the egalitarian aims of a republic. The underlying attitudes of the ***Tradiciones peruanas,*** however, are multifaceted and very frequently reveal a liberal and contemporary spirit. With obvious affection Palma reconstructs a Peruvian colonial world vividly alive with ambitious officials, cunning clergy, coquettish, seductive women, strutting Spaniards. It is a cape and sword epoch of passion and intrigue, of superstition where the Devil stalks, of processions and deceits and religious devotion. What Palma re-creates with intricate sensitivity is the seething New World scene, swathed in Spanish cloaks. But subtle comparisons of the astute, wily "criollos" ["Creoles"] and mestizos with the vain Spanish "hidalgos" ["noblemen"] show his sympathy for the rebellious "criollo" rather than for the Spaniard. He lauds the cleverness of the "limeño" ["native Limean"] bellringer who comes out victorious against a pretentious viceroy; or the successful protests by the "limeñas" against viceroys, archbishops, and even an edict of Felipe II legislating against "la saya y el manto" ["the skirt and the mantle"], the distinct dress of the "tapadas" ["veiled women"]; or the young boy from Arequipa who bests the Spanish Archbishop and years later becomes the twentieth Archbishop of Lima and one of the great men of independence. The most interesting and beautiful women are from Lima, not those who arrived from Spain. The most vivid scenes take place in the streets of Lima and not in the stately palace of a surrogate king. Palma smiles slyly but fondly at the pomposity and pride of the viceroyalty.

The hum of activity and the murmur of conversations which emanate from the *Tradiciones* bring a spicy perfume of the past, undiluted by idealization. Archbishops and viceroys live again; Martín de Porres scatters his miracles; La Perricholi

Caricature of Palma. From Ricardo Palma, *by José Miguel Oviedo. Editorial Universitaria de Buenos Aires, 1965.* © *1965 Editorial Universitaria de Buenos Aires.*

entices Viceroy Amat and scandalizes the aristocracy. Haughty nobles, potbellied monks, and discontented shrimp-sellers jostle each other in the crowded pages. Palma knows the origin of countless street names in Lima, why the Church of San Pedro has three doors, how the Jesuits schemed to get an estate away from the Paulist fathers, why pregnant women were allowed to roam through monasteries, why neither viceroy nor archbishop can use a parasol in religious processions, how the ceremonies of Holy Thursday began in Lima, when the first bullfights were fought, and the history of the first olive trees. He describes in detail the excitement at the arrival of Spanish ships bearing news from Spain, the stir over the constant excommunications, the feuds over the right of asylum. Nothing pleases Palma more than to spy on the intrigues of the viceroy's court, or to come upon scandals of the convent, or to delve into the enmity among religious orders. Palma's historic past is without idealism. He views the Church, the Jesuits, the colonial institutions with amusement, irreverence, and irony. His sarcasm stings, but it does not wound deeply. The tone is popular, and Palma neither moralizes seriously nor attempts to extract deep philosophic lessons from history.

A multiplicity of perspectives govern Palma's attitudes toward the colonial past. As a "limeño" he takes great pride in the viceroyalty which brought honor and glory to the City of Kings. Yet he shows little nostalgic longing to return to viceregal times. On occasion a faint wistfulness passes through the work, inevitable, surely, in both the artist who misses grace and elegance in his prosaic surroundings and in the political man of his times, anguished by the present. But any wistfulness comes wrapped in fine irony. Thus with straight face Palma relates a seventeenth century dispute over whose carriage should give way in a narrow street—the one belonging to the second Marqués de Santiago, or the one belonging to the first Conde de Sierrabella (**"Un litigio original"**). All Lima's nobility becomes involved, which gives Palma the opportunity to present pages of noble titles in Lima, plus each family coat of arms. Straightforwardly he announces that his exhaustive investigations have never come upon a Palma! A citizen of the republic did not need titles, but more than once Palma's obscure origins had been jolted by the hierarchal structures of Lima's society.

Palma saw the foibles of society and was sometimes wary. At the same time his whimsical spirit, seeking the humorous in the human, allowed spontaneous, irrepressible humor to ripple through the *Tradiciones*. These facets of sparkling wit belong to the festive air of coastal Peru and to the languid atmosphere of Lima. Palma is an authentic "criollo" with the "lisura" of Lima on his lips—the "lisura," that graceful maliciousness with which the "limeño" has greeted life since colonial times. It has enabled him to be satiric while smiling, to exaggerate with delicacy, to be provocative while maintaining his exterior decorum. (The "lisura" of the viceroyalty was an acceptable satire of customs and prejudices and provided a lighter side to the excessive formalism of the epoch.) Palma's "tradición" is tinged with a mischievous, even salacious flavor which may take on picaresque coloration. Peruvian picaros ("mataperros criollos"), however, have greater subtlety and certain aristocratic attitudes not present in their Spanish counterparts, and their jesting and joking were not meant to inflict injury. The "limeña" note, so evident in Palma, stems from a long line of Peruvian satirists, and Palma is the continuation of this native trait as he encases graceful "limeña" satire in lasting artistic form.

In the soft, sensuous ambiance of Lima there is a frivolous vision of life which brings the light joviality to Palma's prose. The humor can be straight-faced, teasing, tart, malicious. The grief of Doña Violante de Ribera is treated with concern: "A cadaver in the room of a noble and reputable young lady is an unwelcome guest." (**"La monja de la llave"**) The love between a young Inca princess and a handsome Spanish captain leads to amorous meetings. Palma advises his readers to read the first pastoral idyl they can find in order to form a correct idea of their transports of love. And then immediately to drink a glass of water in order not to gag from so much syrup. (**"Hermosa entre las hermosas"**) He is amused by the pretentious dolt who began a sermon: "Our Lord Jesus Christ said, and in my opinion He said it very well . . ." (**"Historia de una excomunión"**) He characterizes María Abascal as what is understood by the term "an aristocratic courtesan," that is, a "horizontal" of high tone. (**"María Abascal"**)

Nowhere is the irony more subtle and fine than in Palma's discreet irreverence. With candor he relates the miracles which abounded on all sides. "Yo ni lo niego ni lo afirmo" ["I neither deny nor affirm it"], he assures the reader after relating the feat of Fray Gómez, who, according to the Franciscan chronicles, flew through the air. Without overt comment he describes the situation of a mason in Lima who fell from a wall and was left suspended in the air while Fray Martín de Porres, under sentence not to perform more miracles, went to ask his superior for permission. Behind the mask of innocent acceptance the reader glimpses the smiling irony. Other "tra-

diciones" exhibit more open humor in their irreverence toward bishops, saints, virgins, and even Christ Himself. In **"Un pronóstico cumplido"** Palma explains earnestly that flattery will continue on in heaven. Why, it will be necessary to applaud the trills of the seraphim with great enthusiasm and to give loud kisses to the stem of the lilies that St. Joseph carries! **"Apocalíptica"** quotes God as saying: "Ya no aguanto más a esa canalla ingrata que sólo me proporciona desazones. Convoca, hijo, a Juicio Final" ["I will no longer suffer this ungrateful rabble who only give me annoyance. Son, I invoke the Final Judgment"]. But although God fumes and the trumpet player tires, the "limeños" never bestir themselves to get to the Final Judgment. "¡Válganos Santa Pereza!" Christ and His apostles appear in unexpected places, "montados sobre la cruz de los calzones, o sea en el rucio de nuestro padre San Francisco" ["mounted on the cross of trousers, or maybe in the grey hair of our father Saint Francis"] (**"Refranero limeño"**), or trudging across the Peruvian sands on their way to Ica. Conversations between the Savior and St. Peter are blunt. "Cuidado, Pedro, con tener malas pulgas y cortar orejas. Tus genialidades nos ponen siempre en compromisos" ["Careful, Peter, about being in a bad mood and cutting off ears. Your eccentricities always embarrass us"]. (**"Dónde y cómo el diablo perdió el poncho"**) On occasion Palma just misses being sacrilegious because of the ingenuous attitude he adopts. Such an attitude also enables him to discuss solemnly the salubrious effects of the Devil, or to relate an Indian catechumen's opinion of the Mass: "Tiene de todo su poquito. Su poquito de comer, su poquito de beber y su poquito de dormir" ["Overall, it has a little bit. A little bit of eating, a little bit of drinking, and a little bit of sleeping"]. (**"Una aventura amorosa del Padre Chuecas"**) Only occasionally does Palma's light irreverence toward the Church and religion veer in the direction of sarcastic anticlericalism. Then it is the Jesuits among the religious orders who receive the brunt of his jokes. In the main, however, Palma reveals a skeptical but benevolent attitude, one of fine doubt, perhaps more of the human than the divine.

Palma is unequaled in the grace and spice with which he portrays the women of his *Tradiciones peruanas*. A "limeño" must be gallant, an expert in matters of love, a connoisseur of the ladies. Palma plays his role to the hilt. In his flattering tributes to feminine beauty, coupled with his bantering, impious outlook toward its effect on men, he represents the attitude of his century, the "beloved torment" attitude in direct opposition to the unisex ideas of the late twentieth century. Woman is an essential element of the *Tradiciones*. Palma worships beauty and youth first; he is respectful toward mothers (and few are unworthy); he is indulgent toward the Perricholi and her sisters; he is dubious about those who enter the religious life; he is acrid toward mothers-in-law; he dislikes old women. Palma paints with great detail the physical aspects of the women who interest him. (Such detail is not wasted on men.) The seduction of feminine beauty begins with the eyes: Doña Violante de Ribera was a "limeña" beauty with "eyes blacker than a bad intention." Leonorcica Michel had "eyes with more questions and answers than the catechism." Then the velvet skin, the lips redder than wild cherries, the flowing hair, the tiny feet. How Palma enjoys the attributes of Eve's daughters! Visitación has a tiny and tempting waist with that look-at-me but do-not-touch air. . . . Mariquita Martínez was one of those "limeñas" who possess more grace in walking than a bishop in confirming. Mariquita Castellanos: A royal lass indeed. . . . The fruit of Paradise depends on age, on her "twenty Aprils" or her "seventeen springs." On the other hand, he is unimpressed by those who "give the flesh to the Devil and later offer the bones to

God.'' And he deals harshly with the serpents in Paradise, that is, the ''mothers-in-law.'' Above all, Palma admires femininity, ''la mujer-mujer'' [''the woman-woman''] of Rosa Campusano, the favorite of San Martín, rather than Manuela Sáenz, the ''mujer-hombre'' [''the woman-man''] of Bolívar. (**'''La Protectora' y 'La Libertadora'''**)

Palma uses language appropriate to the social class of the woman and according to the quality of character. The frequent diminutives not only denote endearing attributes of the person herself, but the fondness and fascination of the author. Virtue, purity, fidelity of wives and widows, and the abnegation of mothers are highly lauded. At the same time marriage remains a trap which the adroit male should seek to avoid. And a deceived husband who does not avenge himself merits no respect! Palma is never more effective than when he is revealing a slightly licentious story. The obsession of the theme of honor, revolving around a woman, vies with Golden Age theater.

Palma's attitudes toward women are highly conventional. Yet even here there are stirrings of flexible, even non-traditional thinking. His women can be coquettish, clever, winsome, frivolous; but reflecting his New World perspectives, it is always the vivacious, bewitching ''limeña'' who holds the place of honor in the vast procession of women who file through the pages of the **Tradiciones**. Nonetheless, he often criticizes the indolence characteristic of many ''limeñas,'' while he applauds those who stand up to the authorities, particularly viceroys and archbishops. There is also a certain grudging admiration for the spirit of those who avenge their dishonor either by cleverly trapping the errant male or by cruelly slaying him. And all the adoration of feminine pulchritude does not prevent Palma from voicing his disapproval of the atrocious feminine education in all eras.

Not far removed from colonial times, Palma's generation lived without the yoke of Spanish government but still within the confines of Spanish influence. For Palma, political independence did not mean a severance from Spanish culture and tradition to which he adhered with pride. His Hispanism, however, never takes precedence over his Americanism, nor confuses his identity. The Palma who fought valiantly against Spanish dreams of reconquest in 1866 is the same Palma who traveled eagerly to Spain to embrace with warmth the writers he had admired through his lifetime.

Palma's Americanism is particularly evident in his attitude toward the language held in common by America and Spain. Before the Real Academia Española de la Lengua in 1892 he presented his argument for the admission of some 350 Americanisms into the **Diccionario de la lengua española** on the grounds of their longstanding use by Spanish-American writers and by the general public. In Palma's view, the Spanish language should provide a strong link between the two peoples, cemented and enriched by an understanding and an acceptance of American contributions. Conversely, he was completely opposed to the increasing influence of French on the language. In his plea for unity of vocabulary he reflects the thought of many American men of culture belonging to his epoch who deplored the splintering effects which the separation from Spain had had on the language.

In his **Tradiciones** Palma deliberately uses popular language and archaisms, neologisms and the traditional, Spanish-American and Spanish. The language of the ''tradición'' sparkles with diminutives, elegance, proverbs, erudition, even street vocabulary, and thus is connected to all levels of society. Palma possesses a rich vocabulary encompassing the classical and the colloquial, and his concern with language, plus his versatility, enable him to use encrusted words of the *Siglo de Oro* as naturally as American, particularly Peruvian, expressions.

The flavor of spontaneous speech forms the stylistic basis of the ''tradición,'' which sets it apart from the language of both the neo-classicist and the romantic. The reader seems to hear rather than to see the words. The syntax, which is usually rigorously pure, may follow oral use at appropriate times. Metaphorical and picturesque properties of speech contribute to the local, ''limeña'' essence, while archaic expressions, which Palma constantly uses, contribute an air of antiquity. Palma is an intuitive rather than a formal linguist. Specialists in the field will say later that he was inaccurate in the archaisms he used to create verisimilitude, but this has little importance over and against his artistic success in making the past stir with life. The undiminished stock of proverbs and sayings, which represent collective popular wisdom, fascinated Palma for their linguistic and historical interest and especially as a colonial heritage which continued in his own era. He considered himself an authority on the popular language of old Lima, and he always defended the popular voice against the academician. ''Se trata de un limeñismo, sobre cuya propiedad o impropiedad solo los de la parroquia tenemos voz y voto'' [''It is about Lima-ism, and only we who are from the parish have a voice and a vote over its propriety or impropriety''].

Palma saw his **Tradiciones peruanas** in a patriotic light and even attributed a social role to them. He believed that America had not formed an appreciative awareness of its past and that the fanciful trappings of his new genre would enhance its image. Palma was able to see the poetry inherent in the Peruvian past at a time when others of his generation were steeped in devotion to a European medieval past that was not even their own, and where many, trying to remain faithful to a romantic-liberal creed, feigned contempt toward everything about the viceroyalty because it represented oppression and political dependence. On the other hand, with the advance of the century a deep nostalgia enveloped many Peruvian writers, particularly poets, who wrapped themselves in the cult of Perricholism and viceregal courtliness without the human dimensions of Palma's **Tradiciones**.

Peruvian attitudes toward Palma's concepts of their past underwent various revisions. During his lifetime Palma enjoyed the deep affection and respect of his countrymen, and his **Tradiciones** were a perennial success. At the same time when the battle lines between the native and the colonial were being drawn, Palma's work was pushed into the colonial ranks, and to many he became a reactionary. The chief instigator of this view was Manuel González Prada, harsh critic of Peru's social, religious, and political traditions. In his desire for a complete restructuring of the country, González Prada castigated Peruvian literature which he believed fostered a nostalgic love of the past and a consequent disinterest in Peru's present and future. His attacks began in 1886, and they peaked in 1888 with a speech in which he condemned the ''tradición'' (without mention of Palma's name) as a monstrous falsification of history. He ridiculed the content. . . . And he rejected false styles. . . . (pp. 285-92)

Palma was fully aware that many aspects of the colonial era had only assumed different guises in his own contemporary world. He treated this with sarcastic wit and a subtlety apparently missed by some of his contemporaries. He spins tales around public figures of the past whose attributes can be applied to public figures of his day. He constantly draws pungent comparisons between the two epochs: an excommunication in those days was as frightening as "our mass meetings." The election of an abbess in the eighteenth century caused factions and had the same impact as a change of president has in "our republican era." Professional weepers of colonial times have disappeared, to be replaced by something worse: the obituaries that appear in the papers "today." Sometimes the comment is biting: he describes a rowdy group in the early seventeenth century being taken off to the Pescadería prison, where "in our democratic days" liberals and conservatives serve time in loving companionship with bandits. Far from being slavishly enamored of the past, or escaping into remote times to avoid the present, Palma's keen nineteenth century eyes peer at the historical process. At the slightest provocation he sets the reality of the present against the past, and, as narrator, he moves easily backward and forward in time. (In the midst of mentioning the important people in Spain who received boxes of chocolate from the Jesuits in Cuzco, he adds that he will not give a list as interminable as the kicks that the congresses give to that old bird called the Constitution. That's the reason she can't give birth to anything . . . And the story of the Jesuits continues ["**El chocolate de los jesuitas**"]). In politics and in conscience Palma is a liberal. Imbued with the spirit of independence, he puts his faith in the fundamental morality and good judgment of the "pueblo" ["people"]. His popular roots and liberal critiques are present in his *Tradiciones* together with his love of the colonial world, and the paradoxical qualities contribute to their delight.

The originality of the "tradición" as a literary form should also be included as an expression of Palma's unfettered spirit. He considered himself the initiator of a new literary genre, an opinion which can be accepted in the sense that his "tradición," although heir of many literary strains, has no model. Loosened from the tangle of antecedents, Palma's "tradición" floats freely in the literary currents. The lack of false idealism, the range of characters from all social classes, and the popular and colloquial language fall within the reality of the current Peruvian panorama. At the same time Palma's refined irony and his power of fantasy elevate the "tradición" to an imaginative and creative category. Palma began his "tradición" in the early years of independence, and his new genre contributed to the evolution of American literature in the process of separating from its Spanish roots. Of all the nineteenth century literature written before modernism, only the *Tradiciones peruanas* and the gaucho poetry of Argentina and Uruguay stand out as original American contributions.

Palma's originality does not, of course, cancel certain limitations in his prose. His themes are local, not universal. His spirit is vivacious but not profound. His historical concepts lack objectivity. Too large a measure of his work at one time will cloy. It is curious that his chief defect is also one of his chief attributes: his "limeña" vision which colors his *Tradiciones* so delightfully but also reduces them entirely to one small portion of the world. Nevertheless, the expression of this parochial vision spread the fame of Lima far and wide, and through his *Tradiciones peruanas* Palma succeeded in folding a poetic past around his beloved city which enabled it to take its place among other great cities of the world. Indeed, for many years "lo peruano," to the outsider, meant Lima, as seen in the concepts of Peru held by Unamuno, Valera, and other Spanish writers.

Within the development of Peruvian literature, the combination of conservative and liberal attitudes and perspectives in Palma's

Tradiciones provides a starting point for an appreciation of the complex mixtures that make up Peruvian society. Thoroughly at home in Lima, Palma focuses his *Tradiciones* on the capital from which all Peruvian culture had radiated since the time of its founding. While he gives no evidence of the confusion and tensions which grip the later "serrano" writers, he does incorporate a "criollismo" and "mestizaje" of the coastal area of Peru. Adding the spirit of the Andean provinces with antipodal aspects of Peru will be the arduous task of the Peruvian writers who come after him.

A contemporary Peruvian of his time, with pride in the past and confidence in the future, Palma contributed greatly to the development of a national consciousness. His completely Peruvian, "limeño" spirit, which might have limited his effectiveness, opened the door of fame. In turn, this international eminence as a Peruvian writer brought a sense of pride and self-confidence to a nation groping for identity. The lesson was not lost that the grace, the charm, the sparkling wit, the malicious joy sprang from Palma's Peruvian essence. (pp. 292-94)

> *Phyllis Rodriguez-Peralta, "Liberal Undercurrents in Palma's 'Tradiciones peruanas'," in* Revista de Estudios Hispanicos, *Vol. XV, No. 2, May, 1981, pp. 283-97.*

ROY L. TANNER (essay date 1986)

[*Tanner, an American critic who specializes in Latin American literature, is the author of* The Humor of Irony and Satire in the "Tradiciones peruanas." *In the following excerpt from that work, he discusses various forms of humor used in the* Tradiciones peruanas. *Translations in brackets are those of the critic.*]

To write about humor in the *Tradiciones peruanas* is akin to writing about water in the sea, so omnipresent is it in that collection of historical anecdotes. Rarely does a critic of Ricardo Palma fail to comment on at least one of its facets. "Our great humorous epic, our human comedy," "the comical epic of our history"—such references abound, along with allusions to Palma's "salty, earthy humor," to his "ironique légèreté" ["ironic lightness"] and to "his humorous vision of the past." Ventura García Calderón maintains that "to laugh and to make us laugh is the preferential mission of the chronicler," while Palma's granddaughter, who prepared the Aguilar edition of his complete works, asserts, and with justifiable admiration, that her grandfather sometimes "conducts himself as the most consummate humorist, in a way that has no parallel in the Spanish literature of his time." In full agreement with such analyses, the *tradicionista* himself has confessed: "Mi idiosincracia literaria es humorística, y quizá algo volteriana" ["My literary idiosyncracy is humorous, and perhaps somewhat Voltairian"]. (p. 4)

It has been suggested that "a humorist, as an artist, is born with that gift; strictly as a writer, he makes himself, he polishes, and at the same time 'makes' his attitude" [Santiago Vilas, *El humor y la novela española contemporánea*]. Palma exemplified this observation by Vilas explicitly. Though born a legitimate heir to Peruvian *lisura*, "that graceful maliciousness" that constitutes "the Peruvian way of making literature," and with an apparently innate genius for that clever Limean wit, he had to apply himself diligently in order to find the appropriate aesthetic pathway along which to channel it. He worked and reworked his stories with great patience while acclimatizing and immersing himself in the lexicon and the spirit of the language, especially as manifest in classical Spanish authors.

Later he returned to his initial *tradiciones,* retouching and re-vitalizing them with the humor, irony, and spontaneity so typical of his mature style.

Therein lies one of the keys to his success. In order to achieve its greatest effect, particularly in the spoken tongue, humor requires a spontaneity and a natural wit often lost in belabored writings. Palma's anecdotes, however, though exceedingly polished and reconsidered by the author, are alive with the naturalness of a conversational tone essential to the full expression and conveyance of humor.

Within limits one can find "a certain distinctive individuality that marks the humor of each country" [Stephen Leacock, *Humor: Its Theory and Technique*]. Palma's humor exhibits two veins, as suggested earlier in this chapter—Peruvian *lisura* and a particularly Spanish hue. As a disciple of Miguel de Cervantes, he became saturated with the latter's mode of speech as well as with the speech of Quevedo. In a fashion those great masters guided him in the solidification of his style and his humorous perspective of life. One must underscore as equally significant the influence of Peruvian satire. It informs his perception and, guided by the examples of the Spanish classicists, asserts itself in every facet of his work. (pp. 5-6)

A genuine humorist fulfills simultaneous roles as a critical spectator of life and as an artist. As spectator, he contemplates and interprets the whole gamut of human activity from a set philosophical perspective. Having viewed and experienced life, he has adopted "an attitude toward life," a weltanschauung, that for him constitutes "an art for existing." Master of his perspective, he discerns the imperfections in humanity and the seeming paradoxes of existence and responds to them artistically, sometimes suggesting solutions (humorist-moralist), sometimes limiting himself to pure aesthetic delight (humorist-artist).

Palma takes both stances. He criticizes, ironizes, satirizes, or trivializes as occasion and his "comic muse" demand, but always with a strict awareness of the stylistic mold in which he wishes his humor cast. Federico de Onís, in evaluating the novels of Galdós, could also be speaking of Palma's anecdotes when he says [in an untranslated Spanish article], "There is always present as a permanent characteristic of unity a tone in the expression and a way of seeing the world and of feeling life that have a clearly humorous character, a simple, natural, juicy, human humor that resembles that of Cervantes more than does that of any other author." Thus, filtered through the eyes of the *tradicionista,* the colonial era, the Republic, and, in effect, humanity in general take on life and substance under Palma's ironic burst.

The perspective of the humorist derives in part from a firm posture of independence. Like other humorists, Palma championed freedom of conscience and thought. And while he basked in the broader opportunities for expression afforded by ironic humor, Palma, the "unobserved observer," scrutinized and illuminated the multifarious activities of Peruvian society—past and present—according to the free-flowing inspiration permitted by his conception of life. The precise nature of that conception or ideological stance vis-à-vis both the viceroyalty and the republic will become clear as we proceed in our analysis. A true *humorista,* Palma sought "through a realistic vision of existence . . . the exaltation of the human spirit in its free will." In part, however, his recourse to humor and to irony also functioned as a defensive measure. Palma was sensitive to criticism and to his possible lack of popularity; as Jean

Lamore points out, "That particular sensitivity to the criticisms and barbs of younger authors is combated by humor."

In addition, the assassination of President José Balta in 1872, the Sánchez Carrión-Monteagudo affair of the same decade, and the loss of his home and library in 1881, along with other disquieting experiences, had led him to seek further refuge both in the past and in the light skepticism of humorous irony and satire. Each orientation enhanced his role as an independent spectator, relatively free from the barbs of contemporaries and from the philosophical uneasiness that would have accompanied a more serious evaluation of life's inconsistencies and incompatibilities. Of course, another motivation in the adoption of humor as the mainstay of his style and his tone relates to his avid desire to disseminate Peruvian history among his compatriots; his way of sweetening the pill, as he phrased it, so that the *pueblo* would not flee from the imprint of its past. (pp. 6-7)

Now, what can we say concerning the humor of the *Tradiciones peruanas*? First of all, Palma, rather than presenting a single signal, offers a full spectrum of tonalities. From a central attitude that engenders within him a tendency to detect readily in all things "the jocose side of life," his "waggish muse" radiates in all directions. Almost every adjective in the critic's arsenal has been or could be applied to his humor. On the one hand, the *tradiciones* smack of *humoricidad* [which the critic characterizes elsewhere as "the common, practical, realistic aspect of humor"], with an abundance of jests, jokes, frivolous asides, and a regular light banter, an inclination to make light of everything under the sun. As Esmeralda Gijón Zapata has said of Tirso de Molina, his humor "allows nothing to escape which has any handle on which to attach laughter." On the other hand, there hovers over the *tradiciones* a veil of irony that infuses nearly all of them with what Juan Remos terms "a subtle, penetrating humor." This pervasive irony oscillates between pure *socarronería* [subtle irony] and biting satire and frequently evidences both spontaneous wit and substantive perspective. Indeed, perhaps more than any other single facet, Palma's mastery of ironic constructions endows his writing with its distinctive quality. (p. 10)

Humor lies latent in all things, but it takes the rays of a singular humorous attitude to awaken the comic potentiality therein. As Palma focused his own festive, smiling, Creole perspective on the intimacies and the surface features of Peruvian history, he enlivened them with the grade of comicity or *humorismo* [humor deriving from relativity, perspective, and skepticism] they naturally elicited from him. A majority of his comments, however, are couched in a spirit of benevolent sympathy and tolerance that often renders his barbs harmless. Palma's humor breathes this aura of basic human understanding, making it less caustic in general than otherwise might be the case. The *tradiciones* merge tenderness and mordacity, cultivating "the happy doctrine of the joke that does not quite mistreat, of the irony that slides in the midst of a cascade of words that play among themselves testing hues."

Nevertheless, all is not libertine laughter or sportful evocation. The humor of the *Tradiciones peruanas* is designed to teach, to instruct, to motivate, and to criticize at various levels. At the most obvious, Palma wields humor as a bait to attract his countrymen to the perusal of Peruvian history. On another level, as an ironist-satirist with a sympathetic vein, he seeks to call attention to many deficiencies, follies, and injustices by evoking amusement, smiles, or scorn. It is to this level that some point as proof or justification of their perception of Palma as subversive or as antiestablishment. (p. 11)

Over the years Ricardo Palma's works have elicited cries ranging from anti-republic to anti-Spanish, with many gradations in between. In a letter written to Vicente Barrantes in 1890 Palma called attention to Barrante's persistent allusions to his "anti-españolismo" and then interjected, "Por Dios, señor don Vicente! En mi tierra me acusan de lo contrario" ["Good God, señor don Vicente! In my country they accuse me of the opposite"]. Principal among the latter accusers was Manuel González Prada, who, beginning in 1886, launched an energetic campaign to discredit on many fronts the preceding generation, Palma included. While belittling the latter's style, he pounded on the absence of ideas of present and future significance in the *tradición,* in essence terming it a monstrous falsification of history created by a reactionary. Rufino Blanco Fombona perpetuated this view in his prologue to *Páginas libres* in 1915 and in his own work, *Grandes escritores de América,* two years later. "Palma is a Hispanizer, a retarder, a servile spirit, a man of the colonies" who seeks to preserve the memory of domination in his yearning for chains and for the whip. (Of course, Palma's irritating marginal notes in one of Blanco Fombona's books in the National Library did not help matters any.) At the opposite end of the pendulum stand Haya de la Torre, Mariátegui, Luis Alberto Sánchez, and others who underscore the critical portrayal of both the viceroyalty and the republic by the *tradicionista.* Says Mariátegui: "His gibing cheerfully gnaws at the prestige of the viceroyalty and the aristocracy. He translates the waggish discontent of the *creole demos* . . . Palma harbored a latent rancor against the reactionary aristocracy of yore."

In addition to these two perspectives, there are many critics who place greatest emphasis on Palma's nationalism, lauding his exaltation of the native land. These critics tend to play down his liberalism and skepticism, sometimes intentionally, sometimes because they have not analyzed carefully enough. This variance between those who pass over his freethinking spirit and those who stress it was brought to light in 1933 on the occasion of the hundredth anniversary of his birth when a lecture by Jorge Guillermo Leguía on Palma's liberal tendencies was eliminated from the collection of papers published as a tribute to him at that time.

The truth of the matter naturally draws and blends assertions from both parties, discarding their respective singleness of focus. Palma, a true mestizo, was pulled and influenced by a number of attitudes. On the one hand, he loved the colonial era for its historical and human dimension as a key antecedent to present nationality. On the other hand, he used the *tradición* to chide and to attack folly and injustice, both in the viceroyalty and among his own contemporaries. Palma was stiffly jolted by reality on many occasions. As the victim of venomous attacks in public, of "gossip, envy, everyone's looking out for himself," and as a witness of "the meanness of national life, public immorality, ingratitude, and the misunderstanding of the people," the Peruvian author had been wounded deeply in his sensitivity. These experiences led to a disenchantment that manifested itself in the irony and the ironic satire that constitute such a significant component of his style and tone.

As several critics have touched on briefly . . . the *Tradiciones peruanas* reveal to the careful reader an abundant number of between-the-lines statements that ironically and/or satirically draw comparisons between the private and public deficiencies of the viceroyalty and those of the nineteenth century. To label

Palma a subversive on the basis of these allusions, however, is to employ an overly harsh and unduly connotative term. Palma's liberal, reformist, patriotic, freedom-loving stance is never placed in question. Democracy and republican independence are clearly not abandoned. However, the various power elites in Lima deserved upbraiding on many points, most of which were echoes of injustices of the colonial past. Palma's irony and satire humorously but clearly denounce these shortcomings. Nevertheless, his irony does not suggest subversion in the sense of overthrow; rather, it admonishes repentance, adherence to basic morality and wisdom, and true democratic progress.

In addition, as further manifestation of his fundamental perception of right and wrong, and despite his epicurean bent, the Peruvian author almost exclusively underscores in his anecdotes the triumph of virtue over vice or at least the punishment and the remorse associated with evil acts. (pp. 11-13)

As mentioned before, Palma's humor partakes of many of the characteristics normally associated with the Creole nature, particularly in its coastal, Limean variety. In varying grades and shades both approaches to humor—Creole and Limean—embody *lisura,* satire, irony, *socarronería,* and irreverence presented in a mocking, mischievous tone. Manuel Beltroy, on the occasion of the *tradicionista*'s death, sums up the relationship in this way: "The Peruvian creole temperament, bantering and happy, sly and frivolous, epicurean and fanatical, frolicsome and versatile, found its finished, complete concretion in Palma's temperament and its most faithful expression in the *Tradiciones Peruanas.*" All this, however, took time to develop. Early *tradiciones* (in their original versions) reveal little of the subtle irony and light mocking laughter of the majority of the anecdotes. As he matured in his perspective and ability, Palma not only wrote in a more jovial and biting vein but also went back to earlier *tradiciones,* infusing them with the same spirit. The final result, as I have sought to highlight, was the merging in Palma of "wittiness, truth, goodness and poetry," the four cardinal points of humor.

At this juncture we can now look closely at two key areas: the basic material of human existence upon which Palma's humor and irony operate and the techniques adopted to extract most felicitously the comic potential of that material. **Constituents** of the former include the Catholic religion and spiritual life; marriage; sex; literature, particularly colonial poetry; women; public life, with its plethora of officials and professionals; societal and economic phenomena; types, in an endless string from the ingenuous Indian to the lustful avaricious viceroy; and language.

The techniques or stylistic processes comprise some that are broad and many that are specific. Among those of a general nature we could best begin by signaling the overall tone or atmosphere of the *Tradiciones peruanas.* Eastman has explained, "no reputation is more secure, once it is established, than that of the national humorist or comedian." Once he is known and people know what to expect from him, just the mention of his name will predispose them to laugh. The same applies to Palma and his works. Ever since the confirmation of their popularity, a mere allusion to the *tradiciones* has sufficed to stimulate in the initiated reader an anticipation or readiness for the inevitable tickling of Don Ricardo's banter. In this way the general atmosphere of the stories enhances the effectiveness of the mirth therein.

A second overarching facilitator of humor concerns the effect of the unexpected, indirect revelation of often unarticulated truths. Horace speaks of telling the truth with a laugh or with a jest, and satirists have practiced this art for centuries. Indeed, the revelation of truth without fear is a very pleasurable experience constituting "a chief source of the joy motive in popular jokes." Throughout the *tradiciones,* Palma availed himself of these facts, teasing the reader's funny bone while illuminating through irony certainties often hushed in normal social intercourse. Closely aligned with this is another general approach to humor practiced by the *tradicionista,* namely, the use of sudden, surprising deviations or jolts in the logical flow and order of ideas. (pp. 14-15)

[It] does not surprise us to learn that a large portion of [Palma's] humor is rooted in the able maneuvering of the language. . . . It is true that situational humor exists, but the maximum realization of humor in the *tradiciones* clearly rests on style imbued with irony: "Finally, the style of the ***Tradiciones*** is the best test of Palma's humor. . . . That extremely rich prose . . . is by itself an invitation to rejoice" [Porras Barrenechea, *Tres en sayas*].

A panoramic overview of Palma's techniques in regard to humor renders patent this assertion. Such a scan places in bold relief comparison, metaphor, circumlocution, wordplay, the modification of set phrases and commonplaces, caricature, the presentation of types, hyperbole, the incongruent joining of words or situational and character elements, dialogue, the insertion of colloquial terms, the colloquialization of sacred things, the softening of truculent, tragic scenes through euphemism, and playing with names. Intimately and inevitably bonded to Palma's humor one also continually discovers irony, satire, and the never-distant subjective presence of the narrator.

Immediately apparent is the fact that the bearers of comicity just listed, rather than revolving in isolated orbits around the aesthetic nucleus of the ***Tradiciones peruanas,*** complement each other in mutual and in interrelated associations. For instance, inherent in humorous comparisons we often observe puns, caricature, metaphor, hyperbole, irony, satire, and periphrasis. Similarly, humor based on wordplay often crossbreeds with caricature, satire, irony, simile, metaphor, exaggeration, religious allusion, and surprise. The interdependencies are numerous. Like a juggler, Palma manipulates and interweaves them, achieving in the process the renowed weave that typifies what we now envision as a *"tradición peruana."* (pp. 15-16)

Roy L. Tanner, "Introduction," in his The Humor of Irony and Satire in the "Tradiciones peruanas," *University of Missouri Press, 1986, pp. 1-16.*

ADDITIONAL BIBLIOGRAPHY

Arora, Shirley L. *Proverbial Comparisons in Ricardo Palma's "Tradiciones peruanas."* Berkeley and Los Angeles: University of California Press, 1966, 198 p.

  Uses the *Tradiciones peruanas* to study proverbs and cliches in Peruvian common speech.

Compton, Merlin D. *Ricardo Palma.* Boston: Twayne Publishers, 1982, 168 p.

  General survey of Palma's life and work, with emphasis on his development of the *tradicion* and its portrayal of Peruvian history.

Englekirk, John E. Review of *Epistolario de Ricardo Palma,* edited by Augusta and Renée Palma. *The Hispanic American Historical Review* XXXI, No. 1 (February 1951): 132-34.

  Applauds the publication of a selection of Palma's letters.

Franco, Jean. "Literature and Nationalism." In her *An Introduction to Spanish-American Literature,* pp. 46-73. Cambridge, England: Cambridge University Press, 1969.

  Includes discussion of the irony and humor of Palma's *Tradiciones peruanas.*

Guice, G. Norman. Review of *Ricardo Palma: Cartas ineditas,* edited by Rubén Vargas Ugarte. *The Hispanic American Historical Review* XLV, No. 2 (May 1965): 323-25.

  Discusses sixty letters written by Palma between 1880 and 1913, with attention given to Palma's intense patriotism during the War of the Pacific and to his distinctive writing style, which made it possible for the editor of the volume to identify anonymous wartime correspondence as Palma's.

Hall, Nancy Abraham. "Ricardo Palma's 'El Peje Chico'." *Romance Notes* XXII, No. 1 (Fall 1981): 32-36.

  Compares Palma's *tradicion* "El peje chico" with two of its historical sources.

Morris, Robert S. "Ricardo Palma and the Contemporary Peruvian Theatre." *Romance Notes* XIV, No. 3 (Spring 1973): 465-68.

  Examines Palma's influence on modern Peruvian dramatists Sebastian Salazar Bondy and Julio Ramon Ribeyro.

Schraibman, Joseph. "An Unpublished Letter from Galdós to Ricardo Palma." *Hispanic Review* XXXII, No. 1 (January 1964): 65-68.

  Prints a letter in Spanish written by Benito Pérez Galdós to Palma in 1901, praising his *tradiciones,* particularly one entitled "Amor de madre," and proposing a dramatic adaptation of the story.

Stowell, Ernest. "Ricardo Palma and the Legal Profession." *Hispania* XXV, No. 2 (May 1942): 158-60.

  Examines Palma's satirical treatment of lawyers, judges, and officers of the court in the *Tradiciones peruanas.*

Tanner, Roy L. "Ricardo Palma's Rhetorical Debt to Miguel de Cervantes." *Revista de Estudios Hispanicos* XVII, No. 3 (October 1983): 345-61.

  Compares the literary technique of Palma's *tradiciones* with that of Cervantes's *Don Quixote.*

———. "Ricardo Palma and Francisco de Quevedo: A Case of Rhetorical Affinity and Debt." *Kentucky Romance Quarterly* 31, No. 4 (1984): 423-35.

  Discusses stylistic similarities between Palma's writing and that of Francisco de Quevedo.

Terry, Edward D. Review of *Tradiciones peruanas,* by Ricardo Palma, edited by Pamela Francis. *Hispania* 54, No. 1 (March 1970): 232-33.

  Commends a reprint of fourteen of Palma's *tradiciones* for valuable supplementary notes, topical inclusiveness, and judicious selection.

Torres-Ríoseco, Arturo. "The Romantic Upheaval in Spanish America." In his *The Epic of Latin American Literature,* pp. 44-85. New York and London: Oxford University Press, 1942.

  Includes discussion of Palma's literary career.

Alexandros Papadiamantis

1851-1911

Greek novelist and short story writer.

One of the most prominent Greek fiction writers of the late nineteenth and early twentieth centuries, Papadiamantis is best known as a chronicler of life on his native island of Skiathos. In over two hundred short stories and several novels, he portrayed the lives of farmers, sailors, monks, fishermen, housewives, and other humble people, combining lyric descriptions of the island with realistic depictions of the harsh lives of the villagers. Pervaded by the author's love for the Greek landscape, people, and culture, these stories earned Papadiamantis a reputation as "the quintessential Greek writer."

Papadiamantis's mother was the daughter of a prominent family of landowners and sailors, his father a Greek Orthodox priest. After undertaking his early education at schools in Skiathos, Skopelos, and Athens, Papadiamantis enrolled at the University of Athens to study philology, but was forced by financial necessity to leave the university without completing a degree. Thereafter he earned a meager living translating French and English literature into Greek and writing serial novels and short stories for newspapers and literary journals. Despite the widespread recognition he eventually gained for his writings, Papadiamantis shunned all publicity and led a secluded life. He died in 1911.

Papadiamantis's first works of fiction were historical and adventure novels set in various eras of Greek history. While popular with readers, these novels have generally been dismissed by critics as immature and artistically weak, and his reputation rests almost entirely on his novels and short stories set in Skiathos. In these works Papadiamantis combined elements of the Greek oral and literary traditions, faithful portrayals of the lives and customs of the island's inhabitants, and explorations of current social issues, focusing on such subjects as emigration, poverty, and familial relations. His best-known work, the novel *He phonissa* (*The Murderess*), examines the problem of the subservient position of women in Greece, depicting a woman who murders young girls in an attempt to save them from the harsh future awaiting them as wives and mothers. Other works depicting life on Skiathos demonstrate Papadiamantis's deep religious convictions and contain frequent biblical allusions; many of them, such as "Christmas Bread," are based on church holidays. Although Papadiamantis has frequently been criticized for artistic failings, including sloppy prose, the random mixture of colloquial and literary language, and poor narrative construction, many critics maintain that these flaws are more than offset by the evocative charm and poignancy of his works, which made him one of the most popular authors in his homeland at the turn of the century.

*PRINCIPAL WORKS

I metanastis (novel) 1879-80; published in journal
    Neologos
I embori ton ethnon (novel) 1882-83; published in journal
    Mi hanese
I yiftopoula (novel) 1884; published in journal *Akropolis*
Christos Milionis (novel) 1885; published in journal *Estia*

Ta rhodin' akroyalia (novel) 1908-09; published in
    journal *I nea zoi*
He phonissa (novel) 1912
    [*The Murderess*, 1977]
Ta apanta. 6 vols. (short stories and novels) 1954-55
Tales from a Greek Island (short stories) 1987

*Papadiamantis's works were first published in magazines and newspapers and did not appear in book form until after his death.

C. TH. DIMARAS (essay date 1948)

[*Dimaras is a Greek critic. In the following excerpt from his* History of Modern Greek Literature, *first published in Greek in 1948, he analyzes technical aspects of Papadiamantis's fiction and discusses the change in his critical reputation since his death.*]

[Papadiamantis's] novels were juvenilia, ambitious compositions which were not supported by sufficient preparation. In any case, they exhibited an effort toward composition which Papadiamantis quickly abandoned. Later, what we still call short stories were only short narratives depicting certain moments of life or presenting some psychological episode and a study of manners. At times they were composed only of descriptions. Papadiamantis was fond of minute details in his descriptions and often interrupted the unity of his narrative by introducing an extravagant proportion of descriptions. His heroes came from the island environment and usually expressed the ordinary pacifist mood of these inhabitants. Papadiamantis was sympathetic to these simple people, not only conforming to the mode of his times, but also because these men were in accord with his own states of soul. However, the folklore element abounds in his work, and, if an intention at psychological analysis was not apparent, and if a diffuse lyricism did not run throughout his work, we could say that it set the tone.

The folkloristic element emerged from a true familiarity of the author with his subject. He lived the life he depicted; he had observed the manners carefully and with love; his descriptions, when he succeeded in elevating them as an objective narrator, constituted faithful portrayals of life and the mentality of the inhabitants of his own island. More often, however, the narrator interposed with commentaries and gave to the work an edifying tone that detracted from the benevolence and native wit Papadiamantis had for his heroes. His psychological analysis was usually understated because often his characters were voluntarily comic. They had imprecise contours, they were neutral, because that is how their creator wanted them. Moreover, the types present little variety: there are three or four men, the same number of women, and only the names change. Sometimes, stronger personalities appeared, as the one in *The Murderess*. In this novelette, Papadiamantis presented a woman whose sadism, her perverse mysticism, led to a series of infanticides. As for lyricism, the particular atmosphere that Papadiamantis created in his short stories consisted of nostalgia, reverie, reminiscence, and religiosity. His technique was simple, always the same; in its repetitiveness, it became monotonous. The author projected himself indirectly in the narration in order to express his own emotional world. All this, however, was offered in a harmonious reproduction of the atmosphere of Greek folk life and especially that of the Greek islands.

When one reads a short story by Papadiamantis, he is charmed by the material and by its presentation. When he reads two stories, the impression is attenuated. When he reads many, the impression disappears, not only because of the monotonous technique, but also because the same themes and motifs are encountered: there is neither development, nor even restoration. A closed world, pleasant on first contact but oppressive in the long run, exists in all his stories. Furthermore, the entire prose work of Papadiamantis, if one excepts his early novels, is marked by a total negligence, which is contrary to all notion of art. Style, expression, and language are governed by chance; he had no success in this sense. The narrator's intervention becomes burdensome and awkward, an insipid play on words, references to events that are about to follow, inversions, parentheses, points of suspension, exclamations—all the defects of careless writing are constantly found in his work. The verbal expression presents the same defects; it is cursorily written and lacking in limpidity; the distribution of parts is defective. Sometimes, the first reading does not suffice to give each verb its complements. At other times, we have the absence of the principal after a hypothetical proposition. Adverbs often are placed at random; adjectives are poor and conventional or so rare and elegant that they evoke no response in the reader.

This evaluation of Papadiamantis, to a great extent, can be considered an expression of today's opinion. Among the first to examine his work critically were Gregory Xenopoulos, who published a brilliant critical work the year before Papadiamantis died, and Kostas Hadzopoulos, whose study appeared in 1914. But, while he was alive, a legend was created around him, whose origin should somehow be explained. He was known for his purist language, bad technique, and folklore; that is, those qualities essential to reconciling the undistinguished society in which he lived and all that was essential to be reconciled with the intellectuals who warred against the demotic and simultaneously praised the study of neo-Hellenic manners. Papadiamantis was read with pleasure by men who were not accustomed to good quality writing or one for which any preparation was required. It was natural that the generation which considered Souris a great poet should consider Papadiamantis a great prose writer; the significance of art existed only in the other camp, with those who labored to create, who struggled to climb slowly in an environment of public indifference and disapprobation by the intellectuals, who considered themselves as depositories of tradition. Poverty was characterized as sobriety, the recondite was called art, punning was considered wit.

However, even later, other generations and other intellectuals who confronted the Greek literary situation with awareness and responsibility praised Papadiamantis extensively. The "nationalist" line, which began with Perikles Yannopoulos, could not but cherish the sensitive painter of the Greek island atmosphere, the glorifier of Greek tradition, the scorner of new trends imported from the continent. Photos Politis was also fond of Papadiamantis for the same reason. He found the simple narrator's purity of spirit and respite from the astute efforts, the rationalizations, and the experiences of more recent writers:

> He carried in his work a Greek conviction and sentiment. An authentic Greek and a powerful writer,

he produced pages of admirable purity and moral force, while he himself was devoured by nostalgia for a remote fairy-like island, bathed in blue light, where the plains spoke and where the grottos chanted funereal lamentations, where the flowers, the trees, and the birds scattered gaiety and where men were true children of God.

Admiration for Papadiamantis became profoundly rooted in Greek letters. It was thirty years after his death before many voices, more or less courageously and more or less clearly, tended to re-establish a more accurate hierarchy in the new Greek prose. (pp. 390-93)

> *C. Th. Dimaras, "Prose, We Want Prose!—Prose," in his* A History of Modern Greek Literature, *translated by Mary P. Gianos, State University of New York Press, 1972, pp. 379-93.*

LINOS POLITIS (essay date 1973)

[*In the following discussion of Papadiamantis's fiction, Politis assesses artistic merits and shortcomings of his works.*]

[Papadiamantis] made his appearance with historical and adventure novels, but then went over to the "genre" story, to which he devoted himself almost exclusively for a quarter of a century. His tales, which exceed 200 in number, are not on the same level; many are only hasty sketches or "snapshots," others are more like essays than stories. But the successful stories are many and remarkable. Almost all of them describe events and human characters to be found on his island, Skiathos; and the writer's homesickness gives them life and movement. Nostalgia is the permanent basic element in Papadiamantis; it is his strength and his weakness. Since his own time his work has been the object of criticism, which sometimes went so far as excessive praise and admiration, and at others erred as far in the opposite direction by underestimating him. Hostile criticism picked on the loose construction of his stories, the absence of plan, the lack of artistic intention. In a large degree these objections are sound; but the lack of construction is usually owing to the nature of his nostalgia and reverie; the ideas, not bound by any predetermined plan, follow the course of reverie—and his very lack of connection is a virtue and has charm. As with many painters, Papadiamantis's main strength lay in the free sketch. On the other hand, beyond in an underlying tendency for the "genre" style, he had caught many aspects of the modern Greek character that are not easily caught, and had captured something of what might be called "modern Greek popular mythology." His childhood years on the island, his bond through his father, a priest, and through other members of his family, with the world of Orthodoxy (he himself was a cantor, and he loved to take part in all-night services), his retiring life in Athens, and his companionship with humble people, all give an authority to his accounts. They go deeper than mere "genre" tales, or folkloristic studies, and it is this that his supporters admired.

In language, unlike many others of his generation, Papadiamantis made no decisive step from katharevousa to demotic. His katharevousa, however, is entirely personal, individual, and inconsistent. What has been said about the influence of the language of the Church upon Papadiamantis is irresponsible and without proof. I should say there were three levels in his language: in dialogue he uses the popular spoken language, almost photographically recorded, and often with idioms from Skiathos. In the narration there is another language, based indeed on katharevousa, but with an admixture of many de-motic elements (and this is his most individual style); finally there is a pure katharevousa, the traditional prose language of the earlier generation, which Papadiamantis reserves for his descriptions and his lyrical digressions.

From his abundant output we may set aside stories that are hardly more than mediocre. Before 1900, "**The Homesick Woman**" and "**Round the Lake**" stand out, the latter for its strikingly poetical tone; so does the long story "**Love in the Snow**" with its lyrical melancholy. After 1900 the lyric tone dominates, and to this period belong the much-read "**Dream on the Wave,**" "**Reverie on 15 August,**" and the longest of them, which is like a lyric confession, *Rosy Shores*. But the work of his last decade, if not the most personal, is the most powerful: *The Murderess*. The central figure in this long story is Frangogiannoù (the murderess); she is now sixty years old and, as she thinks over the past, she realizes that woman is always a slave, first to her parents, then to her husband, then to her children, and then to their children. Thus she conceives the idea of killing little girls, to spare them all this trouble. With this fixed idea in her mind she accomplishes a series of murders; the police are after her, she seeks sanctuary in a church near the sea, and drowns "on an isthmus that joined the rock of the hermitage with the mainland, halfway between divine and human justice." *The Murderess* is a powerful work; this woman with her perverted mind, who puts herself outside the human society, is an enigmatic figure and altogether unlike the islanders who people the other stories; they may be crafty, but are always good-hearted. The psychological description is given with a quite different fullness; the construction is compact and more care is taken over the artistic execution. (pp. 167-69)

> *Linos Politis, "Prose After 1880: The 'Genre' Story, the Language Question and Psycharis," in his A History of Modern Greek Literature, Oxford at the Clarendon Press, Oxford, 1973, pp. 164-78.*

PETER LEVI (essay date 1981)

[*Levi is an English poet, novelist, travel writer, and translator of Russian and Greek literature into English. In the following excerpt from the introduction to his translation of* The Murderess, *he examines theme and technique in the novel.*]

In some ways Papadiamantis was a very naive writer. In his style the many mingled elements, the genuine folklore and the dryads in which he all but believes, the realism and the exoticism, the narrative gift and the excessively romantic lyricism, make it impossible to disentangle his virtues from his vices as a writer. They are also extremely hard to render in modern English. His language and tone have many changes. He is a parodist and a satirist and also a recorder of dialect. He belongs uniquely to a particular moment in Greek development, in the troubled history of the Greek language and the first emergence of its modern literature. At the same time he is inevitably the civilized observer of a retarded world. Athens in the nineties was not London or Paris, though one can smell in his writing more than a whiff of European influence from the mid-century, but the island world that Papadiamantis described was pro-vincial in a far deeper sense. Skiathos was fifty times further behind the Athens of that time than Athens was behind Paris or London.

This novel makes it clear that Papadiamantis wrote about a world to which he was born, an island of which he knew every stick and stone, every legend and every piece of gossip. For most of us that passionate genuineness does an important ser-vice. It fills with realism and with thrilling interest the some-what shadowy period of early modern Greek history. But that is not the point of the book, any more than the similar service that Thomas Hardy does in English—and for which today we greatly value, even overvalue, his novels—provided the mo-mentum of *Tess* or of *Jude the Obscure*. In fact Hardy and Papadiamantis in their different spheres have a striking number of elements in common, even to the extent of a certain nec-essary awkwardness and naivety.

The motive force of *The Murderess* is certainly to be found in the history and the tragic paradox of the central character. Papadiamantis was a religious man; he had tried his vocation as a monk on Athos. But no religious solution is offered. Religion in his novel is used simply to deepen the tragic tone. Nor is any human or secular solution offered. What happens, with the whole weight of what leads to it, is like a wild scream of protest. Is the murderess mad? Sleepless, worn out by life, half-mad in the end, exalted by madness only as a tragic heroine is exalted. I assume that Papadiamantis knew the Medea of Euripides as well as he knew nineteenth-century novelists.

The mechanism of the story is quite simple. Papadiamantis was a magnificent writer of short stories and essentially this is a very long short story. The old woman, whose background and whose whole life are made clear to us with an economy that one notices only in retrospect, is driven to despair about the fate of women in Greek island communities like her own. Girls are such a burden to their mothers they would really be better dead. Papadiamantis writes with particular horror of the dowry system, which incidentally has not died to this day. We are led to consider back street abortions, superstitions, the lack of doctors, the idiocy of officials, the corruption of the new, "liberated" middle class, and the fate of poor families. Greece has altered of course, but a lot of this is still recognizable, at least in remote places. But the key of the story is the obligation on the poorest women and the poorest families to scrape to-gether marriage settlements for every girl born.

Social progress is not offered as a palliative. Indeed it is prog-ress which has done some of the harm. Earlier or later in history there might be different problems: the tax officers take over from the bandits, and the local girls "take on confidence," without learning anything at school. At this given moment, the old woman is ground between an upper and a lower millstone. Maybe the monks in their monastery are happy, because they bring no children into the world? Not even Papadiamantis can really believe that. It was a passing thought, like the aspiration to fly away like a bird and be at peace. The hermit on his rock and the monastic gardener with his verses from the psalm are like similar figures in Shakespeare. They define a world, they may even play a role, but they are not really characters in the same sense as those that human passion haunts. (pp. ix-xi)

> *Peter Levi, in an introduction to* The Murderess *by Alexandros Papadiamantis, translated by Peter Levi, Writers and Readers Publishing Cooperative Society Ltd., 1983, pp. ix-xiii.*

MICHAEL H. STONE (essay date 1983)

[*In the following excerpt, Stone unfavorably reviews* The Mur-deress.]

Occasionally, new writers, or old writers discovered, receive acclaim because of the freshness of their message, the style of their prose or simply because of the subject matter. Regrettably the discovery of Alexandros Papadiamantis, author of *The Murderess,* will not bring with it any commendation. (p. 127)

The Murderess is a dull tale about a widow on a Greek island who cares for the children of her daughters. At the turn of the century life in Greece was harsh and the dowry system was an added burden to families with girls. Frankojannou, or old Hadoula, virtually the only character, reacts violently to both the cruelty of life on her island and the unjust system of dowry. The author attempts to imply that she is mad, mentally, but he is not very convincing. Moreover, the author inadequately expounds upon key elements in Greek society, specifically, religious superstition and the cultural dictates of a chauvinistic society upon its women.

This overly long short story does, however, have some rather descriptive passages of the island's physical characteristics, which, if one is familiar with Greece, are very real. There just is not enough to put in a Michelin Tour Guide, however.

The Murderess lacks force and has an insouciant approach toward providing local color. (pp. 127-28)

> *Michael H. Stone, in a review of ''The Murderess,''*
> *in* Best Sellers, *Vol. 43, No. 4, July, 1983, pp. 127-28.*

THEOFANIS G. STAVROU (essay date 1986)

[*Stavrou is a Greek-born American historian and critic specializing in Russia and the Middle East. In the following excerpt, he surveys Papadiamantis's fiction.*]

There is a tendency to divide Papadiamantis' literary output into two main categories. The first one spans the years from 1879 to 1887, when he published what are usually described as his historical novels—*The Immigrant Woman, The Merchants of Nations,* and *The Gypsy Girl.* A fourth work, *Christos Milionis* is sometimes viewed as concluding the cycle of the historical novels and sometimes as the transition point to the next period when Papadiamantis devoted himself entirely to ethographic short stories, 170 of them, some maintain. The one major exception is his best known work, *The Murderess,* serialized in 1903 and described by the author as a social novel.

There has also been a tendency to be harshly critical of Papadiamantis' accomplishments during the first period. The author was still searching, critics claim, and they argue that his indebtedness to European models is all too obvious. They recognize his power of description but they all point to his ethographic stories as his great literary accomplishment. Legitimate as these observations may be, unfortunately they obscure the fact that Papadiamantis' novels touch on themes of central significance to him and which reoccur frequently in his short stories. (p. 74)

The plot of [his first historical novel, *The Immigrant Woman*] is the aftermath of the plague that hit Marseilles in 1720 with disastrous results for the Greek community there including the parents of the heroine. The orphaned young woman is then brought back to Smyrna by two captains from Skiathos, father and son, who knew her father. In Smyrna the son marries her, abandons her and when he returns from Marseilles finds her dead. Soon thereafter he, too, disappears. The story has some powerful scenes but what distinguishes it is Papadiamantis' treatment of its theme about immigration—one of the most agonizing themes in Greek history from classical times to the present, which has drained the country of human resources and

which manifested itself with vengeance during Papadiamantis' time. It is a theme or motif which is treated with great artistry by Papadiamantis in over thirty of his short stories. What is important to note is that from his very first work, Papadiamantis, who is usually referred to as an ethographer, focuses on basic social and political problems and their consequences.

This becomes more evident in his second historical novel, *The Merchants of Nations,*... in which he unleashes criticism against plutocracy, the root of all evil especially for young nations. Even though the plot of this work is in the middle ages when Venice ruled the Mediterranean, Papadiamantis transfers the lesson to the Greece of his day when political and economic self interests obstruct the implementation of useful reforms.... His preoccupation with political and social injustice will surface in many of his short stories, especially **''The Spoilers of the Land.''** *The Merchants of Nations* is also a satire against Catholicism and an indictment of the abuses of Venice in the Aegean.

Papadiamantis injects an aspect of political anxiety in his third historical novel, *The Gypsy Girl.*... Written nearly a quarter of a century before the epic poem by Kostis Palamas, *The Twelve Words of the Gypsy,* Papadiamantis' work focuses on the uncertainty and anxiety experienced by Greek society during the last years of the Byzantine Empire. Introducing flashback technique, he captures and maintains the interest of the reader, as the Gypsy girl is stolen from the palace in Constantinople, brought to Monemvasia in the Peloponnese accompanied by the gypsies who reared her and ultimately introducing Plethon Gemistos, the neoplatonic philosopher, who established himself in Mystras near Sparta seeking to replace Christianity with classical philosophical ideas if Greece were to be saved. Furthermore, Gemistos urged Greece's reconciliation with or return to Europe. The careful student of modern Greece cannot help but note the theme which preoccupied Papadiamantis for the rest of his life—the question of political and cultural orientation.

With *Christos Milionis,*... Papadiamantis moves chronologically into the modern period and concentrates on the relationship between Greeks and Turks during Ottoman rule on the eve of the Greek War of Independence. The story was inspired by a popular song about the life and death of Milionis confronting the Turks in the area of Akarnania. It abounds in description of the klephtic world, and in this regard it is justifiably considered as the ''transition'' work between the historical novel and the ethographic short stories of Papadiamantis. It is a rather long story and for this reason is often grouped together as one of five works usually referred to as Papadiamantis' novels. Besides *Christos Milionis,* they are *The Spoilers of the Land, Guard over the Quarantined Ship, The Murderess* and *The Rosy Shorelines.*

The Spoilers of the Land are, of course, the politicians deceiving the common people with campaign promises, bribes and divisive techniques all leading to strife and corruption at a time when the nation was passing through one of its most crucial phases and leading to the disastrous war with Turkey in 1897. It is his first major work which could be described as a social satire. Another novel, *Guard over the Quarantined Ship,* is partly satirical but basically a tragedy. It is the moving story of a mother who is determined at any cost to see her son who is quarantined on boats offshore because of a cholera epidemic, the quarantine or ''forbidden ships.'' waiting like the carriers of death offshore near the island. The mother disguises herself as a guard and manages to see and help save her son. As has been pointed out, the story could be called *A Mother's Love* or *The Chronicle of the Cholera.* It contains some of his finest pages and his characters are well developed. Above all, it portrays human reaction, noble and ignoble, when confronting such crisis.

Ten years after **Guard over the Quarantined Ship,** Papadiamantis produced what is generally accepted as his masterpiece, **The Murderess,** which the author described as a social novel and as such it has been viewed ever since. It may also be viewed as the author's attempt to redeem himself in a major way as a mature artist. We must remember that during this period he was expected to produce chiefly short stories, three to fifteen pages in length. With **The Murderess,** he vindicated himself by demonstrating his ability to rise beyond mere ethography and to engage in complex psychographic presentation of plot and character. The social message of the story was unmistakably clear. It was dictated by a set of social and economic conditions to which Papadiamantis could relate only too painfully. His four sisters were all without husbands. Three never married and the one that did marry lost her husband to madness. The other three never had a chance because they failed to amass the indispensable dowry, the prerequisite for arranged marriages. Putting it more accurately, Papadiamantis, as the oldest brother, failed to provide it for them. He therefore exposed this social institution under whose curse the female population of the island suffered from birth to death in utter enslavement and humiliation. When life has no meaning or purpose, the question of putting an end to it becomes a logical conclusion. This certainly is the conclusion reached by old Frangoyannou, one of the most unforgettable characters in all of his work. As she reviewed her own life, she realized again that in her entire life she had done nothing but serve somebody else: "When she was a young child she served her parents. When she got married she became her husband's slave. . . . When she had children she became their slave and when her children acquired their own children, she again became a servant to her grandchildren." And as she observed little girls and reflected that they would grow up to follow the same miserable path of life, she systematically and calculatingly proceeded to murder them and save them from their destiny. It is a frightful story handled expertly by a craftsman of the word. It is difficult to know precisely whether the author wanted to present the murderess as the embodiment of evil, who simply could not but commit the crimes, as some maintain, or whether her deeds are acts of mercy to free human beings—little girls—from a social trap they could not otherwise escape. Or, is it, in the final analysis, a question of choice between accepting one's lot patiently until this earthly sojourn ends, or trying to rectify it by rational means. After all, Papadiamantis chose the names of his characters carefully, and it is conceivable that he might have had something specific in mind when he named the murderess Frangoyannou, "Frank" meaning European. In any event, whether sympathetically treated or not, in the end Frangoyannou must pay for her crimes to satisfy both divine and human justice. It has been suggested that the influence of Dostoevsky, whose *Crime and Punishment* Papadiamantis had translated earlier, must have been considerable. Other influences could have been French and Scandinavian novels of similar bent which the Greeks avidly translated and read at the turn of the century. The question of borrowing and influences aside, what is significant is that the author, as was his style, drew on a local incident and through his art addressed a more complex personal and social predicament.

Papadiamantis also called his last novel, **The Rosy Shorelines,** a social novel. . . . The tile of the work suggests ethographic content, and it contains such beautiful descriptions that even Constantine Cavafy was impressed. But the descriptions are supplemented with dialogues on important social issues which lend the novel special strength.

Periodization is especially difficult for Papadiamantis' short stories. They all basically emerge from a familiar atmosphere, and taken collectively they reflect Skiathos and Greece from 1887 when he wrote **"Christmas Bread,"** to 1910 when a sick man and only months before his death he wrote **"Repercussions of the Mind."** In fact, some maintain that it is possible to recapture the Papadiamantis' ethos with almost any of his representative stories. However, it is important to keep in mind that it is not merely th deliberate description of nature bordering on physiolatry, or the churches with their saints and incenses, the olive presses and the windmill that make his work unforgettable. Rather, it is his characters, drawn from a limited environment to be sure, but so convincingly portrayed and so terribly human, that animate the ethographic canvas of Papadiamantis. They range from the village priest, the monk, and other clerical types to the industrious citizen, the parasite, the drunkard, the officials, the usurers, the sailors, the immigrants, lovers against love, the children; and the women characters ranging from the "murderess" type and the treacherous mother-in-law and foster mother to the most exemplary ones, from the housewife and compassionate grandmother and godmother, to the faithful betrothed defying the ravages of time, and the young widow of the village priest who was not supposed to remarry but ultimately yielded to love.

A list of titles of the most representative of his numerous short stories will evoke some of the images of this canvas. Following **"Christmas Bread,"** short stories appeared in relative rapidity: **"The Maid," "The Gleaner," "Poor Saint," "I Mavromantilou," "Summer-Eros," "The American," "The Dreamer," "Christ in the Castle," "The Monk," "All around the Lagoon," "The Easter Cantor," "Love in the Snow," "I Glykofilousa," "Eros-Hero," "Goutou-Goupatou," "Demons in the Stream," "Dream on the Wave," "I Pharmakolytria," "Fortune from America," "Under the Royal Oak," "The Witches," "Woman Wading," "Reverie on the Fifteenth of August," "The Dirge of the Feal,"** and **"The Dead Traveler."** Some of them were commissioned or written entirely with religious holidays in mind. In fact, Papadiamantis introduced the "eortastiko" or holiday story in Greece, something similar to Dickens' Christmas stories. He was often compared to Dickens much to his chagrin. These became Papadiamantis' most anxiously awaited stories. They deal mostly with the Christmas, New Year and Easter holiday cycles although other important religious holidays were often used as pretext for this type of story.

Among the long list of Papadiamantis' short stories the following may be examined both for content and style. The **"Christmas Bread,"** with which he started his "ethography" period, is the story of a scheming mother-in-law who is trying to separate her son from his virtuous wife who unfortunately cannot bear any grandchildren for her. When she failed to convince her sailor son to divorce her, the mother-in-law decided to kill the young wife by poisoning the "Christmas Bread" which she presented to her while the son was at sea. Unsuspecting, the young wife went to church to take communion. Her husband returned unexpectedly from the sea voyage, and she ran home from church to set a table for him but stayed only for a while because church was not over yet. While alone, the husband ate the poisoned bread. In the meantime, his mother learned that her son had returned. She, too, ran to welcome him, found him dead on the floor, and realized much to her shock that she had killed him. This is the beginning, in modern Greek literature, of the exploration of family relations through the character of the bad mother-in-law. In an introductory note, Papadiamantis suggested that this was a topic deserving further exploration and many young writers heeded his advice. He also intimated that the character of the bad foster mother provided many opportunities for highlighting contemporary social problems. By contrast, old Sophoula Sarantanou in, **"The Last Godchild,"** who could not have children of her own, chooses to baptize several of them—forty to be precise—and as their godmother she assumes maternal duties displaying generosity and tenderness, filling the home with laughter and joy, especially during the holidays—all this, against her husband's disapproval. The tragic death of the last godchild, whom she named after her, accidentally drowned in a well, robs the old godmother of her special joy but only temporarily for "At every Easter she sits and makes the holiday bread for little Sophoula, who wanted to play 'hide and seek' and her voice like the chirping of birds echoes in her soul. . . . She makes the holiday bread and throws it in the well and bends down in order to enjoy the lost angelic face and to breathe the inexplicable fragrance coming up from the water as incense from an innocent soul." This story has been described as a "symphony of angels" and it is only surpassed in power of description and the victory of the holiday spirit against all adversity by Papadiamantis' **"The Maid."** The latter is the name of the boat, the only property of a poor veteran seawolf who at the end of his life is pensionless. He has his little boat and his little daughter, Ouranio. He overloads the boat with Christmas supplies. News reaches the little girl that the boat has sunk on Christmas Eve. But miraculously, after fighting the waves all night his life was spared, and the Christmas joy of little Ouranio was complete. Father and daughter have the best Christmas of their lives in their humble hut. These themes, revealing an inner joy and triumph in the midst of misery and poverty, recur in most of the holiday stories like **"The Gleaner," "Easter in the Country," "Greek Easter,"** and **"Children's Easter."** All these stories relate the hard existence for the islanders—many of whom are forced to leave to improve their lot and support their families. But those left behind, especially the women, assume the heavy burden of bringing up the children alone and enduring misery. And so Papadiamantis links these social and economic problems to the immigration movement, the hope and the drain of the nation. He touched on this problem in *The Immigrant Woman,* but he provides a closer description of the problem in **"The Gleaner"** and especially **"The American,"** "the ballad of the diaspora," as it has been described. It is the story of Mothonios who immigrated to America, spent twenty years of life there, made a fortune, but in the process lost his youth and his language. But the yearning for his village lingers on. When he returns, his parents are dead, his ancestral home is in ruins and most of the villagers do not recognize him. He discovers that the girl he left behind is still waiting, like a modern Penelope, even though many had asked to marry her. She lives and mourns with her mother, who at Christmas time refuses to let children come and sing carols because "nobody" lives there. When Mothonios appears and they get married after twenty years, the house is flooded with lights and the children are invited to sing. One of the most successful and best known stories of Papadiamantis, it is indispensable reading for those who want to appreciate the motives and the consequences of the immigration movement to the United States. "So much world is consumed in America," as one of the

characters put it. The agonies connected with the immigration problem are touched upon in several other stories but is dealt with again in some detail in the **"Fortune from America."** (pp. 74-81)

The "eortastika" or holiday stories of Papadiamantis are typical of the world with which he is often identified but they are not limited to holiday descriptions. They are a comprehensive commentary on the lives of the Skiathites and, by extension, of most modern Greeks at the turn of the century. There is an inevitable interrelationship among the most important short stories of Papadiamantis between religious holidays, the struggle for survival, and love in the countryside and town. In the latter category, Papadiamantis has produced some of the most sensitive descriptions of idyllic scenes, as in **"Summer-Eros"** which takes place in full-blooming May, and in **"The Dreamer,"** the story of a young woman who, in the absence of a dowry, married an older man, well established, but hardly able to provide more than fatherly care. She is consumed by the dream for the life that she could have had if she had married somebody younger, like the young student who falls in love with her and with whom she escapes temporarily in a small boat at night only to return to her destined relationship, leaving the young student in a state of despondency. A variety of this theme of unfulfilled love manifests itself in **"Eros-Hero,"** and especially in **"All around the Lagoon,"** where the author indulges in a matchless description of the island while reminiscing about his youthful experiences there and especially his secret love for Polymnia whom he never conquered but whom he likens, in his description, to the breath of the sea breeze. If all of Papadiamantis' works were lost except **"All around the Lagoon,"** it would still be possible to capture the essence of his world. The same interrelationship can be noticed when he writes stories or poems to his favorite Madonnas: the "Glykofilousa," the "tender-loving" mother of God in whose care mortals bring their problems; the "Katevodotra," the one that keeps a protective watch over the sailors as they leave the island; the "Pharmakolytria," the one who can be counted upon to put an end to the bitter agonies of those in love; or the Madonna of Kounistra and of Kehrias to whom he feels especially attached. From all of them he expects some kind of liberation or redemption. This attempt at liberation was tried by the three women in **"The Witches"** one moon-flooded evening when, totally naked in a field, they employed their magical practices while one was kneeling on the ground, another half bent and the third standing up. The first did not want to have to give birth to girls, the next wanted to turn her lover's mind and the third wanted to stop the magic spell of her rival. Priest Parthenis encounters them during these rites. It is rather surprising that scene could take place on the island of Skiathos a century ago. It is an effort to describe the blend of the sensual and the religious while focusing on the measures to which the islanders had to resort in order to escape from their limited, predestined world.

Two other stories alone justify the position Papadiamantis has been accorded in modern Greek literature. They are, **"Love in the Snow,"** and **"The Dirge of the Feal."** They summarize as well as bracket his themes and symbols and they stand as landmarks of his ascent to artistic perfection. Above all, they both deal with the question of redemption at the end of a harsh existence. In some parts, the symbolism in the stories is highly autobiographical.

"Love in the Snow" is rather Dostoevskian in its prothesis or mood. It is a melancholy reflection of Old Yannios's torturous life. His fortune is gone and his wife and only child are dead. His old cloak is the only piece of clothing left from before his misfortune. No longer young or handsome, he is totally alone in the world and tries to forget the past by drinking and by falling in love with a talkative neighboring lady who does not respond. It is the heart of winter—Christmas—and snowing. In his stupor, he decides to knock on the door of his neighbor, but instead staggers and falls on the snow. Nobody notices him, and the snow falls on him and piles up a few inches becoming a sheet, a shroud. And symbolically Papadiamantis concludes, "And old Yannios became all white and slept under the snow so as not to appear naked and loose, he and his life, and his deeds, in the presence of the Way, the Light and Life."

Similarly, **"The Dirge of the Feal,"** which Jean Moréas called a "masterpiece of world literature," deals with the pain inflicted on human beings during the course of their lives. Old woman Loukena, who had lost five children, was doing her washing by the sea, when her granddaughter Akrivoula fell from a cliff and drowned. She had lost her way, diverted by the music of a young shepherd boy, and when she fell nobody saw her. Only the feal, who also had been charmed by the music of the young shepherd and had come near the shallow water, found the drowned body of poor Akrivoula and began to mourn her. The mourning of the seal was translated into human tongue by a fisherman versed in the language of the seals. It ended, wondering, "if the sufferings and the misery of the world will ever come to an end." (pp. 82-4)

Alexandros Papadiamantis, the "saint of modern Greek letters," stood alone in word and deed following the canons he set for his life. He imitated no one and no one imitated him. He remains inimitable partly because of his unique literary expression. . . . His durability is in many respects a "cultural mystery," for as Odysseus Elytis suggested, he pillars on which Papadiamantis built his edifice have already been demolished by industrialism and secularism, and one would have thought that he, too, would have been lost and forgotten. Yet he is very much with us. (p. 95)

> *Theofanis G. Stavrou, "Alexandros Papadiamantis: A Greek Writer against the Current," in* A Greek Diptych: Dionysios Solomos and Alexandros Papadiamantis *by Louis Coutelle, Theofanis G. Stavrou and David R. Weinberg, Nostos, 1986, pp. 63-97.*

DAVID R. WEINBERG (essay date 1986)

[*Weinberg is an American critic. In the following excerpt, he analyzes characteristic elements of Papadiamantis's fiction in an attempt to explain the widespread appeal of his works.*]

Alexandros Papadiamantis over the seventy-five years since his death has been revered as one of Greece's greatest modern writers. The reverence for Alexandros Papadiamantis has been, and is, something special and quite unique. There exists an indefinable aura about Papadiamantis. In Greece, even if one has not read any of his short stories, one grows up in a cultural environment having absorbed the idea that Alexandros Papadiamantis is one of Greece's literary heroes. (p. 99)

Now it is the task of the literary critics to tell us why. This, for the most part, they have not done. George Valetas, the great Papadiamantis scholar, deplored this situation years ago when he wrote:

> The bibliography concerning his life and work is enormous and surprises by its extent and variety. Yet,

substantive it is not, only a pile of chaff. The greater part of the bibliography on Papadiamantis consists of occasional articles, announcements, accounts, annals, scholia, opinions, poems, descriptions, anecdotes, information, recollections, obituaries. The serious critical articles are few. They can be counted on the fingers. . . . In all the publications there is worship, praise, attempts at judgement, much subjectivism.

That was 1955. The situation has changed considerably since, especially in the work of Triantaphyllopoulos and others. But one of the reasons for the early lack of good scholarship on the literary art of Alexandros Papadiamantis is that substantive criticism was derailed by the language question. Papadiamantis wrote in what we describe as a *mihti,* a mixture of the purist langauge—the *katharevousa,* and the demotic. And he was writing at a time when the great controversy was raging as to which literary language was the most appropriate for the newly resurrected nation: the *katharevousa* which is related to the ancient tradition or the demotic, the language of the people. Critics, therefore, spent their time debating whether Papadiamantis was a katharevousian or a demoticist. Partisans on each side claimed him as their own and each could support their claim because of the *mihti.*

Of course, the place to have looked for the literary art of Alexandros Papadiamantis was not in a language controversy, but in the language of the texts themselves. We shall take this approach.

But let us begin with the metaphysical. Namely, these feelings of reverence for Papadiamantis and see if we can substantiate them. I believe Papadiamantis' effect on us is based on the fact that Papadiamantis is a quintessential Greek author—perhaps the quintessential Greek writer. This is something we feel instinctively. But I believe we can analyze why. If we were to compose a table of elements, however incomplete, much like the Periodic Table of the Elements, which itself is incomplete, we would identify the following, each with equal "atomic" weight:

a) Papadiamantis' love for the land and its history.

b) His love for the Greek people, especially the common folk.

c) Papadiamantis' love for the Greek ethos—its culture, customs, beliefs, legends, and sentiments.

d) His love for the Greek religion and the traditions of Orthodoxy.

e) His love for the Greek language.

Together, these elements become amalgamated into a universe which is the universe of the collected writings—over 180 short stories and novels—any one of which is a microcosm of the whole.

And finally, this univese is held together, if we can continue the metaphor, by an irreducible axiom, a world view (again one quintessentially Greek) which I call the "tragic perspective," that tragic perception of the human condition which has tinged Greek literature for over 4,000 years, expressed in Papadiamantis' own words as . . .

> As if there were ever an end
> to the misfortune and sorrows of this world.

Now the place to examine this universe and all the elements therein is, of course, the writings themselves. Since we cannot deal with 180 stories and since each is a microcosm of the others, let me choose one written at the height of Papadiamantis' powers, a work considered Papadiamantis' great masterpiece, yes, *The Murderess*. (pp. 100-02)

[*The Murderess*] is the story of a poor peasant woman, Hadoula Frangoyannou, whose life epitomizes that axiom of "endless misfortune and sorrows."

The first chapters find her keeping nightly vigil beside the cradle of her sick infant granddaughter. And during these long nights, the whole of her life passes in reverie and reminiscence through her mind. "She sees it was nothing other than serving others. When she was a child, she served her parents. When she married, she became a slave to her husband . . . ; when she had children, she became their maid; when her children had children, she became again the maidservant of her grandchildren."

She remembers her own mother's poverty and hardships, but especially she recalls overhearing her conversations with neighbor mothers and grandmothers about "the great surplus of young girls," the "conditions of poverty and want," "the demands of suitors," "the doweries" and "the suffering to establish the weaker sex."

She recalls her own marriage. How "they matched her up and married her off, endowered her with the ramshackle house in old uninhabited Castle and the uncultivated melon patch in the wilds of the island's northern confines, and the wild field disputed by the neighbor and the church."

She recalls the emigration of her sons. Her first at twenty "left for America and after two letters was never heard from again. Three years later her second boy . . . a grown young man, also embarked. . ."

Then one night "enervated by all these thoughts, inundated by waves of memory,. . . and overcome by the turmoil and tempest of her existence. . ., she leans over the cradle, forces two long, rough fingers into the infant's mouth to 'shut it up'. Then fingers out of the small mouth, which stopped breathing, she seizes the baby's neck and squeezes it for a few seconds."

Guilt ridden and ashamed in front of her daughter, she seeks relief in the country and makes her way to an old abandoned monastery which lies concealed in the hills. There, in the deserted and ruined chapel of St. John the Hidden, where it was the custom to confess one's most secret deeds, she lights a candle, kneels and prostrates herself before the half-destroyed fresco of St. John and says:

> If I've done right, St. John, give me a sign today . . .
> that I might do a good deed, a charitable act, so as
> to calm my poor heart and soul!

Returning to the valley, she comes to a farmstead and finds two little girls playing by a cistern full of water. "There!. . . you've given me the sign, St. John. . . . What a relief it would be for their poor parents if they were to fall into that cistern. . ." and she subsequently drowns them.

Thus continues a series of murders, all young girls or infant girls, which to her warped but sincere mind is done with God's blessing.

The police finally suspect her, she flees into the mountains where she continues the infanticides among the shepherds. After much suffering, deprivation and torment, she desperately tries to reach an old chapel which stands on a sea-battered rock at the end of a causeway. This hermitage could provide her safe sanctuary. With the gendarmes at her heels, she attempts the crossing as the tide is rolling in. She loses her footing. At the instant just before she drowns, "Frangoyannou's glance falls upon the Bostani, the deserted northwestern palisade where, for dowry, she had received a field, when as a young girl, she had been given, matched and married away by her parents."

"Oh! My dowry!" she said.

These were her last words.

And the story ends this way:

> Old Hadoula found death in the passage to St. Savior,
> on the neck of sand joining the rock of the hermitage
> to the land, half-way in the road between the justice
> of man and the justice of God.

(pp. 102-04)

Even from this short summary, I think we can see how Papadiamantis has poured the elements we have enumerated into this story. He has poured the landscape of his beloved island, (never mentioned by name and therefore universalized as Greece.) He has poured the chapels and monasteries which dot the hills and mountains, and the traditions of Greek Orthodoxy associated with each; the toil and torment of the poor; the status of women, the legacy of the dowry system; the emigrations abroad—in short, the Greek experience distilled.

The distillation we realize, of course, is a literary distillation which creates a world, a universe with which we can sense with verity the essence of a culture and a people. But it is illusion. It is artifice only made possible by a writer who has complete control of his language.

Yet in a statistical study I made of the *mihti*, relating to the language question, the details of which are too complex and technical to review here, I found some surprising results; that the character of Papadiamantis's *mihti* is a result of random and haphazard selection of language. That's quite a statement to make about a great writer, that his style is a result of random and haphazard selection of language!

Let me cite a textual illustration from that study: In chapter one of *The Murderess*, Papadiamantis is describing Hadoula Frangoyannou's parents. We might expect a paring of the parental forms: "mother" and "father," or "mama" and "papa," or "ma" and "pa.". . . [Instead we find "pater"] paired with "mana." Now "pater" which is Byzantine Greek meaning "father," is actually ancient even Homeric, while "mana," "mother" is modern demotic. That's like writing: Her "Sire" was such and such; her "mommy" was thus and so. (pp. 104-05)

[This] is the kind of random mixing of forms that is so characteristic of Papadiamantis' style. But we know that statistics are often deceiving. We also know that no writer, especially a great writer can succeed with a totally haphazard and random style. There has to be a guiding principle at work, one which functions either consciously or unconsciously.

The fact is that there is an interesting stability and consistency about Papadiamantis' *mihti* which the critics seem not to have noticed—an evenness as to the proportion of the *katharevousa* to the demotic throughout the prose. No single paragraph or section of the narratives (excluding dialogue, of course) "degenerates," so to speak into the demotic. So the principle at work behind random selection is an overriding sense of never allowing the writing to become too demoticized.

But the more important question is that of the aesthetics of this style, which brings us to the central dichotomy in the bibliography. Throughout the criticism there is generally great praise for the fiction; the style, however, receives cool reception. Some critics found his language "tiring." Others found his language "unaesthetic," though many of these judgements were biased by partisanship in the language controversy.

I believe Papadiamantis' style must be evaluated as to the success of its purpose. In examining his fiction, I find not only a master storyteller, but a writer in command of his language, however "mixed." There is in the Papadiamantis style that uniqueness and power of expression which only great writers impose on the structures within which they are confined. The fact that Papadiamantis may have randomly chosen between purist and demotic forms says nothing about the power of the words themselves to evoke and express what is intended. Since throughout the criticism there is great praise for unique works of fiction like *The Murderess,* it can only mean that the *mihti* does not destroy the illusion of reality necessary to all great art.

In appraising the aesthetics of the prose, it may be well to remind ourselves that Papadiamantis was also a poet whose collected poems number close to fifty, for his prose it seems to me, contains many of the elements we associate with poetry: nature painting, rhythmic line supported by alliteration, biblical reference and allusion, synthesis of the physical environment with the emotional state of characters, and philosophic comment.

Here, for example, is beautiful nature painting together with a synthesis of Hadoula's emotional state and the natural environment. In the story, Hadoula, now a fugitive from the police, exhausted after days and nights of wandering from place to place in the mountains where she had fled, comes one morning to a deep grotto-like depression in the earth surrounded by greenery, trees and ivy. She descends into it to hide and rest. Day is breaking and Papadiamantis describes the sunrise and its transformation of both her hiding place and her spirit:

> At that moment, the sun came up. The disc emerged out of the waves opposite, out of the distant ocean and from her shelter Hadoula could see a long strand. Birds of the echoing rocky mountain crags, circling above her, shrieked long caws while in the valley's groves and small woods birds sang joyous melodies.
>
> One warm ray, coming from afar, from the flaming sea, penetrated the thick foliage and ivy covering of the tormented woman's refuge, causing the morning dew to glisten like lots of pearls, in a shower of emerald peplum, and all the shiver of dampness and all the cold of livid fear fled, bringing for the time being, hope and encouragement.

Even in translation one can't imagine prose closer to poetry. In Papadiamantis' fictions there are many such poetic passages where atmosphere and natural surroundings are grafted to events and the psychological state of characters. In fact, I might say, it is a major characteristic of the prose. Without a doubt, it is the result of Papadiamantis having so completely absorbed the atmosphere and the landscape of his native island during boyhood. The caves, the grottoes, the cliffs, the mountains, the sea-coves and the legend-laden ghost town of the old abandoned Castle were the playgrounds of the writer to be.

Part of that landscape was also the religious life of the island with its myriad chapels, churches, and monasteries, each with its own saint name, each having its own celebrations and traditions. Papadiamantis' father was a psalmist and cleric of the island and led a religious life in those monasteries and chapels which he served. Young Alexandros often accompanied his

father, and soon learned by heart the *troparia,* those short fourth and fifth century hymns.

This early association with psalm, hymn, and *troparia* no doubt schooled Papadiamantis' poetic abilities. It not only affected his poetical works, but his prose style as well. Characteristic are those long descriptive sentences with rhythmic movement and sweep that carry the reader over beautiful terrain, as we have just seen.

Papadiamantis' religious background also accounts for the way in which he introduces biblical Greek as easily as he does the demotic. This poetic element of using biblical reference and allusion was second nature to him.

In chapter one of *The Murderess* for example, during the description of Hadoula's nightly vigils, we are suddenly reading:

> She gave not sleep to her eyes
> Nor slumber to her eyelids . . .

which is a direct quote from Psalm 132:4. It is so close to the *katharevousa* which surrounds it that one hardly notices it.

Later there is an interlude in *The Murderess* where Papadiamantis uses biblical text to tragicomic advantage. Hadoula, exhausted from running place to place, stops by a cool spring to drink some water. There she meets an old monk, Father Josaphat, who tends the garden at a nearby monastery. As he approaches to fill a water jug, he sees Frangoyannou and bids her a good morning. She tells the priest of her suffering but he answers her from his own world of biblical quotation:

> "What brings you here, my good woman? Something troubles you I see. . ."
>
> "Ach! Father Josaphat," lamented Frangoyannou effusively "If I were a bird I'd fly away,"
>
> "'O that I had wings as those of a dove,'" said Father Josaphat, remembering the chants.
>
> "Father, I want to leave this world . . . I can't suffer any longer."
>
> "'I have fled afar off and lodged in the wilderness,'" said the old monk again.
>
> "My life is in turmoil, Father, and I'm greatly distressed."
>
> "May God deliver you, my daughter, 'from distress of spirit and tempest,'" added the monk continuing the chant.
>
> "I can't escape hate, maliciousness and jealousy. . ."
>
> "'Destroy, O Lord, and divide their tongues: for I have seen iniquity and gainsaying in the city,'" concluded Father Josaphat.

Then after filling his water jug, he said:

> "If you pass by our gardens, good woman, call on me so as I may offer you a lettuce and some beans."

And he left.

Perhaps the "tragicomic" or "humor" should be added to our incomplete table of elements. This sad philosopher, this man whose prose sustains that "tragic perspective," was also a writer whose observation of human behavior and society did not exclude the satiric or the humorous. (pp. 106-09)

And finally there are those poetic and very engaging moments of philosophical discourse. Though we might expect, from the demands of realism, that peasant characters would express themselves in the demotic, they usually articulate Papadiamantis' innermost thoughts and beliefs in "high" literary language. Hadoula Frangoyannou, for example, whose language in the dialogue is as colloquial and "unlearned" as we might expect from a poor peasant woman, speaks to us about the world and its miseries in a most learned tongue. Here is the passage shortly after her meeting with the monk. Even in English translation it sounds learned:

> As she climbed the opposite ridge, beyond the gardens, above the stream, she heard the small bell of the monastery toll sweetly, humbly, monotonously, awakening the echoes of the mountains, and stirring the gentle wind. It was therefore midnight, hour of the Midnight Office, hour of Matins! How happy they were, these men, who, early in their youth by divine inspiration had the prescience to do what was best—not to bring, that is, others into the world ill-fated! . . . after that, everything is secondary. . . .

But the *katharevousa,* among the modern Greek languages, is certainly the most appropriate for philosophic thought—rich in abstract terms and directly related to the ancient tradition.

All this illustrates that Palamas, a poet himself, understood and expressed about the capriciousness of Papadiamantis' *mihti* when he said, "that Papadiamantis changes grammar, style, language in accordance with his circumstance, taste, disposition. . . ." In choosing *katharevousa* for philosophic comment, demotic for colloquial expression in dialogue, and *mihti* for narration in-between Papadiamantis demonstrates the poet's instinct for just that: matching grammar, style, and language to circumstance, taste, and disposition.

In our table of elements we listed Papadiamantis' love for the Greek language. This means, the entire historical spectrum—ancient, biblical, Byzantine, modern. Unlike the writers of his time whose fashion it was to exclude language in order to "purify" language, Papadiamantis' intent was to include, to embrace the historical spectrum. His intent is not only illustrated by the inclusion of the biblical, as we have seen, but by the practice of including the indigenous language of his beloved island. (pp. 111-12)

In this way he was also *malliarist* in spirit [In a footnote Weinberg explains that the term *malliarist* "(literally 'hairy') is a derisive name given by the purists to those grammarians and writers attempting to systematize the demotic language."]; exhibiting the desire to preserve the native language as the malliarists had done, especially Nikos Kazantzakis, who deliberately collected words from the villages and the islands and included them in his writing with the aim of preserving them.

Papadiamantis was by no means unaware of the language controversy swirling around him. He just chose to ignore it, because he chose to express himself in a manner in harmony with his sensibilities and background. Any other manner would have been for him false, synthetic, and insincere. His background was itself a mixture: aristocratic but poor; island provincial, but worldly in vision; educated, but with empathy for the peasant, the unskilled and the unschooled. (p. 112)

Having endeavored in this lecture to analyse Papadiamantis' "Greekness," in the final analysis we realize that his legacy, like that of all great writers, is of universal character and significance. This is because Papadiamantis, like all great writers, belongs to that high priesthood we call *dáskalos*—"teacher." Papadiamantis' writings, which are tempered only by a soft-

ening strain of romanticism, for the most part belong to that category of fiction we call realism and social satire. As such, they instruct—for they lay bare the human condition, so that with understanding and compassion, we can perhaps improve it. (p. 113)

> *David R. Weinberg, "The Literary Art of Alexandros Papadiamantis," in* A Greek Diptych: Dionysios Solomos and Alexandros Papadiamantis *by Louis Coutelle, Theofanis G. Stavrou, and David R. Weinberg, Nostos, 1986, pp. 99-113.*

GEORGE ECONOMOU (essay date 1987)

[Economou is an American poet, translator, and critic. In the following excerpt, he reviews the short story collection Tales from a Greek Island.*]*

In his provocative essay "The Storyteller," the critic Walter Benjamin identifies two spheres of life, the agricultural and the merchant seafaring, as the sources of two major groups of storytellers. Though he was never a farmer or a sailor, Alexandros Papadiamantis, the son of a Greek Orthodox priest from the Aegean island of Skiathos, grounded his tales of the lives of his fellow islanders in these two primary activities of Greek life.

Perhaps that is why, despite the fact that his work has not always elicited high praise from his country's literary establishment in the past, more recently certain poets like Constantine Cavafy, George Seferis and Odysseus Elytis have responded positively to his writings. They have especially expressed appreciation for his distinctive use of language, powers of simple narration and masterly blending of the cruel exigencies and exquisite natural surroundings of a way of life that resonates with folkways, myth and religious sensibility.

With his place among Greece's modern writers now secure, Papadiamantis merits the attention of the larger audience that translation into English gives him. His novella, *The Murderess,* . . . should be required reading for anyone with an interest in the European prototypes of feminist writing. Now, *Tales from a Greek Island* offers 12 more astutely selected examples of Papadiamantis's depiction of late-19th-century Greek life. This selection from his nearly 200 works of short fiction, most of which deal with the hardships and joys of the insular community of Skiathos, shows the full range of his skill in combining realism and symbolism; it demonstrates, too, his ability to draw and establish characters with seemingly effortless precision, and to endow his narratives with a universality that allows some of his stories to transcend their regionalism.

By leaping back to a mythic source, his tales also often deepen their dual effect of timelessness and continuity. Elements from Greek myth and legend are so deftly introduced into his plots and characters that they seem more the result of direct observation than of literary invention. For example, in the final tale of the volume, **"The American: A Christmas Story,"** Papadiamantis plays a variation on the ancient theme of the hero's return, skillfully deploying throughout the plot a subtle set of parallels with the second half of Homer's *Odyssey.*

While the tales will challenge and delight a new readership, it is the women in these stories who most strongly claim our attention. Papadiamantis paints a vivid picture of the deprivations and severe limitations that 19th-century village customs (such as the rigid dowry system) imposed on their lives. At the same time, he portrays their courage, ingenuity and endurance with unusual fidelity and a matter-of-factness that might chill a contemporary reader. These women may be Penelope's daughters, but a different world requires that they summon and use (with greater need and poignancy than do their male counterparts) the legacy of survivorship from father Odysseus.

Papadiamantis, who divided his bachelor's life as a writer between Athens and his beloved Skiathos, reveals both conservative and traditionally religious convictions in his works. Yet, like Balzac and Dostoyevsky, he is capable of the ironic detachment that can reveal a character's inability to live up to the ideals of a deeply traditional ethos. As a writer committed to a realistic rendition of a locale and its inhabitants, he has also been compared with Thomas Hardy.

> *George Economou, ''The Joy of Skiathos,'' in* The New York Times Book Review, *August 30, 1987, p. 14.*

Luigi Pirandello

1867-1936

For further discussion of Pirandello's career, see *TCLC*, Vol. 4.

Italian dramatist, short story writer, novelist, critic, and poet.

One of the most important dramatists of the twentieth century, Pirandello prompted a reevaluation of traditional stagecraft through his innovative use of philosophical themes and experimentation with dramatic structure. Obsessed by the relationship of reality to appearances and of sanity to madness, he often portrayed characters who adopt multiple identities, or "masks," in an effort to reconcile social demands with personal needs. He was closely associated with the Theater of the Grotesque, a dramatic school that stressed the paradoxes and contradictions of life, and was also deeply concerned with making literature a more truthful and effective means for conveying human experience. Toward this end he developed the aesthetic theory of "humorism," which he defined as a mingling of comedy and tragedy to produce simultaneous emotional awareness of both of these aspects of the human condition.

Pirandello was born in Sicily to a prosperous sulphur merchant. Although his father initially sent him to study commerce at the local technical institute, Pirandello lacked interest in the subject and transferred to an academic secondary school, where he excelled in oratory and literature. He began writing at a young age, and by the time he was twelve had produced his first play, *Barbaro,* with siblings and friends. He also wrote poetry and fiction, publishing his first poem in 1883 and his first story a year later. After graduation, Pirandello attended universities in Palermo, Rome, and finally Bonn, where he earned a doctorate in Romance philology. He then returned to Rome, living on a remittance from his father while trying to establish himself as a writer. After his father arranged Pirandello's marriage to Antonietta Portulano, the daughter of a business partner, the couple settled together in Rome and had three children. To support his family, Pirandello was forced to increase his literary output and to take a position as professor at a women's normal school. In 1904 he realized his first critical success with the novel *Il fu Mattia Pascal (The Late Mattia Pascal),* but this was overshadowed when his father's sulphur mines, in which Pirandello was heavily invested, were destroyed in a flood. All of Pirandello's wealth, including his wife's dowry, was wiped out. Upon hearing the news, Antonietta suffered an emotional collapse; she subsequently became obsessively jealous and delusional. Although subjected to relentless accusations and abuse, Pirandello refused to have his wife committed; instead, he took refuge in his study, where he lost himself in writing short stories, novels, and essays. He also wrote several plays, but was unable to get them produced.

The stress under which Pirandello lived was exacerbated when Italy entered World War I and his son was imprisoned in an Austrian POW camp. At the same time, Pirandello's wife became increasingly hostile and threatening, until at last he was forced to have her institutionalized. More than ever Pirandello turned to his writing for consolation. His biographer Gaspare Giudice wrote that "the sudden awareness that his own distress coincided with the laceration of the world outside, the corre-

spondence of the absurd public agony with his own private pain, the confirmation that everything was vain and iniquitous" led Pirandello to produce the plays on which his fame would later rest. This period of intense creativity lasted from 1916 to 1922 and culminated in the production of his two greatest works: the dramas *Sei personaggi in cerca d'autore (Six Characters in Search of an Author)* and *Enrico IV (Henry IV).* Pirandello quickly went from being an author with a respectable but modest reputation to being one of the major literary figures in Italy. He took advantage of this public prominence to help Benito Mussolini and his Fascist Party endure a desperate crisis. In 1924 a leading member of the opposition, Giacomo Matteotti, was brutally assassinated by supporters of Mussolini. The Fascist Party was discredited, and Mussolini was nearly forced to resign, when Pirandello chose to join the Party as ostentatiously as he could. In a letter to the pro-Fascist paper *L'imperio,* he asked to join the Party and pledged his "humble obedience" to Mussolini. Mussolini, showing his appreciation for the gesture of support, provided funds for the Arts Theater that Pirandello had established. Pirandello, as producer and director, saw many of his plays first performed in this theater, and he took his company on tour throughout the world. However, the Arts Theater never achieved financial success and was dissolved in 1928. Frustrated by the failure of his theater, by his unsuccessful attempts to establish a government-sponsored

National Theater in Rome, and by the decreasing popularity of his plays, Pirandello lived in self-imposed exile for the next five years. In 1934 he was awarded the Nobel Prize in literature, which he donated a year later to support the Italian invasion of Ethiopia. He continued to write as his health gradually deteriorated, and he died in December 1936.

Pirandello's early works were strongly influenced by verism, an Italian naturalist movement led by Giovanni Verga. Writing in his native Sicilian dialect, Pirandello skillfully described the landscape and inhabitants of Sicily. While his first successful novel, *The Late Mattia Pascal,* displays a naturalistic style, it also suggests the philosophical themes of his later work. Portraying a man who assumes a false identity in order to escape the circumstances of his life, *The Late Mattia Pascal* deals with the relationship of personal identity to the social definition of an individual. Pirandello's last novel, *Uno, nessuno e centomila (One, None, and a Hundred Thousand),* expands upon this theme by examining Vitangelo Moscarda's efforts to free himself from the restrictions of his social identity. Unlike Mattia Pascal, who after abandoning his social identity painfully realizes that it is impossible to establish a new one, Moscarda seeks to rid himself permanently of those characteristics by which others have identified him. Pirandello's techniques of characterization parallel the struggles of his protagonists to deconstruct their superficial identities: instead of constructing a coherent character through a cumulative revelation of detail, Pirandello first described a character in superficial terms and then later contradicted what he had written. In his essay *L'umorismo (On Humor),* which he dedicated "To the Memory of Mattia Pascal, Librarian," Pirandello articulated the major aesthetic principle that guided his work. Pirandello's theory of humorism is based upon his vision of the conflict between surface appearances and deeper realities. According to Pirandello, when an opposition exists between a character's situation and an audience's expectations, the audience gains an "awareness" of this opposition, and the situation appears comic. When the audience additionally recognizes a character's suffering beneath the comic appearance, the audience gains a "sentiment" or "feeling" of this opposition. Catharsis occurs when, through a combination of opposing reactions, the audience achieves both a compassionate understanding of the character's situation in the fictional world and a deeper insight into the real world. Pirandello was thus more interested in the audience's direct emotional experience of the theater than in the purely abstract and philosophical aspects of his plays.

Pirandello described his dramatic works as a "theater of mirrors" in which the audience sees what passes on stage as a reflection of their own lives: when his characters doubt their own perceptions of themselves, the audience experiences a simultaneous crisis of self-perception. In questioning the distinction between sanity and madness, Pirandello attacked abstract models of objective reality and theories of a static human personality. For these reasons, many critics have labelled him a pessimist and a relativist; others, noting the strong sense of compassion that Pirandello conveys for his characters, contend that Pirandello is not preaching a definable ideology, but is simply expressing his acute consciousness of the absurdities and paradoxes of human life. As Pirandello explained: "My works are born from live images which are the perennial source of art, but these images pass through a veil of concepts which have taken hold of me. My works of art are never concepts trying to express themselves through images. On the contrary. They *are* images, often very vivid images of life, which, fos-

tered by the labors of my mind, assume universal significance quite on their own, through the formal unity of art."

In his most famous play, *Six Characters in Search of an Author,* Pirandello described the plight of six characters who interrupt the rehearsal of another Pirandello play to demand that their stories be acted out. His acknowledgement of the stage as the location of a theatrical performance—a place where life is only simulated—startled audiences and critics alike and heralded the self-conscious use of the theater that is a hallmark of modernist drama. Summarizing the effect of Pirandello's play, Antonio Illiano has written that the "sudden and unexpected appearance of live characters, who claimed to belong to the stage and could actually be seen and heard, was like a bombshell that blew out the last and weary residues of the old realistic drama." At the first performance of the play in Rome, the audience was so infuriated that a general riot broke out that lasted well into the night. The play was next performed several months later in Milan, but after the notoriety of the play's earlier performance, as well as the intervening publication of the text, the audience came knowing what to expect and the performance was a triumphant success which soon spread to theaters throughout the world. Pirandello's new technique created an ironic parallel between the relationship of the six characters to the stage manager and actors on the one hand, and the relationship of the performance of *Six Characters* to the actual audience on the other. When the characters argue that they are more real than the stage manager because their lives are fixed and unchanging in the roles that they eternally relive, they are actually challenging the audience's belief in the stable reality of their own personalities. Pirandello followed the success of *Six Characters* with *Henry IV,* which many critics consider his greatest work. Written four years after he had his wife committed, *Henry IV* is the last and most eloquent expression of the theme of madness that had been prevalent in Pirandello's personal life and in his art. It uses none of the modernistic dramatic techniques of *Six Characters* and instead draws upon and enriches classical dramatic patterns; the influence of *Hamlet* is especially evident. The play depicts a man who, as the result of an injury suffered at the hands of a rival, believes he is Henry IV. Eventually, he regains his sanity but in a fit of rage kills his rival, so that he must feign continued madness if he wants to avoid the consequences of his deed. Considered an apology for madness, *Henry IV* examines the practical reasons that make insanity and the construction of illusions the only logical response to a reality that is too painful to bear.

After writing *Henry IV,* Pirandello read a discussion of his plays in Adriano Tilgher's *Studi sul teatro contemporaneo* (1923), and the remainder of his career as a playwright was influenced by this critic's perception of his work. Tilgher saw in Pirandello's dramas a consistent and compelling philosophical formula which explained the often confusing and contradictory elements of these works. Tilgher wrote: "The philosophy implicit in Pirandello's art revolved round the fundamental dualism of Life and Form: Life, perpetually mobile and fluid, which cannot help developing into a form, although it deeply resents all form; and Form which determines Life, by giving it rigid and precise borders, and freezes it, suppressing its restless motion." Pirandello was pleased by the academic authority that Tilgher's essay gave to his dramas, and he was stimulated to approach more intently the life-form dichotomy in his works. Many critics blamed this objective for the decline in the quality of Pirandello's later plays, which were viewed as overly intellectual, obscure, and lacking emotional vitality. Tilgher himself later wrote that "it would have been better if Pirandello had never read my essay. It is never good for a writer to be too conscious of his inner world, and my essay fixed Pirandello's world in such clear and well-defined terms that Pirandello must have felt imprisoned in it, hence his protests that he was an artist and not a philosopher . . . and hence his attempts to escape. But the more he tried to escape from the critical pigeon-holes into which I had placed him the more he shut himself into them." Pirandello was bitterly disappointed by the critical and popular failure of his later dramas, a disappointment only partially mitigated by the Nobel Prize. However, after his death critics began to question the utility and appropriateness of the life-form dichotomy as the principal critical approach to Pirandello's works, and the rise of existentialist theory and of the Theater of the Absurd did much to alter the context of the debate on Pirandello.

Pirandello is today viewed with a more sophisticated appreciation for his philosophical themes and with near universal esteem for all his works, including his later dramas. What was previously scorned as overly intellectual and incoherent is now respected for its provocative treatment of relativism and antirationalism. Pirandello foresaw the abatement of the critical controversy that he inspired during his lifetime, and looked to that time when his works would be judged according to the artistic terms in which they were created: "The commotion aroused almost everywhere [by my work] is not the ideal environment for it. For me it is no more than a pledge for the future. Before it is attacked, as every human creation inevitably is, the meaningless clamour around it must be silenced; and there will be a moment when, in the first lull it will come to life . . . clear as it once was in my mind when I contemplated it in its finished form and, for an instant, thought it perfect."

(See also *Contemporary Authors*, Vol. 104.)

PRINCIPAL WORKS

Mal giocondo (poetry) 1889
Amori senza amore (short stories) 1894
Beffe della morte e della vita (short stories) 1902
Bianche e nere (short stories) 1904
Il fu Mattia Pascal (novel) 1904
  [*The Late Mattia Pascal*, 1923]
Erma bifronte (short stories) 1906
L'esclusa (novel) 1908
  [*The Outcast*, 1925]
L'umorismo (essay) 1908
  [*On Humor*, 1974]
I vecchi e i giovani (novel) 1913
  [*The Old and the Young*, 1928]
Liolà (drama) 1916
  [*Liolà* published in *Naked Masks*, 1952]
Si gira (novel) 1916
  [*Shoot! The Notebooks of Serafino Gubbio,
    Cinematograph Operator*, 1926]
Così è (se vi pare) (drama) 1917
  [*Right You Are! (If You Think So)* published in *Three
    Plays*, 1922]
Il piacere dell'onestà (drama) 1917
  [*The Pleasure of Honesty* published in *Each in His Own
    Way, and Two Other Plays*, 1923]
Il carnevale dei morti (short stories) 1919
L'uomo, la bestia e la virtù (drama) 1919

Sei personaggi in cerca d'autore (drama) 1921
  [*Six Characters in Search of an Author* published in *Three
    Plays*, 1922]
Enrico IV (drama) 1922
  [*Henry IV* published in *Three Plays*, 1922]
Novelle per un anno. 15 vols. (short stories) 1922-37
Vestire gli ignudi (drama) 1922
  [*Naked* published in *Each in His Own Way, and Two
    Other Plays*, 1923]
Ciascuno a suo modo (drama) 1924
  [*Each in His Own Way* published in *Each in His Own
    Way, and Two Other Plays*, 1923]
Uno, nessuno e centomila (novel) 1926
  [*One, None, and a Hundred Thousand*, 1933]
Come tu mi vuoi (drama) 1930
  [*As You Desire Me*, 1931]
Maschere nude. 10 vols. (dramas) 1930-38
Questa sera si recita a soggetto (drama) 1930
  [*Tonight We Improvise*, 1932]
*Horse in the Moon (short stories) 1932
*Better Think Twice about It, and Twelve Other Stories
  (short stories) 1933
*The Naked Truth, and Eleven Other Stories (short stories)
  1934
I giganti della montagna (drama) 1937
  [*The Mountain Giants* published in *The Mountain Giants,
    and Other Plays*, 1958]
*The Medals, and Other Stories (short stories) 1939
Short Stories (short stories) 1959
Short Stories (short stories) 1965

*These stories have been selected from the series *Novelle per un anno*.

ADRIANO TILGHER (essay date 1923)

[*Tilgher was an Italian philosopher and critic whose analysis of Pirandello's works in* Studi sul teatro contemporaneo *(1923) established the main tradition of Pirandello criticism and influenced Pirandello's own writing. In the following excerpt from that work, Tilgher examines Pirandello's worldview as it is presented in his writings.*]

(1) What, in Pirandello's view, distinguishes man from the other beings of nature? This, and only this: that man lives and feels himself live, while the other beings of nature just live, live purely and simply. The tree, for instance, lives completely immersed in its own vital sense; its existence equals the slow and dark succession of vital vicissitudes in it; sun, moon, wind and earth surround it, but it sees and knows nothing of them: it senses them, of course, but only insofar as they become states of its own being, from which it fails to distinguish itself. Since it knows nothing of anything else, the tree knows nothing of itself as different from anything else.

(2) But in man, no matter how uncouth, life splits in two: even to the most uncouth of men it is essential to be and to know that he is, to live and to know that he lives. In man, life has projected and detached from itself as its own opposite something that Pirandello calls the feeling of life and that I would call, in philosophically stricter terms, consciousness, reflection, thought. In such detachment, with the attendant delusion of assuming as objectively and externally existing reality this mutable inner feeling of life, there lies the first cause of human

misery. For once it has detached itself from life, the feeling of life (or consciousness as we may call it) by filtering through the brain tends to cool off, to clarify and idealize itself; from the particular, changeable, ephemeral state it was, it will eventually crystallize into a general, abstract idea (see Pirandello's essay *L'umorismo.*)

(3) Having risen through logical abstraction to its own second power, having become reflective thought, the feeling of life tends to confine life within fixed boundaries, to channel it between chosen banks, to pour it into stiff, definitive molds: the concepts and ideals of our spirit, the conventions, mores, traditions, and laws of society. That causes a basic dualism. On the one hand, blind, dumb Life will keep darkly flowing in eternal restlessness through each moment's renewals. On the other hand, a world of crystallized Forms, a system of constructions, will strive to dam up and compress that ever-flowing turmoil. "Everything, every object, every life carries with it the penalty of its form, the pain of being so and never otherwise, until it crumbles into ashes" (see the short story **"Candelora"** [**"Candlemas"**]). "Every form is death. We are all beings caught in a trap, detached from the unceasing flux, and fixed to death" (see the short story **"La trappola"** [**"The Trap"**]).

(4) Most men live within those frozen forms, without even so much as surmising that a dark, furious ocean may stir under them. But in some men, thought, that very activity which, lightning-like in its mystery, has split life asunder, separates from the forms into which life's hot flux has clotted and perceives them for what they really are: merely ephemeral constructions, under which the tide of life roars unconstrained by any human illusion. In the man who has achieved this deliverance from the forms of life, any human construction arouses a sense of contrast which topples it under his very eyes. There is something comical and grievous at the same time in that crash. The crash is comical because it lays bare the intrinsic unreality of human constructions, but grievous too, because, however flimsy, the demolished structure did afford man a shelter from the mad storm of life.

In such intimate mixture of laughter and tears, of comedy and sadness, is humor as Pirandello feels it to be and defines it. "I see something like a labyrinth, where through so many crisscrossing paths our soul rambles without ever finding a way out. And in this labyrinth I see a double herma which laughs from one face and weeps from the other, laughs indeed from one face at the weeping of the twin, opposite one" (see *Erma bifronte* [*Two-faced Herma*], preface). Since humor is the attitude of the man whose thought, having attained self-consciousness, has broken through the screens of conceptual constructions to look out on life's abysmal tide of tumultuous incoherence, it has to be an essentially cerebral state of mind. Humor and cerebralism: all of Pirandello's art is summarized in these two words.

(5) Therefore, antithesis is the basic law of his art. The customary relationships of human existence are triumphantly subverted. Among the comedies, *Pensaci, Giacomino!* (*Think It Over, Giacomino!*) features a husband intentionally forcing the (to him only too well known) young lover of his wife to come back to her, while *L'uomo, la bestia e la virtù* (*Man, Beast and Virtue*) shows a lover dragging the betrayed husband back to the marriage bed. *Ma non è una cosa seria* (*It Can't Be Serious*) deals with marriage as an antidote against the danger of marriage. Of the short stories, **"Da sé"** (**"By Himself"**) presents the supposedly dead man who traipses to the graveyard thereby enjoying many things which are lost on quick and dead alike. **"Nené e Niní"** (**"Nené and Niní"**) acquaints us with two little orphans who bring ruin to a whole series of stepfathers and stepmothers. **"Canta l'epistola"** (**"Sing the Epistle"**) develops the motif of a mortal duel caused by the plucking of a leaf of grass. **"Il dovere del medico"** (**"The Physician's Duty"**) tells the story of a doctor who, from sheer sense of duty, lets his patient bleed to death, then in **"Prima notte"** (**"First Wedding Night"**) we see two newlyweds spend their first wedding night weeping respectively on the grave of her fiancé and of his first wife; finally, **"L'illustre estinto"** (**"The Illustrious Deceased"**) (to put an end to our practically inexhaustible examples) is the tale of an illustrious deceased who gets a hidden burial by night, like a dog, while a perfect nobody receives honors and gifts in his place.

(6) Dualism of Life and Form (or Construction); the necessity for Life to sink into a Form without possibly ever being exhausted by it: here is the fundamental motif underlying all of Pirandello's work in such a way as to organize it into a strict unity of vision. That suffices to show the remarkable modern relevance of this writer of ours. All of modern philosophy, from Kant on, rises from this deep insight into the dualism between absolutely spontaneous Life, which in its perennial upsurge of freedom keeps creating the new, and the constructed Forms or molds which tend to imprison that upsurge, with the result that Life every time shatters those molds to dissolve them and go beyond in its tireless creativity. The whole history of modern philosophy is the progressive deepening of this basic intuition into self-possessed clarity. To the eyes of an artist like Pirandello, who lives on just such an intuition, reality will appear dramatic at its very roots, the essence of drama lying in the struggle between Life's primal nakedness and the garments or masks with which men must by all means insist on clothing it. *La vita nuda* (*Naked Life*), *Maschere nude* (*Naked Masks*). The very titles of his works are telling.

(7) To enjoy Life in its infinite nakedness and freedom, outside all constructed forms into which society, history, and the events of each individual existence have channeled its course, is impossible. Mattia Pascal tried that, who, palming himself off as dead and changing name and aspect, believed he could start a new life, in the enthusiasm of a boundless liberty. He learned at his own expense that, having cut himself off from all social forms and conventions, he was only allowed to witness other people's life as a foreign spectator, without any further possibility to mingle with it and enjoy its fullness. Since he had estranged himself from the forms of Life, it now no longer conceded itself to him except superficially, externally. And when, surrendering to its call, he deluded himself that he could plunge again into the river of Life to be enveloped by its waves, that river rejected him, and again at his own expense he learned that it is not possible to act as living and dead at the same time. Thus in despair he resolved to stage a resurrection—too late to sit down again at the banquet of existence, in time only to see others partake of it (see the novel *Il fu Mattia Pascal* [*The Late Mattia Pascal*]). Of course it is possible to estrange oneself from the forms of Life, but only on condition that one gives up living.

(8) To accept the Forms of constructions into which Life has been forced; to participate in them with heartfelt belief and yet avoid crystallizing oneself in one of them or in one of their systems, but to retain so much spiritual fusion or fluidity that one's soul may go on from form to form without finally coagulating in any, without fearing the impurities it inevitably

carries along in its ceaseless flow, since that very flowing will purify it: here is the practical wisdom of life. It is a wisdom of precarious value, far from insuring perfect happiness, since some form may always emerge to obstruct so firmly the soul streaming at white heat that the latter fails to melt the obstacle and finally subsides into it, stifled.

That is the case of Corrado Selmi of *I vecchi e i giovani (The Old and the Young)*, in whom Pirandello has embodied this refreshing ideal of wisdom. Corrado has to commit suicide one day when certain past actions of his come to light, because these actions, for all the redeeming freshness of life he had put in them and the good he thus managed to spread around by their means or in their spite, do appear vile and dishonorable to society that looks at them from the outside.

(9) But Selmi's idea of practical wisdom can only be achieved by a soul endowed with the strength to pass on from form to form without either being imprisoned in any one of them or losing in the passage the sustenance of its vital illusion. That means a soul capable of attaining in itself a balance between Life and Form and of dwelling there contentedly. But whoever radically lives by the Pirandellian insight that any Form must always be a limiting determination and therefore a denial of Life . . . will have only two choices left. Either (like the Vitangelo Moscarda of *Uno, nessuno e centomila [One, No One and a Hundred Thousand]*) he can try and live Life in its absolute primeval nakedness, beyond all forms and constructions, focusing on a vibrantly fleeting present, experiencing time moment by moment, without even thinking of time in the process for that would mean to construe it, to give it a form and thus limit and stifle it (This is an enactment of Bergson's intutionalism, with a timeless *pure present* substituted for *pure duration*. Such an ideal of life is, however, attainable at the limit, i.e., practically unattainable.);

(10) or else, having discovered the provisional nature of Forms along with the impossibility to do without them, the ineluctable penalty one will eventually have to pay for the Form that Life donned or let itself be dressed in, one can renounce life: and that is the case of Don Cosmo Laurentano of *I vecchi e i giovani (The Old and the Young)*.

> "One thing only is sad, my friends: to have seen through the game! I mean the game of this mocking devil who hides within each of us and has his fun projecting for us as external reality what, shortly after, he himself will expose as our own delusion, laughing at the pains we took for it and laughing also . . . at our failure to delude ourselves, since outside these delusions there is no reality left. . . . And so don't complain! Do trouble yourselves with your endeavors, without thinking that it all will lead to no conclusion. If it does not conclude, it means that it should not conclude, and that it is therefore useless to seek a conclusion. We must live, that is, we must delude ourselves; leave free play to the mocking devil within us. . . ."

· · · · ·

(25) Just because the Pirandellian Weltanschauung does not admit of one reason, of one logic, and of one law, but of as many as there are individuals, and indeed as many for the same individual as feeling creates in its endless variations, each character from his own viewpoint is right, and no such thing exists as one higher point of view from which to judge all others. Thus in the end Pirandello does not judge, absolve, or condemn any of his characters; rather, his judgment is implied in the portrayal he gives of them and of their actions' consequences.

That makes for a firmly immanent morality, to the absolute exclusion of any reference to transcendent norms. For each one, the judgment is implicitly given by the results of his actions.

Thus, for instance, not one word of condemnation is ever uttered by Pirandello on his many fictive women, even though, personifying blind instinct unrestrained by reason and thought, they seem to be crazy, amoral, conscienceless creatures, addicted to orgies of sensual cerebralism as well as to hangover nausea and horror of it, with sudden yearnings for purity and motherhood. Such are Silia of *Il giuoco delle parti (Each in His Role)*, Beatrice of *Il berretto a sonagli (Cap and Bells)*, Fulvia of *Come prima, meglio di prima (As Well as Before, Better than Before)*, the Stepdaughter of *Sei personaggi in cerca d'autore (Six Characters in Search of an Author)*, the Murdered Woman of the "lay mystery" *All'uscita (At the Exit)*, Ersilia of *Vestire gli ignudi (Naked)*, all of them full of hatred against the man each confronts (respectively Leone, Ciampa, Silvio, the Father, the Fat Man) since he embodies what is directly contrary to them: order, reason, pondering calm, and prudence.

(26) In the Pirandellian view of things, Life must needs give itself a Form and withal not exhaust itself therein. Also, in the human world the creator of Form is thought. Thus, while with other artists conscious thought only accompanies the unfolding of inner events from the outside, and throws on them a cold superficial light, so that drama is generated and consummated exclusively in the emotive sphere, the possible intervention of thought never being crucial, with Pirandello thought finds its way into every moment of psychological becoming.

His characters justify, condemn, criticize themselves in the very act of living through their torments; they don't just feel, they reason rightly or absurdly on their feelings, and in so doing transfer them from the level of mere emotionality to a level of higher, more truly human complexity. Man after all is not just feeling, but also and especially thought, and he reasons, whether rightly or absurdly, especially when he suffers. Feelings, passions, affections are always thrown into perspective by thought which colors and imbues them with itself, yet by the same token it, in turn, is colored by them and warmed by their flame. Thought here is life and drama, and takes shape gradually through ceaseless lacerations and contrasts. We thus have cerebralism, of course, but one and the same with the torment and passion of drama. Thinking thought, which is activity unfolding through continuous struggles and wounds, places itself at the center of art's world: with Pirandello, dialectic becomes poetry.

(27) Pirandello's art, chronologically as well as ideally contemporary to the great idealist revolution that took place in Italy and Europe at the beginning of this century, carries over into art the anti-rationalism which fills modern philosophy and is now culminating into Relativism. Pirandello's art is anti-rationalist not because it denies or ignores thought to the total benefit of feeling, passion, and affections, but rather because it installs thought at the very center of the world as a live power fighting with the rebellious powers of Life. Anti-rationalist (or anti-intellectualist) do I call it, because it denies that a complete, self-contained and wholly determined order of truth preexists thought, as if the only thing left for thought itself to do were humbly to take notice of preordained truth and bow to it; yet it is a thought-affirming art, instinct with the drama of thinking thought. . . .

Thought actually leavens Life. Therefore, while for other writers reality is massively compact and monolithically rigid, given once for all, with Pirandello it flakes off into several levels which in turn then endlessly complicate one another. Not only what is commonly called real is such, but also, and with the same right, whatever appears to be real in the warmth of a feeling. A deeply dreamed dream (as in the short story **"La realtà del sogno"** [**"The Reality of Dream"**]), a memory (as in the short story **"Piuma"** [**"Feather"**]), or a fantasy (as in the short stories, **"Se . . ."** [**"If"**], **"Rimedio: La geografia"** [**"The Remedy: Geography"**], **"Il treno ha fischiato"** [**"The Train Whistled"**]) are as real to him who intensely lives them as this thick world of things and people to which alone we usually ascribe the name of reality. As a consequence, what is real to one person may not be to another, or may be real to still another in a different way, and what was reality to the same man fades off in his eyes once the engendering sentiment has failed. Jocularly, the short story **"Il pipistrello"** (**"The Bat"**) tells of one such clash between different levels of reality, and of the attendant troubles.

(28) Two plays by Pirandello above all show this living dialectic of Spirit in action: *La ragione degli altri* (*Other People's Point of View*) and *Sei personaggi in cerca d'autore* (*Six Characters in Search of an Author*). In *La ragione degli altri* a situation has arisen whose inner logic by its own unfolding determines the action's development and leads the characters to the only admissible end. The central character, Livia (who is fully aware of the situation's logic), has broken off with her husband Leonardo upon learning of a mistress, Elena, who has borne him a daughter. The weary mistress would like to send her husband back to her, and she is willing to forgive him, on one condition, however: that Elena surrenders to her the child to be raised as Livia's own daughter, in the comforts destitute Elena cannot give her. Elena took Leonardo away from her as a husband, and she is returning him as a father; well then, let the father either stay with his child's mother, or come back to his lawful wife, but with the child. To have him back only by half, a husband with herself and a father with the other woman, will never do. "Where the children are, there is the home!" and Leonardo had no children from Livia. "Two homes, that is out! I here and your daughter there, that is out!"

Such is the situation, of which Livia represents and interprets the inner logic, for her feeling has risen to the highest degree of rationality. Around her and the other characters move on different levels, all of them lower than Livia's: in all of them passion to some extent dominates reason. Each of them defends a particular right of his: Elena, as the mother she is, wants to send Leonardo back to Livia, but to keep the child; Guglielmo, as the father-in-law, regardless of the child, wants Leonardo to be reconciled to his daughter Livia, or else Livia to return to her parental home; Leonardo claims his right as a husband in love with his wife again and as a father who won't ever give up the child. The action is continuous dialectic, through which all these one-sided rights and reasons gradually become aware of their one-sidedness to yield finally to the right and reason of Livia, which contains them all and is therefore superior to all, for it interprets the good of the child, the strongest right and need. Livia is of course taking her mother away from the little girl, but she is giving her another, equally affectionate one, along with the father, and wealth and a name for good measure.

(29) In *La ragione degli altri* (*Other People's Point of View*) we see a dialectic operate whereby a higher truth or reason conquers the lower ones. In *Sei personaggi in cerca d'autore* (*Six Characters in Search of an Author*) we see the very dialectic

of truth or illusion taking shape. In this admirable play, which takes its cue from a motif outlined in the short story, **"La tragedia di un personaggio"** (**"The Tragedy of a Character"**), Pirandello wants to portray scenically the laboring process whereby the riot of phantoms born by the artist's imagination, throbbing with life as they no doubt are yet at first still confused, dark and chaotically unaccomplished, aspires to a final composure in whose encompassing harmony what had initially flashed in the artist's mind as faintly distinguishable splotches of color may find the proper balance in an ample, luminous, well organized picture.

One is born a fictional character as one is born stone, plant, or animal, and if the really of the character is an illusion, any reality will likewise turn out to be an illusion once the animating feeling has changed. Who was born a character, then, has even more life than the so-called really existing men, for they change in every way from day to day, and pass and die, while the fictional character, instead, has his own incorruptible life, eternally fixed in his nature's unchangeable essential traits. "Nature uses the instrument of imagination to pursue its own creative work on a higher level." And once he is created, the character detaches himself from his author, lives by himself and imposes his will on the creator, who must follow and let him do as he pleases. One day six characters, whom their author had sketched and provisionally composed in an undeveloped, unfinished scenic plot, turn to a *stage manager* to propose that he allow them to act out onstage the drama irrepressibly stirring within them.

Not all of these characters are equally achieved. Two, the main ones (*Father and Stepdaughter*), are very close to accomplished artistic achievement, some other instead is little more than brute nature, blind impression of life (the *Mother*), still another (the *Son*) is lyrically achieved and rebels against a dramatic enactment. These six characters in search of an author do not, then, share the same level of consciousness: they are the scenic realization of the several levels of consciousness on which an artist's imagination has dwelt. Pirandello's play would realize in scenic terms the process of coalescence leading to the work of art, the transition from life to art, from impression to intuition and finally expression. The turmoil of scarcely sketched phantoms who, full of an incoercible life the author gave them and cannot withdraw, play at overpowering one another, at securing each the center of the whole work and drawing to themselves all the interest of the *stage manager,* is very well rendered through a broken, panting dialogue. Pirandello has deeply seen that right here, in this *eccentricity* (literally meant), in this blind rushing to develop to the bitter end each separate seminal motif lies the whole essence of Nature or Life, what distinguishes it from Spirit, Art, which instead is coordination, synthesis, discipline, and thus choice and conscious sacrifice.

But this, which should be the play's central motif and indeed dominates it throughout Act I, finds no adequate development in Acts II and III, where we do not see, in scenic terms, the passage of characters from a lower to a higher level, for they fail to proceed from confusion to order, from chaos to artistic cosmos. Who was nature remains nature, who was realized only lyrically remains so. The play cannot come to light. Why? Because the *son* rebels against acting his role in the play, he is not cut out for scenes. The play fails, because instead of a coordinating spirit the characters meet a mediocre manager who tries to improvise it, and no work of art is to be improvised; it cannot be a mediocre manager, with no artistic experience or depth, a manager who sees only the so-called requirements of theater, to set up in a few hours a play needing no less than a painstaking elaboration. Yet this seems to me a particular reason, devoid of universal value and incapable of demonstrating anything. What universal meaning can be inferred from the fact that a tradesman of theater is unable to bring to fruition a theme left in its inchoate phase? To lead to complete expression of characters in whom whatever life was infused has not yet expressed itself?

In Acts II and III the dominant motif of the play interweaves with the one of the distortion actual life undergoes when passing into the mirror of art (a motif which reappears in Act I of *Vestire gli ignudi* [*Naked*]). In Act II there operates again the evil mirror which sends back to the individual his own unrecognizable image. For when they see the actors, exclusively preoccupied with the scenic truth to be achieved, repeat their own gestures and those words they had uttered in the urgency of unstilled passion, the characters no longer recognize themselves, and in their bewilderment, they burst into laughter or despair. The mirror is in this case the art of the stage (though whatever is said of it can be said of art in general), and when it is reflected in it, actual life in the common sense of the word, the life of interest and passion, appears to itself distorted and false. But by dwelling at length on this theme, Pirandello unknowingly transforms his characters (who should be more or less achieved artistic phantoms) into real beings, and by thus transferring them from the level of imagination onto the level of actual life he splits the play at the seams.

But there is still a third motif which interferes with the others to the play's detriment. Of the six characters in search of an author, each one already knows what will happen to himself and to the others: they have the total vision of their destiny. For instance, whenever the *father* and the *stepdaughter* place themselves at a certain point of the story and try to pick its thread up from there, there is present to the scene the *mother* who already knows how it will end, and in her foreknowledge she is induced not to witness the action passively, but to implore that she be spared the horrible spectacle about to take place. Thus sentimental considerations may emerge to trouble, tentatively, the necessary architecture of a work of art, which has its own inner logic not to be disturbed by any regard for the spectators' tender hearts. But this motif should have been developed much more deeply and with greater emphasis. Besides, Act III after all only treads in the footsteps of Act II, and the end of the play is quite absurd; it's any old epilogue, stuck there just to wind things up and let the curtain fall.

Yet despite these structural faults the play does remain the strongest attempt in Europe so far to realize scenically a process of pure states of mind, by analyzing and projecting onto the stage the various levels and phases of one stream of consciousness. The attempt had already been made by others in Italy, but never with such violence and daring ambition. The drama the six characters carry inside without yet managing to express it. . .is typically Pirandellian. The hints we get of it, broken, uncorrelated and confused as they must needs be, since they constitute a sketch and not an accomplished work of art, still have as much tragic power as one can imagine.

(30) The dangers such a theater incurs are intrinsic to its very nature, and the word *cerebralism* may sum them up (meaning, this time, arid intellectualistic contrivance). Of course it cannot be denied that Pirandello's characters look too much alike; rather than various characters, they seem one and the same character placed in ever different yet identical situations. Of course the progress of Pirandellian art moves not toward enrichment but toward the greater deepening of one and the same Weltanschauung. As all of Pirandello's work tends to the theater, so all his theater tends to one perfect work totally expressing the Pirandellian intuition of life, like a pyramid tending to one point into which everything underneath may converge and be resolved.

Often the play is the belabored and gray scenic dressing of an abstract reflection or of a situational device which preceded and replaced dramatic vision. Figures then become skeletal, frozen in a grimace, stuck in a mania which is the wooden covering of a set theme. Artistic value in those cases finds refuge entirely in the details of some scene. Words, circumscribed in their common meaning, are pale and deprived of imaginative radiance. The pattern will usually consist of a weird picturesque preparation serving to introduce abstract cogitations on a psychological or metaphysical truth.

But there are the plays born of a lively and powerful dramatic vision, to which abstract meditation is coeval and not preconceived: first of all, *Enrico IV* (*Henry IV*); then *Sei personaggi in cerca d'autore* (*Six Characters in Search of an Author*); *Il berretto a sonagli* (*Cap and Bells*); *Così è (se vi pare)* (*It Is So, if You Think So*); *Il piacere dell'onestà* (*The Pleasure of Honesty*); and, some notches down, *Pensaci, Giacomino!* (*Think It Over, Giacomino!*); *L'innesto* (*The Grafting*); *Come prima, meglio di prima* (*As Well as Before, Better than Before*); *Vestire gli ignudi* (*Naked*). Here whatever may be wooden or skeletal is a function of the peculiar dramatic insight, but under that deathly cold one senses the deep subterranean throb of life which finally breaks through; the frozen spasm will then melt into tears. Remaining always very simple (in fact the most sober and bare, the farthest from literary artifice, the most truly spoken idiom ever heard on our stages), the language of these plays is nimble, witty, juicy, bursting with vitality; dialogue is concise, detailed, unornate, and its fresh, relevant imagery admirably helps it to match the sinuosities of psychological becoming.

(31) And all the art of this great writer seems to be caught in a magnificent ascending movement. It seems to me that he is gradually liberating himself from the biggest flaw of his first theatrical works: what I once called, in *Voci del tempo* (*Voices of Our Time*), the imbalance between the smallness of results, all steeped in the particular, and the metaphysical grandiosity of Pirandello's preliminary intentions. It's an imbalance between the grandeur of such intentions and the story which should have expressed them scenically, usually a story of hopelessly pathetic petty bourgeois creatures living in backwoods small towns, of little boardinghouse tenants, of people catering to village clubs, in a bleak, depressing atmosphere.

How on earth, for instance, can we recognize the universal drama of self-knowledge as death (*As Well as Before, Better than Before*) in the story of courtesan Fulvia who, after many years spent in shameful abjection away from her husband's home, returns there to contemplate herself in the image her daughter Livia has conceived of her through blessed ignorance of her real identity as a person or as a mother? Or, again, in the story of State Councillor Martino Lori, who after six years of unbelievable gullibility wakes up to the fact that neither wife nor daughter were ever his own? The sorrow of the wretched man in Act III of *Tutto per bene* (*All for the Best*) is doubtless heartbreaking, but to share it we must postulate on his part an absolutely incredible, or at least unique blindness, which removes him from our compassion into a kind of estrangement.

Surely, even in these first plays, when the meaning Pirandello wants to squeeze from the story and the story itself succeed in finding their harmony we get actual masterpieces like *Il berretto a sonagli* (*Cap and Bells*). Where this harmony is not reached, beauty takes refuge in the details of some scene or character, mostly in the final scenes, when the mask drops and lays bare a sorrowing visage. But in *Six Characters* and in *Henry IV* the metaphysical urge shatters the puny frames which once throttled it, and it gets free play in ampler vicissitudes. The drama throbs with stronger life, its underlying metaphysical torment conquers an apter expression. The motifs are still the same, but tragedy unfolds in a higher, purer atmosphere. And Pirandello has not yet said his last word. He seems now to become increasingly aware of his original dramatic potential.

The first progress of the Sicilian artist took place when, having gone beyond the phase of the peasant short story in Verga's regional-naturalist mood, and beyond the subsequent phase of the ironic, skeptical short story based on manipulation of incident, and having passed from small- and large-scale fiction to the theater, he managed to integrate dramatically those motifs which in his earlier works of fiction lay side-to-side without substantial correlation, like gunpowder lacking a spark to fire it. In the production antedating *The Late Mattia Pascal* the synthesis of Pirandello's special humor is not yet really achieved. Pirandello endeavors to attain the artistic effect through a pessimistic narrative form in Verga's dramatic style, but intellectual negation prevents him from sharing wholeheartedly the anguish of his creatures. He would have us experience as drama what in his mind has been already overcome in a kind of philosophically resigned humor. In this phase of his art feeling and thought are juxtaposed rather than fused, and disturb each other.

This state of mind finds its most felicitous expression in *The Late Mattia Pascal,* where sorrow is overcome in the resigned acceptance of its absolute uselessness. After this novel, the art of Pirandello develops in such a way as to make ever more intimate the synthesis of its two basic elements, so that thought will be born along with feeling as its accompanying shadow. Live anguish gradually sheds any ironic felicity, any expressive indifference and intermediate nuance, to embody itself in ever leaner and more convulsed forms. That is when Pirandellian drama rises, from an intimate need. A second progress is now being made by the artist, who tends to clench the expression of his authentic dramatic center in all its purity and metaphysical universality. The progress made to date is the sure promise of the inevitably forthcoming masterpiece, in which Pirandello's vision of life will fully possess and express itself.

So far, one thing is sure: that with Pirandello for the first time Italian literature discovers how the spirit, far from being the simple, two-dimensional entity it once believed, is a chasm unfathomable by the eye, an unexplored region sounding with strange voices, streaked by phantasmagorias, peopled with monsters, where truth and error, reality and make-believe, wakefulness and dream, good and evil struggle forever tangling in the shadow of mystery. (pp. 20-34)

> *Adriano Tilgher, "Life versus Form," translated by Glauco Cambon, in* Pirandello: A Collection of Critical Essays, *edited by Glauco Cambon, Prentice-Hall, Inc., 1967, pp. 19-34.*

LUIGI PIRANDELLO   (essay date 1925)

[*In the following essay, Pirandello discusses the process of artistic creation that produced* Six Characters in Search of an Author *and how it relates to the themes of the play.*]

I had to, to escape from . . . well, that is what I am going to explain.

As I have written elsewhere, the lively little maid servant who for years and years now (though it seems as though it were only since yesterday) has been waiting on my writing, is for all that not so new at her work. She is often of a somewhat scornful and jesting humor, this *Fantasia* of mine. If, now and then, she is of a humor to dress in black, there is no denying that her solemn apparel is often extremely odd. But if you think that this is her usual style of dress, you are very much mistaken. Time and time again I've seen her put her hand in her pocket and pull out a fool's cap, red as a cox-comb, and all a-jingle with its tiny bells. This she claps on her head, and off she goes! Here today, and somewhere else tomorrow!—And she persists in bringing back with her the most disgruntled beings imaginable and filling up my house with them—men, women and children, all involved in the most extraordinary and complicated situations—their plans frustrated, their hopes deluded—in short, people it is often very uncomfortable to deal with.

Well, a few years ago *Fantasia* was unfortunately inspired—or it may have been just an unlucky whim on her part—to unload a whole family on me. I don't know where in the world she had fished these people up from, but she insisted that they were material for a perfectly gorgeous novel.

A man of about fifty, in black coat, light trousers, his eyebrows drawn into a painful frown, and in his eyes an expression mortified yet obstinate; a poor woman in widow's weeds, leading a little girl of about four by one hand and a boy of ten or so by the other; a pert, bold young miss, also in black, but an equivocal and brazen black it seemed, as she moved about in a constant flutter of disdainful biting merriment at the expense of the older man; and a young fellow of twenty-odd who stood apart from the others, seemingly locked within himself, as

Autographed handbill for three comedies by Pirandello. Instituto di Studi Pirandelliani, Roma.

though holding the rest in utter scorn . . . in short, the Six Characters just as they appear on the stage at the beginning of my play. At once they began telling me their misfortunes, first one, then another, each in turn silencing all the rest, as each in turn shouted out his story; and there they were flourishing their scattered passions in my face, just as in the play they flourish them in the face of the thoroughly misunderstanding Manager.

Can an author ever tell how and why his imagination gives birth to a certain character? The mystery of artistic creation is the mystery of birth itself.

A woman may desire a child, but the desire, however intense it may be, does not suffice to create; and then one fine day she discovers that her desire is to be realized, but she cannot tell at what precise moment the life within her came into being. And in just the same way the artist, who gathers within himself innumerable germs of life, can never say how, or why, or at what precise moment one of these particles of life has lodged in his imagination, there to become a living creature inhabiting a plane of life superior to our voluble and vain daily existence.

Well, all I can say is that, without my having sought them at all, there they were, those six characters you now can see on the stage, so alive you could touch them, so alive you could fairly hear them breathe. And there they stood, each with his secret torment, but bound to all the others by birth and by the tie of events experienced together, waiting for me to let them into the world of art by making of their persons, their passions, and their vicissitudes, a novel, a play, at the very least a short story.

They had come into the world alive and they wanted to live. Now no matter how strikingly individualized a character may be, I have never represented man, woman, or child, for the mere pleasure of representation. I have never related a single experience for the mere pleasure of relating it; I have never described a landscape for the mere pleasure of describing it.

There are authors—and they are not so few—who *do* write for the pleasure they take in the writing alone, and who look for no other satisfaction. Such writers one might describe as historical.

But there are others who, in addition to deriving the pleasure I have described, feel a spiritual need that will not permit them to use characters, events, or scenes which are not impregnated, so to speak, with a special sense of life that gives them a universal significance and value. Such writers are, properly speaking, philosophical. And to this latter group I have the misfortune to belong.

I hate symbolic art, for it makes a mechanical structure, an allegory, out of all representation, destroying its spontaneity, reducing the creative impulse to an empty and short-sighted effort; for the mere fact of giving an allegorical meaning to what is being represented indicates that the representation proper is held in low esteem, as having in itself no truth, whether real or imaginary. Such a representation has been prepared simply for the purpose of demonstrating some moral truth. But the spiritual need I referred to a moment ago cannot be satisfied by allegorical symbolism, except in the rare instances where, as in Ariosto, the motive is lofty irony. For the latter derives from a concept, or rather *is* a concept that is trying to become an image; but the former, on the contrary, tries to find in the image itself, which should be alive and spontaneous in every aspect of its expression, a meaning that will give it significance.

Now, for all my prying and searching, I could not succeed in finding any such meaning in these "characters." And I concluded therefore that there was no particular obligation on my part to give them the life for which they were clamoring.

"I have already tormented my readers with hundreds and hundreds of stories," I thought to myself. "Why should I bother them with an account of these six unfortunates, and their wretched plight?"

And acting on this feeling, I pushed them out of the way. Or rather, I did everything I could to get them out of the way.

But one doesn't give life to a character for nothing!

These creatures of my brain were not living *my* life any longer: they were already living a life of their own, and it was now beyond my power to deny them a life which was no longer in my control.

Persisting in my intention of driving them out of my mind, I found to my consternation that almost completely detached as they were now from any supporting narrative, emerging miraculously from the pages of the book containing them, they went right on living their own lives; from which at certain moments during the day they would turn aside to confront me in the solitude of my study. Now one, now another, now two of them together, would come to tempt me and propose scenes that I was to set down in dramatic form or simply describe; and they were always at great pains to point out the effects to be derived from their suggestions, and the singular and novel turn that some unique situation might take and the interest it would arouse, and so on, and so on.

For a moment I would give in; and this momentary weakening, this brief surrender, was enough for them to draw out of me additional life, and naturally with every particle of life that they thus acquired they grew all the better able to convince me, their powers of persuasion growing with their life, increasing as the life in them increased. And so it became more and more difficult for me to get rid of them in proportion as it became easier for them to appear before me and tempt me. Finally, as I have already suggested, they became an obsession—until suddenly I thought of a means of getting out of my predicament.

"Why not," thought I, "represent this unique situation—an author refusing to accept certain characters born of his imagination, while the characters themselves obstinately refuse to be shut out from the world of art, once they have received this gift of life? These characters are already completely detached from me, and living their own lives; they speak and move; and so, in the struggle to live that they have persistently maintained against me they have become dramatic characters, characters who can move and speak of their own initiative. They already see themselves in that light; they have learnt to defend themselves against me; they will learn how to defend themselves against others. So why not let them go where the characters of a play usually go to attain full and complete life—on a stage? Let's see what will happen then!"

Well, that's what I did. And of course things turned out just as they had to turn out: there was a mixture of the tragic and the comic, of the fantastic and the real, in a situation as humorous as it was novel and complicated. The play all of itself, by means of the breathing, speaking, moving characters in it, who carry the action and suffer its conflicts and clashes in their own persons, demands to be acted at any cost. It is the vain attempt to improvise on the stage the carrying out of this demand that constitutes the comedy.

First, the surprise of the company of actors who are rehearsing on a stage littered with sets and properties, a surprise mixed with incredulity at seeing those six characters appear on the stage and announce that they are looking for an author; then the mother's sudden faint and the instinctive interest of the actors in the tragedies they sense in her and in other members of that strange family; then the confused, ambiguous conflict that unexpectedly takes possession of that empty stage so little prepared to receive it; and, finally, little by little, the rising tide of that interest as the conflicting passions of father, step-daughter, son, and mother, break out and try to dominate each the other with tragic and lacerating fury.

And, lo, those six characters who had of their own initiative stepped up on the stage, suddenly find in themselves that sense of universal significance which I had at first sought in vain; they find it in the excitement of the desperate struggle each character carries on with the others and in the struggle that all of them together carry on with the Manager and the Actors who fail to understand them.

Unintentionally, without knowing it, each one of them, in defending himself against the accusations of the others, under the pressure of his agitation gives out as his own vivid passion and torment, passions and torments that for years have been those of my own being; the impossibility (we take it as a heart-rending deception) of establishing a mutual understanding on the empty abstractions of words; the multiple personality of every one of us, a composite with as many faces as there are possibilities of being in each of us; and finally the tragic conflict between Life, which is forever fluid, forever in flux, and Form, which hardens Life into immutable shapes from which Life itself withdraws.

Two of those characters in particular, the Father and the Daughter, recur again and again to the frightful and unchangeable fixity of their form in which both see the essence of their being perpetually imprisoned; for the one that unalterable shape is punishment, for the other vengeance; and this form, which is themselves, they defend against the vapid jests and the meaningless chatter of the actors, trying to make the commonplace Manager accept it, while he of course is intent on changing it and adapting it to the so-called requirements of the theatre.

The six characters are not seemingly all in the same stage of formation. This is not because some of them are of first, and some of secondary, importance, finished pictures and studies in the rough. That would be nothing more than the most elementary sort of perspective, necessary to any architectural composition of scene or narrative. Neither is it because they are not all completely formed for the purposes they serve. All six are at the same stage of artistic realization and all six are on the same plane of reality—and this is the strange part of the play. Yet the Father and the Step-Daughter, and also the Son, are realized as *mind,* while the Mother is *nature;* and the Boy who looks on and makes gestures, and the Child, both absolutely inert, are no more than onlookers taking part by their presence merely. This creates a perspective of another sort. Unconsciously I had felt that I must realize some of the characters (artistically speaking) more completely, others less so, barely suggesting others still as elements of a story to be narrated or represented; those who are most intensely alive, the Father and Step-Daughter, naturally come forward and direct and drag along the almost dead weight of the others; of whom

one, the Son, is reluctant, while the Mother, like a resigned victim, stands between those two small creatures, the children, who have scarcely any being except that of appearance, and who need to be led by the hand.

And that is just how they ought to appear—in the stage of creation arrived at in the author's imagination at the moment he attempts to drive them away from him.

When I stop to think of it, to understand this artistic necessity, and then unconsciously to comply with it and resolve it by means of this perspective seem to me nothing short of a miracle. The truth of the matter is that the play was conceived in one of those moments of illumination when the imagination acts with untrammelled spontaneity, and when, for a wonder, all the faculties of the mind are working together in a superb harmony. No human brain, coldly attacking this problem, could ever have succeeded, no matter how hard it tried, in grasping and satisfying all the necessities of this form. Therefore whatever I may say in order to throw light on its significance and importance should not be interpreted as something I thought out before I set to work—as a defence of that work in short; but as a progressive discovery which little by little I have been able to make and which I shall certainly never complete in the brief span of my mortal life.

I have tried to represent six characters in search of an author. Their play does not take shape precisely because the author they are looking for fails them; and the play actually presented consists of their vain attempt to induce him to satisfy their wishes—by giving them a play, a comedy, to act; but the play is a tragedy also, because these six characters fail of attaining their purpose. The author turns them down!

But can an author represent a character even while he is refusing to deal with him? It seems clear enough that, in order to represent a character, an author must first welcome him into his imagination before he can "express" him. And that is what I did. I took those six characters in and realized them; but I took them in and realized them *as having been turned down.*

But let us understand precisely what it was that was turned down; not the characters evidently, but their play—the very thing that interested them above all else, of course. But it didn't interest me at all, for the reasons I have pointed out.

And what, for a character in a play, constitutes his comedy or tragedy as the case may be?

Every creature born of the imagination, every being art creates, must have his own play, that is to say, a play of which he is the hero and for which he is the dominating character. That play is the *raison d'être* of that particular character; it is his life process; it is necessary for his existence.

So far as the six were concerned, I accepted their existence: but I refused the reason for their existence; I accepted the organism as it had developed but in place of its own function I assigned to it another more complex function in which its own original function scarcely figured at all. A terrible and desperate situation for both of them, Father and Step-Daughter, for of all the six it was they who were most eager to live, who were most fully conscious of being characters, that is to say, absolutely dependent on a play, on their own play, since that is the only one they are capable of imagining. Yet that is the play that is turned down! An impossible situation in short, a situation they must get out of at any cost for it is a matter of life and death. True, I did give them another *raison d'être* than their own, another function—nothing less than the "impossible'' situation, the dramatic situation, which consists of being turned down and in search of an author; but they cannot even suspect—since they already have a life of their own—that this has now become their real reason for being, and a sufficient cause for their existence. If anyone should tell them so they wouldn't believe it;—how is it possible to believe that the only reason for one's existence resides wholly in a ceaseless torment that seems as unjust as it is unexplainable?

I cannot imagine therefore why I was found fault with because the character of the Father, instead of remaining what he should have been, went beyond his own characteristics and rôle as a character, at times trespassing on the author's own activities and adopting them as his own. I, who can understand those who do not understand me, see plainly enough that the blame comes from the fact that this character gives out as his own a work of the spirit that is recognized as being mine. That he does so is perfectly natural and of no significance whatever. This travail of spirit in the character of the Father derives from causes and reasons which have nothing to do with the drama of my personal experience—a consideration which of itself would rob the criticism in question of all semblance of consistency. However, I wish further to make it plain that the inherent activity of my mind—an activity that I have every right to let one of the characters reflect provided I make it organic—is one thing; while the activity my mind carries on for the purpose of realizing this work, the activity which succeeds finally in giving shape to the play of those six characters in search of an author, is quite another. If the Father participated in this activity, if he helped to form the play the essence of which is the authorlessness of those six characters, why then— then only!—would one be justified in saying that the Father is at times the author himself, and is therefore not what he should be! But the Father exists as a character in search of an author: he suffers that destiny, he does not create it; he endures it as an inexplicable fatality, and the situation in which he finds himself is one against which he rebels with all his strength, trying to remedy it; he is therefore really a character in search of an author and nothing more, even though he does express as though it were his own the activity of my mind. If he really did share in the author's activity that fatality would be easily explained; that is to say he would be admitted—as an *unadmitted* character—into the very centre and core of the poet's creative imagination, and would no longer have any cause to feel despair because he could not find anyone to affirm and compose his life as a character; I mean that he would accept willingly enough the *raison d'être* given him by the author and would without a moment's hesitation throw his own overboard, promptly consigning the Manager and the Actors, to whom he had appealed as his only recourse, to the devil.

There is one character, the Mother, on the other hand, to whom the mere fact of having life, considered as an end in itself, is not of the slightest importance. For she never doubts for a moment that she is already alive, nor does it ever occur to her to inquire in what respect and why she is alive. In other words she is not aware of being a character, for she is never, not even for a single moment, detached from her ''part.'' She doesn't even know she has a ''part.''

This makes her perfectly organic. In fact, her rôle as mother does not permit her to be mentally active. And she has no ''mind;'' she lives in a stream of feeling that never ceases, so that she cannot become conscious of her own life, that is to say, of her being a character. But for all that, even she, in her own way and for her own ends, is searching for an author. At

a certain moment she seems pleased at being brought before the Manager. Because she hopes to gain more life through him? No; but because she hopes the Manager will give her a scene to act with her son, a scene into which she would put a large part of her own life. But the scene does not exist: it has never nor could it ever have taken place. That shows to what a degree she is unaware of being a character, unaware that is, of the life she may possess, fixed and determined moment by moment in every gesture and in every word she speaks.

She comes on the stage with the others, but she does not know what she is being made to do. Apparently she imagines that the mania for life which is constantly assailing her husband and daughter, and on account of which she too is dragged on to a stage is nothing more than another of the usual incomprehensible eccentricities of that cruelly tormenting and cruelly tormented husband of hers, or—and this is what for her makes it so frightful—another questionable move on the part of her poor erring daughter. She is entirely passive. The circumstances of her life and what they have come to mean in her eyes, her own nature, are all given by the other characters, never by herself, and only once as her natural instinct rises up rebelliously in her does she contradict them to make it clear that she had no intention of abandoning either her husband or her son; but that the child was taken away from her and that her husband forced her to abandon him. She is able to set you right on questions of fact, but she does not know and she cannot explain anything else.

Briefly, she is *nature*, nature fixed in the form of a mother.

As to the new kind of satisfaction I found in this character, I must say a word. Nearly all my critics, instead of defining the Mother as un-human—this seems to be the peculiar and incorrigible nature of all my characters without exception—have been good enough to note ''with unaffected pleasure'' that at last my imagination had given birth to an extraordinary *human* character. This unlooked for praise I explain in this fashion: my poor Mother is tightly bound to her natural function as mother, and cannot possibly function mentally or spiritually; that is to say, being hardly more than a piece of flesh living completely in the functions of bearing, suckling, nursing and loving her progeny without ever needing to use her brain, she realizes in herself the perfectly typical ''human being!'' Of course! For nothing is more superfluous in the human organism than the mind!

My critics expected with this praise to dismiss the Mother and made no attempt to penetrate to the kernel of poetic values this character possesses in the play. A ''most human'' figure, yes, since the character entirely lacks mental activity, that is to say, is unaware of being what she is and takes no interest in explaining to herself how it happens that she is as she is. But the fact that she does not know she is a character in a play does not prevent her from being one. That is her dramatic situation in my **Six Characters**. And the most vivid expression of this situation flashes out in her cry to the Manager when he tells her to pause and consider that as all these things she is relating have already occurred they should not cause her to weep afresh. ''No, it is happening now, it is always happening! My torture is not feigned! I am alive, I feel every moment of my torment. My torment too is alive and in every breath I draw!''—She feels all this, without understanding it, as something inexplicable therefore: but she feels it with such terrible force that it does not even occur to her that it could be explained to her or to the others. She feels it—that suffices. She feels it as grief, and this grief at once cries out. And that is how she reflects the hardening of her life in a form—the same thing that in quite another fashion torments the Father and the Daughter. With them it is mind; with her, nature. The mind rebels and tries to draw whatever advantage it can from its torment; but nature, unless stimulated by the senses, can only weep.

The conflict between Life and Form is inexorably a condition of the spiritual order; it is also inherent in the natural order. Life, which abandons its fluidity in order to become fixed in our bodily form, little by little kills its form. In the irreparable and continuous aging of our bodies the nature fixed in those particular forms has an eternal cause for complaint. The Mother's plaint is both passive and perpetual. Revealed through three different faces, made significant in three distinct and simultaneous conflicts, it is in this play that the dramatic struggle between Life and Form finds its most complete expression. Moreover, in that poignant outburst of hers to the Manager, the Mother also brings out the particular significance of the form of life created by the human spirit: that is to say, the artistic form—a form which does not congeal, which does not kill, its own life and which life does not devour. If the Father and the Daughter were to begin their scene a hundred thousand times, invariably, at the appointed moment, in the second when the life of the work of art is to be expressed by the Mother's cry, that cry would resound—unchangeable and unchanging in form, not as a mechanical repetition is unchanging, a repetition required by external forces, but alive and as though new each time, and each time suddenly born to live forever—embalmed alive in imperishable fixity! Always, when we open the *comedy,* we find the living Francesca confessing her sweet sin to Dante; and though we should read that passage a hundred thousand times in succession, Francesca will still a hundred thousand times repeat her words, not mechanically, but as though each time were the first, and with such vivid and sudden passion that the poet each time will turn faint with his emotion!

All that lives, by the sheer fact of living, has a form and so must die; all except the work of art which, on the contrary, lives forever insofar as it is form.

The birth of a creation of the human imagination, that step across the threshold from nothingness to eternity, can occur suddenly, when some necessity has served as its matrix. In a play that is imagined a character does and says whatever is necessary, he is born just the character he ought to be. That is how Madame Pace comes to life among the six characters, with all the effect of a miracle or a surpassingly clever trick realistically portrayed. But it isn't a trick. That is a real birth, and the new character is alive, not because the character was alive before, but because successfully ushered into life, as required by the very fact of her being a character—she is obliged to be as she is. As she steps on the scene there is a break therefore, a sudden change in the planes of reality on the stage, because a character can come to life that way only in the imagination of the poet and not on the boards of the stage itself. Without anyone's noticing it, I suddenly changed the nature of the scene; at that precise moment I took it back into my imagination but without removing it from the sight of the audience; that is to say, instead of the stage. I showed them my imagination in the act of creating, as though it were a kind of stage. The sudden and uncontrollable transformation of some form of appearance from one plane of reality to another is a miracle of the same kind as that accomplished by the Saint who animates his statue, which for that moment is certainly neither of wood nor of stone. But it is not an arbitrary kind of miracle. That stage, since it receives the imagined reality of the six characters, does not exist of itself as a fixed and immutable fact, just as nothing in the play exists in advance—everything is actually in the making, everything about it moves and changes, always impromptu, always tentative. Even the plane of reality in which all this formless life moves and flows in its eager search for form is thus organically displaced. When I conceived of having Madame Pace come to life then and there on that stage, I felt sure I could carry out my conception, and I did so; if I had noticed that this sudden birth suddenly and in a twinkling broke in upon and gave another shape to the plane of reality of the scene, I would certainly never have attempted it, for I would have been appalled by its apparent lack of logic, which would have thus have inflicted an unfortunate injury on the beauty of my play. But the fervor of my imagination saved me; because, in the face of a deceptive logic, that fantastic coming to life is demanded by an artistic necessity that is mysteriously and organically correlated with the life of the whole work.

When anyone tells me that my play is not as good as it might be because, instead of being smooth and stately, it is chaotic in expression, and sins by its romanticism, I am forced to smile.

I can understand of course why this criticism is made. As I have written this play, the dramatic presentation of the six characters appears tumultuous and unruly. It never proceeds in an orderly fashion: it lacks logical development—there is no stringing together of events. True enough! Had I gone out to look for it with a lantern I could not have found a more disorderly, eccentric, capricious and complicated manner, a more *romantic* manner, in short, of presenting the drama in which the six characters are involved. True again! But as it happens, that is not the play I have presented. The play I am dealing with is quite another play—I need not repeat what that play is! But aside from the various excellences to be found in it according to one's taste, it contains a sustained satire of romantic methods; for while my characters are in such a fever to outdo themselves in the parts each of them has in one play— their play, I am presenting them as characters in another play— my play! This they neither know nor suspect. As a result the extreme agitation their passions cause in them—a trait of romantic treatment—is humorously superimposed on sheer void. And the play of the six characters, represented not as it would have been composed by my imagination if my imagination had accepted it, could not have a place in my work except as a "situation" to be developed somehow or other, and could not come out except in eruptive, incoherent commands, in violent short-cuts, chaotically, in short, perpetually interrupted, led off the track, contradicted, actually *denied* by one of its characters, and not even seen by two of them!

One of the characters—the Son, who denies the conflict which makes him a "character"—derives his importance, his "substantiality," from the fact, not that he is a character in the play-in-the-making,—for he scarcely appears at all in that capacity—but that he is a character in my representation of the play-in-the-making. He is in short the only one who lives as a "character in search of an author" and nothing else; to such a degree that the author he is looking for is not a dramatic author. This too could not very well be otherwise. Moreover, not only is the attitude of this character completely organic in my conception, but he heightens the general confusion and disorder, besides being another element of romantic contrast.

It was precisely this organic and natural chaos that I had to represent. But to depict chaos does not mean that one must proceed chaotically, romantically! The method I have used is the very opposite of chaotic. It is clear, simple, and orderly, as is evident from the way the plot, the characters, the several planes of reality, imaginary and real, the dramatic and comic values, have all been accepted by the play-going publics of the world; and for those who have eyes to see further the play contains still other values, by no means the usual values, and of no mean scope. Great is the confusion of tongues among men if there are words in which criticisms of this nature can find expression. The confusion is the confusion of the law of order itself which this play of mine observes in every particular, and which makes it a classical and typical play, while at the same time forbidding its ultimate catastrophe to find expression in a single word. It is made clear to everyone witnessing the play that Life cannot be created by artifice, that the play of the six characters, lacking as it does an author to nourish it in the womb of his spirit, cannot be represented for the vulgar satisfaction of someone who wishes merely to know how an event developed. This event is recorded by the Son in the material succession of its moments, but it is entirely devoid of meaning and therefore does not need even a human voice to express it; but, with its own material voice, and for the simple reason that the event had happened before, it happens again. Ugly and useless, catastrophe swoops down with the detonation of a weapon—a piece of mechanism—on the stage, shattering and throwing to the four winds the sterile attempt of characters and actors to make their play without the help of the poet.

If I dare not heed the statement which G. B. Shaw has seen fit to make—that *Six Characters in Search of an Author* is the most original and dynamic play ever written in any nation, or at any time, whether ancient or modern—I can at least feel in all conscience that the appearance of the *Six Characters* marks a date in the history of the Italian theatre which it will not be possible for the supporters of the "old" drama to ignore. (pp. 36-52)

Luigi Pirandello, "*Pirandello Confesses . . . ,*" in The Virginia Quarterly Review, *Vol. 1, No. 1, April, 1925, pp. 36-52.*

WALTER STARKIE (essay date 1926)

[*Starkie was an Irish critic and literary historian who specialized in Romance languages and gypsy folklore. In the following excerpt from his study* Luigi Pirandello *(1926), he examines thematic and stylistic elements of Pirandello's short stories.*]

Italy is the country *par excellence* for the short story, and from Boccaccio to Pirandello, Italian authors have always known how to adapt their inspiration to this most difficult form of literature. English writers have never been able to make a complete success of the short-story form. The neatness of finish, the lightness of touch, the vivid style, seem far truer to the genius of Latin peoples, whose qualities are of the spontaneous kind. Northern nations produce novel writers in abundance, because in the North men brood over their sorrows and there is calculation even in their joy. Just as their lives in sunless climes are governed by will-power, so their literature is above all things an expression of their inner thoughts, an analysis of their passions. In the South, where the sun shines and where men's passions rise high, happiness, as Nietzsche once said, is short, sudden and without reprieve. There is less calculation and analysis, and more spontaneity. There is less sustained effort, but more frequent flashes of inspiration. This is especially true of Pirandello. In his longer novels there are many prolix passages which fatigue even the most hardened Piran-

dellian. In his short stories, on the other hand, Pirandello is rarely prolix, and he has a variety of methods of treatment worthy of Guy de Maupassant. But it is only the outer technique that resembles the Parisian writer: whereas Maupassant the malicious and sarcastic novelist deserves, according to Croce, the name of ingenuous poet, Pirandello must not be considered thus. The adjective "ingenuous" is the antithesis to his self-conscious art. Maupassant suffers and rejoices with his characters—he is all sensibility. Pirandello rarely shows any pity openly. The pity we feel for his characters is derived from our sense of pain at the heartlessness of the author. Both authors are profoundly pessimistic and a-religious. God is absent from both, and we have a sense of desolation and sadness. Guy de Maupassant watches the sad destiny of humanity with pity and with composed serenity; Pirandello is never serene, because he suffers ceaselessly in himself. He is more egotistical than Maupassant and thinks for ever of his own woes, not of those of his characters. Every short story of Pirandello is, as it were, a myth in the Platonic sense, to explain his subjective philosophy. And this philosophy is the philosophy of the individual, because Pirandello, like most of the moderns, would deny that there is a real world of things and persons, existing by itself outside the spirit which knows it. Like Maupassant, Pirandello would refuse to be called a realist, saying that "the great artists are those who display to other men their illusion," but he would go farther in his statement. For him the world is only a dream, a mirage, a phenomenon, an image created by our spirit. There are no such things as fixed characters, for life is ever changing, ever ebbing and flowing. Thus we find it very difficult to seize hold of these characters: they often resemble those modernist pictures wherein the painter has tried to paint the subjects in motion. It is for this reason that Pirandello is a symbol of all our present age: his fantastic stories are symbols of the struggle that goes on ceaselessly in all the minds of modern men. There is no dolorous serenity in his work, because the mind of to-day cannot rest: there are few men of flesh and bone in his novels, because flesh and bone are of no account. The world of Pirandello resembles that of Lucretius: shimmering myriads of atoms that combine by chance with one another and produce now a tree, now a man, now a beast—all according to the rules of chance.

Pirandello has been unceasing in his production of short stories ever since the first years of the present century. In these stories we can see his evolution as an artist. In the earlier collections, such as *Quand'ero matto, Bianche e nere, Erma bifronte, La vita nuda* and *Terzetti,* many of these stories are . . . Sicilian. They are in many cases simple and unaffected in style and purged of rhetoric, as if he had attempted to cultivate the short rhythmic style of Maupassant. Gradually then we notice a tendency to prolixity and rhetoric—towards dialogue which announced the future dramatist. In many of the later volumes of stories, such as *Berecche e la guerra* and *Il carnevale dei Morti,* the story is the merest excuse for long pieces of tortuous sophistry. (pp. 112-14)

First of all let us consider some stories in the earlier editions which might seem to reappear again and again with slight variations through the author's entire production. One of his favourite plots for his short stories is to show how "the best-laid plans of mice and men gang aft agley." In "**La vita nuda**" ("**Life in Its Nakedness**"), a story which has given its name to a volume, a young girl whose fiancé on the eve of the wedding has died suddenly, visits a sculptor to order a memorial in honour of the dead man. Stricken with grief, her one thought is to symbolize eternally her sorrows by representing

Life in the form of a young girl resigning herself to the embraces of Death, represented as a skeleton holding out the bridal ring. At first, under the influence of sorrow, the lady insists, contrary to the wishes of the sculptor, that the figure of Life should be clothed, but later on, when she falls in love with the sculptor's friend and her recollection of the dead fiancé has begun to fade, she insists that Life should be shown in its symbolic nakedness resisting the contact of Death.

On other occasions Pirandello takes the opposite course, and makes his characters lament over the past that will never return. In **"Prima notte"** . . . , he describes the marriage between Lisi Chirico and Marastella, village folk of Sicily. Lisi was a widower, and Marastella had been in love with a youth who perished in a shipwreck. The bridal couple spend their first night in the graveyard; she weeps over the tomb of her lost love, he calls on his dead wife by name: "The moon gazed from heaven down on the little graveyard in the uplands. She alone on that fragrant April night saw these two black shadows on the yellow little path near two tombs. Don Lisi, bending over the grave of his first wife, sobbed: 'Nunzia, Nunzia, do you hear me?'"

Such a story, in spite of the morbid and rather unnatural thesis it develops, is a good illustration of Pirandello's power. More than most modern authors he is able to convey to his readers a haunting sensation of sadness that does not leave us even when we have laid aside the book. Lisi Chirico and Marastella are not normal human beings: they are too neurotic, too highly strung for country folk; but so subtly does the author paint the background that they stand out in bold relief. And this skill of the author in drawing his background does not appear by direct touches, after the manner of a Thomas Hardy. Except for the last few lines which we have quoted there is no pictorial description. We infer the setting of the story from the dialogue bandied about by the characters. Pirandello's skill in producing the atmosphere he requires for his story or drama recalls the methods adopted by Jacinto Benavente, another master of the indirect description. As in the case of Benavente, too, if we probe deeply the mind of our Pirandello, we reach sentimentality—a modern sentimentality which hides away from the light of day and erects a structure of irony and cynicism as a barrier to protect its sensitiveness. The last story we treated showed traces of the sentimental, but perhaps the most characteristic example occurs in the story, **"Il lume dell' altra casa,"** from the collection *Terzetti*. Tullio Butti, the hero, like eighty per cent of the Pirandello heroes, is a queer, grotesque fellow. It is a good thing that the world of Pirandello is the stuff of dreams: what a miserable state real life would be if all men were like Mattia Pascal or Tullio Butti! Tullio Butti seemed to have a feeling of rancour against life. Nobody was ever able to make him take any interest in anything or relax his sullen, introspective gaze. Even his talkative landlady and her daughter were unable to humanize him. From the window of his room Tullio could see into the house at the opposite side of the street. In the evening, looking out at the windows of the house, he saw a family sitting round the dinner-table, and at the head sat the father and mother. The children were waiting in eager impatience for their food to be served. All were laughing gaily, and the mother and father laughed too. Every evening Tullio sat in darkness and gazed at the lighted window opposite, and it became his one joy in life. But the inquisitive daughter of his landlady, noticing that he used to remain hours in his room without a light, did a very excusable thing under the circumstances: she looked through the keyhole and saw Tullio standing gazing at the lit-up window. And forthwith she rushed off in hot haste to her mother to relate that he was in love with

Margherita Masci, the lady opposite. Soon afterwards Tullio saw with surprise his own landlady enter the room opposite when the husband was not there and talk to the lady. The same evening, as a result of that conversation, the lady came to the window and whispered across to him good night. From that day onwards Tullio did not wait eagerly in his room for the illumination of the window opposite: nay, he waited impatiently until that light should be extinguished. With terrible suddenness the passion of love raged in the heart of that man who had been for so long a stranger to life. He left his lodgings, and on the same day as he left, the tidings came that the lady opposite had abandoned her husband and three children. Tullio's room remained empty for some months, but one evening he returned bringing the lady with him. She begged for leave to stand at the window and look across at the other house, where sat the sad father surrounded by the three downcast children. In this tale there is a warmth of sentiment that is lacking in many of the stories, but even here there is the sting characteristic of Pirandello. The tragedy arises as usual from the meddling curiosity and gossip of people who are not concerned. It is the talkative landlady who lights the fatal fuse. The moral is the same as in countless modern plays where evil gossip breaks up the peace of families.

The same tender sadness appears in **"La camera in attesa"** (contained in the collection *E domani lunedì*). Three sisters and their widowed mother have been awaiting for some years the return of the brother and son, Cesarino, who went off to Tripoli on a military campaign. For fourteen months they have had no news of him, and as a result of repeated inquiry it has been ascertained that Cesarino has not been found among the dead or the wounded or the prisoners. Ever awaiting his return, the four women have kept his room ready for him. Every morning the water in the bottle is changed, the bed is remade, the nightshirt is unfolded, and once a week the old clock is wound up again. Everything is in order for his coming. Nothing shows the time that has elapsed except perhaps the candle, which in weary waiting has grown yellow, for the sisters do not change it as they do the water in the bottle. At first all the neighbours were greatly moved by this case, but little by little their pity cooled and changed to irritation, even in some a certain sense of indignation for what they called play-acting. But the neighbours forget that life only consists in the reality that we give to it. Thus the life that Cesarino continues to have for his mother and sisters may be sufficient for them, owing to the reality of the acts they perform for him here in the room which awaits him, just as it was when he left. The reality of Cesarino's existence remains unalterable in this room of his and in the heart and mind of his mother and sisters, who outside this reality have no other. Time is fixed immutable were it not for Claretta, the betrothed of Cesarino. The thought of her makes the four women note the passing time. In the first days she used to visit them daily, but gradually, as time dragged on, her visits became rarer. The old mother, who counts the days that elapse between each visit, is surprised that whereas the departure of Cesarino seems only yesterday, so much time passes for Claretta. The culminating point of the tragedy arrives when the news is brought that Claretta is getting married. The mothers lies dying; the three daughters look at her with sad envy. She will soon be able to go and see if he is over there; she will be relieved of the anxiety of that long wait: she will reach certainty, but she will not be able to return and tell them. The mother, though she knows for certain that she will find her Cesarino over there, feels a great pity for her daughters, who will remain alone and have such need to believe that he is still alive and will return soon. And thus with her last breath she whispers to them: "You will tell him that I have waited so long." And on that night in the silent house the room is left untouched, the water is not changed, the date on the calendar marks the previous day. "The illusion of life in that room has ceased for one day and it seems for ever." Only the clock continues to speak of time in that endless waiting.

Again and again the same theme recurs in the *novelle* in different forms. "What makes life is the reality which you give to it." Thus the life that Cesarino Mochi's mother and his three sisters live in that room of his is sufficient for them. If you have not seen your son for some years, he will seem different to you when he returns. Not so Cesarino; his reality remains unchangeable there in his room which is set in expectation of his coming. . . . In **"I pensionati della memoria"** (**"The Pensioners of Memory"**), Pirandello treats the same idea, but takes it up where the former story left off. Supposing even that the mother and sisters had been present at the death of Cesarino and had watched his coffin being lowered into the grave, would they not feel that he had departed for ever, never to return? But no, gentlemen, Pirandello tells us that Cesarino's mother and sisters and many of us would find that the dead man comes back behind us to our homes after the funeral. He pretends to be dead within his coffin, but, as far as all of us are concerned, he is not dead. He is here with me just as much as you are, except that he is disillusioned. "His reality has vanished, but which one? Was it the reality that he gave to himself? What could I know of his reality—what do you know about it? I know what I gave to him from my own point of view. His illusion is mine." And yet these people, though I know that they are dead, come back with me to my house. They have not got a reality of their own, mark you; they cannot go where they please, for reality never exists by itself. Their reality now depends on me, and so they must perforce come with me: they are the poor pensioners of my memory. Most people, when friends or relations die, weep for them and remember this or that trait in their character which makes the feeling of bereavement seem greater. But all this feeling of bereavement, this sorrow, is for a reality which they believe to have vanished with the deceased. They have never reflected on the meaning of this reality. Everything for them consists in the existence or in the non-existence of a body. It would be quite enough consolation for these people if we made them believe that the deceased is here no more in bodily form, not because his body is buried in the earth, but because he has gone off on a journey. This will be their consolation. The real reason why we all weep over our dead friend is because he cannot make his presence a reality to us. His eyes are closed, his hands are stiff and cold: he does not hear or perceive us, and it is this insensibility that plunges us in sorrow. Owing to his death our one comfort has departed—the reciprocity of illusion. If he had only gone off on a journey, we could live on in hope like Cesarino's sisters, saying to ourselves: "He thinks of me over there and thus I live for him."

In the stories we have considered there are traces of a kindlier Pirandello. Sometimes he produces a deep emotional effect on his reader when he ceases to try to solve a problem or work out a knotted intrigue. In **"Il ventaglino"** (**"The Little Fan"**) we see a little scene in a public park in Rome on a hot and dusty afternoon in August. So subtle is the author's method of description in this story that we visualize the scene. The park is dusty and the yellow houses nearby are forlorn and desolate; men are slumbering in the sultry atmosphere. On one seat a thin little old man with a yellow handkerchief on his head is reading a paper; nearby a workman out of work sleeps with

his head leaning on his arms. On the other side an old woman listens to the sad tale of a woman nearby, and then departs after giving her a piece of bread. Then there is a red-haired girl who walks up and down impatiently: she is evidently waiting for somebody. All these people Pirandello describes for us impressionistically. Amongst them appears poor Tuta with her baby in her arms. Tuta is alone in the world with her baby. She has but a penny in her pocket and the child is famished. "Not a single person would believe that she was in such hopeless want. She could hardly believe it herself. But it had come to that. She had entered that park to find a shady spot and had loitered there for the past two hours: she could remain on until evening, but then . . . where was she to spend the night with that child in arms? And next day? And the day after that? . . . Ah, Nino, there is nothing for it but the river for both of us." Then Tuta watches mechanically the people crowding into the park in the cool of the evening: children skipping, nurses carrying babies, governesses, soldiers in uniform. Something seemed to change her line of thought. She looked up at the people and smiled. She unbuttoned the neck of her coat and uncovered a little of her white neck. Just then an old man passed by selling paper fans. With her last penny she bought one. Then "opening still more of her blouse and starting to fan slowly her uncovered breast she laughed and began to look invitingly and provokingly at the soldiers who were passing by."

Such a story shows us Pirandello at his best, because in it he avoids any criticism of his characters. He limits himself to exposing objectively the results of his observations. In the majority of the stories the author tries to justify himself, and he insists on criticizing and interpreting his characters to us. In such exquisite stories as **"Il lume dell' altra casa,"** **"La camera in attesa"** or **"Il ventaglino,"** the characters and the atmosphere they create round themselves tell us the inferences to be drawn. Pirandello tells us more about his characters than any preceding novelist: he allows them to blurt out all the thoughts that are passing through their minds. One of the reasons why nearly all his characters are abnormal is because he will not content himself with exposing their exterior, obvious personality, but tries to reach even their subconscious thoughts and actions. Pirandello never stops short at the objective observation of character: irresistibly he is driven on to interpret and comment critically upon the children of his imagination. And this critical and interpretative attitude of mind often chills the inspiration and kills the character. When Pirandello the critic and dilettante metaphysician appears on the scene, Poetry in fright takes to her heels and flees away. . . . [The] whole basis of Futurism consists in pitiless criticism of the past. The Futurists believe that "Passéisme" (one of Marinetti's coined words) is synonymous with all that is evil, because its devotees in their thought and art are incapable of understanding the essence of modern life. It is therefore not surprising that Pirandello's works should be full of the close reasoning and criticism of the modern mind, especially as he himself is a vacillating Futurist—one who belongs to the older generation and yet has found a place at the table of the present-day youths.

Sometimes Pirandello's stories are feasts of dialectic and there is no attempt at weaving a story. They are, as it were, dialogues between the author and himself about metaphysical problems, and no abnormality is too exaggerated to illustrate his point. We find a woman of forty years of age who allowed herself to be seduced by a peasant youth of nineteen and became *enceinte*. Then after marrying him to calm the scandal, she commits suicide rather than allow him to possess her again.

Pirandello as a student in Bonn.

In another story a youth who is in Holy Orders loses his faith and goes back to his country village, to become the butt for the ridicule of all. But he sees the folly of everything and minds not their jeering insults. His sensitive mind becomes pantheistic and turns to all the manifestations of Nature, especially those plants and flowers that bloom for but one short day. The more fragile and humble those plants or insects, the more they excited his compassion and moved him to tears. Sometimes it was an ant or a fly or even a blade of grass. All these tiny things set off the enormous vacuity of the universe, the unknown. For a month he had been watching intently a blade of new grass growing between two stones in a ruined chapel. Every day he went to see it and protect it from marauding goats and sheep. One day he saw a young lady in the chapel, and distractedly she picked the blade of grass and put it in her mouth. Then the youth felt irresistibly impelled to hurl the epithet "stupid" at her. After hearing about this insult, her fiancé challenged the youth to a duel and wounded him fatally. When the priest was hearing the poor boy's confession at the point of death, he asked him why he had acted thus. He replied gently, "Father, for a blade of grass." And all thought that he was continuing still to rave. In other stories Pirandello draws on all his fund of grotesqueness in order to produce his "creepy" effect; peasants filled with insane hatred against rich neighbours who have lately arrived, or else a man who feels such loathing for his wife because of her infidelity that he locks her in the upper part of the house while below he brings in drunken prostitutes to sleep with him. In those stories life seems to be

a hideous nightmare and everything is out of focus. Every character suffers from some fixation to the point of madness. The irony of Pirandello disappears, and all that we see is one of those grinning masks which frighten children. Such stories often produce a terrifying effect on readers, because these abnormal beings have a complete logic of their own—the logic of the madman. More than any writer of to-day Pirandello is able to convey to us the emotion of horror. Let us quote one story called "**E due.**" . . . A young man one evening, while walking on the outskirts of the city near the bridge over the river, sees a man climb on to the parapet, lay down his hat there, and then cast himself into the river. Diego hears the terrible splash in the water beneath—then not a sound—absolute silence on all sides. And yet the man was drowning there beneath him. Why did he not move or shout for help? It was too late. Pirandello in masterly manner suggests the surroundings as they appeared to the horror-struck youth. The houses opposite in darkness, in contrast to the lights of the city: in the silence not a sound except far off the chirrup of crickets, and beneath him he heard the gurgling of the dark waters of the river. And that hat—the hat which the unfortunate man had left on the parapet—it fascinates us as it fascinated Diego: he cannot drive it from his thoughts. Later on we find him on the parapet again. He took off his hat and placed it in the same place as the other had been: "He went to the far side of the lamp to see what his hat looked like on the parapet, under the light of the lamp like the other. He stood for a few moments, leaning over the parapet and looking at it, as if he himself was not there any more. Then suddenly he gave a grim laugh; he saw himself stuck up there like a cat behind the lamp, and his hat was the mouse. . . . Away, away with all this tomfoolery! He climbed over the parapet: he felt his hair stand on end—his hands quivered as they clung tightly on to the ledge. Then he loosened his grip and threw himself into the void." In such a story Pirandello shows qualities of subtle analysis and description which rival Maupassant; it is only at the end, when the character watches itself act, that we see the cloven hoof of the Pirandellian. At other times our author touches the chord of Anatole France and leads us into a garden of Epicurus. The last *novella*, "**All' uscita**" ("**At the Gate**"), of the collection *E domani lunedì* will be a fitting conclusion to our examination of Pirandello's short stories. We are at the gate leading from a cemetery, and we meet the phantoms of the Fat Man and the Philosopher who have recently died. The Philosopher, true to his vocation, starts immediately to weave his sophistries for the benefit of his grosser friend. He will continue for ever in the next world to reason and reason, just as the Fat Man will continue to wear his vesture of adipose tissue. The latter, however, will not be satisfied to be fat: he sees still the little garden of his house in the sunlight, the little pond in the shade with the goldfish swimming about; he smells the fresh perfume of the new leaves and then the red and yellow roses, the geraniums and the carnations. All the philosophy in the world will not prevent the nightingale from singing or these roses from blooming. All these joys made this Fat Man accept the sorrows and the worries in his past life. They enabled him to accept with resignation the caprices of his wife, her infidelities that were legion. Life for him was possible because he had no illusions. He had even been relieved to hear that his wife had a lover, because he knew that all her hatred of him would be transferred to her lover. But that lover is not a fat man: he is jealous, and in one of his fits he will kill his mistress. And lo, she appears, a bloodstained phantom, running along as though pursued by her mad lover. All these phantoms relate their experiences, their desires which have never been satisfied. And death does not solve the riddle, because it is nothing but total disillusion. Thus the end is the same as in Anatole France's story "In the Elysian Fields" when the shades, gathered together in a field of asphodel, converse about death as if they knew nothing of it and were as ignorant of human destinies as when they were still on earth. "It is no doubt," as the smiling cynic Menippus said, "because they still remain human and mortal in some degree. When they shall have entered into immortality, they will not speak or think any more. They will be like the gods." But the philosopher Pirandello will not become a god: he will be left behind at the gate to continue his reasoning for all eternity. (pp. 115-26)

Walter Starkie, in his Luigi Pirandello: 1867-1936, *third edition, University of California Press, 1965, 304 p.*

BENJAMIN CREMIEUX   (essay date 1927)

[*Crémieux was a French critic and friend of Pirandello who translated several of his plays into French. In the following essay, he introduces the theoretical basis and principal themes and techniques of Pirandello's works.*]

The best critical study that has yet been printed on the work of Luigi Pirandello is undoubtedly that of Adriano Tilgher in his *Studi sul teatro contemporaneo.* He describes the rich content of Pirandello's work in an analysis with whose solidity and rigor no fault can be found. "Pirandellism" emerges from this volume systematized in the most coherent and complete way. But however interesting "Pirandellism" may be in itself it would be diminishing Pirandello's own literary stature to reduce him to a mere "ism." One may even ask whether this would not distort the significance of all his work.

"A theatre of ideas"—that was the theme on which French critics rang the changes after the first presentation in Paris of his play, *Six Characters in Search of an Author.* But we must return a negative reply to their suggestions. Pirandello's is, indeed, a theatre that makes you think, but it is not a "theatre of ideas." In the same way, there is no such thing as "Pirandellism" in Pirandello himself, and yet it is quite true that one can extract "Pirandellism" from Pirandello's work.

Pirandello himself has not changed for thirty years. To the people who used to ask him what he was he always replied that he was a "humorist," and one of his first works was indeed a study of humor, in which he set forth clearly those theories of art which he has since developed and deepened without fundamentally altering.

Humor, as Pirandello understands it, has nothing in common with the humor of our gay French authors. It is closer to English humorists of the eighteenth century, closer to the humor of a Stern or a Swift. Yet it does not wholly mingle with humor of this sort. Pirandello's humor is not an art form deliberately chosen by the writer as a result of his own character or personality, or chosen at random. No; genuine, profound, and thoroughgoing humor is a necessity to anyone who has a clear vision of the realities of human life. Most humorists confine themselves to exploiting the feelings of contradiction, to searching for the comic element that sorrow that lies just beneath tears and seeking the sorrow that lies beneath the comic, or else devote themselves to concealing their own keen sensitiveness beneath the ironic modesty of a smile.

True humor, according to Pirandello, takes its rise in man's consciousness of his own existence, in the fundamental truth that a man does not merely live his life but that he also *thinks* his life. Man is both spectator and actor at the same time. This is the one great difference between him and the rest of nature. A tree or an animal lives according to the law of its own existence—governed by the circumstances which affect it; but a man—even the most inferior—not only lives his life, but also has ideas about himself and about his life. The process of living flows ceaselessly on, changing from moment to moment. But the mind of man is not so swift as the process of life itself. Man's images of himself and of his own existence still appear to him to be faithful representations of the world outside, even at that very moment when life has already profoundly changed them. Hence arises a duality between life itself and man's image of it, between the Real and one's idea of the Real, for the latter is no more than the form in which man perceives Reality in order to be able to think it at all. Reality cannot be thought about except when it is given form by the human consciousness.

There are only two ways in which this duality can be done away with: one must either refuse to think about life at all and be content to live his life like a vegetable, or else he must refuse to heed any Reality outside his own mind. The latter attitude is suited to crazy men who pay attention only to their own fixed ideas, and it is suited also to heroes in literature—since they have been created by artists and are stable creatures who cannot change.

Each of these statements might be illustrated by one of Pirandello's plays or stories, and this is equally true of the statements that are to follow. Therefore the first feeling of duality which lies at the basis of humor is, for Pirandello, the basis for any true vision of human life, and so in becoming a humorist Pirandello is indulging in the strictest realism. He does not distort life, nor does he systematize it, as people pretend. He does nothing but keep human life as it is. **Bare Life** is the title of one of his recent collections of stories. **Bare Masques** is the general title that he gives to his plays. He does not condescend to dress up life or prettify it. He shows it as it really is—the perpetual duality between life and man's feeling of it.

The consequences of this never-ending duality are infinite. The four hundred short stories, the five novels, and the twenty-eight plays that Pirandello has written have no object except to illustrate the consequence of this principle; and in taking this course Pirandello, without being aware of it, has come in touch with Bergson's philosophy of change, with Freudianism, with Einstein's relativity, and with Marcel Proust. He has reached the bottom of the great problem which more or less disturbs the philosophers and writers of to-day—I mean the multiplicity of human personalities, the impossibility of communication between human beings, the difficulty of distinguishing between illusion and reality.

Adriano Tilgher has listed, with admirable skill, the principal themes employed by Pirandello. First of all there is a series of single themes to which we have already made allusion: the impossible attempt to live life as it really is, the renunciation of living, the impossibility of watching one's life, the nonexistence of personality, since each individual is a chaos of contradictory forces. After this comes a series of relationships of men among themselves: to be is only to seem, each individual is an island on which one can never land, men can never understand themselves. Third, there are the pieces which have as their fundamental thesis the abyss between the present and the past: man's desire to keep himself as he is while everything is changing around him and in him, the contradiction that exists between an individual man and the idea that other people have of him, the destruction of the mask with which man covers his own face, the acceptance of a mask which others impose by force (as in Pirandello's play about the man who is accused of being a gambler and who in the end has to become one and goes to court to ask for a gambler's license), the revolt of life itself against this mask (as in the third act of the *Pleasure of Honor*), and, finally, the triumph of the irrational.

Although it sometimes happens that dialectic and a kind of spirit of philosophic systematizing dominate some of Pirandello's stories or comedies and reduce them to mere jugglery,—full of skill, no doubt, but without anything genuinely stirring about them,—nevertheless the case is usually just the reverse. Pirandello looks to life itself for his first inspiration, no matter whether he is working on some strange but authentic occurrence, or whether he is deliberately inventing a plot. His plots are often extremely complex and yet so probable that oftentimes real life confirms them. Consider, for example, the adventure in *The Late Mathias Pascal*, which really happened some twenty years after Pirandello's novel had been published. On the bare materials furnished him by his imagination Pirandello works until he has transformed them to accord, not merely with his own personality, but also with each of his characters.

The realism with which Pirandello carefully reproduces the point of view of each of his characters results in extreme unevenness in the course of the dialogue in a story or a play. Remarks whose significance scarcely exceeds the ordinary observations of the entertainers in *La Vie Parisienne* stand side by side with passages whose unexpected quality, keenness, and depth make Pirandello the equal of a Stendhal, a Dostoevskii, or a Proust. Properly considered, this proves that Pirandello is not a dealer in ideas alone, not a mere philosopher, but a creator. He writes at the dictation of his own characters, and he does not endeavor to arrange or clarify what his heroes dictate to him. He simply transcribes faithfully. Hence arises a certain heaviness, sometimes a certain slowness and repetitiousness, but at the same time an extraordinary feeling of life.

The variety of Pirandello's subjects and heroes is amazing. When you have read some twenty or thirty of his ill-matched stories, a sudden crystallization takes place in your mind, and you see the Italy of the days before the war,—all of it,—Italy as it existed from the disaster of Adowa to the gallant entry into the great World War. No one has painted the middle classes of the Italian capital and provinces with more vigor and more truth in all that remarkable mingling of finesse, credulity, passion, positivism, poetry, and pharisaism which makes the Italian one of the most complex and strangest of all the peoples of the new Europe.

There is no need for haste in judging Pirandello. He scorns advertising and allurement. He knows that he is bitter and unpleasant reading, but he knows also how great a lesson of force and of goodness is contained in his work. He knows that he is not merely a destroyer. This life which flees from us without ceasing and which deceives those who think that they have pinned it down once for all—this life a man worthy of the name must bravely construct minute by minute as fair and fine as he can make it for himself and for others. In a large measure the misfortune of mankind is made by man's own intellectual and moral inertia. The territory over which man can exercise his power is very limited: the past is his no longer, the future is not yet his; but he can model the present to suit himself, provided he conforms to the requirements of life—

life, which perpetually changes. A gleam of hope and optimism in the midst of ruins. (pp. 123-26)

> Benjamin Crémieux, "Luigi Pirandello and His Writings," in The Living Age, Vol. 318, No. 4122, July 7, 1927, pp. 123-26.

JOHN GASSNER (essay date 1940)

[*Gassner, a Hungarian-born American scholar, was a great promoter of American theater, particularly the work of Tennessee Williams and Arthur Miller. He edited numerous collections of modern drama and wrote two important dramatic surveys,* Masters of the Drama *(1940) and* Theater in Our Times *(1954). In the following excerpt, he surveys Pirandello's drama.*]

Luigi Pirandello . . . became an important figure in the modern drama by dint of applying a fine intellect to the negativism of his colleagues. His was a highly modern mind replete with the relativistic philosophy and psychiatric science of the twentieth century. In addition, he possessed an original inquiring spirit which after pondering acutely on the relation between the drama and subjective life did not hesitate to break down the last formalities of dramatic structure. The social and political realities which had forced themselves into the modern theatre received scant attention from him, and the situations which he most favored are remote from the cardinal conflicts of the age. Nevertheless, both his disillusionment and his psychology stamp him as an ultra-modern.

Pirandello achieved structure because his temperament, training and private life blended so completely with the "grotesque" dispensation. Born in 1867, in Girgenti, he was a native son of Sicily, the homeland of irascible temperaments and animal passions. Even his able apologist Domenico Vittorini declares, "I should not say that Pirandello is a kindly person." Naturalism flourished on Sicilian soil when Verga and others set down its primitive life. A streak of naturalism appeared in Pirandello in his early works and it is present even in many of his most cerebral efforts, since these also present sordid situations and deal with elemental passions. Incest, prostitution, and suicide appear liberally in *Six Characters in Search of an Author,* for example. Early in life he became violently anti-d'Annunzian. Living in a land of simple peasants over whom hung a "pall of inertia broken by sudden outbursts of jealousy and crime," he could have little patience with d'Annunzio's rococo sentiments and superman-worship. For Pirandello, as for the naturalists, all men were little specks of sensitive flesh, and these specks lived passively in a world over which they could exercise little authority. (pp. 435-36)

[Pirandello] was essentially an anarchist who had no use for society, and above all a pessimist.

He sometimes denied that he was one. But his explanations were exceedingly tenuous. Although he struck a comic note in most of his plays, and called them comedies, his vision was fundamentally tragic. He himself once stated, "I see life as tragedy," and it is not only the tragic content of such plays as *Six Characters in Search of an Author* that confirms this admission. In a foreword to a book about himself he wrote: "I have tried to tell something to other men, without any ambition, except perhaps that of avenging myself for having been born."

His humor throughout is ironic and saturnine; its brilliance owes everything to these attributes. It might be argued that anyone as cerebral as Pirandello, whose plays are full of logistic contortions, is essentially anti-tragic. His characters are the puppets of perverse syllogisms and Stark Young has rightly stressed the fact that they are theatrical abstractions. According to the latter, Pirandello has "transferred to the mind the legs and antics and the inexhaustible vivacity and loneliness and abstraction of the *commedia dell' arte*." A writer who plays with such abstractions would indeed seem to be far removed from the field of tragedy. But had not Pirandello's spiritual parent Chiarelli already made a distinction between "the mask and the face"? Behind Pirandello's defensive *commedia dell' arte* mask it is easy to detect a face contorted with pain and a sense of futility. Did he not himself write in his thirty-fifth year: "Ask the poet what is the saddest sight and he will reply 'It is laughter on the face of a man'." Did he not add, "Who laughs does not know."

Pirandello is, however, an exception to his own axiom: He laughed because he "knew." He "knew" that life is absurd. If, like a Talmudist or a medieval theologian, he took delight in subtle dialectics for its own sake (in Rome and Milan people rioted and fought duels over him on this score), he was also expressing a conviction that nothing in life is certain except its uncertainty. Life possesses only the reality that the mind creates for itself; and the mind creates this reality—a man, to use his phrase, "builds himself up"—in order to defend itself against personal defeat. (pp. 436-37)

Among his early naturalistic sketches is the folk comedy *In a Sanctuary* revolving around a rustic quarrel concerning the intelligence of pigs, and *The Other Son* represents the heartache of a destitute old mother whose son has emigrated from Sicily. *The Patent* is a delightful farce about a poor fellow who is harassed by his neighbors because they consider him a sorcerer. He sues for libel and refuses to be placated by a patient, Pirandellian judge. An accident to the judge's goldfish in open court, however, confirms his reputation as a sorcerer. And by then the desperate and pathetic victim of rumor has decided to capitalize his notoriety. He will make the townspeople pay him to plague their competitors or to ward off evil from themselves by removing himself from their presence. *Sicilian Limes,* written in 1910, is a tender little play. A humble piccolo player who enabled a poor rustic girl to achieve fame as a concert singer visits her in northern Italy in the hope of winning her love. But he departs a painfully disillusioned man when he finds her morally corrupted by her sophisticated circle. A number of other effective pieces in Pirandello's early vein mark him a near master of the one-act form.

However, Pirandello achieved his mark in radically different work, which he anticipated in 1904 with his novel *The Late Mattia Pascal,* the story of a librarian who escapes an unpleasant domestic life by pretending death by drowning and assumes a burdensome new personality. True to his custom of dramatizing his short stories, he wrote *Pensaci, Giacomino! (Think of It, Giacomino!)* in 1914, and many characteristics of his art first came to the fore in this play. It possesses saturnine humor, a perverse character, and logic defensively pursued to extravagant lengths by this person. Old Professor Toti revenges himself upon the school system by marrying a pregnant young girl; now the authorities will have to pay a pension to his widow long after his death! He remains a husband only in appearance, however, while she enjoys the boyish love of young Giacomino. In fact, the husband expects to be betrayed since this marriage is unnatural—"Otherwise, how could I, poor old man that I am, have any peace." He does not mind the gossip of the town, is fond of her lover, and actually forces him to remain true to her. And he is satisfied, despite the laughter of the multitude, since he has saved a girl from prostitution and misery by his behavior. Here already we have Pirandello turning the conventions topsy-turvy, and proving that the socially incorrect view may be the better and more humane one.

The Pleasure of Honesty, in the same year, is another sardonic chuckle. A woman who is distressed by her daughter's unmarried state sanctions her liaison with a Marquis. But Agata becomes pregnant and needs the cloak of honesty which only a husband can supply. A husband is found for her in the person of a lonely and strange individual who agrees to screen the lovers for a consideration because he has no illusions regarding honesty. Yet once the mask of honesty is assumed, he insists that the mummers wear it forever. He insists on the utmost honesty after the marriage, and this cynic succeeds so well in upholding the principle of "honor" that he wins his wife's love and society's esteem.

Cap and Bells in 1915 marked a further step in Pirandellian satire. Men "build themselves up," says Pirandello, and cannot forgive anyone who destroys the role they are playing. "We are all puppets," one of the characters declares, but "we all add another puppet to that one; the puppet that each of us believes himself to be." And everyone wants that second puppet to be inviolable—that is, he wants everyone to respect it. In *Cap and Bells,* the grotesquely ugly bookkeeper Ciampa is not troubled by the knowledge that his wife is betraying him with his employer; why shouldn't she, since he is so ugly, so long as others do not suspect the situation and laugh at him! But when the employer's jealous wife exposes the intrigue and has her husband arrested at Ciampa's house, the situation is impossible not only for this woman who will now have to leave her husband but for Ciampa who is furious at having his "puppet" destroyed. Thereupon he hits upon a solution:—the jealous woman, who is already repenting her hasty deed, must allow herself to be declared insane. Then when the case against her husband is dismissed and Ciampa's honor is saved, she can return from the asylum—"cured." She doesn't fancy the idea, but Ciampa gets his way, and she is carried out of the house shrieking while Ciampa grins contentedly.

From *Cap and Bells* to *Right You Are, if You Think You Are* the way leads to the meaning of truth. After having maintained in *Cap and Bells* that each man creates a suitable mask for himself, Pirandello declared in his new play that we are incapable of penetrating the mystery of another person's identity. This means that we must exercise tolerance toward others; that is, we must respect their deepest fabrications because we cannot really know the truth about them. Suppose that all records were destroyed by an accident like the earthquake referred to in *Right You Are,* we would then have no way of verifying that people are what they claim to be. To demonstrate this point Pirandello concocted an extravaganza in which the élite of a provincial town are set at loggerheads because Signor Prola does not allow his wife's supposed mother to see her. He claims that the old woman is his mother-in-law only by a first marriage and that she is laboring under the illusion that her daughter is still alive. She, in turn, claims that Signor Prola is suffering from the delusion that his wife died and that the woman he is living with now is his second wife. Prola and his mother-in-law are, however, kind to each other and comparatively happy until the town begins to buzz with scandal. Nor can the town discover the truth since Signora Prola is willing to be a second wife to her husband and a daughter to the old lady. The point is not only that we cannot discover the identity of Signora Prola, but that it is unnecessary to do so. Illusion is a bitter necessity to at least one of the principals of this play, and it must be respected. The town is consequently satirized for its idle curiosity. Judged by realistic standards, **Right You Are** is of course preposterous, but accepted as a philosophical extravaganza it is neatly pointed, and it comes close to Aristophanic humor. Its real shortcoming is the thinness of the plot.

Thereafter many of Pirandello's plays were only comic or serious variations on the relativity of reality or the "drama of being and seeming," as Vittorini calls it. Dual personality is the theme of **Signora Morli One and Two,** in which a woman reveals different features to the gay husband who abandoned her and to the grave lawyer who protected and made her his wife in all but name. Dualism also appears in **As You Desire Me.** Here the characters alternately defend and accuse a woman who was responsible for a friend's suicide, and since each disputant wins his opponent over to the opposite position the woman's guilt can never be determined. Such is the value of men's opinions of each other or even of themselves.

In **Naked** a pathetic creature clothes herself with illusions in the hope of concealing her frustrations and inner poverty. The nurse Ersilia who has made what she believes to be a successful attempt at suicide tells a newspaper reporter that she is dying for love because she wants to be interesting to herself before the end. She recovers, however, and upon being wooed by the repentant lover who had abandoned her she confesses that he means nothing to her; she did not try to commit suicide for him and she will have nothing to do with him. These and other revelations culminate in everybody attacking her. She had only wished to die clothed in a beautiful romance which had been beyond her reach in life, but now she is accused of immorality and imposture. Stripped "naked" by others who fail to comprehend the complexity of human motives and finding herself forced back into the colorless reality from which she had tried to escape, she attempts suicide for a second time and dies.

The ultimate in self-delusion, however, is insanity, and it is with good reason that Pirandello put much of his best dramatic talent into his treatment of that theme. **Henry IV** is the tragedy of a complex and painful character who lost his mind after falling from his horse at the conclusion of a masquerade. A wealthy relative coddles his illusion that he is the medieval German emperor Henry IV and surrounds him with a grotesque retinue. After twelve years he recovers sanity but pretends insanity because the real world, in which he found so much perfidy and lost the woman he loved, is a poor substitute for the illusory one. When this woman and his rival, who had caused his fall out of jealousy, appear together, "Henry IV" wounds him mortally. Now, however, the pretence of madness is more imperative than ever if he is to escape the legal consequences of his vengeance, and he must remain Henry IV for the rest of his life. The challenge of the play lies in its hero's deliberate renunciation of reality as something too painful to bear. Without this nihilistic animus, **Henry IV** would be an inexcusably contrived melodrama. With it, the play is still contrived—but for a purpose. This is hardly sufficient to place it among the world's major plays, but owing to its bitter intensity and unique background it is one of the most powerful of Pirandello's work.

Finally Pirandello's foray into mirrors through which even Carroll's Alice did not venture also led him to question the adequacy of art. He devoted several plays to the problem and provided contradictory answers. **When One Is Somebody** is the tragedy of a famous writer who is compelled to remain in the mold which he created for himself by his works. Although a noble love rejuvenates him to the extent of giving him a new literary style and a fresh vitality which no one would have associated with him, society will not allow him to leave the prison walls of his fame. He must not violate the style which made him famous! In **Trovarsi** a famous actress cannot surrender her stage personality; she loses her lover, who resents the similarity between her public and her intimate behavior, but gains the seemingly greater gratification of remaining an artist.

As a rule, moreover, Pirandello expressed a strong dissatisfaction with art, complaining that it fell so short of the truth. In this he was not, however, echoing the complaint of the naturalists against those writers who failed to photograph factual reality. He was indeed genuinely displeased with conventional theatricality and satirized it mercilessly. But his basic disaffection arose from the fact that life, which is constantly changing, is invariably distorted or killed when presented on the stage. Human motives, too, are multifarious and cannot be reduced to a simple formula for a public impatient with subtleties. Pirandello, therefore, either denies the validity of all drama or calls upon it to become as fragmentary, relative and fluid as life itself.

In **Tonight We Improvise,** which describes a play in the making, he contrasts the intense aliveness of the characters with the artificiality to which the stage reduces them. Here the actors lose themselves in their role so completely that they crack the mold into which a fussy stage director tries to place them. Pirandello, who had a penchant for unconventional dramatic devices and prided himself on the ingenuity of his plots, found ample opportunity to exercise this talent in his critiques of the drama. He reached the peak of dramatic originality and critical profundity in the well-known **Six Characters in Search of an Author.**

Here the characters lead an independent life because their author failed to complete their story. They invade a rehearsal of another Pirandellian play and insist upon playing out the life that is theirs. Constantly interrupting the stage manager and the actors, disapproving narrow stage interpretations and insisting upon explaining themselves, they break down the structure of the play until it becomes a series of alternately comic and tragic fragments. Here Pirandello has, so to speak, written a play to end all plays. And all this from the fact that life, with its subjective complexity and irrationality, defies the glib interpretations of the stage and its actors.

One character protests to the director and the actors: "Of my nausea, of all the reasons, one crueler and viler than another, which have made this of me, have made me just as I am, you would like to make a sentimental, romantic concoction." No naturalist could have made a severer charge against formal dramaturgy. Moreover, the *dramatis personae* are "characters"—that is, they are stamped with certain characteristics which create their own situations regardless of the intentions of their creator: When a character is born he acquires immediately such an independence from his author that we can all imagine him in situations in which the author never thought of placing him, and he assumes of his own initiative a significance that his author never dreamt of lending him.

The drama which the six characters insist upon acting out in defiance of all the contrivances favored by the ordinary theatre is a nightmare of sordid situations and self-torment. The Father, who came to believe that his gentle wife was more in rapport with his humble secretary than with himself, set up a home for them. The family does not credit this motive and suspects that he wanted to rid himself of his wife; and no doubt his motivation was more complex than he can possibly understand or acknowledge. He kept the Son for himself, and the latter grew up into a lonely, embittered youth. After the clerk's death the Mother, who bore him three children, disappeared with her new family, and the Father met his Stepdaughter only years later in a disreputable establishment. He was prevented from committing incest only because his wife who saw the Father and the Stepdaughter together warned them. The Father took the family back with him, but since then their hearts have been consumed with shame, sorrow, and exasperation. The legitimate Son resents the presence of the Mother's illegitimate children, the Mother is passively miserable, her adolescent Boy broods upon suicide, the Father is constantly apologizing, and the Stepdaughter cannot ever forgive him or overcome her disgust. Ultimately the Mother's youngest child is drowned, the Boy shoots himself, and the characters run off the stage in confusion.

Try to make a neat little play out of all this, Pirandello seems to say! This is life! The tragedy of the six characters can never be completely dramatized because their motives are so mixed; because some of them—the Mother and the Son—do not explain themselves sufficiently; because others—the youngest child and the Boy—are inarticulate. Moreover, some of them are too passionately eager to justify themselves and are too bedeviled to stay within the playwright's frame. Many of the tendencies of the twentieth century—its impatience with formal art, its investigation of the nebulous but explosive unconscious, and its relativist philosophy—are caught in this work. *Six Characters in Search of an Author* is as important as a monument to the intellectual activity of an age as it is original and harrowing. And it is harrowing despite comic details because Pirandello's puppets are intensely, if fragmentarily, alive. Only in some unnecessarily metaphysical passages which produce more confusion than profundity can the play be said to fall short of complete realization.

Pirandello reached his high point with this work, written in 1921. Numerous other variations on his favorite themes merely displayed his ingenuity, and a few full-length dramas of womanhood (*As Well as Before, Either of One or of No One, Other People's Point of View,* and *The Wives' Friend*) are in the main only conventionally affecting. He repeated himself, lapsed into sterile cerebration, and generally missed the attribute of living characterization which distinguishes the work of most masters of the drama. His sardonic viewpoint too often evoked puppets and snarled his plots until both became mere contrivances. Only the power of his intellect set him above the mere artificers of the theatre. (pp. 438-44)

His work remains a monument to the questioning and self-tormenting human intellect which is at war not only with the world, the flesh and the devil but with its own limitations. Once the intellect has conquered problem after problem without solving the greatest question of all—namely, whether it is real itself rather than illusory—it reaches an impasse. Pirandello is the poet of that impasse. He is also the culmination of centuries of intellectual progress which have failed to make life basically more reasonable or satisfactory. He ends with a question mark. (pp. 444-45)

John Gassner, "Latin Postscripts—Benavente and Pirandello," in his Masters of the Drama, *third edition, Dover Publications, Inc., 1954, pp. 424-45.*

RENATO POGGIOLI (essay date 1958)

[*Poggioli was an Italian-born American critic and translator. Much of his critical writing is concerned with Russian literature, including* The Poets of Russia: 1890-1930 *(1960), which is one of the most important examinations of this literary era. In the following excerpt, he examines several major philosophical issues in Pirandello's work, including reason and logic, human guilt and eternal judgment, and the divisibility of personality.*]

Logic, or reason, according to the classics of philosophy, had always had a universal value, equally valid for each *individual of the human race*. By this universality, reason had acquired a transcendental essence. The Encyclopedists and the Illuminists adored it with the same faith that they ridiculed, as evidence of moral disease or a product of ignorance, in the believers in positivistic religions. Their spiritual children, the Jacobins, dreamed at the height of the Terror, of making of reason a goddess.

Pirandello does not believe in reason as an absolute and transcendental value. Since he sees logic everywhere, he cannot consider it an eternal and superior value. Between him and the theologians of reason lie romantic thought and modern relativism. At the most, he considers it as a social function. It may render the social life of man easier (or more complicated), but it will never be the basis of a moral code.

Man knows and feels that logic and reason are not beyond, but within himself. He realizes their existence only by introspection. He exploits them without having much respect for them. He uses them to defend himself against others and, above all, against himself, as well as to assert his own personality, to give color and taste to his interior life. He considers them, at the same time, the justification and the instrument of his happiness.

For the "modern" man, therefore, reason is a practical activity or, if the term did not sound contradictory, a sentimental activity. But to the "ancients" it was a moral, rather than a practical guide. For Kant, universality of reason is the basis of the categorical imperative of the conscience, which teaches man to direct his actions according to a principle that might become a universal rule. Socrates teaches the same truth. For Kant and Socrates, reason determines the action, guides the will, gives a general and moral sanction to the work of the individual.

From this classic rationalism determining morality, we have reached modern rationalism (which some dissenting critic may call intellectualism) of which Pirandello is one of the greatest interpreters. Actually, in his work logic is only a reasoning machine which spins its wheels in the void, or turns them without gaining ground, eroding and sharpening itself in a continuous, useless attrition.

The machine which is out of order in Pirandello's world, a world equally dominated by logic and instinct, is the will. In his characters, logic has become a second nature, another instinct. When Pirandello was narrating his life to his future biographer, he said he had been born in the country, near a wood that the Sicilians, in Biblical style, had named Chaos. Not only had he been born, but he lived, thought and worked in chaos, because chaos signifies a universe regulated neither by man nor by God, a cosmic jungle where the will either does not exist or cannot operate.

The chaotic nature of reason, undisciplined by any law, the slave to the whims of instinct, and like it, bound by the vain, strenuous pursuit of happiness, is the predominant motif of Pirandellos's works. Very few critics have realized this fact. Most of them have stopped at that point where reason itself, in the futility of its search, becomes the cause of unhappiness.

In the first place, logic attempts to furnish the individual with the weapons he needs in his fight against society. Its first duty is to provide man with social respectability. Before it becomes the source of individual illusions, logic is to be regarded as a machine rationalizing what every man conceals deep in his subconscious because, according to society's judgment, it is shameful or mean. But man, by acting his social role, comes to believe it to be real and often confuses the mask he wears with his real features. Logic has become a true logic of the irrational. The romantics and the analytical novelists had already written of the "logic of passions," or to use another romantic phrase, the logic which through the constant supply of a vital warmth becomes the "eloquence of the passions."

Dialectic and eloquence, the latter the body and clothing of the first, are terms which occur frequently in a discussion of Pirandello. Reason always attempts to convince others or itself. Recalling the image of the unfortunate lawyer of **"The Jar,"** we see that in Pirandello the unfortunate man is his own lawyer, now defending, now accusing himself, often doing both with such detachment as to regard himself a legal case. Pirandello's characters do nothing but accuse or defend themselves before a hypothetical tribunal. When their dialectic reaches the level of confession, we see Pirandello in his greatest and most human light, and all sophism disappears in a yearning for purification. But even then the confession of his characters does not resemble that of a guilty man or of a sinner who is elated by the humiliation of an act of mystic contrition, as happens in the great Russian novels. They are not inspired by God, but by an obscure fatality to which they are subject. In this sense, the writer who resembles Pirandello most is Franz Kafka who is haunted by the life of the conscience, not as a confession, but as a ceaseless trial.

The "demon" of logic and reason in Pirandello is much more powerful and diverse than is the intelligent, indulgent one Socrates heard within himself, in whose advice he found the inspiration of truth and the words for explaining it. It is not a demon, as understood by the Greeks, but the devil himself, as conceived by Christianity. The Evil One who does not convince, but seduces; the Serpent of the Garden of Evil, the one who called sin the tree of knowledge. Pirandello's demon belongs to the same race as the demon in Dante's *Inferno,* who fights with an angel for the soul of a sinner. He succeeds finally in winning it with brief, brilliant reasoning and then says to the angel, with an ironic smile: "Thou didst not think I possessed such logic."

In the lucid, sceptical spirit of Pirandello, whom thought and imagination had led beyond the circle of his father's faith, this conception of intellectual guilt is a profound reminiscence of Christianity. Original sin is the corruption of the conscience. It is the sin of pride; from it arises some of the greatness and all of the misery of man. The Christian considers it sin and describes it. For Pirandello, it is sin transformed into sorrow and therefore he regards it with mixed pity and horror. But in the face of the nobility which every human sorrow arouses, the pity in Pirandello's world overcomes the horror. As long as the struggle between pity and horror continues, we have the Pirandello of comedy and farce, humorous and grotesque. But when pity wins the battle, his art substitutes for the comic mask of buffoonery the severe and solemn mask of tragedy. Then

the teaching of the poet who may seem one of the most cruel and violent critics of humanity rings out like the evangelical words: "Judge not."

All the sadder and more profound characters appearing in his works seem to repeat those great words. They no longer seem Catholic, because they rebel against being judged and condemned for eternity according to their "deeds." Even Jean-Jacques Rousseau, who regarded the Calvinistic conception of grace as a convenient spiritual alibi, refused to be judged according to his deeds. His narcissism led him to believe that man can be saved by the mystic merits of his personality, if he possess a sensitive soul, satisfied with the peaceful contemplation and adoration of itself. In this doctrine, that very pride constitutes election and predestination. It is, in short, a new idolatry.

However, Pirandello's man not only rebels against being judged according to his deeds: he does not even want to be judged for the real or apparent virtues of his soul. He knows that his feelings and thoughts are just as weak and subject to the same slavery as his body. While Rousseau's man seems to say: "Forgive us our sins and love our soul," Pirandello's man whispers, cries out and repeats: "Judge us not. There is nothing in us worth saving!" When he is not swept on by the flow of sentiment, Pirandello's man feels his soul, his intelligence and his body overwhelmed by an absolute, unique feeling of shame.

Most of the time, Pirandello's characters try vainly to fight it. Sometimes they reveal it cruelly in the souls and lives of their fellowmen. Sometimes they bare it in themselves with such great sincerity that it seems like immodesty. The feeling of shame dominates them because of the instinct of modesty which is still strong and deep in their nature, as it was in the soul of Verga's Sicilians. Pirandello shows that moral modesty is similar to physical modesty. "Each of us, sir," the Father tells the Manager in *Six Characters,* "in society, before the others, is clothed in dignity." The moral and social logic proves that the soul, too, possesses a body, a body it must conceal. The garment which hides the body of the soul is falsehood. But shame or life almost always destroys this mask. There lies the tragedy of existence which inspired Pirandello with the paradoxical and meaningful title under which he has gathered together the body of his dramatic works, *Naked Masks.* This idea of mask and of nakedness has always tormented his imagination and is manifest in other titles, such as *Life in Its Nakedness* and *Clothe the Naked.* The lack of physical modesty and the unexpected half-nakedness have been permanent elements of vulgar humor from the earlier farces to modern pochades. But from these offences done to modesty Pirandello has drawn all the grotesque, tragic-comic play of his humor, symbolized by the hook which the Father in *Six Characters* describes. In his Stepdaughter's eyes, the Father will always remain caught on the hook, as Dostoevsky would say, of "an obscene episode:" "She then insists on attaching to me a reality which I could never expect to assume for her in a fleeting, shameful moment of my life." He will console himself with the fact that, in her eyes, he has lost forever social honor, the reason for life, or what the hero of another play of the same title calls "the pleasure of respectability."

The Father of *Six Characters* is one of Pirandello's many creations who, in the ceaseless process of living, defend themselves by denying the judge the right to condemn them. They seem to be telling him: Either you are one of us, and therefore you cannot condemn us or, if you are different, you cannot understand nor judge us. Anyhow, you could not condemn a soul or a life eternally because of one cheap and vulgar incident. "A fact," Pirandello says elsewhere, "is like a sack which will not stand up when it is empty. In order to make it stand up, we must put into it the reason and sentiment which caused it to exist." An artist may possibly discover the sentiments and reason which impart the essence and the value to a given fact, but a judge never. The judge looks on the accused or guilty man as an individual, that is, as something integral and permanent. Pirandello and his characters, instead, are perpetually haunted by the many and fleeting aspects of personality. Under the disintegrating force of logic and life, the human personality dissolves into a sort of atmospheric dust, filled with countless grains and atoms now disappearing into the shade, now revealed in different colours and vibrations in response to the particular sunray which falls on them. In Pirandellos's own words, man is at the same time "One, No One, and a Hundred Thousand."

Borgese was the first critic who contrasted Leibnitz's idea of the monad with Pirandello's conception of the infinite divisibility of personality. We can extend the comparison still further and assert that Pirandello does not believe in pre-established harmony, but in a pre-established dis-harmony.

But this profound mistrust in the harmony of life, this basic doubt which is a fundamental of Pirandello's art, is not the doubt of a Mephistopheles which denies all human values. Pirandello's characters arrive at the denial of all truth only because they are pursuing, anxiously and desperately, *the* truth. Although his art often reveals the humorous or the grotesque, it is never cynical or damning, but almost always pathetic and tragic. For this reason, Starkie's likening of Pirandello to Dean Swift is not sound.

The fundamental austerity of his spirit withstands even the difficult trial of the obscene elements in his works. In some, for example in *Man, Beast and Virtue* or even in *Liolà*, the plot revives situations found in the old Italian short stories from Boccaccio to Bandello, or in the plays of the 16th century from Aretino to Bibbiena. But Pirandello emphasizes the humorous element in such a way as to give the impression that the good-natured licentiousness of the classics has been contaminated or vulgarized by the "gags" of the commedia dell'arte. As in Machiavelli's *Mandragola*, the saraband of the passions is not observed with any kind indulgence, but with a detached clarity which actually becomes disgust and contempt. By presenting this aspect of the exciting, shameful adventure in the intricate jungle of consciousness and instinct, the author of the *Novelle per un anno* may be considered the author of *The Thousand and One Nights* of the modern soul. Similarly, the complicated, mysterious plots of the longer stories and of the *novelle* read like the countless installments of a serial murder story of the subconscious.

Because it is a continuous process of argument and questioning, Pirandello's style seems like the faithful transcription of thought born and evolved only to be expressed orally. Like lava, it is shaped by internal fire. Pirandello the writer is at times nothing but the feverish stenographer of a rapid, violent voice dictating to him from within himself and he seeks to reproduce its constant crescendo, its reticences and pauses, its interjections of surprise and doubt. Because of this oral element, Pirandello's thought does not proceed by synthesis, but by syncopes, and that explains the frequency of pauses and dashes on his pages.

The balance between dialogue and narration weighs in favor of the second, in his novels and short stories as well as in his

plays. The brief moments of pure action develop much as in a moving picture (Pirandello showed some curiosity and mistrust toward this new art in his novel *Si gira*), but the core of the story or novel is the meditation which either proceeds or follows the action. The drama is nothing but dialogue. According to Valéry, rhyme and verse are the exclusive characters of poetry. For Pirandello, the alternate beats of conversation and arguments become more important than the speakers and assume the real rôles of protagonist and antagonist. Thus Pirandello reminds us that, as etymology teaches, dialogue and dialectics are one and the same word.

The conversational bent of his imagination is revealed in his titles. Almost always they have the quality of an interruption, of a proverb used to silence or finish off one's opponent, or of a bitter and wise "last word" offered by a sceptical spirit as advice or admonition: *All for the Best; Each in His Own Way; Each of Us His Own Part; Think It Over, Giacomino; Right You Are, if You Think You Are; As You Desire Me; We Do Not Know How; But It Is Not Serious; Same as Before, Perhaps Better;* and so on.

The inquiring nature of his inspiration endows his writing with a constant spirit of research, not scientific or chemical research, but the magic, vain seeking of the alchemist for the philosopher's stone. It is in this constant moving from formulae to experience, in the intertwining of hypothesis and supposition that his thought assumes a tortuous pattern suggesting to Starkie his clever reference to Hamlet's remark: "All is oblique," and which reminds us also of Ibsen's myth in *Peer Gynt*. "The great curved one."

In Pirandello's world, life and death become true theatrical climaxes, taking the form of human reactions to biological catastrophes. Truly biological is that conception which envisages man in a continuous process of transformation and destruction of an infinite number of spiritual cells, this process either stimulated by the germs of logic, or destroyed by its microbes. This associative and disassociative nature of intelligence also continuously creates and destroys the ties between man and man, "Men gather together only to fight," says one of the heroes of *La nuova colonia (The New Colony)*, an imaginative drama about the founding of a new Utopian town by a group of outlaws. In this play, the complete failure of the enterprise proves that the religion of the group (of the masses) is destroyed by a spirit which does not even believe in the religion of the individual.

The idea that there can be no progress, deriving unquestionably from Catholic doctrine, is deeply rooted in the Italian spirit. Christian progress is individual, but it has meaning and form only in God, that is, beyond the earthly life. Before Baudelaire, Giacomo Leopardi had ironically praised "magnificent, progressive destinies." Pirandello understands life as a succession of rises and falls, and doubts the possibility of any final, perfect ascension. The spirit can achieve stability only on the plane of art. But art, as well as logic, aims at creating a vital illusion, although it creates that illusion without any practical end in view. It is the one pure, unhindered and free form of the intelligence. The artist alone has the right to believe in and respect the phantoms of his imagination, precisely because they are not used for any purpose, because they hide nothing, they are not machines or masks, but real and true creatures. It is in this sense that Pirandello reconciles himself, through a profound historical synthesis, with the major tradition of Italian culture, that is, the primacy of art over all other activities of the human spirit. Pirandello does not affirm such primacy in the humanistic terms of Croce, nor in the aesthetic narcissism of d'Annunzio. He states it humbly, like the workman who sees himself subordinate to the beautiful work he has created with his own hands. The centre of his art is always its humanity. Unlike Ortega y Gasset, he never aimed at the "dehumanizing of art." The heroism and nobility of his life as an artist lie in his constant search for characters who are real people, not merely reflections of people. It was modesty, not pride, that prompted him to entitle his most famous work *Six Characters in Search of an Author.* In reality, he was an author who constantly sought new characters. And it is through them that he will acquire an immortality less ephemeral than that which he attained in his lifetime through his successes on the stage, the award of the Nobel Prize, or his membership in the Royal Academy of Italy. (pp. 38-47)

Renato Poggioli, "Pirandello in Retrospect," in Italian Quarterly, Vol. 1, No. 4, Winter, 1958, pp. 19-47.

AURELIU WEISS   (essay date 1964)

[*Weiss is the author of* Le theatre de Luigi Pirandello *(1964). In the following excerpt from a translated portion of that work, he demonstrates the influence of Pirandello's philosophical convictions and dramatic theories on his dramatic technique.*]

Pirandello's masterful dramatic technique stands in sharp contrast to the wariness of his thought and the relativism of the human truths he presents. Scepticism usually begets a certain amount of detachment toward human weaknesses. By and by weariness, disillusion, and contempt build a wall between the thinker and life. But human nature follows mysterious ways and the most cynical of men may feel an overwhelming desire to confide in other men and to pour out his disillusions, his defeats, and his philosophical conclusions.

Pirandello was such a man. He had observed the damage wrought by illusions and the nefarious power of unreality. To him life was a huge stage where grotesquely masked characters play parts for which they had never been cast. The actors remain unaware of the silent drama until a pain intense beyond all expectation tears off the masks and reveals their naked faces. This view of life as a miscast tragedy came to him through an insight which determined the orientation of his life. It permeates all his works; the same concern, the same characters, the same ideas, and almost the same words come back again and again as variations on a theme. Death interrupted him while he was still hard at work.

What had he left unsaid? Wasn't *Henry IV* his dramatic "Summa" as *One, None, and a Hundred Thousand* was his last will and testament in the novel? He derided human certainty and denounced the fragility of the truth (which he thought was the same as the lie). He had no hope for a world irretrievably lost in error and injustice and condemned never to know its real face. Was he trying then, like the sceptics of ancient Greece, to invite his audience to compete with his own negativism in order to find in the discipline of logical argument the only solid point in a tottering universe? Whatever the answer to this question, one paradoxical fact remains: the playwright and novelist who was convinced that any communication between men is based on misunderstanding felt compelled to proclaim his doubts to an audience which he pictured in his works as an amorphous gathering of anonymous beings, incapable of understanding themselves and even less the desires and personalities of others.

The need for something to believe led him to put his faith in the usefulness and legitimacy of doubt, a creed he shared with all the sceptics. Guillaume Guizot accurately defined their position as "doubt refusing to doubt itself and claiming as its own the certainty it refuses to everything else."

Pirandello's ideas are of major importance to our private and social life. They should have precipitated an upheaval in our family and social relationships. They did not and we may wonder why. It certainly was not for lack of trying. But the human mind will act only on certain ideas among all those which are offered to it. What kind of consistent action can be taken on the basis of a philosophy which leaves nothing but a gaping hole in the place of what it has destroyed? At best this philosophy can induce a few to walk close to the edge of the abyss. But why should anybody take the risk of falling? There was no promise of any discovery at the bottom, except that of the same fallacies which were at the rim.

The truth of what he said is easily verified, but it concerns each instant, each gesture of man in his social relationships. Nobody could ever conceive of a revolution at the level of such details. To people who live in a society, the rules of the social game seem as natural and matter of fact as the air they breathe. Pirandello's mistake was to direct his address to a world which wants to live and act, even at the cost of allegiance to man-made idols and mass-produced "truths.". . .

Pirandello was often accused of being more a philosopher than an artist. To this unfair accusation he reacted violently by asserting again and again that he was neither an intellectual nor a "mind-controlled" writer. He admitted that a number of ideas flowed along with his creative work, but as tributary streams. He defined himself as one of the writers who:

> . . .besides the pleasure of telling a tale, feels a deeper spiritual need: that of letting come to life only those characters, plots and landscapes which are permeated with a special sense of life which gives them a universal value. Such writers are born philosophers. I have the misfortune to be one of them.
>
> (Preface to *Six Characters*)

After a conversation with Pirandello, Alfred Mortier recorded the following impressions:

> For a long time he has been considered as an intellectual and controlled by intellect in his writing. After listening to him, I see him as a visionary and a man haunted by his own creations. They obsess him without respite until he has put them down in writing. The dialectician comes in later. It would be more accurate to say that among the creatures who wander in his head, there is always one who happens to be a dialectician and gives to his work an intellectual and sometimes artificial character.

In fact, there were no successive phases in his creative process. Imagination and intellect worked simultaneously, the latter being only a modality of perception. . . .

It must be admitted, however, that his protagonists were all born with a strong family likeness and that a number of them are characterized by the need to analyze themselves and to establish philosophical relationships between themselves and other men. Sometimes, as in *Each in His Own Way*, the spectator finds himself in the core of Pirandello's thought from the very first lines of the dialogue. Were it not for his flair for dramatic dialogue, we could swear that we are witnessing a dispute between philosophers and that the whole point is to show the victory of the author's idea. His need for tossing ideas all around the stage is so compelling that one or two characters usually have to summarize the situation in terms of the philosophical implications of the development of the plot.

It is not easy to define Pirandello's philosophy. It bears some resemblance to that of Pyrrhon, the Greek philosopher, but mostly on the point that our sensations and opinions are neither real nor false since there is no substantial difference between truth and untruth. "On certain questions there is no difference between being right or being wrong," says a character in *The Reason of Others* (*La ragione degli altri*). However, Pirandello refuses to be caught in the swamps of negative abstractions and in *Each in His Own Way*, Diego says: "Outside of specific and concrete cases in life, there are a number of abstract principles on which we can agree."

Moreover, in direct opposition to the Pyrrhonian attitude, Pirandello never tries to avoid the anguish resulting from intellectual speculation. Instead of striving to remain unmoved and impassive, like the sceptics, the Italian author, speaking as Diego, declares: "I have dug inside my soul and made it into the burrows of a mole." (pp. 30-3)

Pirandello's ideas were not new. Bergson had already expressed them when he opposed life and form and gave his definition of the word "form." In his "Essay on the Immediate Data of Consciousness," published in 1888, he showed feeling as "something alive, which grows and changes continually." He added: "We are facing a shadow of ourselves: we think we have analyzed our feeling but we have only found a substitution; we have replaced it by a juxtaposition of lifeless stages of being which it is possible to translate into words." Later, in *Creative Evolution*, published in 1907, Bergson expressed the same idea:

> Life is evolution. We concentrate a definite period of this evolution in a stable image which we call form and, when the change has become substantial enough to shake the happy inertia of our perceptions, we say that the form has changed. But in reality the form changes at every instant. I should rather say that there is no form since form is immobile and reality is constant change. The constant change of form is reality: form is but an instant taken during a transition. Here again our perceptions succeed in crystalizing into discontinuous images the fluid continuity of reality.

No formula could summarize more clearly Pirandello's thought. However, even though Bergson is the father of the idea, Pirandello is the first to have given it artistic expression and social significance. And what is more important: to be expressed on the stage this idea needed a complete revision of the traditional stage rules. It meant a complete revolution in the old dramatic structure based on the consistency and permanence of the characteristics of the individual.

This is not to say that the multi-faceted aspects of human personality had not been dealt with on the stage before. Strindberg attempted to depict this constant change in his dreamlike dramas. A marginal note from *The Dream Play* reads as follows: "The characters split, they become double, they multiply, dissolve, scatter and regroup again. But one single consciousness, the dreamer's, rules them all."

Strindberg had influenced the German Expressionists. Reinhard Sorge, Franz Werfel, and Ernst Toller strove to represent the multiple images of one single individual or one human group. In Toller's *Masses and Man*, the Woman, her Husband and the Nameless One each show multiple images of a single individual. There are other parallels with Pirandello. For example, one of Strindberg's favorite tricks was to unmask his characters at one specific moment of the action. In *The Pelican* the word "unmasking" is specifically used. Pirandello knew Strindberg's theatre, but his tack was different. On a number of important points, their views were opposed. Pirandello never shared Strindberg's hatred for women, although he had much better reasons for such extreme feelings. His own vision of man's inconsistency is quite different from Strindberg's and those Expressionists who preserved the immobility of the traditional dramatic character while splitting his personality. Audience and readers were aware that they were dealing with one single personality shown under different and even contradictory aspects. However, each of these aspects remained distinct from the others as an unchangeable trait of character. Nothing ever suggested the continuous fluidity of human personality submitted to an infinity of determining causes.

Strindberg and the German Impressionists considered dream as indispensable to the atmosphere of their creations. In his drama *Paul among the Jews*, Franz Werfel said that dream is a deeper reconstruction of individual life. That is why so many ghosts appear in Strindberg's *Road to Damascus*. Magic rites and incantations create a mysterious atmosphere with the help of appropriate settings, light, and stage motions. Life becomes dream, and what happens on stage is far removed from the daily life of the audience and beyond any tangible reality.

Pirandello was quite willing to make use of dreams but he was not, like Strindberg, frightened by solitude. He could have agreed with the Swedish playwright's statement that ". . . one always meets somebody in the middle of solitude. I am not sure whether it is myself that I see, but in solitude one is not alone. The air swells and gives birth to invisible beings whom one can feel present and alive" (*Road to Damascus*). But Pirandello's critical mind knew how to control the ghosts and how to make them into deeply human creatures. From the creation of his phantoms he drew an almost voluptuous pleasure which fed his inspiration.

The distinguishing mark of the Sicilian playwright is that he did not slice off the different facets of human personality. He showed them as an uninterrupted stream, forever changing but essentially one. . . .

He expressed simply and clearly what the Expressionists were trying to say in a contorted, forced, and painful language. In this he proved himself to be a Latin. Bitterness might have been in his heart, but a smile remained on his lips, even for his most frightening revelations. . . .

But this is not the most important contribution of his theatre. His true innovation and one with far-reaching consequences is the elimination of characters from his plays. Characters are the very foundation of traditional drama, and Pirandello's theatre is a constant denial of the existence of such a thing as a character.

Louis Gillet noticed it:

> His vision of the soul as a mobile substance, a stream of phenomena, an elusive, fluid, scattered something in constant evolution . . . is at the very opposite of the classical concept of the character, according to which everything is consistent.

When the usual relationship between objects is warped, as happens in Pirandello's world, everything seems uncertain and elusive. The familiar landmarks disappear and our imagination can roam wild. In this subtle game of the intellect, everything becomes possible and anything can be proved.

Such a concept cannot be expressed through the traditional forms. It needs its own style. The function of words is to express concepts and thus to crystallize them. How is it possible to find words fluid enough to communicate the ceaseless motion of human personality? It is possible to overcome the fixity which is the very nature of words? . . . What was needed to succeed in such an enterprise? The first step was to strike an initial blow strong enough to shatter our certainty. The second was to create an atmosphere where reality would become less concrete and where illusion could play freely and gently worm its way into the audience's consciousness. No longer sure of anything, the spectator could accept as normal the oscillation between reality and illusion.

Pirandello set to work with determination. His plays are full of contradictory interpretations and demonstrations of directly opposite propositions. Recurring imbroglios destroy certainty and confuse logic while eeriness invades reality and works on our sensitivity. Truth borrows the glamor of fiction.

Obviously the old routines of stage convention had to be upset. Hence the criticisms and accusations of inability to portray life. Even in Italy, where he was one of a long line of playwrights working on parallel lines, he met with sharp criticism. At the peak of his productivity, he was accused by Lucien Gennari of being a dilettante whose works were not even finished and who ignored the most basic rules of dramatic structure, leaving his plays like "houses without walls." . . .

Before Pirandello, the *raison d'être* of the dramatic climax was to bring about the characteristic resolution of the hero's personality. The situations were of no interest except for their impact on the life of the characters. This point of view has no meaning in Pirandello's theatre—it contradicts his basic concept. "Let me laugh," says one of his heroes, "Characters? Where do you find characters in life? . . . only the word exists and the point is to show that it has no meaning." A character with precise contours does not exist in real life. The truth we apprehend through the senses cannot enlighten us on reality because our spiritual retina retains images which no longer exist. Our judgment of "reality" is based on delayed images . . . so that what we call "characteristic traits" are but temporary reactions to specific circumstances which change and call forth new and different reactions.

The climax of traditional drama is the confirmation of the hero's characters as presented in what precedes the climax; the conflict in Pirandello's theatre liberates the character from any conformism and allows him to follow his natural reflexes: he is not the same, he becomes another man.

If we accept this point of view as valid, we are faced with the question of what to think of the great figures created by poetic imagination. Can we say that King Lear, Don Quixote, Don Juan, Tartuffe, are deceitful fictions without human reality? Are they only a few moments of their lives, arbitrarily immobilized like the images of a film when the camera has temporarily stopped? We are forced to this conclusion if we agree with the protagonist of *Six Characters*:

> The drama . . . is all there . . . in the awareness that we have to be one, when we are a hundred, a thousand, that we are as many times one as there are potentialities within ourselves. With this man, I am somebody, with this other man I am somebody else. And all the time we believe that we remain the same

with all, the same "one" we think we are in all our actions. . . .

Why then had Pirandello declared, "After Shakespeare, Ibsen is, in my opinion, the greatest playwright"? This is an expression of respect and admiration, but how is it possible to respect and admire something which is false and artificial? For indeed Shakespeare's and Ibsen's characters are eminently consistent in their distinctive traits. Yet it is well known that *Hamlet* had an influence on the genesis of *Henry IV*.

To resolve the paradox we have to accept the idea that no matter how different playwrights may be in their concepts, they have to submit to similar rules when they want to express those concepts on the stage. . . . In a detailed comparison of Pirandello's novels and short stories with the plays they inspired, Paolantonacci brings out the difference between Pirandello-novelist and Pirandello-playwright in these terms:

> The playwright has none of the clearcut and consistent pessimism which is so evident in the novels and short stories. The original characters and plots are warped and, more serious treason, the very meaning of the original text is altered. Pirandello sensed the necessity of this treason because the original creations were absolutely irreconciliable with the necessities of the traditional theatre.

On the stage, life must be crystallized into a few well-chosen traits. Similarly, poetic thought is a prisoner of the written words necessary to its expression.

In his "Essay on the Immediate Data of Consciousness," Bergson wrote:

> *Language convinces us that our sensations never vary* and it even deceives us concerning the character of the sensation we feel. In short, the clearly delineated words, the brutal words which register what is most stable, most common, and, as a consequence, most impersonal in the delicate and elusive impressions of our individual consciousness . . . these words would turn against the very sensation which gave them birth and *even though they were invented to express the instability of the sensation, they would immediately communicate to it their own stability.*

Pirandello proved that he was fully aware of this process of immobilization. In *Six Characters* the Father says to the Manager, "Our reality does not change; it can't change! It can't be other than what it is, because it is already fixed forever. It's terrible. Ours is an immutable reality." He proceeds to make a distinction between artistic creation and life: ". . . your reality is a mere transitory and fleeting illusion." . . .

It is easy to imagine the difficulty of translating to the stage the constant fluidity of life. Benjamin Crémieux has given the following portrait of the ideal human being as seen by Pirandello: "It is the character who is endowed with enough moral and psychological agility to mold consciously the shape of each second of his life, and to be ready the next second to renounce this transitory shape in order to make fresh contact with life." This psychological "actualism" constitutes for Pirandello the only truth. No playwright has ever been able to ignore the laws of artistic creation in order to represent such fluidity. Pirandello conformed to the rules, like everybody else.

In *Six Characters* the only thing he shows us through authentic stage technique is one moment of the Father's life which is, in his own words, "suspended, caught up in the air on a kind of hook." But to make the audience understand that this "suspended" movement is unique, Pirandello explains it in an ex-

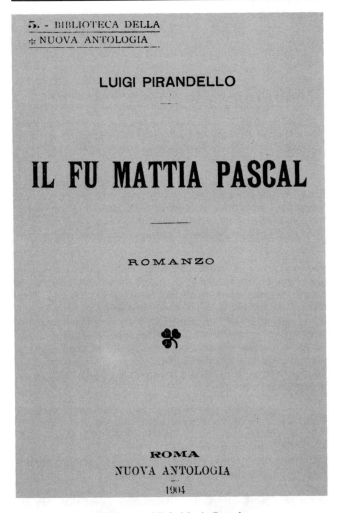

Title page of Il fu Mattia Pascal.

position interrupted by the dialogue, then taken up again with renewed insistence. The "suspended" moment itself is extremely dramatic, but the exposure which goes along with it is not. It could just as well be a separate comment on the dramatic action.

To put his creations on the stage, Pirandello was faced with the task of giving shape, substance and purpose to beings which according to his own beliefs, had no fixed form, no substance, and no final goal except death. This is the reason why he hesitated so long before writing for the theatre and why he felt he could not succeed. For years he considered the theatre as an inferior genre because of its restrictive rules.

In *Six Characters,* he instinctively dramatizes the commentary by setting it in opposition to the Manager and the Actors, thus creating a parallel conflict. But to preserve the unity of the action, he progressively brings closer and closer the dramatic and the ideologic conflicts until they merge as one.

It is well done but somewhat too obvious. It is evident that the thought could be expressed fully only through the commentary explaining the action. We can see here the difference between the "moment," which is motion, color, and life, and the interpretation of the fact, which is analysis. The "moment" has a dramatic value in itself, whereas the parallel ideological conflict draws its life and its justification from its association

with the "moment" and survives on the stage only as long as it seems to merge with the action.

Another factor to consider is that Pirandello was a convinced positivist. Notably absent from his theatre are the mysterious forces which defy all physical laws, the lucid and shrewd half-madman, the seraphic woman endowed with a strange charm, which are the common fare of fantastic literature. In Pirandello, the dream becomes lucid, realistic, and mercilessly logical. This may be the most important contribution of his genius. He has taken from the dream its esoteric character and has replaced it with a realistic element. Stripped of all magic, the fantastic penetrates the reality of life, permeates the concepts of justice, morality, and reason. As if under a magic wand, reality springs from fiction, logic and oddity, and certainty from doubt.

This type of surrealism with roots deep into solid ground is typically Mediterranean, and is also represented by other Italian writers. Gianfranco Contini has defined it as "an attempt to get rid of the intellect through eminently intellectual processes." . . . Pirandello's surrealism was complemented by a very special type of "logic." In *Six Characters,* the Father indulges in a brilliant debate to persuade the Manager and the Actors to let the Characters play their parts. Later, he gives a tightly logical demonstration of the fluidity of human personality and of the inability of man to understand man. We are forced to realize that we are not dealing with pre-determined characters who belong in a finished play, as we were led to believe. These characters are their own masters, they can act and think in the middle of circumstances not imagined by their author. Consequently, they are no longer stage characters whose life is determined by a specific ploy, they have become the heroes of a parallel intrigue added and juxtaposed to their original life. It is easy to see that Pirandellian logic is built on contradictions.

The logical structure of **Henry IV** is equally baffling, even though it is Pirandello's best play. Henry IV has recovered his sanity after a long period of madness. His love of years ago is rekindled and in a fit of retrospective jealousy he kills the man who had been his mistress' lover while he was insane. Ashamed, shattered by this explosion of hatred, he realizes that he cannot catch up with the stream of life which has kept flowing while he was in retirement, and decides to take shelter in a deliberately simulated madness.

It could indeed be a solution, wise or absurd. But one may wonder why this shrewd man, this perfect simulator and excellent actor who is remarkably wise to the world, seems to be completely unaware of the enormous risk he is running and believes himself safe. A crime has been committed; the least that society can do is to confine him to an asylum for the criminally insane. Yet, there he is, convinced that all his troubles are over and that he will now be free to build the life of his choice. The Father in **Six Characters** explains his actions in logically acceptable terms. So does Hamlet. We are far from a satisfactory explanation in the case of Henry. We can understand why he will go on simulating madness *after* the crime. But how can he explain the eight years of simulated insanity which preceded the murder? Only a purely philosophical and poetical reason could be offered as an answer.

Pirandello used to say that "a fact can be absurd in real life but not in art." His theatre demonstrates that often in life a fact seems absurd because we do not know all the circumstances. The function of art is often to clear up this sort of misunderstanding by putting the facts in their proper setting.

But what kind of natural, acceptable circumstances can explain a deliberately chosen simulation kept up for eight years? Art and life have this in common: what is *necessary* is held as true. And it is precisely the necessity of Henry's choice of insanity which is not justified, or at least not sufficiently justified.

Brutus and Hamlet simulated madness; but they had a purpose. Their success depended on the perfection of the simulation. The ruse was temporary and necessary to the achievement of a goal. In simulating madness Henry wants simply to isolate himself from society and time. Was it necessary to simulate madness for eight years to reach this goal? However, Pirandello's technique is such that the audience does not have the time nor the inclination to indulge in these critical considerations. If some of the spectators should question the credibility of the hero's behavior, Pirandello could always counter with a quotation from Sarcey, "An audience does not worry about the verisimilitude of a story if they are moved deeply enough. A reader thinks, an audience feels. . . . [it] is there to be moved and entertained." . . .

Pirandello was a sensitive visionary, but from his youth, he had shown an interest and an affinity for the positivist theories which were being propounded in Western Europe. In the name of lucidity he destroyed the ghosts he had created and at the same time suffered from their destruction. The ghosts kept coming back and haunting him, surging in his mind with an irresistible force. The game was endless. He never knew any respite in the fight between his positivist mind and the dreams of his imagination. The more he wanted to know, to understand, and to explain, the more he felt condemned to an endless search plagued by the curse of his imaginary world.

All of his moral strength was needed to struggle against the spiritual nihilism which was waiting at the end of his path. But he was defeating his own purpose. He fought against untruth while questioning the existence and the possibility of any valid truth. He aspired after a life based on natural data but never could define such a life or even have a glimmer of what it could be. He coined the expression "to build oneself." "Each one of us tries to create his own personality and his own life with the same faculties the poet uses to create his work of art," says one of his characters in *Tonight We Improvise.*

Unfortunately, the concrete application of this idea proved to be rather unsuccessful. Donata, in *To Find Oneself,* has composed her life according to the patterns of the characters she played on the stage. When she wants to free herself from these patterns, she discovers that it is only on the stage that her life can be created "freely," that is by escaping from her own existence through a transfiguration. Some consider this solution as a triumph of creative freedom. But it is in fact nothing but the sacrifice of a life which Donata wished to be her own but remains the shadow of her parts. Similarly, Henry IV finds "freedom" in playing a part: that of a madman. "It is very hard to be cured from scepticism; one gets mired into it by the very efforts one makes to get out of it," said Ernest Renan. Such was the case of Pirandello. He could entertain no illusion about the final result of the fight between the positive forces of life, which try to escape from all restrictions, and the dark forces constantly misleading us. He had no choice but to indulge in "a delicate and clever melancholy which freezes the smile and brings dignity to the jester by turning him into a humorist." This form of humor is the expression of an intelligence which, having reached the end of its speculations, can only laugh at itself and at the same time at all the sorrows, all the errors, all the weaknesses of humanity. (pp. 36-45)

Auréliu Weiss, "The Remorseless Rush of Time," edited and translated by Simone Sanzenbach, in The Tulane Drama Review, *Vol. 10, No. 3, Spring, 1966, pp. 30-45.*

ANTONIO ILLIANO   (essay date 1967)

[*Illiano is an Italian-born American educator and critic and the translator of Pirandello's* L'umorismo *into English. In the following excerpt, he addresses thematic elements of* Six Characters in Search of an Author.]

A little less than half a century ago there appeared on stage in Rome one of the most brilliant pieces of deviltry in modern literature, Pirandello's *Six Characters in Search of an Author.* It created such a stir that in less than three years it was translated in many languages and performed all over Europe and in New York.

The sudden and unexpected appearance of live characters, who claimed to belong on the stage and could actually be seen and heard, was like a bombshell that blew out the last and weary residues of the old realistic drama. It took everybody by surprise—and confused, as it still does today, both audiences and critics. But the novelty of the invention is so stimulating, and its great inherent theatricality so skillfully handled, that the play seldom fails to provide even the most sophisticated audiences with a fresh, though not easily definable, type of cathartic experience. (p. 1)

Now who are these six characters and where do they come from? They appear on a stage where a company is about to begin rehearsals for a new play, Pirandello's *Il giuoco delle parti.* They interrupt, claiming that they are really six most interesting characters, side-tracked, however, in the sense that their original author first conceived them "alive," and then *did not want* or was no longer able materially to write them down in a work of art. They repeatedly assert that they are more real than the actors themselves, since, having been created, they now have a reality of their own, independent of their author. Consequently, they are now looking for a writer willing to put them into a book, and for a company of actors who will actualize and materialize their drama.

This extremely explosive beginning sets off a most complex series of chain reactions, developing in all directions, all intricately woven in a spinning rhapsody of polemics, contrasts, misunderstandings, disquisitions, and heated feelings; a rhapsody ending in true agreement with Hegel's theory of the drama, that is, not ending at all. (p. 2)

After being exposed to such an elaborate treatment, the listener or spectator cannot help feeling that he has just been taken for a most intriguing ride, and deposited exactly where he started out. The next thing that comes to mind is the concern—critical and methodological—that unless one is extremely cautious about it all, the very same excursion is bound to start all over again. Clearly, the play has several meanings, several layers of reality adding up to an unconcluded and unconcluding plurality. In spite of a seemingly philosophical surface, it does not try to preach any moral or philosophy, not excluding skepticism. A definition of the *Six Characters,* if it were at all possible, must take into account the fact that the play is, first and foremost, a highly sophisticated and artistic re-enactment of relativism-in-the-making. It is, therefore, amusing to see how many critics, lured by Pirandello's deceitful disorder, either plunge into it and drown, or somehow skirt about on a slippery edge—and in both cases, missing the point, that the play, like life itself, is a many colored thing which refuses to be neatly pigeonholed. (pp. 2-3)

To understand the complex machinery of the *Six Characters* we must adopt a new critical perspective, a perspective that may enable us to face directly Pirandello's *forma mentis,* the inner generator of the energy and life of his art. A few questions concerning the so-called reality and autonomy of the characters may come in very handy at this point, to start us on our new itinerary.

First of all, is it true that the characters are more real than the actors, as they claim to be throughout the play? At this point perhaps we should briefly clarify the meaning and function of the actors as Pirandello uses them in this play. Obviously, they represent here the people of flesh and blood, physical life. As such—though fictitious figures themselves, in so far as they were conceived by the playwright for the story line of his comedy—we tend to see them in terms of a non-mythical world, and accept them not merely as plausible symbols but as real and actual human beings.

But in the case of Pirandello's characters, who are presented as neither the people conceived by the author for his play, nor as actors representing people, what shall we say about *them*? How can we describe or classify them? Again, is it true that these characters are more real than the actors?

The answer to this question will vary according to the meaning we attribute to the adjective *reale.* If we take *reale* to refer to that which is "physical, having a body," the answer is obviously negative. Here only the actors have physical substance, possess bodies, and are, therefore, real. If, on the other hand, we interpret *reale* in the philosophical sense of "pertinent to the *res* itself," and therefore substantial and everlasting, then the answer is affirmative; the characters *are* more real than the actors.

Now, this duplicity of *reale* is definitely no mere coincidence. It is, on the contrary, cleverly used with ambivalent purpose, and becomes one of the main sources of ambiguity in the comedy. In fact, if we switch the question around and ask, "are the actors more real than the characters?," we stumble on the same horns of the dilemma, but in reverse. We answer with an affirmative in the sense that the actors refer to people endowed with physical consistency; and we answer in the negative because people are changeable and perishable. It is an insoluble dichotomy, and one that can turn into a most perplexing predicament; so that many observers and readers become easy prey to Pirandello's mix-up, and instinctively pose the question, "but then what is more real than what?" In utter seriousness, they consequently start looking for an answer that does not exist, without realizing that the author is asking the very same moot question, but for artistic purposes. They then take for granted that the characters are the symbols of art, and conclude that, when Pirandello says that they are more real than the actors, he actually means that art is superior to life.

Seen in the varied *spectrum* of meanings which the *Six Characters in Search of an Author* implies, this last interpretation is not an impossible one, provided it does not become too rigid and exclusive. As many writers have been fond of quoting, "life is brief and art is long." Life has one kind of reality, a transient one—since man is mortal, but art has another kind, since it can outlast its creation, and achieve a permanence we call perennial.

The main reason why it is difficult to wrap up the *Six Characters* in one sweeping generalization is that the characters themselves were not meant to be symbols. The actors, yes, may be taken to represent human nature with all its predicaments. But the characters were conceived, to use Pirandello's own definition of them, as *realtà create,* that is, as concepts stripped of all symbolizing vestment, as bare concepts and not personages symbolizing concepts. One may here indulge in a bit of sophistry and go so far as to say that they are indeed symbols, but symbols symbolizing lack of symbolism, nakedness. But we should rather stick with Ortega y Gasset's clear and articulate formulation, that "the traditional playwright expects us to take his personages for persons and their gestures for indications of a 'human' drama. Whereas here [in the *Six Characters*] our interest is aroused by some personages as such— that is, as ideas or pure patterns."

A very important question now arises as to what happens to these concepts, once they have been created; how does the playwright handle them?

Pirandello says that the creatures of his inspiration, once conceived, achieve a complete autonomy. We could agree with his pretense if we equate this alleged independence with its aesthetic value, that is, if we take the autonomy of the characters to mean their artistic liveliness and effectiveness. To be sure, clean-cut detachment between creator and creature is a Utopian mirage, one that has always attracted the naive idealist. Giving characters an independent kind of realism is an extremely refined device in literature, one we may say began with Cervantes, with whom Pirandello was quite familiar, and a device easily recognized in the work of many writers since. Here is, for instance, what some of them have said about it: "My notion always is that, when I have made people play out the play, it is, as it were, their business to do it and not mine." (Dickens) "Often my characters astonish me by doing or saying things I had not expected—yes, they can sometimes turn my original scheme upside down, the devils!" (Ibsen) "There is always a regular army of people in my brain begging to be summoned forth, and only waiting for the word to be given." (Chekhov) Or take Turgenev, who once said that an author must cut the navel-string between himself and the offspring of his imagination.

But it is one thing to talk about creative theories and another to actualize them on the artistic plane. And no other writer has brought this technique into the open and made it serve so successfully, as both Unamuno in the novel and Pirandello in the theatre. To be sure, in both these two authors there is an epistemological and ontological preoccupation, in so far as the question "Who and what are the characters?" is another way of asking "Who and what am I?," "Who and what are you?" etc. And, in both of them, the personages involved in their stories are involved in nothing more nor less than a stubborn and hopeless attempt to escape being dominated by their authors. . . . As for the desperate lot of the *Six Characters,* one needs only to survey their existence briefly.

It all started one day when Fantasy, the "maidservant" of Pirandello's art, inexplicably gave birth to six characters. It is not hard to accept this basic fact. These figures, however, have a very peculiar birth defect—one not readily seen. They are deprived of the consciousness of their true paternity: they know they are characters, they know they are rejected characters, they believe they were created and then deserted by some author, but they are completely unaware of the most crucial truth of all, namely, that their blood is truly Pirandellian. Once deprived of their identity, it is easy for the author to have them do whatever he likes. So he has them knock at his door and persistently beg him to write them down, in a play or novel. Not a chance. For a while, he argues he has to find a meaning for them, a meaning that would justify their artistic existence. Till finally, he has another spark of genius: Why not represent them just as they are, as rejected and unfinished: *This* may well be their meaning! So he grants them a fake passport, so to speak, and makes them believe that they are free to go and search for their promised land. So the six fools walk onto a stage, eager and desperate to achieve what they don't realize is unattainable, that is, what has *a priori* been decreed as such by their creator. On that stage, which the author has purposely chosen for them, because it is totally unprepared to receive them, they come to face with a most exasperating failure. But this is not all. Not by any means. Where is the author, while both actors and characters engage in a dialogue or cross purposes? Hiding and unseen, the author is watching all of them perform, and writing down his own play: The *Six Characters in Search of an Author.* It turns out that the poor stooges, while trying to enact their own suffering drama, have been used for a completely different purpose, one they do not and cannot suspect.

Are we still to speak of "autonomy" of the characters? Indeed, if we insisted in doing so, we would not only yield to easy and idle labelling, but, what is more revelant, we would dangerously hinder our penetration and understanding of the tragic *substratum* of the play.

To a large extent, the Pirandello touch here is romantic irony straight from the books of Heine, Tieck, Jean Paul Richter and F. Schlegel, to mention but a few of the German Romantics with whom Pirandello was well acquainted. To get closer to the truth, we should say that it is romantic irony highly tinged with Kleist's *Marionettentheater.* In Pirandello, however, the romantic view disintegrates through multiplicity, contradiction and ambiguity, as has happened with other writers in the same tradition. One of the first to attain a lucid perception of Pirandello's modernity was Yeats, who, grouping him together with Pound, Eliot and Joyce, once said that they ". . . break up the logical processes of thought, by flooding them with associated ideas or words that seem to drift into the mind by chance," and even more brilliantly remarked that in them "there is hatred of the abstract. . . . The intellect turns upon itself."

Pirandello's work, however, is not only the product of a literary tradition aware of the spiritual crisis faced in a modern culture, but indeed reflects what must be regarded as the peculiarly original structure of his mind, namely, the motivations which make him acutely conscious and perceptive of the absurdities and paradoxes of human tragicomedy. We said at the beginning that the reader or spectator experiences an uneasy sense of repetition and uncertainty. Now this feeling cannot be explained away in terms of romantic irony alone.

Romantic irony may be illustrated by the author who first creates and then deflates or destroys his creation. Whereas in Pirandello, once the process has started, it remains open to further dialectical developments. So that we have not only inversion or reversion, but also inversion of inversion, reversion of reversion.

Yeats sharply intuited the extend and importance of this phenomenon, when he spoke of the intellect that turns upon itself, and it is regrettable that he did not elaborate on this statement. An essay attempting to show in what way the intellect turns

upon itself in Joyce, Eliot, Pound and Pirandello, could prove to be a most challenging study in comparative literature. Here one can only outline how the creative intellect, conscious of its powers, becomes a witness to itself in Pirandello's mind. There, in Pirandello's mind, the inversion in the creative process takes place as a work of reflection, an active and vigilant force which is at the basis of Pirandello's art and of his theory of humor.

In 1908, long before he became famous as a playwright, he had written a very important essay called *L'umorismo,* an exposition of his *poetica* and of his *Weltanschauung,* on which he was to build most of his future work. Any serious attempt to penetrate Pirandello's world should necessarily begin with an attentive and thorough study of this essay. (pp. 3-9)

"Humor" has a particular meaning and value for Pirandello. With him, the comic view may have the most serious of undertones. What seems humorous on the surface is revealed as a matter of sorrow and pain, and far from comic, underneath. To support this view, Pirandello gives us a striking example in an old lady with dyed hair, dressed like a young girl and wearing heavy make-up. At first sight she makes people laugh because she does not look as an old lady is supposed to: comedy consists of this awareness of the contrary. At this point, however, Pirandello's reflection interferes to tell us that the old lady is aware of being ridiculous, but is willing to deceive herself, by believing that the artifice of appearance will help her keep the affections of a younger husband. Well, if reflection comes to suggest all this, then there is nothing left to laugh about; on the contrary, the picture becomes quite sad. "From that *awareness of the contrary,* [reflection] has made me shift to the *sentimento del contrario.*" Here we finally hit the mark of Pirandello's *forma mentis:* the sentiment of the contrary. This is the essence of true humor. Human beings do not accept reality as animals do; they question it, but cannot find a clear purpose and explanation. So . . . they invent fictions that may give life some meaning, vain and illusory as it may be. Humor is like a restless little devil who comes to break them to pieces, so that we can see how, behind the Vanity Fair, *panta rei,* everything flows, in a steady uninterrupted stream.

This sentiment of the contrary was inborn in Pirandello. We can trace it as far back as his childhood, but in order to realize what a deep and moving force it was, we need only glance at a few of his titles. The very first Pirandellian published work is a collection of poems in his early youth called *Mal giocondo,* which reminds one of Heine's tortured wit. Years later other works came out with titles like *Fuori di chiave, Il fu Mattia Pascal, Erma bifronte, Maschere nude,* etc. And what about the play here discussed, the *Six Characters in Search of an Author,* in which, beginning with the title, there is nothing that cannot be inverted or reversed? It should perhaps be clearer now what it is that Pirandello means when, in the *Preface,* he defines this drama as "a mixture of tragic and comic, fantastic and realistic, in a humoristic situation quite new and infinitely complex."

Many critics are attracted by the plentiful philosophical disquisitions scattered throughout his work and to the idea that the true nature of Pirandello is that of a philosopher. On this assumption they then proceed to reconstruct and reorganize his *Weltanschauung* into a well wrought and neatly chiselled system. Nothing could be more erroneous and impractical. Like all great artists, Pirandello has the qualities of a thinker, though not a completely original one. Actually, his thought is asystematic *a priori,* based on analysis and not synthesis, on fracture and multiplicity and not on unity; and his thinking is not separable from the process of artistic creation.

Finally, Pirandello's constant reflection and anayltic drive should not be mistaken as motivated by sheer cerebrality. They are, instead, the product of deep suffering and overwhelming compassion for mankind's uneviable lot in a world of flux and misery. Speaking of himself and of his art, Pirandello once said: "To live before a looking glass is not possible. Try to look at yourself in a mirror while you are crying for your deepest sorrow, or while you are laughing for your merriest joy and your tears and your laughter will stop suddenly." And then he added polemically: ". . . only a few—not entirely dazzled by the shining of that mirror—have so far succeeded in seeing the amount of real sorrow and of human suffering which this 'overbrained humorist' has succeeded in putting into his dramas and comedies." (pp. 9-11)

> Antonio Illiano, "Pirandello's 'Six Characters in Search of an Author': A Comedy in the Making," in *Italica, Vol. XLIV, No. 1, March, 1967, pp. 1-12.*

JØRN MOESTRUP (essay date 1972)

[*In the following excerpt, Moestrup surveys Pirandello's lyric poetry.*]

The poems Pirandello wrote both before and after the turn of the century are poor, which shows that it is the genre, not the stage of development, that is responsible. It is impossible to find any real explanation, and it only remains to face the fact that Pirandello was not a lyric poet despite the persistence with which he continued to write verse. His dialogic and conversational style is alien to lyric poetry and he characteristically had no contact with the best of what was being written at the time.

A contributory factor to the weakness of his poems is the arbitrariness of his form. His use of metre and verse form is casual and the content of his poems could have been expressed just as well in prose, which, according to the standards of his contemporaries, was a fatal deficiency. The Symbolists cultivated the detail as a meaningful unit; the individual word is not merely a part of the whole; it is itself a microcosm with its own particular expressiveness. To ignore this is a deadly sin, which Pirandello commits in all his poems. His lack of feeling for what was vital in the poetry of the time appears in some derogatory remarks about Verlaine and Mallarmé. In *Art and Conscience Today* he reiterates the indignant philistine's opinion of Verlaine without commentary and as an established fact: Verlaine is degenerate, a vagabond, criminal and it has previously been stated in a disparaging tone that he belongs to the so-called Symbolist school. In **"To Next Summer,"** a poem written in 1896, he is ironic at the expense of Verlaine and Mallarmé, who are lumped together with D'Annunzio. (pp. 20-1)

Pirandello's début as a writer, his first collection of poems [*Mal giocondo*], is of special interest despite the modest quality of the poems. The book is carefully composed: between the introductory and the concluding poems there are five sections; each section has its title and the middle section is very suitably called "Intermezzo" ("Intermezzo lieto"). The introductory poem is an invocation to art, which is having a difficult time in a period dominated by science and violent social change, and the concluding poem contains the young poet's programme for the future. Each of the five sections has its own character and is different from the others in content and tone, but this

is only natural, as they are not particularly homogeneous. The first group, "Romanzi," treats of youthful striving for the ideal, which can have various forms. At times it is identified with love, but it always represents something higher than everyday life. This striving is always threatened by disillusion, the feeling that there is nothing "higher," and that it is in vain to seek for it. Total impotence and pessimism prevail in poems V and XI, but on the whole the first group is pervaded by an atmosphere of passionate hope.—A different and contrasting attitude is to be found in the fourth section, "Poems of the Moment" ("Momentanee"), which is a long imitation of Leopardi both in content and tone. In these short poems Pirandello imitates the tragic hopelessness, *l'infinita vanitá di tutto*, both resigned and deeply felt, that is so characteristic of Leopardi. The second section, "Comic Poems" ("Allegre"), is the weakest. Pirandello tries to write a number of grotesque and sardonically humorous poems, but the attempt at humour is merely irritating and tedious. In the third section, "Carefree Intermezzo," the mood of the first section is resumed in a calmer tone. The theme of love and nature as man's ideal refuge reappears, but as an idyll that has little in common with the excited mood of the first section.—The concluding group, "Sad" ("Triste"), takes up a new theme and consists of satirical poems on social subjects. Pirandello is now involved; he puts away his pessimism and wishes to play his part in the improvement of social conditions. But there is an undertone of desperation in the poems, which are the expression of an act of will, and latent despair can be felt lurking in the background.

From the above it can be seen that, despite its schematic plan, the collection is far from being homogeneous and balanced. The great variation is an expression of uncertainty rather than of formal and conceptual wealth. It is clear that this book contains many of the elements that were later to appear in his writing. They can be taken as an indication that Pirandello did not develop: in his very first poems, it is maintained, the basic features of the works that become world-famous are to be found. It cannot be right, however, to isolate these individual features; what is important is the way in which they are combined and the emphasis they are given as parts of a whole. From this point of view the Pirandello who wrote in the 1890s is quite different from the short story writer of 1910 or the dramatist of 1920.

What is characteristic of Pirandello before he reached the age of thirty is the lack of a synthesis. As yet he has found neither form nor content. It is not difficult to identify his starting point—his passionate moral and philosophical engagement—and see it as the psychological and conceptual raw material of his later masterpieces. Intense feeling is a constitutional element of his writing from the very beginning, but in his early work the lack of an object, a point of balance, is felt; at one moment the tone is that of violent enthusiasm, at the next almost zum Tode betrübt ["mortally grieved"]. The intellectual content is not in balance; there is a conflict between optimism and pessimism, and since it is unresolved there is a lack of unity.—It is difficult to distinguish between the ethical and the philosophical elements in Pirandello's work. His search for an explanation of life and the result of this search decide his attitude to action and to passing judgement on action. (pp. 22-4)

The title is a direct expression of the contrasts that were characteristic of Pirandello at this time. It is difficult to render it in English. *Male* means illness, both physical and spiritual. It is paired with the adjective *giocondo*, gay, carefree, and the title expresses the form of youthful, therefore pleasurable in itself, pain that is to be found in the poems. Pirandello was aware of his dilemma.

Pirandello's second collection of poems [*Gea's Easter*] is quite different from the first. It is an ovation to Gea's Easter, the Spring, one of the transient pleasures that life offers mankind. Some lines from poem XIII might serve as its motto: "Take from each transient hour / all the joy you know." It starts with the decision to live in the present without thought for the future which will only bring unhappiness and death. One must forget what is to come and enjoy youth, nature and love.—This attitude is totally alien to Pirandello and there is something hectic and forced about the poems with their constant undertone of melancholy. The poems are technically primitive and there are innumerable literary echoes. The collection is short, consisting of 27 pages compared to the 68 pages of *Mal giocondo.*"

1896 saw the appearance in Rome of a not particularly noteworthy translation by Pirandello of Goethe's *Roman Elegies*. In the previous year his *Rhineland Elegies* had provided an Italian counterpart. The earliest of these poems had been written several years before during his stay in Germany. There is nothing essentially new in these poems. They are largely autobiographical and describe Pirandello's experiences in Bonn and his reactions to this new environment. The winter atmosphere on the Rhine both fascinated and repelled him; in the mist and cold he dreams of the light in Italy. Pirandello never had any intimate contact with Germany; his stay in Bonn gave him a certain understanding of the differences between the mentalities of Northern and Southern Europe. This is to be seen at various places in his work, for example in the short story "Far Away" ("Lontano"), but despite initial admiration he had little liking for Northern European ways of thinking and living. He never felt that basic sympathy—which does not exclude criticism on certain points—for the new conditions, which is inseparable from intimate participation in a new environment.

In style the elegies resemble the previous poems; there is no attempt at simplification and the diction is still that of classical Italian poetry with its special vocabulary and uninhibited changes in word order.

Shawm was published in 1901. It is short (27 pages), but considerably longer than the 16 elegies (12 pages). A large part of the book consists of an epic poem, *Padron Dio* (roughly: *God Owns Everything*) (14 pages), the subject of which Pirandello had treated in a short story two years previously. It is a novelettish story about a tramp, who goes round to the rich claiming that he is God's tax collector.—This form of sentimental humour characterizes most of the other poems in the collection. In all of them natural objects are anthropomorphized—an almond tree with snow on it, a sunset, the wind and the clouds, and so on. There is one important innovation. Pirandello has now definitely given up the language of classical poetry and aims at simplicity and naturalness. This happens first in the lyrical poems; the narrative poem *Pier Gudrò*, written in 1894, and *Padron Dio* do not count in this change, since the epic had a different tradition. This definitive abandonment of a specialised vocabulary, in which Italian lyric poetry was still rooted, is an important element in the process by which Pirandello matured as an artist, a process which was concluded by the end of the century. This change is yet another criterion for distinguishing between the first and the second period in Pirandello's work.

Pier Gudrò (13 pages) was published in 1894. It is a short epic poem, the main character of which is a preparatory sketch of a figure who later appears in the novel *The Old and the Young* (written between 1906 and 1908) under the name of Mauro Mortara. The poem is a sentimental, romantic and politically reactionary tale about a patriot of the years 1848 and 1859. Despite his age he is immediately ready to go to war for his country once again and is indignant at the anti-national position of the Socialists. His three medals from the war of liberation are what he values most in life.—What is interesting in this stylistically simple verse narrative is the political content, which confirms that Pirandello had already formed the attitudes he maintained throughout his life and which ended in open adherence to Fascism. (pp. 24-7)

The last of Pirandello's collections of poems [*False Notes*] consists largely of poems written between 1900 and 1910, but also contains a number of older poems. . . . The tone oscillates between various shades of irony, and common to most of the poems is the philosophical perspective they open up. This is often expressed by means of characteristically bizarre and comic imagery, which seldom has the desired effect. The introductory poem "Prelude" is an example: in it the poem compares himself with a conductor, whose orchestra suddenly begins to play false after a mysterious lady, thin and without eyes (= Death), has concealed herself in the contrabass. This kind of metaphor imparts a crossword-puzzle character to the poems, and matters are not improved when they are constructed in such a way that the concluding point is intended to compress the main content of the poem into one symbol. This structure is used to excellent effect in the short stories, but in the poems it seems forced. As in his earlier poetry no special use is made of the genre. The conceptual content is the same as that found in his prose, but Pirandello gains nothing from his verse form.—The familiar themes appear time and time again: the idea of death, the infinite smallness of the world in space, life as suffering, the impossibility of understanding its meaning, the necessity of resignation. Sometimes, as in poems like "Looking at the Sea" ("Guardando il mare") and "Clouds" ("Nuvole") a bizarrely desperate disgust is expressed. In the poem "Meeting" ("Convegno"), first printed in 1901, the theme is that of remorseless change in a person's life. The author has a meeting with his previous selves, those from Bonn, Palermo and other places, and feels that he has nothing in common with them. The typical dichotomy of resignation/revolt is expressed in an outburst shortly before he shoos his other selves away; he says that he has nothing to regret: "I hate to remember and complain" ("odio il rimpianto"), but reviewing his metamorphoses in the first part of the poem, he writes about one of them: "Ah, whoever happened to meet in Palermo / my other self / that my life's / best time / still enjoys there . . . " "I limp / where he flew / and patch up the person he created."

A concentrated retrospective account of his own life is to be found in one of the score of poems which, though written between 1900 and 1910, were not included in *False Notes*. . . . The poem is entitled "Spectacles" ("Gli occhiali,") and consists of four four-line verses with seven syllables in each line: "I once had a pair of green spectacles; I saw the earth green and gay and was happy // then I meet a certain gentleman who looks absentminded and sad. "Green," he says. "Oh dear, you're ruining your eyes. // Take mine instead and then you'll see things as they are." I took them, believed him and saw everything black. // I soon got tired of the earth that was made in that way, threw away the glasses, and since then I have seen nothing. //"

With its sharp humor, its bizarre but formula-like structure the poem is characteristic of Pirandello's last collection of poems, in which oddly enough it was not included.

One of the poems written in this decade is an epigram written on the occasion of the bicentenary of Goldon's death. It gives Pirandello an opportunity to air his dissatisfaction with the popularity achieved by Ibsen's drama in Italy:

> Witty soul, Latin soul,
> Do you know that your country is celebrating you, in
>   gratitude?
> but Osvald from Norway has taken up lodgings
> at Mirandolina's inn.

(pp. 79-81)

Jørn Moestrup, in his The Structural Patterns of
Pirandello's Work, *Odense University Press, 1972,
294 p.*

RENATE MATTHAEI   (essay date 1973)

[*In the following excerpt, Matthaei explicates* Henry IV.]

Of the plays that made Pirandello famous, *Henry IV* is the most conventional in form. It was written in 1921, the same year *Six Characters* was premiered, but displays none of the dramatic devices of that play. Pirandello evidently found the correct dramatic form for *Henry IV* at the first attempt. This was not difficult, for the story underlying this play is comparatively simple, and at no point does it transcend the classical dramatic pattern. On the contrary, it so enriches it that life itself can be turned directly into theater, something that appeared impossible with *Six Characters*.

Henry IV is the typical eccentric who seeks refuge in a fiction because of a failed human relationship that humiliates him. He assumes an attitude of madness that makes right lie on his side. Thus he solves his conflict in the simplest way possible—by suppressing his personal past. The new assumed past then enables him to conceal his painful role of unhappy lover behind the more glittering and universally recognized role of the humiliated Henry IV.

The theater is exactly suited to such an exchange of roles. It provides all the means for creating a perfect illusion—costume, scenery, drama. And the catastrophe itself then follows as a necessary consequence of the confrontation with the other players who represent both the past and present reality—life itself that has been suppressed.

Thus we have a situation that can clearly be surveyed internally as well as externally. The tension lies entirely in the psychological, which is unlike what is normally thought of as real Pirandellian drama. Pirandello's psychology, like that of Strindberg, is permeated by the morbid. It has its rightful place right on the stage. In disguise, which is an indication of motivation, it can communicate itself and become comprehensible. Thus it is no longer—as is usual with Pirandello—an insoluble metaphysical secret.

The motivation is shown so clearly only because it is itself a theatrical stereotype. The story pattern that underlies this "historical" pseudotragedy is the usual triangular one of love, jealousy, and revenge—a Sicilian melodrama, as Eric Bentley called it, or, if you like, an opera libretto. Pirandello used the story only to provide a trauma for his protagonist. The theme itself did not interest him. He was interested only in the reaction to it of the character—the flight from humiliation into madness.

By contrast with *Six Characters*, who seek in vain for a role in which to lodge their trauma, the person of Henry IV disappears in the role. But the person also wants to get out of it. This is where the drama begins—at the point of crisis where the character wants to return from total illusion to reality and is given the possibility of doing so by external agents, the visits of the doctor, his former mistress, and his rival.

The encounter with the persons who were guilty of bringing about his original trauma unbalances the firmly established illusionary world of Henry IV. It begins to let in light, to take on a twilight existence. And only through this does life return and make the dramatic action possible.

The doctor feels he understands this instability. He decides that the picture of Henry IV's beloved, which hangs in the throne room as sign of his fixation, must come alive in Frida, dressed up for the part, and make possible the transition to truth.

Pirandello's usual tendency to let his plays explain themselves here becomes the whole principle that makes up the plot. Both sides see through the fiction and use it to further their own purposes. For the visitors it is a weapon against madness, for Henry IV an instrument of revenge.

In the great revelation scene in the second act, Henry IV admits the reasons for his playacting to one of his privy councilors. Because he cannot and will not conform, he forces the others to enter his world of illusion, making them into puppets. In this way he wins back the freedom of his own subjectivity. The others had earlier amused themselves at his expense. Now it is his turn to amuse himself at their expense. But at the same time he remains the prisoner of his self-chosen ceremonial. Because of the alienation of his past he cannot communicate himself, and his revenge remains a dumb one. His act of pretence seems to be fragmented within itself and is overburdened with diffuse emotions that seek relief in constantly new forms.

This division within himself gives rise to a drama of immense oppressiveness. His entrance, delayed over two lengthy introductory scenes, is frightening—and pompous. Flanked by two of his councilors who carry crown, scepter, and the globe with the cross, he enters the throne room in masklike dress.

He is "nearly fifty, very pale, gray-haired. But the hair on his temple and forehead is patently dyed blond, in a downright childish way. His face is tragically pale, his cheeks rouged. His eyes have a fixed stare. He bears himself with an affected humility. Over his kingly attire he wears the hairshirt as Henry IV wore at Canossa." Like his external appearance, his speech is ambiguous—at the same time very formal and spontaneous, declared commitment and affected declamation.

The guests, who appear before him in the dress of Henry IV's period, are his puppets, whom he lets dance on the strings of his caprice, taking their disguise seriously at one moment, seeing through it the next. He talks about the intrigues of the bishops, the slander against his holy mother Agnes. Then suddenly he breaks out of his role. Pointing to his dyed hair, he tells his former beloved that he does this for her sake.

It is no longer possible at this point to distinguish what is truth and what pretence—both are blurred. But even as he breaks out of his role, he is still acting. His naturalness is stylized; his pathos and his gestures those of a tragedian playing Hamlet. At the end of the scene Henry IV points "almost in fear" to his picture, which, together with that of his beloved, hangs in the throne room and depicts them in historical costume. For a moment there seems to become visible through his mask the real human being imprisoned in his fixation. But straightaway he disappears again in a terrifying pantomime of madness.

He notices his rival, Belcredi, who has come closer. To everyone's astonishment and horror, he runs to the throne, where his crown is lying, snatches it up, and hides it under his cowl. Then, after bowing several times with a crafty smile, he disappears.

This exaggerated reversion into madness reveals Henry IV's real sickness. He is no longer capable of articulating his position. At the approach of his rival, he backs into his world of illusion, which is the only place where he can be master of himself. For to acknowledge reality means, for him, to admit his defeat and expose to ridicule his own absurdity. He would be stripped. Thus, he retreats all the more violently into his disguise, which lends significance to his socially unrecognized introversion and frees him from the knowledge of his own banality.

The rejected metaphysical aspect here creeps back in again. Essentially, it is what makes Henry IV's love impossible. "One wasn't to toy with him," says the marchesa about her rejected lover. "There is nothing more funny. If men could only see themselves with this look of eternity in their eyes! It has always made me laugh so much."

Henry IV now projects this sense of the eternal, which the marchesa rejected.

Within the framework of the medieval order, which he as emperor represents, he makes his own feelings absolutely binding. They do not admit of any questioning. From this position he tyrannizes over his surroundings.

But he pays for his dominion with his "life." Because he cannot leave his imaginary world without losing his intoxicating sense of power, he attempts the opposite—to pull outside life forcibly into his illusion. When the stratagem with Frida in costume in the final scene is to give him back the "sense for the distance of time," he takes illusion for reality. He draws Frida to himself: "The dream has become alive with you. More alive than ever. Up there you were an image. Now you have been made a living person. You're mine. You're mine. I have a right to you."

But this time, too, it is Belcredi who opposes this fallacious claim. In all things, he is the opposite of Henry IV—sober and flexible, a champion of reality, who has never insisted on being taken seriously and thus won the woman he loved and acquired a natural authority. At this point he jumps at Henry IV and protests. Like the others, he has learned from the councilors that Henry IV only pretends to be mad. And for him the pretense has now come to an end. He is not in fancy dress, and he demands from Henry IV a statement of the truth. "You're not a madman."

In that same moment, when he is forced into a confrontation with reality, the feelings of revenge that Henry IV had nurtured for twenty years in the role he had assumed, break out of control. In a flash he draws the sword from the side of one of his councilors and drives it into Belcredi's body.

The deliberately provoked crisis does not take Henry IV out of his isolation. But it does, for the first time, reveal its real extent. The protest against his surroundings shows itself to be fatal, not only for the others but also for himself. Belcredi dies. And with his death Henry IV also destroys the possibility of a new life for himself, a life that recognizes the truth and is free from illusion. He has to go on playing the part of madman, to confirm the judgment of those around him, whom he had previously made game of, that he is a puppet, totally alienated, receiving his principles of action solely from without, from society.

More strongly than in his other plays Pirandello criticizes, with this conclusion, a mode of behavior that defends itself from the recognition of reality by the illusion of a closed system. The seemingly eccentric case of Henry IV becomes a general pattern of alienation, of the isolation from life brought about by adherence to ideologies, by the dictates of society, by illusion-making, and by the pathos of introversion. With almost clinical exactness Pirandello showed how society's system of coercion brings about the disintegration of the personality, which moves from deliberate madness to instinct-driven, uncontrollable crime.

Possessing these traits, the figure of Henry IV seems like a conjuration of the fascist phenomenon. The protagonist's behavior exemplifies the sickness of a society that found its expression in the dictatorship of Mussolini at the very time that Pirandello wrote this play.

Pirandello saw these connections very clearsightedly. He criticized the power complex as irrational impulse, as illusionary superstructure to the psychic defect. He demythologized the "hero," whom he put into a drama that is a parody of both a tragedy and a historical play. He constructed what looks like a powerful personality but reveals itself as one lacking in awareness and being dominated by a mechanical dependence on the subconscious and the demands of the environment.

But despite all critical detachment, Pirandello loved his protagonist. And this too alludes to his later ambivalent attitude to fascism. Henry IV is shown not as a bugaboo but as a monster who towers over the others in grandeur, power, and self-sufficiency. There is around him an aura of a deeper, more general justification, the melancholy fascination of suffering that is the symptom of a basically nihilistic devaluation of values.

For Pirandello, Henry IV expresses the spirit of his period with more awareness than do his opponents. This gives him a kind of superiority. He knows that his costume is the "obvious and freely chosen ridiculous distortion of that endless masquerade, which dupes and enslaves us when we disguise ourselves as what we believe ourselves to be—without knowing it."

"Life is one huge puppet show." This was Pirandello's view even when he was only nineteen. It was a favorite formula that he repeated with constantly new variations. When Henry IV speaks like this, it is Pirandello speaking through him. Pirandello did of course criticize the ensuing act of murder. But it also provided him with his argument: that in a world without context and meaning, the need for self-realization leads of necessity to violence.

Thus by the detour of unmasking, Henry IV arrives at a new mythos. In his wrong he is right—because circumstances want it so. That circumstances too can be changed remains outside his experience. That is why the end changes nothing. It only comes back all the more strongly to its point of departure. His life remains without a future, a stagnating self-enclosed vision of chaos and emptiness. (pp. 103-11)

Renate Matthaei, in his Luigi Pirandello, *translated by Simon and Erika Young, Frederick Ungar Publishing Co., 1973, 184 p.*

ROGER W. OLIVER (essay date 1979)

[*In the following excerpt, Oliver discusses the major ideas in Pirandello's essay* L'umorismo *and their relevance to the interpretation of his drama.*]

L'umorismo, the most complete enunciation of Pirandello's aesthetic principles, was first written in 1908 and then revised and reissued in 1920. These dates are important. They indicate that although Pirandello first published the essay before he began his playwriting career—basing its chapters on a series of lectures he delivered at the girls' school where he was teaching—he returned to the essay, revising and enlarging it, after he had written over a dozen plays. Also significant is the fact that the revision was published only a year before he wrote *Sei personaggi in cerca d'autore (Six Characters in Search of An Author)* and two years before *Enrico IV (Henry IV),* two of his greatest plays. Thus, in the middle of his career as a dramatist, Pirandello returned to his essay on humor, an essay that is not written specifically about drama but that sheds a great deal of light on his practice as a playwright.

The essence of *L'umorismo,* a treatise that includes a linguistic, historical, and comparative analysis of the word "humor," is captured in an often quoted description of an old lady and, more important, in the humorist's response to her:

> I see an old woman, with her hair dyed, greasy all over with who knows what kind of horrible concoction, awkwardly made up with rouge and dressed in youthful clothes. I begin to laugh. I become *aware* that this old woman is the *opposite* of what a respectable old woman should be. I can thus, after this first superficial encounter, stop myself at this comic impression. The comic is exactly this, an *awareness* of the *opposite.* But now, if reflection intervenes and suggests to me that this old woman probably does not experience any pleasure in dressing up this way, like a parrot, but that perhaps she suffers and does this only because she is pitifully deceiving herself that, dressed as she is, hiding her wrinkles and white hairs, she will succeed in keeping the love of a husband much younger than herself, then after realizing this I am no longer able to laugh, as I did before, because this reflection has worked on me and made me go beyond the first impression, or rather, made me look more deeply within myself. From the first awareness of the opposite I have made myself pass to this *sentiment* or *feeling of the opposite.* And this is all the difference between the comic and the humorous.

This graphic image of the old woman illustrates the dual focus of Pirandello's interest and his art. He begins with a careful description of the old woman's physical appearance, then moves from the objective phenomenon of the woman to his subjective apprehension of her, defining his apprehension in two stages. The first is a purely intellectual awareness of the surface, a reaction to incongruity that yields laughter. The second is an emotional understanding that combines thought and feeling in a perception of what might lie beneath that surface. This second level causes the laughter to cease, replacing it with compassion, and perhaps even tears. It is not the old woman but the perception of her that has altered, encompassing first the comic and then the more serious potentialities of the experience.

A closer investigation of this image of the old woman can lead us to a way of approaching Pirandello as a dramatic artist. The woman is a theatrical rather than a literary creation. She does not tell us about her life and the motivations that led to her actions of dyeing her hair, using excessive makeup and dressing in clothes more suitable for a younger woman. We see only her present state and must surmise the actions that created that state, like the dyeing of the hair. The motivations for her actions must also be surmised by those who observe her, her "audience." There is no outside source to provide background information. If the audience's impression of her changes, it is only because that change has occurred in the observer's mind after further reflection on the image she presents.

Moreover, her attempt to cheat reality and the way others perceive her is a theatrical trick. The old woman has used makeup and costume, two of the basic tools of the theater, to alter her physical appearance. She is creating a role, a character different from herself. Like an actress in a third-rate provincial company, however, she has performed the job poorly. Instead of convincing her audience, she has called attention not only to herself but to her use of makeup. She has revealed her identity as role player, and she is laughed at because she has done it so self-consciously.

Once the old woman's appearance elicits the response of laughter, the emphasis shifts to the person observing here, from the actress to the audience. That audience has been amused by her bungled makeup job. On reflection, is it possible, after all, that she is aware of what she has done? She may realize the ridiculousness of her persona and yet have decided that it is worth the risk in order to keep the man she loves. She has not intended the laughter and thus has failed in at least part of her deception. The existence of a deeper reason for the old woman's actions, and the possible self-realization of her grotesque image, however, has altered the way she is perceived. She may have neither this motivation nor this insight into her position, but if her observer endows her with it, then his apprehension of her will change whether she is correctly understood or not.

The complexity of *umorismo* as defined by Pirandello is therefore rooted in its ability to extend beyond one kind of perception to another perception that challenges and modifies the first. The comic is based on the *avvertimento del contrario,* the awareness of an opposite. This awareness of a superficial incongruity involves an outside standard, the "what a respectable woman should be" of the quotation. Humor, on the other had, is *il sentimento del contrario,* the feeling or sentiment of an opposite, and involves a comparison of two personal reactions. The humorist and, by extension, the audience members who are convinced by the playwright that they should view an action or a character as humorous, are thus moving beyond the apparently comic surface to the pain that may be concealed below. As this pain is revealed, a compassionate response is elicited, even though the awareness of the initial comic reaction remains, however inappropriate it may now be. Since the feeling of the second response is built on the previous comic awareness of incongruity, that comic response remains important, not only as the catalyst of *umorismo,* but as an integral part of it.

This conflict between surface appearance and deeper realities becomes the basis for both subject matter and dramatic technique. Previous discussions of the essay have focused on the former use, providing the source of the illusion-reality dialectic identified as one of Pirandello's primary concerns. His discussion in *L'umorismo* of another related dialectic, this one between life and form, has provided another wellspring for those critics trying to define a philosophical position in the plays:

> Life is a continuous flux that we try to stop, to fix in stable and determinate forms, both inside and out-

side of ourselves, because we are already fixed forms, forms that move in the midst of other immobile forms and that follow the flow of life until the movement stiffens, slows down and then stops. The forms in which we try to arrest and fix in ourselves this continual flux are the concepts and ideals by which we wish to preserve, in a coherent manner, all the fictions we create for ourselves, the conditions and the state in which we try to achieve stability. But inside of us, in what we call the soul, and that is the life in us, the flux continues, undetected, running under the dams and past the limits that we impose in creating a conscience and constructing a personality. In certain tempestuous moments, under attack from this flux, all of these forms of ours collapse miserably; and even the part that does not run under the dams and outside the limits, but discovers itself to us distinctly and thus is channeled into the feelings and duties that we impose upon ourselves in the habits we have marked out, at certain moments of overflow, even these parts exceed the blanks and upset everything.

There are some people who have restless spirits that are almost constantly amorphous and thus scornful of ever coagulating or solidifying into this or that form of personality. But even for those people who are much more tranquil, who are set into one kind of form or another, the amorphous state is still possible—the flux of life is in everything.

Although it may appear that Pirandello is positing a philosophical or even psychological system, these ideas were presented more in the hope of making his needs as an artist more clear. The conflict between the forms and concepts used to create order and the sense of freedom and change that appear essential to life is less interesting to Pirandello as an abstract dialectic than as a concrete manifestation in humor behavior. Because some people like the old lady create fictions or forms in an attempt to deal with life, to alter how they are perceived and how they see the world, the artist must explore both the nature of the phenomena and their consequences. Any position of relativism, based on the suggestion that an individual's personality is multifaceted and ever changing, is then presented, not as an abstract generalization, but as a perception into human nature dramatized for an audience through characters. The impulse toward generalization comes in the mind of the audience rather than in the words of the playwright. The old woman remains a concrete theatrical image even if the response to her undergoes change and analysis.

The idea of life opposing form given here is not a particularly original one. In discussing the flux of life, Pirandello is alluding to a concept similar to the élan vital of Henri Bergson and the life force of Friedrich Nietzsche and later George Bernard Shaw. In fact, most of the concepts in Pirandello's *L'umorismo* and plays were not original. The work of Sigmund Freud had revealed the multi-dimensionality of the personality, as well as the unconscious, while the formulations of Albert Einstein were defining relativity. Georg W. F. Hegel's "levels of consciousness" also can be found in the matrix of ideas from which Pirandello drew. It is in his transformation of these thoughts from the level of theory to that of artistic creation that Pirandello demonstrates his originality.

The difficulty of perception and the need for the complexity of humoristic vision can perhaps best be illustrated through Pirandello himself. In 1921 and 1923, respectively, an Italian critic, Adriano Tilgher, published two collections of essays, *Voci del tèmpo (Voices of the Time)* and *Studi sul teatro con-*

temporáneo (Studies in Contemporary Theater) [see excerpt dated 1923], where he lavishly praised Pirandello and used the life-form dichotomy of *L'umorismo* to explicate the plays. Pirandello, the victim of outrageous critical and public reaction, expressed his gratitude to Tilgher for clarifying his work but was perhaps overanxious to be appreciated. What had been posited by Pirandello as one part of an approach to life was now adopted as the way of interpreting his dramatic work. (pp. 1-6)

Another interpreter, the Italian director Luigi Squarzina, artistic director of the Teatro Stábile di Roma, vigorously challenges the Tilgherian dichotomy. For Squarzina, the key lies in Pirandello's presentation of a series of changing perspectives, making him "one of the first European writers to contribute to the fragmentation of traditional structures." As Squarzina sees it, this fragmentation goes far beyond Tilgher's life-form dialectic, as the following statement concerning his production of *Ciascuno a suo modo (Each in His Own Way)* makes clear:

> By moving continuously from identification to alienation and back to identification again, we presented Pirandello's reality as a playing with mirrors, as I think Pirandello really wanted it to be, but never as a Manichean dichotomy of reality—like A and B, black and white—never.

Although the life-form dichotomy can sometimes be used to describe the conflict between emotion and intellect that Pirandello often explores, as well as the conflict between a role and the person underneath, Squarzina is correct in arguing that the play's complexity surpasses the simplicity of Tilgher's formulation. His insistence on dealing with the attempt of forms to organize the life spirit—a spirit that tries to assert its freedom by breaking through those formal restrictions—also places excessive emphasis on the theoretical substratum of the plays, an emphasis that overlooks the theatrical images and relationships that are of primary importance.

When Squarzina writes of mirrors in connection with Pirandello's plays, he refers to an image that is ultimately much more important to an understanding of Pirandello's dramaturgy than the life-form dialectic. Pirandello himself defined the mirror as the principle of his theater aesthetic in the following terms:

> When a man lives, he lives and does not see himself. Well, put a mirror before him and make him see himself in the act of living, under the sway of his passions: either he remains astonished and dumbfounded at his own appearance, or else he turns away his eyes so as not to see himself, or else in disgust he spits at his image, or again clinches his fist to break it; and if he had been weeping, he can weep no more; if he had been laughing, he can laugh no more, and so on. In a word, there arises a crisis, and that crisis is my theater.

Actually, there are two crises in the *teatro dello spècchio* (theater of the mirror): one onstage and one in the auditorium. They are both crises of perception, however, and it is the relationship between the two, explored with great care, that establishes both Pirandello's dramaturgy and his vision of life as well. For Pirandello is ultimately much more concerned with perception than with metaphysics. The conflict between forms and a life force coursing underneath is subsidiary to the conflict between how the individual perceives the world and how others apprehend the same phenomenon.

The first crisis, involving the characters onstage, occurs when they are forced to confront something they have attempted to avoid looking at in the past and are forced to move from one level of perception to another. This confrontation may be beneficial, even though painful, or it may be disastrous, destroying an illusion that is necessary for the continuation of life. Pirandello is not an ideologue. He is not advocating the destruction of all forms, of all fictions, of all illusions. In fact, his sharpest criticism is reserved for those characters who insist on interfering with the private affairs of others, despite the possible harm they might cause. Thus, the exposure to Delia Moreno and Michele Rocca, two of the central characters of *Each in His Own Way,* that their mutual hatred is really a mask covering their love, is a necessary crisis, while the agony to which he group of gossips subjects the newly arrived Ponza-Frola family in *Cosí è (se vi pare) (That's the Way Things Are—If They Seem that Way to You)* is not.

The second kind of crisis is focused on the audience, when the playwright as humorist tries to get the spectators to make the same leap from the *avvertimento* to the *sentimento* level. The play has been a mirror of a particular aspect of life. Yet the audience's response should not stop with an examination of the characters, even if that examination probes beneath the dramatic surface to the reality of the stage life, making the connection between the ideas and emotions of the characters. The mirror in which other people's lives were reflected should now reflect something of the audience's own life. Through the crisis precipitated on stage another crisis should be caused in the spectator. If he identified with a character who was deceiving himself or wrongfully seeking information that was of no concern to him, then the revelation offered by the play can be personalized by the playgoer. Just as characters should have been presented with images that will penetrate through the intellectual conceits constituting the surface of their reality, so the audience should react in the same way. Once those characters have left the stage, the mirror reflects back to the audience images of themselves, as they confront their relationship with what they have just seen, as well as the reality of their own lives.

Sometimes Pirandello creates certain expectations in his audience by trapping them into identifying with characters who are searching for the wrong information or are engaged in dangerous pursuits. When those characters are frustrated, so is the audience. If Pirandello has functioned as a true humorist, however, the spectator's initial anger and frustration will not be his final reaction to the play. A member of the audience expecting to be told "the truth" about the family relationship between Signor and Signora Ponza and Signora Frola in *That's the Way Things Are* may, upon reflection, feel an empathy with the family's sorrow, leading to a realization that such information is certainly not the focal point of the play. A reversal will occur that will be the essence of humor. As Pirandello writes in *L'umorismo:*

> Every sentiment, every thought, every impulse that springs up in the humorist immediately splits itself into its opposite: every yes also becomes a no that in the end comes to assume the same value as the yes. Perhaps the humorist may pretend sometimes to hold only one position: inside of him, however, the other sentiment that at first doesn't seem to have the courage to reveal itself speaks to him; it speaks to him and begins to move him; now with a timid excuse, then with a shrewd reflection that deflates the seriousness of the situation and leads to laughter.

The serious may lead to the comic, the comic to the serious. Life, particularly as seen by an Italian, is tremendously volatile. Pirandello's plays thus suggest the constant possibility of reversal both in their subject matter and in the dramatic technique employed to communicate this insight to an audience. (pp. 7-10)

In dramatizing his insights on the stage, Pirandello's technique as a humorist differs from the one often employed by other literary and dramatic artists. Instead of trying to create a character and make him coherent through the cumulative revelation of information, adding more and more details until a portrait is completed, he creates a superficial image of that character and then tries to break it down. In Pirandello's works, first impressions are almost always contradicted later. The appearance expressed by an accumulation of surface detail must be penetrated, since the reality covered by that detail may be the opposite of what is first seen.

In this same way Pirandello's plays begin with the dominant theatrical convention of his day, that of psychological realism. A drawing room, a salon in a villa, eventually the theater stage itself becomes the location of his drama. Yet the vision dramatized is not that of familiar reality but of life unmasked by the humorist and then reflected back to an audience in a mirror showing an altered image. This new vision, attempting to engender in the audience the "sentiment of the contrary," may thus contradict the old, comfortable representation it is used to seeing, just as Pirandello's dramaturgy seems at first to be "realistic" and then fragments into something seen from new and different perspectives.

The surface appearance the humorist must penetrate is often, in Pirandello's plays, a conscious construct intended to deceive or distract. To define the process whereby characters—and, by extension, the theatergoers whose reality they mirror—try to make themselves into something that will pass as a coherent and consistent personality, he uses the term *costruirsi (to build oneself up).* The key to the process of *costruirsi* is the desire to create a persona, an image, that will cover over those very incongruities that the humorist seeks to expose. An appearance of unity is created to cover the reality of multiplicity. A character tries to hide the inconsistencies of his personality behind an image, a persona that will project the part of himself he wants to be seen, the part that he has built up.

The word used most often to describe these personae is "masks," and indeed the title chosen for Pirandello's total collection of dramatic work is *Maschere nude (Naked Masks).* There are many ways in which characters (and the people they reflect) can use these masks. A mask can be a fiction created as part of a *costruzióne,* of which the person using it is constantly aware. It can also be a fiction that comes to be believed in by the individual as his true reality. A mask can also be a construct that is forced upon the person by society in order to protect itself, especially if that person's behavior threatens to endanger the established order.

Pirandello does not take one consistent attitude toward the masks employed by his characters. The mask can be a protective as well as a destructive mechanism for both the individual and society. It is the humorist's job, with his mirror and the crisis it causes, to bring new insight when all perspective on the use of the mask has been lost, either by those who are wearing it or, as in the case of the group of gossips in *That's the Way Things Are,* those who capriciously try to tear it off without anticipating the possible consequences.

The very terms that Pirandello uses to express his vision of life suggest the close ties between that vision and the medium of the theater he has chosen to express it. . . . [The] key terms of *L'umorismo*—especially *maschera* (mask), *spècchio* (mirror), and *costruirsi*—are all close to the basic act of theater as a reenactment of life. Pirandello even uses these words as an integral part of his drama, with the characters actually referring to masks and mirrors. By structuring the characters' relationships with each other through these devices, Pirandello attempts to present his audience with a vision of itself that will generate awareness of the presence of these "theatrical" devices in nontheatrical circumstances; that is, in everyday life. (pp. 11-13)

The metaphor of the mask as a theatrical role suggests how the theater serves as mirror of reality, as re-creator of life's actions and people. It also predicates the opposite insight, that life itself is intensely theatrical, with individuals adopting masks in order to perform roles that will create an illusion for others and even for themselves. If theater is the illusion of reality, then very often so is life itself. Theater reflects life, and life theater, with both using roles, masks, makeup, and costumes to create the perception of another reality. The theater of the mirror thus becomes mutually reflective, with each mirror pointed at the other, so that at times there is great confusion over which is originating and which is reflecting, a confusion that is at the center of Pirandello's art.

If the actor's presentation of a character can be compared to the assumption of a mask, then it can also be linked to Pirandello's concept of the process of *costruirsi*. I do not think it is purely coincidental that the Russian actor Konstantin Stanislavski entitled one of his books *Building a Character,* for the whole process of the creation of a character is an act of construction. The actor begins with the foundation of the playwright's words and ideas; he then uses his imagination, intelligence, and physical skill to build up his vision of that character. Just as a person does not construct his character in a vacuum, so the actor must take into consideration what his fellow actors are doing and how his individual work fits into the overall design of the play as conceived by playwright and director.

Pirandello's self-proclaimed role as humorist makes the choice of his theatrical technique almost inevitable. As a humorist he often strips his characters of their illusions, their *costruzióne,* so that they must face the reality of their existence. In the same way he approaches the theatrical process—the relationship between audience and presentation—and strips away some of the illusion. In certain plays actors are called actors, and the stage is acknowledged in its true identity. Since Pirandello has written a play, there is still some illusion involved, but there is also more acknowledgment of the reality of the audience's presence in a theater than had been customary in the plays written previously. (p. 14)

Pirandello's self-conscious use of his medium . . . firmly places him within the realm of the Modernist approach to artistic creation. As defined by Clement Greenberg in his important essay "Modernist Painting," the distinguishing characteristic of the Modern in art is the artist's acknowledgment that he is working in his own medium. Instead of denying or camouflaging the materials at his disposal, he accepts and even emphasizes them. As Greenberg writes. "The essence of Modernism lies, as I see it, in the use of the characteristic methods of a discipline to criticize the discipline itself—not in order to subvert it, but to entrench it more firmly in its area of competence." (p. 16)

In the theater, the first step toward the Modernism discussed by Greenberg is the acknowledgment of the theater stage as the location of the play's action. Although later playwrights like Samuel Beckett, Eugène Ionesco, and Jean Genet go further in presenting more subtle exploration of what Peter Brook calls "the empty space" of the theater, it is Pirandello, with his raised curtain and empty stage greeting the incoming audience of *Six Characters in Search of an Author,* who really heralds the arrival of Modernism in the theater. Although it is true that Bertolt Brecht soon experimented in a similar way with his "alienation technique," distancing both actor and audience from the realistic illusion of the play, it is Pirandello's theatricalism, despite its retention of certain illusory practices, that forged the bonds between the two sides of the footlights and made the Modernist theater possible. (p. 17)

The humoristic artist, in whatever medium, goes beyond the comic and/or satiric perception of illusions. He tries to penetrate beneath the surface of these illusions in order to understand them in all their complexity. Most important, the humorist wants to see how and why these illusions come to be. It is this very search for complexity, and the understanding of this complexity, that produces the compassion that sets his work apart from the comic and satiric writers. Pirandello wants to undress his characters, not to laugh at or scorn them, but to come to terms with the "real" person, in all of his or her humanity. When this real person is seen, the combination of laughter and tears is the appropriate response. *Umorismo* is thus especially necessary in the twentieth century, where the human condition is perceived as an end in itself rather than as part of a larger process in which actions might be given meaning or justification by reference to some religious or cosmic process.

The theater becomes the best way of communicating this humoristic vision to others precisely because it presents the body as well as the soul of its characters. A first impression can be created by the visual appearance of a character in a certain milieu, an impression that can be contradicted by what the character later reveals through actions and the response of others. Since one illusion—that of actor as character, of stage setting as real place—is already being created, the atmosphere for the exploration of these and other illusions has been established. The connection between the illusion of the theater and the illusions of everyday life can be made without much preparation, because the art of acting, the creation of a role, a "mask," is so close to the vision of life suggested in the essay. (pp. 18-19)

Pirandello further merges his aesthetic, as formulated in *L'umorismo,* and his dramatic practice by structuring his plays in such a way that if the audience members do not follow his clues and perceive humoristically, they will miss the very point he is making. Those theatergoers, including critics, who stop at the intellectual aspects of Pirandello's plays, fail to penetrate the surface of his work. Humanity may try to live rationally, under the rule of logic, but when a person is in "the act of living," he or she often acts under the sway of passion. Many of the so-called philosophical speeches in Pirandello's plays, particularly those of the Father in *Six Characters,* are in reality deeply felt attempts to justify actions that were prompted by the dominance of emotion over intellect. Pirandello is investigating human nature as a complete organism, an organism that has both emotional-sentimental and rational-intellectual sides, and he accomplishes this by engaging his audience on both of these levels. These two sides often come into conflict with each other, and out of this crisis, referred to as *il senti-*

mento del contrario, comes the core of the theatrical work under discussion here.

Pirandello's theater, a mirror that attempts to penetrate through the facades built by people in order to reflect the reality of their inner being, does not present an exact replica of that image. It distorts, transforms, and selects. Ideas are exaggerated into bloodless abstractions, emotions into melodrama. In exploring the primal conflict between the two sides of human nature, Pirandello, as artist, emphasizes the extremities of the duality. There is also a cumulative effect. If the intellect has dominated, then emotional pressures build until they finally erupt with great force. The enormity of the passionate outburst may then require sophisticated intellectualization in order to supply the self-justification necessary to maintain the vision of self necessary for survival.

Pirandello is really too complex a playwright to settle for delivering a message in his work. Yet if one can be conjectured, it is less concerned with the ideas of the plays—illusion versus reality, the difficulty of establishing one truth, one personality, or one vision of life—than with the process of perception that is at the basis of his dramaturgy. The humorist does not stop at surface appearances—at what may first seem to be—but continues to look, to examine, to be open to feelings as well as thought. In doing this he often reverses his first perception, exchanging it for a deeper insight, one that combines both sides of human nature and that often results in a compassion missing from the initial response. Pirandello chooses a dramatic technique that challenges the validity of first impressions by an interpenetration of theater and life, his mirror and what it reflects. In creating a self-conscious, Modernist theater, he is paradoxically creating an art that penetrates into the truth of life, where the practices and ideas of the theater have become more and more central to human relationships. Pirandello's art ultimately merges subject matter and form, so that they, like thought and emotion, theater and life, and the comic and tragic response, interpenetrate to comment on and enrich each other, creating the complexity that is both Pirandello's intention and his achievement. (pp. 20-1)

> *Roger W. Oliver, in his* Dreams of Passion: The Theatre of Luigi Pirandello, *New York University Press, 1979, 167 p.*

OLGA RAGUSA (essay date 1980)

[*In the following excerpt, Ragusa notes the importance of Pirandello's one-act plays as a key to understanding his dramas, analyzes his female characters, and examines the plays he designated "modern myths."*]

[From] its beginnings Pirandello's theatre had contacts outside the *teatri stabili* and the main acting companies.

The premières of *La morsa* and *Lumíe di Sicilia,* of *Il dovere del medico* and *La patente,* took place thanks to "little" theatres, . . . [and most of Pirandello's dialect production fell] outside the main line of Italian theatrical life at the time. In 1922-3 there was the premiere of *L'uomo dal fiore in bocca* at the Teatro degli Indipendenti, directed by Anton Giulio Bragaglia pithily described as "by temperament unconventional." There was also a performance of *All'uscita,* presented as part of a "tri-synthesis" together with Marinetti's *Bianca e Rosso* and the pantomime *Malagueña* interpreted by Jia Ruskaja. . . . This brings us practically to the eve of the foundation of the Teatro d'Arte and its opening performance of yet another ex-

perimental one-act play *Sagra del Signore della nave.* . . . (pp. 172-73)

This rapid review of Pirandello's contacts with experimental theatre establishes the potential importance of the one-act plays as a key to his entire production. The one-act plays not only span his entire career as a playwright but, synchronically considered, they form an exceptionally interesting unit, whose various implications have however been completely overlooked. The situation stems both from the lack of critical attention accorded this minor genre in general—a step-child even more than the short story has been—and from the predominantly thematic approach which has prevailed in Pirandello studies. Moreover, information about the one-act plays is less readily available than for the three-act ones, except perhaps for *L'uomo dal fiore in bocca* which is often ranked with the masterpieces. One of the difficulties arises at the moment of production itself and casts its shadow over the subsequent history of reception and assessment. A one-act play alone does not constitute an evening at the theatre. It must always be given together with some other performance. . . . The play(s), dance(s), song(s) accompanying it no doubt interfere with sustained and focused attention. Yet, at the same time, they provide a new and unusual context within which to situate the work, a context which is not limited to textual material. In Pirandello studies these contexts have rarely been stated and never explored. And yet, with the exception of the trilogy of the theatre-within-the-theatre, the one-act plays offer an almost text-book illustration of Pirandello's interest in transcending the limitations of a given medium, be it written narrative or traditional drama. From the

Pirandello with his grandchildren in 1934. Photo collection Dr. Alfredo Zennaro.

short stories turned plays as "novelle sceneggiate" ("dramatized short stories"—this is how the first version of the play *La patente* was designated) a direct line leads to the much later public readings of Pirandello stories, the musical versions of some of the plays, and the adaptations of both narrative and drama for the screen, the radio, and after his death television.

But there can be no doubt that the most important aspect of Pirandello's later years was his encounter with Marta Abba, the third "actor" [after Angelo Musco and Ruggero Ruggeri] to have had a determining role in the conception and fashioning of his theatre. Once again works would come into being in which the "character" did not exist prior to the actor who was to impersonate him, where a "part" did not exist prior to the assignment of that part, where there was a minimum in break of continuity between the play as it was in the author's mind and as it would be on stage. (pp. 173-74)

Abba made her debut in Rome on 22 April 1925 in the Pirandellian play *Nostra Dea*—whose protagonist changes personality with every change in dress—written by Massimo Bontempelli, one of the co-founders of the Teatro d'Arte and leading Italian modernist. . . . By mid-June she had played in *Enrico IV* and *Sei personaggi*. Bontempelli writes that this performance (the first directed by Pirandello himself) was "a completely new interpretation of that masterpiece"—referring, no doubt, to the specially prepared final, revised version of the play . . .— and that Abba brought to the role of the Stepdaughter "the restlessness, the mysterious self-flagellation that constitute the very personal, unique foundation of her artistic personality." It was not until 1927, however, that she was to act in a play written expressly for her by Pirandello: *Diana e la Tuda* and *L'amica delle mogli*. By that time she had added or was about to add to her repertoire the roles of Signora Frola in *Così è (se vi pare)*, Ersilia in *Vestire gli ignudi*, Evelina in *La signora Morli, una e due*, Agata in *Il piacere dell'onestà*, Silia in *Il giuoco delle parti*, and Fulvia in *Come prima, meglio di prima*. (She had played Gasparina in *Ma non è una cosa seria* earlier, even before being called to Rome.) The London *Times* critic who reviewed the 1925 performances of Pirandello's Company on tour was struck by Abba's versatility: she "showed herself as clever at representing dowagers [Signora Frola] as the young heroines [the Stepdaughter and Ersilia] for which hitherto she had been cast." Of her interpretation of Dea, Silvio D'Amico had written: "We came to know in turn a roughish, passive, tender, dreamy, treacherous, composed and suppliant Abba." More than anyone else she succeeded in achieving Pirandello's wished for, complete identification between actor and role . . . to the point that she is reported to have been in the habit of tacking up on her dressing room door not her own name but the name of the character she was playing.

Much—perhaps too much—has been written about Pirandello's male characters. *The* Pirandellian character, suffering *raisonneur* or character in search of an author, is always understood to be a male character. But if instead of starting with the premise of a certain predetermined development in Pirandello's work and fitting Mattia Pascal and Ciampa, Baldovino, and Chiàrchiaro, Serafino Gubbio and Signor Ponza, "Enrico IV" and the Father into it, we were to start with a phenomenology of characters, a kind of mammoth Cast of Characters of the men, women and children that populate the world of his narrative and drama, we would find how large and varied is the part women play in it. They represent not only the other half of mankind, but are far less homogeneous as a group than Nicola Ciarletta implies when, basing himself on a selective

sample, he characterizes Pirandello's women as "without country—they could be equally well Sicilian or German—stateless, without passport, tied to the power of men who can construct or destroy them, raise them or debase them, give them a name or take it away again." . . . Though there are those that are little more than part of a setting—signora Agazzi and her entourage in *Così è (se vi pare)*, la Barbetti in *Tutto per bene*, zia Nifa and comare Gesa in *Liolà*—others have destiny, sometimes, as in the case of signora Ponza, all the more rock firm for being so drastically understated. In the plays that Pirandello wrote for Marta Abba—*La nuova colonia, Lazzaro, Come tu mi vuoi, Trovarsi, Quando si è qualcuno,* in addition to those already mentioned—and in those that she made hers through repeated performance, we are of course not dealing with chorus figures but with protagonists, protagonists who came on stage well after Pirandello had abandoned the regional world of his early drama and had already created those ambiguous female characters who, as in *La ragione degli altri*, proved stumbling-blocks on the way to success. (pp. 174-76)

Of the first two plays that Pirandello wrote for Marta Abba, *L'amica delle mogli* belongs to what are commonly thought of as the minor works, while *Diana e la Tuda*, one of only three plays he designated a tragedy, stood so high in his estimate that in the final collection of *Maschere nude* he placed it immediately after the three plays of the theatre-within-the-theatre and *Enrico IV*. There is one structural feature that sets these two plays (as it does *La ragione degli altri* for that matter) apart from the [plays written for] . . . Ruggeri: the protagonist—to whom the title directs attention—appears on stage without elaborate preparation, without doubts or questions regarding her identity, which imposes itself instead with the incontrovertible evidence of a physical fact: "Entra Marta," we read in the stage directions for *L'amica delle mogli.*

> E bellissima; fulva; occhi di mare, liquidi, pieni di luce. Ha ventiquattr'anni: contegno, non rigido, ma riserbatissimo, che non impedisce affatto però la pura espressione della più nobile grazia femminile.

> ("Enter Martha. She is very beautiful, with tawny hair and sea-coloured dewy eyes, flooded with light. She is 24. She is reserved but not stiff, and her bearing does not in any way inhibit the purest expression of feminine grace and nobility.")

And in the stage directions for *Diana e la Tuda*, as Tuda appears from behind the curtain which had shielded her from view while she was posing, we read:

> È giovanissima e di meravigliosa bellezza. Capelli fulvi, ricciuti, pettinati alla greca. Occhi verdi, lunghi, grandi e lucenti, che ora, nella passione, s'intorbidano come acqua di lago; ora nella serenità, si fermano a guardare limpidi e dolci come un'alba lunare; ora nella tristezza, hanno l'opacità dolente della turchese.

> ("She is very young and marvellously beautiful. She has tawny curly hair dressed in Greek style. Long green eyes, large and shining. They grow cloudy like the waters of a lake, in passion; in peace and tranquility, they are still, transparent and tender like the light of the rising moon; in sadness, they are mournfully lustreless like turquoise."). . .

(pp. 176-77)

Like *Enrico IV* (and *Il giuoco delle parti*), *Diana e la Tuda* ends with an act of murder. The murderer is Nono Giuncano, a sculptor who, in an impetus of rebellion and in his quest for the immediacy of life, gave up his art by smashing the statues in his study. When the play opens, he is trying to dissuade the much younger Sirio Dossi from continuing work on a statue of Diana for which the young, beautiful, and very much alive Tuda—she is holding a bunch of grapes in one hand and a sandwich in the other when she first appears—is posing. The stage directions describe Giuncano as in his sixties, gloomy and restless, with white dishevelled hair and beard but youthful, piercing eyes in contrast to a lined and wasted face. He has, in other words, the attributes of the troubled, divided Pirandellian hero. But as the title indicates, he is not the protagonist of the play. This creates an imbalance or a lack of focus absent from the plays written for Ruggeri. In comparison to those plays, *Diana e la Tuda* is simpler. In it, too, there is preceding action (Giuncano had befriended Sirio when he was a boy and there is even a hint that the two are father and son), but its disclosure is not tortured and torturing as in those plays. *Diana e la Tuda* lacks their complicated time perspective, the revelation of time past, the searing *anagnorisis*. Our expectation of finding a protagonist-centred play is further disappointed when we discover that the title itself is misleading in this respect. It is the closest Pirandello has come to naming a play after a woman, an impression strengthened by its proximity to *Enrico IV* in the table of contents of *Maschere nude*. But the two female names refer one to the representation of the mythological goddess as statue and the other, preceded by the familiar, almost condescending *la,* to the artist's model. Thus they stand not for two persons or even two things (Diana as an object and *la* Tuda as an object) but for a relationship: the relationship between the work of art and reality, or between Form and Life to use Tilgher's terminology, which is appropriate here. We are back with the more typical, epigrammatic Pirandellian titles which point to an underlying idea or express a gnomic judgement.

But in *Diana e la Tuda* story and idea do not merge as successfully as in *Cosí è (se vi pare)*, *Sei personaggi*, or *Vestire gli ignudi*. The untidiness of passion, which in Pirandello is never far beneath the surface of ratiocination, here bursts forth with particular virulence and sullies the stark monochrome of an extraordinary expressionistic setting: the studio's white walls, the black rug and furniture, the plaster casts of various Diana statues, the enormous, black shadow of the posing Tuda projected against the wall. Like "Enrico IV" and Belcredi, Giuncano and Sirio are rivals (in both plays the word "cimentare" ("to provoke") recurs as the linguistic clue to the structural parallel just before the *dénouement*). While the old Giuncano, approaching the final and irreversible rigidity of death, opts for life, for the wonder of red poppies growing for no one but themselves on an abandoned field (a parallel to the dying Tommaso's vision of blades of grass in the early *Il dovere del medico*) or for Pygmalion's miracle which would discompose the statue into a living, moving woman (like others of Pirandello's protagonists Giuncano is looking for a "remedy," an incandescent substance which could flow through marble like blood), Sirio is unrelenting in his pursuit of the completion and perfection of his work, after which he plans to commit suicide.... Tuda loves Sirio who, intent on his project, can love neither her nor anyone else, and she does not love Giuncano who both loves and understands her. (Twice she playfully kisses Giuncano in Act I, the consummate playwright's touch to hint at what the "correct" pairing-off would be.) Worse still, Tuda loves Sirio the man, not Sirio the sculptor. The human sentiment with its unpredictable impulses, its rootedness in the world of everyday experience, thus deflects the direction of the play and introduces petty jealousies (Tuda's "betrayal" of Sirio with the painter Caravani for whose grotesque, vulgar

interpretation of Diana she also poses; the rivalry between Tuda and Sirio's mistress Sara Mendel) and the variegated activities connected with a successful model's life (a busy scene with dressmaker and milliner; an encounter with the "witches," aged former models who come to warm themselves at the embers in Sirio's stove) into what is on another level the lonely Promethean struggle between artist and work. At the end, events accelerate and Giuncano, true to the model of "Enrico," but without the added burden or illumination of insanity, kills his rival, Tuda is robbed of any possibility of self-realization, of "consisting," to use a Pirandellian term, of having life, that is, as either woman or statue, person or character. In the bleak ending of the play, which finds Giuncano and Tuda separated, each in his own annihilation, Tuda, like Ersilia in *Vestire gli ignudi,* assumes responsibility for what has happened: "Ucciso per me, per me che ho la colpa di tutto!" ("He has been killed for (through) me who am to blame for everything!"). Her failure has been one of compassionate understanding and self-sacrifice. The run-down, emaciated, prematurely aged woman into whom she has turned, with hard glassy eyes and clenched hands that she can no longer relax (a challenging interpretation for Abba the actress!) is an emblem parallel to that of the veiled signora Ponza at the end of *Cosí è (se vi pare):* "Io, io sì, di tutto—perchè non seppi essere quella per cui lui mi aveva voluto!" ("Yes, I, I am to blame for everything because I was not able to be the one that he wanted!"). Once more we hear that statement of supreme acquiescence and almost mystical merging by which the creature accepts the imprint of the maker, man accepts the will of God, which is one of the most powerful motifs in Pirandello's work and is the culturally conditioned underpinning of his yearning and straining for unity.

This brings us to the last area in Pirandello's production to which attention should be drawn: the plays that he designated as "miti moderni" ["modern myths"]. In 1931 he published the first act of *I giganti della montagna* (left unfinished at his death) under the title of *I fantasmi*. In the introductory note he established the existence of a second trilogy in his work, a parallel to the theatre-within-the-theatre: *Lazzaro,* the religious myth; *La nuova colonia,* the social myth; *I giganti,* the art myth. What exactly Pirandello meant by myth is a moot point, although the reversed chronological order in which he cites the first two—*La nuova colonia* was actually conceived and executed before *Lazzaro*—would seem to indicate that he had in mind some global view of mankind's progress, probably derived from his early acquaintance with German Romantic thought and more recently reinforced by his contacts with theatrical and artistic life in France and Germany (Pitoëff and Reinhardt). "Myth" is one of those "very significant" and "very difficult" words that Raymond Williams has written about in *Keywords*. From what was once a negative term for a lie or an untruth, it has become a highly charged expression of approbation for the imaginative capacities of man, conceived not so much as the gift of an individual but of a whole people or race. While myth may be a story, it may also be a perspective or a mode of consciousness. In both instances, the primitive—whether cultural or psychological—is privileged. The world of myth is not only the world of fiction, but the world of archetypal images beneath and beyond the civilizing force of logic. In addressing an international meeting on the theatre in 1934, Pirandello showed how all-embracing his concept of theatre had become, encompassing not only the "pantheatricalism" of Nikolaj Evreinov but having recaptured also the original idea of theatre as public ritual and religious ceremonial. "Il teatro propone," he said, quasi a vero e proprio giudizio pubblico le azioni umane quali veramente sono, nella realtà schietta e eterna che la fantasia dei poeti crea ad esempio ed ammonimento della vita naturale cotidiana e confusa: libero e umano giudizio che efficacemente richiama la coscienza degli stessi giudici a una vita morale sempre piú alta e esigente.

("The theatre proposes, as though to true and proper judgement, human actions as they really are, in the genuine and eternal reality which is created by the imagination of poets to be example and admonition to natural life in its everdayness and confusion: a free and human judgement which effectively calls back the judges themselves to an ever higher and more exigent moral life.")

The early spectators and reviewers of the myths—of *La nuova colonia* and *Lazzaro* to be precise, for *I giganti della montagna* had a different history—knew as little about nascent studies of myth as the spectators and reviewers who had first rejected *Sei personaggi* had known about a tradition of the play-within-the-play in the history of drama. Sandro D'Amico recalls that to the public that had just mastered Tilgher's interpretation, the "new" Pirandello appeared to have undergone "a kind of senile conversion," that his "pervasive optimism" was as difficult to digest as his pessimism had been. Subsequent criticism, too, has maintained a negative view. Together with the rest of Pirandello's post-1923 production, the myths have been given short shrift. Once again, Pirandello's "philosophy"—his ideas on nature, science, religion, morality, society, art . . . —attracted more attention than his "art." Specifically, under Fascism the myths tended to be studied to determine whether or not they conformed to orthodox ideology while, since, Marxian criticism has used them to show how reactionary Pirandello's model of human progress is, inasmuch as he is deaf to the class struggle and depends on accommodation and illusion for whatever personal and social reconciliation he can envisage. The absence of any but the most meagre theatrical history for *La nuova colonia* and *Lazzaro* has made the situation particularly difficult for these two plays, by keeping occasions for a fresh view to a minimum. We must more or less accept on trust Bragaglia's opinion that *La nuova colonia* is "an absolute masterpiece in Pirandello's theatre." (Again the case of *I giganti* is different for its status of unfinished work has exercised a special fascination on directors and producers and it has been performed more frequently and under better conditions than the others.)

To come to *La nuova colonia* directly after *Diana e la Tuda* is to be struck by the vast world of difference between the two. Not only are the setting and the social class of the protagonists different, but it is as though the individual "hero," the character seeking centre-stage to plead his "reason," had been pushed back and almost completely reabsorbed into the chorus or crowd from which he had initially emerged. In terms of the social ladder sketched by Verga in the Preface to *I Malavoglia,* we are back "in those lower spheres in which the mechanism of the passions is less complicated." But *La nuova colonia* also differs from the more or less contemporary *Questa sera si recita a soggetto,* to which it is rarely related since the chronological proximity is lost sight of when the latter is grouped (as done by Pirandello himself) with the plays of the theatre-within-the-theatre. Franca Angelini has suggested that Pirandello's myths are to be placed in the context of Bontempelli's and of the latter's call for a theatre to educate the masses, to capture, as he wrote in 1933, that "atmosphere of a beginning (*primordio* is his word) which fate has assigned to our time."

There can be no doubt that Bontempelli is thinking of the new historical epoch ushered in by the Fascist revolution, but it is also true that the very words "primordial" or "primeval" carry with them a reference to origin: for Pirandello, his Sicilian origins.

In both *La nuova colonia* and *Questa sera* we find again, in contrast to *Diana e la Tuda,* Pirandello's well-known Sicilian subject-matter. Sicily provides the inner story of the play-within-the-play in *Questa sera,* and though this story is not set as precisely as *Liolà's* had been (in the countryside of Agrigento, complete with the dialect that is spoken there and no where else), it is still a story of characters identifiable by their *état civil* ["civil state"], with recognizable names and documentable pedigrees. The distancing effect is supplied by the outer story—the plan for a performance based on improvisation rather than a script—and this outer "story" is of course in the very vanguard of the theatrical experimentation of Modernism. In *La nuova colonia* the curtain rises on a tavern scene in a sea-faring town of the South; it might well be in Sicily but not necessarily so, for there is nothing geographically localized in the setting of the circumstances of the different characters who gather there. And the distancing effect achieved by this initial indeterminateness is reinforced when only one character (the tavern keeper) has the individual identity bestowed by a name and surname. All the others are known by given names, nicknames, and diminutives, differentiating them at the very primitive level of distinguishing characteristics perceived and verbalized in a closed and limited social environment. We are indeed in the world of myth and not of history, or to put it in terms of Pirandello's total production, we are in the world of *Sagra del Signore della nave, La favola del figlio cambiato, All'uscita,* and *I giganti della montagna.* In the first, the scene is a village festival and the people who congregate there are, with one exception, known only by their trade, profession, or status. In the second, the scene is a theatrical space with its possibility for changes in scenery, and the characters belong to the world of the fairy-tale: the prince and the changeling, the mother and the witch. In the third, we are on a country road against a cemetery wall; and the characters are "Appearances" and "Aspects of Life"—and it is not insignificant that the play, first written in 1916, should have been placed in *Maschere nude* (a collection arranged thematically and not chronologically) at the head of the last group of plays, immediately preceding *La nuova colonia.* In the fourth, finally, we are in an indeterminate place, "al limite, fra la favola e la realtà" ("at the boundary line, between fable and reality"), and the characters are the Scalognati [the unlucky ones, ex-variety actors who have escaped from ordinary life], the members of the Countess's Acting Company (she is Ilse, "la fata amica" ["the fairy friend"], who had already appeared fleetingly in *Arte e coscienza d'oggi*), and beings described simply as Apparitions, the angel Centuno, and puppets (*fantocci*)—a strange assortment indeed to appear on the stage that had through most of Pirandello's career been occupied by characters who "imitated" men and women of the real world, even though they had often had, in their opposition to one another, an ontological function.

The later Pirandello is the most difficult one—difficult because he has not been studied enough, because he is unfamiliar, and especially because the many layers of his previous production, achieved step by step over a period of about fifty years, reappear and coexist in any one of the plays in an ever-changing configuration: recognizable character types and situations that ask to be understood anew both in spite of and because of their background. If we come to these plays by way of the earlier ones, we may be disturbed by similarities that yet do not conform to the familiar pattern. If we come to them directly, discounting the earlier ones, we risk finding ourselves faced by a short-hand—Pirandello's achieved personal self-expression—for which we lack the key. They represent a challenge which has barely begun to be taken up. (pp. 177-83)

Olga Ragusa, in her Luigi Pirandello: An Approach to His Theatre, *Edinburgh University Press, 1980, 198 p.*

ADDITIONAL BIBLIOGRAPHY

Alley, John. "French Periodical Criticism of Pirandello's Plays." *Italica* XXV, No. 2 (June 1948): 138-49.
    Describes the critical reception of Pirandello's drama in France.

Aste, Mario. "Two Short Stories of Pirandello: Their Sources and Their Relationship to the Essay *Umorismo.*" *Perspectives on Contemporary Literature* 7 (1981): 64-72.
    Compares two of Pirandello's short stories, "I galletti del bottaio" and "Il gatto, un cardellino e le stelle," to their respective sources and comments on the relevance of *L'umorismo* to the themes of the story.

Bassnett-McGuire, Susan. *Luigi Pirandello.* New York: Grove Press, 1983, 190 p.
    Thematic exploration of Pirandello's drama.

Bentley, Eric. *The Pirandello Commentaries.* Evanston: Northwestern University Press, 1986, 119 p.
    Includes ten essays written between 1946 and 1986 by a prominent critic and translator of Pirandello's works.

Bergin, Thomas G. "Luigi Pirandello: Pathfinder—and More." *Books Abroad* 41, No. 4 (Autumn 1967): 413-14.
    Acknowledges the lasting influence of Pirandello's dramatic themes and techniques but argues that Pirandello will be most remembered for the sensitive portrayal of the human condition in his fiction.

Biasin, Gian-Paolo. "Strategies of the Anti-hero: Svevo, Pirandello, and Montale." In *Italian Literature: Roots and Branches,* edited by Giose Rimanelli and Kenneth John Atchity, pp. 363-81. New Haven: Yale University Press, 1976.
    Describes the character Vitangelo Moscarda from *Uno, nessuno e centomila* as a classic example of an anti-hero.

Bishop, Thomas. *Pirandello and the French Theater.* New York: New York University Press, 1960, 170 p.
    Traces Pirandello's influence on the major French playwrights of the twentieth century.

Buck, Philo M., Jr. "Futility in Masquerade: Luigi Pirandello." In his *Directions in Contemporary Literature,* pp. 79-100. New York: Oxford University Press, 1942.
    Treats the major themes in Pirandello's drama.

Cambon, Glauco, ed. *Pirandello: A Collection of Critical Essays.* Englewood Cliffs, N.J.: Prentice-Hall, 1967, 182 p.
    Contains thirteen essays by prominent critics. Included are an abridged English translation of Adriano Tilgher's important essay in *Studi sul teatro contemporaneo;* "The Techniques of the Unseizable," by Auréliu Weiss; and "Pirandello's Drama of Revolt," by Robert Brustein.

Canadian Journal of Italian Studies 6, No. 22-3 (1983): 155 p.
    Special issue containing sixteen articles and bibliographies on Pirandello in Italian and English.

Chandler, Frank W. "The Philosophic Pirandello." In his *Modern Continental Playwrights,* pp. 573-95. New York: Harper & Brothers, 1931.

General overview of Pirandello's drama.

Clark, Hoover W. "Existentialism and Pirandello's *Sei Personaggi.*" *Italica* XLIII (1966): 276-84.
    Compares existentialist elements in *Sei personaggi* with the tenets of modern existentialist thought.

Costa, Orazio. "The Italian Directors Face to Face with Pirandello." *World Theatre* XVI, No. 3 (May-June 1967): 248-55.
    Holds that Pirandello renovated the dramatic conventions of his day. Costa relies on his experience in directing Pirandello's plays to develop his argument.

Della Fazia, Alla. "Pirandello's Mirror Theater." *Renascence* XV, No. 2 (Fall 1962): 37-40.
    Examines the function of mirror imagery in Pirandello's drama.

Della Terza, Dante. "On Pirandello's Humorism." In *Veins of Humor,* edited by Harry Levin, pp. 17-33. Cambridge: Harvard University Press, 1972.
    Discusses Pirandello's theory of humor as put forth in *L'umorismo* and its application to his work.

Fabbri, Diego. "A Rip in a Paper Sky." *World Theatre* XVI, No. 3 (May-June 1967): 218-23.
    Examines Pirandello's original dramatic techniques and notes that his greatness lies in the tragic vision by which he produces catharsis in his audiences and readers.

Fergusson, Francis. "The Theatricality of Shaw and Pirandello." In his *The Idea of a Theatre,* pp. 178-93. Princeton: Princeton University Press, 1949.
    Praises *Six Characters in Search of an Author* for its sophisticated subversion of the limiting conventions imposed on theater by modern realism.

Giudice, Gaspare. *Pirandello: A Biography,* translated by Alastair Hamilton. Oxford: Oxford University Press, 1975, 221 p.
    Abridged translation of the standard critical biography.

Golino, Carlo L. "Pirandello's Least Known Novel." *Italica* XXVI, No. 4 (December 1949): 263-68.
    Explicates Pirandello's novel *Suo marito* (1911).

Hamilton, Clayton. "Luigi Pirandello and Maurice Maeterlinck." In his *Conversations on Contemporary Drama,* pp. 150-74. New York: MacMillan Co., 1925.
    Argues that Pirandello's plays fail because they do not provide the stable characters that audiences of drama expect.

Heffner, Hubert C. "Pirandello and the Nature of Man." In *Modern Drama: Essays in Criticism,* edited by Travis Bogard and William I. Oliver, pp. 255-75. London: Oxford University Press, 1965.
    Disputes the view that "dissolution of the ego" is Pirandello's most important contribution to modern drama. Heffner analyzes elements of dramatic characterization and human personality in order to demonstrate that "the ego does not disappear in Pirandello's character; it grows more complex, taking on some of the aspects of change which we find in human personality."

Italica XLIV, No. 1 (March 1967): 1-60.
    Issue containing several Italian and English articles on Pirandello, including "Pirandello's *Six Characters in Search of an Author: A Comedy in the Making,*" by Antonio Illiano; "Pirandello and the Puppet World," by Douglas Radcliff-Umstead; and "Pirandello and Azorin," by Wilma Newberry.

Krutch, Joseph Wood. "Pirandello and the Dissolution of the Ego." In his *"Modernism" in Modern Drama,* pp. 65-87. Ithaca: Cornell University Press, 1953.
    Examines Pirandello's denial of the existence of a consistent human personality.

Lavrin, Janko. "Luigi Pirandello." In his *Aspects of Modernism: From Wilde to Pirandello,* pp. 231-47. London: Stanley Nott, 1935.
    Discusses the major themes in Pirandello's drama.

Lucas, F. L. "Part IV—Luigi Pirandello." In his *The Drama of Chekhov, Synge, Yeats, and Pirandello*, pp. 358-438. London: Cassell, 1963.
Brief essays on each of Pirandello's plays.

Lucente, Gregory L. "'Non conclude': Self-Consciousness and the Boundaries of Modernism in Pirandello's Narrative." In *Criticism* XXVI, No. 1 (Winter 1984): pp. 21-47.
Probes the development of Pirandello's philosophical ideas and literary aesthetics in two of his novels: *The Late Mattia Pascal* and *One, None, and a Hundred Thousand*.

Phelps, Ruth Shepard. "Pirandello's Plays." In her *Italian Silhouettes*, pp. 116-41. New York: Alfred A. Knopf, 1924.
Overview of Pirandello's drama.

Piccoli, Raffaello. "Italian Letter." *The Dial* LXXVIII (January 1925): 43-50.
Criticizes Pirandello's work, concluding that its attack on absolutes is antithetical to poetic imagination. Piccoli attributes Pirandello's popular and critical success to a general deterioration of Italian culture during the modern era.

Radcliff-Umstead, Douglas. *The Mirror of Our Anguish: A Study of Luigi Pirandello's Narrative Writings*. London: Associated University Press, 1978, 329 p.
Examines the major themes and techniques of Pirandello's fiction.

Ragusa, Olga. "Pirandello's Haunted House." *Studies in Short Fiction* X, No. 3 (Summer 1973): 235-42.
Explicates the short story "La casa del Granella."

Review of National Literatures 14 (1987): 190 p.
Special issue devoted to Pirandello. Contains nine articles, including "Pirandello's Introduction to the Italian Theater," by Anne Paolucci; "Pirandello's Scandalous Docile Bodies," by Jennifer Stone; and "*Six Characters*: An American Opera," by Antonio Illiano.

Rey, John B. "Pirandello's 'Last' Play: Some Notes on *The Mountain Giants*." *Modern Drama* XX, No. 4 (December 1977): 413-20.
Offers an explanation of why Pirandello never finished *The Mountains Giants*.

Sogliuzzo, A. Richard. *Luigi Pirandello, Director: The Playwright in the Theatre*. Metuchen, N.J.: Scarecrow Press, 1982, 274 p.
Describes how Pirandello's consciousness of the demands of theatrical production influenced the creation of his plays.

Thompson, Alan Reynolds. "The Pirandellian Universe." In his *The Dry Mock: A Study of Irony in Drama*, pp. 65-79. Berkeley: University of California Press, 1948.
Maintains that Pirandello's humorism, evident in Six *Characters in Search of an Author* and *Henry IV*, is essentially "Romantic irony."

Trilling, Lionel. "Luigi Pirandello: *Six Characters in Search of an Author, A Comedy in the Making*." In his *Prefaces to the Experience of Literature*, pp. 45-50. New York: Harcourt Brace Jovanovich, 1979.
Argues that *Six Characters* is the most "elaborate and brilliant" dramatic comparison of the reality of the stage to the reality of life.

Williams, Raymond. "Luigi Pirandello." In his *Drama from Ibsen to Eliot*, pp. 185-95. London: Chatto & Windus, 1965.
Examines how Pirandello's drama destroyed the "illusion of reality" that had been the foundation of naturalist drama.

Henrik Pontoppidan

1857-1943

(Also wrote under the pseudonyms Rusticus and Urbanus) Danish novelist, short story writer, dramatist, and memoirist.

Considered the foremost Danish novelist of the late nineteenth century, Pontoppidan examined the cultural effects of changing class structures, sexual mores, and values during a period of transition in Danish society. Often described as a Naturalist, Pontoppidan was one of the first Danish novelists to depict the suffering of the peasantry seriously and with compassion, criticizing the idealistic and ineffectual attempts of the upper class to implement educational and political reforms. Throughout his fiction Pontoppidan satirized utopianism, whether it appeared as a neo-Rousseauistic celebration of rural life or as simple-minded liberalism, and he continually depicted the disillusion resulting from social ideals. This theme is developed most elaborately in the three cycles of novels upon which Pontoppidan's reputation is based: *Det forjættede land (The Promised Land), Lykke-Per,* and *De dødes rige.* Although not widely read outside Denmark today, Pontoppidan's work was so esteemed during his lifetime that he received the Nobel Prize in literature for 1917.

Pontoppidan was born in Fredericia, Denmark, into a prominent Lutheran family which for generations had produced theologians and scholars. Both his father and grandfather had been Lutheran clergymen, and Pontoppidan was expected to continue the family tradition. When he was six Pontoppidan moved with his family to Randers, where he attended a Latin school and excelled in mathematics. It was his facility with this subject, together with a distaste for the restrictive lifestyle of a Lutheran cleric, that led him to apply to Copenhagen's Polytechnical Institute in 1873. Biographers note that Pontoppidan's rejection of religious life and decision to study engineering resemble the choices of the main character in his eight-volume novel cycle *Lykke-Per.* While at school, Pontoppidan began to read such authors as Søren Kierkegaard, Fyodor Dostoevsky, and Friedrich Nietzsche, and in 1876 he began writing dramas. Realizing he preferred literature to engineering, he withdrew from school in 1877 in order to pursue a literary career. To support himself, he taught natural science at a Grundtvigian folk school, a rural high school which was part of a nationalistic and religious movement inspired by N. F. S. Grundtvig, who propagated an idealized image of both the natural life of the peasant and the potential of popular education to unify rural and urban Denmark. In sympathy with agrarian life and the suffering of the poor, Pontoppidan wrote stories portraying the peasantry as victims of social and economic forces. Representative of his work of this period is the story "Et endligt," which relates the lack of compassion displayed by several town leaders for a dying man whose family is destitute, therein presenting an indictment of the upper class for its callous response to the impoverishment of Denmark's rural population. In 1881 Pontoppidan published his first collection of short stories, *Stækkede vinger.* With the royalties advanced him, he quit teaching and married a woman of the peasant class. The marriage ended in divorce eleven years later, and biographers speculate that Pontoppidan's personal failure to live out the Grundtvigian ideal in his own life by becoming a farmer and

marrying a peasant woman led him to condemn such attempts in his fiction, which is often concerned with the subject of misalliance.

Called a "literature of social consciousness," the fiction Pontoppidan produced during the 1880s treats concerns that became central to his work. The novel *Isbjørnen,* for example, examines the social and political malaise of the rural population of Denmark, while *Mimoser (The Apothecary's Daughter)* traces the dissolution of two marriages as a result of the change in sexual morals occurring in Denmark in the 1880s. Pontoppidan also continued to describe the injustices experienced by the poor in short stories, including those collected in *Skyer* and *Fra hytterne.*

Upon divorcing his first wife in 1892, Pontoppidan married a woman from his own social class. With his new wife he moved to Copenhagen, where he became part of a group of free-thinking artists and intellectuals that had formed around the literary critic Georg Brandes, whose critical principles were founded on a rejection of religion as a source of ethical guidance and a concommitant faith in reason and science as a guide to moral decisions. By 1912, however, Pontoppidan had become disillusioned with the social and political effects of liberal attitudes and policies he believed were typified by Brandes. In his memoirs, he wrote: "Is it not on the whole one of our most unfortunate delusions that we in our conscience—that attic full of all kinds of old, hidden superstitions and long superseded prejudices—that we in the spectral voice from that sepulchre possess a divine guide through life's labyrinth, a guide in whom we can put greater trust than in the supreme human good: our reason?'' Pontoppidan continued to publish throughout his long life; he died in Copenhagen at the age of eighty-six.

Analyzing the effects of social changes on late-nineteenth-century Danish society, Pontoppidan's work was concerned with the hypocrisies, abuses, and unrealistic attitudes he found in the major social movements of his age. His first extensive treatment of the effects of social reformists, *The Promised Land*, portrays the Grundtvigians, who endeavored to end poverty and illiteracy through an educational system meant to bring together cultured urbanites and the rural populace. Pontoppidan regarded the efforts of the Grundtvigians as unnatural, naive, and overly ambitious. He believed that because the Grundtvigians refused to acknowledge the limitations imposed on a person by heredity, they naively assumed they could effect dramatic social changes by means of superficial social reforms. Representing what Pontoppidan considered the naive Grundtvigian response to the plight of the poor, the main character of the novel cycle neglects his duties as a husband and as the pastor of a village church in order to devote himself to the political cause of the peasants, but his unrealistic attitude toward the poor only leads to his personal ruin. Unlike Pontoppidan's earlier portrayals, his depiction of the lower classes in this novel cycle has been described as unsympathetic. Whereas in ''Et endligt'' his attack had focused on the self-absorbed wealthy Danes as the source of the problems of the poor in Denmark, the emphasis by now has shifted to include the peasants as a class of self-seekers. In *The Promised Land* the rural populus is depicted as a cunning faction of society which makes great demands on the aid supplied by the church, abusing what it views as hypocritical charity that is dispensed solely to gain additional votes for the parish. This change in Pontoppidan's attitude toward the peasantry is considered indicative of the development in his work from examining the effects of social ills to focusing on the underlying causes he believed originated in the character of the Danish people. In his next major novel cycle, *Lykke-Per*, a talented young engineering student displays attitudes and opinions that reflect those current in Copenhagen during the 1880s. Specifically, Per adopts the prevailing assumption of intellectuals living in the capital that Denmark was a backward country requiring intense technological development in order to compete with the great industrialized nations of the West. Per makes the simplistic supposition that Denmark's problems will be solved with the construction of an immense and overly complex canal system of his design. Eventually he is forced to realize, however, that the project is not economically feasible, and his misjudgment is meant to represent the ill-conceived ambitions of Danish society as a whole. In *Lykke-Per* Pontoppidan wrote: ''It is as if some hidden disease consumed the strength of the nation, sucked out the marrow of its best youth, and exposed the country as booty to the lust of foreign conquest.''

Disillusion with facile solutions to social problems also pervades Pontoppidan's last novel cycle, *De dødes rige*, an analysis of the aftermath of the successful democratic movement in Denmark between 1900 and 1910, when an emerging liberalism had minimized the importance of traditional values such as marriage and family life without providing an adequate substitute. Pontoppidan expressed his antipathy for such trends, particularly the libertinism advocated by Brandes, who wrote

that increased intellectual productivity is dependent upon ''the most uninhibited freedom within the realm of Eros.'' Abandoning a sustained focus on any single character, *De dødes rige* presents a comprehensive view of the many popular movements originating in Denmark at the turn of the century. In studies of his works, Pontoppidan has been repeatedly praised for his ability to portray the effects this rapid social transformation had on individuals living at the time. As H. G. Topsöe-Jensen has written: ''No other of the newer Danish authors has been able to present such a complete picture of his time, its intellectual movements, and its human types.''

PRINCIPAL WORKS

Staekkede vinger   (short stories)   1881
Landsbybilleder   (short stories)   1883
Sandinge menighed   (novel)   1883
Ung elskov   (novel)   1885; revised edition, 1906
Mimoser   (novel)   1886
   [*The Apothecary's Daughter*, 1890]
Fra hytterne   (short stories)   1887
Isbjørnen   (novel)   1887
Skyer   (short stories)   1890
Muld   (novel)   1891; revised edition, 1898
   [*Emanuel; or, Children of the Soil*, 1896]
Det forjættede land   (novel)   1892; revised edition, 1898
   [*The Promised Land*, 1896]
Den gamle Adam   (novel)   1894
Nattevagt   (novel)   1894
Dommens dag   (novel)   1895; revised edition, 1898
Lykke-Per. 8 vols.   (novel)   1898-1904; revised editions,
   1905 and 1908
Fortællinger   (short stories and novellas)   1899
Det ideale hjem   (novel)   1900
Lille rødhaette   (novel)   1900
Asgaardsrejen   (drama)   1902
Den kongelige gaest   (novel)   1908
   [*The Royal Guest* published in *The Royal Guest, and
      Other Classical Danish Narrative*, 1977]
†*Torben og jytte*   (novel)   1912; revised edition, 1917
†*Storeholt*   (novel)   1913; revised edition, 1917
†*Toldere og syndere*   (novel)   1914; revised edition, 1917
†*Enslevs død*   (novel)   1915; revised edition, 1917
†*Favsingholm*   (novel)   1916; revised edition, 1917
''A Fisher Nest''   (short story)   1927; published in journal
   The American-Scandinavian Review
Mands himmerig   (novel)   1927
''Eagle's Flight''   (short story)   1929; published in journal
   The American-Scandinavian Review
Undervejs til mig selv   (memoirs)   1943
''Gallows Hill at Ilum''   (short story)   1971; published in
   Anthology of Danish Literature

*These works comprise the novel cycle *Det forjættede land*.

†These works comprise the novel cycle *De dødes rige*.

WILLIAM MORTON PAYNE   (essay date 1896)

[*The longtime literary editor for several Chicago publications, Payne reviewed books for twenty-three years at the* Dial, *one of America's most influential journals of literature and opinion in the early twentieth century. In the following excerpt, he discusses the importance of the Grundtvigian movement as the backdrop for* The Promised Land.]

Herr Pontoppidan's [*Emanuel; or, Children of the Soil*] is the first part of a sort of novel-trilogy, in which the author has sought to exhibit the after-effects of the Grundtvigian movement that stirred Danish society to its foundations in the fifties and sixties. It is to be hoped that **The Promised Land** and **The Day of Judgment,** the two remaining sections of the trilogy, will also soon be put into English. The movement which will always be known by the name of Bishop Grundtvig was a religious revival and something more. It aimed to substitute a living Christianity for the dull formalism that had taken hold of the church in Denmark, and at the same time to awaken the historical consciousness of the Scandinavian people by reviving an interest in their magnificent inheritance of myth and tradition. It also aimed to exalt the peasant as the finest, because the least sophisticated, element of the Scandinavian character. We say Scandinavian rather than Danish of set purpose, because Grundtvig's influence was felt throughout the three countries, and because he never ceased to urge their union. The novel now under discussion deals with the seventies,—when Grundtvig was no more, although his spirit was still abroad— and pictures for us the life of a small peasant community hopelessly estranged from the State Church, yet eager for spiritual guidance. The generous soul of the pastor soon brings him into sympathy with the aspirations of his people; he marries a girl of peasant extraction, and breaks with his ecclesiastical superior. At the last moment, the intervention of Bishop Monrad, who is wise enough to see and correctly interpret the signs of the times, persuades the hero to remain in the Church, leaving him free to work out his ideals under the protection of the organization. This hasty outline can give but an imperfect notion of what the reader will find to be a very genuine and charming book, fresh in its interest and valuable as a means of acquaintance with the intimate life of one of the most interesting of European peoples.

William Morton Payne, in a review of "Emanuel; or, Children of the Soil," in The Dial, *Vol. XXI, No. 244, August 16, 1896, p. 92.*

THE NATION, NEW YORK   (essay date 1896)

[*In the following excerpt, the critic unfavorably reviews* The Promised Land.]

Henrik Pontoppidan's story [*The Promised Land*] treats of an interesting period in Danish history about twenty years ago, when, to the freeing of the peasants from serfdom nearly a century before, succeeded the movement to free their minds from ignorance as well as their bodies from slavery. The establishment of "people's high schools" for the encouragement of an enthusiastic patriotism was the great work of Bishop Grundtvig in the beginning of the century, and the influence of this institution, as well as of a popular religious movement, is seen reflected in the twin villages of Pontoppidan's story. To our thinking, the facts of the case, as stated in the preface, are more interesting than the novel, which, however patriotic, moves but listlessly for the general reader. The aristocratic priest, his democratic curate, the heresies of a preaching weaver, the manners and customs of a not too interesting peasantry, lists of their clothes, food, and amusements, with the final triumph of the plebeian over the patrician idea, are the leading features of a book more significant to students of Danish progress than to seekers after an entertaining novel.

A review of "The Promised Land," in The Nation, *New York, Vol. LXIII, No. 1627, September 3, 1896, p. 181.*

J. G. ROBERTSON   (essay date 1920)

[*In the following excerpt from an essay originally published in 1920, Robertson examines the theme of disillusionment in Pontoppidan's three novel cycles.*]

Det forjættede land appeared after [Henrik Pontoppidan] had served a long apprenticeship in short stories and sketches of peasant life. In these stories, ***Landsbybilleder (Pictures from Country Towns)***, ***Fra hytterne (From the Hovels)***, ***Skyer (Clouds)***, we see him gradually feeling his way through a literature of peasant stories richer than any other in Europe, to an art and style of his own. A comparison with the older and more complacent work of Winther, Schandorph and even Blicher, shows how wide a gap separates the art of a generation ago from that of to-day, while even the vigorous romantic realism of Björnson seems to grow, by juxtaposition with Pontoppidan's, a little more romantic and a little less real. But Pontoppidan's horizon is narrow; his view, as he himself tells us, is limited "by what one can see from a Zealand hill''; and this narrowness of outlook has to some extent passed over into *Det forjættede land*. The book is long, wearisomely long, being in reality three books fused into one. It is a novel of the provinces, in which Copenhagen is only a very distant speck on the horizon; a novel about peasants and pastors; and although Pontoppidan's competency to paint the Danish peasant cannot be impugned, although he knows the Danish clergy as no other, from the Copenhagen bishop to the wandering revivalist or the "stickit minister'' who becomes a "polar bear'' in his Greenland exile (*Isbjørnen*), this does not relieve the book of a certain drab monotony. Grundtvigian efforts at enlightenment stamp it as a picture of the eighties of last century, and supply an element of healthier idealism; but even this is neutralized by the author's Flaubertian dislike of the province, which he but ill succeeds in concealing. The story of *Det forjættede land* is summed up by the inscription, which Pastor Petersen, the spokesman of a redeeming sanity, says should be put upon the hero's grave:

> Here lies Don Quixote's double, Emanuel Hansted by name, who was born to be an honest man, but regarded himself as a prophet and a saint; who in consequence clothed himself in the garb of a herdsman, and held every inspiration that occurred to him to be a special call of Heaven; who bungled everything that passed through his hands. . . . but, notwithstanding, regarded himself to the last as chosen by Providence to prepare for the coming of the millennium.

Det forjættede land is a sombre book, a story of that hardest of all tragic fates, disillusionment. The moral, if one may speak of a moral in a writer so studiously amoral as Pontoppidan, is that the idealists and dreamers, the geniuses of the world, are hopelessly in the wrong; that the price must inevitably be paid by all who, either by their gifts or their ambitions, dare to raise themselves above their fellows. That Pontoppidan has been influenced by Ibsen's *Brand* is hardly to be gainsaid; Emanuel is a prose Brand, Brand in a specifically realistic milieu, a Brand in whom all the torments to which such a nature is exposed are relentlessly laid bare, as they could not be in five acts of trochaic verse. The pitiful sacrifice of Emanuel's child has clearly been suggested by the similar incident in Ibsen's drama.

Disillusionment, too, is the theme of *Lykke-Per;* but *Lykke-Per* is planned on a much broader basis, and is more closely knit together than its predecessor. It seems to me, indeed, easily the most powerful novel of modern Denmark, and even a landmark in the development of realistic fiction in Europe. Pontoppidan's horizon had widened; one sees it in the more varied range of the shorter stories which preceded and accompanied *Lykke-Per.* To these belong the little story **"Orneflugt"** (**"Eagle's Flight"**), to which [Poul Carit] Andersen gives typical significance, as containing the quintessence of Pontoppidan's art. Here, as in most of his work at this time, he is clearly searching for new moral values—"the rights of passion and the great emotions." This is to be seen in the story entitled *Mimoser* (*Mimosas*), on which the controversies evoked by the *Doll's House* and Björnson's *Gauntlet* have left their mark. Or again, he may seek new social and political ideals, as in *Nattevagt* (*Nightwatch*), *Den gamle Adam* (*The Old Adam*), and *Det ideale hjem* (*The Ideal Home*), with its fantastic plea for a new society built up on matriarchal principles. As a story, *Lille rødhætte* (*Little Red Riding Hood*), the title of which is apt to mislead, is, of all that Pontoppidan wrote in what might be called his *Lykke-Per* period, likely to make the deepest impression on the reader.

Lykke-Per is, no doubt, an intimately personal book, how personal it would not be fair to Pontoppidan the artist to attempt to gauge. But the Latinized name of the hero, Per Sidenius, is significant; he, too, like the author himself, is a pastor's son; he, too, comes to Copenhagen to become an engineer, and fails. Unlike its predecessor, *Lykke-Per* plays largely in the Danish capital, although Copenhagen is rather one-sidedly represented by Jewish circles. Pontoppidan's realism is extraordinary in its minute detail, and in its ruthlessness—that inevitable accompaniment of the art of seeing things exactly as they are. The book is studded with portraits of contemporaries: in Dr Nathan, for instance, Georg Brandes is depicted with a vividness which no mere description can convey; Enevoldsen is the master-spirit of the previous generation, J. P. Jacobsen; and Holger Drachmann, Pontoppidan's chief antagonist in the Danish literary world, is not forgotten. Essentially true, too, is the picture of the "Gjennembrud"—the "breakthrough"—in Danish thought and literature in the eighties and nineties of last century, and of that conflict—by no means confined to Denmark—between industrialism and science (of which Sidenius is the self-constituted champion) on the one hand, and the ideal claims of poetry on the other. But against this background a tragic fate is unrolled. *Lykke-Per* is the book of a man who is at war with life, but his is not one of those great inspiring wars, that lift men to a higher plane; it is a bitterly cynical war. Even Emanuel Hansted, with all his quixotry, has more of the redeeming qualities of the tragic hero than Per Sidenius. Sidenius is a "problematic nature," but of a much more complicated and subtle kind than that of the hero of Spielhagen's famous novel, which held the mirror up to the Europe of seventy years ago; he is the Aladdin of Oehlenschläger transported to a very modern world; an Aladdin in the most realistic surroundings, an Aladdin spiritualized by the delicate art of *Niels Lyhne,* and decked out with something of the fantasy of that other Aladdin of the north, Peer Gynt. Good fortune falls to Sidenius just as the oranges fell into Aladdin's turban; but he, too, is powerless to make that good fortune his own. The simple truth is summed up in one sentence: "If, in spite of all the success he enjoyed, he had not been happy, it was because he *would* not, in the ordinary sense of the word, be happy."

Although Pontoppidan holds no flattering mirror up to Danish national characteristics, his *Lykke-Per* is, none the less, a deeply national book; in spite of much that is distorted and exaggerated, it does reflect the Danish temperament, "the passionless Danish folk with the pale eyes and the timid soul," as it had never before been reflected.

> Thus it had always been in Denmark. One generation after the other grew up, red-cheeked and clear-eyed, free-minded and strong; and one generation after the other has sunk into the grave, broken, bent, always vanquished. It is as if some hidden disease consumed the strength of the nation, sucked out the marrow of its best youth, and exposed the country as booty to the lust of foreign conquest.

These heroes of Pontoppidan's are tragic figures, not because they do not get what they want: on the contrary, in one sense they all enter their "promised land": but they are disillusioned when they get there. *Lykke-Per* is one long tragedy of the lucky mortal who gets all he wants. It is the tragedy of the will which set in seriously, far back in the nineteenth century in European literature, with Grillparzer in Austria. This is what constitutes Pontoppidan's pessimism: his tragedies are not tragedies of heroism spent in vain, or of superhuman renunciation, but of the failure to respond to success, to act, to seize the fleeting moment, to admit the happiness that stands waiting on the threshold. Sidenius goes out into the world with great gifts and sincere intentions; he is buffeted, crushed, jeered at, disillusioned: life grinds the spirit out of him: he does not die fighting, like Emanuel Hansted—even if it be only fighting windmills—with the halo of sanctity around him, but in abnegation and spiritual paralysis.

The most recent phase of Pontoppidan's development is represented by a long novel, the last volume of which appeared after the curtain had risen on the Great War. In some respects, *De dødes rige* has less claim to be regarded as a single book than its predecessor; it is rather a cycle of stories held together with difficulty by the continuity of the characters. Indeed, the first two sections give the impression that, when they were written, they were not meant to converge at all, and that the connection was really an afterthought. But apart from this lack of unity, the new novel is a finer and maturer work. It is, none the less, true to the old realism; perhaps truer than before; but the ruthless element has been eliminated; the persistent "j'accuse" of *Lykke-Per* has disappeared. The pictures of Denmark—and they range from Funen in the south to Jutland in the north, and again to Copenhagen—are extraordinarily delicate and clear. I cannot think of any other modern Danish book that makes the poetry of Copenhagen so real to us as this; the Copenhagen of sea-mists creeping up from the Sound, of overcrowded streets, glistening in the lamp-light; its noisy trams and drab suburbs with the work-people tramping homeward. We get to know the Danish Rigsdag, the Copenhagen newspaper offices; one could point to the very house on the St. Annæ Plads where the great Enslev died: the flat in the Drönningens Tværgade where Jytte Abildgaard and her mother lived.

The "Danish folk with the pale eyes" is here seen from a new angle; seen in its political life. Enslev, the political leader, is, no doubt, under something of a disguise, Sverdrup. The portraits of this book surpass in psychological delicacy those of the earlier novels; in fact, one recognizes certain types of figures which had already appeared in other books, but which are here raised to a higher artistic power; for instance, the fine figure of the rebel priest, Mads Vestrup. Torben Dihmer, who may be called the hero only in so far as he is the most persistent male figure throughout the book, is one of the most complex portraits in Pontoppidan's gallery; and the charming Jytte Abildgaard is far more living than the often theatrical Jacobe of *Lykke-Per.*

The hero of *Lykke-Per* in a moment of introspective clairvoyance realizes that "there is no other hell than that which men, in their fear of ghosts, make for themselves"; and that he is himself but a ghost, wearing out his life in the vain fight with incorporeal shadows. This thought is followed out in the last book. The kingdom of the dead is the kingdom of the past, of the people and things that have been, and are now but memories. The world has become the dream; the real the unreal; life is a mere blind fighting of the air, and Torben Dihmer comes back from this world as from a journey in the kingdom of the dead, back to the one reality of his own lonely life. If *Det forjættede land* is a kind of *Brand* in Pontoppidan's work, and *Lykke-Per* is his *Peer Gynt,* here he has reached the stage of *When We Dead Awaken*—awaken from the kingdom of the dead to a new kingdom of the living. *De dødes rige* is a mellower, less rasping book for delicate nerves than *Lykke-Per;* a gentler renunciation lies over it; but the pessimism, if less militant, is unabated.

I have spent so much time over these three long books, that it is impossible to do justice to the fine art of Pontoppidan's smaller pictures; but there are some wonderful stories among these, the early ones romantically exuberant in youthful spirits, the later ones reflecting the darkening mood, the problem and the conflict. One of the sources of charm in these stories, as in the larger books—for they do not pretend to charm by wit or brilliancy of style—is a striking freshness of situation. Things happen here which in no way conflict with probability, and which yet never happened before in fiction. Who, for instance, can forget that scene where Sidenius goes down to the wharf to accompany his mother's coffin to its last resting-place in Jutland, and sees it hoisted into the hold like any other bale or packing-case? This originality of outlook on the facts of life is perhaps what best maintains the interest in the loosely bound fabric of *De dødes rige;* there is hardly an incident here which is not stamped with this peculiar distinction. The shorter stories show more clearly Pontoppidan's personal conviction on matters of "actual" interest; his antipathy, for instance, to anything that savours of lyricism or romanticism; his democratic faith in the future of the proletariat, and his—for an imaginative writer strangely incongruous—hope in the ultimate triumph of scientific materialism over poetry: even his Tolstoi-like contempt for art. But it matters little whether such views are the author's or not, or whether they appeal to us or not; it is the great impersonal art of his books that matters. It has been urged that, with M. Rolland's *Jean Christophe,* the age of the old Flaubertian realism has definitely passed. I am not so sure of it. In these books, at least, are revealed new potentialities of the old realism, potentialities that rest on the spiritual and the psychological, no less than in the faithful reflection of real things. (pp. 247-54)

J. G. Robertson, "Henrik Pontoppidan," in his Essays and Addresses on Literature, 1935. *Reprint by Books for Libraries Press, 1968; distributed by Arno Press, Inc., pp. 245-54.*

OSCAR GEISMAR (essay date 1933)

[*In the following excerpt, Geismar discusses Pontoppidan as a transitional author whose work reflects the social and political changes of his era.*]

Henrik Pontoppidan has often been extolled as the unprejudiced and dispassionate observer and the cold, clear writer, but this estimate rests upon a misunderstanding. He has persistently avoided admitting the multitude to the secret emotions of his soul, but this aristocratic reserve does not reach down to the depths of his being. In his case the saying that still waters run deep holds good. It is also true that his treatment of the Danish language brings him into kinship with the older line of Danish prose writers. Gently, but coolly too, the words flow from his pen. They record rather than paint. But if one listens attentively one perceives that this wise and clear speech bears a message from an unquiet heart. There is passion hidden beneath the smooth surface.

The Denmark which Henrik Pontoppidan and his contemporaries inherited when they made their appearance about 1880 was a Denmark of defeat. The shadow of Dybbøl Hill lay over them. The intellectual renaissance under Georg Brandes and his closest followers was still in progress, but the next decade drove in the sense of defeat unmercifully and those men, who in their youth had felt it burn into their hearts, never forgot that experience. Their world was bounded by Herman Bang's *Generations without Hope* and Henrik Pontoppidan's *The Kingdom of the Dead.* Bang found relief for his soul in tears of pity, but Pontoppidan was seized with terror before the impending destruction; a lurking fear of ghosts lies concealed behind all his utterances. Goaded on by this fear, he scanned the nation for possible signs of spring. He discovered none, and it is this destitution which has made of him the great castigator and prophet of doom.

It is unjust to him to interpret this censorious attitude of his merely as the intellectual aristocrat's scorn for the mob. It was so with Georg Brandes but not with Henrik Pontoppidan. He always possessed within himself so much of Grundtvig's spirit that the ties which bound him indissolubly to his people never sundered. As with the Old Testament prophets, the scourge with which he chastened his contemporaries cut deepest into his own heart. It was appropriate, too, that when the day of reunion dawned after the World War he should give the most affecting expression to the joy of meeting:

> It sounds just like a fairy tale, a story from days of old,
> A stolen daughter, deeply mourned, returns safe to the fold. . . .
> Clad in white and red thou comest, smiling towards us on thy way,
> Hail to thee, our mother's darling, in the dawn of a new day!

Family affiliation could not give the young Henrik Pontoppidan the shelter and support which even the most self-reliant need. So there remained to him the nation which just in these years needed to be raised up again after the mutilation it had suffered in the defeat. The eighteen-eighties were the days of intransigence in political struggles, but they were also the auspicious springtime for the schools of Grundtvig and Brandes. (pp. 7-9)

Grundtvig himself had his life firmly rooted in profound religious experiences and his eager participation in national and educational life was inextricably bound up with that faith and that hope which his Christianity yielded him. Gradually, however, as this so-called Grundtvigism spread more and more and branched out in various directions, the national side of the movement frequently came to stand on its own feet; but at the same time it undeniably lost most of its power and vigor. For Henrik Pontoppidan, Grundtvigism was never really much more than the great means to the desired end—popular revolt, the lever by which the Danish peasantry was to be raised up to political and intellectual equality with the other ranks of the kingdom. He devoted some of the best years of his youth to an attempt to carry out this gigantic task.

As he himself acknowledges in his great novel cycle, *The Promised Land,* the attempt failed, and as a disappointed man he pulled his tent pegs out of the Danish peasant soil to fix them elsewhere. Why was it a failure? Chiefly, I suppose, because he had made only the surface of Grundtvigism his own. A cut flower soon wilts. But deeper reasons were also operating here. What was aimed at in those days was nothing less than a fusion of the classes of society, if not economically, at least nationally and socially. When it really came to the point, the whole movement was opposed to Pontoppidan's aristocratic artist's soul. It became obvious that his faith in the shibboleths refused to be transmuted into everyday facts. This tragedy, much of which is of a very intimate character, is treated of in *The Promised Land.*

As a work of art in the broad style, this novel is perhaps to be regarded primarily as a portrayal of civilization. Pontoppidan has always despised the artistic preoccupation with words and tones. Art for art's sake was not his motto. When he wrote it was always with some definite end in view and this purpose is the hidden secret of his books. In this book he proposes to write the threnody of Grundtvigism. It, too, was a piece of romanticism and as such without vitality. For the sake of the cause he unfolds his gigantic canvas to the view of all good people. The execution of the painting is here as elsewhere in this writer lacking in finish, but to make up for this it is singularly vivid. And perhaps the tragic gleam which plays over the fate of its main characters will preserve it from the early death which otherwise awaits all representations of contemporary life.

From Grundtvig the road led to Brandes. Similarly in *Lucky Per,* the hero, Per Sidenius, flees from his Grundtvigian home to fight his way up through the half-Semitic world of Copenhagen radicalism, where, although his works are comparatively unknown, the name of Georg Brandes is the great battle-cry. One is forced to admire the dazzling virtuosity with which Pontoppidan succeeds in animating the whole of this milieu differing so vastly as it does from the scene of *The Promised Land.* The sureness with which he has seized and rendered the peculiar characteristics of the Jewish race is most extraordinary. It is the Copenhagen of the 'nineties that meets the reader's eye, radiant still in its newly inherited riches, defiantly ensconced in its independent scepticism, but like an exotic plant in inhospitable soil doomed to wither.

Less interest attaches to the hero's many and grievous afflictions, and that in spite of the fact that behind his figure one catches more than a glimpse of the Danish-born pastor's son, Henrik Pontoppidan, who was likewise unable to find his abiding-place in the ranks of Brandes. Although his fate fills many long pages, Per Sidenius is not a great figure. One suspects, too, from the main outlines of the book, that his flight from home is more of a romantic gesture than a deliberate and considered step. In spite of the radical war paint he is a Sidenius to the bottom of his soul. Uprooted from his native soil, he must end in solitude. The new may attract him but it has no power to hold him.

This was precisely the case with Pontoppidan. Brandes also repelled him, and gradually, as he saw the fruits which the

newly planted tree was bearing, despondency and resentment filled his heart. In what is for him a surprisingly frank poem he gives expression to just these feelings regarding Georg Brandes: "The tree of freedom which he planted in the land is now poisoning the people with worm-eaten fruits." With this bitter experience behind him, Pontoppidan became what he now is: the great recluse who from the depths of his soul thirsts for friendly intercourse. With the eyes of a caged eagle he gazes about him for signs of spring but finds none.

At one stage he returned briefly to the interest of his youth—politics. In the meantime the change of system had brought the Left into power. Perhaps the new Denmark was to be born in the hall of the Folketing. But again despondency seized him. It is this man's fate that in whatsoever direction he looks his disconsolate wrath goes in advance like a consuming flame and parches the country until it is a wilderness. If Grundtvigism was bad and Brandes worse, the Denmark of the new century was in truth worst of all. If it were to have a general title it must be: *The Kingdom of the Dead.*

It cannot be denied that in his last great work one perceives in quite a different way from in *The Promised Land* and *Lucky Per* that the author does not feel himself co-responsible and is therefore not sympathetic. The book is not the confession of an accomplice but the indictment of a judge. Coupled with this is the fact that the mass effect completely subordinates the interest in the individual. Now the depiction of mass movements belongs to the province of the historian of culture. The stuff of art is man, the individual, even if they do perhaps make their appearance now and then in the plural. There is scarcely a single character in *The Kingdom of the Dead* drawn with so masterly a stroke as to be unforgettable, and as a picture of the age the book will probably be forgotten with the age it mirrors.

If we think back over the series of Henrik Pontoppidan's works, of which only the most important are mentioned here, and center them about the personality from which they have proceeded, the author appears before our eyes in lofty remoteness, grimly pronouncing judgment, pitilessly probing. Now and then, however, his voice trembles, for he is in the same boat himself and is wracked with fear at the threatening catastrophe. For the sake of this tremble in his voice we take courage and venture to attest our love for him. As artist he does not rank among the greatest, but in a remarkable age of transition he has lived the fate of his people with a sensitive soul and has recorded what he has experienced in clear and intelligible Danish. Concealed in these records lies the ultimate significance of Henrik Pontoppidan. (pp. 10-12)

Oscar Geismar, "Henrik Pontoppidan," in The American-Scandinavian Review, *Vol. XXI, No. 1, January, 1933, pp. 7-12.*

W. GLYN JONES (essay date 1957)

[*Jones is an English educator and critic who has written and lectured on Scandinavian literature. In the following excerpt, he offers an overview of Pontoppidan's major works.*]

Throughout his life Pontoppidan viewed the Denmark he knew with a profound sense of tragedy; he saw it as a land of decadence and self-seeking, a mere caricature of the land that had once ruled the Baltic and whose influence had been felt far beyond, and it is in the light of this that his writings must be judged. For different as such works as *Landsbybilleder* (*Pictures from the Villages*) and *De dødes rige* (*The Realm of the Dead*) are from each other, they are both products of this same feeling in the author. He spent his life looking for the cause of the dearth which he saw around him, and his search goes from the purely superficial judgement of the early short stories with their crass naturalism and their agitation for better material conditions to the profound studies of the Danish national character as Pontoppidan conceived it in the great novels of his mature period.

In his very earliest work he is content to view the poverty which was so widespread in the country districts and to see in the abolition of this the final solution to Denmark's misery. In these—for the most part short stories—he cries shame on the upper classes for their lack of interest in the conditions of those less well off than they, condemning the treatment accorded to those no longer able to take care of themselves, and crying in despair at the irreverence with which even their dead are treated when the poor child's grave is dug up to make room for the nobility.

Pontoppidan was in fact the first Danish novelist to deal seriously with the conditions of the poor, and in so doing he made way for authors such as Aakjaer and Skjoldborg who devoted most of their energies (at least in their prose writings) to the same thing. With Pontoppidan, however, social criticism of this sort was only a passing phase: he quickly perceived that the real cause of Denmark's ills lay below the surface, and accordingly there are signs even in these early works of the approaching moral criticism of the Danish people which was to dominate the main part of his writings, and in which complacency, self-seeking and the lack of a sense of reality are revealed as the principal weaknesses of the Danish nation. For instance, he does not criticize the farmers merely because of the way in which they treat their inferiors, because of the accommodation they offer them and the way in which they speak to them, but in a work such as *Sandinge menighed* (*The Parish of Sandinge*) he goes on to contrast the misery of Lone with the "happy, well-fed farmers" in their meeting-house, singing joyful hymns and oblivious of the grim reality around them; and in *Idyl* he even develops this theme further by telling how the farmer's comfort is not disturbed, but on the contrary is increased, by the "cheerful" sound of the threshing being done by the poor farm labourer while he himself is resting during the winter evenings.

From this attack on complacency in one particular class it is not a very far cry to an attack on the Danish national character as a whole as envisaged by Pontoppidan, and already in "**En fiskerrede**" (translated as "**A Fisher Nest**") he shows the first signs of this attack. In this story he censures the modern population, not because they plunder a ship, but for the despicable, underhand way in which they do it, contrasting it violently with the manly way in which they would have done it a couple of centuries before. Here, then, for the first time, Pontoppidan deals with the decadence which he sees in modern Denmark.

It is, however, in *Skyer* (*Clouds*) that this thought finds its full expression, in such stories as "**Ilum galgebakke**" ("**The Gallows Hill at Ilum**"), showing how the peasants of olden days reacted to oppression, and contrasting this with the way in which the modern farmers react to the new oppression of an autocratic government—by holding meetings and talking about it. This collection of stories is almost entirely concerned with situations arising from the provisional laws which were enforced by the Cabinet despite opposition from the Folketing, and Pontoppidan emphasizes throughout the contrast between

what the Danes say they will do and what they actually do. Both violent hatred of the Conservative Party and the Prime Minister, Estrup, and an air of disappointment, almost of melancholy, are apparent in the stories, but any remaining doubts as to Pontoppidan's essential demand are removed on reading his cry for "a brand new people" in "**To gange mødt**" ("**Twice Me**"). Bad as the government might be, the ultimate remedy is in the hands of the people themselves, but they show themselves incapable of applying it.

That Pontoppidan longs for spiritual renewal—or at least a change of heart—in the Danes is already apparent in the early novel *Isbjørnen* (*The Polar Bear*), in which Pontoppidan might almost be said to have found his "new people"—in Greenland. He spends much of his time extolling the Greenlanders for their simple virtues, only to compare and contrast them with the Danes as Thorkild Müller finds them on his return home—oppressed, but unwilling to do anything about it, even to the extent of thinking that Müller is mad when he refuses to oppress them and demand his tithes. These Danish farmers cut poor figures at the side of their Greenlandic neighbours who still retain the qualities which were once to be found in Denmark and which Pontoppidan now seeks in vain.

These themes are continued and developed in the first major novel, *Det forjættede land* (*The Promised Land*), which marks both the culmination of Pontoppidan's early work dealing especially with rural conditions and the beginning of a new approach to the subject. Published in three parts, from 1891 to 1895, it is naturally a much more profound study than the earlier works and in it we reach the decisive stage in the development from a superficial, material criticism to a moral one, and also the development from works dealing essentially with the people as a conception to novels in which the interest is centred on the individual. It is none the less a judgement, a moral judgement of the Danish nation as a whole, dealing with people from all parts of the country, all classes and all political parties; it may well be considered as a first analysis of the deeper-lying causes of the decadence about which Pontoppidan is so much concerned. Apart from Hansine and possibly her father and mother, there is scarcely a person in this book whom Pontoppidan does not condemn in one way or another. Not that all the characters are equally despicable: Provst Tønnesen and Pastor Petersen are not exactly admirable characters, but Pontoppidan has a certain amount of respect for them. Tønnesen is what he says he is, and even though in the first book, *Muld* (*Soil*), Pontoppidan has to put him in an unfavourable light in order to gain our sympathy for Emanuel and his new friends, he treats him on the whole as a worthy enemy. Indeed, on the occasion of the bishop's visit one cannot help feeling that the author grudgingly admires Tønnesen's outspokenness in the discussion on politics, in which the bishop has earlier played a rather unfortunate role.

With its profoundly pessimistic view of the Danish nation *Det forjættede land* can easily be interpreted as a negative work, attacking everything and everyone, and offering no solution. But Pontoppidan is in fact quite positive in it, for he is fighting for a principle in the abstract; his characters have no principle at all, no life force, and that is what he deplores in them. In its portrayal of people of this sort *Det forjættede land* is closely linked to such early works as *Skyer* and points the way forward to such novels as *De dødes rige*.

As in *Skyer* the reaction of the ordinary people to the provisional laws is also dealt with here, but the author's criticism of them is even more biting, and considerably more subtle. With bitter irony Pontoppidan juxtaposes the people's mourning at the funeral of Emanuel's son and their curiosity and impatience to learn the result of the previous day's debate in the Rigsdag; and when the news arrives, they completely forget the occasion which has brought them together; the heartbroken father is forgotten; his sermon is scarcely heard; hardly has the earth been cast on to the coffin before the "mourners" are on their way home, loudly condemning the action of the government. But it is not many days before their zeal is spent, and they decide to wait and see what happens before resorting to any sort of violent demonstration. The author's scorn for these tactics of wait and see is amply displayed in the scene portraying the meeting of the local council. And arising out of this situation is yet another charge of self-seeking, this time with the bishop as the scapegoat. He has contrived to get himself elected to the Folketing by taking Emanuel's part against Tønnesen and thereby gaining the support of the local population; it is suggested that he should attend the protest meetings (which are the sum total of the people's anger and resentment) organized after the proclamation of the provisional laws, but he prefers to maintain what he calls his "Archimedean standpoint, outside the political parties." The bishop is not referred to often, but by means of an episode of this nature Pontoppidan contrives to make him into a symbol of the instability and selfishness which he is attacking.

So much for the people as a whole. What then of the individuals themselves? Throughout **Muld** Hans Jensen is a staunch supporter of Provst Tønnesen and an opponent of Væver Hansen and his party, but by the second volume of the trilogy he has seen his advantage in changing colours and becoming "the well-known leader of the farmers, Hans Jensen from Vejlby." Niels Damgaard is different, but no better, hiding his ambition under a cloak of piety and following the fashion by starting yet another religious sect based on a new interpretation of the ritual of baptism. Pontoppidan goes to considerable pains to show the development of his hypocrisy. If we examine the local grocer or either of the school teachers, we shall find the same sorts of traits in all of them.

There are, however, one or two characters who command our respect if not our affection, a number, that is, who cannot be classed entirely as self-seekers. Væver Hansen is the most striking of these. He is not an attractive person, nor can it be suggested that he is acting entirely from idealistic motives; but Pontoppidan goes to the trouble of explaining his actions against a background of past wrongs to his father and a resultant desire for revenge. He has a strong will and strength of purpose, and on that account alone we have to respect him, even if it is not easy to decide exactly what his aim is.

And then there is Aggerbølle, the veterinary surgeon who ruins himself through his love of card-playing. In a way he is a foil to Emanuel, like him having come to the country full of romantic hopes and fancies, and like him having been completely disappointed and disillusioned by the experiment. He is portrayed as a weak character, but he is not despicable in the way that so many of the others are, and when he talks of evil spirits in the air, one cannot help feeling that it is Pontoppidan himself speaking. It is worthy of note in this connexion that Aggerbølle is looked down on by the rest of the "respectable" population; they certainly give him sufficient economic help to keep him off the parish, but it is with considerable condescension. With all his faults, Aggerbølle is better in the eyes of the author than any of the others in the village, and consequently his humiliation is seen in a tragic light.

These are, however, only occasional exceptions to the general charge against the Danes, which in this work is extended so as to embrace a class for whom Pontoppidan has previously shown considerable sympathy: the poor. In fact, from being an oppressed class in his early works, they have now become a class of self-seekers as much as anyone. Svend Øl and Per Brændevin, with whom Pontoppidan is most concerned, come to Emanuel's evening gatherings, not so much out of a genuine desire to take part as on account of their just having received some poor-aid which Emanuel has arranged for them—they feel that if they come and show their gratitude there might be more for them at a later date. Very little sympathy is betrayed for their community as a whole, and although the section dealing with a visit Emanuel pays to them contains a full description of squalor and misery, the tone is very different from that in the short stories. No longer are Pontoppidan's paupers deserving, but lazy and greedy, unwilling to help themselves, ungrateful drunkards who believe the parish has been charitable to them merely because it wanted to keep them out of the workhouse and so keep their votes for the day when they would be needed for the farmers' candidates. Pontoppidan might very well have suggested this in his early work, but there is no indication whatever of its being true in this case, and it is quite apparent that he is in fact deliberately limiting what he has said before. Until now he has tended to define good and bad according to their social standing, but this is no longer true, and class differences play a considerably less important part in the rest of Pontoppidan's production. We are aware of poverty and riches, but they cease to have any significance.

It was at this time (1894) that Pontoppidan published **Nattevagt** (**Vigil**), that is to say just before the last book of the trilogy, entitled **Dommens dag** (**The Day of Judgment**), in which he completely leaves the last vestiges of what we for the sake of convenience may call "social criticism" and concentrates more on the personal tragedy of Emanuel Hansted and the Babel-like discord within the various sectarian movements in Denmark. This was in its turn followed by a series of non-critical, semi-romantic short novels. **Nattevagt** is normally considered a work in which Pontoppidan reasserts in the strongest possible terms the charges and the methods he has used in his early work, using Jørgen Hallager as his mouthpiece. But the mention of Hallager as a photographic retoucher in **Lykke-Per** (**Lucky Peter**), seems rather to indicate the failure of his attitude and the failure, therefore, of Pontoppidan's former critical attitude towards society, and **Nattevagt** must in fact be considered a transitional work heralding a new phase in Pontoppidan's production. In the scene where Thorkild Drehling, who is a much more attractive person than Hallager, comes to say goodbye to his colleague, there is a violent discussion in which they both state their attitudes. Jørgen Hallager's are those to which Pontoppidan has adhered in the past; Thorkild Drehling's are those to which he is going to adhere in the future:

> I know that you can meet sorrows and disappointments in life which hurt you far more than hunger and cold. . . . Just look down any street and notice the faces you meet there. For every one that is marked by anxiety for his next meal, overwork or any other form of hardship you will find ten, indeed twenty, in whom you can read as from an open book of the thousand and one secret worries which harass mankind without taking rank and condition into account; indeed they are perhaps felt most of all by those to whom life appears to have been most gracious . . . sorrows caused by love, worry on account of one's parents, loneliness, tiredness of life, fear of death, fear of life, what have you.

That this is the statement of a new programme is quite apparent from the following works, all of which deal with these new aspects of human suffering. In *Det forjættede land* Pontoppidan has already been approaching this new treatment of human beings; it is as though he has been coming to the conclusion that the material improvements with which he originally sought to improve society in fact must occupy a secondary place, that individual problems can be of much greater importance. The following works all deal with the private affairs of these individuals, even though they are seen against the background of a society which still fills Pontoppidan with disgust; even *Lykke-Per* with all its breadth is fundamentally a personal story. A more "social" note is certainly struck again in *Mands himmerig* (*Man's Heaven*), but the personal element still plays a much more important role than it used to, and the book has nothing whatever to do with the material welfare of any part of society.

Self-seeking continues to play a dominant role in the later works, and Pontoppidan even develops this theme in some respects. In *Lykke-Per* for instance the press emerges as one of the causes of the low morale in Denmark; as it grows in power it could obviously have an enormous influence for good, but it prefers to pander to the public taste in order to drag the public in the direction in which it wants to go when the time comes to vote. This is indicated through the figure of Dyring in *Lykke-Per;* it is developed in *De dødes rige* in the portrayal of the party press as envisaged by Pontoppidan, and more especially in the way in which it makes use of Mads Vestrup; and it achieves its fullest expression in *Mands himmerig*, which deals exclusively with the press, the weakness and self-seeking of those who control it and profess to have the well-being of Denmark at heart, and the way in which the one man who tries to awaken the Danes is hated by all and finally wears himself to death in his efforts.

Another theme which is developed to a considerable extent in the later works is the hollowness of the Church, against which he makes the same charges as against the individual. Pontoppidan, having been brought up in a strict, and perhaps rather narrow home, had quickly reacted against the claims of the Church and of Christianity as a whole. In his early works he criticizes the Danish State Church for its insufficiency, but generally speaking he does not develop his attitude to it in these books, preferring instead to deal with the sectarian activity, which at that time was so widespread in Denmark. He views it with complete scepticism, as is perhaps best seen in *Det forjættede land*. Now, however, he shows an ever-increasing interest in the State Church, and in *De dødes rige* he tries to deal it its death blow. What has previously been attributed to insufficiency is now put down to self-seeking, which when found in the Church seems to be even worse than in the individual. In this book Pontoppidan seems to be dogged by a fear of the increasing power of the State Church and its priests, all of whom are fighting for their own private views—as he maintained in his lecture **"Kirken og dens mænd"** (**"The Church and Its Men"**) in 1914—and none of whom have undergone a religious experience. The climax of this gigantic attack on the State Church is reached in the portrayal of the manner in which it deals with Mads Vestrup, in whom Pontoppidan sees a priest who has undergone the experience which the others lack. It is a mark of the bitter irony of the novel that Vestrup's rivals, the State Church party, silence him by pretending they are going to employ him on work to which a priest is more suited. The final picture of Mads Vestrup, defeated, collecting articles on church affairs and not being allowed to write any

himself, is one of the most harrowing scenes Pontoppidan ever wrote, and it is perhaps a shame that he did not leave it at this instead of letting Vestrup die suddenly and then contrasting his funeral with that of the upstart millionaire, Søholm. The Church is a perennial theme in Pontoppidan's work, but it cannot be said that it is a central theme; it is rather treated as another reflection of the Danish national character, and as such it is dealt with in the same way as individuals, and charged with the same vices.

Pontoppidan's other main charge against the Danes, their lifelessness and lack of a sense of reality, is also developed in the later novels. In *Lykke-Per* this characteristic is contrasted with the virility of the Jewish circles in Copenhagen, of whom Pontoppidan gives a vivid, although perhaps slightly idealized, portrayal. As a link between the two sides of society we have Per Sidenius, the Dane engaged to the Jewish girl, trying to deny his own nature, desperately endeavouring to escape the inheritance which he has received from his forefathers, most of them pastors in the Danish State Church. But Per is himself in fact a symbol of the Danish character; he fails in his engagement; he is weak when on the point of really achieving something and getting at least a part of his plan for a new bonded harbour and a canal system in Jutland accepted; he is reminded of his inheritance and gives up the whole scheme, which is later copied by a mere sycophant. It is to some extent open to discussion whether Per's own story is tragic or not, whether, in fact, he must be considered a failure, or whether he must be thought of as having achieved the peace of mind which he has longed for throughout the novel. In fact it is a combination of both, but tragic it is, as it must be when seen from Pontoppidan's own point of view. Per lacks the virility the author is seeking, and although he most certainly does achieve peace of mind as a philosophizing road-mender in the north of Jutland, he is most certainly a failure, for he only achieves this serenity by renouncing the very virtues which have been on the point of raising him above the level of the average Dane.

This is the factor which distinguishes him so sharply from Torben Dihmer in *De dødes rige,* who also withdraws from society and finds peace and consolation in an invalid existence, cut off from all human intercourse. But Per withdraws because of a weakness in himself, whereas Dihmer does so out of sheer disgust with the society around him. Per symbolizes the Danish character, but Dihmer represents rather the desire to reform it which seems doomed to failure.

De dødes rige, the third of Pontoppidan's great novels, is in some ways the finest of them, but it is certainly the most bitter. It bears scarcely a trace of the violence of Pontoppidan's early works, being the considered opinion of a mature individual. But the theme is the same as in the others: a cry of despair at the futility which is so apparent in Denmark. The author is still looking for virility and honesty, and this is the cause of one of the most interesting of all his portraits of a priest. Mads Vestrup is honest, and this, if not his belief, earns him the respect of the author. He is one of the very few of Pontoppidan's priests who gain our sympathy, and unlike Emanuel Hansted, another who is certainly true to his ideals, he is close to reality throughout. He knows the Danes for what they are, and, like the author himself, he tries to shake them into a consciousness of their situation. But he fails; and as a mark of his contempt Pontoppidan symbolically lets Torben Dihmer renounce the medicine which alone can keep him alive in "the realm of the dead."

There is a quite unified development in Pontoppidan's work. In his search for the cause of the dearth which he sees around him—and as such his work must fundamentally be considered—he looks first at the superficialities and then proceeds to a much more profound analysis in which he discerns two main causes of evil: the Danish lack of a sense of reality, and self-seeking, two themes which can easily be traced throughout his work; and they can also throw light on much that otherwise is ambiguous in the extreme. As the author proceeds from a material judgement to a moral one it becomes easier for him to see and appreciate the ''non-material'' sufferings that he has not mentioned before—and so we are presented with such characters as Jakobe in *Lykke-Per* and Torben Dihmer, Jytte Abildgaard and Mads Vestrup in *De dødes rige*. And at the same time as the personal element plays a larger and larger part, class distinctions, which are of supreme importance in the earlier work, disappear almost entirely.

Because Pontoppidan is so preoccupied with things so specifically Danish, some knowledge of Danish history and culture from 1880 to 1920 is really necessary in order fully to appreciate the depth of his thought. None the less it ought to be possible for the foreign reader to appreciate the subtleties of his portrayals and the force behind them, and this is to some extent borne out by the numerous translations of his works which do in fact exist in languages other than English. He must have been a considerable success in Germany where most of his works are available in translation. Many, too, are translated into Swedish and Dutch, and further away from the Germanic tradition there are numerous translations into Polish and Hungarian, and rather fewer into Russian. Apart from two books from *Det forjættede land* the only works available in English are two of his shorter novels and two short stories. It seems unfortunate that a writer of Pontoppidan's stature should be virtually unknown here despite his having shared the Nobel Prize for Literature with another Dane (Karl Gjellerup) in 1917, and despite the great influence which he has exerted on the Danish prose of this century. Nexø's novel *Pelle Erobreren* (*Pelle the Conqueror*) was dedicated to ''The master, Henrik Pontoppidan,'' and without him it is unlikely that the realist novels of the twentieth century, which are among the truly great achievements of modern Danish literature, would ever have existed in their present form. (pp. 376-83)

*W. Glyn Jones, ''Henrik Pontoppidan (1857-1943),''
in* The Modern Language Review, *Vol. LII, No. 3,
July, 1957, pp. 376-83.*

ERNST EKMAN   (essay date 1957)

*[In the following excerpt, Ekman examines Pontoppidan's fiction
as criticism of modern Danish society.]*

Henrik Pontoppidan was born in Fredericia in 1857 and died in Ordrup near Copenhagen in 1943. His lifetime covered the major part of the period which saw Denmark's change from a seventeenth century political system to a modern democratic state and from a poor agricultural country to a prosperous and partially industrialized model agrarian state. He was witness to two military invasions from the south, in 1865 and 1940, as well as to cultural invasions of ideas and new forms of literature which, in the 1870's and 1880's, came through the doors opened wider by Georg Brandes and produced an intellectual awakening throughout Scandinavia. Having observed radical changes in both the face and mind of Denmark, Pon-

toppidan set himself the task of describing in novels these changes and their consequences.

Pontoppidan was a productive writer who had his literary début in 1881 and continued writing until his death sixty-two years later. He wrote in almost every literary genre; short stories, reviews, political articles, tourist propaganda, poetry, weekly columns in newspapers, and, most important of all, novels. Deploring the slipshod, he wrote slowly, carefully, and well—with a marvelous sense of the plasticity of the Danish language. His aim in his novels was to present things in a realistic manner, but his common sense prevented him from wandering in the direction of naturalistic excesses while his aesthetic sense and deep knowledge of human psychology would not let him be a simple journalist.

The late nineteenth and early twentieth centuries are filled with the names of Scandinavian authors of international fame: Ibsen, Bjørnson, Kielland, Lie, Garborg, Strindberg, Heidenstam, Lagerlöf, Brandes, and Bang, to name but a few. Pontoppidan, in my opinion, belongs on this Parnassus but, despite the fact that he was granted half the Nobel Prize for Literature in 1917, his fame has not spread far outside the Scandinavian countries. Part of the reason for this is that he has not been sufficiently translated. To be sure his three major novels have appeared in German translations, but none has come out in French, and only two parts of the first have been translated into English. Pontoppidan is an important author who, unfortunately, remains relatively unknown. Even in Denmark his circle of readers has never been particularly large, and just as he seems to have been quite unaffected by literary currents about him, so also he does not seem to have influenced in any important way other writers. The proletarian novelist Martin Andersen Nexø, who dedicated his first important novel ''Til Mesteren Henrik Pontoppidan,'' is the exception proving the rule. Perhaps the basic clue to his lack of popularity can be found in his skill in analyzing Danish national character and characters. For many he seemed cold and unfeeling; his objectivity and scepticism having obscured his deep understanding of and sympathy for humanity.

Det forjættede land (The Promised Land), Lykke-Per (Lucky Peter), and *De dødes rige (The Kingdom of the Dead)* are Pontoppidan's most important novels and cover roughly the period from 1870-1914. They provide sources, in the words of one critic, for the ''political and literary, religious and secular history of Denmark in town and country during the last two generations.'' If Pontoppidan is considered as a critic of Danish society, *Lykke-Per* and *De dødes rige* are the most important of the three novels. To be sure, Pontoppidan's analyses of Grundtvigianism, the people's college movement, and the peasantry in *Det forjættede land* are of interest, but these issues do not have the same universal applicability as those presented in the other two novels. Some impression of Pontoppidan's general attitude toward these subjects can, however, be gained from a passage in *Lykke-Per:* ''Nonetheless the broad-backed Danish peasant sat on his farm with an unchallenged feeling of being the nation's marrow, its principal source of power, and its hope for the future. It was a concept that, in the course of the century, had become a national dogma which the Grundtvigian People's College had finally sanctified. From Skagen to Gedser town and country were united in awe-inspired worship of butter and pork in the good old land of the Danes.''

The Pontoppidans, the name is a Latinization of Broby, are an old and distinguished Danish clerical family, and the author's own father held several livings in the Established (Lutheran)

Church of Denmark. But Henrik Pontoppidan reacted early in life against the conventional and intellectually and emotionally unsatisfying religion of his home. This reaction is mirrored in *Lykke-Per* when the chief character, Per Sidenius, who is also a clergyman's son, is caught stealing apples. In the presence of his many brothers and sisters at the dinner table, he is solemnly rebuked by his stern father and reminded of the commandment "Thou shalt not steal!" Despite the assurance that his father's words are for his own good and have been said in order to prevent his ending as "that evil brother over whom the Lord pronounced His frightful curse, 'A fugitive and a vagabond shalt thou be in the earth'," this psychological torture leads the young man into an enduring hatred of his family. For Per Sidenius, an intelligent and independent child, the Church of his fathers becomes anathema and the enemy that must be defeated and destroyed before a new age of science and progress can be ushered in. It should be emphasized that, at this point, Pontoppidan identifies himself closely with his hero.

In *De dødes rige,* Mads Vestrup, a pious and exceptionally sincere and devoted rural pastor, succumbs to a temptation of the flesh. With Christian humility he begs forgiveness of his bishop but to no avail, and he is defrocked. He becomes a wandering revivalist preacher who thunders against the abuses of the Church and its compromises with the world. In some of Vestrup's colorful sermons, the reader senses Pontoppidan's own disdain of the self-righteousness of the Church which preaches forgiveness and practices hypocrisy.

In *Lykke-Per* the Church is a bastion of ignorance and oppression, but the very violence with which Per Sidenius reacts against Christian symbols is an indication that he, like Pontoppidan, cannot break completely with his past. At one point he flies into a rage upon hearing church bells, draws a revolver and shoots hysterically at an image of the Virgin on an Austrian mountainside. Yet by a quirk of Fortune he later becomes the son-in-law of a representative of one direction of late nineteenth century physical Christianity, Pastor Blomberg. Blomberg preaches Christianity without pain, the Sermon on the Mount but not the Crucifixion. He is, in short, Grundtvigian rather than Kierkegaardian. Life is no great problem for him, and the faith he preaches is sufficient to meet the minor difficulties he and his followers are liable to encounter in their oversimplified, uncomplicated, and unsophisticated world. Blomberg's faith is in the beauty of nature and the efficacy of psalm-singing in keeping God's sheep content with their lot in the world. His faith is sincere, open, unintellectual, and shallow. There are no harsh words about sin and repentance in his sermons but rather an emphasis on the love of Jesus, on an optimistic kind of *Christentum durch Freude.*

For Per, Blomberg's answer to the religious question is lighter and easier to swallow than the harsh, cold, and doctrinal Lutheranism of his childhood, but he does not fail to note that there is a good deal of the old self-righteousness even in this new Wesleyan Christianity. This is shown in Blomberg's condescending attitude towards his fellow pastor, Fjaltring, who has none of Blomberg's charming ways to attract people to his church but who possesses an intellectual depth and spiritual understanding lacking in Blomberg. Fjaltring feels that:

> One couldn't even use a phrase like fear of God about the Christians these days when they amicably took Our Lord by the arm and, with a patronizing air, or, when moved, with a childish infatuation threw themselves around His neck. Obviously referring to Pastor Blomberg, he spoke contemptuously of "our good-natured Grundtvigian Christianity" which was in the

process of becoming the national Christianity of the country . . . and which, even in religious matters, sought out the idyllic and replaced the passion of faith with lyric poetry.

Pontoppidan's views on the social gospel can be seen in his portrayal of Pastor Gaardbo in *De dødes rige.* Gaardbo is a representative of a religious response to anti-clericalism. His first concern is with the poor, and his aim is to translate Christian principles into daily action both locally and nationally. To him it seems as if the materialist forces of Danish liberalism can best be conquered by translating the social gospel into political action, and he backs the formation of a church party which elects him to parliament. In the end he develops into a kind of theocrat. Meanwhile he displays the same intolerance of other views found in Per's father and Pastor Blomberg, and his lack of understanding of his fellows and narrow righteousness cause his fiancée to commit suicide and separate him from his twin brother for a long period of time. On every level Pontoppidan has examined the Danish Church and organized Christianity in general and found little to praise and much to criticize.

Per Sidenius early makes up his mind to enter the field farthest removed from theology, and any of the humanities for that matter, engineering. He enrolls at the Copenhagen Institute of Technology fully determined to conquer the world with his technical achievements. (Pontoppidan himself attended the Institute.) He had imagined that the far-famed school would be: "A kind of temple . . . where the future happiness and prosperity of a liberated mankind would be forged with the lightning and thunder of the spirit, and he found a grim and unsightly building in the shadow of an old episcopal mansion and within it a collection of dark and depressing rooms where some young men stood bent over small paper-covered tables while others sat with long pipes and read their notebooks or played cards on the sly." He found no inspiration in the teachers, a motley and unwholesome-looking group, most of whom were disinterested both in the students and what they were attempting to teach them. Per had imagined engineers as conquerors of nature and as adventurous explorers, but he found that the average engineer was only: "an ordinary office worker, a calculating machine endowed with a conscience, a living painting. . . . The greater part of his fellow students . . . dreamed only of . . . reaching . . . a position in the Civil Service that would permit them to set themselves up with a little household in a little house with a little garden and then, after forty years of faithful service, retirement with a little pension and a little badge of distinction." Per does not wish to become a part of this earthbound mob with their prosaic dreams for the future, and he spends almost all of his time working on an ambitious canal project to turn Jutland into a new commercial and industrial center. Finally he takes his ideas to a professor to ask his advice and opinion on the plans and drawings. It does not take long for the professor, "with the unpleasant ability which old teachers develop in the course of the years," to point out an error in the calculations and to counsel the younger man to spend his time on his studies rather than on fanciful projects.

The result is that Per gives up any idea of taking the engineer's examination and turns his back on the established school system with its dull and insensitive teachers and its intellectually lazy students and determines to proceed in the world without the dubious benefits of further education. An older man expresses Per's contempt for the Institute of Technology and society in general in words which might be pertinent in other places as well: "Everything at the present time is organized to encourage mediocrity. There is no longer any room for the exceptions, no understanding of, indeed not even any desire for, the unusual, the progressive, the pioneering intelligence.'' Per has found life to be an eternal struggle between the older and the younger generations with all power in the hands of the former. Pontoppidan, the prophet of the individual against the mass, finds little comfort in the Danish educational system of the late nineteenth century.

Pontoppidan knew at first hand the newspaper world, having been a writer for several of the most important newspapers of the Danish capital, and it is of interest to note his severe criticism of the press. His descriptions of Danish journalism in the two novels under discussion indicate that he did not believe that the newspaper is or can be an intelligent organ for the disinterested shaping of public opinion. In *Lykke-Per* the financier Max Bernhardt has controlling interests in several papers and is able to use them to further his own financial projects. If announcement of a new stock issue is given to the press along with money for advertisements, favorable mention can be assured. Journalism has, in short, prostituted itself, and this has terrible consequences, for (according to Pontoppidan) we live in the age of the journalist; the man with a smattering of knowledge and an unerring sense of what the mob wants to read. In *Lykke-Per* the journalist Dyring is distinguished only by an incredible ability to adjust himself immediately to any situation by sensing in which direction the wind is blowing. He is stolid and unoriginal, possessing neither talents nor vices and is properly scolded by his old-fashioned uncle: ''You can't take life seriously. For you and your materialistic, unpatriotic, and godless bunch life is nothing but a good or a bad joke. Your country's afflictions, the distress of the population, political misfortunes, war, pestilence, and fire—everything for you is only material for entertainment, food for the columns, a prey for your hired pen.'' In *De dødes rige* Dyring has a spiritual brother in the form of Samuelsen, editor of the leading newspaper of the Left. Samuelsen's devotion to the political cause of the Left is in direct proportion to the number of advertisements in the paper. When revenues fall off, Samuelsen does not hesitate to accept a secure and rewarding position as editor of a conservative newspaper. In Pontoppidan's Denmark, the journalist has no real opinions of his own; he writes what the hand that feeds him expects him to write, and, to judge from the descriptions of interviews, he writes neither well nor accurately.

Pontoppidan does not stop with journalism but includes also perceptive comments on contemporary figures in Danish literary and artistic life. His views on the important critic Georg Brandes, whom he calls Dr. Nathan in *Lyyke-Per,* are worth noting:

> He was small in size, and in general people found his face unattractive. . . . It was most handsome when he was listening, for then its expression was enlivened by that which was most important to him—his thirst for knowledge, his unmeasurable desire . . . or lust for learning. His indiscriminate animation had contributed . . . to the opposition and aversion with which he had been met. Time after time it had alienated friends and natural allies by violating Nordic-Germanic ideas of masculine dignity. . . . He had his spiritual roots in Romance civilization and his predilections for the refinements of French taste (he had also displayed this as a young man by taking on a certain external elegance) made him immediately suspect among his countrymen, not the least in the learned world.

Almost all Scandinavian writers of the late nineteenth century were influenced by Georg Brandes, but none of them evaulated him with the critical skill of Pontoppidan.

> To be sure he possessed brilliant talents, but he was not what generally is understood by the word ''genius,'' no self-esteeming spirit, no new creator. Compared with home-grown originals like Grundtvig or Kierkegaard, he could even seem to lack any truly deep distinction. . . . As if with hundreds of eyes he scanned the literatures of all countries and all times, leaping with unfailing instinct on all that could serve as a stimulant back in Denmark and producing a sometimes bitter and sometimes sweetly spiced tonic for Danish youth.

In Pontoppidan's opinion, Brandes acted as a necessary catalyst in Danish literature. Social radicals accepted him as a hero or deified him, and religious conservatives were spurred on to greater activity: ''In a good many of these he had really managed to arouse the active passion and the fanatic fervor that he had sought in vain to instill in his partisans.''

The difficulties for Brandesianism in late nineteenth century Denmark were many for: ''What there was of culture in the people belonged almost exclusively to the Church.'' In fact, the victory of rationalism in Denmark was far from complete: ''The religious counter-offensive was still not widely noticed in the capital where people's minds were too much taken up with the newly created business whirl. Out in the provinces, on the other hand, and especially in the country, the new religious movement silently grew stronger and assembled around parsonages and People's Colleges like an army around its fortresses.''

One of the factors influencing public reaction to Brandes was based on religion: ''That the man was a Jew had contributed to Per's never having felt a desire to acquire more detailed information about him. He wasn't at all fond of this strange tribe of people.'' The problem of the Jew in Denmark is a central one in *Lykke-Per.* Jakobe Salomon, a key figure in the novel, is the step-daughter of a wealthy and influential Jewish financier. From her school days on she found her Jewish background a hindrance to making and keeping friends. Although not at all religious, the coldness and cruelty of a society that has constantly reminded her of her strangeness has made her feel bonds of unity with other Jews who are victims of outrageous crimes committed by Christians, rather than of mere prejudice. Pontoppidan's picture of the Jews is both sympathetic and understanding. His descriptions of Jewish family life are warmly and well done, just as his analysis of Danish anti-semitism is both revealing and interesting. Some of the reaction against the Jews is on patriotic grounds; the Colonel who fought in both wars against the Germans, hates the Jews because of their connections with Germany. Per's family hates them for not having accepted Jesus as the Messiah. In *Lykke-Per,* however, most Danes are anti-semitic out of simple jealousy for the prominent positions held by certain Jews. The painter Fritjof calls Denmark ''the new Jew-land'' but revises his opinion when a Jewish merchant purchases several of his paintings at a good price and thereafter he speaks respectfully of Jews as ''bearers of culture.''

Pontoppidan does not seem as tolerant of the Danish businessman as he is of Danish Jews. In *De dødes rige* the self-made coffee millionaire Søholm is the epitome of the modern big businessman. Everywhere in Copenhagen electric signs flash on and off informing the public that Søholm's coffee is the cheapest and the best. This modern day highwayman is personally ruthless and even brutal to his own family. In a weak moment when he fears death he attempts to buy off God by promising a considerable donation to the Church, but upon recovery he reduces the contribution to insignificance. In effect, Søholm worships financial success as the highest possible human achievement and represents the triumph of modern barbarism. On the other hand, Pontoppidan does demonstrate a certain amount of sympathy for the "matadors of the Stock Exchange" who try to make their fortunes in a gentlemanly fashion and who are almost to be pitied in their dread of unfavorable publicity and their constant desire to be accepted as respectable members of society.

The social radicals making up the Bohemia of Copenhagen also come in for Pontoppidan's criticism. Per Sidenius is at first amused by: "These curious people who could get fired up over a combination of colors and talk themselves into ecstasy because of four rhymed lines—as if the welfare of all mankind depended on their correct understanding." Later the radicalism of the Bohemians, which accompanies their over-developed aesthetic sensitivity, seems to Per to stem more from a stubborn desire to be different than from any strong convictions. The independence of the opinions of society which the Bohemians claim is, according to Pontoppidan, illusory, and they are actually lost souls who have found no substitute for the rejected opinions and ideas of the society from which they have divorced themselves. In essence, the liberated spirits, the Bohemians are the most unfree of all men, for they must seek an audience for their works of art among the public they supposedly despise and at the same time constantly feel the pressure of intense professional jealousy within their own ranks.

The Copenhagen of Kierkegaard had had no Bohemia, but the Danish capital of the last decades of the nineteenth century was in the process of becoming a world city and, in relation to the countryside, a large head on a small body. Pontoppidan finds the pressures for conformity in dress, manner of speech, and even thinking in Copenhagen very depressing. Per's disillusionment with the society of the capital is complete and he sees those who surround him as: "nothing more than self-righteous Sideniuses who plastered over their petty bourgeois timidity with a Pharisaic overbearing scorn for the glory and splendor of this world." Per is, however, intoxicated at the beginning with Bismarckian Berlin: "There is something about the life and noise here that electrifies me from the inside out. . . . What are these great cities but tremendous turbines drawing in the streams of people and then spewing them out again after having deprived them of their ergs? What a concentration of living power! There is really something elevating about feeling the floor under one's feet tremble with the discharged energy of two million people." Later he sees the towns as a blot on the country side and looks with dismay at the specialization Which modern urban industrial society has made necessary. Per Sidenius (and Pontoppidan) cannot feel at ease among the: "Technicians of the kind that world competition has produced; men with a phenomenal professional knowledge in a single and, most frequently, limited field who are, on the other hand, quite lacking in knowledge outside their speciality and generally denuded of all interests not tied to the fight for existence and personal well-being." In Pontoppidan's view, these highly-trained professional idiots are creating a world over which they have no control and about which they have no understanding. Each expert proceeds on his own level without any overall organization and, as more and more "progress" is achieved, it becomes increasingly difficult for any one person or group

of persons to have a comprehensive and reasonable view of modern life.

If life in urban industrial centers in the late nineteenth century was unsatisfying, life in a provincial town in the 1880's was even worse. The description of a party at the home of the apothecary in a small town in Jutland is one example: "No one's enjoyment of the party was diminished because the food was not exactly prepared by a master chef and the contents of the bottles in no way corresponded to the distinguished names on the labels. These were not people with fastidious palates. . . . After dinner, the gathering divided, in the customary provincial manner, with the ladies remaining in the living room while the gentlemen retired to the office to smoke tobacco and give the conversation freer reins. Here they liberated themselves comfortably from the last bit of social restraint and told dirty stories, drank liqueurs, enjoyed their belches, and half-dozed." There is, in fact, little to recommend the society of the small town and Per finds that: "Since he lacked the prerequisites to be able to judge them as individuals, they all seemed to him to be exactly the same. Everywhere he saw only the distinguishing characteristics of the class: the avarice, the petty dogmatism . . . all of those ignoble characteristics that are bred in narrow and out-of-the-way communities."

In Pontoppidan's view, modern man and modern society in all of its forms are fundamentally incompatible. In *Lykke-Per* and *De dødes rige* he serves up a varied *smørrebrød* of Danes from every class of society. On each level, life presents the same dilemma: the impossibility of a proper adjustment between the past, representing the totality of man's previous experience in living with himself, and the present which is unfolding at such a rapid rate that no one can comprehend it. The exit for most modern men, at least in the novels of Pontoppidan, seems to be some form of oversimplification. The middle-aged product of a distinguished family, Neergaard, can find no means of escape but suicide when his empty-headed and thoroughly meaningless mistress abandons him for a younger man. His philosophy of life is summed up in the following words: "The chains we men are not born with we put on ourselves during the long course of our lives. We are and we remain slaves. We only feel comfortable in bolts and irons."

In *De dødes rige* the young, intelligent, and emancipated Jytte Abildgaard is quite incapable of being happy and can neither love nor truly be loved. She is acquainted with life but does not really know it and therefore finds her existence boring; this despite her rich and varied education. She can analyze rationally even her own courtship, but her rationalism does not save her from a foolish marriage to a fashionable painter who has distinguished himself more in the boudoir than the studio. Their marriage is a proof that life is, in fact, both boring and meaningless. When Jytte discovers her husband's infidelity during her pregnancy, she leaves him and dies soon after the death of the child, summing up her life in the words: "Yes, now I'm dying, Meta, but then I've never really lived."

Seen with Pontoppidan's eyes, the first decade of the twentieth century is an age of disillusionment. Having given up the solace to be found in the hope of salvation offered by the Church, man has now also lost his faith in progress and in the eventual triumph of science and reason. Some people grasp at straws, like the health faddists in *De dødes rige* who seek to find happiness in eating vegetables or performing exercises. Others relax into a permanent ennui enlivened sporadically by the amusement provided by acrobats, trained animals, or cabaret singers. According to Pontoppidan, conversation in the beau monde of the decade before the first World War has the character of concurrent monologues rather than of an exchange of ideas by two minds meeting on approximately the same level.

Some men are too intelligent to relax or to grasp at straws. One such person is the liberal Zaun who possesses both wit and ideals. Unfortunately, however, he lacks force of character and is incapable of putting his ideas into action. He knows the political situation in every country in the world and feverishly speculates on what effect the fall of a minister of the interior in Bulgaria or Uruguay will have on the election prospects of the Danish Left. Zaun understands problems but can do nothing to help solve them. The result for him is an insomnia that Pontoppidan diagnoses as the incapability of escaping at any time from the pressing problems of a world that is rapidly falling apart.

Pontoppidan offers no solutions. The career of the liberal leader Enslev, a composite of several contemporary Danish politicians, in *De dødes rige* offers proof that politics are, indeed, quite hopeless. One follows Enslev in his development from a fire-eating and idealistic young writer attacking the vices of reactionary Denmark to the old and honored leader of the Left whose ideals have become tarnished by power, and, in fact, quite unimportant. A modern politician, says Pontoppidan, has little use for ideas or ideals and must pay first attention to political strategy and expediency. In his last years, Enslev is a demagogue who loses control of his party, splits it, and suffers defeat only to be honored after his death as a real champion of the people.

The society Henrik Pontoppidan has described is sick and, in his opinion, there is no cure for his illness. He might be accused of being a social historian without any social consciousness, of being a person lacking any feeling of the necessity of group cooperation to reach a desirable goal. Actually, the heroes of *Lykke-Per* and *De dødes rige* resolve their incompatibility with society by becoming virtual hermits. It would seem, from their examples, that Pontoppidan thinks that the best way to cope with modern life is to have as little as possible to do with it. But Pontoppidan was a writer and not a reformer or preacher, and whether one accepts or rejects his iconoclastic and highly individualistic views, no one who reads *Lykke-Per* and *De dødes rige* can deny that he has presented in these novels an interesting and penetrating critique of Danish society in the late nineteenth and early twentieth centuries. (pp. 170-83)

> Ernst Ekman, "Henrik Pontoppidan as a Critic of Modern Danish Society," in Scandinavian Studies, Vol. 29, No. 3, August, 1957, pp. 170-83.

BØRGE GEDSØ MADSEN (essay date 1965)

[*Madsen is an American educator and critic with a specialty in Scandinavian literature. In the following essay, he contrasts the two main characters in Pontoppidan's novel cycles* The Promised Land *and* Lykke-Per.]

In 1875 in the preface to the second edition of *Catiline*, Henrik Ibsen wrote among other things the following: "Much around which my later writings center, the contradiction between ability and desire, between will and possibility, the intermingled tragedy and comedy in humanity and in the individual,—appeared already here in vague foreshadowings. . . ."

These words of Ibsen's are singularly apt when they are applied to the fantast characters which are so frequently encountered in the Danish novel of the nineteenth and the twentieth cen-

turies. One predominant characteristic of the Danish fantast figures is a feeling of impotence stemming from failure to follow some kind of calling or, more simply, from frustrated attempts at living a fruitful, energetic human life. Thus we find, for example, the fantast as would-be scholar and lover in the character of Magister Claudius in Poul Martin Møller's *En dansk Students Eventyr*. In Jacobsen's *Niels Lyhne* the daydreaming Niels is the fantast viewed as impotent poet and atheist, while Herman Bang's William Høg in *Haabløse Slægter* is portrayed as the ambitious but untalented actor. In Johannes V. Jensen's *Kongens Fald* the self-doubting fantast Christian II is shown to be unfit for the role of king and leader of men. And in the novel trilogy *Det forjættede land* . . . Henrik Pontoppidan has subjected the fantast as would-be prophet to a close scrutiny.

At the end of *Det forjættede land* its main character, Emanuel Hansted is described as "the ghost of Don Quixote." Throughout the novel Emanuel Hansted is conceived and portrayed consistently by Pontoppidan as a Don Quixote, a lonely, romantic, impractical idealist who is constantly foiled and eventually defeated in his encounters with reality. He is one of the most fully developed fantast characters in the Danish novel. His *Fantasteri* manifests itself mainly in two ways: in his aspirations as prophet and saint, and in his romantic, almost Rousseauistic, cult of the Danish peasant in whom he, naïvely, sees the bearer of a folk culture which will prove more viable than the effete, decadent urban civilization.

The seed of Emanuel Hansted's *Fantasteri* is laid in early childhood. As in the case of J. P. Jacobsen's Niels Lyhne and Herman Bang's William Høg. Pontoppidan stresses the great (dangerous) influence exerted by the mother on the fantast-to-be. When Emanuel was a boy, his mother would tell him legends and fairy tales about warriors and princes who under the banner of Christ went out into the world to fight for truth and justice. Later in life he is convinced that in that early period of his existence he received the dedication to become a minister. He believes that his fate was settled from childhood. When his fantast mother dies, after having lost her reason, Emanuel feels misunderstood and lonely in his father's house.

Emanuel Hansted's feeling of loneliness, which follows him as a shadow wherever he moves, is the reason for his seeking contact with the peasant population and with nature. Fleeing worldly, sophisticated life in Copenhagen which repels him by its emptiness, he obtains a position as curate in the country and sees it as his mission to awaken the spirit of Christ in the peasantry. To save *himself* he furthermore desires fervently to establish personal contact with the peasants who seem to him, the product of overcivilization, much more wholesome and noble than the tainted city dwellers. Emanuel carries his overstrained desire for identification with the peasants so far as to marry a peasant girl, Hansine, who to his infatuated eyes seems to "resemble nature."

As a genuine fantast Pontoppidan's Emanuel Hansted has no sense of reality. His head is in the clouds, his feet barely touching the ground. The peasants in his parish are not so much wholesome, noble children of God as materialistic, politicizing realists who plan to use Emanuel as a pawn in tactical maneuvers of their own. His marriage to Hansine proves to be a mistake. In spite of a temporary mutual attraction, they are fundamentally incompatible, uncongenial natures. As their marriage slowly disintegrates, Emanuel is drawn helplessly and pathetically to the elegant Ragnhild Tønnesen who represents the milieu he tried to escape by leaving Copenhagen. Early in

Volume II of the trilogy, Emanuel's religious *Fantasteri* is fully developed. This is illustrated graphically by his attitude toward his son's illness. For two years "Gutten" has been suffering from an ear infection which is becoming increasingly serious. But Emanuel, serenely confident that God will make everything right in the end, remains impervious to Hansine's repeated pleas that they seek medical advice. When he finally reluctantly agrees to call a doctor, it is too late, and the boy dies. The heartbroken Emanuel now accuses himself of having shown no confidence in God, that is to say because he did call the doctor in the end instead of trustingly letting things take their course. *Not for one moment* does he reprove himself for not having called the doctor while there was still time. He has lost contact with reality, is completely in the power of his fantastic notions, but all the time—to be sure—motivated by the most "idealistic" considerations.

The titles of the three volumes in Pontoppidan's trilogy are: *Muld (Mould); Det forjættede land (The Promised Land);* and *Dommens dag (Judgment Day). Mould* refers to the layers of earth, that is the rural population, which thus far to a large extent have been left uncultivated, and which through cultivation (education) may perhaps be made to yield considerable harvests. *The Promised Land* is the field of communication and love which Emanuel hopes to establish between himself and the peasants, but which never materializes. In the last volume, *Judgment Day,* judgment is pronounced on the fantast Emanuel Hansted by Pontoppidan's partial mouthpiece Pastor Petersen, called Rüdesheimer.

In *Judgment Day* Emanuel Hansted works himself more and more deeply into his religious *Fantasteri* and finally dies in insanity, as his mother had done before him. At the end of Volume II, *The Promised Land,* he had become separated from Hansine and the children. His congregation, led by the scheming Weaver Hansen, had turned against him and mocked him openly, as he admonished them to lead a life of purity. In the third volume of the trilogy Emanuel gradually comes to see all his sufferings not as a punishment from God but on the contrary as a blessing, a divine distinction bestowed on him. He gathers around him a little group of fanatics to whom he seems like a prophet or a saint. Among these Emanuel works certain "miracles": a hopeless alcoholic is cured of his disease; a woman fatally ill with cancer of the stomach, who had kept the village awake at night with her screams of pain, now comes to see the pains as divine blessings and offers prayers of thanks to God for this special grace that her illness now seems. To Emanuel the final, decisive proof of the rightness of his calling is the letter he receives from Hansine in which she tells him that their marriage must be dissolved. Emanuel, like Christ, is now completely alone, distinguished by God for his sacred mission, as he believes. By this time, however, he is so distraught by mental torment and physical exhaustion that he loses his mind. When, at the end of the novel, he tries to speak at a meeting, he breaks down and can only exclaim sobbingly: "My God! My God! Why hast Thou forsaken me?" Shortly before this happens, Emanuel has had a vision of his dead mother who appeared before him and gave him her blessing. The son, who in childhood was launched on his fateful career as a prophet by his over-strained mother, is joined in the end by this mother. The author's point is made with didactic clarity: the religious fantast has come full circle.

In the severe judgment which Pastor Rüdesheimer pronounces on Emanuel at the end of *Judgment Day,* he says among other things the following:

> The worst fault of people nowadays is that they totally lack a sense of humor. Rightly considered Emanuel Hansted's efforts have been essentially laughable, his life a series of low-comedy scenes. With all justice it might, some day when he dies, be written on his tombstone: Here lies Don Quixote's ghost, Emanuel Hansted by name, who was born to be an honest curate but believed himself to be a prophet and a saint; who therefore donned a herdsman's garb and considered every impulsive idea a special calling from heaven; who consistently bungled everything he took hold of, left his wife and neglected his children, but nonetheless until the end regarded himself as the one chosen by Providence, the one who would prepare the advent of the millennium and proclaim God's judgment on men.

Speaking with considerable violence and indignation, Pastor Rüdesheimer expands his criticism of the individual Emanuel Hansted into a general denunciation of religious *Fantasteri* in Denmark in modern times. Generalizations about the last two decades of the nineteenth century abound in his long speech at the end of the novel. Not only Emanuel Hansted but also his mother have the excuse that they are "the children of an affected age, of a confused century which, like no century before it, has cultivated simplicity and put a premium on foolishness . . . a century in which overstrained ideas, hysterical lamentation and all sorts of hot-air eccentricity are admired as expressions of true, divine genius." On Judgment Day Emanuel Hansted may claim as "extenuating circumstance" that he was a "result of our time's unhealthily inflated emotional life, a product of the process of lyrical putrefaction in which the society of the old world is being destroyed." Later the Pastor sarcastically observes that though he has heard much about the modern "break-through" in science, literature, and the arts, he is unable to see that anything has been broken through, or that anything new has emerged. He goes on to say: "At any rate I still see the same superstitious glorification of our abnormally developed emotional life, the same hysterical worshipping of passion, exaggeration, and affection *(Fusentasteri).* It even seems to me that in recent years the disease has spread in a sinister way, that the fungus of lyricism has penetrated to the very marrow of the people itself."

As counterparts to the idealistic but headless fantast Emanuel Hansted, Pontoppidan has placed in his novel the two characters Pastor Rüdesheimer and Hansine. Rüdesheimer's philosophy is common sense and moderation in all things, including religion. He himself has lived through periods of religious crisis full of anguished speculation; but he has emerged from them with the simple wisdom for himself and his congregation that happiness lies in rendering to the world what belongs to the world and to God what belongs to God. During the week one should work and enjoy the simple pleasures of life in moderation; on Sunday one should go to church like a child, trusting in the fatherly love of God—and let it go at that! Excesses, either in the direction of debauchery or asceticism, are not for Pastor Rüdesheimer. After many years of marriage to Emanuel, the healthy, down-to-earth Hansine wakes up to a feeling of deep shame when she finally realizes to what extent she has been misled. Toward the end Pontoppidan writes about her that she has now put aside the vain dreams of youth.

> She had learned that happiness in life consisted in having your root in your own soil and in growing in the light of the homely sky—how low and oppressive and sunless it might be. Never—not even in her loneliness out by the sea, separated from husband and children—had she felt a homelessness so depressing

as the one that had confused her mind in Vejlby parsonage.

Det forjættede land is in many ways a didactic novel, a frontal attack on the Danish *Fantasteri* as it manifests itself in religion, particularly within the Grundtvigian sect. Occasionally Pontoppidan is carried away by his didactic purposes, and when this happens Emanuel Hansted becomes less credible as an individual, a denfenseless target for the author's satire. To be sure the first volume of the trilogy had suggested in several ways that Emanuel was something of a *Sværmer,* but the reader is totally unprepared for the kind of otherworldliness that Emanuel betrays in the opening pages of the second volume. To convince Hansine that they should let God or Nature take care of Gutten's illness, Emanuel cites a couple of case histories from his own schooldays: two boys were suffering from an eye complaint; one was treated by a doctor and became blind; the other was left alone and lived forever after with the finest pair of eyes one could imagine. *Quod erat demonstrandum:* one should never let a doctor treat an illness! This is not only a credible degree of impracticability on the part of the fantast hero, it is a kind of stupid fanaticism, a lack of ordinary intelligence and common sense which nothing in the first volume had indicated that Emanuel was capable of. It is planted there by Pontoppidan for satirical purposes, to expose Emanuel as an incorrigible fantast.

This is not to say, however, that Emanuel's fate leaves us unmoved. Fumbling, egocentric, and pathetic as he often is, he is not without a certain tragic grandeur at the end in his Christ-like isolation. He bears a strong resemblance to other idealistic fantasts in Scandinavian literature—Ibsen's Brand and Bjørnson's Pastor Sang in *Over Evne I.* Like them Emanuel Hansted fails, but like them he fails nobly.

Where Emanuel Hansted fails, Per Sidenius in ***Lykke-Per*** . . . succeeds, though only after a long struggle of liberation. Emanuel Hansted is destroyed by his religious *Fantasteri* but Per Sidenius eventually overcomes *his* in his final victory over the "Sidenius heritage" which has haunted him like a ghost through most of his life. Early in childhood the defiant Per begins his rebellion against the Sidenius heritage, the joyless pietistic Christianity of his parents. The climax of this rebellion is marked by the scene in the Swiss Alps where he in youthful bravado fires a shot at the crucifix and dares the "ghosts" to pursue him with their rumbling. But in the following chapters of ***Lykke-Per*** the ghosts of the past begin to assert their power over him. He is strongly affected by the "beautiful" Christian deaths of his parents; feelings of guilt because of his coldness toward them manifest themselves; he loses interest in his grand canal project, interest in fighting for it, boasting to his fiancée Jakobe of his lack of "vanity." For a while he is tempted by Pastor Blomberg's happy form of Christianity and fascinated by the life-denying, almost masochistic religion of the somber pastor Fjaltring. During his religious crisis Per seems to the atheistic, Jewish Jakobe a typical Danish fantast. In a letter to him she tries to analyze his temperament and writes among other things the following:

> How different from most of his contemporaries he might seem to be . . . he still was a genuine son of his country, a full-fledged child of the passionless Danish people with the pale eyes and the timid souls . . . the hill trolls who could not look toward the sun without sneezing; who only came to life in the dusk when they were sitting on their hillocks conjuring up bright visions in the evening clouds as solace and comfort for their oppressed minds . . . a

people of gnomes with big, thoughtful heads but the weak limbs of a child. . . .

But these words contain only part of the truth about Per. They must be contrasted with Per's final action: his leaving wife and children (partly for the sake of their happiness) to find out who he really is in isolation and self-examination. Jakobe's characterization of him must also be contrasted with some of the entries in Per's diary found after his death by one of his friends. The following passage is particularly significant:

> Without the primitive natural impulse, the self-creating power which manifests itself in passion—whether it be turned outwards toward reality or inwards toward thought or upwards toward dream—and without a great, indeed fantastic courage to *will* oneself in divine nakedness, nobody achieves real freedom. Therefore I consider myself fortunate that I lived in an age which called forth this impulse and strengthened this courage. Otherwise I would have become an incomplete man, a Sidenius, all my life.

Two worlds are contrasted in ***Lykke-Per*** with Per Sidenius as the connecting link between them: the Sidenius world with its joyless form of Christianity and the world of the atheistic Copenhagen Jews, "nature's children," as they are called, "untainted by a heaven and a hell." In the course of the novel Per moves from the Sidenius world toward the world of nature's children. Whether he has completely eradicated every trace of the Sidenius philosophy in himself may, perhaps, be doubted—his motives for leaving his wife and children are complex. But in his final belief in "wise, generous nature which compensates on one hand what we lose on the other," Per Sidenius has achieved at least a partial victory. In his determined attempt at self-understanding and self-realization, the fantast has partially corrected himself of his *Fantasteri.* In ***Det forjættede land*** Emanuel Hansted, who is completely devoid of self-knowledge, wanders around in a vicious circle which eventually cuts him off from reality so that he succumbs in madness and despair. In ***Lykke-Per,*** too, the Sidenius heritage threatens to become a vicious circle, but Per manages to break out of it before it closes around him. In increased self-knowledge Per finds the fulcrum from which he can support his life and accept reality. (pp. 227-35)

> *Børge Gedsø Madsen, "Henrik Pontoppidan's Emanuel Hansted and Per Sidenius," in Scandinavian Studies, edited by Carl F. Bayerschmidt and Erik J. Friis, University of Washington Press, 1965, pp. 227-35.*

KENNETH H. OBER   (essay date 1978)

[*In the following excerpt, Ober presents an atypical reading of* The Kingdom of the Dead, *maintaining that Pontoppidan's characterization creates a mythic dimension in this work that transcends the social novel.*]

Pontoppidan's *De dødes rige* . . . is most frequently interpreted primarily in relation to its social criticism, and the pessimism in the novel is derived from Pontoppidan's doomsday view of Danish society of the time. Within the framework of this critical view, however, most of the characters and their actions seem rather formless and inconclusive; their personalities seem unfinished and blurred and appear at times to merge and overlap. Thus the characterizations of the two pastors, Johannes Gaardbo and Mads Vestrup, tend to blur into each other, and Mads Vestrup sometimes suggests a reversed and distorted image of Johannes Gaardbo; the physicians Asmus Hagen and Povl

Gaardbo echo this relationship; and the politicians Tyge Enslev and John Hagen repeat it once again. It is perhaps significant that the major characters who fall outside this pattern are the most central ones, Jytte Abildgaard and her one-time fiancé Torben Dihmer. Jytte, perhaps *the* major character of the novel, is the human thread that connects and interrelates the other characters; Torben, though also an all-pervasive presence in the novel, has a curiously passive role, rather above and outside the work, and he, alone of all the chief characters, takes no really active part in the development of the novel. It is also significant that, although virtually all the central characters in the end suffer failure and tragedy, only Jytte and Torben are capable of foreseeing their own physical destruction. Jytte senses that her marriage with Karsten From, the woman-chasing painter, may destroy her, and she accepts her fate since she is powerless to resist it, while Torben deliberately stops the treatment for his disease with the full knowledge that the disease will then slowly kill him.

A possible key to the apparent unclear differentiation of the other major characters may be provided in the first book of the novel, where Jytte, musing over her ambiguous relationship to Torben, alludes to the Greek myth of the androgynous original human creature, a myth which her father had once told to her. . . . On a personal and individual level—leaving aside Pontoppidan's social criticism—this myth, which is referred to by Jytte at crucial times in the course of the novel, offers the solution to the personal tragedy of each of the principal characters; the sum of these tragedies makes up the pessimistic tone of the entire work.

There are, however, two levels to the interpretation of the incomplete nature of the personalities of these characters. One level repeats the sexual incompleteness implied in Torben and Jytte, but the other and more important level, which has nothing to do with sex, involves a fatal lack or flaw in the character of each—a lack supplied by the "other half," by the personality of the alter ego of each. On the first level, the personal tragedies of Jytte and Torben, and their wasted lives, are the direct result of Jytte's failure or inability to acknowledge and accept her physical and spiritual oneness with Torben, and their tragedy is mirrored or caricatured again and again in the fates of the other characters.

Thus the immediate cause of the first "downfall," that of the poor, uncultured fundamentalist country pastor Mads Vestrup, is the past failure on his and Oleane Staun's part to recognize and accept each other as soul mates. They had grown up together and had been young sweethearts, but had been separated and had each married unsatisfactorily. When they again meet, their old love is revived. Oleane, at least, recognizes—too late—that they had been destined for each other, for when Mads, during the early stages of their renewed love, finds her weeping and asks why, she answers, "Du veed det jo godt, Mads Vestrup! Det skulde ha' været vos to!" As a result of the discovery of his affair with Oleane, Vestrup loses his post as pastor, which is his only source of income, and the series of events which lead eventually to his spiritual surrender and to his death is begun.

Vestrup's fellow pastor, Johannes Gaardbo, the nephew of the democratic party's leader Tyge Enslev, also forfeits his chance for personal happiness and fulfillment as the result of his failure to recognize and accept the love of his fiancée, his cousin Rosalie. She drowns two months before their scheduled wedding, and Johannes's brother Povl, a doctor, in investigating her "accidental" death finds a letter she had written which

proves her death to have been suicide. She has been unable to live with Johannes's uncompromising, inhuman demands in the name of religion. The disclosure of her suicide is only gradually made during the novel, but Povl discovers that Johannes has really known the truth from the first, but has hidden it even from himself. Povl has long been aware of his brother's destructive influence on others, all due to Johannes's fanatical religious beliefs, and Povl repeatedly terms Johannes a "Varulv" and a sick man.

John Hagen, the pitifully ridiculous "Jægermester," Jytte's cousin and a member of the landed aristocracy, also owes his personal tragedy to his having chosen the wrong mate in Vilhelmine Søholm, the beautiful but vulgar and shallow daughter of the brutal "Grosserer" Søholm, the parvenu millionaire. Vilhelmine married John only for the sake of an alliance with an old, aristocratic family. Only when John has lost literally everything—his fortune, his family estate (which Søholm buys), his political position, his wife (who has for some time almost openly carried on an affair with "Skovtaksator" Frandsen), and even his sanity—does he eventually find his true mate in Mariane Wamberg, the coproprietress of the boarding house where John has been placed after his release from the hospital.

The party leader Tyge Enslev ultimately sees his career wrecked (and dies), not least because he as a young man was prevented from union with the woman who should have been his life's companion—Jytte's mother. The immediate cause of his being ousted as leader of the party he had spent his life building is his failure to accept the advice and good offices of Jytte's mother at a time of crisis. Enslev had met her years before in the provinces, in the early years of her own marriage, and he had been instrumental in having her husband elected to the Rigsdag so that she would have to move to Copenhagen and thus would be in his reach. She, however, had always been too naive to understand Enslev's motives, and they had remained only friends.

The more important level of interpretation of the incomplete self, however, is indicated by the fact that Pontoppidan's major characters, with the exception of Jytte and Torben themselves, are divided, on the basis of profession, into pairs—the pastors Johannes Gaardbo and Mads Vestrup, the physicians Asmus Hagen and Povl Gaardbo, the politicians Tyge Enslev and John Hagen. The first-named member of each pair seems more dignified and serious, and, at first glance, more sympathetically presented by the author, while the second member seems a distortion, almost a caricature of the first. A closer examination, however, reveals that the "caricature" in each instance possesses human qualities which the "serious" character lacks. All are ultimately failures in some sense, even Asmus Hagen, the apparently successful one of the six. His failure is the least obvious, since his is the least profoundly drawn of all the six portraits. In addition to the division by profession, there is an intricate network of interlocking and overlapping relationships among these six—Johannes Gaardbo and Povl Gaardbo are twin brothers, Tyge Enslev is their uncle, Asmus Hagen and John Hagen are brothers, Johannes Gaardbo and Mads Vestrup are both ultimately crushed by becoming involved in the political life surrounding Enslev. Further, the adversary relationship of rationalism vs. religion, introduced early in the novel through Asmus Hagen and Mads Vestrup, is reflected and focused in Povl Gaardbo and Johannes Gaardbo. In the case of each of the three pairs, one member has a tragic flaw or lack of a quality which the other member possesses. In one sense, even Jytte reflects this duality, and is paired with Meta,

Povl Gaardbo's wife, each possessing an essential quality which the other lacks—Meta has the ability to submerge herself in devotion to other human beings, and Jytte possesses the ability to analyze herself and her own actions; Meta is a natural mother, while Jytte has no desire for children, and indeed dies as a result of complications arising in childbirth.

The "twin" pastors, Mads Vestrup and Johannes Gaardbo, are equally sincere in their religious beliefs, and since each is utterly convinced of his own righteousness, they are equally intolerant of the beliefs of others. Thus they are both religious fanatics, but they differ in that Mads Vestrup has demonstrated that he possesses a saving human weakness—the ability to reject other human beings who sincerely love him. He has brought about the wreck of his professional career by being unable to resist Oleane Staun's love, and he freely sacrifices himself for his wife and children. Johannes Gaardbo, on the other hand, has been the direct cause of the death of Rosalie, the girl who loved him, and he alienates and rejects his own brother. While Johannes is psychologically more complex than Mads, he is also prone to self-deception; Mads, though the simpler of the two, does not have this fault. Unlike Mads, Johannes has not redeemed himself by "falling." Mads, for his part, lacks Johannes's power of establishing rational understanding with other human beings on various levels; in fact, on an individual plane, Mads is unable to communicate rationally with anyone except his wife, and she plays no real role in the novel. For a short time Mads is able to interest and attract people at his religious meetings, but this is primarily because of his novelty, and public interest soon wanes. In spite of his unattractive appearance and manners, however, Mads demands our sympathies much more than does Johannes, because Mads sacrifices himself, while Johannes sacrifices others. Each of the two has a fundamental flaw which causes his personal tragedy—the lack of a quality which the other possesses. Together, they would combine the rational with the human.

Of the two physicians, Asmus Hagen and Povl Gaardbo, the deficiencies of the first are not quite so apparent as those of the second. Asmus is aristocratic, rich, and successful in a worldly sense; he is also unquestionably an extremely highly skilled medical scientist. Povl, on the other hand, is of humble origin, poor, and, in the eyes of the world at least, a professional failure. Further, he has the family's hereditary deformity of a lame foot, a family trait he shares with Enslev. Still, Asmus, even though through his science he temporarily cures Torben Dihmer, represents a total reliance on human science, and he exhibits little or no sign of true humanity. The reader sees no side of his personality except his professional self, while Povl, who is initially presented in an unattractive light (as is Mads Vestrup), is repeatedly shown with his loving wife and ever-growing family. Povl is uncompromising in his adherence to his personal code; for example, he refuses to prescribe medicines and drugs when he believes they are not necessary, although he knows this act will mean the destruction of his professional position. Asmus's successful colleagues in medicine, on the other hand, do not hesitate to cater to the petty wishes and whims of the rich and powerful Søholm, and liberally and unnecessarily prescribe pain-killing drugs for him. Again, the apparently more successful and socially acceptable of the incomplete pair of "twins" is the one who lacks the saving trait of humanity, and with all his medical mastery, Asmus is unable to save two of the people closest to him—Torben Dihmer and Jytte's mother—from death. In the one case his humanity is insufficient to give Torben a reason for

living, and in the other case his medical science proves powerless. Thus he too is a failure, and in a larger sense than his (at first glance) far less attractive "twin." Again, each member of the pair possesses a quality, the lack of which causes the personal failure and tragedy of the other.

The leader of the democratic party, Tyge Enslev, and his reflection John Hagen continue the pattern. Enslev engineers John's entry into politics for reasons of political expedience rather than for any personal qualifications on John's part. Indeed, John is patently ill qualified; he is silly, fatuous, childish, and sexually immature (his voice, which is that of a boy at the age of puberty, is repeatedly pointed out; in light of this, and the fact that there have been no further children, there is perhaps a question as to the paternity of his wife's child who died early). Once again, the less conspicuously successful of the "pair" seems at first by far the less attractive, and Enslev by contrast is at first portrayed as a powerful and imposing personality, an indestructible and tireless force in the national political life. But as the novel develops, Enslev is revealed as lacking in genuine human compassion and understanding, a deficiency he thus shares with the other two apparently successful members of the "pairs"—witness his early loveless marriage, his public repudiation of his young mistress, who commits suicide (the frequency of incidental suicides in the novel is striking—Jytte's brother, Johannes Gaardbo's fiancée, Enslev's mistress, each, even Rosalie's, disposed of in a few lines, each caused by a love disappointed through the inhuman behavior of one of the lovers), and more conspicuously his often brutal treatment of the faithful Frøken Evaldsen, who has sacrificed her reputation and social position in her lifelong devotion to him as his mistress and his virtual slave. This "tragic flaw" once again is instrumental in bringing about the failure of the apparently more praise-worthy member of the "pair," and the gradual shift of the reader's sympathies over to the other, ostensibly weaker "twin." John Hagen is shattered precisely because he possesses the human weakness of being able to sacrifice himself in love, even though the object of his love, Vilhelmine Søholm, is not worthy of such devotion—she has been carrying on her long-standing affair with Frandsen virtually under her husband's nose, and, with the aid of her father's money and influence, she avoids any taint of guilt resulting from her husband's discovery of the affair (even John is eventually convinced that he did not actually witness his wife's deception), and divorces John after his mental collapse, having appropriated his title and his family estate.

The application of the extended myth of the divided self to Pontoppidan's delineation of his characters adds a new interest and a new dimension to the characterizations themselves and removes the atmosphere of incompleteness which seems otherwise to surround them. In addition to contributing a new depth to the novel and increasing interest in the fates of the characters, this interpretation adds an almost mythic quality to what critics have too readily labelled as a social novel. Like *Det forjættede land* and *Lykke-Per, De dødes rige* has a philosophical substance that transcends a mere picture of the times. (pp. 396-402)

Kenneth H. Ober, "The Incomplete Self in Pontoppidan's 'De Dødes Rige'," in Scandinavian Studies, *Vol. 50, No. 4, Autumn, 1978, pp. 396-402.*

CHARLOTTE SCHIANDER GRAY   (essay date 1979)

[*In the following excerpt, Gray focuses on Pontoppidan's evolution as a writer, observing a shift from an emphasis on social injustices in his early work to a more limited focus on the problems and psychology of individuals in his later work.*]

Several of Pontoppidan's early short stories deal with social inequality and injustice. *Sandige menighed* . . . , *Landsbybilleder* . . . , and *Fra hytterne* . . . were pioneering short stories in "the modern breakthrough" because of their realism in the social description. Pontoppidan was unique among the bourgeois writers in his proproletarian attitude and focus on material conditions. . . . (p. 274)

But already in these stories the origin of social inequality is traced to the individual character or metaphysical systems or both. In **"Knokkelmanden"** potential social criticism is finally undercut with a reference to a certain eternal metaphysical order. In **"Vandreren"** the narrator concludes with the statement that material conditions essentially remain unchanged. The old class difference between estate owner and peasant has been replaced with a new one between farmer and country proletariat. The same attitude in **"Naadsensbrød"** leads to a description where both old and new are deplorable. One kind of suppression is replaced with a new kind—to the undialectical observer suppression is the nature of social relations, and its concrete historical manifestations are rendered irrelevant.

The major reason for this superficial and static understanding of the social relationships can be found in Pontoppidan's bourgeois ideology. The decisive factor is then not that Pontoppidan is concerned with inequality, but from which point of view he approaches the social problems. This point of view may be defined by help of Georg Lukács's terms "kritischer Realismus" and "sozialistischer Realismus," which designate respectively whether the social conditions are described "von aussen" or "von innen." The bourgeois point of view is "von aussen" and is individualistic. It moves from the individual towards society because it separates the individual from society. This is in contrast to the viewpoint "von innen," which finds the Archimedean point within the social contradictions and then bases its typology on an analysis of these contradictions. The bourgeois point of view is psychological and moralistic, excluding the social dynamics within which the psychological development takes place. The one-sided individual orientation precludes any understanding of the constant social and psychological interaction.

The bourgeois viewpoint "von aussen" may be described in its class context as the perspective which is limited to the circulation sphere. The circulation sphere represents the level of the market where commodities including labor power are "freely" exchanged. When the bourgeois experience is limited to the circulation sphere, it leads to a perspective which views social dynamics as consisting entirely of human interaction and behavior. This ideological approach neglects production relations and thus the basis by which society is produced and reproduced—and therefore changes. The reification of morality and the individualization of social relations both preclude the vision of a collective transformation of the social order. The bourgeois social concern is transformed, as in the case of Pontoppidan, into pessimism, escapism, and mysticism.

Pontoppidan's essentially ahistorical view of society has a decisive impact on his concept of the human being and its activities. The fact that society is perceived as static leads to a condemning description of Emanuel Hansted's and Væver Hansen's fruitless political endeavors in *Det forjættede land.* Emanuel is described as a fantast in his attempt to reach beyond the ideology of his class, and the weaver, who will not relinquish

the social struggle, is attributed the role of an unscrupulous scoundrel. Action is discredited and mystified, its content is rendered irrelevant, and action now merely reflects the inner disharmony or hatred of a person—an obvious example of the psychologizing of what is part of a social dynamic.

The static view of society is passed on to the characters. When there is no interaction between a character and society, there is no prospect of new experiences and therefore no possibility of personal development. Already Emanuel's activity caused a fatal transgression of his "natural" condition, and Lykke-Per's "development" was merely apparent. (pp. 274-76)

When social culture is deprived of its dynamic content, some other "power" must explain cause and effect. In *Lykke-Per* and *De dødes rige* the protagonists' nature becomes fate; development is predestined. The contrast to Emanuel's unsuccessful striving in *Det forjættede land* is the "rootedness" of Hansine, the peasant-born wife of Emanuel. Hansine's harmonious life in "egen Jordbund" becomes the alternative to social change, and her life-style the postulated solution to painful striving for change within society. . . . (p. 276)

The static view of society and the human being becomes the root of a dehumanized philosophy and a decreased egalitarian attitude. When the life of a character is considered predetermined, the quest for improved conditions for the individual becomes irrelevant. Taken out of its social context, human potential is estranged into some abstract, universal quality. The content of human life is predestined in the universal "harmony" as shown in *De dødes rige,* which centers around the story of Søren Smed, who tries to alter his fate, and the strife and disharmony his act causes for his descendants.

Bertha Abildgaard is one of the spokespersons for this deterministic philosophy. She views herself as part of a great impersonal universe which rests in itself with a balance of its own. The universe contains an equal amount of happiness and sorrow, and each person must strive not to disturb this equilibrium. As Bertha Abildgaard has had a happy marriage, the universal balance now requires her suffering. . . . If a person's life does not "cancel out," the descendants are presented with the remainder. . . . This fatalism, which was the philosophy in accordance with feudal society, now revives what in the bourgeois context is an obsolete aristocratic character trait such as Torben Dihmer's stoic endurance.

Pontoppidan denies the effect of material conditions; instead, he focuses his criticism on abstract moral qualities of his characters. His early social protest is transformed into an alienated moralizing. However, since the impacts of social reality cannot be overlooked, they have to be reinterpreted. The obstacles to a fuller and more human life are not derived from social relations and alienation, but they are part of "the order of nature." The social, horizontal dynamic has been turned into a vertical, static order.

It is, of course, possible to break away from a class-defined ideology, and Pontoppidan's early rebellion against his background and his concern with social injustice did contain such a potential. When Pontoppidan did not succeed, his failure can be traced to powerful psychological factors as well as to the particular historical development of the capitalist system which Pontoppidan experienced.

In the so-called "modern breakthrough" the leading writers dissociated themselves from the capitalistic bourgeoisie in a radical bourgeois criticism deriving its ideas from the French revolution of 1879. The principal class basis for this ideology was the agrarian petite bourgeoisie with whom Pontoppidan identified—Pontoppidan himself lived in the countryside under very modest circumstances. But when the small independent farmers followed their material interest and began to cooperate with the capitalistic bourgeoisie, economic gain and security rendered Pontoppidan's valued concepts of freedom and equality irrelevant.

As an "independent" writer Pontoppidan now dissociated himself from the liberal ideology and from the materialistic pursuit of the farmers. Since Pontoppidan could not identify with the budding carriers of socialist thought, however, he remained isolated from the then progressive ideas, with the result that his protest lost a historical and concrete basis and therefore content. In his growing disillusion with the capitalistic development and its impact on the human being, Pontoppidan then replaced his liberal ideas with his parental ideology, with its focus on spiritual values and asceticism.

The change from a partly objective and activity-oriented attitude towards the material conditions to a nonrational spiritualism and asceticism may then be explained as Pontoppidan's resignation and identification with the predominant ideas in the bourgeois ideology, as it was mediated through his father and further developed under the pressure of the intensified monopolistic, capitalistic society. While the former attitude represents the opposition of the son against the family tradition, the latter is the result of his identification with it. It is thus implied that a liberation from the father could have resulted in a transgression of the ideological limitation.

Pontoppidan's description of the formation of the superego is analogous in the novel *Lyyke-Per* and his autobiography. The varying depth and subtleness of the two works has to do with Pontoppidan's reserved attitude towards the autobiographical genre, but the two works agree in their description of the authoritarian father-image. The father is portrayed as very strict and reserved but authentic and humble at heart—character traits which Freud emphasizes as the result of the formation of a strict superego. Pontoppidan describes his childhood home as severe and joyless, and he stresses the influence of the father and *his* family background upon the atmosphere of the home. (pp. 276-78)

The concrete biographical facts furnish sufficient evidence to substantiate Pontoppidan's representation of a somber atmosphere. The Pontoppidan family descended from the feudal bourgeoisie, including several famous clergymen. Under the changing conditions of the emerging capitalistic society, the social status of the clerical family was declining. . . . Pontoppidan's father came from a large, poor clerical family, and when finally a clergyman himself, the father had to support the widow of the previous clergyman while his own offspring increased to the number of sixteen.

The hard physical and psychical conditions broke down the parents while Henrik was still a child. The father became almost blind, with the result that Henrik had to read aloud to him. The mother, weakened by the many childbirths, often had to remain in bed for long periods. In 1864, when Henrik was seven, the war against Germany led to the invasion and lodging of German officers in the family home. If the social conditions of the parents were precarious, this added national humiliation was hard to endure. Henrik suffered only indirectly—through his parents—from the German invasion, but he personally had to go through the traumatic experience of losing a beloved one-

year-old sister as well as two younger siblings. Freud stresses the importance of such a loss.

It is not surprising that Pontoppidan experienced his childhood home as a place of want and restriction. Neither his need for reasurring love and attention nor his drive for self-expression could be fulfilled. The lack of love and affection runs like a leitmotif through the two childhood descriptions. In *Drengeaar* Pontoppidan expresses his past longing for some immediate and physical contact with his father. . . . (pp. 278-79)

When Lykke-Per rebels against this puritan and ascetic home, the father's reaction confirms both the son's want as well as his dependency. The son is refused the kind of unconditional, immediate love he desires; instead a distorted kind of "love," developed out of the historical and social situation of the father, is thrust upon him. (p. 279)

The immediate effect of the father's authoritarian methods towards the son is the estrangement of the latter. In his autobiography, Pontoppidan several times stresses his feeling of being an outsider, a stranger in his milieu. . . .

The suppression at home led to Pontoppidan's search for outlets for his libido outside of the sphere of the home. His only possibility in this respect became nature. Wandering in nature connotated freedom and adventure—adventure became the key word symbolizing the opposite of what the home represented. . . .

When the son rebelled against the dominance of his father by choosing the engineering career, the latter was also viewed in the enchanted light of adventure. Both in the autobiography and in *Lykke-Per* the engineer is portrayed as an adventurer. (p. 280)

When the son seeks nature for his self-realization, he loses his father's protection and becomes vulnerable to the dangers of nature. The engineer not only seeks adventure, he also seeks to bring nature under control, to master it. However, parallel with the internalization of conscience, nature achieves a deeper meaning to the son. Nature is no longer merely a physical outer source of pleasure or danger, nature now also becomes an inner power to be reckoned with. As the tendency for internalization is intensified, geographical nature obtains increased symbolic significance. If the father once offered protection from outer dangers, the son's superego now guards him from his inner nature—his sexuality.

When Lykke-Per's father died, Lykke-Per realized the powerlessness of the engineer towards nature. Pontoppidan likewise rejected the engineering career after the death of his father but also after personally having been confronted with death during his mountaineering in Switzerland, when he was forced to overnight alone in the snow. In the autobiography Pontoppidan does not connect this event directly with his decision to abandon his engineering studies, but it is possible that he, in the autobiography, has "forgotten" the psychological relation. The engineering career had no impact on nature's great power, neither did it offer any answer to the vital questions in life.

Freud has pointed out how the death of the father intensifies the power of conscience. Lyyke-Per's changing attitude becomes apparent after the death of his father. His attraction towards the pleasures of life, whether material comfort, good food and luxury in the Salomon household, or his sexual life with Jacobe and later in his marriage with Inger, is imperceptibly turned into disgust. With the internalizing of the strict authority Per's ascetic attitude grows to the extent that Per "enjoyed" suffering. His model becomes the clergyman Fjaltring, who cultivated want and suffering. (pp. 280-81)

The suppression of instinctual drives naturally causes a problematic sexual sphere in Pontoppidan's works. One manifestation of sexuality as ambiguous and sinful is the recurrence of descriptions where sexuality is connected with death. Per's relationship to Mrs. Engelhardt is an example hereof. After Per has been making love with her; he is struck by the thought that the body of her previous lover was hardly cold in the grave. Overwhelmed by guilt feelings, Per jumps out of the bed, projecting what is now his disgust onto Mrs. Engelhardt. From then on Per's sexuality remains problematic. (pp. 281-82)

Freud's distinction between two primary instincts—Eros and a death instinct—in the (bourgeois) character structure, is clearly illustrated in Pontoppidan's works. The drive towards death arises out of the conflicts between superego, ego, and id. The coercions upon the ego by the socialized superego and the pressure of the uncivilized id interact in a disharmonious struggle, causing both the urge towards violent aggression as well as the longing for peace and harmony—two aspects of death. (p. 282)

The longing for peace and oblivion is connected with the nature sphere in a manner that conveys the longing for Nirvana, a flight from the unresolved conflicts of life. In Pontoppidan's literary universe the nature sphere progressively manifests itself as a disguised realm of death. In Pontoppidan's three major novels the protagonists all suffer from a weakened Eros and they all internalize their frustration into self-destruction and a longing for peace like the one found in the prenatal womb.

The immateriality of the nature sphere points to the fact that nature, which originally was meant as an alternative to the ascetic atmosphere of the clerical home, has assumed the content it was meant to replace. What Lykke-Per posts as an alternative to the ideas of the father turns out to be repetition under the disguise of the nature form. According to Pontoppidan's explicit statement Lykke-Per does not possess guilt feelings; instead, he believes in the harmonizing effect of nature. However, the so-called built in harmony of nature as it is described in *Lykke-Per* and *De dødes rige* is the equivalent of fate. Pontoppidan compares the nature instinct, which guides Per, with fate, and according to Freud fate is a transcription of parental authority; in a religious context fate equals providence. (pp. 282-83)

The ideology of a providence is basically common for Pontoppidan and his father. The difference is not qualitative but quantitative and reflects the intensified alienation under the capitalistic system. Whereas the father's providence still functions as part of culture and its institutions, Pontoppidan's providence has been estranged from society into a "natural" power. Pontoppidan's "solution" bears evidence to the intensified isolation and mystification of the individual in the advanced capitalistic system.

The precondition for a more objective view of society and oneself involves the understanding and at least partial liberation from the parental authority. As long as the son remains chained to the father, he will internalize the conflicts arising out of the social circumstances and fall prey to irrationalism. A deeper knowledge of the social and psychological interaction is the indispensable prerequisite for the development of an understanding of and a will power towards change.

The historical conditions alter and the forms of suppression with them; the strict authority of the puritanical father has been replaced with other often impenetrable authorities in the present consumer society. However, Pontoppidan's quest for liberation—in both its progressive and regressive tendencies—offer deep insights to the contemporary reader—still trapped in the shackles of ideology. (p. 283)

> *Charlotte Schiander Gray, "From Opposition to Identification: Social and Psychological Structure behind Henrik Pontoppidan's Literary Development," in* Scandinavian Studies, *Vol. 51, No. 3, Summer, 1979, pp. 273-84.*

P. M. MITCHELL (essay date 1979)

[*Mitchell is an American educator and critic with a specialty in Danish literature. In the following excerpt from his biographical and critical study of Pontoppidan, he discusses four phases in Pontoppidan's literary career.*]

In retrospect one can conveniently divide Pontoppidan's work into four periods. One might speak of major strands of narrative art in the same sense that Knut Ahnlund did in his Swedish dissertation on Pontoppidan in 1956, although the present review of Pontoppidan's oeuvre does not make the same substantial divisions or temporal subdivisions as does Ahnlund.

In the first instance, Pontoppidan was one with his time in reacting against social injustice. He represented that direction of *belles lettres* in the 1880s labelled "naturalistic," which saw in daily life, even if it be humdrum existence, subject matter quite as worthy of treatment as was adventure or romance. The naturalists argued that it is less of an effort to portray the unusual and the exciting or to produce a variant of the *Wunschbild*—the dream of an exciting life and successful achievement, an escape from reality—than comprehensibly to depict what can be seen every day. We have observed that Pontoppidan did not write about the indigent but hard-working peasant merely because that was an unworked narrative vein any more than he wanted simply to suggest a rural idyll or to admire the honesty and uprightness of the exploited tiller of the soil. He wrote both because he perceived what hitherto had been overlooked and because he hoped to arouse his readers to a new cognition of social conditions. He was motivated both by indignation and the desire through the printed word to help the less fortunate. At the same time he was writing, new problems of urbanization and industrialization were making themselves felt elsewhere, but he was independent of the advocates of political reform. He might have heard of Marx, but he never read Marx. He was clearly an independent observer seeking a philosophical position of his own.

The social criticism was not confined to a note of distress evoked by the oppression of small folk in the countryside. Pontoppidan took a broader view. In particular, the position of the church was brought into question and the irritating self-satisfaction of the Grundtvigian movement was made apparent. There was, further, an awareness of the contrast between town and country, between the governors and the governed, although Pontoppidan levelled no partisan charges and made no specific suggestions for change. He espoused no party platform.

A skepticism toward organized religion is noticeable from the start in Pontoppidan's writing. This characteristic is easily explained. Although Pontoppidan was the son of a conservative Lutheran clergyman, his modern orientation and interest in the natural sciences and engineering did not permit him to accept without question the traditional faith. As a consequence, the entire metaphysical structure of Lutheran Christianity threatened to come tumbling down, leaving the individual in a state of chaos. The skeptical, naturalistic social awareness of the young Pontoppidan moved him into a position where he himself had to seek to reestablish a belief; he must create his own metaphysical pattern. At this juncture he wrote his critical, social novel *Det forjættede land (The Promised Land)*. But the promised land was reached neither by the leading character of the book nor by its author. Indeed, *The Promised Land* is philosophically a monument to failure, to the inability of the old order to adjust to new times or to accept a new reality. It is no accident that the central character of the novel is a clergyman, and a fool in more than one sense of the word: he is naive, he is ignorant, he is selfish.

Coexistent with Pontoppidan's social indignation and his skepticism toward the traditional state and church was the second strand: his patriotism, his predilection for life in Denmark. At every point in his career as a writer, he evinced appreciation for the Danish landscape. Even when he used descriptions of nature for an ironic purpose (as so frequently was the case), he nevertheless preserved an intimate relationship and a receptive attitude toward nature in his homeland. Pontoppidan travelled and lived abroad a great deal, particularly in Germany, Italy, and Norway, but when he left Denmark, it was not to flee the country or to seek some better spot on earth, some ideal land which possessed those virtues which Denmark lacked. Experiences abroad were interesting and enlightening, but Denmark remained for him the norm of existence.

Pontoppidan was sensitive to all aspects of landscape and seascape. With an unsurpassed freshness, he could describe them both in their infinite variations. Early criticism of Pontoppidan regularly identified him as a naturalist. On the basis of his transmutation of landscapes into words, he might well be classified as an impressionist, but such a label would have to be burdened with so many reservations that it really would lose all validity. The young Pontoppidan could just as easily be labelled a "nature writer" since he was so often concerned with the natural scene and addressed himself to an accurate portrayal of what he observed. No wonder, then, that he was asked to contribute chapters on various parts of Denmark to a monumental topographical work of the day. Just as Pontoppidan could illustrate the social conduct of Danish peasants naturalistically, so too was he able to look upon the Danish landscape with fresh eyes. Moreover, he was able to combine the depiction of social conditions and the depiction of landscape so that the one suggested the other, as is so strikingly the case at the beginning of the story **"Gallows Hill at Ilum"** in the collection *Skyer*.

In the course of the 1890s the third strand of his oeuvre becomes prominent: the need to establish a life philosophy. As this demand became more insistent for Pontoppidan, he subjugated his tendency to description and observation of the surroundings to philosophical reflection and to the need of the individual to find himself and to assess his relationships with other human beings. The sublimated account of this struggle constitutes Pontoppidan's *magnum opus*, *Lykke-Per*, in which autobiographical elements predominate at the beginning of the narrative, so convincingly that the reader finds the story less of a construct than might otherwise be the case. Pontoppidan was exposing a sensitive nerve of his own experience, although there can be no equation of Per Sidenius ("Lykke Per") with Pontoppidan himself. The social order is no longer being ques-

tioned so sharply, but attention is called to the individual's right to affect the lives of other human beings. The sins of pride, arrogance, and ambition are flayed so that the reader recognizes in Per Sidenius his own failings. Per's discovery of himself is convoluted and Pontoppidan does not endeavor to address himself solely to the ethical point of his tale. He views the hero in a historical context: he has been born into a certain society; his efforts to remold society according to his self-centered ideas and needs are unsuccessful; and he withdraws from society in order to find himself. He has unhappy experiences in the basic situations of the human being: as a child vis-à-vis his parents, brothers, and sisters; as a schoolchild and student; as a lover, husband, and father. He was not only a failure in all these situations; he failed to satisfy his own ambitions and to achieve worldly success. Only when he discovered that the ambitions themselves were defective and that worldly success ultimately failed to provide satisfaction, was he in a position to take on a new role in society, and at this juncture, Pontoppidan let "Lykke-Per" die. His creator could, however, apply some of his acquired wisdom and the life philosophy that experience, reflection, and cognition had given him. Addressing himself to the basic questions of individual human life, he could now view situations through the lens of his newly gained perception. Incidentally, the Faustian message of altruistic endeavor is educible from *Lykke-Per*, although Per himself did not realize it. That was left to his abandoned fiancée, Jakobè Salomon, who was something of an outsider in Danish society because of her Jewish heritage. Per Sidenius finally found himself, but it cost him a life to do so and he served no purpose outside himself. Jakobè Salomon was herself, and devoted all her energies to making for a better society.

Some of the situations and ideas of *Lykke-Per* appear in other narratives by Pontoppidan, but the core of his novel is the questioning of certain conditions that occur in Western civilization, in particular the relationship between man and woman, especially within a marriage. To be sure, this element is not peculiar to Henrik Pontoppidan; it was a part of the dialectic and ratiocination of the time. From the 1870s on, the questions of the ideal marriage, of women's rights, and of sexual mores had been under increasingly intense discussion, in particular the matter of sexual morality evoked a kind of drawn battle in Scandinavia. In his books, although less in public debate, Pontoppidan took his stand among the radical forces that questioned traditional marriage. Pontoppidan even suggested a rather grotesque alternative to marriage (in *Det ideale hjem—The Ideal Home*). He went along with those who abjured hypocrisy with regard to sexual morality and who excused, if they did not advocate, free love. Several pathetic life stories are found in Pontoppidan's short novels that touch upon issues that were troubling both Scandinavian and the larger European society. The complex of questions that can be identified with this aspect of Pontoppidan's career is less easy to confine temporally. One of the short novels . . . (*Den gamle Adam—The Old Adam*) is in part the story of a marriage broken up by a man's attraction to a goose of a young woman, but the possible rights of passion and free love are still the subject of the last of the "short novels," *Et kærlighedseventyr (A Love Story)*. And the possibility of a satisfactory solution was less likely in the first novel dealing with the rights of Eros than in the last, twenty-five years later.

The fourth and final strand of Pontoppidan's creativity is represented by the five-volume novel *De dødes rige (The Realm of the Dead)* in which all of the motifs and ideas that had been touched upon, hitherto once more found expression. On the one hand, it is a picture of the times, a chronicle of the early years of the twentieth century, but on the other, it is a warning to Pontoppidan's countrymen about the forces which threatened to constrict, change, or destroy their world. The narrative does not concentrate upon an individual; to a certain extent it may be called a collective novel (a term of more recent vintage). The social situation being depicted is more important than the fate of any individual. There is, however, much interrelationship of the characters, as much as in a drama by Ibsen, where characters are skilfully and artfully, but also artificially, interdependent. Their interdependence in Pontoppidan's novel is sufficiently complex and well-grounded that the reader does not find it forced and unacceptable. Pontoppidan delineates multiple levels of society: none is without its problems. The older Pontoppidan viewed society as a whole, but it was Danish and not just any Western society which he analyzed in exemplary fashion.

There was no new phase generated in Pontoppidan's work after World War I. A return to his biographical point of origin was gradual, and perhaps inevitable in an author who was still writing as a septuagenarian and octogenarian. Between 1938 and 1943 he produced memoirs which, without being particularly revelatory, tell something about his earlier years and corroborate various theses regarding the genesis of some of his work. Neither at the beginning nor at the end of his career was Pontoppidan satisfied with the state of the world, but, writing in 1943 a few months before his death at the age of eighty-six, he was not dissatisfied with himself for what he had tried to accomplish. He knew that he had done his share toward the emancipation of the human spirit. (pp. 138-44)

P. M. Mitchell, in his Henrik Pontoppidan, *Twayne Publishers, 1979, 158 p.*

ADDITIONAL BIBLIOGRAPHY

Review of *The Promised Land*, by Henrik Pontoppidan. *The Athenaeum*, No. 3616 (13 February 1897): 210.
   Approbatory review of *The Promised Land*. The critic states: "Pontoppidan possesses many of the qualities which should make him popular with all classes of the English public. His art is cheerful, sane, and healthy; he is a genuine humourist, with a keen eye, but also an indulgent smile, for the foibles of his fellows; and his simple, concise, and pregnant style, pointed with light irony and graceful satire, reminding one especially of Guy de Maupassant, especially in his shorter stories, is that of the true *raconteur*."

Bach, Giovanni. "Danish Literature." In his *The History of the Scandinavian Literatures*, pp. 161-220. 1938. Reprint. Port Washington, N.Y.: Kennikat Press, 1966.
   Survey of the ways in which Pontoppidan's fiction serves as an indictment of Danish society.

Clausen, Julius. "Novels and Memoirs in Denmark." *The American-Scandinavian Review* XXII, No. 1 (March 1934): 59-63.
   Favorable review of *Drengeaar*, the first volume of Pontoppidan's memoirs.

Jones, W. Glyn. "Henrik Pontoppidan (1857-1943)." *The Modern Language Review* LII, No. 3 (July 1957): 376-83.
   Provides an overview of Pontoppidan's career as a fiction writer and social critic, finding his early work "superficial" in its critique of Danish society and his later work more profound in its focus on Denmark's underlying moral and spiritual problems.

———. "Henrik Pontoppidan, the Church and Christianity after 1900." *Scandinavian Studies* 30, No. 4 (November 1958): 191-97.
   Analyzes Pontoppidan's view of the Lutheran church as exemplary of his attitude toward Denmark in general. Jones contends: "If we take [Pontoppidan's] work as being largely a criticism of the Danish character—and such an interpretation seems to be valid, even in the light of recent research—then the Lutheran Church must be seen as an agent which fosters precisely those characteristics which Pontoppidan sees as dangerous: their daydreaming, their emotionalism, their mental well-being (which he expressly condemns in *Lykke-Per* as leading to mental and spiritual stagnation)."

———. "*Det forjættede land* and *Fremskridt* as Social Novels: A Comparison." *Scandinavian Studies* 37, No. 1 (February 1965): 77-90.
   Compares Pontoppidan with a conservative Danish writer, Jakob Knudsen, to demonstrate that Pontoppidan subordinated social issues to his study of individual psychology and national identity.

Larsen, Hanna Astrup. "Pontoppidan of Denmark." *The American-Scandinavian Review* XXXI, No. 3 (September 1943): 231-39.
   Discusses the social context of Pontoppidan's fiction.

Marble, Annie Russell. "A Group of Winners—Novelists and Poets: Henrik Pontoppidan." In her *The Nobel Prize Winners in Literature*, pp. 197-201. New York: D. Appleton and Co., 1925.
   Argues that although Pontoppidan wrote realistic fiction, he was essentially an idealist.

Mitchell, P.M., and Ober, Kenneth H., eds. Introduction to *The Royal Guest, and Other Classical Danish Narrative*, pp. 1-22. Chicago: University of Chicago Press, 1977.
   Discusses social criticism in Pontoppidan's fiction.

Rossel, Sven H. "Nordic Literature in the 1880s: Henrik Pontoppidan." In his *A History of Scandinavian Literature, 1870-1980*, pp. 40-4. Minneapolis: University of Minneapolis Press, 1982.
   Survey of Pontoppidan's work.

Topsöe-Jensen, H. G. "Naturalism: Denmark." In his *Scandinavian Literature from Brandes to Our Day*, translated by Isaac Anderson, pp. 65-84. New York: W. W. Norton & Co., 1929.
   Survey of Pontoppidan's fiction.

Raymond Radiguet

1903-1923

French novelist, short story writer, poet, dramatist, and essayist.

Radiguet's renown as one of the most talented French writers of the early twentieth century is based upon his two novels, *Le diable au corps (The Devil in the Flesh)* and *Le bal du comte d'Orgel (The Count's Ball),* both written before he was twenty years old. While his earliest writings mimicked the experimental techniques that dominated French literature of the period, Radiguet adopted a more classical style in his later prose and poetry; his novels, in particular, have been praised for relating the psychology and actions of characters in a direct, unadorned manner that is frequently described as "austere." Critics have also applauded Radiguet's understated style, and while several have noted that the author's youth is apparent in the sometimes moralistic tone of his novels, it is generally agreed that his portrayals of adolescent psychology are among the most insightful in modern literature.

The son of a political cartoonist, Radiguet grew up in the Paris suburb of Parc St. Maur, on the Marne river. He attended the local primary school and the Lycée Charlemagne in Paris, where he established a reputation as a brilliant but unruly student. By the time he was fourteen years old his attendance was so sporadic that his father withdrew him from school altogether and attempted to conduct his education at home. However, the task proved unmanageable and was quickly abandoned, leaving Radiguet free to pursue his own interests at the age of fifteen. Fascinated with literature, Radiguet began to compose poems and essays, using his father's friendship with newspaper editor André Salmon to obtain his first writing assignments. Within a short time his essays were appearing in Salmon's *L'intransigeant* and other Paris newspapers, while his poetry was being published in the avant-garde journals *Sic, 391,* and *Littérature.* Such exposure brought Radiguet's work to the attention of the Dadaists, who dominated the Parisian avant garde at the time; recognizing the young man's literary talent, they quickly accepted him into their coterie. Radiguet's most significant literary affiliation was with the controversial, iconoclastic poet Jean Cocteau, who had worked briefly with the Dadaists but had abandoned their nihilistic philosophy and radical literary experiments for a more traditional aestheticism. Radiguet was similarly inclined toward a more formal approach—although his first poems imitated the experimentalism of Guillaume Apollinaire, he cited the classicists François de Malherbe and Jean de La Fontaine as his poetic models—and allied himself with Cocteau from their first meeting in 1919, a decision that shaped the course of his short literary career.

An established artist and Radiguet's elder by some fourteen years, Cocteau was instrumental in the publication of Radiguet's work: in 1920 he arranged for the release of the first of Radiguet's three volumes of poetry, *Les joues en feu (Cheeks on Fire),* and two years later he persuaded his own publisher to accept *The Devil in the Flesh* even though the novel was not yet finished. Cocteau also claimed to have been the guiding influence in the creation of *The Count's Ball,* encouraging and often forcing the younger man to write when he was tempted to engage in what Cocteau considered frivolous activities. De-

From Gli Inediti, by Raymond Radiguet. Guanda, 1967. © by Guanda editore, Parma.

spite such efforts, Radiguet remained a rebellious youth and worked only intermittently on his second novel during 1923; in March he was much distracted by the fanfare that accompanied the publication of *The Devil in the Flesh,* and contemporaries report that he spent much of the remainder of that year attempting to free himself from Cocteau's personal and professional domination. Nevertheless, Radiguet traveled with Cocteau to the south of France during August and September of 1923 and there contracted the typhoid infection that claimed his life three months later. *The Count's Ball,* completed shortly before Radiguet's death and proofread by Cocteau, was published in 1924.

Cocteau asserted that *The Count's Ball* represented the fulfillment of the literary promise only partially realized in *The Devil in the Flesh;* however, most critics consider the earlier novel to be by far the better of the two. The story of an affair between a fifteen-year-old boy and the nineteen-year-old wife of a soldier fighting in the First World War, *The Devil in the Flesh* presents a realistic and intellectually sophisticated portrait of adolescent psychology, concentrating on the insecurity, prurient compulsions, and latent cruelty of the male protagonist. Critics agree that the veracity of this portrait stems in part from Radiguet's proximity to his subject matter, being little more than an adolescent himself and having had similar liaisons with older women, but they further note that Radiguet's profound comprehension of his own psychology and his ability to convey that awareness are clearly the marks of a gifted writer. Moreover, Radiguet's descriptions of the boy's feelings are only one of the many highly regarded aspects of the novel, which has been applauded for its complex portrayal of the older lover, its skillful evocation of the atmosphere of wartime France, and its lucid prose style.

Radiguet's classicist tendencies, apparent in the narrative simplicity of *The Devil in the Flesh,* are more pronounced in *The Count's Ball,* for which he borrowed the plot of Madame de Lafayette's seventeenth-century classic *La princesse de Clèves* as well as her understated, ironic prose style. Like *La princesse de Clèves, The Count's Ball* depicts the growing love between a married woman, Mahaut d'Orgel, and one of her husband's friends. However, Radiguet changed Madame de Lafayette's story, in which the husband is completely unaware of the unconsummated affair until his wife confides in him, to include malicious manipulation of the lovers by Mahaut's well-bred but puerilely decadent husband, and in so doing created an indictment of the excesses of aristocratic society. Radiguet explained that he wished to create a novel that would explore "romantic psychology" in the context of a particular social milieu but that the book would not be a "description of society." Critics agree that Radiguet achieved this goal, concurring with Anthony West that *The Count's Ball* "is a love story first and last."

Hailed at his death as an "infant genius," Radiguet remains a widely respected novelist. His current reputation, however, depends less upon the surprise evoked by his precocity than upon his literary talents, which are considered equal to those of the most esteemed modern prose writers. In particular, *The Devil in the Flesh* has been acknowledged as one of the most adept explorations of adolescent psychology ever accomplished, comparable to James Joyce's *Portrait of the Artist as a Young Man* and to Alain-Fournier's *Le grand Meaulnes.*

(See also *Dictionary of Literary Biography,* Vol. 65: *French Novelists, 1900-1930.*)

PRINCIPAL WORKS

Les joues en feu (poetry) 1920; also published as *Les joues en feu* [enlarged edition], 1925
 [*Cheeks on Fire,* 1976]
Devoirs de vacances (poetry) 1921
Les Pelican (drama) 1921
 [*The Pelicans* published in *Modern French Plays,* 1975]
Le diable au corps (novel) 1923
 [*The Devil in the Flesh,* 1932]
Le bal du comte d'Orgel (novel) 1924
 [*Ball at Count d'Orgel's,* 1929; also translated as *The Count's Ball,* 1929; also *Count d'Orgel,* 1952; also *Count d'Orgel Opens the Ball,* 1952]
Oeuvres complètes. 2 vols. (novels, poetry, short stories, drama, and essays) 1959

RAYMOND RADIGUET (essay date 1923)

[*In the following excerpt from an essay that first appeared in 1923, Radiguet comments on the style and subject matter of his poetry.*]

My fondness for clarity is too strong to keep silent about the mysteries concealed in [my] poems, or to pretend to be unaware of their existence. These mysteries in no way emerge from an aesthetic, nor are they the result of some wager. I shall never find a justification for them where one would ordinarily look, and why should I authorise an obscurity cultivated by some of my predecessors? If I am to be blamed or praised, no one but me deserves the praise or blame. My poems are the natural expression of a blend of reticence and a hiddenness proper to the age at which they were written. If everything is not clear, there is no point in accusing my favorite poets. Because it is Ronsard, Chénier, Malherbe, La Fontaine, Tristan l'Hermite who taught me what poetry is. If I dip into the works of more recent poets, I have not been able to draw any lesson from them, and there is not even one that I would like to imitate. Some wretched masters have taught a whole generation of youth that to get to the heart of things one must strip poems of all their trappings, and that in removing the obstacles one gets closer to the poetry.

Is it an uncommon modesty that makes a poet confess that the most certain interest in his work is doubtlessly psychological in nature? *Cheeks on Fire* might throw light on a mysterious moment: the Birth of Venus, which must not be confused with the Birth of Love. It is before or after the heart that our senses awaken, never at the same time. In addition, these poems do not seem frivolous to me after writing **The Devil in the Flesh**, that drama of the fore-season of the heart. Old men will perhaps reproach me, as they have done before, for lacking youth. One would astound their romantic notions by telling them that they only depreciate and misrepresent things in wishing them to be other than they are, even when we wish them to be more beautiful. Perhaps they will also accuse me of libertinism. The optical error which makes people judge a work as licentious when everything is told purely and simply earned my first novel many readers. I hope they were disappointed. But should one even inquire?

Daphnis and Chloë, the most chaste novel in the world, is it not one of those books that schoolboys read in secret? And more men than one would believe remain schoolboys all their lives. Prurient curiosity and schoolboy sniggers! How many people have been able to dispense with them with the years?

Among the other things that might mislead the attentive reader, I would like to prevent at least one from doing so. After he has read the first half of [*Cheeks on Fire*] and understood that the author intends for each poem a particular shape, he will be surprised to see me adopt a form, no doubt elastic enough in its monotony, but at least, at a glance, quite repetitious. It is because all these octosyllabic poems, rhymed when they sang to me, derive from the same source of inspiration. They were written in March and April, 1921, on the shores of the Mediterranean. On its ancient shores, to this naive inhabitant of the Ile-de-France, mythology showed itself living and naked. After the nymphs of the Marne, seeing Venus in her bath is enough to turn your head. It is in some of these poems that the most greedy sensuality is least hidden. Then we see the singular apparition of Venus gently disappearing. (pp. 9-11)

> *Raymond Radiguet, in a foreword to his* Cheeks on Fire: Collected Poems, *translated by Alan Stone, John Calder, 1976, pp. 9-11.*

JEAN COCTEAU (essay date 1924)

[*A French author, Cocteau has been called a Renaissance man for his varied work in twentieth-century avant-garde liter-*

ature, music, drama, painting, ballet, and film. As a young man Cocteau began experimenting with the infinite possibilities of art freed from rigid restrictions, experiments which often offended contemporary sensibilities and led to his being labeled an enfant terrible. *Throughout his life his single goal as an artist was to shock and surprise the complacent, and while his iconoclastic approach to art frequently elicited denunciations of his works, he also won wide respect for the vigor and sophistication of his ideas. In the following essay, which first appeared as the preface to the French edition of* The Count's Ball *in 1924, Cocteau assesses Radiguet's talent and provides quotations from Radiguet's unpublished notes.*]

Raymond Radiguet was born on June 18, 1903; he died without knowing it on December 12, 1923, after a miraculous life.

The tribunal of letters has decided that he had a cold heart. Raymond Radiguet's heart was hard. His diamond-like heart did not react to minor experiences. It needed fire and other diamonds. It neglected the rest.

Do not rail against fate; do not speak of injustice. He belonged to the tragic race of those whose life unrolls too rapidly to the very end.

"True presentiments," he wrote at the end of *The Devil Within*,

> are formed in the depths that exist far below the level of our conscious minds. Hence, we are apt to misinterpret the acts they lead us to perform. . . . A disorderly man is about to die. Though he does not suspect that his end is near, he suddenly imposes order on himself. His life changes. He files away his papers; he rises early and goes to bed before midnight; he forsakes his vices. His friends congratulate themselves. And when his death occurs brutally, it seems all the more unjust because of what had gone before. *He was going to be happy.*

For the last four months, Raymond Radiguet had been growing methodical: he slept; he filed away his notes; he recopied his manuscripts.

I was fool enough to rejoice. I had mistaken for a condition of feverish disorder something that was really the cold complexity of a machine to engrave crystal.

Here are his last words:

"Listen," he said to me on December 9, "I have something terrible to tell you. In three days I am going to be shot by the soldiers of God." Then, seeing that I was holding back my tears, and that I was trying to invent a more favorable diagnosis of his case, he added, "Your diagnosis isn't so good as my own. The order has been given. I heard the order."

Later on he said: "There is a color that moves, and there are people hidden in the color."

I asked him if I should drive them away. He answered, "You can't drive them away because you don't see the color."

After these words, he relapsed into a sort of coma. He moved his lips; he spoke our names; he looked with surprise at his mother, his father, his own hands.

Raymond Radiguet is beginning.

For he left three books behind him: a volume of unpublished poems, *The Devil Within*, which is a masterpiece of promise, and the fulfillment of that promise in *The Count's Ball*.

One is rather appalled by a boy of twenty who publishes the sort of book that can't be written at his age. The dead of

yesterday are eternal. The young novelist who wrote *The Count's Ball* is the ageless author of a dateless book.

He had begun gathering his material in 1921. Two years later, before sending the manuscript to the printer, he tore up his notes. However, I found a dozen lines preserved in an envelope, and thinking them precious, I am transcribing them here:

THE COUNT'S BALL

A novel in which only the psychology will be romantic.

The only imaginative effort will be applied, not to exterior events, but to the analysis of emotions.

This novel of chaste love will be as salacious in its own way as the most unchaste novel. The style will be careless, since elegance should always have the look of being ill-dressed.

As for the background:

The "society" atmosphere is favorable to the flowering of certain emotions, but the book will not be a description of society. In this respect it will differ from Proust. The background, in reality, is of no importance.

He finished this novel in the country, toward the end of September, 1923. The proofs reached him in the hotel room where he lay stricken with fever. He had determined to make no revisions.

In spite of Raymond Radiguet's repugnance for everything monstrous or unnatural and his dislike for infant prodigies—at fifteen, he claimed to be four years older—I ought to mention that his poems were written between fourteen and seventeen, his first novel between sixteen and eighteen, and *The Count's Ball* between eighteen and twenty.

His death robbed us of his memoirs, three short stories, a vast appendix to *The Devil Within* (he planned to call it *Ile de France, Ile d'Amour*), and *Charles d'Orléans*, a historical tableau which would have been as purely imaginative as the false autobiography of his first novel.

The only honor I claim for myself is that of having given Raymond Radiguet, during his brief life, the illustrious place that was conferred on him by his death. (pp. v-xi)

P.S.—The following notes, which confirm two passages in my preface, were found among the papers of Raymond Radiguet:

(1)

[No date]

ABOUT *THE DEVIL WITHIN*

People have insisted on finding confessions in my book. What an error! Priests are thoroughly familiar with this psychological trait, which is often observed in women and adolescent boys—I mean the habit of making false confessions, in which one accuses oneself of crimes that have never been committed, out of pride. Everything is false in *The Devil,* and for two reasons: first, to give it the relief of a novel, and second, to depict the psychology of the young hero. This sort of braggadocio is part of his character.

(2)

September, 1920

"These prodigies of youthful genius who, in a very few years, become prodigies of stupidity!"

Most families possess their infant prodigy. They have invented the word. And certainly there are real infant prodigies, just as there are adult prodigies. They are very rarely the same. Age counts for nothing. It is Rimbaud's work, and not the age at which he produced it, that astonishes me. All the great poets wrote at seventeen. The greatest are those who succeed in making us forget their age.

M. Paul Valéry, when asked why he wrote, answered, "Out of weakness."

I believe on the contrary that not writing would be the real weakness. Did Rimbaud cease to write because he doubted himself and wished his reputation to rest on what he had done already? I don't think so. One can always do better. But those timid people who don't dare to publish their work until they have "done better" should not take this as an excuse for their weakness. For, in a certain more subtle sense, one never does better and one never does worse.

(pp. xii-xiv)

> *Jean Cocteau, in a preface to* The Count's Ball *by Raymond Radiguet, translated by Malcolm Cowley, W. W. Norton & Company, Inc., 1929, pp. v-xiv.*

JACQUES RIVIÈRE (essay date 1924?)

[*Rivière was a widely esteemed French critic who served as editor of the* Nouvelle revue française *from 1919 until his death in 1925, publishing the work of such major twentieth-century authors as Marcel Proust and James Joyce. In addition, he wrote a number of highly regarded literary studies, and his analyses of the works of Proust are considered particularly important. In the following excerpt, Rivière discusses the psychological acuity of Radiguet's works, noting that, while displaying a certain perceptiveness, they are neither as complex nor as surprisingly precocious as many critics contend.*]

Had Raymond Radiguet lived, would he ever have taken his place among the great explorers of the human heart? Would he ever have revealed to us any of its unknown aspects? Would he ever have brought about any progress, ever truly have made any advances into that concrete, yet plastic matter of the soul, the matter which both appeals for understanding and rejects it? Nothing in what he has left us gives us any right to affirm that he would have done so.

It is not my purpose to dispute either the value or, especially, the quality of these *reliquiae*. But, after all, we must first note that the psychological perspicacity of Radiguet was still under tutelage at the time of his death; he was using it only in certain directions, directions that, since they had already been noted by preceding geniuses, were not conventional but traditional.

I have never understood very well how the *Diable au corps* could have created that almost unnatural impression of precocity which revolted and repelled certain readers. The cynicism with which this book was sprinkled rather than impregnated revealed the youth rather than the maturity of its author. Fundamentally there was nothing abnormal, no view of feelings that went beyond the conventions of his age. The feelings themselves were absolutely "contemporary" with the characters described: naïveté was obliterated rather than absent. There was not anything really extraordinary in this book excepting its accuracy and its discretion.

In the *Bal du comte d'Orgel* we now find proof that Radiguet was not a prodigy, a phenomenon, but a writer of great sensitivity, a writer with some weaknesses against which he was struggling by the study of the masters, and consequently, a writer of promise. In this book, the path along which he ad-

vances, so to speak, is even more narrow. He now seeks direction and support not only from the French psychological tradition in general but, more specifically, from Madame de La Fayette. We must not expect to see him penetrate any thicket, struggle through it, make cuttings, make clearings.

But within the frame that he allows himself, his personal intuition functions delightfully and with true simplicity. With an unswerving eye, he discovers the feelings of Madame d'Orgel, of François de Séryeuse, he brings out their gestures and their thoughts, one by one, with his own hand.

To be sure, it cannot be said that he follows the great inner detours or the meanders of character. (His characters remain very slightly individualized.) But each point he touches upon is on the vein; we are carried along by the constant detection of true feelings. And the fact that the feelings are always noble does not once make us want to suspect them.

There is nothing I admire in this book more than the perfect accuracy of its predictable analysis. But to understand the value of such a quality, let us stop and think of the immense jumble of psychology that we have been forced to accumulate through that taste for the extraordinary which we inherited from romanticism. Beside the truly powerful and instructive descriptions—descriptions that, precisely, have integrated aberrations into human nature—of a Proust or a Gide, how many false perversions have been abundantly studied! How much inhumanity has been presented in horrible magnification! (pp. 222-23)

For say what we may, love—the love that we feel, that we give—remains the greatest good of man. And those who cannot experience it have the right to nothing—except regret.

I am not exaggerating my thought. However hideous may be the subject, in psychology I shall always give the advantage to discovery—provided that it is indeed discovery and that it strikes us not merely with stupefaction but also with conviction. However, the *Bal du comte d'Orgel* perhaps reintroduces to the portrayal of the passions certain qualities of measure and proportion that there would be some danger in allowing to disappear; it reminds us of the importance, the greatness, of normal feelings. This very brief book, entirely composed of chaste sparks, can encourage those who think that a certain human proclivity must be espoused if one wants the investigation of the inner world to remain touching and to lead once more to the sublime. (pp. 223-24)

> *Jacques Rivière, "In Defence of Literature: 'Le Bal du comte d'Orgel'," in his* The Ideal Reader: Selected Essays, *edited and translated by Blanche A. Price, Meridian Books, 1960. Reprint by Harvill Press, 1962, pp. 222-24.*

DOUGLAS GARMAN (essay date 1925)

[*In the following excerpt, Garman praises* The Count's Ball *while noting that the author's youth is apparent in the sententious tone of the novel.*]

When Raymond Radiguet died in 1923, he had already written a book of poems, *Les joues en feu . . .*, and two novels, *Le diable au corps* and *Le bal du comte d'Orgel*. Yet though he was only twenty when he died, his last book shows no signs of that usually irritating anomaly, *l'enfant prodige*. As he wrote of Rimbaud:

> L'âge n'est rien. C'est l'œuvre et non l'âge auquel
> il l'écrivit qui m'étonne. . . . On fait toujours mieux.

Mais que les timides qui n'osent pas montrer leurs œuvres en attendant de faire mieux ne trouvent pas ici une excuse à leur faiblesse. Car dans un certain sens plus subtil, on ne fait jamais mieux, on ne fait jamais plus ma!

["Age is nothing. It is the work and not the age at which he wrote it that astounds me. . . . One can always do better. But timid writers who dare not show their work while they wait to do better must not find in this an excuse for their weakness. For in a certain more subtle sense one can never do better and one can never do worse"].

It is in this subtle sense that one perceives the value of Radiguet's work.

Le diable au corps is the story of a young boy's precocious love for a woman older than he and married, but the vigour and sincerity with which it is told rid it of the mawkishness that was to be expected. It is not a really remarkable book but it shows great promise and, in *Le bal du comte d'Orgel,* that promise is in great part fulfilled. How well Radiguet understood what he wished to do may be realised from his note apropos of *Le Bal:* "Roman où c'est la psychologie qui est romanesque" ["Novel in which it is the psychology that is romantic"]. For this is his achievement—to have written a novel dependent for its success, not on its plot, but on the *romance of the mind*. He is not concerned, as are so many of his contemporaries, with the sophisticated exploitation of intricate, unusual psychology, but writes with the candour of an assimilated sophistication, only possible to the great. The ingenuousness which at first strikes one, does not affect "ces profondeurs que notre esprit ne visite pas, où se forment les vrais pressentiments" ["those depths which our spirit never visits, where true presentiments form"]. He is sure of his content: only in his expression of it is he sometimes naively uncertain. There is nothing strained about his writing, none of the *préciosité* of, for instance, M. Morand, whose brilliance so often dissembles an emotional and psychological hysteria. Radiguet's tendency to be sententious is essentially a youthful fault. When he writes of the insipid, worldly Paul Robin, "Ne pas vouloir être dupe, c'était sa maladie" ["Not wanting to be a dupe, that was his malady"], he utters an astute criticism, but it should not have been necessary to add, "C'est la maladie du siècle" ["It is the malady of the age"]. To do so detracts from the force of his remark, and in the same way his generalisation of the characters in the admirable scene on *le train des théâtres* ["theater crowd"], dulls the vivacity of his portraiture.

For the rest, *Le bal du comte d'Orgel* is a slight, but remarkable, novel. The scantiness of *décor* is justified by its effect—calculated by Radiguet—of accentuating the drama of the two personalities, Mahaut and François. It is regrettable that French literature, in its present state of somewhat unhealthy, in-bred sophistication, should have been deprived of such an invigorating influence, but there is no doubt that Radiguet has already made himself felt, and his book should certainly be read by those English people who wish to understand contemporary French mentality. (pp. 325-26)

> *Douglas Garman, in a review of "Le bal du comte d'Orgel," in* The Calendar of Modern Letters, *Vol. 1, No. 4, June, 1925, pp. 325-26.*

GEOFFREY STONE (essay date 1932)

[*In the following excerpt, Stone commends the artistic and intellectual maturity of* The Devil in the Flesh.]

Raymond Radiguet's life lasted not much longer than Chatterton's. The fact predisposes one to go to his work as *curiosa,* but a reading of it proves that it may be judged by higher standards. It is a favourite device of reviewers to compare certain books to etchings, and, if none of the staleness of the figure will attach to the novel, we might say that *The Devil in the Flesh* is like an expert dry-point; there is the same economy without any fashionable "starkness," the same intimacy of work done with speed that comes from decision rather than slovenly haste, and the same quickening of the imagination. It is that decision, the complete lack of adolescent groping, which is the chiefest of Radiguet's talents; and, though the sureness of his strokes is aided by the cruelty of adolescent egoism, it is to his credit that he progresses beyond this partial insensitivity and never uses it to obtain a *frisson noveau* ["new thrill"]. The book is mature, but it could have been written by no one but a prodigy. This is not to contradict the statement that the novel may be judged aside from its creator's years: it means that we get all the vividness of a tale by one who, in its very center, still could see the wood for all the trees.

The book has been called classic, and, if we take classic to mean a quality of restraint and a concern with the central, then this story of the adulterous love of a sixteen-year old boy and a girl of nineteen deserves the description. Precocious sex experience is rare enough to make it a sensational theme for literature, yet Radiguet—dealing with a prodigy who, like most brilliant children, combines sharpness of intellect with an uncertainty of emotion and a solipsistic attitude that would be neurotic in an adult—soon penetrates to the abiding aspects of love, and the beauty and sanity of his work lie in the clarity with which he reveals the growth of love, jealousy and a sense of responsibility in the boy's mind. The tale is moving because here first love—under exceptional circumstances, it is true—is shown as more than a ripple on a pool of shallow emotions; it is the chief means of proving that the pool is deep and cannot be explored without danger. And the mature and masculine nature of the book issues from the implicit affirmation that this danger, however fearsome, must not be shirked if life is to be more than a skimming of surfaces. If these words bear a dull weightiness of tone, they do not reflect the light expertness and the fresh charm of experience first encountered which this unusual novel holds.

> *Geoffrey Stone, in a review of "The Devil in the Flesh," in* The Bookman, *London, Vol. LXXV, No. 1, April, 1932, p. 112.*

LAWRENCE LEIGHTON (essay date 1932)

[*In the following excerpt, Leighton praises Radiguet for the acute analyses of emotions in his novels.*]

Radiguet's first novel, *Le diable au corps,* is the story of an adulterous passion. The hero and heroine are young, the hero too young to take part in the war in which the heroine's husband is fighting. Both the age of the protagonists and the milieu in which their history is exposed are abnormal. Radiguet warns us of that fact, devoting a slow series of chapters to the establishment of the feverish lassitude that qualified the life of those for whom the war was only distant alarms. But his triumph is that out of singular conditions there emanates the conviction that the truth of these hearts is universal, that in spite of the forced maturity of the hero, the absence of the husband, and the peculiarities of the daily life—even with a wholly different set of accidental *données*—the hero's heart and soul would have changed and developed as it did, and that the misery and unhappiness that met this pair was necessary and inevitable. This furtive and impossible quasi-Arcadian romance, actuated by the hero's egotism and by the stupid errors of two sets of parents, pursues a normal course which convinces us of the reality of the fable. The progression in the hero's attitude towards the husband from a grotesque chivalry to a waspish hate, the growth of his egotism from a simple desire to play the "man" to an arrogance that turns in a cruelly selfish fashion against his partner; these are developments of character that bear the mark of authenticity. The drama is not a tragedy; there is no attempt to persuade us that the hero is *chrestos* ["virtuous"], rather it is a complete and subtle illustration of the hero's statement, "Mon amour sophistiquait tout" ["My love clouded everything"]. That concept alone shows us that we are in a more recognizably human world than that of *A Farewell to Arms.* The death of the heroine is perhaps not justifiable as an event, any more than is Catherine's in Hemingway's novel; it is much more satisfactory as a symbol and aesthetically truer than Hemingway's effort to extract extra tears.

His second novel, ***Le bal du comte d'Orgel,*** is a comedy of masks and concealment, joined with a comedy (a *comédie larmoyante* ["tearful comedy"] one might say) of restraint. The formula is again adultery, but an adulterous love which is barely recognized, and is renounced before consummation. The author's interest is not centered in the evil results of disordered passion, but in its effect upon the sincerity of his actors. This question of sincerity is so dominant as to render the minor characters types of sincerity or insincerity. One of the minor agents, Paul Robin, a young diplomat, who serves as a foil for the hero, is so neatly presented in a passage of exquisite subtlety, that quotation is justifiable:

> Those who do not perceive the deeper qualities, who let themselves be fooled by the surface of things are like timid bathers afraid of venturing beyond their depth. Paul thought he had achieved a character for himself; in reality he had merely surrendered to the vices which were invading him little by little. However, he found it more convenient to have people believe that he was acting through policy than to confess that it was merely through weakness. Prudent almost to cowardice, he frequented many different circles; he considered it wise to have a foothold everywhere. When following such tactics, one is always in danger of losing one's balance. . . . "Not to be duped" was the disease of Paul Robin. It is the disease of the century. It can sometimes bring one to the point of duping others. Every organ grows or is atrophied because of its activity or inactivity. By dint of distrusting his heart, he had lost most of it. He thought that he was hardening himself, inuring himself to life, whereas in reality he was being self-destroyed. Mistaking completely the goal to be obtained, he enjoyed this slow suicide more than anything else in his character. He believed that it was a means to a better life. But so far people have found only one method of keeping the heart from beating, and that is death.

Set off against this perfect *poseur* are the naïve honesty of the hero and the more perfect sincerity, that comes of breeding and suffering, in the character of Prince Naroumof, the Russian émigré who serves almost as a tragic chorus to the piece. The reader's chief interest is in the heroine. Simple and good, the strange attraction that she feels for the hero causes her, in her turn, to assume a mask, but her honesty forces her, unable to play a rôle, to unmask; in the process she has discovered her

husband's mask. The situation in its comic implications remotely resembles *The Doll's House,* but Radiguet escapes the necessity of the mock-tragic conclusion that is forced upon Ibsen by Nora's essential triviality. The Countess d'Orgel might have been insipid except that, as Radiguet says, "les manoeuvres inconscientes d'une âme pure sont encore plus singulières que les combinaisons du vice ["the unconscious workings of a pure spirit are more peculiar than the contrivances of vice"]. The comedy which encloses this book indicates a finer tact than Fitzgerald has when in *The Great Gatsby* he demands a greater emotional load than his characters will bear.

The milieu of *Le bal* is the milieu of Proust, but the difference between the two uses made of the Faubourg St. Germain is significant. Proust loved his background for its own sake; his genius as a novelist included the talents of a scene-painter and a ballet-master. One is afraid that it requires only a change in fashion to outmode much of *le côte de Guermantes,* just as Cooper's virgin forests are outmoded. Of course there is much in Proust's background that is vital, and it is the significant social setting which Radiguet has used as a frame, religious and social conventions which tell us a great deal about his characters before they act, which immediately give his characters depth and perspective, and which impart to their actions meanings and connotations which thicken the texture of the novel. It is this feeling for characters in the round who are natural and human because they are part of a recognizable social organism, which we feel to be lacking in our American novelists. We appreciate their difficulty: American society is more disordered and flowing than in older countries; James complained that we have no Ascot, no Epsom. Still institutions and conventions do exist here, and their use would imply more and interest us more than the use of the caravan society of *The Sun Also Rises,* which leaves us too much at the mercy of the idiosyncratic conventions of an individual author.

With the appreciation of the value of a social establishment, in integrating and realizing the novel for the reader, goes a feeling for the continuity of human experience. This feeling works in two ways. Most deeply, it endows the writer with an attention to history, an awareness of tradition, and a regard for the future. More immediately to our purpose, it gives the characters in his works a guarantee of their being in time, as the use of social conventions guarantees their being in space. In other words, in a good novel, characters do not come from nowhere, and they depart from the book upon a projection of possible future existence. It is this illusion which is saved by Radiguet and which is lost by our American authors. (pp. 533-37)

> *Lawrence Leighton, "An Autopsy and a Prescription," in* The Hound & Horn, *Vol. V, No. 4, July-September, 1932, pp. 519-39.*

HENRI PEYRE (essay date 1944)

[*Peyre is a French-born critic who has lived and taught in the United States for most of his career. One of the foremost American critics of French literature, he has written extensively on modern French literature in works that blend superb scholarship with a clear style accessible to the nonspecialist reader, most notably in* French Novelists of Today (*rev. ed. 1967*). *Peyre is a staunch defender of traditional forms of literature that examine the meaning of life in modern society and the role of individual destiny in an indifferent universe; he dislikes experimentalism for its own sake, noting that "many experimenters are the martyrs of a lost cause." In the following excerpt from the text of a lecture deliv-*]

ered in 1944, Peyre praises Radiguet's sensitive and realistic portrayal of adolescence in The Devil in the Flesh.]

Raymond Radiguet owes his survival to two slim, youthful, yet extraordinarily precocious, novels. Death carried him off at the age of twenty. Whether he would have matured into a full-blown novelist, creating a world of his own and perhaps rivaling Stendhal, or would have lapsed into overconscious analysis and the tricks of a moralist writing novels in the classical tradition must remain matter for speculation. It is dangerous for a gifted writer not to have passed through a romantic phase, with some unsure or bad taste, an unpruned growth of sentiments and unruly emotions, and an undisciplined abundance. But it would be ungracious to be squeamish about the achievement of Radiguet. Many Frenchmen consider his *Bal du comte d'Orgel* a masterpiece to be ranked with *La Princesse de Clèves,* which was obviously Radiguet's model. We do not, and we confess that our disbelief when reading that novel is constantly aroused by the author's intrusions into his narrative and by the sententious tone of these reflections of a very young man who thinks he has nothing more to learn about life and love. But *Le diable au corps* is a minor masterpiece of French fiction in this century, and it inspired one of the best French films of the last twenty years. Radiguet, born in 1903 in the suburbs of Paris, along the river Marne, which serves to endow his novel with reality and with poetry, composed some delicate and strange poems when he was fifteen; they were collected in *Les joues en feu.* They do not warrant comparison with Rimbaud's far more powerful genius, but they reveal a combination of sensitiveness, restraint, and familiar irony, the original vein of the year 1920 and those following, as the postwar poetry of Max Jacob and Jean Cocteau, Radiguet's two sponsors, was to demonstrate. *Le diable au corps* appeared in 1923 and was translated into English in 1932. On December 12, 1923, Raymond Radiguet died of typhoid fever. Three days earlier he had whispered to his friend Jean Cocteau: "Listen to something dreadful. In three days, I shall be shot by the soldiers of God." Cocteau, Lacretelle, and Mauriac mourned him as one of the "inheritors of unfulfilled renown." Aldous Huxley, prefacing Kay Boyle's translation of *Le diable au corps* recalled young Mozart and remarked that the author "set out in possession of those literary virtues with which most writers end."

Precocious as he was, Radiguet could not but write an autobiographical novel under a disguise. But most of the usual faults of adolescent writing have been avoided by the youthful author, except a tendency to summarize the lessons of his experience in those neat, imperious maxims of which French novelists have always been fond. The book has been called a "*Daphnis and Chloé* in modern dress," and the author himself mentions the falsely naïve Greek pastoral that his mistress and he are living over again. But the idyl becomes a tragic one, and the adolescent blends cynicism and cruelty with tenderness. It assumes universal value by the remarkable talent for selection of significant details displayed by an author in his teens who had read Mme de la Fayette, Stendhal, and perhaps Mérimée. It is the definitive portrayal of the adolescent in wartime, rushed into manhood and unequal to the emotional demands and responsibilities thrust upon him.

War is mentioned in the opening sentence of the book; to the boys then entering their teens, it was a four-year holiday, with freedom prematurely won from their parents, who spoiled their sons, threatened by the draft; the young women, temporarily deprived of their husbands, were prompt to initiate these youngsters to love.

The narrator is still a child who has to creep out of his home stealthily at night for his first rendezvous and to forge lies to conceal that he has missed school. He tries hard to appear cynical, but he faints when he watches, with the crowd of his little town, a mad woman leap from the roof of a house. He meets Marthe, who is a few years older, engaged to an officer, and very much of a "petite bourgeoise." A common interest in literature arouses their curiosity about each other. He skips school to accompany her when she buys furniture for her future home. He imposes his own taste upon her, and he naïvely wonders at her feminine pleasure in yielding to his self-assured male reasoning. He meets her again after she has married, having been invited to look at the bedroom decoration he selected for her. He has now lost his pose and his cynicism in playing at inspiring love. He is the shy and clumsy adolescent, fearful of the mystery in the woman, intimidated by his own body and the gestures of profanation that love seems to require. She leads him tenderly to physical union, after the subtle gradation from "vous" to "tu," from respect to carnal union, and from passion to the tenderness that outlives and justifies the physical passion. Some details of the idyl, such as the basket filled with eatables that the boy had to accept from his mother; his fear of ridicule; his arrival, soaked from the rain, when Marthe has to make him undress and don her husband's dressing gown; the fire of olivewood beside which they lie down in silence—all are exquisitely selected and treated with skill.

But the adolescent is still a child intent upon breaking up his toy and killing his happiness. There is no sense of sin or remorse in him, but an unexplained cruelty, as of a boy bent on hurting his devoted mother and jealously picking quarrels on the flimsiest pretexts. A demon of analysis, instilled by literature, makes him question whether he really loves her. He becomes impatient over her angelic look when she wakes up beside him or after she has become pregnant. Their love, meanwhile, has become a scandal in the little suburban town. She must go and stay with her family. Once Marthe and he attempt a trip to Paris for a night; in an unforgettable scene of boyish cruelty, he makes her walk for hours (she is then pregnant) in search of a hotel, while he is too shy to ask for a double room. She catches a lung affliction and dies soon after. Her young lover faints when his younger brothers break the news to him. "My jealousy," he confesses when tragedy has at last overwhelmed him, "pursued her even in the grave, and I hoped that there would be nothing after death." He understands that he was probably never really happy but that he loved Marthe profoundly, even if their love was doomed in advance by all the conventions of their class and the ineluctable necessities of life.

Le diable au corps, which is strikingly but unfaithfully rendered by *Devil in the Flesh* (for neither the suggestion of flesh nor that of the Devil as evil is connoted by the French phrase, whose meaning is closer to being full of devilment and restlessly sowing one's wild oats), cannot be ranked with the more mature and relentless analytical novels of French literature, of which *Adolphe* is the prototype. Its study of analysis of love and of a self-tormenting adolescent hurting the woman who has unreservedly given herself to him shows flashes of deep insight, but it is not woven into a finished artistic whole, as are Gide's shorter novels or Proust's poetical developments. It is remarkable for its restraint and its structural organization, with episodes, concrete details, and symbolic incidents marking the phases of an implacable tragedy of love and death. Except for the few unpleasant didactic remarks strewn here and there, the novel stands out for its perfect naturalness; the adolescent and the woman accept themselves as they are, submit to their love and its consequences, quietly ignore and challenge society, and reach a bareness in stating their feelings, as they discover them, which was to remain unequaled in the novels of the decade 1920-30.

There is more tenderness and more sincerity, more art, in its naïve excess of sophistication, and more mystery in this little book than in most of the more ambitious volumes of Romains, Duhamel, and even Martin du Gard. Once again, a novel may survive owing to the restrained poetry that breaks through in patches in spite of the author's endeavor to be a detached and lucid moralist. Radiguet's promises were great indeed. Like Rimbaud, to whom he is often and unfairly compared, like Cocteau himself, who became, for a brief while, a convert following Radiguet's death, the author of *Le diable au corps* was athirst for purity when he analyzed himself and others most mercilessly, a fallen angel or, as Cocteau put it, a glove of heaven:

> You know what I call "gloves of heaven": To touch us without soiling itself heaven sometimes puts on gloves. Radiguet was a glove of heaven. His form fitted heaven like a glove. When heaven takes out its hand, it is death.

>   (pp. 62-5)

> *Henri Peyre, "Martin du Gard, Duhamel, Romains, Radiguet," in his* The Contemporary French Novel, *Oxford University Press, 1955, pp. 38-66.*

FRANÇOIS MAURIAC   (essay date 1949)

[*Mauriac was a distinguished French novelist, dramatist, journalist, and critic whose numerous works reflect his distinctly Roman Catholic perspective. This perspective is particularly evident in Mauriac's fiction, where the subject of sin predominates. A Nobel laureate and member of the prestigious Académie Française, Mauriac also earned wide respect for his penetrating, often controversial social and literary commentaries, and while he frequently placed himself in opposition to the dominant intellectual trends of his time, he nevertheless retained the esteem of his peers. In the following excerpt from an essay originally published in 1949, Mauriac pronounces* The Count's Ball *a masterpiece.*]

Was Raymond Radiguet an infant prodigy? He was, at any rate, prodigiously lucid, a lucidity without equal at so early an age. Those of us who were imprudent enough to publish books at twenty, have later recognized how their first youth deformed the world and themselves. Not any more than a dead man has come back to describe to us what was going on beyond the tomb, has any boy before Radiguet revealed to us the secret of his youth; we were reduced to our memories which are touched-up photographs. His work owes its shocking appearance to this lack of retouching, because nothing resembles cynicism more than clairvoyance.

So *The Devil in the Body* shocked, and it also upsets the numerous race of those who do not like rising suns. But, they told themselves, in order to take heart again, the property of a miracle lies in its not renewing itself; and here is a boy who is emptying his school-bag before us; his experience is too short for him to find much to say to us . . . Alas! On December 12, 1923, they could add "Raymond Radiguet will not tell us anything more." . . .

Yet, here is *Count d'Orgel's Ball.* Did Radiguet know in advance he should not lose any time? It was enough for him to

pass through the world without saying anything, to pick up that splendid booty. Being in a hurry, he did not take the trouble to disguise the face of his models; and *Count d'Orgel's Ball* will give those who enjoy the game of removing masks amusement in so doing; but let them not stop there. There is no book which deserves less than that one to be called a novel of real persons, or which attains more surely the universal.

To write *Count d'Orgel's Ball* at the age of twenty, it is not enough to be generously endowed with the rarest gifts; one must have reflected over his trade; and it is praiseworthy that, while still so young, Radiguet knew how to bring out the two laws of the novel, essential, according to us . . . "a novel in which it is the psychology that is romantic," he himself wrote regarding the *Ball*; "the whole effort of the imagination is applied there, not to external happenings, but to the analysis of feelings." Does the psychological novel differ from the novel of adventure? "In nothing; it is the same thing," answers Radiguet, and he proves it. *Count d'Orgel's Ball* offers more vicissitudes and keeps us more breathless than any book full of intrigues, yet everything goes on inside the beings. What is called a novel of adventure, which is only an artificial entangling of circumstances, can indeed divert us, in the Pascalian sense of the word, that is, turn us away from ourselves. However, it is within ourselves that our adventure, the only drama that interests us is being played, and it is for the true artist to lead us to it. I would swear that of all his works, Monsieur Pierre Benoît looks upon his *Mademoiselle de la Ferté* with the most favor.

As for the second law whose acquaintance permits a boy to write that masterpiece of stature, *Count d'Orgel's Ball,* Radiguet's age and the conditions of his life would, it seems, have rendered its discovery singularly difficult. He said of his book: "A chaste novel of love, as improper as the most impure novel. . . ." To evaluate justly such a discovery, we must remember the apparent disorder in which that brief life burnt itself out. Discipline was not the order of the day in the society in which Radiguet moved. Listen how Jean Cocteau relates the "apparition" of that strange child nourished on the extreme left of letters, and who, more than any one of us, deserves the epithet of classic.

> . . . Raymond Radiguet appeared. He was fifteen and claimed to be eighteen, which confuses his biographers. He never had his hair cut. He was near-sighted, almost blind and rarely opened his mouth. The first time he came to see me, sent by Max Jacob, I was told: "In the waiting-room, there is a child with a cane. . . ." As he lived at Saint-Maur Park, along the Marne, we called him the miracle of the Marne. He seldom went home, slept anywhere at all, on the ground, on tables, with the painters of Montparnasse and Montmartre. Sometimes he pulled out of his pocket a dirty little torn piece of paper. The scrap was passed around and they read a poem as fresh as a seashell or a bunch of currants.

Not ony did Radiguet live in that anarchy, but he saw the success too of the newly arrived in Letters, almost all busy in depicting men and women whose sole vocation was pleasure. Anyone else would have entrusted himself to Morand's furrow, and, without doubt, would have been lost in it. Nothing, in our opinion, demonstrates better the extraordinary merit of Morand than the interest he forces us to take in creatures so stripped as his, and in whom passion runs up against nothing. In Morand, no possible conflict; and besides we don't even think of it, dazzled by pictures, intoxicated by odors, bathed in an atmosphere that satisfies our joy. With erotism lying in wait, in which so many young talented men of to-day have come to flounder, Paul Morand walks along the cliff and avoids falling in. Radiguet, too, does not even permit it to approach. If he had the devil in his body, look how austere the principles of his art were.

"Atmosphere useful for the unfolding of certain sentiments," he writes in the margin of *The Ball*, "but it is not a painting of the world." It is because he could permit himself the luxury of scorning the scenery; he shows us souls.

In Mahaut d'Orgel, Radiguet's heroine, purity of heart gives importance to love. Her conjugal tenderness and her ignorance of passion prevent her from recognizing the delightful invasion of it. Her purity even drags her down dangerous steps. The richer our moral life is, the more complicated our sentiments, and the more their interpretation demands of both simplicity and subtilty. Radiguet shows us, through glass, the workings of hearts entirely engaged in deceiving themselves. "This is what they think they are discovering in themselves. This is what is really going on," he seems to tell us. All his art as a novelist is based on that formula. Perhaps he is too much the master of his creatures; they never drag him along; they follow in a straight line, from which we sometimes wish they would deviate; one would say it was a spring that is extended in accordance with wise foresight . . . but it is the attribute of a passion that leads everything to itself, to regulate all our acts with an aim to satisfying them; passion, to a certain degree, mechanizes us. That is what was very well seen by Radiguet who would quickly have acquired more suppleness. Such as it is, his work is enough for us, his elders; the cause is clear, that child was a master. (pp. 120-23)

François Mauriac, "Radiguet," in his Men I Hold Great, *translated by Elsie Pell, Philosophical Library, 1951, pp. 120-23.*

ANTHONY WEST (essay date 1953)

[*The son of Rebecca West and H. G. Wells, West is an English author who has written several novels concerned with the moral, social, psychological, and political disruptions of the twentieth century. As a critic he has written a study of D. H. Lawrence in addition to many reviews published in various magazines. In the following excerpt, West examines the artistry of Radiguet's novels.*]

[*The Devil in the Flesh*] is a novel that goes beyond the achievement of most novelists, and it is today as fresh, as funny, and as moving as if it had been written yesterday. It has left its date behind and become literature. A piece of romantic realism about a love affair between two very young French people during the 1914-18 war, written immediately after its end, *The Devil in the Flesh* is a most remarkable evocation of the atmosphere of civilian life in wartime. Many people have tried to describe the infection of orderly private lives by public disorders, but few have succeeded so completely, and fewer still have so successfully described the curious satisfaction that the true egotist finds in maintaining the tension of a love affair that is bound to go badly wrong in the long run. The hero is intoxicated by the approaching disaster and gives himself up to it with the feckless delight of a breakable child sliding downstairs on a tea tray toward a hallway full of breakable objects. Over and above this, there is a lyricism in the Marne scenes that recalls de Maupassant's boating stories but is more pleasing, because Radiguet had a warmer heart. Its warmth is even more evident in *Count d'Orgel*, in which he used an entirely different style and employed the even, wittily understated narrative technique developed by Mme. de Lafayette, which is all coolness and detached elegance.

> M. de Nemours' love for Madame de Clèves was so violent in its first stages that he could take no interest in the other women he used to love, with some of whom he had kept in touch while he was away. Indeed he quite forgot all about them.

These lines from *The Princess of Clèves* announce the beginning of one of the most convincing stories of devotion and enduring love in any novel. Their flatness is deceptive, since they constitute both a highly romantic statement about emotion and a tightly packed piece of realism, which leaves no room for doubt as to the kind of amorist that M. de Nemours has been and that Mme. de Clèves will, naturally enough, suppose him still to be. These two sentences are the pivot on which *The Princess of Clèves* will turn. *Count d'Orgel* turns on a pivot of the same kind. The Count's wife does not wish to be unfaithful to him, and François de Séryeuse, who loves her, does not wish to be disloyal to him, but smallness of mind provides the Count with an immunity to fidelity and to loyalty, as some people have immunity to disease.

> Earlier, brief infidelities to his wife did not give Orgel a moment's hesitation. That she knew nothing about them was enough to quiet his conscience. He was

A drawing of Radiguet done by Cocteau. Copyright ARS N.Y./SPADEM, 1988.

not overcome by passionate desires and did not derive very much pleasure from these small deceptions. It was from a sense of duty, if this is not too strong an expression, that Orgel had been unfaithful to Mahaut. It was part of his career as a man of fashion.

This compactness spares one a great deal of realistic snuffing around the couches and lightly rumpled beds on which the Count has demonstrated his littleness of spirit; the banal conversations, the comings and goings in discreetly indiscreet hotels and apartments, the creaking machinery of the amorist's contrivances all lie between the lines as sharply defined as if they had been described. The story gains by this swift passage to the one vital point—that they do not even interest the Count himself. The same deftness is employed when it is discovered by chance that the Countess and M. de Séryeuse are cousins. The Countess is enormously relieved; because M. de Séryeuse is a relative, she can allow him to come closer to her with propriety, and as the blood relationship is recognized, the possibility of adultery seems to recede. It will help her to conceal her real feeling toward him. The Count, who is a snob in the manner of M. de Charlus, talks about the cousinship all through dinner; he, too, is pleased to find that his friend is one of the family.

> The news spread quickly to the servants' quarters.
>
> "In the long run the Count must have found it more convenient," said the footman sententiously.
>
> The pantry is not far from the drawing room. This servant initiated the scandal: he formulated what was first whispered and then said out loud.

With extraordinary deftness, a dozen scenes describing the spread of a rumor have been eliminated. The Countess's illusion of security has also been destroyed; the cousinship that she relied on as a concealment in fact makes her secret feelings public property and takes her another step toward admission of her love.

However admirable these technical excellencies, it is not for them that most people will enjoy the book. They will find their pleasure in the simple fact that it is a love story first and last, filled with the atmosphere of Paris at a time when Paris was filled with brilliance and genius. (pp. 125-26)

> *Anthony West, "Amour and Antiques," in* The New Yorker, *Vol. XXIX, No. 6, March 28, 1953, pp. 125-27.*

WALLACE FOWLIE (essay date 1953)

[*Fowlie is among the most respected and comprehensive scholars of French literature. His work includes translations of major poets and dramatists of France (Molière, Charles Baudelaire, Arthur Rimbaud, Paul Claudel, Saint-John Perse) and critical studies of the major figures and movements of modern French letters (Stéphane Mallarmé, Marcel Proust, André Gide, the Surrealists, among many others). Broad intellectual and artistic sympathies, along with an acute sensitivity for French writing and a first-hand understanding of literary creativity (he is the author of a novel and poetry collections in both French and English), are among the qualities that make Fowlie an indispensible guide for the student of French literature. In the following excerpt, Fowlie views Radiguet's works in the context of literary trends of the early twentieth century.*]

Before writing his two novels, Raymond Radiguet practiced with poems (*Les joues en feu*), composed in accordance with a type of preciosity which is difficult to define or describe.

They bear some analogy with the early poems of Cocteau and with the paintings of Marie Laurençin. One might place them midway between the cubists and the art of the *fauves*. They are written with so few words and they combine so ingeniously a formal elegance with licentiousness that the term "classical" or "post-classical" would not be inappropriate to apply to this youthful art. Radiguet first excelled in a form of wit which the French literary tradition has always esteemed. It is the skill in using a word which will say one thing and imply another. It is almost the practice of the metaphor, the uniting of two seemingly disparate and contradictory terms. Radiguet once acknowledged that his models were La Fontaine and Malherbe [see excerpt dated 1923]. His poems, not so successful as those of Max Jacob and Apollinaire, belong to their tradition—it is Cocteau's also—which banished the mysteriousness of symbolism in order to rediscover the more direct spiritual quality of things, their bareness, their provocative freshness. Contemporary with the cubist movement in painting, this art of poetry was a worldly sophisticated heritage from earlier periods when French intelligence had enjoyed great freedom and suppleness within the formal limits of madrigals, anagrams, sonnets and songs. (pp. 527-28)

More deeply and more subtly than other books of the early '20's, Radiguet's two novels, and especially *Le bal du comte d'Orgel*, depict the new "mal du siècle" which had broken out during the years following the war. *Le diable au corps* involves a study of the sense of limitless freedom felt by the young, and *Le bal* analyses the sense of bewilderment which resulted from this very freedom. Radiguet himself defined *Le bal* as a novel in which the adventure element is the psychology: "Roman où c'est la psychologie qui est romanesque" ["Novel in which it is the psychology that is romantic"]. The analysis in the novel is not carried out in order to reach its own truth, but rather for what it reveals about the hero who is analysing himself and others. It is a means to provide his portrait of the hero rather than to judge him.

Count d'Orgel bears a close affinity with the 17th century *Princesse de Clèves* of Mme. de La Fayette. It appears that Radiguet did not conceal from his friends his deliberate intention of using the model of the classical work. Both novels are stories of a wholly admirable woman who loves in different ways but incompatibly two men. In Radiguet's novel the passionate love which Mahaut feels for her husband diminishes through the course of the book until it becomes a conventional attachment. The purity of her heart, from beginning to end, testifies to the significance of her love. Yet it is this very purity of heart which leads her close to great peril. Mahaut is the wife of Count Anne d'Orgel. They participate in the wordliness of Paris society, quite comparable to the court life background of Mme de La Fayette's novel. The third character, François de Séryeuse, is a friend of Count d'Orgel. The love he feels for Mahaut and her love for him exist at the beginning of the book and do not change. By the last scene, Mahaut and her husband are seated in the same room, but they are actually in two different planets. "Count d'Orgel had observed nothing of the transformation that had taken place before his eyes. Instead of addressing a frenzied creature, he was now talking to a statue."

Radiguet exercises control over his characters at some distance from them. He is almost too much their master. Their own speeches reveal what they discover about themselves and then Radiguet intervenes to tell us what is really transpiring. The importance of the book is perhaps in its philosophy of love.

When we learn that Mahaut is deeply in love with her husband, we have a first intimation about Radiguet's fundamental pessimism, because Count d'Orgel is a shallow character who obviously is not in love with his wife. At the moment in the story when Anne d'Orgel discovers that Mahaut and François are cousins, he forces them to embrace. They are embarrassed, but they perform the ritual of the kiss and laugh over it. With such a scene, Radiguet's belief that love, rather than joining two beings, separates them, becomes clear. Behind the remarkable chastity of the novel, lies a concealed sensuality which is totally reckless. Radiguet himself has said about his novel: "Roman d'amour chaste, aussi scabreux que le roman le moins chaste" ["This novel of chaste love will be as salacious in its own way as the most unchaste novel"]. By the end of the story, we realize we have passed through many peripeteia all of which transpired within the hearts of the characters. Radiguet discovers the sentiments of Mahaut and François by looking at them steadily and directly. He releases their thoughts and gestures in methodical fashion as if he were performing a series of tricks. The book has an acrobatic sense of proportion in its brevity, its swiftness, and the chastity of its concealed fire.

The "ball," referred to in the French title, is to be a masked ball. It does not take place during the novel, but the characters are planning to attend it. Their costumes obviously will symbolize the parts they can't play in real life or the parts they don't realize they are playing. D'Orgel himself, for example, has no conception of the jealousy he feels for François de Séryeuse. Passion, whether recognized or not, tends to mechanize its victims. The adolescent hero of Radiguet's first novel, *Le diable au corps*, wore a deliberate mask of virile maturity during the course of his love experience. Physical suffering, even sadism, and cynicism characterize *Le diable*, but all that is absent from *Le bal*, where the attitude toward love has deepened at the expense of appearing more hopeless, more tragically pessimistic.

La princesse de Clèves may well be the model for *Count d'Orgel*. Gide has pointed out that the Radiguet novel was strongly influenced by *Les Pléides* of Gobineau. It is not extraordinary that a novelist, at the age of twenty, leaned heavily on other works. Proust learned how to write by composing his "pastiches" and Mallarmé's first poems were cast in Baudelairian form. What is extraordinary is the deftness and the precision of Radiguet's writing, its competency which is executed almost as if it were a wager. The sentences have a colorless purity and create an effect totally different from that of the far more romantic and diffuse novel of Alain-Fournier, *Le grand Meaulnes*. This letter held an important place in the French novel during the '20's and '30's (it was published in 1913), but today it seems to be losing out in favor of such works as *Count d'Orgel* and *Les enfants teribles* of Cocteau. Radiguet and Cocteau are close in their common dislike for the pretentious, the loquacious, the tiresome. Their purely descriptive passages are more swift and condensed than the swiftest in Stendhal. They are most skilful in their depiction of brief moments, brief encounters. They are interested primarily in taking candid camera shots of man's adventure. Pictures which will relieve the monotony of a too familiar story.

The theme of love in Radiguet is at all times comparable to the high moral conception of love in the tragedies of Racine or in the novel of Mme de La Fayette. And yet, it bears analogies with the theme of love in the work of Cocteau, for whom love is never a moral problem, but rather a willfulness to explore and a curiosity. Passion for Cocteau is almost always the capacity of being enchanted, of being bewitched. I suspect that the meaning of love is more dramatic and more tragic in Radiguet, but very often his treatment of it in *Le bal* resembles a strange fascination for the perilous, for the properties of an object like that snowball in which the pupil Dargelos had concealed a stone. In their will to avoid the monotony of the novel and the inherent heaviness of its form, both Cocteau and Radiguet created semi-mythological characters who do not have the same need of speech and action as ordinary creatures. It is enough to see them briefly, in a brilliant setting.

It is claimed that the new element of poetry which so often participates in the form of the modern novel is generally expressed in the "atmosphere" of the story. The French writer has always had traditionally another use for his treatment of the poetic. This trait, which is almost an idiosyncrasy, is illustrated in Raymond Radiguet's second novel. It is poetry conceived of as a source of truth, as a means of knowledge. What is poetic in Racine, for example, is quite different from what is poetic in Shakespeare. The poetic in Mallarmé is not the poetic in Hopkins. I am trying to say that there is an important idiosyncratic element of the poetic in French art which is not materially poetic. In *Count d'Orgel*, Radiguet actually refers to the type of poetic beauty which comes from the description of atmosphere and from the analysis of imprecise states of feeling, and he announces that another kind of poetry is to be found in the notation of the precise and the direct. It is a form of art which sustains and deepens intelligibility, exemplified in the best pages of Baudelaire, Rimbaud and Claudel. The art of Stendhal, whose novels have been exceptionally enjoyed in the 20th century, has some of this poetic element which is a concentration or a denuding, a swift precise expression of critical judgment. Stendhal sees more than he feels, but he remains in the tradition of the French moralists, of Mme de La Fayette, of Choderlos de Laclos, and in the category of French artists, where we would place Radiguet, who give primacy to the senses and the reason of man. (pp. 529-32)

Wallace Fowlie, "Raymond Radiguet (1903-1923)," in The Sewanee Review, *Vol. LXI, No. 3, July-September, 1953, pp. 527-32.*

WILLIAM JAY SMITH (essay date 1954)

[*Smith is a prolific American poet, critic, and translator whose contributions to the field of contemporary verse have been widely applauded for their clarity and structural simplicity. Using traditional forms and themes derived from classical literature, he has placed himself outside the dominant modernist trends in poetry, and his technique has been widely praised by those who disapprove of what they consider the increasing obscurity of contemporary poetic expression. Smith is also recognized for his scholarly achievements, which include critical essays on English and French literature and translations of the works of French poets Valery Larbaud and Jules Laforgue. In the following excerpt, he discusses Radiguet's classical approach to poetry.*]

In the poems of that young genius, Raymond Radiguet, one finds the same qualities of disarming candor, quiet, penetrating vision, and cool self-possession that have made his novels famous. He seems to have had from the very beginning a strong sense of the deepest classical tradition in French literature: his model in prose was Mme. de Lafayette, author of the most classical of French novels, *La Princesse de Clèves;* his models in poetry were Ronsard, Malherbe, La Fontaine. Radiguet could lay claim also to the sure, unfettered brilliance of youth. He died in 1923 at the age of twenty; all his poems were written between 1917 and 1921, between the ages of fourteen and eighteen.

"The Language of Flowers or Stars," one of his earliest works, sets down so modestly the awakening of the senses that the poem almost passes us by. The words evoke such a still, breathless atmosphere that they seem to communicate without being spoken. There is in these lines something shimmering, fresh, and resonant. It is as if a child had made some astonishing pronouncement without quite realizing the depths to which he had reached. **"To a Nude Walking,"** which resembles one of the songs of Ronsard, has all the directness, the classical control the writer admired: "Racine, at first, seems less audacious than Rimbaud. The daring of Racine is simply more refined than that of Rimbaud, for it pushes modesty to the point of going completely unnoticed."

It is perhaps significant that Radiguet, in **"The Language of Flowers or Stars,"** should, in a sense, have domesticated the months of the year. To the very young the domestic scene possesses mythical dimensions which it loses as one grows older: beasts sleep in the child's bed, knights breakfast at his table, the fabulous is everywhere around him. And so it is that classical myths come to life again and again in terms of the ordinary and everyday. Radiguet sought out banality in order to come to terms with it, to raise it to the power of dream. "The striving for banality," he wrote, "will ward off strangeness, which is always detestable. That queerness which spoils much of Rimbaud one never finds in Ronsard." **"The Flower Girl"** is the tale of Leda and the Swan in reverse: the Swan is abducted, the heavenly creature made at home. The world of the Swan is the limitless realm of adventure; its reality is supplied by the child's vision, it is fed as the Swan is fed. If the celluloid toy lives and breathes, it does so through the child's sense of play, a faculty which in the adult becomes the freedom of the imagination. With Radiguet, on the edge of adulthood, play and imagination are interlocked in a very remarkable fashion. This rare combination lies behind the peculiar understatement and wit of this early sketch; it gives it the same luminous quality one remarks in the author's more important work.

Raymond Radiguet was aware that more than the record of a youthful heartbeat is demanded of writing for it to live. On the subject of the young writer, he said: "It is a commonplace, and consequently an inescapable truth that to write one must have lived. But what I would like to know is at what age one has the right to say: 'I have lived.' Does not this simple past logically imply death? For my part, I believe that at any age, and at the very earliest age, one has both lived and begun to live. However that may be, it does not seem to me impertinent to lay claim to the right of utilizing one's memories of one's first years before one's last memories have arrived. Not that we condemn the powerful charm there is in speaking of dawn on the evening of a fine day, but different as it is, the interest is no less in speaking of it without waiting for night."

Radiguet did not wait for night. He spoke of the dawn, but he had what great writers, young or old, possess: the vision of the whole day, which is life. (pp. 289-90)

> William Jay Smith, "A Note on Radiguet," in Accent, Vol. XIV, No. 4, Autumn, 1954, pp. 289-90.

H. A. BOURAOUI (essay date 1973)

[*Bouraoui is a Tunisian-born Canadian poet and critic. In the following excerpt, he maintains that the protagonist of* The Devil in the Flesh *exemplifies certain features of Radiguet's personal aesthetic philosophy.*]

Raymond Radiguet's *Le diable au corps* can be read as a simple novel of adolescence during a period of social upheaval brought about by the First World War, but its scope is really far more ambitious than such an interpretation would indicate. We are conscious throughout the novel that, in the hero-narrator, we are dealing with a very special individual, a would-be poet or dramatist who tries to make his life a work of art. Young, untutored, and inexperienced as he is, he is no mere plaything of fate and larger social forces; he also tries to be a shaper and manipulator of them. He not only seeks to affirm his own identity in the face of society, but also, by means of the continuing dialectic between the individual and his surroundings, to fit both himself and his milieu into a specifically *aesthetic* entity. The society we witness, on the other hand, unlike the individualistic hero, is abstract, generalized, almost universalized. Radiguet seems to suggest that the hero's ultimate defeat would be the fate of a certain poetic temperament in any age, and that the obstacles presented by this particular World War I era are little different from those of any other period. For these reasons, the most fruitful means of examining the novel would seem to be aesthetic, rather than ethical or sociological, although the latter two contribute subtly and intrinsically to the former.

In attempting to perform his feat of aesthetic ordering, the hero uses two modes: poetic and dramatic. The poetic is rendered by the metaphorical patternings of the novel, which suggest the narrator's desire to see the world of matter as essentially malleable. The dramatic is evidenced by the theatricality and melodramatic preconceptions on which he bases his first love affair. Radiguet underlines throughout the inadequacies and false imaginings in which these two modes are rooted. Yet his sympathies remain much more clearly with the hero, who at least yearns to create beauty, than with the aesthetically blind bourgeois society surrounding him. At times, indeed, it is difficult to separate Radiguet's creativity from that of his hero, except that through the form of the novel he attempts to detach and objectify his own misgivings about his most appropriate mode of expression. It will be crucial for us to determine how and why he has chosen to accommodate these two principal elements of poetry and drama within the framework of a novel, and whether he succeeds thereby in adding a new dimension to the art of fiction, or whether the result remains on the level of an interesting experiment. David Noakes remarks that, although Radiguet's gifts were essentially poetic, the lyrical expression of his novels succeeds far more notably than his verse; Noakes adds that it was Jean Cocteau who persuaded his friend "qu'il y avait en lui une poésie qui demandait une forme ostensiblement non-poétique" ["that there was in him a poetry which demanded an ostensibly nonpoetic form"]. In perceiving the implications of this idea for the modern novel, the young Radiguet shared the interests of Joyce, Virginia Woolf, Proust, and Alain-Fournier.

A key image which the narrator propounds at the beginning of the novel crystallizes both his strengths and his flaws, and predicts the causes of his failure to shape reality, with any degree of permanence, according to his needs. He defines himself in his relation to the *monde des objets* ["world of objects"] as a kind of cat which sees a bit of cheese under glass: "Je n'ai jamais été un rêveur. Ce qui semble rêve aux autres, plus crédules, me paraissait à moi aussi réel que le fromage au chat, malgré la cloche de verre. Pourtant la cloche existe. La cloche se cassant, le chat en profite. . . ." ["I have never been a dreamer. What seems like a dream to others, who are more credulous, seemed to me as real as the cheese is to the cat in spite of the bell jar. Nevertheless, the bell jar exists. When the glass breaks, the cat profits. . . ."] The cat is to the cheese as the artist is to his work, or the dramatist to his play. But the narrator is not only the playwright; he is also the protagonist of his own drama. He is a romantic and a sensualist. For him, the "dream" has a tactile existence and is therefore attainable. In this, he is at one with his culture heroes, Baudelaire and Rimbaud. But he forgets that if the war permits the cat to reach the tempting "cheese," Marthe, it also marks the end of Marthe's virginity by precipitating her early marriage to a soldier, Jacques.

Had the hero ears to hear, other *cloches* ["bells"] and *sonnettes* ["chimes"] sound a warning to him throughout of the threatening, cynical, and only at times indifferent presence of the "glass screen" of society. At the beginning of their liaison, he proceeds cautiously to avoid publicity, "pour ne point ébranler la cloche de la grille" ["so as not to jar the bell at the gate"], and he fears that he will "prendre les sonnettes pour des commutateurs" ["mistake the chimes for the light switches"]. A *sonnette* also marks the end of their first night of love when, ironically, Marthe's mother arrives to accompany her daughter to mass. And at the end of the novel, before hearing the bells announcing the armistice, the hero listens anxiously for the sound of the *sonnette* which may bring news of Marthe and their baby. Finally, the armistice bells announce the end of their idyll and the restoration of order: "mes oreilles, un jour, entendirent des cloches. C'étaient celles de l'armistice" ["my ears, one day, heard bells. They were those of the armistice"].

Marthe's room, moreover, becomes an extension of this almost invisible "cloche" of the resistant outside world. When the protagonists feel most secure and isolated within their "cocoon," they are actually most surrounded by a public—Jacques, their parents, the Marins, who live downstairs and spy on them. For the hero the glass is invisible, but it is nonetheless there. The war seems to shatter the glass so that he, the cat, can reach the tempting "fromage." But in reality there is only a crack which is soon repaired when the war ends, making of his "triumph" a mere passing illusion.

For many readers, as for the narrator, the atmosphere under the "cloche" at times is almost claustrophobic rather than lyrical. We seem rarely to escape a kind of imprisonment in Marthe's bedroom, and can readily sympathize with the narrator-hero when he exclaims at one point, separated from his mistress, that it is a relief to sleep alone. Radiguet is perhaps suggesting that the egoism of the romantic poet has too little of the "human" about it, is too little tied to reality, too much to intense emotion that cannot be sustained.

An apparently extraneous incident early in the novel actually represents a further extension of the narrator's "cloche" image, whose relevance to his own fate becomes evident only later on. He relates a vivid boyhood memory of a neighbor's maid who goes mad, climbs up on the roof, provides entertainment for the local spectators, and finally leaps to her death on the stones below. For the onlookers, the woman's death becomes their own little drama "in the air" which they can witness without any emotional involvement, as they are later to witness the hero's love affair with Marthe. They can "boo" the Maréchauds and applaud the speech of the "charitable" woman with impunity, and the whole episode is set up for us, as for them, with an elaborate *mise en scène*. Their responses present an effective distillation of social attitudes brought to bear upon

the individual whose behavior deviates from the norm. The maid's "escape" from the enclosed house to the roof is analogous to the narrator's later attempt to break through the glass "cloche" imprisoning what he takes to be a form of lyric happiness. Her public scandal and shameful death resemble those of Marthe later on, whose straying from the normal bourgeois path becomes a public spectacle before everyone but Jacques, whom society protects to the end. The hero's mother, in fact, describes Marthe as "une folle" ["a mad woman"]. The maid's derangement may also suggest the hero's own *dérèglement des sens* ["derangement of the senses"]—only his is conscious and in the manner of Rimbaud or Baudelaire.

Like his parents later on, the Maréchauds, who employ the maid, simply avert their eyes from the catastrophe. If their reaction cannot simply be described as indifference, it is, at the most, embarrassment at exposure to public obloquy or ridicule, whereas the narrator is touched by an element of tragedy in the death of a woman suffering in isolation amidst all the publicity, just as he and Marthe are later to suffer. . . . (pp. 64-7)

Two major patterns of imagery are also introduced in this incident and later internalized by the narrator so as to translate his poetic vision. The *pompiers* ["firemen"], all "volontaires," who "leur travail fini, viendront éteindre l'incendie, s'il ne s'est pas éteint de lui-même" ["their work finished, will come to extinguish the fire, if it has not extinguished itself"], not only underline the ridiculous aspect of the maid's death (and foreshadow the absurdities of the two childish lovers), but also reveal the human helplessness to cope with the fire of passion which dominates the book. Fire metaphorically suggests not only the outer war surrounding the lovers, but also the inner war in their souls. It implies at the same time the fire of love and the flames of hell, of the "diable au corps." Water imagery, on the other hand, suggests the transiency both of passion and of outer and inner warfare. In this instance, the maid's figurative "shipwreck" also foreshadows that of the lovers. Paradoxically, the shipwreck image not only implies destruction, but also, because it is of the very essence of poetry, reveals the working of the narrator's creativity: "Je pensai à quelque fille, capitaine corsaire, restant seule sur son bateau qui sombre" ["I thought of some girl, a corsair captain, staying alone on her sinking boat"]. Here, as later, however, the hero in his arrogance overestimates the capacity of his senses to endure such poetic pain, for both he and his father are "bouleversés" ["flabbergasted"] by the sight, and what is created does not quite balance what is destroyed.

A later scene more directly involving the lovers parallels the episode of the maid's death in that it reveals the ambivalent permissive-repressive reactions of a bourgeois "audience" toward a dramatic "spectacle." It also illustrates the narrator's flair for the dramatic in both its tragic and farcical veins. If, in these "petites villes de banlieue" ["suburban small towns"] there is a fear of the "qu'en-dira-t-on" ["what will people say"], of "racontars" ["gossips"], there is also a fascination with the "doings" of those who have dared to reject their moral conditioning, even a reluctant envy of them, and an attempt to reach a cheap "catharsis" analogous to that attained painlessly by identifying with characters in a play.

This attitude reaches a climax when the Marins, the family of the retired municipal counselor who own Marthe's house and live on the first floor, decide to have a party whose hidden purpose is very different from its stated intention, which is to encourage M. Marin's "rentrée politique" ["political comeback"]. It is to be a "raout-surprise" ["surprise party"], and is intended to dramatize or utilize as a public spectacle for the edification of the guests the love affair taking place overhead. Madame Marin, we are told, needs only the baton of the stage director to complete the picture. M. Marin's willingness to publicize the peccadilloes of others for personal profit is the other side of the coin from the Maréchauds' fear of public scandal, and resembles the self-interest of the "charitable" woman's husband in the earlier scene. The narrator reminds us pointedly that these representatives of public order, the municipal counselors, "jouent toujours un rôle dans mes aventures" ["always played a role in my adventures."]. But the two protagonists carry off the triumph, for their discretion creates a new drama in which the Marins are made to appear ridiculous before their friends, and the bourgeois attempts to create art fail miserably.

Although the narrator's peculiar genius succeeds in this episode in polarizing his own poetic drama and the Marins' cheap sensationalism, his creative autonomy is not always so clear-cut. Indeed, even here, his dramatic success is completely dependent on the Marins' abortive attempt to titillate their "public." We are constantly reminded that he can exercise his creativity only under the protective shield of the "cloche," and that the bourgeois world of his parents, of the school, of the village shapes his poetry at least as much as he does. As he indicates at the beginning of the novel, a bourgeois morality encourages sensuality rather than killing it, but a distorted sensuality.

The narrator's conception of poetry and drama diverges from that of his parents and friends in that it involves a deeper and more natural commitment. For instance, when he is expelled from school, he immediately demonstrates a Rousseauistic preference for quests into nature with his friend René (perhaps also a Romantic echo from Chateaubriand). He is deluded principally in his faith that one *can* return to nature in total artistic autonomy. As his parents' distorted vision is actually a prerequisite for his own poetry, so is World War I symbolic of the external forces operative on him when he least suspects it. The war is the precondition permitting his love affair, since his youth exempts him from the draft. Yet, since its effect on his life is one of absence rather than presence, he is easily tempted to forget its existence. We can visualize it on the very periphery of his life, with Marthe's room at the center, surrounded first by the ordinary life of the village, and only then, unseen and largely unheard at the center, by the war.

But the insularity of this lyric love, or poetic creation, at the center depends on the continuation of the war and is not exempt from that larger warfare which is a permanent condition of human existence. The war serves as an ominous background reminding us of the ephemeral aspect of both love and poetry. In its literal sense World War I is merely the catalyst that triggers the narrator's poetry and, at the same time, the adult bourgeois world's attempts to create a rational order to repress the adolescent poetry. For the narrator, pastoral scenes along the Marne create an effect of peace, of an idyllic existence, even though he knows the war is virtually on his doorstep. Any glimpses he has of the war are fleeting and seem somehow unreal. Characteristically, he views them, through inexperienced eyes, as a play put on for his amusement or as an encouragement of his own heroic posturings. Soldiers on a train provide a theatrical spectacle for those, like himself, who are too young for the army, and a sentinel makes his initial amatory exploit seem more dangerous than it really is. The nearest the war actually gets to him is through the *sound* (perhaps comparable to the *cloches* and *sonnettes* as a reminder of that reality which hems in his dreamworld) of a distant cannon.

For a time he toys with the idea that the war may legitimize their affair by killing Jacques, but both he and Marthe are too good-natured really to hope for this. Moreover, they realize they actually need him: were it not for Jacques, Marthe would still be living with her parents, and the narrator, who is a minor, could not even see her. Therefore the same circumstance—his youth and exemption from the draft—furthers their affair and ultimately puts an end to it. But perhaps its very brevity and intensity are of the very essence of poetry. (pp. 67-70)

The narrator's youth, like the war and his dependence on the adult world, points up the ironic discrepancy between his expectations of total creative freedom and the very real, resistant materials with which he has to work. His age represents both his poetic strength and his weakness, and in that sense it is the key to the whole novel. Some of his reactions to love are still infantile. For instance, after he has played at "l'école buissonnière" ["hooky"] with Marthe and enjoyed the liberty, he begins to enjoy freedom for its own sake and to continue playing hooky without her. He sees Marthe rather childishly, not as a fellow human being, but as "un jouet qui se donne lui-même" ["a toy which gives itself."] The egocentrism of youth is difficult to separate from that of the romantic poet. Like Julien Sorel, he is a complete novice whose early abortive attempts at love-making have their ridiculous aspect. For instance, Marthe, who is supposedly an experienced nineteen, is finally forced to make him the present of a robe to remind him that he has been altogether too discreet and timid. And when he takes off for his first night of love, using as a pretext an early-morning walk with René, his mother packs a picnic basket, and he sees himself not as a romantic hero, but as a curious compound of Red Riding Hood and Prince Charming, a comic figure misplaced in a fairy tale—"ce Prince Charming, un panier de ménagère à son bras" ["this Prince Charming, a picnic basket on his arm."] Marthe has to take the initiative and seduce him almost maternally. And when it is all over, they both cry like two children. Similarly, his boasting to René that he does not really love her has in it not so much of cowardice as of adolescent fanfaronade. (pp. 70-1)

Paradoxically, the poetic dimension of the novel grows out of the absurd contradictions between the lovers' real situation and their lyric aspirations. The hero is intensely concerned with words and gestures, with finding an adequate means of communication to transcend these absurdities by locking himself and Marthe within a private world of his own creation. Even his first abortive attempt at reaching a young female classmate was in epistolary form, conveyed by an underclassman named "Messager." Silence at first is a problem between himself and Marthe, and even the "moyens de correspondre aussi grossiers que la parole ou le geste" ["means of correspondence as vulgar as words or gestures"] would be better. He does not know how to address Marthe, whether to "tutoyer" her, "construisant mes phrases de façon à ne pas lui parler directement" ["constructing my sentences in such a way as not to address her directly"]. Unlike Marthe, he recognizes the impossibility of total frankness between two human beings. He does, however, admire her love letter at one point, forgetting that "aucun genre épistolaire n'est moins difficile: il n'y est besoin que d'amour" ["no epistolary genre is less difficult: there is need there only for love"].

His imagination is, moreover, essentially bookish. He models his love story on the only "experience" he has had, his adult readings, often misunderstood or confused with a child's fairy tales. He is an avid reader who counts two hundred books that pass through his hands during the vacation. This avidity perhaps accounts for his inability to perceive the difference between dream and accessible, tactile reality. Like Constant's Adolphe, he is excited at the idea of having adventures and, as we have seen in the incident of the bonne ["maid"], is constantly in search of the "poésie des choses" ["poetry of things"].

His literary taste becomes clear when he attempts to teach Marthe and create her after his own image. She is his *medium* of expression even more than she is his mistress. They both discover a liking for Baudelaire and Verlaine, whom Jacques disapproves of. The narrator increasingly directs her taste toward the "poètes maudits," particularly when he introduces her to Rimbaud's *Une Saison en Enfer,* whose title is close to Radiguet's own. In fact, it would be no exaggeration to say that his literary affinities lead them to a veritable debauch. He constantly uses art as a frame, comparing, for instance, their relationship to that of Daphnis and Chloe. (pp. 71-2)

These attitudes suggest the strengths as well as the weaknesses of his creative drive. It is rooted, as it was for Rimbaud, in *vertige,* in the *dérèglement des sens,* and in egoism; worst of all, it violates the "otherness of the other," as a confusion of art with life will always do. Radiguet himself, on the other hand, as Noakes remarks, seems to be moving at this time from Rimbaud's influence toward the classical restraint of Mallarmé. For the narrator, love is a projection of his own ego, a form of narcissism. But its lyrical quality and innocence render the reader essentially sympathetic to it. Its childish thoughtlessness is comparable to that of the narrator's sisters who set out to carry pears to the wounded soldiers: "Quand elles arrivaient à J . . . , les paniers étaient presque vides" ["when they arrived at J . . . , the baskets were nearly empty"]. He speaks of Marthe proudly early in the novel, as Adolphe and Valmont did of their mistresses, as "le seul amour qui eût été digne de moi" ["the only love that had been worthy of me"]. In fact, he defines love explicitly at one point as "l'égoisme à deux" ["egotism for two"], which "sacrifie tout à soi, et vit de mensonges" ["sacrifices all to itself, and lives on lies"]. It is he, however, who teaches her to lie. Speaking throughout in the past tense, he recognizes that his supposed "clairvoyance" about her motives was really just another form of self-projection. When Marthe rebukes him for the purely sensual episode with Svéa, he turns the tables and arrogantly accuses her of "froideur" ["coldness"] for not being sufficiently jealous. Not only Marthe, but their child becomes for him a kind of *dédoublement* ["duplication"] of himself.

Love is for him the highest of the art forms, to be equated with poetry; but he sees true poetry as narcissistic and therefore "maudite": "elle [Marthe] était comme ces poètes qui savent que la vraie poésie est chose 'maudite', mais qui, malgré leur certitude, souffrent parfois de ne pas obtenir les suffrages qu'ils méprisent" ["she . . . was like those poets who know that true poetry is an accursed thing but who, despite their conviction, suffer at times from not achieving the suffering they despise"]. In other words, this poetry is antisocial; at the same time it suffers from the want of a sympathetic audience and is therefore dependent on the applause or calumny of spectators from the outside world. Love is inseparable from hate, because both are forms of egoism which seek to create others in their own image. . . . (p. 73)

Like his creator Radiguet, the hero sometimes seems uncertain what is to be his chosen form, as flashes of poetic insight are joined not by a sustained narrative thread, but by unconvincing theatrical climaxes. His drama, like his poetry, is a curious compound of the vertiginous, egocentric, and melodramatic. It constantly fails to take cognizance of the real world, which is particularly conspicuous when the hero imagines the ever-manageable Jacques walking in with a revolver in the middle of their tryst, prepared, like a character in a bad play, to shoot the lovers. He seeks to create a poetic, romantic drama in the manner of *Ruy Blas* by setting the stage, furnishing even the properties, and experimenting with all the types from the tragedy of the insane maid to the farce of the "raout-surprise." He is constantly manipulating others, from Marthe to his parents to René. We soon become aware that for him life is a series of games and stratagems, just as the war is, for an inexperienced boy, a series of complicated maneuvers by toy soldiers. Art is for him a substitute for life, not an imitation of it, for it has been his only preparation for the adult experience into which he has been hurled. From this fact arise the contradictions and instability of the world he creates, so that we have the impression of walking on shifting sands. When he criticizes his "œuvre"—Marthe's room and, by extension, Marthe herself—for these very contradictions, it is solely from the aesthetic point of view: "je fus à la fois heureux et malheureux, comme un dramaturge qui, voyant sa pièce, y découvre trop tard des fautes" ["I was at once happy and unhappy, like a dramatist who, seeing his play, discovers his mistakes too late"]. But he fails to perceive the most serious fault of all, that his creation lacks any roots in reality.

The imagery and the artistic frame do nevertheless create a kind of art work, however flawed. Marthe herself is an artist of sorts—she paints water colors—but they are poor and she is much more the narrator's work of art than her own. He steers her steadily away from her bourgeois values into a kind of revolt which is first literary, then emotional—an unnatural progression, to be sure. But there *is* love between them, not the mere sensuality of the forbidden fruit he tastes with Svéa. Their child represents a kind of triumph for him. Although Radiguet never names his hero, leaving the subject open to poetic suggestiveness, the child carries his name and continues the adventure. Marthe calls for the hero with her dying breath, but Jacques thinks it is the child she wants.

Marthe and the hero are a kind of latter-day "Paul et Virginie," although there are also striking resemblances to Rousseau's *La Nouvelle Héloïse* and to Adam and Eve in the Garden of Eden. The poetry he espouses is clearly romantic; their love is an attempt to return to nature and live with the simplicity of flowers and animals. Thus, for him, gardening is also a creative act and an egocentric one for he feels "le même orgueil d'homme, si enivrant, à étancher la soif de la terre, des fleurs suppliantes, qu'à satisfaire le désir d'une femme" ["the same manly pride as intoxicating at quenching the thirst of the soil, of the supplicating flowers, as at satisfying the desire of a woman"]. But a storm is always threatening, and the baby is born in January, midwinter, instead of March, early spring. It is premature, like their love, and must be protected by society in the form of a *couveuse* ["incubator"]. If the love affair is initiated with a bouquet of roses, they are later reminded that roses have all too short a season.

The water and fire images, in particular, warn us of the transiency of this lyric love. It resembles a "château de sable" ["sandcastle"] which the tide may carry away, and the narrator occasionally feels "mal de mer" ["sea sick"], or that he has been "jeté à l'eau" ["thrown into the water"]. The aesthetic, romantic order fed by the literal fire, or by the war, is also flickering and temporary, and both are aware that they are playing with fire and may get burned. (pp. 74-5)

Whatever there is of truth in his vision, Radiguet seems to conclude on a note of pessimism as to the viability of the Rousseauistic poetic ideal. The hero's "paresse" ["lassitude"] throughout the book, his timidity, the fact that he does nothing to win Marthe before she marries, his dependence on her energy, and his constant reversals of attitude toward her are signs not only of his immaturity, but also of a poetry which lacks control, which sees itself as a passive receiver of sensations. It may well be that Radiguet sees *all* such poetry as escapist and immature. He has apparently used *Paul et Virginie* as his model in creating a study of men as children left on their own with an expectation of total freedom to create—in this, perhaps, all poets are children. When war temporarily destroys social order, they are free to return to nature. But their triumph is, if not illusory, at least temporary, and is enveloped in the larger frame, the "cloche de verre" ["bell jar"] without which human society cannot exist.

Whether this is also the fate of Radiguet's own creation, *Le diable au corps*, is not so clear. If his hero has tried to create lyric poetry or drama, he has himself chosen to create a novel incorporating certain aspects of the other two genres. This may in itself imply an awareness of the weaknesses inherent in his hero's poetic vision and an attempt to establish a greater distance from the lyric center of the work, ostensibly the hero's creation, by enclosing it in his own creation, the "cloche de verre" of an extended narrative. His own search for a more objective, permanent form may explain his frequently ironic attitude toward his hero. But his stance is not consistently ironic, and the book remains an uneasy amalgam of disparate forms. The hero seems to represent the romantic, "maudit" ["accursed"], vertiginous stage of Radiguet's own career, whereas the essential qualities of the novel itself are classical: "mesure, fraîcheur, distinction" ["measure, freshness, distinction"], says Frédéric Lefèver, while Paul Valéry remarks on its "netteté" ["clarity"], its "marche directe et décidée" ["direct and resolute progression"] and its "dessin suffisant" ["sufficient design"], and Henri Massis speaks of "cette technique, cette philosophie, cette mesure" ["this technique, this philosophy, this measure"], and "cette pénétration du réel" ["that penetration of the real"]. Apparently Radiguet had, by the time of writing the novel, rejected in part the influence of Romanticism and of Rimbaud, but had not yet succeeded in creating his own aesthetic creed and its characteristic form.

Viewed from this angle, Radiguet's work, while minor, belongs to more to the simple "roman d'adolescence" than Proust's *A la recherche du temps perdu* or Alain-Fournier's *Le Grand Meaulnes*. Like these, it is an experiment which attempts to penetrate to the very roots of the function of the novel and to establish its fruitful relation to the other genres. If Proust's mode of exploiting the lyrical was to incorporate *poèmes en prose* ["prose poems"] at crucial points in the text, Alain-Fournier's was to bathe the reader in a particular poetic ambience resulting from linked images and from his hero's dynamic attempts to shape reality. The result in the former case is a poetic novel; in the latter, a *poème romancé* ["novelized poem"]. In the case of Radiguet the seams still show between and among the genres he is exploring, and the transition is not complete. We are left with a set of single vivid poetic images

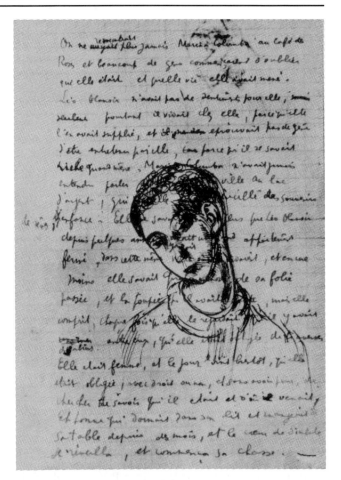

Manuscript page with a drawing by Radiguet. From Gli Inediti, *by Raymond Radiguet. Guanda, 1967. © by Ugo Guanda editore, Parma.*

which are only pasted together, not fused, and with jarringly melodramatic episodes. The quasi-ironic, quasi-sympathetic tone that pervades the book leaves us in some doubt as to the author's intention and to his success in "distancing" himself from the work. Like his hero, he seems sometimes to enclose us under glass in a claustrophobic world rather than extending the realm of the poetic imagination. But *Le diable au corps* was, after all, a first novel and a courageous attempt to break down some of the traditional barriers to the free functioning of fiction. (pp. 75-7)

> H. A. Bouraoui, "Radiguet's 'Le diable au corps': Beneath the Glass Cage of Form," in Modern Language Quarterly, *Vol. 34, No. 1, March, 1973, pp. 64-77.*

PHILIPPE R. PEREBINOSSOFF   (essay date 1976)

[*In the following excerpt, Perebinossoff examines the attempts of Count d'Orgel in* The Count's Ball *to manipulate others, drawing parallels between his machinations and the controlling force exerted by a theatrical director.*]

Raymond Radiguet in *Le bal du comte d'Orgel* reveals Anne d'Orgel's proclivity for exercising control over others by emphasizing his involvement in theatricals. Count d'Orgel's obsession with theatrical intrigues defines his character. He is an impresario who creates scenarios he wills upon others. He manipulates the emotions of his wife Mahaut and their friend François in order to satisfy his craving for a director's control over a performance he has formulated. The consequences of his penchant for theatricals do not concern him. All that matters is that he be amused and that he remain in complete control. Radiguet's use of theatricals allows him to place Anne in a dramatic situation which enables François, as well as the reader, to comprehend the system of priorities by which Anne arranges his life.

As Radiguet shows, Anne's orientation and approach to life are essentially theatrical. Radiguet describes Anne's voice as possessing that sharp tone "conservé au théâtre" ["reserved for the theater"]. When Mahaut suggests that they take a ride late one night, Anne reacts by adopting "le visage stupide des comédiens qui expriment l'étonnement" ["the stupid face of comedians expressing astonishment"]. He exaggerates his response with stock facial contortions to indicate he thinks his wife has taken leave of her senses. He overacts as if he were performing in a broad *Boulevard* farce or in a silent movie. A dandy, Anne even evaluates war as he would a performance: "la guerre l'avait *amusé*" ["the war amused him"] because it enabled him to mix with different social classes, something he continues to attempt when he devotes his energies to his favorite pastime, the planning and execution of a costume ball.

Anne totally ignores the possible consequences of his amusements. He prefers to view an intrigue as an "innocente plaisanterie" ["harmless joke"]. His pleasure is paramount and he categorically refuses to accept responsibility for the consequences of his *divertissements*. Radiguet introduces Anne to the reader at the Médrano Circus, an appropriate locale for an *au courant* Parisian in 1920—one recalls, for example, Cocteau's fascination with the trapeze artist Barbette in the early '20s. At the Circus, Anne decides to play a joke on Paul Robin, a casual acquaintance. Paul is at the Circus with François de Séryeuse, someone Anne has never met. To tease Paul, whom he sees as a social climber, Anne approaches François during the intermission while both of them are backstage visiting the clowns, and asks him to participate in a dupery. At Anne's suggestion, they pretend to be friends of long standing to annoy Paul, who had sought to keep Anne and Mahaut to himself.

Through the farce, Anne and François become friends. Their participation in the dupery cuts through the standard preliminaries of friendship. Radiguet writes, "Ils se sentaient complices. Ils étaient leurs propres dupes, car ayant décidé de faire croire à Robin qu'ils se connaissaient de longue date, ils le croyaient eux-mêmes" ["They were their own dupes, since, having decided to make Robin believe that they had known each other a long time, they believed it themselves"]. Playing the role of friends, they become friends. Role-playing and acting "as if" cause the imposture to become reality.

Once the initial contact between them has been made, Anne "adopts" François. He repeatedly invites François to dinner and grants him the privileges of an esteemed intimate. Describing Anne's adoption of friends, Radiguet writes, "Il 'adoptait' les gens, plus qu'il ne se liait avec eux. En retour, il exigeait beaucoup. Il entendait un peu diriger. Il exerçait un contrôle." ["He 'adopted' people, more than linking himself to them. In return he demanded much. He understood directing a little. He exercised control"]. Flattered by the Count's persistent manifestations of friendship, François quickly plunges into the midst of a complicated situation.

Anne exercises his control by encouraging a romantic attachment between François and his wife. His main reason for seeking to supervise an infatuation between them is that he needs to have others admire his wife to stimulate his own interest in her. As a spectator watching François pay homage to Mahaut, Anne "lui en trouva plus de saveur, comme si elle eût été la femme d'un autre" ["found her more exciting, as though she had been the wife of another"]. Alone with Mahaut, Anne experiences "la mélancolie." An evening at home with her does not provide him with the excitement he needs. Radiguet notes that ". . . Anne d'Orgel n'était à l'aise que dans une atmosphère factice, dans des pièces violemment éclairées, pleins de monde" ["Anne d'Orgel was only at ease in a factitious atmosphere, in brightly lit rooms, filled with people"]. Anne needs an audience. Although he might never openly admit to himself that he is deliberately attempting to make François fall in love with Mahaut, all of Anne's actions support such an interpretation. Anne requires the titillation such an intrigue or game provides.

Count d'Orgel's means of nurturing an infatuation between François and Mahaut are related to theatricals. At a party following the Médrano Circus, he concocts a love potion supposedly similar to the one shared by Tristan and Isolde—a potion which only François and Mahaut drink. When Anne discovers that Mahaut and François are distant cousins, he is overjoyed by this *coup de théâtre*. Encouraging greater familiarity between them, he insists that François kiss his new-found cousin. This *coup de théâtre* is an integral part of his scenario to bring Mahaut and François closer to one another.

Radiguet frequently states that Mahaut is in love with her husband and that François' initial interest in her contains no hint of deceit or treachery. Radiguet, however, also describes François as carefree and lazy, and as such he is ill-equipped to resist Anne's manipulative actions. After the Count has fostered the intimacy, François holds Mahaut's hand in Anne's carriage twice, first by mistake and the second time intentionally. Anne observes the second instance. He is shaken by the discovery, but when Mahaut tells him about it without knowing that he has observed the act, his face takes on an expression of joy. When she asks him what she should do, he tells her to ignore it. Anne switches from concern to joy because he knows he still controls her: she tells him of her own volition. Once his control is reestablished, he readily accepts François' seeming violation of their friendship because it suits him to have François infatuated with his wife. Any feelings of anxiety Mahaut might be experiencing are of no concern to him as long as he feels himself to be in complete control.

Mahaut and François' friendship and subsequent infatuation are so intimately connected to Anne's control that when they are alone, they find that they are unable to say very much to one another. Anne's absence makes them uncomfortable: "Il semblait à chacun qu'il fallait jouer un rôle et qu'ils avaient négligé de l'apprendre" ["It seemed to each of them that it was necessary to play a role and that they had failed to learn it"]. Both are lost without a scenario to perform and without Anne to direct them. They are incapable of relating to one another without him.

Mahaut suffers greatly as a result of Anne's "adoption" of François. About the time she is forced to admit to herself that she loves François, Anne decides to give a masked ball, ostensibly to amuse her. Mahaut is against having the ball, because it would necessitate even closer contact with François than usual, but Anne insists. Anne will not allow anything to inhibit his pursuit of pleasure. Anne's insistence that the ball be given and the anxiety she experiences over her attachment to François cause Mahaut a great deal of torment. Using another theatre metaphor, Radiguet writes, "Sa personne tout entière reflétait le cruel combat dont elle était le théâtre" ["Her whole body reflected the cruel struggle for which she was the theatre"]. Her psyche becomes a battleground for Count d'Orgel's entertainments—first, his manipulation of the romance, and second, his staging of the masked ball.

The rehearsal for the ball is the key event in the novel. Through the rehearsal, Radiguet shows the extent of Anne's obsession with theatrics and establishes the system of priorities by which Anne organizes his life. By means of François' reactions to Anne's frenzy while planning the ball, Radiguet is able to comment on François' maturation process. Through the rehearsal, François sees Anne for what he is.

The arrival of an unexpected guest at the rehearsal causes Anne to fear that the evening's entertainment will be ruined. The guest, Prince Naroumof, has recently been exiled from Russia, and Anne fears that a discussion of Naroumof's political misfortunes will thwart his intention of spending the evening reviewing the preparations for the ball. As the rehearsal is his overriding concern, he decides to keep Naroumof in the background and not to make any fuss over him or to pay him any particular attention; in other words, Anne assigns him a supporting rather than a starring role in his evening's entertainment. Count d'Orgel fears that the mention of political realities will supplant his attempts to create a world of illusion out of costumes, dancing, and role playing.

Throughout the rehearsal, Count d'Orgel devotes himself entirely to the preparations for the ball. He works "comme un diable" ["like a devil"], and is angry that Mahaut does not give him as much support as he wants. For example, when Mahaut's anxiety over François' presence causes her to faint, Anne is furious with her for interrupting his party. Taking complete control of the evening's agenda, Anne announces the evening's festivities as if he were presenting a series of tableaux, much in the manner of a Broadway director staging "numbers." For example, the passing from dinner to the discussion of the ball becomes "un changement de spectacle" ["a change of spectacle"]. Trying on various costumes awakens "en Anne la passion la plus profonde des hommes de sa classe, à travers les siècles: celle du déguisement" ["in Anne the most profound passion of men of his class throughout the centuries: that of disguise"]. Radiguet employs an established aristocratic activity, dressing up for masked balls, to establish the peculiarities of his main character's personality.

The Count's frenetic behavior at the rehearsal causes François to reevaluate his opinion of him. He watches Anne change scarves: "Pour la première fois, il ne vit plus en Anne cette espèce de supériorité qu'il lui accordait d'office. Il le jugea. Il le trouvait puéril" ["For the first time, he no longer saw in Anne that sort of superiority that he had accorded him out of duty. He judged him. He found him childish"]; watching Anne and the other guests fight over jeweled pieces of cloth, François comes to hate them: "Il ne désirait être rien d'autre que lui-même" ["he wanted to be nothing but himself"] and he despises their role-switching and inconsistencies.

Anne totally forgets himself amidst the "bacchanale improvisée": "Son visage montrait la fièvre des enfants excités par le jeu" ["His face showed the fever of children excited by the game"]. Made dizzy by all the excitement, he runs in and out

of the room, each time reappearing with a new costume. He is incapable of checking the flow of passions that such activities arouse within him. Along with the inconsistency in character which François equates with repeated costume changes, Anne displays the kind of unleashed passion which Plato and other critics of the theatre associated with theatrical activities. Anne gets so carried away that he dons Naroumof's Tyrolian hat and executes a Russian dance. Prince Naroumof is not amused by the performance. He is convinced that the war must have made everyone crazy. Naroumof represents order amidst the chaos of Anne's theatrical evening.

Anne refuses to take Mahaut seriously when she confesses her love for François after the rehearsal. He tells her that she must be feeling ill or nervous, and he treats her like a child who does not know what she is talking about. He reacts only when she tells him that she has written to François' mother describing the situation; he pauses and answers, "'C'est absurde . . . Il faut que nous cherchions un moyen de tout réparer'." ["'It's absurd . . . we must seek a means of fixing everything'"]. He is not at all concerned with his wife's feelings about a situation he has created. What concerns him are the social implications of the letter to François' mother. To avoid any hint of scandal or gossip, he decides that François' *must* come to the ball, that he *must* continue to be a part of their entourage, and that Mahaut *must* select his costume for the ball. Anne has made his decision. Appearances and the dictates of form take priority over Mahaut's feelings. Count d'Orgel believes that what takes place in public is all that matters—only what takes place in public can pass for reality.

Anne's concern with form necessitates that Mahaut follow his instructions to prevent the possibility of a scandal. His obsessive involvement with the theatrical entertainments which are such an integral part of his life may have temporarily caused him to lose control at the rehearsal, but he is nevertheless able to regain his control when he feels threatened by a potential scandal. As he leaves Mahaut after deciding what she will have to do, in the last sentence of the book, he directs her, "'Et maintenant, Mahaut, dormez! Je le veux'" ["'And now Mahaut, sleep! I want you to'"]. Anne is fully in control. He has prepared a script to resolve the potentially scandalous results of his "innocente plaisanterie" ["harmless joke"] and Mahaut is forced to perform his scenario.

The novel gains thematic unity and power through Radiguet's skillful use of theatrical imagery. All of the characters in Radiguet's carefully structured novel are affected by Anne's vision of life as a game of illusion and role-playing. He manipulates the lives of the people around him in order to preserve his theatrical vision of the world. Through Radiguet's narrative technique, the reader's developing antipathy for Anne parallels François' disillusionment with the puerile aspects of Anne's character revealed through his fascination with theatrical amusements. (pp. 131-36)

> *Philippe R. Perebinossoff, "Amusement and Control: The Theatricals of Raymond Radiguet's Count d'Orgel," in* Romance Notes, *Vol. XVII, No. 2, Winter, 1976, pp. 131-36.*

MARTIN TURNELL   (essay date 1978)

> [*An English critic, Turnell has written widely on French literature and has made significant translations of the works of Jean-Paul Sartre, Guy de Maupassant, Blaise Pascal, and Paul Valéry. In the following excerpt, he analyzes and compares* The Devil in the

Flesh *and* The Count's Ball, *finding the former to be the more sophisticated of the two novels.*]

"I shall be severely reproached for what I have done," runs the opening sentence of **Le diable au corps.**

> But how can I help it? Was it my fault that I was twelve years old a few months before the war broke out? The difficulties that I encountered during that extraordinary period were no doubt of a kind which no one ever experienced at that age; but since there is nothing on earth which in spite of appearances is strong enough to age us, it was as a child that I behaved in an adventure which would have embarrassed a grown man. I am not the only one. And my friends will retain a memory of the period which is not the same as that of their elders. Let those who are already feeling angry with me realise that the war was for so many young boys a four-year holiday.

It is an admirable start and touches on some of the main issues. Radiguet's achievement lies in the veracity and convincingness with which he presents a child's vision of the world and his refusal to allow the naked vision to be toned down or blurred by empty moralising or by literary tricks borrowed from the repertoire of other writers. He writes with a child's vividness and directness, and he reveals the child's ruthless disregard for other peoples' feelings. It follows that it is not sufficient to describe the novel, as has been done, as "le seul livre *vrai que nous ayons sur l'adolescence*" ["the only *true* book on adolescence we have"]. What is outstanding is that the story of an adolescent love affair is told by an adolescent with the power and psychological insight which belong to a gifted and mature novelist.

We must go on to say that too little attention has been paid to the setting and structure of the novel. Wartime France means that there will be a relaxation of discipline and that children will be able to behave more or less as they choose during what appears to them something like an exceptionally long holiday, but which may well end in disaster for them (as it does for the narrator) simply on account of the slackening of discipline.

Radiguet enlarges on the situation by the ingenious use of the images of the cat, which are particularly effective in a novel about adolescent love:

> Mes parents condamnaient plutôt la camaraderie mixte. La sensualité qui naît avec nous et se manifeste encore aveugle, y gagna au lieu d'y perdre.
>
> Je n'ai jamais été un rêveur. Ce qui semble rêve aux autres, plus crédules, me paraissait à moi aussi réel que le fromage au chat, malgré la cloche de verre. Pourtant la cloche existe.
>
> La cloche se cassant, le chat en profite, même si ce sont ses maîtres qui la cassent, et s'y coupent les mains.
>
> Les vraies vacances approchaient, et je m'en occupais fort peu puisque c'était pour moi le même régime. Le chat regardait toujours le fromage sous la cloche. Mais vint la guerre. Elle brisa la cloche. Les maîtres eurent d'autres chats à fouetter et le chat se réjouit.
>
> (My parents were more or less opposed to boys and girls going about together. Sensuality, which is in us from birth and makes its appearance while still blind, increases in us rather than diminishes.
>
> I have never been a dreamer. What seems like a dream to others, who are more credulous, seemed to me to be as real as the cheese is to a cat in spite of the glass dome over the cheese platter. Nevertheless the dome exists.
>
> When the dome breaks, the cat benefits, even if it is its masters who break it and cut their hands.
>
> The real holidays were approaching, and I paid little attention to them because for me it was the same régime. The cat went on looking at the cheese under the dome. Then came the war. She broke the dome. The masters had other cats to flog and the cat rejoiced.)

In what is really a piece of self-criticism, the narrator sees himself as a cat mischievously trying to find a way of extracting cheese from under the dome in order to have a pleasant little meal consisting, significantly in view of what is to come, of the masters' food. The second part of the first cat image is an indication of the way in which discipline will be neglected by masters whose clumsiness or blunders lead to the breaking of the dome for the benefit of the cat and damage to themselves. The last image shows that once war has broken out, it is the "cat" who breaks the dome and can do so with impunity because the "masters" are taken up with wartime activities and are treating the enemy as "the other cats."

The image of the cat looking hungrily at the cheese which it is prevented from reaching by the glass dome stands of course for an adolescent looking hungrily at a girl, even if his "sensuality," which is inborn like a cat's taste for cheese, is still "blind," but is unable to reach her because she is carefully protected under the "dome" which is her parents' home. The war will have the same effect as the smashing of the "dome," except that fortunately for the couple there will be no actual "smashing." After her marriage the girl will go to live in her husband's flat. She will naturally be alone because the husband will spend most of his time at the front, but she will take a major step in developing the love affair by inviting the "cat" to visit her in the new "dome." Her family will know virtually nothing about the liaison even in its last stages and the narrator's own family will turn a blind eye and refuse to intervene. (pp. 264-66)

The narrator meets Marthe for the first time in 1917, when the two families are on a Sunday outing together. The couple discuss Baudelaire and Verlaine, the poets they admire, but of whom Marthe's fiancé and her parents disapprove. This prompts the observation:

> I was glad to find that we had a secret, and I, who am timid, began to feel tyrannical.

"Timid" and "tyrannical" are keywords. They reflect the vacillations and doubts about the narrator's real feelings for Marthe and the aggressiveness which is characteristic of a child and will play an important part in the novel. He keeps on repeating to himself at the first meeting that Marthe does not "intimidate" him and that he is only prevented from kissing her by the presence of her parents, then admits:

> What luck that I was not alone with her! For I still should not have dared to kiss her, and there would have been no excuse.
>
> That's how the timid person cheats.

He soon moves in the opposite direction and displays the "tyrannical" element. He has seen some of Marthe's water colours before the meeting which her father had brought to his parents' house so that they could be used for a wartime charity. The attraction that he had come to feel for her does not prevent him from remarking candidly in recalling them:

> Ces aquarelles était sans nulle recherche; on y sentait la bonne élève du cours de dessin, tirant la langue, léchant les pinceaux.
>
> (These water colours were without any studied elegance; they gave the impression of a good pupil at a drawing class, sticking out her tongue, licking the brushes.)

When he happens to meet Marthe unexpectedly in Paris on his way to school, decides to play truant and accepts her invitation to help her choose furniture for the marriage flat, he says:

> Cette obligation d'accompagner Marthe m'apparut comme une malchance. Il fallait donc l'aider à choisir une chambre pour elle et un autre! Puis, j'entrevis le moyen de choisir une chambre pour Marthe et pour moi. . . .
>
> Son fiancé goûtáit le style Louis XV.
>
> Le mauvais goût de Marthe était autre; elle aurait plutôt versé dans le japonais. Il me fallut donc les combattre tous les deux. . . .
>
> J'étais parvenu à transformer, meuble à meuble, ce mariage d'amour, ou plutôt d'amourette, en un mariage de raison, et lequel!
>
> (The obligation to accompany Marthe seemed to me unfortunate. It meant helping her to choose a room for herself and another! Then I saw the means of choosing a room for Marthe and for me. . . .
>
> Her fiancé's taste was for the style Louis XV.
>
> Marthe's bad taste was of another kind; she was rather inclined to go in for the Japanese. It was therefore necessary for me to combat the pair of them. . .
>
> I succeeded in transforming, piece by piece, this love marriage, or rather this marriage of infatuation, into a marriage of reason—and what a one!

The first thing that strikes us in this passage is the statement that "I saw the means of choosing a room for Marthe and for me," which is exactly what happened. We can go on to observe that although his comments might be described as brazen, there is nothing that is really heartless about the narrator. We shall find that as his feeling for Marthe deepens, he will revoke his criticisms and will even regret his own taste for the furniture that he helped to choose, dismissing it as "odious" and saying that it was not chosen for his pleasure, but simply in order to "displease Jacques." We also find that he is completely honest and never attempts to conceal from himself or excuse the harshness that he not infrequently displays towards Marthe. (pp. 267-68)

What makes this novel virtually unique is the extraordinary insight that the novelist displays when he eventually came to reveal the complexity of the feelings of the adolescent lovers.

> My clear-sightedness was only a more dangerous form of my ingenuousness. . . . This pretended insight obscured everything from me, made me doubt Marthe. Or rather, I doubted myself, not finding myself worthy of her. Even if I had had a thousand more proofs of her love, I should not have been less unhappy.

We must go on to observe that the initial attraction, which seems to have been something like a youthful flirtation on the narrator's part, or so he believed for a time, gradually changes into a much deeper feeling which is both emotional and physical:

> However, there was another thing which ought to have made me understand my true feelings. When I met Marthe a few months ago, my pretended love did not prevent me from judging her, from finding ugly most of the things that she found beautiful, and from thinking that most of the things she said were infantile. Now, if I did not think like her, I told myself that I was wrong. After the crudity of my first inclinations, it was the gentleness of a deeper feeling which deceived me. . . . I began to feel respect for Marthe because I was beginning to love her.

His first view of Marthe's poor taste and childish talk was no doubt correct and a sign of the narrator's far greater intelligence, but it has been obscured by something like genuine love—genuine because of the respect that he feels for the loved one. The paradox lies in the fact that it is an illusion about her abilities which begins to reveal his real feelings to himself.

We observe that the word "beginning" turns up again in the last sentence. The narrator's illusion that he does not love Marthe any longer or, in another place, that his love for her is "dead," is only completely dissipated when they begin to make love, first by kisses provoked by Marthe, then by intercourse. I suggested that the use of the "cat" image at the beginning of the novel was peculiarly suitable in a novel about adolescent love. The same is true of the images of the magnet and the alarm clock which are used to describe the last two stages of becoming lovers:

> Un jour que je m'approchais trop sans pourtant que mon visage touchât le sien, je fus comme une aiguille qui dépasse d'un millimêtre la zone interdite et appartient à l'aimant.
>
> J'embrassai Marthe sur l'épaule. Elle ne s'éveilla pas. Un second baiser, moins chaste, agit avec la violence d'un réveillematin. Elle sursauta, et, se frottant les yeux, me couvrit de baisers, comme quelqu'un qu'on aime et qu'on retrouve dans son lit après avoir rêvé qu'il est mort.
>
> (One day I moved too close, but without my face touching hers. I was like a needle which goes a fraction of an inch beyond the forbidden zone and is caught by the magnet.
>
> I kissed Marthe on the shoulder, but she did not wake. A second and less chaste kiss acted with the violence of an alarm clock. She shot up and, wiping her eyes, covered me with kisses, like someone whom one loves and whom one finds in one's bed after dreaming that he is dead.)

It is characteristic of some of the great French novelists that their work often contains phrases which might have come from one of the seventeenth-century maxim writers. They are not abstract pronouncements; they spring directly from the contemplation of experience and are nearly always dramatically appropriate. The maturity which they distil contributes largely to the sense of maturity which belongs peculiarly to the French novel. Although, as already suggested, the images of the magnet and the alarm clock are peculiarly suitable to the account of two adolescents becoming lovers, later in the novel we shall come across what we are inclined to call mature maxims because they show that the adolescents have reached something like a state of maturity in their love.

The passage describing the way in which the narrator's kiss "acted with the violence of an alarm clock" deals with something that happened on the morning after the night of love-making for the first time. In the middle of the night there had been a touch of something like black comedy. The narrator had turned up at Marthe's flat entirely unexpectedly:

> I opened the door and whispered "Marthe?"
>
> "Rather than give me a fright like that," she answered, "you could very well have put off coming till the morning. You've got your leave a week early then?"
>
> She thought that I was Jacques.

The brutal way in which she addresses her imagined husband naturally reminds us of the occasion on which she shocked the narrator by flinging one of her husband's unread letters into the fire, which may in spite of himself have been responsible for his treatment of one of her letters which caused him so much emotion. It shows that the "tyrannical" element was not confined to the male lover, though the woman only uses it with her husband. Although I observed earlier that there would be no smashing of a "dome" to bring the two lovers together and that Marthe herself would invite the narrator into the new "dome," his unexpected arrival on this occasion, which leads to love-making for the first time, reminds us not only of the "cat" breaking the glass dome and presumably thoroughly enjoying the "cheese," but also of the narrator's remark, when he was helping to choose the marriage furniture, that he saw "the means of choosing a room for Marthe and me." For it becomes of course the room where, in spite of what the narrator calls "ma timidité maladive" ["my sickly timidity"], love-making will take place on innumerable occasions. (pp. 271-74)

We have seen that something like borrowings of seventeenth-century maxims is part of Radiguet's inheritance. It makes his comment on the first kiss far more pregnant than the corresponding observation on love-making:

> La saveur du premier baiser m'avait déçu comme un fruit que l'on goûte pour la première fois. Ce n'est pas dans la nouveauté, c'est dans l'habitude que nous trouvons les plus grands plaisirs.
>
> (The taste of the first kiss disappointed me like a fruit that one tastes for the first time. It is not novelty, but habit which provides the greatest pleasure.)

"Habit" is an important word and will turn out to have a dual meaning.

The temporary separation of the couple when the husband is home on leave prompts the narrator to remark with another use of homely comparisons:

> What worried me most was the fast imposed on my senses. My restlessness was the same as that of a pianist without a piano or a smoker without cigarettes.

The passage brings home the highly amorous nature of his attraction for Marthe and the "habit" it has become through the husband's absence. His susceptibility is underlined by the way in which he agrees, during one of these separations, to put the fidelity of his friend René's mistress to the test and is promptly seduced by her. It is also underlined by his own unsuccessful attempt to seduce Marthe's Swedish girl friend. . . . (pp. 275-76)

Marthe is as susceptible as the narrator, and the way in which they indulge themselves as soon as the husband is out of the way again leads to something on the part of the narrator which is like a temporary loss of appetite through over-eating and illustrates the other implications of "habit."

> In bed beside her, the desire which seized me from moment to moment to be in bed alone, at my parents' home, made me see the unbearableness of life together. On the other hand, I could not imagine life without Marthe. I was beginning to know the chastisement of adultery.

It is another example of his insight and the remarkable clarity and brevity with which it is expressed. It is a reaction from which even adult lovers, whether married or not, do not always escape. What Radiguet does, as usual, is to emphasise the adolescent nature of the experience by references to the narrator's desire to escape, to be alone, and his nervousness at the prospect of "life together." It is capped by his inability even to "imagine life without Marthe," which exposes or sums up the complexity of his feelings in a mere five lines.

What emerges is that the state of confusion which followed love-making becomes permanent. Love continues to grow; there are periods of happiness; but fears for the future, internal conflicts on the part of the narrator, the mixture of "timid" and "tyrannical" impulses persist. The discovery that Marthe is pregnant produces characteristic reactions:

> L'instinct est notre guide; un guide qui nous conduit à notre perte. Hier, Marthe redoutait que sa grossesse nous éloignât l'un de l'autre. Aujourd'hui, qu'elle ne m'avait tant aimé, elle croyait que mon amour grandissait comme le sien. Moi, hier, repoussant cet enfant, je commençais aujourd'hui à l'aimer et j'ôtais de l'amour à Marthe, de même qu'au début de notre liaison mon coeur lui donnait ce qu'il retirait aux autres.
>
> (Instinct is our guide; a guide which leads to our fall. Yesterday, Marthe feared that her pregnancy would separate us from one another. Today, when she had never loved me so much, she believed that my love was growing like hers. I, who after repelling the child yesterday, today was beginning to feel love for it and took away love from Marthe in the same way that at the beginning of our liaison my heart gave her what it had taken away from others.)

The first sentence is an admirable example of what I have described as "mature maxims." Whatever the intention, its appearance in the present context seems to indicate that pregnancy, which is undoubtedly the fruit of "instinct," will lead to tragedy, and that is what will happen.

The narrator's change from "repelling" to "loving" the coming child, of which he is already convinced that he is the father, shows that on this occasion the novelist deliberately emphasises the closeness of the structure of his work by comparing the way in which at the beginning he took away love from other people to give it to Marthe and is now doing the opposite by taking away some of his love for her and giving it to the child. Nor should we overlook the reappearance of the word "beginning," which reflects alternately movements towards and away from Marthe. (pp. 276-77)

The last stages of the novel are the most moving and in some respects the most striking:

> Maintenant Marthe ne m'était pas seulement la plus aimée, ce qui ne veut pas dire la mieux aimée des maîtresses, mais elle me tenait lieu de tout. . . .
>
> L'amour aneschésiait en moi tout ce qui n'était pas Marthe.

(Now Marthe was not only my most loved, which is not to say the best loved of mistresses, but she took the place of everything for me. . . .

Love had anaesthetized in me everything that was not Marthe.)

The two passages may create the impression that their love has become absolute, but it would be misleading. We have seen that in spite of everything the narrator's vacillations, his internal conflicts, his fears of the future and uncertainties about his own feelings have never been eliminated. The important words are not "the best loved of mistresses" in the first of the two passages. It means that though the narrator is completely absorbed by his attitude to Marthe and is indifferent to everything and everybody else, it is not the absolute love of a mature man. It remains the powerful attraction of an adolescent, reminding us of the contradiction of the "unbearableness of life together" and the narrator's inability to "imagine life without Marthe." For true love means the complete unity of the couple, which depends on the internal unity of each of them—something which is never achieved by the narrator.

"The storm is approaching," we are told elliptically. It will be remembered that in the novel's opening passage the narrator attached special importance to the effect of war, which meant that children escaped normal discipline and found themselves on a "four-year holiday." What emerges is that the realisation that the free period was limited is responsible for the uncertainty about his future which continually haunts the narrator. It is expressed with remarkable effectiveness a little over halfway through the novel:

> Notre union était donc à la merci de la paix, du retour définitif des troupes. Qu'il chasse sa femme, elle me resterait. Qu'il la garde, je me sentais incapable de la lui reprendre de force. Notre bonheur était un château de sable. Mais ici la marée n'étant pas à heure fixe, j'espérais qu'elle monterait le plus tard possible.

> (Our union was therefore at the mercy of peace, the final return of the troops. Let him [Jacques] drive his wife away, she would remain with me. Let him keep her, I felt incapable of taking her from him by force. Our happiness was a castle of sand. But here the tide not having a fixed time, I hoped it would rise as late as possible.)

It is clear that the narrator sees no hope of Jacques abandoning his wife. This means that his own union will come to grief with "the final return of the troops." It is summed up brilliantly by the use of the sea image in the last two sentences, in which happiness is reduced to a "castle of sand" which will obviously be washed away when the tide rises. The result is that the only consolation can be a delay in the rising of the tide, which fortunately for him has no "fixed time." In other words, the adolescent lover hopes that instead of victory and peace, war will go on!

The statement that "The storm is approaching" refers to two factors: the knowledge that the armistice is very near (meaning that the "tide" is about to "rise" and wash away the "castle") and the belated attempt of the narrator's father to stop the pair spending nights together. The narrator is prepared to defy his father, but Marthe opposes him and threatens to move to her parents' home. The narrator then proposes that they shall go to Paris and spend a night at an hotel, comparing the couple to "children upright on a chair and proud to be a head and shoulders above the grown-up people." Marthe does not like the idea of going to Paris, but gives way to her lover. The visit to Paris turns out to be another mixture of the "timid" and the "tyrannical" on the part of the narrator, but this time the order is reversed. He is "tyrannical" in insisting that they should go together to Paris, but "timid" in his repeated pretence that he was unable to obtain a room at any of the hotels, where he simply pretends to make enquiries on his own while Marthe remains in the street. The result is that they are obliged to abandon the plan to stay the night, owing to the narrator's absurd "timidity" in not applying for a room at any of the hotels he visits, with the result that they return home in a miserable state. "Marthe," we are told, "in a corner of the carriage, exhausted, terrified, her teeth rattling, *understood everything*." She may, he adds, have been able to see that "there could be no other issue except death."

That is precisely what happened. "This night of the hotels," he says, "was decisive." The narrator finds her ill in bed the next morning. The doctor has to be called in. She is moved to her parents' house and eventually dies after the birth of her child without her lover ever seeing her again. (pp. 279-81)

Although Radiguet was "severely reproached for what he had done" by some of his first critics and though the narrator might fairly be called an *enfant terrible,* there is nothing "heartless" or "cynical" or "immoral" about the novel itself. Its great originality lies in the contrast between the immaturity of the child's reactions, with the jealous hope that there is no afterlife for his mistress as the outstanding example, and the absolute maturity with which they are presented. If the novel makes a painful impression it is because of the frankness and the veracity with which it describes the child's behaviour, the refusal to allow it to be blurred or toned down by sentimentality or empty moralising, and the honesty with which the child admits his faults. It is, indeed, the mastery with which Radiguet presents a picture of adolescent love in a way in which it had never been done before that makes *Le diable au corps* a unique work.

For a writer whose first novel is outstanding, the second presents a special problem. He naturally tries to improve on what may be a masterpiece, but can never be sure of succeeding or even producing anything which equals his first work, reminding us of the vast gap between Benjamin Constant's *Adolphe,* which was published in 1816, and his *Cécile,* which had to wait until 1951 for publication. There was a time when *Le diable au corps* was treated as an extremely promising first novel or, as Cocteau put it in his preface to the second novel, a "masterpiece of promise," with "the promise fulfilled" in *Le bal du comte d'Orgel.*

With the passing of time there has been a change of view. *Le bal du comte d'Orgel* is a highly talented novel, in which Radiguet becomes the omniscient novelist instead of the autobiographical novelist, is much more sophisticated than *Le diable au corps,* and there are even moments when we have the impression that it is more mature, but it has nothing like the same impact as the first novel. The feeling or, as one is tempted to call it, the illusion of greater maturity is easily explained. When he began his second novel Radiguet, who was a precocious child, was at least two years older, had mixed freely with literary society, had seen more of life and, as we shall find, chose very different protagonists from those of his first novel. The impact of *Le diable au corps* is naturally the result not simply of talent, but of the strongly personal element in the story and the narrator's use of the first-person singular. Although the love story in *Le bal du comte d'Orgel* reveals great insight and is decidedly moving, it is much less personal and has a detachment that reminds us of *La Princesse de Clèves*, which was a major influence on the work.

A young man named François de Séryeuse meets the Comte d'Orgel and his wife and becomes one of their friends. François and Mahaut fall in love, but remain chaste, with the result that Radiguet's 'scabrous' only applies to their feelings and not to their behaviour. The couple are, indeed, profoundly disturbed to find themselves in love. They are careful never to make a declaration to one another. The furthest that they go is an occasional polite kiss on the cheeks. The first causes embarrassment because it is instigated by the husband, who convinces himself for social reasons that the pair are cousins.

In spite of the differences, the two novels are clearly a pair. The illicit love affair of the two adolescents belonging to the bourgeoisie is matched by the chaste love affair of two people who are older, more responsible and belong to a higher class of society. We have seen the importance of the setting of the wartime period in *Le diable au corps*. The setting of the postwar period in *Le bal du comte d'Orgel* is also important and in some respects more far-reaching.

Although Radiguet deals like his great predecessor with high society, he is no imitator. The skill is apparent from the way in which he brings out the decline which has taken place since the seventeenth-century. When we set Mme de La Fayette's portrait of M. de Nemours beside Radiguet's of the Comte d'Orgel, we begin to see what has happened:

> Mais ce prince était un chef-d'oeuvre de la nature; ce qu'il avait de moins admirable, c'était d'être l'homme du monde le mieux fait et le plus beau. Ce qui le mettait au-dessus des autres était une valeur incomparable et un agrément dans son esprit, dans son visage et dans ses actions que l'on n'a jamais vu qu'à lui seul.

> Le Comte Anne d'Orgel était jeune; il venait d'avoir trente ans. On ne savait de quoi se gloire, ou du moins son extraordinaire position était faite. Son nom n'y entrait pas pour grand'chose, tant, même chez ceux qu'hypnotise un nom, le talent prime tout. Mais, il faut le reconnaître, ses qualités, n'étaient que celles de sa race, et un talent mondain.

> (But this prince was a masterpiece of nature; what was least admirable was to be a man of the world with the best figure and the handsomest face. What put him above everybody else was his incomparable gallantry and a charm of mind, face and action which nobody had ever seen except in him alone.)

> (Comte Anne d'Orgel was young; he had just become thirty. No one knew what had gone to the making of his great reputation, or at least his extraordinary position. His name played no great part in it because talent comes first even among those who are hypnotised by a name. But, as we must realize, his qualities were only those of race and his social talent.)

There is immense conviction behind Mme de La Fayette's "chef-d'oeuvre de la nature" and "valeur incomparable," which we do not find in the portrait of the count. Radiguet speaks of his "gloire," using the popular seventeenth-century term, feels at once that it will not do, changes it to "extraordinaire position," and concludes that it must be due to "ses qualités [qui] n'étaient que celles de sa race" and "talent mondain," which suggests nothing more than birth and the position that it gives him in smart society. The truth is that the old Europe has gone and that when applied to the count the famous seventeenth-century word reverberates hollowly in the void. A new word will be added which seems to echo it and at the same time undermines it. It is "frivolités."

Comte Anne d'Orgel is charming, but incorrigibly frivolous. His role is twofold. He is the husband in a triangular love affair, but he is also a symbolical figure. He is the usurper, the representative of the social class which has retained its privileges and its pride, but lost the functions which justified them. In this way he is the link between the personal and the social themes. The king and his court, which were the pivot of Mme de La Fayette's complicated hierarchy, have vanished. The royal tournaments and the court balls, where her characters distinguished themselves, have been replaced by the Médrano Circus, the *dancing* at Robinson, or the fancy-dress ball which is rehearsed but does not take place in the novel, in spite of its title.

The novel is constructed with the same skill as *Le diable au corps*. It begins with something like a psychological portrait of Mahaut. It goes on to look at the history of her family, which will help to explain the peculiarities of her psychology and reminds us of Radiguet's treatment of the prewar period in the first novel. Mahaut married Anne d'Orgel when she was eighteen. We learn, significantly, that "She fell madly in love with her husband who in return showed her great gratitude and the warmest friendship which he himself took for love." We are then told something about his family.

The Orgels' meeting with François, which takes place in the first chapter, introduces us to some of the minor characters who contribute to the picture of post-war society, but are naturally much more individualist than the minor characters in *Le diable au corps*. (pp. 279-86)

In the opening paragraph, we are told of Mahaut.

> Les mouvements d'un coeur comme celui de la comtesse d'Orgel sont-ils surannés? Un tel mélange du devoir et de la mollesse semblera peut-être de nos jours, incroyable, même chez une personne de race et une créole. Ne serait-ce plutôt que l'attention se détourne de la pureté sous prétexte qu'elle offre moins de saveur que le désordre?

> Mais les manoeuvres inconscientes d'une âme pure sont encore plus singulières que les combinaisons du vice. C'est ce que nous répondrons aux femmes, qui, les unes, trouveront Mme d'Orgel trop honnête, et les autres trop facile.

> (Are the movements of a heart like the Comtesse d'Orgel's old-fashioned? Such a mixture of a sense of duty and weakness will perhaps appear in these days to be unbelievable, even in a person of breeding and a Creole. Might this not be rather because attention turns away from purity on the same pretext that it offers less savour than irregularity?

> But the unconscious manoeuvres of a pure soul are still more unusual than combinations of vice. That will be our reply to women, some of whom will find Mme d'Orgel too virtuous and others too susceptible.)

"Surannés" is one of the focal words of the novel. The ambiguity is intentional. The novel sets out to explore certain feelings which to the present day appear old-fashioned, to analyse their composition and to see whether they are authentic. It is a characteristic of Radiguet's style that while the tone of the passage is necessarily ambiguous, the vocabulary is extremely precise. (pp. 286-87)

Altogether the two paragraphs form a plan in which the key words and phrases show the direction in which the novel will move and the way in which feelings will be explored. It can, as we shall see, be summed up by a phrase which is used in a different context near the end of the novel: "bizarreries du coeur" ["peculiarities of the heart"].

This takes us next to the analysis of François' attachment to Mahaut:

> L'amour venait de s'installer en lui à une profondeur où lui-même ne pouvait descendre. François de Séryeuse, comme beaucoup d'êtres très jeunes, était ainsi machiné qu'il ne percevait que ses sensations les plus vives, c'est-à-dire les plus grossières. Un désir mauvais l'eût autrement remué que la naissance de cet amour.
>
> C'est lorsqu'un mal entre en nous, que nous nous croyons en danger. Dès qu'il sera installé, nous pourrons faire bon ménage avec lui, voire même ne pas soupçonner sa présence. François ne pouvait se mentir plus longtemps, ni boucher ses oreilles à la rumeur qui montait. Il ne savait même pas s'il aimait Mme d'Orgel, et de quoi au juste il pouvait l'accuser; mais certes la responsable c'était elle, et personne d'autre.
>
> (Love had taken root in him at a depth to which he himself could not penetrate. François de Séryeuse like many other very young men was so constituted that he was only aware of his most vivid, that is to say, his coarsest sensations. An evil desire would have affected him very differently from the birth of his love.
>
> It is when an evil enters us that we imagine ourselves in danger, but as soon as it has taken root, we can settle down comfortably with it and without even suspecting its presence. François could not go on lying to himself any longer or close his ears to the rising sound. He did not even know whether he loved Mme d'Orgel, and of exactly what he could accuse her; but certainly she was the person responsible and nobody else.)

The interest of the passage lies in the skill with which the novelist shows us François' feelings functioning simultaneously at two different levels, described as "une profondeur où lui-même ne pouvait descendre" and "ses sensations . . . les plus grossières." The most complex word is "un désir mauvais." The birth of his love for Mahaut is not "evil" since he was not aware that he was in love, and we know that their "purity" will always prevent them from becoming lovers in the practical sense. The feeling, however, is "evil" in the sense that he has fallen in love with another man's wife. Although he still does not know whether he loves Mahaut, reminding us of the vacillations of the narrator in *Le diable au corps*, he feels that something is wrong and that it is she alone who is responsible. (pp. 287-88)

There has been a comparatively early breakdown, or partial breakdown, in François' resistance. The breakdown in Mahaut's comes a good deal later, but is complete and much more disturbing than François':

> Les mots ont une grande puissance. Mme d'Orgel s'était cru d'attribuer une prédilection pour François le sens qu'elle voulait. Ainsi avait-elle moins combattu un sentiment que la crainte de lui donner son véritable nom.
>
> Ayant jusqu'ici mené de front le devoir et l'amour, elle avait pu imaginer, dans sa pureté, que les sen-timents interdits sont sans douceur. Elle avait donc mal interprété le sien envers François, car il lui était doux. Aujourd'hui ce sentiment, couvé, nourri, grandi dans l'ombre, venait de se faire reconnaître.
>
> Mauhaut dut s'avouer qu'elle aimait François.
>
> (Words have great power. Mme d'Orgel believed herself free to interpret her predilection for François in the way she wanted. This meant that she struggled less against a feeling than the fear of giving it its true name.
>
> Up to this point by matching duty and love, she had imagined in her purity that forbidden feelings are without sweetness. She had therefore misinterpreted her own feeling for François because of its sweetness. Today a feeling which had been hatched, nourished and had grown up in the dark compelled recognition.
>
> Mahaut had to admit to herself that she was in love with François.)

It is another example of the complexity of the protagonists' minds, or what Radiguet calls in his first chapter "the unconscious manoeuvring of a pure soul." For Mahaut the confusion between word and thing, between "feeling" and "fear," leads us to the illusory balance of "duty" and "love," which is supported by a further misunderstanding. For it is Mahaut's own "purity" which prevents her from interpreting her feelings correctly and it is only at this late stage that she comes to realise that "forbidden feelings" are not necessarily disagreeable and gives them their "true name." What is clearly highly original is the way in which Radiguet shows the difference between real and imagined feelings. (pp. 290-91)

The dinner party at which the Comte d'Orgel and his friends plan, or rather rehearse, the fancy-dress ball is the climax and illustrates all Radiguet's gifts as a novelist:

> Hester Wayne, with a notebook on her lap, drew a picture of shapeless costumes. Hortense d'Austerlitz went in for improvisation on herself. She ransacked the drawing-room, used a lampshade as a hat, tried out the endless masquerades which aroused in Anne the profoundest passion of men of his class throughout the centuries: the passion for disguise.

"Disguise" is the focal word of the passage and underlines the novel's principal theme. Its meaning is twofold, or perhaps we should say manifold. It stands for the protagonists' unsuccessful attempts to "disguise" their real feelings from themselves, to make all feelings and all actions conform at least outwardly to the pattern imposed on the aristocratic society to which they belong. It is also an ironical reference to the opposite tendency which is found in some of the characters, including the count: the desire to escape temporarily from their official selves by putting on fancy dress and giving full rein to "frivolity," which is what happens at the dinner party, with some disturbing results.

The decisive event is the unexpected arrival of Prince Naroumov, an old friend of the count's and a Russian refugee who has lost everything in the Revolution. His arrival causes an immediate feeling of gloom. In a moment of aberration, or extreme "frivolity," the count puts on Naroumov's hat and does a few steps of a Russian dance:

> "Excuse me," Naroumov said. "That's my hat. It was given to me by some Austrian friends who had nothing else to offer."

A horrible chill paralysed the whole company. In the uproar they had forgotten the presence of Naroumov. He now assumed the aspect of a judge who was calling scoffers to order and reminding them of the respect due to misfortune.

Naroumov is another symbolic figure, a visitant from a country where an aristocratic society, which had lost its moral fibre and surrendered to "frivolity," had been swept away. He is clearly intended as a foil to the count, as a warning voice calling, or attempting to call, a supposedly doomed society back to seriousness and reality. Although he is a righteous man who has been ruined by the Revolution, his attitude remains profoundly charitable. He feels no bitterness towards the revolutionaries and has no sympathy for Hester Wayne, the American guest, when she says to him: "How you must loathe those Bolshevists."

When he says to himself, "War has made the whole world go mad," he is quietly pronouncing a verdict not merely on the society portrayed in the novel, but on the world to which they belong and reveals himself as a "judge calling the scoffers to order." (pp. 292-93)

Radiguet keeps the wife's confession to her husband, which corresponds in a way to the Princesse de Clèves' *aveu* to her husband, for the last pages. The results are very different. The Prince de Clèves dies of a broken heart, but in spite of this the Princesse de Clèves refuses to marry M. de Nemours and retires to a convent. The count is shaken, but promptly begins to close his eyes to what he has heard:

> "It's absurd. . . . We must look for a way of putting everything right."

His first move is paradoxical, but is characteristic of a man who has mysteriously been made to fall in love with his wife by another man's love for her before he comes to learn about it. He promptly says that François will be coming to the ball. He goes further and adds: "François must be with us when we make our entry into the ball. You shall choose a costume for him"—a particular engaging suggestion for the reader! (pp. 293-94)

It remains to add that though there has been no suggestion that *Le bal du comte d'Orgel* is in any way an unfinished novel, we cannot help speculating out of curiosity about what the protagonists' future would have been. We know that the Comte d'Orgel has belatedly fallen in love with his wife and we know that François and Mahaut would never have committed adultery. The assumption is that the husband and wife would have continued to live together with increased pleasure on the husband's part and probably less on the wife's part, while at most the relations between her and François would have turned into something like an *amitié amoureuse* ["loving friendship"] which might have continued if he had married somebody else. For only if the husband had died could the two chaste lovers have become husband and wife themselves. (p. 294)

When we look at Cocteau's contrast between "roots" and "flower" in Radiguet's two novels, we see that it is misleading. A careful reading shows that Radiguet's primary concern in both of them was with the "roots" of being, which makes them a pair. A novel about a violent and illicit love affair ending in tragedy is naturally disturbing. A novel about chaste lovers who do not give in is stimulating or, one might even say, uplifting, considering that most French novelists deal with falls. Our impression that in *Le bal du comte d'Orgel* we are looking at an elegant "flower" is naturally strengthened when

the chaste lovers are living in a society that, in spite of "frivolities," is remarkable for its grace and an absence of anything like the "tyrannical" impulses, which applies even more strongly to Radiguet's world than to Mme de La Fayette's. Our verdict must therefore be that the "phenomenon" or, I prefer to call him, the "infant prodigy," was the author of two of the outstanding psychological novels of his day, and it is sad to think that he was taken away from us at the age of twenty. (pp. 295-96)

> Martin Turnell, "Raymond Radiguet," in his The Rise of the French Novel: Marivaux, Crébillon fils, Rousseau, Stendhal, Flaubert, Alain-Fournier, Raymond Radiguet, *New Directions, 1978, pp. 257-96.*

JAMES P. McNAB (essay date 1984)

[*In the following excerpt, McNab provides an analysis of Radiguet's novels, finding in* The Devil in the Flesh *a convincing portrait of romantic love, while observing that* The Count's Ball *reflects the author's conservative political and aesthetic views.*]

The story told in *Devil in the Flesh* is simple and even banal. It describes the circumstances leading up to, in the course of, and following a love affair between the unnamed first-person narrator, who is a mere youth, and his mistress, Marthe. Marthe is three years older than he. She marries Jacques, a soldier at the front, whom she scarcely knows, and with whom she does not find happiness. The liaison is conducted in the Marne region, specifically in the *départements* of Seine, Seine and Marne, and Seine and Oise, as well as in Paris. The events described go from the narrator's childhood, when he is twelve, in March 1914, until a few months after the Armistice, around March 1919. The end of the war brings the end of the liaison, and also the death of Marthe in childbirth. The husband assumes that this son—fathered in fact by the narrator—is his own. The narrator, saddened but wiser, detects some pattern to life as he views Jacques:

> I wished to see the man to whom Marthe had pledged her troth.
>
> Holding my breath and walking on tiptoe, I made for the open door. I got there just in time to hear:
>
> "My wife died calling his name. Poor child! Isn't he my only reason for living?"
>
> Upon seeing the dignity of this widower, and how he mastered his grief, I understood that in the long run order takes care of things. Hadn't I just learned that Marthe had died calling my name, and that my son would have an orderly existence.

Radiguet himself expressed strong feelings of distaste for the nineteenth century and in particular for the realist movement. But there is about *Devil in the Flesh* an appearance of truth; it gives an impression of experience lived, of verisimilitude. It is true that the story provides little information about material circumstances such as income earned, clothes worn, height, weight, or appearance of the principal protagonists: in other words Radiguet does not present his characters in the detailed manner of a Stendhal or a Balzac, let alone a Zola. He appears to respect his own intention, which was to subordinate all of the material conditions of the tale to the treatment of love. In this respect, he returns to a tradition that goes back to the seventeenth century, but which has been followed by other later writers also, including talents as diverse as Laclos, Benjamin Constant, and Eugène Fromentin, whose works Radiguet knew. One must therefore ask, in the face of the remarkable paucity of detail—absolutely no description of how the narrator looks, no mention of his name and, similarly, very few details indeed about Marthe's appearance—what it is that gives this work such a ring of truth, such an air of authenticity.

There is, in the first place, a very effective and astute presentation of both space and time in *Devil in the Flesh* and these combine to thrust the reader into a three-dimensional world that successfully imitates reality. The names of places, all located in a well-defined, specific geographic area, press upon us. La Varenne, Chennevières, Ormesson, Sucy, Lagny, Meaux, Brunoy, Mandres all appear, then reappear or disappear, described briefly, but with just enough accuracy and telling appropriateness to give weight and credibility to the action. We learn, for example, that the narrator would go with his companions and play his mischievous games "upon the slopes of Chennevières." This may be the sketchiest of descriptions; but like all the others, it is accurate; Chennevières's most distinctive characteristic is that it does stand relatively high on a plateau, looking down upon the Marne. Elsewhere, the narrator expresses his dream of staying in Mandres, with Marthe, because it is a town where roses are grown, and, every night, a train leaves there, with a load of the flowers; this image had always fired his imagination. This may seem irrelevant. But it is not. It rings true, if one realizes that the full name of Mandres—never spelled out in *Devil in the Flesh*—is in fact Mandres-les-Roses. It is not of course in any single, brief description that Radiguet endows his narrative with a substantive, substantial background. It is rather in the accumulation of such brief notations that he provides what Stendhal called "little, true facts" forming a coherent and convincing overall picture. Even in the case of two towns the names of which are not given, Radiguet effectively gives an impression of authenticity. The two are identified simply as F . . . and J. . . . One obvious reason for their being presented only by initial letters is that Radiguet wishes to give the impression of protecting the identity of the two protagonists in this love story. The narrator lives in F . . ., while Marthe's home is in J. . . . In fact, however, if one really wishes to identify their real-life, geographic counterparts, they appear to exist: Parc Saint-Maur (F . . .) and Champigny (J . . .). A number of details given in the novel seem to indicate these two towns. They are two kilometers apart, there is a railway bridge at Champigny, and the military trains passed by there during the war.

Perhaps the single most effective technique used by Radiguet to reinforce the impression of verisimilitude is the constantly mentioned, ineluctable presence of the Marne, the river itself, acting as an effective counterpoint to the foreground events and action. We have the impression that it is always there, flowing gently, a kind of muted commentary. When the narrator witnesses a death and faints, his father takes him to the Marne to recover: ". . . he bore me off to the edge of the Marne. We remained there very late, in silence, lying in the grass." Here is the first mention of the narrator's hometown: "We lived in F . . . on the banks of the Marne" and of Marthe's house: "Marthe lived in J . . ., her street led down to the Marne." When he goes to her home, here is how he finds his way: "I followed the Marne," and one walk among many, taken alongside the river: "Around five, we went for a walk alongside the river." Even when the narrator imagines a hypothetical death-scene for his mistress, the river is part of it: "She would go to the edge of the Marne, catch cold, then die." There are many more examples. It is surely more than a coincidence, moreover, that the very consonance of the heroine's name—Marthe—is as close as a name can be to that of the river Marne and that both are close indeed to the word

"mater" or "maternal." Each is, in its way, an archetypal, maternal, soothing presence.

In combination with the identification of place, Radiguet's very specific naming of dates and hours and moments makes for a very convincing narrative. These are never obtrusive. Nonetheless, dates and numbers are presented with quite astonishing frequency throughout *Devil in the Flesh,* giving it a most impressive specificity. Again and again, we are reminded of the day, the month, the year, or the time of day. We are told the age of the narrator, or that of Marthe. But Radiguet is extremely clever in the way in which he presents this information. It is never allowed to dominate the narrative, so that the story might turn into a report or a chronicle. Instead, it emerges inconspicuously. For example, the narrator describes the events leading up to his first making love with Marthe. He compares himself and her to Daphnis and Chloé. He slips in some quite detailed information by way of describing a dressing-gown that she offers him, as a form of invitation to make love to her: "On the day of my sixteenth birthday, in the month of March 1918, begging me not to get angry, Marthe made me a present of a dressing-gown resembling her own, which she wanted to see me wear when I was with her."

It is of course possible to set Radiguet's own life and the events of *Devil in the Flesh* side by side, in order to see to what extent the latter follows the former. In fact with the major exception of the conclusion, where Marthe dies in the novel, but Radiguet's mistress did not in the "real world," the two follow largely parallel paths. Certainly Radiguet is disingenuous in alleging that *Devil in the Flesh,* avoiding the mood of "anxiety," which was so fashionable in this period, also should not be seen as an autobiography or confession:

> Will the reader be astonished to find in a book about adolescence none of that famous "anxiety" so in fashion in the last few years? But for the hero of *Devil in the Flesh* (who should not be confused with the author, notwithstanding the use of "I"), the interest is elsewhere. This interest arises more from the circumstances than from the hero himself. In the book, you see the freedom and idleness brought on by the war forming a young boy and killing a young woman. This little love-novel is not a confession, least of all when it most appears to be one. It is an all too human failing to believe only in the sincerity of someone who accuses himself; so, since the novel demands contrasts rarely to be found in life, it is natural that what is in fact a false autobiography should seem most true.

Most of the novel is, in point of fact, autobiographical. Ultimately, however, it is the quality of Radiguet's writing, and not just the quality of his experience, that has allowed the work to survive. It is as experience transformed and shaped into a self-sufficient, aesthetically satisfying narrative that *Devil in the Flesh* must be examined. It is in the context of literature, rather than that of life or raw experience that its most important qualities emerge.

In order to understand the fictional point of view given in the novel, one must listen carefully to its very first lines: "I am going to leave myself open to many reproaches. Yet what can I do about it? Is it my fault if I had my twelfth birthday a few months before the declaration of war." From the very beginning, the narrator makes it perfectly clear that his point of view will be that of a child, not an adult. Consequently, the war will mean something quite different for him from what it does for a grown-up person. One must then ask oneself just what the war did mean for him. It is described as "this extraordinary period" and as a "four-year summer holiday." Whereas for most people war is the most unavoidable and drastic reality, bringing death and suffering in its wake, it is; for the narrator, something totally different. It is, on the contrary, a removal of and from customary reality. It is a set of extraordinary circumstances rendering possible events that otherwise could not take place. To be sure the war as war does enter the picture: "We could hear the cannon. There was fighting close to Meaux. People were even saying that some Uhlans had been captured near Lagny, fifteen kilometers from home." There are a number of such descriptions. But war in this novel is important not as history, pressing down with all its weight upon the lives of the protagonists. On the contrary, it frees the narrator from normal constraints, liberates him into a world where his scope for action is greater than in time of peace, and is the agent by which the weight of real life and responsibility is removed from his shoulders. It causes the barriers to come tumbling down. The narrator compares himself to a cat, attentively watching a piece of cheese under a glass dome. In effect, the war broke the glass dome: "I never have been a dreamer. What seems dreamlike to others more credulous than myself struck me as being as real as is the cheese for the cat, in spite of that glass dome. And yet the dome does exist. With the breaking of the dome, the cat seizes the opportunity, even if it is the masters who break it and cut their hands on it." In other words this is the story not of "the masters who cut their hands"—the adults engaged in war—but of the cat and the forbidden cheese: the child given the opportunity to do something that is normally unattainable.

When times are extraordinary, as they are here, it becomes perfectly normal for extraordinary occurrences to take place. We know that these extraordinary happenings will be possible only for as long as the war lasts. They begin with it, and end with its conclusion. The time it covers is not that of normal experience for the boy—it abstracts him from normal reality—instead, time is perceived as a series of moments of heightened perception and deepened significance. The first such moment suggests the uncanniness, strangeness, and ultimate impermanence of the world the narrator is about to enter. For adults, the imminence of war is suggested by the Caillaux affair (Caillaux was accused of corresponding with the enemy) and the assassination of Archduke Franz Ferdinand in Sarajevo. But the narrator's perception is neither political or historic: it is, rather, personal. Standing on the threshold of a new life, separating a prosaic past from a poetic future, is a suicide he witnessed. On the eve of July 14, 1914, a neighbor's maid climbed on the roof of her employer's house. While the latter, a town councilor named Maréchaud, overcome by the ignominy of the situation, hid in his house, the maid hurled imprecations at the crowd below, which was torn between the temptation of the nearby fair and the spectacle of the maid on the roof. She remained there from two o'clock in the afternoon until late in the evening, defying all the efforts of the firemen to rescue her. Finally, quite insane but somehow satisfied by the performance she had given, she plunged to her death, before the horrified gaze of the narrator, looking on with his father. The boy fainted and was taken to the edge of the Marne to recover.

The incident of the maid's death is significant for a number of reasons. There is, in the first place, the intrusion of the extraordinary into the banal life of a quiet town. Throughout Radiguet's critical essays, there is a sense of the need to endow recent events with a character of mythology, and indeed to search out supernal reality in apparently trite circumstances.

This suicide is just an example of what Radiguet would call a mythical event, Joyce an epiphany, and Baudelaire a solemnity. Its profound significance might be hard to elucidate, but it is nonetheless real. In the words of the narrator: "If I insist upon such an episode, it is because it sheds light better than any other on that strange period of war, and shows how, more than the picturesque features of things, it was their poetry that impressed me." The maid, moreover, in uttering her incomprehensible words, is Cassandra-like, a figure of prophecy of dire events, whom nobody understands. Her very death, after a day of what might be called "entertainment," as she performed on the roof, is a "paradigm" for the narrator's perception of the war: four years of holidays, followed by a death—that of Marthe. Moreover this episode appears particularly appropriate as a model for many of the relationships presented in the novel. With the disappearance of paternal authority during the war, the men are at the front or, like the narrator's father, less strict than they would normally be, because of the circumstances: a world of freedom, but disorder and confusion are also allowed to develop. Maréchaud hides while his housemaid "performs" and then dies. Witchlike, she has prophesied a period of anarchy, a troubled time; like the witches of *Macbeth* announcing the start of an extraordinary period: "The charm's wound up," the maid sets the stage, prepares the reader for the unusual.

As though to enhance the extraordinary, uncanny, or mythical attributes of the incident involving Maréchaud and his maid, he is made into a grotesque figure, at home in a romance or a fairy tale. He is described as "a grotesque little man, a dwarf with a white goatee, wearing a hood." He is toadlike. And yet, as the elected officer of his fellow citizens, he represents and symbolizes his society. In fact, the relationship of the narrator to most figures of authority in this novel is an adversary relationship. We are confronted here, in a story ostensibly about life in the Marne in the course of World War I, with many echoes of traditional romance, going back to the tale of Tristan and Iseult. With the incident involving the suicide, *Devil in the Flesh* ceases to be simply a "confession" about a specific set of events in the Marne and becomes more than that; it is simultaneously a contemporary romance, whose time-frame is partly "July 14, 1914," etc., but also the "once upon a time" of a fairy tale or the *in ille tempore* of myth or legend. (pp. 74-81)

With *Devil in the Flesh,* Raymond Radiguet achieved a prodigious tour de force, a novel that is on the whole very successful at a time when novels were considered to be discredited. At the age of seventeen, he proved that the novel could still capture all the subtleties of a complex psychology in the twentieth century. Still more remarkable is the fact that, drawing upon the raw experience of his own life, he created a coherent work of art having much in common with medieval literary forms. To be sure, he must have examined other models with great care. One thinks in particular of Laclos's *Les liaisons dangereuses,* Fromentin's *Dominique,* and more particularly Benjamin Constant's *Adolphe;* the latter was reprinted twice in 1920, more than a hundred years after it first appeared, and appears to have been known to Radiguet. Certainly Radiguet seems to have profited from a close reading of the epistolary novel *Les liaisons dangereuses,* or of novels in which letters play an important part, such as *Adolphe.* Letters are used to extremely good effect in *Devil in the Flesh.* They are in no way obtrusive; but they are present throughout the narrative. A letter announces the marriage of Jacques and Marthe to the narrator. One month later, it is in a letter that Marthe urges him to come to see her and complains about his neglect of her.

Jacques writes to Marthe every day, and she tosses these letters into the fire, as she lies alongside the narrator. When Jacques writes disconsolately to say how easy it would be to die, it is the narrator who dictates to Marthe the tender letter she sends in reply! When Marthe's parents perceive that the narrator is writing to her, they burn his letters before her very eyes! And it is with a joyful letter that Marthe announces the birth of their son.

The letters in *Devil in the Flesh* serve several useful functions. In the first place, Jacques's frequent letters serve as a counterpoise to the love affair between the narrator and Marthe. Whereas they live in the present, his letters are a constant reminder that the past and the future do exist, that there is an outside world that must inevitably encroach upon them. In burning his letters, Marthe in effect banishes concerns other than her present love. But the narrator's unease or disquiet remains. He cannot forget that Jacques was there before him, and will no doubt be there again. They do indeed bring to life the possibility of this threat, with Jacques's writing to indicate that he will be brought back wounded from the front, and will be passing through the town of J. . . .

In addition, the letters in this novel underline a rather basic pessimism regarding human communication. At the beginning of their love affair, Marthe writes letters that are admirable; the text of these is not given at all. At this point a perfect harmony or symmetry is suggested in the relationship. In most cases, however, the letters reveal flawed communication of one sort or another. In almost every case, the letters bring out a fundamental asymmetry or disparity or distance between the writer and the recipient or addressee. Jacques sends tender letters that are burned. Those he receives are dictated by his wife's lover. When Marthe lies dying, the narrator begins an angry letter of insult that becomes a letter of apology. His letters are burned by Marthe's parents. Earlier, Marthe had justly accused him of betraying her with her friend Svea. But the narrator writes a deceitful letter that convinces Marthe her fears are unfounded, and this induces her to write to her landlady to announce that the narrator should be allowed to visit her apartment with anyone he wishes. The love shared by Marthe and the narrator briefly lifts them to a plane of existence where there is no need for formal communication, verbal or written. But, when letters are written, they more often than not involve deceit, misunderstanding, or disappointment.

From a strictly technical, narrative point of view, the letters do seem useful and even necessary. The danger of monotony in *Devil in the Flesh* is real but never realized. The point of view of the first-person narrator is of necessity limited. In effect, in beginning the affair with Marthe, he withdraws into a small world: a tiny cast of characters, a small stage, one main preoccupation, love. Thanks to the letters, other characters are brought into the action: Jacques especially, but also the parents of both protagonists, and the larger outside world are brought into focus and made to seem real.

The borrowings in *Devil in the Flesh* are relatively minor and the originality of the work is considerable. Radiguet denied himself the use of picturesque detail to hold the reader's attention; for example, we know nothing about the lovers' appearance, nothing about what becomes of the youth after his affair, not even his name! Nonetheless, he is complex: perverse and naive, he is endowed with life thanks to Radiguet's art. Similarly, we scarcely see Jacques Lacombe, except through Marthe, who is herself a shadowy or evanescent figure, or through the letters they exchange. But he too is brought to life

by the author. Finally, even the Marne, as river and region, is a real presence, and almost a "character" in *Devil in the Flesh*: both poetic and true to life, a suitable setting and an appropriate complement. (pp. 90-2)

[Although *Le bal du comte d'Orgel*], Radiguet's second novel, also tells the story of the burgeoning of an adulterous love affair, it is in fact quite different from the first, and indeed from any other novel of the time. (p. 93)

Written in the third person, not the first, *Count d'Orgel* takes place in the postwar Parisian world in 1920, presenting the essentially aristocratic company that is grouped around the Count d'Orgel and his wife, Mahaut, who is of a very distinguished noble house, the Grimoard de la Verberie. Having left France in the seventeenth century for Martinique, her family had come back at the turn of the twentieth, in 1902. Whereas the love affair in *Devil in the Flesh* completed a cycle that included the death and the birth of a child, that which is described in *Count d'Orgel* remains unconsummated, potential, virtual, and platonic. Radiguet may well have been following here the pattern established by the seventeenth-century novel *The Princess of Cleves*, by Mme de Lafayette, which was said to be a model for him. Be that as it may, the young François de Séryeuse, who is of noble origin also, falls in love with Mahaut and she with him. Toward the end of the work, each learns indirectly that this love is returned, but the actual ending of the story offers neither solution nor resolution. The Count d'Orgel, a somewhat fatuous figure as a rule, summons up authority when he learns of the love shared by François and Mahaut. He does not try to dismiss the man. Instead, he insists that François should still be among the guests at the count's forthcoming fancy dress ball, the "Ball" of the French title, and that the embarrassing situation must be patched over. The final words of the novel are his, to his wife: "And now, Mahaut, sleep. This I command." One can only speculate about further relations among the three, but it seems clear that they will be unhappy. There is no sense of that restoration of order or of an "orderly existence" to be found at the end of *Devil in the Flesh*. (pp. 93-4)

Within *Count d'Orgel* there are two time-frames, not one. The actual events take place over an eight-month period. It is too easy to ignore the fact that the characters' conduct in this period is very much conditioned and colored by the past: not just their own, but their ancestors', a historical past. This forms a second, essential time-frame. One critic, failing to perceive this, asserts that "the first pages of the novel, on the origin of the Grimoard (Mahaut's family) are hardly comprehensible and strike us as being without a real connection with the remainder of the narrative. Mahaut, as we see her, has nothing in common with the existentialist protagonist, self-created and free; instead, she is the latest in a line, the depository of traits that have been transmitted over hundreds of years. Her voice is that of her race, for example, as her husband's is that of his:

> Her speech had something harsh about it; graceful but stern, it appeared rough, masculine to the uninitiated. More than features, voice reveals race. The same kind of naiveté would have led people to think Anne's voice effeminate. His was a family voice, a voice that is still to be found in the theater.

The very differences that set her apart temperamentally from her husband are not individual differences, but ancestral; whereas she belongs to the feudal, landed aristocracy, he is the scion of a family that had always been at court. His perception of reality is limited to what happens in public; his greatest fear is of scandal, and there is in fact a world of difference between him and his wife: all the difference between Versailles (his natural habitat) and a medieval feudal castle (hers). As a result, her seriousness, like his frivolity, are inherited traits, shared by their respective families. It becomes clear, then, that the first pages of the novel are anything but irrelevant or extraneous. In fact, if one looks closely enough, it may be possible to predict an unhappy fate for Mahaut after the actual conclusion of the novel. One of her ancestors was Josephine. She, like Mahaut, had gone to France from Martinique. Her unhappiness in marriage (first with the Viscount Beauharnais, then with Napoleon) may well be construed as prefiguring Mahaut's own misfortune in love.

Mahaut is not the only character for whom the past shapes the present. The very first mention of Anne d'Orgel in the novel underlines not his appearance or "individuality," but his name, "a fairly good name in France." This sets the pattern of a man who inherits the past and displays it in his thoughts and deeds. He impresses those who come into contact with him, and this faculty stems from his race: "his qualities were just those of his race." The perfect courtier in a century without a king, Anne remains comfortable only when he is surrounded by people, in the artificial atmosphere that prevailed at court: "It was not a lack of heart, but Anne d'Orgel was at ease only in an artificial atmosphere, in the blinding light of a room full of people." Such a man brings to bear upon life a perspective unlike that of another. Like the courtier at Versailles in the seventeenth century, Anne considers conversation an art of the highest importance, at its best a "masterpiece." His childlike joy in preparing for the masked ball is no merely personal idiosyncrasy; the preparatory activities "awoke in Anne the most profound passion of the men of his class through the centuries: that of disguise." We come to realize that differences that have been centuries in the making open a huge gap in understanding between Anne and Mahaut. Her passion elicits no equivalent response in him. At first, she had fallen passionately in love with Anne. He is a stranger to intimacy, and it is only when he sees his wife with François, at a distance, as it were, or as "another" woman, that he comes to love her: "That day her husband had longed for her as though she were not his wife." At the end, Mahaut is appalled by her passion for François, for she fears its radical consequences, whereas Anne's concern is only to maintain appearances, to act as if nothing untoward had occurred.

It would not be extreme to assert that Radiguet, in *Count d'Orgel,* presents a race or class theory of psychology. He does so without solemnity, invokes no scientific theory to justify his point of view, and is extremely deft in his presentation of character. The portraits are more reminiscent of a seventeenth-century moralist such as La Bruyère—especially since Radiguet also makes much use of the maxim, a common classical device—than they are of sketches by Balzac, Taine, Zola, or any other "scientific" determinists. Nonetheless the author applies his theory or technique consistently across the board, to all of the characters. François, for example, is granted access to noble houses because of a certain family air of nobility. Neither he nor his hosts are consciously aware of this: but it exists. His mother, for her part, thinks that she behaves like a woman of the middle class. But her noble origins transpire in her deeds in spite of herself, *noblesse oblige:* "Associating only with them, Mme de Séryeuse finally adopted the prejudices of the old bourgeoisie against the aristocracy without realizing that she was condemning her own people. Nonetheless she was forever acting in a way that revealed her breeding.

Among the relatively minor characters also, ancestry will out. Princess Hortense d'Austerlitz owes her gusto and common touch to her family antecedents: she was of recent nobility, that created by Napoleon, while earlier her family had been butchers. The Persian prince, Mirza, reveals his race involuntarily: "His race would emerge when one least expected it." Similarly, although Naroumov's sensitivity is shaped by the suffering he has known, it is also a product of his origins.

The least sympathetic portrayals in the novel are reserved for the two commoners, Paul Robin and Hester Wayne. Whereas all of the others are very much "children" of the *ancien régime*—prerevolutionary times—these two are not provided with a substantial past. Paul is a product of the nineteenth century and, claims the narrator, more's the pity. A rather ridiculous descendant of Rastignac or of Julien Sorel, Paul is a social climber, eager to succeed, to see and be seen: "Unburdened of all that foolish literature, a production of the nineteenth century, how charming he might have been." We know nothing of Hester Wayne's childhood or parents, let alone her more distant ancestry. She is repeatedly described as the "American woman." She is a shrill, vulgar seductress, a negative counterpoint to Mahaut's purity. She is thought beautiful by her contemporaries, but the narrator considers this assessment to be flawed, a misperception. By implication, the aesthetic standards of the time—1920—are not to be trusted. A truer beauty is that of François's mother, who at thirty-seven "looked like French women of the sixteenth century." In a vulgar age, however, it is Hester Wayne and not Mme de Séryeuse who is found attractive by the majority.

Underlying Radiguet's character portrayal is a rather deep pessimism, which shows itself in a number of ways. The very element of fatality implied by the weight of the past upon the present is in itself pessimistic. Radiguet's characters, laden with their ancestry, are far from being free agents. Throughout the novel, there is a pattern of unhappiness, especially in marriage. Indeed, there is in *Count d'Orgel* no example of a long, lasting, loving marital relationship. Some of the marital misfortunes stretch the reader's credulity. For example, not only is the Persian prince Mirza a widower, but even his fifteen-year-old niece has been widowed.

The world in miniature represented by the Count d'Orgel and his entourage, noble, elitist conservators of the past, is shown to be threatened and vulnerable in the novel. Naroumov is the best illustration of the ruin that threatens. He loses everything in the Boshevik Revolution and now cuts a pathetic if moving figure. Much earlier, the French Revolution had led to Napoleon and the sudden elevation of thousands of commoners to the nobility: "This outlandish masquerade, when people changed names as readily as one puts on a false nose, wounded them." On the very edge of this society, threatening to encroach still further upon it and eventually to cause it to disappear, is the larger, leveling society of the people. It is presented strikingly when the count and his friends, heading out of Paris for the Robinson dancing establishment, are obliged to stop at the porte d'Orléans when a car breaks down. A crowd is lined up outside: "A procession of cars was waiting to start up again. . . . The gaping people who made up this impudent line pressed their noses against the windows of the vehicles, so as to take a better look at their owners. The women pretended to find this ordeal charming." While there is no real danger in this encounter, it is one of several episodes showing the huge gap between the classes.

When set alongside let us say *The Conquerors* (1928), by André Malraux, *Count d'Orgel* strikes us as an extraordinarily reactionary novel. Malraux's characters come to life in or date from the turbulence of the historical present: "A general strike is ordered in Canton." How far is Radiguet from this conception! His characters are antihistorical and anachronistic. They, petrified in the present, are heirs to the past; indeed, they are little more than filters or foci through which the past is allowed to seep. In a sense, the action is reaction, for it is a denial of the present and of history since the French Revolution. The diachronic sequence—the eight months of the foreground action—is accompanied by the indispensable, synchronic, and analeptic weight of the past. Each character is an heir, drawing consciously or unwittingly, for good or ill, upon the tradition he or she embodies.

Radiguet wrote *Count d'Orgel* when he was in contact with a number of partisans of the extreme right-wing movement known as *Action Française,* and the conclusion appears inescapable that such intercourse helped shape the values that underpin his novel.

Count d'Orgel is by no means obtrusively ideological. The fiction carries its ideas and values, or is borne by them, gracefully. The philosophical statement does not stand out as ungainly excrescence or awkward digression, as it does in some of the novels of the Goncourt brothers, or even certain works by Sartre, for example. Instead, it is assimilated into the work, to be an implicit part of it. In its major features, however, it is a more subtle, less forthright echo of much of the conservative doctrine enunciated by Charles Maurras, the leading figure of the very influential *Action Française.*

In part, Maurras's profound antipathy toward revolution, and the French Revolution especially, was based upon his complete devotion to the past. Whereas the revolutionary wished to eradicate the past, in order to start anew, Maurras repeatedly voiced his ardent desire to revalidate the prerevolutionary past, and not repudiate it. Repeatedly he underlined the fact that man is an heir and exhorted his fellow countrymen not to forget the past: "Do not forget: that is the point of departure of all order and of all law." By the same token, he loathed the "revolutionary Beast," which brought anarchy in its tracks. Maurras believed strongly in immutable essences, immutable nature, and in particular in unchanging, essential human nature. In social terms, this expressed itself in an advocacy of rank and hierarchy, and a belief in the hereditary aristocracy. Authority, in Maurras's words, "is born." The quality of the leading class was grounded specifically in its rank; so, he wished above all to reintroduce and enforce this rank and hierarchy. Maurras was very distrustful of the nineteenth century and its ideals, from democracy to competitiveness and ambition. He was equally distrustful of foreign influences, be they American, German, or Jewish.

While Radiguet does not go so far as to advocate the return of the monarchy—as Maurras does—and does not show the same antipathy toward foreigners—and Germans in particular—as Maurras, his characters in *Count d'Orgel* embody many of Maurras's principal ideas. Their lives are colored, shaped, and conditioned by those of their forebears, to whom an indelible, straight line connects them. Radiguet's commitment, like that of Maurras, is to an essentialist psychology: that is, his characters' essence is very real and precedes their existence. Radiguet is as far from existentialism as possible. Similarly, he is as far removed as possible from a Balzac or a Stendhal. His characters have nothing in common with the strenuous, striving, struggling, and scheming end-oriented activities of a Vautrin, a Julien Sorel, or a Rastignac, viewing Paris as a possible booty. The two exceptions in *Count d'Orgel,* Paul Robin and Hester Wayne, who are deprived of a past, are condemned to be free in a different sense from that proposed by Sartre. They do not achieve lucidity and dignity accompanied by anguish; on the contrary, lacking tradition and lineage as a guide, heirs to no long and legitimate tradition, they are misguided, arbitrary, and simply wrong in their values, opinions, and judgments.

Within the context of Radiguet's apparent conservatism, his assessment of the novel of love as "profoundly, gravely frivolous" is more than a superficial *boutade.* Applying himself to the analysis of feelings, and not external events, success, or ambition, he gives his characters the opportunity to reveal these feelings. By our contemporary standards of goal-setting, the pursuit of material well-being, and the striving after power or success, the activities in which the Count d'Orgel and his companions indulge are frivolous, of little consequence or importance. But, insofar as these characters escape these contemporary standards and hark back to a much earlier period, their activities are appropriate to them, reveal them in their essence, and are, accordingly, important. This "frivolity" is a less structured, more informal, but equally revealing equivalent of the ball: the paradigm of the life led by an exclusive group whose roots are in the customs of the *ancien régime.* (pp. 103-09)

James P. McNab, in his Raymond Radiguet, *Twayne Publishers, 1984, 169 p.*

LEON S. ROUDIEZ (essay date 1985)

[*Roudiez is an American critic and educator whose special area of study is modern French fiction. In the following excerpt, he employs a Freudian approach in an analysis of* The Devil in the Flesh.]

"It behoveth us live merrily, nor hath any other occasion caused us flee from yonder miseries." Those words, found in the First Day of Boccaccio's *Decameron,* are echoed by the "quatre ans de grandes vacances" caused by the war, as stated at the end of the first paragraph in *Le diable au corps.* Radiguet's phrase gave currency to the traditional reading of the novel, a perfectly plausible one (especially to the extent that "plausible" implies conformity with dominant ideology). Henri Peyre summed up such a reading felicitously when he characterized the fiction as "the definitive portrayal of the adolescent in wartime, rushed into manhood and unequal to the emotional demands and responsibilities thrust upon him." I do not wish to push the analogy with the *Decameron* any further: it does serve to remove the First World War from Radiguet's novel as a specific historical referent while maintaining it as an awesome presence of death, a catalyst for eroticism, even though that presence is first concentrated in one character, Jacques, before engulfing another, Marthe. Freud, writing at the time of the same war, said that it laid bare the primal man in each of us. The words may seem too strong in the present context, but the war did lay bare an adolescent's eroticism and its attendant cruelty.

Both are implicitly present in the image that is stated twice at the narrative's outset: the cat and the bell jar. It is an ambivalent image, like almost everything else in the novel. On a first level it is somewhat obvious and unproductive. As the adults have broken the jar and hurt themselves in so doing, the cat, that is, the narrator and other adolescents, are free to enjoy things that are normally forbidden. That gives a particular emphasis to the notion of "grandes vacances," but nothing more. The jar, however, is a container and, in Freudian symbolism, may represent the female organ; the breaking of the jar would correspond to the tearing of the hymen, but no blood is mentioned because the narrator is not responsible—Marthe is no longer a virgin when he sleeps with her. Cats have traditionally been associated with darkness, sensuality, and death. Thus, on that second level, the image becomes much more pertinent to the narration. It is Jacques who has broken the jar, and his being a soldier in wartime links him with death. The narrator is both resentful and grateful; grateful because both Jacques's act and the state of war have made possible the affair with Marthe, resentful because he knows he would not have had the courage to do it himself (one will recall how little initiative he displays in his dealings with Marthe and her own reproachful gift of a dressing gown, which he recognizes as a *praetexta*—her reproach for his wishing "rien d'autre que ces fiançailles éternelles" ["nothing other than this eternal betrothal"]).

As I proceed beyond the introductory pages, I am struck by several particularities of the text. First, there is a chronological imbalance that appears to invalidate the initial image. The "grandes vacances," inspite of what the narrator says, were not caused by the war, for one year before its start he had begun a series of "fausses vacances," the period during which he does not go to the *lycée*. Then, when he begins commuting to Paris with his friend René in order to attend classes at Henri-IV he notes simply, "Trois ans se passèrent ainsi" ("Three years passed in this manner")—and reveals no significant instance of misconduct. He does have semi-innocent fun (which he calls *polissonnerie*) with girls of his age and class, but no war was ever necessary for that. Nor is it the war that disrupts the narrator's family life; the father is not drafted, there is no mention of any relative being killed or wounded. The irregularities or disruptions in his studies are also independent of the war. Actually, the main narrative begins in April, 1917, when he meets Marthe Grangier, and is brought to a conclusion early in 1919 with the death of Marthe. My second-level reading of the bell jar metaphor, emphasizing sexuality and death, is thus congruent with the stress laid on this aspect of the narrative.

The second particularity I notice is the symmetrical articulation of the text. There is, for instance, the incident of the schoolboy, the narrator, who sends a letter to a little girl in another class only to have it intercepted by her parents, and the ensuing embarrassment to nimself and others. Toward the end of the novel, his letters to Marthe are intercepted by her parents, and when he is summoned by her mother he again feels like a schoolboy. The day he spends with Marthe in Paris choosing the furnishings that will fill the apartment (and especially the bedroom) where she is to live—the sexual symbolism of which is similar to that of the bell jar and constitutes a positive event from that point of view (he fills the female matrix with his own substance, making her refuse Jacques's)—is echoed by their trip to Paris in search of a hotel room, a sexual quest that is no longer symbolic, a search that ends in failure and a premonition of death. A different kind of symbolism becomes apparent when one adds to the Freudian equivalence between room and woman the more traditional interpretation: as an enclosure, the room may be viewed as sacred space, here that of marriage, from which he is barred on account of Jacques's presence. There are other such correspondences, usually antithetical (thus redoubling the imbalance I previously noted), such as the scandal provoked by thc Maréchaud's maid as opposed to the Marin's failure to provide their guests with the

one they promised. Emblematic of such oppositions is the contrast between a very early statement, "les troubles qui me vinrent de cette période extraordinaire" ("The disorders that arose from this extraordinary time"), and the one that appears in the last paragraph of the novel "l'ordre, à la longue, se met de lui-même autour des choses" ("order, in the long run, arranges things"). I shall now move on to a third category of phenomena that are basically of a textual nature, for they will help put everything else into sharper focus.

What dominates the novel textually is the presence of the letter "m" and the set constituted by the letters "m" plus a vowel plus "r." In other words, as the narrative proceeds, it finds itself coming more and more under the spell of the phrase, "Marthe la morte" (even though it is not literally present in the novel). While the narrator is first motivated by erotic desire, it is gradually death that he wishes for the woman he loves, death and oblivion: "Oui, c'est bien le néant que je désirais pour Marthe...." ("Yes, it was really nothingness that I wished for Marthe"). It should also be remembered that when he first meets Marthe, during an outing with his and her parents, they walk along a small river called Morbras, the first syllable of which sounds exactly like the French word for death. When Marthe leaves to spend some time in Granville, the association between absence and death is stronger than one would normally expect. As Marthe asks the narrator to go to her apartment he says he is reminded of his aunt asking him to visit the tomb of his grandmother. The next paragraph continues to link dead person and absent mistress, Marthe's bedroom and cemetery.

Marthe, however, is not simply the stereotyped "woman he loves." Etymologically, the name can be traced back to an Aramaic word meaning lady or mistress, and this leads me to suggest that Marthe really represents Woman rather than *a* woman. Incidentally, this concern for the meaning of proper names is justified by Radiguet himself when, on the occasion of the incident I mentioned above, the narrator asks a classmate named Messager to convey a letter to the girl he had become interested in. He says he did not pick him on account of his name, but Radiguet chose (or maintained) that name just the same. One should also note that Marthe's name has four letters in common with that of the river Marne and especially that the first three are identical. The narrative involving Marthe is clearly set against the background of the Marne. After she marries she goes to live close to the river; when the narrator goes to spend his first night with her, he follows the bank of the river. Earlier, when he would go to read books in his father's rowboat, he was too scared to take it away from its mooring, and now when he goes boating with Marthe it is she who does the rowing thus suggesting that the river is her domain. The narrative also includes an indication that the two words function in similar fashion. When the narrator first mentions the Marne he points out that his sisters, when referring to the Seine river, call it "une Marne" because it is a word meaning river rather than the name of *a* river. In similar fashion, later in the novel, Marthe's spinster sister-in-law refers to "une Marthe." The link between Marthe and Marne allows me to take one step further thanks to the symbolic association between water and mother: to the narrator Marthe is not only Woman but also Mother. In the context of *Le diable au corps'* narrative this is reinforced by the meaning of the noun "marne," which corresponds to the English "marl," a mixture of clay and calcium carbonate used to fertilize certain types of soil. Furthermore, the connection is made in the narrative itself; the night of their first intercourse, as the narrator arrives soaking wet because of the rain and Marthe urges him to take off his wet clothes so as not to catch cold, he notes, "ce déshabillage prenait un sens maternel" ("this undressing took on a maternal meaning"). After they make love he sees her transfigured and is surprised that her face is not surrounded with a halo "comme dans les tableaux religieux" ("as in religious paintings")—for one second, she is the Holy Mother. When they eventually realize that she has become pregnant the narrator makes an explicit identification: "Hélas! Marthe n'était plus ma maîtresse mais une mère" ("Alas! Marthe was no longer my mistress, but a mother"). The shift is symbolically completed at the end of the novel after the baby is born and turns out to be a boy—Marthe gives it the narrator's name. It is the name she calls out when she dies; one cannot be sure whom she calls, son or lover, and it does not really matter. It seems hardly necessary to point out that the French word for "mother" shares the same initial pattern as the word for death and the name of Marthe and the river Marne: "m" plus vowel plus "r."

Consciously or not, Radiguet inscribed the same pattern quite frequently into the novel's text. The council whose maid goes berserk is named Maréchaud; the one who lives under Marthe's apartment is Marin. The first time the narrator sees Marthe she is standing on a *marchepied* on the train bringing her to La Varenne. When they part he says he will come to see her the following Thursday and lend her a couple of books, but he cannot bear to wait that long and on Tuesday (*mardi*) he takes the books to her. His birthday comes in March (*mars*) and during that same month he and Marthe first make love together; their child, prematurely born the following January, was due in March. Early in their love-making she asks him to brand her (*marquer*) and when she is pregnant he remarks that he has done so, but in the worst possible way. My point in noting these occurrences is to suggest a kind of obsession, on the part of the writing subject, with that syllable on account of the stress it lays on the notions of Woman, Mother, and Death. In similar fashion, the reader's attention is, through the repetition of that syllable, drawn to the connections I have been making. Whether or not a reader actually make the connections depends on the attentiveness of his or her reading as well as sensitivity to textual matters.

I shall now examine several incidents or statements in *Le diable au corps* in the light of the foregoing observations. First, there is the story of the Maréchaud's maid, which the narrator calls his first memory of the war, although it took place on the eve of July 14th, 1914, couple of weeks before the war actually started. He relates it after he has alluded to the war's beginning and told of minor events in the family occurring toward the end of August: the chronological imbalance is thus compounded. The incident can be read as apparently intended, a poetic transposition of the strangeness and horror that characterize times of war. It is nevertheless more pertinent to the major narrative line, the story of Marthe, of which it is almost a mise-en-abyme. It is centered on a young woman, apparently gone mad, who cavorts on the roof of her employers' house, thus causing a public scandal that the latter try to ignore. Likewise, the public display by Marthe of her affection for the narrator on a Sunday afternoon shocks those who know her ("Ils durent y voir une fanfaronnade" ["They must have thought I was boasting"] he says), and eventually the ultimate scandal, Marthe giving birth to the narrator's child, will be hushed up by her family and their doctor. The voice of the woman on the roof is described as inhuman, throaty, exceedingly soft, and later when the narrator, out of prudence, refrains for a while from spending the night with Marthe he is relieved at not having

to hear a comedian's angelic voice, who seems "chaque matin sortir de l'audelà" ("each morning to come from the beyond"). The scandal caused by the Maréchaud's maid is highlighted by activities connected with France's national holiday, and that caused by Marthe's behavior is made worse because her husband is in the army in time of war. Most importantly, the incident suggests the stereotyped association between women and madness (the narrator says his mother "me voyait perdu par une folle" ["thought me corrupted by a madwoman"]) and the narrator watches her as if under a spell. After she finally jumps off the roof he falls in a faint just as he will experience what he calls a syncope after the death of Marthe. Going back home with his father he imagines seeing the ghost of the maid; it is only Maréchaud himself, in his night dress, "contemplant les dégâts, sa marquise, ses tuiles, ses pelouses, ses massifs, ses marches couvertes de sang, son prestige détruit" ("contemplating the damage, his marquee, his tiles, his lawn, his flower beds, his steps covered with blood, his demolished prestige"). That will also be the narrator's unstated condition at the end or, rather, that is what he surveys as he writes his version of the story: the crumbling of his adolescence at the hands of Marthe.

The Maréchaud episode introduces another couple, a nameless one. They are political opponents who attempt to capitalize on the Maréchauds' plight. She makes a hypocritical speech, quoted in full, and the people assembled to watch the spectacle are not impressed. Moments later the husband makes his speech, which is not quoted, and the people applaud. This is typical of the difference in treatment accorded men and women throughout the book. In addition, the other women involved are mothers.

In the early pages of *Le diable au corps* the narrator mentions both his parents in seemingly objective fashion, but closeness to his father is emphasized. On the Sunday of the meeting with Marthe, both families are included. His own mother, however, is unaccountably absent: she has been erased from the text. Of Marthe's mother, he says that she disliked her at once; the father, on the other hand, seemed "un brave homme" ("a fine man"). The narrator's first statement to Marthe, intended as a gallantry, is: "Vous ressemblez peu à madame votre mère ("You don't resemble your mother"). After his liaison with Marthe has been consummated, he notes the difference in his parents' attitude: the father not only tolerates the situation, he seems inwardly pleased, while the mother is both jealous of Marthe whom she consequently dislikes and worried about what people will say. When Jacques comes home on leave and Marthe behaves strangely, her mother decides to take her back. She refuses to have a bed set up for Jacques in her room. Her father thinks her attitude absurd and her mother points out to him and to her son-in-law "qu'ils ne comprenaient rien à la délicatesse féminine" "that they understood nothing of feminine delicacy"). Irony readily comes through such a seemingly objective account, for both narrator and reader know there is no delicacy involved but a growing dislike for Jacques as a result of her passion for the narrator. The result is to downgrade the notion of "feminine delicacy" and Madame Grangier as well. In subsequent episodes of the narrative she is treated in similar fashion: she eventually discovers the truth but says nothing for fear of magnifying the scandal. She stupidly harrasses her daughter, at the same time secretly admiring her for having done what she herself had never dared. Like Marthe's father, Jacques's is termed a "brave homme." His mother, like "toutes les mères," disapproves of her daughter-in-law. In the last pages of the book, the narrator alludes to the distance that separates him from his mother. As he collapses, she takes over: "Les yeux secs, elle me soigna froidement, tendrement, comme s'il se fût agi d'une scarlatine" ("With dry eyes, she nursed me, coldly, tenderly, as if it were a case of scarlet fever"). In other words, she did her duty and she did it in a way that bespeaks authority and competence.

He is, on the contrary, very close to his father. The latter is clear-sighted, not easily fooled. He is indulgent to the point of encouraging his son's whims. His displays of severity are followed by forgiveness, and he tends to let his son do whatever he wishes. When things appear to be getting out of hand, he threatens to have Marthe prosecuted for abducting a minor, but he of course does nothing. Earlier, when he decides to remove his son from school, it is his wife who notifies the principal and chooses the time for doing it. The father is obviously lacking in authority. The observations he makes to his son are sad, while his wife's remarks are sarcastic. He is weak, but his son understands him—undoubtedly a "brave homme" like the others.

In short, the men, including Jacques (who is just an unfortunate victim) are treated more sympathetically in the narrative of *Le diable au corps* than the women, especially when the latter are mothers. And Marthe who is both, actually and symbolically, is treated worst of all. Where love is concerned the narrator is ambiguous or even contradictory. On a number of occasions he speaks of his love for Marthe, but he also says that it weakened in the presence of the slightest obstacle and is seized with panic at the thought that Jacques might allow himself to be killed. He admits that what seemed like a display of passion to Marthe, when he kissed her as she was rowing the boat, was "surtout la manie de déranger" ("above all the need to disturb"); he recognizes that his attitude is that of a libertine and compares his voluptuousness to the behavior of a drug addict. Actually, his problem is that he cannot stop thinking of himself; he does get at the contents of the bell jar, and self-gratification is his overriding aim.

The narrative of the day on which Marthe enters the picture is vaguely reminiscent of Stendhal's account of Madame de Reynal, as the object of Julien Sorel's first advances, but the narrator lacks Sorel's purposefulness. And as the beginning of the novel clearly indicates, his adolescent eroticism had already been aroused before his meeting Marthe; she intensifies it by providing a willing and then a loving object. The narrator deludes himself in calling his own feeling love. Radiguet in turn might well have suffered from the same delusion, for he referred to *Le diable au corps* as "ce drame de l'avant-saison de l'amour" ("this drama of the beginning of love") thus allowing both the conventional reading and the present one. One might say, if one were dealing with actual persons, that the narrator's ego drive is too strong, and this would account for the presence of the death drive to which I also alluded. One will recall that when he thinks Jacques has returned unexpectedly, he hopes the outraged husband will kill both Marthe and himself. I have already pointed to a weakness in his sexual drive; there is something about the Mother that disturbs him and affects his emotional relationship with Woman. Add a weak father who fails to exert his authority, and one understands the narrator's statement, "Sans doute sommes-nous tous des Narcisse" ("Undoubtedly we are all Narcissus"). As Julia Kristeva recently put it, "N'est-il pas vrai que la narcissique, tel quel, est précisément quelqu'un incapable d'amour?" ("Isn't the narcissist, precisely, someone who is incapable of love?"). Radiguet's narrator practices eroticism, but he cannot find an object of love outside of himself. Hence his unwitting cruelty.

In conclusion, my revisiting *Le diable au corps* has convinced me that, rather than a classical narrative endowed with universal value, it is a very particular text that wrestles with the consequences of the narrator's poorly resolved Oedipus complex. As to the connection between Radiguet and the narrator, since I have neither the space nor the competence to analyze that relationship in any adequate fashion, I shall leave it to psychoanalysts to probe such a complex matter: they need only follow the trail that Radiguet has blazed for them. (pp. 251-59)

> Leon S. Roudiez, "Radiguet Revisited," in Studies in Twentieth Century Literature, *Vol. 9, No. 2, Spring, 1985, pp. 251-60.*

ADDITIONAL BIBLIOGRAPHY

Cantwell, Robert. "Polishing Our Bicycles." *New Republic* LXX, No. 905 (6 April 1932): 214-15.
    Discusses Radiguet's technique of juxtaposing his characters' immature moral dilemmas with larger, more important conflicts.

Cocteau, Jean. "Raymond Radiguet." In his *Professional Secrets*, pp. 94-9. New York: Farrar, Straus, and Giroux, 1970.
    Anecdotal account of Cocteau's five-year relationship with Radiguet.

Crosland, Margaret. *Raymond Radiguet: A Biographical Study with Selections from His Work*. London: Owen, 1976, 153 p.
    Combines biographical data drawn from French sources with excerpts of Radiguet's unpublished texts.

Huxley, Aldous. Introduction to *The Devil in the Flesh*, by Raymond Radiguet, pp. v-vii. New York: H. Smith, 1932.
    Comments on the rarity of Radiguet's precocious literary talent, noting that *The Devil in the Flesh* "is a good book, when one remembers the author's age, extraordinary in being so mature, so finished, so complete. . . . Radiguet set out in possession of those literary virtues with which most writers painfully end."

"Precocious Lovers." *New York Times Book Review* (6 March 1932): 18.
    Review of *The Devil in the Flesh* in which the critic asserts that "although some of the praise which [Radiguet] has drawn may be attributed to faddism and to the gaping wonderment we always accord to infant genius, there is no doubt that this 'marvelous boy' had gained, before he died, a remarkable intuitive knowledge of human emotions and a still more remarkable style."

Niess, Robert J. "Some 'Mal Mariées' of the Early Twentieth Century." *Kentucky Romance Quarterly*, No. 2 (1978): 205-12.
    Includes Marthe of *The Devil in the Flesh* in a discussion of ill-treated women in early-twentieth-century French novels.

Raymond, John. "New Novels." *New Statesman and Nation* XLIV, No. 118 (9 August 1952): 167.
    Review of *Count d'Orgel Opens the Ball* in which Raymond judges the novel one of the best love stories ever written.

Redman, Ben Ray. "The Youngest Classic." *New York Herald Tribune Books* 8, No. 27 (13 March 1932): 2.
    Review of *The Devil in the Flesh*. Redman concludes: "the born artist has sternly shaped the stuff of adolescence into pure literature."

Robinson, Christopher. "The Cult of Youth." In his *French Literature in the Twentieth Century*, pp. 82-108. London: David & Charles, 1980.
    Discusses Radiguet's novels in the context of the proliferation of adolescent-oriented literature during the period from 1890 to 1930.

Steegmuller, Francis. "Inventing the Twenties." In his *Cocteau*, pp. 217-317. Boston: Little, Brown, and Co., 1970.
    Extensive discussion of Radiguet's involvement with Cocteau.

Jānis Rainis

1865-1929

(Pseudonym of Jānis Pliekšans) Latvian poet and dramatist.

Important both as a political activist and as a writer, Rainis was the most prominent figure in Latvian literature during the first three decades of the twentieth century. His poetry and dramas were strongly nationalistic, combining Latvian folklore and history with advocacy of Latvian independence from Russian and German domination. As a translator of works from twenty-two languages into Latvian, Rainis is credited with elevating Latvian literature by introducing to his compatriots the more mature literatures of Europe. Described by Zenta Maurina as "a living synthesis between East and West," Rainis is one of the few Latvian authors to earn an international reputation.

The son of an estate overseer, Rainis was born in 1865. After completing his primary and secondary education in Latvia, he attended the University of St. Petersburg, graduating with a degree in law. He began his literary career in 1891 as editor of the influential political newspaper *Dienas lapa,* in which he promoted social reform and Latvian independence from Russian rule. A member of the liberal political movement New Current, Rainis was arrested in 1897 for his political activities and was exiled for six years, first to Pskov, then to Slobodsk. While in exile he wrote poetry and completed a translation of Johann Wolfgang von Goethe's *Faust.* His first published poetry collections—*Tālas noskaņas zilā vakarā* (1903) and *Vētras sēja* (1905)—gained him a critical reputation as Latvia's preeminent lyric poet and won him a large popular following for their passionate protests against oppression. After the 1905 Revolution, Rainis was forced to flee Latvia to avoid political persecution. He spent the next fourteen years in Switzerland, where he wrote his most important works. In 1918 Latvia was proclaimed an independent state, and Rainis returned to his homeland. For the rest of his life he continued to write while holding prominent positions in the Social Democratic Party and national government, including those of member of parliament and minister of education. Rainis also helped found the Riga Art Theater in 1920, and he served as director of the Latvian National Theater from 1921 to 1925. He died in 1929.

Rainis's work was primarily didactic in intent. As he wrote: "A great work must be done: to bring light to our brothers, to lead the nation toward a brighter, happier future. . . . The highest goal [is] development of the nation." Throughout his career, Rainis wrote poetry celebrating his homeland and advocating political action. While *Tālas noskaņas zilā vakarā* and *Vētras sēja* were written to inspire the struggle for national liberation, *Tie, kas neaizmirst* commemorated the participants in the failed 1905 revolution and *Sveika, brīvā Latvija!* hailed the attainment of Latvian independence. In other collections, such as *Gals un sākums,* Rainis treated personal and philosophical themes, including loneliness, the bitterness of exile, the place of the individual in society, the relationship of humanity to nature, and human destiny.

In addition to poetry, Rainis was the author of fifteen dramas, most of which are written in blank verse. Many are based on episodes from Latvian history, such as *Rīgas, ragana,* which

Courtesy of Rolfs Ekmanis

describes the attack on the city of Riga by Peter the Great in 1710. Others draw on subjects from Latvian folklore, including the highly regarded *Uguns un nakts* (*Fire and Night*). Recounting a battle between the legendary Latvian hero Bearslayer and the evil Black Knight, *Fire and Night,* in the words of Emma S. Richards, calls for "spiritual regeneration by means of the eternal struggle between the primordial forces of good and evil." Rainis's *Jāzeps un viņa brāļi* (*The Sons of Jacob*), is generally considered his best play. Based on the biblical story of Joseph and his brothers, *The Sons of Jacob* is especially praised for its psychological insight and intensity of feeling.

Rolfs Ekmanis has written that "although Rainis often advanced theses, he knew how to distinguish between aesthetic and moral values," and most critics concur that Rainis's works successfully combine social advocacy with poetic artistry. Stressing humanistic ideals, his writings have also been praised for transcending their basis in Latvian culture to appeal to universal human emotions.

PRINCIPAL WORKS

Tālas noskaņas zilā vakarā (poetry) 1903
Vētras sēja (poetry) 1905
Uguns un nakts (drama) 1907
 [*Fire and Night*, 1981]

379

Klusā grāmata (poetry) 1909; also published as *Vēja
    nestas lapas,* 1910
Indulis un Ārija (drama) 1911
Tie, kas neaizmirst (poetry) 1911
Gals un sākums (poetry) 1912
Pūt, vējiņi! (drama) 1913
Jāzeps un viņa brāļi (drama) 1919
    [*The Sons of Jacob,* 1924; also published as *Joseph and
        His Brothers,* 1965]
Spēlēju, dancoju (drama) 1919
Sveika, brīvā Latvija! (poetry) 1919
Mīla stipŗāka par nāvi (drama) 1927
Rīgas, ragana (drama) 1928
Raksti. 17 vols. (poetry and dramas) 1952-65

GRACE RHYS   (essay date 1924)

[*Rhys is the translator of* The Sons of Jacob. *In the following
excerpt from her introduction to that work, she notes the play's
principal themes and artistic merits.*]

Rainis has poured all the passion of the persecuted exile into
his study of Joseph [in *The Sons of Jacob*]. But he is a dramatist
par excellence, which means he can enter into the soul of every
one of his characters, animating them towards their actions,
from within. Each of the brothers is separately studied, as
anyone who troubles to read the book of Genesis will find out.

It is characteristic of his method that he takes old vessels and
fills them with new contents. Thus in this play of Joseph we
may find three themes:—the terrible drama lifted from the Bible
and made very actual: within that is the drama personal to
himself of the revolt against tyranny: the ordeal of the reformer.
A third idea informs the whole play; throughout it the corn is
used, and finely used, as a symbol: the tiller of the ground
despises the nomad; the new civilisation wars against the old.
One might almost dare to add that behind this struggle seems
to lurk the idea of the warring love, the foreseeing wisdom,
that is to conquer the bitterness of the earth and its ancient sin.

It is quite worth while to compare Rainis' play with that of
the poet Charles Wells, whose play of *Joseph and His Brethren,*
published exactly a hundred years ago, had a belated success
when republished with an introduction by Swinburne fifty-two
years later. Bland enough the cruel story appears, pale and
colourless the characters, in comparison with the sharp strokes,
the close psychology of the Latvian poet. There is, of course,
in Wells' verse, more of what I may call poetic revelling—
more of the cult, the leisurely flowering of beauty. The intensity
of Rainis exhales a far different atmosphere; there is a strength
and even a terror in his work which makes the sudden twist at
the end, away from history, and into a curious, purely psychological conclusion, all the more striking and unexpected.
(pp. xii-xiii)

> *Grace Rhys, in an introduction to* The Sons of Jacob
> *by J. Rainis, translated by Grace Rhys, J. M. Dent
> & Sons Ltd., 1924, pp. v-xiii.*

JĀNIS RUDZĪTIS   (essay date 1953)

[*In the following excerpt, Rudzītis outlines Rainis's career and
notes principal elements of his works.*]

Jānis Rainis (Janis Pliekšans) is the leading figure in Latvian
literature, being a part of its classic background, and undoubtedly the best known Latvian author abroad. . . . His literary
career began with a splendid translation of Goethe's *Faust*
which was followed by the original verse, chiefly lyrical. His
remarkable poems and dramas in verse, especially his tragedies, made him the founder of the Latvian classical drama. In
the center of his philosophical contemplations there is usually
an individual in absolute loneliness. The problems of his poems
and drama are in fact the solutions of the attitude of such an
individual toward the opposite sex, society, state, mankind and
the universe. He was non-sectarian, but he expressed ideas of
a cosmic religion. His belief in immortality was founded on
the doctrines of Heraklit about the eternal rhythm. As a reg-
ulating force in all human relations he advocated the idea of
human love in its highest sense. His conceptions are expressed
in symbols. His style is laconic, lapidary, and at the same time
very coloristic. The power to combine the ideas and exquisite
lyric note with the strong drive of deeply philosophical thoughts
was one of his most significant gifts. Most of his excellent
dramas are built upon events in Latvian history. Among them
there is a verse drama *Uguns un nakts* (*Fire and Night*), based
on the life of the Latvian mythological hero Lacplesis, the
characters being poetical symbols. The drama is really a revelation about the past, present and future of Latvian history.
All in all, Rainis was among the first poets who visualized
Latvia as an independent state. (p. 259)

> *Jānis Rudzītis, "Literature and Drama," in* Cross
> Road Country: Latvia, *edited by Edgars Andersons,
> Latvju Grāmata, 1953, pp. 253-68.*

VITAUTS KALVE   (essay date 1954)

[*In the following excerpt, Kalve notes several characteristics of
Rainis's poetry and dramas.*]

[Rainis] divides existence into a variety of opposites (as shown
by the titles of his works: *Uguns un nakts* [*Fire and Night*],
Gals un sākums [*The End and the Beginning*], *Jāzeps un viņa
brāļi* [*Joseph and his Brothers*]; the latter characterizes the
irreconcilable conflict between the individual and society), but
he conceives these opposites—following the example set by
Hegel—as being engaged in an eternal dialectical struggle which
leads to syntheses out of which emerge new opposites, and so
forth for ever, in an everlasting rhythm which is the meaning
and the life of existence. Rainis's point of departure is the
value of the human soul in itself; he magnifies this value in
accordance with the Nietzschean conception of the absolute
value of individuality and of the individual's loneliness.

"Kalnā kāpējs" ("The Mountaineer").

Thy loneliness shall grow from year to year,
Friends sleeping under wooden crosses;
Few wayfarers to give thee friendly cheer,
Few blossoms midst the scanty mosses.

These, too, shall go, thy path ascending,
And glacial silence woo thy losses—
No respite here, no rapt unbending:

Behold, o wanderer, the snow-swept crest,
While earthly yearnings scourge thy turbulent breast!

Rainis goes still further and seeks, in ever changing ways, the
fulfilment of the individual soul through its fusion with society
into a more complete whole (this is at times organically conceived as the Latvian nation). These are the ideas he introduces

again and again in his lyrics and his tragedies. Reconciliation and fulfilment are the essence of Rainis's conception of life, although in his most significant work (*Jāzeps un viņa brāļi*) he finally shows that reconciliation and fulfilment belong to the mystical beyond, outside the confines of this life.

Being a constructive thinker, Rainis . . . paid great attention to the construction of his poetry, and he was the first to achieve a highly concentrated mode of expression. He took over, in its entirety, the tradition of the poetry of the National Awakening—on the one hand, he made full use of its motifs and, on the other, he endeavoured to revive the metrical form, diction and structure of the Latvian folk-song. The fundamental principle of his poetry was: an old song to new tunes. Rainis's achievements were greater than those of his predecessors chiefly because his dialectic thinking corresponds to the dialectics of the folk-songs. (pp. 119-20)

> *Vitauts Kalve, "The Period of Exploring Problems,"*
> in Latvian Literature, *by Janis Andrups and Vitauts*
> *Kalve, translated by Ruth Speirs, M. Goppers, 1954,*
> *pp. 113-26.*

ZENTA MAURINA (essay date 1968)

[Maurina was a Latvian-born fiction writer, biographer, and critic. In the following excerpt, he places Rainis's works in the Latvian literary tradition and discusses Joseph and His Brothers.]

If the poet is the voice and the central core of a nation, the interpreter of the soul of his people, . . . Jānis Rainis must be such a one. As a living synthesis of West and East his mind embraced wide horizons. Though he was at home in seven languages and translated into Latvian poetry from twenty-two languages, he wrote his own plays and poems in Latvian only. German and Russian schools, imprisonment and exile could not silence the springs of his native Latvian. He raised up ancient traditions from out of the very depths of the past and endowed with new life the figure of the Latvian national hero Lāčplēsis, the bearkiller, who not only assumes power through the blood of his defeated enemies but by his direct and close ties with mother earth.

The characteristically Latvian themes [combine] . . . in the poems and plays of Jānis Rainis: he who tramples down others humiliates himself; he who elevates others to a higher plane, elevates himself as well—this is the leading and central theme of his works. While he enriched the Latvian language, the most sacred of words for him was mankind. His tragedy *Joseph and His Brothers* has little in common with the biblical story and nothing at all with Thomas Mann's novel, yet it takes on the same meaning for Latvians as does Goethe's *Faust* for the Germans and Western Europeans. The ideal mode of life for Joseph is work on the land: "He that passes like a sun-stream over the wheat. . . ." The substance of the tragedy is contained in Joseph's journey towards self-perfection which leads him across chasms of despair into foreign and alien lands and equally across the abyss of irresistible desire for vengeance. Joseph follows the road which Dina pointed out to him, Dina who came to him in the desert when he tended the sheep in order to warn him of the malice of his brothers and to give herself to him. She was not afraid of the wild animals, nor of the roughness of his brothers who behaved more cruelly than the

beasts. The invisible talisman which she leaves him before she meets death speaks:

> But love asks nothing, only gives and gives
> It recompenses hate; why, if it were
> As high as a mountain and as deep as an open grave.
> Sun with her gold would cover over the mountain
> And fill the grave.

Out of hatred and envy Joseph is thrown into the grave of death, but he escapes and wins the highest honours and respect in the land of Egypt. His brothers emigrate to Egypt during the years of hunger and starvation and implore him for bread, having no one else to turn to. Two emotions dominate Joseph's struggle: to take revenge or to pardon; this struggle marks the drama's climax with consummate mastery of language. Himself an exile, Rainis has woven personal experiences into his work, as Joseph comes to understand the futility of all earthly endeavor. Though he cannot forget he nonetheless forgives his brothers, but can feel no bond between them. He gives his starving brothers bread and resigns his high office. Dressed in an old shepherd's cloak he leaves Potipha in order to find inward purification and fulfilment in solitude. The murders or suicides usual in tragedies do not occur, but we are made to feel the stages of loneliness of one who gives himself away.

Fifteen years have now passed, and Dina remains as alive within his heart as when she first came into the desert to meet him, then a shepherd. He now feels able to carry out her directions:

> I see you again, my homeland—there's the cliff!
> And there above—Dina—thither I climb—
> Dying—I die not—the messengers of the sun
> Fasten their eager wings upon my feet,
> Inviting me to the day-illuminated heights!
> Oh, then I'll fight my battle over again.
> Until my strength is melted in the sun,
> Until the Universe and I are one.
> Then falls the wall that rears between me and men,
> Between the good and the evil, the live and the dead.
> Then I'll come back, and bring the sun with me!

(In the original, Joseph's monologue ends with the key Latvian word Sun.)

> *Zenta Maurina, "The White Gown: Variations on*
> *Latvian Themes," translated by Karl W. Maurer, in*
> MOSAIC: A Journal for the Comparative Study of
> Literature and Ideas, *Special Issue: The Literature*
> *of Small Countries, Vol. I, No. 3, April, 1968, pp.*
> *70-82.*

ARVIDS ZIEDONIS, JR. (essay date 1969)

[A Latvian-born American critic specializing in Baltic literature, Ziedonis is the editor of the Journal of Baltic Studies *and the author of* The Religious Philosophy of Jānis Rainis. *In the following excerpt from that work, he examines the religious ideas expressed in* Fire and Night *and* Joseph and His Brothers.]

Rainis developed his first major play, *Fire and Night,* which was written between 1903 and 1905, from Pumpurs' epic legend of *Lacplesis*. He included the Kurbad legends and others and gave added philosophical and spiritual symbolism to this drama. All characters are symbolical.

Rainis has used here the popular legendary hero Lacplesis, fighter of evil and oppression; but he has portrayed him with much greater depth than Pumpurs had achieved. In this way, also the legendary Spidola and Kangars have been further developed. Although the play is based purely on legends, it touches various eras of Latvian history from the time of early feudalism (approx. 700 A.D.) up to the 1905 revolution, when this work was written. (p. 132)

This drama describes the primitive struggle between the forces of fire and night, as they exist in their original state of dialectical opposition and as they progress through various stages of freedom—original, moral and spiritual—which, in a positive sense, lead to man's spiritual liberation and eventual synthesis of the dialectic; while, in a negative sense, by abusing the freedom, man experiences slavery and destruction, and he also inflicts suffering upon others.

Spidola and Lacplesis symbolize the eternal forces of life: the spiritual and the physical. Both of these forces are present in man in a seemingly dialectical opposition until they reach inner union and harmony.

In the primitive state, the spiritual force does not have direction: Spidola in the beginning is fickle, irrational, undecided, constantly changing like a snake between good and evil. In this state she has complete freedom: She can grant herself anything that she wishes and needs no other power. She is ruled by her own passions and impulses which can be constructive or destructive: "I am free and for my own sake." In this sense, Rainis is in agreement with [Nicolas] Berdyaev, who believes that the first freedom is uncreated: "In the beginning there existed meonic freedom, which is interpreted as an urge to be. Because it was freedom, it contained within itself the possibility of both good and evil."

Rainis talks of the "urge to be" in his poem "Whenever I woke from a dream . . .":

> Only an urge I felt, as from earth's fire,
> Which burns unkindled since eternity.

This urge to be (Let there be light!), this spiritual spark from the eternal fire is Spidola—shining brightly but unconsciously through her own desire to be, to grow, to assert herself:

> I am I, I come of my own,
> I go of my own, I know not where,—
> Wherever I want—
> I shine from my own light,
> I, Spidola,
> Fire is my father,
> From the innermost earth's eternal flame
> The burning soul of all of life,—

Jacob Boehme, who belongs to the realm of mystical rather than systematic theologians, calls this beginning the primeval will—"Ungrund." (pp. 146-47)

The primeval will, according to Boehme, manifested itself in a dynamic dialectic, which resulted in a three-fold movement of the trinitarian Godhead; but in Berdyaev, according to Matthew Spinka, this primeval freedom is not found in the Godhead, as in Boehme, but rather in the Ungrund, in the primeval freedom. Berdyaev states that this first kind of freedom is prior to good and evil and determines their choice. It is the primeval, irrational, dark and undetermined freedom. It lies outside of God, outside of being; it is pre-existent to all being which is already determined. (p. 148)

Rainis, a contemporary of Berdyaev, holds the same view that not God but man himself should be blamed for the good or the evil which exists in the world. In this freedom, there is also beauty, expressed in creativity. Spidola is the inner self, the spiritual self—the light that shines from within. As the symbol

of light, she is in constant struggle with the opposite—darkness, which is ignorance and unawareness, evil.

When the Black Knight commands her to entangle the hero Lacplesis and to distract him from his goal, Spidola defies his orders and points out that she is free to make her own choice. Here Rainis indicates that man is capable of becoming either good or evil; it is man's own free choice. When evil is imposed on Spidola by force, her rebellion results in good action; whereas Dostoevsky's character in the *Notes from the Underground* becomes mean and spiteful when society forces him to conform: "I am a sick man . . . I am a spiteful man. No, I am not a pleasant man at all!" Berdyaev says that man will do anything in rebellion to some kind of life which is imposed upon him by force: He will put up with suffering and will be ready to disrupt the whole rational order of life for the sake of asserting his free will. Rainis shows that this first kind of freedom lets man choose between good and evil and that man has in this freedom the liberty for the acceptance of God. He shows that the original freedom does not guarantee by any means that man will choose to do good, as is evident in Spidola's capricious behavior during the first and second acts. The outcome may be a choice for discord and hatred, a choice for evil; on the other hand, it could be a choice for growth spiritually and for concern towards others in love. The reason for this dialectic is that this original freedom has not been sanctified in live. Berdyaev says that "it has not been illuminated by the inner light of truth."

Only at the end of the third act, when Spidola realizes how deeply she has hurt Lacplesis by permitting innocent suffering to come upon his people and Laimdota, who is also dear to her because "she is a part of me," Spidola stops toying with life and remains in deep thought over Lacplesis' warning:

> See that your own goals become lucid
> Through your own beauty!

Out of this contemplation, Spidola makes her decision rationally and morally: She must save Lacplesis from the power of evil! This decision Spidola made in the second kind of freedom, moral freedom, which is the rational choice between good and evil. At this stage, she decides to subordinate Lacplesis, the physical force, under her control. Through this act, Rainis emphasizes his conviction that the spirit should rule, not the body: The higher nature should control the lower nature of man.

In his most primitive state, Lacplesis is purely physical, animal-like (with bear-ears). He is determined by his mission, which he follows stubbornly, in a one-sided manner. Nothing else catches his attention: Like Luther's "horse"—he looks neither right nor left. This physical force, according to Rainis, is as eternal as is the spiritual force of life:

> You are from eternity, just as I am;
> We are the branches of the same root,
> Together to us belongs victory,
> Only by us our rule can be broken.

Spidola encourages Lacplesis that together they will be mighty and eternal. He should just obey her and do what she asks of him; and, in overcoming her greatest enemy, absolute evil and darkness, she will become free and eternal—the ruler of heaven and of the earth. In overcoming Lacplesis' physical strength, in subordinating it to her spiritual strength, she will lift him, transform him into life in eternity.

At this time, Lacplesis is still unconscious of his eternal nature; he realizes only his own strength. Relying completely on this strength, he seeks to solve all problems by himself. He is afraid of Spidola and seeks to gain victory without becoming involved with her. He is conscious only of his goal: "You will have to fight against all evil." Contrary to Greek thought, Rainis believes that the body is basically good.

Evil, for Rainis, is nothing else than the abuse of freedom on the part of man. If man decides to do evil, by abusing his moral freedom for selfish motives and calculations, he becomes a slave to his sin. When Kangars tells Spidola that he has sold himself to the devil, she replies in disgust: "You slave!" Kangars here compares with Goethe's Faust, who has sold himself to the devil in return for worldly pleasures. Rainis says that for this reason Faust causes unjust suffering to all that come in contact with him—Margaret, her mother, and her brother. Berdyaev, too, says than an immoral man is no longer free and that he will inflict upon the world suffering, oppression and injustice. Kangars tries to justify his actions, saying to Spidola: "I sold myself to hell for you—" But she replies: "Oh, not for me, for money."

Whereas in Goethe's *Faust* Margaret had compassion on Faust and redeemed him through her love when she saw his remorse, Rainis leads Kangars to destruction because Kangars is unable to love anyone: He seeks to gain Spidola's love through trickery, through calculations—for his selfish gain. Throughout the play, Kangars implores Spidola to give up Lacplesis and to accept his "love." He promises to make her his queen and let her rule over him, but each time Spidola turns away in disgust because in such proposals Kangars is not sincere. On the Island of Death, when Kangars thinks that Spidola has been weakened, he proudly declares: "I shall trample you under my heel!" Kangars seeks the wisdom of Spidola so that he could become more powerful and oppress the people with greater cunning, as he had promised to the devil:

Spidola: Tell him what he has sold
  For the money of hell and honor among fools.
First devil: He fell to the ground and promised
  That he will betray his own people—fie!
Second devil: He fell to the ground and promised
  That he will destroy her heroes,—fie!
Third devil:
  That he will make them listen to oppressors,—fie!
Fourth devil:
  That he will kill and torture the fighters for freedom,—fie!
Fifth devil:
  That all he will put into chains of slavery,—fie!
Sixth devil:
  That every free spirit he will suppress,—fie!
Seventh devil:
  That every living soul he will starve to death,—fie!

Through this conversation, Rainis shows how the unconscious thoughts and desires of the traitor are brought to consciousness. Through *Uguns un nakts (Fire and Night)*, Rainis tried to expose the traitors of the nation. He showed the people how history was affected by the abuse of freedom by individuals or groups of individuals motivated by selfishness to sacrifice their own conscience. Much suffering was caused throughout the centuries by people like Kangars, who did not care about the welfare of society but made deals with foreigners for the sake of personal gain. Whereas in Pumpurs' *Lacplesis* all chieftains stand united behind their hero, Rainis emphasizes division among the chieftains and brings out their distorted character, which hindered the hero and the people from attaining national unity and freedom. Rainis concludes that all social evils are man-made.

Also, there is an indication of Rainis' conviction that man is not subject to "blind fate" (determinism), as the Black Knight tries to convince Spidola, "This is what fate destines you to do." Rather, it is a question of whether man is willing to accept fate "blindly," or whether he is willing to overcome his circumstances. Men and nations are not determined by blind fate if they are culturally and spiritually alert and if they are united in their efforts. As such, they are able to shape their history, with the help of the Absolute (God), whom Rainis interprets, in this case, as the objective justice (in opposition to blind justice, which is injustice, caused by man through the abuse of moral freedom). Therefore, the fate of the nation is each man's responsibility.

Rainis emphasizes that freedom is short-lived, unless it is spiritual and responsible freedom. Thus he distinguishes the outer and the inner freedom. The outer freedom is political freedom, which is temporal if based merely on crude might. It must be combined with the inner freedom, the freedom of the spirit, which is eternal, to have a more lasting effect. Lacplesis tells Spidola on the Island of Death:

> When happy and free will be Latvia,
> Then will my task be completed.

Spidola assures him that he can attain such a goal on the Island of Death: It is only a temporal goal. Throughout the play Rainis shows that the physical force alone is insufficient for overcoming the evil forces of life: Man needs to cultivate the soul, the heart and the mind—the spirit. Without these, he will tire in the struggle and become discouraged; life will overcome him. In this state, man seeks only immediate goals. He is drawn downward into everyday life, into the common life of pleasures and immediate satisfactions. He wants to be finished with his task and then rest from his labors in peace and contentment. From these discouragements and fruitless struggles, Lacplesis realizes his deep longing for peace when he encounters Spidola on the Island of Death:

> I have always avoided you,
> We were deadly enemies,
> But strange longings,—who can explain—
> Have always pulled me to you;
> What I have always avoided to want
> Here in Death Island should I attain:
> To sleep and to cease,
> To fall into eternal unconsciousness—

Lacplesis mistakenly thinks that his seemingly contradictory longing for Spidola is the longing for peace. Lacplesis imagines that she is static peace. Contrary to some philosophers, who imagined that spiritual freedom was static freedom, Rainis asserts that it is dynamic energy, mystical and unfathomable, of the spiritual world. It is not inactivity, asceticism or forgetfulness. This wish for forgetfulness in the sleep of nonexistence finds its parallel in Hamlet's struggle of "to be or not to be":

>   . . . To die, to sleep;
> No more; and, by a sleep to say we end
> The heart-ache and the thousand natural shocks
> That flesh is heir to, 'tis a consummation
> Devoutly to be wished. . . .

But Rainis explains through Spidola's words that the spirit of man does not seek rest; rather, he is always willing to go on in creativity (The spirit is willing, but the flesh is weak.) and in constant change for new goals. Like Dante's Beatrice, Spidola calls Lacplesis on to greater spiritual heights:

> Does not your longing reach beyond Laimdota?
> Not further, through the ages, to eternity?
> This is not the end of your goal,
> If further leads you on my voice—
> Come, Lacplesis!
> . . . .
> Only he who achieves the great inner freedom
> Is able to enter into the great life.
> You toiled only to fulfill your task,
> That is why you tired in your efforts;
> Only in my beauty you would find
> Eternal strength and wholeness.

Lacplesis cannot comprehend as yet Spidola's mysterious words. He cannot understand her riddles when she explains to him that in losing herself she gains herself and becomes eternal, and that this is also what he should do. It is significant that during this conversation on the Island of Death Spidola is invisible; she is pure spirit, seated in the mythological apple tree. The body only subconsciously feels the need for the spirit, while the spirit constantly seeks to establish conscious balance and harmony—God seeks man.

Once this union is achieved between the body and the spirit, when Lacplesis drinks of the water of life, a new power surges up within him: a new strength rejuvenates him; it is something which he had not felt so long (spiritual strength, rebirth). Through this rebirth, Spidola joyously announces that now Lacplesis belongs to her and that she will protect him and bring him to the diamond mountain, where there is true light, warmth, joy (enlightenment, Nirvana). He who seeks this mountain becomes detached from everything that is on this earth—love and hate, everything that is crude and low. The sun she will put in his hair, and from its white rays will be fashioned his garments. But this is not all: She will lead him on to the beginnings of life, to the beginnings of creation, to the mystery of life (the Absolute). This is the fulfillment of spiritual freedom.

Now that this spiritual union has been attained, Spidola becomes visible in her glory and brilliance; Lacplesis looks with awe at her beauty. Through this and various other works, especially poems, Rainis extolls the beauty of man's spirit, its mystery, its unfathomable power, which is a spark of the Absolute. Spidola urges Lacplesis also to eat her apple, and then their union would be complete; but Lacplesis is afraid that then he would have to die. The apple, as in the Bible, here signifies the fruit of wisdom and of death. Life is a mystery. Ultimate wisdom can be known to man only after death. In answer to Lacplesis' fears, Spidola explains that in drinking of the spring of life, he has already died to this earth. Having awakened to spiritual life, mere physical existence will not seem attractive to him any more. Lacplesis does not realize that with Spidola he has attained the state of detached attachment, and attached detachment. He is no longer satisfied with being completely physically attached, but he has not broken the "silken thread" which still connects him with life. He can be creative and make life a beautiful dream. Spidola explains that she is eternity, who has come to fulfill the earth and to make it beautiful, creative:

> I can change reality into a dream,—
> Your awakening will be beautiful as a dream,
> Your most beautiful dream will become reality.

Lacplesis has just tasted of spiritual life and has just become aware of its power; yet, he is still so earthly, so attached to the primeval force, the powers of the unconscious, which is symbolized in his bear-ears, that all of Spidola's words are riddles to him. Thinking that she would make any of his dreams become reality, he is lulled into the false security of relying on Spidola's help to accomplish his goals for him:

> I did not accomplish what I set out to do,
> Give me, (then), your apple of death!

Berdyaev states that this second kind of freedom is not only of God, but also of man. Man makes his choice independently from God. Sometimes man is only too ready to shift it to stronger shoulders. Dostoevsky expressed this thought similarly in "The Grand Inquisitor": People do not want this kind of freedom, which is a great burden. They want security, the tangible rather than the mystery of the unknown. The Grand Inquisitor says to Christ: "Didst Thou forget that man prefers peace, and even death, to freedom of choice in the knowledge of good and evil? . . . Oh, we shall persuade them that they will only become free when they renounce their freedom to us and submit to us." Rainis realized that in the dialectic between the spiritual and the physical forces in man the spiritual constantly seeks liberation—freedom from the earthly ties. It achieves the greatest strength after death. But man must know when to turn back, as the Buddha turned back after his enlightenment. He returned to his people to help them and to share with them that which he experienced. If he had died before that, he would have thrown himself away; Rainis says that for a hero or for a spiritual leader of the people that is the greatest sin. Spidola says of Lacplesis, in contempt: "He has thrown himself away—that is the greatest sin!" Rainis condemns such freedom without responsibility. When man seeks the "easy way out" to the solution of his problems, when he loses his love for life and seeks only after-life, man commits the greatest sin—he throws himself away and ignores his purpose here.

When Lacplesis spits out the apple and awakens, Kangars realizes that he must destroy the union between Spidola and Lacplesis; otherwise he himself will not prevail. But the inner harmony of man cannot be destroyed by any outer forces. Only man himself can break this union and become fragmented, one-sided, alienated, incomplete. Spidola had declared this to Lacplesis before:

> Together to us belongs victory,
> Only by us our rule can be broken.

This union can be compared to the experience of Job; no outside force could affect him as long as he was whole within and as long as he sensed his union with God. When through treachery Lacplesis is persuaded to strike the spring with his sword, he cuts himself off from this spiritual union; he becomes separated from eternity:

> You cut off your road to eternity!
> Your courage evaporated like air.
> You are no longer the strongest!

Rainis here points out that this separation has grave consequences: Not only does man regress to meaninglessness, he also cuts off his road to eternity. While no outward forces could separate him (Nothing can separate us from the love of God—St. Paul), inner separation excludes man from his "self"—his eternal spirit. As their paths are again separated, Spidola says that she will have to return to her domain of the spirit alone, because the people will not seek any more the spiritual life. Lacplesis, without her, will be overcome by the forces of darkness if he remains merely physical, without the power of the spirit. Then all life will die out. But, in love, Spidola makes her decision: She will give up her rule in heaven and die in the shape of a mortal so that Lacplesis (earthly life) will be saved from destruction by the evil forces (Kangars):

> This cannot be,—fate wants to divide us,
> In mortal shape I want to die
> And guard you and remain with you,
> E'en though I lose my heavenly rule!

Overwhelmed at her love, Lacplesis asks her to remain in heaven, for now he knows that she is truly divine; he is not worthy of her great sacrifice. But gratefully Lacplesis obeys her wish, and she comes to him freely in love and humility, in tenderness and beauty, which is greater than before. In joy, Lacplesis tells his people:

> Here is your deliverer,
> Mighty Spidola!
> For you she sacrificed herself,
> Giving up her heavenly kingdom.

Rainis sees the third freedom, the spiritual freedom, as the synthesis of the dialectic through love. In this evolvement between the spirit and the body can be detected various stages: 1. sin (striking out against the spirit—lower nature against higher nature), 2. the fall (separation from the spirit), 3. suffering (agony through awareness of separation, fear and remorse) and 4. the redemption through love (recognition of the spirit as divine, which empties itself and returns in sacrificial love so that both the spirit and the body would again be whole). (pp. 148-62)

[Rainis] believed that through active, sacrificial love, which crystallizes the mind, the heart and the soul, man would attain the final fulfillment and reach the third stage of freedom, spiritual freedom. The nation had to go through suffering to become unified. Spidola says in the third act, the beginning of oppression, that she has put Laimdota and all others on the "same boat to experience common sorrows and common joys, so that their souls would melt into one." Through such a purge also Spidola and Lacplesis experience greater clarity: "Change toward clarity!" Constant change and re-examination brings Spidola to the realization of her purpose in life. Lacplesis, too, realized the new strength which came to him through union with the spiritual, the divine, the eternal: it is the creation of a new being. Rainis calls it "the new man." His dynamic energy comes from active love, which, to Rainis, is the greatest force.

Berdyaev calls this new man the new spiritual man, who comes into being through the divine-human mystery of the two natures of Christ:

> To receive the freedom of Christ is not only to receive
> the freedom of God but to receive also, by partaking
> of Christ's human nature, that freedom which enables
> man to turn to God. It is thus the power of becoming
> God's free sons and so making that loving response
> to God which He needs.

In Christ, according to Berdyaev, is the source of freedom of the whole human race, not only of the eternal Adam but of the spiritual Adam, of Eternal Man—Christ. He is the unifying force. The solution to the problem of human freedom, therefore, lies in the dogma of the divine-human nature of Christ. Through the divine-human mystery of the two natures of Christ, consequently, can be explained the two natures of the new spiritual man.

Where Berdyaev says "Christ," Rainis puts the concept "active, sacrificial love." Rainis speaks of God, the Absolute, the divine spirit, which is transcendent and also immanent in man—in his inner self—but he does not stress Christ or the triune God. It could be said that Rainis saw in each man who had come to spiritual awareness and who was striving for inner fulfillment a Christ-like figure, who wholeheartedly responded to the love of God. This concept, however, must not be understood in the traditional sense, for then we leave out sin. In this respect, Rainis felt that Faust was closer to man's real nature; but even he could not be accepted as an all-inclusive type— only as an individual. Modern man could not accept renewal through magic; he must seek natural renewal—in free nature and in love:

> Faust is closer to us than Christ, for in Christ we
> find not a single sin, not a single weakness. He is
> too much God, and it is easy for him to be holy and
> to proclaim holiness. Each of us, wretched human
> beings, falls and sins because we are completely base
> and mean; and from us is demanded that which is
> even difficult for God to fulfill. Faust, at least, is
> human. And if, through honest striving, he has attained the highest level of humanity, then we, too,
> can attain it, no matter how sinful and petty we are.
> Also, Faust started too late, when all his strength
> had been exhausted and when he was no longer able
> to absorb within himself all of life and to develop
> his personality. But it is easy for Faust to get out of
> this predicament: The old witch takes from him thirty
> years of his life, and he becomes rejuvenated. In our
> enlightened age, this is no longer possible. Here we
> must seek other and completely different, natural means
> for renewal—in free nature and in love.

Rainis says that while man talks in selected, noble, grand expressions about the fulfillment and wholeness of man between two human beings, about the spiritual growth through common thoughts and feelings, which increases the strength of each individual, in nature this is only a common, self-evident occurrence; for the specific individual it means renewal and further creativity. Could not man also understand life with such loftiness and unconcern? "This loftiness, this natural explanation for all things, not through supernatural but through natural causes—is already the real truth." On this truth, as Rainis saw it and interpreted it, he based his natural religion. Through the interaction of the spiritual and the physical, life is renewed and results in further creativity.

Through the sacrifice of Spidola (the lofty spirit, the beauty of the human soul), Lacplesis (unconcerned physical nature) will go not to his death but to birth, to a new beginning. Even though basically the dialectic exists, it is overcome through love, kindness and grace, as Spidola explains her contradictory nature to Kangars:

> The noble one, even in hate is to be loved,
> Neither by you, nor the black one to be overcome.

Spidola reacts with hatred and open revolt when the physical force reigns; however, when she reigns, she guards Lacplesis with love, kindness and grace. Both of these forces are constantly present in man also in the spiritual freedom: Man is, at the same time, a sinner and a saint. Rainis believed that love is the strongest force. In active love, man can change his environment and, most important, also himself: "Change, and change your own self upwards!" Even though harmony could be attained in life, final union and complete fulfillment are possible only in death. In the face of death, man turns inward and, in a moment of truth, he achieves great clarity, overgrowing his previous cycle and entering into a higher stage of development. Such a transformation occurred in Lacplesis and

Spidola on the Island of Death. In the final act, again in the face of death, Lacplesis sees clearly his temporal goal—Laimdota—and his eternal goal—Spidola. He achieves his final consummation with the spiritual goal. Rainis believed that when one goal has been attained there is always another ahead. Life is constant struggle.

Spidola and Lacplesis grew through constant struggles and through love, and gradually they eliminated their extreme polarities and approximated the state of inner harmony: Spidola gave up her divine detachment and uncontrolled demonic tendencies, growing in love toward a meaningful life; Lacplesis became detached from the primeval, purely physical, earthly nature growing in the realization of brotherhood among men and nations. If interpreted from the point of view of Rainis' natural religion, this could mean that the spirit grew toward greater clarity and purpose by eliminating unattainable supernatural beliefs; while, through evolution, the physical man lost the narrowness of his goals and envisioned brotherhood with other nations for a more abundant life. In both cases, this harmony was achieved through their willingness to die to their own selves, in sacrificial love and in a heroic spirit, constantly changing and improving toward wholeness.

Rainis sought to influence his audience through the portrayal of this inner transformation of the heroes in order to initiate in them the desire for spiritual growth and wholeness in their own lives for "only he who achieves inner freedom can enter into the great life." Even though Lacplesis falls into the river with his last enemy, there is a feeling of hope and assurance that he will go not to death but to new life. (pp. 162-67)

What to the Germans is Goethe's *Faust* to the Latvians is *Uguns un nakts*. In both of these plays are portrayed definite national character traits. Goethe had taken the legend of Faust from various writers before him, had combined several motifs and had given them greater importance and purpose. Rainis, too, combined several sources and created something completely new, original and nationally characteristic. It is Rainis' most important work in his cycle of legendary Latvian plays. (p. 167)

[*Joseph and His Brothers*] is considered one of Rainis' major works, if not the major work. It took Rainis about thirteen years to crystallize his philosophical and religious thoughts in this play while he worked on and completed *The Golden Horse, Indulis and Arija* and *Blow, Wind!* Rainis himself stated in his introductory remarks, which he added in 1925, that the source of the play is biblical and that he has not willfully changed its content. He also mentions that he tried to use Hebrew and Egyptian idiomatic expressions. . . . *Joseph and His Brothers* is Rainis' first tragedy in the humanity cycle. Later works are *Ilya of Murom* (*Ilja Muromietis,* a play dealing with Russian folklore) and several fragments of other plays. (p. 244)

Like Indulis, [in *Indulis and Arija*], Joseph, too, had a complete rapport with God in his youth when he was at home with his father. Joseph seemed to be the personification of love itself even though his brothers were unkind to him and, in their jealousy, mistreated him. Joseph could not penetrate into their evil world even though he constantly tried to make peace with them. "With love I want to gain their love," is the leitmotif, which goes through this whole play. Not hate against hate, but love against hate.

Dina, Joseph's great love, urges him to be patient with his brothers, saying that love cannot be taken as one wants: It can be given only.

> Oh, love asks not, it just gives and gives,
> And thus it recompenses all the brothers' hate.

> Hate is high as a mountain, deep as a pit—
> Yet love is so much greater: Like the sun,
> It covers up the mountain and fills the pit.

Here Rainis brings out the purpose of love—to bring forth good fruits, to be like a tree, which constantly adds new leaves, to be always new, constantly renewing itself in life, in love, as from a hidden spring. . . . (p. 245)

Having told Joseph of the danger which awaits him, Dina gives her dagger to him so that he may protect himself (thinking not of her own protection):

> This my gift is higher than my love.
> With it, I give you back to yourself.

Here Rainis points out that love is the greatest when it is given freely, without any selfishness or attachment. Through her death, Dina frees Joseph from any attachment to her, unless he freely chooses to love her. Dostoevsky expressed this kind of love, which is given freely, in the "Grand Inquisitor," through Christ: "Freely I want man to follow me." Dina knows that she is going to her death: "To the high rock, which even the mountain goat cannot ascend, there shall I climb. There the sun (God) will take me back; there my flesh will go back to the earth; and my breath will rise up to you, who are in the sun."

After Dina has gone away, the brothers arrive and gradually make preparations for their evil deed—to kill Joseph and, thus, to hurt their father. In dreams, there is communion with the Absolute, a revelation of His will; therefore, the wicked brothers think that by destroying Joseph they will also destroy their father's belief in dreams:

> No! Neither hope nor you shall live!
> Then he will understand what your dreams have been!
> From this time on, let no man build on dreams.

What would a man be without dreams? Desperation would overtake him. Levi knows this is the worst punishment, which he can inflict upon his father. But Joseph still insists that his dreams will come true:

> You've tied my body, you can't tie my hopes!
> . . . I hope on my spirit,
> Which is a part of God's great dream!

Like Indulis, Joseph, too, has to rely on his wisdom, his spirit, and on God's great dream, of which he is an active part. Rainis very explicitly states here his own conviction that no powers of evil can destroy that which God has intended to be; and, a part of God's plan is man's spirit, which cannot be destroyed. But man has to respond to God's plan. Rainis emphasizes that God's plan for Joseph also works in Egypt. The people joyfully greet Joseph, called by them "Nofer," the good one, saying:

> Hail to you! Hail! Our great lord Nofer, hail!
> You are the ruler of the fertile earth,
> Both of the Upper lands and of the Lower.
> You are the lord of the four gates of the earth!
> Commander of the sword and of the lash!
> The opener and closer of the Nile!
> Sower of the grain and also reaper!
> Quencher of thirst, and appeaser of our hunger!
> Hail, praise and blessing to the Sun-god's chosen!

Here Rainis repeats his conviction of the universality of God: The chosen of the Lord of Israel is also the chosen of the Sun-god of Egypt; therefore, it is the same God, called only by different names.

From all over the lands, people come and ask Nofer to be merciful and to give them bread. Joseph says, "I'll give you bread. What will you give to me?" And the people shout:

> Take all, take everything, just give us bread!
> Take our wives, children, cattle, gods!
> Take ourselves as slaves, just give us bread!

Here, the call for bread Rainis interprets similarly to Dostoevsky. The Grand Inquisitor tells Christ that the people do not want freedom; all they want is bread. Freedom is a burden to them: "Make us your slaves, but feed us!"

Even though Joseph feels that he and his work in Egypt have been blessed, there is no real joy; he cannot find rest, for deep within him is an unquenched thirst for justice. When he asks Potiphar, the wise man, what he should do, Potiphar advises him:

> Why ask of us? Seek for yourself until you find it:
> He who was humbled more than man may be
> Must rise above that which man was able to attain.

In this answer, Potiphar tells Joseph that he must seek for himself until he arrives at the answer, which he alone can supply; for no one knows really how Joseph feels, nor what has happened to him. Each man reacts differently to a given situation; therefore, his solution is individual. Rainis here is somewhat different from the biblical teaching, which states that "he who humbles himself will be exalted," which implies only passive response. Someone else will exalt him. Rainis, however, says that "he who has been humbled below human dignity must himself, by his own efforts, seek out the causes and gain an insight from the occurrence by searching for the truth and by examining his own heart; and then he must grow spiritually to new heights, which he has been unable to reach before." Another thought, closely connected, is that in this process of seeking justice, truth and dignity, one must inevitably endure suffering, which chastizes the human soul and makes it more beautiful.

Upon the appearance of the brothers in Egypt, there begins the struggle between them and Joseph to unearth the truth, to dig up the past, so that through justice reconciliation could be established. Not only are the brothers gradually and reluctantly forced to confess their dark sins, but Joseph, too, brings out his "skeleton from the closet," which he had kept from Asnath for about a decade: It is the black shirt of his revenge, which pierced his heart with thorns from the pit, into which his brothers had thrown him, and which poisoned the clear waters of his soul. Asnath reproves Joseph that he had never told her of this shirt, which was between them and secretly kept them apart. But Joseph explains that he took off that shirt when Asnath was given to him like wondrous happiness; nevertheless, happiness is unable to erase unhappiness. Asnath says lovingly that, if only she had known before of this, she could have overcome his hate with her love, but now this hate will destroy them.

Joseph is determined to fight fire with fire, thorns with thorns until revenge itself will be erased and good and evil will become harmonious:

> I struggled to forget, but eternally it pierced me;
> Again I must put on this old black shirt.
> When shall I take it off? Along with life?
> Let thorn pierce thorn, till both are blunt!
> Let wounds be closed with other wounds!
> The shirt of thorns I shall remove
> Revenge itself when is erased,
> When good with evil shall become harmonious.

But Asnath sadly replies, "Oh Nofer, they can be harmonious only in death!" "So be it, then!" replies Joseph. "I control myself, and I become myself. Calmly I calculate what shall accomplish my plan: They shall go home and take with them their money. They will be caught! The sound of each coin will send them into terror; each bite of bread will choke in their throats, and the dust of my wheat shall smother their joy; their suffering of a few weeks will repay mine over these many years. But the debt will be erased only when all of their wicked clan will be destroyed." Joseph has sunk low, indeed; through calm calculations he is devising a plan to make his brothers suffer, just as they calculated when they made preparations to go to the pit at Sichem.

Joseph, however, has a different motive: He seeks to make them suffer not only for the sake of suffering, but also for the sake of changing them. This is the only thing which he has not tried before. It seems to him the last desperate attempt to destroy the evil in their hearts. If his love to them could not attain this goal, then let it be "an eye for an eye, and a tooth for a tooth." He has to meet them on their own level, as in his recent dream the firmament descended over the mountains and made them flat, and finally it embraced them on the lowness of the earth. Joseph's struggle is similar to Hamlet's, who sought peace but finally had to resort to revenge through calculations and trickery to meet his wicked uncle on the same low level. In this revenge, however, Joseph realizes also his own growth: "I control myself and become my own."

The fourth act takes place in a closed court of Joseph's palace. Tables have been set for the Feast of the Dead, an Egyptian festival. As the brothers arrive in Egypt for the second time, they are received cordially and are invited to the feast. The brothers confess that they have found their money in their bags of grain, but they are assured by the keeper of the house that they have nothing to fear if their conscience is clear. Still, they wonder about the changed atmosphere of sudden kindness.

Joseph and Asnath are in the court to see if everything is ready for the feast. "For the Festival of Peace, Nofer!—Because finally your heart has found peace," says Asnath. As Joseph remains alone, he reminisces over what has happened to him since he had sent his brothers away with money in their bags to hurt them, to make them fearful, and to send them into despair. What has happened to him? It seems to him that greater suffering has overcome his own soul: In his heart revenge has been replaced by compassion—what his mind had planned has been opposed by his heart. Good and evil are struggling within himself:

> Oh, heart of mine!
> Oh heart, you go your own compassionate way!
> Have all my sufferings become indifferent to you?
> Look here: For years I've gnawed myself—and you?
> You pitied those that caused my suffering.
> Are you so weak? Are you incapable of hate?
> You fan the flowers, but you break not trees;
> Like the mountain storms do in my fatherland?
> Yet, I know it's not weakness—I don't understand.
> Within you lives a strength, ill-inclined to me,
> —But still it's mine,—And, still, it's rooted elsewhere—
> Am I really my own?

Joseph here talks of the inner strength, as it was similarly experienced by Indulis. Here Rainis identifies this strength even more definitely with the Absolute, expressing man's dependence upon a power, which is mightier than man is himself. At times, this power seems even ill-inclined to man's passions and calculations, which fragment him. This power seeks to establish harmony and wholeness, creating compassion and love, which overcomes hate and revenge. Through Joseph's own suffering, in grief, his compassion has overcome his passion, as it similarly expressed in the teachings of the Buddha: "Let a man overcome anger by love, let him overcome evil by good; let him overcome the greedy by liberality, the liar by truth!"

"Now there is peace," realizes Joseph. He hopes that his brothers, too, will have mellowed by their anguish. What neither time, nor fate, nor happiness could overcome has happened through Joseph's grief and inner struggle: Again he can say and feel the words "beloved brothers." Joseph has regained his inner balance. He is able to guide and inspire others; again he can truly participate in others' joy. No longer are his words of goodness and of kindness mere words—they are reflected in his heart. Only one thing remains: justice. He must attain his justice and also justice for his brothers. Here Rainis is convinced that true justice cannot be attained without the remorse and the longing for forgiveness in both parties. Joseph's remorse is not sufficient; there must be remorse also in his brothers. Joseph seeks Potiphar's advice about this justice:

> You have told me:
> Let yourself be wronged, for you are great?
> And Potiphar concludes:
> —Do not protect yourself, for you are strong.
> This is the law of ancient virtue,
> Which Kachemna gave us a thousand years ago—
> When in the third rule he was the ninth ruler,
> Again a thousand years passed by—
> And in the fifth rule was the ruler Asa.
> Then Ptah-hotep, his wise man, wrote it down—

Potiphar's interpretation here is similar to that of the New Testament: When a man strikes you, turn the other cheek. Rainis could not accept such passive love. For him, love had to be active, transforming the individual himself and others: "Change, and change your own self upward!" For this reason, Joseph declares to Potiphar:

> I seek no more revenge—all I ask for
> Is only justice.—Will you deny this, too.

Potiphar reminds him that he should not ask for any reward for his striving and struggling, nor for the years of hardship, which he had to endure. Joseph accepts all these requirements. Nothing does he ask for himself, but he cannot compromise his sense of justice: "Now all I ask is justice." Rainis here expresses the Hebrews' deep feeling for justice—objective justice—which was their highest goal as it is also his. Jehovah is the God of Justice.

While Potiphar (representative of passive religious love) tries to dismiss Joseph's need for justice, the latter says that he must have this justice for the sake of harmony and balance in life: heaven and earth can remain only when they are in balance, and time and the soul can rest only in harmony. Only when the brothers will have changed their lives will Joseph, too, have attained harmony. In Potiphar's understanding, this harmony lies therein that everything passes on, the good and the bad; and, in their passing on, there is created balance between them. There cannot be revenge for them later, for then the situation has changed, and revenge is no longer relevant. The present has nothing in common with the past, for everything passes and ceases to be. Potiphar here represents Rainis' view of constant change and transformation of everything in life. Joseph here represents the Western, more masculine world with its determination for justice, equality, law and order; Potiphar,

on the other hand, represents the Eastern, more feminine world, which in greater harmony accepts life for what it is, treasures this great gift and accepts as part of life also suffering, for which balance and harmony will be established through time and life itself. There seems to be a greater appreciation of grace in the Eastern world, and this grace is also more dominant in Christianity. Through the dialogue between Joseph and Potiphar, both become changed: In the end, Potiphar realizes the greatness in Joseph's quest for justice, while Joseph accepts the fact that past wrongs cannot be atoned for; therefore, man should live in harmony and love with others right now, in the present, to avoid undue suffering. Joseph, in the end, embraces both views—Eastern and Western—and merges them into one.

The greatness of Joseph is that he is the embodiment of both good and evil, hate and love. The inner struggle of his life is due to the fact that he is driven by both of these forces: the force that calls him to revenge and justice and the force that makes him want to forgive. Through his struggle and search, Joseph has reached the realization that forgiveness cannot be achieved or granted by a third party; nor can he simply dismiss the whole subject and state that he has forgiven; he feels that true forgiveness calls for inner struggle, inner search and a definite conviction of remorse in both parties: Only when there is a spirit of remorse and a change of heart can true reconciliation be achieved. (pp. 245-56)

Rainis sets the stage for the transformation of the brothers: Joseph invites them to the banquet, where they are treated with kindness, which makes them feel extremely uncomfortable. The brothers feel that something terrible must be in store for them.

Before Joseph attacks them, however, Asnath sings the song of harvest, showing how Joseph is going to sacrifice himself for others, reminding him that this must be done through love:

> Osiris is the swelled ear of grain, which is tied to Isiris, the earth. The reaper cuts and separates them, the sower throws them into the wind. Seth hacks Osiris into pieces, scattering the shreds as the sower sows the wheat. Isis receives them and gathers them and makes them alive in the mystery of love. The grain drops into the soil and disappears. But other grain is ground to flour and pushed into the heat, then removed and once again pushed into the heat, until it has changed; and it is eaten up. And yet, it returns to the earth, as all return to the mother. The grain which had disappeared into the earth becomes alive from the warm rays of the sun. When it is unable to rise itself, it sends forth shoots, from his body and fruit, to rise up; it breaks the black walls of the grave and comes forth and sees the new sun; but the old body perishes, as does all other flesh since Ra; and it returns like boats to the shore. . . . Great cycles are drawn by the sun Ammon-Ra, and in eternal growth and in eternal change, through countless sufferings you must die so that life would rise! You are the god Nuter, the young green; through you will grow the grain of a hundred nations. . . . My hacked-up Osiris, you will grow!

Here Rainis has masterfully portrayed the harvest of life, death and the rebirth of man. Osiris is hacked to pieces, but he becomes whole again in the mystery of love, to come forth in a new sun—after-life. Rainis distinguishes the two-fold purpose of man's life: Some grain disappears into the soil for the new cycle, while other grain is ground and heated and eaten up—chastised and changed and used up by others, for the benefit of others, and also for his own soul. Rainis believed that the old body returned to dust, but some new form, like shoots from the grain, would break forth and reach after-life. A certain mystery underlies the interpretation—the mystery of love. In the next cycle, the fruits live on in future generations as their inheritance from the past, and also as man's own spiritual manifestation in eternity. All living things are constantly involved in eternal change and growth, in death and in life. Rainis points out that Joseph must sacrifice himself for the good of mankind, for the enlightenment of others. He is no longer motivated by revenge and ancient hate, but by "ancient love," which is his fond memory of his father and of Dina. Through compassion, Joseph seeks to bring his brothers back to true life to make them whole.

First, Joseph confronts them with an image of his own suffering so that they might clearly see their sin: When the statue of Osiris is carried through the hall, according to ancient tradition, the guests and Joseph's brother notice that it is really a boy, who is wrapped with thorns, not a wooden statue; with terror they recall how they had thrown Joseph into the pit, together with thorns, so that he would cry louder.

As they seek to leave, Joseph asks them to stay; and he explains that the festival reminds the people of death and of the final judgment: For the good, there will be reward in heaven, but the evil ones will be questioned and judged (referring to his later interrogations of them). Forty-two deadly sins will question such a one whether he is guilty of any of them. If he is guilty, his heart will be taken away, for the heart is the core of the strength of life (through sin man is separated from God); and this heart will be thrown into the depths of hell (unresolved guilt). In the night, the evil ones will have to descend the steps to the bottom of hell, through demons and all kinds of terrors. Here is a parallel with Dante's description of hell and its terrors; however, Rainis has interpreted hell as inner hell (man's search for his heart—for God—for redemption), while Dante interpreted it as outer hell (afflictions of the body through torture, filth, and fire). Dr. Kroner points out that "Dante's picture of hell is deficient because he did not sufficiently understand this truth that the guilty man had to see his own transgression; the punishments, therefore, depicted by him do not appear quite adequate." Rainis, in his interpretation here, shows a greater insight than Dante. By bringing the brothers to the awareness of death and judgment, Joseph tries to make them realize that there is still time to change—to repent.

Through the interrogation, which follows, the brothers still remain stubborn. They do not want to bring up their past. Even though they now realize their sins, they do not want to confess them. Because their hearts are hardened, it takes them much longer than it took Joseph to feel remorse. When Asnath asks Joseph just to forgive them: "Your justice—only to forgive, to pity" Joseph states his understanding of the purpose of forgiveness:

> What is the meaning of forgiveness?
> To say that evil is good? To become evil oneself?
> No, to take evil and to change it into good is to forgive.
> For otherwise beasts will devour men,
> And mankind will deny itself
> And crush the shoots which aspire toward good.
> The earth will open and forth will come the dragon—evil.

Here Rainis points out that the purpose of forgiveness is to change evil into good. In order to do this, man must be heroic, and he must always actively participate in the struggle between good and evil. The evil man must "die to his old self" and change his whole being to a new way of life. Rainis cannot accept that evil can simply be erased and forgotten; it must be overcome consciously.

Even though the interrogations create a great strain on Joseph—he must turn away so that they would not see his tears—finally, at the third interrogation Reuben takes the blame upon himself, saying that he is guilty and that he will accept his punishment; the others, however, should be allowed to go home. But Joseph is not satisfied with such an easy answer to the problem; he wants all of them to realize their guilt and to become changed through remorse.

Still they are stubborn: Only a Jew should judge a Jew. Rainis here parallels Joseph's suffering to the countless sufferings of his people, who never received justice because they had no rights. And, in indignation, Rainis says through Joseph:

> Was not your brother, whom you murdered
> Also a man?—or just a Jew?—Did he not
> As a man feel pain? Or does it hurt
> A Jew less than any other man when he is cut?—
> Cannot I also as a man
> Demand for his suffering expiation?
> —And judge you here as man judges man?
> —Not only as a Jew a Jew?

Rainis here emphasizes that for the sake of humanity, there must be objective justice, which sees the worth of each individual. Why should there be a differentiation when it comes to the distribution of justice? Afraid, the brothers still seek excuses for their actions, saying that whatever happened has happened as it should have been. God himself let it happen, and Joseph should not question them about it. Rainis believed in the mystery of fate, the activity of God in man's life; however, here he points out the weakness of the excuse of people who try to blame God for their own misdeeds, ignorance, and negligence. Another points out that if their brother had been more upright, he would not have fallen. This is another fallacy. Right cannot always prevail over might, in a sense of physical endurance.

Finally the brothers agree that there is one who could judge them, but he is dead. Then Joseph reveals himself: "I am the dead man! I am—Joseph!" The brothers fall back is if struck by lightning. By making himself known, Joseph has smitten them. When in *Don Giovanni*, Mozart's opera, the ghost of the father appears in the last act, Don Giovanni is judged and is sent to hell; however, Joseph's revelation to his brothers, in compassion, creates in them remorse and the longing for forgiveness. In accordance with his dream, Joseph (the firmament) has descended over his brothers (the mountains) and has crushed their false justice (their hardened hearts), embracing them in their remorse (on the lowness of the earth). The brothers fall down on their knees, afraid to come close to him. But Joseph, seeing their fear, goes to each of them and kisses them. In deep emotion, the brothers weep as if in great pain. Joseph now realizes that all is fulfilled. This was his mission for them:

> Oh, in your great weeping all is atoned for,
> Oh, evil, through remorse, turns into good,—
> To life now comes even your own justice.

Joseph now realizes that never can evil done be all repaid; neither can the good be repaid when time has gone by; therefore men should love each other and work together while there is still time. What Rainis is trying to say is that man should live his life fully every moment, every hour, for nothing can be made up later. Often it is too late. Life should be spontaneous, fresh, exciting, creative, mysterious, full of love—not calculated, bit by bit.

Seeing how the brothers try to be kind and loving to him and to each other, Joseph feels that his mission is fulfilled at this particular time. Now his spirit looks forward to new vistas: to seek the great justice beyond death. Joseph feels that he is no longer a Jew, neither is he an Egyptian. He has surpassed the narrow boundaries of tribes and nations. Giving to his tribe the land of Goshen, Joseph bids them fare-well:

> To you the whole world I return
> And keep for myself only my soul!
> I go away, so I can find myself.

Potiphar realizes that "since a thousand years nothing like this has happened, since even Kachemna!" As the brothers and the people of Egypt bless Joseph, he looks into the distance and says ecstatically:

> Again I see my homeland:
> There's the high cliff—there's Dina, there I'll climb—
> Dying—I shall not die—the messengers of the sun
> Will under my feet their winged covers spread,
> Into the bright land of the sun they'll carry me;
> There I will go to fight in a new struggle:
> My own light I shall merge with the sun,
> I shall come into harmony with the universe.
> Not to scorn the world, but to understand it;
> With generations I'll be one and gain peace,
> There will be no more walls between self and other,
> Between just, unjust,—between to be or not to be,
> And then I shall come back and bring to you the sun.

Joseph's "Faustian" soul is not satisfied even after having attained his own peace and that of his brothers, as long as there is suffering in mankind, which results from wrong principles and from the lack of objective justice. For the final truth and the great justice, which can be found only beyond death and which is hidden by the mystery of love, Joseph is willing to go even through death. Dina, as his "Beatrice" or "Margaret," leads him on and guides him toward his final enlightenment.

As Joseph walks away, Potiphar realizes that through Joseph's life the people have become renewed:

> You have enlarged the narrow bounds of people;
> You chastise without club, you shoot without a bow,
> You change him who encounters you,
> You are he who renews in us eternity!

Rainis shows that Joseph, as a seeker, lives between the present and the world of his dreams, in which reflect the present and the future. There is something eternal in his soul which does not let him rest on his accomplishments: "Das Werdende, das ewig wirkt und lebt," the eternal force within him, spurs Joseph on to greater harmony than he can achieve on earth, where there will be no more walls between self and other, between just and unjust, between to be or not to be. The last phrase, of course, reminds one of Shakespeare's famous words of Hamlet. Indeed, Joseph's problem is like the problem of Hamlet, who seeks synthesis between just and unjust, between to be or not to be. While, however, Hamlet dies by someone else's hand, after having achieved a sense of clarity and revenge, Joseph remains active after his struggle with his brothers. He is not satisfied with his victory but seeks an even greater clarity and understanding, which would benefit not only him and his immediate problems but which would help all mankind: ". . . And then I shall come back and bring to you the sun." It seems that here is expressed also Rainis' socialistic idealism: not only

to fulfill oneself in after-life, where there are no boundaries between the opposites of this world, but also to go into a new struggle for clarity, which would benefit all mankind. Even beyond this earthly life, Joseph feels responsible to society.

In summary, at the core of the play is Joseph's hardening of heart against his brothers, against all of life. Revenge was all that he could think of and dream of in the midst of joy, happiness, love and prosperity. In this lies Joseph's tragedy. Only when he is confronted again with the past can Joseph resolve his problem: Neither time, nor love, nor anything else in the whole world could quench his thirst for revenge and for justice. Joseph realizes that his brothers, too, have suffered; they cannot bear to talk of their sins. Each time that Joseph brings up the subject they beg him to stop. But this does not help Joseph to overcome his feeling of revenge. Only when he himself suffers for having unjustly hurt them, after he has sent them away with the money and the chalice in their bags, can Joseph say that he felt so much sadder. In compassion, Joseph can again say "beloved brothers," even with his heart. In order to help his brothers, Joseph knows that he must yet go another step: He must awaken in them remorse and a desire for forgiveness. This finally leads to reconciliation and a new life in wholeness and in love. Through Joseph's realization of sin and redemption, remorse and forgiveness, finally the realization of the truth of life makes Joseph spiritually free to go on to greater heights in the life of the spirit. (Here is a parallel to the New Testament: "Seek and you will find . . ." and "The truth will make you free.").

The story of Joseph is a story of exile and a reunification, not only with his brothers but also with the Absolute. Joseph knew through his dreams that God had great plans for him: He would give him all the land to rule, and all would bow down before him. In Egypt, however, when he is a ruler and all the people bow down before him, Joseph finds no real joy in his heart. He feels this is not the work for which God has intended him. Outside of his native land, Joseph feels exiled, torn from his roots—his father, his tribe, his faith and his work. In his loneliness, Joseph does not any more feel so close to God as he did before, and slowly revenge seeps into his heart. For seventeen years, the black shirt of thorns pieces not only his body but also his heart. Only when Joseph is spiritually reconciled with his brothers does he realize that this was God's mission for him, and that now he is ready to go further and search for the final unification of mankind in order to overcome the prejudices between nationalities, races and creeds, which create divisions and walls between individuals. (pp. 256-66)

> *Arvids Ziedonis, Jr., in his* The Religious Philosophy of Jānis Rainis: Latvian Poet, *Latvju Grāmata, 1969, 344 p.*

EMMA S. RICHARDS   (essay date 1974)

[*In the following excerpt, Richards demonstrates an affinity between Rainis's poetry and that of the English Romantic poets.*]

A study of the Latvian poet Jānis Rainis [*The Religious Philosophy of Janis Rainis*, by Arvids Ziedonis, Jr.; see excerpt dated 1969] . . . offers to the West a good example of the reciprocal nature of literature and history and shows the paralleling and echoing of literary themes over a diverse period of time and place. The work of Rainis, largely unknown to readers of English and American literature, opens the prospect of perceiving the range and spread of ideas considered peculiar to the Romantic epoch of the early nineteenth century

(1798-1832), suggesting, at the same time, the infectious quality of literary ideas and literary forms.

The complexity of events that comprise the background of Rainis's life evoked responses in him strongly analogous to the thought of many of the English Romantic poets, including Blake, Wordsworth, and Shelley. Born in 1865, Rainis grew up in the years when radical and revolutionary movements were troubling Europe, stirring nationalist and populist quickenings against oppressive and tyrannical rule. Like many other intellectuals, Rainis found his life's work in the patriotic utterances of poetry, folk song, and drama, as well as in the polemics of social and political reform in the cause of Latvian independence. (p. 126)

Like the Romantic poets, Rainis inculcated through his plays and poems a spirit of resistance to tyrannical rule. His method included the use of myth and folk tale as a reminder of the unique culture of Latvia. He too felt the need to keep alive in his people the spirit of freedom and independence. As a student of history and literature, he suggests in his diaries that it is the function of the poet to describe his age, to show the relationship among events, and to place them in such perspective that it will be seen how the present derives from the past and, in turn, shapes the future. It is the poet who thus becomes a "shaper" and "creator" of his own time.

In his book on Rainis, Arvids Ziedonis shows how the theme of national independence develops in the plays and poems of the years prior to the short-lived revolution of 1905 and also in the years thereafter. In *Fire and Night,* one of a cycle of plays designed to inspire his people in freeing themselves from the autocracy of the landed gentry and the Tsar, Rainis creates a tale involving mythic elements. A legendary hero, Lāčplēsis, "bearslayer," is sent by Pērkons, the Lord of creation, to the castle of Spīdola, emblem of spiritual light. In a struggle with the evil Black Knight, both warriors fall over a cliff and Laimdota, symbol of Latvia, must save Lāčplēsis. Eventually, Lāčplēsis realizes his life must include two goals—the temporal one of union with Laimdota and the eternal one of union with Spīdola. Written between the years 1903 and 1905, the play calls for a spiritual regeneration by means of the eternal struggle between the primordial forces of good and evil. Despite the mythical characters and the fantastic trappings of air-borne carriage, aereal music, and magic sword, the play conveys strongly the note of moral and spiritual struggle.

A poetry collection, *Sowing the Storm,* also written in anticipation of the revolution of 1905, expresses the joy of a new epoch of self-determination for Latvia. Unfortunately, the attempt at revolution by Latvia failed, and the punitive measures of the Russians, aided by the Germans, resulted in the death of some two thousand of the Latvian population, the burning of many homes, and the devastation of the land, with Rainis and his wife Aspazija, however, escaping to Switzerland, where they remained in exile for fifteen years. Rainis continued his resistance with the publication of numerous satirical and poetical pieces. Such a collection of poetry, *The Quiet Book,* for example, though confiscated, expresses despair over the failure to achieve liberation and the return of oppression.

In the years of exile, Rainis suffered the hardships of illness, depression, and domestic difficulties. He knew intimately the bitterness of solitude. Nevertheless, this period was also one of self-examination and meditation during which he gained insights on the imperatives of man's inner spiritual life. These philosophical and religious thoughts found their way into the collection of poems entitled *The End and the Beginning,* which examines the course of human destiny from birth to death, the relation of man with nature, and the growth of self-awareness of the soul. (pp. 129-30)

In his early years as newspaper editor, [Rainis] had formulated his theory of literature, a theory which suggests its functional use in the life of a people: "A great work must be done: to bring light to our brothers, to lead the nation toward a brighter, happier future. . . . The highest goal—development of the nation, which must be furthered with all means, with an alert mind—even 'if we have to suffer the consequences'." Like the earlier Romantics, Rainis dedicated himself to the task of writing, as a force in effecting a national liberation, a national freedom resting on the concern for individual freedom as well.

Inevitably such philosophical attitudes embrace not only political but religious idealism as well. In his study of folk literature, Rainis perceived something of the power of the ancient religious truths. He saw that Latvian mythology consists of a poetry of "ethical and virtuous character, based on the merger of nature with life." In the love of nature exhibited in the myths he felt the parallel with the religion of the East—Shinto and Hindu—and became convinced also of the power of this ancient literature to influence the life of his own time. For that reason, he incorporated the ancient myth with its "love for life, joy in work and in the beauty of nature" as a "wisdom of the past to guide his people in the present and to influence them for generations to come."

A hallmark of Romanticism is its special view of nature as a religious or quasi-religious force, dynamic in its effect on the life of mankind. Wordsworth, as the epitome of the nature poet, was profoundly interested in the interaction of mind with nature and centered his poetic belief on this concept. As a student of psychology, he believed that a reciprocal relation exists between the mind and the world of nature, the mind both receiving and creating impressions of beauty. Physical nature, with Wordsworth, thus possesses the power of awakening the sensibilities and shaping the moral awareness of mankind. (pp. 130-31)

Through reading Latvian mythology, Rainis came to view the cosmos as a composite of various attitudes of divine creation. These manifestations were in themselves regarded as minor divinities—"gods of the sky, of woods, and fields." His play *Indulis and Arija,* semi-historical and legendary, interprets nature in both pagan and Christian terms. Indulis, in a ritual of sun worship, addresses himself to God. He seeks help from nature in the blue anemone that he presses to his wound; he calls upon the oakbranches as living protector. In constructing his characters, Rainis attributes to them a philosophy that regards the earth as sacred, the natural world, both beautiful and terrifying, both comforting and awesome, imbued with the mysterious force of God. (pp. 131-32)

Myth [was utilized by the Romantic poets] for the purpose of plot and character and for atmospheric feelings of the supernatural. The use of myth conveys also the symbolic struggles of good and evil. The use of myth explores the psyche in an effort to perceive the workings of creative artists and to perceive new artistic patterns. By means of myth, thus, Romantic poets created a new interest in physical nature as a source of vitalistic energy, and in human nature and the psyche as reservoirs of unconscious ideas potent for artistic creativity, as well as possible new arenas for discovery of age-old archetypalist patterns.

The new ideas associated with the theories of mind and the nature of imagination and the subconscious which entered English poetry in this period correlates with [an] interest in German writers. (p. 132)

[The] "German" fad drew England into the mainstream of Continental literature and may, thus, represent the source held in common—the link between the West and the East of the Baltic States, accounting for the resemblances in Jānis Rainis of the earlier Romantic poets. The intellectual ferment of the Romantic epoch in England, signalled by the revolutionary ideas on the social scene and the unorthodox views on religion and nature, involved also new views for literature. Experimentation with the traditional literary forms and structures of ballad, sonnet, ode, and blank verse narrative occurred in new or modified ways, involving the language of the "common man" as appropriate diction for poetry. Whatever the literary form or adaptation, however, the focus rested on the inner gaze, the subjective feeling, the personality of the artist, and on the view of nature as an organic part of the life of man.

With Rainis, as Ziedonis suggests, the main preoccupation developed from the special events of his time. His work necessarily encompasses the more limited range of the functional purpose of teaching, inspiring, and generating the forces of morale for the struggles of national liberation. Perhaps another study in English is due to enlarge the acquaintance of the West with Rainis as an artist and critic, providing material on his theory of poetry, his interest in and handling of metrical forms, his ideas on artistic composition and on the philosophy of the creative imagination—these may be subjects for future explorations for students of literature and subjects for future analysis of the relationship of literature and history. (pp. 133-34)

> *Emma S. Richards, "English Romanticism and the Latvian Poet Jānis Rainis," in* Journal of Baltic Studies, *Vol. V, No. 2, Summer, 1974, pp. 126-35.*

ROLFS EKMANIS   (essay date 1978)

[*In the following excerpt, Ekmanis surveys Rainis's career.*]

[Janis Rainis was] the focal point of Latvian literary and intellectual history during the first three decades of this century. . . . His place still today is unquestionable as the greatest Latvian poet of this century—Latvians of all ranks would say their greatest writer, deserving to be compared with the greatest names in world literature, is Rainis. The essayist Zenta Maurina calls Rainis "the voice and the central core of a nation, the interpreter of the soul of his people" [see excerpt dated 1968]. Rainis substantially enriched Latvian literature and brought it up to the level of that of West European literature. Brilliant and strongly individualistic, he is the best example in modern Latvian letters of the organic relationship between talent shaped by tradition and talent creating tradition. (p. 69)

Rainis' masterful translations gave great works of world literature their footing in Latvia and proved that the Latvian language could be an instrument of unusual emotional and intellectual experiences. Thoroughly familiar with European literature, continually drawing attention to European literary

achievements and deriding local dilettantism, Rainis, nevertheless, did not fail to understand national values, and for his cultural work found inspirations on Latvian territory, in Latvian history and folklore. With the first two collections, *Tālas noskaņas zilā vakarā* (*Distant Moods in a Blue Evening*) and *Vētras sēja* (*Sowing the Storm*), which heralded a new age in Latvian poetry and established his pre-eminence as a lyric poet, Rainis proved himself an exquisite technician in verse, possessing a fastidious sense of form and poetic diction. He was consistently successful with formal innovations. Because of his concise and terse, yet colorful and mellow mode of expression, the poet preferred an abbreviated sonnet form consisting of nine lines in iambic pentameter (the "Rainis' stanza"). Rainis' poems, revealing his own voice in its majestic and everyday perspective, provoked the most unusual response, because they were unrivalled for their passionate and rebellious protest against oppression. He was at once regarded as an apostle of freedom. In the next three volumes *Jaunais spēks* (*New Strength*), *Klusā grāmata* (*The Silent Book*—officially banned by the censors in 1909, it was republished in 1910 as *Vēja nestas lapas—Leaves Driven by the Wind*), and *Tie, kas neaizmirst* (*Those Who Do Not Forget*), we find fiery verse striving to strengthen the national spirit of his compatriots who took part in the abortive 1905 revolt against Tsarist autocracy. In the allegoric poem *Ave, sol!*, Rainis extolls the forces of light and wisdom symbolized by the sun. Into his most intellectual poetry collection, *Gals un sākums* (*End and Beginning*), the poet projected the spiritual and social crisis of his own individuality and that of his nation, which in turn indicated the underlying restlessness of a whole civilization. One solution recommended there is the acceptance of perpetual changeability—a theme which often appeared in his dramas. Latvia's attainment of independence in 1918 was greeted by Rainis with two memorable volumes, *Sveika, brīvā Latvija!* (*I Salute You, Free Latvia!*), and *Daugava*, containing many verses which were and have remained a reveille and a hope in the hearts of Latvians for the last fifty years. Many more notable collections of verse followed (some published posthumously) with lyrical poems exceedingly variegated and rich in themes. Although Rainis often advanced theses, he knew how to distinguish between aesthetic and moral values, and accepted their interdependence.

Most of Rainis' fifteen dramas (all but two written in blank verse) espoused national causes and drew heavily on Latvian history and particularly folklore. A dramatist *par excellence*, Rainis, however, stepped out of the circle of national creeds and appealed to universal human emotions. He who tramples down on others humiliates himself as well—this the leading and central theme of Rainis' plays. The most sacred word for him was mankind. Rainis' *Uguns un nakts* (*Fire and Night*), one of the most esteemed works in Latvian literature, is built around the ancient popular legend about the Latvian epic hero Lāčplēsis ("Bearslayer")—who not only assumes power through the blood of his defeated enemies, but by his direct and close ties with mother earth—and his struggle with the Black Knight. The theme of freedom is prevalent in this play. The interest in the symbolic continues in *Zelta zirgs* (*The Golden Steed*), based on an Estonian version of the folk tale about the princess who slept for seven years, with much admixture of Rainis' own incidents and details. The humble and altruistic Antiņš, at the beginning held in contempt for his fancied stupidity, is seen in all the glory of undaunted courage in time of crisis. In *Indulis un Ārija*, set in a more authentic distant past of the Baltics, the clash between democratic ideas and despotic autocracy is accompanied by the theme of the "eternally feminine." *Pūt, vējiņi!* (*Blow, Winds!*), described by the author himself as a "consequence of the atmosphere of exile and reflections on its psychology," follows the highly stylized trochaic tetrameter of folk songs. Somber mysticism and numerous elusive symbols and allegories characterize his *Spēlēju, dancoju* (*I Played, I Danced*). This fairy play in verse, full of demons, witches and hobgoblins, is perhaps Rainis' most original drama. *Jāzeps un viņa brāļi* (*Joseph and His Brothers*) is usually considered Rainis' greatest drama because of the striking emotional-psychological treatment given its characters. According to Zenta Mauriņa, this play, expressing Rainis' awareness of universal communion and the irreconcilable conflict between the individual and society, takes on the same meaning for Latvians as does Goethe's *Faust* for the Germans. Though based on a Biblical narrative, it has little in common with the Biblical story and nothing at all with Thomas Mann's trilogy *Joseph und seine Brüder*. While in *Krauklītis* (*The Little Raven*) Rainis drew heavily on Latvian ritual folk lyrics including ancient wedding songs, *Ilja Muromietis* is a dramatization of Russian heroic epic songs. In the latter, the hero Ilja of Murom, a variant of Rainis great anchorites, turns into stone because he fails to understand the law of "dialectical movement." The subject of *Rīgas ragana* (*The Witch from Riga*) concerns the taking of Riga by Peter the Great in 1710. The entire play, based on historical facts and folk legends, is a symbolic warning of Russian aggression. The prose tragedy *Mīla stiprāka par nāvi* (*Love Is More Powerful than Death*) is devoted to the highly dramatic legend about Maija Greif from Turaida which had inspired several works of literature since 1848, by both Latvian and Baltic German writers. Five of Rainis' dramas have been set as operas and his lyrics have also attracted composers. (pp. 70-2)

> *Rolfs Ekmanis, "Literary Scene in Latvia during the*
> *First Year of Soviet Rule, 1940-1941," in his* Latvian
> Literature under the Soviets: 1940-1975, *Nordland*
> *Publishing Company, 1978, pp. 38-78.*

ADDITIONAL BIBLIOGRAPHY

Rubulis, Aleksis. "Latvian Literature: National Literature." In his *Baltic Literature*, pp. 115-59. Notre Dame: University of Notre Dame Press, 1970.
> Brief biographical and critical sketch.

"Jānis Rainis." *Soviet Literature*, No. 10 (1975): 161-63.
> Reprints two letters from Rainis to the writers Nikolajs Helmanis and Ansis Gulbis.

Stulpāns, Jeronims. Afterword to *Lauztās Priedes*, by J. Rainis, pp. 116-18. Riga, Latvia: Izdevniecība Liesma, 1965.
> Praises *Lauztās Priedes* as a hymn to the socialist revolution in Latvia. Stulpans quotes Andrejs Upits's contention that "in beauty and inspired revolutionary force, no other poem in all Latvian lyrical poetry is comparable to these immortal lines" and maintains that "Rainis was ever loyal to the Revolution, to Socialism. . . . He marches with all those who are united in the great struggle for mankind's happiness."

Ziedonis, Arvids, Jr. "The Controversy about the Poet Jānis Rainis." In *First Conference on Baltic Studies*, edited by Ivar Ivask, pp. 81-2. Tacoma, Wash.: Association for the Advancement of Baltic Studies, 1969.
> Decries critical commentary on Rainis as "superficial and fragmentary," maintaining that critics of varying political and religious perspectives have routinely oversimplified the philosophy expressed in his writings in order to claim him as a proponent of their own views.

———. "The Influence of Jānis Rainis on Writers in Soviet Latvia." *Journal of Baltic Studies* VI, Nos. 2-3 (Summer-Fall 1975): 141-52.
> Discusses Rainis's critical reputation and influence on younger Latvian writers.

Thomas (Clayton) Wolfe

1900-1938

American novelist, short story writer, dramatist, essayist, and poet.

The following entry presents criticism of Wolfe's novel *Look Homeward, Angel*. For a discussion of Wolfe's complete career, see *TCLC,* Volumes 4 and 13.

Wolfe's first novel, *Look Homeward, Angel,* is an evocative portrayal of a young man's coming of age. Based on the author's childhood and youth in the town of Asheville, North Carolina, this work is so faithful to the unappealing as well as the admirable traits of its characters that the people of Wolfe's hometown considered it a personal attack on them. Commentators have often viewed *Look Homeward, Angel* as an unfocused melange of incidents and emotions, although some critics have disagreed with this characterization, noting structural elements that serve to unify Wolfe's novel. Important among these are three central thematic concepts: the preexistence of a person's consciousness before birth, the isolation of the individual, and a romantic fatalism which holds that all human behavior is determined by natural causes and is thus unchangeable. While such themes emphasize the strong feeling of desperation and melancholy in *Look Homeward, Angel,* Wolfe also offered a sense of hope in his celebration of sensual life and affirmation of self-knowledge as a means to personal fulfillment. Published to mixed reviews and critically dismissed for several years after Wolfe's death, *Look Homeward, Angel* has since gained recognition as a major American novel.

Wolfe began *Look Homeward, Angel* in 1926, the year after he met Aline Bernstein, a New York stage designer who supported him financially and emotionally during its composition. She had convinced him to abandon writing drama, an enterprise in which he had been unsuccessfully engaged for several years, and with her encouragement Wolfe began a novel tentatively titled "The Building of a Wall." The finished manuscript, the title of which had become "O Lost!" was accepted by Scribner's in 1928, with the proviso that the lengthy work be editorially pruned and the title changed. With this process Wolfe began a professional and personal relationship with Scribner's editor Maxwell Perkins. Perkins persuaded Wolfe to cut a lengthy section at the beginning of the book which chronicled the ancestors of its principal characters, the Gant family, but beyond this concession Wolfe seemed incapable of revising his work without adding pages of new material; eventually, Perkins himself had to assume much of the responsibility for paring the manuscript. Although the text underwent significant editorial change, it required far less alteration than did any of Wolfe's later novels, which editors constructed from Wolfe's voluminous outpouring of autobiographical prose. The novel, retitled *Look Homeward, Angel* after a phrase from John Milton's elegy "Lycidas," was published in 1929.

Look Homeward, Angel is an example of the bildungsroman, a novelistic form in which a young protagonist grows from innocence to maturity. The bildungsroman is often autobiographical and frequently depicts the young author's rejection of social conventions and institutions and decision to become a writer. In *Look Homeward, Angel,* Wolfe portrays Eugene

Gant, Wolfe's fictional alter ego, from infancy to the age of twenty, when he is preparing to enter Harvard. In the course of the narrative, Eugene confronts his sexual awakening, struggles for independence from his family, and sees his much-loved brother Ben die. The climax of the novel focuses on Ben's death, an occurrence that has a tremendous effect on Eugene; the final chapter, the supernatural dimension of which stands in contrast to the rigid naturalism of the rest of the novel, portrays the ghost of Ben returning to Eugene and making him recognize that the answers he seeks can be found only within himself. Conspicuous among the achievements of *Look Homeward, Angel* are Wolfe's remarkable character portrayals, particularly his depiction of Eugene's father and mother, W. O. and Eliza Gant. W. O. Gant is a loud, energetic, openly lecherous, and self-pitying man who fully dominates his family even as he feels restricted by it. Eliza, who always refers to her husband as "Mr. Gant," is puritanical and penurious, and mothers her children to the point of suffocation, especially Eugene, her youngest child, who sleeps in her bed until he is nine years old and whom Eliza calls "baby" even when he is an adult.

Wolfe begins *Look Homeward, Angel* with a manifesto of determinism, writing: "Each of us is all the sums he has not counted: subtract us into nakedness and night again, and you shall see begin in Crete four thousand years ago the love that ended yesterday in Texas,'' and concluding that ''each moment is the fruit of forty thousand years.'' Although *Look Homeward, Angel* is deterministic in principle, much of the conflict in the novel revolves around Eugene's violent reaction against, rather than resigned acceptance of, his surroundings, his family, and his life. The loneliness and sense of loss Eugene experiences as a result of this conflict reflect two other primary themes of the novel: the solitude of the individual and the preexistence of personal consciousness before birth. Wolfe wrote in a letter to his sister Mabel that the dominant message of his book was ''that men are strangers, that they are lonely and forsaken, that they are in exile on this earth, that they are born, live, and die alone.'' Throughout his life Wolfe felt socially inadequate and alone, and he instilled in Eugene the same sense of isolation; in fact, critics point out that every member of the Gant family appears separate and detached, either by temperament, hostility, or the inability to communicate fully with one another. While Wolfe shared with other modern writers the belief that the loneliness of the individual was, at bottom, a universal and irreparable condition, his assertion of the preexistence of personal consciousness was more idiosyncratic. Critics point out that Wolfe's failure to reconcile such a belief with his deterministic vision of humanity creates an interesting thematic tension in the novel. The concept of preexistence allowed Wolfe to portray even the infant Eugene as possessing an adult intelligence. Thus, through the use of interior monologue, Wolfe could convey Eugene's reactions to his surroundings without the restrictions an author would normally encounter in portraying the viewpoint of a child. The concept of preexistence was appropriated for more than technical reasons, however: it also justifies Wolfe's evocation of an undefined sense of loss in the character of Eugene. This sense of loss is construed as the individual's memory of a paradise which existed before physical existence. In the face of determinism, loneliness, and loss, Wolfe nevertheless achieved a sense of hope in *Look Homeward, Angel*. The decision reached by Eugene at the conclusion of the novel—that one must look into oneself to discover freedom and peace—stands as a counterpoint and possible resolution to the deterministic vision of the beginning; as Eugene's brother Ben tells him, ''*You* are your world.''

Look Homeward, Angel met with mixed reviews when it was first published. Although immediately acclaimed by some critics as a brilliant contribution to American literature, an approximately equal number of critics disparaged the novel. The negative reviews can be divided into two categories, the first consisting of the reactions of primarily Southern critics who considered the novel an unprincipled attack on Wolfe's family, his hometown of Asheville, and, by extension, the South itself. A second group of critics disparaged the novel for what they considered offensive subject matter and a juvenile emotionalism in which the response of the protagonist to every experience is so uniformly intense that distinctions are lost between weighty and trivial matters. Later critics began to summarily dismiss Wolfe's work, particularly as his subsequent novels made it clear that he was incapable of writing anything but autobiography so ill-disguised that even names were often only moderately changed—W. O. Wolfe became W. O. Gant; Julia Elizabeth Wolfe, Eliza Gant; Ben Wolfe, Ben Gant— and that a great deal of editorial intervention was necessary to arrange coherent narratives from Wolfe's fragmented and voluminous memoirs. Bernard DeVoto, in a famous essay entitled ''Genius Is Not Enough,'' acknowledged Wolfe's talent but asserted that such talent was insufficient to produce great literature if the writer had no artistic control or

vision of anything but his own life. This reaction was typical until the middle 1950s, when critics who had enjoyed reading *Look Homeward, Angel* in their youth became part of the critical establishment. Prominent among these was C. Hugh Holman, whose essay ''The Loneliness at the Core'' pointed out the central theme of isolation to which the book's audience, composed largely of young adults, responds. Gradually, a re-evaluation of Wolfe's work took place, resulting in discussion of various aspects of *Look Homeward, Angel*, such as its humor, philosophical assumptions, symbolism, and the psychology of its main character and, implicitly, of Wolfe himself.

Recent critics have utilized various methodologies to examine *Look Homeward, Angel*, two of the most important being the identification of recurring symbolic elements in the work and the analysis of the psychologies of the characters. Elaborate patterns of symbolism have been traced through the novel, the most obvious of which are first encountered in the introductory prose poem, in which ''a stone, a leaf, an unfound door'' are all invoked, and are throughout the text repeatedly evoked, as symbols associated with Eugene's sense of loss and indefinite desire. The theme of isolation is also introduced in the prose poem, and the final sentence, ''O lost, and by the wind grieved, ghost, come back again,'' is repeated wholly or in part as a leitmotif at several points in the narrative. The web of symbolism is one element Wolfe used to unify an otherwise episodic novel and to reinforce his subjects of loneliness, loss, and the desire for escape. These subjects are tellingly examined by psychological critics, who contend that studying Wolfe's autobiographical characters and the circumstances of his life as revealed in his novels can aid in understanding Wolfe and explain his achievements and limitations as a writer.

Look Homeward, Angel is generally regarded as Wolfe's most complete and greatest work, the one in which his energy and lyric prose are most evident and successful. While flawed by exaggerated emotion and unrevised autobiographical material, the novel is rich in sensual detail and passionate intensity and is increasingly recognized as one of the most important novels in twentieth-century American literature.

(See also *Contemporary Authors*, Vol. 9; *Dictionary of Literary Biography*, Vol. 9: *American Novelists 1910-1945; Dictionary of Literary Biography Yearbook: 1985;* and *Dictionary of Literary Biography Documentary Series*, Vol. 2.)

BASIL DAVENPORT   (essay date 1929)

[*Davenport is an American educator, critic, and editor who has compiled numerous anthologies of science fiction and fantasy. In the following essay, he compares Wolfe to French satirist François Rabelais, finding that both authors combined sensitivity with a great appetite for life.*]

If it were customary to head reviews with a motto, like a chapter of Walter Scott, a review of *Look Homeward, Angel* might well take a phrase from Mr. Arthur Machen's *The Secret Glory*: ''*C'est Maître François! Maître François en très mauvais humeur peut-être, mais Maître François tout de même!*'' [''That's Master François! Master François in very bad humor, perhaps, but Master François all the same!''] The analogy must not be pushed too far; there are of course many important differences, notably a violent emotional intensity in Mr. Wolfe that is entirely lacking in Rabelais, but they have the same fundamental and most unusual quality, a robust sensitiveness. Extraordinary keenness of perception usually makes a character like Roderick Usher or Des Esseintes, or, in real life, Proust, one who is forced to shut himself away from bright lights, loud sounds, and strong feelings, and occupies himself with infinitely cautious and delicate experiments upon himself. But Mr. Wolfe, like Rabelais, though plainly odors and colors and all stimuli affect him more intensely than most people, is happily able to devour sensations with an enormous vigor; his perceptions have a rare combination of fineness and largeness.

In manner, Mr. Wolfe is most akin to James Joyce, somewhere between the ascetic beauty of the *Portrait of the Artist as a Young Man* and the unpruned fecundity of *Ulysses*; but he resembles many other people by turns. His hero, Eugene Gant, amuses himself by registering at country hotels as John Milton or William Blake, or by asking for a cup of cold water and blessing the giver in his Father's name; so Mr. Wolfe amuses himself by writing here in the manner of one author and there of another. He will suddenly fall into a dada fantasia, such as often appears in *transition,* as:

> A woman sobbed and collapsed in a faint. She was immediately carried out by two Boy Scouts . . . who administered first aid to her in the rest-room, one of them hastily kindling a crackling fire of pine boughs by striking two flints together, while the other made a tourniquet, and tied several knots in his handkerchief,—

and so on, and half a dozen pages later he will enumerate, in the painfully unimaginative manner of "An American Tragedy," the real holdings of Mrs. Gant:

"There were, besides, three good building-lots on Merrion Avenue valued at $2,000 apiece, or at $5,500 for all three; the house on Woodson Street valued at $5,000," and so on for a page and a half. That is, it seems to be the great gift of Mr. Wolfe that everything is interesting, valuable, and significant to him. It must be confessed that he has just missed the greatest of gifts, that of being able to convey his interest to the ordinary reader.

Upon what was his vitality nourished? Rabelais fed on all the fulness of the French Renaissance, a dawn in which it was bliss to be alive; what would he have been like if he had been a poor boy in a small southern town, with a drunken father, a shrewish mother, and a family of quarreling brothers and sisters? Mr. Wolfe's answer seems to be that, in his childhood at least, he would have done unexpectedly well. Eugene, in pitifully cramped surroundings, somehow has a greater fulness of life than most boys have. From his father, especially, he draws some sense of Dionysian madness, of Falstaffian greatness. The teaching he has is very bad, but he gets somewhere, from it or from himself, a real feeling for Latin and Greek. His first money is earned on a paper route that takes him through the negro quarter, his first knowledge of women comes from a negress who is in arrears to his company, yet he is never without a sense of the wonder and pain of desire and hunger. Years ago Mr. Tarkington said: "There's just as many kinds of people in Kokomo as there is in Pekin," but he carried little conviction, for his melodrama was too obviously arranged. It is Mr. Wolfe's contribution that he has drawn an unsparing picture of character and emotion. For those who can see it, there is everywhere a wealth of vitality that is almost enough.

But it is the little less, after all, and his town grows more insufficient as Eugene grows older. There is one chapter, in

manner probably inspired by *The Waste Land,* describing an afternoon in the square, with a running comment of quotations.

> "Give me a dope, too."
>
> "I don't want anything," said Pudge Carr. Such drinks as made them nobly wild, not mad. . . .
>
> Mrs. Thelma Jarvis, the milliner, drew, in one swizzling guzzle, the last beaded chain of linked sweetness long drawn out from the bottom of her glass. Drink to me only with thine eyes. . . . She writhed carefully among the crowded tables, with a low rich murmur of contrition. Her voice was ever soft, gentle, and low—an excellent thing in a woman. The high light chatter of the tables dropped as she went by. For God's sake, hold your tongue and let me love!

It is good enough, the town and the soda-water, but it should be so much better! A great company of poets are called on to set the beauties of the world against their pitiful analogues in Altamont. Mr. Wolfe's criticism of the narrowness of his hero's surroundings is the more bitter because he has done it such abundant justice.

The bitterness grows when Eugene goes to the state university. Here Eugene, developing rapidly, becomes more difficult to understand, more difficult perhaps for his author to picture. It is often observable in books that begin with the birth of a boy that they grow confused as he approaches the age of the author. Here too the goat-foot that always belongs to the followers of Joyce is shown. Eugene becomes morbidly conscious of his physique, and yet unnaturally neglectful of it. He does not have his teeth filled or his hair cut; he does not bathe. He is naturally not popular, and he resents his want of popularity, in a way that is not far short of megalomania; he revolts against American sanitation and cleanliness, declaring that health is for fools, and great men have always shown signs in their lined faces of the disease of genius. Now this is hardly comprehensible, and hence hardly credible, even when the first two thirds of the book has given one the will to be as sympathetic as possible. There are possible reasons for Eugene's cult of dirt, ranging from a subconscious fear of impotence and a confused desire to be like the Horatian he-goat, *elentis mariti* (there is something like that in Mr. D. H. Lawrence), to a rankling sense of social inferiority, perverted by a fierce pride into a resolve to emulate the Fraternity Row aristocracy in nothing, not even in cleanliness (there is something like that in Mr. Wilbur Daniel Steele's *Meat*), through a dozen others. But Eugene here is not clear, as if Mr. Wolfe did not understand him, or understood him too well to think him worth explaining.

In the end Eugene is left wondering, with the same sense of the loneliness and greatness of the soul that informs the book from the beginning. ***Look Homeward, Angel*** though it has the faults of luxuriousness, has the great virtue that it always has the vision of something half-comprehensible behind the humdrum life, and that in the reading it carries conviction with it.

> *Basil Davenport, " 'C'est Maître François'," in* The Saturday Review of Literature, *Vol. 6, No. 22, December 21, 1929, p. 584.*

MARGERY LATIMER   (essay date 1929)

[*In the following excerpt from an essay first published in 1929, Latimer praises* Look Homeward, Angel *for its narrative energy and the vitality of its characters.*]

Sometimes an intense shock or a pain that has to be endured will give you a monstrous delight in life, as if the cautious habitual self in you had had its death blow and you were thrown out of yourself into the universe. [*Look Homeward, Angel*] is like that. There is such mammoth appreciation of experience and of living that the intention of the novel cannot be articulated. It comes through to you like fumes or like one supreme mood of courage that you can never forget, and with it all the awe, the defilement and grandeur of actual life. Mr. Wolfe makes you experience a family through twenty years of its existence. He gives the disharmony, the joy, the hideous wastefulness and the needless suffering, and yet not once do you dare shrink from life and not once are you plastered with resentment and loathing for reality and experience. The author has stated in his introduction that he wrote this book with strong joy, not counting the costs, and I believe it. He also has said he tried to comprehend his people not by telling what they did but what they should have done.

This "should-have-done" is the lyrical, subtle part of the book that comes to you in moments of peril. Ben, the elder brother, finally dies. He has never been educated because of his mother's iron determination to own all the real estate in Altamont and his father's riotous capacity for enjoyment. His whole being has been at the mercy of his parent's whims and the working out of their characters. As he dies the terrible vanity of the family rises above the calamity, their desire to vindicate themselves shuts him out of the world and finally, as they reveal themselves, you reach the rock bottom of their characters—innocence. Compared to some rational, ideal pattern of living they are mad, insane, as innocent as animals who kill each other for food and cannot do otherwise.

> Then, over the ugly clamor of their dissension, over the rasp and snarl of their nerves, they heard the low mutter of Ben's expiring breath. The light had been reshaded; he lay like his own shadow, in all his fierce gray lonely beauty. And as they looked and saw his bright eyes already blurred with death, and saw the feeble beating flutter of his poor thin breast, the strange wonder, the dark rich miracle of his life surged over them its enormous loveliness. They grew quiet and calm, they plunged below all the splintered wreckage of their lives, they drew together in a superb communion of love and valiance, beyond horror and confusion, beyond death!

Eugene, the youngest son, suddenly understands and possesses his family for a moment. As he looks at his brother he thinks, "That was not all! That really was not all!" And you think, reading, "O lost! that part of people that cannot be understood or possessed or expressed, O lost world of people—each one mysterious." But every act of these people is inevitable, so are their clothes, so are their words. Stevie, for example, "J. T. Collins, that's who! He's only worth about two hundred thousand. 'Steve,' he said, just like that, 'if I had your brains'—he would continue in this way with moody self-satisfaction, painting a picture of future success when all who scorned him now would flock to his standard." And Eliza at the very beginning does not need to be described when she says, "If I'd been there, you can bet your bottom dollar there'd been no loss. Or, it'd be on the other side." And then Gant, who part of the time is "picked foul and witless from the cobbles" and the rest of the time is making his house roar with fires and rich talk, making the outside of his house rich with vines and carving angels on grave stones. Or he is bringing into the warm kitchen great bundles of meat.

In them all, like the vast crude breathing of the earth, is their will to live. Mr. Wolfe describes with monstrous torrential joy the sensual delights of eating. He isn't content to describe a meal in a sentence, but he uses a page, bringing the food before you until it is so tangible it is intolerable, until it is so rich and abundant that it pierces you with awe of life. All the time you are eating that food as if it were actual. He describes the monstrous pleasures of the body in the same way until there is a gigantic picture of living flesh enjoying the universe. But like a Greek chorus or an angelic whisper from the centre of this excess are the words, "O lost!"

The story is always present. There is always the tremendous excitement of the life of this family, of what they will do and say and feel. Eugene, who in the author's mind is the central character of the book, is interesting only in connection with his family. The story is really the family with its distorted relationships shadowed by their angelic possibilities. Each person is a distinct reality but they are bound together, and when they are sundered the life of the book dwindles. Eugene at college is not as interesting or as real as Eugene the paper boy trying to collect from the prostitutes in Niggertown. But Eugene's life away from his family is only one hundred pages or so, and the fact that Ben's death marks the highest point in feeling and interest does not diminish the value of the book as a whole. The author proudly and naively says "It sometimes seems to me that this book presents a picture of American life that I have never seen elsewhere." I agree with him, and if I could create now one magic word that would make everyone want to read the book I would write it down and be utterly satisfied. (pp. 10-12)

Margery Latimer, "The American Family," in The Merrill Studies in "Look Homeward, Angel," *edited by Paschal Reeves, Charles E. Merrill Publishing Company, 1970, pp. 10-12.*

JONATHAN DANIELS   (essay date 1929)

[*Daniels was an American journalist, historian, novelist, and critic. In the following excerpt from a review first published in 1929, he characterizes* Look Homeward, Angel *as a bitter attack by Wolfe on his hometown and family.*]

More than a novel, Thomas Wolfe's first book, *Look Homeward, Angel,* is the record of the revolt of a young spirit. Tom Wolfe, once of Asheville, has gone the way of rebels and in a sense this first novel of his is the reign of terror of his talent. Against the Victorian morality and the Bourbon aristocracy of the South, he has turned in all his fury and the result is not a book that will please the South in general and North Carolina in particular. Here is a young man, hurt by something that he loved, turning in his sensitive fury and spitting on that thing. In *Look Homeward, Angel,* North Carolina, and the South are spat upon.

In this novel which is admittedly autobiographical in some part, the author Wolfe says of his hero who is easily identifiable with Wolfe:

> His feeling for the South was not so much historic as it was of the core and dark romanticism. . . . Finally, it occurred to him that these people had given him nothing, that neither their love nor their hatred could injure him, that he owed them nothing, and he determined that he would say so, and repay their insolence with a curse. And he did.

Look Homeward, Angel is that curse. And in just so far as the curse has entered into the creation, his work has been injured but it is a novel fine enough to show that once Mr. Wolfe has got this little score paid off to his own country he should be able to move on in greater serenity of spirit.

And there may be injustice in calling this book that curse. It is not impossible that he merely chose for artistic reasons the device of writing about North Carolina and North Carolina people through the Gant family, of Altamont (Asheville). Seeing any section through the Gant family would be like looking upon that section through the barred windows of a madhouse. In such a case the hysteria of the madhouse is apt to color the whole country outside. So it is here.

It is a book written in a poetic realism, the poetry of dissolution and decay, of life rotting from the womb, of death full of lush fecundity. The book is sensuous rather than cerebral. It pictures a life without dignity—cruel and ugly and touched only by a half-mad beauty. It moves slowly but at almost hysterical tension through twenty years of the life of the lower middle class Gant family, a life stirred only by the raw lusts for food and drink and sex and property. And this picture of the Gants is a cruel picture, drawn not in sympathy but in bitterness. Only one character in the whole book, the perpetually doomed [Ben] is drawn with tenderness and feeling.

In photographic detail the Gants are presented through 626 pages of quarrelling life. W. O. Gant, the father, is a wanderer, tombstonemaker, a selfish and self-pitying, bombastic drunkard. The mother, Eliza Pentland Gant, is a stingy, petty woman, avaricious member of the acquisitive mountain Pentlands. There are the children: Daisy, who is an unimportant figure of a girl; Helen, like her father but wiser and kinder; Steve, who is a hopeless degenerate; Luke, the buffoon; Grove, who dies in childhood; Ben, the doomed one, a night worker hungry for beauty and dignity; and Eugene, the hero, a strange figure of sensitiveness, aspiration and inferiority. And beside them are innumerable minor characters, prostitutes, white and black; loose women, Negroes and dope-fiends, drunken doctors, tuberculars, newsboys and teachers.

The book moves slowly with a somewhat too diffused point of view. There is hardly any growth in character but only growing details and passing time. The novel, with its central scene set in Asheville, moves in the South from Maryland to New Orleans and west to St. Louis. There are Negroes in it and cavaliers and all the other figures of Southern legend but the sense of reality is not in them. They are all figments of the Gant madness.

It is a book which shines too steadily with the brilliance of lurid details of blood and sex and cruelty. There is beauty in it but it is not a beautiful book. Mr. Wolfe writes with a splendid vividness but there is a heavy quality of sameness in so much stark color. The whole book seems somehow the work of a man who is staring rather than seeing.

In many places Mr. Wolfe has taken no pains adequately to disguise the autobiographical material set down as fiction. His very disguises seem made to point at the true facts. Asheville people will undoubtedly recognize factual material which escapes other readers, and no one who attended the University of North Carolina contemporaneously with Wolfe can miss the almost pure reporting which he presents in the story of his life there. (pp. 2-4)

Jonathan Daniels, ''Wolfe's First Is Novel of Revolt:
Former Asheville Writer Turns in Fury upon N.C.

Thomas Wolfe's parents, Julia and W. O. Wolfe. North Carolina Collection, UNC Library, Chapel Hill.

and the South,'' in Thomas Wolfe: The Critical Reception, edited by Paschal Reeves, David Lewis, 1974, pp. 2-4.

THE TIMES LITERARY SUPPLEMENT   (essay date 1930)

[In the following excerpt, the critic discusses the emotional force of Look Homeward, Angel.]

Mr. Thomas Wolfe's novel, **Look Homeward Angel,** was obviously written as the result of tremendous internal pressure. It is a first novel and very long, following a boy's emergence from childhood and imprisonment in the bosom of an extraordinary family to manhood and independence. Such Odysseys of youth are not uncommon; and by this time the crudities of the American scene are so familiar that the strange squalid-extravagant life of the Gant family in the hill town of Altamont, here described in profuse detail, will hold no particular surprise; what is amazing is the pressure under which this narrative is shot forth. To use a homely American metaphor, it might be called a ''gusher''; for Mr. Wolfe's words come spouting up with all the force of a subterranean flood now at last breaking through the overlying strata of repression. Such native force is rare in England now; and it is impossible to regard this unstinting output of magnificent, raw vigour without a thrill and a hope that it will be channelled to great art. The present book is not great art; but its promise and its power are so extraordinary that we dwell upon them rather than upon the details of its story.

Whether or no the family life of the Gants—the Bacchic flaming father everlastingly at odds with the tight-lipped avaricious mother nursing her secret pain in dumbness, the worthless Steve, the thwarted secretive Ben, the Cheery "go-getter" Luke, and the passionately serving Helen—was Mr. Wolfe's own or no, there can be no doubt that he is Eugene, the last born, who saw the light while Gant the father was booming eloquent curses outside the bedroom door, and who grew up with the taints of the Gant and Pentland blood in his body, and in his soul the sensuality, the aimlessness of his mother's family and the ache for wandering, the almost demoniac power of fantasy and the sense of being a stranger in an alien world which stamped his drunken but gigantically moulded father. It is the story of a boy's escape from a thralldom to which his own nature is much as circumstances subjected him. His mother's avarice, it is true, keeps him in the low boarding house that she, though rich in real property, keeps penuriously, forces him to sell newspapers at dawn before going to school, cuts short his schooldays and sends him to the State university too soon. But it is the influence of the blood which makes him return again and again willingly to that home of strife and discomfort, bound together by its very hatreds, until its fibres are at last rent apart by the death from pneumonia of Ben—a passage of remarkable power—while Gant curses, Eliza purses her tight lips and the others wrangle hideously round the dying man. The words of Ben's last moment give a measure of Mr. Wolfe's power over words when shaken, as he is often shaken, by a spasm of emotion:—

> Suddenly, marvellously, as if his resurrection and rebirth had come upon him, Ben drew upon the air in a long and powerful respiration; his grey eyes opened. Filled with a terrible vision of all life in the one moment, he seemed to rise forward bodilessly from his pillows without support—a flame, a light, a glory—joined at length in death to the dark spirit who had brooded upon each footstep of his lonely adventure on earth; and, casting the fierce sword of his glance with utter and final comprehension upon the room haunted with its grey pageantry of cheap loves and dull consciences and on all those uncertain summers of waste and confusion fading now from the bright window of his eyes, he passed instantly, scornful and unafraid, as he had lived, into the shades of death.

This is not merely an eloquent passage, it is summary and judgment of what has been fairly set out with intense vividness before.

This intensity of apprehension, whether sensuous or imaginative, is Eugene's mark in the novel, as it is Mr. Wolfe's in the performance. We do not need the catalogues, remarkable in themselves, of the books on which Eugene fed his voracious fancy or the rich foods on which the elder Gant, in the great days, gorged his sons and daughters: Mr. Wolfe reveals himself as one who has fed upon honeydew and everything else under the sun. And his most astonishing passages, crammed though they are with the clangorous echoes of English poetry and prose, too often falling into sheer metre, come when, in contemplation of his past, he sends out a cry of lyrical agony for lost beauty. One might take to pieces the paragraph on spring that begins: "Yes, and in that month when Proserpine comes back, and Ceres' dead heart rekindles, when all the woods are a tender smoky blur, and birds no bigger than a budding leaf dart through the singing trees''; or that other beginning: "In

the cruel volcano of the boy's mind, the little brier moths of his idolatry wavered in to their strange marriage and were consumed''; one might trace the echoes and point out the faults, but the Marlowesque energy and beauty of them has already made such work vain. What is going to be done with this great talent, so hard, so sensual, so unsentimental, so easily comprehending and describing every sordidness of the flesh and spirit, so proudly rising to the heights? Knowing the times and the temptations of the times, we may well watch its fresh emergence with anxiety: for if Mr. Wolfe can be wasted, there is no hope for to-day.

A review of "Look Homeward, Angel," in The Times Literary Supplement, *No. 1486, July 24, 1930, p. 608.*

STRINGFELLOW BARR   (essay date 1930)

[Barr was an American historian, novelist, and critic. In the following excerpt from a review originally published in the Virginia Quarterly Review *in 1930, he contrasts* Look Homeward, Angel *with other novels written about the South.]*

Stark Young's *River House* and Thomas Wolfe's *Look Homeward, Angel* are both novels about the South written by Southerners. But a foreigner would not readily discover in the two books reflections of the same civilization. *River House* is a backward glance at a dying culture submerged and overwhelmed not merely by America but by its own Americanized youth. *Look Homeward, Angel* is the saga of a human soul, the soul of a boy who happened to grow up in North Carolina. (p. 18)

I should call *Look Homeward, Angel* the work of a genius, but that the word is somewhat overworn of late. In any case I believe it is the South's first contribution to world literature. I am aware that "Uncle Remus" is read wherever English is spoken and that in our own generation writers like DuBose Heyward and Julia Peterkin have created real literature. But it seems to me extremely significant that generally speaking the Southern writer has had to turn to the negro when he wanted to paint life as it is. The life of the white Southerner has been for political and traditional reasons so compact of legal fictions and dying social shibboleths that it has been difficult to do anything with it unless one sentimentalized. Even *River House* had to be composed in a minor key, perhaps the only key available to a defeated culture. Thomas Wolfe, on the other hand, has constructed a really tremendous novel out of the mean and sordid life of a North Carolina town. A lesser artist looking on that scene, would have become excitedly denunciatory or triumphantly analytical and would have discovered in it no more than another Zenith City or another Winesburg, Ohio. What Mr. Wolfe beheld was the travail of the human spirit, blind to its own stupidities, its cowardice, its lusts. His novel is of epic proportions, physically and spiritually.

His hero's father "reeled down across the continent" from Pennsylvania to North Carolina and spawned a family of children as terrifyingly different from each other as most brothers and sisters really are: Helen, with her tempestuous affections and antagonisms and her inherited bibulous tendencies; Luke, with his genius for acquaintance and his incapacity for real feeling; Steve, whining, boasting, and stinking of nicotine; Eugene, about whom this epic really centers; Ben, with this fierce spiritual isolation, perpetually murmuring over his shoulder to his particular angel: "God! Listen to that, won't you!" Above them all the father, W. O. Gant, towers like the elder

Karamazov, screaming profanity and obscenity at his wife and children, reciting eternally from Shakespeare and a dozen other bards, roaring for every one's pity, drinking himself into cancer, and being hauled out of brothels by his eldest son.

Which of Thomas Wolfe's particular skills has contributed most to this book's making? Over and over again his prose slips into sheer poetry. Over and over again one ironic sentence creates a character. But above all his loving pity for all of lost humanity gives his work that religious quality one gets in Dostoevsky.

Does Mr. Wolfe add anything to our comprehension of the South? It is a difficult question to answer. His book is not about the South of Major Dandridge at all. Indeed, that Old South is not very obvious to anybody who ever saw "Altamont," which is the name Mr. Wolfe gives his native Asheville. The Gants are certainly not typical of the Southern upper class, though neither are they quite what that upper class means by "common." They are socially unclassifiable. *Look Homeward, Angel* is not concerned with the problem of a surviving Southern culture. When its author mentions the South it is chiefly to speak of "the exquisite summer of the South," the "opulent South," or the "fabulous South." The natural beauty of the land lies deep in his blood but the politico-social problems of its people touch him scarcely at all.

I do not believe that Mr. Wolfe's novel has invalidated one iota the significance of whatever the Old South produced of human beauty; and I am certain that Mr. Wolfe himself would feel soiled at being thought of as a "debunker." But I do think that he is the first novelist of the new dispensation in the Southern States, the first to grow up sufficiently outside of River House to look with a child's eyes at the life about him. Whenever, as in Poland or Italy or Ireland, the sense of a culture distorted by outside pressure has directed the artist's eyes to programs like national resurgence, the highest art has been the chief sufferer. The South has labored precisely under that handicap; unable to recapture a social synthesis that Reconstruction had destroyed, it had not the heart, or the stomach either, to adopt frankly the American solution of life. Nor has Mr. Wolfe adopted it, but his conflict is no longer the political conflict of the South and the North but the artistic conflict of his own spirit with the souls about him. With *Look Homeward, Angel* the South has contributed to the literature of the world a novel, strongly provincial in its flavor, universal in its terrible tragedy. (pp. 18-20)

Stringfellow Barr, "The Dandridges and the Gants," in The Merrill Studies in "Look Homeward, Angel," *edited by Paschal Reeves, Charles E. Merrill Publishing Company, 1970, pp. 18-20.*

THOMAS WOLFE   (essay date 1936)

[*In the following excerpt from* The Story of a Novel, *Wolfe recounts the experience of writing* Look Homeward, Angel *and discusses reaction to the novel in his hometown of Asheville, North Carolina.*]

I don't know how I became a writer, but I think it was because of a certain force in me that had to write and that finally burst through and found a channel. My people were of the working class of people. My father, a stonecutter, was a man with a great respect and veneration for literature. He had a tremendous memory, and he loved poetry, and the poetry that he loved best was naturally of the rhetorical kind that such a man would like. Nevertheless it was good poetry, Hamlet's Soliloquy, *Macbeth*, Mark Antony's Funeral Oration, Grey's "Elegy," and all the rest of it. I heard it all as a child; I memorized and learned it all.

He sent me to college to the state university. The desire to write, which had been strong during all my days in high school, grew stronger still. I was editor of the college paper, the college magazine, etc., and in my last year or two I was a member of a course in playwriting which had just been established there. I wrote several little one-act plays, still thinking I would become a lawyer or a newspaper man, never daring to believe I could seriously become a writer. Then I went to Harvard, wrote some more plays there, became obsessed with the idea that I had to be a playwright, left Harvard, had my plays rejected, and finally in the autumn of 1926, how, why, or in what manner I have never exactly been able to determine, but probably because the force in me that had to write at length sought out its channel, I began to write my first book in London. I was living all alone at that time. I had two rooms—a bedroom and a sitting room—in a little square in Chelsea in which all the houses had that familiar, smoked brick and cream-yellow-plaster look of London houses. They looked exactly alike.

As I say, I was living alone at that time and in a foreign country. I did not know why I was there or what the direction of my life should be, and that was the way I began to write my book. I think that is one of the hardest times a writer goes through. There is no standard, no outward judgment, by which he can measure what he has done. By day I would write for hours in big ledgers which I had bought for the purpose; then at night I would lie in bed and fold my hands behind my head and think of what I had done that day and hear the solid, leather footbeat of the London bobby as he came by my window, and remember that I was born in North Carolina and wonder why the hell I was now in London lying in the darkened bed, and thinking about words I had that day put down on paper. I would get a great, hollow, utterly futile feeling inside me, and then I would get up and switch on the light and read the words I had written that day, and then I would wonder: why am I here now? why have I come?

By day there would be the great, dull roar of London, the gold, yellow, foggy light you have there in October. The man-swarmed and old, weblike, smoky London! And I loved the place, and I loathed it and abhorred it. I knew no one there, and I had been a child in North Carolina long ago, and I was living there in two rooms in the huge octopal and illimitable web of that overwhelming city. I did not know why I had come, why I was there.

I worked there every day with such feelings as I have described, and came back to America in the winter and worked here. I would teach all day and write all night, and finally about two and a half years after I had begun the book in London, I finished it in New York.

I should like to tell about this, too. I was very young at the time, and I had the kind of wild, exultant vigor which a man has at that period of his life. The book took hold of me and possessed me. In a way, I think it shaped itself. Like every young man, I was strongly under the influence of writers I admired. One of the chief writers at that time was Mr. James Joyce with his book *Ulysses*. The book that I was writing was much influenced, I believe, by his own book, and yet the powerful energy and fire of my own youth played over and, I think, possessed it all. Like Mr. Joyce, I wrote about things that I had known, the immediate life and experience that had been familiar to me in my childhood. Unlike Mr. Joyce, I had no literary experience. I had never had anything published before. My feeling toward writers, publishers, books, that whole fabulous far-away world, was almost as romantically unreal as when I was a child. And yet my book, the characters with which I had peopled it, the color and the weather of the universe which I had created, had possessed me, and so I wrote and wrote with that bright flame with which a young man writes who never has been published, and who yet is sure all will be good and must go well. This is a curious thing and hard to tell about, yet easy to understand in every writer's mind. I wanted fame, as every youth who ever wrote must want it, and yet fame was a shining, bright, and most uncertain thing.

The book [*Look Homeward, Angel*] was finished in my twenty-eighth year. I knew no publishers and no writers. A friend of mine took the huge manuscript—it was about 350,000 words long—and sent it to a publisher whom she knew. In a few days, a week or two, I received an answer from this man saying that the book could not be published. The gist of what he said was that his house had published several books like it the year before, that all of them had failed, and that, further, the book in its present form was so amateurish, autobiographical, and unskilful that a publisher could not risk a chance on it. I was, myself, so depressed and weary by this time, the illusion of creation which had sustained me for two and a half years had so far worn off, that I believed what the man said. At that time I was a teacher in one of New York's great universities, and when the year came to a close, I went abroad. It was only after I had been abroad almost six months that news came to me from another publisher in America that he had read my manuscript and would like to talk to me about it as soon as I came home.

I came home on New Year's Day that year. The next day I called up the publisher who had written me. He asked me if I would come to his office and talk to him. I went at once, and before I had left his office that morning, I had signed a contract and had a check for five hundred dollars in my hand.

It was the first time, so far as I can remember, that any one had concretely suggested to me that anything I had written was worth as much as fifteen cents, and I know that I left the publisher's office that day and entered into the great swarm of men and women who passed constantly along Fifth Avenue at 48th Street and presently I found myself at 110th Street, and from that day to this I have never known how I got there.

For the next six or eight months I taught at the university and worked upon the manuscript of my book with this editor. The book appeared in the month of October, 1929. The whole experience still had elements of that dream-like terror and unreality that writing had had for me when I had first begun it seriously and had lain in my room in London with my hands below my head and thought, why am I here? The awful, utter nakedness of print, that thing which is for all of us so namelessly akin to shame, came closer day by day. That I had wanted this exposure, I could not believe. It seemed to me that I had shamelessly exposed myself and yet that subtle drug of my desire and my creating held me with a serpent's eye, and I could do no other. I turned at last to this editor who had worked with me and found me, and I asked him if he could foretell the end and verdict of my labor. He said that he would rather tell me nothing, that he could not prophesy or know what profit I would have. He said, "All that I know is that they cannot let it go, they cannot ignore it. The book will find its way."

And that fairly describes what happened. I have read in recent months that this first book was received with what is called a "storm of critical applause," but this really did not happen. It got some wonderful reviews in some places; it got some unfavorable reviews in others, but it unquestionably did have a good reception for a first book, and what was best of all, as time went on, it continued to make friends among people who read books. It continued to sell over a period of four or five years in the publisher's edition, and later in a cheaper edition, The Modern Library, it renewed its life and began to sell again. The upshot of it was that after the publication of this book in the autumn of 1929, I found myself with a position as a writer. (pp. 4-13)

I had not foreseen one fact which becomes absolutely plain after a man has written a book, but which he cannot foresee until he has written one. This fact is that one writes a book not in order to remember it, but in order to forget it, and now this fact was evident. As soon as the book was in print, I began to forget about it, I wanted to forget about it, I didn't want people to talk to me or question me about it. I just wanted them to leave me alone and shut up about it. And yet I longed desperately for my book's success. I wanted it to have the position of proud esteem and honor in the world that I longed for it to have—I wanted, in short, to be a successful and a famous man, and I wanted to lead the same kind of obscure and private life I'd always had and not to be told about my fame and success.

From this problem, another painful and difficult situation was produced. I had written my book, more or less, directly from the experience of my own life, and, furthermore, I now think that I may have written it with a certain naked intensity of spirit which is likely to characterize the earliest work of a young writer. At any rate, I can honestly say that I did not foresee what was to happen. I was surprised not only by the kind of response my book had with the critics and the general public, I was most of all surprised with the response it had in my native town. I had thought there might be a hundred people in that town who would read the book, but if there were a hundred outside of the negro population, the blind, and the positively illiterate who did not read it, I do not know where they are. For months the town seethed with a fury of resentment which I had not believed possible. The book was denounced from the pulpit by the ministers of the leading churches. Men collected on street corners to denounce it. For weeks the women's clubs, bridge parties, teas, receptions, book clubs, the whole complex fabric of a small town's social life was absorbed by an outraged clamor. I received anonymous letters full of vilification and abuse, one which threatened to kill me if I came back home, others which were merely obscene. One venerable old lady, whom I had known all my life, wrote me that although she had never believed in lynch law, she would do nothing to prevent a mob from dragging my "big overgroan karkus" across the public square. She informed me further, that my mother had taken to her bed "as white as a ghost" and would "never rise from it again."

There were many other venomous attacks from my home town and for the first time I learned another lesson which every young writer has got to learn. And that lesson is the naked, blazing power of print. At that time it was for me a bewildering and almost overwhelming situation. My joy at the success my book had won was mixed with bitter chagrin at its reception in my native town. And yet I think I learned something from that experience, too. For the first time I was forced to consider squarely this problem: where does the material of an artist come from? What are the proper uses of that material, and how far must his freedom in the use of that material be controlled by his responsibility as a member of society? This is a difficult problem, and I have by no means come to the bottom of it yet. Perhaps I never shall, but as a result of all the distress which I suffered at that time and which others may have suffered on account of me, I have done much thinking and arrived at certain conclusions.

My book was what is often referred to as an autobiographical novel. I protested against this term in a preface to the book upon the grounds that any serious work of creation is of necessity autobiographical and that few more autobiographical works than *Gulliver's Travels* have ever been written. I added that Dr. Johnson had remarked that a man might turn over half the volumes in his library to make a single book, and that in a similar way, a novelist might turn over half the characters in his native town to make a single figure for his novel. In spite of this the people in my native town were not persuaded or appeased, and the charge of autobiography was brought against me in many other places.

As I have said, my conviction is that all serious creative work must be at bottom autobiographical, and that a man must use the material and experience of his own life if he is to create anything that has substantial value. But I also believe now that the young writer is often led through inexperience to a use of the materials of life which are, perhaps, somewhat too naked and direct for the purpose of a work of art. The thing a young writer is likely to do is to confuse the limits between actuality and reality. He tends unconsciously to describe an event in such a way because it actually happened that way, and from an artistic point of view, I can now see that this is wrong. It is not, for example, important that one remembers a beautiful woman of easy virtue as having come from the state of Kentucky in the year 1907. She could perfectly well have come from Idaho or Texas or Nova Scotia. The important thing really is only to express as well as possible the character and quality of the beautiful woman of easy virtue. But the young writer, chained to fact and to his own inexperience, as yet unliberated by maturity, is likely to argue, "she must be described as coming from Kentucky because that is where she actually did come from."

In spite of this, it is impossible for a man who has the stuff of creation in him to make a literal transcription of his own experience. Everything in a work of art is changed and transfigured by the personality of the artist. And as far as my own first book is concerned, I can truthfully say that I do not believe that there is a single page of it that is true to fact. And from this circumstance, also, I learned another curious thing about writing. For although my book was not true to fact, it was true to the general experience of the town I came from and I hope, of course, to the general experience of all men living. The best way I can describe the situation is this: it was as if I were a sculptor who had found a certain kind of clay with which to model. Now a farmer who knew well the neighborhood from which this clay had come might pass by and find the sculptor at his work and say to him, "I know the farm from which you got that clay." But it would be unfair of him to say, "I know the figure, too." Now I think what happened in my native town is that having seen the clay, they became immediately convinced that they recognized the figure, too, and the results of this misconception were so painful and ludicrous that the telling of it is almost past belief.

It was my experience to be assured by people from my native town not only that they remembered incidents and characters in my first book, which may have had some basis in actuality, but also that they remembered incidents which so far as I know had no historical basis whatever. For example, there was one scene in the book in which a stonecutter is represented as selling to a notorious woman of the town a statue of a marble angel which he has treasured for many years. So far as I know, there was no basis in fact for this story, and yet I was informed by several people later that they not only remembered the incident perfectly, but had actually been witnesses to the transaction. Nor was this the end of the story. I heard that one of the newspapers sent a reporter and a photographer to the cemetery and a photograph was printed in the paper with a statement to the effect that the angel was the now famous angel which had stood upon the stonecutter's porch for so many years and had given the title to my book. The unfortunate part of this proceeding was that I had never seen or heard of this angel before, and that this angel was, in fact, erected over the grave of a well known Methodist lady who had died a few years before and that her indignant family had immediately written the paper to demand a retraction of its story, saying that their mother had been in no way connected with the infamous book or the infamous angel which had given the infamous book its name. Such, then, were some of the unforeseen difficulties with which I was confronted after the publication of my first book. (pp. 16-25)

Thomas Wolfe, in his The Story of a Novel, *1936. Reprint by Charles Scribner's Sons, 1949, 93 p.*

CARL VAN DOREN (essay date 1940)

[*Van Doren is considered one of the most perceptive American critics of the first half of the twentieth century. He worked for many years as a professor of English at Columbia University and served as literary editor and critic at the* Nation *and the* Century *during the 1920s. A founder of the Literary Guild and author or editor of several American literary histories, Van Doren was also a critically acclaimed historian and biographer. In the following excerpt, he discusses Wolfe's portrayal of the Gant family in* Look Homeward, Angel.]

[In *Look Homeward, Angel*, Wolfe] had been so true to the customary life of his native Asheville (called Altamont in the novel) that the town angrily recognized itself; and he had drawn the Gant and Pentland families of the novel from actual Wolfes and Westalls. *Look Homeward, Angel* is a family chronicle, ranging wide enough to include all the kinsmen and working close enough to show each of them in individual detail. There was a difference between Wolfe and any of the recent novelists who had studied American families in fiction. Instead of writing dryly or cynically, as if to reduce families to the bores and pests it was fashionable to consider them, Wolfe wrote with magnificence. No matter how unpleasant some of the Gants might be, or how appalling, they were not dull. Wolfe in reproducing or creating had not once looked at them with cold disinterested eyes, but with the clannish loyalty in which particular or temporary hatreds cannot bar out a general love. He enjoyed the living reality of the Gants, even if he could not approve their characters. The avarice of Eliza Pentland the mother (Wolfe's own mother was Julia Elizabeth Westall) seems a credible obsession. The roaring violence of Oliver Gant the father (Wolfe's own father was named William Oliver) is gorgeous rather than monstrous. The elder Gant is central to *Look Homeward, Angel* as to the later novels. "The deepest search in life, it seemed to me," Wolfe wrote in *The Story of a Novel,* "the thing that in one way or another was central to all living was man's search to find a father; not merely the father of his flesh, not merely the lost father of his youth, but the image of a strength and wisdom external to his need and superior to his hunger, to which the belief and power of his own life could be united." In *Look Homeward, Angel* Wolfe was searching for the truth about the physical father of Eugene Gant—or of Thomas Wolfe. The story of Eugene, which Wolfe had set out to tell, must be traced back of him to the father in whom his stormy nature had begun. As to Eugene, he belonged to a type often celebrated in contemporary novels: the talented youth trying to rise from more or less commonplace circumstances. But Eugene transcends the restless type by being its most superb example in his time: perhaps mad but certainly magnificent. (pp. 344-45)

> *Carl Van Doren, "New Realisms," in his* The American Novel: 1789-1939, *revised edition, The Macmillan Company, 1940, pp. 334-48.*

HERBERT J. MULLER (essay date 1947)

[*Muller is an American historian and critic who has written on such diverse topics as philosophy, history, modern technology, politics, religion, and their various relationships with and effects on literature. In the following excerpt from his book-length study of Wolfe, Muller discusses the autobiographical nature of* Look Homeward, Angel *as a fault and negatively evaluates the character of Eugene as well as Wolfe's grandiose expression of emotion in the novel.*]

[One] may grant Wolfe that all serious fiction is autobiographical, in that it is written out of the author's deepest experience. Nevertheless one must add that hardly any other novelist has used his own experience so directly and so exclusively. On his first trip to Europe, Wolfe kept assuring his mother that he was "writing it all up." He was always writing up his history, and then worrying over the problem of how to fit it all into his novels. Edward C. Aswell, his last editor, remarks that he was amazed to find, after he had removed all the extraneous matter, that the rest of the manuscript fell into a perfect shape, and that all Wolfe's novels together become in effect "one book"; he describes this "unity" as an "extraordinary literary achievement." There is indeed a unity. But aside from the fact that Aswell had to remove the extraneous matter himself, this is scarcely extraordinary, nor is it strictly a *literary* achievement. The unity is primarily that of a life, a personality. It might almost be reduced to the statement that all of Wolfe's work was written by Wolfe, and chiefly about Wolfe; it might be found as well in the volume of his letters to his mother.

I should not insist upon this distinction merely out of a desire to be scrupulous or conscientiously critical. The issue here is not the academic question of whether Wolfe's sprawling books are "really" novels at all; it is not a matter of definition, of failure to disguise his materials or to get them into a conventional form. Rather, it is Wolfe's prolonged inability to dominate his materials, to master any kind of form. This inability either to escape or to command his own life history is the immediate sign and source of his faults as an artist. They are grievous faults, as he himself admitted; they are also typically American, and symptomatic of an age of disorder; they are finally the measure of his growth, as the index of all he had to outgrow. On all counts they need to be seen clearly for what they are, and not dressed up as qualities of his original genius.

In simple kindness as well as justice to Wolfe, it is well to begin by saying the worst.

The notorious diffuseness of his lengthy novels is accordingly quite different from the sprawl of Balzac, Dickens, Zola, Melville, or Tolstoy. It is due in part to his youthful obsession with sheer quantity or extent of experience, and his youthful passion for "expressing it all"—everything must be told, nothing implied. More significantly, it is due to the absence of a clear intention or design. The old masters were careless, but they were seldom confused; they could be leisurely and digress freely because they knew where they were going, had something to digress from. Wolfe, on the other hand, always felt swamped by his material, because of his teeming memory. He conceived his main problem as not how to select, to shape, but how to get it all in, to let it flow freely. Hence he got far too much in, and despite all his anguish it flowed much too freely, because his memory was in fact teeming. (pp. 26-8)

Wolfe is much too prone to invoke instead of to render, to tell us what to feel instead of building the feeling, and to be carried away by a train of feeling started off by mere habit or verbal association instead of by fresh perception. Even apart from the stereotyped rhythms and images, and from the too fancy feathers in his cap, his habit of deserting his characters is another

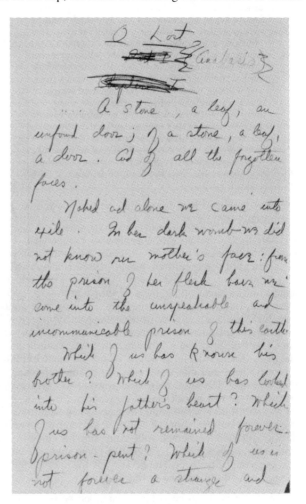

First manuscript page of Look Homeward, Angel. *Reproduced by permission of Paul Gitlin, Administrator of the Estate of Thomas Wolfe.*

sign of self-indulgence, lack of fidelity to his main task as a novelist.

This undisciplined self-expression is the more conspicuous because it is such a tumultuous, violent, extravagantly emotional self that Wolfe is expressing; and so we have to put up with the notorious excesses of Eugene Gant. Eugene is forever beside himself, which is where he wants to be. He ''yells,'' ''howls,'' ''bellows madly,'' ''snarls like a wild beast''; he is repeatedly ''choked with fury,'' ''white with constricted rage,'' ''frantic with horror''; when he broods in silence it is to contemplate things ''intolerable,'' ''implacable,'' ''unutterable''; when he nevertheless utters the unutterable, his favorite adjectives are ''wild,'' ''tortured,'' ''demented,'' ''demonic,'' ''maniacal''; and at the end of such bouts with himself or the world, he ''beats his knuckles bloody on the stamped-out walls.'' Extensive quotation is needless and depressing; one passage will give the idea:

> Now a huge, naked, and intolerable shame and horror pressed down on Eugene with a crushing and palpable weight out of the wet, gray skies of autumn. The hideous gray stuff filled him from brain to bowels, was everywhere and in everything about him so that he breathed it out of the air, felt it like a naked stare from walls and houses and the faces of the people, tasted it on his lips, and endured it in the screaming and sickened dissonance of ten thousand writhing nerves so that he could no longer sit, rest, or find oblivion, exhaustion, forgetfulness or repose anywhere he went, or release from the wild unrest that drove him constantly about. . . . He saw the whole earth with the sick eyes, the sick heart, the sick flesh, and writhing nerves of this gray accursed weight of shame and horror in which his life lay drowned, and from which it seemed he could never more emerge to know the music of health and joy and power again; and from which, likewise, he could not die, but must live hideously and miserably the rest of his days, like a man doomed to live forever in a state of retching and abominable nausea of heart, brain, bowels, flesh and spirit.

What has happened here is that Eugene has just received his first rejection slip.

It is safe to say that all this is somewhat exaggerated. Even without the testimony of Wolfe's friends, we would guess that he experienced some mild emotions, uttered some casual remarks, left some walls unbloodied. Likewise we would discount some passages on the basis of simple arithmetic. While at Harvard, Eugene reads like a madman, ''tearing the entrails'' from 2,000 books a year (''deliberately the number is set low''); but a few pages later we are told that he was also spending ''thousands of good hours'' thinking about a certain waitress. The more serious trouble, however, is that too much of all this is literally true, and that Wolfe was not deliberately exaggerating for effect. His faults may be summed up as a remorseless excess, but he had in fact been a very excessive young man. He was still full of mixed emotions, some deep and brooding, others touchy or moody, but all boiling at the same temperature. He was still more concerned with expressing his emotion than with understanding it; or he hoped to come upon an understanding simply by overwriting. He felt the more intensely because he still did not know what to think.

Hence Wolfe is apt to be at his worst when he is alone with his hero, writing directly of the inner world in which presumably are to be found the important meanings of his life story. To many readers, Eugene Gant is the least interesting and least convincing of Wolfe's major characters. His rages and despairs become more tiresome because we seldom really see him; he is a disembodied passion, an incessant blaze and blare without shape or substance. And when the outer world is presented directly as he sees it, it may also take on a violent monotony and finally become unrecognizable. Here, for example, is Eugene's impression of New York in one of his black moods:

> Around him in the streets, again, as winter came, he heard a million words of hate and death: a million words of snarl and sneer and empty threat, of foul mistrust and lying slander: already he had come to see the poisonous images of death and hatred in the lives of a million people—he saw with what corrupt and venomous joy they seized on every story of man's dishonor, defeat, or sorrow, with what vicious jibe and jeer they greeted any evidence of mercy, honesty, or love.

Of this, all one can say is that it isn't so.

Altogether, there is no question of Wolfe's passionate sincerity, his agonized effort to be utterly ''true and honest and courageous.'' There is also no question that truth-telling is an even more arduous business than he at first conceived. If he often reveals more about himself than he intends, making an embarrassing show of his naïveté, he often reveals considerably less than he intends, exposing but not elucidating. If he is being honest and courageous in exposing so much, he nevertheless finds it too easy to let go, to indulge in the luxury of all this passion; to forego this luxury would have cost him still more anguish. His limitations may be exposed most clearly on his own ground, by setting his novels beside such other autobiographical novels as *Sons and Lovers, Of Human Bondage, The Portrait of the Artist as a Young Man* and *Remembrance of Things Past*. In these the hero is a creation, not a *nom de plume,* and his life a work of art, not a flood of memories. In this company Wolfe appears a very artless young man. (pp. 33-7)

> *Herbert J. Muller, in his* Thomas Wolfe, *New Directions Books, 1947, 196 p.*

MAXWELL E. PERKINS   (essay date 1947)

> [*Associated with the publishing house of Charles Scribner's Sons from 1910 until his death in 1947, Perkins is considered to have been one of the greatest American editors of the twentieth century. Gifted with shrewdness, sensitivity, patience, and a single-minded devotion to his profession, he discovered and maintained long editor-author relationships with such eminent writers as F. Scott Fitzgerald, Ernest Hemingway, and Thomas Wolfe, among many others. In the following excerpt from an essay which originally appeared in the* Harvard Library Bulletin *in 1947, Perkins relates his first acquaintance with the manuscript of* Look Homeward, Angel *and with Wolfe, and writes of the process of editing the novel.*]

The first time I heard of Thomas Wolfe I had a sense of foreboding. I who loved the man say this. Every good thing that comes is accompanied by trouble. It was in 1928 when Madeleine Boyd, a literary agent, came in. She talked of several manuscripts which did not much interest me, but frequently interrupted herself to tell of a wonderful novel about an American boy. I several times said to her, ''Why don't you bring it in here, Madeleine?'' and she seemed to evade the question. But finally she said, ''I will bring it, if you promise to read every word of it.'' I did promise, but she told me other things that made me realize that Wolfe was a turbulent spirit, and that we were in for turbulence. When the manuscript came, I was fascinated by the first scene where Eugene's father, Oliver W. Gant, with his brother, two little boys, stood by a roadside in Pennsylvania and saw a division of Lee's Army on the march to Gettysburg.

But then there came some ninety-odd pages about Oliver Gant's life in Newport News, and Baltimore, and elsewhere. All this was what Wolfe had heard, and had no actual association with which to reconcile it, and it was inferior to the first episode, and in fact to all the rest of the book. I was turned off to other work and gave the manuscript to Wallace Meyer, thinking, "Here is another promising novel that probably will come to nothing." Then Meyer showed me that wonderful night scene in the cafe where Ben was with the Doctors, and Horse Hines, the undertaker, came in. I dropped everything and began to read again, and all of us were reading the book simultaneously, you might say, including John Hall Wheelock, and there never was the slightest disagreement among us as to its importance.

After some correspondence between me and Wolfe, and between him and Madeleine Boyd, from which we learned how at the October Fair in Germany he had been almost beaten to death—when I realized again that we had a Moby Dick to deal with—Wolfe arrived in New York and stood in the doorway of my boxstall of an office leaning against the door jamb. When I looked up and saw his wild hair and bright countenance—although he was so altogether different physically—I thought of Shelley. *He* was fair, but his hair was wild, and his face was bright and his head disproportionately small.

We then began to work upon the book and the first thing we did, to give it unity, was to cut out that wonderful scene it began with and the ninety-odd pages that followed, because it seemed to me, and he agreed, that the whole tale should be unfolded through the memories and senses of the boy, Eugene, who was born in Asheville. We both thought that the story was compassed by that child's realization; that it was life and the world as he came to realize them. When he had tried to go back into the life of his father before he arrived in Asheville, without the inherent memory of events, the reality and the poignance were diminished—but for years it was on my conscience that I had persuaded Tom to cut out that first scene of the two little boys on the roadside with Gettysburg impending.

And then what happened? In *Of Time and the River* he brought the scene back to greater effect when old Gant was dying on the gallery of the hospital in Baltimore and in memory recalled his olden days. After that occurred I felt much less anxiety in suggesting cuts: I began then to realize that nothing Wolfe wrote was ever lost, that omissions from one book were restored in a later one. An extreme example of this is the fact that the whole second half of *The Web and the Rock* was originally intended to be the concluding episode in *Of Time and the River*. But most, and perhaps almost all, of those early incidents of Gant's life were worked into *The Web and the Rock* and *You Can't Go Home Again*.

I had realized, for Tom had prefaced his manuscript with a statement to that effect, that *Look Homeward, Angel* was autobiographical, but I had come to think of it as being so in the sense that *David Copperfield* is, or *War and Peace*, or *Pendennis*. But when we were working together, I suddenly saw that it was often almost literally autobiographical—that these people in it were his people. I am sure my face took on a look of alarm, and Tom saw it and he said, "But Mr. Perkins, you don't understand. I think these people are *great* people and that they should be told about." He was right. He had written

a great book, and it had to be taken substantially as it was. And in truth, the extent of cutting in that book has somehow come to be greatly exaggerated. Really, it was more a matter of reorganization. For instance, Tom had that wonderful episode when Gant came back from his far-wandering and rode in early morning on the trolley car through the town and heard about who had died and who had been born and saw all the scenes that were so familiar to Tom or Eugene, as the old trolley rumbled along. This was immediately followed by an episode of a similar kind where Eugene, with his friends, walked home from school through the town of Asheville. That was presented in a Joycean way, but it was the same sort of thing—some one going through the town and through his perceptions revealing it to the reader. By putting these episodes next to each other the effect of each was diminished, and I think we gave both much greater value by separating them. We did a great deal of detailed cutting, but it was such things as that I speak of that constituted perhaps the greater part of the work. (pp. 81-3)

Maxwell E. Perkins, "Thomas Wolfe," in Thomas Wolfe: A Collection of Critical Essays, *edited by Louis D. Rubin, Jr., Prentice-Hall, 1973, pp. 80-8.*

HUGH HOLMAN   (essay date 1955)

[*Holman was an American detective novelist and critic whose works focus predominantly on the fiction of Southern writers, particularly Ellen Glasgow, William Faulkner, Flannery O'Connor, and Thomas Wolfe. He edited several notable collections of Wolfe's writings, including* The Short Novels of Thomas Wolfe *(1961) and* The Letters of Thomas Wolfe to His Mother *(1968). In the following essay, Holman disputes traditional views of* Look Homeward, Angel *and discusses the book as a profound depiction of loneliness and isolation.*]

Thomas Wolfe's *Look Homeward, Angel* fell on critically evil days, and they have taken their toll of its reputation, if not of its steadily increasing number of readers. It was published the month of the 1929 stock market crash, lived the first decade of its existence in the sociological and Marxist-minded thirties, and presented to politically sensitive critics a hero of whom its author approvingly wrote: ". . . he did not care under what form of government he lived—Republican, Democrat, Tory, Socialist, or Bolshevist. . . . He did not want to reform the world, or to make it a better place to live in." That hero, Eugene Gant, was hardly in tune with the intellectual temper of his times.

It is a frankly autobiographical book, "a story of the buried life," written by a man who, by his own confession, "failed to finish a single book of . . . [Henry] James." Yet its whole existence has been during a time when the technical and formal considerations of Henry James have triumphantly established themselves as the proper criteria for fiction. For a book largely devoid of the traditional fictional or dramatic structure, almost naïvely innocent of "crucial plot," and seemingly dedicated to the lyrical expression of emotion not very tranquilly recollected, the age of Jamesian criticism has proved patronizingly hostile.

As Herbert Muller, by no means an unfriendly critic of Wolfe, has said:

> His limitations may be exposed most clearly on his own ground, by setting his novels beside such other autobiographical novels as *Sons and Lovers, Of Human Bondage, The Portrait of the Artist as a Young*

Man and *Remembrance of Things Past*. In these the hero is a creation, not a *nom de plume*, and his life a work of art, not a flood of memories. In this company Wolfe appears a very artless young man [see excerpt dated 1947].

In such a context of critical opinion it has required effort to maintain a serious attitude toward Wolfe and his first book, *Look Homeward, Angel*, which is almost universally acknowledged to be his best novel—effort that few serious critics have made.

I believe that my experience is fairly typical. I belong to the generation that read *Look Homeward, Angel* when it was new and they were very young. It wove for me an evocative spell as complete as any book ever has. It seemed to me that this was not a book; it was life and life as I knew it. I brought to it, a very young book, the naïve and uncritical response of the very young. Such an attitude did not survive, and in a very few years I became aware of the irresponsibility, the rhetorical excess, and the formless confusion of the book.

To go back to *Look Homeward, Angel* in 1955 and seriously to read it has been an experience in some ways as startling as the initial reading was, and it has made me aware that it is a different book from what I had thought and a much better one.

The standard view of *Look Homeward, Angel* has assumed one of three attitudes: that literal autobiography very thinly disguised constitutes the important portion of the book; that what form it has was given it by the editor Maxwell Perkins rather than its author; and that the book is most interesting in terms of Wolfe's acknowledged and pervasive debt to James Joyce.

The first attitude has resulted in a mass of biographical data, but, as Louis D. Rubin has recently pointed out, the value of the book must ultimately be determined in terms of its quality as *novel* rather than its accuracy as personal history. The second attitude reached the epitome of critical severity with Bernard DeVoto's ''Genius is not Enough'' [see Wolfe entry in *TCLC*, Vol. 1], and Wolfe is today generally credited with the major, if not the sole part in determining the form of his first two books.

The debt to Joyce, although everywhere obvious, seems to me almost nowhere truly significant. The least admirable portions of *Look Homeward, Angel* are those very portions where the ghost of *Ulysses* hovers visibly on the sidelines—portions such as the well-known record of the schoolboys' trip home from school, with its ironic pattern of mixed quotation so reminiscent of Joyce.

I think the first thing that strikes the mature reader who goes back to *Look Homeward, Angel* is the realization that it is a book enriched by a wealth of humor and saved from mawkishness by a pervasive comic spirit. This quality of the book is usually lost on its young readers, because the young very seldom see much amusing in themselves. Yet everywhere in this book one is aware that it is a very young book, not because its attitudes are themselves very young, but because it is a record of the inner and outer life of a very young boy.

The author looks back at youth with longing and love, but also with a steady but tolerant amusement. This is nowhere more apparent than in the hyperbolically presented day-dreams of ''Bruce-Eugene'' and in the very youthful posturing of the college student so earnestly set upon dramatizing himself. The humor is itself sometimes very poor and very seldom of the highest order. It is satire directed with crude bluntness; it is hyperbole lacking in finesse; it is *reductio ad absurdum* without philosophical seriousness. Wolfe is not a great comic writer, but his comic sense gives distance and depth to his picture of his youthful self.

For all its rhetorical exclamation about emotion, *Look Homeward, Angel* is a book firmly fixed in a sharply realized and realistically presented social environment. The book comes to us almost entirely through Eugene Gant's perceptions, but what he perceives is very often Altamont and Pulpit Hill (Asheville and Chapel Hill, N.C.) and he perceives them with a wealth of accurate detail. At this stage of his career, Thomas Wolfe had few serious pronouncements to make about man as a social animal (in his later career he was to attempt to make many), but he had a realist's view of his world.

It is a view colored, too, by a broadly Agrarian attitude, however much he was contemptuous of the Agrarians as a group. His picture of Altamont is a picture of a place mad with money and size, of a people submerging everything of value in valueless wealth. This view, the sword on which Eliza Gant is first hoist and then eviscerated, extends from the family to the life of the town and finally to the imagery of the whole book. As an example (and it is but one of hundreds), when he hears his idol-brother Ben talking sententious businessman nonsense, ''Eugene writhed to hear the fierce condor prattle this stale hash of the canny millionaires, like any obedient parrot in a teller's cage.''

Further, we perceive as a rediscovery that beneath the extravagant rhetoric, the badly and baldly rhythmic passages—the ones that eager young men reprint as bad free verse—there is a truly lyric quality in Wolfe's writing. With an abnormally keen memory for sensory perceptions, what Wolfe called his ''more than ordinary . . . power to evoke and bring back the odors, sounds, colors, shapes, and feel of things with concrete vividness,'' he is able to bring to bear vicariously on our five senses the precise content of a given scene and to make it poignantly and palpably real.

And here he works, not as a rhetorician asking us to imagine an emotion, but as an imagist rubbing ''the thing'' against our exposed nerve ends and thereby calling forth the feeling. It is, perhaps, in this ability to use authentically ''the thing'' to evoke emotion that the finest aspect of Wolfe's very uneven talent appears.

A new look at *Look Homeward, Angel* shows us that it is a book, not only of Eugene's ''buried life,'' but one about tragic loneliness. Few lonelier pictures exist than the ones here that show the insularity within which Eliza and W. O. Gant live. This W. O. Gant, a rich and hungry man in spirit, who was never called by his wife Eliza anything except ''Mr. Gant,'' strove by rhetoric, invective, alcohol, and lust to make somehow an impress on the unresponsive world around him. He is the ultimate tragic center of a book which deals with spiritual isolation almost everywhere.

Certainly the book lacks formal novelistic structure. If its core, as I believe, is W. O. Gant, then it contains a wealth of unresolved irrelevancy. If its central pattern is somehow linked up with brother Ben, as Wolfe seems to feel that it is, then we must regretfully assert that Brother Ben is a failure, the only really dead person in a book noteworthy for the vitality of its characters.

Yet *Look Homeward, Angel* has a consistency and an integrity of its own. In a way different from those indicated above, it presents a world. And as we survey that world and its characteristics, it begins to appear very much like the universe of that surprisingly modern eighteenth century figure, Laurence Sterne; and the thought impresses itself upon us that Thomas Wolfe has created for Eugene Gant a Shandean world and that his book has something of the inspired illogic of the universe of Walter Shandy and Uncle Toby.

Both *Look Homeward, Angel* and *Tristram Shandy* defy formal analysis. Both are concerned with the education of the very young. Both see that education as essentially the product of the impact of the world outside upon the young mind. Both describe that education through memories in maturity. And both gain a certain quality of detachment through the comic or amused presentation of material, although Sterne's humor is better than Wolfe's and more pervasively a portion of his book.

Both Eugene and Tristram are the products of mismatched parents, both pairs of whom exist in their eternally separate worlds. Both heroes have older brothers who die; both are given to rhetorical excesses; both have a tendency toward unsatisfied concupiscence; and both embarrass us by "snickering," as Thackeray pointed out about Sterne. But these are superficial similarities; more real ones exist in method, language, and theme.

Look Homeward, Angel and *Tristram Shandy* are both ostensibly about their heroes, are records of these heroes' "life and opinions," yet neither Eugene nor Tristram is as real as other characters in their books. Uncle Toby, "My Father," and to a certain extent "My Mother" dominate *Tristram Shandy* and overshadow its narrator-hero. W. O. Gant, Eliza Gant, and Helen Gant dominate *Look Homeward, Angel,* and beside them the viewpoint character, Eugene, pales into comparative unreality. Furthermore, both books are family novels, peculiarly rich in brilliantly realized, hyperbolically presented familial portraits.

Both Wolfe and Sterne were adept at the precise, fact-laden description in which the thing evokes the feeling. Both were given to the representation of emotional excess in terms of heightened sensibility. Sterne is famous for this characteristic; in Wolfe, one needs only to look at the Laura James sequence to see the "novel of sensibility" present with us again.

Both men were remarkably proficient at capturing the individual cadences of human speech and reproducing them with sharp accuracy, and both delighted in the rhetorically extravagant; so that their works present, not a unified style, but a medley of styles.

But most significantly of all, both Wolfe and Sterne were oppressed with the tragic sense of human insularity, with the ineffable loneliness at the core of all human life. Walter Shandy sought a word to communicate with wife and brother, and he sought in vain. His wife walked in inarticulate silence beside him. Eugene Gant was striving for "a stone, a leaf, an unfound door." W. O. Gant, with all his exuberance and overbrimming life, remained "Mr. Gant" to a wife who never understood "save in incommunicable gleams."

And the whole problem of life, loneliness, and memory with which in their different ways these two books are concerned is for both writers bound up in the mystery of time and memory. Uncle Toby and Tristram, as well as Sterne, brood amusingly and seriously about kinds of time. For Wolfe and his hero, Time is the great unanswerable mystery and villain of life.

The world of Eugene Gant is a Shandean world. And in that inconsistent, unbalanced, illogical, incongruous, incomplete, and lonely universe, the secret of *Look Homeward, Angel*'s sprawling formlessness, its unevenness, and its passages of colossal failure and of splendid success exist.

Unless we demand that all novels be neat and concise, *Look Homeward, Angel* has much to offer us still: a clear, detailed picture of a town; two extravagantly drawn but very living people, Eliza and W. O. Gant; a comic sense that lends aesthetic distance; a poignantly lyrical expression of the physical world of youth; and a picture of the individual's incommunicable loneliness. (pp. 16-17)

> Hugh Holman, "The Loneliness at the Core," in
> The New Republic, *Vol. 133, No. 15, October 10,*
> *1955, pp. 16-17.*

BRUCE R. McELDERRY, JR.   (essay date 1955)

[*McElderry was an American educator and literary critic whose critical studies focus predominantly on the works of such American realists as Mark Twain, Henry James, and Thomas Wolfe. In the following essay, first published in 1955, he examines humor in* Look Homeward, Angel.]

When Wolfe's first novel appeared in 1929 it contrasted sharply with the drab realism and despairing naturalism so prevalent in the decade since the war. The really typical book of 1929 was Ernest Hemingway's *Farewell to Arms,* which leaves its central figure numb with grief for his dead wartime love, without a shred of faith in life, in country, or in himself. *Look Homeward, Angel* was a different book. With confident good humor it turned back to an older America, primarily to the America of 1900 to 1917. That older America, as Wolfe represented it, was far from ideal. It was provincial, it was naïve, it was crude. But it was exuberantly alive, and it believed in itself. It was that belief in itself that America needed to recover in the nineteen-thirties, and the popularity of Wolfe's books in the ten years from 1929 to 1939 is a testimony to the service he rendered. His untimely death in 1938 cast a Keatsian halo around his memory, and in 1939 Wolfe was a minor literary cult.

The Keatsian halo has proved unfortunate, for it has prevented recognition of Wolfe as one of the finest humorous writers in America since Mark Twain, perhaps even better than Twain in range and variety. *A Subtreasury of American Humor* (1941), for example, included no selection from Wolfe. There has been an overzealous concern with the "serious" side of his work: the autobiographical nature of his fiction, the importance of editorial revision by Max Perkins, the question of whether Wolfe developed an adequate "philosophy," and the extent to which he mastered artistic form. It is time to re-read *Look Homeward, Angel,* his best novel, not so much as the agonizing search for maturity by an adolescent genius, as for the wonderful gallery of comic characters remembered and created from Wolfe's journey through the early years of this century. Eugene Gant's struggle to escape from family and environment is a thoroughly American pattern, and it gives intelligible direction to the story, but it is not the main attraction, any more than the freeing of the negro slave Jim is the main attraction of *Huckleberry Finn.* In both books it is the rich panorama and the lively episodes that enthrall.

In the comfortable old times pictured in *Look Homeward, Angel* a boy's heroes were Theodore Roosevelt, Admiral Dewey, and

Woodrow Wilson. William Jennings Bryan actually appears in one scene of the novel, sonorously praising to a newspaper reporter the charms of Altamont (Asheville). Veterans of the Civil War looked back over the long years with sad pride, and the Spanish-American War was a recent event, of glorious memory. Ridpath's *History of the World* was serious reading, and for entertainment there were dozens of Alger books with alliterative titles like *Sink or Swim,* the endless adventures of the Rover Boys, and *Stover at Yale.* It was the era of the *Police Gazette,* the minstrel show, and the early silent movies. Young people of a certain age—and older ones, too—sang "I Wonder Who's Kissing Her Now," "Till the Sands of the Desert Grow Cold," and "The End of a Perfect Day." All these delights, and many more, are set down in Wolfe's novel as they really were. They are amusing, as old snapshots always are, but they are true, too, and they are worth remembering without the malice that so distorts Sinclair Lewis's description of provincial America in *Main Street.*

It is the tolerance, the lack of malice, that gives distinction to Wolfe's humor in this novel. In this he is often superior to Twain, for much of Twain's humor is overshadowed by his obvious desire to score off somebody else as more stupid than himself, or sometimes to get even with himself for being stupid. Either way the temptation to bludgeon his way is strong. Wolfe is more natural, and more varied. How easily he gets his effect as he describes the meeting of Eliza Pentland and W. O. Gant. Eliza introduces herself as a representative of the Larkin Publishing Company:

> She spoke the words proudly, with dignified gusto. Merciful God! A book-agent! thought Gant.
>
> "We are offering," said Eliza, opening a huge yellow book with a fancy design of spears and flags and laurel wreaths, "a book of poems called *Gems of Verse for Hearth and Fireside* as well as *Larkin's Domestic Doctor and Book of Household Remedies,* giving directions for the cure and prevention of over five hundred diseases."
>
> "Well," said Gant, with a faint grin, wetting his big thumb briefly, "I ought to find one that I've got out of that."
>
> "Why, yes," said Eliza, nodding smartly, "as the fellows says, you can read poetry for the good of your soul and Larkin for the good of your body."

This is humor drawn from nature, requiring nothing but selection and the restraint of accurate reporting. Another passage illustrates humorous interpretation. Gant has just called his four sons for breakfast:

> "When I was your age, I had milked four cows, done all the chores, and walked eight miles through the snow by this time."
>
> Indeed, when he described his early schooling he furnished a landscape that was constantly three feet deep in snow, and frozen hard. He seemed never to have attended school save under polar conditions.

Sometimes the humorous effect is finely dramatic, as when one of Gant's sprees makes it appear that he is actually dead. Eugene's brother Ben turns to Eliza in fright:

> "Well," she said, picking her language with deliberate choosiness, "the pitcher went to the well once too often. I knew it would happen sooner or later."
>
> Through a slotted eye Gant glared murderously at her. Judicially, with folded hands, she studied him.

> Her calm eye caught the slow movement of a stealthy inhalation.
>
> "You get his purse, son, and any papers he may have," she directed. "I'll call the undertaker."
>
> With an infuriate scream the dead awakened.
>
> "I thought that would bring you to," she said complacently. He scrambled to his feet.
>
> "You hell-hound!" he yelled. "You would drink my heart's blood. You are without mercy and without pity—inhuman and bloody monster that you are."

Subtler, however, is the remarkable scene in which "Queen" Elizabeth, the town madam, orders from Gant a tombstone for one of her girls:

> "And she was such a fine girl, Mr. Gant," said Elizabeth, weeping softly. "She had such a bright future before her. She had more opportunities than I ever had, and I suppose you know"—she spoke modestly—"what I've done."

Elizabeth insists on purchasing the angel, Gant's favorite piece of statuary, and together they select a suitable inscription for the young prostitute's monument:

> She went away in beauty's flower,
> Before her youth was spent;
> Ere life and love had lived their hour
> God called her, and she went.

No excerpt can convey a sense of the delicate balance that prevents this scene from falling into burlesque. Gant and Elizabeth are humorous characters in a humorous situation. Wolfe lets them have their scene without satirical interjections.

Old man Gant is Wolfe's greatest character, and it is time to recognize him as one of the most varied comic characters in American literature. Beside him, Twain's Beriah Sellers is a shallow and tiresome stereotype. Gant's feud with Eliza is counterpointed by his even greater rage at her brother, Major Will Pentland. Gant's tirades, his passion for food and drink, his fear of the automobile he absentmindedly purchased, his unblinking support of the temperance movement, his pride in his children—these are but a few of the comic materials. But Gant is not the only source of humor. Eliza herself, literal-minded and obsessed with greed, is a wonderful foil to her turbulent husband. When Gant returned without warning from his long ramble in the west she "explains" his return:

> "I was saying to Steve last night, 'It wouldn't surprise me if your papa would come rolling in at any minute now'—I just had a feeling. I don't know what you'd call it," she said, her face plucked inward by her sudden fabrication of legend, "but it's pretty strange when you come to think about it. I was in Garret's the other day ordering some things, some vanilla extract, soda, and a pound of coffee. . . ."
>
> Jesus God! thought Gant. It's begun again.

Besides Gant and Eliza, there is young Luke Gant, energetically stuttering the townspeople into buying the *Saturday Evening Post.* There are Doc Maguire and Horse Hines (the undertaker), frequently found at Uneeda Lunch No. 3. There are Eugene's teachers: Mr. Leonard clumsily justifying the study of the classics he so unimaginatively taught; Professor Torrington, the pompous Rhodes Scholar who thought Barrie more important than Shaw; and Buck Benson, who said, "Mister Gant, you make me so damned mad I could throw you out the window,'' but left Eugene with a permanent love of Greek. There is a wonderful account of a Shakespeare pageant (1916):

> The pageant had opened with the Voices of Past and Present—voices a trifle out of harmony with the tenor of the event—but necessary to the commercial success of the enterprise. These voices now moved voicelessly past—four frightened sales-ladies from Schwartzberg's, clad decently in cheese-cloth and sandals, who came by bearing the banner of their concern. Or, as the doctor's more eloquent iambics had it:
>
> > Fair Commerce, sister of the arts, thou, too,
> > Shalt take thy lawful place upon our stage.
>
> They came and passed: Ginsberg's—''the glass of fashion and the mould of form''; Bradley the Grocer—''When first Pomona held her fruity horn''; The Buick Agency—''the chariots of Oxus and of Ind.''

And—years before Walter Mitty—there are the skillful parodies of youthful daydreaming in which Eugene Gant sees himself as Mainwaring the young minister, declaring his love to Grace the beautiful parishioner before he goes ''out west''; as Bruce Glendenning, the beachcomber who saves Veronica from a band of yelling natives; and as ''The Dixie Ghost,'' beating Faro Jim to the draw.

Despite these shining riches, there remains what Kipling called ''The Conundrum of the Workshops.'' The work may be clever, striking, human—but ''Is it Art?'' It is a hard question with respect to humor. Even admirers of Dickens are embarrassed by it. And as for *Huckleberry Finn*, Twain himself authorized the shooting of persons attempting to find a motive, moral, or plot in it. It is generally thought that without these you cannot have Art. Whether they are in fact present in *Huckleberry Finn* I shall not go into, but motive, moral, and plot are reasonably in evidence in *Look Homeward, Angel*. Eugene Gant is a sensitive boy, and his journey to adulthood has point and interest. For readers today it has more point than Huck's journey on the raft. At any rate it is a more difficult journey, for Twain took care that Huck never underwent the pangs of adolescence, in which, as Keats said, ''the soul is in ferment.'' Whatever defects in Art there may be, *Look Homeward, Angel* has many pages as funny as any in the *Subtreasury of American Humor*. If we begin with them, and tolerantly recognize that the perfect novel has not yet been written, we may come to agree with Wolfe's mother. After she read her son's novel she said: ''It's not bad at all—not bad at all.'' (pp. 189-94)

> *Bruce R. McElderry, Jr., ''The Durable Humor of 'Look Homeward, Angel','' in* Thomas Wolfe: Three Decades of Criticism, *edited by Leslie A. Field, New York University Press, 1968, pp. 189-94.*

LOUIS D. RUBIN, JR. (essay date 1955)

[*Rubin is an American critic and educator who has written and edited numerous studies of Southern literature. In the following excerpt, he examines Wolfe's view of his hometown in his letters and in* Look Homeward, Angel, *and discusses the town's reaction to the novel upon its publication.*]

Wolfe left Asheville in 1920—the departure is described in the first pages of *Of Time and the River*—and his first letters home indicate enthusiasm for Harvard and his work there in Professor George Pierce Baker's ''47'' Workshop, and only a mild interest in Mrs. Wolfe's Asheville doings in the real-estate business. From the first he showed a zeal to distinguish himself in

the eyes of the home folks, along with confidence that he would do so without any great difficulty. But as several years elapsed and Wolfe began to realize that it was not to be so easy as all that, we encounter a new tone in the letters to his mother. Commencing about 1923, he begins to show some anxiety over what Asheville and Asheville's citizens think of him. Living as he was largely off his mother's generosity, he resents the need to justify himself commercially, as he feels he must do, in the eyes of the family back home.

It is coincident with this development that there begins to appear in the letters the first criticism of Asheville and its ways. Once the criticism starts coming, however, it comes thick and fast. The letters written during the period 1923-27 are full of it. For the most part they are personal complaints, no doubt heavily influenced in their tone by what Norman Foerster has termed ''the prevailing spirit of naturalism abroad in literary circles at the time.'' In lambasting Asheville for his mother, Wolfe follows the Sinclair Lewis line of reasoning: Asheville is so busy with business pursuits that it has no time for art and beauty. There is much smiting of boobs, in the style of H. L. Mencken, as for example when he wrote his mother in 1923 that the plays he was going to write would not

> be suited to the tender bellies of old maids, sweet young girls, or Baptist ministers but they will be true and honest and courageous, and the rest doesn't matter. . . . I have stepped on toes right and left—I spared Boston with its nigger-sentimentalists no more than the South, which I love, but which I am nevertheless pounding. I am not interested in writing what our pot-bellied members of the Rotary and Kiwanis call a ''good show''—I want to know life and understand it and interpret it without fear or favor. . . .

> I will step on toes, I will not hesitate to say what I think of those people who shout ''Progress, Progress, Progress''—when what they mean is more Ford automobiles, more Rotary clubs, more Baptist Ladies Social unions. I will say that ''Greater Asheville'' does not necessarily mean ''100,000 by 1930,'' that we are not necessarily 4 times as civilized as our grandfathers because we go four times as fast in automobiles, because our buildings are four times as tall. What I shall try to get into their dusty, little pint-measure minds is that a full belly, a good automobile, paved streets, and so on, do not make them one whit better or finer,—that there is beauty in this world,—beauty even in this wilderness of ugliness and provincialism that is at present our country, beauty and spirit which will make us men instead of cheap Board of Trade Boosters, and blatant pamphleteers. . . .

Asheville was unable to appreciate beauty—and young men who believed in it, that was the trouble: ''If I really succeed, by the only standard that counts,—my own,—namely by writing a fine and noble play or book, worthy of my best, they would not understand what I had done, and would no doubt be a little bored by the result,—preferring *Parlor, Bedroom, and Bath,* or the poetry of Edgar A. Guest, or Dr. Frank Crane, and so on.''

Wolfe was never a Nashville-type Agrarian; the Nashville group didn't like him too much and he didn't like them. The Agrarians at various times criticized Wolfe's work, and he replied in kind in *The Web and the Rock*. But Wolfe was certainly as hostile as the Agrarians were to the New South of investment and factories and real-estate speculation. Unlike the Nashville group, however, he was not often disposed to recognize any great decline in the New South from the old, pre-industrial South. He would not have agreed with Allen Tate that "the Southern man of letters cannot permit himself to look upon the old system from a purely social point of view, or from the economic view; to him it must seem better than the system that destroyed it, better, too, than any system with which the present planners, Marxian or any color, wish to replace the present order." Wolfe thought almost entirely in terms of the artist, especially during the 1920's, and he hardly considered the rural South any more tolerant of or sympathetic toward true artists than the Kiwanians and Rotarians. (pp. 79-81)

The attitude toward Altamount of Eugene Gant, in *Look Homeward, Angel,* is much the same as that reflected in the letters of the 1920's. Eugene Gant is the artist growing up among the insensitive townsfolk, including his mother's family, who are too busy hoarding, sleeping, and feeding to recognize or understand his genius. His father had come among these same townsfolk and succumbed, selling his prized stone angel to adorn the grave of a whorehouse resident. Eugene will not do this; he will go forth instead to the shining city of light and culture, where his true brilliance will be recognized.

In the course of the novel a great deal of sarcasm is aimed at the commercial mind. Wolfe's concern with it, however, is not so much because he thinks that land speculators and money grubbers are evil, but because businessmen are insensitive to the merits of beauty and artists. Even Ben Gant, the Wolfean symbol of wasted youth in an alien and loveless world, does not suffer because of the commercial mores of Asheville. Rather it is the *personal* stinginess of Eliza and W. O. Gant that sends Ben out at a too-early age to earn a living. In his tirades, Ben blames not the community's economic philosophy, but that of his parents. "The value of a dollar! By God, I know the value of a dollar better than you do," Ben tells Eliza. "I've had a little something out of mine, at any rate. What have you had out of yours? I'd like to know that. What the hell's good has it ever been to any one? Will you tell me that?" If Ben is the victim of materialism, it is his parents' personal materialism. It is not the town that makes them that way. Eugene, of course, will escape. He will leave Altamont, and the family. But at this time Wolfe never seemed to draw a connection between Eliza Gant's ways and larger happenings in the community.

Look Homeward, Angel was published in October of 1929. Its arrival coincided with the stock market collapse. Both events made tremendous impressions on Asheville, already hard hit by the collapse of the real estate boom in 1927, and on Thomas Wolfe. "His own book," writes Jonathan Daniels, "written with the same eager fury which his mother gave to real estate, hit the town almost like the collapse of the real estate boom and left people almost as naked. And it made nobody so hurt and naked as himself—in loneliness under anger—even if the book also clothed him, at last, with the appreciation he so much wanted and which his work so deserved." An Asheville newspaperman has recently described the impact of the book on the town in 1929:

> The newspapers broke the news that Sunday morning to a city whose people had gone through the real estate boom-and-bust cycle of the middle 1920's, but were yet to travel the valley of stern personal and civic discipline imposed by bank failures and the great depression. It was a much more neighborly town than it is today and the people were proud, sensitive, and independent.
>
> The reaction was natural—as natural as sunshine and rain, a fact not clearly understood by people else-

where. It followed the pattern of people everywhere when they consider themselves affronted or are placed on the defensive. . . .

The reaction of the community was not organized. It was simply the sum of its many parts, the personal viewpoints of the citizens. Depending on the individual, they expressed hurt, shock, anger, irritation, resentment, indignation, or disgust. They felt the mores of the community had been violated; that Tom had been disloyal to his own family, to his friends, and to his native city. His characters and incidents, they said, had been too thinly disguised.

Some were loud in their expressions of opinions, others whispered, some laughed. It is possible, also, that some were disappointed when they could not identify themselves as characters in the book.

In *The Story of a Novel,* Wolfe himself describes Asheville's reaction to *Look Homeward, Angel*:

> For months the town seethed with a fury of resentment which I had not believed possible. The book was denounced from the pulpit by the ministers of the leading churches. Men collected on street corners to denounce it. For weeks the women's clubs, bridge parties, teas, receptions, book clubs, the whole complex fabric of a small town's social life was absorbed by an outraged clamor. I received anonymous letters full of vilification and abuse, one which threatened to kill me if I came back home, others which were merely obscene. One venerable old lady, whom I had known all my life, wrote me that although she had never believed in lynch law, she would do nothing to prevent a mob from dragging my "big overgroan karkus" across the public square. She informed me further, that my mother had taken to her bed "as white as a ghost" and would "never rise from it again."

Asheville soon became too pre-occupied with the devastating effects of the depression to worry much about Thomas Wolfe, however. As George W. McCoy remarks, "the people of Asheville turned their major attention to the struggle for economic survival after banks failed and the depression came." Jonathan Daniels also describes the crash in Asheville quite vigorously:

> The mayor was run out of office by clamoring citizens, a good many of whom had participated in the mess which made the mayor's perhaps corrupt use of city funds to save the bank seem necessary. The bank president, who was the town's first citizen in politics and finance, went down to Raleigh to become a convict. Six months after the bank failed, the ex-mayor went to the men's room on the floor above his law office and with a 45-caliber revolver—and approximately as Tom has described it in *You Can't Go Home Again*—blew half his head and brains all over the room. Also, as Tom wrote, a blind man found the body when he went in the room and stumbled against something on his way to the urinal.

If Asheville soon became too busy to concern itself overly much with Wolfe, the converse was by no means true. The reception accorded *Look Homeward, Angel* by his home town came with considerable impact for Wolfe. Formerly he had felt himself separated from the city because he was an Artist, and Asheville's grubbing minds could not recognize true art. He had gone forth into exile as Stephen Dedalus did, to live in silence, exile, and cunning while for the millionth time (though the first time in just this way, of course) he would forge in the smithy of his soul the uncreated conscience of his

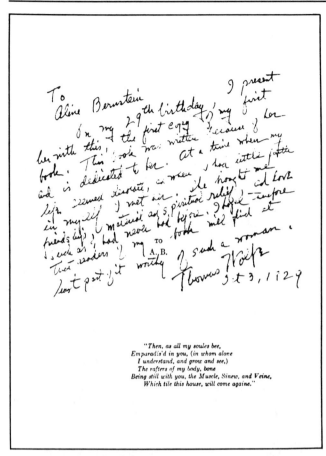

Inscription to Aline Bernstein in the first copy of Look Homeward, Angel. *Reproduced by permission of Paul Gitlin, Administrator of the Estate of Thomas Wolfe.*

"Then, as all my soules bee,
Emparadis'd in you, (in whom alone
I understand, and grow and see,)
The rafters of my body, bone
Being still with you, the Muscle, Sinew, and Veine,
Which tile this house, will come againe."

race. Now, however, instead of himself having imposed the artistic exile, he was declared by the townsfolk to be morally and socially undesirable, a traitor to all who loved him and whom he loved. Asheville's citizenry had in effect told him that he was henceforth no son of theirs, and that he was to go and never darken their door again—something quite different from any self-assumed artistic isolation for someone like Wolfe, to whom the oft-denounced ties of home and the past were nevertheless so important.

The truth is that Wolfe had never for a moment given up the idea that his home town would recognize him as the genius he knew he was. His book was in this respect designed to show the folks back home what he could do. It was Wolfe's *apologia pro vita sua,* and his claim to importance in the eyes of Asheville. In *You Can't Go Home Again* Wolfe describes George Webber's visit to Libya Hill just before publication of his first novel, "Home to Our Mountains," a visit quite similar to one that Wolfe himself made to Asheville while *Look Homeward, Angel* was on the presses: "He had the feeling, therefore, that in the eyes of his own people he had 'arrived.' He was no longer a queer young fellow who had consumed his substance in the deluded hope that he was—oh, loaded word!—'a writer.' He *was* a writer. He was not only a writer, but a writer who was about to be published, and by the ancient and honorable James Rodney & Co.''

Thus the hostile reception accorded his masterwork by his home town profoundly disappointed Wolfe. Instead of being hailed

as the poet and genius of the mountain country, he was reviled as a traitor to it. (pp. 85-9)

Louis D. Rubin, Jr., in his Thomas Wolfe: The Weather of His Youth, *Louisiana State University Press, 1955, 183 p.*

FLOYD C. WATKINS (essay date 1957)

[*Watkins is an American educator and critic specializing in Southern writers. In the following excerpt from his acclaimed critical work* Thomas Wolfe's Characters, *he discusses the background of Asheville, North Carolina, and Wolfe's depiction of the town as Altamont in* Look Homeward, Angel.]

Wolfe's description in *You Can't Go Home Again* of the publication of the first novel of Monk Webber is . . . autobiographical. Webber has, says Wolfe, written about his home town "with a nakedness and directness which, up to that time, had been rare in American fiction." *Rare,* probably not in artistic realism, but in truth: Theodore Dreiser, Sinclair Lewis, and James T. Farrell had been most devastatingly direct in their treatments of fictional people. The truth of this phrase seems to have stuck in Wolfe's mind, because exactly two hundred pages later in the same novel Webber again thinks about his having written with "naked directness and reality that was rather rare in books."

The basic factors in Wolfe's writings and in any evaluation of them are his family, his community, and his university; and these elements are with him much more determining forces than they are with most writers. The history and customs of his subjects called for "naked directness" and realism, satire, and idol-breaking. Asheville and the many crosscurrents of life there to be observed are the very matrix of his art.

The mountains surrounding the town on all sides may have hemmed in life, as Wolfe said in *Look Homeward, Angel,* but certainly they did not dam it out. The story of Asheville essentially is one of the influx of the world. The mountaineer girl now has her mail-order dress and a radio, perhaps even television, and the strains of popular songs like "I Love Paris" prove that an alien culture has been carried into the homes of those whom W. O. Gant calls "mountain grills." But the distant lure of the hills long ago established such precedents. The ancestors of these very mountaineers were drawn to the site of Asheville by the wonders of the Blue Ridge ranges as they could be seen from the Piedmont region of North Carolina. Wild and strong-blooded frontiersmen, who were the forerunners of the modern far and lost hillmen, dispersed the wilder Indians, but in western North Carolina there are more survivals of the older cultures than are to be found in other regions of America. The reservation of the Cherokee Indians is not far from Asheville, and the Indian woman with a papoose on her back and a small tribe of little Indians beside her is still to be seen occasionally in the streets of the town.

These elements of the far and lost mingle with some of the most cosmopolitan Americans, the sport-shirted, tired, surly tourists and the bright businessmen who minister to their needs. The influx began significantly with George Vanderbilt, that most famous of all the tourists who have gravitated to what Ashevillians like to call "The Land of the Sky." In most of his works Wolfe has described the vast estates and the castle of this son of one of the greatest of the American robber barons after the Civil War. For five years, between 1890 and 1895, Vanderbilt was constructing that magnificent, depressing, unhomelike, forbidding 125-room castle, set in the midst of a huge estate that in 1905 consisted of one hundred and forty thousand acres of land once owned by Anglo-Saxon mountaineers, who could never have dreamed of such opulence. Thus, Asheville now, as in Tom Wolfe's youth, can display the primitive and proverbial log cabin culturally juxtaposed with Vanderbilt's medieval castle and its imported collections of priceless European plunder. There are Italian marble lions of the sixteenth century, carvings of the knightly and aristocratic "Return from the Chase" and of scenes from Wagner's operas, gold and silk tapestries that depict the loves of Venus and Mars and that probably bedecked the tent of Francis I at the Field of the Cloth of Gold, the chess table in which Napoleon's heart rested as it was reportedly smuggled into France after his death, a library of twenty thousand ornately printed and lavishly bound volumes, and the furnishings of Cardinal Richelieu. "And in a curious way that great estate had shaped the whole life of the town," Wolfe himself observed in *Of Time and the River*. "At the heart of the town's desire was the life of that great house." What an empty heart and desire and house!

This is but one of the structures built in Asheville by the newcomer barons of America. There is also the tremendous Grove Park Inn, built by the developer of Dr. Grove's chill tonic. Asheville is today partly a conglomeration of tourist motels and partly a site of relics of a more glorious and exploited past. The Asheville-Biltmore College has been established in Overlook or "Seely's Castle," built by the daughter and son-in-law of E. W. Grove at a cost of several hundred thousand dollars. Modeled on the Forde Abbey, twenty-five miles from London, the building was left incomplete exactly as the abbey was so that the copying would be exact. It was constructed by Italian workmen after they had finished the Grove Park Inn.

One who tours this city, which is a relic of a bygone age of American attempts to become aristocratic, feels somehow that the mountaineer culture in its very simplicity was superior and that somehow here is a symbol of the picture of Altamont and Asheville's tragic flaw. It is also, one must not forget, the raw material of Wolfe's works. The intercourse of Asheville with the tourists begot the boom and resulted in the prostitution of the mountains and the simplicity of the life they had fostered. And there is still the mark of illegitimacy on the children they have bred. Those boarders leisurely rocking on the front porch of Eliza Gant's Dixieland were tourists paying their currency for the hospitality of a prosperous descendant of the hill-bound. The very blood of Tom Wolfe was a mixture of the drifting Yankee lured by the wonders of the mountains and of one of the mountaineers from "over yonder in Zebulon," who sold books to the tourists and the newcomers, who married out of the tribe to the Yankee, who catered to tourist boarders, and who speculated in land that constantly rose in price because of the hopes of more tourist trade.

This is the material and the conflict, the source of the poetry, the memory, and the rhetoric. Cosmopolitan and provincial Asheville gave Wolfe his background, furnished the mores of his novels, and gave him his subjects and his characters. Perhaps Asheville and his mother provided him with his tradition and his constant provincialism, his desire to come home again. With its tales of far-off wonders, as described by the tourists, the town and the blood of his father gave him his wanderlust. There were reasons for his being torn, attracted, and repelled. It was his very nature and the nature of his town and of his family.

The character of the town also intruded into the Wolfe and Gant family. The bourgeois character of the invading tourists perhaps explains the excessive concern of some of them for social standing. "I don't believe in cheap things"—this is a standard they often reiterate. Helen Gant is shocked when she realizes that her dying father's best friends are the honest, common working men who cluster together away from the prominent citizens when they visit him during his last sickness in *Of Time and the River*. That Puritan strain in the mountaineer is an innate characteristic of the Pentlands, the Gants, and Aunt Maw of the Webber cycle. The primitiveness and the luxury of Asheville are both to be found in the Old Kentucky Home, now a shrine to Wolfe's memory. An old, intricately fashioned sterling silver coffee urn stands in the dining room, and from its table the modern tourist can see the primitive kitchen with several wrought-iron wood stoves. On the wall hangs a beautiful piece of china that Mr. Wolfe bought especially to hang his watch on at night, but it contrasts strangely with the cheap iron beds of the many bedrooms. Such incongruence might be illustrated over and over, for it was a basic characteristic of Tom Wolfe's surroundings. The Old Kentucky Home is so much like Dixieland that one who enters the house for the first time feels as if he were rereading the book. Wolfe has described minutely and accurately the rooms and the furniture of the old boardinghouse.

In the final analysis, *Look Homeward, Angel* is a portrait not only of the ego of Wolfe but also of a Southern town. The unbelievably large number of characters does indicate that he succeeded in portraying, as George Webber wishes to do, "the whole town from which he came, and all the people in it just as he had known them." This book was but a beginning, and all the other novels, even those after the change from the Gant to the Webber hero and family, continue to portray the same town, the same places and people.

Altamont is a portrait of a town that is as fully populated as Spoon River or Main Street or Winesburg, Ohio. Wolfe's writings are at times just as satiric, just as realistic, and just as bold as those of the most caustic Midwesterners, and this is what was to make the people of Asheville run mad with anger. There are, however, additional qualities in his writings that are not to be found in the books about the other imaginative towns. Masters, Lewis, and Anderson forgot the poetry and the innate goodness and mystery of man found in the simple folk of the local colorists; but Tom Wolfe, unlike most of his contemporaries, was able to conjoin realistic descriptions with some feeling, goodness with depravity. This achievement, perhaps, accounts for his great popularity among the American middle class, who have not yet turned naturalistic or esoteric.

Wolfe saw poetry and romance and nobility in the citizens of his town, and the almost unalleviated sterility of Lewis' Main Street is not to be found in Altamont. Despite the burliness and bawdiness of Doc McGuire, for example, there is a strain of great nobility in his rather depraved soul, as there is also in the honorable but dishonored aristocrats of Faulkner's Yoknapatawpha. No character with the vitality and gusto of McGuire and old Gant or with the brusqueness and love of Ben ever lived in Main Street.

Young Eugene Gant does hear the locomotive whistles calling him to wander, but Tom Wolfe the wanderer died while he had in progress a book on the Southern mountaineers. Their vitality served him as literary raw material all his life. Even his accounts of life in Brooklyn and at Harvard reveal a satire and a barrenness of incident and romance that are never to be found in the sections of his books about North Carolina and the South. No Altamontian ladles out his life in coffee spoons. One need not be a Confederate to deplore sometimes his failure to concentrate entirely on the land of his birth. It gave him the richest material he ever used, and *Look Homeward, Angel,* the only novel entirely with a Southern setting, remains his best book perhaps because comparatively he failed with alien people, settings, and materials.

Besides the appeal of exaggerated, comic, robust, tragic, and absurd characters, Wolfe permeated his works with a lyric strain that caused great admiration despite the lack of discipline. Often his poetry files off the edge of the satire and mysteriously contributes the feeling that regardless of satire, the portrait is essentially one of love. Two volumes of collected poetic passages from his works and the admiration of his readers testify to his lyricism, demonstrable from the poetic prose on the flyleaf of *Look Homeward, Angel* to the lyrical lament about the death of his brother Ben. Wolfe added much satire and lyricism by numerous quotations from the great poetry of all ages. Nearly every one of the forty-two pages in chapters XXIII and XXIV has several quotations lifted from great poems. With a peculiar aptness and irony, Wolfe succeeded in making the borrowed verses comment on characters in Altamont. Negro laundresses at work, for example, are described in terms of one of Herrick's love lyrics: they plunge "their wet arms into the liquefactions of their clothes."

The books Wolfe read as a child and the motion pictures he saw also compose part of the background of the novel. Probably that cheap fiction which causes the dreamy young Eugene to think of himself as the heroic Bruce Eugene is taken literally and specifically from the pulp fiction of the time. The *Asheville Citizen* in 1914, for example, ran as a serial novel Harold MacGrath's *The Adventures of Kathlyn.* The hero, John Bruce, who saves Kathlyn in India, may have stayed in Wolfe's mind and served as the inspiration for the great Bruce that causes young Gant to call himself Bruce Eugene.

The description of the old silent wild western that Eugene has just seen with his father follows with the usual minutiae of detail many aspects of *The Fugitive,* a 1916 western starring the famous William S. Hart. Many of the actions and characters are almost identical in the motion picture and the novel, but apparently Wolfe also used vivid portions of other old westerns that he had seen as a child. The result of the combination is a paradoxical blending of satire on early movies and the wonders of romantic boyhood.

All these elements enter the lifelike portrait of youth spent in Asheville. And most of them point to a sympathy with the provincial, the rural, and the small town that was seldom to be encountered when *Look Homeward, Angel* appeared in 1929. It is no wonder that a cosmopolitan and urbane Fitzgerald thought Wolfe was wasting his time. Rather, the wonder is that Wolfe did not agree. (pp. 30-7)

> *Floyd C. Watkins, in his* Thomas Wolfe's Characters: Portraits from Life, *University of Oklahoma Press, 1957, 194 p.*

RICHARD WALSER   (essay date 1961)

[*Walser is an American biographer and critic specializing in writers native to the state of North Carolina. In the following excerpt from his study* Thomas Wolfe: An Introduction and an Interpretation, *he examines the themes, symbolism, and poetic prose style of* Look Homeward, Angel.]

Look Homeward, Angel carries as its subtitle "A Story of the Buried Life." What did Wolfe mean by this? Evidently the phrase was borrowed from Matthew Arnold's short poem beginning "Light flows our war of mocking words," in which Arnold comments on that part of man's life hidden behind the disguises he wears and on his inability, except in moments of love, to reveal himself. This buried life, even so, is the real one, the essential one which lends meaning to existence. Wolfe extended this notion into what he called his "plan" for the book. Before the novel was accepted for publication, he wrote that in it "There are two essential movements—one outward and one downward. The outward movement describes the effort of a child, a boy, and a youth for release, freedom, and loneliness in new lands. . . . The downward movement is represented by a constant excavation into the buried life of a group of people, and describes the cyclic curve of a family's life— genesis, union, decay, and dissolution." The buried life was a secret life, and though even Gant and Eliza had such a side, it is mainly Eugene, and to a lesser degree, Ben, who are shown to be strangers to the world.

With Eugene the secret life had much to do with imagination, by means of which he daydreamed of huge ships and faraway cities and lands which opened out. In his imagination there was belief in the great virtues: tenderness and gentleness, beauty and love and goodness, valiance and glory. There were more intense moments like the one in which he lusciously imagined himself the only male in a town of pretty women whence all the men had fled, and how he would loot the shops and cellars and fulfill all his sensuous desires. There were more comical moments in which he saw himself as "Ace Gant, the falcon of the skies, with 63 Huns to his credit by his nineteenth year." And there were the more honest moments when he admitted "the wild confusion of adolescence, the sexual nightmares of puberty, the grief, the fear, the shame in which a boy broods over the dark world of his desire," when "every boy, caged in from confession by his fear, is to himself a monster."

The essence of the buried life was a continuation of prenatal existence. If Wolfe borrowed Arnold's phrase for his subtitle, he was even more influenced by the Neoplatonic romanticism of Wordsworth and Coleridge. In the prose-poem facing the first chapter are these well remembered words: "Naked and alone we came into exile. In her dark womb we did not know our mother's face: from the prison of her flesh have we come into the unspeakable and incommunicable prison of this earth." Eugene was born trailing Wordsworthian clouds of glory, but all too soon he was suspended in time, caught in life's prisonhouse, and the sound of the great bell ringing underseas was dimmer and dimmer. As time went on, the prison house became more stifling, and though he sought to escape the prison gates, he came to realize that his incarceration was complete and he found comfort in the fantasy of the buried life. Thus walled in, he projected "an acceptable counterfeit of himself which would protect him from intrusion." At birth he knew the word— "the lost key opening the prison gates, the lane-end into heaven"—but eventually, like all who are born, he forgot it.

Re-echoes of pre-existence and the buried life persist throughout the novel and give it unity. To go a step further, [W. P.] Albrecht contends that Wolfe utilized, besides the pre-existence-and-return myth, other Platonic contrasts: dark and light, many and one, isolation and union, imprisonment and freedom, shadow and reality. His study and love of the romantic poets left their mark.

While the subtitle and opening sentences of *Look Homeward, Angel* established a mood for the story to follow, they do not state a theme. Almost from the first days when Wolfe started writing the novel, there was no doubt in his mind what his intent would be. Though the materials would come from his own life, he planned to tell, he wrote Mrs. Roberts, "the story of a powerful creative element trying to work its way toward an essential isolation; a creative solitude; a secret life—its fierce struggles to wall this part of its life away from birth, first against the public and savage glare of an unbalanced, nervous brawling family group; later against school, society, all the barbarous invasions of the world." The words are clear. Wolfe was then twenty-five years old; his young spirit was being assailed by the world which he had sought outside his mountains; he needed at that moment for the past to be caught, as it was with Proust, through memory; and he felt the necessity to put down on paper the agony of his present problem.

The pith of any work of fiction is conflict. Eugene Gant's conflict was one between himself and world, between himself and family, school, and society. He struggled against a father whose artistic nature he thought had been wasted, against a mother whose love he believed he had lost, against brothers and sisters who had succumbed to the pressures and been defeated. Inwardly he took up arms against a home town which he felt was united to destroy him. He was determined to keep his individuality intact.

Eugene's fight is all the more difficult because he was constantly aware that, in spite of his strong resolution to preserve his self, the elements of Chance were operating full time. Eugene had only to go back in memory to know that "the loss or gain of a moment, the turn of the head, the enormous and aimless impulsion of accident, had thrust into the blazing heat of him." And so it would go on, each moment being the culmination of thousands and thousands of years. Cause led on to Cause, and Man's life was not ordered by mind and reason but was the frenzied fumbling of Chance, Variety, and Fate. If the battle was unequal, the best one could do was to isolate himself—to "wall" himself in—and "escape" into life, not from it.

Like all young men, Eugene pondered the reasons why life should be this way, but these occasions were rare. Generally they came in fancied seconds when Time was suspended and no-Time took over. Eugene would see a woman from a train window, and suddenly the train was motionless, the woman was frozen without movement, and Time was stopped. The reader of *Look Homeward, Angel* may recall that the instant after W. O. Gant had sold the angel to Queen Elizabeth, he stood upon the steps of his stonecutter's shop and the pulsing fountain in the public square was held in photographic fixity. Where was man headed? "Where now? Where after? Where then?" There was no answer. Only death was sure.

Throughout the novel, the mood and theme are enriched by a number of symbols which must be understood if the poetic nature of the fiction is to be fully realized. A translation of poetic symbols is not always easy, and the reason is aptly given by Richard Chase in *The American Novel and Its Tradition*:

> . . . a poetic symbol not only *means* something, it *is* something—namely an autonomous truth which has been discovered in the process by which the symbol emerged in the context of the poem. If it still permits us to think of it as an ordinary symbol—as something that stands for something else—we see that it does not point to anything easy to express. Rather, it sug-

gests several meanings. . . . Furthermore, the "poetry" of a novel will probably reside less in the language than in the rhythm and relation of picture, scene, character, and action. . . .

This is especially true of Wolfe, where the symbolic words *are* something at the same time they carry another intention. Moreover, like the whale in Melville, the intention is constantly shifting, rarely static.

A good example is the Angel of the title. Here are the lines from Milton's "Lycidas":

> Or whether thou [the poet's college friend who has drowned], to our moist vows denied,
>
> > Sleep'st by the fable of Bellerus old,
> > Where the great Vision of the guarded mount
> > Looks toward Namancos and Bayona's hold.
> > Look homeward, Angel, now, and melt with ruth:
> > And, O ye dolphins, waft the hapless youth.

Here Milton invokes the protector angel St. Michael to turn from foreign threats in order to weep for a disaster at home. The same meaning may be applied to Wolfe's novel. Heaven is urged to look toward home and "melt with ruth" rather than gaze afar for tragic possibilities. Altamont and the Gant family have their own pathetic lives. This poetic interpretation of the word *angel* is balanced by a palpable image: the stone angel on the porch of Gant's shop. This angel, which Wolfe wrote was responsible for his title, "had come from Carrara in Italy, and it held a stone lily delicately in one hand. The other hand was lifted in benediction, it was poised clumsily upon the ball of one phthisic foot, and its stupid white face wore a smile of soft stone idiocy." As a youth in Baltimore, Gant had seen such an angel and had then yearned to carve a similar one and thus release evidence of the creative urge within him. He never learned to carve such an angel; the artistic impulse burned and died as the prisonhouse closed about him in the philistine confines of Altamont. In this instance, the angel is the symbol of the creativity which, though throbbing, is suppressed in most men.

A third and more compelling interpretation, and in no way unconnected with the other two, is the angel of Ben and Eugene. Wolfe generally substituted the word ghost, the ghost being the spirit from some pre-existence. "O lost, and by the wind grieved, ghost, come back again," Wolfe reiterated. The ghost is a lonely spirit. It is sometimes synonymous with the loss of innocence as when, after Eugene's first visit to a prostitute, he "was haunted by his own lost ghost: he knew it to be irrecoverable." But the angel-ghost image, like any wraith, shifts and changes. Often it stands for corporeal life, which is not real at all, but a zombie taking the place of the real. At such times the ghost wails for a return into life from exile. The ghost therefore is lost. Eugene, himself a ghost, seeks the way of returning. "The way is here, Eugene. Have you forgotten? The leaf, the rock, the wail of light. Lift up the rock, Eugene, the leaf, the stone, the unfound door. Return, return." Then, after Ben's death, Ben *becomes* Eugene's ghost, and Ben's answer to the question "Where is the world?" is the simple one "*You* are your world." In that last chapter, the dead Ben finally has life, and he is therefore no longer a ghost. The stone angels begin to move, and with them Eugene believes himself freed. The ghost-angel reappears as creative power. . . .

Often in the same context as the angel is the triple symbol "a stone, a leaf, a door." In *The Prelude*, Wordsworth writes of "a tree, a stone, a withered leaf," a phrasing upon which Wolfe apparently based his refrain. In his novels, the *stone* is reminiscent of Gant's angel and its metaphorical meaning for the artist; it is also the solid element in life's uncertain transformations. The *leaf*—the "withered leaf"—is, by way of contrast, consonant with decay and death. The most frequently used of the three words is the *door,* and the search for the door, which, if one could find and enter it, would mean artistic and spiritual fulfillment.

There are many other ringing words, of course. The train, with its apostrophe to America and to America's unknown people and places, sometimes becomes for Eugene the "gateway to the lost world." More than any other symbol, the train is Wolfe's signature, as the star is Robert Frost's.

And there are the mountains, which represent Eugene's bound-in life and his desire for escape.

All of these symbols are tied in with Wolfe's mood and theme, culminating in Eugene's conviction "that men do not escape from life because life is dull, but that life escapes from men because men are little."

The symbols are interwoven into the prose paragraphs, and when the reader comes upon them, they are like the soft low notes of a musical instrument, sounding to remind him that outside the story of written words is a meaning deeper and more profound than the progressive narrative before him.

Wolfe's search for America is less evident in **Look Homeward, Angel** than in the later books. In his first novel he was so concerned with an examination of his youth that he had not yet projected his subject matter very far beyond Altamont and Old Catawba. The country out there was largely *terra incognita.* Still there are hints that the stretch of America was in his mind. Gant's trip to California by train called forth a rhapsodic passage. When Eugene takes a trip down into South Carolina (by train, of course), there in the nighttime beyond the windows was "the American earth—rude, immeasurable, formless, mighty."

If the quest of America was yet to come, not so Wolfe's discovery of poetry. Fully does **Look Homeward, Angel** deserve the rather generally agreed-upon opinion that it is the most lyrical novel ever written by an American. There are many ways in which Wolfe used poetry. Besides the rhythmic lines, the colorful phrasing, the symbolic images, and the leitmotifs, Wolfe picked up from Joyce a method of using well-known phrases from classical poetry, verbatim or in paraphrase, to balance Eugene's everyday world. In this fashion was Eugene able to rout his enemies in secret and to comment upon the commonplace. For instance, noticing a streetcleaner at his vulgar labor (in that most Joycean of chapters, number 24), the boy's mind runs to Gray's line, "Let not Ambition mock their useful toil." Taunted by his friend's reasoning that it paid to be a Christian because church membership was good for business, Eugene thinks with Coleridge: "To walk together to the kirk, with a goodly company."

Such a scheme is not, of course, inherently poetic. More to the point is the chapter on Ben's funeral (number 37), where Wolfe leaves prose far behind, and even poetry merges into music. Like the last scene of *Götterdämmerung,* a whole symphony of themes is repeated and pulsed toward the transcendent triumph of life over death.

In the last chapter, the meeting of Eugene with Ben's ghost provides Wolfe with an opportunity to drift into pure fantasy; and to match the fantasy are the cadenced phrases and suggestive terms. "I shall lift no stone upon the hills," Eugene says

to the ghost in nonrealistic expression; "I shall find no door in any city. But in the city of myself, upon the continent of my soul, I shall find the forgotten language, the lost world, a door where I may enter, and music strange as any ever sounded; I shall haunt you, ghost, along the labyrinthine ways until—until? O Ben, my ghost, an answer?"

Wolfe's use of poetry must take into account, too, his dithyrambic paragraphs which delight in sensuous impressions. Sound and sight passages are not unusual in prose fiction, but Wolfe is one of the few writers for whom the pleasures of smell can be prolonged for page after page. All the senses are keenly at work in his descriptions of food, in which sections even Dickens is rivaled. Here is a delectable account succinctly covering a day at the Gant household:

> In the morning they rose in a house pungent with breakfast cookery, and they sat at a smoking table loaded with brains and eggs, ham, hot biscuits, fried apples seething in their gummed syrups, honey, golden butter, fried steak, scalding coffee. Or there were stacked batter-cakes, rum-colored molasses, fragrant brown sausages, a bowl of wet cherries, plums, fat juicy bacon, jam. At the mid-day meal, they ate heavily: a huge hot roast of beef, fat buttered lima-beans, tender corn smoking on the cob, thick red slabs of sliced tomatoes, rough savory spinach, hot yellow corn-bread, flaky biscuits, a deep-dish peach and apple cobbler spiced with cinnamon, tender cabbage, deep glass dishes piled with preserved fruits—cherries, pears, peaches. At night they might eat fried steak, hot squares of grits fried in egg and butter, pork-chops, fish, young fried chicken.

If such a passage is less than lyric poetry, it must be remembered that Wolfe had many styles at his command. Poetry and realism are inextricably compounded in the slice-of-life portions of the book, especially when they concern the early morning activities of various folk in Altamont. At such times Wolfe wrote in Joycean sentences to his heart's content.

When in a jolly mood, Wolfe could turn to parody and, particularly when he was telling of Eugene's daydreams, mock the sentimental fiction which went for literature in Altamont. Or he could ridicule the stupid social-column writing of the newspaper, as here:

> Members of the Younger Set were charmingly entertained last night at a dinner dance given at Snotwood, the beautiful residence of Mr. and Mrs. Clarence Firkins, in honor of their youngest daughter, Gladys, who made her debutt this season. Mr. and Mrs. Firkins, accompanied by their daughter, greeted each of the arriving guests at the threshold in a manner reviving the finest old traditions of Southern aristocracy, while Mrs. Firkins' accomplished sister, Miss Catherine Hipkiss, affectionately known to members of the local younger set as Roaring Kate, supervised the checking of overcoats, evening wraps, jockstraps, and jewelry. . . .

The account continues in this vein, but the paragraph is enough to toss to the winds the claims of those who affirm that Wolfe was without humor.

The central and simplest theme of **Look Homeward, Angel** is the revolt of the individual from the small town, a theme uppermost in the minds of other writers of the 1920's—Zona Gale, Sherwood Anderson, and Sinclair Lewis, to name a few. But unlike the works of these authors, **Look Homeward, Angel** was written at a time when the clouds of glory had not entirely passed away, at a time before the prison house had completely closed in. The stars were right; the union of Boy and Man was as nearly perfect as could ever be expected, and from this union came a lyrical quality rare in fiction. (pp. 61-8, 70)

Richard Walser, in his Thomas Wolfe: An Introduction and Interpretation, Barnes & Noble, Inc., 1961, 152 p.

RICHARD S. KENNEDY (essay date 1962)

[Kennedy is an American critic and biographer whose studies of Thomas Wolfe and E. E. Cummings are highly acclaimed. Since the 1970s he has edited and published several collections of Wolfe's uncollected writings. In the following excerpt, Kennedy examines the dual narratives of Look Homeward, Angel, one concerning Eugene Gant's development and the other recounting the Gant family history, within the context of two philosophical bases which underlie the novel: a naturalistic view of reality and the Platonic idea of preexistence.]

Look Homeward, Angel is that work which Wolfe assured Professor Baker he would write "for [his] souls ease and comfort."

Stepping far beyond his attempt to present the cross section of a town in Welcome to Our City, he created an elaborate microcosm in which to place his autobiographical hero, Eugene Gant. He assembled a throng of characters, ranging from briefly glimpsed citizens, who are sharply caricatured, to those figures closest to Eugene, who are as fully alive as any literary creations can be, well-defined, yet containing a mixture of good and evil, strength and weakness, capacity and limitation. By means of symbol and allusion, he enlarged his scene beyond the family circle and town life to keep the history of man before us. More than this, he circumscribed the whole spectacle with a cosmic view that dominates the book.

Critics have commented extensively on Wolfe's characterizations in Look Homeward, Angel, delivering their just appreciations of the vigorous Gant, theatrical in his bluster; the patient, grasping Eliza, her mind a sea of trivia; the impulsive, generous Helen; and the brooding, nocturnal Ben. They have drawn conclusions about the author's life from the character of Eugene and from his relations with his family. They have discussed the book as the first movement in Wolfe's four-novel symphony of life. But of the order of his little universe in his first work, of the structure and unity of Look Homeward, Angel, the only long novel that Wolfe brought to completion himself, nothing has been said. And unless we recognize the three separate planes of statement that Wolfe has fused into a unified narrative, we not only fail to appreciate the fullness and the seriousness of his achievement but we even fall short of grasping the full meaning of his book.

The central narrative presents the story of the growth of Eugene Gant toward a freedom from forces deterring him from the best fulfillment of his nature and, more positively, toward a realization of what life means within the world scheme that Wolfe sets up. Wolfe has embedded this central narrative within a family chronicle in which Eugene plays his small part. From the very outset, Wolfe had this much of his plan in mind, as we see from the letter he sent Mrs. Roberts from Bath:

... its unity is simply this: I am telling the story of a powerful creative element trying to work its way toward an essential isolation; a creative solitude—a secret life—its fierce struggles to wall this part of its life away from birth—first against the public and savage glare of an unbalanced, nervous brawling family group; later against school, society, all the barbarous invasions of the world. In a way, the book marks a progression toward freedom; in a way toward bondage. . . . Just subordinate and leading up to this main theme is as desperate and bitter a story of a contest between two people as you ever knew—a man and his wife—the one with an inbred, and also an instinctive, terror and hatred of property; the other with a growing mounting lust for ownership that finally is tinged with mania—a struggle that ends in decay, death, desolation.

As he worked, his plans enlarged. He placed these two narrative elements within a double framework of ideas. The greater presents an all-inclusive view of the universe, and the lesser deals with individual man's place within this universe.

The larger and more general framework is Wolfe's biological interpretation of life—vitalism, emergent evolution, or creative evolution. . . . [This] philosophy possibly grew from seeds planted by Professor Horace Williams in lectures at Chapel Hill, but it seems more likely to have taken shape from Bernard Shaw and H. G. Wells, especially from Wells's novel, The Undying Fire. Wolfe incorporates this view of life in his book, but since he is a novelist, not a philosophical essayist, the creative evolutionary theory is implied rather than expounded in Look Homeward, Angel. The theory, based on a distinction between life and matter, may be summed up briefly in this way: Matter existed before organism, but when conditions permitted, life began (no attempt is made to explain how) and undertook its evolutionary climb, making use of matter for sustenance and for body. Organism, guided by Life Force, the essence of life, evolved from a microscopic blob, through an animal without a backbone, to man, and is still moving onward, though its destiny is unknown. Although life moves forward through what seems to be blind-chance struggle, its ruthless and apparently wasteful progress has a certainty of purpose that is beyond our comprehension. Since Life Force, living in matter and with the help of matter, adapts matter to its own ends, it represents a super-will in the universe. Man's role in the evolutionary progress is unspecified. Although man houses a larger share of the energy of life than lower forms of organism, this power is, in Wolfe's eyes, a magnificent but tragic gift.

In tracing the growth of Eugene, Wolfe treats the idea of the Life Urge within the body very much like the Jungian concept of libido, which goes beyond the sexual emphasis of Freud's use of the term to become a kind of life energy. In fact, psychoanalytic concepts color the book throughout. Wolfe probes the psychic recesses of Eugene, of W. O. and Eliza Gant. He employs sea and grotto imagery. Certainly he makes Eugene's Oedipal attachment to his mother an important feature of his narrative. It is clear that he developed a ready familiarity with depth psychology during the time he knew Aline Bernstein.

In Look Homeward, Angel Wolfe begins his presentation of the vitalistic world view on the title page. In the motto, "At one time the earth was probably a white-hot sphere like the sun," we have initial matter, the earliest stage of man's known universe before it was invested with life. Then as we begin Chapter I, we are immediately confronted with life and its progress, for the white-hot sphere has long since cooled, thus allowing the Life Principle to enter on the scene and to combine with matter.

But the purposive character of Wolfe's view of life is not explicitly stated at the outset; it is not revealed until the last chapter. In the beginning, Wolfe emphasizes the "waste and loss'' that surround life's movement and change; and throughout the narrative, he repeatedly asserts the power that ''the dark miracle of chance'' exercises upon the course of the Life Urge.

The early statements about chance gradually mingle with reflections on Fate, especially in Eliza's murky observations of the tide of events surrounding her family. At the death of her son Grover, we see her grim acceptance of life's harshness: ''. . . she had looked cleanly, without pretense for the first time, upon the inexorable tides of Necessity, and . . . she was sorry for all who had lived, were living, or would live, fanning with their prayers the useless altar flames, suppliant with their hopes to an unwitting spirit, casting the tiny rockets of their beliefs against remote eternity, and hoping for grace, guidance, and delivery upon the spinning and forgotten cinder of this earth.'' In other places Wolfe introduces phrases reminiscent of Hardy that imply plan in terms of chaos: ''blundering destiny,'' ''aimless impulsion of accident,'' ''on the hairline of million-minded impulse, destiny bore down on his life again,'' and so on. Occasionally when he uses the word Chance, Wolfe might easily have substituted the word Fate—for example, in the child Eugene's earliest interpretation of life: ''The fusion of the two strong egotisms, Eliza's inbrooding and Gant's expanding outward, made of him a fanatical zealot in the religion of Chance. Beyond all misuse, waste, pain, tragedy, death, confusion, unswerving necessity was on the rails, not a sparrow fell through the air but that its repercussion acted on his life. . . .''

In combining, and at times confusing, the ideas of Chance and Necessity, Wolfe presents all the appearances of a formidable determinism operating on men's lives. In granting Chance a part to play, he emphasizes man's limited understanding of any purpose that Life Force may be working out.

In the concluding scene of *Look Homeward, Angel,* Wolfe reveals his view of life in the meeting between Eugene and the returned ghost of his brother, Ben. Eugene, seeking an answer to the meaning of life, is raised to a God-like stature, and he sees a vision of life in which only the Life Urge is eternal, striving to fulfill its unnamed purpose over the centuries as civilizations rise and fall:

> . . . he saw the fabulous lost cities, buried in the drifted silt of the earth—Thebes, the seven-gated, and all the temples of the Daulian and Phocian lands, and all Oenotria to the Tyrrhene gulf. Sunk in the burial-urn of earth he saw the vanished cultures: the strange sourceless glory of the Incas, the fragments of lost epics on a broken shard of Gnossic pottery. . . .
>
> He saw the billion living of the earth, the thousand billion dead: seas were withered, deserts flooded, mountains drowned; and gods and demons came out of the South, and ruled above the little rocket-flare of centuries, and sank—came to their Northern Lights of death, the muttering death-flared dusk of the completed gods.
>
> But amid the fumbling march of races to extinction, the giant rhythms of the earth remained. The seasons passed in their majestic processionals, the germinal Spring returned forever on the land,—new crops, new men, new harvests, and new gods.

Wolfe combines other ideas with this basic conception of life. Although his eclecticism does not make for perfect coherence, the sweep of his ideas is impressive and it adds weight to his narrative. Since the concept of a developing universe invites

contemplation of the problem of time, three of these ideas center on the time element that accompanies the evolutionary march of the Life Principle: the question of the inheritance from time past, the question of the present existence of past moments, and the question of fixity and change.

Wolfe feels that the individual is a representative of all his forebears and all the experience that has formed their lives: ''we are the sum of all the moments of our lives'' and ''each moment is the fruit of forty thousand years.'' One of the dilemmas of the boy Eugene is presented by the opposing traits he inherited from his parents. He finds in himself not only his father's desire to wander but his mother's affinity for home, not only the Gant liberality but the Pentland stinginess, not only the Gant realism but the Pentland superstition and mysticism. This conflict is developed more specifically in Wolfe's later books.

The idea that life is an accumulation of moments into one moment goes beyond the question of the inheritance of the past to put before us the question of the present existence of past moments. Eugene first senses the accumulation in his own life when he is twelve years old: ''I am, he thought, a part of all that I have touched and that has touched me, which having for me no existence save that which I gave to it, became other than itself by being mixed with what I then was, and is now still otherwise, having fused with what I now am, which is itself a cumulation of what I have been becoming.'' And throughout the book he yearns to recall a past moment or a forgotten face. In the concluding scene, he is allowed a vision of earlier stages of his own life, all simultaneously ''printed in the air.'' He sees a selection of the moments that made up his life, his comings and goings through the town square. The scene was probably suggested by Bergson's ''cinématographique'' analogy of time and life: although the analytical intellect perceives separate moments as snapshots, they are actually part of the ever-moving stuff in the cinema of life.

Eugene is also obsessed with the problem of fixity and change: ''He did not understand change, he did not understand growth. He stared at his framed baby picture in the parlor, and turned away sick with fear and the effort to touch, retain, grasp himself for only a moment.'' Wolfe occasionally introduces the grasping of a present moment while time and all activity remain at a standsill. These time-stops, similar to the transcendental moments of the Romantic poets, go beyond the universe of Life Force with its ceaseless change. Wolfe describes the experience when the boy Eugene, passing through Georgia on a train, glances out of the window to see a woman leaning in a cabin door:

> It was as if God had lifted his baton sharply above the endless orchestration of the seas, and the eternal movement had stopped, suspended in the timeless architecture of the absolute. Or like those motion pictures that describe the movements of a swimmer making a dive or a horse taking a hedge—movement is petrified suddenly in mid-air, the inexorable completion of an act is arrested. Then, completing its parabola, the suspended body plops down into the pool. Only, these images that burnt in him existed without beginning or ending, without the essential structure of time. Fixed in no-time, the slattern vanished, fixed without a moment of transition.

Here we do not have a moment treated as an accumulation of the past. This phenomenon is a ''terrible moment of immobility stamped with eternity in which, passing life at great speed, the observer and the observed seem frozen in time." These time-stops are glimpses into another world.

This brings us to the second framework of ideas that gives *Look Homeward, Angel* additional technical richness and further philosophic depth. In dealing with individual man's place in the universe of Necessity and Chance, Wolfe makes use of the Platonic myth of pre-existence. In the Platonic scheme as set forth in the *Phaedo, Meno, Timaeus*, and other dialogues, man's spirit leaves the real and unchanging world of immortality and enters a mortal body at the time of birth. During its temporary exile in the imperfect world of grief and change, man's spirit yearns to return to the divine world of reality. Wolfe had been familiar with the idea of prenatal life ever since he had translated Plato in his Greek classes at Chapel Hill. In addition, he had heard the doctrine in the classrooms of John Livingston Lowes at Harvard. (The idea made its deepest impression upon him, however, in Wordsworth's great ode, "Intimations of Immortality from Recollections of Early Childhood," for *Look Homeward, Angel* abounds with echoes from this poem.

Wolfe introduces the idea of pre-existence when Eugene is brought into the world in Chapter IV. The infant remembers the former life, but he gradually adjusts to the present life as growth and sensation drive out the memory of pre-existence. For Eugene's faint remembrance of the former life, Wolfe usually employs the symbol of undersea sound: "He had been sent from one mystery into another: Somewhere within or without his consciousness he heard a great bell ringing faintly, as if it sounded undersea, and as he listened, the ghost of memory walked through his mind, and for a moment he felt that he had almost recovered what he had lost." Other symbolic sounds are musical, varying from a full orchestration to the notes of far-off horns.

To sum up, Wolfe views man as a creature not only with a body molded by Life Force, activated by Life Force, and bearing the seeds of Life Force but also with a spirit "trailing clouds of glory . . . from God who is our home." Man's physical life is subject to the determinism of Life Force, which threads its way through a world of chance, but his spirit represents a free will operating within these limitations, an individuality which can respond intellectually and emotionally, make choices, and strive to achieve an understanding of life's complexities. This dualism of the physical and spiritual, of the ideas of creative evolution and of pre-existence, sets up an ideological conflict within the book. One group of ideas acknowledges a world of accumulation and change; the other assumes the existence of a timeless, ideal world. The human dilemma between what is and what ought to be, between two kinds of reality, is what Eugene Gant must face. Wolfe introduces this painfully complex problem in the proem which precedes Chapter I, and he develops it throughout his pages. (pp. 124-30)

Richard S. Kennedy, in his The Window of Memory: The Literary Career of Thomas Wolfe, *The University of North Carolina Press, 1962, 461 p.*

RICHARD S. KENNEDY (essay date 1964)

[*In the following excerpt from an essay first published in 1964, Kennedy examines the literary style of* Look Homeward, Angel.]

[The] American writer has a good knack for taking lowly materials and surrounding them with an aura of the great and important. Melville takes a rough crew and an odoriferous whaling vessel and by means of style and structure creates a prose epic. Tennessee Williams takes a nymphomaniac and a thug and with symbol and technical manipulation creates a profound and moving tragedy. Wolfe takes the story of a lower-middle-class boy who lives in a Southern town and creates a novel of development that transcends its restricted lineaments. By various devices, Wolfe enlarges his scene beyond the family circle and beyond town life to make us aware that Eugene is part of a very large and complex world and that he is one of the participants in the history of man. Style is one of the means by which he creates a sense of variety and abundance in the book, for Wolfe has a variety of styles that he employs.

One of the narrative styles may be described as rich, sometimes overflorid, arranged in long, loose sentences, frequently made up of elements piled in a series:

> Eugene was loose now in the limitless meadows of sensation: his sensory equipment was so complete that at the moment of perception of a single thing, the whole background of color, warmth, odor, sound, taste established itself, so that later, the breath of hot dandelion brought back the grass-warm banks of Spring, a day, a place, the rustling of young leaves [;] or a page of a book, the thin exotic smell of tangerine, the wintry bite of great apples; or, as with *Gulliver's Travels*, a bright windy day in March, the spurting moments of warmth, the drip and reek of the earth-thaw, the feel of the fire.

When the diction is concrete, as it is in this example, the style is very effective, particularly for communicating an atmosphere of plenitude—of a world that has so much in it that because of abundance itself it must be very good.

At times, Wolfe's prose takes on some of the qualities of the poetry of the Imagists. There are passages which are simple, metaphorical, and rhythmical in which an impression in the mind of Eugene is carried vividly to us—as, for example, when the boy thinks of his brother:

> My Brother Ben's face, thought Eugene, is like a piece of slightly yellow ivory; his high white head is knotted fiercely by his old man's scowl; his mouth is like a knife, his smile the flicker of light across a blade. His face is like a blade, and a knife, and a flicker of light: it is delicate and fierce, and scowls beautifully forever, and when he fastens his hard white fingers and his scowling eyes upon a thing he wants to fix, he sniffs with sharp and private concentration through his long pointed nose.

The effect of passages like this is to create the impression that life is full of vivid little moments of illumination which can be responded to and experienced intensely.

I have called passages like these poetic because they have rhythm and highly charged language, but they are just one of Wolfe's characteristic ways of saying things. There are times, however, when he is consciously being "poetic": that is when he writes short, set pieces (he later called them dithyrambs) that have an elevated manner and a formality of address and of arrangement in his sentences. We find these inserted in various places in the book. Here is one which Wolfe has placed at the end of a scene about Eugene's first love-affair:

> Come up into the hills, O my young love. Return! O lost, and by the wind grieved, ghost, come back again, as first I knew you in the timeless valley, where we shall feel ourselves anew, bedded on magic in the month of June. There was a place where all

the sun went glistering in your hair, and from the hill we could have put a finger on a star. Where is the day that melted into one rich noise? Where is the music of your flesh, the rhyme of your teeth, the dainty languor of your legs, your small firm arms, your slender fingers, to be bitten like an apple, and the little cherry-teats of your white breasts? And where are all the tiny wires of finespun maidenhair? Quick are the months of earth, and quick the teeth that fed upon this loveliness. You who were made for music, will hear music no more: in your dark house the winds are silent.

When a prose lyric like this elegy is very personal to Wolfe, it is an intrusion, but one would never want to banish it. It becomes a memorable passage. It remains a beautiful excrescence on the work. Its general function then is only its presence as part of the encyclopedic profusion of the book. More often, such passages are formal apostrophes, and the effect is rather of oratory than poetry. The reader has a feeling that a public spokesman is giving voice to a communal emotion or attitude. Again there is a sense of a larger world which surrounds the hero and with which he must come to terms.

There are other passages in which the style combines both the grand and the commonplace. The effect is to elevate or to ennoble the commonplace. When old Mr. Gant returns from a trip and looks over the home town, Wolfe begins the whole section with an epic style, even employing epithet: ''How looked the home-earth then to Gant the Far-Wanderer?'' The verbal contrasts that Wolfe plays with are many: he combines the rich and the spare; he exaggerates and then follows up with understatement; he joins the majestic and the vulgar, the formal and the colloquial. The effects are varied. Sometimes he is highly comical. At other times, he makes ordinary details seem to be recurrences in the endless cycles of time. For example, here is a passage which makes use of mythological allusion and high flown language about the coming of spring—when little boys play games in the street:

> Yes, and in the month when Proserpine comes back, and Ceres' dead heart rekindles, when all the woods are a tender smoky blur, and birds no bigger than a budding leaf dart through the singing trees, and when odorous tar comes spongy in the streets, and boys roll balls of it upon their tongues, and they are lumpy with tops and agated marbles; and there is blasting thunder in the night, and the soaking millionfooted rain. . . .

In *Look Homeward, Angel* style is used for depth as well as for breadth. Wolfe uses the stream-of-consciousness style quite frequently in the book—usually a series of phrases and images that are supposed to represent the thought-stream of the characters. Here is an example. But I will spell out the movement of thought before quoting it. Old Mr. Gant is riding through Altamont. He thinks of some of the chamber of commerce booster slogans about the town. His thought jumps to Los Angeles and its growth. He thinks then of Mr. Bowman who lives in California and who used to be in love with Mrs. Gant. This makes him think about himself and an experience with a woman in New Orleans. This then makes him remember a time long ago in New Orleans when he was robbed in a hotel room. He thinks of prostitutes in New Orleans. He then thinks of fictional heroines in stories about New Orleans. This makes him spin out a fantasy in which he plays a heroic part.

> America's Switzerland. The Beautiful Land of the Sky. Jesus God! Old Bowman said he'll be a rich man some day. Built up all the way to Pasadena.

Come on out. Too late now. Think he was in love with her. No matter. Too old. Wants her out there. No fool like——— White bellies of the fish. A spring somewhere to wash me through. Clean as a baby once more. New Orleans, the night Jim Corbett knocked out John L. Sullivan. The man who tried to rob me. My clothes and my watch. Five blocks down Canal Street in my nightgown. Two A.M. Threw them all in a heap—watch landed on top. Fight in my room. Town full of crooks and pickpockets for prizefight. Make good story. Policeman half hour later. They come out and beg you to come in. Frenchwomen. Creoles. Beautiful Creole heiress. Steamboat race. Captain, they are gaining. I will not be beaten. Out of wood. Use the bacon she said proudly. There was a terrific explosion. He got her as she sank the third time and swam to shore.

Stream-of-consciousness passages amplify the characterizations in a book. But the general impression of the excursions through the minds of the characters in *Look Homeward, Angel* is that the hidden life of the psyche, the buried life as Wolfe calls it, is teeming with activity and that human life, such as that developing in Eugene, is a mysterious but wonderful thing.

These are some examples of the narrative styles. The presence of many different dialogue styles, of course, increases the stylistic variety, particularly because most of the characters are quite distinctive in the way they speak: W. O. Gant is full of exaggeration and rhetorical flourish; Mrs. Gant carries on in the rambling, interminable manner of free association; Ben is sharp and laconic; Luke stutters. In addition there are the currents and eddies of talk in the town—the words of clerks, servants, loafers, politicians, gatherers at the lunch counters. Much of this town talk, seemingly insignificant, is like that in Wilder's *Our Town*: it reflects the rhythms of life, comings and goings, deaths and entrances. Moreover, it is good talk, with a marked colloquial flavor. Here, for example, is Gant on the streetcar:

> ''Jim Bowles died while you were gone, I reckon,'' said the motorman.
>
> ''What!'' howled Gant. ''Merciful God!'' he clucked mournfully downward. ''What did he die of?'' he asked.
>
> ''Pneumonia,'' said the motorman. ''He was dead four days after he was took down.''
>
> ''Why, he was a big healthy man in the prime of life,'' said Gant. ''I was talking to him the day before I went away,'' he lied convincing himself permanently that this was true. ''He looked as if he had never known a day's sickness in his life.''
>
> ''He went home one Friday night with a chill,'' said the motorman, ''and the next Tuesday he was gone.''

Beyond this, *Look Homeward, Angel* has a number of other evidences of Wolfe's linguistic interest such as parodies of pulp fiction stories with Eugene as the hero—like the one about Bruce-Eugene Glendenning, international vagabond, who fights off the dangerous natives, and keeps back two cartridges for himself and the beautiful Veronica Mullins; or Eugene's fantasies when he comes from the motion picture theater—Eugene Gant, the Dixie Ghost, who shoots it out with Faro Jim in the Triple Y Saloon. In this book, Wolfe plays with language in dozens of ways.

What I have been trying to establish is that by means of style Wolfe had done two important things. First, he has provided a swirl of experience around his hero and made the whole experience of life and of growing up seem exciting and valuable. Second, the linguistic variety has contributed to the complexity of the little universe in which Wolfe has placed Eugene Gant and which the boy is trying to understand. In his search for understanding, Eugene has been impelled to look to the city and its crowded streets and to the multiplicity of social experience that travel and wandering seem to offer. But at the end of the book, the ghost of his brother Ben, returned from the dead, tells Eugene that he is wrong. Eugene should look inside himself for the way to understanding. "*You* are your world," says Ben. The quality and the amplitude of that world has been partly conveyed to us by means of style. (pp. 85-90)

> *Richard S. Kennedy, "Wolfe's 'Look Homeward, Angel' as a Novel of Development," in* The Merrill Studies in "Look Homeward, Angel," *edited by Paschal Reeves, Charles E. Merrill Publishing Company, 1970, pp. 82-90.*

THOMAS C. MOSER (essay date 1965)

[*Moser is an American educator and critic. In the following excerpt, he discusses Wolfe's romantic portrayal of Eugene and his vivid characterizations of the other Gants in* Look Homeward, Angel.]

Readers over thirty find Thomas Wolfe difficult to appreciate—not to understand but to appreciate. He often writes very badly, even in *Look Homeward, Angel,* the most finished of his novels. As Faulkner said, Wolfe throws away style and coherence. One recalls that embarrassing passage early in the novel where the infant hero, Eugene Gant, in his crib, thinks of

> the discomfort, weakness, dumbness, the infinite misunderstanding he would have to endure. . . . He grew sick as he thought of the weary distance before him, the lack of co-ordination of the centres of control, the undisciplined and rowdy bladder, the helpless exhibition he was forced to give in the company of his sniggering, pawing brothers and sisters, dried, cleaned, revolved before them. . . .

He understood that "no one ever comes really to know anyone," that "caught in that insoluble prison of being, we escape it never. . . . Never, never, never, never, never." As he looked at the "huge leering heads that bent hideously into his crib, . . . his brain went black with terror." This passage has been called the "silliest" in serious fiction, not merely because of the gross violation of probability, but because of the sentimentality, the unmotivated hysteria, and, simply, the ineptitude: inserting the five famous "nevers" from *King Lear,* using such a melodramatic cliché as "his brain went black with terror."

Although *Look Homeward, Angel* is his most unified novel, much of the unity is superficial, imposed gratuitously by the subject matter. A middle-class boy, growing up in a small American city, follows an almost predictable series of experiences. Despite Wolfe's frequent assertions of connections, one feels very little sense of growth in the main character, of relations between characters, or of the impact of event upon character. Although the dramatized incidents are often utterly persuasive, even very moving, their effects upon the characters are not realized. Wolfe is a perfect example of Hemingway's famous statement: "You'll lose it if you talk about it." When Eugene argues with his mother, when he loses his girl friend, when his roommate dies—in each case Wolfe talks about the painful effects, and each time he loses much of the feeling created by the dramatized scene. The dialogue and the gestures

are just right; the hero's thoughts and the author's comments are often wrong.

Failing so radically in the two crucial artistic requirements of style and coherence, surely Wolfe deserves our indifference. But he does not always fail in these matters, and he succeeds brilliantly in other ways. If we let his weaknesses obscure his strengths, the fault may lie, after all, with ourselves. According to the publisher,

> Each new generation as it comes along rediscovers and claims this book for its own. For Wolfe wrote about youth, and he spoke to youth more convincingly than any American writer has ever done.

To appreciate Wolfe older readers must be willing to recall their own youth sympathetically and to look again at the world with youthful eyes—eyes that, despite the distortions of sentimentality, may see in some ways more clearly than those of age.

Why do academic critics disapprove of Wolfe? Partly, at least, because Wolfe did not write the kind of book an American novelist of the 1920's *ought* to have written. Somehow, Wolfe ought to have written in the tradition of Flaubert and James and Conrad, the tradition of exquisite craftsmanship. Hemingway and Fitzgerald are the obvious exemplars. Or, Wolfe should have been an experimenter in technique, like Joyce and Faulkner. Although Wolfe deeply admired Conrad and Joyce, he wrote very old-fashioned novels, a mélange of the picaresque—Fielding, Dickens, Twain—and of the spiritual autobiography—the English romantics, Melville, Whitman.

But if Wolfe's manner is old-fashioned, his matter belongs to our century. When the wisest man in Conrad's *Lord Jim* is asked to diagnose the hero's ailment, he replies: "I understand very well. He is romantic." Conrad's subject, the youthful, romantic egoist, is Wolfe's subject. The hero of *Look Homeward, Angel* has affinities, too, with Fitzgerald's Jay Gatsby and with Faulkner's Quentin Compson in *The Sound and the Fury*. But there is an important difference. These other novelists keep their romantic heroes in check: Conrad and Fitzgerald through a subordinate, ironic narrator; Faulkner through the perspectives of other characters, other points of view. But Thomas Wolfe—Eugene Gant—simply expresses, expresses, expresses his romantic emotions.

> I intend to wreak out my soul on paper and express it all. This is what my life means to me: I am at the mercy of this thing and I will do it or die.

Look Homeward, Angel begins with a kind of prose poem:

> . . . a stone, a leaf, an unfound door; of a stone, a leaf, a door. . . . we seek the great forgotten language, the lost lane-end into heaven, a stone, a leaf, an unfound door. Where? When?

Like many romantic tales, then, this is the story of a quest, a quest that can never be successfully completed. Just as Gatsby forever pursues the green light, so Eugene Gant's quest finds its symbol in the leaf, stone, and door. Eugene is full of "desire and longing" for some vague perfection never precisely located. As a boy growing up in an isolated provincial town, Eugene often believes his "happy land" lies outside the cup of the mountains, perhaps in the deep South, burning "like Dark Helen in [his] blood," or perhaps in some "golden city." Since the railroad train is his means of escape, train whistles have a special poignancy for him. More frequently, Eugene locates his happy land in the world of imagination, dreams, and artistic creation. He seems to place this in a wonderful cave, entered through an underground passage:

> He groped for the doorless land of faery, that illimitable haunted country that opened somewhere below a leaf or a stone.

Again, Eugene's quest leads toward communication with another person, with his dearest brother, Ben, or with his beloved Laura James. Here, the door leads not to an underground faeryland but rather through the barrier separating personalities. Often, borrowing Wordsworth's notion of a prenatal paradise, Wolfe locates his goal in the past, either in some heaven where he lived before birth or in the actual past of his childhood. Finally, at the very end of the novel, Eugene says that he has found his happy land:

> . . . in the city of myself, upon the continent of my soul I shall find the forgotten language, the lost world, a door where I may enter.

Self-knowledge, then, appears to be the key to the door. Or rather, the door seems to open upon the individual's inner, buried life.

Although Wolfe asserts that the quest has ended, and although at times Eugene glimpses his goal, the prevailing mood of the hero is frustration. Note that the initial prose poem is less about the quest than about loneliness and loss.

> Which of us has known his brother? Which of us has looked into his father's heart? Which of us has not remained forever prison-pent? Which of us is not forever a stranger and alone? . . . O lost, and by the wind grieved, ghost, come back again.

As a matter of fact, Wolfe's first title for the novel was "O, Lost," and the second, "Alone, Alone." The title he finally chose comes from John Milton's elegy, "Lycidas," in which the poet asks the angel, St. Michael, to look back toward England and melt with pity at the spectacle of a promising young man's death by drowning. While Fitzgerald portrays Gatsby as a young man with an "extraordinary gift for hope," Eugene and Wolfe recognize that utter loneliness is man's lot and that ceaseless change, immutable Time, and Death inevitably frustrate longings for the happy land.

The circumstances of Wolfe's own life make this obsession with change and loss quite comprehensible. One of his earliest memories was the death of his brother Grover, when Wolfe was only four. At six came the wrench of having to leave the warm center of his life, his father's house, for the impersonal, transient chaos of his mother's boardinghouse. Much later he wrote:

> I was without a home—a vagabond since I was seven—with two roofs and no home. . . . I think I learned about being alone when I was a child . . . and I think that I have known about it ever since.

It is hardly surprising that he describes Eugene as "a stranger in a noisy inn." Eugene sees little evidence that anyone else transcends loneliness. He and his brothers and sisters feel only embarrassment when they watch their father's clumsy attempts to embrace their mother: "Aw, Papa, don't." Wolfe used to say that the most tragic event of his life was the death, when he was eighteen, of his favorite brother, Ben. But perhaps even more important was the constant awesome sense of his father's ultimate end, the awareness that the most vital, heroic figure in his life was doomed.

Furthermore, the town in which Wolfe grew up was also undergoing convulsive change. Asheville, North Carolina (Altamont in the novel), is not quite a typical Southern town. Although it underwent the pain of the post-Civil War era, its location high in the Appalachian Mountains gives it a climate that attracted people from the outside world. By the turn of the century, Asheville had become an important health resort and a popular vacation spot. Northern millionaires settled in Asheville, real estate values soared, and the population doubled. Wolfe grew up in an environment that displayed simultaneously Southern defeat and Northern "progress," Southern poverty and Northern materialism. Every year he saw another piece of his cherished past obliterated, until finally his father's tombstone shop gave way to a skyscraper.

Although the themes of loneliness and loss are enormously important to Wolfe, their mere expression does not contribute great significance to the novel. Aching so to be happy and knowing that he cannot, Eugene responds in an adolescent way: he feels sorry for himself. Moreover, the older he becomes the more naked is the self-pity and the less interesting the central character. When Wolfe writes badly, the subject is almost always Eugene. (pp. 207-12)

Wolfe's greatest triumph in **Look Homeward, Angel** is, of course, the re-creation of his own family, the Gants. Although Eugene at some point hates every member of the family, Wolfe himself loves these creations: "to me . . . they were the greatest people I had ever known. . . . If I could get my magnificent people on paper as they were. . . ." Magnificent they are, and emphatically a *family*: "They had twisted the design of all orderly life, because there was in them a mad, original, disturbing quality." Above all, there is their fantastic energy: they appear to live without need of sleep; they are all compulsive talkers, whether in the slow, deliberate utterances of Eliza, or the idiotic outbursts of Luke, the engineering student: "He was not an electrical engineer—he was electrical energy." In Helen the "hysteria of constant excitement" lurks. Like Eugene, they are all embarked on a quest though, except perhaps for old Gant, none of them seems quite aware of the fact. Helen instinctively gropes "toward a center of life and purpose to which she [can] fasten her energy." Ben, so ironic, disdainful, and independent, tries to get at life by reading the success sermons of millionaires in the *Post*.

Despite their consistent family resemblances, the Gants are all brilliantly defined, their differences made unmistakably sharp. The mother and father live vibrantly in their own right; at the same time, they unobtrusively symbolize the two central, conflicting forces in the novel: the human quest and its inevitable frustration. Wolfe draws W. O. Gant in wonderful broad strokes: the long frame, the large hands, the great blade of a nose, the cold, uneasy eyes, the faint, sly grin at the corners of the thin mouth. Gant, a Northerner in the South, married to a woman he does not understand, longing to carve an angel's head, but unable to, desiring to be a Far Wanderer but tied to his family and home. Gant is "a stranger in a strange land." Sporadically drunk and disorderly, he is nevertheless the artist striving to impose order on a changing world. Gant brings a kind of ritual to their wild family life. Combining Shakespearean rhetoric with Southern political oratory, he delivers to wife and children carefully rehearsed speeches, full of invective, at appointed hours of the day. He yells:

> We will freeze in this hellish, damnable, cruel and God-forsaken climate. Does Brother Will care? Does Brother Jim care? Did the Old Hog, your miserable

old father, care? Merciful God! I have fallen into the
hands of fiends incarnate, more savage, more cruel,
more abominable than the beasts of the field. Hell-
hounds that they are, they will sit by and gloat at my
agony until I am done to death.

Although the hand of death is ever upon him, he remains a
fount of energy: he is the great provider, buying whole hogs
from the butcher, and a marvelous gardener: "The earth was
spermy for him like a big woman." Gant builds roaring fires;
his neighbors can tell he is at home by the thick column of
smoke from the chimney. He is the source of sexual energy:
twice-married father of eight, old rooster frequenting Elizabeth's brothel, pursuer of colored cooks and middle-aged widows, he is held in high esteem even by the Temperance Ladies
of the First Baptist Church. To his children he is simply man
as hero:

> swinging violently back and forth in a stout rocker,
> [he spits] clean and powerful spurts of tobacco-juice
> over his son's head into the hissing fire.

Eliza is her husband's antithesis. He disdains ownership, spends
lavishly, and talks rapidly. She, on the other hand, saves bits
of string; has a "powerful germinal instinct for property . . .
[; and likes] "to take her time" [and come] "to the point after
interminable divagations down all the lane-ends of memory
and overtone, feasting upon the golden pageant of all she had
ever said, done, felt, thought, seen or replied, with egocentric
delight." Her memory moves over the ocean bed of events
like a great octopus. To Gant, and at times to all the rest of
the family, she seems to symbolize the immutable Time and
inert matter that will inevitably frustrate man's romantic quest.
Yet she, too, is emphatically human as she stands perpetually
over the spitting grease, her nose "stove-red," her hands chapped
with hard work and covered with glycerine, her body "clothed
in a tattered old sweater and indefinable under-lappings."

Wolfe particularly establishes her humanity in his account of
the death of Ben, surely the best prose that he ever wrote. Here
is language so accurate that it makes the reader see poor Ben
in his last moments, language full of feeling yet seldom sentimental:

> the sallow yellow tint of his face had turned grey:
> out of this granite tint of death, lit by two red flags
> of fever, the stiff black furze of a three-day beard
> was growing . . . it recalled the corrupt vitality of
> hair, which can grow from a rotting corpse.

Wolfe brings the whole family together for the death: Helen
contradicting herself, vibrating between rage at Eliza's ineptitude in the emergency and pity because Ben has rejected his
mother; senile Gant, weeping in his rocker at the foot of Ben's
bed, and employing his old rhetoric not to eulogize his son but
to pity himself:

> O Jesus! I can't bear it! . . . How are we ever going
> to face this fearful and croo-el winter? It'll cost a
> thousand dollars before we're through burying him. . . .

Helen actually shaking him in fury right in the death chamber.

> And Eliza, now that [Ben] could deny her no longer . . .
> sitting near his head beside him, clutching his cold
> hand between her rough worn palms.

Even when Ben is apparently rigid in death, he asserts his
vitality:

> suddenly, marvelously, as if his resurrection and re-
> birth had come upon him, Ben drew upon the air in
> a long and powerful respiration; his grey eyes opened.

Filled with a terrible vision of all life in the one
moment, he seemed to rise forward bodilessly from
his pillows without support—a flame, a light, a glory—
joined at length in death to the dark spirit who had
brooded upon each footstep of his lonely adventure
on earth.

But this is not all. Daringly, Wolfe follows the tragic account
of Ben's death with a chapter full of eating and of comedy
which ends in the funeral parlor of "Horse" Hines, beside
Ben's embalmed corpse. Overcome with pride, Hines explains
his artistry, how he has tried to do Ben justice. When Luke
finds Ben a trifle pale, Hines whips out a rouge-stick and
sketches a "ghastly rose-hued mockery of life and health"
upon the dead grey cheeks. "Did you ever see anything more
natural in your life?" Eugene notes "with a sort of tenderness . . . the earnestness and pride in the long horse-face." But
the "dogs of laughter" tug at Eugene's throat, he slides gently
off his chair, slowly unbuttoning his vest, languidly loosening
his tie. He gurgles helplessly, and Luke looks on all a-grin.
That Wolfe should introduce a comic note here is perfectly
appropriate. It has been said that the essence of comedy is
"human life-feeling." Wolfe, for all his loneliness, self-pity,
and despair, affirmed life. He managed to pack a very great
deal of this "human life-feeling" into *Look Homeward, Angel*.
For this reason and despite countless obvious faults, the novel
endures, and Wolfe appears to have conquered his old enemy
Time, after all. (pp. 214-18)

> *Thomas C. Moser, "Thomas Wolfe: 'Look Home-
> ward, Angel',"* in The American Novel: From James
> Fenimore Cooper to William Faulkner, *edited by
> Wallace Stegner, Basic Books, Inc., Publishers, 1965,
> pp. 206-18.*

JOHN S. HILL (essay date 1965)

[*Hill is an American educator, short story writer, and critic. In
the following essay, first published in 1965, he disputes critical
interpretations that are based on the title of* Look Homeward,
Angel.]

It is readily agreed that Chapter 40 of Thomas Wolfe's *Look
Homeward, Angel* is both the goal of the novel and the summation of its author's philosophy. Less agreed upon is the
interpretation of this final chapter. The disagreement rises from
a faulty explanation of the roles of Eugene and Ben Gant,
which, in turn, rests on the misinterpretation of the title. The
premise underlying the two erroneous views is, simply: that
because Wolfe took this title from Milton's "Lycidas" he also
took the explanation. In reality, although Milton can claim the
title, it is Wordsworth and Coleridge who claim the content
and who influence the final meaning.

The importance of "Lycidas" is further reduced by the history
of the novel's title. When Wolfe began writing it in July, 1926,
he considered calling the novel *The Building of a Wall*. In
November, 1926, he made a list of "'Possible titles': *The
Building of a Wall; Young Poseidon, Poseidon's Harbor,* or
Theseus . . . and *The Hills Beyond Pentland. . . .* By June,
1927, he was considering *Alone, Alone. . . .*" By September,
1927, he settled upon *O, Lost!* It was under this title that the
novel was accepted on January 7, 1929, by Scribner's. It was
several months later, in the spring of 1929, that Wolfe renamed
the novel *Look Homeward, Angel*.

Generally it is valid to assume that because a novelist uses a
quotation for his title it is possible to interpret much of the

novel in light of the source for the title, as is the case with John Steinbeck's *The Grapes of Wrath* or Ernest Hemingway's *For Whom the Bell Tolls,* to cite only two examples. But with **Look Homeward, Angel** the case is different. And it is precisely this difference which has caused misreading of the final, climactic chapter.

While a graduate student at Harvard, Wolfe studied "The Poets of the Romantic Period" under John Livingston Lowes; Lowes later "praised his thesis on 'The Supernatural in the Poetry and Philosophy of Coleridge.'" Among what Wolfe called "much of the best that has ever been written," he placed "Coleridge (including the essays)." Further, "*The Ancient Mariner* was to become his favorite poem."

Wolfe's motto for the novel, "a stone, leaf, a door," leads one to Wordsworth's line, "Which, from a tree, a stone, a withered leaf," in *The Prelude* (III, 163). Moreover, the theme of the novel calls to mind Wordsworth's "Ode: Intimations of Immortality from Recollections of Early Childhood" (especially lines 64-65: "But trailing clouds of glory do we come / From God, who is our home"") and "My Heart Leaps Up When I Behold" (particularly line seven: "The Child is father of the Man"). Further, "Wolfe's fiction constitutes a search for lost time . . ." and in this respect "Wolfe is close to Wordsworth."

It seems rather obvious that the influence of Wordsworth and Coleridge takes precedence over that of Milton, but this fact is usually mislaid and the final chapter is all too often explained in the light of "Lycidas."

In Chapter 40 of **Look Homeward, Angel,** Eugene Gant encounters the ghost of Ben, his recently deceased older brother, at 3:15 a.m. on the porch of their father's stonecutter's shop, which faces the town square. Throughout the novel, Ben and Eugene are much alike: each represents the individual frustrated in his desire to join his personality to those of all others about him, in his desire to recapture the once better time (so Wolfe believed) from which each one comes, and in his desire to break down the door that prevents man from joining the human race (defined as a single communicating unit) and learning about his own place in the sun.

If one reads this final chapter with "Lycidas" in mind, he will equate Wolfe's refrain, "O Lost, and by the wind grieved, ghost, come back again," with Ben only. From this point it is but a step to an interpretation such as this:

> By analogy Ben's role in **Look Homeward, Angel** would seem to be the angel's, while Eugene is Lycidas; but throughout the novel Ben is also a ghost in that, like every person, he cannot be known even to his brother. In the last chapter he is restored to a "life" he did not have while alive; he is no longer a ghost because no longer a stranger. At the same time he is also an angel in the sense that he can now direct Eugene home. "*You* are your world," says Ben to Eugene, directing him to the bright world of fused experience. Ben is not explicitly named "angel," but the identification is further implied by the stone angels' coming to life when Ben returns.

As one of Wolfe's editors has stated, "he wrote with singleness of purpose, trying to catch in words and fix upon the printed page something deep and dark . . . in human nature." This "something deep" is man's memory (which grows ever dimmer as he ages) of the better land from which he comes; the "something dark" is the steadily growing realization that he cannot return to that land, that home. As such, the now lost land of pre-existence becomes rather like a ghost, and it is for this "lost, and by the wind grieved, ghost" that Eugene yearns. Thus, as will be shown, Eugene and the ghost are synonymous.

Such a reading as this eliminates Ben as *the* ghost; however, he may (for lack of a better term) be called *a* ghost, for such is the accepted term for an apparition. As a ghost, he is like the ghost of Hamlet's father: he imparts information; he does not become the principal character.

There is more than this to Ben's role, however. Throughout the novel, Ben is as alone as Eugene. When he dies, he is still alone. When he returns, it is not merely as an informative ghost but as a part of Eugene himself, as a symbol of what Eugene has discovered through Ben's death.

The apparition of Ben itself limits its role. When Eugene asks "which of us is the ghost" the apparition does not answer. But only a moment later it says, "Fool . . . I tell you I am not a ghost." It is the apparition which asks "what do you want to remember?" and forces Eugene to acknowledge that "'There is something I have lost and have forgotten.' . . . A Stone, a leaf, an unfound door." In an episode "unwoven from lost time," Eugene sees that

> Ben, in a thousand moments, walked the Square: Ben of the lost years, the forgotten days, the unremembered hours . . . .
>
> And as Eugene watched . . . he saw himself—his son, his boy, his lost and virgin flesh—come over past the fountain. . . . And as he passed the porch where he sat watching, he saw the lost child-face. . . . Eugene leaped to the railing.
>
> "You! You! My Son! My child! Come back! Come back!"

The child is father of the man, yes, but the memory of the child steadily grows fainter until memory is gone. "Home" to Eugene Gant is both the land of pre-existence and his own childhood—that is, childhood as a symbol of hope, of dreams. Heretofore he has always looked to this home. Now, however, his "meeting with knowledge" (the ghost of Ben) gives him a new home to look toward: himself.

The fact that the influence upon Wolfe was that of Wordsworth and Coleridge rather than of Milton; the fact that the title was selected after, not before, the novel was written; the fact that the apparition of Ben is a dramatic picturing of Eugene's realization of certain knowledge; and the fact that the ghost of Ben eliminates itself as a ghost—all these facts show that it is Eugene, not Ben, who is the subject of the refrain, "O Lost, and by the wind grieved, ghost, come back again." Eugene *is* the ghost insofar as the ghost is a projection of himself—that is, of his past. The lost ghost is the wispy memory of a once better existence, of a far better place now grown so dim in memory that it may as well be grieved for only by the wind. Thus the grieved-for past (the ghost) and Eugene (whose past it is) are synonymous.

Because the refrain applies so thoroughly to Eugene, it may be assumed that the "Angel" of the title does too. This assumption is correct. To revert to Wordsworth for a moment: the already quoted line, "But trailing clouds of glory do we come / From God who is our home," indicates what Wolfe first means by "home" and "look homeward." Further, is not an angel "From God"? Is not an angel one who trails "clouds of glory"? And if Eugene is the one who seeks this pre-existence, is he not clearly the angel? Additional proof is that Eugene is the innocent who receives knowledge; he is the primary seeker in the novel; he is the one who looks homeward, both to the home that is pre-existence and, later, to home that is in himself. Chapter 40 details the acquisition of knowledge by Eugene—it is not Ben who looks homeward, for Ben is already there. It is Eugene Gant who is told to "Look homeward, angel" and who discovers where that home lies. After all, it is not Ben who "turns his eyes upon the distant soaring ranges."

In Chapter 35, just after Ben dies, Wolfe writes that Ben "lived here a stranger, trying to recapture the music of the lost world, trying to recall the great forgotten language, the lost faces, the stone, the leaf, the door." Far more important, Wolfe also states: "We can believe in the nothingness of life, we can believe in the nothingness of death and of life after death—but who can believe in the nothingness of Ben?"

Obviously, not Eugene. Nor does he believe in the nothingness of himself. This fact is revealed in Chapter 40. The apparition tells Eugene, "*You* are your world" and "*this* is life." At this point, Eugene "stood upon the ramparts of his soul, before the lost land of himself" and he realizes that "no leaf hangs for me in the forest; I shall lift no stone upon the hills; I shall find no door in any city. But in the city of myself, upon the continent of my soul, I shall find the forgotten language, the lost world, a door where I may enter, and music strange as any ever sounded." The novel's final paragraph reinforces the fact that Eugene has new hope, that he has found that the home he must look toward is, indeed, himself: "Yet, as he stood for the last time by the angels of his father's porch, it seemed as if the Square already were far and lost; or, I should say, he was like a man who stands upon a hill above the town he has left, yet does not say 'The town is near', but turns his eyes upon the distant soaring ranges."

Throughout the first thirty-nine chapters of *Look Homeward, Angel,* Eugene Gant longs for the home from which he came. In Chapter 40 he discovers that he holds the answers to his questions within himself. He learns this through the apparition of Ben, which is a dramatic projection of his own thoughts and his conclusions about them. Eugene accepts this knowledge, as all men must, and faces the future with confidence. Eugene, who did not believe in the nothingness of Ben, certainly does not, in the final summary, believe in the nothingness of Eugene Gant, either. (pp. 134-39)

John S. Hill, "Eugene Gant and the Ghost of Ben," in The Merrill Studies in "Look Homeward, Angel," *edited by Paschal Reeves, Charles E. Merrill Publishing Company, 1970, pp. 134-39.*

MORRIS BEJA (essay date 1971)

[*Beja is an American educator, short story writer, and critic specializing in twentieth-century literature. In the following excerpt from his* Epiphany in the Modern Novel, *he discusses Wolfe's use of epiphanies, which he defines as "sudden illuminations produced by apparently trivial, even seemingly arbitrary, causes," as an important narrative device in* Look Homeward, Angel.]

It would be pointless for me to trace the pattern of epiphanies in *Look Homeward, Angel,* or in any of Wolfe's novels . . . , for the simple reason that there really is no pattern. Yet a chronological examination of his work does have value in suggesting how thoroughly moments of passionate illumination pervade it, how related they are to his basic notions of art and the artist, and especially in showing how his views toward the use of the epiphanies of his own past developed and changed.

Early in *Look Homeward, Angel*—as in *A Portrait of the Artist,* with its opening scene of Stephen creating a rhyme out of the demand that he "apologise"—we are given an epiphany that strongly hints at the hero's vocation as an artist. The incident occurs at school, where all the children have been able to learn how to write except Eugene, who draws only jagged lines and is unable even to see any difference. One day his friend Max looks at Eugene's sheet and, commenting that "That ain't writin'," scrawls a correct copy of the exercise on the paper; somehow this act suddenly causes Eugene to write out the words too—"in letters fairer and finer than his friend's"—and to go on hurriedly to copy the subsequent pages, as the two boys react "with that clear wonder by which children accept miracles."

> "That's writin' now," said Max. But they kept the mystery caged between them.
>
> Eugene thought of this event later; always he could feel the opening gates in him, the plunge of the tide, the escape; but it happened like this one day at once. Still midget-near the live pelt of the earth, he saw many things that he kept in fearful secret, knowing that revelation would be punished with ridicule.

Though this episode, like the one in the *Portrait,* may be regarded as revelatory primarily for the author and the reader,

Dust jacket of the first printing of Look Homeward, Angel, *by Thomas Wolfe. Copyright 1929 Charles Scribner's Sons. Copyright renewed © 1957 Edward C. Ashwell, Administrator, C.T.A. and/or Fred W. Wolfe. Reprinted with the permission of Charles Scribner's Sons, an imprint of Macmillan Publishing Company.*

it does provide a mysterious new awareness for the two boys as well; and it is immediately followed by another revelation which they—"midget-near the live pelt of the earth," or trailing clouds of glory as it were—cannot communicate and so keep secret: but this time it is a vision of the hidden presence of evil in the world. Watching some workers repair a broken water main in one of the town streets, Eugene and Max are standing next to a fissure in the earth, a window that opens "on some dark subterranean passage," when they suddenly see gliding past them "an enormous serpent" which vanishes into the earth behind the working men, seen only by the terrified children and never revealed by them.

Such scenes appear throughout the novel, and many of them seem based on Wolfe's own memories; but art reflects the mind and world of its creator in more ways than one, so in *Look Homeward, Angel* a large number of the purely imaginary incidents, too, involve the recollection or recapture of lost time by various characters themselves. Oliver Gant goes though such a moment when, to his dismay, the local madam buys his statue of an angel for a prostitute's grave. The importance to Gant of this angel has been prepared for by the first epiphany in the novel—one that also dealt with the discovery of artistic longings. Gant, fifteen years old, was walking along a street in Philadelphia when he saw a statue of an angel outside a stone cutter's shop, and it instilled a lifelong desire "to wreak something dark and unspeakable in him into cold stone," to "carve an angel's head," to "seek the great forgotten language, the lost lane-end into heaven." The angel purchased by the madam has been imported from Italy, but it is as close as Gant has ever come to carving his own angel and to finding the forgotten language. As he and the madam conclude their transaction, their thoughts turning to the years that have gone by since their youth, they look out upon the town square, where everything seems suddenly "frozen in a picture":

> And in that second the slow pulse of the fountain was suspended, life was held, like an arrested gesture, in photographic abeyance, and Gant felt himself alone move deathward in a world of seemings as, in 1910, a man might find himself again in a picture taken on the grounds of the Chicago Fair, when he was thirty and his mustache black, and, noting the bustled ladies and the derbied men fixed in the second's pullulation, remember the dead instant, seek beyond the borders for what was there. . . .

"Where now?" Wolfe asks, "Where after? Where then?"

At the end of the novel, Gant's son Eugene sees in the same square a vision of his whole past life; in general radiance and significance, that final vision and the others I have cited are exceptions to most of the epiphanies in the book, which are plentiful and often individually very effective, but which too frequently have no real function in relation to the rest of the novel. They reveal a good deal about specific people, but little in regard to comprehensive themes, and sometimes they even seem like merely irrelevant intrusions. Occasionally, however, a moment of revelation will not only give us insight into Wolfe's characters, but also serve broader purposes of form by bringing together various themes or threads in the story—as with Eugene's climatic experience at the very end, the evening before he is to leave Altamont.

The vision of Ben concludes the novel with a forecast of the future, but it serves primarily as a summary of the past. The nature of that summary seems meant to illustrate Wolfe's assertion in his note to the reader that "we are the sum of all

the moments of our lives"; gazing upon the town square, Eugene feels that he sees all his younger selves evoked before him:

> And for a moment all the silver space was printed with the thousand forms of himself and Ben. There, by the corner in from Academy Street, Eugene watched his own approach; there, by the City Hall, he strode with lifted knees; there, by the curb upon the step, he stood, peopling the night with the great lost legion of himself—the thousand forms that came, that passed, that wove and shifted in unending change, and that remained unchanging Him.
>
> And through the Square, unwoven from lost time, the fierce bright horde of Ben spun in and out its deathless loom. Ben, in a thousand moments, walked the Square: Ben of the lost years, the forgotten days, the unremembered hours. . . .
>
> And now the Square was thronging with their lost bright shapes, and all the minutes of lost time collected and stood still. Then, shot from them with projectile speed, the Square shrank down the rails of destiny, and was vanished with all things done, with all forgotten shapes of himself and Ben.

When the images of the past have disappeared, Eugene experiences another "moment of terrible vision," this time of "his foiled quest of himself," of the same hunger that has "darkened his father's eyes to impalpable desire for wrought stone and the head of an angel"; we are thus brought back to the first epiphany in the novel. Ben reveals in an "apexical summation" that what Eugene seeks must be found within himself ("*You* are your world"), and that the object of his quest—"the forgotten language, the lost world"—involves the past as much as the future. But it is forward that Eugene tries to look as he expresses in his final words his confidence that he will someday find what he desires, just as at the end of *The Story of a Novel* Wolfe himself is confident that we shall all "find the tongue, the language, and the conscience that as men and artists we have got to have." The last chapter of the novel has generally suggested the visions in Joyce's Nighttown episode in *Ulysses*; but it is Stephen's affirmation on the last page of the *Portrait*—that, as artificer, he will forge the uncreated conscience of his race—that is called to mind by the last page of *Look Homeward, Angel,* with the young artist's determination to attain what his father has sought but never found in the carved angel: "the forgotten language, the lost world." (pp. 159-62)

> *Morris Beja, "Thomas Wolfe: The Escapes of Time and Memory," in his* Epiphany in the Modern Novel, *University of Washington Press, 1971, pp. 148-81.*

JOHN HAGAN (essay date 1981)

[*In the following excerpt, Hagan traces a unifying thematic and symbolic structure throughout the narrative of* Look Homeward, Angel.]

One of the main reasons for [the] comparative neglect [of *Look Homeward, Angel*], I believe, is the still prevailing notion that Wolfe's first novel, though undeniably powerful in some respects, is mere "formless autobiography," the product of a *naïf* who had no "ideas" and only a rudimentary technique. To be sure, Wolfe was hardly a flawless writer, and the pattern of his book is not of the tightest; its structure could never be called rigorously Jamesian. But organic unity, formal cohesion, and thematic control of a larger and looser kind—of a sort to be found, for instance, in *Moby-Dick, Bleak House,* and *War and Peace*—are demonstrably present. Accordingly, . . . I should like to show how the novel's various themes, images, and symbols are integrated in a rich, complex, many-layered whole, and reach their appropriate culmination in the brilliant and extremely moving last chapter.

Drawing upon late nineteenth- and early twentieth-century concepts earlier embodied in fiction by writers like Zola, Hardy, and Dreiser, the narrator of **Look Homeward, Angel** boldly sketches in the famous opening three paragraphs an uncompromisingly deterministic picture of the human condition which becomes a leitmotif throughout. Wolfe's protagonist, Eugene Gant himself, shares these ideas. Lacking any firm, traditional religious beliefs, he becomes early in life a "fanatical zealot in the religion of Chance," the secular faith of the philosophical mechanist. Moreover, though there is, after all, good fortune as well as bad, the novel's conception of determinism, like that of the Naturalists in general, tends to be bleakly pessimistic. At the time of the death by typhoid fever of his eldest son, Grover, at the St. Louis Fair in 1904, W. O. Gant feels the dreadful power of "the inexorable tides of Necessity." Later, a conspicuous and embarrassing skin irritation which Eugene has inherited from his mother's family convinces the young man that "there was no escape" from his biological heritage; he was "touched with the terrible destiny of his blood, caught in the trap of himself and the Pentlands, with the little flower of sin and darkness on his neck. . . ."

Heredity and other deterministic forces—variously called "destiny," "chance," "necessity," and "accident"—thus constitute a "trap" within which Eugene feels himself confined. At the same time, one of the very traits he has inherited from his father makes it impossible for him to resign himself to such a condition. This trait is his enormous, "Rabelaisian" lust for life and boundless exuberance, his surging energy and huge, "Faustian" hunger, under the compulsion of which he is ready to hurl himself against whatever constrains him from devouring experience to the utmost. The whole thrust of his life, therefore, becomes a heroic struggle for freedom, for if heredity and other deterministic forces themselves cannot be overcome, he never loses his faith that there are many other thwarting circumstances, analogous to them, which can be. His very first bid for liberation takes place only a few months after his second birthday when he slips away from his negligent baby-sitter into the driveway of a wealthy neighbor and is almost trampled by a horse drawing a grocery wagon. "It was his first escape," the narrator points out, and he "carried the mark of the centaur [on his forehead] for many years." The image of the centaur as a symbol of liberation also appears in Chapter 29 in Eugene's "whinnying squeal—the centaur-cry of man or beast, trying to unburden its overladen heart in one blast of pain and joy and passion," and again in Chapter 39 in the description of him as "a centaur, moon-eyed and wild of mane, torn apart with hunger for the golden world." Still other metaphors of his desire for physical and spiritual escape are among the novel's most pervasive tropes—that of trains (on which he and others travel or whose haunting whistles, bells, and rumbling wheels he hears from a distance); that of the "door"; and that of "journeys," "quests," and, above all, "voyages," of which the comic antithesis is the intellectual incompetence of his eccentric school-teacher, John Dorsey Leonard, who "skirted Virgil because . . . [he] was a bad sailor—he was not at all sure of Virgilian navigation. He hated exploration. He distrusted voyages."

From one point of view, of course, the quest for liberation marks Eugene as a late avatar of the archetypal Romantic rebel and outsider, individualist and man of feeling, metaphysical seeker and poet. Indeed, one of the paradoxical features of his consciousness is the way in which early nineteenth-century Romanticism and late nineteenth-century Pessimistic Determinism meet in it and clash. The coexistence in the same character of these different kinds of sensibility—the Romantic-poetic and the Naturalistic-scientific—is one of the chief sources of the novel's dramatic tension. But it is not only the quest for liberation that links Eugene with the early Romantics and their typical heroes and plots. He is a Romantic in a more specific way, which we may loosely call "mystical," and which, as many recent critics have pointed out, is associated with the Platonic and Neoplatonic doctrine of "pre-existence" as developed by Wordsworth in his great ode, "Intimations of Immortality." On one level at least, the "home" of the title toward which the angel is implored to look is the life before birth, where alone can be found the true home of the spirit. An even more obvious reference to this realm is the fourth paragraph of the famous lyrical prose-poem which serves as an epigraph to Part One of the novel and supplies a recurrent refrain: "Remembering speechlessly we seek the great forgotten language, the lost lane-end into heaven, a stone, a leaf, an unfound door." The "door," which Wolfe often uses as a symbol of escape in general, here acquires the additional, fairy-tale-like meaning of an entrance specifically into the paradise of pre-existence—an entrance whose location is also marked by the "stone" and the "leaf." Finally, Eugene's recollections of this paradise—of which there are several scattered throughout the book—are defined by two other important images, those of sound (voices, bells, or music) and water: "somewhere within or without his consciousness he heard a great bell ringing faintly, as if it sounded undersea, and as he listened, the ghost of memory walked through his mind, and for a moment he felt that he had almost recovered what he had lost."

Now, the point to be made about these mystical experiences is that, far from being merely "poetic" embellishments or merely exotic indicators of Eugene's "sensitivity," they provide every phase of the central story of his quest for liberation with a crucial frame of reference. In opposition to the bleak, deterministic prison-house of "destiny," "chance," "necessity," and "accident" in general and various other constricting circumstances in particular, they feed Eugene's passionate and, at bottom, religious yearning for transcendence, for escape into beauty and order, permanence and perfection—his desire, in a word, for an Earthly Paradise. For although **Look Homeward, Angel** is in many ways a Naturalistic novel, its protagonist is an imaginative young man of torrential vitality and idealism for whom a Naturalistic view of life can never be enough. His gargantuan hunger for this-worldly experience in all its manifestations coexists with a profound need to believe that such experience can be fabulous and enchanted, and provide a genuine "home" for his heart's desire. The other-worldly realm of pre-existence and the ecstasy which recollection of it arouses become for him not only an image of paradise lost, but a model, an archetype, of the paradise which can be regained in the here and now. For no matter how often he is made aware of "the nightmare cruelty of life," Eugene remains to the end a "Myth-maker," a visionary, a romancer, an American Adam, who is always seeking to return to the paradise from which he feels he has been expelled.

Specifically, his efforts to preserve his poetic conception of experience in the face of circumstances that are always threatening to destroy it consist of various struggles—carried on more or less simultaneously in complex counterpoint—to achieve some measure of ideal existence by escaping from five major constraining conditions: loneliness, family, hometown, native region, and (taken together) time and death. The first four of these quests terminate in his decision at the end of the novel to go to Harvard, and the last in his discovery at the same point of his vocation as an artist, a discovery which resolves at the deepest level the other quests as well.

Eugene's sense of the lost paradise of pre-existence is one of the main sources of the intense feelings of loneliness which he begins to have even as an infant. But his loneliness is also due to more ordinary causes, typical of many other *Bildungsromane*. For both his temperament and his values effectively isolate him from everyone in his family (except his older brother, Ben) and from most of his fellows in school and college too. During his Freshman year at the state university, in particular, he is so "desperately lonely" that "he saw himself in his clown's trappings and thought of his former vision of success and honor with a lacerating self-contempt." The clown image, in fact, is one of the novel's chief symbols of his loneliness in general, just as that of the centaur is of his quest for liberation. Terrified by the seemingly huge size of the family members bending over his crib, "he saw himself an inarticulate stranger, an amusing little clown, to be dandled and nursed by these enormous and remote figures." And many years later, when participating in a ludicrous Shakespeare Tercentenary pageant, he is dressed by the Leonards in "a full baggy clown's suit, of green linen" that prostrates the spectators in "wild, earthshaking, thundercuffing" laughter.

His quests to escape from this loneliness take three main directions: for the knowledge and stimulus to his imagination which can be gained from books; for "life" itself, which is to be found only outside of books; and for self-acceptance and independence. In each of these kinds of experience he seeks a "door" that will admit him to that fabulous and ideal "home"— that paradise of pre-existence regained on earth—for which he so painfully yearns, and in the possibility of which he never loses his faith.

One of his earliest desires is for the knowledge which can be acquired from speech and reading, for while he is still in his crib he realizes precociously that "his first escape must come through language." Books, he soon learns, can liberate him from his loneliness because they introduce his vivid imagination to a "vast, enchanting, but unperplexing world" outside the confines of his narrow, immediate surroundings. Great teachers partake of the same glow for him. His years at the Leonards' private school "bloomed like golden apples," because "the school had become the centre of his heart and life— Margaret Leonard his spiritual mother." To her "he turned his face up . . . as a prisoner who recovers light," convinced that "the way through the passage to India, that he had never been able to find, would now be charted for him."

Ever since childhood, Eugene's voracious reading in cheap fiction has also been providing him with another mode of escape from loneliness in self-flattering daydreams. Several of these fantasies are of high adventure or of grandiose achievements which win him acclaim or power. He rivals his mother's epic acquisitiveness in visions of princely wealth, and compensates for his clumsiness on the playing-field by imagining himself performing "heroic game-saving" feats of athletic prowess. Especially comic are his fantasies of glory at the time of America's entrance into the First World War, in which he

is debarred from participating because of his youth: "he longed for that subtle distinction, that air of having lived and suffered that could only be attained by a wooden leg, a rebuilt nose, or the seared scar of a bullet across his temple." Even after the war is over, delusions of grandeur of still other kinds afford him an escape from his loneliness—now become almost paranoid—when he revels in thoughts of himself as "Senator Gant, Governor Gant, President Gant . . . Jesus-of-Nazareth Gant," and the like.

Eugene's daydreams are also often highly erotic. For sex too can be an escape from loneliness into a kind of glory, provided, of course, that it is sanctified by "love" and the woman, however passionate, is "pure." Although Eugene's lust is strong, his romantic, idealistic temperament makes it impossible for him to be satisfied with "pagan love" alone. Building elaborate structures of wishful thinking on the basis of popular society novels and the silent movies, he imagines preposterously elegant men and women making love "in kid gloves, to the accompaniment of subtle repartee . . . beyond all the laws of nature . . . exquisitely and incorruptibly," and himself as "Bruce-Eugene" or "The Dixie-Ghost," the noble, unblemished hero who never fails to enjoy the delights of passion with the most beautiful and ardent yet virtuous women.

More importantly, his quest for liberation from loneliness eventually takes him from books into "life" itself, when he comes to believe that the marvelous can be found in "real" (as distinct from merely imaginary) experience too—that the Ideal and the Actual, Romance and Reality, are one. "Facts" which fail to conform to this belief simply cease to be "facts" at all for him. Even when he learns certain unpleasant truths about Mrs. Leonard and her relatives, for example, he flatly refuses to believe them: "all the facts that leveled Margaret down to life . . . were as unreal and horrible as a nightmare. . . . Eugene believed in the glory and the gold." In the same way, after he has lost faith in the bookish teachings of Vergil Weldon, his professor of philosophy at Pulpit Hill, he is sustained by his conviction that "the world was full of pleasant places, enchanted places, if he could only go and find them. . . . He always felt sure things would be better elsewhere." Thus, "he was devoured by a vast strange hunger for life"; "the world lay before him for his picking"—not, as for Adam and Eve, a world radically different from Eden, but an Eden itself, "full of opulent cities, golden vintages, glorious triumphs, lovely women, full of a thousand unmet and magnificent possibilities. Nothing was dull or tarnished. The strange enchanted coasts were unvisited. He was young and he could never die." By the end of the novel, to be sure, he has not given up his quest for formal learning, for he is about to leave for graduate study at Harvard. But Harvard has come to mean much more to him than books; it too is a part of fabulous, liberating "life": "it was not the name of a university—it was rich magic, wealth, elegance, joy. . . . And he felt somehow that it gave a reason, a goal of profit, to his wild ecstasy."

Meanwhile, during the summer following his first year at Pulpit Hill, his quest for a paradise in "real life" has also resulted in a romance with one of his mother's boarders, named Laura James. No less than his earlier erotic fantasies that were fed by books, the two main parts into which Chapter 30, which records their brief love affair, is divided are dominated by imagery of enchantment. In the first, he and Laura declare their love for one another in what might be the preternatural, mythical realm of one of his favorite poets—that "chief prince of the moon and magic"—Coleridge. "The moonlight fell upon the earth like a magic unearthly dawn. It wiped away all rawness, it hid all sores. It gave all common and familiar things . . . a uniform bloom of wonder.'' As the pair embrace, Eugene's ''limbs'' are ''numbed'' by a ''passion . . . governed by a religious ecstasy''; and, after they have parted for the night, he falls asleep to the sound of a cock's ''distant elfin minstrelsy.'' Equally idyllic, though taking place in daylight, is the scene in the second part of the chapter, in which Eugene and Laura picnic on the following afternoon in a cove in the hills. The comparison of her body to a ''Maenad's'' which might ''grow into the tree again'' unmistakably links her to ''the flitting wood-girls growing into bark'' who have appeared earlier in one of Eugene's recollections of pre-existence. The setting too is a counterpart of the pre-natal realm—a landscape which combines features of pagan pastoral, the Biblical Paradise, and fairy tale. Here, forgetting the passage of time and the ''pain and conflict'' of the town, which ''lay in another unthinkable world,'' the lovers ''clung together in that bright moment of wonder . . . believing all they said.''

Laura, of course, ultimately puts Eugene's trust to a severe test: in their Eden there is a ''snake,'' both literal and figurative. The young girl betrays ''the apple tree, the singing, and the gold,'' because she has been secretly engaged to someone else, and only a few days after leaving Altamont marries him. Eugene is crushed; having sought escape from loneliness in a ''real life'' paradise of love, he appears to have been left more lonely than before. Nevertheless, he soon recovers: his very loss of Laura, together with other experiences, teaches him that there is yet another way in which loneliness can be escaped—a way already suggested by his juvenile fantasies of demonic ''isolation and dominance over sea and land . . . victorious dark all-seeing isolation'' and of ''opulent solitude'' (reminiscent again of pre-existence) in ''kingdoms under the sea, on windy crags, and . . . [in] the deep elf kingdoms of the earth's core.'' For if there are many times when he finds his loneliness and the self-contempt it can breed an intolerable bondage, there are others when he eagerly embraces the proud self-acceptance which can be fostered by loneliness itself, and rejoices in his solitary state as a field for the development and display of heroic independence.

During his last year at the state university his hope of finding a ''vast Utopia of . . . loneliness'' reaches its climax. Although he is troubled at first by a repetition of the students' mockery, and driven almost mad with shame by the Pentland rash, which has appeared on his neck and made him absurdly conscious of all his other physical blemishes, he eventually begins ''to take a terrible joy in his taint,'' because he has come to believe that the truly great men of the world have also been ''tainted''— ''wasted and devoured by the beautiful disease of thought and passion.'' By thus persuading himself of his kinship with such ''lords of the earth,'' ''Eugene escaped forever from the good and the pretty, into a dark land that is forbidden to the sterilized,'' wherein ''he felt that . . . there was in him a health that was greater than they could ever know.'' In more appealingly modest and comically self-ironic moods, he even achieves enough objectivity to live comfortably with the heretofore intolerable idea that he may not be the genius he has always liked to think himself after all: ''over that final hedge [of self-knowledge], he thought, not death, as I once believed— but new life—and new lands.'' The magic of one such ''new land,'' Harvard, consists precisely in his faith that there he will be able to cultivate his ''proud loneliness'' to the fullest. (pp. 266-74)

The most inclusive trap from which Eugene's quest for an Earthly Paradise compels him to seek escape, of course, is that of time and death, the ultimate expression of those blind, remorseless laws of ''destiny,'' ''change,'' ''accident,'' and ''necessity'' that govern the godless, naturalistic universe as a whole. Personal encounters with the agonizingly protracted dying of his father and the deaths of his brother Grover, his college roommate (Bob Sterling), Laura James, and especially his beloved Ben assure that a dread of mutability and mortality is never far from his mind. Indeed, his sensitivity to the brevity of human life, to the ''lostness'' and dreamlike strangeness of the past, and to the dizzying rush of himself and the world he has known to extinction and oblivion is shown in many ways throughout the novel to be extremely acute. It is a vital element in his insatiable energy and partakes of the same intensity, for life and joy are precious to him, as they were for Keats, precisely because he knows they are so fleeting. His loneliness, insofar as it springs from a sense of expulsion from the timeless paradise of pre-existence into the temporal world, is directly related to the same awareness, and the latter encompasses and exacerbates his sense of entrapment by family, hometown, and native region as well. Futhermore, as I shall show, a complete resolution of his quests to escape from these other traps can come only when he is able to meet the supreme test of conquering time and death themselves.

This conquest is achieved when he discovers his vocation as an artist in the novel's last chapter—a discovery toward which numerous signs (e.g., his precocious interest in language, his ravenous love of reading, his maturing critical powers and taste, his rich fantasy life, and his actual writings) have been steadily pointing the way. Before looking at the chapter in detail, however, we must consider for a moment how an earlier one prepares for it. This is the famous Chapter 36 which describes Eugene and his brother Luke's visit to Horse Hines's mortuary, where they view Ben's corpse and make arrangements for his funeral, and which reaches its grotesque climax when the undertaker, regarding with great complacency the job of embalming he has done, decides that he needs to apply only one last touch to make his work of ''art'' perfect:

> ''Just a moment!'' said Horse Hines quickly, lifting a finger. Briskly he took a stick of rouge from his pocket, stepped forward, and deftly, swiftly, sketched upon the dead gray cheeks a ghastly rose-hued mockery of life and health.
>
> ''There!'' he said, with deep satisfaction; and, rougestick in hand, head critically cocked, like a painter before his canvas, he stepped back into the terrible staring prison of their horror.
>
> ''There are artists, boys, in every profession. . . . Did you ever see anything more natural in your life? . . . That's art, boys!''

At this point Eugene, unable to contain himself any longer, falls to the floor, almost strangling with laughter, and screams, '''A-r-t! Yes! Yes! That's it!''' Needless to say, the episode is a masterpiece of macabre comedy—and an especially bold one at that, since it follows almost immediately the magnificent, extremely moving account of Ben's death. But it also makes a serious point, which can easily be missed, in relation to Eugene's discovery of his vocation. For when Hines attempts to give the appearance of ''life and health'' to Ben's corpse, he is only trying to perform, in however bizarre and parodic a way, that very function of triumphing over time and death which belongs to genuine art itself, and Eugene, in crying out hysterically as he does, seems to recognize this fact. The moment thus becomes for the young man an epiphany, completing his earlier recognitions of the power of Gant's stonecutting and of Homer's poetry to transcend flux, and leading directly to the resolution of his own quest for transcendence in Chapter 40.

The action of this last chapter falls into four main parts, the first three recapitulating matters which the novel has considered earlier. Thus, the opening passage reminds us of Eugene's unusually powerful imagination by showing how, after arriving at his father's shop on the eve of his departure for Harvard, he conjures up Ben's "ghost" and imparts life and animation to Gant's stone angels. The second part of the chapter then dramatizes once more the power of Eugene's phenomenal memory, which calls forth into the Square "the thousand forms of himself and Ben" as they were in childhood, and for an instant holds in radiant stasis "all the minutes of lost time." Eugene also hints to the "ghost" of Ben how he has experienced faint memories of the even further past of pre-existence, and recalls having had such recollections as a child. In turn, this awareness of time, loss, and death leads immediately into the third part of the chapter where, in a "vision" of history which echoes Shelley's "Ozymandias," Eugene perceives again the tragic ephemerality of mankind in general in contrast to the permanence of the earth itself.

Finally, the fourth—and most difficult—part of the last chapter consists almost entirely of a still more "terrible vision" of Eugene's own personal future—a vision in which he sees that all of his quests for the Earthly Paradise have ended only in frustration and defeat. He also sees himself as turning at this same time to Ben for an answer: where are "'an end to hunger, and the happy land?'" "'Where is the world'" he is seeking? Ben's elliptical reply is that "'There is no happy land. There is no end to hunger. . . . *You* are your world'." That is, to find what he is searching for his brother must explore himself, for this is the only reality which is accessible and knowable to him. Apparently misunderstanding this advice, Eugene resolves in despair to give up his quest entirely and simply wait for the final, inevitable voyage into the "'one land unvisited,'" death itself. But now Ben reiterates what he has just said, and Eugene, at last grasping the point, is marvelously revived. "'Fool,' said Ben, '*this* is life. You have been nowhere!'" Besides death, "'there is one voyage, the first, the last, the only one'" still left—the voyage into himself—and Eugene immediately and exultantly vows to embark on it. How this journey will end he doesn't know, for when he asks Ben the vision suddenly fades away. But no matter; Eugene has been strengthened by his brother's counsel, and, as dawn comes and the ghost of Ben disappears and the angels are once more frozen in their places, he turns with bold, new confidence to his departure for Harvard and the beginning of his great voyage of self-discovery.

The question to be asked, of course, is what this whole episode means in relation to the quest pattern of the novel in general and the quest for transcendence of time and death in particular. Most obviously, the chapter is an allegory of education and hence a microcosm of the *Bildungsroman* pattern which governs the book as a whole: Eugene is the pupil and the "ghost" of Ben is the teacher; whereas previously the former has learned from experience, here he learns from his brother. But what he learns now is that he must give his quests a vital new direction. Heretofore, looking "homeward" has meant seeking for the Earthly Paradise in the world outside himself: as an escape from loneliness he has sought it in books, "life," and physical

isolation; as an escape from his family, Altamont, and the South, he has sought it in far and exotic places; and as an escape from time and death he has sought it in consoling thoughts of Ben's liberation from suffering, of his resurrection in the form of the flowers which grow above his grave, and in scenes like those glimpsed from the windows of speeding trains, which create an illusion of timelessness. Now, however, under Ben's tutelage, he understands that he must seek the Earthly Paradise—look for his spiritual "home"—somewhere else as well. For if death is in Arcadia (the traditional meaning of the Latin motto, "*Et ego in Arcadia*," which crosses his mind at one point in his conversation with Ben's "ghost"), in another sense Arcadia is a deathless place within himself, and there he must go to find it.

But what exactly does discovering himself mean? What is the nature of the self which we may presume Eugene will eventually find? The language which both he and the narrator use to describe "the lost land of himself" is practically identical with that which is used elsewhere in the novel to describe the paradisaical realm of pre-existence. Any full recovery of pre-natal memories, however—not to mention a return to the pre-natal life itself—is of course impossible, for these memories are, by their very nature, fleeting and elusive, and, according to Wordsworth, become progressively more so as the child grows into youth and adulthood. Like all his other quests, therefore, Eugene's quest for his hidden self can only be for some metaphorical equivalent of the pre-natal paradise. What, then, is this something?

Although Wolfe does not explicitly tell us, the answer is clearly implied by the last chapter in its first three sections, which show how Eugene, who is painfully aware of the tragic ephemerality of man and his works, and longs to achieve the permanence, immutability, and timelessness symbolized by the enduring earth and the realm of pre-existence, does actually triumph over time and death for a moment by the power of his imagination and memory, working together, to call back the past, raise the dead (Ben), and animate the lifeless angels. And what are imagination and memory for Wolfe if not the essential components of art itself, without which, indeed, the achievements of imagination and memory can only be fleeting? As memory immortalizes the past, so art must immortalize memory. Art, in fact, is doubly symbolized in the last chapter: first (and as elsewhere), by the angels themselves—those replicas of the angel which W. O. Gant, the artist *manqué*, saw as a boy in Baltimore and has futilely longed all his life to carve—and then by the fact that Eugene's imagination brings those angels to life, making them *his* creations, *his* works of art, just as, in bringing to life on the same occasion his earlier self through memory, he has created "his son, his boy." By thus symbolically dramatizing the power of art to triumph over the flux of life and render it timeless and beautiful, the first three sections of Chapter 40 implicitly provide the reader with the answer to the question which, in the last section, Eugene fails to get from Ben: what he will ultimately discover as he pursues his "ghost along the labyrinthine ways" will be the enormous creative resources of his imagination and memory—in short, nothing less than his vocation as an artist. It is in the direction of this discovery that he has been moving throughout his story.

With the forthcoming discovery of his artistic vocation, then, Eugene will have achieved, in the only way possible for him, his quest for liberation from time and death. But, by the same token, this discovery will permit a resolution of all his other quests too, and is thus ultimately the controlling theme of the entire novel. For Eugene will be able to escape from the traps of loneliness, family, town, and region, and pursue his quest for the Earthly Paradise, not only in the ways we have already seen, but by making them the very subject of his art—by transcending them through a supreme act of re-creation. Heretofore, he has failed to understand this. Early in the novel, for example, when he tried to avoid facing the unpleasant truths which he had come to learn about Margaret Leonard and her relatives, and which he feared might plunge her "in the defiling stream of life," he believed mistakenly that "it was not truth that men live for—the creative men—but for falsehood," and at the time of Ben's death he regretted that he and his brother had spent their lives in the "mean cramped huddle of brick and stone" that is Altamont, instead of in more glamorous and exotic places like "Gath or Ispahan . . . Corinth or Byzantium." During his conversation with Ben's "ghost" in Chapter 40 he makes this last point again, when he insists that stone angels should not walk in such an unremarkable place as Altamont's Square, but only " 'in Babylon! In Thebes! In all the other places'." Beauty may be truth, and truth beauty, he is saying, but not here! Similarly, the name of Harvard appeals to him not only because the university it designates is far away, but because it is "enchanted" and sounds to him "like Cairo and Damascus." He has yet to learn what the narrator, paraphrasing Romantics like Wordsworth, Coleridge, and Carlyle, has known from the beginning—that "it is the union of the ordinary and the miraculous that makes wonder."—When he does discover that it is art which can effect this union, he will have come to know at the same time that the "door" to the Earthly Paradise can be found anywhere—even in ugly, humdrum Altamont—through the exercise of his creative power itself. Whereas Ben, who is "lost" and can find no "door" because he has felt neglected by his family, acquired no satisfying vocation, and failed to discover any meaning in life as a whole, willingly embraces death as an escape from his frustrations and torments, Eugene will both find himself and affirm life by recapturing the past—including Ben himself—in timeless artistic form. As he once suspected on his trip to Charleston, Eugene now knows that "his gateway to the lost world" really lies behind him in the experiences he has already had and those waiting to be shaped by his hand. Thus, although in the last paragraph of the novel, the town Square already seems "far and lost" to him, and he has become "like a man who . . . turns his eyes upon the distant soaring ranges," he and the angel of the title—which has now become his muse—will ultimately "look homeward" in the broadest sense of all, by immortalizing the family, the town, the region, and his own life there in art. (pp. 279-85)

John Hagan, "Structure, Theme, and Metaphor in Thomas Wolfe's 'Look Homeward, Angel'," in American Literature, Vol. 53, No. 2, May, 1981, pp. 266-85.

DARLENE H. UNRUE (essay date 1985)

[*In the following excerpt, Unrue discusses affinities between* Look Homeward, Angel *and the Gothic novel.*]

Perhaps one of the reasons for the personal appeal of Wolfe, and of *Look Homeward, Angel* especially, is that Wolfe is more than simply a lyrical writer, and *Look Homeward, Angel* is more than merely a romantic novel. A closer look reveals that it abounds in archetypal Gothic images that appeal to readers subliminally; it shares with other Southern Gothic works the significant elements of both Southern and Gothic setting (bells,

darkness, wind, a decaying mansion, labyrinths, an abyss, and eerie music), a quest, imprisonment, a ghost, and themes of isolation and fear of annihilation.

The matrix of prototypical Gothic novels is a journey that leads to knowledge. Usually the journey is made by a virtuous heroine or a noble hero, or later is undertaken by a brooding villain-hero. The journey, often into strange lands, includes imprisonment along the way and confrontations with numerous dangers and evils, usually within the labyrinths and cellars of Gothic castles; but the more serious and horrifying the journey, the greater the victory if and when the sadder but wiser traveler returns home. Thus, the journey becomes an archetypal quest. The Gothic quest differs from the more general romantic quest primarily by the intensity of the extreme experiences completed against the backdrop of thunder and lightning, howling winds, wailing ghosts, and screeching demons, all of which are archetypes, some psychoanalysts believe, for the anxieties and fears of us all.

Look Homeward, Angel superficially is concerned with an actual world of people, buildings, and social problems; it is concerned more specifically with the quest, or initiation, of the novel's hero, Eugene Gant. Having been alienated from his mother and having lost his dear brother Ben, Eugene at the end of the novel finally understands that he must break irrevocably with his family and go out into the world on his own. But the process that has led to that awareness has been a long and agonizing spiritual journey. In order to evoke the intensity of the suffering, Wolfe has drawn heavily upon stock Gothic images, relying upon their psychological weight to carry much of the meaning of the story.

Just as many an imprisoned Gothic hero has contemplated his sad fate, an adolescent Eugene recalls infant impressions of being imprisoned, not within a gloomy castle, but first within a crib and second within a physical self:

> And left alone to sleep within a shuttered room, with the thick sunlight printed in bars upon the floor, unfathomable loneliness and sadness crept through him: he saw his life down the solemn vista of a forest aisle, and he knew he would always be the sad one: caged in that little round of skull, imprisoned in that beating and most secret heart, his life must always walk down lonely passages. Lost. His brain went black with terror. He saw himself an inarticulate stranger, an amusing little clown, to be dandled and nursed by these enormous and remote figures. He had been sent from one mystery into another: somewhere within or without his consciousness . . . he heard a great bell ringing faintly, as if it sounded undersea, and as he listened, the ghost of memory walked through his mind, and for a moment he felt that he had almost recovered what he had lost.

That passage is permeated with a feeling of isolation and terror evoked by the images of prison bars, lonely, dark passages, a distant bell, and a ghost (even if only the ghost of memory). It is significant that the passage can be compared fruitfully with a passage from Maturin's classic Gothic work *Melmoth the Wanderer* (1820). In the early work John Melmoth has extracted from the Englishman Stanton's manuscript an account of the latter's discovery that he is imprisoned in a madhouse. Stanton sees that he is alone, hears bells, and discovers that the door to his room is locked. He calls aloud, and his voice is echoed by many others "in tones so wild and discordant" that he stops in "involuntary terror." As the day goes on and as his loneliness and fear increase, he tries the window, seeing for the first time that it is grated. As he looks out into the humanless courtyard, he sickens with ''unspeakable horror'' and sits down miserably in ''complete darkness.'' When he shakes the door ''with desperate strength'' and utters ''the most frightful cries, mixed with expostulations and commands,'' his cries are echoed by maniacs' malignant voices, which sound like ''wild and infernal yells of joy.''

Both Wolfe's passage and Maturin's are imbued with what Denis de Rougemont has called ''night mysticism'' and with what Elizabeth Kerr has called the ''dream side of the psyche, the essence of Gothicism which reveals the instinctual unconscious aspects of the psyche and abounds in literal and figurative dream-nightmare imagery effects.'' Eugene's infant reveries also contain two of the three kinds of images Irving Malin deals with in *New American Gothic,* the ''voyage into the forest'' and also, as in Stanton's account, the enclosing place that represents retreat or imprisonment or both. As a variation of the second kind of image, Malin refers to the ''other room'' in the haunted castle which is the ''final door through which the ghost-like forces march.'' It is a variation on the haunted castle itself, what Malin calls ''the metaphor of confining narcissism, the private world.'' For literal examples of the metaphor, he refers to Faulkner's insane asylum at Jackson that shuts up Benjy Compson and Darl Bundren, the jail in Jefferson, and Miss Reba's brothel in Memphis. Of course, Stanton is in a real madhouse, and Eugene is in a crib in the family home. Yet both Maturin and Wolfe, as well as Faulkner, have chosen the same motifs to translate those feelings of isolation, imprisonment, and terror into terms the reader can understand.

The dominant symbol and the focus of Gothic literature is the castle, or its equivalent, what G. R. Thompson terms ''the most obvious single objective correlative'' derived from *The Castle of Otranto* and indeed ''suggested by the term 'Gothic''' itself. The haunted castle is the other image that Malin considers, and he notes that in American Gothic ''the 'castle' must be less ancient and magnificent and may be merely a ruined mansion like Faulkner's Old Frenchman's place or the Sutpen mansion.'' The equivalent in *Look Homeward, Angel* is Dixieland (perhaps its very name suggests that like Emily Grierson's decayed mansion it, too, is a symbol of the Old South). Not precisely a mansion, it is the creaking old boarding house of which Eugene's mother, Eliza, is the proprietress. It is the edifice that contains Eugene's crib, and it is also that with which Eugene identifies his physical self in a brilliant illustration of a Jungian archetype. Eugene refers often to ''the bleak horror'' of Dixieland and thinks of it as the catalyst for his own infinite loneliness and the symbol of his spiritual imprisonment. The boarding house and his awareness of isolation blend in one passage which mirrors the terrors of his mind. Eugene has drunk himself into a stupor with a concoction of gin, rye, and bourbon:

> Then a divine paralysis crept through his flesh. His limbs were numb, his tongue thickened until he could not bend it to the cunning sounds of words. He spoke aloud, repeating difficult phrases over and over, filled with wild laughter and delight at his effort. Behind his drunken body his brain hung poised like a falcon, looking on him with scorn, with tenderness, looking on all laughter with grief and pity. There lay in him something that could not be seen and could not be touched, which was above and beyond him—an eye within an eye, a brain above a brain, the stranger that dwelt in him and regarded him and was him and that he did not know. But, thought he, I am alone now in this house; if I can come to know him, I will.

> He got up, and reeled out of the alien presences of light and warmth in the kitchen; he went out into the hall where a dim light burned and the high walls gave back their grave-damp chill. This, he thought, is the house.

That passage exhibits clearly the way in which the fear of external dangers, common in some early Gothic fiction, has become exclusively the fear of internal, or psychological, dangers. And the physical Gothic castle has become here the physical, conscious self.

The old Gothic fiction was filled with extraordinary plights that evoked awesome fears. One common fear was that of annihilation, especially as a result of falling from great heights into black and bottomless pits. Often the castle, established high on an Alpine peak, provided the means of developing that kind of fear, and often a gaping chasm either within the edifice, as in Poe's ''The Pit and the Pendulum,'' or in the mountain terrain, evoked the terror. One of the most dramatic scenes of all of Gothic fiction occurs at the end of Lewis's *The Monk* (1796) when the demon hurls Ambrosio into a mountain abyss:

> Darting his talons into the monk's shaven crown, he sprang with him from the rock. The caves and mountains rang with Ambrosio's shrieks. The demon continued to soar aloft, till reaching a dreadful height, he released the sufferer. Headlong fell the monk through the airy waste; the sharp point of a rock received him; and he rolled from precipice to precipice, till bruised and mangled, he rested on the river's banks.

Wolfe also finds useful the image of the chasm or the pit inhabited by demons. Wolfe's pit, like that of the best of the older Gothic works, is a symbol for the fear of annihilation or the fear of the unknown side of the psyche. Eugene is especially susceptible to these horrifying fantasies when he is an impressionable boy, struggling to find meaning in his cruel existence. One passage is extraordinarily reminiscent of Lewis's passage:

> And when the bells broke through the drowning winds at night, his demon rushed into his heart, bursting all cords that held him to the earth, promising him isolation and dominance over sea and land, inhabitation of the dark: he looked down on the whirling disk of dark forest and field, sloped over singing pines upon a huddled town, and carried its grated guarded fires against its own roofs, swerving and pouncing with his haltered storm upon their doomed and flaming walls, howling with thin laughter above their stricken heads and, fiend-voiced, calling down the bullet wind.

Another such passage occurs when Eugene and his sister Daisy attend a fair in St. Louis. Daisy in ''furtive cat-cruelty'' has taken Eugene with her into ''the insane horrors of the scenic railway,'' and ''they plunge bottomlessly from light into roaring blackness.'' When the blackness does yield, it is to ''gloom peopled with huge painted grotesques, the red maws of fiendish heads, the cunning appearances of death, nightmare, and madness.'' As the car rolls ''downward from one lighted cavern to another,'' he hears laughter like that in Stanton's madhouse and in which his sister joins. He is paralyzed by the belief that he has ''surrenderd all his hope'' to ''the lewd torture of demons masked in human flesh,'' and as he and Daisy emerge into the ''warm and practical sunlight,'' he is ''half-sensible'' and ''purple with gasping terror.'' Eugene's fears can be recognized as irrational, based not upon the threat of external dangers but rather upon his internal fear of self-confrontation.

Many evocative passages in **Look Homeward, Angel** suggest the older Gothic works. For example, when the adolescent Eugene is sent to Niggertown to "capture" a new servant, he searches "fetid cellars" through "all the rank labyrinths." He suffers profoundly in isolation with his emerging psyche, and in one passage he thinks of himself as "holding in fief the storm and the dark and all the black powers of wizardry" as he crouches "against a lonely storm-swept house"; he feels a touch and looks "haunter-haunted, pursuer-pursued, into the green corrupted hell-face of malignant death." Both those passages might be compared, for example, with one from Walpole's *The Castle of Otranto* (1764), in which Isabella flees into the depths of the castle from the villainous Manfred. The castle's decay, darkness, and deep caverns symbolize Isabella's fear of the unknown just as the images in Wolfe's passage symbolize Eugene's fear of his unknown self.

Such Gothic passages occur regularly in **Look Homeward, Angel,** but perhaps the strongest Gothic link in the novel, and the inspiration for some of Wolfe's most poetic writing, is the presence of a ghost. In the older Gothic fiction the ghost followed an ancient literary tradition, having appeared in the Greek and French classical drama, in English drama, and in folklore. Like all facets of the ancient world, the ghost is admired by the Gothic writer, who uses the spectre primarily for any of three reasons: to create an atmosphere of fear, to reveal information, or to make a moral statement that could not be made without the help of a *deus ex machina*. A typical Gothic ghost is that which appears in Clara Reeve's *The Old English Baron* (1778); Sir Philip Harclay, returning to England after thirty years in French and Mohammedan wars, is visited by the ghost of his best friend and provided sufficient information to avenge the wrongs that have been brought upon his house in his absence.

The ghost in **Look Homeward, Angel** is the spirit of Eugene's brother Ben, whom Eugene frequently identifies as his other self. Darkness and wind attend Eugene's calling upon the ghost ("O lost, and by the wind grieved, ghost come back again!"). When the ghost comes, like many a Gothic ghost, it comes to instruct. The ghost of Ben tells Eugene that a physical journey in search of self-knowledge—in search of reality—is futile. In answer to Eugene's question "Where is the world?" the ghost of Ben replies, "Nowhere. You are your world."

Throughout the last pages of the novel Eugene confuses the ghost of Ben with his own spirit. And his seeking of that ghost/spirit is the psychological equivalent of the search for a "father," a source of strength. A final passage in this novel illustrates well one of the modern directions of the Gothic. These thoughts are Eugene's:

> O sudden and impalpable faun, lost in the thickets of myself. I will hunt you down until you cease to haunt my eyes with hunger. I heard your foot-falls in the desert, I saw your shadow in old buried years, I heard your laughter running down a million streets, but I did not find you there. And no leaf hangs for me in the forest; I shall lift no stone upon the hills; I shall find no door in any city. But in the city of myself, upon the continent of my soul, I shall find the forgotten language, the lost world, a door where I may enter, and music strange as any ever sounded; I shall haunt you, ghost, along the labyrinthine ways until—until? O Ben, my ghost an answer?

In this passage Thomas Wolfe has used the images of labyrinths without doors, ghosts, and strange music to dramatize his hero's search for self-knowledge and deliverance—a psychological search, but also a twentieth-century version of the old Gothic quest.

It remains to consider Wolfe in comparison with other Southern Gothic writers in order to determine what he shares with them and what he does not. Elizabeth Kerr concludes that the South provided William Faulkner and other Southern writers with "a reality which could be depicted with the strong contrasts of the Gothic genre to reveal social and psychological truths less accessible to purely objective and realistic treatment." She goes on to say that "with a foundation of realistic displacement which conceals Gothic structure beneath the representation of modern society, all the strategies of point of view, discontinuity, ironic inversion, exaggeration, and parody are employed to give new meaning to old formulas."

There were elements in the South of the 1920s that made it ripe for Gothic fiction, and there were circumstances in Thomas Wolfe's experience that made him turn naturally in **Look Homeward, Angel** to Gothic motifs and symbols. Modern Southern Gothic writers, unlike their ancestor Poe, have not set their works in "the misty mid regions of Weir" or exclusively in the landscape of the soul. In this respect the family line runs more clearly from George Washington Cable than from Poe. One of the characteristics of Southern Gothic writing is that it often concerns itself with time and place as well as with horror. In "A Rose for Emily," for example, Faulkner devotes his entire long second paragraph to establishing the exact setting. And Wolfe, like Cable, Faulkner, and other Southern Gothicists, provides in **Look Homeward, Angel** a strong sense of time and place. Like Miss Emily's decayed ancestral home, Dixieland is described in realistic detail as a big "frame house of eighteen or twenty drafty high-ceilinged rooms"; "rambling, unplanned, gabular" and "painted a dirty yellow," it later is referred to by Eugene as "the tomb."

Setting thus becomes crucial to the thematic development of much of Southern Gothic. Edward Stone believes that setting is crucial because the real setting, in the midst of social turmoil, is that against which Southern Gothic writers are reacting and which they embroider upon with Gothic images. The 1920s indeed were a period of rampant industrialism in the South and of a transformation of traditional social structures; the times would have been unduly troubling to a sensitive and poetic young person. In discussing the development of American Gothic fiction Stone also describes one of the common themes as the frightening burden of an isolated and alienated sensibility exploring its own emotions and one of the Gothic terrors as the vision of a landscape ravaged by modern industrialism. The incessant theme of loneliness and alienation in **Look Homeward, Angel,** expressed by the pervasive repetition of the "O Lost!" motif, can be traced to both these sources.

Thus, the young and sensitive Thomas Wolfe, writing in the upper South in the 1920s, was trying to work out through art his search for himself and his revulsion for the change that was taking place in his society. A part of the repugnance of Dixieland, a repugnance so strong that it evokes nightmare terrors, is that it represents the opposite of what Eugene wants. He wants aesthetic nourishment, and Dixieland is an ugly symbol of twentieth-century American capitalism and of his mother's total absorption in the profit motive. He fears imprisonment in Dixieland in that he fears imprisonment in a materialistic society that does not allow the poetic soul to flower. It is understandable that he responds childishly to the train whistle that will take him out of it; in his ignorance he fails to see that the train shares many of the characteristics of Dixieland. Ironically, it is the train, often a symbol of twentieth-century industrialism and progress, that obsesses him as the means of escape to knowledge, at least until the ghost of Ben tells him not to look outward for life's meaning but to look within.

The infant, child, and adolescent Eugene Gant, trying to find his way in the spiritual landscape of terrors and horrors, confronts his world's absurdities in grotesque characters and nightmares which will continue through the twentieth century into the theatre of the absurd and into the novels of black humorists like Pynchon, Barth, and Vonnegut. Thomas Wolfe and other writers who have sought to present in fiction man's searches and his internal terrors have turned frequently to the iconography of the Gothic. Because each human being's inner kingdom is private, there is no absolute description that will render it intelligible to the reader. The Gothic symbol, with its inherent wealth of emotion, has offered writers one means by which to give form to the abstract hope of fulfillment and the fear of annihilation, a hope and a fear that form the underlying conflict in such Southern American fiction. It is significant that after **Look Homeward, Angel,** when Wolfe was finished with his theme of initiation, when his autobiographical hero Eugene Gant had found his ghost within at the same time that he repudiated the materialism of his society, Wolfe turned naturally away from the Gothic; in subsequent novels he embraced a wider romantic mode as his hero confronted a larger social perspective than that of Altamont, a perspective that focused on a landscape more eternal than the dreamlit Gothic region of the soul. (pp. 48-55)

> *Darlene H. Unrue, "The Gothic Matrix of 'Look Homeward, Angel'," in* Critical Essays on Thomas Wolfe, *edited by John S. Phillipson, G. K. Hall & Co., 1985, pp. 48-56.*

ADDITIONAL BIBLIOGRAPHY

Burgum, Edwin Berry. "Thomas Wolfe's Discovery of America." In his *The Novel and the World's Dilemma*, pp. 302-21. New York: Oxford University Press, 1947.
> Discusses Wolfe's progression from personal to social concerns in *Look Homeward, Angel*.

Carpenter, Frederic I. "Thomas Wolfe: The Autobiography of an Idea." In his *American Literature and the Dream*, pp. 155-56. New York: Philosophical Library, 1955.
> Interprets Wolfe's major novels as allegorical representations of the development of American democracy, and *Look Homeward, Angel* as portraying the struggle between North and South, as well as between materialism and freedom.

Champion, Myra, comp. *The Lost World of Thomas Wolfe*. Asheville: Privately printed, 1970, unpaged.
> Collection of photographs of people and places fictionalized in Wolfe's novels.

Church, Margaret. "Thomas Wolfe: Dark Time." *PMLA* LXIV, No. 4 (September 1949): 629-38.
> Compares Wolfe's view of time and memory with that of Marcel Proust.

Evans, Elizabeth. "*Look Homeward, Angel* and *Of Time and the River*: 'The Apple Tree, the Singing, and the Gold.'" In her *Thomas Wolfe*, pp. 35-63. New York: Frederick Ungar Publishing Co., 1984.
> Recounts the writing of Wolfe's first two novels and public reaction to them.

Falk, Robert P. "Thomas Wolfe and the Critics." *College English* 5, No. 4 (January 1944): 186-92.

Discusses early criticism of Wolfe, faulting excesses of both praise and denunciation of his work, and demonstrating that he was the object of such extreme views because he stood outside any established critical tradition.

Field, Leslie A., ed. *Thomas Wolfe: Three Decades of Criticism*. New York: New York University Press, 1968, 304 p.
> Includes essays on *Look Homeward, Angel* by Bruce R. McElderry, Jr. and Richard S. Kennedy, as well as thirteen essays on Wolfe's major themes and style and a selected bibliography of Wolfe criticism.

Geismar, Maxwell. "Thomas Wolfe: The Unfound Door." In his *Writers in Crisis: The American Novel, 1925-1940*, pp. 187-235. New York: Hill and Wang, 1947.
> Discusses *Look Homeward, Angel* as an accurate portrait of the society in which Wolfe grew up and as an illustration of the lost paradise theme in literature.

Hilfer, Anthony Channell. "Wolfe's Altamont: The Mimesis of Being." *The Georgia Review*, XVIII, No. 4 (Winter 1964): 451-56.
> Examines Wolfe's realistic representation of his life in chapter XIV of *Look Homeward, Angel*.

Holman, C. Hugh, ed. "Part Three: Reviews of *Look Homeward, Angel*." In *The World of Thomas Wolfe*, pp. 54-63. New York: Charles Scribner's Sons, 1962.
> Reprints excerpts from three essays on *Look Homeward, Angel*: "C'est maître François," by Basil Davenport (see excerpt dated 1929); "The Loneliness at the Core," by C. Hugh Holman (see excerpt dated 1955); and "Thomas Wolfe and the Kicking Season," by Pamela Hansford Johnson (see entry below).

Johnson, Pamela Hansford. "The Story of Eugene Gant." In her *Hungry Gulliver: An English Critical Appraisal of Thomas Wolfe*, pp. 40-66. New York and London: Charles Scribner's Sons, 1948.
> Recounts the development of Eugene through *Look Homeward, Angel* and *Of Time and the River*. This is the earliest book-length critical work on Wolfe.

——. "Thomas Wolfe and the Kicking Season." *Encounter* XII, No. 4 (April 1959): 77-80.
> Assesses the primary objections to Wolfe's writing, judges that despite his faults he was a great artist, and offers the supposition that the dismissal of Wolfe as an important writer may be only a temporary critical phenomenon.

Kennedy, Richard S. "Thomas Wolfe and the American Experience." *Modern Fiction Studies* XI, No. 3 (Autumn 1965): 219-33.
> Discusses the personal notebooks, used in the composition of *Look Homeward, Angel*, in which Wolfe jotted down observations and notes to himself and wrote first drafts of fiction and letters.

McElderry, B. R., Jr. *Thomas Wolfe*. New York: Twayne Publishers, 1964, 207 p.
> Discusses various aspects of *Look Homeward, Angel*, including its characters, structure, lyrical style, and autobiographical character.

Phillipson, John S. *Thomas Wolfe: A Reference Guide*. Boston: G. K. Hall & Co., 1977, 218 p.
> Annotated bibliography of Wolfe criticism.

Reaver, J. Russell and Strozier, Robert I. "Thomas Wolfe and Death." *The Georgia Review* XVI, No. 3 (Fall 1962): 330-50.
> Discusses Eugene Gant's evolving view of death in *Look Homeward, Angel*, contrasting his youthful fear of death with his later acceptance of it, an acceptance that is also reflected in Wolfe's later novels.

Reeves, Paschal, ed. "*Look Homeward, Angel*." In *Thomas Wolfe: The Critical Reception*, pp. 1-30. New York: David Lewis, 1974.
> Reprints twenty-five early reviews of *Look Homeward, Angel*, and offers a checklist of twelve additional reviews.

Rubin, Louis D., Jr., ed. *Thomas Wolfe: A Collection of Critical Essays*. Englewood Cliffs, N.J., 1973, 182 p.

Includes an essay by Thomas C. Moser devoted to *Look Homeward, Angel* and several general essays that include criticism on *Look Homeward, Angel*.

Snyder, William U. *Thomas Wolfe: Ulysses and Narcissus*. Athens: Ohio University Press, 1971, 234 p.
Psychoanalytical study of Wolfe's relationships with men and with women as evidenced by *Look Homeward, Angel* and Wolfe's other novels. Snyder relates the nature of these relationships to Wolfe's compulsive, autobiographical manner of writing.

Turnbull, Andrew. "Aline" and "Arrival." In his *Thomas Wolfe,* pp. 96-126 and 127-53. New York: Charles Scribner's Sons, 1967.
Recounts Wolfe's relationship with Aline Bernstein during the composition of *Look Homeward, Angel* and his relationship with Max Perkins during its editing and publication.

Walser, Richard, ed. *The Enigma of Thomas Wolfe: Biographical and Critical Selections*. Cambridge: Harvard University Press, 1953, 313 p.
Includes essays on *Look Homeward, Angel* by Edward C. Aswell and Maxwell Geismar, as well as twenty-four essays devoted to other novels or to the accomplishments of Wolfe's whole body of work.

———. "The Angel and the Ghost." In *Thomas Wolfe and the Glass of Time,* edited by Paschal Reeves, pp. 45-77. Athens: University of Georgia Press, 1971.
Contrasts the symbolism of the angel and the ghost in *Look Homeward, Angel*.

Appendix

The following is a listing of all sources used in Volume 29 of *Twentieth-Century Literary Criticism*. Included in this list are all copyright and reprint rights and acknowledgments for those essays for which permission was obtained. Every effort has been made to trace copyright, but if omissions have been made, please let us know.

THE EXCERPTS IN TCLC, VOLUME 29, WERE REPRINTED FROM THE FOLLOWING BOOKS:

Allen, Walter. From *Joyce Cary*. The British Council, 1953.

Anderson-Imbert, Enrique. From *Spanish-American Literature: A History*. Translated by John V. Falconieri. Wayne State University Press, 1963. Copyright © 1963 by Wayne State University Press. All rights reserved. Reprinted by permission of the Wayne State University Press and the author.

Beja, Morris. From *Epiphany in the Modern Novel*. University of Washington Press, 1971. All rights reserved. Reprinted by permission of the publisher.

Bloom, Robert. From *The Indeterminate World: A Study of the Novels of Joyce Cary*. University of Pennsylvania Press, 1962. © 1962, by the Trustees of the University of Pennsylvania. Reprinted by permission of the publisher.

Borges, Jorge Luis. From *Other Inquisitions: 1937-1952*. Translated by Ruth L. C. Simms. University of Texas Press, 1964. Copyright © 1964 by the University of Texas Press. All rights reserved. Reprinted by permission of the publisher.

Brent, Albert. From *Leopoldo Alas and "La Regenta": A Study in Nineteenth Century Spanish Prose Fiction*. The Curators of the University of Missouri, 1951.

Brod, Max. From *Franz Kafka: A Biography*. Translated by G. Humphreys Roberts and Richard Winston. Schocken Books, 1947. Copyright 1937 by Heinr, Mercy Sohn, Prague. Copyright 1947 by Schocken Books, Inc. Copyright © 1960, renewed 1975 by Schocken Books, Inc. Reprinted by permission of Schocken Books, published by Pantheon Books, a Division of Random House, Inc.

Cocteau, Jean. From a preface to *The Count's Ball*. By Raymond Radiguet, translated by Malcolm Cowley. Norton, 1929. Copyright, 1929 W. W. Norton & Company, Inc. Renewed 1957 by Malcolm Cowley. Reprinted by permission of W. W. Norton & Company, Inc.

Coester, Alfred. From *The Literary History of Spanish America*. Macmillan, 1916. Copyright 1916 by Macmillan Publishing Company. Copyright renewed 1944 by Alfred Coester.

Dauvin, René. From " 'The Trial': Its Meaning," translated by Martin Nozick, in *Franz Kafka Today*. Edited by Angel Flores and Homer Swander. The University of Wisconsin Press, 1958. Copyright © 1958, renewed 1986 by the Regents of the University of Wisconsin. Reprinted by permission of the publisher.

De Onís, Harriet. From an introduction to *The Knights of the Cape and Thirty-Seven Other Selections from the "Tradiciones peruanas" of Ricardo Palma*. Edited and translated by Harriet de Onís. Knopf, 1945. Copyright 1945, renewed 1972 by Alfred A. Knopf, Inc. All rights reserved. Reprinted by permission of the publisher.

DeVoto, Bernard. From *The Letters of Bernard DeVoto*. Edited by Wallace Stegner. Doubleday, 1975. Copyright © 1975 by Avis DeVoto, as Executrix of the Estate of Bernard DeVoto and Wallace Stegner. All rights reserved. Reprinted by permission of Doubleday, a division of Bantam, Doubleday, Dell Publishing Group, Inc.

Dimaris, C. Th. From *A History of Modern Greek Literature*. Translated by Mary P. Gianos. State University of New York Press, 1972. Translation © 1972 State University of New York. All rights reserved. Reprinted by permission of the publisher.

Ekmanis, Rolfs. From *Latvian Literature under the Soviets: 1940-1975*. Nordland Publishing Company, 1978. © copyright 1978 by Buecher-Vertriehsanstalt. All rights reserved. Reprinted by permission of BVA.

Eoff, Sherman H. From *The Modern Spanish Novel: Comparative Essays Examining the Philosophical Impact of Science on Fiction*. New York University Press, 1961. © 1961 by New York University. Reprinted by permission of the publisher.

Finney, Brian. From *The Inner I: British Literary Autobiography of the Twentieth Century*. Oxford University Press, 1985. Copyright © 1985 by Brian Finney. All rights reserved. Reprinted by permission of Oxford University Press, Inc. In Canada by A. D. Peters & Co. Ltd.

Flint, Jack M. From *The Prose Works of Roberto Arlt: A Thematic Approach*. University of Durham, 1985. © Jack M. Flint 1985. Reprinted by permission of the author.

Ford, Ford Madox. From *Portraits from Life: Memories and Criticisms*. Houghton Mifflin Company, 1937. Copyright, 1936 and 1937, by Ford Madox Ford. Renewed 1964 by Janice Biala. All rights reserved. Reprinted by permission of Janice Biala.

Foster, David William. From *Currents in the Contemporary Argentine Novel: Arlt, Mallea, Sabato, and Cortázar*. University of Missouri Press, 1975. Copyright © 1975 by The Curators of the University of Missouri. All rights reserved. Reprinted by permission of the publisher.

Frederick, John T. From *William Henry Hudson*. Twayne, 1972. Copyright 1972 by Twayne Publishers. All rights reserved. Reprinted with the permission of Twayne Publishers, Inc., a division of G. K. Hall & Co., Boston.

Galsworthy, John. From an introduction to *Green Mansions: A Romance of the Tropical Forest*. By William Henry Hudson. Knopf, 1916. Introduction copyright 1916, renewed 1944 by Alfred A. Knopf, Inc. Reprinted by permission of the publisher.

Peyre, Henri. From *The Contemporary French Novel*. Oxford University Press, 1955. Copyright © 1955 by Oxford University Press, Inc. Renewed 1983 by Henri Peyre. Reprinted by permission of the publisher.

Politis, Linos. From *A History of Modern Greek Literature*. Oxford at the Clarendon Press, 1973. © Oxford University Press, 1973. Reprinted by permission of Oxford University Press.

Politzer, Heinz. From *Franz Kafka: Parable and Paradox*. Revised edition. Cornell University Press, 1966. © 1962, copyright © 1966 by Cornell University. Used by permission of the publisher, Cornell University Press.

Radiguet, Raymond. From *Cheeks on Fire: Collected Poems*. Translated by Alan Stone. Calder, 1976. © English translation John Calder 1976. All rights reserved. Reprinted by permission of John Calder (Publishers) Ltd., London.

Ragusa, Olga. From *Luigi Pirandello: An Approach to His Theatre*. Edinburgh University Press, 1980. Reprinted by permission of the publisher.

Rahv, Philip. From *Image and Idea: Fourteen Essays on Literary Themes*. New Directions, 1949. Copyright 1949 by Philip Rahv. Renewed 1976 by Betty T. Rahv. Reprinted by permission of the Literary Estate of Philip Rahv.

Reiss, H. S. From "Eine Neuordnung der Werke Kafkas? Zu zwei Aufsätzen von Herman Uyttersprot," in *Franz Kafka*. Ergänzter Neudruck. Lambert Schneider, 1956. Translated for this publication by Noel Barstad. Translation © 1988 by Gale Research Inc. Translated and reprinted by permission of Verlag Lambert Schneider, Heidelberg.

Rhys, Grace. From an introduction to *The Sons of Jacob*. By J. Rainis, translated by Grace Rhys. J. M. Dent & Sons Ltd., 1924.

Riviere, Jacques. From *The Ideal Reader: Selected Essays*. Edited and translated by Blanche A. Price. Meridian Books, 1960. Originally published as "Le bal du Comte d'Orgel," in *Nouvelle revue Française*, June, 1924. © by Librairie Gallimard, 1924. Reprinted by permission of Georges Borchardt Inc.

Roby, Kinley E. From *Joyce Cary*. Twayne, 1984. Copyright 1984 by Twayne Publishers. All rights reserved. Reprinted with the permission of Twayne Publishers, a division of G. K. Hall & Co., Boston.

Roosevelt, Theodore. From "An Introductory Note," in *The Purple Land: Being the Narrative of One Richard Lamb's Adventures in the Banda Orientál, in South America, as Told by Himself*. By W. H. Hudson. E. P. Dutton and Company, 1916.

Ronner, Amy D. From *W. H. Hudson: The Man, the Novelist, the Naturalist*. AMS Press, 1986. Copyright © 1986 by AMS Press, Inc. All rights reserved. Reprinted by permission of the publisher.

Rubin, Louis D., Jr. From *Thomas Wolfe: The Weather of His Youth*. Louisiana State University Press, 1955.

Rudzītis, Jānis. From "Literature and Drama," in *Cross Road Country: Latvia*. Edited by Edgars Andersons. Latvju Grāmata, 1953.

Rutherford, John. From an introduction to *La Regenta*. By Leopoldo Alas, translated by John Rutherford. The University of Georgia Press, 1984. © 1984 the University of Georgia Press. All rights reserved. Reprinted by permission of the publisher.

Sawey, Orlan. From *Bernard DeVoto*. Twayne, 1969. Copyright 1969 by Twayne Publishers. All rights reserved. Reprinted with the permission of Twayne Publishers, Inc., a division of G. K. Hall & Co., Boston.

Singer, Carl S. From "The Examined Life," in *Approaches to the Twentieth-Century Novel*. Edited by John Unterecker. Thomas Y. Crowell Company, 1965. Copyright © 1965 by Harper & Row, Publishers, Inc. All rights reserved. Reprinted by permission of the publisher.

Sokel, Walter H. From "The Programme of K.'s Court: Oedipal and Existential Meanings of 'The Trial'," in *On Kafka: Semi- Centenary Perspectives*. Edited by Franz Kuna. Barnes & Noble Books, 1976. Copyright © 1976 Elek Books Ltd. All rights reserved. Reprinted by permission of Grafton Books, a division of the Collins Publishing Group.

Spaini, Alberto. From " 'The Trial'," translated by John Glynn Conley, in *The Kafka Problem*. Edited by Angel Flores. New Directions, 1946. Copyright 1946, renewed 1974, by New Directions Publishing Corporation. Reprinted by permission of the editor.

Starkie, Walter. From *Luigi Pirandello*. J. M. Dent & Sons Limited, 1926.

Stavrou, Theofanis G. From "Alexandros Papadiamantis: A Greek Writer against the Current," in *A Greek Diptych: Dionysios Solomos and Alexandros Papadiamantis*. By Louis Coutelle, Theofanis G. Stavrou, and David R. Weinberg. Nostos, 1986. Copyright © 1986 Nostos. All rights reserved. Reprinted by permission of the publisher.

Tanner, Roy L. From *The Humor of Irony and Satire in the "Tradiciones peruanas."* University of Missouri Press, 1986. Copyright 1986 by The Curators of the University of Missouri. All rights reserved. Reprinted by permission of the publisher.

Thorlby, Anthony. From *Kafka: A Study*. Rowman and Littlefield, 1972. © Anthony Thorlby 1972. Reprinted by permission of the publisher.

Tilgher, Adriano. From "Life versus Form," translated by Glauco Cambon, in *Pirandello: A Collection of Critical Essays*. Edited by Glauco Cambon. Prentice-Hall, 1967. Copyright © 1967 by Prentice-Hall, Inc. All rights reserved. Reprinted by permission of the Literary Estate of Glauco Cambon.

Trench, Herbert. From an introduction to *The Death of the Gods*. By Dmitri Merejkowski. Translated by Herbert Trench. G. P. Putnam's Sons, 1901.

Turnell, Martin. From *The Rise of the French Novel: Marivaux, Crebillon fils, Rousseau, Stendhal, Flaubert, Alain-Fournier, Raymond Radiguet*. New Directions, 1978. Copyright © 1978 by Martin Turnell. Reprinted by permission of New Directions Publishing Corporation.

Umphrey, G. W. From an introduction to *Tradiciones peruanas*. By Ricardo Palma, edited by G. W. Umphrey. Benj. H. Sanborn & Co., 1936.

Unrue, Darlene H. From "The Gothic Matrix of 'Look Homeward, Angel'," in *Critical Essays on Thomas Wolfe*. Edited by John S. Phillipson. G. K. Hall & Co., 1985. © Darlene H. Unrue, 1984. Reprinted with the permission of the publisher.

Uyttersprot, Herman. From " 'The Trial': Its Structure," translated by Konrad Gries, Edmund P. Kurz, and Inge Liebe, in *Franz Kafka Today*. Edited by Angel Flores and Homer Swander. The University of Wisconsin Press, 1958. Copyright © 1958, renewed 1968 by the Regents of the University of Wisconsin. Reprinted by permission of the publisher.

Van Doren, Carl. From *The American Novel: 1789-1939*. Revised edition. The Macmillan Company, 1940. Copyright 1921, 1940 by Macmillan Publishing Company. Renewed 1949 by Carl Van Doren. Renewed © 1968 by Anne Van Doren Ross, Barbara Van Doren Klaw and Margaret Van Doren Bevans. Reprinted with permission of Macmillan Publishing Company.

Walser, Richard. From *Thomas Wolfe: An Introduction and Interpretation*. Barnes & Noble, 1961. © copyright, 1961 by Barnes & Noble, Inc. All rights reserved. Reprinted by permission of the publisher.

Watkins, Floyd C. From *Thomas Wolfe's Characters: Portraits from Life*. University of Oklahoma Press, 1957. Copyright 1957 by the University of Oklahoma Press. Renewed 1985 by Floyd C. Watkins. Reprinted by permission of the author.

Weinberg, David R. From "The Literary Art of Alexandros Papadiamantis," in *A Greek Diptych: Dionysios Solomos and Alexandros Papadiamantis*. By Louis Coutelle, Theofanis G. Stavrou, and David R. Weinberg. Nostos, 1986. Copyright © 1986 Nostos. All rights reserved. Reprinted by permission of the publisher.

Wilson, Edmund. From *The Shores of Light: A Literary Chronicle of the Twenties and Thirties*. Farrar, Straus and Giroux, 1952. Copyright 1952 by Edmund Wilson. Renewed 1980 by Helen Miranda Wilson. All rights reserved. Reprinted by permission of Farrar, Straus and Giroux, Inc.

Wolfe, Thomas. From *The Story of a Novel*. Scribner's, 1936. Copyright 1936 Charles Scribner's Sons. Copyright renewed © 1964 Paul Gitlin Administrator C.T.A. Reprinted with the permission of Charles Scribner's Sons, an imprint of Macmillan Publishing Company.

Wright, Andrew. From *Joyce Cary: A Preface to His Novels*. Harper & Row, 1958, Chatto & Windus, 1958. Copyright © 1958, renewed 1986 by Andrew Wright. Reprinted by permission of Harper & Row, Publishers, Inc. In Canada by the author and Chatto & Windus.

Ziedonis, Arvids, Jr. From *The Religious Philosophy of Jānis Rainis: Latvian Poet*. Latvju Gramata, 1969. Copyright © 1968 by Arvids Ziedonis, Jr. All rights reserved. Reprinted by permission of the author.